Colonel St

Colonel Stuart Tootal has ~~served~~ ~~in~~ ...eland, the Gulf War and during the invasion of Iraq. He also served in the MOD, for which he was awarded the OBE. On leaving the Army, he set up the 3 PARA Afghan Trust charity. He now works in the corporate security sector.

Praise for *Danger Close*:

'At ... mander telling us the cold, harsh truth about this ... xcellent and compelling read' Andy McNab

'Too... e perspective of a man in charge . . . he tells the story... Wars are invariably muddles, but Tootal details a sh... prehensive one' Max Hastings, *Sunday Times*

...rst-hand account of the realities of frontline co... start of the bitterest war that Britain has fought ...ons' Patrick Bishop, author of *3 PARA*

'... r commander to provide an account of the fi... al's book is refreshingly free of the gung-ho m... sentimentality that afflicts other lesser entries of the genre' *Sunday Tribune*

Danger Close

Commanding 3 PARA in Afghanistan

COLONEL STUART TOOTAL
DSO OBE

JOHN MURRAY

First published in Great Britain in 2009 by John Murray (Publishers)
An Hachette UK Company

First published in paperback in 2010

1

© Colonel Stuart Tootal 2009

The right of Colonel Stuart Tootal to be identified as the Author of the Work has been asserted
by him in accordance with the Copyright, Designs and Patents Act 1988.

A CIP catalogue record for this title is available from the British Library

ISBN 978-1-84854-258-7

Typeset in Monotype Bembo by Servis Filmsetting Ltd, Stockport, Cheshire

Printed and bound by Clays Ltd, St Ives plc

John Murray policy is to use papers that are natural, renewable and recyclable products and made
from wood grown in sustainable forests. The logging and manufacturing processes are expected to
conform to the environmental regulations of the country of origin.

John Murray (Publishers)
338 Euston Road
London NW1 3BH

www.johnmurray.co.uk

For Jacko

Private Damian Jackson
3 PARA. Killed in action
5 July 2006 (aged 19).

Contents

Maps

UZBEKISTA

INDIAN OCEAN

TURKMENISTAN

JOWZJAN   BALKH

FARYAB   SAMA

SAR-E POL

BADGHIS

BAMIAN

HERAT

GHOWR   ORUZGAN

IRAN

GH

FARAH

ZABOL

Lashkar
Gah

Kaf

NIMRUZ

KANDAHAR

HELMAND

P

N

	International Boundary
	Province Boundary

0   100   200 km

0   100   200 mi

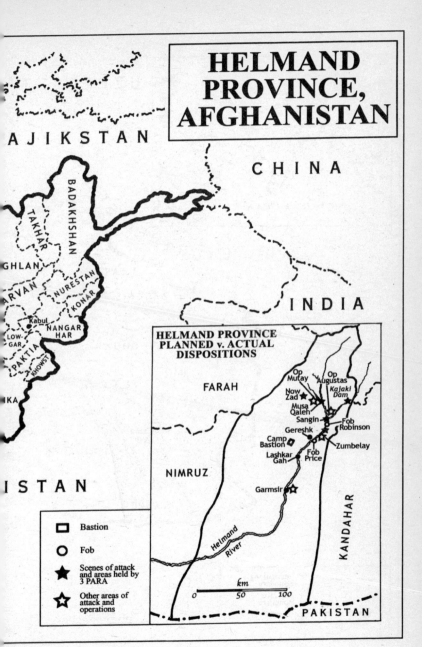

HELMAND PROVINCE, AFGHANISTAN

AJIKSTAN

CHINA

BADAKHSHAN

TAKHAR

GHLAN

ARVAN

NURESTAN

KONAR

Kabul

LOW-GAR

NANGAR
HAR

PAKTIA

KHOWST

KA

INDIA

ISTAN

HELMAND PROVINCE
PLANNED v. ACTUAL
DISPOSITIONS

FARAH

Op
Mutay

Op
Augustas

Now
Zad

Kajaki
Dam

Musa
Qaleh

Sangin

Fob
Robinson

Gereshk

Camp
Bastion

Zumbelay

Lashkar
Gah

Fob
Price

NIMRUZ

Garmsir

KANDAHAR

	Bastion
	Fob
★	Scenes of attack and areas held by 3 PARA
☆	Other areas of attack and operations

Helmand
River

km

0   50   100

PAKISTAN

Preface

In April 2006 the 1,200 soldiers of the 3 PARA Battle Group started their journey to southern Afghanistan. They were the first British unit to be sent into the lawless province of Helmand. Forecast as the start of a three-year commitment to bring much-needed stability to a country ravaged by thirty years of war, their deployment was heralded as a peace support mission. Some who made the decision to send us hoped it would be completed without a shot being fired, but the Taliban thought differently. During its six-month tour of duty, 3 PARA fired over 479,000 rounds of ammunition in a level of sustained combat that had not been seen by the British Army since the end of the Korean War. The action took place across wild desert plains and among the foothills of the Hindu Kush. In the oppressive heat of the Afghan summer, the Battle Group fought desperately to defend a disparate number of isolated district centres against relentless attacks. Undermanned and suffering from critical equipment shortages, the intensity of the conflict stretched resources to breaking point as 3 PARA became involved in a deadly battle of attrition against a resurgent Taliban determined to drive British troops from Helmand. But it was the raw courage and fighting spirit of British soldiers that forced the Taliban to blink first. After months of vicious close-quarter fighting they won the break-in phase of the battle for Helmand in an unforgiving campaign that larger British forces continue to fight today.

The award of over thirty decorations for gallantry, including a posthumous Victoria Cross and George Cross, bears testimony to the intensity of the combat and the selfless bravery of an extraordinary band of brothers. However, as in all wars, there was a price to pay. Fifteen members of the Battle Group were killed in action and another forty-six were wounded in battle. This is their story, told both from my own perspective and that of many of those whom I was fortunate enough to know and command. It says something of the impact on their families and on those whose loved ones did not return. I have attempted to capture the essence of the fighting at the sharp end: the sights, sounds and smell of combat through a variety of different landscapes. I have also tried to provide an insight into the bigger picture issues and the difficult life-and-death decisions that were made. The following pages chart the highs and lows the Battle Group experienced and also deal with the consequences of doing the nation's bidding, both on and off the battlefield. They say something of a peacetime society where the implications of war are often poorly understood and where there have been far too many incidents of poor treatment of those who suffer the mental and physical scars of battle. But ultimately this book is about the ordinary paratrooper and soldier in battle, their remarkable fortitude, their will to combat, the privations they faced and how they accepted risk and loss as part of the business that they are in. Having once been a soldier, writing *Danger Close* has been both an emotional and cathartic experience; my one hope is that I have done justice to those with whom I was privileged enough to serve.

Introduction

The Dawn of Battle

The engines of the twin rotors of the Chinook helicopter screamed for power and the fuselage vibrated violently as we lifted off from our base in the middle of the Helmand desert. We were a four-ship helicopter formation carrying 150 members of my Battle Group. Each man carried in excess of 60 pounds of equipment and was crammed into the tightly packed interiors. The American-built heavy-lift CH-47 Chinooks were the workhorses of our RAF helicopter fleet, affectionately known as cabs by the men who flew them. They were escorted by two Apache AH-64 gunships piloted by men of the Army Air Corps. The Apaches were our muscle, each capable of delivering a devastating fire of hundreds of 30mm cannon shells from its nose gun, explosive-tipped rockets from its side-mounted pods and Hellfire 'fire and forget' missiles which could flatten a small building.

The force being lifted consisted of my Battle Group Tactical Headquarters (known as Tac), two platoons of A Company, a fire support group of machine gunners, a Royal Engineers search team and a squad of men from the Afghan Army. Full to capacity, and with every seat taken, my men sat on the floor with their legs astride the man in front. Each man was festooned with individual assault gear, belts of ammunition, scaling ladders and automatic weapons. As we gained altitude and headed out across the open desert the thick fog of fine swirling sand kicked up by the rotor blades and the caustic smell of aviation fuel were blown from the confines of the fuselage. It was replaced by a perceptible atmosphere of enthusiastic apprehension. I could see it etched on the faces of my men as they nestled among their comrades. Encased in their combat body armour and wearing lightweight Para helmets, each man was deep in his own private thoughts as they set about mentally preparing themselves for the unknown of the lawless northern interior of Helmand Province.

As we flew over the security of Camp Bastion's razor-wired perimeter and headed north across the empty desert, I ran through the plan in my head. Codenamed Operation Mutay, it was our first deliberately planned helicopter air-assault mission since arriving in Afghanistan a few weeks previously. It had been billed as a simple enough affair by our superior UK Task Force headquarters located in Kandahar. We were to conduct an operation to cordon and search a compound that a local Taliban commander was known to have frequented. We hoped to apprehend him, but, if not, a search of the compound might yield useful intelligence, as well as insurgent weapons and equipment. Intelligence reports indicated that the target area was expected to be quiet. This seemed to have been confirmed by the fact that we had recently occupied the nearby district centre (district administrative offices) in the town of Now Zad to prevent it falling to the Taliban. Since B Company's arrival there a few days previously, insurgent attacks against the Afghan police garrison had ceased. B Company's subsequent security patrols into the town had gone unmolested and I had been able to relieve them with a smaller force from the Gurkha Company originally assigned to guard Camp Bastion. This all seemed to support the assessment we had been given that the Taliban had withdrawn from the area.

As the assault group flew towards the target area twenty minutes' flying time from Bastion, I knew that other members of my Battle Group would be driving towards supporting positions from the district centre in Now Zad. The Patrols Platoon and a platoon of Gurkhas would provide outer cordon depth positions around the general area of the target compound to provide additional security for the operation. Once in position they would allow the helicopter-borne troops to air-assault close to the compound and establish an inner security cordon immediately around it. Once cleared by A Company, the search team would then be able to search the compound. It was the sort of thing we had done on many occasions in Iraq and Northern Ireland and I remember thinking that it all sounded simple enough.

Five minutes out from the target landing zone (LZ) and the outer cordon troops reported that they were driving into position. The Gurkhas moved out of the district centre in Land-Rovers equipped with heavy machine guns. They headed north accompanied by a number of local Afghan National Policemen, known as the ANP. The Patrols Platoon moved to the south in eight other WMIKS, Land-Rovers so called because of the heavy .50-calibre machine guns fixed on Weapon Mount Installation Kits. Each heavy machine gun fired half-inch bullets that were capable of cutting a man in half. A bonnet-mounted 7.62mm General Purpose Machine Gun (GPMG) provided additional fire support from the front seat commander's position.

I leaned into the space between the two pilots in my cab. The sun shimmered through the cockpit window and I could see the two Apache helicopters take station in over-watch, hovering positions from which they would be able to deliver devastating firepower with their Hellfire missiles and 30mm cannons should we need their fire support. In the distance, and slightly below them, the other three CH-47s were stacked in a diagonal approach attitude one after the other and were beginning their run into the target area. As my helicopter remained in an offset holding pattern, I allowed myself a moment to savour the warm feeling of satisfaction associated with seeing a plan unfolding as intended. Everybody was in position and we would reach our planned H Hour, the designated time when an operation is due to start. I smiled to myself; things were on track and appeared to be going well.

The radio communication nets went quiet as the pilots in the other three Chinooks concentrated for a fast assault landing approach into the LZ. This was a critical phase of the operation: the aircraft would not only be vulnerable to enemy fire as they landed, but the downwash from their blades would kick up a dust cloud that would induce zero visibility for the last 40 feet of their descent. They would land hard, fast and blind. They were not only susceptible to being riddled by hostile gunfire or RPG rounds, but they also ran the very real risk of a collision with the ground, or each other, as they landed in the thick, swirling sand cloud known as a brown-out. I thought of my men in the back of the cabs; each would be tense with the last few moments to landing, eagerly waiting for the wheels to touch down. An instant later the rear ramp would be lowered, allowing them to clear the fuselage in seconds. They would be glad to get out on to the ground, their destiny finally decoupled from the dangers of being confined in the cramped interiors of an aircraft carrying several thousand litres of highly flammable aviation fuel.

Suddenly static burst into my headset and I distinctly heard the faint, but frantic, words of 'Contact! Contact!' Shit. Shit. Some of my troops were already in an engagement with the enemy. With the assault helicopters still in the process of committing themselves into the LZ it meant that things had already started to go badly wrong.

The picture was unclear, but I could hear snatches of one of the tactical air controller's desperate appeals for close air support. From the call signs I could hear, I knew that both platoons moving to the outer cordon positions had been ambushed. The pilot of my aircraft was trying to talk to the Apaches, fly his aircraft and tell me what he was picking up over the radio, as I could only hear agitated snatches of radio traffic. I told him to overfly the area so that I could get 'eyes on' to see what was happening on the ground below me. Out of the starboard gunner's hatch I could make out several of our vehicles in a wide, dry watercourse of a wadi. They were stationary and their positioning suggested that they had been halted in a hurry. But we were still at several thousand feet and I could discern little else. I desperately wanted to get lower to see more, but my pilot rightly wanted to maintain altitude to keep us out of the range of enemy small-arms fire.

I frantically thought about what to do. It was too late to call off the three CH-47s, as they had already committed themselves to running into the target area and we could not raise them on the net anyway. I wanted someone to tell me what was going on and what I should be doing about it. But I could only communicate over the intercom with the pilot and the snatches of transmission I could hear from the ground were broken and intermittent. Focus, think about your options! I grabbed Captain Rob Musetti, my fire support commander sitting in a seat by the starboard door gunner. I tried to brief him over the roar of the aircraft's engines. Despite shouting myself hoarse, I could barely make myself heard. I hastily scribbled a note on a small piece of card: 'Both outer call signs in contact.' But without a headset, Rob had even less of an idea about what was going on than I did. He looked bemused, clearly aware that something was amiss but it was obvious that we weren't going to have a meaningful discussion.

My mind raced. Should we land and commit the one immediately available reserve we had into a confused situation? Should we stay on station and wait for the situation to clarify itself? Or should we return to my headquarters at Bastion to try to gain a better understanding of the situation and gather reinforcements?

Meanwhile the battle a few thousand feet below me was unfolding. The Gurkha Platoon had been ambushed in the wadi with RPG rounds and bullets glancing off their vehicles. One of their accompanying Afghan policemen had been hit and badly wounded. Leaving their radios behind them, and under withering fire, the Gurkhas had been forced to abandon their WMIKs to fight among the tight-knit alleyways and high mud walls in the compounds that surrounded the wadi. The Taliban were firing from dug-in positions that had clearly been prepared to cover such an approach. Two kilometres to their south the Patrols Platoon had also run into a series of ambushes. Returning fire, they fought through each engagement in an attempt to reach their cordon positions only to come under contact again. In the process Private Ali was knocked backwards by two enemy bullets that hit his magazines and ignited the tracer rounds inside them. A Company had landed and had come under sporadic fire on the LZ. They had initially fought off a number of Taliban who had engaged them and then managed to secure the compound.

But I was unaware of the precise nature of events on the ground, and my mind continued to race as I thought about the implications of the various options regarding the call I knew I had to make. Then I heard just what I didn't need to hear from the pilot, Lieutenant Nichol Benzie, who was flying our aircraft: 'Colonel, we are five minutes to bingo fuel. You need to make a decision about what you want to do.' Shit. Staying on task circling above the contact was no longer an option. We were approaching a critical fuel situation and we either had to land into the fight below us or return to Bastion to refuel and gather reinforcements. Time was ticking by fast; I was blind and had no situational awareness of what was going on; I couldn't communicate with anyone on the ground, but I had to make a decision.

Leadership in war is a complex business, often necessitating decisions be made on the basis of imperfect information where there is no time for prevarication. It requires judgement and intuition regarding events that are unclear and where the consequences often have life-or-death implications. But leading men in combat and making command decisions are also the essence of what every commander aspires to do; suddenly I wasn't so sure. As those precious moments slipped by and I agonized about the choices I faced, the military maxim of 'Beware what you wish for' crossed my mind. Bugger that, I thought, this is what I get paid for; time to decide. I flicked the switch on my intercom: 'Land on.'

Due to the shortage of aircrew gunners at the time, I manned the CH-47's port M60 machine gun as we ran into the LZ. Traversing it across its arcs, I noticed the pop and smoke of an explosion and saw armed figures suddenly appearing among the undergrowth as we swept over the hedgerows and ditches below us. I beaded the weapon's sight of the M60 on them, but relaxed my grip on the triggers with relief when I recognized one of the men as a paratrooper from A Company. The aircraft landed with a thump and we ran off the tailgate. I managed to make the customary thumbs up to the tailgate gunner as we left the cab, not sure whether it was for his confidence or mine, and entered a blizzard of swirling sand and uncertainty.

I

3 PARA

Angels with Dirty Faces

Bloody marvellous, I thought as I walked out of the Chief of the General Staff's (CGS) marbled office in Whitehall. As well as being head of the Army, General Sir Mike Jackson was also the Colonel Commandant of the Parachute Regiment. Through gravelled tones and cigar smoke, he had informed me that I was going to be the next commanding officer (CO) of the regiment's 3rd Battalion, better known as 3 PARA. I was elated. To me command of an infantry unit, especially a Para battalion, was the apogee of a soldier's military career. However, getting selected to command hadn't been a foregone conclusion. There was some stiff competition for the post and coming originally from a Scottish infantry regiment, I had been something of an outsider. 'Jacko' mentioned that my selection was still subject to official approval at an Army appointments board. Just before I left his office he told me not to tell anyone 'except your good lady wife of course'. Although I had a serious girlfriend, in an Army still founded on the tradition that single officers unmarried in their late thirties are considered to be somewhat suspect, I wasn't about to tell him that I wasn't married.

I had taken a rather convoluted route to command a Para battalion. Born into a family with an air force background, my lineage might have suggested that I should have joined the RAF. My grandfather had been a wartime pilot and was a twenty-six-year-old flight lieutenant when he was killed flying a Halifax bomber over Germany in 1945. My father had also been a military aviator, spending twenty years in the RAF before taking early retirement as a group captain. Although I joined the RAF section of my boarding school's Combined Cadet Force, I had been brought up on a diet of war comics and Action Man. As a small boy, playing soldiers was what I enjoyed doing most and it bred an affinity for becoming one when I grew up. However, I knew relatively little about the Army and more distant maternal family connections influenced my decision to join a Scottish infantry regiment.

In 1988 I joined the 1st Battalion the Queen's Own Highlanders in Germany after completing officer training at Sandhurst. The Cold War was in its death throes and life in the British Army of the Rhine soon became dispiritingly predictable. The majority of the battalion's time was spent fixing ageing armoured vehicles, most of which had entered service before I was born. Time not spent tinkering on the tank park was taken up with orderly officer duties, where a young subaltern engaged in the unexciting tasks of inspecting guards, checking stores and endlessly cleaning one's parade dress. This was punctuated by unimaginative and mundane exercises where we spent interminable hours driving across the West German plain in vehicles that wheezed to a halt with impressive regularity. Living in armoured personnel carriers for weeks on end, we rarely dismounted to conduct proper infantry training and became preoccupied with keeping our antiquated equipment on the road. When it did come, light relief to the monotony of soldiering in Germany came in the form of emergency tours to Northern Ireland and the 1991 Gulf War.

Patrolling the streets of the province's divided sectarian community in West Belfast in 1989 was my first exposure to operational soldiering. In the late 1980s soldiers and policemen were still being killed by the IRA and the ever present danger of terrorist attack provided an exciting edge after the drudgery of Germany. Shootings and bombings occurred on an intermittent basis and for the first time I noticed how the soldiers I commanded looked to young officers to make decisions in conjunction with sound advice from the more experienced non-commissioned officers (NCOs). It was a junior commander's war and I relished every moment of it.

Deployment to the Gulf a year later was a stark contrast to conducting internal security duties in Northern Ireland. I was commanding the battalion's platoon of armoured reconnaissance vehicles, and we were attached to the headquarters of the 1st (UK) Armoured Division. I remember waiting to cross the Saudi Arabian border into Iraq and the ground shaking as heavy US B-52 bombers pulverized enemy positions ahead of us. During the 100 hours of battle that followed to liberate Kuwait, we witnessed the carnage of war at first hand. The burnt-out hulks of Iraqi tanks and human remains littered the desert. The culmination of the division's rapid advance brought us to the main Kuwait City to Basra road. Aptly named the Highway of Death, allied airpower had got there before us. They had caught the remnants of the Iraqi Army as it attempted to retreat north. Hundreds of scorched and smashed vehicles were strung out along the crater-marked road as far as the eye could see. The engines of some of the undamaged vehicles were still running and it was an apocalyptic scene; the greasy smoke of burning oil fields cast a black cloud above us and the stench of death was everywhere. As we viewed the widespread devastation and did what we could to treat some of the survivors, I was struck by the fact that there is no glory in war when one surveys its aftermath.

Operations in Northern Ireland and the Gulf were but brief interludes. All too quickly they were once again replaced by conventional peacetime soldiering in places such as Germany and desk-bound staff appointments in the UK. I became increasingly conscious of the need to find more demanding pursuits if I was to stay in the Army. Commitments in the Balkans would no doubt have taken me out of Germany, but operations in places like Bosnia had settled into routine peace-keeping duties that were of little appeal. When I was afforded the opportunity to be seconded to command a rifle company in the Parachute Regiment as an alternative to returning to serve more time in Germany, I jumped at the chance.

The Parachute Regiment's status as an elite unit allows it to select and train only the toughest of candidates. With the exception of that conducted by the SAS, the Paras' selection training is recognized as being the hardest in the British Army. But the key to the success of the regiment is the calibre of the men who make up its ranks. The Paras are the only regiment in the British Army that requires its recruits to undergo a rigorous selection course; known as P Company, it is the benchmark entry standard into the elite and sets them apart. The gruelling assessment course consists of two parts. The build-up phase is designed to improve a trainee's fitness and endurance, while the test phase gauges the individual's determination, team spirit, aggressiveness and behaviour under stress. It assesses whether an individual has the self-discipline and motivation required to serve with Airborne Forces. The tests are physically and mentally demanding. They stretch each candidate to the limit and decide whether an aspiring Parachute Regiment recruit is good enough to wear the distinctive maroon beret.

Nothing in a Para's training is done without a purpose and each event of Test Week is designed to simulate a particular battle activity and the hardships associated with airborne operations. Having inserted into an area by parachute, Paras are rarely expected to have much in the way of vehicle support. They must fight on their feet and tab to an objective carrying all their equipment with them. Thus the emphasis of P Company is placed on tabbing, the crucial ability to traverse the rough terrain of a battlefield on foot, at speed and while carrying a heavy pack and weapon. As well as conducting timed battle marches over hilly country at muscle-aching pace, the aspiring recruit must also pass an aerial assault course, known as the Trainasium, where misplaced footing could lead to the prospect of a fall and serious injury. Other tests include completing an arduous 1.8-mile cross-country course attached to a log the size of a telegraph pole by a length of rope to simulate a team resupply of heavy ammunition. 'Coming off the log' is a cardinal sin and is likely to lead to failure. Another event is called milling, a form of boxing where each candidate is expected to unleash sixty seconds of controlled aggression on his opponent by landing as many blows on him as possible. Sixteen-ounce boxing gloves and head guards are worn, but relentless attack is the objective. The Parachute Regiment is the only conventional unit in the Army that practises milling and most recruits finish covered in blood. When I did it aged twenty-nine I was no exception.

I can remember stepping into the arena where my fight took place. The blood of those who had already completed their milling session was spattered across the floor; the referee from the P Company staff was also covered in it. When you are told to fight you attempt to unleash hell on your opponent. You don't try to box, you just keep hitting him, you don't give quarter and you don't take defensive or evasive measures: if you do, you will fail. I fought a Sapper corporal from the backstreets of Manchester; he was several inches taller than me and had been deliberately chosen to fight me. My misfortune in being drawn against him was not only due to my comparative lack of physical stature, but also due to the fact that I was an officer. One of a party selected to fight the officers on the course, my opponent had been revved up by the P Company sergeant major. He had declared that this was their 'one chance to legally hit an officer'. He told them not to waste it, stating that he wanted to see our blood on the floor.

My opponent set about doing just that. Given the adrenaline that was pumping through my body, I didn't expect the first blows to hurt as they landed square on my nose, jaw and the sides of my head. But they did, each one a blinding flash of light and pain. I milled back furiously, my arms rotating like windmills. My nose was bleeding, my right eye was cut and my contact lenses had long since been knocked out. Sixty seconds of unabated, mutual unrestrained aggression seemed like a lifetime; when it was over I was absolutely knackered. I was covered in blood and I had lost, but I had also demonstrated an ability to keep going forward and show that I could take damage. Battered and beaten, I had passed the test, as putting me into a position to face superior odds and carry on while getting hurt was exactly the point. I took some mild satisfaction that I had at least blackened one of my opponent's eyes.

If the recruit survives the endless tabs, Trainasium, log race and the milling, he still has to pass an 18-mile endurance march over mountains and a team race carrying a stretcher weighing 160 pounds over a 5-mile cross-country course. The stretcher race is designed to replicate evacuating a casualty under battle conditions and, as in all P Company events, it is conducted at a breakneck pace and no one is expected to walk. Even if candidates get to the end of Test Week, they still have to face being told whether they have performed well enough to earn the right to wear the maroon beret. In the particular case of officers, passing the physical aspects of the tests is not enough. Officers are also assessed on their aggressive leadership ability and those who are not seen to go the extra distance to motivate and lead other candidates will fail. Regardless of rank, the average pass rate for a successful Para recruit is under 40 per cent. Attempts to increase the pass rate by reducing standards have been vigorously resisted and it is a quality line that is fiercely guarded.

My own experience of P Company taught me that there is no such thing as an average Para recruit. They are all different, which is one of the key strengths of the regiment. However, common character traits of a successful recruit are that they are mentally robust and have a keen determination to succeed. Without these they will not pass. A very fit recruit might fail P Company because he stops when his body is in pain and it is telling him to give up. However, an averagely fit recruit can pass the same course because he has the guts and determination to ignore the pain and keep going with all he has got. P Company not only sets the benchmark entry standard, but it also provides a thread of shared experience that ties all members of the Parachute Regiment together. Regardless of rank or seniority, each paratrooper knows that the comrades he serves alongside have been through it, which generates a status of elite membership based on common self-sacrifice and mutual trust and respect. However, while passing P Company earns the individual the right to wear the maroon beret, it is not an end in itself. Full club membership rests on passing subsequent parachute training.

A trainee must complete eight static line jumps from a C-130 Hercules aircraft, including one at night. The challenge of passing the basic parachute course is mental rather than physical. Parachuting may be the Paras' preferred method of battlefield entry, but it is a stressful and fear-inducing activity. Paratroopers must learn to cope with the anxiety of a forthcoming jump. For me it was always a remote nagging sensation that started as we prepared our equipment and walked up the tailgate ramp into the back of a waiting Hercules. It increased as the aircraft took off and began to approach the drop zone (DZ). I would experience an appreciable dread as the Parachute Jump Instructors (PJIs) told us to stand up and fit our equipment in the back of the aircraft.

Often being the senior officer aboard, I was expected to jump first. Thoughts of obstacle hazards on the DZ and emergency situations would fill my head as the para doors were opened and I was greeted by the blast of the slipstream. The PJIs would shout to be heard over the roar of the four turbo-prop engines as they checked our kit and hooked up our static lines. At the front of a 'stick' of forty-four paratroopers I would be manoeuvred into the open door, one hand across my emergency reserve and one foot forward on the jump step. As my eyes fastened on the dispatch light, my peripheral vision would be filled by the ground rushing past several hundred feet below. Apprehension would suddenly be replaced by a feeling of aggressive determination, the atmosphere of the moment of leading men out of the door, the need to focus on drills and the desire to get the jump done. The dispatch light would flash 'red on' to indicate the aircraft was making its final run in to the DZ at 800 feet. Twenty seconds later it would flash 'green on'. Instantaneously the PJI would shout 'Go!' and I would be out of the door and tumbling in the aircraft's slipstream.

As I desperately tried to keep my feet and knees together to avoid causing the rigging lines of my chute to twist, the static line would snap open a billowing canopy of silk which would be followed by a heartening jerk. Sudden relief that I had a properly functioning parachute would be almost immediately replaced by the need to steer away from other jumpers. A collision with any one of them risked provoking the collapse of a chute. Once in clear airspace, heavy equipment containers fastened to waists and legs are released to dangle weightlessly below each jumper on a 10-metre strop. But the elation of an open parachute, avoidance of collision and the momentary joy of floating in the air are all too quickly replaced by the imminent prospect of landing. The ground seems to rush up to meet you at alarming speed. You try to assess your drift, then give up and adopt a tight position and prepare to accept the landing. It arrives a moment later with a sudden crunch capable of knocking the air from your lungs. I always landed like a sack of potatoes, but if I managed to walk off the DZ without significant injury I was content to consider it a successful jump.

Unlike sports parachuting, military jumping is an unpleasant process. Anxiety concerning potential injury or death is accompanied by having to endure the hot and cramped conditions in the back of an aircraft. Eighty-eight men together with their equipment are wedged in like sardines, each man's legs interlocking with those of the paratrooper sitting opposite him. The low-level flight to the DZ might take several hours and airsickness afflicts most as the aircraft flies low level all the way to the target area. The unpleasantness is compounded by having to stand up inside the fuselage in full kit weighing anything up to 140 pounds, for up to forty-five backbreaking minutes as the aircraft twists and turns to make its final approach. To refuse to jump is a court martial offence, but refusals are rare, as those who are likely to do so will have been weeded out during training. Few Paras enjoy the experience of parachuting, but all of them have proved that they are prepared to conquer personal fear and go through the door of uncertainty when required.

The Paras' potency also stems from being able to draw on their short but impressive history. What the regiment has achieved in just over sixty years since its formation provides a founding base for the continuing ethos of the Paras. It is inculcated in recruits from the moment their training starts. They are consistently reminded of the fact that they were a force raised in 1940 to operate cut-off behind enemy lines, outnumbered and where the odds would be stacked against them. The fact that the golden thread of the regiment's past is still so recent gives it a greater significance than that of older regiments, where memories of what was achieved at Waterloo are of little relevance to young soldiers. Many of the veterans of famous Parachute Regiment battles such as Normandy and Arnhem are still living and regularly mingle with today's paratroopers at pass-off parades and regimental events. Evidence of the importance of the regiment's past achievements is also reflected in the behaviour of the serving soldiers. Unlike other regiments, the single soldiers adorn their rooms with regimental emblems and montages of past endeavours. In addition, many paratroopers have the regimental cap badge tattooed on the top of their right arm to provide an enduring reminder of who they are both to themselves and to others.

The Parachute Regiment's training, history and fierce professional pride made it an obvious solution to my aspirations to engage in a more ambitious form of soldiering. However, my initial jubilation at being seconded to the Paras having already passed P Company was checked by the daunting prospect of joining a new and very different military club to the one I had been used to. Driving down to Dover one sunny autumn morning in 2000 was akin to going to a new school on the first day of term. I tried to suppress the butterflies in my stomach as I drove up the steep hill by Dover Castle which was the home of the regiment's 1st Battalion.

I need not have worried. I had joined my own regiment at a time when it was still traditional for more senior officers not to talk to a new officer during his first six months in the mess. The ethos in 1 PARA was completely different and I was made to feel welcome from the moment I arrived. The members of the battalion who I met first were the Late Entry officers. Joining as private soldiers, or what the regiment refers to as Toms, each had been commissioned from the ranks and had a minimum of twenty years' individual experience from across the regiment's three battalions. As Toms or junior NCOs, each of the men I met that first morning had fought through the gorse line at Goose Green with 2 PARA, or had climbed the rocky slopes to fight on Mount Longdon with 3 PARA during the Falklands War. Their experience gave them every reason to doubt me as an outsider, yet they immediately took me into both their company and confidence. It was something that set the more general tone of my arrival and was to last for the three years of my tour with 1 PARA. It also reflected one of the Parachute Regiment's key strengths of diversity. An eclectic mix of people, they have a progressive willingness to take in outsiders; when I joined 1 PARA, six other officers in the battalion had started their careers in other regiments, including the commanding officer.

Taking over command of the ninety-odd paratroopers that made up B Company 1 PARA was equally heartening and it felt like coming home. The soldiers I commanded were bound together by common characteristics of being fit and highly motivated. They had an edifying propensity to talk endlessly about going on operations and being 'Ally'. In essence this meant having a certain martial coolness and taking pride in looking and acting like a paratrooper. No one seemed to care about your heritage, as long as you didn't harp on about it and you were fit, good at your job and cared about the blokes. There were no armoured vehicles to maintain, duties were kept to a practical minimum and eschewed ceremonial bull. The training was also imaginative and demanding. My time in 1 PARA took me back to Northern Ireland for other emergency tours and we conducted exciting exercises using live ammunition in Kenya and Oman. Serving in 1 PARA also took me back to Iraq in 2003 during the invasion to remove Saddam Hussein. Although it came late in the day, my experiences of serving with 1 PARA were all that I expected soldiering to be. Consequently, it felt like a natural process to transfer to permanent membership of the regiment towards the completion of my tour as a major.

Leaving 1 PARA ended with promotion to lieutenant colonel. After completing a 6-month visiting fellowship at King's College I assumed the post of Military Assistant to the Assistant Chief of the General Staff. My boss was Major General David Richards, who was Mike Jackson's right-hand man in the MOD and was later to command all NATO troops in Afghanistan, including 3 PARA. But taking over command of 3 PARA was still over a year away and my duties as his military assistant were to keep me extremely busy. At the time we were in the process of re-organizing the infantry regiments, fighting hard to minimize the impact of the MOD's continual cost-cutting exercises and dealing with the ministerial fallout of fighting a vicious insurgency in Iraq. However, my thoughts were never far away from the prospect of getting back to field soldiering and becoming CO of a Para battalion. In fact I thought about it constantly. It was a very bright spot on the horizon amid a sea of ministerial bureaucracy driven by process-obsessed senior civil servants. I was still a long way away from the coal face of real soldiering but I knew that I was going back to it. Tubes and buses as a means of getting to and from work were soon replaced by running to and from the MOD with a weighted pack on my back. As I struggled to manage a training regime around long office hours, I marvelled at how much fitness I had lost since wearing a suit in Whitehall.

Had I joined the Paras at the start of my career I might have expected to have served in all three of the Parachute Regiment's regular battalions. Having not done so, 3 PARA was an unknown quantity and I set about trying to get a feel for the nature of the unit I was about to command. If you took off a paratrooper's DZ flash (a coloured square patch of cloth sewn on to the right arm to mark members of individual battalions on a parachute drop zone), you might not see any appreciable difference between them. The Paras' basic ethos, physical toughness and high standards of robust soldiering are the same, but in the collective identity of a battalion differences do exist. The unique nature of 3 PARA went beyond the mere fact that they wore a distinctive emerald-green DZ flash. I knew that 3 PARA enjoyed a reputation for being the wildest of the regiment's battalions. Although widely respected for its high standards of professionalism and preference for field soldiering, it had a tradition of having an even more relaxed attitude to discipline and dress and an intolerance of military bullshit than 1 and 2 PARA. These attributes were captured in the battalion's nickname of Grungie 3. When I sought the advice of several senior Parachute Regiment officers who had already commanded Para units, virtually all of them commented that they considered 3 PARA to be a particular command challenge compared to the other battalions in the regiment.

It was a reputation that was well known throughout the rest of the Army and was reflected in the legendary antics of the infamous 3 PARA Mortar Platoon. The heavy weapons platoons of any Para battalion enjoy a particular inner sense of identity based on their specialization and relative maturity compared to the more junior Toms in the rifle companies. In 3 PARA's case this was especially true of the Mortar Platoon, where every member who served in Afghanistan has '3 PARA Mortars' tattooed on their wrists. Once famous for their wild parties, a certain gay abandon of normal conventions and breaches of discipline, the myth was founded on events long past. However, it still managed to attract several non-specific mentions on my CO Designates Course which was designed to prepare lieutenant colonels like me for command of their units. I wasn't sure whether to be quietly proud or somewhat alarmed that no other student's future command was getting mentioned. I decided on the former, believing that it is perhaps better to command a battalion that has a reputation rather than a unit without one. Nevertheless I drove through the gates of 3 PARA for the first time with a certain amount of trepidation: taking command of any unit is a daunting challenge, but assuming charge of the freewheeling, wild-child battalion that 3 PARA was vaunted as being was something else.

Added to this, 3 PARA had been warned off to be ready for

operations in Afghanistan. Rumour of an impending deployment had been rife since the start of the year and had been building during my last few months in the MOD. The government had announced its intention to shift the focus of the UK's military effort in Afghanistan to Helmand Province in the lawless south of the country. Two months before joining the battalion, it had finally been confirmed in military circles that 3 PARA would be the first UK Battle Group to deploy into the area. The precise dates of our deployment were still to be confirmed, as an official announcement by John Reid, the Secretary of State for Defence, was still to be made in Parliament. The delay in the announcement was subject to diplomatic negotiations with some of our European partners, many of whom were less than convinced about deploying into the more dangerous south. However, what I did know was that we would be expected to begin operations in Helmand some time in the early spring of 2006.

The uncertainty of our deployment combined with the unknown quantity of my new command was not helped by the fact that, with the exception of the Regimental Sergeant Major (RSM), I knew virtually no one in 3 PARA. Nigel Bishop was thirty-nine years old and had been my company sergeant major in 1 PARA. We had served together in Northern Ireland in 2001 and in Iraq two years later. 'Bish' was a committed professional. He had initially joined 3 PARA as a new recruit fresh from the regiment's training depot in 1983. He had arrived at a time when 3 PARA's exploits in the South Atlantic were still a central part of the battalion's identity. Those who joined after the conflict felt a sense of inadequacy for not having been there. Bish felt it particularly because he joined 4 Platoon in B Company whose platoon sergeant, Ian McKay, had won the VC. McKay died along with many others of the platoon fighting on Mount Longdon. By the end of his first year in 3 PARA Bish had managed to prove that he was a capable young soldier and became accepted by the Falkland veterans. I rather hoped that it might take their new CO a little less time to fit in.

I arrived at the battalion's barracks in Colchester at the end of October 2005 and soon began to realize that there was nothing wrong with 3 PARA's reputation, as some of those whom I had consulted suggested. Within the first week I had visited each of the battalion's six companies and I had also spoken to each of the battalion's three messes, made up of the corporals, SNCOs and officers respectively. I had also addressed the whole battalion to tell them who I was, what I expected of them and what we would be doing to prepare for operations in Afghanistan in the coming months. Speaking to the massed ranks of several hundred paratroopers assembled before me might have seemed like a nerve-racking experience. But it wasn't; I wanted to be there and relished my good fortune at being CO of 3 PARA. The one matter that might have concerned me was my own personal foot-drill. Marching in step, halting and turning about with parade square regulation was something I had always been crap at from the day I started my Army career at Sandhurst. However, I was at 3 PARA now and it was a relief to know that I could dispense with having any anxieties about it. In essence foot-drill was not something they did much of and certainly not something they put any great store by.

When I came to address the battalion for the first time I had a feel for the manner of the men I commanded. They were different, even from their equally professionally committed regular sister battalions, 1 and 2 PARA. Self-assured and freewheeling in their approach, they cared passionately about what was important in soldiering and disregarded the unimportant. They were my type of soldiers and I was now one of them. In essence they were my 'angels with dirty faces'; relaxed in style, their attitude to soldiering appealed to me. All they wanted to do was go on operations and be tested in combat; like all Paras it was what they had joined the Parachute Regiment to do. Different though they were from the rest of the pack, if they had any malaise it was nothing to do with their diversity or approach. What they suffered from was a concern that the impending deployment to Afghanistan would turn out to be a disappointment.

The men of 3 PARA had also taken part in the 2003 invasion of Iraq and had been disappointed by their experiences there. It had been billed as a combat operation, but they saw relatively little of the action and felt that their combat talents had been wasted. As a result, they were wary of having high expectations for Afghanistan. Many were concerned that it was being billed as a peace support operation. Their disappointment with Iraq and concerns that Afghanistan might turn out to be another damp squib reflected a general frustration in the regiment, as it had seen relatively little action since the Falklands War in 1982.

The regiment had not deployed during the first Gulf War and had not been involved in operations in Bosnia with the rest of the Army in the mid-1990s. The balance had been addressed to some extent by 1 PARA's operations in Kosovo and Sierra Leone in 1999 and 2000 and 2 PARA's deployments to Macedonia in 2001 and Kabul in 2002. However, despite two commendable but brief actions, fought by A Company 1 PARA against the Westside Boys in Sierra Leone and C Company of the same battalion in Iraq in the last few days of their tour, these events had fallen short of the combat operations that Paras aspired to be part of.

At the time we knew little of the prevailing circumstances in Afghanistan. Reports from British military planners already based there suggested the area we were to deploy into was relatively peaceful. At the time I shared the same nagging doubt of my soldiers that Afghanistan could turn out to be another anticlimax. This was not helped by a comment made by John Reid in March 2006, a month before 3 PARA deployed. In an interview with BBC Radio 4's *Today* programme he stated that: 'If we are here [in Afghanistan] for three years to accomplish our mission and have not fired a shot at the end of it, we would be very happy indeed.' Events were to prove that he could not have been more wrong.

2

Afghanistan

On initial inspection, Afghanistan has little to commend it as a country worth fighting and dying for. Located in one of the most inhospitable and remote corners of the earth, it is the world's fifth poorest state and has become synonymous with instability, terrorism and war. It is a land of rugged mountains and dusty desert plains, where the winters are bitterly cold and the summers are blisteringly hot. It possesses few of the prerequisites of a modern nation-state. There are no railways, no national health system and the road network is restricted to one two-lane potholed circular highway. Racked by crippling poverty, a quarter of Afghan children die before reaching the age of five and 75 per cent of its population are illiterate, including many of its government officials. Afghanistan is a country of some 32 million souls made up of different tribal races of Tajiks, Uzbeks, Hazaras and Pashtuns. Fractured by ethnic and complex tribal divisions, they are a people bred of a tradition of hostility to central authority. Even with the presence of over 50,000 NATO troops, the writ of the Afghan government and the rule of law extend little beyond the capital of Kabul. Unity of national purpose is infrequent and brief; when it comes, it has taken the form of bloody resistance to outside interference.

Yet in geopolitical terms, Afghanistan has long been an area of global strategic interest. Sitting at the crossroads of Asia, the armies of Alexander the Great, the Arab Empire and Genghis Khan have all passed its way. Its borders were born of the imperial squabbles of the Great Game between Russia and Britain in the nineteenth century. But like many armies before them, the British Army's previous interventions in Afghanistan have echoed with failure and less than successful conclusions. The First Anglo-Afghan War (1839–42) resulted in the humiliating retreat from Kabul and the destruction of an entire British force. The second, between 1878 and 1880, saw the rout of a British brigade, while the third, in 1919, ended in inconclusive skirmishing with rugged Pashtun tribesmen along the North-West Frontier. Followed by the bloody Soviet occupation in 1979 and their ignominious withdrawal a decade later, these more modern incursions suggest that Afghanistan is a place where the normal rules of great power intervention do not apply. But after al-Qaeda's attack on the Twin Towers in September 2001, Afghanistan once again attracted international attention.

With the fall of the Taliban regime at the end of 2001, as a consequence of America's hunt for Osama bin Laden, NATO agreed to take command of an international stabilization force in 2003. Known as ISAF (International Security Assistance Force), the force was centred on Kabul and included a British infantry battalion. Initially, NATO's mission remained confined to the capital and was kept separate from the American counter-terrorist operation in the south and east of the country. However, in opening up a second front of the war on terror in Iraq, the US took its eye off the ball in Afghanistan. Failing to stabilize a country in desperate need of reconstruction and development after three decades of war, it allowed a resurgent Taliban to return. Having already expanded into the north and west of Afghanistan, NATO agreed to extend its mission into the lawless and more violent south and east of the country. NATO troops would first assume responsibility from the Americans in an area known as Regional Command South. This included the provinces of Oruzgan, Zabol, Kandahar and Helmand and was to be completed by August 2006.

The decision to send 3 PARA to Afghanistan formed part of Britain's agreement to switch its military contribution from Kabul and send a United Kingdom Task Force (UKTF) of 3,700 troops to Helmand Province. The troops were drawn from 16 Air Assault Brigade with 3 PARA providing the infantry element of the force. As well as its normal complement of three rifle companies and specialist platoons of heavy machine guns, anti-tank missiles, mortars, reconnaissance patrols and snipers, the battalion expanded to become an all-arms unit of nearly 1,200 personnel. Two troops of Sappers from 51 Air Assault Squadron of the Royal Engineers provided demolition and construction capabilities. Communication experts came from the Royal Signals, and combat medic technicians from the Royal Army Medical Corps (RAMC) reinforced 3 PARA's own medics. The artillery was made up of a battery of six 105mm Light Gun howitzers from 7th Parachute Regiment Royal Horse Artillery (7 RHA). D Squadron of the Household Cavalry Regiment, equipped with Scimitar reconnaissance vehicles and Spartan personnel carriers, provided a light armoured capability, which was further strengthened by a mechanized infantry platoon from the fledgling Estonian Army. As an airborne unit, the Battle Group would move by CH-47 Chinook troop-carrying helicopters. It would fight in conjunction with airpower and artillery, which would be coordinated by Fire Support Teams (FSTs) of forward air and ground fire controllers from both the Army and RAF. Close air support was provided by A-10 tank-buster aircraft and AC-130 Hercules Spectre gunships from the US Air Force. Other NATO countries also provided fixed-wing air support, including Harrier jets from the RAF. Apache helicopter gunships from 9 Regiment Army Air Corps provided further firepower.

With the exception of 16 Brigade's Pathfinder reconnaissance platoon and small teams sent to mentor the Afghan National Army (ANA), the Battle Group constituted the fighting element of the UK force. But while the formation of the Battle Group would enhance 3 PARA's ability to respond robustly if attacked, the mission was conceived as a peace support operation. Any use of force was seen as a last resort and actually having to hunt down the Taliban was not part of the mission. Instead our intended role was to provide security to protect the development and reconstruction efforts of the Provincial Reconstruction Team (PRT) that would deploy with the task force. This was made up of both military elements and development specialists from the Department for International Development (DFID) and the Foreign and Commonwealth Office (FCO). It was hoped that their efforts would win over the loyalty of the majority population of the Pashtun people and allow the government in Kabul to extend its authority into the province. Intelligence reports as to the reception we would receive when we deployed into Helmand were patchy and inconsistent. However, most assessed that Helmand was relatively peaceful. At one planning meeting conducted in Kandahar before the deployment I presented my proposals in the event of being attacked. At the end of it, I was taken aside by a Royal Marines colonel who worked for the UK's Permanent Joint Headquarters (PJHQ) who were responsible for planning the overall UK deployment. He told me that I shouldn't worry too much, as he did not anticipate there being any trouble from the Taliban in Helmand.

I reflected on his assessment as I boarded the aircraft that was taking me back to the UK. I had just spent two days in the neighbouring province of Zabol where US forces were being attacked by the Taliban on a routine basis. The PJHQ team were adamant that the situation in Helmand was very different. As we taxied to our take-off point, the repatriation service for a Canadian soldier who had been killed in action was taking place. His flag-draped coffin was being carried up the rear ramp of a waiting C-130 Hercules with a white-robed chaplain officiating over the first stage of his final journey home. In the background fighter jets were screaming down the main runway on their way to a 'Troops in Contact' situation, or what the Americans called a TiC. My mind clouded with doubts as I watched the red-hot glow of their engine exhausts disappear into the night on their way to help someone in trouble. I thought about what I had seen and heard in a country with a history of fierce resistance to foreign intervention. It made me doubt that the Taliban had such notions of there being any sort of peace to be kept.

Lessons of history and a potentially flawed mission concept were not my only concerns: I was also vexed that part of the UK's mission was the stated intent of eradicating the cultivation of opium poppies. Ninety-three per cent of the world's opium comes from Afghanistan, with half of the crop being grown in Helmand. Most of it enters Western cities in the form of heroin and it feeds the habit of 95 per cent of Britain's addicts. Eradication might have provided a compelling additional motive for intervention in Helmand, but in an agrarian society of dirt-poor farmers, most of the population have little alternative to growing opium. Trapped in a cycle of poverty, intimidation and feudal drug-crop bondage to those who rule with the gun, many are forced to grow poppies. I did not doubt that the opium trade helped fuel the Taliban insurgency by providing money for arms and insurgent operations, but my concern was that the political imperative of eradication ignored the impact it would have on the people who grew it. I raised this issue with the Whitehall officials who briefed us on the mission. I asked them how we would be able to gain the consent of the people if we were seen to support operations that threatened the very basis of their livelihood. Despite these concerns, the advocates of official policy insisted that reducing the production of opium was an essential part of the mission. However, they were not going to be one of the poor buggers at the sharp end, reaping the consequences of a policy that threatened to drive every Afghan dependent on poppy production into the arms of the Taliban.

It was clear that the struggle that we were about to become engaged in would be psychological as well as physical; it would be a battle for the hearts and minds of the people. I doubted whether eradication would help achieve this. We would be operating in a guerrilla landscape, where our protagonist lived and operated among the civilian population. He would be indistinct from them until he decided to attack us. He would do so at a moment of his own choosing, before melting back into the obscurity of the community from whence he had come. While we would be constrained by the norms and conventions of war, such as the Geneva

Convention, the insurgent would not. The local population would be their support base. They would provide him with shelter, supplies and information. He would win their favour through popular appeal, propaganda or intimidation. If we fired at him and in the process hit civilians, we would lend support to his claim to be defending the people from an external aggressor. But in turn he would not be immune to using civilians as deliberate human shields or punishing them savagely for supporting foreign troops.

Operating in an alien culture where they are unaware of who is friend and who is foe, death for a British soldier may be just around the corner. A seemingly benign situation can change into an extremely dangerous one in a heartbeat. Is the car approaching the patrol at speed driven by a suicide bomber? Is he ignoring the warning signs because he is an illiterate farmer who fails to appreciate the apparent perception of threat his actions are generating, or is he intent on blowing himself and the patrol to kingdom come? The soldier who has to make the right split-second decision of whether to open fire or not might be eighteen years old, but there is no time to refer the fast-developing situation to higher authority; he has to decide. How he reacts is compounded by the fact that he may not have slept for days, he may be scared and suffering from combat fatigue. This is a snapshot of the type of environment modern soldiers are expected to operate in. It places the most enormous pressures upon them, but despite the relative immaturity and limited world view of many of them, soldiers are expected to get it right regardless of the complex and challenging situations they face. I doubted that Afghanistan would be any different.

Lacking a clear, defined picture of exactly what might await us, we prepared to do everything. Our training took us from the frozen moorland streams and forestry blocks of Northumberland to the rocky desert of Oman. We focused on re-honing the basic skills of field-craft, shooting and combat first aid, as well as progressively building up training that integrated all elements of the

Battle Group together. The artillery of I Battery fired over open gun sights in support of live firing company attacks and the Engineers practised their infantry skills. We placed an increased emphasis on fitness to improve our endurance to cope with the rigours of climate and fatigue. We paid particular attention to the issue of the Rules of Engagement (ROE) so soldiers would know exactly when they could and could not fire their weapons. I wanted my soldiers to have the confidence to open fire when necessary and without hesitation. But I also wanted them to be clear on the constraints and know that any abuse of a civilian or captured insurgent would not be tolerated. I based this aspect on a number of scenarios.

One hypothetical example involved a soldier advancing through a village at night where intelligence reports indicated a high threat of attack. In the shadows he sees an individual who lifts what looks like a weapon towards him. There is no time to shout a warning and the soldier fires and hits the target. The figure turns out to be a shepherd armed only with his crook. As tragic as the action would have been, I told my soldiers that I would support them in such a situation if an individual honestly believed that his life, and those of others, had been under threat at the time. However, I also told them that if in the same situation they had decided not to fire, but then kicked the shit out of the shepherd for giving them a scare, they would find themselves in front of a court martial for abuse. It was a clear message and I felt that my soldiers understood and accepted it.

We also based much of the training on the experience of visiting the Americans in Zabol. We built mock Afghan compounds using hessian cloth and poles to replicate high mud-walled enclosures of small one-storey buildings. This allowed us to practise patrolling in a village environment, where the soldiers used the Pashtun phrases they had learned and practised showing respect for the customary norms of an Islamic society. Paratroopers played angry elders, weeping women and enjoyed putting their comrades under pressure to see how they would react.

We pored over maps and set about learning as much as we could of the terrain over which we would operate. Sandwiched between Kandahar Province to its east and the empty quarter of Nimruz Province running to the Iranian border in the west, Helmand is principally a landscape of flat, featureless desert that extends southward to its border with Pakistan. To its north, the rugged mountains of the Hindu Kush begin to rise sharply and unannounced from the desert plateau. The mountains' melt waters feed the Helmand River that cuts a diagonal line down its centre from the north-east to the south-west. It brings the one source of nature's life-blood to the population of a million-odd people scattered among the villages that cling to its fringes and tributary wadis. The river flows all year and its water is sucked out by wells and irrigation ditches to feed belts of fertile land that extend for a few hundred metres on either side of its banks. These are the only areas that can support life and the thin riverside strips of countryside resemble a sun-baked version of the Norman bocage of fruit orchards, cultivated fields and hedged banks among a myriad interconnecting mud-walled alleyways and lanes that criss-cross between the village compounds.

The only tarmac road in Afghanistan cuts Helmand at its mid-northern point. Highway One provides a tenuous link to Kandahar City and Herat to its north-west. To the south of the road lie the provincial capital of Lashkar Gah and the second city of Gereshk. As the province's major population centres, these two towns were initially considered as the principal focus of our operations. But 100 kilometres to the more barren north of the road lie the towns of Now Zad, Musa Qaleh, Sangin and the Kajaki Dam complex. The three towns are situated in the heartland of the Pashtun tribal areas that defy provincial government control from Lashkar Gah. Whoever held them would be seen to have de facto control of the north of the province. The significance of the Kajaki Dam lay in the fact that its ageing hydro turbines provided the one source of electric power to Helmand and much of Kandahar Province. If it fell to the Taliban it would enable them to place a stranglehold on much of the region. The remoteness of these locations and their strategic draw were to make them the future pressure points of our operation. They were to become the scenes of vicious fighting in the months ahead and were to witness much bloodshed. But as I sat in Colchester their significance to our operations lay in the future. As I studied maps and intelligence reports about Helmand, the enormity of the task the Battle Group faced began to dawn on me. Even if our operations could be limited to the region around Lashkar Gah and Gereshk as planned, it was still a huge area for the limited number of troops that I would have at my disposal.

I had no doubt of the Battle Group's potency if all its assets were concentrated together. But the plan was that the Battle Group be split up into three individual company groups. One would garrison a Forward Operating Base (known as a FOB) at Gereshk, one would operate from our desert base at Camp Bastion and would be sent out to secure areas for the PRT's development operations. The third would be held in reserve in the event of either of the other two requiring reinforcement. We would be stretched very thinly. Despite being reinforced by a platoon of infantry from the Royal Irish Regiment and thirty men from 4 PARA, the regiment's TA Battalion, we would still deploy seventy-five soldiers short of our full complement of infantry.

The command structure that we would operate under also had a number of deficiencies. Although the headquarters of the UKTF was made up of staff officers from 16 Air Assault Brigade, it was not going to be led by their normal brigade commander, Brigadier Ed Butler. Command had instead been given to Colonel Charlie Knaggs. Knaggs was an Irish Guardsman who had been brought in at short notice because the UKTF would be subordinate to a Canadian multinational brigade commanded by a Canadian brigadier called David Fraser. The MOD and PJHQ felt that it would be inappropriate for a British brigadier to work to a Canadian one, so they appointed Knaggs because of his subordinate rank as a colonel. Butler still deployed to Afghanistan as the senior British representative, but, much to his chagrin, was given no tactical control of UK troops. It was a confusing command arrangement. In essence it meant that I had three bosses to work to: Butler because he was the senior British officer and my normal boss, Fraser because he was the multinational commander and Knaggs because he was my immediate superior officer. It would not be an easy arrangement for Knaggs either. He would have to take orders from Fraser, but would then have to get them endorsed by Butler. To make the issue even more complicated, Fraser reserved the right to give me direct orders as one of his multinational Battle Group commanders without reference to Knaggs. I in turn would then still have to get Butler's endorsement as the senior British officer who was expected to clear the political use of UK troops with PJHQ.

I felt for Butler. He had been my immediate boss since arriving in 3 PARA and his frustration at not being able to command his own brigade that he had trained and prepared was an understandable source of personal irritation. Over the months before the deployment we had built up a good relationship based on mutual trust. He had a level of highly relevant operational experience and I respected his judgement, but my command link to him would now be convoluted rather than direct. At forty-four he was one of the Army's youngest and brightest brigadiers and had lobbied unsuccessfully against the decision to split him away from tactical command of the troops on the ground. Butler had already seen active service in Afghanistan and had a hands-on approach to soldiering that appealed. Although self-assured, and despite his experience, he was always willing to listen to the advice of others and demonstrated an obvious interest in the welfare of the ordinary soldiers under his command. However, his role in Afghanistan would base him in Kabul and divorce him from direct command of front-line operations. I would still have access to him, but I would have to work through the sensitive layers of two other senior officers, which would require diplomacy and tact. Designed to meet the political expediencies of multinational sensitivities, it was not a logical command arrangement that would have been recognized in any decent military staff college.

Besides the lack of manpower and overly complex command structure, we had not received our full allocation of specialized communications and electrical equipment that we knew would be vital for operating in Helmand. I was also convinced that the six Chinook troop-carrying helicopters and their authorized flying hours that were being made available for the operation were insufficient. As well as hindering operational flexibility, the lack of helicopters would increase risk. It would force greater reliance on vehicles and if we were forced to drive when we should be flying we would be more vulnerable to mines and roadside bombs. The issue was raised up the chain of command and supported by Butler, but it fell on deaf ears in the MOD and PJHQ. I thought it a sufficiently serious matter to raise with the Prince of Wales when he came to visit the battalion two months before our departure.

Before leaving, the Prince asked me if I had any concerns about the forthcoming operation. 'Sir, among other things we don't have enough helicopter flying hours for what we need to do and that is going to increase risk,' I said. The Prince asked me if I wanted him to raise it with the Secretary of State. I paused for a moment. I realized that I would be breaching the chain of command which wouldn't take kindly to a mere lieutenant colonel raising such issues with a prince. 'Sir, I would be very grateful if you would.' The Prince of Wales rang John Reid the next day, which was a Saturday. By Monday the shit had hit the fan in the MOD and cascaded back down to me. The Prince's intervention didn't lead to an increase in flying hours, but plenty of people in the ministry were upset with me from the Secretary of State down. I got a mild bollocking, but a more severe rebuke was forestalled by Ed Butler, my brigade commander, who shared the concern about helicopters. Perhaps more significantly, General Sir Mike Jackson spoke up in my defence.

Notwithstanding these concerns, by the end of March we were trained, packed and ready to go, but we would not be deploying together. PJHQ planned to send 3 PARA into theatre a company group at a time, with the other attached arms following on there-after. It meant that the Battle Group would not be complete in Afghanistan until July. A concern that insufficient logistics and accommodation would be in place to support us was cited as the reason for the delay. To me it seemed to smack of over-caution. Operations are always subject to the art of what is logistically feas-ible, but we were an expeditionary army and I was content to begin operations with a minimum logistic footprint. I needed to have all my combat power available even if that meant being a little less comfortable. We were Paras after all and were prepared to rough it if we had to. But my arguments to fly everyone in together were ignored and it meant that I had to make the difficult decision as to which company would deploy first. I elected to take my Tactical Headquarters party (Tac) with A Company Group and the reconnaissance Patrols Platoon in first, much to the chagrin of the other elements of the Battle Group which would have to follow on later.

For those of us who would deploy first, the final few days before our departure were filled with last-minute preparations and saying goodbye. People wrote their wills, updated their personal insur-ance, completed next-of-kin cards, received final inoculations and spent precious time with family and friends. I spent an evening briefing the wives of the soldiers. I wanted to tell them something about where their husbands would be going and what we would be doing. It was a difficult balancing act: while I didn't want to alarm them, I also didn't want to mislead them about what we might be entering into. I said that we weren't going looking for trouble, but that we were more than capable of looking after ourselves if we came across it. I concentrated on explaining the stated mission and focused on how our task was to spread goodwill, win consent and provide security for development and reconstruction. We were about to find out if our stated mission and intelligence assessments stacked up to reality.

3

Mission Creep

We landed under the cover of darkness, the lights of our C-17 transport aircraft switched off to assist in countering the surface-to-air missile threat as we descended into Kandahar Airfield (KAF). I sat with helmet and body armour on and pushed myself back into my seat, hoping that the C-17's anti-aircraft missile system was as good as the RAF claimed it to be. The threat was brought home to me by the sudden lunge of the aircraft as it made a steep dive approach for an ear-popping tactical landing. I watched the stripped-down hulk of the Chinook we carried in the cargo hold sway and strain against its restraining chains as the C-17's nose tipped violently forward. The Chinook was one of six helicopters that we would rely on to move around Helmand Province. Its arrival promised a busy few days and nights for the RAF engineers who would work flat out in the baking heat to refit its 60-foot rotor blades. The Chinooks would provide part of the resupply chain to our new desert base of Camp Bastion located 140 kilometres to the west of KAF. They would also provide the lifeline to the isolated FOBs from which my companies would patrol. The sudden bump of the C-17's landing gear and the slackening of the restraining chains indicated that we had arrived in Kandahar.

The airfield was to the south of Kandahar, Afghanistan's second city and the spiritual home of the Taliban, where the one-eyed cleric Mullah Omar had started his radical Islamic movement in 1994. His initial motivation had been to rid the city of brutal mujahideen warlords. Once loosely united against the common foe of the Soviets, the various guerrilla commanders had soon begun fighting each other during the civil war that followed the Russian withdrawal. Their methods were vicious and they extorted the local people for their own aims. Stringing up two feuding mujahideen commanders from the barrel of a tank for their part in the kidnapping and raping of a small child, Omar's vigilante actions gained popular support from a Kandahari population sick of anarchy and lawlessness. With a growing basis of mass appeal and the aid of Pakistan's intelligence services, the Taliban eventually swept to power capturing Kabul from the Northern Alliance two years later. The brief respite from the lawlessness of mujahideen infighting was soon replaced by the oppressive rule of Omar's regime and the Taliban's fanatical application of sharia law, which was to bring misery to millions of Afghans.

But this was before 9/11 and America's intervention in Afghanistan. The main hangar at KAF still bore the pockmarked bullet holes of the Taliban's last desperate stand against the US-backed Northern Alliance forces in December 2001. The new occupants were now American servicemen in T-shirts and desert combat fatigues who sweated in the heat to service helicopters. The scattered remains of the wreckage of Soviet aircraft added to the feel of previous ownership of another age, as did the mines that remained in the more distant edges of the runway. There they remained as potential hazards to the unwary military jogger who ignored the small red triangular signs that warned of their presence.

With the departure of its previous occupants, KAF had become a thriving military commune of multinational forces. Americans, British, Canadians, Dutch and Romanians all held tenancy. It was constructed with the single pursuit of preventing a return of the Taliban and had no real sense of permanence about it. Prefabricated buildings and the thousands of ISO shipping containers that lined dusty roads gave the place an air of an international Wild West gold-rush town. The plywood structures, vehicle parks and vast rows of tented accommodation were punctuated with the odd pizza outlet or Green Bean café. There was also a barber's shop, where the tired-looking Ukrainian female hairdressers gave the impression of having travelled too far and seen too much. These snatches of home-like comfort seemed to be the single most important obsession for many of the thousands of allied rear-echelon support troops based there. To me KAF had little to commend it and I developed a loathing of the place as soon as we arrived. My abiding memory was of the dust and the pervasive smell of human shit. The latter was particularly powerful if the wind blew from the west where a vast pool of human excreta churned in an open sewage treatment plant. It was strong enough to make you gag even when some way away from it. Rumour had it that a Romanian soldier had swum the 50 metres across the pool for the sum of $500. Perhaps it was the result of spending too much time in KAF. We would be only too glad to get out of the place and deploy forward to our own camp in Helmand Province following several days of briefing and planning.

After a night of getting used to the sights and sounds of KAF and breathing its unpleasant air, my planning team linked up with the UKTF headquarters for an initial briefing. In line with the plan already drawn up by the PJHQ team sent forward to Afghanistan before our arrival, UKTF envisaged that our opera-tions would be restricted to a limited geographical area of Helmand. Extending from Camp Bastion in the west to the town of Gereshk, 40 kilometres to its east, and to Lashkar Gah, another 40 kilometres to the south, this area formed a triangular shape on a map. The 'Triangle' represented less than a sixth of the total area of Helmand, but included the province's major population centres. It was also where the limited authority of the provincial Afghan government was most established. Consequently, it was decided that the reconstruction efforts should be concentrated there. Limiting operations to the Triangle also reflected the fact that 3 PARA currently had only one company group in Afghanistan. The other two companies were not due to arrive until the end of June and the rest of the Battle Group's artillery and light armour would not arrive until early July. It was decided that my one available company would occupy an FOB near Gereshk (FOB Price) and concentrate on patrolling into the town. Once again I voiced my concern about the delayed arrival of the rest of the Battle Group which meant that we would lack the means to reinforce any troops that ran into trouble with the Taliban. But PJHQ were adamant that the full deployment would remain spread over the coming months.

PJHQ were also still wedded to the view that Helmand was relatively quiet. This optimism ignored the fact that the province was an unknown quantity of ungoverned space. The authority of the provincial government did not extend beyond Lashkar Gah. Consequently, there had been no one to challenge the Taliban and the tribal warlords who exploited the drugs trade. The province had a nominal Afghan National Police force, but the majority of ANP were actually a corrupt ragtag collection of tribal militiamen who owed their allegiance to their clan chiefs. A small American PRT had worked out of Lashkar Gah. Driving around in Humvees, it had come under sporadic attack on at least one occasion, but it was not charged with establishing a permanent presence of authority to challenge those who ruled by the gun.

This uneasy status quo was fundamentally altered by the appointment of a new provincial governor called Mohammed Daud. An engineer by trade and lacking any influence with the local tribes, he became increasingly frustrated by the slow arrival of the UK troops. After the murder of four of his district administrators in the north of the province, he was determined to flex his muscles. A month before we landed in KAF he established an ANA FOB in the heart of the Sangin Valley 90 kilometres to the north of Highway One. It was located just to the south of the town of Sangin. The town was the urban centre of the opium trade in Helmand and the base threatened the autonomy of those involved in the production and distribution of the drug. A coalition of the Taliban and hostile local tribes had threatened to overrun the base. On two occasions they had massed to attack and the situation had only been restored by the timely reinforcement by an infantry company from a Canadian armoured infantry unit based in Kandahar. The establishment of the base was part of a sequence of events that was to lead inextricably to drawing the British out of the Triangle into the more dangerous north.

Even though we had only arrived in limited numbers, there was increasing pressure for us to take over command of the base. My problem was that I had insufficient troops to relieve the Canadians and meet my commitments in Gereshk. I also wanted to avoid having to guard another location where 50 per cent of the allotted troops would find themselves being tied up in static force protection duties. Additionally, I was concerned as to whether we had the necessary helicopters or flying hours to keep the base properly supplied. I discussed this with the UKTF staff who agreed with the need to get the deployment of my complete Battle Group brought forward. They also left me with the task of working out how I could provide a security effect in the Sangin Valley without getting fixed into guarding and supplying another base. Our mission was already becoming increasingly ambiguous. PJHQ clung stubbornly to the view that we should be restricted to conducting peace support-type operations in the Triangle, while the prevailing geopolitical situation suggested otherwise. The majority of my Battle Group was still sitting in the UK and the lure of Sangin was a potentially dangerous prospect. Although I didn't have the necessary troops to do much about it, Sangin was intimately connected with the security of the rest of the province and I knew that we could not ignore it. Uncertainty and resource scarcity were becoming constant themes of the operation. It was something that we were getting used to and I consoled myself that at least we would be getting away from the ever-present stench of KAF's sewage works.

After a week of constant re-planning in KAF, it was good to leave the place eventually and head to our base at Bastion. Our new home was not yet complete, but I saw it as preferable to KAF. The airfield had come under a number of night-time rocket attacks while we were there. They were largely ineffective, but did nothing for a decent night's sleep, which was fast becoming a premium. If the rocket impacted somewhere within the perimeter the explosion would wake you up. The attack siren and over-excited people thumping on your door to tell you to get to the shelters would then keep you from getting back to sleep. Lack of rest bred a fatalistic streak in me and I always elected to stay in the 'safety' of my lightweight sleeping bag. Although lacking blast protection, it provided a brief respite from the interminable planning and briefings that extended late into the night.

We flew west over dramatic sand dunes that were painted an ochreous red by the early morning rays of the sun. Each dune cast a shadow that made the terrain seem like a shifting sea of sand that had become frozen in time. As the desert slipped past beneath us Afghanistan's history of foreign intervention weighed on my mind. While still at school, I remembered the beginning of the Soviet occupation in 1979 and their ignominious withdrawal ten years later. As an undergraduate I had attended lectures given by ITN's correspondent Sandy Gall about reporting and living with the mujahideen in the 1980s. He had also briefed the officers' mess in Colchester before we left for Helmand. Although our mission was very different, it was strange to think that we were now where the Russians had failed. In turn I thought about the British Army's own history of involvement in Afghanistan. I conjured up an image of the 44th Regiment's last stand on an isolated icy rocky outcrop at Gandamak during the First Anglo-Afghan War in 1842, so dramatically captured in oil by William Barnes Wollen's famous painting which hangs in the museum of the Essex Regiment. I thought of Wollen's canvas depicting doomed British redcoats huddled together as the last remnants of the Army's inglorious retreat from Kabul. In their midst an officer with the Queen's Colour wrapped inside his tunic steadies his men, as knife-wielding, black-robed Afghans surge up the slopes to hack them to pieces amid the snow and haze of musket powder smoke.

Our route out to Helmand also took us over the former battlefield of Maiwand, where a British force under General George Burrows had been annihilated by an Afghan army during the Second Anglo-Afghan War in 1880. The final leg of our flight took us over the town of Gereshk, where the Battle Group's A Company was now based having deployed forward from KAF a few days before. Through one of the Perspex portholes of our helicopter I caught a brief glimpse of the large mud-walled structure of the fort where a small British garrison had been besieged for sixty-three days in the same year. It was finally relieved by Lord Roberts's epic march through the summer's scorching heat to avenge Burrows's defeat at Maiwand.

The Soviet invasion demonstrated Afghanistan's continuing geopolitical importance, but now the Afghans' jezails and Martini-Henry rifles had been replaced by AK-47s. This Russian-designed automatic weapon was the ubiquitous weapon of choice of the Taliban and the rugged Pashtun tribes that make up the majority of Afghans in southern Afghanistan. War against the Soviets had also supplied and taught them to use other modern weapons of war: mines, RPG launchers that could propel a rocket grenade several hundred metres and could destroy a tank, as well as mortars and roadside bombs. The tradition of Afghan fighting prowess and access to these weapon systems made me wonder what our own future held for us.

Discerning the Taliban from simple armed tribesmen and pro-government militia would be an incredibly difficult task. The Taliban wore no uniforms and were made up of a complex pot-pourri of guerrilla fighters whose motivations and groupings varied. There is a popular misconception that the Taliban wear distinctive black turbans, but this ignores the fact that it is also the chosen headdress of many of the policemen and tribal militiamen with whom we were to work. Additionally, some of the Taliban's younger foot soldiers wore no turbans at all. The Taliban's ranks undoubtedly included ideologically committed fighters who took their orders from the movement's senior commanders based across the border in the Pakistani city of Quetta. But this hardcore element was indistinguishable from the local fighters made up of poor rural farmers. In essence these farmers provided part-time fighters, or what we came to refer to as the '$10 Taliban'. They might attack for reasons of money, intimidation or a fear that their culture of independence and their reliance on opium production were under threat. Additionally, tribal affiliations and feuds emanating from the Pashtunwali code of blood debt and martial honour, so deeply ingrained in the Afghan psyche, might also provide the motivation to fight us. I put these thoughts to the back of my mind as our helicopter bled altitude and dropped to 50 feet for a 'nap of the earth' approach into Camp Bastion that had begun to loom as a hazy smudge on the horizon.

4

Hearts and Minds

Our helicopter kicked up a cloud of brown swirling grit as we skirted Bastion's perimeter of high-banked sand and an outer fence of razor-wire coils. It was obvious that the camp was still in the process of construction and represented a 2-square-kilometre building site. The place was a hive of building activity and the unloading of stores and equipment. Some arrived by C-130 Hercules on a rough desert strip by the side of the camp. The heavily laden transport aircraft gouged deep furrows in its crushed stone gravel surface when they landed, often shredding the tyres of their undercarriage in the process. The less valuable commodities, such as food, bottled water and the heaviest equipment, were brought in overland by Afghan haulage contractors in their 'Jinglie' trucks. Each truck was adorned with brightly painted symbols and garish charms which jingled and shone in the desert sun as they made their tortuous journey along Highway One from Kandahar. The road was prone to ambush but, despite the risks, the contractors were paid good money and kept on coming.

I toured the camp with Bish and visited the field surgical hospital. As we looked round the tented wards we were impressed by the facilities and the professionalism of the medical staff, although I hoped that we would not be putting much business their way. It was late morning as we left to head back to our headquarters tent, known as the JOC, which stood for Joint Operations Centre, and was located at the other end of the camp. Although still only April, the heat was oppressive and the rising temperature summoned up what the Afghans called the 100-Day Wind from the surrounding

Dasht-e Margo, which in Pashtu means the Desert of Death. It would blow incessantly from the south-east for the next twelve weeks. Gathering speed, it would cast up rising dust devils high into the sky. These swirling columns of sand could knock a man over and the wind covered everything in a thin layer of talcum-powder-fine sand. It matted hair with grit and clogged air-conditioning units which struggled to remain operational in the scorching heat.

The JOC would become the control centre for all 3 PARA's operations. Consisting of two long tents, it became increasingly more crowded as new members of the headquarters staff turned up to fight for space among the long folding tables, collapsible canvas chairs, computer systems and map boards that lined its sides. At one end of the tent a large rough-hewn wooden 'bird table' had been constructed by the Engineers. Situated close to the various radio nets, it was spread with maps and constituted the central hub of the headquarters from which operations were planned and coordinated. The air conditioning groaned and failed in the first few days and the heat became unbearable, especially when the tents were crammed with nearly a hundred people who attended daily briefings, planned, organized logistics and manned the communications systems. Apart from the mist of sand that blew in from every pore in the canvas sides, the air was filled with the sound of crackling radio nets and the thump of generators.

The sand and the heat were to become a factor in every aspect of living in Bastion. But, as the camp began to grow, its occupants could benefit from living in a secure environment with freshly cooked meals, access to the internet, phones, makeshift gyms and regular showers. All these facilities could be used when people were not on guard duty, manning operation centres, servicing vehicles or conducting operations beyond the confines of the perimeter. However, with the exception of the logistic support troops, the vast majority of the Battle Group would soon find themselves spending little time at Bastion. Instead they would live in Forward Operating Bases (FOBs), in Afghan district centres or from the vehicles in which they patrolled the desert. The relative creature comforts of Bastion would rarely be available to these soldiers. Instead austere conditions and constant danger would become the daily fare of the environment in which they lived.

With four days to go before our first patrol, I spent my time overseeing the continued planning, shuttling back to KAF for update briefings and hosting what was to become a continual stream of visiting VIPs who all wanted to come and look at Bastion. The Secretary of State for Defence was one of the first to arrive. I spent about an hour briefing John Reid, who chastized me playfully about raising the issue of the lack of helicopters with the Prince of Wales. Reid rang me out of the blue a few days later to ask me if our communications systems were robust enough for the task of operating over the long distances we would be expected to cover. He was due to brief the families of the six Royal Military Police soldiers who had been killed in Iraq in June 2003. At the inquest into their deaths the coroner's findings had criticized the lack of available radios, which might have allowed them to call for help when the Iraqi police station they were working in was taken over by an armed Iraqi mob that subsequently murdered them. Reid wanted to be able to tell the families that lessons had been learned and the Army now had adequate radios in place. I told him that our communications systems were more robust, but reiterated the point I had made during his visit, that we were still short of many satellite radios. He focused on my comment of improved robustness, but said nothing about the outstanding shortages before he rang off. I had been with 1 PARA as the second-in-command in Iraq when the six Royal Military Police had been killed. I had attended the coroner's inquest in October as a witness. That night I noted the conversation in my diary and wondered whether I would be attending future coroner's inquests as a CO.

The morning of 29th April dawned clear and bright, like most other days in Bastion, although by midday the air would be full of sand which would reduce visibility to some 20 metres and blot out the sun. What was different about the 29th was that it was the anniversary of the fall of the Taliban and the date of our first patrol into Gereshk. I had already flown down to join A Company in FOB Price the day before, as Tac and I would be going out with them to get a feel for the ground. After being briefed by Will Pike who commanded A Company, I set off to the ranges with Tac to check-fire our weapons on the base's makeshift range. I noticed a small group of other British soldiers who were also zeroing their weapons.

One made a point of introducing himself to me and immediately started with a charming apology. He was a friend of one of my other company commanders and had lobbied hard to get a slot with 3 PARA as a company second-in-command; I was short of one and he came highly recommended so he was offered the job. However, at short notice a vacancy in his old unit turned up which offered him the chance to deploy to Afghanistan with them. Consequently, we were still short of a deputy for B Company. I had been disappointed by his sudden change of heart that left us down a key commander, but I understood his decision; every soldier wants to deploy on operations with his own unit and mates he knows and trusts. Additionally, I was won over by his Irish charm and the fact that he had the balls to come and speak to me when he could have said nothing and I would have had no idea who he was. The meeting stuck in my mind because the next time I was to come across this affable Irishman it would be in far more tragic circumstances.

The next day the patrol set down next to a large mud-walled compound on the outskirts of Gereshk. The downwash of the rotor blades kicked up dust and debris and scattered it around the compound. Goats dashed for cover and a donkey brayed frantically as the mechanical monster roared into their midst from the sky. Local Afghans came to their doors and looked at us with astonishment, as I hoped the reed-matted rooftops on their outhouses would survive our arrival. As the helicopter departed we waited for A Company's troops to fan out and secure our route to the town's hospital. A small boy rushed up to us with a jug of water. A broad smile broke out on his face as we made a show of accepting his hospitality by washing our faces and hands in the cool liquid. We thanked him in Pashtu and began moving out of the compound once A Company reported that they were in position. He ran proudly back to his father who acknowledged our gratitude. However unannounced and unorthodox our visit to his compound had been, the Pashtunwali code of *Melmastia*, which meant showing all visitors hospitality, appeared to have been satisfied.

We patrolled along the town's main street in soft desert hats with our Para helmets slung in order not to appear threatening. I moved with my Tac group of key staff officers, signallers and immediate force protection among a bustling traffic of white Toyota Corollas, minibuses, motorbikes and donkeys. We passed open-fronted shops which seemed to sell everything from food produce to transistor radios. Small, angelic-looking children went barefoot on the stony ground as they gathered around us. Excited by our presence, they asked for sweets and took an intrigued interest in looking through our rifle sights. We greeted everyone we met, aware that this would have been the first foreign foot patrol most of the inhabitants of Gereshk were likely to have seen since the days of the Russian occupation.

Our salutations of *Salaam alaikum* were met by some with the customary response of *Alaikum es salaam*, the right hand spread to the chest, and the odd handshake. Other people watched as we passed; some smiled and waved as they went about their daily business. Old men, all wearing beards and black or white turbans, sat on their haunches drinking tea from small glass cups. Some smoked and others fingered prayer beads. Their look was one of mildly interested curiosity. No doubt they had seen soldiers of many different armies pass this way before. However, the expression on the faces of the younger men caught my attention. They tended to be dark looks of suspicion and hostility; few were prepared to return our salaams. They lounged in the background looking menacing. A few solitary individuals watched and followed us from a distance either on motorbikes or on foot. They stopped occasionally to speak into mobile phones; it was obvious that we were being 'dicked', a term borrowed from experiences in Northern Ireland where local inhabitants kept tabs on a patrol in Republican areas and reported its movements to the IRA. Did these men represent our first encounter with the Taliban? It was impossible to tell.

The women were the one element of the population that ignored us completely. We didn't see their faces; shrouded head to foot in burkas of light powder blue, they looked out on the world from behind the meshed eye slits of their veils. They followed dutifully a few paces behind their menfolk or scurried past without sparing us a second glance. To do so would have incurred the wrath of their male relatives. Any engagement with us, or any other unrelated man, would be seen as besmirching family honour and could have resulted in a savage beating, or worse.

We found the hospital quickly enough. It lay behind a thick iron gate in the middle of a shady compound off the main street by the side of the canal. The canal drew water from the Helmand River that cut north to south through the town. We loitered dutifully at the bottom of the steps while we waited for the hospital administrator to come and meet us. His hooked nose and dark olive skin suggested he was a Pashtun, but he wore western clothes, a doctor's white overcoat and spoke excellent English. He willingly invited us into his facility. I left my rifle at the door and entered with Harvey Pynn, the unit's medical officer, and Major Chris Warhurst, who was the Engineers' squadron commander. We were given a short tour of the hospital wards and a small operating theatre. It was basic but functional. At the end of the tour I asked the doctor about his concerns as we drank sweetened black chai (tea) from the small glass cups that we had been given.

The doctor mentioned that he had difficulty accessing basic drugs, and that the hospital had no modern washing facilities so everything had to be done by hand. We had all noticed the soiled

sheets in the ward we had visited but asked why the large industrial washing machine we had passed in a corridor was still sitting
in its cellophane wrapping. He told us that it had been given to the
hospital by the US government agency USAID, but that they had
failed to install it before the American PRT had withdrawn from
Helmand. Chris Warhurst chipped in that some of his Engineers
were dual trained as plumbers and electricians and he was pretty
confident that he could get it working. Harvey Pynn also said that
he could afford to provide many of the drugs the hospital needed
from our own supplies. The doctor nodded enthusiastically and
we all felt elated. Within the space of a few hours on the ground
we had identified a quick-impact project that would make a small
but near-immediate difference to the lives of some of the locals.
Additionally, it could be delivered from the Battle Group's own
resources.

The rest of the patrol was uneventful. We visited the main ANP
police station and met the police chief before patrolling back to
FOB Price on foot. As we climbed out of the town we passed one
of the ANP checkpoints on Highway One. The policemen wore
uniforms and allowed the traffic to pass unmolested. No doubt
when we were out of sight, they were likely to slip back into civilian clothes and extort bribes again. The corruption among the
ANP was endemic and it made us all wonder how we could ever
help the Afghan government win the consent of its people when
it had a police force that was little better than a bunch of bandits.

My thoughts about the ANP were quickly replaced by the sheer
mental effort of moving through the oppressive midday heat on
foot. Wearing body armour with ceramic bulletproof plates, plus
water, ammunition and weapons, each man carried in excess of 50
pounds in weight. Those with radios carried nearer 70 pounds. I
noticed how I quickly began to lose situational awareness of what
was going on around me, as I concentrated on putting one foot in
front of the other. FOB Price's watchtower loomed in the hazy
distance 5 kilometres away across the sun-baked and featureless
gravel plain. As the sweat ran in a constant stream under our body

armour we sipped persistently from the tube-fed CamelBaks on our backs, but the FOB didn't seem to get any closer.

The first patrol into Gereshk might have been uneventful but 150 kilometres to our north events were unfolding that heralded the end of the poppy season and the start of the fighting season. With the final gathering of the opium sap, the Taliban were beginning to call on the services of tribal males of fighting age who were no longer needed to work in the fields. While we were tabbing out of Gereshk, the isolated northern town of Bagran had fallen to the Taliban. A day later an ANA convoy on Highway One was hit by an improvised explosive device (IED) on the outskirts of Gereshk. Four Afghan soldiers were killed and another three were injured. I was walking past the medical centre when the casualties were being brought in. The grisly residue of the body parts of the dead were being lifted out of the back of an ANA pick-up truck. They had been placed in large surgical bags and the face of the severed head of one Afghan soldier stared back at me through the transparent green plastic. It was a sobering reminder of the human cost of conflict and I saw it register on the living faces of two of my young Toms who were passing in the opposite direction. It focused my mind on the fact that Afghanistan was a dangerous place and that we couldn't afford to take anything for granted. This was brought home to us the next day when the second patrol we conducted came under fire as we left the town.

In comparison to the battles that were to follow, the incident was of little significance. But it confirmed that not everyone welcomed our presence. However, I felt that a significant proportion of Afghans would be willing to support our efforts to help their government if we could demonstrate that we could bring security and development to their society. The reconstruction and development of Helmand Province was going to be a mammoth and long-term task. However, 'quick-impact projects', like getting the washing machine working, could go a long way to gaining goodwill and consent. They would help develop relationships, understanding of our mission and demonstrate that promises of helping to provide a better life were more than just empty rhetoric. Like the finite supply of goodwill that existed at the start of the invasion of Iraq, the support of those Afghans willing to give us a chance to make a difference would quickly evaporate if we weren't seen to deliver tangible improvements.

Our one concrete act of goodwill from that first patrol would be worth more than a thousand empty promises. Consequently, DFID's reaction to our proposed project at the hospital caught me by surprise. I was informed that it was not UK policy for the Battle Group to get involved in such issues. I was even more surprised when I was told that no one else was going to do it either. The department countered with thin arguments that any small-scale immediate help on our part would generate a dependency culture among the Afghans. They also maintained that it would raise ethical issues of the military being seen to get involved and further argued that such work should be left to the non-governmental organizations (NGOs). I told them that I didn't mind who did it as long as someone did. However, the NGOs were incapable of doing anything about it as most had stopped working in Helmand as a result of the prevailing security situation.

I was dismayed. Such viewpoints were based on DFID's limited experience in places such as Africa and the Balkans. But Afghanistan wasn't Africa or Bosnia and their edict bore no resemblance to the reality of conditions on the ground. They naively assumed that the Afghans would wait patiently for the promise of long-term social and economic development and reconstruction once security had been established. It was an attitude summed up by one DFID official who commented that they 'didn't do bricks and mortar'. But lofty ideals of an intangible Western-style society with a functioning bureaucracy, national health service, women's rights and higher education meant little to a populace where the majority of government officials couldn't read, village schools were burnt to the ground by the Taliban and the most basic ailments went untreated because of a lack of access to drugs. Perhaps I shouldn't have been surprised by DFID's attitudes given that their personnel were not allowed by FCO policy to go beyond Lashkar Gah, where the security situation was relatively benign. Consequently, they were never in a position to assess a situation on the ground, having seen it themselves. Two months later DFID were to withdraw their personnel from Helmand altogether, having never visited the hospital.

Where we had failed to gain traction with DFID, PJHQ had at least begun to recognize the changing dynamics in Helmand and speeded up the deployment of the rest of the Battle Group. B and C companies arrived in May with a troop of gunners. But the rest of the artillery and light amour would not arrive until July. The companies were beefed up with a Fire Support Group (FSG) of heavy machine guns, snipers and Javelin missile anti-tank launchers. C Company replaced A Company patrolling in Gereshk and B Company's platoons were used to provide small immediate reaction forces. One platoon was used to provide the Helmand Reaction Force (HRF) and to escort the Medical Emergency Resuscitation Team (MERT). This consisted of an anaesthetist and other specialist medical personnel who were on standby to fly out with the casualty evacuation helicopter to stabilize casualties during the flight back to surgery in Bastion. A second platoon was held at KAF and could only be released for use by the Canadian brigade headquarters. This meant that A Company were my only uncommitted forces.

Although we had only patrolled into Gereshk, the first three weeks in Helmand had passed in a blur of frantic planning activity. Constant briefings, readjustment of force groupings and replanning had meant that the headquarters staff had got very little sleep. The troops in the companies fared little better. People were constantly stood up for missions, given orders and then stood down again in response to changing threats and newly emerging tasks. My problem was that I had precious few troops to meet them. Even when the rest of the Battle Group arrived I would only ever be able to field a few hundred boots on the ground at any one time. This number would be reduced further as two weeks of R and R kicked in and routine illness, injury and combat casualties started to take their toll. It was a reality the governor, Mohammed Daud, found hard to grasp. He had envisaged that all the 3,000-odd UK troops would be available to fight. However, the vast majority of them were support troops in the form of medics, headquarters staff, logisticians and technicians. Spread between Kabul, Kandahar and Helmand, their job was to sustain the fighting troops. Of the entire British force the ratio of support troops to fighting personnel who could be expected to fire their weapons was probably less than 3:1. With the changing threat in the north, it meant that we had to rely on the ANA. But they were still arriving from Kabul, were not trained fully and lacked much of their equipment. Regardless of these shortfalls, they were sent to relieve the Canadians in FOB Robinson, 7 kilometres to the south of Sangin.

Just before last light on 17 May reports began to come in that Musa Qaleh was under attack. The town's district centre was in danger of falling to the Taliban and over thirty of the ANP defending the compound had been killed. The situation was temporarily restored by the dispatch of 200 pro-government militiamen supported by the UKTF's Pathfinder Platoon. The attempt to take Musa Qaleh was a clear indication that the Taliban had launched a concerted effort to challenge Kabul's authority and kick the British out of Helmand.

If anyone wanted confirmation that the poppy season was over and the fighting had started, it came two days later when a French military convoy was ambushed as it attempted to make its way from the Kajaki Dam down to FOB Robinson. It was a costly mistake that left three Frenchmen dead and led to the subsequent killing of a score of ANA soldiers. The survivors had made it to FOB Robinson where they had been picked up and flown to Bastion. Two of the French officers came into the JOC to give us an indication of exactly where they had been ambushed. Clearly suffering from battle shock, they had difficulty pointing out the precise location of where they had lost men and vehicles. We gathered round the bird table to listen to their story. They had just rounded a bend when the first AK bullets began to smack into the side of their trucks. Following standard anti-ambush operating procedures, they had attempted to drive through the killing area. But the ambush extended for virtually the whole 7 kilometres of the route down to Sangin. As they pressed on they faced an increasing gauntlet as every 'man and woman' seemed to come out of their compounds to fire at them. The added complication was that twelve of the ANA soldiers who had been with them were missing.

Will Pike was tasked to fly out with A Company and attempt to recover any sensitive equipment and casualties he could find. Lacking precise locations they overflew the length of the route. But with darkness approaching and running short of fuel, they were forced to turn back empty-handed. The search resumed the next morning. They located and destroyed some of the vehicles, but there was no sign of the dead Frenchmen. Before returning to Bastion, Will was also tasked to look for the missing ANA soldiers, who had managed to make radio contact with their headquarters. Located on a lonely hilltop, they reported that they were surrounded by Taliban and were running low on ammunition. Without a map they were unable to confirm their position. The forlorn group of men were asked to describe their location, but without coordinates it was like looking for a needle in a haystack among the rugged peaks of the Sangin Valley. The Chinooks circled likely areas to no avail until the radio contact went dead. It was a salient lesson against using predictable routes that invited ambush. Sadly it was a mistake that was to be repeated.

Several days later it was reported that the town of Now Zad was about to fall and Daud was keen to get British troops up there as fast as possible. I gave Major Giles Timms a warning order that the task was likely to fall to him and what he had left of B Company. Then I dashed off to grab my kit and make my way to the incoming helicopter that had been sent to pick us up for an emergency meeting at UKTF headquarters. After arriving in Lashkar Gah, we were briefed by Charlie Knaggs on the situation. The twenty ANP in Now Zad's district centre were claiming that they were about to be overrun and Knaggs wanted me to come up with a plan to establish a 'platoon house' in the town. He believed the presence of thirty-odd British soldiers would bolster the mettle of the ANP. Butler was there too, but he was keen to demonstrate that he was keeping out of the tactical business and allowed Knaggs to lead. Darkness had already fallen and there was no time to eat. I asked him to give me four hours to conduct my estimate before I back-briefed him on my plan. We then started to work through the night.

We briefed Knaggs and Butler four hours later. I made the point that defending the district centre compound would take more than a platoon. Having studied detailed air photographs, I realized that all thirty men would be required to guard the place. It also needed a quick reaction force to fight off attacks and reinforce vulnerable points, and sufficient troops to conduct local security patrols and build up its defences. The troops stationed there would be vulnerable and isolated. They would need to be able to operate as an independent sub-unit capable of holding out on their own until reinforcements could be sent to relieve them. This required specialist communications back-up, in-place logistics, medical support including a qualified military doctor, a mortar team to provide fire support and an FST to call in close air support if required.

In short, it needed all I had left of B Company. In an ideal world I would have liked to have given them an additional platoon, but there was none to spare and they would have to go as they were. I said I was confident that we could hold the compound. But I pointed out that it would stretch the Battle Group and fix troops to another static location at the expense of having an effect elsewhere. Additionally, more of our precious helicopter hours would be burnt up keeping the compound supplied with rations and ammunition. My one condition of taking the place on was that the UKTF found B Company a doctor to go with them.

If someone got hit, they would be at the end of a fragile evacuation chain and having a doctor attached to them would improve their chances of staying alive until the casualty evacuation helicopter got to them. Knaggs and Butler accepted what I had to say and agreed to get us a doctor, but stressed the political importance of being seen to support Daud. Despite my reservations at the tactical level, I understood the bigger picture imperative of backing up the governor. They asked when B Company could go. 'The company is already standing by and the assets are in place to lift them. Let me get back to Bastion and give them final confirmatory orders and we can be on our way,' I replied.

I flew up with B Company. Like most provincial Afghan towns in Helmand, Now Zad is a nondescript collection of flat compounds built of mud bricks. The dusty main street was flanked by an assortment of small open-fronted shops. Most of them were trading and, with the exception of the barefoot children, the townspeople went about their business seemingly unconcerned by our presence. There was not much evidence to suggest that the ANP were about to be overrun, although many of them had fled. Some had since returned including the district police chief, Hajji. I went round the sangars, which were built-up defensive positions of sandbags, breeze blocks and wood, that B Company had started to construct and spoke to the blokes. I noticed some empty AK-47 cases, indicating that there had been some fighting, but there weren't enough to suggest that a full-scale battle had taken place.

I chatted to a TA soldier from 4 PARA who had put his struggling acting career on hold to come out to Afghanistan with 3 PARA. It was a bizarre situation. He sat on a sandbag with his GPMG covering the street below us. While he talked of the few bit-parts he had got in soaps like *EastEnders* and whether he might do better to take up a career in law, a donkey and cart passed below and a small scruffy Afghan child called up to us. In the distance the bright orange globe of the setting sun began to sink below the rocky skyline and the Muslim call for prayer echoed out across the town. It all seemed a long way from the sets of Albert Square.

I had supper with Hajji later that night. As we sat cross-legged and ate a very palatable goat stew with thin leavened nan bread, he talked of his desire to use our helicopters and jets to help him hunt down the Taliban. He maintained that they had left the town but believed that they lurked in the surrounding countryside. He seemed unconcerned about socio-economic issues, such as education, which was strange since all the town's schools had been closed or burnt down by the Taliban. He dismissed my suggestion that we should hold a *shura*, the Afghan word for meeting, with the local tribal elders. He argued that all of them had recently fled the town and would be too frightened to talk to us. Hajji did not necessarily strike me as a man who could be trusted, but I agreed that we would conduct joint patrols with his motley crew of ANP who, since B Company's arrival, had abrogated complete responsibility for defending the compound. I noticed the adolescent who served us chai. He had foppish henna-dyed hair that fell over eyes that had been highlighted with make-up. His enhanced femininity stood out in contrast to the rugged Pashtun features of the rest of the ANP and suggested he was Hajji's catamite. He was probably a local boy and I doubted he was a willing volunteer for the role, which would have done little to enhance the legitimacy of Hajji in the eyes of the townspeople.

While B Company watched and waited in Now Zad, the rest of the Battle Group continued to respond to the whims of Daud. On 24 May A Company had flown a rescue mission to extract one of the governor's supporters from the Bagran Valley after he claimed that he was being surrounded by Taliban. Again this consumed scarce helicopter hours and we were becoming increasingly reactive to events. I wondered whether we had got too closely into bed with the governor and were in danger of chasing shadows. We were deviating from the principle of using our forces to have an effect in one area which could then be secured for development. In response to pressure from Daud, Knaggs was also talking about establishing platoon houses in Musa Qaleh and at the Kajaki Dam as both areas were perceived to be under increasing threat. I didn't doubt it, but our resources were finite and were already dangerously overstretched.

3 PARA were also coming under increasing pressure from the Americans to contribute to Operation Mountain Thrust, the brainchild of Major General Ben Freakly. He was responsible for overseeing the conduct of all military operations in southern Afghanistan before the US handed over to NATO command. Freakly was David Fraser's boss and he wanted to clear the Taliban out of Helmand Province in a series of search and destroy operations before ISAF took over. An American battalion was already operating between Musa Qaleh and Bagran, but Freakly wanted the Brits to target some of the Taliban leaders who were believed to be hiding out in farmers' compounds to the south of the US troops. They were considered to be 'high-value targets' and it was assessed that each had a band of hardcore fighters who would fight to the death to prevent their commanders from being captured.

We were continually stood up and then stood down from conducting a number of raids to kill or capture insurgent commanders. Each involved lengthy planning sessions, only to be called off after hours of painstaking staff work had been put into planning each mission. Freakly also wanted to get British troops up to the Kajaki Dam to relieve an American company that had moved into Musa Qaleh. I conducted reconnaissance missions to both locations, which only served to confirm that I would need a company to hold each of them. However, with what was left of B Company in Now Zad and C Company in Gereshk, I had only A Company's two platoons of infantry, an FSG and one section of mortar barrels left uncommitted.

In order to free up more troops we stripped men from the Gurkha Company which was tasked with guarding Bastion. Replacing them with support troops and soldiers from a Danish squadron that had been attached to UKTF, we formed two additional platoons of infantry. One was sent to take over from Giles

Timms's men in Now Zad which had remained relatively quiet since his arrival. The other was sent up to reinforce the ANA troops and the troop of guns that were in FOB Robinson. Freeing up B Company from Now Zad meant that I had the makings of a second sub-unit available for operations. It would allow the Battle Group to contribute one company for strike operations as part of Mountain Thrust and dispatch another one to Musa Qaleh if we had to.

5

The Hornets' Nest

Of all the strike options that we worked up, Operation Mutay was the most straightforward and represented the most efficient use of the scarce resources available. This dictated its selection from a host of other targets we had looked at. The location of the target compound was only 3 kilometres from Now Zad, which meant it could be used as a launching pad for the outer cordon and would help us to achieve surprise. I could use the Gurkha Platoon stationed there to drive the short distance to provide an outer security cordon position to the north. They could take Hajji's ANP with them to provide the important Afghan face to the operation, although to preserve security they wouldn't tell him what we were about until just before they left. The Patrols Platoon could also stage through the district centre the night before. This would allow them to move smartly in their WMIKs to secure the southern cordon position the next morning. Consequently, we could snap the outer cordon ring shut quickly before inserting A Company by helicopter a few minutes later to secure the compound for the Engineers' search team.

This provided us with the best chance of catching the targeted Taliban leader if he was at home. Intelligence also suggested that the man we were after would have only a few of his fighters with him, as it was believed that the bulk of the insurgents had been dispersed by the arrival of British troops at the district centre. Based on this assessment I was confident that we had sufficient troops to provide the net to capture them and the necessary combat power to overmatch them if they decided to fight. What

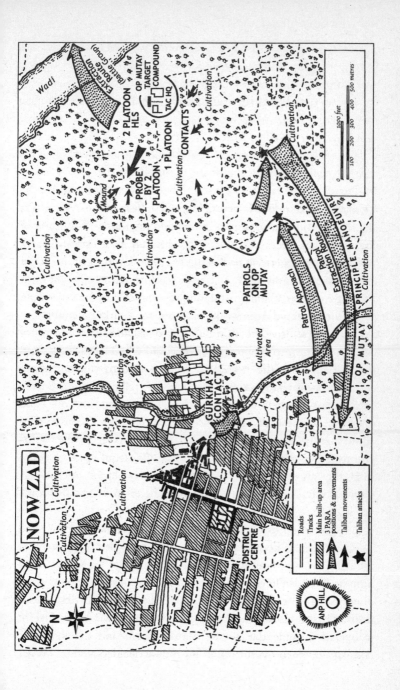

I didn't realize was that the intelligence we had been given was wrong and the Taliban leader we were after had all his fighters with him. By the time we had made the decision to launch the operation the intelligence had already been revised to indicate that over sixty Taliban were well established in the area. The revised estimate never reached us.

The Taliban picked up the movement of the vehicles from the district centre in Now Zad from the moment they drove out of the gate. They had posted men who had been monitoring our presence in the district centre since the first troops had arrived there. But this was unknown to the Gurkhas. As the Taliban spotters reported the Gurkhas' movements on their 'push to talk' radios, other fighters were rushing to grab AKs and RPGs and get to the routes the troops were likely to use. The surrounding vegetation, compound walls and ditches dictated that any vehicle movement would be constrained to only a limited number of approaches. If the Taliban moved fast enough they could ambush them. Two Russian-made belt-fed PKM machine guns were moved to cover the exit junction of a dry wadi bed that the Gurkhas had begun to move into.

Another group of ten to twelve Taliban moved at right angles across a cultivated field in an attempt to cut off the Patrols Platoon as they drove down a narrow track flanked by a long mud wall. The open field on the other side of the track was impassable to wheeled vehicles because the ploughed earth furrows had been baked as hard as concrete by the scorching sun. The terrain was hideous and lay in stark contrast to the empty desert the platoon had previously driven across to get up to Now Zad. Using the cover of thick hedges, walls and irrigation ditches that criss-crossed the area, the insurgents moved undetected into their battle positions. They primed their RPG launchers and slipped off the safety catches of their AK-47s. The thump and crack of bullets over their heads and the wushing fizz of RPGs would be the first indication of the dangerous nature of the situation my troops had driven into.

Captain Mark Swann urged his men to move quickly. He felt

that the plan hinged on getting his Patrols Platoon WMIKs into position quickly and he could already hear the approaching helicopters that were carrying A Company. Suddenly his lead WMIK came under contact, and Lance Corporal Hughes saw the attackers. His .50 Cal kicked into life; then it stopped as the first few rounds of faulty ammunition fouled in the barrel. Corporal 'Ray' Davis filled the gap as he poured back fire at five Taliban gunmen with the GMPG mounted on the front of his bonnet. He managed to account for two of them before extracting back out of the killing zone. Swann was still desperate to get to his allocated position and sought to find another route, but the difficult terrain meant that he was stuck to using the track and the Taliban knew it. He dismounted half of his men to protect the vehicles as they pushed forward again.

Corporal Atwell spotted more Taliban moving through an orchard towards the patrol when the whole treeline on their right appeared to erupt in a blaze of muzzle flashes. Davis and Atwell were already returning fire from their vehicles. Private Ross refused to take cover as he pumped rounds from his .50 Cal at an RPG gunner he had spotted. The words 'Contact left, rapid fire!' crackled in Private Rowel's headset as he got a couple of rounds off from his own vehicle's .50 Cal before it stopped. He couldn't re-cock it and screamed at his driver, Private Webley, to get on the front-mounted GPMG. In the ensuing chaos, Swann was yelling orders into his radio telling his men to drive through the ambush site. As he did so bullets thumped past and RPGs scythed into the roadside trees, cutting down branches that landed among the vehicles. While the platoon returned fire, Flight Lieutenant Matt Carter, the Patrols Platoon Joint Terminal Attack Controller (JTAC), was in the process of fighting back with his radio as he called in one of the hovering Apache helicopters.

Channelled by the banks of the wadi, the Gurkhas were unable to bring their heavy .50 Cal machine guns to bear when the Taliban manning the PKMs opened up on them. They were forced to abandon their vehicles as bullets smacked around them and an RPG round glanced off the bonnet of the lead WMIK. One of the accompanying ANP was hit in the stomach and was dragged into cover as one of his police comrades sprayed the contents of his weapon in the direction of the insurgents. Some of the Taliban fighters had moved more slowly than others; one was cut down by Rifleman Yonzon as he emerged from the entrance of a building with an RPG launcher on his shoulder. The Gurkhas were also calling in air support, but their JTAC, Lieutenant Barry de Gode, was having trouble getting one of the radios to work. It had initially been left in one of the stricken vehicles, but the patrol commander, Lieutenant Paul Hollingshead, had braved the fire to retrieve it. AK-47 rounds were punching into the mud wall where the troops had taken cover when de Gode eventually got the radio working. He popped a red smoke grenade to assist the pilot in spotting his location.

As the Apache pilot looked down at the contact site his monocular vision sight automatically slaved the barrel of his helicopter's cannon on to where he was looking. Confident he could discern friendly forces from the enemy, his number two lined up the video cross-hair sight of the cannon on the coordinates de Gode had given him. The Taliban appeared as dark silhouettes against the cold grey background of the sighting systems screen. He squeezed the trigger and 130 30mm rounds began ripping through the trees into the insurgents. The storm of fire from the Apache allowed Paul Hollingshead to rally his men. They fired and manoeuvred their way back across the wadi, regained their vehicles and extracted back to the district centre.

The Apache in action above the Patrols Platoon also assisted them in their break clean from the first contact. They reorganized by a large compound. The vehicles formed a rough defensive perimeter with weapons facing outwards over the fields of dry poppy stalks which now burnt fiercely, having been ignited by RPG and tracer rounds. Swann heard the other contacts around him: the Gurkhas in the wadi to his north and the crackle of small-arms fire to his east indicated A Company's helicopters had also come under fire as they landed. Swann was still determined to get to his cordon positions, but more Taliban were moving against him and another firefight broke out. Private Ali was suddenly flung backwards by two AK bullets that tore into his chest webbing. They struck his magazines and ignited the tracer rounds inside them. Corporal Berry kicked dirt over him to put out the fire as Lance Corporal Clayton dragged him back into cover.

Matt Carter was trying to vector the Apaches on to the new threat, but neither he nor the pilots could get a precise fix on the Taliban. Carter was concerned about the cannon fire hitting their own people and wouldn't clear the helicopters in until he could give them a precise target indication. Ali was convinced that he had spotted them and was shouting for an AT-4. Private Dewhurst ran back to his vehicle to get him one of the light anti-tank weapons Ali intended to use as a high-explosive pointer. Although having been hit minutes previously, Ali positioned himself in clear view of the enemy with the rocket launcher balanced on his shoulder. He seemed to take an age to fire it and Swann shouted at him to get on with it. Ali told him that he wanted to make the shot count. It did. Both the pilots and Carter saw the strike and a stream of 30mm cannon shells streaked on to the telltale smoke signature rising from where Ali's rocket had landed. The firefight abruptly died out and the Patrols Platoon cleared forward and entered a compound. It was splashed with blood and the trails of crimson-stained sand indicated where the Taliban had dragged their dead and wounded away.

Landing a few hundred metres away, A Company were unaware of the contacts against the Gurkhas and the Patrols Platoon until the leading men of 1 Platoon also came under brief sporadic fire as they exited the Chinook. Corporal 'Prigg' Poll led his section to engage two gunmen who were shooting at them from between the broken gaps of a mud wall. They returned fire and followed them up into a compound. Privates Damien Jackson and 'Monk' Randle entered to be greeted by a group of women and children. Some panicked on the appearance of the two soldiers, others milled around, but the presence of the civilians prevented the two young paratroopers from firing, allowing the Taliban to make good their escape from the rear of the compound.

Concerned about becoming separated from the rest of the platoon, Poll decided to pull his section back to the landing point. But 1 Platoon had been dropped off in the wrong location and were half a kilometre from where they should have been put down. They could still hear the contact raging against the Patrols Platoon as they closed into the cover of a long wall. The platoon sergeant, Dan Jarvie, and Lieutenant Hugo Farmer worked out where they were. Having got their bearings, they headed north through an orchard towards where 2 Platoon had landed. Taking lead point with his section, Corporal Prigg Poll spotted a lone individual observing the platoon from a doorway. He was armed, but kept his AK by his side. He could have been a Talib, perhaps one of those who had engaged them? But in a land where everyone had a gun, he could equally have been a simple farmer looking to his family's security. Poll held his fire and the Afghan watched the platoon move off towards their correct location.

By the time my CH-47 touched down next to the compound, 2 Platoon had already secured and cleared it. It felt good to be on the ground, but now I needed to find out what was happening. The frantic snatches of the JTAC's radio traffic I had heard coming across the Chinook's intercom had told me that the outer cordon troops were in contacts. But I didn't know what their status was and knew virtually nothing else about what had being going on as I circled overhead. I linked up with Will Pike who gave me a situational report. From what Will told me, I was confident that we could hold the compound and complete the search mission. With the arrival of Captain Rob Musetti's additional machine guns aboard my helicopter, I assessed that we had sufficient troops to form a defensive perimeter that could keep the Taliban at bay. The Taliban leader we were after was obviously away from the compound directing the attacks against us, but a search might still yield useful intelligence and weapons.

My immediate concern was with what was happening to the Patrols Platoon and the Gurkhas. We had all been taken by surprise by the close, hemmed-in nature of the surrounding countryside. The open desert had been replaced by a relative oasis of orchards, grass banks of thick vegetation and deep water-filled ditches that bounded small patchwork fields. It was what the military called 'close country'. It was also a guerrilla fighter's paradise, as it made any vehicle movement unprotected by dismounted infantry extremely vulnerable to ambush. I wanted both vehicle-mounted platoons to break out into the relative safety of more open country where they could take advantage of the range of their heavier weapons systems. To try to reach us would only invite further attack. We couldn't get communications with the Gurkhas, but I managed to raise the Patrols on the net and spoke to Lance Corporal White who was Mark Swann's signaller. Swann was disappointed, his men were buzzing from the firefight and he wanted to get into a position where he could support me. However, he knew that it was the right call and started his withdrawal out to the desert in the west. Will's signaller, Lance Corporal Shorthouse, shouted over that he had finally made contact with the Gurkhas and I was relieved when he informed me that they had managed to withdraw back to the district centre. Now I could focus on the immediate task at hand without having to worry about fighting two other separate battles.

Before visiting the compound to check on the progress of the search, I turned my attention to how we would extract off the ground when it was finished. The countryside was too close to plan a helicopter pick-up from around the compound. We would have to move several kilometres to a safer pick-up point out in the surrounding desert. I consulted my map and selected a route west to where the Patrols Platoon would be able to secure an LZ for the helicopters. I briefed the plan to Will and Captain Matt Taylor. Matt had just stepped up to the operation officer position. This was his first op, but he questioned my extraction plan suggesting it might be better to choose a shorter route across a dry wadi to the east. I saw the merits in his proposal, although the Patrols Platoon wouldn't be in a position to secure an LZ. But having to cross less ground, where our movement would be constricted and every wall or grassy bank could conceal a group of insurgents waiting to ambush us, was a better idea. I told Matt that we would go with his plan and to get Bastion to brief the pilots to be on call to fly to an LZ to the east. I winked at Matt: 'Questioning the CO on your first trip out as the new ops boy, eh?' Taylor was over 6 foot and built like an ox, but he looked down and smiled shyly. He had made a good call and he knew that I valued him for it.

I entered the compound through a low, blue-painted wooden door that had seen better days. Weeds struggled out of the dry mud floor of the rubbish-strewn courtyard and the odd sorry-looking chicken pecked among it. Captain Jon Evett's Engineers were busily conducting the search of the internal rough mud-bricked buildings and he told me he would need at least four hours to do it properly. I updated him on what had being going on outside the compound and asked him to go as fast as he could. I spoke to an ANA officer whose men were keeping watch over the family who had been in the compound when we entered. They now sat huddled in a corner next to a large bundle of dried poppy canes; the women were shrouded in scarves. I averted my gaze from them and offered my salaams to the oldest man present, a gap-toothed, wizened individual, who returned my greetings. Through an interpreter, I apologized for the intrusion and explained why we were in his compound and that we meant him and his family no harm. I said that we came in peace and were there to help the Afghan people at the behest of the government. He told me that the Taliban had made him let them use his compound, but had now gone.

As I left the compound and went to look at some of A Company's positions I reflected on how incongruous my words must have sounded given the firefights that heralded our arrival. The blokes of A Company were in good heart, but virtually all of them mentioned their surprise at the close nature of the surrounding countryside. A number pointed out the irrigation ditches which formed tunnels deep enough for a man to move through undetected and the high walls that all offered favourable cover for an approaching attacker. As I headed back towards the compound the snap and crack of rifle fire suggested that 1 Platoon were in action again as the Taliban began to probe our positions.

Corporal Poll's section had taken up a position behind a wall facing east. He reported hearing Afghan voices coming from the other side. Lance Corporal 'Billy' Smart and Private Monk Randle took up fire positions over the wall and issued a challenge to two Afghan males armed with AK-47s and an RPG. When one of them raised his AK against them, Smart and Randle fired and dropped both of them. But they didn't see their comrades around a corner and their actions invited a heavy weight of return fire which zipped over their heads. Private Damien Jackson pumped a couple of grenade rounds at them from the under-slung grenade launcher fitted to the bottom of his rifle, which allowed Smart and Randle to get into cover. Poll managed to shoot and kill another enemy fighter before dropping back into a small alleyway. His platoon commander agreed to allow him to make a left-flanking attack to roll up the remaining Taliban, whom Poll suspected had taken shelter in a nearby compound. Private McKinley heard the firefight, but could see nothing through the thick vegetation. Climbing a tree to get a better look, he spotted an insurgent crossing a small wall. He beaded the insurgent with the black tip of his telescopic rifle sight and counted the nine rounds he squeezed off against him. The man crumpled. Alerted to his presence in the tree, other Taliban opened up against him. McKinley scrambled back down to the ground as enemy bullets chopped into the branches above him.

Taking a gun group of GPMGs with him, Poll called on all single men of his section to follow him and pushed through the undergrowth to a compound. He came under contact and attempted to get through a small gap in a wall but the weight of fire pushed him back. Farmer closed up to his point section commander. Suddenly explosions erupted around them as the Taliban tossed grenades over the top of the wall. Luckily for Poll and Farmer the grenades fell on broken ground. The folds in the earth absorbed the blast and channelled the lethal lumps of fragmented metal harmlessly above their heads. Private Lanaghan was close enough to hear Poll shout, 'Fucking hell, they are throwing fucking grenades at us!' He was also close enough to feel the shock waves of the explosions. Poll and Farmer knew that there were women and children in the compound, which prevented them from throwing grenades back at them for fear of causing casualties among the innocent. By the time they had forced their way into the compound the Taliban had withdrawn by a rear exit, leaving the civilians and a number of panicking livestock behind them. Poll was having a bad day: as well as getting shot at and blown up, he had also been stung by a wasp and kicked by a cow.

As the noise of the exchange of fire and the crump of grenades echoed across the fields, I looked at my watch; we had been on the ground for almost four hours. It was about 1500 hours and the sun was already beginning to slip towards the western horizon. The vegetation obscured most of the fighting and the odd stray round zipped above our heads. I was content to let Pike fight his platoons as I planned the next stage of disengaging from the battle and how we would get to a safe LZ to extract from.

I was becoming concerned at how long the search of the compound was taking. The nature of the surrounding countryside was making fighting off the Taliban's attacks hard enough by daylight, but it would become a nightmare when night fell. I urged the search team to get a move on. Jon Evett said he needed another hour and a half. I gave him forty-five minutes and told him that we were racing against the onset of darkness. I passed 2 Platoon, who were itching to get into the fight and had not fired a round since landing. They were snapping that 1 Platoon were getting all the action, but they were about to get what they wished for. A radio report came in indicating that the Taliban commander we were looking for might be located to the south-east of our position. The contacts against 1 Platoon had died down and it was a possible indication that the enemy were shifting their effort to take us on from a different direction. I spoke to Will Pike and ordered him to send 2 Platoon to clear to the south-east, but I impressed upon him the need not to let them get decisively engaged in a firefight that would then become difficult to break off when we needed to extract. Last light was a little over three hours away and I was mindful that we would have to move to the LZ sooner rather than later.

Trying to keep some form of tactical formation while cross-graining the tyranny of a terrain of mud-walled alleyways and irrigation ditches was like completing a rural assault course. The short assault-scaling ladders 2 Platoon carried assisted their passage. But even when they moved across relatively flat ground the concrete hardness of the ploughed ruts threatened to break ankles when they crossed it at speed. Each man was encumbered with between 50 and 60 pounds of kit, not including the weapon systems that they carried and the body armour that encased them in the sweltering heat. Although the sun was dipping, it was still 40°C in the shade. Corporal Tam McDermott led the point section. He paused as they came to a wide, open field and allowed his platoon commander, Tom Fehley, to catch up.

Recognizing the danger of crossing the open terrain, Fehley ordered McDermott to go firm and adopt a static position to provide covering fire while he ordered Corporal Scott McCloughlan's section to clear the orchard on the other side. Fehley agreed to let McCloughlan flank left round the open field to avoid the exposed ground. McCloughlan selected a route that brought the section to an alleyway blocked in on either side by high compound walls. He moved cautiously into the alleyway with his lead scout, Private Dale Tyler. Noting movement 100 metres to his front, he dropped to one knee. Suddenly the whole alley was riddled with enemy machine-gun fire. Rounds struck into the walls around McCloughlan and Dale as both returned fire. Dale loosed off a couple of UGL rounds as they withdrew back to where they had started, firing as they went. By the time they got back to the rest of the section, the whole of the orchard on the other side of the field had opened up. Other Taliban fighters blazed away at the two forward sections, their bullets thudding into the mud earthworks and slicing through the vegetation they were using for cover.

McDermott was ordered to take over from McCloughlan and make another attempt to probe left, but the Taliban were bent on making their own efforts to outflank the platoon. Prudently, McDermott had placed privates 'Zippy' Owen and 'Flash' Gordon with two GPMGs to guard against this threat. It meant that both men had to adopt an exposed position and rounds kicked up the dirt around them as they hammered back with their belt-fed machine guns. Although it kept the Taliban from taking advantage of the open flank, the weight of fire McDermott was taking as he crawled forward eventually forced him back.

With the left approach closed as an option, Fehley ordered McCloughlan to try to find an approach on the right flank towards a small mound of higher ground. Seeing two men appear on the grassy hillock, McCloughlan's section shook out into assault formation. Unable to identify the positive presence of any weapons, McCloughlan ordered his men to hold their fire as he moved forward to investigate. He moved cautiously, his weapon in his shoulder at the 'watch and shoot' alert position. He scanned the men through his rifle sight; he was close enough to see the expressions on their bearded faces. Both men wore black turbans and the traditional shalwar-kameez. As he inched forward AKs concealed in the long flowing material of their dress were brought to bear against him. His safety-catch already off, McCloughlan's finger squeezed and released against his trigger, the firing mechanism spat bullets and automatically cocked and re-cocked as his rounds cut down the two men.

I had been sitting by the side of the compound mentally willing the search team to hurry up as 2 Platoon had begun to move off. I heard the first contact; the firing seemed to be much closer. I decided to get forward and marry up with the company commander to find out what was going on. I passed the word to Tac; we re-chambered rounds and checked our gear. As we broke cover round the side of the compound, rounds whizzed past us and cracked over our heads, showering us with small branches and twigs. We dropped back behind the wall and decided to move round from the other side of the building. I left Matt to man the Tac Sat radio as we patrolled forward and told him to keep the JOC at Bastion updated. There was no fire on the opposite side, but Will Pike suddenly appeared from a flank and warned us that we were heading straight towards the enemy less than a few hundred metres away. We pulled back.

Rounds were now landing regularly around the compound and I told Matt, who was standing up in full view, to get down; I noted the edge in my own voice. The pressure was beginning to build. I had spent all day waiting to hear the fateful words of 'man down' come across the net. Getting a casualty out of the close-knit terrain would be a nightmare. It would take a complete section of eight men to carry him back to the emergency LZ by the compound, which would denude our defences considerably. Additionally, calling a helicopter close in to the compound would invite having it shot down. I checked the premonition forming in my mind and for the first time that day I felt physically scared. There was a tightening in my chest under my body armour and my mind clouded with doubts as to whether we would actually make it out in one piece: 2 Platoon were still significantly engaged, the extraction phase was risky and darkness was approaching. I chastised myself; my job was to make sure that we got everyone out and self-doubt wouldn't help that. I knew that I needed to occupy my mind with activity.

I went to see how Evett's men were doing and was relieved to be told that his search team were almost finished. I re-briefed Pike and Taylor on the extraction phase, stressing the importance of making sure 2 Platoon started to break their contact. I looked across at Bish; as the RSM he would play a vital role in the physical mechanics of the withdrawal, and he would also have the immediate responsibility of making sure that no one was left behind. I knew that he would be all over it and I took confidence from the expression of sheer professional determination on his face. Matt squared away the detail of calling in the choppers from Bastion; the trigger would be the break clean of 2 Platoon. It was good to be busy again and I went over to the Regimental Aid Post (RAP) to see the wounded prisoner who had been brought in. He had been apprehended as a youth tried to get him out of the fighting in a wheelbarrow. His lower legs were badly shot up, but he hardly winced as our doctor applied morphine, re-aligned one of his shattered bones and checked the bleeding. He would be a burden during the extraction. But even if he was a Talib, his best chance of survival was with us and the proper medical care he would receive at Bastion. As I watched Captain Harvey Pynn work on his mangled limbs, it made me think what hard bastards these people were.

To McCloughlan it felt like the whole 2 Platoon contact had lasted no more than five minutes; in fact it had been two hours since he first came under fire in the alleyway. Darkness was falling and the search had been completed. Will Pike ordered 2 Platoon to withdraw back to the compound for the extraction, but the firefight was still raging across the open field. The Apaches had been firing in support, but a heavier weight of fire was required to break the contact and allow the platoon to disengage. Corporal of Horse Fry was the JTAC with Fehley; he talked one of the circling A-10s on to the Taliban in the orchard. We had American close-air-support aircraft overhead all day, including a large black B-1 bomber, but the close proximity of civilians had prevented us from asking them to drop bombs. Fry called for cannon fire, marked his target and popped smoke. I heard the rattling fire of the GE and Hughes Chain Gun mounted in the nose of the A-10 before I saw the aircraft. Initially I thought it was a Taliban heavy machine gun; then I heard the after-whirr of the rotating barrels as the tank-buster aircraft banked and turned away. It is a terrible modern-day equivalent of an aerial-mounted Gatling gun. Firing

30mm tungsten-tipped cannon shells at 100 rounds per second, it brassed up the orchard with a devastating weight of lethal fire. One minute there had been trees there and the next they had disappeared in spouting eruptions of earth and sparks along with the Taliban. It was danger close fire delivered at less than 75 metres from the forward line of 2 Platoon's own positions in the full knowledge that its proximity to our own troops meant that there was a real and accepted risk that it might hit them. But the American pilots were good and it provided Fehley's men with a vital breathing space to disengage and withdraw back to the compound.

The extraction phase was uneventful. I had expected the Taliban to follow us up as we crossed the shallow wadi bed to our east and struck out into some open high ground in the desert to secure a pick-up LZ. I had also expected them to try to shoot down the four CH-47s as the helicopters flew low along the tree-line of the wadi that we had left 700 metres behind us. They were a welcome sight but my heart missed a beat as I saw how close they flew to the line of thick vegetation. We covered it with our machine guns, but the Taliban stayed quiet. Perhaps they had had enough and were pleased to see us go and be left in peace to lick their wounds.

The plan was that I would lift off with Tac in the last aircraft, but my chalk of waiting men was the closest to the first cab that landed. I wanted the helicopters to spend no more than twenty seconds on the ground; any longer would significantly increase their exposure to taking fire. Consequently, I wasn't going to change the load order at the last minute. Lifting off as part of the first pair, we circled overhead as the other two aircraft came in to make their pick-up. It took less than a couple of minutes, but it seemed like an agonizing age. I wanted to know that we had got every man into the helicopters; the prospect of finding that we had left someone behind once we got back to Bastion was too much of an unimaginable horror. I asked my pilot to get the aircrew of the other aircraft to do a head check. He came back to me quickly:

'All complete, Colonel.' 'Do it once more, please, and tell them to take their time to double-check,' I said. The second answer came back as an affirmative and I acknowledged the pilot's request to head back to Bastion. I stripped off my webbing and body armour and flopped down into one of the nylon web-strapped seats; I was absolutely knackered.

There was a perceptible buzz about the place when we got back to Bastion. I asked Will Pike to gather the company briefly on the side of the landing site; they wouldn't want a long speech from me, but I wanted to tell them that they had done well. Major Stu Russell, the quartermaster, came out of the JOC and pumped my hand as I drew up in a Pinzgauer truck. Stu had fought through the gorse line at the Battle of Goose Green with 2 PARA in 1982; he had also survived the IRA's bloody bombing at Warren Point which had killed eighteen of his company: he knew what combat was like. The atmosphere in the JOC was electric. My second-in-command, Huw Williams, had also been fretting about getting us out. The relief on his face was obvious and he broke out into a broad grin. The blokes who had done the actual fighting felt it too. All through the evening people came up to them, slapped them on the back and asked them what it was like, a tinge of jealousy in their voices. I felt the onset of the fatigue and drain of emotional energy that follow a post-combat experience, but the day wasn't yet over and I wanted to maintain the momentum. I asked Huw to get all the commanders together once they had eaten for an After Action Review (AAR). We needed to capture the lessons from all the corporals up while it was still fresh in their minds.

The search of the compound had yielded little of real value: the Engineers found a few AK magazines, a bag of bullets and an old grenade. They also found several kilograms of sticky black opium resin. Official policy dictated that we should have seized it, but we weren't there to deprive a family of their livelihood and I made a point of having it handed back to the headman. Although we found little in the compound, we learned many important lessons from the 'Battle of Mutay'. Key points came out in the AAR, although as young officers, planning staff, junior NCOs and aircrew gave their analysis of events, I noted how different accounts of the same action varied. After the strain of combat an individual's memory is random and selective. People tend to focus on fragmentary images and the overall context and precise sequence of events are often lost. However, allowing each man to talk in turn provided a collective synthesis of accuracy. It was probably also an inadvertent form of stress decompression.

The professional skills and drills of the junior commanders and Toms had carried the day, but the vulnerability of vehicles operating without infantry support in close country was highlighted, as was the need to dominate the high ground and have our mortar support with us. The speed at which the enemy organized against us also demonstrated just how impressive their dicking system was. Although 100 kilometres away, they were likely to have picked up the movement of the helicopters from Bastion; four CH-47s lifting off at once and heading in one direction was probably an indicator that something was afoot. The message could have crossed the desert by mobile phone and then been relayed across the valleys to every Taliban stronghold to our north.

But the key lesson was our own lack of timely passage of intelligence. Available information that could have alerted us to the greater presence of Taliban fighters was not passed to the Battle Group. Although we had secure telephones in the JOC they didn't have the right official security classification, so the information sat at Lashkar Gah. I saw it for myself when I flew down the next day. The image of the scale of assessed enemy activity took my breath away when I saw it laid out in front of me. But I didn't see the point of getting angry about it when I spoke to an apologetic intelligence staff at UKTF. 'Next time, sod the regulations about the phones. If it's urgent please just pass the information on to us,' I said.

After Mutay everything changed. Any preconceived wishful thinking about conducting a peace support operation fell away. The penny was finally beginning to drop in Whitehall and PJHQ that we were engaged in countering a full-blown insurgency, against a ruthless and determined enemy. Our assessment that we had killed about twenty of them during Mutay was confirmed when we received a report that twenty-one Taliban fighters had been buried in a cemetery in the Sangin Valley the next day. Given the weight of fire that was exchanged, I was amazed that we hadn't lost anyone. The Toms' superior field-craft played its part, as did the relatively poor marksmanship of the insurgents. But I thought of Private Bash Ali being saved by his magazines and numerous other accounts of close calls; Lady Luck had also been on our side. I suppressed a naive thought that 'maybe, just maybe', we might be able to complete the tour without suffering any casualties. But from then on I knew that every time we went out we would have to be prepared to expect the same reception. Losing some people was likely to be an unpalatable inevitability of the business we were in. I received a handwritten letter from a retired Parachute Regiment general a few days later. He praised the bravery of my soldiers, but warned me to steel myself against the inevitable. Sadly, both he and I were to be proved right in the days ahead.

6

Reaction and Proaction

I was at KAF when initial reports of the first UK casualty came in. I had been attending a meeting with David Fraser and was in the process of back-briefing our discussion to Ed Butler who was down from Kabul. The first reports indicated that a number of personnel had been wounded. Then news came that Captain Jim Philippson had been killed. Jim was twenty-nine and was a 7 RHA officer serving with the team mentoring the ANA Kandak at FOB Robinson. Unbeknown to anyone in the JOC at Bastion, the commander at the FOB had sent out a patrol to recover a Desert Hawk Unmanned Aerial Vehicle (UAV) that had crashed on the far bank of the Helmand River. The small, remotely piloted UAV belonged to 18 Battery Royal Artillery that provided surveillance support to all elements of the UKTF. It carried a camera that beamed back live video images of the ground to a control station in the FOB. The patrol set out a couple of hours before last light. They used the local makeshift ferry to cross the river on the outskirts of Sangin. They had probably been dicked from the minute they left the FOB. Having failed to find the UAV, they used the ferry to cross back to the home bank. As they started to return along the same route they were ambushed on a high-banked levee track. Lance Bombardier Mason from I Battery was hit in the chest. As darkness fell, the patrol's medic fired off the first six magazines from his SA80 rifle to protect him, as the stricken troops waited for help.

Jim Philippson was part of the first relief force which was hastily put together to go to their aid. He was hit by Taliban fire and killed instantly as he moved across a field towards the ambush site. Under the covering fire of artillery from the FOB, his comrades managed to carry his body back to the vehicles that they had dismounted from at the side of the field. A second relief force was quickly dispatched from the FOB, but it too came under contact. Sergeant Major Andy Stockton of 18 Battery had the lower part of his arm severed by an RPG round. With his remaining good arm he continued to return fire with his pistol from his vehicle as they drove along the levee to the ambushed vehicles. As he did so he shouted at his young driver to stop flapping and concentrate on the driving; the last thing he wanted to do was have a crash to add to his problems.

The HRF was dispatched with the casevac helicopter to make a risky landing to pick up the wounded. The Taliban were still concealed somewhere in the blackness and could bring the aircraft under fire at any moment. It spent the minimum time on the ground and the pilot kept the power on so that he could make a rapid lift-off once the injured men were aboard. Mason was stretchered on to the back, but Stockton refused assistance. He walked up the helicopter's ramp calmly smoking a cigarette with his arm hanging off. B Company had been on standby, but as the attack against the ambush site went quiet it was decided to delay flying them in until first light the next morning. It had been a necessary risk to send the casevac helicopter into an unsecured LZ at night, but sending B Company into a confused situation increased the risk of having a helicopter shot down. With the casualties off the ground, and having been beefed up by Sergeant Major Stockton's men, the remaining troops would have to wait for relief.

Within minutes of arriving back in Bastion, Sergeant Major Stockton was on an operating table in the field hospital. The skill of the military surgeons undoubtedly saved his life, but his wounds were too serious to save his arm. The next day B Company flew in, married up with the vehicles on the levee and escorted them back to the FOB. The incident had been a sobering lesson in the danger of using vehicles to drive along an obvious route. It also remained questionable whether the risk of searching for the UAV was worth the life of a brave and popular officer. Like the French ambush, it highlighted the need to coordinate the movement of all patrols with the JOC at Bastion. We had been concerned about the danger of other units moving around Helmand without any reference either to us or the UKTF since our arrival. The point had been made to the Canadian multinational headquarters in Kandahar on numerous occasions, but it was a lesson that was not to be learned until two more tragic incidents cost the lives of other soldiers.

The first incident occurred two days later on 13 June. An American logistics convoy was ambushed on a track that passed through a small village on the route between Gereshk and Musa Qaleh. It was meant to be delivering supplies to US troops participating in Operation Mountain Thrust. But the commander had become disorientated; it was a costly error of navigation. Driving backwards and forwards past the village in an attempt to regain its bearings, the convoy inadvertently gave the Taliban time to organize themselves against it and they hit the convoy with a fusillade of RPG and automatic fire. US Apaches were called in and broke up the attack, but not before one American soldier was killed and a logistics truck and a Humvee had been destroyed. The first we heard of the presence of the convoy was when we were tasked to be prepared to respond to the ambush. A Company was placed on fifteen minutes' notice to move and got the call to fly out at 1600 hours. We had learned the lesson from Mutay and this time they took their section of two 81mm mortar barrels with them.

Landing at an offset LZ far enough away to avoid being fired on, A Company made their way to the ambush site where the surviving US personnel were still milling around in the contact area. They had been there for over an hour, but were too dazed by their experience to move to a safer place. Their vehicles were drawn up in a line and smoke billowed in dying wisps from the burnt-out

Humvee. The Taliban had withdrawn but were still close by. An Apache hovered low overhead to find them and narrowly missed being shot down by an RPG round that sailed past its rear rotor tail. Will Pike had a face-to-face conversation with the US commander and took control of the situation.

He gathered the survivors and their working vehicles and moved them off to the relative safety of the higher ground of a doughnut-shaped feature a few hundred metres away from the village. The position Pike selected wasn't ideal, as it was still exposed to the closer country of vegetation and compounds around them. But with the onset of darkness, it would have to do; he needed to go firm and wait it out until an expected American relief column arrived to recover their people. The company formed a defensive perimeter. The digging was hard and the Toms could make only shallow impressions in the rocky ground. Three of the armoured Humvees with their .50 Cal machine guns were used to bolster the defences. The rest of the American logisticians were too shaken to take an active role and were placed in the central depression of the mount with the remainder of their vehicles. The dead US soldier remained strapped to the outside of one of the Humvees where he had been placed by his comrades for the move up to the feature. WO2 Mick Turner, who was standing in as the company sergeant major, asked the Americans if he could place the dead man in a body bag and put him in one of the vehicles. He doubted the macabre image could be doing much for their morale. Having prepared the position as best they could, the men of A Company then watched and waited for darkness to fall.

Twenty minutes after last light it started. Muzzle flashes lit up the murky shadows around the mound. Tracer fire streaked angrily over the tops of the shallow depressions the soldiers had scraped into the ground to give them a modicum of protection. A heavy Russian DShK machine gun opened up from their twelve o'clock position in a small wood line and a volley of RPGs followed. One of the RPGs passed low over the head of Corporal

Planning operations during a quiet period in the JOC. From left to right: the author; Major Damian Fosmoe (US Army); Major Huw Williams, 3 PARA's second-in-command; and Captain Matt Taylor, the Battle Group Operations Officer

Private Bash Ali of the Patrols Platoon conducting a 'soft hat' patrol in the town of Gereshk. Operations conducted in the north of Helmand were very different affairs from the hearts-and-minds approach that was possible in towns like Gereshk. During Operation Mutay, Ali was struck in the chest by a Taliban bullet. The magazines in his chest webbing stopped the bullet and saved his life

A member of the Patrols Platoon cleans a .50-calibre heavy machine gun mounted on a WMIK Land Rover in Now Zad shortly after B Company occupied the town's district centre in May. The winged Para badge tattoo was sported by many in 3 PARA

The Patrols Platoon fighting to get through to the compound at Mutay outside Now Zad. The fires in the poppy fields in the background have been caused by exploding tracer rounds and RPGs

An orders group outside the compound during Operation Mutay. The author is briefing Major Will Pike surrounded by members of Battle Group 'Tac' HQ

'1,000-yard stare': Private Martin Cork crammed into the back of a Chinook helicopter with other members of A Company, having lifted off the ground after Operation Mutay

A member of the Sniper Platoon looking through the sights of his .338 sniper rifle in a sangar on the Kajaki Ridge. Water from the dammed lake in the background fed the electricity turbines against which the Taliban launched numerous attacks

The wounded son of Dos Mohamed Khan being evacuated from the district centre in Sangin. His rescue was the start of 3 PARA's defence of the town's district centre, which led to withstanding ninety-five days of attacks and resulted in the deaths of six members of the Battle Group and the wounding of many more

A GPMG gunner of 9 (Ranger) Platoon returns fire across a field to cover C Company as they extract from the ambush outside the village of Zumbelay

vate Damian Jackson cko') of A Company ring Operation ntay. He sits next to an -4 anti-tank weapon l his SA80 rifle is fitted h an under-slung nade launcher. Jacko s killed in action in gin on 5 July

Paras from C Company move under fire across the fields outside Zumbelay. Note the burning pieces of RPG shrapnel that have just landed behind the Para to the right of the picture

Sergeant Dan Jarvie, the bombastic and charismatic platoon sergeant of 1 Platoon A Company. He was later mentioned in dispatches for his actions during numerous encounters with the Taliban

Chinook helicopters lift off for an air assault operation from the makeshift helipad of crushed gravel at Camp Bastion. The troops in the foreground are waiting for the returning wave of aircraft to lift. Acute shortages of helicopters meant the Battle Group could never move in one lift

A LAV armoured vehicle from the Canadian Company that temporarily came under command of 3 PARA during Operation Augustus. The vehicles were called 'Green Dragons' by the Taliban who hated their 25mm Bushmaster cannons

Members of 3 PARA under fire on ANP Hill as they defend the district centre at Now Zad from an attack by the Taliban

Battle Group Tactical Headquarters (Tac) on the roof of the district centre in Now Zad during operations to clear the town. Left to right: Major Gary Wilkinson, the artillery battery commander; Captain Nick French, commander of the Mortar Platoon; Sergeant Webb; and Flight Lieutenant Matt Carter. Carter was later awarded a Military Cross for calling in danger close air strikes

RSM John Hardy, an archetypical no-nonsense paratrooper. He cared passionately about the Toms and was affectionately known as 'Uncle John' by the soldiers of 3 PARA

Brigadier Ed Butler, the respected commander of 16 Air Assault Brigade, waiting in the desert to meet the Taliban and Afghan elders to broker the ceasefire agreement at Musa Qaleh in September

Lieutenant General Sir David Richards, the author's old boss and NATO commander of ISAF. He was an inspirational leader and was widely respected by the allies, Afghans and the media

Mark Keenan and detonated against the radiator grille of one of the Humvees. The jagged metal fragments of its warhead spread along the side of the vehicle and sliced into two Americans who had been standing there. Moments previously one of the soldiers had shown a light. It was either a small torch or a match to light a cigarette, but in the blackness it provided a lethal aiming mark.

Private Pete McKinley had been firing his weapon at the muzzle flashes coming from the wood when he heard the frantic cry of 'medic'. Despite the storm of incoming fire, he left his position and sprinted back to the Humvee. One of the Americans had sustained serious wounds to his face, and the other had deep lacerations in his neck. McKinley made an immediate assessment and applied his combat first-aid skills to the more seriously injured man with the facial wounds. Will Pike and Mick Turner arrived with Lance Corporal Paul Roberts, who was the RAMC-qualified Combat Medical Technician attached to A Company. He had been used to working as a small cog in a large medical squadron in Germany staffed by doctors and senior nurses, but he was the most medically qualified individual on the ground that night and he took over command of the incident. Roberts was impressed by McKinley's work and was convinced his prompt intervention saved the American's life. A Company set up an LZ and called in a chopper to lift out the casualties.

The chopper also brought in reinforcements in the form of the HRF. This was Lieutenant Ben Harrop's 7 Platoon from C Company which had been stripped out from Gereshk to make up for manning shortfalls in the troops at Bastion. They brought shovels and sandbags with them to help bolster up the position's limited defences. A-10s and French Mirage fighter-bomber jets came on station intermittently throughout the night, but the troops' close proximity to the village meant that they could not drop bombs and the jet pilots were reluctant to fire their cannon. Whenever there was a gap in the air cover the Taliban would launch another attack to rake the position with fire, forcing A Company to press themselves physically and mentally into the dirt.

It felt to Corporal Scott McLaughlin as if he were digging in with his eyeballs, as the enemy rounds struck close about them. Apaches were dispatched from Bastion in an attempt to break up the attacks. At one point there was a lull in the fighting. Through night vision sights, ten figures wearing burkas were spotted by 3 Section of 1 Platoon moving between two of the compounds from where the Taliban had fired. But in Afghanistan women do not move around at night and they don't carry automatic weapons. Corporal Keenan reported the movement and the whole section opened up as 81mm mortar rounds also rained down among the insurgents.

The heavy machine gun was still causing a serious problem from the wood line. The rounds were coming so close to where Corporal Billy Smith of 2 Section lay in the few inches of shelter he had managed to scratch out from the dirt, that he felt he only had to stick out his hand to catch one. Recognizing the need to do something about it, Corporal Mark Wright ran forward to the position closest to where the fire was coming from. Bullets cracked past him as he made himself visible to get eyes on the target to direct mortar fire. As he fed coordinates to the mortar crews behind him, sights were adjusted and rounds were made ready to drop down the barrels. Satisfied that his teams were 'on', he gave the order 'Five rounds fire for effect' into his radio mike. The bombs slid down the steel tubes and the mortars coughed loudly. The bright flashes from their muzzles momentarily lit up the darkness and the recoil bit their base plates hard down into the stony ground. Ten rounds landed in quick succession as exploding crumps of lethal steel along the treeline. The heavy machine gun fell silent.

A Company spent an uneasy night waiting for the break of first light. Standing to in their positions, they scanned the darkness through helmet-mounted night vision sights and hand-held thermal image devices. The latter could pick up heat sources of anyone moving around in the shadows, but the Taliban had had enough. As the first grey of dawn began to lighten the eastern sky, the company moved off to a safer position 3 kilometres further out into the desert. It brought them to a high plateau where they could see far into the distance. With a clear line of sight across the empty desert they would be able to take on any Taliban before they got close enough to engage them. The insurgents knew it and stayed away. The sun rose and the temperature climbed into the forties. A Company blistered in the searing heat as they waited all day for the US recovery column. They had deployed with 6 litres of water per man, but their CamelBaks were running dry and the water bottles on their belts were empty.

Night had fallen once more when the relief convoy finally arrived. The Americans wanted A Company to stay with them, but they were now out of water and the position was sufficiently well sited to be held by the Americans. The company also needed rest and recuperation for subsequent operations and I agreed to Pike's request to be lifted out. I listened to the noise of the CH-47s' engines as they warmed up and lifted off from Bastion to recover A Company. Then I spent the next hour waiting impatiently to hear the telltale thump of the rotor blades of the returning helicopters that would tell me they had picked up A Company safely.

Having to dispatch A and B companies to dig other people out of trouble only added to the tempo of activity in the Battle Group. We were trying to prepare for follow-up operations in Now Zad and find options to secure Musa Qaleh and the Kajaki Dam. We had also been given three more strike targets to work up and as each one changed we had to start planning over again. Battle Groups are not given medium- or long-term operational planning staff. Consequently, when an operation went live, or we had to react to an event on the ground, we had to stop planning future ops and focus on the situation at hand. I asked for an extra staff major, which would allow us to run both current and future ops planning concurrently, but none was available. A decent night's sleep was becoming a rare commodity and if anyone was getting more than four to five hours a night, then they were doing well. Some planning sessions ran through the night and I would watch weary officers struggle to stay awake during the stifling heat of the next day. Huw Williams and I tried to pace the staff as best we could, but this was not an exercise. Although we were under-manned we had to be able to react to events. If we cut corners and got the planning wrong people could die. It was a responsibility that acted like a moral form of Prozac.

Meanwhile, there had been a realignment of the command chain. I would now work direct to the Canadian brigade com-mander. Charlie Knaggs would focus solely on the PRT and the governor, whose demands took up much of his time and required a significant amount of personal investment. It meant that Ed Butler would take a more direct role at the tactical level. Although David Fraser would give me orders, NATO practice meant that I still had to clear them through the senior British officer. I valued Butler's judgement, so it didn't concern me overly, but it some-times bothered Fraser. Luckily, he was a man I liked and respected, which eased the sensitive line I sometimes had to tread.

On top of this, Butler told me to take over command of FOB Robinson. My problem was that I didn't have a spare major to do it with. The obvious choice was to get a sub-unit commander not directly attached to 3 PARA to do it. There weren't many avail-able, but the one I approached displayed a certain reluctance to take on the task. I later found out that he had sent an e-mail direct to PJHQ complaining that to be given the task would be an improper use of his assets. I was staggered by his behaviour at a time when everyone was doing at least one other person's job and were risking their lives on a daily basis. My adjutant, Captain Chris Prior, jumped at the chance when I said that I would have to give the task to him. It would mean that the never-ceasing administra-tive paper war would have to take a back seat and I would not be able to give Chris a proper headquarters staff of signallers or a senior NCO to act as his deputy. Nonetheless, seeing an opportu-nity to get operational field command, and to be free of the trials of being my Adjutant, Chris was almost out of the door before I had finished briefing him. He went off with a smile on his face to grab his weapon, pack his kit and scrabble around to see if he could scratch a headquarters team together.

The never-ending stream of visitors also added to the frenetic mix. General Richard Dannatt arrived to make his last visit as the Army's Commander-in-Chief before taking over as CGS from Mike Jackson. Visits were a pain, as they detracted from directing and planning operations, but Dannatt said all the right things, listened to what I had to say and made those soldiers whom he spoke to feel valued for what they were doing. He was almost immediately followed by Lieutenant General David Richards, who came down from Kabul where he was getting ready to take over command of ISAF. It was good to see my old boss again. As is his style, he struck up an instant rapport with the Toms, especially Private Bash Ali when he showed him his magazines that had been struck by AK bullets during Mutay. He told everybody how well they were doing and had that special knack of making anyone he spoke to feel as if they were the most important person in the world. He also took the piss out of me, which the blokes loved.

I drove him back to the airstrip on my own and we talked about his concern that we were in danger of getting overly fixed in the district centres. I said I agreed with him and recognized that we were deviating from the simple plan of the inkspot development concept that we had discussed over a pint in a pub in Wiltshire six months previously. I explained my dilemma of meeting increasing commitments with ever-scarcer resources and the paradox of having to establish some permanent presence while still retaining sufficient forces with the freedom to manoeuvre. He was serious for a moment when we stepped out of the Toyota. 'Stuart, your Battle Group is doing brilliantly in difficult circumstances. And you, my friend, keep taking the tablets and keep doing what you are doing.' He smiled as some senior ANA officers approached. Adopting the custom of how Afghan officers greet each other, he hugged them and then turned and hugged me. With that he was gone, striding across the dirt strip to his waiting Hercules whose engine props were already turning. I drove back to the JOC feeling as if someone had just given me a tonic-boosting shot in the arm.

Two days later Des Browne made his first visit to Helmand as the new Secretary of State for Defence. He had flown into Afghanistan direct from Iraq and was no doubt feeling the effects of the heat and jet lag. With his background as a human rights lawyer, I detected that he was not entirely at ease in the company of soldiers. When I briefed him on the Battle Group's operations he pursued an aggressive line of questioning about why we were planning to do strike ops instead of development. He also wanted to know why the military were leading operations rather than the British civilian government ministries. 'Because, sir, this is Afghanistan and we are in the middle of a vicious counter-insurgency. The Taliban are trying to kill my soldiers, which is why we are conducting strike operations when resources permit.' I acknowledged the importance of winning consent and that the non-kinetic aspects of the campaign were vitally important. But I thought I might be pushing the bounds a bit if I said that we were leading because there were over 3,000 soldiers in Afghanistan compared to the number of other government ministry personnel in Helmand, which could be counted on one hand. I could have made the additional point that they didn't get out beyond Lashkar Gah.

After the briefing Des Browne met some of the blokes. While he did so, I spoke to one of his special advisers and asked him if the minister really understood the nature of what we were experiencing. Before he departed, Browne made a point of coming up to me to thank me for what my soldiers were doing and to say how impressed he was with everyone. It was an afterthought that might have been provoked by the tone of my response to his questions, or perhaps the result of a whispered word from his adviser. But I softened a bit. He was knackered, unaccustomed to the heat and had flown halfway round the world. He was new to a very complex job and had a lot on his plate dealing with the implications of being responsible for an Army fighting in both Iraq and

Afghanistan. No doubt he was also suffering from spending the last few days being endlessly bombarded with impenetrable military jargon and unfamiliar place names, as he travelled between the two theatres of operations. I headed back to the JOC to work out how we were going to meet the expanding commitments of future strike operations and taking over Musa Qaleh from the Americans. There was also the pressing concern of defending the Kajaki Dam from the increasing number of Taliban mortar attacks being made against it. I was convinced that if we could get our own mortars on the high ground around the dam before the next attack we might be in a position to catch them in the act and ambush them. Consequently, we decided to put a deliberate plan in place to achieve this by dispatching a small force to Kajaki.

Four nights later we got the message we had all been waiting for. It came across the net, confident, clear and concise: 'Contact Kajaki, wait out!' Matt Taylor's elated repetition of the radio transmission added to the buzz of excitement. I strode towards the map-strewn bird table in the JOC. Others gathered rapidly around the map of the Kajaki Dam that had been carefully prepared in the event of receiving just such a message. Meanwhile, almost 100 kilometres to our north, mortar rounds arced through the night sky to deliver death and destruction among the Taliban's own mortar teams in the river valley below.

The Taliban had fired first and their mortar bombs scattered sparks and shrapnel among Captain Nick French's positions. But Nick's actions matched the Rules of Engagement; as his men had been fired on he was allowed to use his own mortars to respond in kind. The first salvo went wide of the target, but rapid adjustment of the fire coordinates by the forward controllers made the necessary correction. The next salvo landed among the Taliban; the blast of heat and bomb fragments ripped through the fighters, who moments before had been setting up their own weapons and firing against French's position atop the high ridge feature that we had codenamed Sparrow Hawk. The survivors of the second salvo sought cover in a reed bed along the banks of the river. However, it offered them little sanctuary. Obscured from the view of the Mortar Fire Controller, the tripod-mounted GPMGs under the command of Colour Sergeant Schofield kicked into life. Firing at maximum elevation, the tracer of his guns' rounds looped in a high trajectory into the night; burning out at just over 1,000 metres they travelled invisibly over the last 1.5 kilometres to where the insurgents were hiding in the reeds. Delivered at a rate of 750 rounds per minute, the 7.62mm machine-gun bullets sliced into them, forcing out those who had escaped death into another crump of mortar fire. The final bombardment brought the engagement of raining bombs and bullets to a decisive conclusion. The Taliban mortar teams who had attacked the Kajaki team with previous impunity were no more. At least twelve of their number lay dead and several others had been wounded by the ferocity of 3 PARA's counter-fire.

The plan that had been put into action two nights previously had been an outstanding success. The Taliban had followed a pattern of setting up their 82mm Chinese-made mortars in the valley bottom to the south of the Kajaki Dam. They would come at night and fire a salvo of bombs at the compound that housed the US civilian personnel, who supervised the maintenance of the dam's hydro-turbines, and the Afghan security guards. Over the last few weeks insurgent pressure had increased and over half of the guards had deserted. The American company that provided the contractors at the dam were considering pulling their people out. If that happened the dam would be vulnerable to being taken over by the insurgents and the supply of electricity to Helmand and much of Kandahar would be under threat. In response, General Freakly was coming under pressure from the US Embassy to station a British company of infantry there to prevent this from happening. But it was another company that we didn't have.

I had flown up to recce the dam at the beginning of June. We landed on an LZ next to the dam that held back the melt water of the Hindu Kush in a large aqua-blue lake before allowing it to rush through the dam's one working turbine to generate electricity. It then surged as a torrent of white water into the crystal clearness of the Helmand River below. Flanked by high craggy features, the serene beauty of the setting was out of place with the abandoned debris left over from the time when the Soviets held the dam. A large Ukrainian-made crane sat wrecked by the LZ and the surrounding rocky outcrops were dominated by old Russian positions. At the foot of one were the remains of two destroyed Russian T-64 tanks. Their turrets had long been blown off and their burnt-out remains rusted into the sand. The minefields were the other Soviet legacy that littered the surrounding countryside. They had been buried at every likely approach to protect the complex from attack by the mujahideen. Some had been lifted and red-and-white painted stones marked the areas that had been cleared. Moving beyond the stones would invite the danger of stepping on a mine that still lurked beneath the rocky soil.

We were met by John Kranivich, a larger than life ex-US Special Forces soldier who had responsibility for the dam's security. He cradled a snub-nosed AK assault rifle and was glad to see us. As we drove down the track to his compound he filled us in on the Taliban activity that had increased over the last few weeks. They regularly engaged his Afghan guards who manned the positions in the surrounding hilltops. He had originally had over a hundred men, but now he had only seventy. Many had been intimidated by the Taliban who occupied the villages below the dam and controlled Route 611 running up from Sangin 30 kilometres to the south. As we entered his compound we passed a building called the Old Russian House. During the war with the Soviets, the dam had been overrun and the Soviet technicians had made a desperate last stand there. The mujahideen had broken into the ground floor capturing a number of Russians, whose comrades on the upper floor had to listen to their screams as they were tortured to death below them. When the rest of the house eventually fell, the survivors were taken to the dam and fed into the giant metal fans of the turbines. No longer used, the building still bore the battle scars of that terrible and long-forgotten night over twenty years before.

With the tale of the chilling encounter with the mujahideen still on my mind, I was straight up with John and told him that I couldn't spare men to come and guard the complex. However, I said that we could draw up emergency reinforcement plans to come and get him out of trouble if the need arose. John was happy with this, as he was confident that he could hold off any attack for long enough for us to reach him. Matt Taylor and I sketched out some rough contingency options and agreed code words with John. They could be used over his satellite phone in a crisis to dictate exactly how we would arrive and what he would need to do. On our return to Bastion we studied intelligence reports about the attacks. Our analysis suggested that they followed a pattern that made the Taliban vulnerable to ambush. Having conducted the recce to the dam, Matt and I were convinced that we could catch them at their own game. If we could hit them hard enough we might be able to protect the dam without having to station troops there permanently. I gave the task to Captain Nick French who commanded 3 PARA's Mortar Platoon.

Nick was given a small force of two of his mortar teams, a platoon of infantry from B Company and a section of machine guns from one of the FSGs. His temporary command was called French Force. It was infiltrated into the dam complex under cover of darkness in what was made to look like a routine resupply to the twenty ANA who had already been sent up there to bolster the dam's defences. Landing at the LZ, Nick's men manhandled their mortars and machine guns up the steep ground and into position on Sparrow Hawk, which overlooked the dam from the east. There they waited, until the Taliban attacked.

The insurgent attacks against the dam stopped for several weeks thereafter and I was able to withdraw French Force a few days later for use elsewhere. It also negated the need to station a whole company there on a permanent basis. The covert insertion of a temporary force of just forty men had allowed us to deliver the desired effect differently. It made the best use of scarce manpower and the limited resources at our disposal. We had checked the threat against the dam while preserving our freedom of movement. For once we had been allowed to be proactive rather than reactive. However, the elation at the success of forcing the Taliban to react to our decision-making cycle, rather than theirs, was short-lived.

7

Sangin

Everyone from the governor down was delighted by what French Force had achieved at Kajaki on the night of 17 June. But while it temporarily took the pressure off having to station part of the Battle Group permanently at the dam, the requirement to relieve the American troops in Musa Qaleh remained. A Company had been warned off for the task and we were in the process of planning to send them into the town's district centre. Then reports of a more urgent mission began to filter into the JOC. Insurgent activity had been increasing significantly in Sangin and was being exacerbated by local tribal politics. Dos Mohamed Khan was the chief of the Afghan National Department for Security in Helmand and had established his power base in Sangin. Khan was also an Alakazai and his tribe had been seen to prosper under the Karzai regime in Kabul at the expense of other tribes in the Sangin area. His brutal rule had alienated many of the local people and was compounded by the actions of his district chief of police, who had abused his position to abduct and rape children from the town. This provoked an outcry among the inhabitants who besieged him in the local police station. Daud wanted the British to extract him and UKTF became caught on the horns of a dilemma. If they rescued the police chief they would be seen to support the activities of a ruthless criminal. If they didn't rescue him they would be failing to support the governor.

The situation was exacerbated on 18 June when a rival warlord and leader of the Ishakzai tribe capitalized on the growing unrest in the town. With the support of the Taliban he ambushed and

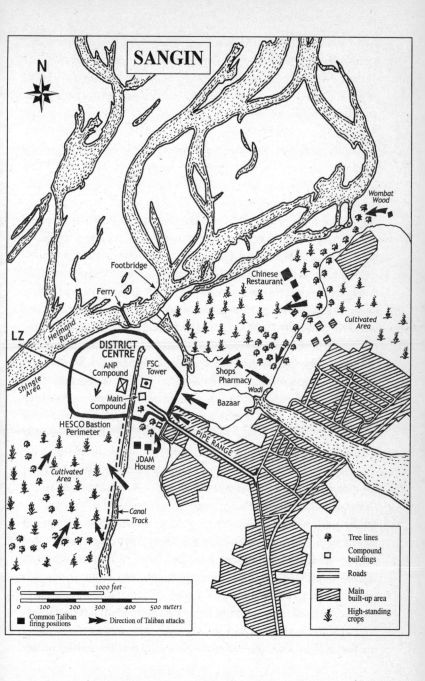

SANGIN

N

Wombat
Wood

Footbridge

Ferry

Chinese
Restaurant

Cultivated
Area

LZ

Helmand Rud

DISTRICT
CENTRE

ANP
Compound

FSC
Tower

Shingle
Area

Main
Compound

Shops
Pharmacy

Wadi

Bazaar

HESCO Bastion
Perimeter

Cultivated
Area

JDAM
House

PIPE RANGE

Canal
Track

0   1000 feet
0   100   200   300   400   500 meters

■ Common Taliban firing positions   ➤ Direction of Taliban attacks

Tree lines

Compound
buildings

Roads

Main
built-up area

High-standing
crops

killed forty of Khan's Alakazai followers. Khan's son was badly wounded in the fighting and Daud wanted the wounded boy and the rest of Khan's followers extracted from Sangin along with the chief of police. The issue of being tainted with supporting the criminal activities of the police chief was resolved when the elders escorted him to FOB Robinson and handed him over to the ANA. However, Khan's wounded son and the rest of his supporters remained in the district centre where they claimed they were about to be overrun by a coalition of hostile tribal factions and insurgents.

The intelligence picture indicated that any British intervention into Sangin would meet with stiff resistance. The risk of having a helicopter shot down as it landed into an unsecured LZ was considered to be severe. Entering Sangin would also consume another company if it became stuck there. With the need to occupy Musa Qaleh still looming on the horizon, there was a danger that the whole of 3 PARA would become fixed in holding static locations. Recognizing the seriousness of the situation, Ed Butler passed the issue up to the British Ambassador in Kabul to get a political decision. In the meantime he asked me to produce a risk assessment of conducting the rescue. He was particularly keen for me to give him my estimate of how many casualties we might take if we had to fight our way in. While discussions were held between Lashkar Gah, Kabul and London, the Battle Group worked up the plan for Sangin. PJHQ and Butler were cognizant of the risk involved but the political imperative dictated that we could not be seen to fail to support the governor's request.

On 19 June I participated in a radio conference with Butler who had flown forward to Lashkar Gah. The conference lasted into the early hours of the next day and Butler was receiving intelligence reports on the situation in Sangin from the governor's office as we spoke. We talked through the casualty estimate I had produced. I reiterated that the best case was that we got to the district centre unmolested and lost no one. The worst case was that we had a helicopter packed with paratroopers shot down; in this scenario we could lose up to fifty people in one go. Butler paused; he knew that I understood the political importance of the mission and I knew that he appreciated the military risks. 'Stuart, we have got reports coming in that the district centre is about to fall. If we are going to reduce the risks to the helicopters we need to use the cover of darkness and go before first light. Given that dawn is less than three hours away, I need to know whether you can launch the mission in the next ninety minutes.' Now it was my turn to pause and I looked at the staff and commanders of A Company who were gathered round the bird table. In essence Butler had given me the final call. 'Brigadier,' I replied, 'give me twenty minutes and I will come back to you with an answer.'

I put down the headset and looked to Huw Williams. 'Do we have everything in place to lift off within the next hour?' I asked. 'We do, Colonel,' he replied. Huw had given me the answer to the practicalities, but he knew that I wasn't looking to him to give me the answer as to whether we should go or not. It was the lives of my men on the line and as their commanding officer it was up to me to decide. I felt the burden of responsibility weigh on my shoulders as we quickly rehashed the pros and cons. Having listened to the views of others, I reflected on the balance of risk. We were here to support the government of Afghanistan; if we didn't go we would fail to do that. If we didn't go now, we would lose the slim element of surprise that we might have and we would probably be pressurized or ordered to go subsequently. Finally, we were Paras and being asked to do difficult and risky things was what we were meant to be about. I gave my decision to the men around me at the bird table; they all accepted it and the rationale that I gave them. I looked at each one as I picked up the headset. I spoke into the mike: 'Brigadier, we will be airborne in an hour.'

I scrambled into the back of the aircraft, the engine exhausts pumping out blasts of hot air as I stepped on to the tailgate. I clambered over the members of my Tac group and the men of one of A Company's platoons as I made my way to the front section by the two side door guns. I put on a headset and listened to the pilots go through their final checks. They were ready to go, but one of the other aircraft reported a technical fault. We sat on the pan with the engines running as we waited for it to be sorted out. It seemed to be taking an age and I considered calling off the mission as the first feeble light of dawn began to creep through the gunner's open hatch. My headset crackled into life and I was told the technical problem was fixed. I gave my acknowledgement and listened to the changing pitch of the engines as the power increased and we began to lift. Matt Taylor looked at me and shouted over the noise of the vibrating cab; he was pumped up and wanted to get it on. I felt a sense of personal guilt for not sharing his youthful enthusiasm. I flicked open my map to double-check the coordinates of the LZ and wondered about the sort of reception we would receive on landing.

As we gained height and headed out across the desert, I stood by the port-side M60 machine gun enjoying the relative cool of the slipstream that blew in through the gunner's open hatch. It provided a brief respite from the stupefying heat of the desert floor a few thousand feet below me. The two-minute warning came over the headset from the pilot. It was immediately followed by the customary two-fingered signal given by the senior air crewman to warn us we were two minutes out from the LZ at Sangin. I rechecked the belt of bullets in the feed tray of the M60, as the troops behind me made last-minute adjustments to kit and checked that their automatic weapons were made ready. The aircraft dropped to low level to make a nap of the earth approach from the western side of the Helmand River. The tension mounted as I felt the acceleration and the tilt of the aircraft, bringing with it the familiar heave in my belly with the sudden loss of altitude. Daylight had broken and the aircraft flew low enough to cast up dancing plumes of sand as old Russian trenches dug in along the heights overlooking the town of Sangin passed beneath us. We dropped over the high ground into the valley below and I saw a momentary flash of aqua blue as we crossed the river and headed to the LZ on the eastern bank. I listened intently on the intercom for the codeword call that the commander of the escorting Apaches would give if he considered that the LZ was cold and safe to land. If he detected the presence of the enemy, he would use another codeword to indicate that the landing area would be hot. He called the LZ cold and we continued to descend. But it didn't mean that the Taliban weren't located in the undergrowth waiting to fire at us during the most vulnerable moments of our descent.

In the final few seconds the smooth beat of the rotor blades slowed to a rhythmic clatter. Nose up and tail down, the aircraft pitched itself into a swirling cloud of dust, followed by the thump of the landing gear as the wheels made contact with the ground. A split second later the tailgate was lowered. Simultaneously, Paras began to run off the ramp and fanned out to take up fire positions forming a V shape beyond the back of the aircraft. All wore goggles and put their heads down to shield themselves from the blast of grit and sand as the aircraft lifted off. Twenty seconds after landing it had gone, leaving us in the silence of the settling dust and the incongruous beauty of our surroundings. We had expected to land under fire, but the scene that greeted us as the dust settled was one of tranquillity. The high reed grass and the green of the trees and fields a few hundred metres off to our right were a stark contrast to the sun-baked yellow-brown monotony of the surrounding desert. A brace of startled marsh snipe broke cover and headed across the river that gurgled leisurely by to our left.

The men of A Company set about readying themselves to move off as a thin early morning mist rose from the river. Tac closed in and established radio contact with Bastion as A Company's lead platoon started moving through the haze towards the district centre. If they came under contact they would call on the support of the two mortars that were setting up next to us. The mortar men were busily checking that potential target grids had been properly plotted into their hand-held fire control computers. As we waited for A Company to secure the district centre and call us forward, I chatted to Corporal Peter Thorpe and Lance Corporal

Jabron Hashmi who were part of a signal detachment attached to the Battle Group. Initial reports indicated that the Taliban had begun to withdraw from the town on our arrival. This appeared to be confirmed by the fact that A Company were able to move into the district centre without coming under fire.

We saw the party we had been sent to rescue as soon as Tac entered the compound on the heels of A Company: a group of twenty or so Afghans. There were more of them than we had anticipated, including a middle-aged relative of Khan's who had been shot through the buttocks. All were dressed in the traditional shalwar-kameez of long, flowing baggy shirts worn over loose-fitting trousers. Younger men carried AK-47s and wore ill-fitting web-strapped pouches for their magazines. The older men wore white and black turbans and long grey beards. Deeply lined faces indicated their seniority and a lifetime of hardship. In their midst was a fourteen-year-old male who lay quietly on a makeshift bed of white sheets. Hit in the stomach by an AK-47 round, this was the district security chief's wounded son who had prompted our mission. He lay uncomplaining as his elder relatives fussed over him and Harvey Pynn checked him out and prepared him for evacuation.

The district centre lay on the eastern bank of the Helmand River on the outskirts of Sangin. It consisted of a typical administrative whitewashed compound. In its centre was an arch-fronted one-storey building and a collection of outhouses surrounded by a high wall. The compound incorporated an orchard and two patches of lawn surrounded by bright Afghan flowers. Next to the compound lay the shell of a large, partially completed structure of two floors, the building work long abandoned. A canal ran off the nearby river and separated the compound from a more modern two-storey building that was the ANP quarters. It was reached from the back of the main compound by crossing a large pipe that acted as a footbridge.

I climbed the crumbling stairs of the half-built building and surveyed the surrounding area from the rooftop, empty AK-47 cases betraying where Khan's militia had fired their weapons against the Taliban. From my vantage point I could see that the collection of buildings that made up the district centre dominated the antiquated ferry-crossing site that had been used by the patrol during their fateful search for the downed UAV. The river bent and flowed towards Gereshk past the open pebble banks where we had landed that morning. There was also a small rickety footbridge that crossed the river and was swept away at the end of each winter when the melt water came. Set among cultivated fields to its north and south, the beginnings of the urban sprawl of the town lay less than 150 metres away on either side of a wide gravel-strewn wadi bed. A group of goat herders milled about in the dry wadi bed and traded some of their flock. To their east a line of shuttered shops and empty market stalls led through the bazaar to the main part of the town. I could make out a road bridge that took Route 611 through the centre of Sangin and a small number of other two-storey buildings that dominated the town's skyline. The odd vehicle moved across the bridge and black figures darted between doorways as if to suggest that the townsfolk of Sangin were alive to our presence.

We roasted for an hour in 46°C of heat as we waited for the incoming helicopters to pick up my Tac party and Khan's sup-porters from a field by the side of the district centre. But it was nothing compared to the conditions A Company would endure. I was leaving them behind with their mortars and machine guns and the RAP; in all, ninety men and a motley crew of about twenty ANP. Daud had promised to send another fifty ANP in three days' time to relieve A Company. But for the moment they would have to make do with the light scales of equipment they had brought in with them. In the days that followed A Company lived off their belt order kit and daysacks until their heavier bergens could be brought forward. Conditions in the centre were austere in the extreme and the company adopted what soldiers call 'hard routine'. The compound had no running water or electricity. The limited water that could be flown forward from Bastion was reserved for drinking purposes only. With the exception of an occasional dip in the canal, there were no washing facilities and the men stopped shaving. They became used to prickly heat as they worked and slept in filthy clothing, in temperatures that reached 50°C. The one latrine consisted of the flat corner of an old storehouse that the ANP used to shit and piss in. To reduce the plague of flies that proliferated in the mass of tight-packed humanity and heat, A Company set up their own latrines using old oil drums near the orchard.

As I left, Pike's men were already preparing defensive positions around the compound. Built for Third World civic administration rather than defence, the district centre was vulnerable and needed to be fortified against attack. We anticipated that the Taliban would soon return and A Company utilized any materials they could lay their hands on to build sangar positions that would act as bunkers for machine guns and missile launchers. Crumbling, locally made breeze blocks were used to build additional walls, and ration boxes were filled with earth in lieu of sandbags. The FSG located their machine guns and Javelin missile launchers on the roof of the two-storey half-built structure. The height of the building would allow their weapons systems to command the surrounding countryside and it quickly became known as the FSG Tower. Before our departure the men of the mortar section were already digging firing pits into the green lawns for their mortar barrels. Nearby in the main compound building Harvey Pynn was turning one of its small dark rooms into an RAP ready to receive casualties.

What started as a rescue mission was the beginning of a much longer commitment to Sangin. The ANP reinforcements that Governor Daud promised to send never arrived and A Company resigned themselves to being in Sangin for considerably more than the three days they had been promised. Daud reluctantly agreed to attend a *shura* with the local elders in the district centre on 24 June, four days after A Company arrived. I flew back into Sangin with Daud's party, which included Charlie Knaggs. The locals reiterated the points that they had already made to Will Pike during a meeting he had held with them on 22 June. In essence they didn't want to see British troops in the town and believed that they should be left to provide their own security. But they mentioned that they would welcome the economic development our presence could bring to Sangin and hinted that they were being intimidated by the Taliban. After Daud's *shura*, the majority of the elders had begun to leave the compound, but as Daud spoke with Charlie Knaggs and me a spokesman for the elders returned. He said that he needed to be given three days to consult with the Taliban and drug warlords about accepting a new chief of police and the presence of British troops. It was agreed that we would not patrol into the town during this period until he came back to us with a response. With that he left, we returned to Bastion with the governor's party and A Company began another period of watching and waiting.

As I flew back on the Chinook I thought about the implications of holding Sangin. I was convinced that we could not sustain Robinson, Gereshk, Now Zad and take on the tasks of holding both Sangin and Musa Qaleh. Although unbeknown to me at the time, we had been sucked into another static commitment that would stretch our thin resources and test our resolve to breaking point. Sangin not only sat in the middle of a confluence of several tribal areas, but it was also the centre of the opium trade in Helmand. These dynamics made the area a volatile melting pot of inter-tribal factionalism, feuding warlords and a place where the Taliban were determined to establish their ascendancy. It also dictated that it would be where the insurgents would focus their main effort in an attempt to break the will of the British commitment to Helmand. Consequently, it was probably the worst place in the province that 3 PARA could have stumbled into. The uneasy peace in Sangin held for two days, with the exception of an isolated shoot against one of the sangars. Then in the early hours of 27 June the fighting started.

I knew it was bad when I was shaken awake and looked up to

see Huw Williams's face looming over me. 'Colonel, you need to come up to the JOC. There has been a contact up in Sangin, there have been casualties and there might be a soldier missing in action.' I fought to clear my mind from the fuddle of sleep as I threw on my uniform. From what Huw told me I knew it wasn't A Company. I glanced at my kit, which was packed ready in a corner of my tent; something told me that I would soon be flying out to Sangin. The situation was unclear when I arrived in the JOC but what we knew was that a Coalition Forces patrol had been involved in a heavy firefight on the southern edges of Sangin. It had been a lift operation to apprehend a Taliban leader. Working out of FOB Robinson they had called on the platoon of Gurkhas stationed there to drive into the outskirts of the town and pick up them and their quarry in Snatch Land-Rovers. The Gurkhas had been ambushed as they drove out to meet the patrol and one of their vehicles had been destroyed by RPGs. As the patrol moved on foot to the pick-up point it had run into the back of the Taliban ambush. A vicious firefight ensued. The patrol managed to fight their way through to the Gurkhas and extract back to the FOB under covering fire provided by the base's artillery. But in the process one member of the patrol had been killed, another wounded and one of their number was unaccounted for.

The report of the contact was the first we knew about the patrol's activities. Following on from the ambush against the French, it was the second incident of coalition forces operating in our patch without our knowledge. But with the possibility that a man was missing in action (MIA) we had to act quickly. If he had been captured by the Taliban, or had gone to ground waiting for rescue, time was of the essence. B Company and the Chinooks had already been stood to. I spoke to the Chief of Staff at UKTF in Kandahar who had also been dragged out of bed. He had no prior knowledge about the patrol and was busily trying to find out more about them from RC-South. Although the picture was still confused, we both knew that we couldn't delay by referring a decision to attempt a rescue operation to higher authority. If we were to have any chance of recovering the MIA we had to launch quickly.

I made the call that we would launch and thirty minutes later we were lifting off from Bastion. We air-assaulted on to an offset LZ on the banks of the Helmand River a kilometre away from the map grid of the ambush site. Daylight was breaking and the Apaches hovered overhead as we waded through a deep tributary stream to a cluster of small compounds on the eastern bank. Tac set up in all-round defence with an FSG and Giles Timms pushed his lead platoon forward to the contact site under the command of Lieutenant Martin Hewitt. I studied my map: the country was close and if we had arrived too late, looking for a missing man among the myriad of farm compounds and irrigation ditches would be an impossible task. Corporal Watt, my signaller, suddenly interrupted my thoughts. 'Sir, 5 Platoon have found them; I'm afraid that they are both dead.' Martin Hewitt's grim discovery answered the question about the missing soldier. He had died fighting bravely alongside his fallen comrade whose own body lay close by. Next to the two men lay a number of Taliban dead which indicated the intensity of the firefight.

The two dead soldiers were placed in body bags and carried back to Tac's location with Company Sergeant Major Willets. The rest of B Company pushed further south down the main road out of Sangin to ensure that sensitive equipment in the Gurkhas' abandoned Snatch was destroyed. A Hellfire missile from one of the Apaches was then fired into the vehicle to complete the task of denying it to the insurgents. I noticed the sobering effect of carrying the dead on the young Toms who lifted the body bags. For most it would have been the first time they had seen British casualties. No doubt it reminded them of their own mortality and the seriousness of the business we were in. For me the incident was particularly poignant, as one of the dead soldiers was the charming Irishman I had met a few weeks before on the firing range in Gereshk.

There was a sombre mood in the helicopter as we flew back to

Bastion with the two body bags placed at our feet on the floor of the cab. I looked across at the liaison officer who had survived the contact and had come with us to help us locate his fallen comrades. I felt for him. His face still betrayed the shock of his experiences; it was the same expression I had seen on the faces of the two French officers after they had been ambushed driving down from Kajaki. Again a patrol had been operating in our battle space without our knowledge. I wondered whether knowing about it in advance might have made a difference. Regardless of the background to the patrol it had brought fighting to Sangin and was to have a profound effect on the troops in the district centre. Later that day an elder came to the compound and told Pike that A Company would be attacked by the Taliban if they stayed in the town. The battle for the district centre was about to begin.

As Will Pike was receiving the elder's warning, Major Paddy Blair was also engaged in dialogue with another local elder 100 kilometres to the south-east in the village of Zumbelay. C Company had set off earlier that morning to conduct a familiarization patrol to the village and gain information on its development needs. They left FOB Price in a convoy of Snatch Land-Rovers and Pinzgauer trucks carrying Blair's company headquarters and 9 (Ranger) Platoon of Royal Irish Regiment that had reinforced 3 PARA at the beginning of the tour, and a section of two mortar barrels. Escorted by an FSG mounted in WMIKs under the command of Captain Alex McKenzie, the men of C Company were glad to be patrolling beyond the confines of Gereshk. They were accompanied by Christina Lamb from the *Sunday Times* and her photographer Justin Sutcliffe. Both journalists were enjoying the carefree company of the men they travelled with. It was a hearts and minds mission and there was no sense that they were going looking for trouble.

Arriving near the outskirts of the village, Blair dismounted and patrolled into its centre on foot with 9 Platoon, a section of snipers and the journalists. The FSG escorted the empty vehicles to a Zulu muster collection point and then moved to some adjacent high ground to the north to cover Blair's move into Zumbelay. Patrolling through open fields criss-crossed by deep irrigation ditches, Blair's men entered the flat, mud-walled compounds of the village. It was unusually quiet. No children gathered to ask for sweets or gawk excitedly at the soldiers who moved through their dusty streets. Apart from a few goat herders who they had passed in the fields there was also a noticeable absence of menfolk. The one local elder they met explained people were away praying at the mosque and suggested that they came back for a *shura* the next day. He offered them no tea as they sat and talked. When Blair and his party got up to leave he recommended they take a short cut back to their vehicles. He indicated the other end of the village where he said they would find a bridge to take them over a wide irrigation channel.

The FSG had lost sight of the foot patrol in the myriad of compounds when they received a radio message to move to a rendezvous point to meet up with Blair's men as they left the village. They had also received a report of a suspicious gathering of armed men in the vicinity. Suddenly there was a large explosion behind the vehicles as the first rocket-propelled grenade landed. It was followed by a swarm of bullets and other RPG warheads. The .50 Cal gunners on the WMIKs hammered back with return fire. Corporal Adams of the Mortar Platoon emptied the contents of his 9mm pistol in the direction of the enemy before scrambling for cover. McKenzie shouted frantic orders to start manoeuvring the vehicles out of the contact area. He had enough time to send a radio message to Blair before he heard another contact unfolding 300 metres away in the fields below him. McKenzie realized that the foot patrol was also being taken on as part of a coordinated attack against both elements of the company. But his immediate concern was to win the firefight against his own attackers and get the Snatches and Pinzgauer trucks to safer ground before he could go and help the foot patrol.

As the dismounted troops moved away from the village they heard the contact raging against the FSG on the high ground.

Minutes later a burst of automatic fire cracked over their heads. Chaos reigned, as they rushed for the cover of the irrigation ditches. Blair fought to regain control of a confused situation. The cohesion of his patrol had been broken in the frantic scramble for the protection of the water channels. His men were split up among the ditches, his FSG were engaged in their own contact and he was being attacked from three different sides. They were in a tight spot. If they stayed where they were they were in danger of being rolled up by the Taliban or being hit by the mortar fire and RPGs that also began to thump down around his men as they sheltered in the ditches. If they moved in isolated groups they would expose themselves to being cut up piecemeal by an enemy who was now less than a few hundred metres from their positions. He needed to coordinate the actions of his disparate sections and get them moving, but the broken ground was preventing his radios from working properly.

His company sergeant major, Mick Bolton, barked orders and junior commanders popped coloured smoke grenades and fired flares to identify their locations. Plumes of the acrid-smelling red and green smoke began to build and swirl in the slight breeze. They attracted the attention of the Taliban, but provided the necessary reference points from which a coordinated response could be made. Commands of 'Rapid fire!' were followed by a crescendo of combined fire of GPMGs, SA80 rifles and Minimi light machine guns. As the heavy weight of fire poured back through the reeds and high grass against the Taliban, the company started to move. Soldiers fired together, then pulled themselves out of the waterlogged ditches to charge across the open ground to the next piece of cover, one section covering the movement of the other, as the process was repeated across sun-baked furrows that threatened to turn ankles. Bolton continued to bark commands: 'Keep moving, keep spread out, get into fucking cover!'

Having been pulled out of one ditch, Christina Lamb pressed herself into the bottom of another, her heart pounding. Every time they moved and sought new cover they seemed to be running into more Taliban intent on killing them. In the pandemonium she had become separated from Justin and feared for his safety. Experienced in covering many war zones, this was the most dangerous situation she had ever been in. She thought of her family safely at home in London and all the things in her life that had been left undone. The significance of the absence of children, the menfolk and the normal Afghan hospitality of offering tea dawned on her. The elder's suggestion of a shorter route had been perfidious, there was no bridge: the men of C Company had been set up. AK rounds chopped into the reeds and the mud of the bank above her head as she prepared to make the next move with the soldiers who protected her.

Not far from where Lamb sheltered, Private Kyle Deerans steadied his breathing and levelled his .338 sniper rifle on a small mound. He settled the cross-hairs of the telescopic sight on a single Taliban fighter as he crested its top. He squeezed the trigger and the heavy-calibre round knocked the man backwards. Another Tom from the Ranger Platoon pushed himself up on his knees and brought his GPMG to bear over the reeds. The belt of 7.62mm bullets jerked violently in his hand as he fired a long burst back towards the Taliban. The company were moving and fighting together, but the Taliban were still closing. Blair had established intermittent radio communications with Bastion and was screaming for air support. The two A-10 aircraft he had been promised had been diverted to a contact in Sangin. He realized that he and his men were going to have to get out of the situation on their own. Blair pressed for fire support from his FSG and the mortar barrels.

Having broken contact and moved the more vulnerable Snatches and Pinzgauer vehicles to safety, Corporal Dennis Mitchell of the Machine Gun Platoon knew where the FSG WMIKs needed to go. To their left there was another ridge that overlooked the field that Blair's men were fighting through. Let's just fucking get there, he thought as the WMIKs were cautiously moved forward in pairs. As they reached the apex of the high ground they looked down to see between ten and fifteen fighters a few hundred metres to their front on the flat ground below the ridge. They were clearly getting ready to ambush the dismounted elements of C Company as they fought their way through the fields. Normal rates of fire went out of the window as the FSG opened up on the group of Taliban with everything they had. The devastating weight of fire from the four WMIKs' .50 Cal heavy machine guns and GPMGs scythed into the insurgents who disappeared in a cloud of dust kicked up by the bullets. The effect of the fire was witnessed by the men of the Ranger Platoon who came across the dismembered remains of the Taliban who had been about to ambush them.

The FSG brought their dismounted comrades some breathing space, but their exposed position on the ridge line attracted fire from another group of Taliban to their left. Their vehicles were rocked by RPG explosions, wheel covers were shredded by shrapnel and one rocket-propelled grenade bounced off the front of McKenzie's WIMK. They pulled back and formed another base line from which they continued to provide covering fire to those stranded in the fields. Corporal Mitchell took advantage of a brief lull in the enemy fire to relieve himself at the side of his vehicle. He glanced to his right and saw McKenzie gesticulating and waving at him to get his WMIK out of the way. He couldn't hear what they were shouting, as he had been deafened by the roar of the .50 Cal that had been firing over his head. He looked to where they were indicating and saw two Taliban firing at him with their AKs. He dived back into his vehicle as their tracer rounds whipped over his head. With a clear line of sight the other WMIKs kicked into life and their heavy machine-gun bullets began flattening a small building the two insurgents had taken cover in.

The supporting fire from the FSG had begun to tip the desperate battle in the fields in Blair's favour. As daylight began to fade two Apaches arrived on station and helped beat the attackers off. The addition of their 30mm cannons to the fire of the FSG allowed Blair to complete a final break clean and link up with his vehicles. A quick head check and hasty redistribution of ammunition was completed. Then the company mounted up and moved out to reorganize in the desert under the cover of darkness. The intervention of the attack helicopters had been timely, as the contact had lasted for three hours and ammunition was beginning to run low. Each of the WMIKs' .50 Cal gunners was on his third or fourth box of ammunition. Thankfully, they had begged and borrowed a large quantity of the half-inch rounds from other NATO forces when they had moved through Gereshk. The experiences of firing the British-issued ammunition and subsequent test firing had proved that it was faulty. Due to poor machine work on the brass cases, the ammunition caused stoppages after one or two rounds had been fired. Had C Company's FSGs been forced to use the standard issue .50 Cal ammunition, the outcome of the engagement might have been very different. But it was aggression, physical fitness combined with junior command grip and accurate shooting that won the day. When fear and danger came to call among the ditches and exposed ridge line, training kicked in and men under fire reacted to the drills that they had been taught. After their safe return to Gereshk in the early hours of the morning, I spoke to Paddy Blair on a secure telephone link to FOB Price. He calmly talked of what had happened, the lessons that had been learned and of how well his men had performed. Just before we finished the conversation he paused, and I could almost see him reflecting at the other end of the line. Then in his characteristic Irish brogue, he added phlegmatically, 'It was a bit cheeky, Colonel; I am amazed that we didn't lose anybody.'

A few days later, Christina Lamb's account of the patrol into Zumbelay appeared as a five-page spread in the *Sunday Times*. Her vivid description of the fighting included dramatic images of the combat that Justin Sutcliffe managed to capture on his camera. The article majored on her personal experiences and the bravery of C Company. In one brief sentence she also raised questions about the nature and strategy of the UK's mission in Helmand. It was not a critical tirade against official policy, but in bringing the fighting she had witnessed to the attention of the British public, she debunked any misconception that the UK was conducting a peace support operation in Afghanistan. I later read the article in Bastion and took no major issue with what she said. However, it provoked an angry response in certain government departments in Whitehall and led to what the press considered an official media blackout on reporters in Helmand. The press saw it as an attempt to prevent further coverage of the fighting from reaching the UK public. The blackout became a media issue in itself as journalists claimed that the government was deliberately trying to hide what was going on in Afghanistan. Officials claimed that restrictions on reporters were being imposed for their own safety. It was a poor argument to present to journalists who accepted the risk of war reporting as a professional occupational hazard. Regardless of the reason, and the fact that I was happy to have the media with us, we were to receive no more embedded reporters until September.

Without access to the front line, the press relied on unsolicited accounts of the fighting drawn from e-mails and the limited and biased testimony of a few individuals who were prepared to breach official regulations and talk to the media. This did little to help the remote and often speculative and sensational reporting. The government's measures in the wake of Zumbelay were a classic example of how not to deal with the media. But the people who suffered most were the families of my soldiers. As reports of the fighting amplified, wives, girlfriends and parents sat at home and became increasingly worried about their loved ones. It was a situation that was not helped by the often distorted versions of events that began to appear on their TV sets and newspapers, especially when the first reports of casualties filtered back to the UK.

8

Incoming

There was a roaring wush as the propellant ignited and blasted the rocket forward from its crude launcher. A little over 2 kilometres away Corporal James Shimmons of the Machine Gun Platoon had no idea that the high-explosive 107mm Chinese-made projectile was inbound to his location on top of the roof of the district centre. He was putting down a shovel he had been using to fill sandbags when it struck the wall of the sniper tower. The rocket passed in front of him and there was a blinding flash which blew him across the roof in a hail of blasted masonry, dust and shrapnel. Shimmons knew that whatever had suddenly shattered the peace of the warm night was big and serious. Amazed that he was still alive, he did an 'immediate fingers and toes check' to see if he had been injured. Then the screaming started.

Virtually every man on the roof had been caught in the blast as the rocket detonated against the wall of the small building on top of the FSG Tower. The 1.2-metre-square concrete structure sheltered the stairs that led up from the ground floor to the large roof. The tower housed A Company's specialist signals team, where corporals Thorpe and Hashmi were preparing to bed down for the night with their Afghan interpreter. On the smaller roof above them, the sniper pair made up of Corporal Hatfield and Private Nixon peered through the night sights of their .388 sniper rifles into the darkness of the night around them. Moments before the rocket struck, Sergeant 'Emlyn' Hughes had walked down the steps of the FSG Tower to have a smoke in the darkened bowels of the building. As he lit his cigarette the world two floors above him exploded.

Those who had merely been caught in the concussion of the explosion or hit by flying masonry were lucky. Private Brown had his leg broken as he was flung backward by the blast, Private Scott's legs were struck by metal fragments and Corporal Hatfield's eardrums were burst. Corporal of Horse Fry and Corporal Cartwright of the FST received more serious shrapnel injuries. Fry's hand had been seriously gashed and his thumb nearly severed; Cartwright received a piece of shrapnel that travelled along the outside of his bowel and became lodged in his pelvis. Serious though the two NCOs' injuries were, they were relatively minor compared to the carnage the rocket inflicted inside the sniper tower itself. Penetrating the wall, the warhead spread its lethal contents among those inside. Within the confined space of the tower, Corporal Peter Thorpe, Lance Corporal Jabron Hashmi and Dawood Amiery, the A Company interpreter, would not have known what hit them.

The attacks against the district centre had started shortly after the elder had come to warn Will Pike. They were intermittent at first; RPG rounds followed by AK fire from the compounds and the row of shops that ran alongside the north of the dry wadi. It initially started as a nightly routine. As muzzle flashes lit up the darkness, men would scramble from their sleeping places on the dusty floor to don body armour and helmets and rush to their stand-to positions. They would return fire with all their weapons systems, including two .50 Cal heavy machine guns that had been flown forward to bolster the defences. The attacks would then peter out as 81mm mortar illumination rounds were fired into the air, their flares casting an eerie light among the shadows as they drifted back to earth under small parachute canopies.

After the first few tentative attacks, they soon started to occur during the day as well. The company took to sleeping by their sangars, often wearing their webbing and body armour in an attempt to catch an hour or two of fitful sleep until the next attack started. But in the first days the Taliban were only testing and counting the defenders' guns; gradually their attacks became bolder. On 30 June two pick-up trucks full of Taliban suddenly drove into the bazaar among the empty market stalls at the other end of the wadi. The GPMGs and .50 Cals kicked into life, sending streams of red tracer rounds into the insurgents and killing several of them before they could get close enough to open fire on the district centre.

On 1 July the Taliban launched a coordinated two-pronged assault. A group of up to twenty fighters attempted to fire and manoeuvre their way across the dry wadi bed, while another group assaulted down the narrow track christened the Pipe Range that led to the gates of the main compound from the east. The attackers were cut down by the company's GPMGs and .50 Cals. Caught in the murderous fire of the open wadi and the confines of the Pipe Range, the insurgents didn't stand a chance. The survivors retreated back into cover leaving their dead behind them. Above them a 500-pound precision-guided Joint Direct Attack Munition (JDAM) was released from the weapon rack under the wing of a circling A-10. The bomb's onboard GPS automatically adjusted the tail fins as it vectored through the air towards its target. They would guide it on to the target coordinates that the pilot had received from the JTAC on the ground and had pumped into the computer in his cockpit seconds before he released the weapon. It found the surviving Taliban in their hiding place with pinpoint accuracy, spewing a fireball and greasy black smoke into the air. Mortar rounds and cannon fire from the Apaches added to the death and destruction visited on the insurgents and they attempted to make good their withdrawal. The attack had been fanatical and daring, but it was amateurish and suicidal in its conception. Coming several days later, the use of the 107mm rocket demonstrated that the Taliban had learned the lessons of costly frontal assaults. It also meant that the ensuing fights around the district centre became less one-sided.

Company Sergeant Major Zac Leong had heard the almighty explosion when the rocket landed. He knew that it was serious before the first report came through the battlefield telephone system that linked the Ops Room to the roof telling them that there were casualties. He charged up the steps with a stretcher party taking Corporal Poll's section with him. They were greeted by a scene of devastation and chaos when they reached the top of the stairs. The interpreter was already dead and the two corporals lay unconscious. Leong's party set about treating and evacuating the wounded men. Sergeant Dan Jarvie rushed to the RAP where Harvey Pynn and his medics, Sergeant Reidy and Corporal Roberts, were getting ready to receive the casualties. Lance Corporal Hashmi was brought in first followed by Corporal Thorpe. Pynn and his team worked desperately to save them as the emergency helicopter was scrambled into the air from Bastion. But despite the medics' tireless efforts, both men were beyond help.

I listened intently to the information coming in about the casualties by the side of the bird table in the JOC at Bastion. My heart sank as their medical categorization quickly changed from T1, which meant gravely wounded and in need of immediate surgery, to T4, which informed us that both men had died. I heard Matt Taylor swear as Huw Williams asked for confirmation. Back in the RAP, Dan Jarvie saw Corporal Cartwright stagger into the aid post doubled up in pain and watched as the medics began to treat his friend. Will Pike pushed for the helicopter to pick up the surviving wounded, but the base was still under fire and Pike knew that he could not guarantee a secure LZ for the helicopter. I asked for medical confirmation of their category status and for Pike's assessment of whether getting them out immediately was critical, or whether they could hang on until a safer daylight extraction could be attempted. Pike responded that they were T2, which meant that they had non-life-threatening injuries, but would still require surgery. He also added that he had spoken to the wounded men and, given the threat to the helicopter, they were all willing to wait for evacuation. It was a tough call. Every commander wants to get his wounded men off the ground. But there was a very real risk of the helicopter being shot down. The lives of the men on board it had to be balanced against the survival of the wounded. With a heavy heart, I gave the word to order the helicopter to turn back.

It was a long night for the men of A Company, particularly for the wounded who waited patiently in the darkness for evacuation. I flew up with my Tac party on the helicopter when dawn broke. We landed in the field next to the district centre, the blades of the helicopter thumping the grass flat. Seconds after we got off the three body bags of the men killed in the rocket attack were carried on board. They were followed by the wounded. I managed to shout a few words of encouragement to Corporal of Horse Fry as he passed me. Then the helicopter was gone, leaving us in the settling dust and grit as it climbed away and headed back to Bastion. I spoke with Sergeant Major Leong who had earned his pay the night before; I noted the blood on his uniform as we patrolled into the district centre from the LZ.

Will Pike met me outside the Ops Room. He updated me on the detail of what had happened and gave me an assessment of his current situation. He had the look of a man who had not slept in days; his face was gaunt and his hair was matted with dried sweat. He was clearly agitated by the predicament he and his men found themselves in, but his words were clear and calm as he talked me through his concerns. I sat back and listened as he outlined how he felt that the company had become dangerously exposed and that more men would die if they stayed in the district centre. He spoke of the porous defences of the compound's perimeter and of the suspected perfidy of the ANP. Daud had still not sent reinforcements and the remaining ANP failed to contribute to the defence of the position. Pike was convinced that they were dicking the movements of his men by giving information to the Taliban. I shared his concerns and trusted his judgement, but I also knew what the political answer would be to any request to withdraw. As we spoke, intelligence reports were coming in that a large attack was being prepared against the compound. I left him to organize his headquarters to prepare to meet the threat.

I went round the positions with Bish to see how the blokes were doing. Bish went one way and I went the other; we agreed to meet in the middle of the position to compare notes. I asked Sergeant Major Leong to accompany me and asked him for his assessment as we headed into the orchard. He told me that things had been hard, but he also made the point of saying that the company was okay and could hang on. They had been fighting off attacks for the last seven days out of fourteen. I doubted any had slept properly in a week. When they weren't fighting, they would have been standing guard and forming work parties to build up their positions. If they tried to snatch a few hours, their fitful slumbers would be broken by the crash of an RPG or the snap of bullets heralding the next assault. They were doing a brilliant job in the most trying of circumstances and I told them so. Each man I spoke to as I walked round the bullet- and rocket-scarred positions wore the stress of the last few days on his face. Apart from the lines of fatigue that were etched on their features they were unshaven and dirty. They had not washed properly since arriving and their combat fatigues were filthy; their sweat-drenched garments had dried on their bodies a hundred times and some were caked in the blood of fallen comrades. My men were exhausted and some were anxious, but morale was remarkably high in the knowledge that this was what they were bred to do. I asked them about what they were going through, listened to their views and reinforced the importance of our task there, however difficult. I thanked the sergeant major and asked him and his men to keep on doing what they were doing.

I met up with Bish and we talked on our own. He shared my opinion that, from walking round and chatting to the men, the company was all right. But he said that they would benefit from being relieved. I agreed and said that I would bring in B Company as soon as possible to give A Company some time out of the line. I went back to the Ops Room and spoke with Will Pike who had just finished giving orders to his command team about their tactics to meet the coming threat. I mentioned my intent to relieve the company and we discussed how the defensive position could be improved. I agreed with his request to bring in Engineer support to build proper sangars, excavate dugouts and build HESCO Bastion blast walls of earth-filled metal cages, which were capable of stopping bullets and RPG rounds. As we spoke men were already making minor makeshift improvements and I suggested to Will that Tac could lend a hand. We offered to finish the work started on a sandbagged emplacement on top of the main one-storey compound building while Will concentrated on completing the organization of his company. I grabbed one of the GPMG gunners to provide us with some local protection and then set off up the short flight of stairs with a spade in my hand.

The emplacement covered one of the southern approaches to the district centre along the canal and into a maize field behind the orchard. We dumped our webbing and weapons by the side of the partially completed sangar and began stripping out shot-up sandbags and refilling them. It was miserably hot as we humped them across the roof, the sweat running down our backs as we worked. The sun was sliding to the west and began to tinge everything it touched in a pink hue that comes with the fading rays of light before the onset of evening. I looked out across the gilded fields and hedge lines on the other side of the LZ and thought evocatively of England. I visualized the sunshine of a summer's evening on leafy church parishes and the first hatch of mayfly that I had already missed.

My thoughts were interrupted by a sharp whip and crack as the first bullets split the air around us. We had positioned the GPMG gunner facing the wrong way. Suddenly I was behind the low wall of sandbags we had built, cocking and firing my weapon out into the field below us. The report of my first round was so close to Warrant Officer Tony Lynch's ear that for an awful second I thought that in my haste to return fire I had hit the one man who was personally responsible for protecting me. I managed an embarrassed apology as he said, 'Fucking hell, Colonel!' and then grinned and started returning fire along with the rest of Tac. I looked to my right and saw Bish lying spreadeagled on the roof as rounds fizzed as they came unnervingly close. I was about to tell him to stop messing about and get behind the sandbags when I saw the bullets lick the dust around him. He was pinned down and the Taliban were trying to bracket him with their rounds. He shouted for covering fire. I changed my magazine and pumped bullets back across the field as fast as I could with the rest of Tac. Bish scrambled for the relative safety of the half-built bunker before picking up his weapon to join in the firefight against the small bobbing black figures obscured by the undergrowth of the hedge line 300 metres away.

The contact stopped as abruptly as it had started; the figures were gone. We all felt elated with the buzz of post-combat euphoria that comes when no one has been hit. But it dawned on me that it was one thing to be shot at once and get away with it. The men of A Company had been doing it day in, day out for the last week. They knew that they would be doing more of it and that some of them would be hit. But for Bish it would be his first and last contact of the tour as his two-year stint as the RSM was due to end. He had been selected for promotion and he was about to return to the UK.

Our brief contact was the start of a night of other attacks as the promised assault against the district centre unfolded. The defenders hammered back at the enemy's muzzle flashes as insurgents fired unseen from behind cover as darkness fell. A 107mm rocket passed overhead, making the sound of a large sky-borne zip as it parted the air above the compound. Rocket-propelled grenades wushed and thumped with a crash of flame and shrapnel as they landed around the position. I listened to the JTAC, Captain Matt Armstrong, talking calmly and with authority to the aircraft that had arrived to provide close air support. Pairs of A-10s flew in, dropped their deadly cargo on the grids that Armstrong fed them and then went off station to refuel. Apaches, mortars and the 105mm guns from FOB Robinson filled the gaps as they sought out the Taliban firing positions. The company headquarters received reports, ordered the resupply of ammunition to the sangars and passed back reports to Bastion.

It was another long night for the men of A Company as they kept the attackers at bay, each man alone with his private thoughts of whether another 107mm rocket might find his location. The air was filled with the staccato chatter of machine guns and the deafening boom of the two mortar barrels each time they fired from the courtyard. The 105mm guns from the battery at Robinson fired numerous danger close missions, where the blast of their shells landed close enough to spray the sangars with shrapnel. Against the cacophony of sound was the dull rhythmic drone of a US AC-130 Spectre gunship as it circled high overhead keeping a lone vigil over the district centre. At intervals the 105mm cannon mounted in its fuselage would boom against an enemy heat source that it had picked up. This lethal version of the four-engined Hercules stayed with us throughout the night, before finally heading for its base with the coming of daylight.

Dawn brought a new, more optimistic perspective that so often comes with the breaking of first light. The attacks had been beaten off and no more casualties were taken. After expecting to be in Sangin for several hours, A Company had been there for two weeks and they were now under constant attack. The defences were poor, promised relief had not arrived and three members of the company had died. Attacks came in day and night and virtually every patrol they sent out resulted in a firefight. At the time, I couldn't promise them when they would be replaced and some talked of the untenable situation they faced, but I knew that it would be politically unacceptable to withdraw. The credibility of the mission and our support for the Afghan government were now on the line. There was no going back. I had no doubt that more men were likely to die, but we would have to tough it out with only the thinly stretched resources we had to hand.

I had spoken of this as I moved round the position from sangar to sangar talking to small groups of my paratroopers. I had to balance my own concerns and their plight against the fact that we were likely to be there for the duration, with all the risks and challenges that holding the district centre entailed. It was my soldiers and not me who were the ones continuously on the front line on a day-in, day-out basis, but they took in what I said. They accepted that I could make no promises and that I needed them to hang on and continue to do just what they were doing. I hoped my presence made a difference, but I was conscious that I was only visiting; getting involved in the firefight the day before while filling sandbags and spending the night with them probably helped. I hoped it showed that, as their commander, I was prepared to lead by example and was willing to face the same risks as my men, however brief my particular exposure to danger had been. Difficult though the position had become, I left with a better confidence regarding the situation in Sangin. I hoped that my men had been able to draw the same level of renewed purpose from me as I had been able to draw from them.

I had been called to attend a meeting with David Fraser at KAF and headed back to Bastion on the helicopter that brought in the first relieving platoon from B Company. The events of the last few days were focused in my mind as I flew to Kandahar on a Hercules transport aircraft from Bastion. Now Zad was also under regular attack and we had had to reinforce it with a second platoon of Gurkhas and another version of French Force. Nick French had set up his mortars on a small hillock a few hundred metres to the south of the district centre which provided a commanding view over the rest of Now Zad. It had formerly been manned by the ANP, which gave it its name of ANP Hill. But its position also made it a target for the Taliban who had brought it under regular mortar fire as they prepared to begin assaults against the district compound. Kajaki was under attack again as well and the American Ambassador had ordered the US contractor personnel to withdraw unless we reinforced the dam with troops. French Force had already been given a warning order to be ready to relocate there on a permanent basis.

An attempt to get a relief column into Musa Qaleh had failed too. Intelligence reports indicated that it was about to run into an ambush as it entered the close country on the only track that led into the town. The convoy commander was Major Gary Wilkinson who would normally have been at my side as my battery commander and fire support adviser. But a shortage of majors within the Battle Group meant that he had been given the task. Gary was prepared to run the gauntlet with the gunners he had taken with him from his gun battery to act as infantry, but I had ordered him to call off the attempt. Instead we had taken the risk of flying in 6 Platoon of B Company into Musa Qaleh to support the Pathfinder Platoon that had already been sent to Musa Qaleh as a temporary measure to relieve the American company that had been based there. Losing 6 Platoon meant that B Company now had fewer troops with which to replace A Company in Sangin.

In short, we were fixed and our resources were stretched to breaking point. The risk of having one of our few helicopters shot down while they kept all the outstations supplied and got their casualties out was severe. I had already discussed this with Lieutenant Colonel Richard Felton who commanded all the UK helicopters in Afghanistan. I agreed with his assessment that losing a Chinook as they began to set patterns of flying into one of the numerous, insecure and predictable LZs was now a matter of when and not if.

The implications of the risks we were taking and the conditions that members of the Battle Group were now living and fighting in were uppermost in my mind when I touched down in KAF. I used the time I had before my meeting with Fraser to seek out Ed Butler who was down from Kabul. He listened sympathetically as I aired my concerns about the risks we were running with becoming fixed and being overstretched. He had heard my views before when I had flown to Kabul a week earlier to attend a meeting of the military element of the Triumvirate which included representatives from DFID and the FCO. At the meeting it had been made clear that my recommendation that we withdraw from Now Zad, as a compensating reduction for taking on Sangin, was deemed to be unacceptable. With the fighting that was now taking place I emphasized that we would have to rely increasingly on firepower to hold the various district centres, with the attendant risk of causing casualties and destruction to the local Afghan people. I also reiterated the point that holding so many outstations would cost the blood of more of my soldiers.

Butler didn't disagree with anything I said. He knew that I understood the political imperative of not withdrawing from what he described as 'strategic pins on the map'. He also accepted that there was little emphasis being placed on development, which was not helped by DFID's unwillingness to consider investing in places like Sangin. Butler said that he would divert Engineer resources to strengthen the defences of the district centre there and that he would take up the issue of the lack of ANP and their behaviour with Daud. He also repeated his view that the Taliban's attacks were a concerted effort to oust the British from Helmand. In the process they were paying a heavy price in the loss of their own fighters. His opinion was backed up by intelligence reports that indicated an increasing number of their wounded were passing back across the Pakistani border for treatment in insurgent-held areas there. There were also reports that the losses were making it difficult for the Taliban to recruit local fighters, who increasingly saw little point in sacrificing themselves on British guns. In essence he saw it as an attritional battle of wills between ourselves and the Taliban. We were going eyeball-to-eyeball with them and over the next few weeks it would be a matter of 'who blinked first'. I told him that he should be confident that it would not be us. Regardless of my concerns, I drew a certain amount of confidence from the fact that I could speak plainly with my superior. He was a combat-experienced commander and was fully cognizant of both the risks and the costs.

As we spoke, the door of the Portakabin office opened and a staff officer from UKTF informed us that we had taken another casualty in Sangin. I resisted the urge to rush immediately to the UKTF Ops Room; Huw was back at Bastion and he would call me if I was needed. I finished the conversation with Butler and excused myself to find out what was happening on the ground. When I got to the Ops Room in the building that UKTF shared with the British logistic component, I was informed that Private Damien Jackson had died of a gunshot wound to the stomach. I got on the phone to Bastion and Huw filled me in on what had happened.

Since B Company's 6 Platoon had been sent to Musa Qaleh, 1 Platoon of A Company had volunteered to stay on in Sangin with B Company to provide them with a third platoon. Although the majority of A Company had flown out, other elements of A Company were also still in the district centre and were due to fly out on the helicopter that would bring in the rest of B Company's men on the morning of 5 July. Giles Timms ordered Hugo Farmer to take 1 Platoon and secure the LZ for the incoming helicopter, while his remaining platoons manned the sangars and provided the standby quick reaction force (QRF). The drill was simple, but an unavoidable pattern had been set and the Taliban knew it, as Farmer's sections fanned out around the landing site. Corporal Poll's 1 Section patrolled south down the track that ran alongside the canal. Poll moved cautiously; he had spotted two Afghans acting suspiciously at the side of the track before darting back across the canal over a small footbridge. His section shook out ready for action and Farmer began to close up with 2 Section in response to Poll's sighting report of a potential threat. As Poll began to push forward with privates Monk Randle, Craig Sharpe and Damien Jackson to investigate, an explosion rocked the ground around him and flung him backwards into a ditch. It was an IED that had been planted by the suspicious Afghans Poll had spotted. The blast knocked Poll out and was followed up by a heavy weight of Kalashnikov and RPG fire from the other side of the canal. The men of his half of the section were caught in the open and Damien Jackson turned and crumpled. Randle grabbed him and dragged him backward across the track towards the ditch as all hell broke loose around him.

It was any commander's worst nightmare: a man down and stuck in the middle of a firefight. The remaining members under the command of Lance Corporal Billy Smart poured fire back at them. Poll came to and was like a man possessed. Standing up, he loosed off 40mm under-slung grenades from the SA80 that Jacko had dropped when he was hit. He discarded the weapon and turned his attention to Jacko. Randle was already trying to stem the bleeding as Poll worked on his breathing. They were joined by Dan Jarvie; as the platoon sergeant his job was to organize the extraction of casualties. Corporal Giles from the medical section took over the treatment. Recognizing that Jacko had gone into shock, Jarvie yelled at him to stay with them while Farmer coordinated the fire and called for an Apache to cover the evacuation back to the district centre. It would be a frantic and almost impossible race against time. They were pinned down and Jacko's life-blood was draining away from an arterial bleed in his abdomen. Sergeant Major Leong arrived with Corporal McDermott's section armed with a stretcher and extra GPMGs. With assistance from the 81mm mortars firing at danger close ranges from the compound less than 250 metres away, 1 Platoon began winning the firefight. Once the majority of their attackers had been killed or suppressed, Jacko was rushed back to the centre on the stretcher over the pipe bridge that crossed the canal and into the RAP. The rest of the platoon extracted back after them, but Jarvie headed out again almost immediately. The LZ was no longer an option for the casualty evacuation helicopter and he needed an alternative site to lift Jacko out. When he got a radio message calling him back, he feared the worst, but desperately hoped that the doc might have managed to stabilize Jacko, perhaps making the need for the helicopter less urgent.

Leong was waiting for Jarvie when he returned. He pulled him aside and told him that Jacko hadn't made it. Pynn had done everything he could for him, but even if he had been alongside him when he had been hit, he wouldn't have been able to stop the bleeding. With the exception of Poll, Jarvie decided not to tell the rest of the platoon. He wanted to keep them focused on reorganizing themselves in case they had to go out again. He then went to have a moment with Jacko in the RAP. To Jarvie, the young soldier he had mentored since he joined the battalion as a brand-new Tom was 'a fucking good lad'. Jarvie had been his platoon sergeant, had nurtured him, watched him get into trouble as a young Tom and seen him mature into one of the more senior members of the platoon. Other soldiers had looked up to him; they turned to him for advice and respected him for his professional dedication to soldiering. Jarvie loved him for his youthful optimism, a buoyant disposition to life that had been cut short four days before his twentieth birthday.

Jarvie discussed with Zac Leong how the news should be broken to the rest of the platoon. As the senior soldier in the company, Leong felt that it was his responsibility to do it. They gathered the boys together and talked of the need to remain focused; Jacko wouldn't have wanted it any other way. Leong reminded them that they were there to fight the Taliban and to remain even-handed in their approach to dealing with the locals. Jarvie could see the determination in the faces of the men who sat in front of him to crack on and get the job done. As he looked at the likes of eighteen-year-old Private Lanaghan and Private Phillips, it made him proud to be their platoon sergeant.

After Hugo Farmer had spoken to his men, they filed into the RAP to pay their respects to Jacko. Lance Corporal Roberts watched them come, and as they looked down on their fallen comrade, he was struck by the closeness of the bond that existed among the Paras as they said goodbye to their mate. Lance Corporal Smart came in last, rested a hand on Jacko then tucked his own maroon beret inside his body bag; he didn't know where Jacko's Para beret was, but he didn't want him to go home without one.

It was early evening. Jacko had been killed in the late morning but I was still in KAF waiting to see David Fraser. I felt rotten about not being with the Battle Group. I had spoken to Giles

Timms on the Tac Sat, but it was managing the morale component by remote control and I wanted to be back with 3 PARA. As I hung round the UKTF hangar, many of the brigade staff came up to me and offered their condolences, but I noted how those of the UK's logistics component kept their distance. I wondered how many of them could immediately pinpoint Sangin on a map. I felt the traditional hostility of those who fight towards those who sustain the fighting rising inside me. The latter are generally held in contempt by those who take the risks of front-line combat duty. They are known disparagingly by combat troops as REMFs, which stands for Rear Echelon Mother Fuckers or what the Gurkha troops called Lungi Fungi which became an adopted term in 3 PARA.

I lumped them in with the 10,000-plus NATO troops who lived inside the airfield, the majority of whom never deployed beyond the confines of the airfield's perimeter. I thought of them working shifts, using the gyms, strutting the airfield boardwalk of pizza huts and frequenting the coffee shops of KAF, when most of my soldiers were sweating in austere conditions and under regular attack in places like Sangin and Now Zad. I didn't doubt that many of them played a vital supporting role and many worked hard to help us. But the common antagonism I felt between teeth and tail was provoked by the thoughtless, unhelpful behaviour of some of those I encountered. At one point during Jacko's contact, an officer of the logistics staff had asked UKTF personnel to keep the noise down. He felt that it was disturbing his daily update briefing taking place in another part of the hangar. It was all I could do to contain my anger as my blokes were fighting for their lives on the ground.

Anxious to get back to Bastion, I managed to find a Lynx utility helicopter heading that way. I went to see Fraser. I apologized that I couldn't hang around any longer for his planned meeting and said that I needed to be back with my Battle Group. He understood and expressed his sorrow for the loss of Jacko. My mind was preoccupied with thoughts of leadership as we flew west into the night. Matt Taylor sat quietly next to me. It was at times like this that commanders earned their pay. Something told me that with the right injection of leadership, compassion and firm guidance about the importance of the mission, the blokes would be fine. They would take the losses in their stride and step back up to the plate.

I talked this through with the new RSM, John Hardy, over a brew and a fag after we landed. I discussed going to see A Company, but he advised against it. 'Not tonight, sir, let them be on their own and get a good night's sleep, then go and see them tomorrow.' I welcomed his words of wisdom. It confirmed that I had made the right choice in selecting him to become my new RSM. John Hardy was the archetypical image of a paratrooper, immensely fit with an imposing presence, his droopy 'tash' curled round either side of his mouth. Uncompromising in his approach, he was known as Uncle John by the blokes and cared passionately about their welfare. He was also a fighting RSM, and carried an under-slung grenade launcher fitted to his rifle with spare grenade rounds strapped to his thigh. Whenever possible he made sure he got forward to use it. When he arrived, I had flown to KAF and it took all Huw Williams's efforts to prevent him from deploying straight up to Sangin with B Company the moment after he had landed at Bastion. He oozed self-confidence and said he only barked for one man, which was the CO. However, despite his unfaltering loyalty, he was always prepared to tell me how it was and I loved him for it.

I missed Bish when he went, as we had gone back a long way. I had said a fond farewell two days previously and was glad we found the time to say goodbye to him publicly. Being pinned down and returning fire had been a fitting way for him to end his career as a Para RSM on being promoted as a Late Entry captain. But now I had a new RSM who, like all good RSMs, was to have a profound and pervasive influence on almost everything that went on in the battalion. He was also to become my friend and closest confidant during the difficult moments in the months that lay ahead.

The next morning I spoke to A Company, conscious that some of them were still in Sangin. It was obvious that they were feeling Jacko's loss, but I detected the grim determination that they shared. We held a ramp ceremony for Jacko shortly afterwards. Although members of A Company wanted to act as pall bearers, John Hardy felt that the company was still too raw and nominated members of Support Company to carry Jacko to the waiting Hercules. The prop wash of the aircraft's engines blasted us with sand and grit as we followed the bearer party to the rear of its lowered tailgate. The logistic HQ at KAF had decreed that repatriation services were only to take place at Kandahar. We ignored the edict and the RAF air-crews screwed the nut to spend a little extra time on the ground at Bastion so that we could say a final farewell to Jacko with some dignity. The RSM and I halted as we watched Jacko's coffin being carried up the ramp and placed in the space between two para doors. As the padre blessed his coffin, I thought that it was a fitting place for a paratrooper to begin his long, final journey home. I watched the faces of the men who had carried him up the ramp. Standing to attention with heads bowed, they strained to listen to the padre make himself heard over the noise of the turning engines; each man alone with his thoughts of loss and saying goodbye.

The short service complete, the party turned smartly and marched back down the ramp. The RSM and I stepped on to the tailgate. We marched the few steps before halting and saluting. We both paused, then turned to our right and returned to join the assembled ranks of those few members of the Battle Group who were not defending the district centres. Standing to attention, we watched the C-130 taxi along the runway before gathering speed to take off. I felt a choking lump in my throat as the aircraft climbed into the sky. The pilot levelled briefly and dipped each of the plane's wings to us as a sign of respect to Jacko and the loss we had suffered. The words of Charles Wolfe's poem, 'The Burial of Sir John Moore at Corunna', rang in my head as I headed back to the JOC and 'thought bitterly of the morrow'.

9

The Manner of Men

The loss of Private Damien Jackson during the attempt to bring in the rest of Giles Timms's men had been a real eye-opener to the harsh realities of Sangin. Compared to what A Company had experienced since the beginning of 3 PARA's tour in Helmand, B Company were relative combat virgins, but their own initiation was not to be long in coming. Unlike A Company, Timms's men knew that their turn of duty in Sangin would be for the duration and they flew into the district centre carrying as much kit as possible. The company's FSG landed at an offset LZ and men like Corporal Dennis Mitchell struggled over the pebbled shale of the riverbank in the blazing heat with over 150 pounds of weight on their backs. As well as humping in their personal weapons, ammunition, three days of rations and water, each man also carried 800 rounds of linked 7.62mm ammo for the GPMGs, an AT4 anti-tank launcher and a plastic 'greenie' container of two 81mm mortar bombs. By the time they reached the compound they were absolutely knackered. Within an hour of Corporal Mitchell's arrival the attacks against B Company started. These set a continuous rhythm of daily attacks that was to go on relentlessly for the next three months as the immediate area around the district centre increasingly became a war zone.

Faced with the overwhelming weight of firepower ranged against them, the Taliban placed an increasing emphasis on the use of 107mm rockets, recoil-less rifles and 82mm Chinese-made mortars to conduct stand-off attacks. Setting up their weapons from a position of cover a kilometre or more from the compound, they would loose off several rounds and then attempt to withdraw before aircraft or artillery could be brought to bear against them. A shady glade of trees 2 kilometres to the north of the compound was a particularly favourite Taliban firing location. To the troops in the compound it became known as Wombat Wood, after an old British recoil-less rifle variant. These stand-off attacks were largely inaccurate, but as the rocket attack that killed the men in the sniper tower demonstrated, the Taliban only needed to be lucky once.

Like A Company, B Company's defence of the district centre relied heavily on the prolific use of artillery support from the light gun battery in FOB Robinson. As the call for fire support came in, the gunners of I Battery would rush to man their 105mm guns. Gun position officers would scream out bearings and elevations, as the long, heavy gun barrels were laid on to the given coordinates. High-explosive shells would then be rammed home into empty breeches, which would snap shut as the gun commanders shouted 'On!' to report that their artillery pieces were ready to fire. Hands were pressed tight against ears to shield them from the deafening roar of each gun, as firing handles were pulled back and 30 pounds of high explosive and metal were sent screaming towards the district centre. The process would be repeated by the sweating gun crews until the bellow of 'Rounds complete!' would announce that another deadly salvo of shells had been fired in support of their beleaguered comrades 7 kilometres away to their north in Sangin. Bombs, rockets and cannon shells from Coalition aircraft added to the lethal mix of projectiles used to break up repeated Taliban attacks. It became a vital lifeline to the defenders, but much of the fire was delivered 'danger close', as shells and bombs vectored in to land within 100 metres of the compound. Men pressed themselves flat at the bottom of their bunkers as incoming rounds landed close enough to spray the fronts of their sangars with red-hot splinters of shrapnel.

Infiltration was another tactic the Taliban used to reduce the effectiveness of our air-delivered munitions and artillery, as they attempted to sneak unseen into attacking positions close to the district centre. One night in the second week of July, a team of ten insurgents used the cover of night to creep through the darkness towards the perimeter. They had skirted round the Pipe Range using the fields and buildings behind the orchard to get within 20 metres of Corporal James Harrop's sangar that covered the south-eastern sector of the compound. All that separated the insurgents from their quarry was a 2-metre-high crumbling mud wall. If they could get to a large gap in the wall undetected, the assault party would be able to launch a vicious surprise attack using their RPGs to destroy the sangar at point-blank range before the defenders knew what had hit them.

On the other side of the wall, Corporal James Harrop cocked his ear to the warm stillness of the night air; could he hear something other than the insects chirping in the background? He physically checked the location of the clacker firing control on the sandbags in front of him. It was attached to a wire that led to the five claymore mines that had been linked together in a daisy chain on the other side of the wall. Harrop peered into the gloom. Suddenly bright flashes lit up the darkness a few metres in front of him, as AK rounds thumped into the sandbags. Harrop hit the bottom of the sangar as the world around him erupted in a bright frenzy of orange flashes and explosions. Instinctively, he reached up above him with one hand. His fingers fumbled for the clacker and closed around the soft green plastic of its grips. He snapped it shut twice to be rewarded by the thunderous crash of the five claymores detonating on the other side of the wall. A split-second interval seemed to occur between each explosion, as their deadly contents of thousands of small steel ball-bearings were blasted into the insurgents. The firing stopped abruptly. From the other side of the wall the Taliban commander was heard screaming into his radio that there were mines everywhere and that all his men were down.

If artillery, bombs and claymores were the blunter instruments used in the defence of Sangin, the employment of snipers provided a more surgical tool. Each of the company groups had a sniper section attached to it consisting of six men from the Battalion's Sniper Platoon. Its members were especially selected and trained. After attending a rigorous ten-week sniper course, they were capable of achieving a one-round, one-hit kill over distances in excess of 1,000 metres with their .338 sniper rifles. The snipers stationed themselves in positions that gave them a commanding view of the ground around the district centre and worked in pairs. The more experienced of the pair would act as the spotter. Using a laser range-finder he would measure the distance to a target, calculate the wind speed and get his 'oppo' to input the data into the Schmidt and Bender telescopic sight of his rifle.

One of their primary tasks was to counter the threat of insurgent gunmen attempting to conduct their own snipes against the soldiers moving around in the district centre. The snipers' precise and lethal effect was demonstrated on numerous occasions. In one particular incident, an intelligence report indicated that a Taliban marksman would attempt a shoot from a given location at a given time. A sniper pair was tasked to cover the likely firing area and neutralize the threat when it materialized. Working from a concealed position, both men scanned the rooftops in the distance. Although over 1,000 metres away, they spotted the slight movement of a weapon being placed on the flat rooftop of one of the two-storey buildings in the town. It was followed by the black silhouette of a lone figure pushing himself up on to the roof. As the bottom half of his torso was raised level with the ledge of the roof, a single shot rang out. The insurgent was flung backwards by the force of the heavy-calibre .388 bullet that struck him in the chest and he slipped from the roof before he had a chance to get his hands on his own weapon.

Despite these successes, the Taliban weren't in any danger of giving up. They continued to conduct attacks against the district centre on an average of four to five times a day. The compound's defences had been improved slightly, but they were still vulnerable. Men continued to be pinned down behind low sandbagged emplacements or had to dive for cover as RPG rounds exploded within the perimeter. The supply bridge to the district centre also remained precarious. Repeated attempts to fly in ammunition and rations had to be aborted as Chinooks came under heavy fire as they tried to get into the LZ by the compound. After ten days of constant attacks the supply situation was exacerbated by a series of severe sandstorms. Visibility dropped to less than 6 metres and flying became impossible.

On 11 July B Company's soldiers were issued with their last day's worth of rations and told to make them last. The next day there was nothing left to issue and the men scavenged for the remnants of ration packs that no one would normally eat. Packets of the disgusting sticky treacle pudding and hardtack brown biscuits were pooled into pathetically small piles. In Corporal Karl Jackson's section this amounted to three boil-in-the-bag sachets of the sickly dessert and a few packets of biscuits. By the end of the day they had only a few of the unappetizing biscuits to feed the whole section of eight men; like the rest of the company they began to try to minimize activity to conserve energy. Drinking water had also run out and men were forced to draw alternative supplies from the canal. Although sterilized and boiled, it was hard to forget that it had passed through the sewage outlets of several thousand people who lived in the upstream villages.

With the weather preventing helicopters from reaching the district centre, an attempt was made to parachute supplies to the beleaguered garrison from a Hercules aircraft on the night of 12 July. The hungry men watched in eager anticipation through their night vision devices as the aircraft flew in from the north. As it approached the DZ marked out on the field by the side of the compound, they willed it to start dropping and watched in dismay as it overshot the DZ. It started its drop too late and the bundles of much-needed rations tumbled out of the back of the aircraft to drift under their parachutes into the middle of the town. Private Thomas Brown accompanied a patrol from 5 Platoon that was sent out to recover the lost stores. His eyes were like 'shit-house rats' as they moved cautiously between buildings looking for the ration containers. In their desperate search to find the food they pushed well beyond the cover of the base's machine guns. As they pressed deeper into the town, dogs began to bark and lights came on in the houses around them. Ravenous as they were, no one wanted to die for a box of boil-in-the-bags and the patrol headed back to the compound empty-handed. They would have to wait for several more days until another method of resupply could be organized.

Sangin was not the only outstation held by 3 PARA that was under pressure: four of the other bases now garrisoned by elements of the Battle Group were also under attack. The Taliban were becoming increasingly bold in Now Zad and their probing attacks and mortar fire against ANP Hill were the prelude to direct assaults against the district centre there. Kajaki was receiving a daily diet of habitual mortar fire, although the high ground occupied by the mortar teams and members of an FSG kept the Taliban from getting too close to the dam. FOB Robinson was also coming under intermittent fire and the insurgents were beginning to attack the Pathfinder Platoon in Musa Qaleh, which was now supported by a troop of gunners acting as infantry, allowing us to withdraw 6 Platoon and send them to join B company in Sangin. Like A Company, the Pathfinders had only expected to be sent to Musa Qaleh as a temporary measure, but instead they had ended up spending weeks there. As the UKTF reconnaissance platoon they were needed elsewhere and the gunners' presence denied the Battle Group a troop of its artillery. I had argued that I could only take full responsibility for holding Musa Qaleh if a compensating reduction in one of the other outstations was made. Given that this was politically unacceptable, UKTF eventually managed to persuade the squadron of Danish reconnaissance troops who were contributing to the UK effort in Helmand to take on the task. The Danes' initial attempts to get through to the Pathfinders failed, but on 26 July they managed to get their column of armoured jeeps and personnel carriers into Musa Qaleh. But the

Pathfinders' attempts to get out met with a series of intense fire-fights and they were forced to withdraw back to the confines of the district centre. Getting them out would be another task that was to fall to the Battle Group.

As resources became spread ever more thinly, the requirement to send people back to the UK on R and R was also beginning to bite. Each soldier was entitled to two weeks' leave during the tour and they were rotated out of Afghanistan in groups of fifty. I had been against the R and R policy from the start, as I knew that it would reduce the Battle Group's manpower even further. But we were directed to do it, the soldiers had been promised it and we were duty bound to make it work. Picking up people from the outstations to meet their R and R flights from Kabul consumed more of the precious helicopter hours. It also entailed risk and individuals fretted about whether the Chinook would make it into their location to get them out in time. R and R was also dependent on the overstretched and ageing RAF air transport fleet. When passenger flights were delayed in either the UK or Kabul the flow of incoming and outgoing troops would overlap. The result was that the Battle Group would end up being short of over 100 personnel who were desperately needed in Helmand.

Despite its other commitments, 3 PARA was also still expected to contribute to US offensive operations as part of Mountain Thrust. On 8 July Major General Ben Freakly flew into Bastion with David Fraser to discuss our next role in the operation. Before he briefed me on our task, I asked him to meet some of the men of A Company. I introduced him to a small collection of 1 Platoon under the shade of a stretched camouflage net. He shook each man by the hand, expressed his sorrow for the recent loss of Damien Jackson and told the assembled men how well they were doing under trying circumstances.

We then gathered with my planning team to pore over maps of the intended target location for the forthcoming raid. We already knew the outline details. Codenamed Operation Augustus, it would be a strike mission to kill or capture a Taliban commander and neutralize his hardcore fighters. Intelligence indicated that the target individual was operating from two compounds several kilometres to the north of Sangin and that we could expect to face up to fifty insurgents who would fight hard to protect their leader. Freakly was convinced that the raid would severely disrupt the Taliban's command chain and would also serve as a warning to less committed insurgents that there was nowhere to hide. With only A Company and the Patrols Platoon not already allocated to defending a static location, I would have to pull C Company out of Gereshk for the operation. Even then I doubted that I had enough troops for the task and Freakly agreed to provide a company of Canadian infantry mounted in light armoured vehicles (LAVs).

I travelled back to Kandahar on board Freakly's command flight of two Black Hawk helicopters. As I sat next to him in the back of one of the choppers, he asked me if there was anything else I needed. I replied that having the aircraft we were travelling in as command platforms for the raid would be extremely useful. He looked at me, smiled and agreed to let me have the two helicopters for the mission.

I spent the next two days in KAF planning the raid and talking it through with the Battle Group's liaison officer at UKTF. Major Nick Copperwaite was normally one of 3 PARA's company commanders but he had been sent to KAF to act as the Battle Group's permanent link to the brigade headquarters. A bright, young and highly capable officer, he kept himself abreast of my thinking and spoke with my authority at UKTF when I wasn't present. He was worth his weight in gold, but he was another high-priced officer who had to be employed away from Bastion. Nick, Matt Taylor and I talked through the operation with the brigade staff long into the night. We ignored an incoming rocket attack, trusting to the inaccuracy of the Taliban as we studied maps and air photographs of the target area. I back-briefed David Fraser on my proposed concept of operations for the raid using a PowerPoint pack of fifty-one slides that the UKTF staff had put together. I pitied the

poor bugger who had worked tirelessly on creating the presentation, as I used only four or five of the most important slides. Fraser
was content to give his consent to the plan and then I took it to
Ed Butler to get his buy-in and the national UK tick.

I noticed the fatigue on his face as we spoke. He had a huge
weight of responsibility on his shoulders and was being pulled
in numerous different directions by the competing, and often contradictory, agendas of others. He had the unenviable task of
attempting to mesh UK military objectives with those of the FCO
and DFID. Although he was only one part of the Triumvirate,
he seemed to be the only one working to try to make a concrete
difference across all the various strands of activity. He also had
to balance national objectives against those of NATO and the
Americans. Butler didn't get on particularly well with Freakly and
I later read that the American general had claimed that he had
come close to punching his British subordinate. Had it come to
blows, my money would have been on Butler.

Having missed another night's sleep, I arrived back in Bastion to
news that the Secretary of State had announced that another 800
troops were to be sent to Afghanistan. As official and media reports
of the intensity of the fighting began to circulate in the UK, it was
recognition of how badly stretched we had become; 3 PARA was
to receive 125 men from the 1st Battalion of the Royal Regiment
of Fusiliers stationed in Cyprus. It was welcome news, but with
the endorsement of the plan for Operation Augustus, our focus
was on the refinement of the mission and the endless series of
last-minute adjustments and briefings.

The plan involved two distinct phases. The first phase was the
flying in of A and C companies to assault the target compounds
to kill or capture the Taliban leader and his fighters. Phase two
involved the move in of the Canadians' LAVs and other Battle
Group elements by road to support the assault. The critical part of
the plan was getting the assault troops in undetected. If they landed
at an offset LZ and then moved in by foot, it was highly likely that
their presence would be discovered and we would lose the element

of surprise. Additionally, the two compounds were surrounded for several kilometres by other compounds and it would be difficult to find an empty piece of desert to land in. Consequently, I had made the decision to land right next to the compounds and assault straight off the back of the helicopters. The Canadians would then drive in from an offset position at high speed to support us. They would bring a section of 3 PARA's Mortar Platoon and the Patrols Platoon with them to give additional support and then provide us with a safe route out to an extraction LZ.

The critical element of the plan of delivering the assault troops to the target objective rested with the men of A Flight of the RAF's 18 (B) Squadron, who crewed the five CH-47 helicopters that we would use for the mission. The flight was commanded by Squadron Leader Mike Woods. As their flight leader, 'Woodsy' had made an immediate difference to the troop-lift helicopter support the Battle Group received from the moment he took over from the flight of Chinook crews they had replaced. Mike was a forthright and energetic Geordie, who made it his business to get involved in the detailed planning of all Battle Group missions. When not flying a mission himself, he was always in the JOC overseeing one of his aircraft's sorties and on hand to give expert advice to the Battle Group staff. He was there because he wanted to get it right and because he cared for his men. Most importantly, Mike and his crews were prepared to breach the rules and take calculated risks to get us to where we needed to go and to pick up casualties. Each time they went out they were pushing the envelope. I never asked them to do the impossible, but the flying we demanded of them was close to it.

Having arrived in May, Mike's team of pilots, loadmasters and air gunners were coming to the end of their eight-week tour of duty before being replaced by a flight from another Chinook squadron in the UK. He and his men had each flown over 100 hours, and the constant demands of operating in extreme flying conditions and regularly coming under fire meant that they needed a break. But it would also mean a vast loss of experience at a time when it was desperately required for Operation Augustus. Ed Butler asked A Flight to stay on to fly the raid and Mike agreed. However, he suggested that his crews should be mixed with the new crews from the UK to spread the experience.

The significance of the threat to the helicopters had been brought home to us two nights previously when an American Chinook was shot down by the Taliban. It had been lifting out a party of US Rangers from a target they had raided close to our own planned objective when it came under withering fire from the surrounding compounds. RPGs and heavy automatic fire sliced through the fuselage, killing the power to the rotors as it began its climb from the LZ. The pilots managed a forced landing, allowing the Rangers and crew to scramble to safety from the severely shot-up aircraft, but it was a sobering reminder of the risks we would be taking.

The assault troops had spent the previous few days rehearsing the drills of how they would break into and clear the compounds. They had been fed intelligence updates on likely dug-in enemy positions identified by satellite photographs and the conditions of the ground that they would be expected to fight across. There had also been numerous postponements, leading many to expect that the op would be cancelled, as we wrangled with the Americans over whether the necessary surveillance aircraft and Predator UAVs would be available. The tension mounted as 13 July dawned, another clear and incredibly hot day; then word came through that the necessary assets would be in place. We were ordered to be ready to launch the next morning; the op was on. Risk was on everyone's mind on the eve of the operation as last-minute refinements were made to the plan and final briefings were given.

With the final components in place I went to my accommodation. I checked, packed and repacked my webbing like hundreds of other men that night in the tents of Bastion as we prepared for battle. Weapons were stripped, cleaned and oiled, grenades were primed ready for use and placed in pouches where they could be easily reached. Extra linked belts of machine-gun ammunition were redistributed and the contents of medical packs inspected. Each man verified the location of his morphine injectors, hoping that he would not have to use them. Men talked among themselves about whether we really would be going and what we were likely to face when we landed. Some took the opportunity to make a call home; sons spoke to mothers, wondering whether they would ever speak to them again. Unable to tell them what they were about to do, many recognized a tone in a voice that indicated that maternal instinct had detected that something was up. Others wrote a last letter home and pressed it on mates asking them to ensure that it was delivered if they didn't make it back. The more experienced soldiers reassured younger ones that they would be all right, half doubting the sincerity of their own words.

I believe that every soldier in my Battle Group experienced fear at some point during the tour and most felt it that night before Augustus. It manifested itself in numerous ways and people dealt with it differently. Most felt it as a mixture of both eagerness and anxiety, especially prior to deliberate Battle Group operations. For me a sense of 'apprehensive enthusiasm' would begin to build the day before a planned operation. I often went to bed to snatch a few hours' sleep, reflecting on the problems that might arise on the morrow. My apprehension would mount as the hours ticked by until my alarm clock went off on the morning of an operation. It would accompany me on the drive to the helipad where the aircraft waited for us in the darkness. It would knot in my belly as the turbines began to whine and the twin rotors of the Chinook started to turn. It would tighten as we walked up the ramp under the heat blast from the engines, tightening once more as they changed pitch and we lifted off. In the back of the aircraft it would mix with a dual sensation of heavier limbs and a dryness of mouth as we approached the last few minutes of the flight to the target area. It was similar to the sensation of being in the back of a Hercules waiting to make a difficult parachute jump when you knew the wind was against you and the back- and leg-breaking hazards on the DZ were numerous. The difference was that there would be a real enemy at the other end intent on doing his best to kill you.

Like most soldiers going into combat, my overriding concern was the fear of failure. Threat to life and limb had its place, but a man's biggest fear about going into battle is concern as to how he is going to behave in front of the group when the lead starts flying. No one wants to let their mates down or be found wanting when it counts. However, what all soldiers hate most is the anticipation of waiting for the unknown. The maxim of 'taking it is not as bad as waiting for it' is absolutely true. As soon as I exited the tailgate on the ground, regardless of what we faced when we got off, the pre-action tension would lift. Suddenly I was busy, I had a job to do and activity would banish the anxiety of waiting. But that night we waited and the dread of an approaching dawn mounted.

As I lay in my camp cot I kept half an eye on the clock by my bedside. Sometimes before an operation, sheer fatigue would not allow anxiety to deny me sleep. But Operation Augustus was different; it had been building for the past few weeks and we knew that it was going to be a big event. Like most of the men in the tents around me, I slept badly and the hand that shook me awake from a fitful doze came all too quickly. Few spoke as they got up, collected their kit together and made their way to the helicopter landing strip. The aircrafts' engines were already burning when we arrived. A and C companies were lined up in their 'chalk sticks'. Lines of men behind each of the waiting helicopters; some men slept and others focused on what was coming. It was the beginning of what we had spent days preparing for and we were pumped up; now all we wanted was to be done with the waiting and get it on. It was a strange relief to be airborne, as I sat in the back of one of the Black Hawks that tucked into station behind the two waves of Chinooks that had already lifted. We flew south for twenty minutes in the opposite direction from the target which was to the north. It was a deliberate part of the deception plan in an attempt to confuse any dickers who might have seen the nine-ship formation of Apaches, Chinooks and Black Hawks take off from Bastion. The other aircraft were unseen in the blackness ahead of me. I felt the turn of the Black Hawk and saw the luminous glow of my compass needle swing north: we were heading towards the target area.

As we got closer, the radio nets in the back of the Black Hawk were alive with air controllers talking the A-10 and AC-130 Spectre gunship pilots on to positions over the target area. Through the headset I could also hear my own headquarters in Bastion relaying information to me. The Predator UAV was picking up movement through its thermal imaging camera. I didn't like what I was hearing. Landing deliberately close to the target compounds where we expected the Taliban commander to be would provide the element of surprise if we arrived undetected. On the other hand, if our presence was detected on the way in we were bound to come under fire as we landed. Bastion was telling me that they were picking up reports of people moving on the LZ; had our impending presence been detected? Ahead of me five Chinooks carrying the assault force of A and C companies were holding off, waiting for me to give them the signal to land.

Minutes ticked by as I tried to get more information from Bastion; the situation was confusing and I desperately wished that I could see the images on the Predator's screen. Loaded in excess of their normal number of passengers, each carrying forty-four heavily laden paratroopers, the Chinooks were operating at the limit of their capacity and burning precious fuel. Mike Woods was watching the dimly lit fuel gauges in the cockpit of his lead aircraft as he waited for my call. He had eight and a half minutes of fuel left; if they dropped below eight minutes they would not have enough fuel to make it back to Bastion and they would have to abort the mission. I needed to make a decision: Do I abort on the assumption that the vital element of surprise has been lost, or do I order the formation to leave its holding pattern and land?

I was conscious of the pressure from the Americans to get this one in. I pressed Bastion for more information. But they didn't have access to the Predator screens that were based in Kandahar and couldn't give me any more clarity on what the UAV was picking up from the ground. I mentally ran through the criteria checklist for making the 'go, no go call' that we had worked up in the planning. If I was uncertain about the security of the LZ, I should either abort or call for suppressive fire to cover us in. But the Rules of Engagement didn't allow for us to start dropping artillery and bombs unless we had positively identified the presence of the enemy. I ordered Major Andy Cash, who was commanding the supporting Apaches, to make a final sweep of the LZ with his own thermal night sight. I heard him confirm the LZ was clear and quiet. He could see nothing and declared the site 'Cold', as fuel gauge needles dipped dangerously close to the abort line. The information I had available to me was far from perfect and I searched my intuition as I made my decision.

With my heart in my mouth, I ordered Mike Woods to lead the rest of the formation in. As my own aircraft banked away to make its run in behind the Chinooks, Matt Taylor thumped my arm and pointed frantically out of the helicopter's starboard window. Streams of red and green tracer fire were arcing through the night sky to where the first of the troop-carrying aircraft was landing on the LZ. It looked like an exercise we might conduct in the UK using live ammunition. But this was no exercise and my troops were being shot at for real as they landed in the back of the tightly packed helicopters. As my American pilot aborted his own run in and banked away, I heard frantic cries over the net: 'Abort, abort! Hot LZ! Hot LZ!' But it was too late. I told my pilot to get us in. 'No way, sir, that is a hot LZ.' No shit. As we circled in the safety of an offset position out in the desert I thought of my men landing in the back of the helicopters and what I had committed them to.

Machine-gun bullets and RPG rockets whipped across the LZ as the first three Chinooks made their landing. The other two aircraft of the second wave were only 30 feet from the ground when they banked away at the last minute. Once one aircraft had been committed to landing, the other pilots in the first wave had to make it in to ensure that a minimum of ninety paratroopers were put on the deck. Any fewer and those who got out would have been outnumbered by the Taliban. However, there was less need to take a risk with the second wave and Mike Woods ordered it to abort as he took his own aircraft into the red-hot LZ. Corporal Graham Groves was standing on the tailgate of one of the second-wave helicopters. He could see the fire coming up to meet his aircraft when he was suddenly thrown violently on to his back as the pilot heaved on his collective to pull the Chinook away from the danger. As Groves scrambled to his feet he looked down at the LZ they had just left. He could see A Company getting out of their cabs into a circle of incoming fire that had opened up all around them. Like the rest of the men in C Company, he was snapping because their aircraft had aborted, and as he flew away he knew that his comrades in A Company would be taking hits.

Nichol Benzie was flying one of the lead Chinooks that had managed to land. As the front wheels of his aircraft went down tracer rounds streamed towards his helicopter. There were four or five firing points to his left and another six or seven opened up from the right. All three of the aircraft's M60 machine guns hammered back in response but they couldn't suppress all the firing points. It was the worst incoming fire Nichol had seen, but he knew that he had to sit there and take it until all the Paras in the back had got off. Mike Woods's aircraft tucked in behind at the six o'clock position, followed by Flight Lieutenant Chris Hasler's Chinook a few seconds later. Amazingly, the first aircraft didn't get hit. Thankfully, the troops in the back were well drilled and cleared the tailgate in under twenty-five seconds, allowing the aircraft to lift off and climb to safety. Had the drills of both the crew and the troops not been so slick there would have been bits of aircraft and Paras spread all across the LZ. As Nichol lifted off an RPG sailed a few feet over the head of his aircraft and another shot underneath its belly. The other aircraft were not so lucky, as the metallic 'thwack, thwack' indicated that the bullets were dancing along the sides of their fuselages. In the back of these aircraft there were scenes of chaos.

In the second Chinook the exit had been equally swift, but not before machine-gun bullets had punched through the fuselage. Sergeant Dan Jarvie had been looking out of the porthole of his aircraft when he saw the fire coming up into the sky towards them as they flew in. He shouted at the blokes: 'Get down, get down!' As he took one last look out before pressing himself against the helicopter's armoured matting he was thinking of his best mate Sergeant 'Ginge' Davis who was aboard one of the other aircraft, hoping that he would be all right. Finding a gap in the armoured matting, one of the bullets hit Private Jones as he made his way towards the tailgate. It struck his upper left arm and exited with enough force to smash through the small personal radio mounted on his chest. A Company's second-in-command, Captain Martin Taylor, was in the process of getting off the tailgate when he heard Jones cry out, 'I've been hit!' In spite of his wound Jones continued to make his way towards the tailgate with the bloodstain spreading on his arm. Taylor told him to stay on board and fly back to Bastion for medical treatment. Jones kept yelling that he was coming with them, he didn't want to miss the action and wanted to get off with his mates, but Taylor gripped him and ordered him stay put before exiting the aircraft himself.

Outside the back of the helicopters all hell was breaking loose. Dan Jarvie was yelling at the top of his voice above the noise of the rotors and incoming fire, telling his men to 'fucking move' and get into the cover of a ditch as they crawled and sprinted across the muddy ground of the LZ. He knew that Jones wasn't with them and heard Corporal Charlie Curnow shouting that Jonesie was down. He expected to see him lying in the field until Taylor told him that he had forced him to stay on board the Chinook that had just lifted.

Recognizing the importance of getting the troops in the back of his helicopter on to the ground, Hasler had pushed on the speed of his aircraft to make it into the LZ. It landed heavily as he pulled up the nose of his overladen Chinook violently to a 25° angle to bleed its forward velocity and drop the rear landing gear on to the ground. For a moment the rear rotor blades spun dangerously close to the mud of the field and one of the back wheels was snapped off by the force of the landing. Inside the aircraft the impact broke the restraining strap along the centre of the fuselage which members of the anti-tank platoon were holding on to. Heavily laden men were thrown bodily to the floor of the tightly packed aircraft. The dim interior lights had been extinguished long before the run in, and now each man struggled desperately to regain his footing in the darkness. They were pinned down by the weight of 70-plus pounds of their strewn equipment and the frenzy of others' thrashing limbs. Each man was intent on only one thing: to get out of the cabs that were acting as bullet magnets to every Taliban fighter who was opening up on them. Bullets pinged off the side of the fuselage as the M60 door gunners thumped rounds back at them.

Even after the main body of troops had cleared the aircraft, Hasler had to keep it on the deck as Colour Sergeant Bell, Sergeant Webb and Flight Lieutenant Matt Carter worked frantically to unload mortar rounds that had been strapped to the tailgate. As the last 'greenie' of mortar bombs was shifted the rear gunner yelled at Hasler to begin lifting. That same instant Bell and Webb spotted two jerry-cans of water further up the cab and raced back to get them. Suddenly aware that the aircraft was lifting, Bell ran down the fuselage and jumped off the tailgate. When he tried to stand up he couldn't and he had to hobble off the LZ using his rifle as a crutch. Sergeant Webb also jumped and the rear M60 caught him a glancing blow as the helicopter lifted. Eyewitness accounts estimate that the helicopter was at least 15 feet from the ground when both men made their leap into the darkness. Colour Sergeant Bell had broken his leg and Sergeant Webb had fractured his hand.

As A Company took cover, the Taliban's positions were being pounded by the Apache and Spectre gunships that were called in by Matt Carter, who had made the jump from the lifting Chinook uninjured. Waiting in a waterlogged ditch, Sergeant Jarvie was getting impatient; he wanted to get cracking and start blowing holes in the compound walls to effect an entry. Fire was still coming into the LZ, but there was now a lot more going out, as aircraft ranged in on the Taliban's positions and A Company's GPMGs were brought into action. Hugo Farmer had pushed forward to the first compound and instructed the Engineers to place a mouse-hole charge that would blow the first entry point through the compound wall. Plastic explosive had been fixed to crossed pieces of wood that would direct the blast into the thick mud structure when placed against it. A second later there was an ear-splitting roar as the charge went off. Normal safety distances went out of the window as Farmer crouched in an irrigation channel a few metres away with his hands pressed tightly against his ears. Concussed by the blast that took the air out of his lungs, Farmer quickly came to his senses and started pushing along the wall looking for the hole. His ears were still ringing when he found the strike mark, but the charge hadn't been powerful enough to blast through the thick, concrete-hard mud. He directed a Tom to batter it through with a sledgehammer and left him swinging madly while he went to see if they could get through the main gates of the compound. Hammers and feet were used to kick in the doors and they were in. Teams of men cleared from room to room, but the Taliban had fled and the compound was deserted.

The LZ was quiet by the time the second wave of Chinooks carrying C Company landed. They had flown to Gereshk to take on board a quick suck of fuel and then returned to clear the second compound. Inside were two dead Taliban who had been firing from the roof when they were hit by an Apache Hellfire missile. There were several rough cotton sacks stuffed with money and sleeping quarters that indicated that the compound had been occupied by a large number of Taliban.

At the time that C Company were landing I still had no idea of the outcome of my decision to commit the helicopters to the LZ. I continued to press for information on the net, but the radios had gone dead. My own aircraft put down ten minutes later into a thick ground mist. The darkness had begun to lift with the coming of dawn and my own fog of war mixed with that swirling around me. We could see no reference points and I cursed as my Tac party gathered together and I waited for my GPS to give me a satellite fix on our position. Through the thinning mist I made out the shape of one of the Canadian armoured vehicles that had raced to the contact point as the Chinooks landed. As I approached the vehicle the now peaceful scene was broken by the swearing of a large moustachioed paratrooper crammed unceremoniously into the back of the infantry carrier. RSM John Hardy was snapping about having to travel ingloriously into his first offensive operation in the back of an armoured vehicle instead of being part of the helicopter air-assault element. He always wanted to be at the thickest part of the action, which explained his bad humour about being assigned to the back of a 'tin box'.

I used C Company to push through several of the surrounding compounds and followed up behind them with Tac. The LAVs pushed out on to our flanks and engaged a number of fleeting targets with their 20mm automatic Bushmaster cannons. There were dug-in positions at the side of many of the compounds and piles of RPG rounds that had been left as the Taliban conducted a hasty withdrawal. C Company also found a vehicle with a number of 107mm rockets inside it, clearly for use against the district centre in Sangin. But the quarry had flown. The risk of bringing the helicopters back in to pick us up was too great and we tabbed out several kilometres to a pre-planned LZ in the desert to the east that had been secured by the Patrols Platoon and mortars. We moved out covered by the Canadians while the dull thud of explosions echoed behind us as the munitions we had found were blown up.

It was oppressively hot as we made the long slog through the blazing heat of the day. The going was arduous; having been pumped up with adrenaline the assault troops were physically exhausted. I noted the fatigue on the faces of those I chatted to when we stopped bent double under heavy loads to catch our breath. But I also noted the buoyant mood and a sense of elation. Everyone had known that Augustus would be risky and the reception on the LZ had brought it home. But the men on those helicopters had conquered their fear; they had met a humbling burden of expectation and had not been found wanting.

IO

Reckon and Risk

The Battle Group returned to Bastion for one night, re-cocked and the next day flew straight into Sangin to conduct an operation to relieve the pressure on the district centre. David Fraser had wanted me to launch immediately from the LZ pick-up that we had tabbed to at the end of the Operation Augustus raid. His message was relayed to me via the pilot while I was still airborne and heading back to Bastion. However, my men were knackered and I insisted that we were allowed to fly back to base, re-brief for the next operation, grab a meal and get a few hours' sleep before air-assaulting into Sangin at first light. Fraser deferred to me as the field commander on the ground and accepted that I was in the best position to judge the condition of my men. The blokes would have done it if I had asked them to, but they were dead tired, having had little to eat and drink since leaving Bastion sixteen hours previously. The morning's excitement on the LZ and the long hot tab out to the pick-up point had also taken their toll. There was no pressing need to get to Sangin that could not wait for twelve hours, especially as B Company was now no longer hungry. The ration situation had been resolved. After the failure to drop supplies by parachute, four American CH-47s had managed to deliver an emergency resupply of food and water the day before the planned Battle Group operation into the town.

Having conducted an AAR for Operation Augustus, I gave confirmatory orders for the next day's Battle Group operation into Sangin. The mission was codenamed Operation Atal and was designed to push the Taliban away from the district centre, consolidate our defences there and secure the area so another *shura* could take place between the governor and the local elders. We would air-assault in two waves of three Chinooks. A Company would land close in to the compound and push north to secure the wadi leading into the town. Half of C Company would fly with them, but would have to wait for the rest of their platoons to fly in on the second wave. They would then push east to secure the portion of the town that dominated the wadi from the south. I would have liked to have flown everybody in one wave, but the Chinooks had taken a battering during Operation Augustus and only three were still serviceable. Flying troops in more than one wave was never ideal, as we would lose the element of surprise once the first helicopters had landed. Second, it prevented us from being able to concentrate our forces. However, once the companies were in place, the Canadians would drive up the wadi in their LAVs and link up in the district centre. We would then remain for two days to allow the *shura* to be held and secure the wadi again for the Canadian LAVs to escort in a large logistics convoy.

The convoy would bring in Engineer stores and earth-moving plant to turn the district centre into a proper fortress. It would also bring in sixty days of food and water to prevent the garrison from running out of supplies in the future. I wanted to bring in a similar supply of ammunition, but there were insufficient stockpiles available in Afghanistan. Consequently, we would have to continue to run the risk of flying in certain ammo types on an incremental basis.

Satisfied that everything was set for the next day, I went to grab a few hours' sleep. I passed Matt Taylor still working at his desk tying the last points of coordinating detail together. I told him he needed to make sure he got some sleep and he promised me that he would. However, driven by the desire to make sure everything was in order, Matt ignored my direction and worked on through the night.

All too quickly my alarm clock peeped at me in the gloom of my tent as 0200 hours came around. I thought of *Groundhog Day* while I pulled on my kit and went to find Tac who were waiting for me to drive to the helicopter landing site. Matt pitched up straight from the JOC and I chastised him mildly for ignoring my orders about getting any sleep. He looked at me sheepishly and smiled; he knew I couldn't fault him for his dedication. As we drove through the fading darkness of Bastion, John Hardy asked me if I had managed to get much sleep. 'Not much,' I said. 'Me neither,' he replied, then fell silent again. In a strange way, it was comforting to know that my redoubtable RSM, who never displayed even a trace of anxiety, might also just be feeling something. The normal emotions ran as we loaded up in the back of the Chinooks and lifted off. I test-fired the port M60 gun and revisited the plan in my head to keep my mind occupied. This time I was convinced we would be taken on as we landed in Sangin, but I was wrong again. With B Company already in the district centre and another 300 paratroopers landing in their midst, the Taliban started to withdraw from their positions. I wondered whether Augustus had put the wind up them, as reports came in that large numbers of fighters were fleeing across the river crossing points to the north and south of the town. Our link up with B Company was unopposed and A and C companies moved through deserted streets, while Tac went into the district centre.

Giles Timms was in chipper form when I saw him. Sporting a beard and wearing desert-issue shorts, he was clearly relishing field command. He took me round the position as we waited for the LAVs to arrive. The smell of soldiers living in the field pervaded the air as we walked and talked. Exhaust fumes of generators mixed with the stink of burnt cordite, while the caustic smell of rations cooking on hexamine burners blended with the odour of latrines and unwashed bodies. Living conditions remained austere, but the morale of his men was exceptionally high. Fighting off several attacks a day meant that sleep was still at a premium, but at one stage there had been a lull of two days in the fighting. Company Sergeant Major Willets told me how the men had become bored and frustrated because all they could do was watch and wait for the attacks to resume. When the next attack came, the men whooped and cheered as they ran up the steps of the FSG Tower to man their sangar positions.

Although they were in high spirits, I apologized to the blokes that we hadn't managed to get rations to them for a few days. I explained why to those I spoke to, but I also made the point that running out of supplies when surrounded was part of our history. When I talked of what conditions must have been like for the paratroopers who held the bridge at Arnhem for nine days against ferocious German assaults, having only planned to hold it for two, in 1944, people got the point that I was making. It didn't make it all right, but, given that the Parachute Regiment's past endeavours are ingrained deeply in today's paratroopers, it helped.

The night I spent in the district centre was warm and quiet. I felt the sweat trickle down my back as I lay on my body armour. Using my webbing for a pillow, I listened to the sounds around me. I could hear the low murmur of men talking in the darkness and the muffled chink of metal on metal as men prepared for a patrol and guard shifts changed over. A faint crackle of static could be heard coming over the radio nets, as if a chorus to the low rhymed chirping of the insects from the orchards and flowerbeds.

Daud and his party turned up the next day for a *shura* with the local leaders after some arm-twisting from Charlie Knaggs to get him to come. The meeting was animated. The elders claimed that the fighting had closed down normal commercial life in the town and there was also some talk of the need for development. But there was no sense of accommodation on either side. Daud argued that the locals must reject the Taliban before development of the town could take place. The elders argued that we should withdraw and that the town was being badly damaged by the bombing.

The lack of development in the town was plainly evident when I accompanied a patrol out on to the ground after the *shura* had finished. I had invited Daud to come with us, saying that with so many of my troops on the ground I was confident that I could assure his protection. However, he seemed uninterested and we went without him. I had no doubt that the fighting had impacted adversely on the local inhabitants, but there was little sign of any bomb damage beyond the immediate buildings around the district centre. Shops were open, some selling Honda motorbikes and others piles of discoloured offal spread on newspaper that attracted swarms of flies as it baked in the heat. We received cautious acknowledgements to our Pashtu greetings as we pressed deeper into the narrow mud streets, though the normal gaggle of barefoot Afghan children was absent. While any real physical evidence of the fighting was limited, the town was a slum. Discarded animal bones littered the alleyways between compounds where they had been thrown by their occupants. There was also an oppressive stench coming from rotting piles of rubbish which had been accumulating long before our first arrival.

As I moved through the streets with Tac, I couldn't help thinking about what we could achieve if we could base more than one company in Sangin on a permanent basis. We could push the Taliban out of the town for good and secure the place for development. But it would take more than 100-odd men to do it and Sangin was only one town and there were many more like it. I knew that once we had withdrawn and the district centre reverted to just one company, the Taliban would return and the fighting would resume.

The effect of our mass arrival was not lost on the ITN journalist John Irvine who had accompanied the *shura* party to Sangin. He came up to me and said how impressed he was with the morale of my soldiers and the fact that we had managed to establish control over the town. He commented that it was in stark contrast to sensational reports that were circulating in the media that compared Sangin to Rorke's Drift. I agreed that the historical analogy to a colonial outpost that was about to be overrun by hordes of Zulus was flawed. It also confirmed in my own mind the value of soldiers talking and the misguided policy of keeping the press away from us. Irvine departed with the *shura* party and the logistic supply convoy arrived the next day.

It drove through Sangin from the east along the wadi secured by A and C companies and was escorted into the district centre by the Patrols Platoon. We had hoped to use the Canadians, but they had been tasked away to restore government control to the town of Garmsir, 100 kilometres to the south of Lashkar Gah. The ANP garrison had withdrawn from it in the face of Taliban attacks and Daud claimed that if it fell, the provincial capital would be next. I was sorry to see Captain Bill Fletcher and his company depart. We had got used to working with the Canadians and I had been impressed by their courage and professionalism.

As we boarded a Chinook to fly back to Bastion the Engineers were already beginning to use the newly arrived plant equipment to fill the HESCO bastion with sand, which would form a solid perimeter around the district centre. I left A Company behind under the temporary command of Major Tris Halse who was standing in for Will Pike who had returned to the UK on an already scheduled posting. Having an additional company operating in support of the troops already stationed there would bolster the position and delay the Taliban's return to Sangin. But it was a temporary measure as the second company would soon be needed elsewhere.

While Sangin was quiet for the moment, the frequency and seriousness of attacks against Now Zad and Musa Qaleh was increasing. In Now Zad the initial attacks that had been directed against ANP Hill had begun to shift to the district centre held by the Gurkhas in the second week of July. The Taliban made their first concerted attack on 12 July. Having ambushed an ANP patrol in the centre of the town, they followed up with RPG and heavy machine-gun fire against the compound. The attack started in the early hours of the morning and went on late into the afternoon, before eventually being broken up by A-10s dropping 500-pound bombs and running in low to strafe the Taliban with cannon fire. Many insurgents were killed, but the attacks continued intermittently for the next few days as the Taliban revised their tactics and prepared to make another assault four days later. Unlike Sangin the district centre in Now Zad was located in a grid of streets in the western part of the town. It was surrounded by walled alley-ways and compounds on three sides with the main street running past its front gate. The insurgents began digging through the walls of the surrounding buildings to create rat runs where they could move close to the sangars unobserved by the Gurkha sentries and circling aircraft.

On 16 July the district centre came under attack from three sides. On the southern side they managed to get into a medical clinic next to the southern compound wall and brought the inside of the base under a withering fire of RPG and AK rounds. In the process Lance Corporal Cook of the Royal Signals was hit in the shoulder. He would survive the wound, but the bullet fragmented and ricocheted inside his body armour causing it to exit from his body in three different places. With only one platoon at his dis-posal and twenty ANA soldiers, the Gurkha company commander, Major Dan Rex, believed that his position was in danger of being overrun. His JTAC, Sergeant Charlie Aggrey, called in a danger close fire mission from one of the supporting Apaches. Aggrey talked the pilot on to the Taliban's location in the clinic. The pilot trusted to the armour of his helicopter as he brought it into a low hover over the district centre. He lined up the sights of his 30mm nose cannon; it swivelled and then kicked into life. Brass cases spewed over the heads of the defenders below him as the pilot sprayed the clinic with cannon fire. Cannon rounds chopped through the concrete and the windows from left to right and the insurgent threat was neutralized in a hail of masonry and explod-ing 30mm shells. For good measure, the Gurkhas followed up by throwing hand grenades over the walls of the compound to catch any retreating Taliban.

In fighting off the attack the Gurkhas used up 80 per cent of their ammunition and the attack also highlighted the vulnerability of holding the district centre with only the forty-odd men that Rex had at his disposal. Consequently, another platoon of Gurkhas were stripped out of the force protection company guarding

Bastion and were sent up to reinforce the district centre. They were also sent mortar barrels and a machine-gun section from the A Company of the Royal Regiment of Fusiliers that had just arrived from Cyprus to bolster the Battle Group.

The addition of the Fusilier FSG gave the Gurkhas their own dedicated mortar fire support, but the Taliban were also using mortars. At first the 82mm Chinese mortar bombs they fired were inaccurate, but their rounds started creeping closer to the district centre as their accuracy improved. On 18 July three rounds landed inside the compound and wounded an ANP policeman. The Taliban were also using their mortars to fire at resupply helicopters that flew into the LZ on the open strip of desert behind ANP Hill. On more than one occasion they landed dangerously close to the Chinooks as they flew in ammunition and lifted out casualties. The improved performance indicated that the insurgents' mortar crews were better trained foreign Jihadi insurgents from Pakistan. The presence of these foreign fighters was also being reported in other areas, as the Taliban moved their men between Now Zad, Musa Qaleh and Sangin. On 22 July reports reached us that fifty fighters had moved into Now Zad. By mid-morning the district centre had started receiving incoming fire. Dan Rex believed the Taliban commanders were meeting in one of the buildings in the town and requested permission to bomb them with a precision-guided JDAM. He was confident that the threat of collateral damage would be minimal and I supported his request, but, despite being under NATO command, UKTF had to clear authority for the strike with PJHQ. By the time I left the JOC at 0200 hours the next morning, a decision on whether we could target the building had still not been made and the fleeting opportunity to destroy the enemy commanders had long gone.

A staff officer in PJHQ was also questioning 3 PARA's need to have a battery of artillery. I was staggered, given how many rounds we were firing to help keep our soldiers alive in Sangin. Perhaps he would like to come out here and get a little combat time in a sangar when it was breaking up an attack with danger close fire, I thought. Spending valuable time answering nugatory questions from a desk-bound officer in the UK was not the only frustrating event to occur that day.

I also attended a meeting I had been called to with General Freakly and some of the UKTF staff in Lashkar Gah. Governor Daud was also present. Due to delays with the helicopter I arrived late and caught the tail end of Daud's complaints that we were not doing enough to counter the Taliban threat. Freakly then followed with a diatribe in which he demanded to know what we were doing to help the governor and accused the 'Brits' of sitting on our butts, while his troops were out fighting the Taliban. He also made the point that even his artillerymen were acting as infantry to take the fight to the enemy. I thought about the gunners of I Battery who until recently had been patrolling the streets of Musa Qaleh. He went on to criticize holding the district centres in Now Zad, Musa Qaleh and Sangin, maintaining that we had become fixed and now lacked the freedom to manoeuvre forces elsewhere to fight the Taliban. I glanced at Daud and thought of the battles we were fighting in these locations, his decisions to send us to them and the ANP reinforcements he had never sent. I also thought about the risks my men had taken on Operation Augustus and the reception we had received on the LZ.

There was a perceptible tension in the air. I paused before I spoke. I mentioned that we too had artillery patrolling in the dismounted combat role. I told him that we were in the district centres because that was where the governor wanted us to be, that we were killing the Taliban in these locations and that we were losing men there doing it. I said that if he wanted us to conduct more manoeuvre operations he needed to tell me which of the district centres he wanted the Battle Group to give up. Major Dave Eastman, a staff officer from the headquarters of UKTF, pitched in to inform him that the UK force was stretched to breaking point meeting all the commitments that the Task Force had undertaken.

There was a brief uneasy silence. Though Dave and I had been respectful of his rank, I suspected that Freakly was not used to dealing with forthright subordinate officers telling him how it was in such a robust fashion. I pressed him for a decision on giving up an outstation. Freakly avoided the question and gave a muted general response about the need to do more. As the meeting broke up, I returned to Bastion reflecting on how doing more with less had become a recurring theme. I also wondered how on earth we were going to sustain what we were already doing.

The arrival of a company from the Fusiliers was a welcome addition, but they would not enable us to do any more. By taking the Gurkhas away from guarding Bastion to garrison Now Zad, our main base was in danger of becoming vulnerable to attack. The gaps in the guard force had been filled temporarily by support personnel, but they were needed to meet the increasing logistical strain of supporting the troops in the field. Equipment needed to be serviced, tonnes of ammunition and stores needed to be loaded forward and medics were required to work in the field hospital, which was now receiving a steady stream of casualties. In short, we needed to pull the Gurkhas back to guard Bastion and we would have to use the Fusilier company to replace them. On 30 July we launched another Battle Group operation using B and C companies to conduct a relief in place between the Fusiliers and the Gurkhas. The operation would include the tracked Scimitar armoured cars and Spartan personnel carriers of D Squadron of the Household Cavalry that had finally arrived in Helmand. They would escort a large resupply convoy up to Now Zad. Once in place they would secure an LZ for B and C companies to air-assault into the empty desert behind the district centre. The Household Cavalry would then conduct a clearance of the town with the companies providing close infantry support to their vehicles as they moved through the close confines of the town's narrow streets. This would then set the conditions for bringing the Fusiliers in and taking the Gurkhas out.

The initial move through Now Zad was uneventful but there was more evidence of the impact of the fighting on the town than there had been in Sangin. The streets were devoid of civilians and the shops were closed. Several had been destroyed by bombs as aircraft sought out the Taliban in their rat runs that they had tunnelled through the interconnecting walls. One of the schools that had already been burnt by the insurgents was now a bombed-out wreck. It consisted of two storeys which made it an obvious point from which to bring the district centre under fire, but it also made it a target for the A-10s.

I was impressed by the length of Dan Rex's beard when he met me at the front gates to the compound. His company having spent the last few weeks largely on their own, he was extremely pleased to see us. I went round the sangars and talked to his Gurkhas. They broke out in broad smiles as I told them how well they had done and kept mentioning the word *shabash*, which is a common Nepali plaudit. They pointed out the strike marks and the near misses of where rounds had struck helmets and weapons systems. But they were glad to be returning to Bastion, as I congratulated them on their bravery. The presence of two companies of Paras and the light armour of D Squadron had flushed the Taliban out of the town and the Gurkha Company was able to move to the pick-up helicopters without incident. Probing attacks began later in the day, but were kept at bay by B Company and the accurate fire of the 30mm Rarden cannons mounted on the Scimitars. C Company and Tac spent the next day rebuilding and improving the damaged sangars as we waited for the Fusiliers to arrive. Again I thought of what could be achieved with the bulk of the Battle Group in one place.

The fly-in of the Fusilier Company and their subsequent takeover of the district centre was uneventful. They brought three full-strength platoons compared to the two the Gurkhas had available to hold the compound. They were also allocated a troop of Scimitars from D Squadron that would stay with them in Now Zad. The four armoured cars were tasked with protecting the LZ and providing fire support with their Rarden cannons from positions around ANP Hill. The insurgents hated the Scimitars, as they

Men of B and C companies collect in a jump-off point in an alleyway in Now Zad before clearing the Taliban out of the town during operations in July

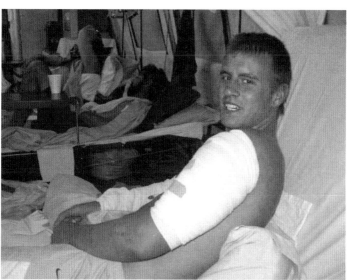

Private Jones in the Bastion Field Hospital after taking a bullet in the arm that penetrated the fuselage of the helicopter he was flying in during the air assault into Operation Augustus

Captain Matt Taylor, the hard-working Operations Officer, mounted on a Household Cavalry Spartan to drive in with B Company to clear the HCR ambush site. Taylor often worked tirelessly through the night to ensure that he got the planning detail of every operation right

Corporal of Horse Mick Flynn's disabled Scimitar at the site of the ambush against D Squadron. The front of the destroyed Spartan personnel carrier can be seen in the foreground. Flynn was later awarded a Military Cross for the part he played in returning to rescue the Spartan's wounded driver

A WMIK of the
Patrols Platoon in
Sangin having driven
hundreds of miles
across the desert to
support a Battle
Group operation in
the town

C Company clear through compounds with fixed bayonets during Operation
Snakebite to relieve troops in the besieged town of Musa Qaleh

A .50 Cal gunner watches and waits on top of his WMIK

A 105mm light gun of 1 Battery 7 RHA fires high-explosive shells from the desert.
The fire support from the artillery was vital to the besieged troops in the district centres

Corporal Bryan Budd of ... Platoon A Company ... outside a sangar in the ... orchard at Sangin. This ... photo was taken a ... month before he was ... killed leading an assault ... on a Taliban position, an ... action that was to lead to ... the posthumous award ... of the Victoria Cross

Private Briggs holding the Taliban bullet that struck the front plate of his body armour during the fighting in the maize fields to recover Corporal Budd's body

Privates Monk Randle and Bally Balenaivalu living in bunkers built by the Engineers to protect against Taliban mortar fire, which became increasingly more lethal

The FSG Tower of the district centre in Sangin looking towards the town's bazaar. Like rest of the compound it steadily became a fortress of sandbagged windows and roofte sangar positions. The comparison between the two pictures indicates how the defenc were improved as the attacks increased

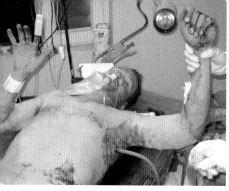

Lieutenant Paul Martin of Easy Company in the Regimental Aid Post in Musa Qaleh after being hit by shrapnel

A Royal Irish Mortar Section of Easy Company lights up the sky from the compound in Musa Qaleh

An RAF Chinook drops supplies on to the LZ at Sangin. The helicopters were a vital lifeline to the troops defending the district centres, but every mission they flew entailed risk and their crews braved repeated Taliban fire to get supplies in and lift casualties out

Sergeant Paddy Caldwell in Sangin with B Company in July before he was struck in the neck by a Taliban bullet during a later Battle Group operation to clear the town

Corporal Zip Lane of A Company receives field promotion to sergeant at Sangin in August

could engage their fighters over long distances, often before they could get within range to fire at the compound. They were equipped with thermal imaging sights which allowed their crews to pick up heat sources of anyone moving in the darkness around them. One night an unsuspecting insurgent was cut in half by a 30mm high-explosive cannon shell as he moved into a firing position over 1,000 metres away from ANP Hill. With the arrival of more men and the addition of light armour, the frequency and intensity of attacks against Now Zad dropped off considerably for the rest of the tour. It had been a more attractive target when it was only lightly garrisoned by the Gurkhas. But once reinforced, it meant that the Taliban would redouble their efforts elsewhere.

The significance of the growing threat against Musa Qaleh resulted in the remaining three troops of D Squadron being ordered away from the Battle Group halfway through the operation in Now Zad. We were due to conduct a Battle Group operation in Musa Qaleh in a few days' time, to get the Pathfinders out and send in British reinforcements to stiffen the resolve of the Danes. But the operation could not be launched until current Battle Group operations had finished in Now Zad. In the interregnum, UKTF directed the Household Cavalry commander to take the rest of his squadron and conduct probing patrols towards the western outskirts of Musa Qaleh. It was felt that the presence of his light armour would relieve some of the pressure the Taliban were applying to the Danes. When Huw Williams informed me of UKTF's decision over the Tac Sat radio I raised my concern that they would be operating without infantry, which would make them vulnerable to attack in close country. I told Huw to tell them to watch themselves. The plumes of dust kicked up by their tracks drifted in the wind as Major Alex Dick's Scimitars and Spartans headed east. I regretted losing them, as their departure would deprive us of the ability to push further into the outskirts of Now Zad to clear any remaining Taliban who were skulking on the fringes of the town. But I also accepted that there was now a greater need to support Musa Qaleh.

Forty-eight hours later swirling pillars of sand were kicked up by the rotor blades of the two Chinooks that also carried us east. As we flew fast and low over the desert I ran through what I knew of the situation we were flying into. One Spartan destroyed by a roadside bomb, a second Scimitar damaged and abandoned in the ambush site, two soldiers reported dead, one severely burnt and one crewman missing. With another suspected MIA, time was against us. The aircraft were flying at their maximum speed of 140 knots, but I willed them to fly faster. A billowing cloud of green smoke marked our LZ next to the squadron's vehicles. We landed on desert tracks to minimize the risk of mines that had already destroyed another Spartan the day before. But that had been an unlucky strike from an old Soviet mine and the crew had managed to walk away from the wreckage unscathed. Alex Dick was waiting to meet us and filled me in on the details of what had happened.

The squadron's move away from Now Zad towards Musa Qaleh had not gone undetected by the enemy. They were lying in wait for them as the lead vehicles pushed into a piece of low ground on the edge of a village. The depression funnelled into a narrow track which was then channelled between two long compound walls that ran for 150 metres before it reached open desert again. The front Scimitar, commanded by Corporal of Horse Flynn, had almost reached the end of the canalized route when he came under RPG and small-arms fire. Returning fire as best he could, he drove out of the ambush to the open desert beyond, hearing a large explosion behind him as he did so. On reaching the relative safety of the open ground he looked back to see the sickening sight of the Spartan that had been following him. It was stationary and burning fiercely.

Flynn turned his vehicle around and headed back into the ambush site. His action attracted another volley of RPG fire which blasted off pieces of the external anti-RPG bar armour that shrouded his vehicle. It protected him and his two crewmen from the impact of the warheads, but the vehicle was forced into a ditch on the side of the track where it became stuck. Still under fire, he ordered his men to dismount and they grabbed their weapons and webbing as they scrambled from the hatches of their disabled Scimitar. They then fought their way back through the ambush site on foot, passing the destroyed wreckage of the Spartan. Flynn saw one of the crew lying in the back of the vehicle and two others lying motionless by its side. All appeared to be dead, but he couldn't see the fourth crew member. Taliban bullets were whipping the desert at his feet and he pushed on to get back to the rest of the squadron who had stopped short of the ambush site on the higher ground. The vehicles of the rest of the squadron were firing at the Taliban to cover Flynn and his crew as they fought their way back to them.

From the hatch of his vehicle, Lance Corporal of Horse Radford spotted movement behind Flynn and his men: one of the bodies they had just passed was still moving. It was the Spartan's driver, Trooper Martyn Compton. Compton had survived the blast that destroyed his vehicle when he saw an RPG heading in his direction. It detonated against the engine next to him and covered him with burning diesel fuel which set his hair and clothing alight. He managed to get out of the wrecked remains of the vehicle, but was shot through the leg as he rolled in the dirt in an attempt to put out the flames before he lost consciousness. Radford jumped from his vehicle and shouted at Flynn as he ran past him to reach Compton. Flynn turned and followed him back to where Compton lay. The two men then picked him up and carried their gravely wounded comrade back to safety as rifle and cannon fire continued to crack and thump around them.

Compton had already been lifted out on a casualty evacuation helicopter by the time I arrived with B Company. I spoke to Flynn and he stated that he was convinced that the other two men were dead, but he could not confirm the location of the third soldier who had been in the back of the Spartan before the ambush. My immediate concern was that he might have survived the blast only to be taken by the Taliban. I gave a set of quick battle orders and ten minutes later we mounted up on the remaining Scimitars and Spartans and headed for the ambush area while artillery suppressed the close country ahead of us. B Company dismounted and cleared either side of the compound walls as the Scimitars covered them in from the high ground. I wanted Giles Timms and his men to secure the area, confirm the location of the missing man and extract the two dead soldiers. I waited with the Scimitars and pressed Timms for information about the MIA. I became impatient; it was taking too long and the Taliban were beginning to probe back into the area of the ambush. I looked at John Hardy and said, 'Let's get down there and see what's happening.' We checked that our weapons were ready and patrolled into the ambush site.

The scene that greeted us was one of complete carnage. The Spartan had been split open and was a mangled wreckage of twisted blackened metal. There was no doubt that the men inside would have died instantly in the blast without knowing what had hit them. One soldier lay on the ground at the back of the vehicle. Another lay inside towards the rear of the troop-carrying compartment. There was no sign of the third. I needed to know whether he might be lying inside, his presence possibly obscured by the collapsed steel plates and burnt-out debris that prevented me from seeing into the forward section of the Spartan. We had to find out; if he wasn't there then we would be into the process of searching every compound and calling in reinforcements to cordon the surrounding area. I heard the crackle of rifle fire in the near distance as we received intelligence reports indicating that the Taliban were reorganizing to attack us. Darkness was only a few hours away and we needed to get moving. I asked a young cavalry officer to head back to his squadron commander. Although keen to get his men out he was understandably shaken and too closely involved. With sporadic fire to our front, Giles Timms had enough to do keeping the area secure and I asked Sergeant Major Willets to go and support him and make sure the blokes were okay. Several were suffering from the heat and I doubted that being so close to the macabre site was doing them much good either.

I looked at John Hardy and we set to work shifting the body of the trapped dead soldier so I could squeeze past him and work my way under the steel plates to get to the front of the vehicle. I pushed my way in, sliding between the contorted metal and the motionless crewman. I heaved against a crumpled armoured hatch and found the remains of the missing soldier. I shouted for Tariq Ahmed, the doctor accompanying us. I wanted him to confirm my assessment that we had accounted for all three crew members. Tariq concurred and we began extracting them. I noted my own sense of clinical detachment as we worked at our grisly task. The firing in the distance and the need to get the job done were uppermost in my mind. I told myself that I could reflect on it later once we had got all our people back to Bastion.

A few hours later I lay on my camp cot unable to blot out the vivid images of what we had seen and done. The sense of clinical detachment I had felt disturbed me as it made me feel like a callous and inhuman bastard. I got up and went to search out John Hardy. We sat and smoked. As the sun dipped towards the distant horizon we talked about the day's events. I told him what was bothering me. John listened, looking at the ground as I spoke. Then he fixed me with his eyes. 'You are the boss, sir, what you did was leading by example. You had responsibility for everyone on the ground today. There were too many people too closely involved. Someone had to step in and get it sorted. Someone needed to be detached and get the job done. That's what you did and it was the right thing to do.' What my RSM said helped me get it straight in my mind. Coming from someone I trusted and who was there at the time, his words made a difference and I felt better for them.

His words also helped me make up my mind about another decision I knew I had to make. I had noticed how people were beginning to suffer increasingly in the heat. Weeks of fighting and living off composite rations were having a debilitating effect. It was not helped by wearing body armour when operating dismounted; troops became fatigued and their situational awareness dropped soon after stepping off the tailgate of a helicopter. They would be fresher and more alert without body armour, so I decided that we wouldn't wear it on the next deliberate operation, although we would continue to wear it for routine patrols round the district centres. I believed that the physical protection that would be lost would be more than made up for by the ability to move faster and remain alert for longer. It also meant that we would use less water, reduce the risk of heat casualties and the subsequent risk to helicopters having to come and pick them up. I talked it through with my commanders and they concurred with my rationale. I got Ed Butler to buy in to my decision and he agreed to keep the heat off me from PJHQ who we knew would be averse to the risk that I had decided to take.

The burden of combat command responsibility weighed heavily on me throughout the tour and virtually everything we did entailed a beltful of risk and uncertainty. It was always there and never went away. It was not something I begrudged, as it came with the turf of being a commanding officer. I occasionally talked to John Hardy about it, as I did after the Household Cavalry ambush. But otherwise I kept the subject largely to myself. My biggest concern was the impact the decisions I took, and the orders I gave, had on the lives of my soldiers. After an incident where someone had been killed or injured, I often asked myself: 'Did we plan it right, could we have done more and what could we have done differently?'

One night I stayed up late smoking with Colonel Matt Maer who had come out to visit from PJHQ. He was a straight-talking individual with an incredibly sharp mind. He combined these qualities with an infectious sense of humour that made it very difficult not to like him. He also had a great deal of relevant combat experience. Matt had commanded his own battalion in Iraq during the Mahdi Army uprising in 2004. His unit had seen some pretty intense fighting for which he was awarded the Distinguished Service Order. His own experiences meant that he knew what command and risk were about. He said some extraordinarily complimentary things about how well the soldiers of the Battle Group were performing under challenging circumstances. Then he stopped and told me there was one thing that I needed to know about my people. As he paused, I wondered what the hell he was about to say. He told me that several members of the Battle Group had come up to him to tell him that they all knew that I took the lives of my men seriously and although I often sent them on dangerous missions, they knew that I never did it lightly. I was aware that Matt was telling me this because it was a ghost he must have grappled with in Iraq, but it was probably the most heartening thing anyone said to me during the whole tour.

I drew on Matt Maer's words when I spoke to Alex Dick after his squadron had driven back into Bastion. He felt responsible for what had happened to his men in the ambush. I told him that it was not his fault and I meant it. He had been under pressure from UKTF to get to the outskirts of Musa Qaleh. He wasn't given any infantry support and had had to take a calculated risk. I told him that it was the nature of war and as commanders we always felt a burden of guilt when bad things happened. I visited his troopers on the vehicle park the next day. Stripped to the waist, they laboured hard in the sun covered in sweat and grease to get their Scimitars and Spartans ready for the Battle Group operation to Musa Qaleh. I talked with them as they serviced their vehicles. They were a tight-knit squadron and every man felt the loss of their comrades. But I was impressed by their fortitude and determination to get back out into the field. Having spoken to them in small groups, I gathered them together and told them that they were doing an excellent job and the light armoured support they provided was making a real difference. I asked them to keep on doing just what they were doing.

I saw them again that evening, the grime of a hard day's toil washed away as they sat in rows for the memorial service for Second Lieutenant Ralph Johnson and Lance Corporal Ross Nicholls, who had died in the Spartan. As I listened to Alex Dick's eulogy for Ralph Johnson I thought of his father in South Africa who would never go hunting on the veldt again with his son. We also commemorated Captain Alex Eida, the artillery forward observation officer, who was travelling in the back of the vehicle. His normal place would have been with the squadron command vehicle, but he had volunteered to go forward with the lead troops so that he could be on hand to call down artillery fire if it was needed. He was a popular officer who had worked with the companies and his loss was felt deeply across the Battle Group.

I was concerned that we might be sending D Squadron back out into the field too soon. Their vehicles were taking a pounding in the harsh environment from driving many miles over difficult and sandy terrain. But we needed them for the next operation to get the Pathfinders out of Musa Qaleh and replace them with another platoon of infantry and a mortar section from the Royal Irish Regiment that had recently arrived from the UK. They weren't additional reinforcements, as they were filling gaps that already existed in the Battle Group. But the Danish squadron had demanded extra troops as a precondition of staying in Musa Qaleh.

Codenamed Operation Snakebite, it would be a complex mission involving a significant number of moving parts. The Patrols Platoon would secure an LZ for B and C companies. Supported by a troop of Canadian LAVs, they would then clear through two villages and a green zone of fields and trees that lay on the western bank of the Musa Qaleh wadi. The Engineers would then clear the track that led from the green zone to the wadi. It was a known ambush site and we anticipated that the route would have IEDs placed on it. The Household Cavalry would then secure a corridor across the large open wadi; simultaneously the Danes would move out of the district centre and secure the street down to the wadi from the eastern side. Once a secure corridor had been established, the Pathfinders would drive out and we would then send the Royal Irish reinforcements and a logistics convoy in to the Danes. The convoy would drive back out once it had dumped its stores and the troops securing the route would then collapse from their protective positions behind it. We would have air cover and a troop of 105mm guns and a mortar section would provide indirect fire support. But as with all the best-laid schemes, not everything went according to plan.

As they moved a day ahead of us, the limited time given to the Household Cavalry to service their vehicles took its toll. Four of the five Scimitars broke down and had to be towed back to Bastion. It meant that the squadron would not be available to support the operation and the task of securing the wadi would have to fall to the Canadian LAVs. Intelligence then indicated that the LZ we had selected might be an old Soviet legacy minefield. There were few alternative landing zones and I decided that the Patrols Platoon would have to do their best to check it before we landed. But they could not do this in darkness and we would have to delay the operation to allow them to do it in daylight. Consequently, the element of surprise of launching before first light was lost. Captain Tom Fehley, who had taken over command of the Patrols Platoon, was concerned about being able to confirm whether the LZ would be clear of mines. I told him that I knew he would not be able to do it properly, as it would take hours and Engineers that we didn't have. I asked him to give me his best assessment when he got there. I would then make the call about the risk of landing the rest of the Battle Group into the LZ.

The possible existence of mines was on my mind as we flew into the LZ in two waves of Chinooks twenty-four hours later. It was a calculated risk and I suppressed the urge to wince as the wheels of my helicopter touched down. No doubt it was on every other man's mind as they stepped off the tailgate and moved to their forming-up positions on the reverse slope of the high ground overlooking the green zone. B Company would move first, but as they married up with the LAVs on their line of departure they came under fire. As they took cover, the LAVs were already returning fire with their 30mm cannons and Matt Carter was calling in an airstrike. He looked at me for clearance to drop. We were under fire and I didn't have time to mess about requesting permission from higher headquarters, so I nodded and told him to call it in. I told Giles Timms to be ready to move his company in a left-flanking attack as soon as the bomb landed.

Ninety seconds later, I heard Matt Carter announce, 'Here she comes!' Released from the weapons rack of an aircraft several thousand feet above us, the small dark shape of the JDAM flashed briefly as it screamed down from the heavens. Earth and rubble heaved up at the sky as the bomb impacted into the target. It was followed by a billowing mushroom cloud of dense black smoke that smudged against the horizon. The noise of the blast wave reached us a split second later and B Company started moving as machine gunners fired them in. I watched B Company assault through a tight cluster of deserted compounds from the left and noticed how much faster they moved without being encumbered by restrictive combat body armour. In response to their rapid movement, I ordered C Company to begin their assault from the right. Paddy Blair was on R and R in the UK, so his company was under the command of Captain Rob Musetti. In anticipation of my order he already had his men ready and waiting to go. I yelled a reminder to watch out for civilians as he cleared through his compounds; unlike B Company's objective we suspected that the compounds to the right were occupied. He yelled back an acknowledgement and then set off after his men. The air was soon filled by the dull thud of mouse-hole charges blasting entry points through walls. After Operation Augustus the charges had been enhanced to penetrate the hard thickness of the mud. But there was no firing or following up with grenades; Rob had briefed his men well about the need to watch out for civilians. They didn't come across any and I marvelled at the locals' uncanny ability to smell trouble and make themselves scarce when the fighting started.

Both companies moved through the green zone with bayonets fixed. The Engineers then cleared the track of several roadside bombs they discovered. With our side of the wadi secure, I gave a radio order to the Danish commander to start securing the street from the district centre on his side of the wadi. He told me that it would take an hour and we fixed an agreed time when he would be in place and we would commence the wadi-crossing phase. As we waited for the Danes to move into position, the artillery rounds were taking time to adjust fire into the wadi to provide the smoke-screen we needed to obscure our movement across it. I tasked Nick French to use his mortars to bridge the gap. Thick white smoke began to billow up from the impacting mortar rounds 200 metres to our front on the far side of the wadi and began to fog into a screen that would mask our activities from likely Taliban positions along the river line. The time on my watch approached the agreed H Hour and I ordered the Canadian LAVs to move out into the wadi and secure a movement corridor across it.

Once the Canadian armoured vehicles were in place I pressed the Danes clearing the street on the opposite side of the wadi. I wanted to know if they were still going to make H Hour. The response was non-committal, but it was clear they were not going to be in place on time. We couldn't begin the next phase of the operation until the Danes were in position and their slow progress began to concern me. The Canadians were under armour and positioned outside the effective range of any Taliban armed with RPGs, but the more time we spent getting the unarmoured vehicles across the wadi, the more time the Taliban would have to move into positions from which they could bring the crossing operation under small-arms fire. Nick French's mortars were also running low on rounds to keep the crossing site obscured with smoke.

The Danes reported that they were finally in position. They had cost us forty-five minutes and we had lost the smokescreen and the proximity of troops in the wadi now precluded the use of artillery. The resupply convoy was already poised to move when the Pathfinders began driving out. I watched them break into the wadi and race across the dried riverbed towards the crossing control point. Each man wore a heavy-set beard that did little to hide the strain of the fifty-two days they had spent in Musa Qaleh. But their faces also showed the elation of finally being able to break free of it. The third vehicle contained their commander, Nick Wight-Boycott. He gave me a flashing grin as he stopped to thank us for getting his men out. He had a long drive ahead of him across the desert to Lashkar Gah, so we kept our conversation short and I wished him luck on his journey. I also wanted to press on with getting the resupply convoy in and out of the compound and ordered Captain Mark Eisler to lead his convoy vehicles across. He had already been briefed that he was to get there, offload his stores, deliver the reinforcements and get back out again as fast as possible. I watched Mark pass me driving the lead Pinzgauer, his face set in grim determination. The rest of the convoy's vehicles disappeared after him into the wadi. There was little to do but sit and wait for him to complete his mission and return with the empty vehicles. I kept glancing at my watch as I contemplated their return and the fact that we had now run out of smoke rounds for the mortars.

Less than an hour later I saw Mark's vehicle break back into the wadi from the far bank. Mark stopped briefly to make his report to me at the crossing point: 'In and out, Colonel, just as you said; all stores and reinforcements delivered.' As Mark headed back up the track to the Battle Group's assembly area I watched the rest of his vehicles cross back to our side. I was relieved to see the last of his vehicles enter the wadi and make its way back towards us. Suddenly there was an ominous crackle of automatic weapons fire. The last WMIK thundered back on to the track on the home bank. It was one of 13 Regiment's vehicles that had driven from Kandahar as an escort for the convoy. The vehicle stopped briefly at the control point. The back of the WMIK was a scene of chaos. At least one man appeared to have been hit and lay on top of another who was screaming. 'Get to the RAP!' I shouted at the driver. Without hesitation, the vehicle took off at speed along the track. Shit, I thought as I yelled at Corporal 'Gorgeous' George Parsons, my signaller, to get on the net and tell Bastion and the RAP that we had inbound casualties. I ordered the Canadians to begin withdrawing and told Tac to start moving too. B and C companies would remain in place holding the home bank until the Canadians were back at the Battle Group assembly area. We set off on foot. It was a fast pace, as we had already spent long enough on the ground and I wanted to get back and find out about the casualties that had been taken in the wadi.

I watched Tariq Ahmed zip up the body of Private Barrie Cutts in the RAP. He had been hit in the head and there was little that could have been done to save him. We carried his body back to the LZ. Mark Eisler was sitting on the sand with the two WMIK crew mates who were visibly shaken by the loss of their friend. Mark was a Late Entry officer, who joined 3 PARA as a Tom and had worked his way up through the ranks. He had fought with the battalion in the Falklands in 1982 and was one of only seven survivors of his platoon who were not hit fighting up the slopes of Mount Longdon. He knew what loss was about and I sat down and listened as he talked to the two young Logistics Corps soldiers. He spoke words of comfort and empathy in a fatherly tone. He brought them out of their shock; he even raised a laugh from them as they talked fondly of the friend they had lost and the sort of bloke he was. I smiled at the young soldiers, as the rhythmic beat of the three Chinooks' rotor blades became louder as they approached the LZ. As they turned it into a blizzard of sand, we picked up Private Cutts and carried him towards the helicopters.

It was another sombre flight back to Bastion with young Barrie Cutts lying at our feet. I watched the starboard gunner glance at his body. I could see in his face a trace of acknowledgement for the risks troops took on the ground once his aircraft had delivered them to an objective. I helped Tac carry Private Cutts to an ambulance that was waiting for us at Bastion. He died under my command following my orders and it was only right that as the commanding officer I should form part of the field bearer party.

11

The Home Front

Even by the standards of the tour, the operational tempo from the middle of July to the beginning of August had been extreme. Including the mission to recover the dead from the Household Cavalry ambush, we had conducted five deliberate Battle Group operations. Each involved several hundred men and the detailed integration of helicopters, artillery, airpower and other multinational forces. At the same time we had defended four outstations against increasingly sophisticated insurgent attacks, contributed troops to the defence of Musa Qaleh and also sent the Patrols Platoon to help relieve the growing pressure on Garmsir. The necessary planning and constant adjustment to rapidly changing situations had been a 24/7 business. Getting a decent night's sleep of more than four to five hours had become a long-forgotten luxury. To a large extent we had become used to it and more than once I noted that personal endurance was the key to sustaining the frenetic pace of activity. However, I could detect an accumulating weariness in the people around me and I also detected it in myself.

After I had debriefed Ed Butler over a phone link to Kandahar following one of the operations, he asked me when I was taking my R and R. I was evasive and mentioned something about there being too much going on. Ed told me that the one direct order he was going to give me while in Afghanistan was that I was to take some leave. No doubt he had a suspicion that I would eschew the opportunity unless ordered to do so. He was probably right, but I also knew that I would benefit from having a break. I discussed when I should go with Huw Williams. As my second-in-command, he would act as the CO while I was away. Huw wanted to take his R and R to get back for his son's first birthday at the end of August so I agreed to take some leave as soon as the operation to relieve Musa Qaleh had been completed. The fact that Andy Cash's Apache squadron was handing over to a replacement squadron from the UK also meant that we anticipated a relative lull in Battle Group operations, as the new pilots need some time to work up to full combat readiness. It meant that I could afford to take ten days' leave and get back in time for Huw to make it home for his son's birthday.

John Hardy knew what was on my mind as he drove me to the airstrip to catch a Hercules flight to Kabul. 'They'll be all right, sir. I know that you won't stop thinking about the Battle Group, but try to and get some sleep.' I handed over my pistol to him and we shook hands. I grabbed my helmet and day sack and walked to the tailgate. I strapped myself in as the aircraft began to taxi and caught a last glimpse of John Hardy before the aircraft's ramp door closed shut. I told myself that they would be okay. My eyes were already drooping by the time the wheels lifted off from the rough desert strip. They opened again as the RAF loadmaster gently shook me awake and told me that we were in Kabul. Our RAF Tri-Star flight back to the UK wasn't until the next day. We were due to spend the night in Camp Souter, the British base in Kabul which was located a short distance from the City's airport. I followed the gaggle of people to a prefab tent that doubled as an arrival lounge; I was in the hands of the Lungi Fungi, those responsible for administrating bully beef and the supply of bullets in the rear and who had little idea of what combat was like. I could sense the messing about was due to begin.

There was no transport to take us to the UK military's logistics base at Camp Souter and no one of any rank to sort it out, except for a poor lance corporal from the Royal Logistics Corps. It had just gone 6 p.m. and his superiors had all knocked it on the head for the night. I told him to get an officer to come and take an interest in finding some transport. Three hours later some vehicles eventually turned up, but by then I had decided to sleep on the floor. The prospect of more waiting around at Souter and having to sit through a health and safety-style camp attack brief was all too much. I was missing the opportunity to sleep between sheets in the officers' mess and drink as many beers as I liked in the bar, but all I was interested in doing was getting home. I fashioned my body armour into a pillow and thought about the stark contrast in conditions and attitudes between the teeth and tail of an army on campaign.

It took several hours to process everybody for the flight the next morning. It amazed me that civil airports could do it within an hour of passengers checking in and yet the RAF made such a hash of it even though they were processing disciplined military personnel. Once eventually on board the Tri-Star, the flight attendants appeared somewhat incongruous as they mimicked the standard civilian in-flight safety brief in their desert flying suits and then added in bits about body armour, helmets and the surface-to-air threat. They were a breed apart from the dust-covered Chinook air crewmen who fought and shared risk with us on a daily basis when they flew into places like Sangin and Now Zad.

The flight back to the UK seemed to take an interminable age as we routed through Cyprus and Germany, but all of a sudden I was outside my quarter in Colchester sniffing the cool air of a late summer's evening. I was unarmed, there was no threat, stinking heat or life-or-death decisions to make. It felt strange and I felt guilty that I was not with the Battle Group. My girlfriend Karin was coming down to join me for a few days before flying to Madrid to see her mother. She hadn't expected me to come back during the tour and had already booked her flight. I told her not to change her plans, as I wanted to get up to the hospital at Selly Oak in Birmingham to see the wounded and planned to do it when she flew to Spain.

We spent four days together on the Norfolk coast. There was a break in the heatwave of that summer and it rained for most of the time. Having not seen rain for four months, I relished the contrast to the constant bright sunlight and dry dust of Helmand. But Afghanistan was always on my mind and my thoughts were filled with what was going on back in 3 PARA. As we walked amid the Austenesque charm of Southwold and along the sandy fringe of beach, I thought of the blokes in the backs of helicopters, the boom of mouse-hole charges and the chatter of machine guns. An annual crabbing competition was taking place. Families and excited children rushed about with orange-hooked twine and plastic buckets. The sun had broken through the clouds and there was a carefree holiday atmosphere that made me wonder if they had any idea of what was going on in Afghanistan. I talked a little of the past four months with Karin, but we both knew that I was going back and I didn't want to alarm her by saying too much. She could sense much of what I didn't say, but kept her concerns to herself. Soon she was heading for Madrid and I was driving my staff car on the M40 towards Birmingham.

I was shocked from the moment I arrived. I had expected to find a proper military wing to the general hospital, run exclusively by military medical personnel for wounded servicemen. But Ward S4, where military patients went for general recovery, was full of civilian patients and staff. Young men wounded in the service of their country, whether in Afghanistan or Iraq, were flanked by geriatric patients and attended to by overworked and, in some cases, disinterested NHS nursing staff. I spotted Warrant Officer Andy Newell from the Pathfinders who had been shot in the arm in Musa Qaleh a week or so earlier. I asked him how things were. 'In truth, sir, shit.' A civilian patient sat a few paces from Andy's bed. He had a problem controlling his bowels and bladder. Andy's complaint was not so much that he wasn't a fellow soldier, but that the nurses were not particularly efficient in cleaning up his mess. Consequently, Andy ended up doing it himself with his one good arm, the other having been fractured in fourteen places by the bullet that had passed through it. It was little wonder that wounded soldiers later contracted MRSA from their time at Selly Oak.

Admittedly, there was no need to clean anything up while I was there, but my informal presence happened to coincide with a visit by the Secretary of State, which, I suspect, contributed to the absence of any human excrement by Andy's bed. I spotted Des Browne from a distance being fussed over by medical staff, but I kept out of his way as I hadn't come to see him. Looking back on it, I regret not accosting him about the poor conditions I had begun to perceive, but he had left by the time I had been exposed to the full extent of the poor care British soldiers were receiving on S4.

I also saw Gunner Knight from I Battery. He had been evacuated with a suspected broken back sustained during operations around Musa Qaleh. He said he didn't know what the extent of the damage to his back was, as the CT scan he had been promised had not materialized. When I asked why, he said he didn't know as no one had bothered to tell him since he had been admitted to the ward several days before. I went up to the central desk in the ward and asked a chap in a white coat if he was the senior medical staff member present. He was evasive at first and then accepted that he might be when I pressed him on his status as a doctor. I asked him about what was happening to Gunner Knight. He said he didn't know and seemed unconcerned. This was until I pointed out that I was Knight's CO and was about to go and find the senior administrator of the hospital and create merry hell if he didn't give me a satisfactory answer. Twenty minutes later the threat produced the answer that the scanner was not working and Gunner Knight's scan would be delayed as a result. I suggested that it might have been prudent to tell Gunner Knight and went over to tell him myself.

When I discussed this matter with the SNCO attached to the ward as the military liaison officer, I asked why he hadn't been able to elicit the information I had just squeezed out of the ward staff. 'Sir, you are a colonel and have rank, I don't. Additionally, you looked in the mood for a fight.' The SNCO in question was not a medical man and undoubtedly was doing his best to make a difference, but he was fighting an uphill battle against bureaucratic indifference and a lack of compassion. He suggested that I might like to hear the experiences of some of the other soldiers who had been wounded in Iraq.

I was introduced to a corporal from an infantry unit who had lost his lower left leg to the tailfin of an RPG in some shitty alleyway in Basra. He was a fit, articulate and enthusiastic young man. On meeting him I was struck by his presence and demeanour that suggested he was not someone who was prone to moaning. He recounted how, after a through-the-knee operation to remove the mangled remains of his lower leg, he had been left unattended to come to from the anaesthetic without any pain relief. While he screamed in agony, it had taken forty-five minutes for the duty doctor to arrive and prescribe the necessary pain inhibitor. During that time he had bitten into his pillow and had trashed his bed space in a futile attempt to subdue the agony that burnt through him. As he did so his wounded ward-mates, on crutches and with drips hanging out of their arms, did what they could to ease his distress until the doctor arrived.

In all I spent five hours in the ward listening to tales of woe from those who had sacrificed much and had been treated with scant regard in return. There was no doubt that the specialist clinical treatment the wounded received was excellent, but the general aftercare was woeful. I heard tales of how a wounded TA soldier had been discharged from the ward in the same filthy and bloody uniform he had been wearing when he was blown up by a roadside bomb that killed a number of his comrades. He had been given a rail warrant and told to get the train back to Scotland. The wounded soldiers were not young men who had been injured as the result of getting pissed and crashing their cars, or people for whom the wheel of misfortune had brought about an unfortunate illness or other injury. They had suffered their wounds as a result of volunteering to put themselves in harm's way in the service of their country. In short, they deserved much better than the disgraceful conditions I witnessed at Selly Oak. How could we ever have let things get so bad? Was this really the supposed better deal we had secured by surrendering our military hospitals in exchange for gaining better clinical experience from the NHS?

I left the ward utterly depressed by what I had seen. To my mind there was no defence for it. I was acutely aware that in a few days' time I would be leading or asking men to go back into combat. Knowing what now awaited them if they were wounded in action caused me profound alarm. As I drove south from Birmingham on my way back to Colchester, I stopped my car on the hard shoulder; I needed a fag. I toyed with the idea of ringing CGS to register my deep concern. I flicked open my mobile and instead rang Matt Maer in PJHQ. I told him what I had seen, how I felt about it and we agreed that I would write a formal letter of complaint to the chain of command when I returned to Afghanistan.

I kept my concerns about what I had seen at Selly Oak to myself when I got back to Colchester and briefed the 3 PARA families a day later. Although I had written to them as part of the monthly 3 PARA families' newsletter that we sent back from Afghanistan, I knew that the wives would be deeply troubled by the sensational news reports that they would have been watching on TV and reading in the press. In general, Army wives are remarkably resilient; they need to be, given the considerable pressures brought about by the demands of supporting their husbands' careers. They become used to the fact that operations and training take their menfolk away from home and entail a degree of risk. But for most of them Afghanistan was different. They knew that it was a shooting war and that members of the Battle Group were being killed and injured on an increasingly regular basis. However, I doubted that many of their husbands, in the telephone calls they made home, would be telling them much of the detail about what was going on, or talked of the risks they were facing. Consequently, for many wives the lurid media coverage was proving to be a real challenge. Often they would hear on the news that a British soldier had been killed in Afghanistan, but they would not know who it was and would grow frantic with worry that it might be their husband or somebody they knew. Every time a wife left the house, or took the kids to school they would dread coming home to see a strange car parked near their house that might be bringing bad news from Helmand. I wanted to reassure my soldiers' loved ones about what we were doing and dampen the over-dramatization of the dangers we were facing. However, I also knew that they would not forgive me for obscuring the truth about the risks involved. It was not an easy balancing act.

I talked in general terms about the harsh conditions and the hazards we faced. But I also told them that morale was incredibly high and that their husbands were relishing the opportunity to do what they had joined the Army for. I majored on the fact that they were exceptionally well trained for the task, that they had good people around them and that we would not take unnecessary risks. I hoped what I said helped put their minds at ease. I used some photographic slides to give them an insight into life in Helmand which I had populated with the grinning faces of men whom I knew were married. I asked for questions at the end and answered each one as honestly as I could. One was from a wife who rightly gave me a bollocking for not mentioning the role and contribution of the Battle Group's exceptionally hard-working chefs.

I took some time to go into the office and visit the Rear Details element of the battalion that had stayed behind to run the domestic base. I talked with members of the Families Office who were doing a brilliant job in looking after the wives and children while the men were away. They provided a vital service, as it meant that those of us in Afghanistan could focus on operations without having to worry about what was happening on the home front. Under the command of Sergeant Major Billy McAleese, Colour Sergeant Neil Wingate and Rosemary Kershaw, the hard-working trio organized trips and parties for the families, sorted out domestic problems and were always there to help and give advice when it was needed.

They also took on the enormous burden of helping to look after the wounded and their next of kin, as well as the families of the soldiers who were killed in action. By the middle of the tour, Billy and Neil were driving from Colchester to Birmingham every other day to see the wounded. They picked up relatives and took the soldiers packs of spare clothes, magazines and wash kits. They assisted the casualty visiting officers who were assigned to look after relatives and organized and attended the repatriations of the fallen. They badgered the hospital staff when needed, filled in many of the gaps in their inadequate welfare system and helped the families take the strain of bereavement or the impact of a serious injury to a son or husband. Billy never switched off his phone. If it rang in the middle of the night he would answer it, drag on his clothing and head out into the darkness to visit a family or head back up to Selly Oak. They played a critical role in keeping the show on the road and were the unsung heroes of the tour.

After a week in the UK, I felt rested. Apart from the general medical treatment of the wounded, I knew that my people on the home front were being looked after. But I felt that I had been away from the Battle Group for far too long. Even though the approaching date of my flight to Afghanistan provoked feelings akin to those of returning to school at the end of a long summer holiday, I wanted to get back and be done with the waiting. I had only heard once from the Battle Group. Unfortunately, it was bad news. Lance Corporal Sean Tansey of the Household Cavalry had been killed in an accident in Sangin. He had been carrying out field repairs under a Scimitar when it collapsed on top of him. Although not a combat death, he died working in an environment that would have not have existed in peacetime and it brought home the general risks a soldier faces, even when not in contact with the enemy. I thought of D Squadron and the likely impact of another death among their number in less than two weeks. It made me even more impatient to get back.

I checked my mobile phone before I went to bed; it was my penultimate night in the UK before heading back to Afghanistan and I was spending it with a friend in Gloucestershire. I checked the mobile again in the morning and there were still no messages. It was a daily routine that I had adopted since arriving back on R and R. Good, I thought: there was nothing from the Rear Details element of 3 PARA in Colchester to suggest anything untoward had happened in Afghanistan while I had been asleep. Content with the thought that no news was good news, I focused on the day ahead, which I would spend visiting my goddaughter, and the prospect of fishing with her father after lunch. The sun was finally shining and I set off in buoyant mood as I drove along a leafy, high-banked lane in the Slad Valley. I was in the heart of Laurie Lee country where he had set and written his famous novel *Cider with Rosie*. The English countryside was at its quintessential best and for a brief moment my mind was a long way away from Afghanistan. What I didn't realize was that as I slept, members of A Company were fighting for their lives in a vicious firefight among the high-standing cornfields to the north of the district centre in Sangin.

As I approached the outskirts of Stroud I felt the ominous buzz of the mobile phone in my pocket. I stopped the car and heard Bish's voice as I pressed it to answer. 'Sir, I am afraid I have got some bad news from Afghanistan: Corporal Budd was killed earlier this morning in a firefight in Sangin.' As I listened to the sketchy details of what had happened the optimism that came with a perfect summer's morning was suddenly banished from my mind. Three hundred miles to my north in North Yorkshire, it was the lack of a telephone call that told Lorena Budd that something was wrong. Calling his wife on the mobile satellite welfare phone in Sangin every Sunday morning was a weekly routine that Bryan Budd had established with Lorena since arriving in Afghanistan. But that Sunday, the black satellite handset lay silent as the men of A Company carried Corporal Budd back to the district centre after a bloody engagement in the maize fields.

12

Crucible of Courage

Bullets zipped through the high-standing maize as the men of Hugo Farmer's platoon thrashed through the vegetation in a desperate effort to get back to the district centre. Farmer struggled to work out where all his men were. Fighting for breath and dripping with sweat, he would pause to speak into his mike to get a location report on each of his isolated sections in an attempt to coordinate their disparate movements. Rounds continued to cut through the leafy screen of crops to his left and his right as the Taliban followed the platoon which tried to make good their withdrawal. Farmer's men would lunge through the rows of plants then stop to set up a snap ambush to catch their pursuers. Each man struggled to regulate his breathing as they adopted hasty fire positions, shouldered weapons and released safety catches. On the order to fire, they poured a heavy weight of lead back in the direction that they had come from. It would gain them a brief respite. But as they began moving again, the resumption of the zip, zip of the bullets cutting through the fibrous maize indicated that the Taliban hadn't given up the chase.

Stationed on the roof of the district centre, the company commander, Major Jamie Loden, knew that his men on the ground were in trouble. Usually his patrols had the upper hand, but this engagement was different. The Taliban were getting better: instead of breaking contact when Farmer's men had first engaged them, they had followed up and were giving battle in a relentless cat-and-mouse chase through the maize crops. As the company commander, Loden's job was to marshal the resources to get his

platoon in the fields out of the shit. He was working the mortar fire controllers hard to rain down supporting fire on the Taliban, but the enemy were too close to Farmer's men and a clear view of who was friend and who was foe was obscured by the thick greenery through which both sides moved. Loden's forward air controller reported that two RAF Harriers were inbound on their way to help. There was a nagging doubt in Loden's mind as to whether they would get there in time, as Farmer and his men continued to race against the insurgents to reach the safety of the earth-filled mesh baskets of the HESCO bastion perimeter.

A Company had begun their second tour of duty in Sangin at the end of July. They went back in under the command of Loden. He had been plucked out of Staff College at short notice to replace Will Pike when illness had prevented Pike's original successor from deploying to Afghanistan. In essence Loden was the new boy and he was prepared to listen to his men who had already spent one tour of duty there. They knew something of what to expect, but they also noticed some changes. In their absence the Engineers had laboured round the clock to turn the district centre increasingly into a fortress. Often coming under fire as they worked, the Sappers had used their earth-moving equipment to throw up a 3-metre-high HESCO bastion perimeter around the compound and the LZ. Topped with razor wire and enhanced with firing platforms for vehicles and men, it was 2 metres wide at its thickest point and was capable of sustaining a direct hit from an RPG or a 107mm rocket. Subterranean bunkers were later dug into the pomegranate orchard to provide protection from mortar fire. The sangars on the FSG Tower and those around the main compound were also in the process of being reinforced by hundreds of additional sandbags. Although much of the work was still to be completed, the district centre was now an urban strongpoint that would not have looked out of place in a conventional battleground, such as Stalingrad. Despite the improved defences, however, the base still came under regular attack and inserting aircraft remained vulnerable to small-arms and RPG fire as they landed into the LZ.

Loden and I both knew that sitting behind the HESCO was not an option. The surrounding area would still need to be dominated by sending out patrols to disrupt the Taliban's attacks, kill their fighters and protect the Engineers as they continued to work on the defences. Additionally, a regular patrol presence outside the district centre was needed to interact with the local population and demonstrate resolve. Loden's immediate challenge was that he was short of manpower. A Company still had only two infantry platoons instead of the normal three. The Royal Irish reinforcement platoon they had hoped to receive had been diverted to support the Danes in Musa Qaleh. It meant that only one platoon could be sent out on patrol at any one time, while the other had to remain in the district centre to man the sangars. The platoons would rotate between the tasks of guarding and patrolling. The platoon on the patrols task was beefed up with a mortar fire controller (MFC) and a dedicated combat medic to increase the chances of survival if someone was hit. The platoon could also call on occasional vehicle support provided by a troop of the Household Cavalry's Scimitars and Spartans, as well as the fire support from WMIKs. But the lack of infantry and the close nature of the terrain restricted vehicle movement to the more open areas around the immediate vicinity of the district centre. If they progressed into the surrounding fields of crops that had grown up to more than 7 feet during the summer, or into the narrow streets, they would be vulnerable to attack. For the majority of any patrol the men on foot would be on their own. They would have to rely on the GPMGs, Minimi light machine guns and under-slung grenade launchers carried by each section, until the MFC could call in indirect fire support or the aircraft came on station.

The improved fortification of the district centre was not the only thing that had altered: the mood of the town and the face of the enemy had also changed since A Company's last stint in Sangin. Private Pete McKinley noticed a perceptible change in the local atmosphere as he patrolled back towards the district centre on 27 July. He was the point man of one of the first patrols to go out on to the ground. The local Afghans appeared edgy as the soldiers passed and they ignored their greetings. Sergeant Dan Jarvie noticed it too. As the patrol moved back into the dry wadi, shopkeepers began hastily to shut up their shops and the streets suddenly cleared of people; it was a clear combat indicator that something was wrong and the patrol went to ground. His senses heightened, McKinley scanned the ground to his front. In his peripheral vision he spotted two gunmen on the rooftops of the shops to his right. He engaged both men with his rifle, hitting one in the face; then the firefight kicked off with a vengeance.

Both sides traded heavy automatic fire as the Taliban opened up from at least three different firing points and the rest of the patrol responded in kind. RPGs thudded into the wadi as Corporal Bryan Budd gathered the rest of his section and sprinted towards the buildings from where the enemy fire was heaviest. There was a sudden yell and sickening crack as one of his men fell. Private 'Eddie' Edwards crumpled into the gravel; the two AK rounds that hit him shattered his femur and opened his inner thigh from his groin to his knee. Braving the incoming rounds, Private Meli Baleinavalu rushed forward to drag Edwards into cover as Budd launched an assault on the buildings and began clearing them with rifle fire and grenades.

In the ensuing mêlée of close-quarter fighting, McKinley was blown on to his back by the blast of an exploding RPG round. After clearing the buildings Budd pulled McKinley to his feet. In the subsequent fighting, at least two more of the insurgents were killed. Edwards was in shock as Jarvie and Corporal Stu Giles began administering first aid. Both men were covered in the frothing blood that squirted from his thigh as they worked frantically to squeeze the wound shut and stem the arterial bleeding. The contact continued to rage around them as a Spartan screamed up the wadi from the district centre to evacuate Edwards and mortar rounds began to crump down on the remaining Taliban. McKinley's prompt engagement of the first two insurgents and follow-up action with Budd undoubtedly forestalled a Taliban ambush. The mortar fire from the compound then ended it. But McKinley had been hit by a piece of shrapnel that penetrated the back of his body armour. He made light of his wound, initially refusing to get into the back of the Spartan with Edwards until the robust intervention of Dan Jarvie convinced him that his evacuation in the armoured vehicle was non-negotiable. Even the redoubtable McKinley recognized that his burly platoon sergeant was in no mood to argue.

Loden had accompanied 1 Platoon to familiarize himself with the ground around the district centre. The patrol provided him with an object lesson in the challenges and risks his men faced on a daily basis when they left the confines of the HESCO bastion perimeter. Any patrol that left the base was immediately dicked. The firefight in the wadi was an indication of just how susceptible his men were to being ambushed. There were only a limited number of routes in and out of the district centre and it was easy for the insurgents to track their movements and lie in wait for them. The contact also demonstrated that the Taliban had continued to adapt and improve their tactics. The number of stand-off attacks against the district centre increased in intensity as the Taliban brought new long-range weapons systems into play. These weapons included 82mm mortars, which had made an appearance in Now Zad, and multi-barrelled rocket launchers that could fire several projectiles at once. The insurgents were also displaying a far greater willingness to engage troops operating outside the base at closer quarters. They would cache their weapons at potential ambush sites in advance. This allowed them to move through the streets undetected and occupy a suitable ambush site once a patrol had been identified. After the attack the weapons would be left in place and the enemy would melt back into the local population.

The improvement in their tactics was a reflection that the inexperienced fighters A Company had first encountered in June had been replaced by a core of battle-hardened guerrillas. It also reflected the fact that the Taliban were finding it more difficult to recruit males from the local population, who had become reluctant to see their men die fighting the British after the insurgents' claim that they would drive them out of Sangin had failed to materialize. The hardcore fighters were more committed to their cause and more fanatical in their approach. Their ranks were also swollen by an increasing number of foreign fighters who brought their combat experience from other conflicts with them.

Being ambushed on 12 August for the first time was a defining moment for Second Lieutenant Andy Mallet who commanded 2 Platoon. He had joined 3 PARA in Afghanistan fresh out of officer training. He had never had the opportunity to train with the battalion before the deployment and the first set of orders he gave to his platoon for a fighting patrol was for real. As he ran through the patrol plan and sketched out the 'actions on' being ambushed and taking a casualty, he left his men in no doubt that he expected to make contact with the enemy. The seriousness of the task was reflected on the faces of his men, such as privates Zippy Owen and Andrew McSweeny, as they listened intently to their brand-new platoon commander. The platoon patrolled into the main bazaar with a number of ANA soldiers and set up a vehicle checkpoint on the main road through Sangin. Mallet let the Afghan soldiers do the talking to the local drivers while his men provided close protection. He knew that he could not remain static for too long, as to do so would invite attack. As his men covered their arcs, the insurgents were already moving unseen against them.

The first indication of the emerging threat came as adults began ushering their children indoors. The patrol collapsed the check-point and headed back into the market. Mallet interpreted the clearing of the streets as a combat indicator and gave orders into his radio mike for his men to be on their guard. The tension mounted as they moved back cautiously towards the district centre, their weapons on their shoulders with safety catches off. Index fingers caressed triggers, as the troops scrutinized every likely ambush point. The welcoming safety of the HESCO perimeter of the base soon came into view less than 100 metres to their front as Mallet's team progressed steadily down the narrow track of the Pipe Range that led to the main gate. His point section had already moved back into the district centre and he had only 30 metres to go. They were almost home.

Suddenly the whole world opened up. Rounds knocked lumps of mud off the surrounding walls and kicked up the dirt at their feet. Mallet heard the wush of an RPG as it landed behind him. It threw up a huge black cloud of smoke and dust, showering his team with shrapnel that sliced off the antenna of his signaller's backpack radio. Knocked down and dazed from his blast, McSweeny came to his senses realizing that he still had a live grenade in his hand. In the chaos he had already pulled the pin before being blown off his feet. He glanced at it briefly and then lobbed it in the direction of his attackers as he scrambled to his feet. Corporal Andy Carr's radio was still working and he immediately started to call down mortar fire from the other side of the HESCO. Mallet's other two sections were already returning rifle and machine-gun fire as friendly 81mm mortar bombs began to thump down danger close. The noise was deafening as rounds and lethal RPG fragments continued to sing among the troops caught in the confined area of the killing zone. The rapid response of the mortars delivered a devastating storm of exploding metal splinters into the Taliban and reduced the amount of fire the patrol was taking. The sections began to peel round each other as they manoeuvred their way out of contact to get back into the district centre.

In all, the ambush had lasted only a few minutes, but to the men who now smoked behind the safety of the HESCO it had lasted an age. Mallet's initial relief that everyone was okay was immediately replaced by disbelief that no one had been hit. As the post-combat euphoria of having survived an engagement without suffering casualties kicked in, Mallet's men began to laugh and joke about their near-death experience. Even Private Owen, who had a reputation for being a serious-minded soldier, went off to clean his GPMG grinning like a Cheshire cat.

The attacks against the two patrols on 27 July and 12 August had been the most serious of numerous encounters with the Taliban. But on both occasions the rapid application of battle drills and sheer tenacity had enabled the platoons to overmatch the insurgents. However, both patrols also highlighted the perils of being forced to patrol along the restricted number of predictable routes which made it easy for the Taliban to dick a platoon. It meant that every time members of A Company moved beyond the HESCO they were likely to be attacked. Consequently, every patrol was treated as an advance to contact and Loden made efforts to come up with novel ways to reduce their vulnerability to ambush. On 14 August, Loden had ordered Hugo Farmer to take his platoon out and blast holes through the walls of the compounds around the district centre using bar mines. Each mine was capable of destroying a main battle tank and contained enough explosive to blow a wide gap through the mud structures. They proved to be better than the underpowered mouse-hole charges and created a gap through which the men could move at ease. Loden's intention was to create alternative routes into the town which would make it more difficult for the Taliban to predict the movements of his men. It was a successful, if noisy, tactic that enabled Farmer to get his men into the centre of Sangin without being tracked in advance by the Taliban. Two and a half days later, 1 Platoon was sent out to make a stealthier attempt to defeat the enemy's dicking screen.

Voices were kept to a whisper as Farmer's men made their last-minute preparations: watches were zeroed, fire plans were confirmed and kit was checked to ensure it would not make telltale rattles or clinks that might give away the presence of the patrol. Final commands were passed down the line from man to man. Cocking handles were slid silently backwards and pushed forwards to chamber rounds to recheck that weapons had been made ready; then Farmer gave word for his point section to start moving out. They slipped through the rear gate built into the HESCO on the river side of the LZ and began to head south into the shadows of the night. They moved slowly, each man concentrating on his footing as they crossed the pebble-strewn flood plain along the riverbank. The world they patrolled into was a contrast of murky green and black as they looked through the monocular scopes of the night vision devices mounted on their helmets. Commands were passed by hand signal as the men patrolled, went to ground and listened for sounds in the blackness around them before moving off again until they reached their laying-up position to wait for the coming of daylight. If their movement out of the district centre had gone undetected they could resume the patrol at first light without being spotted by the dickers, which would reduce the amount of time the insurgents had to organize against them. However, it soon became clear that the Taliban had raised their game one notch further.

As dawn broke, Farmer's men moved from their concealed positions in the dense vegetation. Concurrently, a Scimitar and Spartan moved out of the district centre to distract any watching Taliban spotters. Had Farmer's patrol not been conducting a fighting patrol to look for cached weapons the Taliban had placed ready to engage helicopters landing on the LZ, the scene might have been idyllic. They were surrounded by an exuberance of the greenery of maize crops and vegetable plants bounded by irrigation channels and bushy-topped trees. The early morning sun gilded the high-standing leaves against the growing brilliance of a clear blue sky as a light mist lifted off the river basin. But the peaceful beauty of the scene was lost on the men, who struggled to see further than a few metres to their front as they began to receive reports that their presence might not have gone undetected. They heard a motorbike engine in the near distance and received intelligence reports that the Taliban were looking for the patrol. Some of Farmer's men broke on to a dirt track to see a bike with two Afghans moving slowly towards them. Farmer decided to detain them and take them back to the district centre for questioning. He watched as their hands were secured with plastic cuffs and blacked-out goggles were placed over their eyes to prevent them from picking up information about A Company's defences when they moved back into the base.

Farmer looked away as the men were being detained. Sixty metres off through a gap in the maize he spotted the heads of two more Afghans. Could they be farmers on their way to work in their fields? He looked again and saw four men behind them; he knew there were no fields in the direction they were heading. His suspicions were confirmed as the men moved closer and he spotted that they were wearing webbing and carrying AKs. The insurgents chatted idly, unaware of the proximity of Farmer's men. He had a split-second decision to make: he could either engage them himself or warn the rest of his men. He turned back to face his soldiers, making a thumbs-down signal and pointed to indicate the presence of the enemy in their midst. As he did so the gaze of enemy and foe met through the gaps in the corn. A frozen second of surprise was replaced by a frantic fumbling of weapons and then the shooting started.

Drills kicked in as Farmer's men set about winning the firefight and he shouted orders to launch a hasty platoon attack. His MFC started bringing 81mm bombs down on the Taliban as Farmer crawled along a ditch to within 30 metres of where the enemy had gone to ground and started to throw grenades. As his men laid down suppressive fire, Corporal Budd took his section in a flank-ing attack and the enemy fled. There were no casualties among Farmer's men, but the two detainees had been slow to move from their exposed position and were cut down by their own side's bullets in the opening exchange of fire. The initial contact had been won by 1 Platoon, but they had expended a large quantity of ammunition. They had also lost the element of surprise and were over a kilometre away from the base.

Suspecting that other Taliban would be attempting to move in behind them, Farmer decided to extract back to the district centre. But the Taliban were not about to let them go lightly. They had no idea that the two insurgents who had been apprehended had been killed in the initial firefight and were determined to get their men back and kill some of the patrol in the process. A minute after the patrol began to push back through the maize automatic fire cut through the crops from their right flank, forcing the patrol to take cover in the waterlogged irrigation ditches. As the vegetation above their heads was shredded by incoming bullets, Farmer consulted his map. His horizon was limited to the muddy bank a few metres in front of his face, but he knew that if he pushed north the Taliban would be waiting to ambush his men as they moved through the dense greenery. He decided to alter course and move north-west where he knew that the Household Cavalry's Scimitars had driven out from the district centre on to the relatively open ground by the river. The armoured vehicles were over 1,000 metres away, but if he could get closer to them he could get under the cover of their 30mm Rarden cannons. His men could already hear another group of Taliban beginning to close in behind them and he knew he had to get moving.

Rounds continued to strike into the earth and crack in the air around them as Farmer's men dashed, crawled and waded through the thick plantation. The insurgents were only a few metres from the rear section and their footfalls and breathing were audible to the men they pursued. Farmer put in the first of a series of snap ambushes that cut down the leading Taliban fighters as they closed to within a few metres of where his men had paused to turn and fire. The process was repeated and kept the enemy at bay as the platoon slowly reduced the distance between themselves and the Scimitars that waited to give them covering fire on the edge of the fields. But the Taliban weren't giving up and continued to fire and manoeuvre towards them from the flanks and the rear.

As the deadly cat-and-mouse chase through the maize fields unfolded, Loden's urgent call for air support had finally been answered by the arrival of two RAF Harriers. The pressures the aircrew faced were very different to those of the men on the ground whom they had come to help. Their pressure was to deliver vital fire support when the location of the enemy was not known and the position of friendly troops was difficult to discern. The pilots of the aircraft could see the fields where the contact was raging below them, but they could not distinguish friend from foe among the figures that moved through the maize. The pilots asked for smoke for a point of reference to guide them towards the enemy. Corporal Carr popped a canister that spewed a green cloud of signal smoke, which the pilots spotted. So did the Taliban and it acted like a bullet magnet for their fire.

Suddenly, Carr heard the loudest, but most welcome bang in the world: it was the crack of a 30mm cannon. The patrol had finally broken through the edge of the field and into the more open river line without the help of the Harriers. Carr looked up to see one of the Scimitars firing its Rarden over their heads into the mass of crops behind them. Farmer's men made it into a shallow wadi depression that gave them a degree of cover as tracer continued to spit towards them and rounds ricocheted off the large pebbles. The Scimitar's cannon fire raked into the fields that they had just left and was joined by fire from two WMIKs crewed by the Engineers who had been sent out to reinforce the supporting fire. Mortars and artillery also rained down into the fields as the patrol used the limited cover of the wadi to complete their extraction. Private Jamie Morton was thinking, Fuck, this is cheeky, as rounds struck at his feet as he manoeuvred with the rest of the platoon back to the protection of the base's HESCO bastion perimeter.

Despite the impressive weight of fire, the Taliban were still not backing off and continued to engage the troops as they moved along the wadi. The men on the roof of the district centre also started to come under enemy fire from the town. One of the armoured vehicles shed its track as it manoeuvred into a fire position to cover them. The disabled Spartan attracted the attention of the insurgents and began to receive fire as the crew scrambled for safety. With the break in contact and a clear delineation between friendly and enemy troops on the ground, the Harriers were called back in by the JTAC on the roof of the district centre to drop their ordnance. Loden wanted them to drop their bombs to end the contact and allow him to recover all his troops back into the base. But moving at 600 miles per hour the Harrier pilots were struggling to make out where the enemy were in the thick foliage. The first pilot fired marker rockets to try to get his bearings on the enemy, but they struck the perimeter of the HESCO bastion behind which some of Farmer's men now sheltered. Angry directions from the JTAC on the roof brought the Harrier back on but she was low on fuel and her wing man took over. He dropped one 500-pound bomb 300 metres short of the Taliban, but it caused them to pause. The second 1,000-pound weapon he released was 700 metres off target and landed on the LZ by the district centre. Thankfully, it was a dud and failed to explode. Had it done so the number of friendly casualties it would have caused could have been catastrophic. He was waved off in disgust, but the contact was over. Amazingly, none of Farmer's men had been hit during the engagement that lasted nearly two hours. He and his men were totally knackered. Carrying heavy kit, wearing body armour and helmets, they had fought through nearly 1.5 kilometres of waterlogged ditches, hard rutted ground and thick vegetation in the high summer heat. For most of his already combat-experienced men it had been their worst moment to date since arriving back in Sangin, but fate was to dictate that worse moments were to come.

The shifting nature of the contacts A Company had begun to face later caused Loden to rethink his tactics for patrolling. He consulted his junior commanders to get their views and decided to beef up each patrolling platoon with a fourth section of eight men. Their principal task would be to secure a casualty collection point, as Loden recognized that taking a casualty on patrol would fundamentally alter the dynamics of any engagement. One wounded man would require a whole section to carry and protect him, which would drastically denude a platoon of fighting power. Carrying a fallen comrade under fire is an exacting task and slowing down a patrol's movement would make it vulnerable to taking further casualties. It was also agreed that patrols needed to continue to increase the number of routes they could use and Loden decided to repeat the successful tactic of blowing holes through unoccupied compound walls. On 20 August Loden tasked 1 Platoon with a patrol mission to expand the number of routes to the north of the district centre. It was more open than the area of the Gardens to the south, but it still consisted of a dangerous mix of compound buildings, thick mud walls and a patchwork of high-standing crops. The area was bounded on one side by the Helmand River to the west. To the east a small wadi ran north along the fringes of the main part of the town.

Corporal Guy 'Posh' Roberts had planned to fly out of the district centre on R and R before the patrol. But his helicopter had been delayed so he volunteered to go out with Farmer's men to act as the MFC. He shared the MFC task with Corporal Carr, but felt that it was his turn to go out and he liked the sound of the mission. It was eleven o'clock in the morning as he headed out with Corporal Budd's section. They were tasked to provide right flank protection to the group that would blow the holes through the walls. Budd led his group towards a prominent building called the Chinese Restaurant, so named because of the gaudy lime and pink cement facings that adorned its front. Corporal Andy Waddington moved his men along the river line to provide depth protection and Farmer went with the group that would carry out the explosions. The platoon's initial movement was covered by two WMIKs. One was stationed in the wadi to the front of the district centre and the other tried to cover Waddington's section. But they soon lost sight of the advancing sections as they were swallowed up by the vegetation in the surrounding fields.

Budd's men had gone several hundred metres when he took over as point man of the section; Roberts was just behind him. Budd suddenly stopped in his tracks and gave a thumbs-down signal. He had seen Taliban to the right of his position across a field, but they hadn't seen him. He then made the signal again, showing two fingers to indicate the number of insurgents he had identified. One of the Taliban had a white beard. He was carrying an AK and was looking intently up at the sky. He was distracted by a high-flying aircraft whose engines had masked the approach

of Budd's men. Budd doubled the section back on itself. He
wanted to get a better approach to launch an attack on the men he
had spotted through the edge of the field of high-standing maize.
He gave quick battle orders and shook his front fire team out in
extended line. They slipped their safety catches to the fire position
and pushed through the crops with their weapons pointing
forward.

As the five men broke through the other side of the field the
firing started. One of the WMIKs to the south had been contacted
and the noise of the firing alerted the Taliban Budd had spotted.
The enemy saw the fire team emerge from the crops and started
engaging them. Roberts lost sight of Budd as he became fixated by
trying to hit one of the fighters. The insurgent kept popping up
from behind a wall 15 metres away. Roberts would fire several
rounds to drive him down again as bullets came back in his direction. Frustrated at the limited effect his rifle was having, he
grabbed Private Sharpe's grenade launcher. He fired it at the
Taliban and cursed as he watched the 40mm explosive projectile
sail over his enemy's head. He went to load another of the fat
stubby rounds when he felt a sharp whack on his left side as an AK
round hit him through the open side of his body armour. It felt
like he had been smashed in the chest by a giant baseball bat. He
momentarily thought, What the fuck was that? Then he realized
he had been hit and went down.

Budd's attack had alerted more Taliban in the Chinese Restaurant
who now entered the fray from the left flank. Roberts pressed
himself into the ground as their rounds started spurting into the
earth where he lay. Private Lanaghan grabbed Roberts and started
dragging him back into cover, and as he did so a bullet struck him
in the shoulder and exited through his face; he went down too.
Roberts was convinced that Lanaghan had been killed; the round
had split open his lower face exposing his teeth and covering him
in blood. Then he saw him move and knew he was still alive.
Privates Stevie Halton and Sharpe were the last two standing
members of the team. Halton stood over his stricken mates and

fired short, disciplined bursts back at the Taliban from his belt-fed Minimi machine gun. Sharpe was helping his two wounded comrades when he suddenly dropped to the ground with the wind knocked out of him. He struggled for breath as he frantically pushed a hand under his body armour expecting to feel the warm, sticky sensation of oozing blood. Three of the section were now down but they managed to crawl into the cover of an irrigation ditch. Budd wasn't with them and had last been seen making a lone charge towards the enemy.

Hugo Farmer closed up behind Budd's men with Corporal Charlie Curnow's section. They immediately started treating the wounded. Lanaghan looked in a bad way, but Corporal Billie Owen focused on Roberts, assessing him to be the worst hit. The medic applied a tourniquet to Roberts's arm which cut into his wound; Owen knew he was hurting him, but he had to stem the flow of blood. Sharpe was still in shock and others stripped off his kit looking for an entry wound, but he was lucky. The bullet had hit his ceramic plate in the front of his body armour which stopped the round. Farmer was demanding to know where Budd was. Halton told his boss that the section had lost sight of him as he went right-flanking on his own.

Shit! Farmer thought. One section was out of the game, the rest of his sections were now bogged down in an extended firefight and Corporal Budd was missing. He knew he had to find him as there was no way he was going to leave one of his men behind. He decided to push on with Curnow's section from the right along a small stream and began to creep forward at the head of his men. He came across several dead Taliban and as he looked up he saw weapon muzzles pointing out of a building ahead of him. Constrained by the stream on one side and a wall on the other, he knew that he was in a tight spot even before an enemy machine gun opened up on them. A burst of automatic fire split the air around him and his platoon signaller, Private Briggs, who was standing behind him, screamed out that he had been hit. Briggs had been struck in his ceramic plate and Farmer yelled at him to bug out as he felt a piece of shrapnel bite him in the backside. Curnow was also hit by shrapnel in his lower leg as the three men moved back under covering fire provided by Privates McKinley and Randle.

Loden had launched a Quick Reaction Force (QRF) under Corporal Tam McDermott from 2 Platoon when he heard there were casualties and Sergeant Major Schofield had been sent out with a quad bike and trailer to collect Lanaghan and Roberts. Andy Mallet was champing at the bit to lead the rest of his men out, but Loden was as steady as a rock and held them back until he knew more of the situation he was about to launch them into. When he heard that Farmer had taken more casualties, he launched Mallet. The remaining two sections of 2 Platoon raced out of the district centre with two additional sections made up of military policemen, Engineers and dismounted Household Cavalrymen. They passed Roberts and Lanaghan being carried back on the quad and came across Corporal Curnow sitting by a WMIK that had been disabled in the fighting and was now acting as a casualty collection point. A sporadic engagement was still going on around them as Mallet linked up with Farmer. Farmer briefed Mallet that he wanted him to take his platoon and go left-flanking to try to find Budd. The platoon broke left of the WMIK and came upon an open field. Mallet placed a section with their GPMGs to cover them as they started sprinting across the exposed ground. They had gone only a few steps when they came under fire. The Taliban were firing from loop holes cut into a compound wall, which made it difficult to suppress them. Every time they moved forward they were pinned down and were unable to make any headway. The situation was not helped by the fact that two RAF Harriers, which had arrived overhead, were unable to identify the enemy. Intelligence reports also indicated that more Taliban were being brought into the fight.

Farmer was confident that with the river behind him his rear was secure. Then some insurgents began firing from the reeds along its banks. He was now in the middle of a 360° firefight, but he knew that he had to get Budd back. Farmer ordered Corporal Waddington's section to make another attempt from the right flank, and started to give fire control directions to the two Apaches that had arrived on station. He had learned his lesson about using smoke and popped a signal grenade over a high compound wall to prevent it giving away his position to the Taliban. The pilot asked what effect he wanted them to have on the building that most of the Taliban were firing from. 'Just fucking level it,' Farmer replied.

Hovering at several thousand feet, the Apache Wildman callsigns had a 'God's eye view' of the world beneath them. Although the attack helicopters were sometimes hit, their height and armoured cockpits protected them against small fire. They were also not sweating and slugging it out in the close contact battle like the Paras below them. However, identifying enemy fighters in close proximity to their own troops amongst the dense maize fields was no easy task, particularly if the target indications they were given were frantic and unclear. The front seat commander of the Apaches could hear Farmer's laboured voice in his headset mixed with the crack of bullets and the thump of RPGs in the background. 'Wildman, Wildman, they are in the building! They are in the building!' But which building? Then he saw the telltale wisp of signal smoke that gave him the point of reference that he was looking for.

The target acquisition device system attached to the helmet of the front-seat pilot of the leading attack helicopter slaved the Apache's nose gun on to the Taliban below them. He gave directions to his rear seat pilot to bring the aircraft into the right attack angle. When he was happy that the helicopter was lined up he lazed the target for range with the thumb knobs on the PlayStation-like control system in front of him. The energy of laser reflected back from the wall of the compound from which the Taliban were engaging Farmer's men. It fed back into the onboard weapons computer that automatically adjusted the aim of the cannon. The pilot confirmed the choice of weapon type and verbally rapped out the engagement sequence as he squeezed the trigger on his joystick: 'Good range, engaging with cannon, gun firing.' A killing burst of twenty 30mm rounds streaked away from the barrel of the Apache's cannon to deliver a devastating stream of explosive shells towards the insurgents. As he watched them impact on to the target, he shouted instructions to his pilot to manoeuvre the aircraft so he could adjust his fire: 'Come left, come left, can you see them? There they are! Good range, firing now. Got them!'

As death rained down on the Taliban from above, Corporal Waddington began to probe from the right flank with twelve men. Private Martin Cork pushed through the high-standing maize and thought that this could be his 'last fucking day'. As the section pushed forward, visibility to their front was little more than a few metres. Cork had lost sight of Private 'Jay' Morton in the thick vegetation when he heard him shout, 'Corky, Corky, I have found him!' Bryan Budd was lying face down in a ditch. The body of one dead insurgent lay next to him, with another curled up a little way off. The two men checked for a pulse, but could find none; Bryan Budd had died as he pushed on alone to carry his attack to the enemy. They lifted his body on to the back of Private McManus and ran him back to where Farmer had gathered the remainder of his men.

With the recovery of Budd's body, Farmer reorganized his platoon and started pushing back to the district centre in a coordinated movement with Mallet's platoon. They set off at speed and Farmer was grateful that covering 2 miles of rough terrain in under eighteen minutes wearing battle kit was a standard Parachute Regiment test. The Taliban called in their 82mm mortars and harried them all the way back to the HESCO. As they reached the compound the exploding mortar bombs were landing 40 metres behind them.

As the platoons reorganized themselves in the relative safety of the district centre, the Taliban prepared to launch a 107mm rocket attack on the base. Loden now had US A-10s on station. He cleared the Apaches off to the east. With the airspace now clear, the A-10s made their run in dropping four 500-pound bombs and firing over 1,890 cannon rounds, putting an abrupt end to the Taliban plan of attack.

For the men of A Company, losing Budd was the lowest point. Up until that moment, they had always come out on top in the contacts with the Taliban. Even though seven insurgents had been killed including a senior Taliban commander, and another twelve wounded, it felt as if they had been on the back foot and it was the insurgents who had gained the upper hand. Budd was also an extremely popular and highly respected NCO. His personal gallantry and decision to take the initiative to launch his section into the attack typified the professionalism and courage of Parachute Regiment junior commanders. He was also loved for his humility. Softly spoken and gracious, he was never flustered and took everything in his stride. He was a passionate family man and would often talk about Lorena and Isabelle, his wife and daughter. Lorena was expecting their second child and would give birth to another daughter who would never meet her father. Lance Corporal Mark Keenan was back in the UK on R and R when he heard the news. He was devastated; Budd had been his old section commander and was a good friend. When he arrived back in Sangin a few days later he thought the blokes looked ten years older than when he had left them.

Bryan Budd's loss was felt keenly across the company. Some doubted whether it was worth it and some questioned the effect they were having going out day after day just to get hit. Corporal 'Zip' Lane was standing in as the platoon sergeant for Dan Jarvie who was also on R and R at the time. He knew that some of his men were in shock as he went round and chatted to them. He got them to crack on with routine tasks such as cleaning their weapons and cooking up their rations, recognizing that they needed to be kept busy. Other commanders, such as Loden, Farmer and Mallet, talked to their men too. But the blokes largely dealt with Budd's loss among themselves. Martin Cork and his fellow platoon members felt gutted and deflated. They talked about what had happened, they debated the 'what ifs' and things that might have been done differently. But they knew that they had to accept what had happened and that they still had a job to do. Everyone knew that they would be going back out again. Mallet gave his men a pep talk and stressed the importance of the mission and the need to keep on patrolling. When he finished there was silence, then Private Card, one of the youngest Toms, just said, 'Yeah, okay, boss. No dramas. When are we going back out?'

Hell in a Tight Space

I returned from R and R on 22 August. In addition to the loss of Corporal Budd one other significant thing had changed during the period that I had been away. The Danish contingent had decided to pull out of Musa Qaleh. Since taking over the district centre from the Pathfinders on 25 July, the Danes had taken three casualties, including one soldier who had sustained a serious head injury when he had been hit by a sniper on 2 August. The difficulties associated with his helicopter evacuation had had a profound effect on the Danes. I heard of their anguish about getting their wounded comrade out and remember thinking, welcome to the club. As the risks they faced became more apparent, they had increasingly begun to feel that their position had become untenable. The decision was backed by their government in Copenhagen and was presented to the UKTF as a fait accompli.

With no other forces to replace them, and with little more than forty-eight hours' notice, the task of taking over from the Danes was given to 3 PARA. As I was waiting to board a C-17 transporter to fly back to Kandahar from the UK, Major Adam Jowett was being given a warning order to form an ad hoc company group from anyone who could be spared from the Battle Group. Jowett had been employed in the JOC as a staff officer and relished the sudden, and unexpected, prospect of operational field command. He had two days to cobble his force together. Jowett's new scratch command was called Easy Company, so called in honour of the 101st US Airborne Second World War company depicted in *Band of Brothers*. It also fitted the phonetic alphabetical

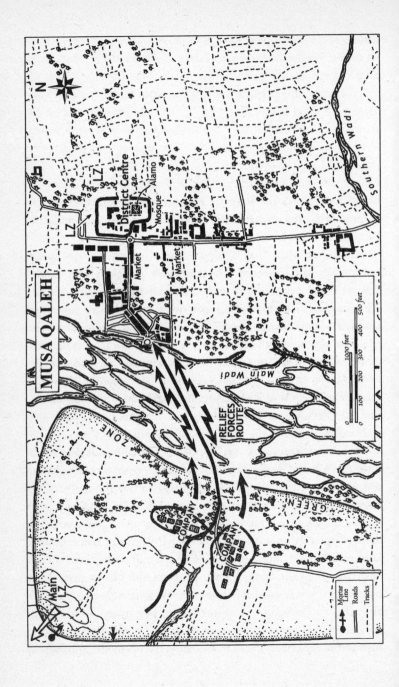

listing of sub-units within 3 PARA. It was based on a small company headquarters consisting of Sergeant Major Scrivener, Sergeant Freddie Kruyer who would act as the intelligence NCO, a signals detachment and a tiny medical team under Captain Mike Stacey who had been offered up by the field hospital in Bastion. Its infantry was made up of the second Royal Irish platoon that had been sent out from the UK and the Irish mortar section and infantry platoon that were already supporting the Danes in Musa Qaleh. Despite losing their platoon Sergeant Ally McKinney, who had also sustained a serious head injury from a sniper's bullet on 9 August, the remaining Irishmen of Somme Platoon would not be coming out when the Danes withdrew.

Musa Qaleh was a hell of a place. I had visited the town's district centre during a recce in May when it was being held by the Americans after the Taliban had first tried to take it from the ANP. The buildings still bore the pockmarked signature of the insurgents' attack where their RPG and AK rounds had struck home. The main administrative building and prison block divided the compound into two parts; the latter was more akin to a twelfth-century Saracen dungeon than a modern-day holding facility. The dilapidated collection of buildings was contained within a 3-metre-high mud-brick wall. A large mosque set in a grove of bushy trees encroached on the confines of the compound on its south-eastern corner. As well as the debris of battle, the place was also strewn with rubbish and human waste. However, it was not the scars of the fighting or filth that attracted my attention. What struck me most about the district centre was its sheer isolation and poor defensive qualities. Unlike Now Zad or Sangin it had no nearby flank or open desert or river line in which reinforcements could be landed or a relief approach could be made. The district centre in Musa Qaleh was situated right in the middle of the town. The compound was abutted by a number of surrounding compounds and narrow alleyways, which provided numerous approaches for an attacker to creep undetected up to the walls. It possessed no natural fields of fire and was too cramped to provide an adequate helicopter landing site within its perimeter. It was also overlooked by several taller buildings which provided elevated platforms from which the insurgents had been able to fire down into the compound.

The town of Musa Qaleh was itself further isolated by a large sprawl of suburban compounds to its north and west and the confluence of two wide wadis to its south and east. The only vehicle access point was from the open desert to the west. But it then ran along a narrow track that was surrounded on either side by orchards and fields; it was ideal ambush country. This green zone had to be traversed before hitting the wadi running north to south along the western edge of the town. Anyone crossing the wadi would then be exposed to the risk of further attack before hitting the edge of the town. Even if it was possible to traverse this route without being attacked, reaching the district centre would still mean running the gauntlet of narrow streets before reaching the front gates. The hairs were standing up on the back of my neck as we drove along the route in three American Humvees that took us back to our helicopter pick-up point out in the desert. None of the inhabitants we passed returned the waves of the US soldiers manning the Humvees' top-cover machine guns. I mused over the vulnerability of the district centre as we drove out of town, crossed the exposed wadi and then travelled through the close country of the green zone. My only distraction was that we would be sitting ducks if the Taliban decided to hit us on the route out. When asked, the US lieutenant in the front of my Humvee informed me that this would be the eighth time he had driven the same route in the last twenty-four hours. I briefly thought about 'nine lives' and hoped for the best. I was relieved to make it back to the LZ in one piece. Although I had only spent a few hours there, Musa Qaleh had a distinctly bad feel to it.

Easy Company flew into Musa Qaleh at the cusp of dawn on 23 August in two Chinooks which were packed to capacity with men and equipment. Every spare space on the two cabs was filled with bundles of sandbags, extra ammunition and medical kit. Jowett knew that he would be operating at the end of a very thin casualty evacuation line and begged, borrowed and stole every additional IV fluid bag, drug and field dressing he could get his hands on. The Taliban saw the aircraft come in and an RPG sailed up to meet them, its projectile bursting in mid-air like flak. There was a crackle of small arms, but the fire was ineffective. Lacking an internal LZ, the helicopters landed outside the district centre on a small adjacent field beyond the walls of the compound. The Danes were exceptionally relieved to see Jowett's men, as the arrival of Easy Company meant that they could leave the hellhole of Musa Qaleh behind them. Including Somme Platoon, made up of the Royal Irish soldiers who had been supporting the Danes, Jowett had eighty-six men to hold the compound. It was a stark comparison to the 140 Danish soldiers and 40-plus armoured vehicles equipped with .50 Cal heavy machine guns that would quit the district centre the next day. Jowett could call on just three un-armoured vehicles and had only two .50 Cal machine guns compared to the eight that the Danes had been able to set up in the sangars. They also had a medical team of twelve people equipped with armoured ambulances; Easy Company had one doctor, two medics and a quad bike.

The operation to extract the Danish squadron was a re-run of the mission 3 PARA had used to get the Pathfinders out of Musa Qaleh. B and C companies once again cleared and held the green zone, while the Household Cavalry secured the wadi and Jowett used his men to picket the narrow streets that led to the dry riverbed. As the Danes drove out, sixty Afghan Standby Police (ASP) drove into the district centre in Hilux trucks. Their arrival was the result of pressure brought by Ed Butler and General David Richards, the new ISAF commander, to persuade the Afghan government to make a greater investment in securing the district centres. It also reflected Richards's concern that the British were becoming dangerously fixed in the isolated northern towns of Helmand, and the beginnings of an initiative to find an Afghan solution to their own security. Regardless of the politics surrounding the arrival of the police they were a welcome addition to the limited forces that Jowett had at his disposal. Coming from Kabul, they were made up of Hazaras and Tajiks. Untainted by local Pashtun tribal affiliations, they were to prove a vast improvement on the local ANP in the other locations held by 3 PARA.

I oversaw the operation from the JOC. Having just stepped off a C-130 at Bastion, it made sense that the mission was led by Huw Williams who had planned it in my absence. Huw was a capable officer and logic dictated that he should command it on the ground, but I spent several anxious hours listening to it unfold on the radios around the bird table, as I sat like an anxious parent waiting for the Battle Group to return. As progress reports crackled over the net, I looked at the brightly coloured pins placed on the map of Helmand Province spread out before me. Each one denoted a fixed location held by 3 PARA and a shiny new pin had been pushed into the grid squares over Musa Qaleh. We were now even more overstretched than when I had left to go on R and R. We had scraped the barrel of our resources to form Easy Company and Musa Qaleh was the last place I would have wanted to put them.

The extraction of the Danes and the insertion of Easy Company were completed without incident. Sporadic contact was made with the Taliban, but they were convincingly overmatched by the presence of the Battle Group and no friendly casualties were taken. Intelligence reports confirmed that the insurgents had mistakenly interpreted seeing so much combat power leave Musa Qaleh as a complete withdrawal of all NATO troops from the district centre. Believing that it was now held solely by Afghan government forces, the Taliban assessed that it would be easily taken and prepared to make a series of concerted efforts to overrun the compound. It was estimated that over 200 Taliban fighters had been brought into the town to make the attempt. However, they reckoned without the presence of the small band of determined men that made up Easy Company.

The first attack began shortly after darkness on 24 August. Jowett's men could see the insurgents darting between the streets less than 100 metres away from their sangar positions as the Taliban manoeuvred into position to bring the base under fire. They attempted to fight their way through the grounds of the mosque. It had been destroyed by a bombing mission called down by the Danes and the heaped mass of rubble and broken masonry provided excellent cover for them to get up close to the compound wall and the front gate. They were beaten back by a combination of the defenders' fire and an F-16 ground-attack jet. One of the insurgents' senior commanders was wounded in the assault and he ordered his men to break off the attack. They withdrew to lick their wounds, leaving some of their dead at the foot of the buckled metal gates at the front of the compound.

The attacks resumed again the next morning as the insurgents fired rockets and RPGs at the district centre. The enemy fire teams were suppressed by an RAF Harrier that strafed them with a ripple of rockets, but one of the Taliban's own 107mm rockets had hit home. It punched its way through three walls before coming to rest under the north-eastern sangar where it failed to detonate. The outpost was temporarily evacuated and the unexploded rocket was given a thirty-minute soak period before the position was reoccupied. Sandbags were piled gingerly around the projectile while the troops who repositioned themselves a few metres from it hoped for the best. The unexploded rocket would remain where it landed for weeks, as Jowett had more pressing issues to deal with. Having sand-bagged the projectile, Jowett began to receive reports that the Taliban were massing in eleven pick-up trucks in the wadi a kilometre to the south of the district centre. A Harrier confirmed their presence but the pilot had difficulty discerning whether the men and vehicles he was seeing were Taliban, as he flashed over them at high-speed altitude. Jowett was convinced that they were and directed the pilot to engage them with two 500-pound bombs. Easy Company's own mortars and a troop of artillery stationed out in the desert joined in the bombardment. Eight of the vehicles were destroyed in a maelstrom of fire and the remaining three were seen fleeing along the wadi. Local reports later vindicated Jowett's decision when they confirmed that many Taliban had been killed in the engagement and another commander had been injured.

The next day the attacks against the district centre dropped off as the insurgents reorganized and brought in reinforcements to replace the losses they had taken in the wadi. The attacks resumed with a vengeance at first light the following day and continued into the evening. It started with a volley of seven RPG rounds from multiple directions, as the Taliban formed up to attack in the streets around the district centre. Cries of 'incoming' and 'stand to, stand to!' sent the men of Easy Company rushing to man their positions and trade fire with the insurgents as they pushed home their assault. At times the enemy were close enough to force the defenders to lean out of their sangars to fire down on them and toss grenades on to them as they dashed along the alleyways below. Jowett requested air support, but was being attacked from so many different directions that he had to prioritize where to call in the A-10s first. The ground-attack jets would line up on coordinates given to them by the JTACs before screaming in to release their lethal loads of bombs and cannon shells along the outsides of the walls of the compound. They blasted down 30mm rounds within 30 metres of the men in the sangars and dropped JDAMs as close as 140 metres away. Having released their ordnance, the pilots would then pull up into a steep climb to circle into position to repeat the cycle and attack the next target they had been given. When they ran low on fuel they would hand over to another pair of aircraft and then ascend to high altitude to suck gas from an air tanker before returning to the fray.

Meanwhile the mortars under Corporal Groves kept up an incessant rate of fire. His crews would adjust their sights, prime the mortar bombs and then drop them down the barrels. Turning away at the last moment, the mortar men would shield their ears with their hands to protect them from the blast as the bottom of the rounds struck the firing pins and were spat high into the sky. The metal tubes would bite back into their dug-in base plates as the process was repeated again and again. The expenditure of small-arms ammunition was equally prolific. While men fired round after round from their rifles and long bursts from their machine guns, others would frantically charge magazines and re-link loose bullets into spare belts of machine-gun ammo. Jowett kept his sniper pair in reserve by the main headquarters building until launching them where the point of pressure was greatest. He launched them many times that day and Corporal Hugh Keir and Private Jared Cleary accounted for many of the enemy with lethal precision fire as they caught insurgents in their cross-hairs. With the exception of the medical team everyone, including Jowett and Sergeant Major Scrivener, fought from their allocated stand to positions. Mike Stacey and his two medics, corporals French and Roberts, readied their gear as the battle raged outside the mud building they had turned into the RAP. The call for their services was not to be long in coming.

Jowett ducked down behind the parapet on the roof of the main headquarters building to change a magazine on his rifle when he heard the call for a medic. He looked to see Ranger Diamond bending over the prostrate form of Lance Corporal John Hetherington. He had been hit by a single AK round that had entered his side below his armpit. They stripped off his body armour and kit, but could find no pulse. As they did so, Corporal French raced out on a quad bike from the medical centre. Lance Corporal Hetherington's limp form was lifted off the roof. He had been one of two men from 14 Signals Regiment who had volunteered to fly out and replace Corporal Thorpe and Lance Corporal Hashmi when they had been killed in Sangin. Tragically, he would make the same journey home that they had made. He was the first of Jowett's men to lose his life in Musa Qaleh and the eleventh member of the Battle Group to die since the beginning of the operation.

Though saddened by the loss of Lance Corporal Hetherington,

Adam Jowett was amazed that more of his men hadn't been hit as he surveyed the aftermath of the battle. It had lasted almost twelve hours and the district centre bore the scars of numerous RPG strikes and sinister black scorched craters where Taliban mortar rounds had landed. The telephone line between the sangars had been cut in several places by shrapnel and every wall was pock-marked with bullet holes. He looked out on to the streets that were littered with Taliban dead. He had ordered that the insurgents were not to be engaged when they collected the wounded and the bodies of their fallen fighters. It was a courtesy of war he doubted would be extended to his men but typified the different conventions of conflict that bound the two sides. However, on this occasion the local dogs had beaten the Taliban to it and began to try to drag the bodies away. Before shots were fired by the sangar sentries to drive the dogs off, two canines tugged at one dead fighter causing his arm to wave as if in a macabre farewell to the men who had killed him.

After each heavy attack, Easy Company would conduct clear-ance patrols to sweep the immediate area around the outside of the district centre. Jowett was able to draw on the local knowledge of the Rangers in Somme Platoon who had done the bulk of the patrolling when the Danes had occupied the compound. They knew where the favourite Taliban firing positions were and would reposition trip flares along likely avenues of approach. Most of the immediate buildings had been badly damaged by the fighting and consisted of a mass of bombed-out shells. The defenders had delib-erately blown out the back of some of the buildings so that enemy gunmen would be silhouetted against the empty background making them easier to see and hit. But it didn't stop the Taliban from using them in subsequent attacks and the casualties that resulted were an indication of their desperation to drive Easy Company out of the district centre. The patrols sometimes found sheets that the insurgents had strung across the gaps that had been created in the buildings in an attempt to mask their movements from the sangars. They also found holes between connecting walls that had been made to provide rat runs to allow the attackers to get closer to the compound without being detected. Some buildings were little more than piles of rubbly mud bricks which were often strewn with the body parts of insurgents. Though the Taliban were prepared to continue to pay a high price in attacking the district centre with their fighters, they were also prepared to rethink their tactics and began to place a greater emphasis on standoff attacks with longer-range weapons. The accuracy of their mortars improved throughout the siege and by its end ninety-six 82mm rounds had landed inside the compound.

On 1 September a barrage of enemy mortar fire began to creep towards the district centre throughout the day. On each occasion the men of Easy Company rushed to their sangars amid shouts of 'incoming!' as the crump and sickening echo of the loud bang that immediately followed it indicated another near miss. In mid-afternoon the sangar on the jail that had become known as the Alamo took a direct hit. Lance Corporal Roberts heard the call come in over the radio in the RAP. He raced to the roof of the Alamo with Corporal French. Corporal Keir and Private Jared Cleary were already treating Ranger Anare Dravia, who had taken the full force of the blast. They knew that they needed to get him off the roof fast. Mortar rounds were still landing in the compound as they carried him past a pile of rubble. Roberts noticed a boot sticking out of it. They cleared away the debris and found Lance Corporal Paul Muirhead, who had a serious head injury. The two medics managed to stem the bleeding to his head and both wounded men were rushed back to the RAP on stretchers. Mike Stacey did all he could for Ranger Dravia, but his wounds had been too grievous. But Corporal Muirhead was still alive and became the focus of the medics' energies as they worked to stabilize him until the arrival of the casualty evacuation helicopter. Jowett had already requested it as soon as he knew he had casualties, but it would not come immediately.

The risk of the casualty evacuation helicopter being shot down had to be balanced against the risk of Corporal Muirhead succumbing to his wounds. The aircraft was already stood to and the aircrew were being briefed as the senior medical officer, Lieutenant Colonel Peter Davis, spoke to me about his chances of survival. If it was assessed that Corporal Muirhead could not wait, we would launch immediately. Davis had been speaking to Mike Stacey on the Tac Sat radio. The two doctors concurred that he could afford to hang on for three hours before his condition deteriorated further. I used this clinical medical opinion to inform my tactical decision that we would use the time to plan and put the necessary risk reduction measures for the helicopter in place. We would wait for darkness when it would be safer to fly in. It would also give us time to coordinate supporting air and ground fire to suppress the Taliban positions that could engage the helicopter. Additionally, it would give Jowett the necessary time to plan a deliberate operation to secure the LZ in the field outside the compound. I briefed the pilot that he was to spend only the absolute minimum of time on the ground necessary for Corporal Muirhead to be loaded and secured on the helicopter. Once Davis, who would fly the casualty mission as the MERT's doctor, confirmed that Corporal Muirhead was safely on board, he was to lift and get the hell out of the fire zone. The pilot took me at my word and ended up lifting so quickly that Stacey was still on the aircraft when it took off. It meant that we would have to fly another nail-biting high-risk insertion to get him back into the district centre early the next morning. Once again the aircraft was fired on, but got in without incident. I left the JOC to grab a couple of hours' sleep before dawn broke, relieved that we had made two sorties into Musa Qaleh without losing a helicopter. As I walked wearily along the plastic duckboards to my tent, I had little idea that we would be flying another such mission before the day was out.

It was mid-afternoon and the mortar round landed with a deafening thump. The hard surface of the roof of the Alamo ensured that its shrapnel spread out to maximum and bloody effect. Kicking up dust and debris, it showered its lethal contents in all directions, the jagged fragments cutting into every individual manning the rooftop sangar. Responding to the call that casualties had been taken, Lance Corporal Paul Roberts once again rushed to the point of the explosion. On his way he passed Lieutenant Paul Martin coming in the other direction. Martin commanded Barossa Platoon of the Royal Irish, and had been hit but insisted that Roberts looked to the other wounded men on the roof. When Roberts got there he was met by a scene of carnage: four men were down. Some lay in shock and others writhed in agony among the dust and broken masonry of the rubble-strewn roof. He set about treating the most seriously wounded first. He knew that he had to act quickly; he needed to stabilize any bleeding and then get them to the RAP as fast as he could. Some were able to help themselves; others needed assistance to get off the roof as other men of Easy Company arrived to help move the wounded.

The first part of his job done, Roberts rushed back to the RAP where he knew Mike Stacey would be in need of his help. As he came through the door, he saw Martin on the raised stretcher and was bloody glad that Bastion had taken the risk to fly Stacey back in earlier that morning. Martin lay stripped to the waist; he had serious fragmentation wounds which had torn into his chest and side. Despite getting to the aid centre under his own steam and turning down medical attention in favour of his men, he was the most badly wounded. Now he was fighting for his life. The razor-sharp metal fragments had lodged near his heart and had shredded his left lung in the process. Still conscious and in much pain, he groaned as the doctor and Roberts turned him over. The removal of the fragments would have to wait until he could be evacuated to the surgical facility at Bastion. As the RAP staff struggled to insert a chest drain that would stop him from drowning in his own blood, the headquarters staff in Bastion had already started planning how they would evacuate Martin and the other four men. Once again we faced the challenge of how to do it without getting a helicopter shot down in the process. Once again I faced the dilemma of balancing the lives of the men on the evacuation helicopter against the life of one man who would clearly die if we didn't make an attempt to evacuate him. I picked up the phone and made the call to the field hospital; I asked to speak to Peter Davis for the second time in as many days.

I watched the surgeons turn over Paul Martin as he lay on the treatment trestle in the pre-operation section of the field hospital. Though less seriously injured, the rest of his men also waited in another part of the hospital to undergo operations to remove shrapnel from their bodies. Martin was still conscious and I winced as his chest drain was adjusted. I noted the bright pool of blood gathering underneath him and thought keenly of the risks we were taking in Musa Qaleh and the difficulty we faced in getting the wounded men out and ammunition into the outstations. In the last four days, Easy Company had lost two men killed and eight men injured, which included Lance Corporal Muirhead who was currently fighting for his life in a hospital he had been evacuated to in Oman. As the medics worked, another of my soldiers was preparing to spend an uncomfortable night in Sangin waiting to be evacuated. Private Spence had lost the top of his finger to a Taliban bullet, but the threat to an aircraft inserting into the district centre meant that he would not be lifted out until just before first light.

I discussed the issue of the risks we were taking with CGS later that night in the JOC. General Richard Dannatt was making his first visit to Afghanistan since becoming the new head of the Army and he listened intently to everything I said. He agreed with my view that the tactical realities of being in places like Musa Qaleh were beginning to outweigh the strategic imperatives of not being seen to withdraw from them. I rehearsed the risk equation I had run through with the staff of losing a helicopter and reiterated that it was a prospect that should be considered as a matter of when and not if. We agreed that if we lost a helicopter, it could be interpreted at the political level as a tactical failure, especially if it was packed with fifty paratroopers on the back. I said that psychologically we were preparing to meet that eventuality and I was confident that we could crack on if it happened, but I explained the additional dilemma if we lost a helicopter on a casualty evacuation mission to Musa Qaleh.

If one Chinook went down over the town, it would take me several hours to launch a ground-based operation to rescue the crew and recover the dead. Easy Company was stretched as it was holding the district centre and lacked the necessary combat power to fight their way through to the crash site. Consequently, I would be forced to launch a helicopter-borne operation using the one immediately available company that was not committed to defending a fixed location. If it landed close into Musa Qaleh, it too ran the risk of having a helicopter shot down and then I would have no one left to go to its immediate rescue. It was a doomsday scenario, but it was a potential risk that could not be ignored and I knew CGS appreciated my candour, as did Ed Butler who listened quietly as I spoke. Ed and I had already discussed the issue. I was aware he and General David Richards were still working hard to find an Afghan solution to Musa Qaleh that would allow us to withdraw without having to surrender the district centre to the Taliban. But there was no immediate prospect of this happening and I knew that in the meantime we would have to carry on as we were.

CGS left Bastion the next day and another nine mortar rounds landed in the district centre in Musa Qaleh. One hit the accommodation where the ASP policemen were sleeping. One was killed and three were injured, one seriously. Once again we went through our risk assessment and another dangerous casualty evacuation mission was flown to Musa Qaleh.

The risk we were facing from the mortars was already on my mind when Intelligence Officer Captain Martin Taylor interrupted my thoughts as I smoked a cigarette outside the JOC. He apologized for the intrusion and I told him not to worry, since it was probably the one time when anyone could have my undivided attention. He asked me if I could spare a few minutes to listen to Sergeant Hughes who had a theory about the mortars and an idea for defeating them. I followed Martin Taylor to the intelligence cell and found Emlyn Hughes poring over a large aerial photograph of Musa Qaleh. He looked up and went straight into it. We were convinced that we had already destroyed several insurgent mortar teams, but the rounds kept on coming. I also knew that we had sent in Engineers to destroy the radio masts in the town that the Taliban had used as aiming markers to line up their mortars to fire into the compound. But Hughes drew on the point to say that the location of the masts dictated the area from where the weapons systems were most likely to be fired. It had caused him to focus on a particular area of compounds.

He had looked at the area again and again until he noticed something unusual about the roofs on a line of buildings. One roof stood out from the regular pattern of the others as it had a strange shadow on it. Hughes was convinced it was a hole that had been deliberately cut into the roof to allow a mortar to be fired through it from the room below. When the location of the building was lined up to where the aiming markers had been, it lay on a direct bearing to the middle of the compound. His suspicions had been confirmed by a more detailed picture he had tasked a Harrier jet to take of the suspicious building. Deep tyre marks in the sand suggested a heavily laden vehicle had been regularly driven to its entrance and were clearly visible in the second photograph he handed me. Hughes was convinced the impressions in the sand were from a vehicle that had been used to transport the mortar team and their weapon. The information was passed on to Jowett who confirmed that there were no civilians living in or around the target building.

Two days later, Hughes's painstaking intelligence work paid off. A loitering A-10 was tasked to check out the building with its surveillance pod when enemy mortar rounds began to impact into the district centre. The pilot spotted a vehicle and a mortar team getting into the back of it to make good their escape. He self-designated the target with his own aircraft's laser and watched the screen in his cockpit flash brightly and then go black as the insurgents were caught in the centre of the exploding precision-guided bomb that he released. The mortar attacks against the district centre dropped off noticeably and Emlyn gave me an embarrassed smile and looked at the floor when I went to congratulate him.

For the men of Easy Company it would not bring an end to the ordeal they faced in Musa Qaleh, however. At the time of the successful strike against the Taliban mortar team, they had spent just over two weeks there. Their occupation of the district centre would last another two months until their most unexpected and unorthodox extraction.

14

The Will to Combat

I woke in the early hours of the morning feeling a distinct chill. It was pitch black outside as I glanced at my watch. The temperature gauge showed that it was still over 20°C, but we had become used to operating in conditions where the temperature never dropped below 35°C and it was definitely getting cooler during the hours of darkness. I opened my trunk and pulled out my lightweight sleeping bag, something that I had not used for the last four and a half months. The Afghan summer might have been coming to an end, but there was no let-up in the tempo of operations. We had fought 315 engagements with the Taliban in which we had fired over 300,000 rounds of ammunition, fired thousands of artillery rounds and dropped nearly 200 bombs. Since the beginning of July we had been suffering an average combat loss rate of four men killed in action and another ten men wounded a month. There were no battle casualty replacements and the shortfalls in manpower we had experienced since the beginning of the tour had never been made good. When we did receive reinforcements, such as the company of Fusiliers or the two extra Royal Irish platoons, they were immediately consumed by the additional tasks of having to hold an increasing number of district centres. Everyone continued to have to do the job of at least one other person as well as their own. After months of the continuous stress of combat and living in the debilitating conditions of heat and austerity, fatigue was becoming a common phenomenon across the Battle Group. In the vernacular of military slang, people were hanging out on their chinstraps.

R and R provided some respite, but as well as exacerbating the manpower situation many found it disruptive both to themselves and their families. Men like Sergeant Darren Hope found it particularly difficult to have to say farewell to his family for a second time when his leave ended. Saying goodbye to his little boy, who said that he wanted to go back with him, was especially hard. Corporal Hugh Keir of the Sniper Platoon didn't enjoy a single moment of his two weeks back in the UK and felt that his family was worse off for it. For many of the wives it disrupted the routine that they had settled into since their husbands had been away. They could never completely relax, knowing that the leave period would end all too quickly and that their menfolk would be going back to the dangers of Afghanistan. As well as having to count the days until their return, those on R and R would feel guilty about being away from their comrades, especially if their platoon or company took losses in their absence. Dan Jarvie felt it as the platoon sergeant of 1 Platoon when Corporal Budd was killed. He flew back into Sangin from the UK the day after the contact in the maize field. As he flew in, his platoon commander was getting on the same helicopter to fly out of the district centre on his R and R. The time that the helicopter could spend on the ground meant that the two men were hardly able to exchange a word to one another. Farmer wanted to stay with his men to lead them through the aftermath of Corporal Budd's loss, but Loden rightly told him to go.

The one man who didn't take R and R was the man who routinely ignored my orders to get some sleep before an operation. Captain Matt Taylor was evasive whenever I brought up the subject about when he was going to take some leave. He relied on my preoccupation not to check on the detail of the R and R plot. By the time I found out that he had no intention of going it was too late, there were no slots left. The fact that he didn't go was probably a poor reflection on me as his commander, but it was also an indication of the level of his dedication and devotion to duty. There is no doubt that soldiers need a rest from constant combat duty, which is why we tried to rotate the companies through the most difficult locations like Sangin. But once they had been given a day or so out of the line in the relative comfort of Bastion, most were good to go again after a shower, some proper food and a decent night's sleep. On one occasion after being relieved in Sangin, B Company spent several days in the camp before their next operation. After three days, even the Toms were coming up to me and impatiently asking when they were going back into the field.

With only two platoons available instead of the normal three, Jamie Loden felt the frustrations of the general lack of manpower more keenly than most of the company commanders. After the loss of Corporal Budd, we had agreed that he would only conduct patrols into Sangin when he had dedicated air cover available. But he knew that if he had more troops he would have been able to have a more dynamic effect against the enemy. He also had to contend with the frustrations of working with the ANP and the ANA. The ANP reinforcements that Governor Daud promised in June had still not materialized and the numbers of ANP already in the district centre had fallen to just seven men. They refused to wear uniforms or conduct joint patrols; Loden was convinced that they were hedging their bets with the Taliban by reporting the company's movements to them. His confidence in their loyalty was not helped by the fact that the Deputy Chief of Police was the brother of the local Taliban commander. Loden spoke to me about this and I agreed we should detain him, but A Company never saw him again and a few days later the rest of the ANP had either joined the Taliban or fled Sangin. The performance of the platoon of ANA in Sangin was little better. Although they wore uniforms and conducted joint patrols with A Company, their commander was corrupt and used his position to extort money from the locals. His removal led to the platoon splitting along tribal lines and a complete breakdown in discipline. Drug taking, sexual abuse of local minors and theft of equipment from the company were common until they were eventually replaced by a more reliable ANA platoon.

Jamie Loden had also been deeply frustrated by the poor support he had received from the RAF Harriers during the contact in the maize fields on 17 August. He summed up some of his frustrations and the dangers his men faced every time they went out on patrol in a private e-mail he sent to a friend the night after Corporal Budd had been killed. The recipient had been a company commander in the Princess of Wales' Royal Regiment, PWRR, who had faced similar challenges in the fighting against the Mahdi uprising in Iraq in 2004. Out of empathy for the situation Jamie found himself in, his friend decided to distribute the e-mail to other colleagues in the Army to help educate them about the harsh realities of modern combat.

The e-mail also ended up in the in-boxes of several senior RAF staff officers in the MOD. What attracted their attention was not the description of the gallantry, austere living conditions and the risk Loden's men were facing on a daily basis. What caught their eye was his comment that the RAF Harriers were 'utterly, utterly useless'. It might have been unfortunate that Loden's adverse comments tarred an entire service, as the support we were receiving from the highly respected RAF Chinook pilots was outstanding. But Loden's opinions were those of a commander and his men who were doing an exceptional job under the most enormous pressures of limited resources and risk. They reflected his view from the very rough end of his particular trench. However, they were not seen that way in the MOD, especially after someone leaked the e-mail to the media, which generated a press storm.

The Chinook crews took it in their stride. Since the tenure of Mike Woods's flight, the Battle Group had developed an extremely solid relationship with the crews who lived, fought and shared risk with us on a routine basis. The fast jet-fighter jocks were less understanding. It was not helped by the fact that we generally preferred the air support of the American A-10s. Though we never met their pilots, we had developed a close rapport when working in the field with them. The support they gave us was awesome and they dug us out of the shit on numerous occasions. Although the A-10 was an older airframe, it was a better ground-attack aircraft than the GR7 Harrier. It was equipped with a very capable surveillance pod that could deliver JDAMs with pinpoint accuracy, helped by the fact that it could fly slower than a Harrier and had better fuel endurance.

Dealing with the sensitivities the e-mail provoked was an unwelcome distraction from the demands of commanding a Battle Group locked in combat. Luckily the senior officers in the Army's chain of command were more sympathetic to Loden's position and the storm in the teacup eventually abated, allowing me to focus on more pressing concerns.

The unexpected intensity of the fighting had exceeded predetermined consumption rates of ammunition and the logistic supply chain was having difficulty keeping up with the prolific expenditure of mortar bombs, missiles and grenades. Planning the UK deployment as a peace support operation meant that insufficient stocks of certain types of ammo had been built up. Shortages were exacerbated by the fact that the logisticians had been slow to adjust their planning tables to meet the growing intensity of the fighting. By 25 August the lack of high-explosive 81mm mortar ammunition had become critical. In Sangin and Musa Qaleh there were fewer than twenty rounds for each mortar barrel; hardly enough to fight off one or two serious attacks. The mortars were vital to the defence of the district centres and we made repeated demands for more ammunition, only to be told that it would take weeks to fly it into Afghanistan from the UK.

We suggested purchasing rounds from the Americans, who used the same 81mm calibre of mortar. We lacked the software to fire their ammunition by our hand-held computerized fire control systems, but we knew that it came with manual conversion tables which would enable us to use it. The answer came back from the UK's logistic HQ in KAF that it would take six weeks to authorize the purchase of foreign stocks. I didn't have six weeks; our barrels could run dry in a matter of hours. I rang Ed Butler and asked him if he could approve an emergency purchase. Much to the chagrin of the logisticians in KAF, he got his staff to make some phone calls and they sent a truck round to a US ammo dump that night. It was loaded up and the ammunition was flown down to Bastion as a priority the next day. From then on, every helicopter flown into Musa Qaleh or Sangin carried sacks of the US ammo, which were packed ready to go on the pad at Bastion. If it was a high-risk casualty mission, the ammo would be hastily kicked off the tailgate as the wounded were brought on board the Chinook. If a man had to be inserted into one of the district centres, he invariably went in carrying two spare rounds in his kit.

It was not only the men and the supply chain that were being pushed to their limits: equipment was suffering too. Every Chinook helicopter was working close to, or in excess of its servicing failure limits to meet the exacting demands of flying near-constant combat operations and their ground crews worked tirelessly to keep them in the air. The fine swirling sand of the desert never stopped blowing and ingressed into engines, instruments and gear mechanisms. The engineers would often have to spend up to four hours washing a main rotor head through with water and grease to remove the fine particles of grit before an engine could be started up.

Keeping the technologically more sophisticated Apache attack helicopters operational was even more of a challenge. The Apache was an answer to a maiden's prayer in terms of its capability, but it had the technical temperament of a finely tuned Ferrari. They couldn't just be started up. When they were required for an operation, one pilot would begin warming up the aircraft and start running system checks while the commander collected the mission brief. He would then sprint from the JOC, climb into the cab and join in the frenetic activity of conducting more system challenge response checks on the flight computer, as the Apache taxied to its take-off point. Day and thermal night sights would have to be bore-sighted for alignment, lasers and missiles would have to be synchronized and digital radios tuned to the correct frequency.

Any of the numerous faults that might appear on the aircraft's computer screen would have to be cleared and painstakingly rechecked. On more than one occasion an Apache would suddenly go non-operational just before mission launch, forcing the crew to unbuckle, scramble into another aircraft and begin the process of detailed technical checks all over again.

Though less sophisticated, the vehicle fleet was also taking a pounding from continuous driving over rugged desert terrain. Clutches were often burnt out in the soft sand and axles broken as WMIKs crossed rocky wadi beds. Vehicle mechanics, such as Corporal Smith of the Royal Electrical and Mechanical Engineers detachment, accompanied long-ranging patrols and crews learned to spot problems early and conduct running repairs in the heat and dust of the field. Spares packs were carried and additional spares, such as complete gearboxes, were flown out by helicopter and changed in place to get a vehicle back on the road again.

Despite the fatigue, lack of sleep and harsh conditions, the will to combat and esprit de corps of the Battle Group remained sky-high. There were momentary dips in morale when losses were sustained, especially among a close-knit platoon or company, but people accepted risk and loss as part of the business that they were in. It was evident during Operation Baghi, which was the next Battle Group operation to Sangin. The stocks of supplies that had previously been built up in the district centre had begun to run low. The threat to inserting helicopters meant that topping up supplies with loads under-slung beneath the Chinooks was an emergency option. Running a vehicle convoy into the base was also dangerous, as it would be vulnerable to ambush as it moved through the town. However, we knew that if we could bridge the Helmand River we could bring in supplies from the empty desert on the west bank.

On 29 August the air-portable ferry bridge that we had requested had arrived in Bastion. It came in sections that could be carried on several trucks. Transporting it up to Sangin would mean running another ground convoy in from the east, but once the bridge was in place we would be able to open up another less risky route into the district centre. Getting the bridge through Sangin would require two infantry companies to secure the route through the town. B Company was available as the Ops 1 Company in Bastion and I would find the second sub-unit of infantry by taking some risk in Gereshk and stripping out C Company for the operation. D Squadron's armoured vehicles would escort the trucks and other supply vehicles through the wadi into the district centre. With the exception of using the Patrols Platoon to secure the high ground that overlooked the river from the east bank, Operation Baghi would be a rerun of the resupply operation that we had conducted in July and there was every chance that the Taliban would be waiting for us.

It was dark as the turbines of the CH-47s began to whine and the troops stirred from where they slumbered in their allotted chalk lines at the back of the aircraft. NCOs counted people off and some smoked a last-minute cigarette. Chinstraps were done up as magazines were pushed home into rifles, bandoliers of spare bullets were adjusted and belts of linked rounds were snapped shut into feed trays. We flew fast and low to beat the coming of dawn, but first light was already breaking as the Chinooks dropped across the river line of the Sangin Valley. With only four aircraft available, we were packed in like sardines. Each man carried two mortar bombs in his back pack and a quad and trailer carrying more rounds was shackled on to the tailgate. There was no room to sit and each man stood pressed up close to the men around him. It was like being on the Tube at rush hour, although adrenaline coursed through us and our thoughts were very different to those of a commuter who had little else to think about other than the drudgery of the day ahead. The M60 gunners traversed their door-mounted weapons across the treelines looking for possible Taliban firing positions as we made the final run into the LZ.

I caught a glimpse of popping brightness and white smoke outside the fuselage through the crush of bodies, as my aircraft suddenly started pumping out its flares. Were they being fired to decoy a heat-seeking missile? Had the Taliban managed to get hold of the weapons that had proved so devastating against Russian helicopters? I trusted the technology of the defensive aid suite to distract any missile that might be in the air from the hot exhausts of the engines, as the pilot went into his evasion drills and banked the aircraft violently left and right. I just caught the final approach warning signal, saw the swirling cloud of brown-out rise up to meet us and inhaled involuntarily as the Chinook spanked into a hard landing on the ground. The force of the impact threw us forward. I suddenly found myself sprawled halfway into the cockpit looking up at the two pilots, the lower part of my body pinned to the floor by members of Tac who had fallen on top of me. Tony Lynch uttered an expletive and managed an apology as we struggled to get up. It was worse for those at the back of the aircraft. The quad bike had broken its shackles and its rider was thrown off as it ran over four of the nearest blokes. Swearing and shouting was audible over the noise of the engines and pandemonium reigned as each man fought against the heavy weight on his back to regain his footing and get off the helicopter.

I spent a nerve-racking few moments, expecting to hear the strike of bullets against the side of the aircraft, as I waited for the seething crush of people to clear the tailgate. It was a relief suddenly to find myself being blasted by the sand and grit outside the helicopter, as the pilot pulled on the power and lifted off. I had landed with C Company along the river line to the south of the district centre. They would clear into the east of the town and B Company would advance into the north. I pushed Tac into the district centre, linked up with a bearded Jamie Loden and headed to the roof.

The message crackled through the net: 'Emerald 6, this is Silver 6. Contact; wait out.' Emerald 6 was my radio call sign, Silver 6 belonged to Giles Timms commanding B Company. It told me that his men had come under fire as they pushed through the same fields in which Corporal Budd had been killed. The point section of his leading platoon under Corporal 'Scottie' Evans had begun to take fire from the Taliban and the rest of 5 Platoon returned fire. I could see the tail end of B Company as they moved through the maize and skirted round compound walls of the farm buildings. A Company's .50 Cal machine guns began to provide covering fire from the roof and their mortars thumped into life from the courtyard below us. Occasional AK bullets began to crack over our heads, as Matt Carter began to cue in close air support for B Company. 'Silver 6, this is Widow 70, you have incoming A-10s and Emerald 6 has given clearance to drop when targets are identified.' Timms replied to Carter: 'Roger. We have enemy engaging us across open ground from the Chinese Restaurant. I want to call in a JDAM strike on to the building and then we will launch an assault using mortars to cover us across the exposed ground.' I acknowledged Timms's plan of attack: 'Silver 6, Emerald 6; copy and roger out.' Timms glanced round the corner of a wall to look at the target across the flat field, and ducked back and swore as an AK round landed close to his head; he waited for the JDAM.

The exploding 500-pound bomb was the signal for Timms to launch his attack. As a black mushroom cloud of dust and debris billowed up in front of them, 4 Platoon assaulted across the open fields. Once they had cleared through the smouldering remains of the Chinese Restaurant, 5 Platoon began their own assault to take some compounds to the right with covering fire provided by two Apaches. Corporal Karl Jackson was moving through some high-standing crops towards the compounds when the fire from the attack helicopters suddenly ceased. The maize provided cover from view, but it would not stop bullets, which began to cut through the vegetation. His men pressed on at the crouch, hoping the rounds wouldn't hit them. The Taliban pulled back, leaving their dead and one wounded fighter behind them, as B Company reached and cleared their objectives.

I had given Giles Timms a large area to cover and he was suffering from his own shortages of manpower: 6 (Guards) Platoon were once again providing the QRF in KAF and his remaining two platoons each had a section away on R and R. He spoke to me on the radio about how he proposed to reposition his forces and clear more compounds to his east. I accepted that he would be spread very thinly and that there would be gaps in his positions. It was not something that was lost on the Taliban who started to infiltrate between his platoons that were now separated by over 500 metres. His men climbed on to some of the rooftops of the buildings in an attempt to be able to cover more ground. Corporal Jackson saw ten insurgents moving back through the fields towards 4 Platoon. He waited for the Taliban to move closer. Then his section opened up on them from the flank with everything they had and he watched the insurgents drop as they were caught in the hail of lead from the section's weapons.

Spread as they were, B Company could not hope to cover all the gaps in their line. One group of Taliban pushed between the platoons undetected and worked their way into a location from where they engaged our position on top of the district centre. The .50 Cals in the two bunkers either side of me pumped their half-inch rounds back towards them. Red streams of GPMG tracer also arced in their direction, as the insurgents' own bullets whip-cracked over our heads. I got on the net and ordered Loden to tell the Engineers assembling the bridge on the riverbank to stop working. Short of infantry, I needed them to conduct a right-flanking attack to kill the infiltrating Taliban. The Sappers dropped their tools, picked up their weapons and went into the assault with covering fire from A Company's machine guns.

I watched them go as RSM Hardy was putting down rounds from a hand-held 51mm mortar. I picked up his UGL and fired a couple of 40mm grenade rounds and watched with grim satisfaction as they landed where his mortar rounds were beginning to pop. The noise was deafening and my ears were already singing with a high-pitched ring, the first indication that they were being permanently damaged by the thundering din on top of the roof. I spared a thought for the blokes who were exposed to the high-frequency assault on their hearing day in and day out for weeks on end. I watched the line of one of the .50 Cal guns and was convinced that they had crossed the imaginary fire control boundary that had been imposed to stop their rounds from landing on B Company. I ordered them to check firing, as a radio call came in from Second Lieutenant Ollie Dale who was commanding 4 Platoon. He politely asked if they could stop firing, because .50 Cal rounds were striking his men's day sacks that they had dropped just to the back of their position.

There was a lull in the fighting and I was confident that B Company were in the best position they were going to be in to hold the area to the immediate north of the wadi. C Company were firm in their positions on rooftops along the main road into Sangin from where they could cover the south-eastern entrance into the main part of the town. A platoon from A Company would cover the last stretch of the wadi into the district centre. The wadi ran over a kilometre to the east of the town and would remain open and exposed. However, this stretch was also its widest point and I told Gary Wilkinson to get his artillery in FOB Robinson to fire smoke rounds into the more exposed areas. The smoke would screen the widest part of the route from the buildings that flanked its more distant fringes. As the white plumes of smoke began to build I ordered the convoy to start moving into Sangin. The Household Cavalry moved first; although distant dots on the horizon, the pillars of sand they kicked up were discernible against the clear blue sky of midday. The dots got larger until the distinct forms of Scimitars and trucks became recognizable as they drew closer. I held my breath as they entered the narrowest and most dangerous part of the route. I willed them on as the first vehicles broke into the bazaar a few hundred metres away from the HESCO bastion perimeter of the district centre. I breathed a sigh of relief as the last vehicle made it into the safety of its confines.

Having been defeated in their first attempts to infiltrate between B Company's platoons holding the area to the north of the wadi, the Taliban started using more covered approaches before re-engaging the troops on the rooftops. Jackson spotted the movement of one group 40 metres from his position and was about to grenade them. Moving up beside him, Sergeant Paddy Caldwell told him to hang on until he brought a mortar fire mission down on them. Paddy was sweating; it was not just the heat that made him perspire, but the fact that he knew he was calling the fire close in to his own position. If he got the coordinates wrong the rounds would land among his men. He gave the order to fire and his men got down on their belt buckles as he counted the seconds of the flight time for the 81mm high-explosive rounds that were already arcing through the air. The mortar bombs came in with a crump and he pushed himself up over the lip of the roof to observe the fall of shot and adjust the rounds. Jackson and his men raised themselves up with him and began to engage the Taliban with their weapons.

As Jackson fired he heard a loud crack that passed him and struck his platoon sergeant in the shoulder. He looked to his right and saw Paddy Caldwell falling backwards in slow motion. Jackson shouted for rapid covering fire from the GPMG and Minimi machine gunners then grabbed Caldwell and dragged him off the roof. He manhandled him into an irrigation ditch and cut off his webbing as he frantically looked for the wound with the help of Corporal Hart, the company medic. The first aid a soldier receives at the point of wounding often makes the vital difference to his subsequent survival. Jackson and Hart knew this, but the new field dressing they used wasn't working, as they couldn't apply the right pressure to stop the bleeding from Caldwell's shoulder. Eventually, they plugged the wound with an older type of bandage and noticed that the round that had struck Caldwell had exited through his neck. As Sergeant Major Willets arrived on a quad bike and trailer, Jackson braved the incoming fire to climb back on the roof to resume command of his section. Willets and Hart lifted Caldwell on to the stretcher on the trailer. Fire continued to rake the whole area and Hart shielded Caldwell with his own body while Willets drove the quad back into the wadi to meet an armoured Sultan ambulance that had been driven out from the district centre by the Household Cavalry to meet them.

I heard the report that B Company had taken a man down and handed over to the battery commander Gary Wilkinson before making my way down the steps of the FSG Tower with RSM Hardy. Paddy Caldwell was being stretchered out of the back of the vehicle as we got down to the courtyard. He was carried into the small cramped RAP in the main compound building. There Tariq Ahmed set about stabilizing him for evacuation while the RSM and I tried to keep him still; he was in pain and kept trying to look up, as he complained about the awkward position he was lying in. We tried to make him more comfortable and reassure him that he was going to be okay. I held his hand and told him that I was there. 'I know it's you, sir, I'm paralysed not blind.' As he spoke, his ability to control his legs was draining away and this feeling was spreading up the rest of his body. As I reached out to hold a drip for one of the medics, I momentarily let go of his hand and noticed how his arm flopped limply back on to the stretcher. The casevac helicopter was already coming in as he was stretch-ered out of the RAP to the LZ. I watched him go, hoping for the best but fearing the worst.

Gary Wilkinson gave me an update on the situation on the ground and Matt Taylor asked me about Paddy. I said that he would be all right and changed the subject, as a 107mm rocket ripped through the air high above us. The attacks had dropped off against B Company, but the Taliban were now focusing their efforts on C Company. The empty trucks belonging to the convoy had got back out of the wadi unmolested with the Household Cavalry in escort. Before they left, the Household Cavalry had fought a series of sharp engagements with some Taliban who had attempted to attack the Engineers who had resumed building the bridge. We had mounted wire-guided Milan anti-tank missiles on their Spartans and they had put them to good use against the insur-gents, who were surprised to find themselves suddenly being blasted by explosive warheads from vehicles that usually mounted nothing heavier than a GPMG. The Engineers had managed to finish constructing the portable ferry bridge and it would be ready to be test-floated the next day.

I decided to pull C Company back into the district centre, as they would need to get ready to stay behind and take over from A Company when the rest of the Battle Group lifted from Sangin once the bridge was operational. I watched the company withdraw back down the line of the wadi. They were followed by the fire of insurgents who took them on from the cover of the narrow alleyways as the platoons pulled back from their positions. A running firefight broke out and the mortars started dropping rounds behind them to cover their move. Those moving along the right-hand side of the wadi had a more sheltered approach, but the men on the left were exposed and I could almost see the rounds skip off the ground at their feet. It was a relief to see them all get behind the safety of the HESCO. They stooped forward like old hags resting on their weapons, each man sucking in lungfuls of air and marvelling at how they hadn't been hit during the frantic extraction down the wadi.

The evening fell calm and warm, the day's fighting over. Despite the presence of a sizable chunk of the Battle Group, the Taliban had stood and fought us all day. It was estimated that they had lost forty men killed in the fighting and another fifty wounded. Although based on intelligence reports, I was always sceptical of the figures and eschewed using body counts as an indication of success. First, they were often inflated: insurgents reported as hit might have been wounded or might simply have taken cover. Second, the body count did nothing to demonstrate whether we were winning the real battle for the hearts and minds of the people. Finally, those we killed were always replaced by others. However, the Taliban's guns fell silent for the next two days. But it had not all been one-sided and I thought of how Paddy Caldwell was doing. Bastion had informed me that he had been flown out to a hospital in Oman. The fact that he had not been airlifted back to the UK concerned me. It made me reflect on the fickle dynam-.

ics of chance in war. Many of my soldiers often remarked how they had just changed a fire position, when seconds later the location they had vacated was raked with fire or hit by an RPG. Why does one bullet narrowly miss a man by a hair's breadth and yet hit another? Why do some rounds pass straight through a soldier causing him comparatively slight injury from which he will recover, when others strike bone and tumble hideously inside the human body causing catastrophic injury?

I also began to notice how easy it was to become complacent about being under fire. Continuous exposure to combat brings with it a familiarity with danger and people learned to tell the difference between incoming and outgoing mortar rounds. It was a standing joke among the veterans of Sangin to laugh and ridicule those who jumped at the loud retort of the mortars being fired from the courtyard, as newcomers often did. They were also able to distinguish between effective fire, which was likely to hit you, and ineffective fire, which would probably not. However, it was a complacency that often annoyed me, even if I was sometimes guilty of it myself. It would vary from person to person and between locations, but I noticed it most in Sangin. I would harangue Toms who walked nonchalantly across the roof of the FSG Tower as rounds cracked a few inches above their heads. Longer-range small-arms fire might often seem innocuous; but it always did until it hit you. It might have looked cool to adopt an attitude of casual indifference, but lethal projectiles are no discriminator of rank, sex or age and I remember thinking that it wouldn't look quite so 'Ally' to have had half your head removed by a stray bullet.

After giving orders to the company commanders and updating the JOC in Bastion on the activities for the next day, I did what hundreds of soldiers were doing around me. I put on a brew to heat up my boil-in-the-bag meal and provide water to make tea, which would be drunk from a home-made mug fashioned from one of the discarded 'greenie' containers used to hold the mortar bombs. I stripped and cleaned my weapons, recharged my magazines and thought about where I would kip down for the night. The pungent smell of cordite still hung in the air when I visited the sangars after finishing my brew. I smoked and spoke to the blokes around me.

I noticed how the men of A Company had bonded after the losses they had suffered in the last few weeks. They were men who had developed a particular closeness through exposure to the constant companionship of death, hardship and everyday thoughts of survival. Despite the rigours of what they had experienced, their morale was sky-high and I marvelled at their continual will to combat. Every young paratrooper wants to be tested in battle. It is what he joined the regiment and trained so hard for. But after the first exposure to combat, any romantic ideals of being a warrior are quickly replaced by the grim realities of war's rough canvas and the true nature of its bloody and brutal business. The impact of the loss of friends, the grip of fear, numbing fatigue and the feeling of being sick with a constant lack of sleep had all formed the tapestry of their daily lives. They were not motivated to keep on going because of abstract sentiments of patriotism. Belief in the cause of what we were doing played a part, but at the worst moments people sometimes began to doubt that. The real motivations were the ethos of the regiment, being paratroopers and loyalty to a small cohesive group that engenders a keen sense of not wanting to let their mates down.

Humour also played a part in the motivation of my soldiers. The nervous emotion of combat often engenders a seemingly incongruous level of humour and sense of the ridiculous that seem absurdly out of kilter with the associated risks of the surrounding environment. Paratroopers often spoke of how they found the immediate aftermath of a near miss, or someone's small mishap under fire, hilarious. It was not uncommon for people to be reduced to fits of giggles after such incidents. It was often an automatic reaction to having survived them and a vital coping mechanism for facing the rigours of the abnormal situation in which they found themselves. Despite the most adverse of conditions and regardless of rank, the banter between officers and men was excellent. The ability to laugh at ourselves and each other served to lighten the seriousness of the grim business we were often engaged in and draw some of the blackness from the sorrow that we suffered.

Men in combat also seek solace from other quarters. For some it is spiritual succour. I noticed how men, regardless of their previous religious conviction, became closer to God when in harm's way. It has often been said that there are no atheists in fox holes and the attendance at Padre Richard Smith's church services increased dramatically. Every memorial service we held at Bastion was always packed to capacity. Sometimes I felt that their function was not so much for the fallen, but for those that they left behind, as they helped provide a point of reference for the living to come to terms with loss and sacrifice. Sergeant Zip Lane never pretended to be massively religious, but he wore a St Christopher and always felt that 'someone upstairs' was looking after him. He also carried a copy of the Paratrooper's Prayer in his notebook and would get 'a real panic on' if he couldn't find it before a patrol. When things got dangerous, Sergeant Hope would think of his family and say a little prayer. He would ask his wife's dead grandmother to look after him, as he was convinced that she would not want her great-grandchildren to lose their dad.

For others superstition had its place and I was no exception. I would always make sure that I had my grubby white leather flying gloves with me on every mission. They had a practical purpose, but I also began to see them as a kind of talisman and wouldn't be without them. I sometimes chided myself for my absurdity, but was quietly relieved to know that others had their own charms. For Sergeant Dan Jarvie it was his threadbare lucky combat shirt, which he wore on every operation even though it was in severe danger of disintegration.

The Battle Group operation brought a temporary lull in the attacks on the district centre and demonstrated the effect of being able to operate with more than one company group in Sangin. It also demonstrated our resolve and created another opportunity to talk to the town's elders. I sent out a message that I wished to hold a *shura* and the next day they came as they had been invited. Unarmed, the thirty or so elders of the town gathered at the front gate; they were wearing shalwar-kameez, turbans and long beards that defined their status as men of tribal influence. I went to greet them, offered my salaams, shook hands with all of them and invited them to sit. It was a surreal moment. These were the people who only a few hours previously we had been fighting. They had spent the last few weeks sending their young men against us to die on our guns and in the storm of our mortar and artillery fire. We were the infidel who had dropped 1,000-pound bombs on them and sprayed them with cannon fire. They were the people who had attacked us relentlessly and had killed some of my soldiers. An image of young Jacko and how his family might be coping with his loss back in Newcastle flashed through my mind. I thought of the sniper tower, only a few feet away from us, where one of their rockets had ended the lives of another three members of the Battle Group. Now we were about to sit down on thick rugs and drink tea together under the shady glade of a large tree in the corner of the compound. The manner and tone were as if we were meeting with civic dignitaries in Colchester. It was cordial and polite, but the seriousness of the agenda was not lost on anyone.

I explained our mission: that we were there at the invitation of the Afghan government to bring security in order that reconstruction and development could start in Sangin. I said that we didn't want to fight, but would continue to respond robustly if attacked. I asked them to help stop the Taliban from launching attacks against us. This immediately brought a chorus of protest. They stated that they were simple farmers who knew nothing of the Taliban. An old man with a wizened and heavily lined face took the lead. He was animated but not aggressive. An interpreter whispered what he was saying into my ear as he spoke. He claimed that the fighting had forced the town's bazaar to shut and that our

Engineers of 51 Squadron begin the construction of the ferry bridge at Sangin. The Sapper on the right wears the heavier body armour, while the one on the left wears the lighter armour favoured by troops when fighting on their feet

The three 3 PARA rifle company commanders on the rooftop at Sangin. Left to right: Major Giles Timms (B Company), Major Jamie Loden (A Company) and Major Paul Blair (C Company). The sniper tower in the background shows where it has been hit by a 107mm rocket

Corporal Mark Wright manning a .50-calibre machine gun on the FSG Tower at Sangin. He later lost his life leading the rescue of wounded comrades from a mine-field at Kajaki. He was awarded the George Cross for his selfless act of bravery

ANA troops return from a patrol with C Company. A Household Cavalry Scimitar follows them in through the HESCO Bastion perimeter at Sangin

othing wrong with the new blokes.' Major Paul Blair briefs new recruits who have just ived in Sangin to join C Company. Having completed basic training they were held in UK until they reached their eighteenth birthdays. Within hours of arriving they were fighting to defend the district centre and Private Hook (centre) was wounded

Engineers often had to fight as infantry. A Sapper GPMG gunner, attached to C Company, returning from a dawn patrol moves along the HESCO Bastion perimeter of the Sangin district centre. By the middle of the summer, virtually every patrol sent out resulted in a contact with the Taliban

A precision-guided JDAM bomb impac[t]
danger close into what became known
JDAM House. Used as a favourite Talib[an]
firing point to engage helicopters comi[ng]
into Sangin, it withstood repeated atten[pts]
to destroy it by bombing. Eventually, it [was]
assaulted by B Company and blown up [by]
the Battle Group's Engineers

The maize fields around the district
centre at Sangin. By July the crops
were 7 feet high and troops patrolling
in them could often hear the Taliban
moving against them only a few
metres away

A Scimitar from D Squadron
Household Cavalry races to find
a vital crossing point on the
Helmand River during the
Battle Group's last operation
in Sangin

The author talking to the Afghan elders and the Taliban at a *shura* in Sangin.
The fighting started again as soon as the talking stopped

Major Adam Jowett, the unflappable commander of Easy Company, says farewell to an Afghan elder at Musa Qaleh after having spent over two months holding the town's district centre against ferocious attacks

The author speaking to the Battle Group at the end of the tour. With the exception of Easy Company, it was the first and last time the complete Battle Group was together before splitting up to fly home

The people who made it all possible. Some of the Toms gathered for the Battle Group photo during the last few days at Bastion

Men of D Company the Gurkha Rifles break from the Battle Group photograph. Originally sent to guard Camp Bastion, manpower shortages meant that they were used to hold the district centre at Now Zad during six weeks of relentless attacks. The company commander Major Dan Rex is in the centre of the photograph

Remembering the British lives lost during the tour, which included fifteen members of the Battle Group

Lorena Budd presents her husband's Victoria Cross to the Parachute Regiment's Museum for safe-keeping

The author returns to Bastion in December 2007. Within a year of this photo being taken names of those killed in action from subsequent battle group were added to all sides of the memorial stone

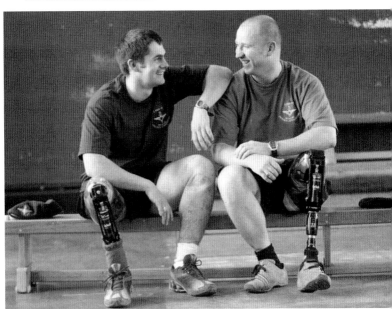

Corporals Stu Hale and Stu Pearson who each lost a leg in the mine strike incident in Kajaki. Both men continued to serve in the regiment. Corporal Hale later returned to Afghanistan with 3 PARA in 2008 on its second tour

bombs were killing innocent civilians. He further stated that we should withdraw and leave the security of Sangin to the town's people. He fingered his prayer beads nervously and occasionally inclined his head to glance at the three younger men who sat behind him. Dressed in black, these men said little, but they appeared to exert a sort of reverence among the older men whose tradition of seniority of age suggested that they should have been their betters.

One of my officers whispered in my other ear that he was convinced that the three younger men were Taliban; he thought he had seen one of them during some of the recent fighting. I focused on the man who spoke, out of deference to his supposed prominence as an elder, but intermittently I fixed my eyes on the three younger men. Although silent, it was clear to me that the old man delivered their message and I wanted them to know that I could see through him. I refuted the claims of civilian casualties, reiterating that we took every measure to avoid them and I was confident in the knowledge that the Taliban would have exploited the situation for their own propaganda had we been inadvertently killing innocent women and children. I reminded the elder that we would continue to kill those who attacked us and would have no compunction in doing so. As I placed an emphasis on this last sentence, I stared at the three men so that they would be clear that my message was for them.

15

Day of Days

His eyes scanned both the ground in front of him and the horizon ahead, as he carefully picked his way down to the gully at the bottom of the Kajaki ridge. His mind was on the mission and his hands grasped the principal weapon of its execution. His .338 sniper rifle was designed to kill a man at over 1,000 metres; Lance Corporal Stu Hale and his fellow members of the Sniper Platoon had demonstrated its lethal use to ranges well beyond that on many occasions. Now this capability was to be used again to attack a Taliban checkpoint that had been set up along the road leading to the Kajaki Dam. It was out of range of the direct fire weapons located on the high feature of the ridge and using the mortars had been ruled out for fear of causing civilian casualties among local Afghans who lived in the surrounding buildings.

Consequently, Hale was leading his small team on a sniper stalk to get into a position close to the Taliban where a precision snipe on to the checkpoint could be made. The sniper team moved forward in tactical bounds, Hale pushing a short distance forward while covered by the Minimi machine gun of Private Harvey behind him. Lance Corporal Hale would then go firm until the rest of his team caught up, then they would repeat the process. Having completed two or three bounds, Hale pushed on again until he came to a small dry wadi in the gully. He hopped across and suddenly found himself being thrown on to his back by some unexplained force. His mind didn't register the explosion, but as he searched for the rifle he had dropped, he noticed one of his fingers hanging off. He looked down and saw that his foot was

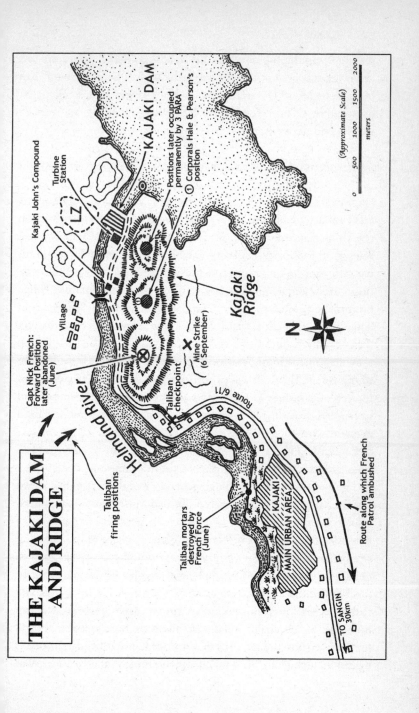

THE KAJAKI DAM AND RIDGE

Capt Nick French: Forward Position later abandoned (June)

Helmand River

Taliban firing positions

Kajaki John's Compound

Turbine Station

LZ

Village

KAJAKI DAM

Positions later occupied permanently by 3 PARA

① Corporals Hale & Pearson's position

Kajaki Ridge

Mine Strike (6 September)

Taliban checkpoint

Route 6/11

Taliban mortars destroyed by French Force (June)

KAJAKI MAIN URBAN AREA

Route along which French Patrol ambushed

TO SANGIN 30km

N

(Approximate Scale)

0   500   1000   1500   2000

meters

missing from the top of where his boot should have been; the rest of his leg was bent at a grotesque right angle where his femur had been shattered. He saw the small black crater and smelled the caustic tang of burnt explosive; it was only then that he realized that he had stepped on an anti-personnel mine.

Hale's sniper team formed part of the forty-strong FSG and mortar section that 3 PARA had sent to defend the dam at Kajaki in early July. The fire group had dug themselves into the steep, craggy ridge line that dominated the dam area and used a combination of Javelin missiles, heavy machine guns and mortars to keep the Taliban at bay. They came under sporadic attack from 107mm rockets and Chinese-made mortar bombs, but their engagements with the insurgents remained long-range stand-off affairs. Hale discussed sending out a sniper stalk to engage a distant Taliban position with his immediate commander, Corporal Stu Pearson. They knew that there was a possible risk of mines. The area was littered with painted red and white stones that warned of their presence and the soldiers used set routes to move between the rocky sangars that had been constructed along the narrow spine of the ridge. But they had spotted a goat track which had been used to place out trip flares at the bottom of the ridge a few hundred metres below them. They had also seen local Afghans moving in the area, which suggested that the proposed path to where Hale intended to take his shot might be clear of mines.

Their positions had been under mortar and RPG fire earlier that day, but the attacks had petered out and Stu Pearson was able to discern the difference when he heard the explosion of the mine in the valley below him. The blast shattered the peace of late morning as it echoed up the sides of the precipitous slopes of the ridge. Hale couldn't believe what had happened to him. His initial thought was that his dreams of joining the SAS were over. Private Harvey rushed over to him and applied a tourniquet to the mangled stump of his leg. He also helped Hale administer his own morphine. Hale felt no pain, but he suspected that it would only be a matter of time before it kicked in; he gritted his teeth against the impending agony. There was a frantic scramble of activity on the ridge line, as the men above the patrol worked out what had happened. Corporal Mark Wright ran from the top of his position by the mortars on the northern part of the ridge towards Stu Pearson's sangar. He shouted to the men around him, including Lance Corporal 'Tugg' Hartley and Corporal Craig who were the FSG's two medics. They took only their weapons and the medical packs: there wasn't time to don body armour or helmets; one of their mates was down and they needed to get to him.

I was in the JOC when the report of the mine strike came over the net at midday. Mark Wright had already sent in a request for an evacuation helicopter. He had considered carrying Hale back up the ridge, but it was a long way and precariously steep. Every time Hale's leg dropped below the horizontal, blood would spurt from the bandaged stump. Getting him back up the goat track would not only take time, but it was also highly likely that any violent movement would lead to him bleeding to death. Wright needed a helicopter to come to where Hale had been hit, but where there was one mine, there were likely to be others. I quickly talked through the options with the headquarters staff who had gathered round the bird table. Bringing a 15-tonne Chinook into the minefield entailed the risk that it would land on a mine or the powerful downwash of its rotor blades would detonate others. The Explosive Ordnance Disposal Engineer adviser in the JOC said it would take several hours to clear a path into the minefield and guarantee that a landing site was free of mines.

We didn't have hours to play with and the obvious solution was to winch Hale directly out of the minefield. The UK didn't have any winch-equipped helicopters in Afghanistan, but we knew that the Americans did. We put in an immediate and urgent request to UKTF for a US HH-60 Black Hawk, but word came back from our higher headquarters that there was likely to be a delay of several hours in getting the necessary NATO release authority. The information was passed to the troops on the ground that a winch helicopter was unlikely to arrive any time soon. We waited for the response, as the message was relayed down to the rescue party from the top of the ridge. The reply came back that they thought there was a chance that a Chinook could get the ramp of its tailgate on to an outcrop of rock close to Hale. If the rescue party could clear a path to the ledge, they believed that they could get Hale out without the helicopter having to land. I knew it was a risky option, but it had to be balanced against the delay in waiting for the Black Hawk and the risk of Hale bleeding to death. I made the decision to send the Chinook. The pilots were briefed on the situation and risks involved and were directed to fly up to Kajaki and react to the signal of the men on the ground.

Soldiers have a deep-rooted pathological hatred of mines. Their use is considered iniquitous, impersonal and indiscriminatory. They could be anywhere, lurking hidden just beneath the surface, waiting for the unwary to tread on them. However, Mark Wright and his party had entered into the mine-strewn ground with complete disregard for their own safety. Now they began an emergency drill of trying to prod the rocky sand around them in an attempt to clear a safe route to where the inbound Chinook might be able to put down. They tried to place their feet on solid rocks as they prodded the earth with anything that came to hand. Stu Pearson was using the metal rod from his rifle cleaning kit. It was difficult to tell whether the resistance a probe encountered was a buried stone or something more deadly. Pearson turned back to walk across the path that he thought he had cleared. Suddenly, he was thrown up and spun round by a violent explosion. Like Hale, he initially felt no pain, but he knew instantly what had happened. Fusilier Andy Barlow rushed over to him and went through the procedure of squeezing off the main artery in the smashed remains of Pearson's left leg with a tourniquet. His right leg was intact, but it looked pretty bad. He injected Pearson with morphine and began treating his other wounds.

The pilot of the Chinook saw green signal smoke rising up from the rescue party's location and lined up his aircraft to land into an offset position. However, the second explosion confirmed in everybody's mind that there were mines everywhere. Additionally, it proved that probing for the mines had not been effective and the route to any LZ was unsafe. Just after the second explosion the heavy clatter of the Chinook rotor blades thumped low over the rescue party. Mark Wright sought to wave it off on the hand-held radio he had with him. The last thing he wanted now was a heavy-lift helicopter trying to land next to them. But his messages had to be relayed to a larger radio set on the ridge and the pilot remained unaware of his desperate message telling him not to come in.

The pilot placed his rear wheels down on the deck but kept his front wheels off the ground to minimize the threat of striking a mine. His rear crewman signalled to the party to bring the casualties to them, but 50 metres of mine-strewn ground still lay between them and safety. The emergency prodding technique had proved ineffective and there was no way that the troops on the ground were going to take the chance of setting off more mines: they waved the helicopter away. The aircraft lifted off, creating a brown storm of dust and debris. Mark Wright was seen to crouch down to shield himself from the blizzard of sand that came towards him; as he did so there was another explosion, most likely caused by rocks or equipment being shifted by the down-draught of the rotors as the Chinook lifted clear of the area. The left-hand side of Mark's chest caught the main force of the blast and shrapnel hit him in the face. In an act of desperate courage, Tugg Hartley threw his medical pack on to the ground in front of him to clear a path of any more mines to get to where Mark Wright lay.

A third man was down; in a matter of minutes another man fell. Andy Barlow moved his foot a few inches backwards as he bent down to pick up a water bottle next to where Pearson lay. The slight movement triggered another explosion that took off one of his legs and hit four other men with steel fragments. Tugg Hartley, Private Dave Prosser and Corporal Craig now all had shrapnel wounds and Mark Wright also sustained further injuries from the fourth blast. Craig struggled back up the goat track, clutching his side where shrapnel had punctured his lung. He managed to make the climb unaided before collapsing at the top of the ridge. Less than an hour had passed since Lance Corporal Hale had stood on the first mine. Six other men were now down and the prospect of rescue was anything but certain.

The messages reporting the additional injuries came across the net one by one in quick succession and Matt Taylor repeated them as they came in: 'Three times T1. . . one times T2,' and then: 'One times T3.' T1 was immediately life-threatening and required priority surgery, T2 meant surgery was required within hours and the T3 was a less serious injury. My blood froze. The dread of hearing that men were down was now coming across the net in spades; they were falling like ninepins. I got back on to the radio and demanded to know when I was going to get my Black Hawk helicopter. I followed it up with a phone call to UKTF. The staff in KAF understood the urgency of the situation and were doing their best to get it released, but I impressed upon them that people were going to die unless someone in the NATO chain of command pulled their finger out.

As I spoke, Matt Taylor was already beginning to decode the Zap numbers that had been sent over the net from Kajaki. They would identify who the men were who had been hit and their blood types, a vital piece of information that the field hospital would require. There was a hushed silence as Taylor began to call them out. People were desperately hoping that it would not be one of their mates. The fact that the identifying numbers had come in so fast was due to Mark Wright. Despite the serious nature of his wounds he remained in command of the rescue party to the end. He made the wounded around him yell them out so that he could pass them on over the radio. Stu Hale could also hear him calmly shouting encouragement to the wounded. There was even an element of humour to lessen the horrors of the situation they were in. Mark Wright joined in the banter as the wounded and those treating them took the piss out of each other. But Mark Wright was fading. He mentioned that he felt cold and that he knew he was going to die. He talked of his parents, his fiancée and their dog. Before losing consciousness he spoke of his uncle who had been a former member of 3 PARA and a major influence in his decision to become a paratrooper himself. He asked someone to tell his uncle that he had been 'a good soldier'.

Three and half hours after the first mine strike two Black Hawks appeared overhead. Each winched down its 'Para Jumper' medic. The men in the minefield screamed at them that there were mines everywhere; they acknowledged the warning with a thumbs up and dropped on to the ground. Moving among the injured, they winched out the most serious casualties first and flew them up to the LZ at the dam where they were transferred to a CH-47 and flown straight to Bastion. Then they went back for the less seriously injured and the five other members of the rescue party who had not been hit. Lance Corporal Hale was still waiting for the pain in his leg to kick in as he watched someone being given emergency resuscitation on the back of the Chinook. He thought it was Dave Prosser, but the medics treating him wouldn't let him look up.

The RSM and I were on the LZ by the field hospital waiting for the Chinook to come in; we went on board as soon as the ramp came down. I stepped over a motionless figure whose upper body was shrouded from view; a discarded oxygen mask and surgical airway lay next to him. We focused on the living as Hale, Pearson and Barlow were carried off with missing limbs and rushed to surgery in the back of the waiting ambulances. John Hardy and I looked at each other before stooping to pull back the shroud. We then lifted the lifeless soldier into a body bag and carried him to an ambulance. The man receiving resuscitation had been Mark Wright, but for him the rescue had come too late.

I drove back from the hospital in the front of the open-top Pinzgauer truck with John Hardy; neither of us spoke as I looked down and felt Mark Wright's blood drying on my hands. At one stage I thought that we were not going to get the men out of the minefield. But any relief I felt was overridden by the sense of loss of one of my soldiers and the grievous wounding of three others whom the surgeons were now working on. It was after 1730 hours, darkness was little less than two hours away and the day was already beginning to cool by the time we got back to the JOC.

Matt Taylor was waiting to meet me and his face said it all before he spoke. 'Colonel, you are not going to believe this, but we have got multiple casualty situations in both Sangin and Musa Qaleh.' Sangin had been engaged by Taliban mortars firing from three different positions and had caused one T1, two T2 and three T3 casualties. Less than five minutes later the district centre in Musa Qaleh had also come under fire and an exploding mortar round caused one T1, three T2 and six T3 casualties among both Easy Company and the ASP. Corporal Graham Groves was on the top of the ANP house when the mortars started to come in against the men of C Company in Sangin. The attack started with small-arms fire and then two mortar bombs landed in the river as others began to creep closer. He felt a sinking lurch in his stomach when he heard the cry for a medic. One of the rounds had landed in the orchard where the bunkers provided the soldiers with a degree of subterranean sanctuary. But the men of 9 (Ranger) Platoon were attending an orders group given by Colour Sergeant Spence. The round caught them in the open, cutting down most of his command team including Lance Corporal Luke McCulloch, who was seriously wounded by a piece of shrapnel that struck him in the back of the head.

We were entering the equation of the mincing machine again. It was exacerbated by the fact that there were now two dangerous locations requiring the launch of casualty evacuation missions. We had only one MERT and one aircraft on short-notice standby to fly it. I picked up the phone that had linked me to the field dressing station. I knew that they were flat out dealing with the mine strike casualties, but I needed a clinical medical assessment to guide my decision as to which district centre to fly to first. The engines of the Chinook were already turning as Lieutenant Colonel Peter Davis arrived in the JOC; as a qualified anaesthetist, he would fly with the MERT. He spoke to each of the doctors over the net and said, 'Sangin first.' Shrapnel from the mortar round that had landed in the compound in Musa Qaleh had ripped into the front part of Ranger Moniasagwa's throat. But Mike Stacey assessed that he was stable and could hang on, so it was decided to attempt to get Corporal McCulloch out first, as his head wound was judged to be more serious.

I looked at Mark Hammond, who was the epitome of a rugged Royal Marines officer and was the pilot who would fly the mission. Shaven-headed and thickset, he was nicknamed 'the School Bully', but the seriousness of what he was about to do was not lost on him. We gathered round the bird table for a last-minute confirmation of the critical mission criteria. Routes and timings were read out and the information was passed on to C Company in Sangin. Ground- and air-fire-support measures to reduce the risk of the helicopter being shot down were hastily rechecked. I looked at my watch as Davis and Hammond left the JOC and headed out to the Chinook; time was of the essence and the clock was ticking. The MERT headed for Sangin and we set about planning the casevac mission to Musa Qaleh.

The nose of the Chinook dropped into the Sangin Valley as Hammond pushed forward on his joystick with his right hand. He gripped the collective with his left and kicked the aircraft's rudder pedals with his feet to bring the Chinook into position to make the final approach into the LZ. Two Apaches had already arrived on station before Hammond began his descent. They hovered above him and searched the ground around the HESCO bastion perimeter for the telltale signs of any heat sources that would betray the presence of Taliban fighters moving into firing positions. The fingers of men of C Company rested on the triggers of their GPMGs and .50 Cal machine guns as they scanned the area from their sangars. They heard the clatter of the rotor blades of the approaching Chinook as an armoured Spartan waited at the side of the LZ with the casualties, ready to drive them out to the helicopter as soon as it landed. The area was quiet and Hammond bled altitude and headed in.

Suddenly, green tracer slashed up towards the aircraft forcing him to bank violently away from the fire that came up from the ground to meet him. He slewed the aircraft and pulled for altitude in a desperate attempt to get away from the bullets that chased after him through the sky. Artillery and mortar rounds began to thump through the air on the way to where the Taliban fired from positions in the fields and compounds to the south of the district centre. Machine guns hammered away at them from the sangars and the circling Apaches raked the insurgents' locations with fire. A second attempt was made and Hammond managed to get the Chinook into the LZ under the cover of the heavy weight of supporting fire that suppressed every likely Taliban firing position. The casualties were loaded into the helicopter and Hammond was already lifting as the Spartan pulled away from the back of the aircraft's tailgate.

With the report that they were 'wheels up' and heading back to Bastion, I left the JOC with the RSM and we headed down to the LZ by the field hospital for the second time that day. Corporal McCulloch looked pretty bad as we carried him off the Chinook that landed twenty minutes later. We placed him carefully into the back of a waiting ambulance. The other injured men were 'walking wounded' and were helped to a second ambulance. John Hardy and I followed them up in the Pinzgauer to the tented entrance of the hospital. Corporal McCulloch had already been taken to the emergency treatment area as I chatted to the less seriously injured while they were being checked out by the nursing staff before being readied for surgery. Peter Davis appeared at my side and told me that despite his best efforts Corporal McCulloch hadn't made it. I thanked him for all he had tried to do and the risks his MERT had faced in flying out to get Corporal McCulloch and the other wounded. Peter Davis had not changed out of his combat webbing. We still had ten wounded men waiting to be evacuated from Musa Qaleh and we both knew that it would not be long before he and Mark Hammond would be flying out again in an attempt to pick them up. Corporal McCulloch was the second of my soldiers to succumb to his wounds, but he would not be the last before the day was out.

Adam Jowett watched the sky over Musa Qaleh for the approach of Mark Hammond's aircraft from the LZ that he had secured with Easy Company outside the district centre. It was a small field sandwiched on three sides by compounds, bushes and trees. His men formed a perimeter around its edges and were already fighting off a number of insurgents who were attempting to work their way towards the open space where they knew the helicopter would try to land. It was just before last light when he saw the dark shape of the Chinook against the fading blue heavens as it flew towards them. As it got closer he heard the boom of RPGs being fired up into the air to meet it and watched the dance of smoke trails which appeared to chase the helicopter across the sky. It banked and turned to avoid them in a desperate attempt to find air space free of the lethal projectiles. The Chinook would turn, pull up and then start to run in again as a relentless stream of rounds and rockets climbed into the sky. Hammond pressed home his attempt as the escorting Apaches pumped rounds from their 30mm cannons at the numerous Taliban positions around the LZ. Jowett saw the Chinook shudder and slow as it came in to the LZ nose up on its final approach. He saw bullets striking into the spinning rotor discs and heard them ping and whine as they were deflected off the turning blades. They thumped into the side of the cab as Jowett yelled into his radio, 'Hot LZ! Hot LZ! Abort! Abort!'

Hammond pulled violently back on his joystick and the engines screamed for power as he went into the emergency abort procedures and fought to lift the 15-tonne airframe out of the storm of incoming rounds. Jowett watched the aircraft gain altitude and limp away towards the east. He was convinced he saw smoke coming from the stricken aircraft and feared that it might go down over the town before it managed to reach the relative safety of the open desert. He shouted into his radio and told Sergeant Major Scrivener to stand to the QRF ready to drive out to the crash site if it fell out of the sky. It would be a desperate measure, as the QRF consisted of fewer than twenty men crammed into two un-armoured light Pinzgauer trucks. He willed it to make it across the rooftops while Ranger Moniasagwa lay on his stretcher still waiting for rescue. Hammond nursed his damaged aircraft back to Bastion, twenty-five minutes' flying time to the south. It was covered with strike marks and had taken rounds in one of its main head rotor assemblies which risked catastrophic mechanical failure. The Chinook wouldn't be going back out again that night, but Hammond, his crew and Peter Davis's MERT would.

Hammond and Davis reported to the JOC while another Chinook was made ready for them. They had already flown two missions under fire. The aircrew were well over their regulation crew-duty hours, but Hammond was adamant that he would try to make another attempt to get the wounded. I spoke to Adam Jowett on the net. He reconfirmed Mike Stacey's assessment that he could keep Moniasagwa stable for a few more hours; after that he would die from his wounds. He had already been lying wounded for over two hours.

Part of the moral component of what makes men fight is that they expect rapid evacuation to immediate medical care and timely surgery if they become wounded. To most soldiers the medical extraction plan is the most important part of the orders they receive for battle. If they get hit, they expect to be looked after. How we would get a casualty from the point of wounding to the surgeon's table was part of the operational planning process that we scrubbed in detail. Consequently, it was not lost on anyone that we were breaching the principle that if a casualty is to stand the best chance of survival he must be lifted to surgery from the point of wounding within two hours. Once again, I was having to balance the lives of the aircrew and the MERT against the life of one of the soldiers who would die if we did not lift him out of Musa Qaleh. The troops in Easy Company were also taking a risk every time they had to push out from the district centre to secure the evacuation LZ.

I told Jowett that I intended to take the time that Stacey's assessment had given us to put the necessary threat-reduction measures in place to minimize the risk of having the helicopter shot down when Hammond went back in. Jowett calmly accepted my decision. I asked him to get round his soldiers and explain my decision; I had no doubt that the grunts in the front line would be cursing those of us ensconced in the safety of the JOC while their comrades suffered and patiently waited to be evacuated. I talked Jowett through the supporting fire package of an AC-130 gunship, A-10s, artillery and Apaches that we were coordinating with the oncoming cover of darkness. I told him that once the package was in place he was to secure the LZ at the last safe moment and then use all the available assets to suppress the Taliban's firing positions. Before I signed off on the radio I said, 'Adam, do what you need to get the helicopter in safely and get the wounded out. If necessary cane the place.'

Three hours later the fire package was set as A-10s, surveillance aircraft and an AC-130 Hercules gunship circled unseen in the night skies over Musa Qaleh. The 105mm gun battery in the desert 12 kilometres to the east of the district centre laid its artillery pieces on to the areas around the LZ and waited for the order to fire. As Hammond once again steered his Chinook towards the town, two Apaches flew thirty seconds ahead of him. To preserve the element of surprise, they would arrive over the compound just as Jowett's men went out to secure the LZ. The Apaches would then provide close-in protective fire to the Chinook as it ran in behind them and dropped down to make its approach into the LZ. The signal came through to the JOC that Hammond was two minutes out. I glanced at my watch as the aircraft began its descent into the danger zone. The atmosphere in the JOC was thick with tension as we waited for reports to come over the radio. I tried to avoid staring at the signaller on the air desk as the seconds ticked by.

Over Musa Qaleh the 105mm rear cannon from the AC-130 boomed in the darkness as it pumped shells down on to the Taliban and artillery fired from the desert. A-10s flew strafing missions, the strike of their 30mm cannon rounds rippling in lines of sparks and metal splinters and 500-pound bombs dropped off their weapon racks. The JTAC in Easy Company was calling down a storm of steel to protect the inserting Chinook, and Hammond dropped from the sky as an inferno raged in a circle around the LZ. The fire was danger close, JDAMs landing within 100 metres of the compound walls and LZ. Jowett's men had been warned to take cover and keep their mouths open as the bombs came in, to reduce the effects of overpressure on their lungs. The blast waves of exploding ordnance were visible to the naked eye as metal fragments travelled out behind them at 1000 metres per second. One unfortunate soldier was blown out of the makeshift latrine as he was forced to make an emergency call of nature. Two 2,000-pound bombs were dropped on a known Taliban forming-up position and debris rained down on the compound for minutes after. The attack helicopters kept a vigil of protective fire with cannons and missiles over the Chinook as they saw it come nose up into the LZ.

'Wheels down,' came the call from the air desk at my right-hand side from where I stood at the bird table. My eyes were fixated on the face of my watch, as the digital seconds started the nerve-racking countdown. Spare mortar ammunition was kicked off the tailgate as the wounded were rushed on to the Chinook. One minute passed by and nothing. Come on, come on, I thought, as I willed the helicopter to lift and get the hell out of there. Nobody spoke and another minute passed. 'Colonel, wheels up from Musa Qaleh,' the air ops officer announced. But the tension wasn't over: it would take another two minutes for the helicopter to climb to a safe altitude out of the threat zone. I was mesmerized by my watch again, as others glanced at the face of the clock mounted over the bank of radios in the JOC. I looked at the air staff; they knew the words I wanted to hear and then they came:

'She's clear, sir.' The wounded had been lifted safely after waiting for seven hours to be evacuated, and the Taliban had been unable to bring their weapons to bear against the Chinook. Easy Company collapsed back into the district centre while small-arms fire and RPG rockets began to strike the compound as the insurgents battered out their frustrations at having missed their prey.

Yet the day wasn't over and the RSM and I turned from the bird table and headed down to the LZ to meet the incoming wounded. Peter Davis gave me the thumbs up as he came off the ramp with Moniasagwa's stretcher; we had got to him in time. Having met them off the tailgate we followed the ambulances to the field hospital. All the operating theatres had been working at full tilt since mid-afternoon. Their trade had not stopped since the first wounded from the minefield had been brought in. Behind the canvas screens of the outer corridor it was like a scene from a butcher's shop. The senior surgeon would pause in his grisly work to update me on how the wounded were doing; three had lost legs and most had undergone surgery to remove shrapnel. Corporal Wright and Lance Corporal Luke McCulloch had died before they arrived at the hospital. Wright's limbs were uninjured and the wounds he sustained indicated that he could not have set off the mine that killed him. We had also received bad news from Oman. Lance Corporal Paul Muirhead had finally lost the battle against the serious head wound he had sustained when an insurgent mortar round landed on the Alamo in Musa Qaleh five days previously.

I spoke to a nurse and walked into the post-op recovery ward, having washed my hands and donned a plastic apron at the entrance. A procedure I had not encountered when visiting Selly Oak. Corporals Pearson and Hale were still sedated; Stu Pearson was coming to, but was still out of it. I moved from his bedside to see Fusilier Andy Barlow lying naked apart from a bloodstained sheet that protected his modesty. I knew it was a stupid question, and I said so when I asked him how he was doing. 'I'm all right, sir; it's the first time I've been legless on the tour since you banned

alcohol!' Andy was nineteen and had just had his left leg amputated above the knee. I didn't know whether to laugh or cry.
Young Barlow's retort had done much to reinvigorate my flagging
spirits as I moved among my horribly wounded soldiers. But I was
still in a sombre mood as I walked through the tented corridor
towards the hospital's entrance. It was late and I needed to get
back to the JOC. As I reached the end of the corridor, there in the
gloom I came across some of the remaining less seriously wounded.
They were waiting patiently for their turn to be attended to while
the more pressing cases were being treated.

At the back of the line sat Private Hook. Hook was a new
recruit who had recently completed his recruit training. His arrival
in Afghanistan the day before had been delayed until he had
reached his eighteenth birthday, which qualified him for active
service. He stood up as I approached and I asked him what was
wrong with him. 'It's my arm, sir. I took a bit of shrapnel from
that mortar that landed in Sangin, but look, sir, it's okay and I can
get back on the next helicopter and rejoin C Company,' he said,
as he waved his wounded arm vigorously above his head. I told
him not to worry too much about that for the time being and to
concentrate on getting his wound looked after. A little later he
went under the surgeon's knife to remove a jagged mortar splinter
from his upper arm.

My penultimate act that night was to attend the last rites given to
Mark Wright. Hours previously, John Hardy and I had lifted his
lifeless body into a body bag on the back of the CH-47's tailgate.
Afterwards I had found a moment to talk with Mark's best friend,
Corporal Lee Parker. For a soldier, the hardest thing is the loss of a
friend. Lee Parker spoke of his fallen comrade, a man he had gone
through training with and had served with side by side for the last
ten years. He told me about Mark's family and how he had been due
to marry his fiancée the month after we got back from Afghanistan;
people I didn't yet know but would soon be writing to later that
morning. I asked Lee if he wanted to come with me to say goodbye
to Mark.

We drove down to the field hospital with John Hardy and made our way to the small tented chapel. Mark's body lay before us, the body bag exposed to show his face and blood-matted blond hair. I can't remember the words the padre used, I know they were appropriate, but I was focused on looking at Mark. He seemed at peace and I thought about what he had done so others might live in that mine-infested gully below the ridge at Kajaki. I thought of his family going about their usual daily routine of a late summer's evening in Edinburgh, not yet aware that their beloved only son was dead and that the planned wedding would never be. I thought of the letters I would have to write and reflected bitterly on the day's bloody events: three men dead and another eighteen wounded.

As we filed out of the makeshift chapel, Corporal Parker stopped to ruffle his dead friend's hair; it was the ultimate act of compassion, love and loss. Witnessing it at the end of that fucking awful day, it very nearly broke me.

Last Acts

The bloody events of 6 September had brought the risks of holding the district centres into sharp relief. It was not something that had been lost on Ed Butler. As the senior commander responsible for the lives of British soldiers, the inability to guarantee the evacuation of casualties from Musa Qaleh and the high threat of losing a helicopter caused him deep concern. He began to question the ethical and military practicalities of continuing to hold the district centre and presented his view to PJHQ that Easy Company should be withdrawn. He had already discussed the matter of giving up Musa Qaleh with the ISAF commander, General David Richards. Richards had never liked the strategy of holding the district centres, but it was something that he had been forced to inherit when he took over command of NATO's operation in Afghanistan. He was also a British officer and was keenly aware of the risks which both Butler and I had spelled out to him. However, he saw any withdrawal as being tantamount to a strategic defeat to the British mission in Helmand and was not prepared to authorize giving up Musa Qaleh. Giving up a district centre would also undermine the authority of the Kabul government that NATO had been sent to support. It was a difficult situation for all concerned, not least the men of Easy Company who were bearing the brunt of political necessity. I knew that David Richards cared passionately about the plight of my soldiers and was working hard to find an alternative Afghan solution to provide security for the district centre. But previous experiences of broken Afghan promises to reinforce Sangin and Now Zad gave me little cause for optimism. I resigned myself to the fact that my men would have to hold out.

The risks associated with the platoon house strategy and the mounting casualty rate had not gone unnoticed in either the corridors of Whitehall or the British press. Since the beginning of August, 3 PARA Battle Group had suffered another eleven men killed in action and another thirty-one had sustained combat injuries. The loss of fourteen servicemen on an RAF Nimrod surveillance aircraft, which crashed near KAF after a refuelling accident on 2 September, compounded the growing realization of the human cost of conducting operations in Afghanistan. The implications of losing a helicopter were being debated at the highest levels in the MOD. Ministers were also appearing on TV to explain why a mission billed as a peace support operation was costing the lives of so many men. The newspapers talked of Afghanistan being a 'death-trap' and used other sensational head-lines, such as 'Soldiers who went to build bridges fight for their lives'. The flawed historical analogy of Rorke's Drift was also being bandied about in the media again. The mistaken policy of imposing a news blackout was coming home to roost, as the British public was fed a daily diet of hand-wringing commentary and government officials struggled to explain the true nature of the mission in Afghanistan.

Lacking access to the front line, the media seized on soldiers' personal accounts of the fighting and the conditions they faced which had managed to find their way into the public domain via YouTube and leaked e-mails. Concerned mothers appeared on TV to talk about their fears for their sons as a result of letters and telephone calls they had received. Home video footage of the fighting taken from 'head-cams' strapped to soldiers' helmets received prime-time viewing when they were aired on news channels. They showed exploding JDAMs, troops clearing com-pounds with bayonets fixed and heavily tattooed muscle-bound Paras returning fire from the district centres. The unofficial expo-sure of some of the realities of the operation in Helmand caused consternation in PJHQ. The growing concern in public quarters was hardly surprising, as officials had done little to try to influence the information campaign.

However, I was surprised by the attitude of some senior serving and retired officers who criticized the scruffy appearance of the soldiers. They failed to appreciate that the heavily bearded Paras who were filmed slugging it out with the Taliban dressed only in T-shirts and flip-flops had just rolled from their sleeping space on the floor to race to a nearby sangar to fight off another attack. Consequently, they did not have the luxury of time to put on anything more than their helmets and combat body armour. The men in 3 PARA always wore full desert battledress on patrols and deliberate operations. But those who criticized from the safety of their armchairs had either never known intensive sustained combat, or had forgotten their experiences. How my men dressed in such circumstances did not concern me; the fact that they could fight was what mattered.

What did concern me, however, was that the material reaching the home front was one-sided and lacked analysis. It was also alarming the families of my soldiers who were glued to their TV screens and becoming desperately worried about their loved ones. We were not being given the chance to tell our own side of the story and put it into perspective. It was an issue that concerned Ed Butler too and he supported my efforts to get a media news team embedded with the Battle Group. Eventually, we overcame the nervousness of many in Whitehall and convinced them that we were in danger of losing the media war.

Bill Neely and Eugene Campbell arrived from ITN on 8 September. Courteous and charming, the two Irishmen immediately struck up a good rapport with the Battle Group. They wanted to get up to Sangin and I was prepared to get them there, but they accepted that the risks of getting a helicopter into the district centre meant that I would not lay on an aircraft just for them. They were prepared to wait for places on the next available flight and were content to film other Battle Group activities in less risky areas during the two weeks that they waited to get in. They spent a day with the Patrols Platoon out in the desert and accompanied A Company on patrol into Gereshk. Getting the ITN crew to Gereshk was central, as it would add some balance to the media coverage by demonstrating that there was at least one place where 3 PARA wasn't fighting.

A Company moved to FOB Price after being relieved in Sangin at the end of August. Patrolling into the town to try to kick-start the thirty-plus quick-impact projects we proposed was an important part of the effort to do some reconstruction and development before the Battle Group left Helmand. Lashkar Gah was the one other area where British troops operated and there was no fighting. There had been the odd suicide bomb and one RPG attack against the PRT headquarters, but these isolated incidents were nothing compared to the fighting in the district centres. But it had not stopped DFID from withdrawing its staff. Little on the development front had been achieved outside Lashkar Gah, but Ed Butler and I were determined that we would try to acomplish something. With DFID's departure it was clear that it would have to be with a military lead. Additional military Engineers had been sent out to bolster UKTF's efforts and the first task was to get them into Gereshk to look at potential security development projects to support the ANP. However, moving to an area where there was no fighting was a stark contrast to being in Sangin where A Company had experienced continuous contact. Some of Jamie Loden's company found it difficult to adjust to an environment where their focus suddenly changed from intensive contact to patrolling in the streets of Gereshk in soft hats, protecting the Engineers and shaking hands with the locals. Some were relieved to be out of Sangin. But some felt guilty that they no longer faced the same level of danger that others members of the Battle Group were experiencing. As far as I was concerned A Company had done their bit.

The start of C Company's tenure in Sangin was no different to

A and B companies' previous tours of duty there. The fact that a new company had taken over in Sangin had not been missed by the Taliban and they immediately set about testing the guns of the new occupants. Corporal Graham Groves had just finished settling his men into the sangars that would be their home for the next six weeks when the attacks started. He looked at his watch; the last helicopter taking A Company out of Sangin had been gone for only forty-five minutes. Like A and B companies before them, Major Paddy Blair's men faced a daily fare of mortars, bullets and rockets as they manned their positions and sent patrols out on to the ground. They were fortunate in having a third platoon with them in the form of 9 (Ranger) Platoon from the Royal Irish Regiment who were caught in the mortar strike in the orchard on 6 September. Since they had lost most of their commanders, Blair ordered Lieutenant Simon Bedford's 7 Platoon to take over their more exposed positions. The men of Groves's section looked at him when he told them that they were to occupy the more vulnerable area where one man had just been killed and five others had been wounded. Without a murmur of complaint they picked up their kit and followed Groves to the bunkers. Two hours later they were joined by volunteers from 9 Platoon who wanted to come back and give 7 Platoon a hand. To men like Groves, the Royal Irish soldiers may not have been Paras, but they were good blokes who had bonded and had become a strong part of C Company.

It took three attempts to get Bill Neely and Eugene Campbell into Sangin. The first two attempts had to be aborted because of the level of fire they attracted as they tried to land into the LZ within the perimeter of the HESCO. On the third attempt they got what they wished for in more ways than one. It was dark when they lifted and Eugene filmed the scene in the back of the helicopter through a night vision device one of the blokes had lent him. The door gunners check-fired their M60s as they flew out over the desert, their weapons spewing sparks and empty cartridges into the night as the Chinooks headed north to Sangin. To reduce the risk of being shot down, the helicopter made for a landing site outside the district centre as dawn was breaking.

The men of C Company were there waiting to meet them, but so were the Taliban. Bullets started to cut across the LZ as the aircraft landed. There were frantic shouts of 'Get out! Get out!' Eugene and Bill grabbed their kit and scrambled off the tailgate. Eugene kept his camera running as stores were hastily unloaded and C Company's reception party poured fire back into the treeline where the Taliban were located. A Spartan armoured vehicle rocked backward as it spat a stream of machine-gun fire into the thick vegetation 250 metres away. RPG rounds, theirs and ours fired by the ANA, crossed in flight as the LZ party disembarked and personnel scrambled to gather equipment from the dust, take cover and assist in returning fire. Eugene's camera was damaged in the chaos as the reception party covered the new arrivals' move to the relative safety of the district centre.

ITN's presence in Sangin captured 3 PARA's exploits there. The footage and reports Bill and Eugene sent back were an instant news splash and provided a graphic exposé into the nature of the fighting the Battle Group were experiencing on a daily basis. But their reports were balanced and the interviews they conducted with members of the Battle Group allowed us to put our side of the story across. It sent an important message back to the people at home: yes, it was intense; yes, the mission had changed; but we were there for a reason, to help the people of Afghanistan against the Taliban. The reports portrayed the mood and spirit of the soldiers; summed up aptly by RSM John Hardy in a powerful piece to camera when he stated, 'It's what we do.'

On 9 September we received intelligence reports that the Taliban were planning a 'spectacular' in Sangin. Two days later C Company called in extensive air support and dropped eleven JDAMs to break up attacks around the district centre. We were also receiving similar reports about Musa Qaleh and two mortar bombs landed outside Jowett's headquarters building. With the majority of my forces fixed in position in the district centres we used the remaining light armoured vehicles of the Household Squadron and the Patrols Platoon to form Manoeuvre Outreach Groups. Known as MOGs, these patrols protected the one artillery battery we had in the desert between Now Zad and Musa Qaleh. Acting as a version of the older Second World War Long-Range Desert Patrols, they also formed mobile groups to interdict the Taliban's movement between the two towns.

We had used the MOGs since July, but we could only launch them when not committed to Battle Group deliberate operations and they were not immune to attack or the ever present danger of mines. On 11 September one of the I Battery's WMIKs supporting the Household Cavalry MOGs to the east of Musa Qaleh ran over a landmine. The WMIK was blown apart injuring three of the gunners who manned it. The most badly injured member of the crew was Bombardier Ben Parkinson who lost both his legs and sustained serious injuries to his head and torso. On 13 September the MOG was attacked with mortar fire and RPGs when they approached an isolated village. There were also attacks against the district centres and Kajaki, but for the first time there were no attacks against Musa Qaleh.

The day before I received a phone call from Ed Butler; it came late at night just as I was about to leave the JOC. He told me that there was a prospect of doing a deal with the local elders in Musa Qaleh. Fed up with the destruction of the Taliban's attacks on the district centre, the people wanted the Taliban to leave the town and were offering to force them out and take responsibility for their own security if we were prepared to withdraw Easy Company. Butler said there was a very good chance of a ceasefire and that a deal was being thrashed out between Richards, President Karzai, Daud and the elders. He wanted me to be prepared to fly out into the desert and secure an area for a *shura* with the locals the next day. The unexpected developments explained why there had been no attacks against Easy Company and stalled the plans we were working up to either withdraw or relieve them depending on the political direction we were waiting to receive. I spoke to

Adam Jowett and directed his men that they were only to fire in self-defence if they came under attack; otherwise they were to hold their weapons tight.

It was a strange turn of events, but we had noticed the beginnings of a general lull in the level of enemy activity in other areas too. Attacks still came in, mainly against Sangin, but since 11 September they were lacklustre affairs that quickly petered out shortly after they had started. It was highly likely that the Taliban were finding it difficult to sustain the level of activity that we had witnessed over the last four and half months. They had lost hundreds of fighters attacking the district centres. The fighting damaged property and had disrupted the lives of the local people who had become increasingly less willing to support the Taliban. The insurgents' credibility had also been damaged. They had not driven the British out, we had held fast and showed no indication that we were about to give up. The locals also wanted to gather in the summer crops, the poppy planting season was already approaching and the continued fighting threatened the ability of the local people to prepare for the coming winter.

I flew out with B Company the next day to the allotted area where the *shura* would take place. Ed Butler came with us and we landed in an LZ secured by the Patrols Platoon and the Household Cavalry. A large camouflage net was set up to provide a meeting place and shade from the fierce desert sun. B Company took up positions around the area from where they would be out of sight from the makeshift pavilion. With everything in place we watched and waited until a distant column of dust heralded the approach of those who came to meet us. They arrived in twelve Hilux pick-up trucks, forty-odd elders dressed in turbans and shalwar-kameez that caught in the wind as we greeted them and ushered them to where our council would take place. The younger age of the men and the black colour of their dress distinguished the Taliban commanders who followed them. As the direct protagonists, neither they nor I spoke. The talking was left to Butler and the elders. The men of age and wisdom said that the Taliban would leave and the elders would guarantee the security of Musa Qaleh if Jowett's men also withdrew. They spoke of the destruction and their desire for peace. Butler proposed a ceasefire between the two sides. If it held and the Taliban left, he said that we would also withdraw our troops. There were no raised voices or threats as we drank tea and the elders accepted the water that they were offered to ease the midday heat. I marvelled at the courteous and surreal exchange of two very different cultures after weeks of fighting and death. The *shura* broke up with handshakes and farewells as the guns of both sides in Musa Qaleh 15 kilometres to our west remained silent.

The coming of the ceasefire was equally surreal to the men of Easy Company. Once the agreement came into effect, Jowett's men didn't fire a single shot. Men used to constant attack and being sick with the loss of sleep, suddenly had to be found things to occupy them. Jowett used the time to rebuild the fortifications, clear up the debris of weeks of fighting, and held inter-platoon sports competitions. The elders came to the district centre every day and talked with Jowett. Unflappable in combat, he turned his abilities to the role of being the commensurate envoy. They could tell that he was an honourable man and he won the elders over with his charm and humility. They were also impressed by the length and thickness of his beard, which in Afghan culture marked him as a man of true stature. The locals brought in fresh produce and goats, which were slaughtered by Sergeant Major Scrivener to provide the first properly cooked meal that the soldiers had eaten in over a month. But the agreement also meant that no helicopters would fly into Musa Qaleh and Jowett received supplies sent by us to the locals. Jowett walked about the town bare-headed carrying only a pistol. One day he came across the freshly dug earth of a mass grave. The elders said that over 200 Taliban fighters had been killed in the fighting and Jowett saw their bodies still being pulled out of the rubble of the town's pulverized buildings two weeks after it had stopped.

The agreement held and its coming marked a continuing drop

in the level of attacks. The nature of the operation was changing and it looked like it was the Taliban who were blinking first in the battle of attrition that had raged since June. Our quietest day was 18 September: there were only two brief attacks, one against the ANP guards on the Kajaki ridge and a single rocket fired from Wombat Wood at the district centre in Sangin. The hint of the coming winter was in the air, but the altering seasons and the lull in the fighting were not the only things that were changing. Elements of 42 Commando, who were due to take over from 3 PARA, had begun to arrive in growing numbers since the middle of September. The Royal Marines were different to Paras: they had an equally strong ethos bred from their tough training, but they were also more regimented in their approach and appearance. I noticed that they all wore the same issued regulation kit, unlike my men who were allowed to wear their own webbing, as long as it was serviceable and enabled them to do the job. They were itching to take over, but I also noted an understandable trepidation regarding what they were about to undertake. I would have been concerned had they not felt it.

Although there had been a perceptible drop in the number of attacks and the ceasefire in Musa Qaleh was holding, the Taliban had not given up. Now Zad, FOB Robinson and Kajaki still came under sporadic fire. The insurgents were also determined to shoot down a helicopter; as the insertion of the ITN crew had demonstrated, every mission flown into Sangin still entailed risk. Although the LZ next to the district centre had been protected by the 3-metre-high HESCO Bastion perimeter of giant earth-filled mesh cradles, the Taliban could still fire over the top of them from a compound across the canal known as JDAM House. It had gained its nickname thanks to the large number of bombs that had been dropped on it in an attempt to flatten it to the ground. But it remained standing and was a favourite location used by the Taliban to engage the Chinooks. Any inserting aircraft was vulnerable to enemy ground fire too as it swept low over the houses and tree-lines to make its final approach.

We attempted to reduce these risks by landing offset from the district centre further down the river line. But the Taliban had got wise to this and had dug in firing positions to cover all likely alternative landing sites. We had already handed over the positions in Kajaki to the Royal Marines as part of a phased handover of our responsibilities to 42 Commando on 26 September. But the handover of Sangin would require one last Battle Group operation to replace C Company with one of their companies and extract the Household Cavalry's troop of Scimitars and Spartans, which would be replaced by the Marines' own light armour. I also wanted to use the operation to clear out the positions the Taliban had dug in the trees along the river line and destroy JDAM House once and for all.

On 29 September 3 PARA launched its last Battle Group operation. We would hand over full command responsibility to the Royal Marines on 6 October, but I was determined that people did not see the operation, codenamed Sara, as the last match of the season. I reminded everyone that we needed to stay focused until the end. We still had six days to go and the tour of Helmand would not be finished until we handed over command. But the fact that it would be 3 PARA's last major act was on everyone's mind as we waited by the LZ in Bastion to board the Chinooks. The normal mix of apprehensive enthusiasm was still there, but it was compounded by the fact that it was likely to be the last major operational push. I told myself that nothing is ever as good or as bad as it first seems as I walked towards my aircraft. The exhausts from the Chinook glowed red-hot as I passed under them and felt the familiar claw tighten in my stomach. I completed the ritual of running the mission through my head as I slapped a belt of bullets in the port M60 and snapped the feed tray cover shut.

Tac would land with B Company who would clear the Taliban's line of trenches and surrounding compounds from the south. C Company would then advance with two platoons out of the district centre to clear the area from the north. The two companies would link up and form a defensive perimeter to allow the

Household Cavalry troops to drive down the river line and ford the Helmand River to a crossing point secured on the other side of the bank by the Patrols Platoon. C Company would then hand over the district centre to the company from 42 Commando and B Company would clear JDAM House before the Engineers came in to blow it up.

The flight in was uneventful. But B Company was soon in contact as they pushed into the treeline of trenches and compounds as daylight began to break. Tac followed them through the tight patchwork of high-standing crops and irrigation ditches. It was difficult to keep sight of the man in front and those on the flanks. I thought of Corporal Budd as we heard the crackle of small-arms fire ahead of us. An RPG round split through the air in the fields above us and B Company's snipers reported hits against Taliban gunmen stationed on a water tower. The fighting was intermittent and the insurgents seemed less willing to contest the ground, as they had been during the previous Battle Group operation at the end of August. C Company also met little opposition as they cleared from the north and linked up with B Company's forward sections.

I heard the engines and squealing tracks of the Household Cavalry moving along the open riverbank behind us as they headed south to find a crossing point. I was relieved when they reported that they had found a fordable stretch of the river and made it across to the Patrols Platoon. It was the part of the operation that concerned me most. The depth of the river had dropped and the ferry bridge we had brought up the month before could now only reach a small island of shale in the middle of the river, but the last stretch beyond the island was still too deep for the armoured vehicles to ford. Had they not found an alternative crossing point in the south they would have been stuck in Sangin.

I ordered the companies to start moving back towards the district centre. Tac moved into the HESCO behind C Company. I moved to the roof to watch B Company's attack on JDAM House.

The intensity of gunfire was already increasing as I climbed the first steps of the FSG Tower. By the time I got to the top Taliban rounds were cracking back overhead and they fizzed and whined when they passed close to the sangars. I heard the boom of grenades as the first sections of B Company went in. Then I heard the radio call of men down.

Corporal Atwell of 6 (Guards) Platoon was tasked with clearing one of the buildings. He pushed himself along the wall at the head of his section. Stopping at an open doorway, he pulled the pin of a grenade and tossed the small metal sphere into the dark of the entrance and flattened himself back against the building. Mistaking the explosion of another nearby grenade for the one Atwell had posted, Captain Guy Lock and Captain Jim Berry advanced on the doorway with their rifles set to automatic. However, Atwell's grenade still fizzed just inside the entrance and then exploded as the two men approached. A fragment caught Atwell's arm as he shot it out as a warning to his platoon commander, but it was too late. Shrapnel tore out from the doorway striking Lock in his arm and shoulder. One fragment hit Berry in the face and penetrated his right eye.

By the time I got down to the LZ a Chinook was already inbound from Bastion. Lock sat against a wall, pale and in shock. Jim Berry was being worked on by two medics. I held the drip they had already got into him as they stripped away his combats to look for more wounds. His right eye was badly cut and he was fitting. The cab came in with a thump 30 metres away and I helped them carry Jim's stretcher to the helicopter.

I was angry that two of my men had been hit so close to the finishing line. I reminded myself that it wasn't over until it was over. C Company was lifting out as the Engineers informed me that JDAM House was now set ready to blow. It had been packed with eighteen bar mines and hundreds of pounds of plastic explosive. I told them to confirm everyone was in cover and then to blow it before the helicopters came back to pick up B Company. I headed back to the roof, and the blast wave washed over me as I got to the top of the tower. A huge geyser of rubble and sand shot into the sky; JDAM House was no more. It would have seemed a more fitting way to end the operation had taking it not led to the wounding of two more of my men. As the last debris fell to earth and the rhythmic beat of the returning Chinooks' rotor blades began to sound in the valley, Jim Berry was fighting for his life on a surgeon's table in Bastion.

With the Marines in place we were ready to lift out of Sangin for the last time. I took one final look at the district centre from the port gunner's hatch. I watched Corporal Stentiford drive Tac's quad bike over the rutted field towards us. The aircraft was already packed with fifty men and the aircrew were impatient to lift; then Stentiford bogged the quad bike. We had already spent too long on the ground. JDAM House had gone, but RPGs were probably already being primed against us. I heard the pilot tell me he needed to lift; I felt myself sigh as I flicked back the intercom switch and said, 'Roger out.' The airframe vibrated violently as the power came on and we climbed from the LZ. I caught a brief glimpse of Corporal Stentiford through the gap in the tail gate as the rear of the aircraft pitched momentarily backwards. He sat on the quad with his arms outstretched as the helicopter lifted away from him; it was like a scene from Oliver Stone's film *Platoon*.

With the exception of Corporal Stentiford, who was eventually picked up after spending five days as a guest of the Marines, it was the end of 3 PARA's time in Sangin. Apart from Easy Company and the Gurkhas, virtually every member of the Battle Group had pulled some duty time there. We had fought in Now Zad, Musa Qaleh, Kajaki, in isolated villages, in the green zones of close country and in the open desert, but the defence of the town's district centre had become the touchstone of faith during 3 PARA's tour. Half the Battle Group's men killed in action had lost their lives there and everybody had a Sangin moment. For some it was the rocket attack that killed corporals Hashmi and Thorpe, for some it was the loss of young Jacko and for others it was the gallant death of Corporal Budd or the mortar strike that killed Corporal McCulloch. The constant attacks, fierce firefights, near misses, danger close fire, fatigue, fear, experience of carrying a fallen comrade and the privations were etched in the memory of all those who occupied a sangar and went out on patrol. In the words of Private Martin Cork, the periods spent in Sangin were the 'crazy times'.

People's experiences were punctuated by highs and lows that created an odd dichotomy: on the one hand the blokes hated Sangin and sometimes questioned their purpose, especially when the casualties and risks mounted. However, it never stopped any of them doing what was asked of them and they saw having fought there as a kind of badge of courage and endurance. That in itself was something that they were proud of. When the soldiers of 3 PARA had first arrived in Sangin the district centre was vulnerable, but it had withstood ninety-five days of sustained attacks and by the time they left the attackers' guns had fallen silent. As B Company and Tac were lifting from inside the HESCO perimeter the Taliban had asked for a ceasefire which came into effect the next day.

The last few days of the tour were spent handing over the other locations of FOB Robinson and FOB Price to the Marines. Having only arrived in July, the Fusiliers would stay in Now Zad under the command of 42 Commando. Easy Company would also be staying. As part of the ceasefire agreement, they would spend another five weeks in Musa Qaleh until their unorthodox extraction in the form of being driven out in vehicles provided by the elders. There was an end-of-term feeling in the air as 3 PARA's sub-units began to return to Bastion. Equipment and stores were checked and signed over to the Marines and personal kit was packed and accommodation swept out. For the first and last time since the beginning of the tour, the Battle Group was together in the same location. I watched them gather for the Battle Group photograph as they arranged themselves on WMIKs and armoured vehicles flanked between two Chinooks matted with oil and sand.

There were over 1,000 soldiers: paratroopers, Irish Rangers, the Estonian Platoon, the Gurkhas who had held Now Zad for the most demanding six weeks, aircrew, gunners, engineers, signallers, medics and cavalrymen from D Squadron.

Regardless of their parent regiment, all of them had served in numerous actions and all had played their part. Many were not infantry men, but every one of them had proved that they were fighters first. The engagements we had fought had been 360° affairs, where there were no safe rear areas. Royal Military Policemen had crewed GPMGs on the rooftop in Sangin, a dentist had carried a resupply of mortar ammunition across an LZ under fire and Engineers had downed tools and gone left-flanking to break up a Taliban attack. It was an awesome sight and the pride I felt for them coursed through every sinew in my body as an Apache hovered in position over the massed ranks and I took my station at the front. The photograph taken, I turned to address them. I spoke of what they had achieved and what they had been through. I told them that I knew it had not been easy, but that they had performed brilliantly. Regardless of the risks, the danger, the lack of resources, shortages of helicopters, hard conditions and uncertainty, they had never failed to deliver. When it really mattered they had stepped up to the plate, they had been counted and had not been found wanting.

The prayers we said at the memorial service we held after the photograph were few and short. We assembled in rough ranks around the Battle Group memorial that had been built by members of the Household Cavalry. It was made of large smooth stones taken from the surrounding desert and cemented together into a narrowing column. On top was placed a simple cross fashioned from 30mm Rarden brass shell casings which reflected the rays of the sun as the padre spoke. I looked at the bowed heads of the soldiers around me as RSM Hardy read out the names engraved on the polished metal plaque that had been fixed to the column. Space had been left for others, that I had no doubt would be filled in the coming months. I thought about the men of the Battle

Group who had been killed as we observed a two-minute silence; names of fourteen soldiers and one Afghan interpreter who would for ever have a place out here in the empty desert, but who would not be coming home with us.

It was also a time to say goodbye to the living as the elements of the Battle Group split up to start the journey home. A Company left in the first phase of the movement plan. They had been first in and had initially borne the brunt of the fighting and it was right that they should be the first ones to go out. But as I said goodbye to them, I reflected that there was no difference between any of my three rifle companies. They had all contributed and in terms of capability and performance I could not tell them apart. I would be flying out with C Company, so I also said goodbye to B Company who would follow on behind us a few days later. Other goodbyes were said to I Battery whose guns had helped keep us alive in places like Musa Qaleh and Sangin. I thanked the Estonians for all they had done. Unlike some of their western European counterparts they had never once shied away from the risks and had always been ready to do more. I also fulfilled a promise that I had made on St Paddy's Day to 9 (Ranger) Platoon when we were training in Oman back in March. I had said I would give them a bottle of Irish whiskey for an excellent platoon night attack they had conducted. I finally met my obligation to them when I handed over a bottle of malt that Bill Neely had given me. Whether part of 9 (Ranger) Platoon or Easy Company, all the Royal Irish soldiers who were attached to 3 PARA had been outstanding. Three of their men had been killed and the number of their wounded ran into double figures, but they never faltered and they had become a respected and integrated part of 3 PARA. Like the rest of the Battle Group team that was now breaking up, I was sad to see them go.

Command passed from 3 PARA to 42 Commando at midday on 6 October. I shook the hand of Matt Holmes their CO, wished him and his men luck and cast my eyes around the JOC for one last time. The report of a contact was already coming in over the radio as I walked towards the door. Had it occurred any earlier, it would have been our 499th engagement with the Taliban. I paused momentarily; it was someone else's show now and we were done.

Coming Home

The pitch of the engines changed as the pilot pushed forward the throttle, released the brakes and the C-130 gunned down the gravel strip to begin its take-off. As the aircraft climbed away from Bastion and headed towards Kabul, beams of bright sunlight shone through the portholes of the fuselage as if to cast a spotlight on to my thoughts. As the floor of the Helmand desert slipped away beneath us, I reflected on what my men had been through and what they had achieved. We had been sent to Afghanistan to bring security and to start reconstruction and development. The mission had been hailed as a peace support operation where it was hoped that we wouldn't fire a shot. But we had found ourselves in the middle of a vicious counter-insurgency and become engaged in an intensity of fighting that had not been experienced by the British Army since the Korean War in the 1950s.

We had fired nearly half a million rounds of ammunition, from machine-gun bullets to anti-tank missiles and high-explosive artillery shells. We had also dropped hundreds of bombs and killed hundreds of Taliban. It was a prolific rate of expenditure, but it reflected the fact that in combat only a very small percentage of bullets fired are actually effective. Even so I marvelled at the extraordinary number of rounds that need to be fired to kill one man. We had expected to do some fighting, but no one anticipated the amount of combat that unfolded. I reminded myself of the military maxim that no plan survives first contact on the ground. I was confident in the knowledge that we had adapted, overcome and had learned to live with the constants of scarce resources, uncertainty and risk. It is what the military does, not least as the battlefield is an inherently chaotic place where nothing goes to plan and everything is down to chance. Success became dependent on making some order out of that chaos. We tried to do it by identifying threats and opportunities and then defeating or exploiting them, by communicating orders to disparate subordinates and then trying to harness the necessary resources to deliver them. It wasn't easy, but then combat never is.

There is no doubt in my mind that our arrival had stirred up a hornet's nest in a province that many had considered quiet until then. But it was only quiet because the Taliban and the drug warlords had been allowed to hold ascendancy there. There was no rule of law, no government authority, and any 'peace' was due to the ruling tyranny and corruption of bandits and insurgents. Although no one ever said it to my face, some safe at home in the bureaucratic corridors of Whitehall later suggested that 3 PARA might have been overly aggressive in its approach. But they were not the ones shedding blood, sweat and tears in the service of their country. The Battle Group did not go looking for trouble. Anyone who thinks that we did has never been in sustained combat, has never risked their life on a daily basis, has never had to make what might possibly be the last call home to a loved one, has never had to pick up the body parts of one of their comrades or zip them into a body bag and has never spent the day covered in the blood of one of their men. My men were also bound by ROE and time and again they checked their fire at personal risk to themselves to avoid causing civilian casualties. Tragically, a small number of civilians were undoubtedly killed in the fighting. However, my soldiers also risked their lives to pick up and treat any locals whether hit by our fire or that of the Taliban, who showed no such compassion or restraint. But regardless of the tragedy that the fighting entailed, anyone who thought that the British were just going to walk into Helmand Province without being challenged was naive and no student of history.

I thought about what we had achieved by the contentious policy of holding so many district centres and the high price my soldiers had paid in holding them. We had gone to places such as Now Zad, Sangin, Kajaki and Musa Qaleh at the behest of the governor, who represented the Afghan government we had been sent to support. Their occupation had fixed us, stretched our limited resources to breaking point and meant that the risk of tactical failure had never been far away, especially if we had lost one of the helicopters that were so vital to sustaining them and getting out our casualties. But had they fallen, the front line of the insurgency would have been in places like Lashkar Gah and Gereshk where there was no fighting and the government held some sway. Holding the district centres also forced a battle of attrition on the Taliban, which they lost. They did not drive us out as they had claimed they would and their credibility in the eyes of the people was damaged in the process. As the ceasefires in Musa Qaleh and Sangin demonstrated, the traditional tribal elders were prepared to exercise their influence and turn away from those who intimidated them with violence. Conversely, the resolve of the UK's commitment to Helmand was demonstrated by the tenacious defence against a concerted onslaught of attacks. We did not win the war, we did not bring about peace or reconstruction, but the successful prosecution of counter-insurgency campaigns is a protracted business and the campaign in Afghanistan is likely to last for decades. Our achievement lay in the fact that we had fought a testing break in battle which permitted the UK to make its entry into Helmand and to set the conditions for subsequent British forces to build on.

The front-end nature of our operation and the reaction it provoked meant that our focus became fighting the Taliban. But I regretted that precious little development and reconstruction had been completed in areas where there had been no fighting, such as Gereshk. In the battle for the hearts and minds of the Afghan people, the limited opportunities that had existed to make a difference had not been seized. The incident of the failure to plumb in the washing machine in Gereshk's hospital, which later provoked a vigorous defence from DFID, was a case in point. But even if arguments for its non-installation, not advocated at the time, had some practical bearing, the complete failure of that one quick-impact project was symptomatic of the malaise and bureaucratic inertia of the whole development programme. Of the thirty other projects that we had identified, all of them lay un-actioned on the numerous forms we had submitted to the PRT. The failure of the development programme was highlighted by the withdrawal of the development civil servants from Lashkar Gah when their efforts were needed most and was typified by the comment from their department that they 'didn't do bricks and mortar'.

Lofty ideals of longer-term development of the instruments of modern government were all very well in a country that had some semblance of peace and a functioning bureaucracy, however corrupt and inefficient, that extended beyond the capital. In Afghanistan, where the writ of the government extends scarcely beyond the environs of Kabul, the people have little time for alien Western concepts of liberal democracy. They live in a society where bricks-and-mortar issues, of basic security, freedom from intimidation and economic betterment are what count. The Battle Group may have assisted in demonstrating Britain's commitment to Afghanistan and enabled some to turn their voices against the Taliban, but in the struggle for the will of its people I felt that we had probably left the majority of Helmand's population still sitting on the fence.

But as we journeyed north and the drab desert became broken by the rocky spines of the Hindu Kush, I reflected mostly on the blood we had expended and the performance of my people. I thought about the remarkable valour of simple men and what they had been through. Most soldiers spend their entire careers waiting to be tested in battle and many never get the chance. But it is one thing to go into combat once and quite another to do it on a sustained basis for months on end. The first battle during Operation Mutay at the beginning of June and the losses we subsequently suffered taught us to beware what every professional soldier wishes for. The casualties and the risks and privations my soldiers endured reinforced the fact that war is not a game. It is a bloody and brutal endeavour, where the price of participation is measured in the unlimited liability of life, limb and sorrow. However, my soldiers coped with shortages, the rigours of the stifling heat and austere living, hunger, prolonged sleep deprivation, the stress of constant risk and the loss of comrades. They went out on patrol again and again in the full knowledge that in places like Sangin they had a 75 per cent chance of being ambushed by the Taliban every time they went out. On occasion I saw real fear in men's eyes when I gave orders for a dangerous mission and I sometimes wondered whether they would be coming back from it. For those who went out, the issue of survival was not lost on them. They too often wondered if they would come back alive, what would happen to their families and whether they should write a last letter home. But the aircrews of the Chinooks, young officers, NCOs and Toms didn't falter. They kept on going out, stoically accepting that loss and risk are part of the business they are in.

For most of us, those six months in Helmand were both the best and the worst of times. When we took casualties, people became close, bonded and dealt with it. But people also got a buzz from doing the job that they had joined the Army to do. The morale and comradeship we enjoyed were exceptional. I saw people grow up and become men. Younger soldiers who might have been a disciplinary challenge to manage in barracks suddenly came into their own in battle.

Nor was there anything wrong with the brand-new blokes. Older generations tend to wonder what the youth of today are coming to. Soldiers are no exception, and senior men often claim that the new generation of recruits are not up to their standards. But despite the fact that new soldiers come from a youth culture marked by the wearing of hoodie tops and eschewing any sense of duty or respect for authority, such views are completely mistaken. Many of my soldiers were eighteen-year-olds fresh from training who came straight out to join us in Afghanistan. Young men like Private Hook who within hours of arriving in Bastion was flying up to Sangin with other new recruits and going straight into a contact. Hours later he was flying back again having been wounded, but he was still adamant that he was ready to return to the company he had only just joined earlier that day. His actions and attitude were a reflection of the other recruits who, with only six months of basic training, were punching well above their weight.

Finally, I reflected on the losses we had suffered and the strange fraternity that we had become. Based on a membership of tough selection, training, attitude and sense of our past, the ethos of 3 PARA had been strong before we had deployed to Helmand. But it had been re-forged in an even stronger metal of kinship through shared hardship and having triumphed in adversity, danger and collective grief. It was a sense of comradeship that binds men together and can only be born through the shared experience of battle. It extended beyond the battalion to the rest of the Battle Group where there was an inclusive membership, because regardless of parent regiment cap badge everyone was valued for bringing something to the table. It was bred from being part of an extraordinary sequence of events and an exceptional endeavour. For those of us in 3 PARA we also felt that we had walked out of the shadows of the exploits of our forebears at places like Arnhem, Suez and the Falklands and could now walk tall in the same light as them. It was a simple comradeship of arms that an outsider who has not lived through similar experiences finds difficult to understand. It was something that was brought home to us as the wheels of the aircraft thumped down on to the tarmac of Kabul airport, and we entered briefly into a very different environment from the one we had just left.

John Hardy and I spent two days waiting at Camp Souter for the RAF Tri-Star that would take us and C Company to Cyprus. It was dead time and it was a peculiar sensation suddenly to have nothing to do. I thought about going to see my old boss across the city in his ISAF headquarters, but David Richards had already been down to say goodbye to us in Bastion and I didn't want to intrude on his time. I also felt no inclination to be among NATO staff officers who drank coffee in their pleasant garden cafeteria, which would not have looked out of place on the King's Road and who got upset when someone suggested that the rabbits which populated the manicured lawns should be shot as vermin. I wandered around the small market set up in Camp Souter that sold imitation muskets and Afghan trinkets. But we hadn't been in Afghanistan on a holiday and I was not predisposed to buy anything. I sat with John Hardy and drank Coke as we watched the logisticians and headquarters staff who worked in the camp drink beer in the bar, play pool and try to chat up the female soldiers. It was a long way from the privations and dangers of northern Helmand.

There were rear-echelon soldiers at Bastion, but they were the medics who looked after our wounded, logisticians who loaded the cargo nets with ammunition at two o'clock in the morning, cooks who manned the sangars when we ran short of manpower and the aircraft technicians who worked through the night to keep aircraft serviceable. Many of them deployed out into the field to provide forward logistic support to the district centres and knew what it was like to be shot at. Even when not deployed, they seemed to be part of the team striving to do their best to make sure that the Battle Group got what it needed to conduct operations. In Kabul there was no stifling heat or dust and the level of risk was much reduced. But it was the difference in attitude that struck me most and I was not surprised to learn that the place had been nicknamed KIA Napa after the Club 18–30 resort. Those around us seemed to have little idea of what the troops in Helmand were going through and most seemed hardly to care.

It was just the same when we staged back through the international airport. Free from the officious logistics staff, who seemed to conspire to make our onward journey as tiresome as possible, we managed to spend a few hours in the bars and the shops behind the main terminal. They were frequented by European soldiers who strutted about in tailored combat fatigues, but who would never venture south to where the real fighting was taking place. I doubt that they could have pointed out on a map the locations of Helmand,

Kandahar and Zabol, where British, Canadian and American soldiers were dying. I watched the men of C Company who sat quietly drinking soft drinks; the RSM had wisely banned drinking alcohol until we reached Cyprus. They were understated, gaunt and, like the rest of us, all they wanted to do was to get home.

We flew via Cyprus, where each of the Battle Group's sub-units were to spend two days 'decompressing'. The original plan had been to spend a week on the island and I had been against it from the start. I knew how the blokes would receive the idea of spending a week of decompression in Cyprus on the way home. They would see it as an unnecessary delay in getting back to the UK and their loved ones. On hearing of the proposal, one Tom suggested that we should call it 'depression'. It was Ed Butler's idea and despite my reservations I knew that it had merit. Butler was drawing on his considerable previous operational experience and realized the importance of men having time to unwind from combat before seeing their families again and returning to normal life. My concerns were twofold. First, I considered a week too long and favoured a shorter in-and-out approach. Second, and of greater concern, I knew that if we were left subject to the vagaries of the RAF's ageing air transport fleet, we could expect to be there for considerably longer than envisaged.

I had discussed my concerns with Ed and also ran them past CGS when he came out to visit. Both were sympathetic. We agreed on a compromise of two days and the provision of a civilian charter aircraft to guarantee being flown out on time. This would allow the blokes to fly in, hand in their kit for laundering, undergo a mandatory stress briefing, hit the beach, get pissed, pick up a clean set of uniform and fly back to the UK the next day. Initial resistance to the civilian flight, by the ever helpful movers in PJHQ, was overcome when I indicated that I would be disappointed if I had to relay their reluctance to meet the requirement back to CGS. Needless to say, we got our chartered flight. In the end the whole thing worked like clockwork. The blokes arrived in Cyprus by midday, they were on the beach by two, the barbecue and beers were available by six and the fighting started by nine. People also got out on time the next day, albeit a little hung over and with the odd black eye.

I walked down the steps of the aircraft when we landed in Cyprus at midday to be met by the RAF station commander. He ushered me and a small number of my staff to the airfield's VIP suite where there was a bottle of champagne waiting for us. It was a kind gesture, but I felt a little awkward as the rest of the blokes trooped off to board coaches that would take them to Bloodhound Camp where their decompression would take place. The camp was an old training site. Situated on the southern tip of the island it was an isolated location and ideal for our needs, as we could be locked down away from the rest of the British military garrison and local inhabitants. The RSM and I drove down to join C Company for their barbecue later that evening. They had handed in their uniforms to the laundry, received a stress counselling briefing and had also managed to spend a few hours on the nearby beach. Now they were dressed in shorts and T-shirts and were drinking copious amounts of beer. They were on excellent form and I wanted to stay and get pissed with them. Prudently, John Hardy suggested it was time to leave after sharing a few beers with the Toms. I didn't want to go, I was enjoying myself and I sensed the real fun was about to start. I reluctantly climbed into the car with my RSM. He was of course right to suggest that we should leave C Company to get on with it and pointed out that it might not be the place for the CO to be.

We left just before it started. The format was roughly the same for all the companies. The chefs would pack up the barbecue and beat a hasty retreat as the first of the food started to sail through the air. Cans of beer then followed, as groups of soldiers grabbed upturned tables to protect themselves and began to return a volley fire of cans and food against their comrades. Company officers and NCOs joined in, and in some case led, the mêlée that erupted like a scene from a Wild West bar-room brawl. There was nothing malicious about it. Men who had not had a drink in months, but had become close through the stress of their recent front-line combat experiences, let off steam in a controlled environment. The companies were left to work it out of their system, although some of the biggest Regimental Police NCOs in the battalion were on hand to curb any wilder excesses and to arrange mini-buses to take the wounded to the nearby A and E to have a few cut heads stitched. When the fighting stopped, they cleared up the mess, resumed drinking and spoke about the battle of Bloodhound Camp they had just had. They also talked of their mates who were not with them, what they had been through and how they felt about it. It was a vital part of the process of coming to terms with their experiences and it was something that needed to happen before they got back to the UK.

The next day, people woke with hangovers, work parties made good the rest of the damage from the night before and people spent a last couple of hours on the beach before picking up their uniforms and heading back to the airport. Padre Richard Smith watched a young soldier laughing and joking with his mates in the surf. The last time he had seen him had been six weeks previously. Then he had spent time with him when he had been frozen in shock and was still covered in the blood of a friend who had been killed in the same vehicle as him.

The fact that Cyprus was such a success was down to the efforts of the staff officers at the headquarters of British Forces in Cyprus. They had been brilliant and laid on water sports and instructors to entertain the troops on the beach and transport to move us around the island. They also left us to our own devices behind the wire at Bloodhound Camp. We were well looked after and it made an important difference. The cabin crew of the civilian charter flight that flew us back to Stansted airport were equally helpful and made a welcome change from the indifference of the RAF flight attendants. They made a fuss of the soldiers and demonstrated a sense of understanding something of what we had experienced. I watched forks of lightning streak down from a leaden grey sky as our aircraft headed over the Mediterranean. A sudden jolt and the smell of burning caused a roar of nervous laughter and cheers as the aircraft was struck by one of the bolts of static energy. I joined in with the incongruous comments of how ironic it would be if, after all that we had been through, our aircraft was suddenly brought down by a lightning strike. However, we made it safely back to the UK and my mobile phone buzzed as I got off the plane in Stansted. In the last six months I had used it only once when back on R and R. I thought of how I hadn't missed it as I picked it up and pressed the button to answer it. It was a call from the media ops officer in 16 Brigade informing me that the Secretary of State and the press would be waiting to meet us when we got back to the barracks in Colchester.

It was the last thing I wanted as I jumped into the staff car with John Hardy and we headed down the A120. I thought about what I would say to the obvious questions I would be asked of what was it like and how did it feel to be back? Did people want to hear about the heat, the danger, the risks, the privations, the grief, the exhilaration, the relief and the fear? I was still wondering where the hell I would start as we pulled in through the gates of the barracks. A military media minder asked us to drive up to the battalion square where the press pack was waiting. We arrived just ahead of the coaches bringing the rest of the blokes to a barrage of cameras and popping flashes. Des Browne was there to greet me as I stepped out of the car. I noticed Karin waiting patiently a few metres behind him; she had been asked to wait while the Secretary of State and the press got their photo opportunity of him welcoming me back. I managed to get in a brief hug with Karin before journalists thrust microphones and lenses in my face and the bombardment of anticipated questions started. I looked over my shoulder and saw the blokes file off the buses. Children and wives rushed to greet their loved ones and small bundles of joy were lifted aloft by their fathers. Although an important part of our return, we could have done without the press scrum, but at least we were home.

Fighting the Peace

I walked round to the side of the bed where Captain Jim Berry could see me with his remaining eye. His head recently shaved, his lack of hair revealed the angry scar of the surgeon's knife that had worked to repair the damage caused by the grenade splinter that had penetrated his brain. Unable to speak because of the tube inserted into his neck, Jim communicated with the aid of a spell card. His fingers drifted over the gridded letters; I asked him to repeat what he was trying to spell, but still couldn't get the meaning of it on his second attempt. His male nurse saw my plight and registered my discomfort at not being able to understand what he was trying to say. Jim spelled his message again and the nurse translated for me: 'Jim says that he is okay, it's good to see you and that he is going to Headley Court.' That short, simple message made my day, as I cast my mind back to the last operation in Sangin when Jim struggled for his life on a stretcher by the LZ and I wondered whether he was going to make it.

With the rest of the battalion on leave, I had spent the time visiting members of the Battle Group whose wounds had brought them home before the rest of us returned. Some of the conditions at Selly Oak had improved since my last visit and there was a noticeable increase in the presence of military medical staff on Ward S4. But not everything had improved. Although S4 was conceived as a dedicated military ward of the larger general hospital, it remained staffed by NHS nurses and civilian patients were still being treated there. One of the wounded told me how he had to listen to an elderly woman scream through the night for her husband as he lay in the darkness wondering whether he would ever walk again. Some of the NHS staff continued to display a marked ignorance of what men wounded in combat had been through.

For Stu Hale, waking up in Selly Oak was almost as traumatic as stepping on the mine in Kajaki. Having been kept sedated since leaving Bastion, he could still feel his right leg. He was unaware of the full extent of his injuries and thought that he had lost only his foot. After coming round in the unfamiliar environment of S4 an NHS care assistant told him to turn over as she wanted to clean him. Hale told her that he didn't want to as he was unsure of how badly hurt he was. In response she simply ripped back the sheets to show him what remained of his right leg; it was the first time he realized that it had been amputated above the knee. Men like Stu Hale and Sergeant Paddy Caldwell deserved better.

Paddy spoke in short rasping breaths when I saw him. He struggled to articulate his words through the ventilator tube in his throat; the Taliban bullet that had exited through his neck had not only taken away the use of his limbs, but also meant that he was no longer able to breathe for himself. He was pitifully thin. His once muscular chest was now emaciated and shallow; it rose and fell weakly in rhythm with the machine that was keeping him alive. 'I regret nothing, sir,' he said. 'I would do it all again if given the chance.' I looked across Paddy to the attractive blonde on his opposite side. Given her attentive nature, I had initially presumed that she was a nurse. However, Mel was Paddy's girlfriend. She had given up her job and the house she rented in Colchester to be constantly at his side since his arrival in Birmingham. Mel had to badger the nurses to change Paddy's urine bags or evacuate his bowels. If they didn't do it, she did it herself, unable to bear seeing the man she loved lying in such a state. Mel didn't really blame the nurses, they were simply too busy and there were never enough of them.

Stu Pearson didn't need a ventilator, but I was fascinated by the small vacuum pump that was attached to the badly damaged tissue of his right leg. Stu talked about Kajaki, the decisions he had made and the chances of success of the vacuum therapy which would determine whether he would keep his remaining leg or whether it would have to be amputated like his left. On his arrival at Birmingham the surgeons were 90 per cent certain that he would lose the other leg. But the small vacuum pump that sucked air and fluid out of his wounds was having a dramatic effect. Deprived of oxygen, Stu's body was encouraged to pump more blood to the damaged tissue. Within days, small spots of flesh began to grow back on what had once been just bone and tendons. Within a week the pink dots had joined up to cover the tendons and facilitate a healing process that meant he would keep his remaining leg. It was testimony to the professionalism of the surgeons in both Birmingham and Bastion but their clinical expertise stood in stark contrast to the general level of post-surgery care the wounded received in Ward S4.

Visiting the wounded on returning from Afghanistan was an experience of mixed emotions. I remained distressed by their suffering and the incidents of sub-optimal treatment that still prevailed. But I was also humbled by their courage and absolute lack of self-pity. Jim Berry was the last of the wounded I visited that day. After seeing Jim I picked up Karin who had been waiting patiently in the corridor. She read me like a book and neither of us spoke as we walked to the car in the gathering darkness of the hospital's grounds. She left me alone with my thoughts as we headed north to meet the families of those men who hadn't managed to pull through.

The Wrights lived in the suburbs of Edinburgh. Scotland's capital city was in the grip of late autumn, the leaves were thick on the ground and the first chill of the coming winter was already in the air; a far cry from the desert heat of Afghanistan. As I walked up the garden path I knew that I didn't want to knock on the door. I was met by Major Gordon Muirhead, a regimental officer who had been appointed as the Casualty Visiting Officer to Mark Wright's family. I was glad that it was Gordon who opened the door. I had been dreading what my first few words might be had it been either of Mark's parents. Gordon ushered me into a neat front room where I was introduced to Bobby and Jem Wright and Gillian, Mark's fiancée. The couple had been due to marry the following month; now the wedding would never take place. Gordon Muirhead had been with the Wright family night and day since they had been given the tragic news that their beloved only son had been killed in the gully beneath the ridge at Kajaki. Gordon managed to keep the conversation light until we sat down for dinner. As the meal drew to a close, I looked at Gordon before asking if the Wrights wished me to talk about the circumstances of Mark's death. As I recounted the events of the day of days, Jem left the table. I looked at Bobby but he asked me to continue, telling me that Jem would still be listening from the front room. When I finished Mark's mother returned. Jem stood looking at me, her hands on the back of a chair as tears rolled down her cheeks. In a faltering voice, she told me that Mark had always wanted to be a paratrooper and knew the risk that went with the job of being a soldier. But she also told me that the son they had waited nine years to have was their life and now he was gone.

Edinburgh was followed by Newcastle, where I explained to Jacko's father that his son hadn't died in vain. Danny Jackson talked of the futility of 'Blair's wars' and I talked of the unlimited liability of being a soldier and that his son wouldn't have wanted to be anywhere else except fighting with his comrades in 3 PARA. The next stage of my journey took me to a new housing estate on the edge of the garrison town of Catterick. The new houses looked oddly out of place in comparison to the dilapidated condition of the surrounding dwellings that made up the rest of the Army estate. I parked my car opposite one of the new houses and wondered whether Lorena Budd was watching my arrival. At least she would be expecting me, unlike the men in suits who she had watched pull up outside the Budd residence two months previously. Then they had come to tell her of her husband's death; then she had been pregnant with their second daughter. We sat in the living room and Lorena spoke of how she was coping with two young children: one who would never see her father again and her newborn daughter who would never have the chance to meet him.

Those killed or injured by bullets and shrapnel were the obvious casualties of the Battle Group. But there were also some who suffered from the more invisible scars of war. I do not believe that there was anyone who was untouched by their time in Afghanistan. The abnormality of combat had become the familiar and routine; on our return the converse was true. As we readjusted to the everyday normality of life in the UK, peacetime society seemed peculiarly alien. Initially I marvelled at life's simple pleasures and sights. People going about their daily business, shopping, commuting to work or pushing their children along crowded high streets without fear for their security: all seemed incongruous compared to our recent experiences. At first I felt strangely naked without my pistol and the focus of a life that revolved round taking risk, making life-or-death decisions and having my kit packed ready for an instant deployment on the back of a Chinook. While nothing at home had changed, what we had been through was a life-forming event and for many of us the experience skewed our immediate world view. Our partners and families recognized the difference in us during the first few months; perhaps a slight edge to a relationship, preoccupation or hyper-arousal to certain smells and sounds, particularly a car back-firing or a door slamming. For most of us the process of normalization took several weeks. It was assisted by the initial decompression in Cyprus and an immediate period spent at work in barracks before heading off on leave. Public reflection was also an important aspect of coming to terms with what we had been through. A memorial service for the dead involving the families and veterans of previous 3 PARA battles and the presentation of campaign medals by the Prince of Wales all played their part. However, for some, the traumatic events of Helmand Province were embedded too deeply in their memory and they began to show symptoms of Post-Traumatic Stress Disorder (PTSD).

Once described as shell shock, PTSD is an extremely complex subject. In simple terms it is an invisible injury of the mind when traumatic experiences remain trapped in a person's memory. Recurring flashbacks, vivid dreams, aggression and dysfunctional behaviour at work and within relationships are some of the main symptoms. To some extent PTSD is the brain's natural reaction to having witnessed life-threatening incidents and/or intense fear and horror. It can affect people differently and it is hard to assess who will suffer and who will remain unscathed. Many people experienced some of the milder symptoms on first returning from Afghanistan, but for most these abated within several weeks. But for a few of my soldiers, returning to a normal life brought no relief and we found ourselves having to address a problem that the military system at large was surprisingly unprepared to deal with. The situation was not helped by the fact that men who are paratroopers have a marked reluctance to let anyone know that they have a problem. We encouraged a culture of openness and understanding, which was helped by the closeness of the relationship between the Toms, SNCOs and officers in the battalion. I was adamant that there should be no stigma attached to it and had numerous discussions with several young soldiers who were profoundly affected by their experiences.

For one young Tom PTSD manifested itself in violence against family members and even complete strangers. It could be set off by the smallest thing: a domestic argument or a minor roadside altercation. In his case he did not throw the first punch, but when faced with a road rage incident during his leave he finished it viciously. With no previous history of violence, he knew he had a problem. His relationships with his girlfriend and family began to break down, he felt short-fused and unable to control his aggression. The soldier concerned sought help and was referred to the military's Department of Community and Mental Health.

However, several of the Toms undergoing psychiatric treatment found it difficult to relate to therapists who had not shared their experiences. Over a fag and a brew, one of them asked me how they could possibly understand what he had been through when the clinician he was seeing had never flown into the Sangin Valley or seen his best mate being killed. Another was sent for treatment at a local branch of the Priory. When I went to visit him I didn't doubt that the centre was doing its best for him, but I couldn't help wondering what a young man who had risked life and limb for his country could have in common with the civilian patients. No doubt professional psychiatric treatment had a positive role to play in helping the relatively few cases of PTSD that we experienced. However, in the opinion of those who suffered, the best form of succour came from being among their mates who were the one body of people who could truly understand what they had lived through.

Within three months of returning from Afghanistan the majority of the battalion's wounded had returned to work at 3 PARA or their parent units. The more seriously wounded continued to receive specialist inpatient care. Corporals Hale and Pearson left Selly Oak and moved to the Defence Medical Rehabilitation Centre at Headley Court near Epsom in Surrey. Located in 85 acres of landscaped gardens, Headley Court is an old converted Elizabethan manor house purchased by the RAF after the Second World War to rehabilitate injured and seriously ill service personnel. The centre is equipped with a hydrotherapy pool, gyms and a prosthetics department with a focus on rehabilitating amputees and individuals with acquired brain and spinal injuries. Drinking tea with Stu Hale and Stu Pearson one afternoon in the centre's refectory, I was struck by the fact that the place was working to its full capacity teaching broken young men to walk on prosthetic limbs and cope with the impact of serious head or back injuries. Designed to accommodate sixty-six patients, every bed space was occupied as the centre sought to deal with numerous casualties from Afghanistan and Iraq; the staff at Headley Court were doing an excellent job but they were clearly stretched.

On 11 January 2007 Paddy Caldwell moved to a specialist NHS spinal unit in Stanmore near London. Suffering from the second case of MRSA he had picked up in Selly Oak, he was put straight into isolation. The care he received at Stanmore was excellent and stood in stark contrast to the treatment he had received on Ward S4 where he had also caught pneumonia. Most importantly, the nursing staff began to educate him about coping with the injury caused by the bullet that had left him paralysed from the shoulders down. Moving to Stanmore meant that Paddy could start to look to a future beyond being confined to a hospital bed. However, the injured would first have to overcome a system that focused on discharging badly wounded servicemen. I was determined that people like Paddy should not be discharged; we were the ones who had broken men like him and I believed that we had a moral responsibility to look after them. Fortunately, it was a sentiment shared by the senior officers in the Army. However, aftercare of wounded soldiers was still orientated around a peacetime structure and was simply not geared up to deal with the level of casualties that were now being sustained routinely in places like Afghanistan and Iraq. Consequently, getting what was right for the long-term wounded had to be driven by myself and Sergeant Major 'Fez' Ferrier, the 3 PARA Welfare Officer and it was a constant struggle.

The first hurdle was convincing the policymakers to issue a dispensation to provide quarters for Paddy and Mel to live in because they weren't married. After a succession of letters, e-mails and telephone calls, it was eventually agreed that the Army would house them when Paddy left hospital in April. Fez Ferrier gained authorization for them to move temporarily into small, cramped quarters until a larger house could be converted to accommodate Paddy's disabilities. In the meantime Stanmore arranged for Paddy to take a number of weekend exeats. However, after spending six months in hospital, the first planned weekend was very nearly cancelled. There was no established system in place to cover the costs of transport, equipment and aftercare once a patient had left hospital, so no one was prepared to fund the £900 to pay for a carer to look after him for the weekend. The money was eventually found, but only after I had produced a cheque from my own bank account to cover the costs, which I think shamed someone into action.

Paddy and Mel eventually moved into the temporary quarters, but the planned conversion of a larger house stretched from two months into five due to numerous bureaucratic delays in authorizing and completing the necessary work. It meant Paddy was confined to living in the front room of their shabby temporary house. He was unable to take a shower or share a bed with his fiancée. It took hours for his carer to get Paddy up and dressed each morning and meant Mel was confined to her bedroom while the daily procedure of ablutions and dressing were completed, or if his urine bag happened to leak. Understandably, they were both visibly distressed and I promised once again to do my utmost to get things moving. After months of infections and tardy treatment in Selly Oak, this was the last thing they needed and it was beginning to put severe strain on their relationship. After having had to explain yet another delay to them for the fifth time, I had had enough of the system. I returned to my office and got on the phone to the welfare people for the umpteenth time. I warned them that if they didn't finally get this sorted there was a chance that the issue might get into the press, which prompted someone to pull their finger out and resolve the delay.

The next day I read a newspaper article in which the MOD claimed that the Military Covenant regarding the nation's moral obligation to look after its soldiers in return for risking life and limb to serve their country was not broken. I doubt whether the Whitehall mandarin who had made the statement had ever visited Paddy or people like Bombardier Ben Parkinson. Ben was the most badly injured of the forty-six men who had been wounded in Helmand. Since the break-up of the Battle Group at the end of the operation he had been looked after by his parent regiment. They, like us, struggled to get what was right for Ben and his family. The mine that Ben's WMIK hit cost him both legs, as well as causing serious internal injuries and brain damage. However, the MOD compensation figure he was awarded was derisory. It was significantly less than the £450,000 awarded to an RAF civilian typist who had sustained a repetitive strain injury to a thumb from using a computer. The MOD's defence of its compensation payments was based on the fact than men like Paddy Caldwell would receive war pensions as well as a lump sum payment. But it was a defence that ignored the full extent of the sacrifice men like them had made. The military career opportunities once open to them were over and so were the job opportunities that would once have been available to them outside the Army. Their plight was not lost on men like generals Richard Dannatt and David Richards who were doing their best behind the scenes to support them. However, they faced an uphill struggle with government officials and ministers who had little understanding of what it meant to risk all for the service of their nation.

Facing a poorly structured and under-resourced welfare system, 3 PARA set up its own charity called the Afghan Trust. The trust set out a charter of obligations for looking after those members of the battalion who had served in Afghanistan. The focus of the trust was to raise money to help look after the long-term wounded and the next of kin of those who lost their lives fighting in Helmand. Funds were generated through sponsored events, such as a charity freefall parachute jump with the Parachute Regiment's Red Devils display team. Sponsored jumpers included Karin, Mark Wright's mother Jem and his fiancée Gillian. Stu Pearson also participated, making his first parachute jump since losing his leg. A later jump with the Red Devils was also made by the Bishop of York which raised £50,000. We gave a number of charity presentations on 3 PARA's tour in the City and at the Chelsea Pensioners' Hospital in London which raised significant amounts of money. Among other things, the fund helped pay for Paddy Caldwell's mobility vehicle, the conversion of a wounded officer's car and donated money to a separate trust fund set up for Bryan Budd's children.

The Afghan Trust was indicative of the fact that a vast proportion of welfare costs for injured servicemen are met by charities rather than through official funding. As well as having our own charity we also drew heavily on the support of the larger service charities, such as the Army Benevolent Fund, which was outstanding in the help that it gave to Paddy Caldwell.

Having to set up the Afghan Trust said much about the existence of a strange dichotomy that exists in the way this nation treats and regards its armed forces. On the one hand I was heartened and impressed by some of the responses we received from members of the public when they found out about what soldiers were going through in Afghanistan and the plight of the injured. Two articles in the *Daily Telegraph* about 3 PARA's wounded generated over £20,000 in donations sent in by concerned readers. Prompted by Ben Parkinson's story, other members of the public set up the Help for Heroes charity to raise millions of pounds to pay for a proper full-length swimming pool at Headley Court.

However, the remarkable outpouring of support contrasted starkly with acts of sheer ignorance and prejudice. Eight months after returning from Afghanistan, my soldiers were still being barred from nightclubs in Colchester on the basis that they were 'squaddies'. One night in July, members of 1 Platoon were turned away from a club. When they explained that they were out to mark the anniversary of Damien Jackson's death in Sangin, the bouncer told them to take their sob stories elsewhere. That same summer, eighty-three residents in a quiet leafy suburb in Leatherhead attempted to block a charity's attempts to buy a house in their street. The house was to be converted for use as accommodation for families visiting soldiers undergoing treatment at Headley Court, but the local residents feared that it would reduce the value of their own homes. In November, reports appeared in the press that mothers at Leatherhead's public swimming pool harangued injured servicemen from the centre who were using the pool to complete a rehabilitation session. Apparently, they complained that the wounded men had not paid to use the pool and the sight of their missing limbs was scaring their children.

Despite the tribulations of returning from Afghanistan, morale in the battalion remained sky-high and revealed the paradox of soldiering. Our experiences had taught us that there is no glamour in war and that it is a hard, dirty and brutal business. But at the same time people had enjoyed the exhilaration of being tested and the euphoria of success. It was something that bound us even more closely together than before, as the fraternity of being a band of brothers was reinforced by the experience of shared endeavour, adversity and collective grief. Modern conflicts are often described as essentially being a company commanders' or a section commanders' war, but the six months that we spent in Helmand defied definition by a particular level of participant. It was everybody's war: every rank and professional trade came under fire and exchanged rounds with the enemy. It bred a corporate sense of group confidence and self-assurance that those who had not been part of a similar event would never completely understand. But it was still evident to outsiders; after visiting the battalion one senior officer remarked how he had seen the light of battle in the eyes of the men that he had spoken to.

I noticed it most when members of 3 PARA went to Buckingham Palace to receive their share of the thirty-two gallantry medals that had been awarded to the Battle Group. We made it a battalion and family event for all the recipients. Regardless of rank we collected in the officers' mess of a nearby barracks, walked to the Palace together and returned there afterwards for lunch. I felt immense pride as the sovereign presented gallantry crosses and medals to the likes of Hugo Farmer, Giles Timms, Paddy Blair, Stu Giles, Stu Pearson, Karl Jackson and Pete McKinley. I also noticed how 3 PARA drew the awe and appreciation of scores of other civilians and military who were being invested as part of the New Year's Honours List. It was a moving day, but tinged with sadness at the absence of two men who had not lived to receive the nation's two highest decorations for gallantry. Corporal Bryan Budd's Victoria Cross, awarded for his gallant lone charge against the Taliban, was collected by his widow, Lorena. Mark Wright's parents and his fiancée made the long trip from Scotland to receive the George Cross awarded to Corporal Mark Wright, who had lost his life at Kajaki so that others might live. Both medals were invested in a private audience with the Queen.

The reputation and sense of collective identity of 3 PARA also had a tangible effect on the new members of the battalion who were keen to prove themselves, and the opportunity to do so would not be far away. Within months of their coming home rumours began to circulate that 3 PARA would be returning to Afghanistan in early 2008. When it was confirmed that we would redeploy with the rest of 16 Air Assault Brigade I was unsure how the battalion would take the news. However, when the official announcement came I noted a perceptible enthusiasm among all those who I spoke to and my mind turned to preparing the battalion to return to war. As the summer of 2007 drew to a close the battalion's retraining was well under way. We had become rusty and the NCOs worked hard at reinforcing the important basics that bitter experience had taught us would keep people alive in combat. The new recruits to 3 PARA made great progress under the direction of their commanders and the more experienced Toms and I marvelled at the high turnover of young soldiers in the rifle companies. Many of those who had served in Afghanistan had been promoted, joined the senior support or D companies, and a few had since left the Army. Taking a straw poll of one of A Company's platoons at the end of a live firing exercise in Wales, I noted that only 25 per cent of the Toms had served in Afghanistan.

I was also aware of fundamental changes in the way in which we were allowed to conduct training. Our deployment had been a unique theatre-entry operation. We were part of the first task force into Helmand and there had been no rule book. We adapted and adjusted to circumstances as we found them on the ground.

By the end of 2007 three other larger brigades had served in Helmand and the red tape surrounding the conduct of operations had grown significantly and a different approach to risk was being enforced. Heavy body armour and standard-issue infantry helmets became compulsory and we were not allowed to train wearing the lighter armour and Para helmets we had previously worn. The standard-issue kit offered better ballistic protection, but it was heavy, ill-fitting and impeded mobility. Troops couldn't adopt proper fire positions wearing it, and it also slowed them down and reduced their endurance: all critical factors in avoiding enemy fire and killing your opponent before he can kill you. However, the policymakers were adamant that we should wear it and banned soldiers from wearing lighter improved ballistic protection even though they were prepared to buy it themselves. The MOD was also unwilling to provide small sonic earplugs to protect my men's hearing from the high-frequency deafness caused by gunfire. Many of them had already suffered irreparable damage in Afghanistan where mortars, RPG blasts and the hammering of machine guns had stripped away their hearing. The system claimed that they should have been wearing the large cumbersome issued ear 'muff' protectors that made wearing a helmet or hearing a radio order impossible. As a result many would be medically downgraded, some risked being medically discharged and all would suffer significantly in later life. The issue of provisioning inexpensive but appropriate ear defence was only addressed in early 2009.

There was a severe shortage too of critical equipment to train on. The battalion had deployed to Helmand with thirty-two WMIKs, the work-horse vehicle of the Battle Group, but all of them had been left behind in Afghanistan. All the battalion's heavy machine guns and night-vision goggles had to be handed over to the receiving unit too. After continual lobbying for WMIKs to train with, two were provided for a two-week period in September to train thirty-odd crews. Eventually, we overcame bureaucratic health and safety concerns and were allowed to adapt some of the battalion's general standard Land-Rovers which shared the same chassis and enabled us to simulate some of the WMIK driver training. It was a skewed approach to risk-taking considering that the MOD was prepared to accept the implications of equipment shortages and send undermanned units into combat, but at the same time it was reluctant to allow commanders the latitude to come up with prudent alternative training methods or allow people to wear decent kit which we already had or they were prepared to buy themselves.

I would not be going back to Afghanistan with the battalion, as I had been selected for promotion and would relinquish command of the battalion in November. But I was sufficiently concerned about the approach to training to raise it publicly with CGS at a conference he held for his commanding officers three weeks before I handed over as CO of 3 PARA.

I stood up among the audience and asked the first question after CGS had finished speaking. I reiterated the things that bothered both me and my soldiers most: the poor treatment of the wounded, the poor accommodation for our families and the lack of decent pay. But I emphasized that what particularly angered them was the complete lack of proper equipment to train with prior to imminent operations in Afghanistan. I made the comment that CGS had put a rather 'positive spin' on his overview of the Army's current equipment programme. I acknowledged that some better equipment was being made available for operations, yet hardly any of it was available for training. Use of the word spin provoked an angry response. I stood my ground, making the point that I was not making a pejorative accusation, but that 'the kit my men didn't have to train on today could result in some of them being killed tomorrow.' CGS's evident irritation with my question wasn't really remarkable given that he already understood the concerns and had taken personal career damage in speaking out publicly about the Army's lack of resources. No doubt he felt as frustrated as I did. But what was remarkable was that none of the other sixty-odd regular commanding officers then asked one question about kit or concerns that they had. No doubt they saw me making a bad career move in attracting the head of the Army's chagrin.

Little did they know that my resignation letter was already typed and was lying on my desk waiting for my signature when I got back to Colchester. I signed the letter the next morning. My reasons for bringing to an end twenty years as a soldier were many and varied. Although I had been selected for promotion and told I would progress further, I knew there was nothing else in the Army that came close to rivalling command of 3 PARA. In both peace and war my experience of being their commanding officer had been exceptional, but it was about to end and the closeness I had enjoyed with soldiers since being a twenty-one-year-old platoon commander was over. Continual cost-cutting and underfunding resulting in shortages of equipment for operations and training and the poor treatment of my wounded had also severely damaged my moral component of being a soldier. Consequently, I was less than sure that progression into the more senior ranks, which seemed to have become increasingly focused on managing the decline of the Army, was what I really wanted.

In the wake of 3 PARA's experiences in Afghanistan and those of other units that followed us, I had also begun to reflect deeply on the level of rewards service personnel received for the risks they took. As well as being poorly looked after when injured, soldiers earn less than the minimum wage, much of their accommodation is sub-standard and their families fare little better. The housing estate my soldiers lived on was one of the worst I had seen. The houses were small and many were in a poor state of repair. The maintenance contract for the upkeep of the houses was subcontracted out and the support the contractors provided was routinely described as woeful. One wife had to wait for months for a boiler to be fixed despite having a small child. Another once told me how she had lived among rats whose urine ran down the walls. Her situation was not deemed an emergency and in the end she had to elicit the help of her husband's fellow paratroopers to come and chase the rodents out.

These problems are compounded by the long absences of partners on operations or training and the fact that wives have to follow husbands when they move postings. As a result, the families were often last in the queue when it came to accessing local public services, such as an appointment with a doctor or a place on the waiting list of a decent school. Soldiers enjoy going on demanding operations and accept risk and loss as part of the business that they are in; retention rates actually improved in the wake of Afghanistan. But I also began to note that an increasing number of soldiers with families were leaving. To a man, they loved the regiment but the stress it was putting on their families was starting to tell and the fundamental problem was that there was little in it for those who kept the home fires burning.

I summed up my concerns surrounding my decision to resign in a personal letter to my brigade commander. I knew I was crossing the Rubicon in writing it, but had no idea of the storm that was about to break. The contents of that personal letter were leaked to the press, and there was a strong rumour that it had occurred at senior levels within the MOD. My resignation appeared as a headline story in a tabloid paper three days later, then featured in all the other national newspapers and on TV. The story ran in the media for most of the next week as it chimed with a leaked report on morale in the Army and public criticisms of the government's handling of defence spending by former military chiefs in the House of Lords. I was genuinely staggered at the interest it generated, although it was unwanted attention as I was focused on handing over command of the battalion. It made for a difficult few days, as I fended off the press and tried to get the MOD press office to come up with some more meaningful and proactive lines, other than the ones that had only succeeded in giving away my private address to the press and dragging Karin into the story.

The battalion was enormously supportive. Informed by the MOD press office that there was likely to be a leak thirty-six hours before the first article appeared, I had decided to speak to the battalion before they read it for themselves in the papers. In outlining my reasons for leaving, I majored on the fact that career progression meant that I could no longer be one of them. They took the point that if I had more 3 PARA time left in me I would not have been resigning. The best thing that anyone said to me during that whole period was when a young Tom came up to me and said: 'Sir, the blokes think what you have done has shown real bollocks and is mega.'

Seven days later I spoke to the collective body of 3 PARA again for the last time. They formed up in the same place where I had first spoken to them when I took over command. It was an enormous effort to hold RSM John Hardy's gaze as he called up the battalion to attention and reported them present and correct to me for the last time. I spoke of all that they had achieved. I told them that they should be rightly proud, that they were of the same stock as the men of Arnhem and Longdon and that they should walk tall and never forget who they were. I also thanked them for all that they had done, the sacrifices they and their families had made and the difficulties they had faced and overcome. I wished them every success on the next tour and started to tell them that my only regret was that I would not be returning to Afghanistan with them; then I faltered, and looked at the ground. They had been my life and soul for the past two years and I was acutely aware that within a few hours they would have a new commanding officer. I forced myself to breathe over a constricting lump in my throat and looked them in the eye for the final time. I took in a deep breath and said that I would look forward to hearing about their future exploits with pride and I hoped one day to see them again on the ground. I turned to return John Hardy's final salute, although this time I couldn't hold his gaze: I turned to my right and headed back to battalion headquarters to clear my desk.

The emotional farewell in Colchester was not to be the last time I saw the battalion before leaving the Army. I completed six months of the post I had been promoted into before becoming a civilian and was charged with delivering the final training exercise for 16 Brigade's deployment back to Afghanistan. One crisp winter's morning in 2008 I was up visiting the brigade training on Salisbury Plain. It was good to be out of my shared broom-cupboard of an office, where the phone didn't work and my aged computer seemed to be continually on the blink. It was obvious who the group of soldiers were by the side of the road as I rounded the corner. Their distinctive appearance, different to others, radiated a sense of professional self-confidence of a body of men who know who they are and what they are about. I saw all this before I registered the distinctive green DZ flash and began to recognize faces. Corporal Stock waved enthusiastically and I stopped for a chat. It was good to be among 3 PARA again, albeit briefly. Although now a newly promoted full colonel, it was the best thing that had happened to me since leaving the battalion back in November. But it was also hard. They were training to go back to Afghanistan and I would not be going with them. They weren't mine any more and now rightly belonged to someone else. I knew that they were in good heart and good hands, but it was still something akin to seeing an old friend sleeping with your ex-wife.

I came across 3 PARA once more before I finally left the Army three months later. I heard the distinctive clatter of the twin-headed rotor blades of a helicopter and the voice of the reporter straining to be heard over the scream of the engines as I listened to my car radio. I heard him mention that he was on the back of a CH-47 with men of 3 PARA flying into an operation during their second tour in Afghanistan. I imagined the blokes in the back, tooled up and ready for action; feeling the lurch of the aircraft as it made its final approach. I thought of the tightening of their bellies as they readied themselves for combat. I was driving along the A303 on my way to my last day of work in the Army, but for a brief moment I was back in Afghanistan with 3 PARA. At the end of the report, I stopped the car on the edge of the road near the ancient stones of Stonehenge. There was a slight spring breeze in the air. As I lit a cigarette I watched the smoke curl over my right arm and cross my winged parachute badge and emerald-green DZ flash of my Para jump smock. Badges I had worn with immense pride for the last two and a half years, but which I would take off for ever at the end of the day. I thought of what it is to have once been a soldier. But mostly I thought of 3 PARA, the blokes, Afghanistan and the men we had lost.

Epilogue

Jim Berry continued to make a miraculous recovery and the last time I saw him he had rejoined his unit. Although suffering from some of the effects of the shrapnel wound to his arm, Captain Guy Lock also continued to serve in the Army, as did Fusilier Andy Barlow and Corporal Stu Pearson, despite having each lost a leg at Kajaki. Sergeant Paddy Caldwell still lives in his converted quarters with Mel, but is adamant that he will not marry her until he has recovered sufficient use of his limbs to stand at the altar. In between intensive physiotherapy sessions to help him realize his goal, he commutes the short distance from his home in his motorized wheelchair to work at the 3 PARA Families Office. Trooper Martyn Compton survived the horrific burns he received in the Household Cavalry ambush to marry the girl he left behind when he went to Afghanistan. The spirit and determination of the severely wounded are a remarkable testimony to those for whom the war they fought in Afghanistan will go on for ever. But for one the hardest hill he would have to climb would be back in Afghanistan.

The last time that Lance Corporal Stu Hale had clambered to the top of the Kajaki ridge he had two legs, but now he climbed with only one. His bandaged stump chafed against the plastic cup of the artificial limb as he laboured with each step. Unable to put his full weight on the bent prosthetic, he had to half hop and half drag it across the steep rocky ground. His mind had been numb as he flew back into the dam area on the back of the Chinook, but as he struggled upwards the recollections of the sniper patrol he led from the ridge two years earlier came flooding back. The dramatic relief of the high ground above the aqua-blue lake that fed the Helmand River began to unlock memories that had been blocked by the trauma of losing his leg and the long road to recovery. He remembered the feeling of dread and isolation after stepping on the mine as he waited for help to reach him and the Black Hawk helicopter that took an age to come. Cresting the top of the ridge he looked down to where the bloody events of that day of days had cost the life of Mark Wright and seriously wounded five other men. He saw Stu Pearson's webbing still lying where it had been discarded after he too stepped on a mine.

But while the debris of that fateful day lay undisturbed, much had changed. Kajaki now had a complete company of soldiers stationed there and the dam had new turbines that 3 PARA had helped to deliver in the last few days of its second tour of duty in September 2008. Where 3 PARA had once operated as a single Battle Group, there were now four British units in Helmand as part of a total force of 8,300 British soldiers. It was a different tour with a different emphasis to the crazy times of the summer of 2006; 3 PARA had operated from Kandahar and, although involved in many engagements, this time they would be bringing all the boys back home again.

Each of the succeeding units had been given more troops and more sophisticated equipment to develop the foundations of the campaign in Afghanistan that 3 PARA laid down. The additional resources had made an impact. Frontal attacks against the district centres in places like Sangin and Musa Qaleh were now a thing of the past. Musa Qaleh had fallen to the Taliban a few months after Easy Company had left. The Taliban had strung up some of the tribal leaders who had negotiated with Adam Jowett, but the town was retaken by British and Afghan forces in December 2007. Like Sangin it is now secured with significantly more troops than the undermanned companies we had available. But while the intense stand-up firefights and mortar bombardments may have ended, they have been replaced by a more frequent use of roadside bombs and suicide bombers. There has been no corresponding increase in helicopters to match the growth in troop numbers, forcing a greater reliance on the use of vehicles which the insurgents have exploited to lethal effect, and Helmand Province remains a deadly place. Over 100 British service personnel have lost their lives since 3 PARA's first tour ended. During the second 16 Air Assault Brigade tour it was the regiment's sister battalion 2 PARA that took the brunt of the casualties, losing fourteen soldiers killed in action with over fifty wounded.

Attitudes to the campaign have also changed. Some senior commanders now talk of unwinnable wars when ours never did. Despite the increase in the number of troops, the insurgency has continued to escalate in the southern and eastern provinces and security in Kabul has deteriorated significantly. However, the war is winnable and it is vitally important that NATO is not allowed to fail in bringing stability to Afghanistan. It is the cradle of 9/11 and remains intrinsically linked to the security of the international community at large. If extremists are not denied ungoverned spaces to operate from in places like Helmand, there will be an appreciable increase in the risk from those who wish to export terrorism to our own streets. Achieving success in Afghanistan is likely to take considerably longer than first envisaged, there will be setbacks and it will be a protracted affair; counter-insurgency campaigns always are. But success will require an even greater investment in troop levels and battle-winning equipment like helicopters. It will require an improved commitment from those NATO nations unwilling to participate in direct combat and a redoubling of effort to increase the capacity of the Afghans' own security forces. The fledgling Afghan Army is a bright spot on the horizon, but it is a nascent force, and a five-year wait for it to increase from its current 68,000 to 134,000 troops is too long.

The international community has to accept that success is likely to fall short of complete victory in conventional terms or the creation of a fully fledged Western-style liberal democracy. Ultimately those who currently resist the central authority from Kabul may even have to become part of a negotiated political solution that is acceptable to the Afghan people and the international community. The majority of the population desperately want peace and security, but many remain on the fence. To win their hearts and minds the current reconstruction and development effort needs to be more vigorous and more visible.

Success also has to be measured in the number of roads and schools that are built, the regeneration of the economy to improve the everyday lives of the Afghans and the creation of viable alternatives to a dependency on opium production. While the conventional military lines of operation are often secondary and subordinate in this area, development agencies like DIFD must be more muscular and risk-orientated if they are to deliver tangible benefits. The UK has invested £600 million in Afghanistan since 2002, but at the time of writing the only school building project in Sangin still remains incomplete two years after 3 PARA fought so hard to keep the Taliban at bay. If the risks are considered too great, then the military must be allowed to take the lead in delivering civil projects and given sufficient finances to do it.

There is no doubt that the overall strategy in Afghanistan is in need of a major overhaul and it remains to be seen whether America's new President can repeat the success of the US Army's surge in Iraq. Gearing up will need to consider all lines of development, take a regional view of working with Afghanistan's neighbours and bind all forty-one participating nations into an agreed stratagem with a unified purpose. It will need to be supported by this country; there will be setbacks and more British servicemen are likely to lose their lives. Consequently, the government will need to do more to convince the public that the blood and treasure that have been, and must continue to be, invested, have not been and will not be in vain. The public information campaign will need to improve and the government must recognize the central role that the media has to play and that keeping them at arm's length is a counter-productive exercise. Operations in the villages, deserts and hills of Afghanistan will require an enduring military presence as, regardless of the increasing technological sophistication of weapons technology, it will remain a boots-on-the-ground intensive activity. The human element, whether in combat or delivering civic assistance, will remain the central dimension. Our service personnel therefore need to be properly equipped, manned, trained and remunerated for the risks, sacrifices and challenges that they will have to continue to face on our behalf.

For many soldiers who have already completed two operations in Afghanistan, their third six-month tour of duty is already on the horizon. The Army has to be properly resourced to ensure that these troops are adequately rested between tours and that their families are looked after. In July 2008 a government Command paper entitled *The Nation's Commitment: Cross-Government Support to our Armed Forces, their Families and Veterans* announced that servicemen and their families would receive priority treatment from the NHS and improved access to public services, such as education and houses. Significantly, it stated that compensation payments to injured personnel would be doubled and men like Bombardier Ben Parkinson finally got a better deal. It chimed with a growing public recognition of what the military does and the unique set of conditions they and their families face at a time when the Military Covenant appears to be increasingly out of kilter with the demands that are being placed upon them. But it has come late in the day and its implementation across all the relevant government departments remains to be seen. Those responsible for ensuring that pledges of obligation are met need to remember that they are not the ones being shot at. They are not the ones who have to zip a fallen comrade into a body bag or answer the questions at a coroner's inquest in front of a dead soldier's family.

Morale on operations was sky-high in 2006 and I believe that remains the case today. Soldiers want to be tested and accept that risk and loss are part of their profession. They don't want the nation's pity, but they do want its support. Yet soldiers still have to share mixed wards with civilians when all the evidence indicates that they recover faster when treated by, and among, their own kind. The MOD is still struggling to grasp the implications of the psychological impact of war on its soldiers. Many of those suffering from PTSD have been medically discharged into a society and health system that are not geared up to look after them. Given that the average incubation period for PTSD is fourteen years, the situation can only get worse, as the demons of thousands of veterans, who have served in places like Iraq and Afghanistan, begin to surface in the future. Although there have been recent pay rises soldiers still need to be paid better when on active service. Even when operational allowances and bonuses are taken into account, a private has to live on less than £20,000 a year. For that they are shot at, bombed, work 24/7 for extended periods and often have to live in a trench. They know what real fear is and live with the physical and psychological consequences of the application of lethal force. They are on call twenty-four hours a day, whether at home or on operations. They do not go on strike, but stand in when others, who earn considerably more than them, do.

Improving the conditions of service and providing the equipment and numbers to ensure operational success at minimum cost will require resources. Current defence spending is unlikely to increase, especially in the prevailing financial climate. But if the military is to provision itself properly from its allocated budget, it must recognize that the strategic landscape has changed. It must restructure to fight the type of wars that it is currently engaged in. This will require a reprioritization and rebalancing of defence spending to end large and expensive Cold War legacy projects. New Typhoon high-altitude fighters currently have no potential adversary. Consequently, their *raison d'être* has become increasingly questionable at a time when there is a severe lack of battlefield helicopters in Helmand.

The lessons of Britain's most recent engagement in Afghanistan have brought about the need for a fundamental reappraisal of the structure and approach of our armed forces. But as this recognition has slowly percolated through to the uppermost echelons of the military establishment, I detect that there are some of them who wish to rewrite the history of events surrounding the Army's effort in Helmand in 2006. Recent comments made to the media regarding mistakes made by soldiers on operations having caused more casualties than the enemy, or that British forces were smug and complacent, suggest a degree of blame is attached to those who risked, and continue to risk, their lives on the ground. This generates a perception of an attempt to shift some of the responsibility from the MOD decision makers. But it ignores the fact that field commanders at the time raised concerns about strategy, the poor reconstruction effort, and made repeated requests for more troops and equipment. They knew what was required and were certainly not smug or complacent. Such criticism also ignores the fact that some notable senior Army officers risked their careers to make these appeals, both before and during the initial deployment to Afghanistan. In truth, those soldiers and officers who fought, and those who continue to fight, are blameless. Instead they do an exceptional job with the limited resources made available to them by the mandarins in Whitehall.

This country owes its soldiers an immense debt of gratitude. Given the risk-averse and self-obsessed nature of modern-day society they are a remarkable fraternity that has demonstrated the strength of character to make something of themselves. Today's young soldiers have witnessed a level of combat experience not seen for two generations and they are every bit as good as their grandfathers and great-grandfathers who fought in the Second World War. The eighteenth-century writer Samuel Johnson once said that 'every man thinks meanly of himself for not having been a soldier'. However, few people step voluntarily into the arena of battle. There is no glamour in it and only those who have done it can comprehend the full nature of the horrors of war. But it is a noble undertaking founded on a culture of normative values of shared endeavour, ethos, mutual trust, regard for the group and self-sacrifice. For me, leaving 3 PARA was the natural order of things, but it meant that membership of an extraordinary band of brothers was over. I was extremely fortunate to have been part of it and to be able to say that I fought and marched with 3 PARA. Sometimes I had to make hard decisions, and people often speak about the loneliness of command, but I can't say that I ever felt lonely as their CO. In the words of Paddy Caldwell, I regret nothing; if I was twenty years younger, I would do it all again.

Honours and Gallantry Awards

Honours and Gallantry Awards made to members of 3 PARA Battle Group and those that worked directly with them during Operation Herrick 4 (April – October 2006):

Victoria Cross

Corporal Bryan James Budd, The Parachute Regiment (killed in action)

George Cross

Corporal Mark William Wright, The Parachute Regiment (killed in action)

Commander of the Order of the British Empire

Brigadier Edward Adam Butler DSO MBE, late The Royal Green Jackets

Officer of the Order of the British Empire

Lieutenant Colonel Richard Friedrich Patrick Felton MBE, Army Air Corps
Colonel Martin Nicholas Nadin, late Royal Army Medical Corps

Member of the Order of the British Empire

Major David James Eastman, Corps of Royal Electrical and Mechanical Engineers

Major Huw Spencer Williams, The Parachute Regiment

Distinguished Service Order

Major Paul Alan Blair, The Parachute Regiment

Lieutenant Colonel Stuart John Craig Tootal OBE, The Parachute Regiment

Conspicuous Gallantry Cross

Lieutenant Hugo James Edward Farmer, The Parachute Regiment

Lance Corporal of Horse Andrew Geoffrey Radford, The Life Guards

Military Cross

Flight Lieutenant Matthew Kenneth Carter, Royal Air Force

Second Lieutenant Oliver Dale, The Parachute Regiment

Corporal of Horse Michael John Flynn CGC, The Blues and Royals

Staff Corporal Shaun Keith Fry, The Life Guards

Corporal Stuart James Giles, The Parachute Regiment

Lance Corporal Karl Wayne Jackson, The Parachute Regiment

Private Peter McKinley, The Parachute Regiment

Major Giles Matthew Timms, The Parachute Regiment

Private Mark James Wilson, The Parachute Regiment

Distinguished Flying Cross

Major Mark Christopher Hammond, Royal Marines

Flying Officer Christopher Michael Haslar, Royal Air Force

Flight Lieutenant Craig Thomas Wilson, Royal Air Force

George Medal

Lance Corporal Paul Hartley, Royal Army Medical Corps

Queen's Gallantry Medal

Corporal Stuart Henry Pearson, The Parachute Regiment

Mention in Despatches

Captain Matthew Anthony William Armstrong, Royal Regiment of Artillery (7 PARA)

Lieutenant Nichol James Emslie Benzie, Royal Navy

Private Jonnie Chad Bevans, The Parachute Regiment

Warrant Officer Class 2 Michael John Bolton, The Parachute Regiment

Warrant Officer Class 2 Karl Terence Brennan, Royal Regiment of Artillery (7 PARA)

Captain Alexander John Eida, Royal Regiment of Artillery (killed in action) (7 PARA)

Captain Mark Richard Eisler, The Parachute Regiment

Lieutenant Thomas David Fehley, The Parachute Regiment

Rifleman Ganesh Gurung, The Royal Gurkha Rifles

Warrant Officer Class 2 Trilochan Gurung, The Royal Gurkha Rifles

Corporal Benjamin Stephen Hall, Royal Army Medical Corps

Private Stephen James Halton, The Parachute Regiment

Lieutenant Martin Joseph Hewitt, The Parachute Regiment

Lieutenant Paul Ronald Hollingshead, The Royal Gurkha Rifles

Sergeant Daniel Jarvie, The Parachute Regiment

Warrant Officer Class 2 Thomas Heron Johnstone, Army Air Corps

Corporal Kailash Khebang, The Royal Gurkha Rifles

Sergeant Carl Frederick Lane, The Parachute Regiment

Warrant Officer Class 2 Zachary Adam Leong, The Parachute Regiment

Captain Alexander James Mackenzie, The Parachute Regiment

Lance Corporal Luke Edward Patrick McCulloch, The Royal Irish Regiment (killed in action)

Warrant Officer Class 1 Christopher Paul Mulhall, Army Air Corps

Rifleman Nabin Rai, The Royal Gurkha Rifles

Warrant Officer Class 2 Andrew Kenneth Schofield, The Parachute
  Regiment
Major Toby Patrick Oughtred Till, Coldstream Guards
Sergeant Daniel Cameron Baxter, Royal Air Force
Sergeant Graham Martin Jones, Royal Air Force
Squadron Leader Michael John Woods, Royal Air Force

Queen's Commendation for Bravery in the Air

Senior Airman Jason Broline, United States Air Force
Staff Sergeant Cameron Hystad, United States Air Force

Queen's Commendation for Valuable Service

Colour Sergeant Stuart Bell, The Parachute Regiment
Captain Nigel John Bishop, The Parachute Regiment
Colonel Charles Peter Huntley Knaggs OBE, late Irish Guards

Acronyms

7 RHA: 7th Regiment Royal Horse Artillery
AAR: After Action Review
ANA: Afghan National Army
ANP: Afghan National Policemen
ASP: Afghan Standby Police
BC: Battery Commander
CGS: Chief of the General Staff
CO: Commanding Officer
DFID: Department for International Development
DZ: Drop Zone
FOB: Forward Operating Base
FSG: Fire Support Group
FST: Fire Support Team
GPMG: General Purpose Machine Gun
HRF: Helmand Reaction Force
IED: Improvised Explosive Device
ISAF: International Security Assistance Force
JDAM: Joint Direct Attack Munition
JOC: Joint Operations Centre
JTAC: Joint Terminal Attack Controller
KAF: Kandahar Airfield
LAVs: Light Armoured Vehicles (Canadian variant)
LZ: Landing Zone
MERT: Medical Emergency Resuscitation Team
MFC: Mortar Fire Controller
MIA: Missing in Action

MOG: Manoeuvre Outreach Group
NCO: Non-Commissioned Officer
NDS: National Department for Security
PJHQ: Permanent Joint Headquarters
PJI: Parachute Jump Instructor
PRT: Provincial Reconstruction Team
PTSD: Post-Traumatic Stress Disorder
QRF: Quick Reaction Force
RAMC: Royal Army Medical Corps
RAP: Regimental Aid Post
RC-S: Regional Command South
RHA: Royal Horse Artillery
RMP: Royal Military Police
ROE: Rules of Engagement
RSM: Regimental Sergeant Major
SNCO: Senior Non-Commissioned Officer
Tac: Battle Group Tactical Headquarters
UAV: Unmanned Aerial Vehicle
UKTF: United Kingdom Task Force
WMIKs: Weapon Mount Installation Kits

Picture Acknowledgements

Captain Andy Blackmore: 1 top. Private Lee Clayton: 1 bottom. Private Martin Cork: 13 middle. © British Crown Copyright/ MOD. Reproduced with the permission of the Controller of Her Majesty's Stationery Office: 12 top, 15 bottom. © British Crown Copyright/MOD. Reproduced with the permission of the Controller of Her Majesty's Stationery Office/photo Sergeant Mike Fletcher: 2 top, 8 middle, 9 top, 11 bottom, 17 top, 21 top, 22 top, 22 middle, 23 top. Captain Hugo Farmer: 9 bottom. Corporal Firth: 12 bottom. Captain Nick French: 4 top, 6 middle, 7 bottom, 10 top, 10 bottom, 15 top. Captain Euan Goodman: 19 top. Private Jamie Stewart Halton: 5 middle. Lance Corporal Lee Hewitson: 2 bottom. Lieutenant Martin Hewitt: 16 top. Mark Jackson: 8 top, 22 bottom. Major Jamie Loden: 13 bottom, 16 bottom. The Daily Telegraph 2007 / Stephen Lock: 24 bottom. 3 PARA Mortar Platoon: 18 top. © Associated Press/photo Musadeq Sadeq: 8 bottom. Captain Mike Stacey: 21 bottom. © Justin Sutcliffe: 5 top, 5 bottom. Captain Martin Taylor: 3 bottom, 6 top, 14 top, 14 bottom. Private Thompson: 11 top. Colonel Stuart Tootal: 13 top, 17 bottom, 24 top. Sergeant Watt: 3 top. Sergeant Peter White: 7 top.

Acknowledgements

Although the events described in this book are as they appeared to me, they also reflect the views and recollections of over one hundred individuals who played a part in this story. The vast majority are soldiers or airmen who fought with, or in support of 3 PARA in 2006. I am indebted to all of them and to the families whom I spoke to; without them and their assistance this book would not have been possible. I would also like to thank Major Jamie Loden for his detailed comments that helped me with some of the accuracy and sequence. The general support and faith of one senior Army officer was particularly important, although he needs no mention here and he knows who he is. My thanks extends to Annabel Merullo, my agent at PFD, who picked up and drove the project late in the day; also to Roland Philipps and the rest of his incredibly enthusiastic, professional and helpful team at John Murray. Patrick Bishop also deserves a mention, as his book *3 PARA* first brought the achievements of my soliders to the attention of the public and played a part in influencing my own decision to write. My final thanks to Karin for her unstinting love and support during both the writing of this book and the events surrounding it.

Index

Read more ...

Michael Jones

LENINGRAD: STATE OF SIEGE

The story of one of the most horrific sieges in history

The siege of Leningrad was an attempt to eradicate the whole
population of a city by starvation. Drawing on eyewitness accounts,
Michael Jones shows Leningrad in its every dimension – the collapse
into looting, criminal gangs and cannibalism, and the courage of
ordinary citizens who drew on their inner resources to inspire,
comfort and help each other. When the 900-day siege ended in 1944,
more than a million people had died. This superbly insightful history
reveals the extremes of both cruelty and goodness that emerge when
ordinary lives are plunged into horror.

'A tribute to the resilience of the human spirit' *Herald*

'Fluently written . . . the uniquely terrible experience of suffering,
especially of 1941–2, is effectively described' *BBC History*

*Order your copy now by calling Bookpoint on 01235 827716 or
visit your local bookshop quoting ISBN 978-0-7195-6942-5
www.johnmurray.co.uk*

PRIVILEGED
SON

Also by Dennis McDougal

The Last Mogul: Lew Wasserman, MCA and the Hidden History of Hollywood
The Yosemite Murders
Mother's Day
In the Best of Families
Angel of Darkness
Fatal Subtraction: How Hollywood Really Does Business (with Pierce O'Donnell

DENNIS McDOUGAL

PRIVILEGED SON

OTIS CHANDLER AND THE
RISE AND FALL OF THE
L.A. TIMES DYNASTY

PERSEUS PUBLISHING
Cambridge, Massachusetts

A CIP record for this book is available from the Library of Congress.
ISBN 0-7382-0270-3

Gift '05

Perseus Publishing is a member of the Perseus Books Group.
Find us on the World Wide Web at http://www.perseuspublishing.com

Perseus Publishing books are available at special discounts for bulk purchases in the U.S. by corporations, institutions, and other organizations. For more information, please contact the Special Markets Department at HarperCollins Publishers, 10 East 53rd Street, New York, NY 10022, or call 212-207-7528.

Text design by Jeff Williams
Set in 10.5-point Simoncini Garamond

1 2 3 4 5 6 7 8 9 10—03 02 01
First printing, April 2001

To my own father, Carl McDougal,
and to Uncle Don, Gheen, Pat, Neal, Fitz, Ray, and Otis—
and all the other fathers of the world who tried mightily
to steer the proper course, live the exemplary life, and be heroic—
and in the end, were only confoundingly, endearingly human,
just as they were supposed to be all along

It's not just what we inherit from our mothers and fathers that haunts us. It's all kinds of old defunct theories, all sorts of old defunct beliefs, and things like that. It's not just that they actually live on in us; they are simply lodged there, and we cannot get rid of them. I've only to pick up a newspaper and I seem to see ghosts gliding between the lines.

—HENRIK IBSEN, *Ghosts*

CONTENTS

ACKNOWLEDGMENTS

IN THESE PAGES, Otis Chandler opened up himself and his family to an outsider's extensive scrutiny for the first time. Otis knew from the outset that he might not always be pleased with my conclusions, and would surely have changed some of the less flattering anecdotes and characterizations had this been his autobiography or even an "authorized" biography with all the pulled punches that such a phrase implies. The telling of part of his tale—including the breakup of his first marriage, the unforeseen tragedy that befell his eldest son, and his ambivalence about losing control of his *Los Angeles Times*—was visibly painful for him to discuss. To his credit, he answered questions even when he did not want them asked in the first place. Though frequently tempted otherwise, Otis was ultimately true to the Jeffersonian principles of Western journalism by which he has conducted most of his professional life: try to tell the truth and let the chips fall where they will.

More than once, his candor has landed Otis Chandler in hot water. Over the years, his closed-mouth relatives have lambasted him mercilessly for speaking his mind, which may account in large part for his reluctance to speak at length to an author before now. For several months in the spring and summer of 2000, Otis met with me weekly—usually on a Tuesday. At one point, several weeks into the project, I suggested *Tuesdays with Otis* as an alternative title for the book. Caution quickly gave way to candor and I soon had the necessary palette from which to paint an accurate portrait of this remarkable, charismatic, and multi-dimensional molder of modern day Los Angeles. To Otis, Bettina, Missy, Harry, Michael, Carolyn, Cathleen, and all the other Chandlers who let down their guard and spoke their truths, I am deeply grateful.

I am also grateful to those who helped me research the earliest years of the Chandler dynasty, particularly Nick Curry, whose exhaustive genealogy of the Chandlers and excavation of much of the existing history of that dominant Southern California clan helped immeasurably in adding resonance and authen-

ticity to the early chapters. Roger McGrath, Ralph Shaffer and Sherman Library director Dr. Bill Hendricks also aided my walk through the early history of Los Angeles and its inextricable relationship to the first three publishers of the *Times*, General Harrison Otis, Harry Chandler and Norman Chandler.

Journalists who mined the Chandler archives before me were generous with both their research and their observations. They included Bob Gottlieb, Charles Rappleye, and Mark Dowie. The research of former *Times* editorial page editor Jim Bassett and the incisive comments of former *Times* editor Nick Williams, both of whom left their posthumous observations buried deep in the *Los Angeles Times* archives, were welcome guideposts through the tumult of the 1960s and 70s at Times Mirror Square. Former Times Mirror executive Peter Fernald and author/photographer Randy Leffingwell helped me pick up the trail through the 1980s and 90s, as did many of my other former colleagues—some named, some anonymous—who labored by my side at the *Times* in the waning days of its golden Otis era.

Thanks to the handful of close friends who read each page for accuracy, syntax, punctuation, and spelling, including Patricia "Babe" McFall, Ms. Julie Payne, my uncle Don McDougal, Pat "Kitty" Broeske, Irv Schwartz, Diane L.M.G. Goldner, Lt. (ret.) John Beshears, my attorney/mensch Pierce O'Donnell, the late and beloved David Levinson, and Irv Letofsky, still the finest newspaper editor I've ever worked with. Or is that, with whom I've ever worked?

My agent and high-heeled henchman Alice Martell saw the worth of the Chandler saga and fought hard to find it a good home. My editor at Perseus Books, Jacqueline Murphy, provided that home, along with patience, passion, and guidance as each chapter rolled off the printer and into a FedEx envelope. Brian Zoccola and Leslie Lazar transcribed dozens upon dozens of hours of interviews. Leslie also helped me keep appointments, write correspondence, and maintain two filing cabinets full of Chandler esoterica, cataloging and keeping them in some sort of passable referential order.

The bedrock foundation upon which all my work rests is still family, starting with my father and mother, Carl and Lola McDougal, and all of my siblings and their mates: Pat and Lynne McDougal, Colleen and Doojie Seliger, and Neal and Jamie McDougal. My children and their spouses validate me in ways that only a proud father can appreciate: Jen and Ray Dominguez, Amy and Mike Riley, Fitz and Sharonne, Andrea and Tim Conklin, and my wonderful bounce-back kid, Kate McDougal. The tonic that keeps me renewed and percolating are the next generation: Meg and Alex, Austin and Cody.

But if the arch of my life and life's work has a keystone, it's my muse and mate, Miss Sharon Marie Murphy. If there's a bigger heart on earth, I don't know who

has it or where it beats. A day doesn't pass that she doesn't teach me again how and why I live. When I wax on pretentiously about how she is the wind beneath my wings, she reminds me instead that she is the fire beneath my butt.

And she's right, you know.

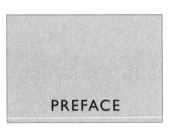

PREFACE

THIS VOLUME BEGAN three years ago as many a Southern California dream often does: over a pricey lunch in a West Hollywood bistro with an agent looking for the Next Big Thing. Somewhere between the arugula salad and the pasta primavera, the conversation turned to the sorry state of the *Los Angeles Times*. As we were both cultural and intellectual snobs, the agent and I spoke of how much better the *New York Times* had become at covering the issues nearest and dearest to our hearts: politics, art, music, literature, and even the movies, which ought to have been the purview of that other *Times,* seeing as how Hollywood was right in its own backyard.

At this point in our conversation, I redoubled my own outrage over the *Los Angeles Times'* spotty and occasionally sycophantic reporting on the entertainment industry. As a staff writer for the *Times* Calendar section throughout the 1980s, I recalled an era when the newspaper's focus on movies and media in general was tough, investigative, anecdotal, and consistently revealing. Something had happened, I railed. The *Times* had never really been the same since Otis Chandler left, and that was a crying shame. The Chandlers, after all, had invented Los Angeles.

My lunch mate sat forward in his seat and asked me if I were not exaggerating. How, he wanted to know, had one family come to create the nation's second largest city? Surely I was kidding him. Like most L.A. residents, my agent friend was an Eastern transplant and knew only the Southern California of recent years. He assumed that L.A. had simply always been here in some form or another. He knew very little of its history outside of Robert Towne's screen roman à clef *Chinatown*, about L.A.'s astonishing wholesale water theft from the Owens Valley nearly 100 years ago. My agent friend had never given the origins of the megalopolis much thought because L.A. was a city without memory. History seemed to have no place here. There were Indians, followed by Spaniards, Mexicans, missions, ranchos, a gold rush, and, then, voila! A city grew like topsy to staggering proportions during the course of the twentieth century. End of story.

Thus, I spent the next hour outlining the saga of General Harrison Otis, Harry Chandler, and the newspaper they created, which defined, promoted, built, and finally controlled Los Angeles. He sat, rapt, at the seldom-told tale of the *Los Angeles Times.*

I had worked for the *Times* for over 15 years, beginning with my first freelance story published in 1976 and ending with my departure from the so-called "Velvet Coffin" in the spring of 1992, just one week ahead of the city's rioting over the acquittal of four white LAPD officers in the Rodney King beating case. I had worked for other newspapers before settling in at Times Mirror Square, but none like the *Times.* I had no way of knowing then, but my tenure there paralleled the last days of the Otis Chandler era—when money was no object in the pursuit of the truth, daily news stories were regarded as literature, and all things seemed possible. I sat at the Round Table of journalism during the final days of Camelot, and had no real appreciation of that singular fact until it was over.

Like my agent friend, I had just assumed that the *Times* had always been there, like L.A. itself. I knew dimly that it had once been regarded as a terrible newspaper from the Great Depression through the early days of the Cold War, but all of that had changed by the time I became a *Times*man. Since the ascendancy of Otis Chandler to the publisher's suite in 1960, there had been balance, style, and grace—a relentless pursuit of excellence—cushioned by more money than any other newspaper earned in America.

But things began to change by the early 1990s. L.A.'s newspaper advertising cornucopia dried up, Southern California defense and aerospace plants shut down, and the eternally expanding *Los Angeles Times* began to shrink. Otis was long gone and, soon, I would be too.

The *Times* subtly evolved from a serious, hard-charging journal of record where a reporter could get a contact high from merely coming to work each day, to a warren where fear for one's livelihood translated itself into timid prose in each day's paper. I watched helplessly as the newspaper rapidly switched from being a "reporter's paper" to a journal rigidly controlled by layer after layer of sycophantic mandarins posing as editors.

In the end, the *Los Angeles Times* made it easy for me to leave. I had recently begun work on my third book, provoking the editors' frustration when I asked for yet another leave of absence. My timing could not have been more perfect because the newspaper that I had grown to believe to be the sin qua non of metropolitan dailies was in the initial throes of what would prove to be a fatal fiscal flu. I joined the first wave of *Times* reporters to accept a handsome buy-out severance package and move on to a new career.

During the years that followed, I wrote three more books, started a magazine, and became a grandfather. It didn't occur to me until the afternoon I lunched with the agent that there might be a book in the history of the *Los Angeles Times.* For one thing, it had been told before, most notably, by author and journalist David Halberstam who included the Chandler saga in *The Powers That Be.* His 1978 tome traced the histories of four major media families, including the Grahams (the *Washington Post*), the Paleys (CBS), and the Luces (*Time* magazine), as well as the Chandlers.

But the story of the *Times* and its founding family has almost always been told piecemeal—even by Halberstam—and never with much candor. Even today the elder Chandlers remain secretive and clannish, equating their vast wealth with smug privilege. Chandlers do not speak to or with the hoi polloi. Otis alone among his cousins will talk about the past but even then, he does so guardedly.

By the time we finished lunch, the agent was enthralled. He babbled about a TV miniseries—a major biopic at the very least. What I had related to him over cappuccino and *creme bruleé* was the kind of grist that simply could not be made up: the rape of the Owens Valley; a labor-management war that led to the dynamiting of a newspaper; a near revolution in Baja California; the construction of hotels, harbors, freeways, airports, and the L.A. Music Center—and all before Otis Chandler even became publisher!

I have come to regard Hollywood—yet another of Harry Chandler's many creations—with the proverbial grain of salt. Its memory is even shorter than its attention span. Hollywood's regard for history is directly proportional to popcorn sales. But the agent's unbridled enthusiasm, fleeting though it may have been, spoke volumes to me about the validity of telling the Chandler saga one more time with feeling. Two years later, as I labored over the first third of the book, the Chandlers sold off their *Times* to the Chicago-based Tribune Company, and the story of their century of domination in Southern California seemed more vital and timely than ever.

It was not just Chinatown. It was a helluva lot more than that, Jake.

Dennis McDougal
January 2001

INTRODUCTION

AT SEVENTY-TWO, Otis Chandler was an outsized man: courtly, craggy, out of sync with the times. He was perhaps better suited to an earlier century when the land was fatter, the men leaner, and the rules of engagement less precise.

It was neither a miracle nor an accident of nature that the broad-shouldered, sandy-haired former publisher of the *Los Angeles Times* more closely resembled a Jack Palance character charging out of the Old West than an aging corporate WASP with one eye on his stock portfolio and the other on the inevitability of his own mortality. Chandler had been defying the odds for seven decades and was used to winning, sometimes by the skin of his large, white teeth.

Once, when he was hardly old enough to climb atop a horse all by himself, he'd been declared dead after being thrown from the saddle. In another close call more than thirty years later, he almost rolled a race car somewhere between 115 and 200 miles per hour and walked away from it, if with a considerable limp. Brushes with death slowed him, but never turned Otis Chandler into a spectator. Grudgingly following doctors' orders, he put in the token recovery time and was back at it again. He had narrowly escaped death in the central African republic of Chad, where Libyan soldiers were butchering Westerners, and the Bering Strait of northern Alaska, where he nearly became a polar bear's entrée.

More recently, in his early sixties, when most men trade in contact sports for something a little less demanding such as golf, Otis had another tundra run-in with a musk ox who gored his shoulder and nearly caused him to bleed to death in the far northern reaches of Canada. But his toughest battle was much closer to home. Seven years earlier, when a routine annual physical revealed that he had prostate cancer, he ordered it cut out of him within twenty-four hours. More than ever, though, Otis Chandler was aware that someday, perhaps sooner than later, he would die.

The founders of the Chandler family fortune, who both died of heart failure, each lived to be eighty. General Harrison Gray Otis, the volcanic first publisher

of the *Los Angeles Times*, expired during one of the hearty regular breakfasts that kept his six-foot frame swollen to 250 pounds. The huge Type-A heart of the patriarch of the Chandler dynasty finally gave out on July 30, 1917, following eighty years of ballsy bluster, blunt battles, and backroom finagling that put his newspaper at the helm of the Los Angeles century. More than once, his great-grandson would concede fondly that he was happy to have inherited some of the General's gusto, but thankful that he did not have his appetite. Following his regular cup of coffee, his Sunday *Times*, and a last platter of eggs, General Otis clapped his hand over his heart and muttered "I am gone" to his maid, Lucy. And then he was.

The deaths of the General's son-in-law Harry Chandler and Harry's son, Norman, the second and third publishers of the *Times* respectively, were neither so quick nor so dramatic. Otis Chandler's paternal grandfather, Harry Chandler, was the shrewd and amoral power broker who was the inspiration for screenwriter Robert Towne's Noah Cross character in *Chinatown*, the classic tale of L.A. corruption and greed. Harry collapsed from a coronary in 1944 after several years of declining health. In 1973, Harry's less nefarious but equally potent heir Norman, Otis Chandler's father, lost a long and painful bout with cancer of the mouth.

From Norman, Otis learned discipline and duty; from Harry, he inherited a taste for patrician poker playing. But it was from his mother that Otis learned a thing or two about patronizing the common man.

Dorothy Buffum Chandler was that singular creature of American capitalism who rises from modest means to tower over all contemporaries as a direct result of money: a classic example of the cultural caste that the French dubbed "nouveau riche." To be sure, Mrs. Chandler was a far more complex woman than Daisy Buchanan of *The Great Gatsby* or Thackery's Becky Sharp, but her roots were much the same. The daughter of an Illinois dry goods dealer who moved to California at the turn of the twentieth century, she was the direct beneficiary of her father's lucky launch of a chain of successful upscale department stores. For sixty years, Buffum's was to Southern California what Gimbel's was to New York.

Her fiscal future secure, "Buff" Chandler rose above education, social station, backbiting in-laws, and her own substantial self-doubts to reign for nearly half a century over L.A. and its *Times* as the city's grande dame. She saved the Hollywood Bowl from the wrecker's ball in the 1950s and created the Los Angeles Music Center in the 1960s, virtually single-handedly. And she groomed her only son early to assume his proper position within her master plan for a Los Angeles that would equal and perhaps even better New York, Washington, and London as centers of art, culture, literature, learning and, above all else, power.

"Remember who you are. Remember what you represent," she drilled her son with such regularity that her echo remained fresh and forceful in Chandler's imagination long after his mother's voice had been silenced forever.

Otis Chandler was the anointed one, the California golden boy whose destiny had been preordained. He would assume the title of fourth publisher of the *Los Angeles Times* and he would remake the newspaper, and the city it helped to create, in his own image. In the space of twenty-five years, the Times Mirror Company that he would inherit from his father and mother would emerge as the richest, most potent media conglomerate in the West: owner of such disparate properties as *Newsday,* New American Library, the *Baltimore Sun*, Harry Abrams Publishing, the *Hartford Courant*, and a bevy of television stations and cable systems. He would shape and redefine Southern California in the final third of the twentieth century, and Buff's influence on him would be as powerful as that of his father and the entire Chandler dynasty. It was imperative that Otis always remember *who he was* and *what he represented.*

But there came a time when Otis Chandler rebelled against filial duty. It arrived later than might have been expected, after he had celebrated nearly thirty years of marriage to the same woman and fathered five children by her, well into his second decade as publisher of the *Times.* But when the moment came, the fourth publisher of the *Los Angeles Times* abdicated his throne, left his marriage, and slowly retreated from his family's Times Mirror empire. Glibly summed up by *Times* metropolitan editor Noel Greenwood at the time:

"Otis has gone surfing, and he's never coming back."

He had set out on his own odyssey to define for himself who he was and what he represented instead of permitting his mother, his father, and all the other Chandlers to do it for him.

He had found some answers, usually more satisfying than they were unsettling. But he was also human, and he possessed a streak to his personality as petty, venal, and hypocritical as any to be found in the Chandler clan. He was a Rolls Royce patrician with the heart of a Harley Davidson. There had been a time in his life when Otis had turned his back on a friend during a serious crisis to save himself. His lust broke many a heart and his lack of compassion could at times be breathtaking. When someone dared criticize him, his temper would simmer before suddenly flaring; and his capacity for revenge could be boundless.

"Both he and his mother were always the victims," wryly observed lifelong friend Bob Emmet. "It was always somebody else's fault."

Yet Emmet, like so many others who had known Otis Chandler over a lifetime, chose to overlook his flaws. So did his first wife, Missy, who stood by helplessly while Otis carried on his flirtations.

"He was spoiled," she said. "He always had to have his way."

And, like the rest of the Chandlers, he was cheap.

"They were the kind of family that would steal the cross from Jesus Christ and leave Him hanging in midair," said a longtime Chandler family historian.

"Otis will step over a $10 bill to pick up a nickel," observed one of his younger relatives.

Although he and Missy were married for nearly thirty years, "I didn't get that much in the divorce," she said. Their wars notwithstanding, Missy has confessed that she sometimes wishes they were still married. His life was always an adventure and the sheer adrenaline rush of just being near him was often enough to balance his sins.

Otis might have faced down lions rather than face his own shortcomings; he might have let greed nearly bury him, as it almost did during the disastrous Geotek affair of the early 1970s; he might have had lust in his heart, rust in his relationships, and dust in his wallet; but he had been born with ink in his veins. Most of all, Otis Chandler was what he had been from the beginning, what he had at last accepted and embraced after years of denial: a newspaperman.

Otis Chandler was a newspaperman, like his father, grandfather, and great-grandfather before him. If history remembered him or any of his forbears, that would be their proper legacy. Newspapermen. To Otis, delivering the news was a sacred trust and no less a professional calling than that of the priesthood. Journalism, after all, was the first draft of history, and history always started with the telling of a story. Dynasties, empires, and great fortunes could be made and lost in a few generations, but their story—their history—would always remain.

And their history always began on the front page.

PART A

The Walrus and the Fox

1881–1930

In all these pregnant years of masterful progress since 1881, the *Los Angeles Times* claims to have had some hand in the superb development of the south—and as it has marched "on and on and on," it has grown from an unpretentious four-page country daily to the expanded state in which it is now seen: the largest newspaper, according to the latest advices, published on the globe.

—Harrison Gray Otis
Sunset Magazine, January 1910

LOS ANGELES DAILY TIMES

Sunday Morning ✳ *December 4, 1881*

News of the Morning

IN THE FIRST-EVER EDITION of the *Los Angeles Times*, readers learned that the Ministerial Association would preach the next Sunday morning against the evils of divorce; that a commodities trader named Mr. E. Germain shipped 720,000 pounds of walnuts to the East Coast during the previous year; and that Sheriff Rowland's six-year-old son broke his arm while crossing the railroad tracks at Spring and Fort Streets.

Readers also learned that, although the Rowland boy was doing fine, a man named Donald from Santa Monica was not; he'd been shot by a Mr. Williams and was not expected to live.

With alarming frequency, Los Angeles residents still settled disputes over land, mining stakes, politics—even divorce and occasional commodities trading—with pistols. Indeed, just two years before the *Times* made its 1881 debut, a reporter for the *Los Angeles Express* settled a tiff with the editor of the rival *Los Angeles Herald* by shooting at him over lunch at the Pico House. He missed, hitting a police major from Compton instead, but apparently did not wound the officer badly enough to merit a jail sentence. The reporter, William A. Spalding, went on to serve briefly as corporate secretary of the *Times* in 1886 before being hired away by the *Herald,* where he became business manager in 1898.

Civilization came late to Southern California and the *Times,* L.A.'s newest four-page broadsheet, duly reported every bloody item, especially if the item happened to involve suspicious doings in Chinatown, as well as the mundane. The

pariahs du jour in L.A., along with vagrant Mission Indians, were Asians with pigtails and a willingness to perform the most demeaning labor at sub-subsistence wages. Able-bodied white men who saw their own wages undercut by the "yellow menace" occasionally lynched them with impunity. From its inception, the *Times* was more sympathetic to the Chinese and other minority races than its rivals were; and it did not favor firearms and lynch mobs as the best solutions to the fledgling city's social ills.

But most of the *Times*' four daily pages in its earliest days weren't devoted to ongoing racial tensions. Most pages contained no news at all. Beginning with its first edition, the *Los Angeles Times* was awash in advertisements: Boarding stables("transient horses and teams a specialty"); hotels ("hot and cold baths free"); blacksmiths ("all work done in a superior manner"); plumbers ("pumps carefully put in"); dentists ("upper or lower set, plain, $10"); psychics, attorneys, preachers, physicians, butchers . . . all paid cash for a few lines of bold-faced type in the *Times*. It was a mark of L.A.'s newfound genteel sophistication that millinery parlors, dressmaker emporia, and Dr. Swan's Remedies for Ladies were also being hawked on the front page. According to one *Times* headline in its first edition, Los Angeles was "rapidly developing into a highly moral town." According to another, L.A. had become a "city of churches."

The city's salutary weather also made typical *Los Angeles Times* headlines during the newspaper's earliest days: Relentlessly upbeat reports brimmed with praise for the wonders the eternal sunshine wrought on the land, which produced bumper crop after bumper crop of every conceivable kind of fruit, nut, and vegetable. According to the *Times*, the semiarid climate also cured all manner of disease, from dropsy to carbuncles to tuberculosis. Best of all, acres of cheap, sunkissed real estate were readily available to sick, snow-weary Easterners who might be passing through and wondering what to do with their life savings.

Los Angeles was undergoing a phenomenal renaissance in 1881. When the *Times* became the city's third daily newspaper, the village known for a century as El Pueblo de Nuestra Señora la Reina de Los Angeles de Porciuncula had finally begun showing signs of shedding a decades-old reputation as the most violent, vicious, amoral settlement of thugs, whores, and thieves west of the Mississippi.

Just a few years earlier, Los Angeles had seen three or four murders every week. Respected East Coast journalist Morrow Mayo dubbed it simply the "Hell-Hole of the West." By 1870, every faith in town except Roman Catholicism had literally boarded up their churches and abandoned L.A. to Satan. On the East Coast, newspapers printed editorials asking whether Los Angeles ought to change its name to Los Diablos.

Most mayhem took place along the quarter-mile corridor of brothels, bars, gambling houses, and opium dens known as Calle de los Negros. Anglicized to "Nigger Alley," Calle de Los Negros was the heartbeat of L.A. and the Gomorrah of the Pacific. Located southeast of the central Plaza de Los Angeles, Nigger Alley had evolved into L.A.'s first Chinatown by the end of the century; it flourished until the 1930s, when it was razed to make way for L.A.'s new Union Station.

But in the mid-1800s, all libidos could still be satisfied for the right price along Nigger Alley, whether the drug of choice was cheap whisky, high-stakes poker, or the black market purchase of another human being to serve as indentured servant, blood sacrifice, or helpless sex slave. Those who weren't felled by rape, homicide, or cirrhosis in downtown Los Angeles could generally count on expiring from the cholera, dysentery, or smallpox that brewed in the *zanjas,* or open-sewer ditches, that fed directly into the city's water supply.

The handful of God-fearing folk who persevered in L.A. during California's first quarter century as the thirty-first State of the Union, however, eventually prevailed over depravity. Slowly, the demons of Nigger Alley died out, disappeared, or moved to more exotic pockets of horror further inland or south of the border in Mexico. Ministers who had earlier abandoned L.A. to the Devil began to return; and the number of churches, schools, and hospitals in Los Angeles gained on the number of dance halls and bordellos.

Racism remained pandemic in the early 1880s, but lynching had begun to fall out of fashion. Although the hundreds of Eastern white settlers now arriving each month on the new Southern Pacific or Santa Fe rail lines continued to hold Mexicans, blacks, Asians, and American Indians in varying degrees of contempt, they rarely favored beating, stoning, dragging, and/or hanging them from the nearest cottonwood, as did the so-called civilized citizens[1] as well as the denizens of Nigger Alley. The law finally superseded mob justice. At the birth of the *Times,* murder—once almost a routine event—now happened only a few times a month, and the guilty parties were often caught, tried, and occasionally even executed—and by the sheriff, not by vigilantes.

Midwestern farmers and their wives had a civilizing effect on L.A. Men aspired to more respectable professions than gambler, thief, or barkeep. Women, too, had more opportunity. Before the waves of western migration brought on by cheap, safe rail transportation, the career paths open to Los Angeles ladies had not advanced much beyond wife or tart.

But during the 1880s renaissance, a clever young woman who had attached herself to an ambitious young man could count on a bright, bountiful future in the county seat of America's last frontier. Consider the case of Miss Eliza Ann

Wetherby and her proud but penniless beau—a nineteenth-century Horatio Alger story if ever there was one.

––––––––––

TWO YEARS BEFORE the beginning of the Civil War, Eliza Wetherby of Lowell, Ohio, married a tall, blond, blue-eyed printer's apprentice who showed little promise of success outside of a florid use of the English language and a brassy ambition that passed in some circles as courage. He also exhibited a bravado that cowed many into believing him a natural born leader. Dreamy Miss Eliza Wetherby fell in love instantly.

His name was Harrison Gray Otis, the youngest of sixteen children born to a God-fearing hardscrabble farm family from the Ohio River Valley. Staunch Methodists and abolitionists, Stephen and Sara Otis could will nothing to their baby boy save a bona fide New England pedigree and a powerful Protestant work ethic. Named for a broadly praised Massachusetts cousin from the previous generation whose conservative Federalist politics had landed him in the Boston mayor's mansion and the U.S. Senate, young Harrison Gray Otis could also point to patriotic firebrand and Revolutionary War hero James Otis as his influential paternal grandfather. The Otis side of his family bequeathed young Harrison not only his lifelong taste for war and all things military but also his political zealotry—which bordered on fanaticism and brought the lucrative patronage that usually went along with supporting the winning political party.

"I absorbed my first political sentiments from my father, who was active in the pre-Republican Liberty Party," Harrison later recalled.

The winning politics practiced by the Ivy League–educated East Coast establishment eluded young Otis, however. Except for three years of basic country schooling, he hadn't the means, the opportunity, or the attention span for the kind of sustained education required of a nineteenth-century machine politician. Otis was restless and wanted to make his fortune. At fourteen, he left home for an apprentice position in the print shop that produced the *Sarahsville Courier*, and he didn't stopped moving until thirty years later, when he and his beloved Eliza finally settled down, 2,500 mile to the west, in that former den of iniquity known as Los Angeles.

Typography was an itinerant's trade in mid–nineteenth-century America, and it allowed Harrison Otis to learn nearly as much about geography as about the newspaper business. Between 1851 and 1856, he worked at several print shops and newspapers throughout the Midwest.

At one of the last of this series of jobs, on the Rock Island *Courier,* Otis went to the editor and demanded that the typographers be allowed to join a union. When

the editor told him no, Otis quit and moved to nearby Davenport, Iowa, to work for another newspaper. The incident set the tone for Otis's lifelong philosophy on employee-management relations: The employee asks and the employer answers. If the employee doesn't like the answer, he leaves.

In 1856, Otis enrolled at Wetherby's Academy in Lowell, Ohio, for some belated formal education; a year later, he attended Granger's Commercial College in Columbus, Ohio, in an attempt to smooth the rough edges of his scant schooling and add some business polish to his skills as a print compositor.

It was in Lowell that he met and courted Eliza Ann Wetherby, the daughter of a wealthy woolen manufacturer and sometimes minister who had opened the academy and named it for himself. Eliza taught there in the 1856–57 school year, when Otis lasted as a student for all of five months. "Lizzie," as Harrison affectionately came to nickname her, was almost four years older and far more sophisticated than her future husband. She fancied herself a poet and even published a rhyme in Horace Greeley's *New York Tribune,* long before she and Harrison heeded Greeley's famous advice to "go west, young man."

The Otises were married in 1859 against Mr. Wetherby's wishes and they did not enjoy much in the way of a dowry. Instead, the couple was "happy and hopeful on $8 a week," as Otis described those days much later in his memoirs. They continued to bounce from town to town, landing briefly in Marietta (Ohio), Louisville, and Chicago, where the antislavery convictions he'd inherited from his parents lured Otis into the passionate presidential politics of 1860. He was an "apprentice" delegate to the 1860 Republican National Convention from Kentucky, and he proudly pointed out for years afterward that he had helped nominate Abraham Lincoln.

But for all his pragmatic optimism and years of experience in printing, when he returned to Ohio and the highly competitive printing business, Harrison Otis remained as dreamily romantic in his own way as his poetess wife was in hers. During a doomed attempt to scrounge newspaper work in Cincinnati, Otis spelled out his wanderlust, his eventual hope for a political windfall, and, above all, his attachment to his young wife in poignant, purple love letters:

Dear, Darling Wife!

The rain might fall ever so fast and the night glow ever so dark, as they do tonight, but if you were close to my heart, no lonely feeling would be there.

Lizzie, it would never do for me to be a missionary, a sailor, or a fisherman, or if I were to turn my attention to any of those occupations you would most certainly have to prepare yourself to be a *voyageur* along with me. I couldn't get on without my wife. If at any future time I should chance to become the recipient of

Presidential favors and be appointed *chargé d'affaires* to the Hottentot Country, or to the Unexplored Region where they converse in the unknown tongue, and live on dirt, I guess you would have to bundle up and charge with me. I couldn't treat with dirt eaters without the aid of my wife.

With the breakout of the Civil War, Otis was among the first to enlist on the side of God, abolition, and President Lincoln, even though Lizzie was about to give birth to their first child. She bore Harrison a son, but the child died within days of its birth. Private Harrison Otis of the 12th Ohio Volunteers hurried back from the front only to see his son buried. Eliza would give him four more daughters—Mabel, Lilian, Marian, and Esther (who also died in infancy)—but there would be no male heir to the future fortunes that the starry-eyed Harrison Gray Otis planned to earn for himself, his wife, and his progeny.

Private Otis distinguished himself on the battlefield; he had at last found a metier in which he excelled without question, despite his meager education and humble beginnings. Twice wounded, he rose through the ranks and seven battlefield promotions to command his own company of Union soldiers at the end of the war. After forty-nine months of continuous service to the Grand Army of the Republic, Major Harrison Gray Otis mustered out in 1865; he was promoted once again following the South's surrender on the recommendation of his commander, Rutherford B. Hayes. For "gallantry and meritorious services," the future U.S. president raised Otis to the rank of lieutenant colonel.

In the arduous years that followed, Harrison hung on tight to his Civil War military service as the proudest moment in an otherwise undistinguished career.[2] As he and Lizzie continued scratching out a living in the printing trade, he vainly insisted on being addressed by friends, peers, and family alike as Colonel Otis, or, simply, the Colonel.

As partners, Harrison and Eliza Otis launched their first newspaper in the years following the war: a "poor little Jim Crow sheet" in Marietta, Ohio, called the *Washington County News*. Their newspaper earned no profits, so Otis subsidized the operation by selling his services as the official reporter for the Ohio State House of Representatives in nearby Columbus. Political patronage within the state capitol paid off further when he dumped the *Washington County News* to accept a job as printing compositor in the Washington, D.C., headquarters of the Government Printing Office, where he joined the International Typographical Union. Later, he moved over to the U.S. Patent Office, where he rose to division chief. By 1870, he had climbed even higher, to foreman, and supervised four hundred employees while earning a salary of $1,800 a year. Harrison Otis might have lived out his life as a comfortable federal bureaucrat had it not been for his

natural restlessness, his gambler's itch, and the inevitable "Get rich quick" appeal of Angora goats.

Like bored middle-aged and middle-class middle managers of any era, Otis skimmed the back pages of magazines and newspaper classifieds for that main-chance business opportunity that would free him from the shackles of daily drudgery and make him independently wealthy. Little luck had come his way during his years in the printing and newspaper trade, and when he came across articles about the exotic appeal of rearing Angora goats, he was intrigued. In 1874, he took a leave of absence from his government job and crossed the country—his first trip west—to investigate the possibility of investing his life savings in a goat farm west of the Baja California coastline on remote and virtually uninhabited Guadalupe Island.

Goats and Guadalupe did not impress him, but California did. As he wrote in a dispatch published in the *Ohio Statesman*, "It is the fattest land I ever was in, by many degrees. Just enough has been done in the way of developing the wonderful, varied and rich resources of Southern California to show what are the mighty possibilities of the section."

Otis returned to Washington, but two years later, he and his family pulled up stakes and returned to California—this time, to Santa Barbara, sixty miles north of Los Angeles. There, William B. Hollister, a fellow former Ohioan and Civil War veteran, offered to stake Otis $6,000 as the new editor and publisher of the *Santa Barbara Press.*

Unlike the Hell-Hole of the West, Santa Barbara had pretensions of civility in 1876, but Otis's chief rival, the *Santa Barbara Daily News,* leaned toward the Democrats in its news columns as well as in its editorial pages, and that meant war to the Colonel. With a bellicose prose style that blended politics and passion with half-truths and full-blown fiction, Harrison Gray Otis jammed his personal point of view into every inch of his staunchly Republican newspaper. Democrats weren't political opponents; they were "hags, harlots, and pollutants." Elections weren't routine political events in a democracy; they were apocalyptic choices between Satan and salvation. In addition to his bristling invective, Otis could also wax on in exaggerated tones about his favorite subjects, regardless of their crackpot nature. And so Santa Barbarans were treated to essays on the probity of planting groves of Australian eucalyptus trees in semiarid Southern California; the remarkable potential in the dry coastal climate for ostrich ranching; and, of course, the unlimited future for those willing to invest in Angora goats.

Balanced to some degree by the poetics of Lizzie Otis, who oversaw the women's pages of her husband's newspapers in the decades that followed, fire-breathing journalism as practiced by Harrison Otis caught public attention—

even if it didn't always rally public support. Although the *Santa Barbara Press* systematically defeated its competition, gobbling up the *Daily News,* the *Advertiser,* and the *Index* over the next two years, the Otises failed to rise to the more genteel levels of Santa Barbara's society and the newspaper remained marginally profitable. By 1878, Otis was turning to his old field commander from his Civil War days for financial aid.

President Rutherford B. Hayes now occupied the White House and, as was the custom of the day, remembered his friends and supporters in the form of plum political appointments. Although Otis didn't delude himself into believing he could land an ambassadorship, he figured that his loyal Republican Party support and his war record had to add up to some kind of cushy job. What he was offered, however, was a slap in the face: the post of the U.S. Treasury Department's official representative in Alaska's Seal Islands; these are located in the Bering Strait, which separates Siberia from Seward's Folly.

Despite its obvious drawbacks, the job did pay well: $10 a day, which could equal a small fortune at the end of a three-year appointment. Otis's duties added up to keeping poachers away from the fur seals and alcohol out of the hands of the Eskimos. On February 13, 1880, Otis wrote his farewell editorial: "On the first day of March, 1880, I will relinquish control of the *Santa Barbara Press*, and transfer it to other hands. Meantime I wish to close up my business here, preparatory to leaving for the far north."

As there was nowhere for Otis to spend his salary in Alaska, he sent it all home to Lizzie; she had remained behind in Santa Barbara with their now-teenaged daughters and struggled to manage the family's newspaper long enough to sell it. Six months after Otis left for Alaska, they got a sobering reminder of just how recently Southern California had emerged from the wild, wild west when Harrison's successor, Theodore M. Glancey, editor of the *Santa Barbara Press,* wrote a searing editorial about a candidate for district attorney—and was shot dead by the candidate in broad daylight in front of the Occidental, Santa Barbara's leading hotel.

In December 1881, Otis returned to Southern California on a brief leave from Alaska. During his stay, he and Lizzie paid a visit to Los Angeles, where Otis was interviewed by a reporter for the town's newest newspaper. Otis, who insisted on being addressed as Colonel, lectured the *Daily Times* correspondent about drunken Indians, punishments for seal poachers, and the primitive, inhospitable climate that would never merit much more than government by force of arms. Colonel Harrison Gray Otis, the soldier who had once fought bitterly to free African American slaves, now advocated the enslavement of Eskimos for their own good.

But Otis conceded that Los Angeles was showing genuine promise as a place civilized enough to settle down in. The town he remembered from his first visit to Southern California as one of the wretched lower rings of Dante's *Inferno* had undergone a considerable transformation in his absence. With the arrival of the Southern Pacific Railroad in 1876, the city boomed. The way station for 5,000 doomed losers had grown to a population of 12,500 and had switched its heartbeat from Nigger Alley to Broadway, southwest of the Plaza, where banks, brokers, and commodity traders had established a new civic center. Adding to this newfound cosmopolitan cachet was an agricultural boom in the surrounding countryside that produced half a million orange trees, wheat fields that yielded 12 million bushels annually, and six wineries that exported 3 million gallons a year to the rest of the United States.

Otis returned to Alaska, but only for a few months. His faithful government service had earned him another government appointment—this time as diplomatic consul to the Southern Pacific paradise of Samoa. By the spring of 1882, Otis was back in Southern California for good; the lure of a brand-new start in the newspaper business in a brand-new L.A. was too seductive. He wired his regrets to Washington, D.C.

With $1,000 he and Lizzie realized from selling the *Santa Barbara Press* and a promise to pay $4,000 more in the years to come, the Otises bought a one-quarter interest in the struggling *Los Angeles Daily Times.* For a salary of $15 a week, Harrison renewed his membership in the rarified world of newspaper publishing and vowed to double or triple the *Times'* daily circulation of four hundred copies. But it was Eliza Otis who gave the family's new business the motto that would endure for a century: "Stand Fast, Stand Firm, Stand Sure, Stand True."

On July 28, 1882, the front page of the *Times* blared: H.G. OTIS TO BECOME PRINTER OF *TIMES.* The Otises had three equal partners in their new enterprise: Jesse Yarnell, Thomas J. Caystile, and S. J. Mathes. A fourth "shadow" partner, A. W. Francisco, one of Colonel Otis's old friends from his Ohio days, agreed to help finance the Otises' end of the partnership.

In the beginning, Mathes ran the *Times'* front office, but it was Harrison and Eliza who supervised ad sales, wrote headlines, drafted editorials, printed and proofed copy, and distributed the final product by 6:00 A.M. every day on the streets of L.A. While Harrison edited and sometimes wrote the front-page news, which included some of the most vitriolic and libelous personal opinions ever printed anywhere, Eliza covered religion, society, fashion, literature, drama, music, and women's issues on the inside pages. She authored several regular columns under the pseudonyms "The Saunterer" and "Susan Sunshine," and at last had a permanent outlet for her poetry:

Oh, you darling pansies!
With your meek little faces,
And your airy, fairy graces,
Filling the garden's quiet places.

The Otises greeted the public; they set type, emptied chamber pots, swept floors. When an occasional fish swam into the flue that carried water from the Los Angeles River into the *Times'* hydropowered printing press, it was Harrison or Eliza who pulled the mutilated trout goo out of the waterwheel. It was no wonder that they behaved in a more proprietary manner toward the newspaper than their three silent partners.

But their *Times* would not remain a mom-and-pop operation for long.

THREE OTHER INVENTIVE EASTERNERS set their own course for Southern California in the early 1880s. Each in his and her own way would soon join Harrison and Eliza Otis in profoundly affecting the future of Los Angeles in the closing years of the nineteenth century. They were quite different from the Otises, just as they were quite different from each other:

Harry Chandler, a tubercular Dartmouth dropout who would develop a Machiavellian instinct for accumulating money and influence once the Southern California sunshine helped him dry his lungs;

Charles F. Lummis, a sickly Harvard-educated romantic fired by dreamy idealism. He had a Victorian novelist's devotion to serpentine phrasings of the English language and an artistic pretension inspired by humanitarian intent—even if it yielded minimal results; and

Helen Hunt Jackson, a poetic widow from Massachusetts whose love of lost causes sparked a Southern California social revolution with sentimental repercussions that still reverberate in L.A. more than a century later.

Of these three new L.A. voices, that of the plump, pretty, patrician Mrs. Jackson was the loudest and most closely listened to in 1882.

"Some day the Los Angeles Chamber of Commerce should erect a great bronze statue of Helen Hunt Jackson at the entrance to Cajon Pass," wrote pioneering L.A. historian Carey McWilliams. "Beneath the statue should be inscribed no flowery dedication, but the simple inscription: 'H. H.—In Gratitude.'"

A Massachusetts literary light who counted Emily Dickinson, Nathaniel Hawthorne, and Henry James among her chums, Jackson was the first Boston Brahmin to widely publicize white America's shameful racism toward the Ameri-

can Indian. In much the same way as fellow Bostonian Harriet Beecher Stowe had rallied the country's conscience twenty-seven years earlier over the plight of African American slaves with the publication of *Uncle Tom's Cabin,* in 1879 Jackson wrote a widely distributed tract titled *A Century of Dishonor*, which blasted the U.S. military's blatant extermination of Indians. The popular pamphlet landed her a presidential appointment as a commissioner of Indian Affairs in 1881—a job that took her, among other places, to Southern California, where she was asked to write a government report on the plight of the few surviving members of the coastal Mission Indian tribes.

Although L.A.'s newly arrived Midwest farm emigrés in 1882 were as repulsed by the stereotypical drunken Indian as they were by the stereotypical shifty-eyed Chinese dope fiend, their collective WASP appetite for dewy-eyed sentiment and frontier romance was as powerful as that of any East Coast desk jockey. The romance of Southern California overrode harsh reality, even when Nigger Alley was staring its newest settlers directly in the face.

Before Mrs. Jackson arrived in L.A. in 1882, the truth about Father Junipero Serra and his greedy entourage of disease-carrying, slave-driving Franciscan monks had already given way to a revisionist history of quaint Mission life: submissive heathens overseen by pious priests in a bountiful primeval setting of olive trees, grape fields, citrus orchards, and semitropical gardens—all shielded inside the sunbaked adobe sanctuary of a California version of Eden.

But Father Serra and his evangelical band of colonial Spanish zealots also brought smallpox, cholera, imprisonment, starvation, torture, and lynching to the Indians; they decimated tribes and reduced the remaining Native American population by more than 90 percent. All this would be carefully excised from California's history texts for most of the next century.

When Helen Hunt Jackson returned to Bostonian civilization after her Southern California sojourn, the Mission myth was intact. In her scathing government report, she failed to mention Franciscan or Roman Catholic culpability; indeed, she assigned most of the blame for Indian subjugation to Mexican *padrones* and the brutish Americans who followed them. But the report was a thimble of kerosene compared to the bucket of napalm that her follow-up novel, *Ramona,* would pour over the flames of white America's guilty conscience.

An Indian tragedy owing a huge debt to the plot of *Romeo and Juliet, Ramona* was Mrs. Jackson's self-described sugarcoated pill designed to expose the wretched mistreatment of Mission Indians to the rest of the world. In unapologetic pop prose, *Ramona* told of the doomed affair between the half-breed Ramona Ortegna and her full-blooded Indian husband, Alessandro. *Ramona* was a prodigious popular success, but it did little to end WASP prejudice. And although the U.S. government continued exploiting Native Americans, *Ramona*

probably did help turn public opinion against the ethnic cleansing of the West. Infamous wholesale slaughters like those at Sand Creek and Wounded Knee came to a halt. Indians were still consigned to wretched reservations where they lived and died in squalid poverty, but genocide was no longer in fashion.

For the hordes of Easterners yet to come, however, *Ramona* and Jackson's equally effusive essays for the popular *Century Magazine*—the *Vanity Fair* of its day—also built expectations of a pastoral early California that never was. Jackson's legacy gave rise to such absolute L.A. fabrications as quaint mestizo mercantilism along Olvera Street, the city's first ethnic theme park built by chamber of commerce entrepreneurs and opened to the public in 1930; to docents reenacting bucolic early California life at the completely reconstructed concrete, lathe-and-plaster "missions" located at San Gabriel and San Fernando; and to a slough of fictitious early California legends, including such early matinee heroes as Zorro, the Cisco Kid, and Joaquin Murietta—a mid–nineteenth-century serial murderer rehabilitated on the silver screen as "The Robin Hood of the West."

This was the already make-believe, culturally skewed young city into which Charles Fletcher Lummis marched during the early weeks of 1885, after 3,507 miles of blisters and bons mots, all of which Colonel Harrison Gray Otis published in the pages of the *Los Angeles Daily Times*.

"Yes, this is a big country," Lummis wrote from Denver.

> You will glibly assent to this hackneyed proposition and assenting will have no more genuine conception of the fact than a hog has of hoopskirts. Now don't fly off and fancy I am asserting anything porcine of your intelligence, for I am not. The simile simply implies that we are all innocent of knowledge in matters whereof we have had no experience. Oh yes, it is true that you have been clear across the continent from Boston to 'Frisco, and after those seven or eight mortal days on the cars you reckon you ought to know how wide the country is. Well, my dear sir or dear madam, I assure you that you haven't the remotest idea.

The ailing and arguably hypochondriac young editor of the *Chillicothe Gazette* in southern Ohio, who said at the time that he suffered from uncontrollable chills and fever and needed a change of climate, had written to Otis that he would walk across America and write his observations for the *Times* along the way if he were assured that there would be a job waiting for him when he arrived in L.A. Harrison Otis accepted this proposal from Lummis two years after buying into the *Times*.

Coining the phrase "See America First," Lummis wrote his transcontinental travelogue as if he were a natural-born booster. He filed dozens of stories, for which he was paid $5 apiece, during his four-and-a-half-month hike from Ohio to

L.A., and as fawning as his prose became with each Western landmark he passed, he saved his warmest gushes for the final few miles. He would never leave Los Angeles and spent the remainder of his life urging the rest of the nation to follow, literally, in his footsteps.

The cross-country stunt built the *Times'* circulation to an unprecedented 2,700 by creating an appetite for the silver-tongued Lummis's running series of dispatches; it turned Lummis into one of Southern California's first modern celebrities in the process.

When he left Chillicothe on September 12, 1884, Lummis was an unknown scholar who suffered from vestigial malaria; seven hundred miles east of L.A., he broke his arm. But as Colonel Otis himself wrote about the tan, fit, and road-toughened Lummis upon his arrival at the San Gabriel Mission on February 1, 1885, he might just as easily have been describing Tom Mix or Wyatt Earp. Lummis was decked out like the hero of some real-life horse opera in "well worn overalls, . . . a dusty white felt hat, with the skin of a rattlesnake for a band, a six shooter in his belt, and a staff in his hand."

Otis had no choice but to hire Lummis on the spot as the *Times'* first city editor; indeed, with the exception of Harrison and Eliza, Lummis was the newspaper's first and only regular working journalist. He personally covered the Apache wars in what was then Arizona Territory, bringing back tales of a vast desert wilderness along the Colorado River where water was plentiful and land was even cheaper that it was in California. Until he quit in 1887 after suffering what he asserted to be a stroke, Lummis worked feverishly to turn the *Times* into L.A.'s newspaper of record.

At the same time, with his echoes of Helen Hunt Jackson's fanciful evocations of the plight of the Indian and the Mission era, Lummis injected as much exotic drama into each day's editions as Colonel Harrison Otis's version of the truth would allow. Unlike his blunt, forceful, and occasionally cruelly sarcastic employer, Lummis used journalism to spellbind his readers as often as he informed and browbeat them. When he had recovered from his "stroke," he edited several magazines over the next thirty years with such names as *Saturday Night, Outlook,* and *Land of Sunshine*, each one hyping the Spanish-flavored Southern California version of the American Dream.

"He wanted Southern Californians to see themselves as moral heirs of Spain," California State Librarian Kevin Starr concluded almost a century later. "He encouraged them to internalize in an American way the aesthetic ancestry of the civilization which had prepared the way for their own."

Ironically, Lummis blamed *Ramona* as the catalyst for turning California's remaining Indian population from "noble savages" into sappy victims in the popular imagination. In his post-*Times* career, Lummis also founded the Southwest

Museum, which still remains one of the most complete repositories of California Indian lore in the world. Even after his departure from the *Times*, Lummis and the Otises remained close.

The most important person by far to arrive in L.A. in the early 1880s—important to every Angeleno and especially important to the Otises—was another sickly soul from the East. He was a skinny nineteen-year-old fruit picker from Landaff, New Hampshire, who rode a Pullman car all the way from Massachusetts in May 1882 to try to reclaim his health in Southern California.

As a Dartmouth freshman, brash young Harry Chandler foolishly tried to impress a cousin on a dare two months into the winter semester by leaping into an icy vat of starch. He immediately came down with pneumonia, from which he slowly recovered, but by springtime his tenacious bronchitis never seemed to improve and he could not step out of the house without convulsing into coughing spasms. Chandler's doctor told him the spasms were so wretched that he had hemorrhaged his lungs and probably didn't have long to live.

Fearing the worst, Chandler's parents followed the newspaper advice that would later be given by Charles Lummis and taken by so many other cold-climate refugees after him: They put their son on the next train to California. At six-foot-two, the blond, blue-eyed Chandler had been a privileged, strapping Ivy League specimen before his illness, but when he arrived in L.A., he was just another miserable, hacking refugee in a Darwinian land where money talked and day laborers listened.

He checked in at a Nigger Alley flophouse, no more than two city blocks away from the two-story brick offices of the *Los Angeles Daily Times*, at the junction of Temple and New High Streets and close to where the U.S. District Courthouse stands today. Chandler didn't try asking for a newspaper job during his first stay in Los Angeles. He spent his early weeks in California feeling sorry for himself; he wandered the downtown streets and peered into store windows, where he caught glimpses of L.A.'s burgeoning abundance. His cough was so bad that no one would hire him. He was even evicted from his boardinghouse because the owner feared that he was contagious.

When he had nearly lost all hope, Harry noticed a photo of a toddler in one of the store windows on Broadway and recognized himself. Back in New Hampshire, his parents had sold his services as a child to early photographers who, in turn, planted his picture on the cover of *All-American Boy* magazine. Now, 3,000 miles away and nearly twenty years later, hacking, threadbare Harry stared at the finely dressed little Harry who had an optimistic smile and sparkling blue eyes planted between healthy baby cheeks. The photo was the epiphany that became a turning point in Harry Chandler's life.

He moved into a tent near the Cahuenga Pass, on the southern edge of the San Fernando Valley some twenty miles from downtown Los Angeles. A sympathetic doctor who also suffered from lung disease was a squatter on the property and allowed Chandler to live there in exchange for help on the small farm he and his wife operated by themselves. Harry regained his health through a daily regimen of breaking horses, tending crops, and picking oranges and grapefruit. In addition to meals, the couple paid Chandler in the form of a percentage of the fruit he picked. He hauled what he couldn't eat to wheat threshers who worked the vast 60,000-acre Isaac Newton Van Nuys ranch a few miles to the northwest. Surprising even himself, Chandler charged $19 a wagon load for the fruit and began to accumulate a small fortune—$2,000 at the end of the first year.

His health restored and a fat nest egg in his pocket, Harry Chandler bid adieu to the doctor and his wife and to Southern California in the fall of 1884. He returned to Dartmouth to live with his grandfather and take his place in the East Coast establishment. But two days after his return, he started coughing blood again; Chandler dropped dreams of Dartmouth a second time and again turned his eyes westward.

Following the short winter of 1884,[3] a few weeks before Charles Fletcher Lummis lumbered into L.A. and took up residence in the editorial offices of the *Los Angeles Daily Times*, Harry Chandler was back on the train headed for Southern California—this time, to stay for good.

CHAPTER 2

SHORTLY AFTER HIS RETURN to L.A., Harry Chandler landed a $12-a-week clerk's job in the *Times* circulation department in 1885, but the job involved brute labor: Harry had to load wagons each morning with bundles of the *Times,* which had grown to eight pages and sold almost 3,000 copies a day, six days a week. Harry's bronchial consumption now appeared to be a permanent part of his past. A robust Chandler had no problem stripping to the waist, smearing ink over his hardening pectorals, and pitching in with the heavy work of bundling and tossing newspaper stacks fresh off the press.

But Harry had no intention of being a loading dock laborer for the rest of his newspaper career. He moved up quickly to *Times* chief of collections, and later to

mail-order manager. Along the way, as always, Harry found side deals to supplement his income.

Using a portion of his $2,000 nest egg, Chandler bought delivery routes for the rival *Herald, Evening Express,* and the *San Diego Union.* Unbeknownst to Colonel Otis, Harry also bought a 1,400-subscriber *Los Angeles Times* delivery route.

In those days, newspaper owners franchised for a price their subscriber distribution to independent contractors. Under such an arrangement, a contractor bought a list of subscribers, hired a delivery crew—usually schoolboys—and collected the delivery fees on a monthly or bimonthly basis for the publisher; the contractor kept an agreed-upon percentage to pay his crew and his contractor's commission.

Although he was integral to the success of any newspaper, the outside distribution contractor nevertheless seldom had anything more than an arm's-length relationship with the stuffy inside editorial and business types. Often, the publisher didn't even know who delivered his newspaper. Delivery in pre-automobile Los Angeles was hard, dusty, dirty work that Harrison and Eliza Otis, now middle-aged, considered beneath them. The increasingly self-absorbed Colonel Otis had no idea that Chandler not only performed his circulation clerk's duties but also delivered the paper to 1,400 subscribers every day; all that concerned Otis was that he heard not a single complaint from a customer.

Echoing his own version New York's Post Office creed about never letting anything prevent him from keeping his appointed rounds, Harry Chandler was a stickler for delivering the *Times*. Distribution was a cash-and-carry business, just as selling grapefruit was, and Harry Chandler understood that the greatest paper in world was as worthless as spoiled tomatoes unless it was delivered on time. That's why, whenever one of his newsboys failed to show up for work, Chandler would mount a horse, ride a bicycle, or even row a boat down the L.A. River during winter flash floods to get those papers to his customers.

Chandler's day started at 4:00 A.M., when as many as fifty newsboys showed up at the *Times* for their newspaper allotments; they paid 2.5 cents per copy and sold them to subscribers or hawked them on the street for a nickel apiece. A hardworking young hustler could earn as much as $1.50 a week and a boss such as Chandler took in $50 to $100 a week. During the rest of the day, Chandler handled routine circulation and accounting duties in his role as a *Times* clerk, then collected the day's cash from his news crews in the early evening.

But his grueling sixteen-hour daily routine was hardly selfless.

As months passed into years, Chandler's nest egg grew; he quietly bought up more independent paper routes—not just for the *Times* but for all three of L.A.'s competing dailies. Before the end of the 1880s, he controlled the distribution of the *Los Angeles Herald* and *Los Angeles Tribune*, as well as the *Times*.

One summer night when the moon was full, Harry had another epiphany. He awoke with a start, ready to get into the yoke for another sixteen-hour day, but his alarm clock said 2:00 A.M., not 4:00 A.M. The moonlight had jarred him awake, and he couldn't go back to sleep. Instead, he got up, dressed, and strolled downtown, toward the *Times*. At First and Spring, he stopped. Across the street stood a long line of men, some sitting on folding stools and some simply sprawled on the sidewalk waiting for the line to move. The line snaked all the way down First Street to Main and disappeared around the corner. Harry estimated the crowd at about four hundred. He crossed the street to investigate.

He learned that the men were waiting for dawn and an opportunity to get first choice at buying a lot in the town site of Alosta, about twenty miles east of L.A. in what is now the city of Glendora, at the base of the San Gabriel Mountains.

"You don't seem to have much to do just now, young feller," remarked one old duffer, who had been standing there for two days. "My son-in-law was supposed to show up here at midnight but he hasn't come and without rest I can't stick it out any longer. I'll give you a dollar an hour if you'll hold my place in line for two hours."

Harry made $2 that night before starting his daily routine at the *Times*, but more important than the extra money was what he learned firsthand about Southern California real estate and the psychology of greed. In the 1880s, undeveloped land in the Los Angeles basin stretched for mile after mile, awaiting anyone with a small nest egg and a strong commitment to turn it into a home, a ranch, a farm, a factory: whatever a man might desire. And yet, men would stand in line for days to pay premium prices for a small slice of land chiefly because they believed every other man wanted the same slice of land.

It was a lesson young Harry Chandler would not soon forget. And the story of that moonlit night became a keystone of the Harry hagiography handed down from Chandler to Chandler for decades thereafter.

Meanwhile, proud, blustering Colonel Otis had immersed himself in municipal politics during the boom years of the mid-1880s and lost sight altogether of the peculiarities of local real estate marketing. All he knew was that subdividers were practically standing in line to buy ads in his *Times* the same way their customers were standing in line to buy lots. The cash rolled in and the Colonel was pleased.

Otis had become a strong, paternalistic bastion of Republican politics in L.A.; he used his newspaper to praise his friends and skewer his enemies. Wearing his newfound respectability in the form of large, well-tailored suits to cover his expanding, lumbering girth, the *Times'* "Walrus," as he was known, did vaguely resemble the arctic mammal that lent him his nickname. The Colonel's dour, melon-shaped head, distinguished by bushy Mephisthophelean eyebrows, a gray

tufted goatee, and long, white mustaches, had become alternately parodied and feared by much of the growing metropolis's citizens.

Regardless of public opinion, one way or the other, Harrison Gray Otis could no longer be ignored. He was the driving pro-business force behind the creation of the powerful Merchants & Manufacturers Association, founded in 1886 to fight off the advances of labor unions. In the same antiunion vein, he cofounded the Los Angeles Chamber of Commerce on October 15, 1888, with Judge Robert M. Widney,[1] dunning its charter members $5 dues per year.

Colonel Otis was no longer a workingman. He was a businessman, and any traffic that he was forced to have with blue-collar types, particularly if they were in his employ, was distasteful to him at best. The high-water mark of Harrison Otis's middle-aged hypocrisy toward the labor movement came on August 5, 1890, when he declared open warfare on his own printers. The International Typographical Union, of which he had once been a card-carrying member, was now his sworn enemy. Although the union helped guarantee the young Otis a job at the Government Printing Office, he had come a long way since then. Otis now controlled a newspaper with an average daily circulation of 6,762 in the fastest growing city in the West; with typical militant intolerance, he labeled those who disagreed with him his foes, especially if he paid their wages.

Almost from the day he first set foot in the *Times* building, Otis had been at odds with his printers. He grudgingly paid them their negotiated raises and met their other demands over the years, but he balked on two key points: "dead heading" and the union's call for a closed shop.

"Dead heading" was the union policy that forced publishers to reset by hand every advertisement or story that came in to a newspaper. In an era when "hot type" printing technology was fast replacing the old method of setting cold type by hand, letter by letter, "dead heading" was both redundant and unnecessarily expensive. One night on deadline, when Otis objected to his printers' resetting a 50,000-character patent medicine ad, the shop foreman threatened:

"All right, there'll be no *Los Angeles Times* in the morning."

Fuming, Otis gave in to the foreman's blackmail, but this was one of the last times he did so. When the union next demanded that lower-paid nonunion printers be barred from working at the *Times,* the choleric Colonel went over the edge. Rather than cave in to ITU Local 174's call for a union shop, Otis locked his printers out. Although his newspaper publishing peers predicted professional suicide, Otis had already made secret arrangements to import "scabs" from Kansas City. The Printers Protective Fraternity, as the nonunion printers called themselves, manned the *Times'* print-setting stalls for the next two years. Otis was so adamant in his antiunion fervor that he not only set up internships for scabs—

these rivaled the ITU's own apprenticeship program—but he paid twice the going rate for his own composing-room crew, just to freeze out the union.

During the generation that followed, dubbed "The 40 Years' War" by such labor movement leaders as Eugene V. Debs and Samuel Gompers, both the newspaper and Harrison Gray Otis would gain a national reputation as standard-bearers of antiunion sentiment; indeed, all attempts to unionize the *Times* were rebuffed until more than fifty years after Otis's death.

In 1890, Otis still had other enemies to vanquish, not least of whom was another Civil War colonel who rivaled Otis not only in military rank but also as a daily newspaper publisher in L.A. Henry H. Boyce was Harrison Gray Otis's avowed archrival, and, worst of all, he was a confounded Democrat.

THE BLOOD FEUD between Colonels Otis and Boyce began in the summer of 1884, six months before Charles Fletcher Lummis limped into town. When Tom Caystile, one of Otis's four partners, died suddenly, Otis smelled opportunity. Harrison and Eliza Otis teamed up with the affluent Colonel Boyce, who had supposedly made a killing in investments back in Ohio, and bought out the *Times*' three remaining owners as well as the dead partner's heirs. The two colonels immediately incorporated both the newspaper and the Mirror Book Bindery where the *Times* was printed each day. It was now the Times Mirror Company,[2] with forty shares of common stock valued at $1,000 a share, which Otis and Boyce split evenly between them.

The following year, in 1885, Los Angeles underwent a boomtown transformation when it ballooned from 12,000 to 100,000 residents. When the Santa Fe Railroad began regular service to L.A. on November 25, 1885, a price war broke out with rival Southern Pacific; as a result, one-way fares from the Midwest and the South began dropping precipitously. At one point, Santa Fe offered Kansas City–to–Los Angeles adult fares for $1, and Midwesterners and Easterners came to Southern California in droves. City directories had to be updated monthly.

Los Angeles County property values also exploded—from $16 million to $107 million—with more than seventy new towns laid out on surveyors' maps. An acre bought for $50 in 1884 was subdivided into five lots that sold for $300 apiece by 1885. Thousands of homesteads were sold on credit, but the newspaper ads that publicized these real estate sales were purchased strictly on a cash basis. The *Times* flourished.

In three years, the Otises' annual gross income nearly doubled, from $64,000 in 1885 to $117,000 by 1888, and the new Times Mirror Company enjoyed a steady

10 percent annual profit margin. It would have been the rosiest period in Colonel Otis's checkered career were it not for Colonel Boyce.

Unlike his previous partners, who had kept their hands off of the news and remained satisfied with the *Times'* ever-increasing profit margin, Boyce fancied himself every bit as much a newspaperman as Otis. If they had agreed on some issues, Boyce's interference might not have been as annoying, but they didn't agree on anything. Boyce's politics favored doing away with national banks, allowing foreigners to own U.S. real estate, granting equal rights to women and, perhaps worst of all, endorsing the right of labor unions to organize and bargain with management. During their brief two-year alliance, the *Times'* partners almost came to blows.

Boyce finally moved to end the partnership by exercising a clause in their agreement that gave Otis a deadline either to sell Boyce his half of the business or to come up with $27,000 to buy him out. Boyce knew the high-living Otises did not have that kind of capital and prepared to take over the *Times.* But at the last minute, Otis called in enough favors from his newfound allies in the L.A. banking and business community to beat Boyce at his own game. Otis forked over $27,000 of borrowed cash and, on April 8, 1886, became the major shareholder of Times Mirror stock.

The first action Otis took as president, general manager, and editor in chief was to drop "Daily" from the paper's name so that it became simply the *Los Angeles Times.* Next, he increased the Times Mirror shares from forty to sixty and used them to raise enough loans to finance construction of a new $50,000 *Times* building. Dubbed "the Fortress" in keeping with the Colonel's relentless military pretense, the new four-story brick-and-granite building at the northeast corner of First and Broadway opened for business in May 1887. Its decorative stone turrets looked down on Civic Center like those of a feudal castle; the state-of-the-art printing presses inside turned out ten times as many copies of the newspaper as the old water-and-fish powered press had.

A bronze eagle perched atop the highest point on the building's battlements glared carnivorously to the south, where every day of the year the railroads dumped future subscribers by the hundreds at the West Coast terminus of the Southern Pacific and Santa Fe lines. Over the entrance was Eliza's motto:

Stand Fast, Stand Firm, Stand Sure, Stand True

The Fortress was the Colonel's pride and joy.

Meanwhile, Colonel Boyce did not take his $27,000 and slink back to Ohio as Otis had hoped. Boyce invested in his own daily, and the *Los Angeles Tribune*[3] quickly became as poisonous a presence in Harrison Otis's L.A. as the typogra-

pher's union. Whatever editorial stance taken by the *Times*, the *Tribune* could be expected to promote the opposite view. When Boyce backed a candidate for California's secretary of state, Otis flatly accused the hapless man of alcoholism, bestiality, fomenting an orgy, and hiring a photographer to preserve his perversions on film. Otis's personal attacks on Boyce were almost as vile. In an editorial published May 28, 1889, Otis denounced his former partner as a "wife-beater, embezzler, hypocrite, thief, pretender, scoundrel and moral leper." He went on to say that "Boyce has swindled his partners in many business deals and stolen soldiers' money entrusted to his care, to be conveyed to families of such soldiers while they were serving in the field."

Boyce accused Otis of extorting $200 in gold from a congressional candidate in exchange for a favorable story; Otis denounced Boyce for allegedly blackmailing a judge for $250 to keep a damaging story out of his *Tribune*. Otis insisted on calling Boyce's *Tribune* the Los Angeles "Trombone." The rivalry grew so serious that *Times* city editor Charles Lummis tussled with Boyce on the street one day; what began as a shouting and shoving match wound up with Lummis beating the rival publisher into submission with his walking cane.

Libel suits flew back and forth while both newspapers' circulation and advertising continued to climb. In 1887, the *Tribune* began publishing seven days a week and the *Times* was quick to follow. In 1888, the *Times* published its first sixteen-page Sunday edition and beat the *Tribune* in the race to become the exclusive West Coast franchise for the Associated Press. As the 1880s gave way to the "Gay '90s," the conflict between Otis's *Times* and Boyce's *Tribune* looked as if it might drag on another twenty years. But Harry Chandler, once a mere circulation clerk for the *Times,* had a solution.

By the time the unassuming Harry Chandler came up with a plan to put Henry Boyce out of business, he had made a habit of surprising the Colonel.

Following his first year of service at the *Times,* Chandler meekly asked to be promoted to circulation manager. He pointed out that he now monopolized most independent newspaper distribution in L.A., including that of the *Herald* and the *Express,* if not the *Tribune.* The naive and obstinate Colonel Otis was not impressed. After all, Chandler ran an army of ragtag newsboys, and what did that prove?

As a demonstration of his power, Chandler sent all the newsboys who delivered the rival *Herald* on a five-day camping holiday in the San Bernardino Mountains, but did not replace them on their paper routes. It also turned out to be their customers' holiday from the *Herald.* None got his paper for a week.

"When the time came to distribute the *Herald*, there weren't any boys to do it," Chandler recounted several years later, "and the confusion was so great for the next few days that the *Times* put on a subscription campaign and got about half the subscribers of the *Herald*."

Otis was impressed. He gave Chandler his promotion to circulation manager. Next time Chandler demanded his stubborn boss's attention, he got it: He was prepared to put Henry Boyce out of business. Otis listened.

"I went to [Colonel] Otis and told him the situation," Chandler recalled.

He said I couldn't do it. I told him I could and not only that, but for the *Times'* sake, I should. My scheme was to starve out the *Tribune*. With two of the three morning papers' distribution systems under my control, it would be simple to play them together against the *Tribune*. If a *Times* subscriber quit, we could swing him to the *Herald*, whereas he might have gone to the *Tribune* if left alone. If a *Herald* subscriber quit, we could swing him to the *Times*. Of course, no one but [Colonel] Otis would know of my connection. The *Herald* routes were to be handled through a dummy.

Chandler's scheme worked so well that Boyce was, indeed, forced into bankruptcy and had to sell his printing presses and other equipment for a fraction of what they were worth. When Otis heard that the *Tribune* had been put up for sale, he gleefully put in a bid, but it arrived too late. The paper and its capital equipment had already been sold, for five cents on the dollar. The buyer was the *Times'* new superintendent of circulation: the guileless young Harry Chandler.

ALTHOUGH HARRY APPEARED TO BE MODEST, he thought of himself as singularly extraordinary. He was more than happy to sell newspapers by the cartload and corner the market using whatever cutthroat methods available, even if he did not read newspapers himself—at least, not in the same studious manner as the Colonel. Harry Chandler's interest in politics was purely pragmatic; the idea of skewering enemies in the pages of the *Times* seemed little more than an exercise in self-indulgent vanity unless one had ulterior motive—and that motive *always* had to be about money.

Chandler's boss, however, had a streak of hubris a mile wide. More than once, principal overrode pragmatism with Colonel Otis. He might easily have lost the advantage he gained during L.A.'s boom-and-bust years of the 1890s had it not been for his new business manager. Harry Chandler was fiscally conservative to such a degree that he could be described as flinty, even cheap, unless he came across a distress sale. When Southern California's economy was a nonstop roller-coaster ride with real estate inflated beyond reason one year and worth nothing the next, Harry Chandler was always there to pick up the bargains; he took care of himself first and his closest business cronies next—if anything was left over once he'd cherry-picked the best deals.

If Harrison Otis was the ponderous and flamboyant Walrus, then Harry Chandler was his penny-pinching Fox. Through an alchemy of perseverance and dumb luck, Colonel Otis had stumbled into his fortune after years of flubs and false starts. But through a combination of hard work, shrewd gambles, and a large dollop of deceptive intent, Harry Chandler began building his fortune while he was still in his twenties. He never pretended to be anything other than what he was: The man after the cash.

At some private level, Harry was also a man of flesh and blood who appreciated women, if not in quite so obvious a manner as he appreciated a dollar. He had taken a bride early in his newspaper career. At twenty-four, the deceptively shy, dimple-chinned Harry Chandler married Magdalena Schlador, the beautiful daughter of a Berlin merchant and sister of one of the other clerks who worked at the *Times*. Although he and Magdalena lived in town on Rosas Street, near the *Times*, Harry was also invested in a three-hundred-acre farm in the outlying hamlet of Burbank; his parents, Moses and Emma Chandler, now having emigrated to Southern California, lived on the farm and raised apricots, peaches, and grapes.

Magdalena gave Harry a daughter, Frances, in 1890; but the first Mrs. Chandler died, apparently from complications from childbirth, two weeks after giving birth to their second daughter, May, in 1892. Whether by chance or by murderous design, as some of Harry's more slanderous detractors suggested in later years, the ambitious young Mr. Chandler was now free to court again. A year and a half after his first wife's death, he married up on the social and business ladder, this time taking the boss's daughter as his bride.

On the afternoon of June 5, 1894, thirty-year-old Harry Chandler wed Emma Marian Otis, twenty-seven, at the Otises' lavish Grand Avenue home. The *Times'* very own "Susan Sunshine" supervised the description of her daughter's wedding ceremony as it appeared on the society page; the piece described the parlor decorations, the guests, and even the subtle particulars of Marian's wedding gown: "The bride, a tall handsome girl, wore a dress of pearl gray silk in the ground of which were woven tiny clusters of pink roses. The dress was trimmed with pink velvet and had bands of duchess lace and soft frills of the same."

The couple honeymooned for a week in San Francisco, then rode the rails back to L.A., where they moved into a new home near the *Times* offices. Harry could stay away from work no longer, but neither could his wife. For the first year, Harry's in-laws from his first marriage lived with the Chandlers to help care for Marian's two new stepdaughters while she worked at the *Times*.[4] Like her mother, Marian was as deeply involved in the family business as her husband was; Harry was a stockholder in his own right who had been quietly acquiring shares for years before marrying the boss's daughter. Marian was also a stockholder, as well as a director of the corporation; her name continued to appear on the *Times'*

masthead as secretary of the Times Mirror Company for many years after her marriage, despite her twin roles as mother to six of her own children and stepmother to Harry's two daughters from his first marriage.

Harry and Marian appeared to be solidly wed during those earliest years, but rumors began swirling around at that time about the Colonel and a twenty-year-old woman who appeared to be his midlife crisis: Ellen Beach Yaw, a lovely young opera singer from the L.A. suburb of Covina. A link between the Colonel and the so-called Covina songbird developed in the early 1890s, when the Colonel called on his wife, Eliza Otis, to write several *Times* articles touting the remarkable soprano voice of "Lark Ellen," as Miss Yaw was known on stage. As time passed, the Colonel's admiring relationship grew noticeably closer. In 1894, he opened and subsidized the Lark Ellen Home for Newsboys in the singer's honor; he ordered his staff to write about her every performance on the road, from New York to London to Vienna. The sheer number of glowing *Times* reviews of Lark Ellen's public appearances became so blatant that letters to the *Times* editors began to make fun of them.

But gossip ended almost as abruptly as the Colonel's passion for Lark Ellen and her music. Whether Eliza put her foot down, or the Colonel simply lost interest, the affair, real or imagined, was over by 1900.[5] As one historian noted more than a half century later: "When she was in England in 1899, Special Correspondence and Direct Wire Dispatches were sent to the *Times*, exclusively, which were costly investments for the newspaper. But mysteriously after this extensive coverage of her activities, the *Times* carried no news of her for over ten years."

FAR FROM LANGUISHING after the union lockout, the *Times* continued to climb steadily in ad sales and circulation. Boycotts and strikes had little effect in L.A., where a frontier mentality persisted long after electricity replaced gas street lights and automobiles begin sharing newly paved streets with horse carts. Colonel Otis's rallying cry of "industrial freedom" struck a chord, even with working men and women whose living standard might have risen with a little union help. As exemplified by the growing antiunion power of the chamber of commerce and the Merchants & Manufacturers' Association, the *Times* was not the only employer in town interested in banishing the unions.

The *Times'* war with its striking printers dragged on, all the way through the 1890s. When ITU organizers threatened to boycott A. Hamburger & Sons, L.A.'s largest department store and one of the *Times'* major advertisers, Hamburger increased its advertising in the *Times* and pointedly offered nonunion overalls at bargain prices. Clerks tracked the customers who bought the overalls; the *Times* then published their names if they were union members to demonstrate the

hypocrisy and weakness of the boycott when it came to a union member's personal greed.

Besides fighting the unions, Otis found another cause célèbre during the 1890s in the Free Harbor League, as well as another high-profile enemy in Collis P. Huntington's Southern Pacific Railroad. Like every right-thinking member of the new Los Angeles Chamber of Commerce, Colonel Otis understood that L.A.'s future as the Pacific Coast behemoth that he hoped the city would eventually become depended in large part on creating a nearby deep-water port. But creating a port where a natural harbor barely existed at all was an expensive proposition and could not be undertaken solely by the city, or even the state of California. L.A. needed enormous underwriting from taxpayers.

With a rail spur already in place from downtown L.A., the coastal settlement of San Pedro twenty miles to the southwest seemed the most likely location for the port, and that is where the *Times* threw its editorial support. But Southern Pacific rail magnate Collis P. Huntington had other ideas. By 1892, he was openly boasting that his connections in Congress would guarantee a deep-water harbor at Santa Monica, where he was already constructing a $1-million pier; he also anticipated the building of a federally financed breakwater at the terminus of his rail line.

During the remainder of the decade, a parade of senators, congressmen, and Washington bureaucrats made the trek to L.A. and visited both San Pedro and Santa Monica to size up which was the better location. Senator William P. Frye of Maine sarcastically summed up most of the East Coast's sentiment to Los Angeles officials: "Well, it seems you have made a great mistake in the location of your city. If you Los Angeles people want a harbor, why not move the city down to San Diego? There is a good harbor there."

Otis and his *Times* were not amused, nor was California's Senator Stephen M. White, who championed the cause of the San Pedro harbor on the floor of the Senate. Otis was instrumental in forming the Free Harbor League, a citizens' lobby that encouraged newly arrived *Times* readers to write to their former congressmen back home in Ohio, Illinois, or Connecticut and urge them to vote for the San Pedro appropriation. For three years, Congress dallied, bottling the appropriation up in committee or tabling it before any final floor vote. But in 1899, the Free Harbor League triumphed. Over Huntington's boasts that he had already sewn up the necessary votes to secure a Santa Monica breakwater, the House and Senate approved $2.9 million for a harbor at San Pedro.[6]

The San Pedro victory marked the pinnacle of Harrison Gray Otis's career and made him a hero twice over in 1899. The former colonel was now General Harrison Gray Otis, and newly returned from a year in the Philippines, just in time to celebrate the dumping of the first shipment of quarried granite into the sea at San

Pedro. On April 27, 1899, Los Angeles celebrated the Free Harbor Jubilee, naming General Otis, now L.A.'s own Spanish American War hero, as the city's chief guest of honor.

The previous June, although he was sixty-one years old and weighed in at a flabby 250 pounds, Harrison Otis convinced President William McKinley, an old crony from his Civil War days, to boost him from the rank of lieutenant colonel to brigadier general and return him to service in the short-lived Spanish American War. Otis led an expeditionary force to the Philippines that arrived just as the war was ending. Despite the Spanish surrender, however, the Americans remained as an occupying army, every bit as colonial-minded as the army they had just defeated. General Otis sent regular dispatches that fully supported U.S. imperialism back to his *Times*. He wrote of the Filipinos with much of the same paternalistic condescension he had once given over to the primitive Eskimos during his Seal Islands sojourn.

"The average Filipino is not a bad fellow, nor wholly without merit or intelligence," Otis wrote in one *Times* editorial. "He certainly has rights to be respected, and I believe that, properly managed, good can be got out of him, both for himself and for the country."

Filipino nationalists, now burdened with a U.S. yoke, were not so smitten with the General's noblesse oblige. A revolutionary force seized the provincial capital of Malolos, sniping at Americans and angrily ordering them to go home. The next *Times* dispatch from Otis now described Filipinos as "ignorant, misguided and bumptious natives."

In the ensuing campaign during the winter of 1899, over one hundred soldiers under General Otis's command were killed. The better-equipped United States Army eventually subdued the Filipino insurrection; it became a war of attrition, and the rebels were now driven back into the jungle. There they fought a protracted guerrilla war that ran hot and cold for the next forty-seven years until the United States at last granted the Philippines their independence.

Harrison Otis had left the Philippines after less than a year and brought home the ultimate military title as his reward. General Otis presided over the Free Harbor Jubilee like a conquering hero; he praised Senator Stephen White for ramming the harbor appropriation through Congress, but also saved a generous helping of praise for himself. He never shed his belief that the spoils always go to the victor: Those who were fit to do so ruled and those who were not were ruled over. That feudalistic philosophy was also a cornerstone of Harry Chandler's Darwinian method of conducting business.

To the General and his new son-in-law, the Free Harbor episode represented far more than a successful lobbying campaign. At the time, Huntington's railroad

was regarded as the single most powerful force in Southern California; that the *Times* had beaten Huntington at his own political game left an indelible impression on the two men who would carry the newspaper into the next century—their century, as it would turn out. Long after the Huntington name faded from all but a few municipal monuments and the Southern Pacific's power had been relegated to footnote status in the history books, the names Otis, Chandler, and the *Times* would continue to dominate the city they helped to create.

In 1898, Harry Chandler was elected vice president and named assistant general manager of the Times Mirror Company; Colonel Otis continued in his role as president and general manager. The following year, Marian gave birth to the first of three Chandler sons. They named him Norman and began grooming him, almost from birth, to assume the helm of the family's newspaper. The *Times,* which had grown and prospered along with the city, now published a Sunday magazine along with a nationally distributed "Mid-Winter Edition," which relentlessly hammered home that Los Angeles had it all: climate, transportation, ocean, mountains, agriculture, wide-open spaces, and so forth.

The special edition, which the *Times* had begun publishing in 1886, had grown replete with positive propaganda about the orange and avocado wonders of sunny Southern California during the 1890s. Thousands of people in the East received free copies, delivered by train, stagecoach, and sailing ship, when the worst of the Canadian snowstorms were pelting Cleveland, Buffalo, Pittsburgh, Philadelphia, and sometimes as far south as Atlanta and Dallas. It became a January tradition. On New Year's Day, when the rest of the country was buttoning up its overcoat, the Mid-Winter Edition reported that the newly settled Los Angeles suburb of Pasadena hosted an annual Tournament of Roses parade down the city's balmy main thoroughfare.[7] The *Times* puffed up every petal so that the miserable Eskimos of Chicago could almost smell the floral displays as they shivered over their copies of the Mid-Winter Edition.

And while Harrison Otis glowed over the glowing "news" columns boosting the utopian dreamscape that was his adopted hometown, Harry Chandler glowed over the enormous number of paid advertisements that made the Mid-Winter Edition the fattest newspaper in the country. And the advertising miracle was not merely confined to the Mid-Winter Edition; by the end of the 1800s, the *Los Angeles Times* carried more advertising lineage than any other newspaper in the United States, a distinction that it would retain for most of the following century.

The *Times* was doing far more than reflect its community, like most comparable newspapers in 1900. The *Times* was creating a major city whose population hit 102,479 at the turn of the century; and General Harrison Otis and his chief aide-de-camp, Harry Chandler, were directing the battle. One point upon which

the quixotic Walrus and the pragmatic Fox agreed, unanimously and without reservation, was that their beloved Los Angeles had everything.

Except water.

CHAPTER 3

CRADLED IN A CRESCENT RANGE of coastal mountains that abuts the Pacific Ocean, Los Angeles was, and is, the heart of a great and unique desert. Visitors invariably buy the vision of a grand, green valley that is immune to the tumble-weed weather and bone-dry landscape that surrounds it. But all this is an illusion, as those who remain for more than a season are made to understand.

The history of Southern California had always been the history of boom and bust that paralleled seasons of flood inevitably followed by seasons of long and merciless drought. The Chumash, Yutah, and Gabrieleno Indians understood these unforgiving cycles and learned to live with them. So did the Franciscan missionaries, the Spanish *padrones*, and the Mexican ranchers who followed them. Each new expeditionary force was itself conquered—first, by the philistines who came after and, second, by the land.

The last wave of such conquering gringos as General Harrison Otis and his shrewd son-in-law, Harry Chandler, saw L.A.'s natural history differently. With the advent of a new century, the Walrus and the Fox had been in residence in Los Angeles long enough to be aware of the region's limits, but they stubbornly believed that can-do Yankee ingenuity could always be counted upon to lick natural obstacles. The team of Otis and Chandler could seduce the masses with tales of Southern California's wonderful climate. Why couldn't they seduce the rain as well?

"There is no need for precipitancy of action, there being no pressing need for immediate extension of irrigation works," Otis editorialized in 1899 in one of the *Times'* regular pitches to grow L.A. ever larger—and never mind its lack of water.

But the natural aquifer beneath the L.A. basin that greedily soaked up sparse storm water each winter had already been tapped far beyond its natural capacity. New settlers had to drill deeper and deeper for the remaining water. At the rate that Los Angeles was growing, city hall's real prognosticators—not the expansionist boosters from the *Times*—gave the region only another five to ten years before the basin began reverting to desert. The utopian trumpeting of the *Times'* Mid-Winter Edition notwithstanding, L.A. had reached its upward limits in sus-

tainable year-round population. Summer drought already demanded water rationing; fines were levied against those misguided city residents who insisted on irrigating their lawns. Something had to be done. But the *Times'* Otis and Chandler were not the men to do it. Fred Eaton and William Mulholland were.

Mulholland was a swashbuckler, tailor-made to conquer the West. An Irish immigrant who sailed the seas, fought Apaches in Texas, and cut timber in northern Michigan before emigrating to Los Angeles in 1877, William Mulholland was a cigar-chomping city ditchdigger who taught himself the science of hydraulics and eventually rose to the position of chief engineer in the Los Angeles City Water Department. At first, he did not see the wisdom of diverting a river to foster L.A.'s expansion, and said as much to the city fathers.

"If you don't get the water, you won't need it," he preached, meaning that the Darwinian economics of water supply and demand would put a top-end limit on how many people would choose to live in Los Angeles. But Fred Eaton, who had preceded Mulholland as superintendent of the Los Angeles Water Department, saw L.A.'s future as a wet dream rather than a dry nightmare.

Elected mayor of L.A. in 1898, Eaton came as close to being a bona fide second-generation Southern California blue blood as any gringo-come-lately; his father, Judge B. S. Eaton, was one of the founders of the patrician L.A. suburb of Pasadena. Most of the male members of Eaton's immediate family were educated as engineers. First as Los Angeles City Engineer and, later, as the city's mayor, Eaton accurately predicted L.A.'s impending water woes as early as the drought of 1892.

During that desperate time, the young city speculated that it might have to import water to prevent disaster, but the nearest rivers with enough to slake the thirst of L.A.'s exploding population appeared to be the Kern or the Colorado, hundreds of inhospitable mountain and desert miles to the north and east. Fred Eaton saw a third possibility. Someday, he said, he would move to the Owens Valley some 250 miles northeast of the city, where water from the Sierra Nevada Mountains ran into the Owens River year round; Eaton calculated that this water could keep Los Angeles wet for a century, maybe longer .

The rains did come again, temporarily tabling the city's water crisis, but more people arrived, too. Eaton knew it was only a matter of time before the temporary crisis became permanent and at the turn of the century, during his tenure as mayor, the drought returned. The city, the *Times,* and Eaton weathered the first several dry years; but in 1903, Eaton told his associates that he was planning to retire and realize his dream of a rancher's life in the Owens Valley.

There, at the base of Mt. Whitney, the highest mountain in the United States at the time, Eaton found the solution to L.A.'s water crisis. As 1920s historian John Steven McGroarty reverently recounted in his hokey three-volume *History of Los*

Angeles County: "There came down from the snows of the High Sierras in the character of a Moses, an old-time lover and long-time resident of Los Angeles who had abandoned his old home town to devote his life to ranching far away to the north among the great mountain peaks of Inyo County. This man was Fred Eaton, sometime city engineer and sometime mayor of Los Angeles."

But McGroarty and a host of other California "historians" during the first half of the twentieth century failed to reveal that two years of scheming, subterfuge, and breathtaking larceny preceded this Old Testament tableau. Eaton was no ogre bent on raping the Owens Valley, but he was no Moses, either. Eaton was a utilitarian, given to rationalizing that the moral high ground always favors the greatest good for the greatest number. The water theft that set the stage for one of the most spectacular real estate ripoffs in U.S. history began with Mayor Eaton's best intentions.

The Owens River fed a ranch that Eaton had his eye on, as well as the ranches of several hundred other cattle and sheep ranchers on the eastern side of the Sierra Nevada. Their fields and orchards extended along a one-hundred-mile stretch between Mammoth Mountain on the north and desert-bound Owens Lake at the south end of a long, broad valley. Nourished by a High Sierra ice pack that never completely melted, the river ran wet and wild year-round and could sustain a city of as many as 3 million were it tamed. But the Owens flowed 250 miles from the Los Angeles city limits and could not be diverted so far from its riverbed.

Or could it?

In 1902, President Theodore Roosevelt had authorized creation of the U.S. Reclamation Service, forerunner of the Department of the Interior's Bureau of Land Reclamation; its mandate was to build such public works projects as dams, aqueducts, and flood control systems that might turn the mostly uninhabitable western United States into arable land. Among other western garden spots, Owens Valley attracted the service's attention: Acres of water seemed wasted as the river flowed unchecked into the saline sands of Owens Lake.

By June 1903, U.S. surveying teams began scouting the valley. Bureau officials were already developing plans for an irrigation system that would capture Owens River water before it percolated into the Mojave Desert; the water would be recycled so that the already rich ranch lands of the valley could sustain even larger herds of cattle and sheep.

Fred Eaton saw a different use for the Owens River. Like 90 percent of his future Owens Valley neighbors, Eaton was more than willing to sign over future water rights to the Reclamation Service on the pretext that the government plan for an irrigation system would benefit all who owned property there. But the former Los Angeles mayor saw no reason why that irrigation system couldn't be stretched

to irrigate another valley halfway across the state. Like a blood transfusion from the living to the nearly dead, the Owens Valley could reinvigorate L.A. and raise the comatose San Fernando Valley water table to unnaturally lush levels.

Although initially scornful about L.A.'s water crisis, General Harrison Otis had done a remarkable about face by 1903. His *Times* was now in perfect agreement with Eaton, but not out of humanitarian angst over the General's dehydrated fellow Angelenos. He had a special interest in bringing water to L.A. by way of the San Fernando Valley, and it had far more to do with greed than with altruism.

How a handful of powerful men led by the owners of the *Times* could pervert the federal government's local irrigation plan into a 250-mile Los Angeles lifeline became a textbook study in mob manipulation, utilitarian theft, and winner-take-all water politics in the arid American West. It began with the formation of a San Fernando land syndicate just four months after the Reclamation Service surveyors descended on Owens Valley. General Otis and his son-in-law, Harry Chandler, founders of that syndicate, depended heavily on secrecy in guaranteeing the rape of Owens Valley. During the next two years, readers of the *Times* would learn regularly and with increasing alarm about the city's dire need for water, but nowhere would they read that the *Times'* publisher and general manager had banded together with seven other power brokers to buy more than 44,000 acres of San Fernando Valley's rocks and chaparral.

The Porter Land & Water Company, which stretched over the present day Northridge section of the San Fernando Valley, supported a few hundred head of cattle and little else; yet in October of 1903, despite the area's wretched possibilities, nine of the wealthiest men in Southern California took a sudden interest in Porter Ranch. Together, they put down 10 percent of the $500,000 asking price for Porter Ranch as an option to buy the arid acreage within three years. The $50,000 check was signed by Brigadier General Harrison Gray Otis.

The General's partners included a *Who's Who* of Southern California's robber barons, many of whom had been arch rivals until they climbed into bed with one another on the San Fernando Valley deal. They were

- Edwin T. Earl, publisher of the *Times'* chief competitor, the *Los Angeles Express;*
- Moses Hazeltine Sherman, a former Arizona schoolteacher who moved to L.A. in 1889, partnered with brother-in-law Eli P. Clark to create the electric Los Angeles Railway Company, and turned a small fortune into millions through real estate speculation;
- Henry E. Huntington, nephew of Southern Pacific's Collis P. Huntington and founder of the Pacific Electric Railway, preeminent foe of Moses Sherman's Los Angeles Electric Railway system;

- Edward H. Harriman, chairman of Union Pacific Railroad and supposedly a bitter opponent of both Sherman and Huntington;
- Joseph Sartori, a founding partner of Security Trust & Savings Bank;
- L. C. Brand of Title Guarantee & Trust Company, Sartori's chief rival; and
- William G. Kerckhoff, millionaire lumberyard magnate who expanded his business operations to utilities and cofounded the precursors of the Southern California Edison Company and the Southern California Gas Company.

The ninth member of the syndicate was *Times* General Manager Harry Chandler, the young man whom General Otis had hired as a circulation clerk almost twenty years earlier, now one of the largest land speculators in the state. The nine Republican political kingmakers of their day together comprised the backbone of the Merchant & Manufacturers Association and the Los Angeles Chamber of Commerce. It further aided their collective cause that Moses Sherman sat as a member of the Los Angeles Water Commission and knew every nuance of Mayor Eaton's master plan to reroute a river halfway across Southern California.

FRED EATON PROBABLY DID NOT personally profit from General Otis's San Fernando Mission Land Company,[1] but only because he believed the profits were to be made at the opposite end of the aqueduct. The ranch Eaton finally decided to purchase was in Long Valley, in the upper reaches of Owens Valley, where a dam could be easily constructed to create a permanent reservoir for Los Angeles water. Eaton figured that whoever owned the reservoir land would also own a veritable gold mine.

But long before he bought that ranch, Eaton pored over property records up and down the valley—all on behalf of the city of Los Angeles—to determine who held water rights and where an aqueduct could best be built to siphon off the Owens and send it spilling off to Los Angeles. When quizzed over his interest in such arcane matters, Eaton told the local record keepers that he was interested in buying retirement property. Later on, he asserted that he was working on behalf of the Reclamation Service which, by this time, had officially changed its name to the Bureau of Reclamation. In a sense, he was not lying; the bureau's engineer, Joseph B. Lippincott, had hired him as a consultant.

If there was a central Iago figure in the Owens River tragedy, it was J. B. Lippincott. Years earlier, while Eaton was still running the Los Angeles City Water Department, he had hired Lippincott. Shortly after the Bureau of Reclamation announced the Owens Valley irrigation project, Lippincott left the city for a position as a bureau engineer—but he did not entirely divorce himself from the Los Ange-

les City Water Department. While nominally overseeing the Owens River irrigation project in his position as a Bureau of Reclamation engineer, Lippincott deputized Eaton as a researcher for the bureau; this post gave the former mayor easy access to records and ample opportunity to buy Owens Valley water rights, right-of-way access, and options on riverfront property for the city of Los Angeles—all on the pretext that he was doing so on behalf of the Bureau of Reclamation.

At the same time, Lippincott produced a feasibility study on behalf of the Los Angeles City Water Commission that condemned the irrigation project as ineffectual; Lippincott's report favored an aqueduct for Los Angeles over a system of reservoirs and irrigation channels for the Owens Valley. Only later, after the Bureau of Reclamation had dropped the project, was it learned that the Water Commission paid Lippincott $2,500—half his annual bureau salary—to produce the report.

Throughout 1904, Eaton quietly bought up over $1 million in Owens Valley water rights and property options; meanwhile, in the Bureau of Reclamation's boardroom, Lippincott systematically torpedoed the very irrigation project that he was supposed to be supervising. A third engineering veteran of the Los Angeles Water Department joined Eaton and Lippincott in their field surveys during that period after finally conceding that Fred Eaton was right: An aqueduct could be built to bring water to L.A. William Mulholland, who had initially argued against such grandiloquent scheming, reluctantly embraced the idea and eventually became the Owens River Aqueduct's loudest and most loyal supporter.

By the spring of 1905, Eaton and his two fellow engineers were ready to start pushing the dominoes that would end drought anxiety forever in Los Angeles. In April, Eaton escorted seven Los Angeles city officials to the town of Independence in the heart of the Owens Valley. Posing as cattle ranchers, the seven officials exercised the land and water options that Eaton had been collecting during the previous year. With the stroke of a pen, L.A. now owned most of the arable land in the Owens Valley.

At about the same time, the San Fernando Mission Land Company exercised its own option and bought the bone-dry Porter Ranch for $500,000—$150,000 down and a mortgage based on future corporate bond sales.[2]

Three months later, on the recommendation of a panel of engineers led by J. B. Lippincott, the Bureau of Reclamation at last abandoned the Owens Valley irrigation project; in less than twenty-four hours, Lippincott quit the bureau and went to work for Mulholland as his chief assistant in the Los Angeles Water Department. Lippincott brought with him two years' worth of bureau-financed maps, survey reports, and engineering studies.

On July 29, 1905, Fred Eaton's carefully crafted cloak of secrecy fell away in the form of a front-page headline in the *Los Angeles Times:* TITANIC PROJECT TO GIVE CITY A RIVER.

Although the citizens of the Owens Valley would later mark that day as the beginning of the end, historian and Los Angeles resident John Steven McGroarty recalled the moment as a celebration: "I well remember that great morning in the month of July when this thrilling dream of the Owens River for Los Angeles was first made public in the columns of *The Times*, where it was published exclusively. The announcement sent a wild thrill through the whole population. And no wonder. Here was deliverance and salvation. It was like that time in Canaan when Joseph's brethren came back from Egypt laden with corn to succor their famine-stricken homes."

Not everyone saw the moment in such glowing biblical terms, including with the *Times*' own rivals. Months earlier, the Los Angeles Water Commission had secretly told all the city's newspaper publishers about Eaton's plan in exchange for their pledge that they wouldn't leak the news until the city had secured all the water rights that it needed in the Owens Valley. When Lippincott bolted from the Bureau of Reclamation, however, General Otis could no longer contain himself; his hubris spewed all over the front page in a geyser of mixed metaphors: "The cable that has held the San Fernando Valley vassal for ten centuries to the arid demon is about to be severed by the magical scimitar of modern engineering skill. . . . The farming lands of the valley will reap as great a blessing from this glorious water enterprise as will the dwellers within the city's gates. Let all the people say 'Amen!'"

Not surprisingly, Edwin T. Earl's afternoon *Los Angeles Express* delivered its own "Amen" in the same basic, if less florid, front-page Owens River story. But the other newspapers in L.A.[3] were caught off guard by the *Times*' scoop—most notably, the morning *Los Angeles Examiner,* which had been competing head-to-head with the *Times* since Hearst had established his L.A. beachhead two years earlier.

In 1903, the split between Otis and the ITU had grown so bitter that ITU president James Lynch implored Hearst to create a new prolabor daily in Los Angeles to go head-to-head with the *Times*. At the time, Hearst was in the midst of creating a nationwide media empire; his prolabor *San Francisco Examiner* was his flagship newspaper. His next conquest was to have been Boston, for which Hearst had already purchased printing presses, but following a pledge from Lynch that L.A. unions would guarantee 40,000 to 50,000 subscribers for at least the first six months of operation, Hearst turned his sights to the south. The presses were installed a few blocks away from the *Times*' "Fortress" and the first issue of the *Los Angeles Examiner* hit the streets on December 12, 1903, amid fireworks and parades, with this front-page pledge to its readers: "The *Examiner* will support with its whole power the proposition that labor is justified in demanding a fair share of

the wealth it produces and its proportion of the country's prosperity. Consequently, the *Examiner* will be the friend of the trades unions, and give them its energetic backing when their cause is just. . . . It shall be its endeavor to bring about better relations between Capital and Labor."

During its first year, the *Examiner* cut deeply into *Times* subscribers and even its advertising, but by the time the Owens Valley story broke, the *Times* had regained its equilibrium. In General Otis's peculiar glee over the proposed aqueduct, *Examiner* editor Henry Loewenthal saw a chance to regain the upper hand; playing on a hunch, he sent two reporters to the San Fernando Valley to snoop.

Loewenthal instructed his reporters that time was of the essence because, as dutifully reported in the *Times*, the Los Angeles City Water Commission was about to tip the final domino in the Eaton-Lippincott conspiracy by putting a $25-million bond issue before the voters on September 7. The ballot referendum would give William Mulholland's water department the money it needed to begin construction on the Owens Valley aqueduct; the *Examiner* had just over a month to find out why General Otis was suddenly so effusive about irrigating the San Fernando Valley.

To make the timing even tighter for the *Examiner*, the *Times* was leading a media-fanned panic over the specter of drought. Although dry summers were not at all unusual, Los Angeles had been without rainfall for four months, and the hottest part of the year was still to come. The *Times* quoted a disingenuous William Mulholland, who pointed to the city's dangerously low reservoir levels and publicly warned that Los Angeles was running out of water. The *Times* did not report that Mulholland had been secretly instructing his workers to dump water from city reservoirs into the Pacific Ocean after midnight, when no one would notice. The *Los Angeles Daily News* did catch Mulholland's minions in the act, however, and reported the strange nocturnal activity, only to be brushed aside by Mulholland's lame excuse that his men were not creating an artificial drought but merely "flushing the system."

Meanwhile, the *Examiner*'s reporters hit pay dirt in the San Fernando Valley. On August 25, Henry Loewenthal published their findings: The newly incorporated San Fernando Mission Land Company, headed by one Harrison Gray Otis, stood to profit the most by the creation of an aqueduct that would effect the rape of the Owens Valley.

Caught with his name on the deed and his hand in the cash register, General Otis maintained that he had pulled out of the deal the previous February, although his son-in-law was still very much a part of the land syndicate. In his *Times*, Otis retaliated the way he always did when confronted with an ugly truth: He fumed, he blustered, he raved, and he sanctimoniously attempted to point an

accusing editorial finger at his accuser, but in this instance the vitriol dripped without effect: "The insane desire of the *Examiner* to discredit certain citizens of Los Angeles has at last led it into the open as a vicious enemy of the city's welfare, its mask of hypocrisy dropped and its convulsed features revealed."

The *Examiner*'s reporting revealed the dirtiest of the litany of dirty little secrets that questionable L.A. Samaritans Fred Eaton, William Mulholland, and J. B. Lippincott had begun piling up two years earlier. Although it remained hard for any Los Angeles newspaper to argue with Eaton's original ideal of using the Owens River as an antidote to L.A.'s water-sapping weather, the *Examiner* found an undeniable hypocrisy in the water's being dumped into the San Fernando Valley, which wasn't even part of the city.[4]

But instead of praising Loewenthal and his reporters for their stunning exposé of General Otis and his *Times*, William Randolph Hearst slapped their wrists.

During the first week of September, just five days before the Owens Valley aqueduct referendum, the legendary publisher left his flagship newspaper, the *San Francisco Examiner*, and rode his private railcar to L.A. When he arrived, the city was in the grip of its usual late summer dry spell. With highs of 101 degrees, the heat in 1905 was particularly oppressive, and it was not much cooler when Hearst met with city officials over the issue of the aqueduct referendum.

There was no love lost between the brash, opportunistic Hearst and the cantankerous and increasingly bilious General Otis. Otis, now sixty-eight, reveled in labeling the forty-two-year-old upstart the "Yellow Yawp" and his union newspaper "Hearst's Howler."

But Hearst found a more pragmatic peer in Otis's assistant general manager, who was only a year younger than Hearst was. While he publicly blasted Hearst, Harry Chandler maintained the moderate backroom persona that his father-in-law did not; he understood that public posturing often meant little when money was at stake—and in the case of the Los Angeles aqueduct, the amount of money at stake was almost unfathomable. To Chandler, it was all a matter of finding out what Hearst wanted and then making a deal.

Money was not so important to Hearst; his mining king father, George Hearst, had left his son a seemingly bottomless pit of cash from his rich ore strikes in the Comstock silver lode, the Homestake gold mine, and the Anaconda copper fields. What was important to William Randolph Hearst was the White House, which he coveted. Presidential politics were very much on his mind when he emerged from his session with L.A.'s leaders, most of whom were Harry Chandler's closest business associates. When he got back to the office, Hearst chastised Loewenthal and wrote the next day's glowing editorial in the *Los Angeles Examiner* himself. Hearst recommended a "yes" vote on the referendum. After

all, L.A. needed the water, he reasoned. It had to come from somewhere and the Owens Valley was half desert anyway.

On September 7, the $25 million aqueduct bond issue passed almost fifteen to one.

The engineering marvel that William Mulholland and his 6,000-man workforce built across the desert over the next seven years was rightfully compared in its scope and skill to the irrigation miracles of ancient Egypt and Rome. When it was finished, the Owens Valley aqueduct stretched over 223 miles, tunneled through two mountain ranges, and drained the Sierra Nevada snowmelt into the dry San Fernando soil between the village of Sylmar and the Granada Hills. As the Inyo *Register* accurately predicted in its own headlines reporting the passage of the Los Angeles bond issue, the aqueduct would "Take Owens River, Lay Lands Waste, Ruin People, Homes and Communities."

Fred Eaton's dream of turning his Long Valley ranch into a Los Angeles Water Department reservoir did not materialize. His old friend William Mulholland held out on Eaton's $1-million asking price, leaving a permanent and bitter rift between the two men.

Mulholland and his chief assistant, Lippincott, were hailed as heroes for nearly twenty years; they became more popular and powerful than any politician in the state. With water, Los Angeles' population reached more than 1 million in Mulholland's lifetime, making it second only to Cairo as the largest desert city on earth. When asked by a *Times* reporter at the height of his popularity whether he would consider running for mayor, the laconic engineer answered that he'd sooner give birth to a porcupine. Like his chief *Times* supporter, Harry Chandler, William Mulholland instinctively understood that real power did not trumpet itself the way politicians did. Real power remained low key, like a cat who pads so lightly that its prey doesn't realize it's being eaten until the cat's jaws are clamped half shut.

IN 1905, THE *TIMES* STOPPED RUNNING ADS on its front page; it no longer had to because the newspaper now grossed over $1 million a year. General Otis could afford to poke a little sardonic fun on his editorial pages as well as use them to scorch his enemies. He welcomed libel suits and reprinted the stories in question when the suits were filed. When one plaintiff won a $1 judgment against the *Times,* the General reported that the man had been "adjudged full compensation for his lost character" and re-ran the original story on the editorial page under the headline "A Low-Priced Character."

A Congregationalist like Eliza, Otis sarcastically blasted the Salvation Army, faith healers, and itinerant ministers as ineffectual con artists. His editorials self-righteously denounced real estate development scams, anti-Chinese prejudice, including WASP boycotts, and bloated government bureaucracy, yet the General saw no hypocrisy in trying to censor public art exhibits for displaying "lewd" paintings. *Suite of the Army,* an oil by William F. Jackson,[5] curator of the Crocker Art Gallery, raised the General's bushy brows when it passed through town because it depicted several young camp followers undressing in an open field to take a bath.

"Modern society demands that people shall be clothed," wrote the General, allowing exceptions only among art more than five hundred years old: "Nudity in art comes down to us from the ancient Greeks and Romans. The standards of society were then vastly different from today. What was quite allowable among those ancient races would now be condemned as worse than savage. In Rome, art flourished most when the Empire was given up to luxury, debauchery and moral decay. . . . But the modern world can and must rise to a higher moral plane in its own affairs."

His taste, he reasoned, ought to be the public's taste, and although there was room for argument (he welcomed opposing views so that he could trample them in print), the General always got the last word.

His fiery editorials notwithstanding, General Otis was beginning to slow down just as his newspaper and the well-watered real estate bonanza it had fostered began to bear fruit. The previous year, he had lost his beloved wife, Eliza, to heart failure; she was seventy-one. In 1906, his eldest daughter, Mrs. Beaulah Lillian (Otis) McPherron, succumbed to tuberculosis at the age of forty-one. His own health was now also beginning to deteriorate. During a visit to Japan in 1906, Otis was hospitalized for more than a month with an unidentified disease. He began a decade of gradual withdrawal from the *Times* by promoting his city editor to managing editor and surrendering control of most of the editorial operation.

Before Eliza's death, the Otises had moved from their grand home on Grand Avenue in downtown Los Angeles to a larger and even grander two-story mission-style estate in developer Gaylord Wilshire's Parkview Estates, on Wilshire Boulevard across the street from Westlake City Park.[6] The General insisted on calling his new home his "Bivouac." When he bought a second home a few years later, further north in the Cahuenga Valley, he dubbed that the "Outpost." The older he got, the more he insisted on labeling everything around him in military terms. When he lost his managing editor in 1904,[7] Otis called the staff together a few months later and commissioned his new editor, Harry Andrews, in a formal

military ceremony. Even his *Times* staff, which was now more than one hundred employees, was his "Phalanx," always poised to go to war.

The enemy was no longer the Confederate soldier, the Spanish sailor, or the Philippine rebel. The enemy was organized labor—more specifically, the organizers of labor. When he spoke of labor leaders like Pullman strike hero Eugene V. Debs or American Federation of Labor president Samuel Gompers, he set aside his usual invective and advocated murder. Although he slowly withdrew from the day in, day out routine at the *Times*, he never surrendered his role as commander in chief of his antilabor "Phalanx." What began as a pressroom floor quarrel over ITU deadheading in the 1880s had escalated to armed combat twenty years later, and the General planned to win that war just as he'd won all the others.

He maintained an arsenal of fifty rifles on hand at the *Times* "Fortress" and put his "Phalanx" through maneuvers from time to time, just to be certain that they could deploy in the event of an attack. Although his employees might have believed the General had slipped into mild dementia, no one dared contradict him. He was deadly serious about defending what was rightfully his. During the early days of the morning *Examiner* when tensions ran high between the union and nonunion newspapers, Otis unlocked the arsenal and ordered the *Times* staff to arm itself and be on alert. To add to his public display of eccentric belligerence, the General took to wearing his uniform and his medals to work, and had small ornamental canon mounted on the hood of the automobile that took him to and from his office.

It was not all Sturm und Drang; along with General Otis's strong public and private views about unions went a reputation that even money-minded Harry Chandler appreciated. Keeping out the unions meant higher profits. Under Harrison Otis's leadership, Southern California labor costs were 30 percent less than anywhere else in the country. Organized labor nationwide began to refer to Los Angeles as "Otistown of the Open Shop"—a derisive epithet that was supposed to mar the region in the eyes of union members as a haven for greedy capitalists who ran sweatshops that exploited the workingman. The cost of living in sunny L.A. was in reality a fraction of that of most weather-bound East Coast cities; thus most Southern California employers could reasonably pay their workforces less, including William Randolph Hearst, whose *San Francisco Examiner* staff earned substantially more than their *Los Angeles Examiner* peers.

But reasonable arguments from either labor or management had been abandoned years earlier. With strikes exploding into outright armed insurrection across the nation—from Chicago's Haymarket riots to the Colorado mining massacres—it was only a matter of time before General Otis's labor baiting and his *Times'* bellicose bellowing would lead to disaster in Southern California.

CHAPTER 4

AT ITS 1907 CONVENTION, the International Typographers Union issued a ringing resolution blasting the *Los Angeles Times* as "the most notorious, most persistent and most unfair enemy of trade unionism on the North American continent." The same year, the American Federation of Labor levied a penny-a-month assessment on its membership to create a war chest for the exclusive purpose of defeating General Harrison Gray Otis and his antiunion open-shop policy.

Like the old warrior that he was, Otis countered each challenge with smug fury. Nothing fazed his *Times*. Although age and infirmity slowed the General's body, his pen was as acid now as it was the first day he had sat in the publisher's office. With each salvo from organized labor, he ordered his "Phalanx" to return fire twofold. He invoked an endless stream of negative euphemisms for organized labor: bullies, anarchists, pinheads, sluggers, brutes, gas-pipe ruffians, union loafers, rowdies, skunks, dynamiters, wolves, beaters up, toughs, roughnecks, union robbers, blacklegs, roughnecks, bums, deadbeats, and even "blatherskites."

The General could not stomach whiners, lollygags, and slackers, but if a man was loyal, talented, and willing to work, he had a lifelong ally in Harrison Gray Otis, as one of his veteran reporters, Harry Carr, attested in his own memoirs:

> The general expected blind loyalty and gave it. One time I had written an interview with a celebrity who denied its truth. The general sent for me. The celebrity sat down, glowering.
>
> "Harry," said the general, "Mr. Blank says you misquoted him. Did he say it or didn't he?"
>
> "He did, sir."
>
> The general grunted and turned back to his work. The celebrity was so incautious as to insist that I had lied. The general struggled to his feet, purple with rage, and yelled until you could hear him two blocks away.
>
> "If you tell me that my men lie, you tell me that I lie! Get out, you . . . "
>
> The world's record for speed across that room is still held by Mr. Blank.

General Otis's antiunion editorials dripped with venomous glee over union-dominated San Francisco, where municipal corruption combined with union graft to create wave after wave of political scandal. Elected officials were regularly

accused, indicted and/or convicted of jury tampering, extortion, and bribery, but not in "Otistown of the Open Shop." Otis declared that so long as the *Times* remained the dominant influence in Los Angeles, labor leaders would have no such impact on city hall.

Bolstered by a roaring economy and the promise of Owens Valley water, the spirit inside the *Times* "Fortress" and the boomtown that had grown up around it was strong, positive, and militant. Sunny Southern California was now the undisputed agricultural center of the United States; the petroleum industry had further fattened the local bottom line ever since E. L. Doheny began sinking the first of more than 1,300 oil wells in 1892. Motion picture production, another thriving new business destined to become a trademark for the new century, also gravitated to L.A., lured as much by its nonunion labor as its nonstop sunlight.

Through the General's eyes, all of Southern California's bounty resulted directly from his *Times'* single-handed decimation of organized labor. Weather and water had something to do with it, naturally, but keeping out the unions remained the key to L.A.'s success; the General would have none of their threats and was rabid on the subject of industrial freedom.

Yet, despite its sarcastic nickname, Los Angeles was not exclusively "Otistown." The same railways that imported thousands of conservative East Coast farm families, retirees, or ranch hands also brought liberals, progressive populists and free-thinking intellectuals as well as contentious factory workers, miners, longshoremen, and carpenters who had tasted the intimidating power that a trade union can have in dealing with an indifferent or recalcitrant employer. The growing power and influence of Hearst's pro-union *Los Angeles Examiner,* which had L.A.'s second-largest circulation by 1910, reflected the growing anti-Otis constituency, and explained in part how Los Angeles could simultaneously be a crucible for socialist politics and the unofficial national headquarters for arch conservative capitalism.

In many ways, Hiram Johnson, a progressive prolabor Republican who swept into the governor's mansion in 1910, personified California's schizophrenic politics. On one side of his platform, Johnson opposed the lobbying tentacles of the Southern Pacific Railway, which continued to dominate Sacramento lawmakers; but on the other side, he favored collective bargaining and a wage earner's basic rights, including the right to sue his employer. Although many employers acted benevolently and could be counted upon to deal with their workers fairly, he warned, others were not benevolent and fair. In one of his most famous campaign speeches, Johnson singled out such an employer in General Harrison Otis, and extemporaneously matched the bitter eloquence of the old warrior's editorials, diatribe for diatribe:

He sits there in senile dementia, with gangrened heart and rotting brain, grimacing at every reform, chattering impotently at all things that are decent, frothing, fuming, violently gibbering, going down to his grave in snarling infamy. This man Otis is the one blot on the banner of Southern California; he is the bar sinister upon your escutcheon. My friends, he is the one thing that all California looks at, when, in looking at Southern California, they see anything that is disgraceful, depraved, corrupt, crooked and putrescent—that is Harrison Gray Otis.

The first years of the twentieth century were a time of class warfare almost unimaginable a hundred years later. Industrialists such as John D. Rockefeller and Henry Ford hired their own small armies of goons to quell strikes and beat back picket lines, often crushing bones and occasionally taking a life in the process. Striking workers fought back with whatever weapons they had at hand. Those police who were not on management's payroll nominally kept order when they could, but the pace at which the civil war spread fast outstripped peacekeepers' resources. Outspent, outmanned, and outarmed, unions increasingly turned to sabotage, arson, and bombing to get their point across.

The International Association of Bridge and Structural Iron Workers led the way, sponsoring nearly seventy bombings between 1907 and 1911. From its headquarters in Indianapolis, the union spread teams of dynamite experts across the country. Not a month passed without an explosion: A steel mill, a bridge, or a stretch of railroad was blown to kingdom come, although no deaths were reported, and injuries were minimal. Although the pattern of destruction was clear enough, the bombers covered their tracks so well that prosecutors could not prove most cases. Getting no help from police, big business turned to private security firms—Pinkerton's National Detective Agency, McPartland Private Detective Agency, and Burns Detectives—to track down the culprits. Their big break came in the autumn of 1910, in the form of an explosion that rocked L.A., its *Times,* and the national labor movement all the way to its roots.

Escalation after escalation marked the months leading to disaster. General Otis's Merchants & Manufacturers Association had assembled a $350,000 war chest the previous spring to fend off a Los Angeles brewers' strike, quell unrest in the leather trade, and undermine a metal workers' union-organizing effort. Mayor George Alexander, a *Times* opponent who had evolved into a Harry Chandler favorite, ordered police to begin enforcing the antipicketing ordinance that had been voted into law by the *Times'* handpicked city council. Although brazenly unconstitutional, the ordinance was used by L.A. police to lock up 470 picketers.

The crackdown backfired, however; union ranks unexpectedly swelled to more than 12,000, unprecedented in open-shop Otistown.

Further widening the gap, the Socialist Party and its leading light, attorney Job Harriman, started gathering serious union support, an indication that General Otis and his *Times* might have gone too far in beating back blue-collar voters. A tubercular Indiana lawyer who had come to L.A. in the 1880s—like Harry Chandler and Charles Lummis—to reclaim his health, the rejuvenated Harriman had moved to San Francisco for several years; he returned to Southern California in 1900 to practice law and socialist politics. By 1910, Harriman began to emerge as a serious contender in the primary mayoral election, which was still over a year away.

The scene was set for a showdown, and at seven minutes after 1:00 A.M. on October 1, 1910, Harrison Gray Otis's "Fortress" erupted in flame and debris. The war between labor and management literally exploded when a time bomb detonated enough dynamite to gut the *Times,* buckling floors, crumbling walls, and tossing tons of printing and typesetting equipment into the air like Tinkertoys. Twenty-one people working to get Saturday's edition of the *Times* out on the streets of L.A. were killed. The explosion was so powerful that it crushed several employees to death instantly; the fast-moving fire that followed cremated more than a dozen others who tried to escape the *Times* building. Among the employees who were burned alive were three editors, five printers, and seven Linotype operators. Of those who did manage to get out, sixteen were injured seriously enough to be hospitalized.

The General was out of town, on his way home by way of Texas from the centennial celebration of Mexican independence in Mexico City. He set out for L.A. immediately after receiving news of the explosion. His son-in-law, who lived a short distance from the newspaper, learned of the disaster within minutes, and arrived at the scene while the fire was still raging.

Night owl Harry Chandler would have been in his office and would certainly have died in the initial blast had Marian Chandler not been in a nagging mood. After he had squired his increasingly matronly wife to and from the theater that Friday evening, he returned to his office for what he said would be just a few minutes of work. When a few minutes turned into a few hours, Marian phoned and asked what had become of him. He would be home soon, he said. When he still hadn't arrived by midnight, she showed up at his office door and ordered him to stop shuffling papers.

"Harry Chandler, if you don't drop everything this very minute and come home with me, I shall never believe you again!" she scolded.

Chandler reluctantly headed home. An hour later, a suitcase of dynamite that had been planted in an ink storage area underneath his office transformed Chan-

dler's side of the building into an inferno; his private secretary, J. Wesley Reaves, was killed instantly.

From the second story of the Chandlers' three-story Fort Moore home just six blocks from the newspaper, eleven-year-old Norman Chandler recalled more than half a century later the haunting tableau that followed the explosion: "I watched from my window a long, long time, and sometimes when I close my eyes now, I can still see the building burning."

General Otis's medieval "Fortress" at First and Broadway had been laid to waste, brick and mortar scattered for blocks around. But with a symbolic glory to which Chandler and the General would point again and again in the months ahead, the wings of the *Times'* bronze eagle remained spread wide and unscathed at the top of one blackened and crumbling wall. Chandler later declared that the sight had inspired him to gather together those uninjured *Times* employees who had assembled outside the ruins and march with them to a *Times* auxiliary plant on Spring Street, four blocks away. There they put out the next day's four-page edition, which carried the defiant headline: UNIONIST BOMBS WRECK THE *TIMES*; MANY SERIOUSLY INJURED.

Harry Andrews, the *Times'* managing editor, wrote in a boxed front-page editorial, "They can kill our men and can wreck our buildings, but by the God above, they cannot kill The *Times.*" When General Otis arrived in town, he ordered that the bombing henceforth be termed in *Times* editorials "The Crime of the Century."

"Oh, you anarchic scum," he wrote in one editorial. "You leeches upon honest labor, you midnight assassins."

But the mayhem did not end that dawn. Shortly after noon, police were called to the home of Felix J. Zeehandelaar, the zealous antilabor secretary of the Merchants and Manufacturers Association. Fifteen sticks of dynamite were wired to an alarm clock set to go off at 1:00 P.M., but the bomber had wound the wire too tightly; the device had been discovered harmlessly ticking beneath Zeehandelaar's bedroom window.

Alarmed by Zeehandelaar's discovery, a caretaker at General Otis's Bivouac[1] made his own inspection and found a suitcase underneath the publisher's bedroom window, ticking off the seconds to 2:00 P.M. At 1:45 P.M., three police officers responded to the caretaker's frantic call. With minutes to spare, one of the officers swiftly carried the suitcase sixty feet away to Wilshire Boulevard. There it detonated, flattening the police with an explosion that left a gaping crater in the road. The force of the explosion broke windows in the General's house, but injured no one, not even the shaken police.

At the urging of Mayor Alexander, the city turned over the blasting caps, the dynamite, and the timing device from the Zeehandelaar bomb to William J.

Burns and his nationally known detective agency with a mandate to get to the bottom of the bombings. The Merchants and Manufacturers Association ponied up another $100,000 in working capital for Burns and attorney Earl Rogers, who had been appointed to help prosecute the dynamiters. General Otis stepped up his editorial campaign, which called for vigilante justice if the police failed to bring the murdering blackguards to justice.

But Socialist Party leader Eugene V. Debs saw a sinister conspiracy in Otis's call to arms and questioned how both he and his son-in-law had just *happened* to be out of the *Times* building when it blew up. Debs, who had run as a Socialist for the U.S. presidency ten years earlier with Job Harriman as his running mate,[2] came to his former comrade's aid by writing a scathing series of speculative articles in the Socialists' weekly newspaper, *Appeal to Reason.* Debs even went so far as to accuse Otis and Chandler of destroying their own building in a bizarre effort to defeat unionism once and for all in Los Angeles.

While Otis and Debs waged their war of words, Burns's detectives were zeroing in on the killers. A month before the blast, on September 4, 1910, a pair of dynamite bombs blew up an ironworks plant and two railroad cars loaded with steel girders in Peoria, Illinois; but, as in the Los Angeles explosions, a third bomb turned out to be a dud. Within a week of the *Times* bombing, Burns's bloodhounds had already made a comparison of the Zeehandelaar bomb and the Peoria dud and found a match: They were both made of the same high-grade dynamite, wired in the same way, and set to go off with the same kind of cheap alarm clocks. The Burns Agency had picked up the scent that would eventually lead it to the Indianapolis headquarters of the Bridge and Structural Iron Workers Union.

ORTIE MCMANIGAL CONSIDERED HIMSELF a professional dynamiter and, as such, saw no reason why he shouldn't enjoy himself between assignments, just as any other professional might; when he arrived in L.A. three months after the *Times* disaster to add a few more conquests to the cause of organized labor, he decided to take the day off before getting down to business. On the day before Christmas, he toured Mission San Gabriel and visited Long Beach before buying a pair of plumes at Crawston Ostrich Farm in South Pasadena and mailing them back home to his wife in Chicago before the post office closed.

A few hours after eating a hearty Christmas Eve dinner, McManigal paid a visit to the Llewellyn Iron Works at the intersection of Redondo and North Main Streets and blew the factory right off the map. In the process, he accidentally exploded a detonating cap that delivered minor cuts to one arm and leg. He opted

to abandon the rest of his assignments, and returned by way of San Francisco to Indiana early the next day.

Dynamiting was not supposed to be so risky—at least it never had been for McManigal. He was careful, he took all the proper precautions, and he enjoyed lots of leisure time between jobs. Upon his arrival in Indianapolis, his immediate boss, Herbert S. Hockin, upbraided him for letting a few flesh wounds slow him down. As supervisor of the union's dynamite operations, Hockin had ordered McManigal to wreck the Los Angeles County Hall of Records and the Alexandria Hotel, as well as another steel mill and the *Times* auxiliary printing plant on Spring Street. Before he left Southern California, McManigal was supposed to have finished the job that had started with the destruction of the *Times* building in October.

Despite Ortie's failure to level a considerable portion of the city, the Llewellyn bombing was quite enough to send a chill through Los Angeles: The *Times* terrorism was not over, an L.A. grand jury was told. Arrests were soon made as far away as Arizona and Arkansas; but those suspects were turned loose nearly as quickly as they were arrested when overzealous local authorities could produce no evidence against them.

As the pro- and antiunion forces of Otistown squared off, Ortie McManigal decided to take a much-needed vacation. He left for northern Wisconsin to do a little deer hunting; an alcoholic, itinerant printer and fellow union bomber named James B. McNamara accompanied him. McNamara's younger brother, John, the widely respected secretary/treasurer of the International Association of Bridge and Structural Iron Workers, ran the union from its Indianapolis headquarters.

McManigal and McNamara had a good enough time together in the Wisconsin woods, but instead of bagging deer, they spent most of their time getting plastered in a cabin that they shared with four other hunters. It was there, during a late-night binge, that McNamara revealed a sorry tale of a union bombing gone awry.

With Ortie as his mentor, McNamara had lately taken up the fine art of destruction, he recounted, and the Los Angeles *Times* had been his first big assignment. McNamara explained in drunken detail to the rest of the hunters how he had been instructed to meet two other West Coast union munitions experts in San Francisco who were to have accompanied him on the outing. When the others got cold feet at the last minute, McNamara proceeded to L.A. on his own. He checked into a downtown hotel under the alias J. B. Bryce and waited until dark to plant three bombs: one outside General Harrison Gray Otis's bedroom window; a second in Felix J. Zeehandelaar's garden; and the third in a narrow street-

level delivery zone behind the *Times* building known by printers, reporters, and Linotype operators as "Ink Alley."

In each instance, McNamara said, there was supposed to be enough dynamite to cause considerable damage, but not enough to destroy an entire building. Mc-Namara, who found his courage inside a whiskey bottle, boasted that he had single-handedly placed each of the three bombs so that they would wreak havoc, but no human misery. That had been the credo of the International Association of Bridge and Structural Iron Workers since Ortie first began bombing three years earlier. The Tatoo Jr. alarm clocks set to detonate the dynamite were set to go off late at night when no one would be nearby to get hurt. McNamara failed to take into account Ink Alley's proximity to natural gas lines, which set off a chain reaction; the flames spread at lightning speed half a city block to the occupied part of the *Times* building.

He never meant anyone to die, McNamara said. The alarm clock in Ink Alley was supposed to go off closer to daylight, around 4:00 A.M., when the *Times* building was virtually vacant. But even though the bomb went off early and he had set it, McNamara was unwilling to take responsibility for the deaths. They rested on the head of General Harrison Gray Otis and his money-grubbing son-in-law, who had fanned the flames of union hatred for so long that the destruction of their headquarters was the inevitable result.

The hunting trip ended with no game but many hangovers. McNamara returned home to Chicago with McManigal. Then the two of them set out on another of their "business" trips, first to Toledo to blow up a building and pick up supplies and later to Detroit to set off another dynamite wake-up call in middle America. It was there, in Detroit's Oxford Hotel during the last week of April 1911, that William J. Burns caught up with them both.

It turned out that among their companions on the hunting trip was an undercover Burns detective who had been tracking Ortie McManigal for weeks; the detective reported directly back to his boss about McNamara's drunken ramblings. The Burns operative also had a clandestine photo taken of McNamara during the trip, which he then shipped to Los Angeles. There, Burns showed the photo to a hotel clerk who identified McNamara as the mysterious J. B. Bryce who had checked in to the hotel the day before the *Times* disaster and hastily checked out the very next morning.

On the strength of McNamara's boozy yarn during the hunting trip and the incriminating photo, Burns hired a pair of Chicago policemen to accompany him to Detroit's Oxford Hotel. There they confronted McNamara and McManigal, who were in the process of putting the finishing touches to another suitcase full of dynamite that they were planning to deliver to a Michigan target.

Although they had neither a warrant nor the local authority to make an arrest, Burns and the Chicago officers seized the suitcase and wrestled the pair out of the hotel. They were hustling them on board a Chicago-bound train when McNamara screamed to a nearby Detroit police officer that he was being kidnapped. The Detroit police briefly detained all five men until McManigal persuaded McNamara to waive extradition. Why McManigal refused to fight Burns and got the reluctant McNamara to go along with him remains one of the central mysteries of the *Times* bombing incident nearly a century later. Everything that followed implied that union bomber Ortie McManigal either decided to switch sides at that moment or had been working on behalf of William J. Burns all along.

When they were back in Chicago, McManigal confessed to Burns his role in the *Times* and Llewellyn Iron Works bombings. Although he maintained that he took his orders from Herbert S. Hockin, McManigal implied in his confession that his partner McNamara's younger brother, John J. McNamara, must have known about the bombings. They were brothers, after all, and the union had been conducting its industrial terrorism campaign for over three years. How could the sober, serious, and scholarly John, a law school graduate and a born labor leader, *not* have known what his alcoholic older sibling was up to?

On the strength of McManigal's confession, Burns sent two of his agents to Indianapolis to confront John McNamara, and within twenty-four hours, all three *Times* bombing suspects had been arrested and put on trains to L.A. under the watchful eyes and threatening presence of Burns's operatives. Meanwhile, Herbert S. Hockin stepped in as the new acting secretary/treasurer of the International Association of Bridge and Structural Iron Workers.

Three days later, on April 26, 1911, the McNamara brothers were booked with considerable fanfare into the Los Angeles County Jail. At the same time, Ortie McManigal was singing like a prosecution canary. He publicly and personally took credit for fifteen bombings throughout the country during the previous three years, but he laid full blame for the murderous *Los Angeles Times* bombing squarely on the shoulders of James B. McNamara and his younger brother, John J. Although McManigal had no direct proof that John McNamara knew about the Hockin-ordered bombings, he recalled for his interrogators the union leader's reaction to the Indianapolis newspaper's headlines about the *Times* bombing the day after twenty-one people died:

"This will make them sit up and take notice and that's what J. B. went out to the coast to do," John McNamara remarked with a smile, according to McManigal.

Both McNamaras repudiated McManigal and declared their innocence. In the weeks that followed, every major figure in organized labor rallied to their cause. Samuel Gompers's American Federation of Labor raised a $190,000 defense fund. Burns was criticized by leaders of organized labor for his extralegal arrest

and extradition tactics; he was also investigated by Congress and indicted on kidnapping charges in Indiana. But the biggest villain in the eyes of labor was General Otis. Even former President Theodore Roosevelt, who deplored the iron workers' bombing tactics and praised William J. Burns for his sleuthing, weighed in on the defense side when he slammed General Otis and his newspaper's irrational antiunion stridency as the root cause of the *Times* tragedy.

On May 5, 1911, based on Ortie McManigal's confession, the Los Angeles grand jury indicted James B. McNamara for the *Times* bombing and his brother John J. McNamara as a coconspirator; McManigal was accused only in the Llewellyn Iron Works bombing. The stage was set. Only one more event was needed for the *Times* trial to become history's most dramatic showdown between union and management: the entrance of Clarence Darrow, the most venerated criminal defense attorney of the young century.

For four decades between the 1890s and the early 1930s, Clarence Darrow defended labor leaders, anarchists, and assorted free thinkers in trials that captured national attention. Darrow successfully defended Eugene V. Debs, president of the American Railway Union, during the Pullman strike of 1894; and three mining union officials accused of paying for the murder of the governor of Idaho thirteen years later in a similar showdown between labor and management. Darrow's fiery courtroom elocution captured the public imagination and defined jurisprudence during the Gilded Age. Wherever he went, newspaper reporters followed. But of all his courtroom appearances, only the famous Scopes Monkey Trial of 1925 exceeded the public frenzy over the trial of the *Times* bombers.

In May 1911, just as the famous lawyer was about to arrive in L.A. from Chicago, the city streets had taken on the trappings of civil war. Twenty thousand McNamara supporters marched on the county jail to denounce General Otis, Harry Chandler, and William J. Burns as schemers bent on crucifying organized labor along with the McNamara brothers. General Otis received regular death threats, which only heightened the decibel level of his *Times* diatribes. The bitter gulf between labor and management spread to every urban center across the nation. From San Francisco to Chicago to Pittsburgh, labor staged mass marches similar to those held in L.A. throughout the spring and into the summer of 1911.

At their July arraignment on murder charges, both McNamaras pleaded innocent. Darrow assembled a defense team of five prominent Southern California attorneys,[3] including Job Harriman, the Socialist Party's candidate for mayor.

The conservative prosecution was all but hand selected by General Otis and Harry Chandler. Since the turn of the century, District Attorney John Fredericks,

who resembled Abraham Lincoln in looks but had the disposition of Boss Tweed, had run the prosecutor's office as if it were a Republican citadel. Fredericks made no secret of his loyalties to Chandler and Moses Sherman, Chandler's chief partner in the real estate development business.

As public sentiment tipped toward the McNamaras, Chandler even tried a tactic that he thought would distance the sycophantic Fredericks—and, thus, the *Times*—from the case: He urged Fredericks to hire an outside prosecutor with no visible ties to General Otis. To ensure public sympathy, the *Times* raised money on behalf of the widows and orphans of the *Times* bombing to pay the prosecutor's salary. Such a move would check organized labor's howls that the McNamaras could never get a fair trial in Los Angeles, Chandler reasoned, and it would also remind a fickle public that the two brothers stood accused of brutally murdering twenty-one innocent men and women. Responding to Chandler's cajoling, Fredericks reluctantly hired former U.S. Attorney Oscar Lawler as a token demonstration of his office's impartiality. But the *Times* widows and orphans didn't pay his salary; the Merchants and Manufacturers Association quietly underwrote Lawler's salary, as it had underwritten that of Earl Rogers.

As flamboyant in his own right as Darrow, Rogers had earned a reputation in the century's first decade as defender of L.A.'s rich and famous. Bankers, oil men, and heirs accused of murdering wives, rivals, and drinking companions invariably turned to Rogers for help. He had been known to elicit gasps from the jury by bringing a victim's crushed skull into the courtroom, by wearing a victim's bloody clothing during closing arguments, and by brandishing a pistol at the prosecution. Rogers's presentation before the grand jury had resulted in the indictments of the McNamaras.

Rounding out the prosecution team were over six hundred detectives whom either Fredericks or Burns had assigned to the case. By contrast, Darrow's defense team made do with just a hundred investigators.

Each side eavesdropped on the other throughout the summer and into the fall. Darrow's telegrams were stolen and his phone conversations were bugged with a crude but effective tap connected to a hidden Dictaphone. His secretary turned out to be a Burns detective and one of Fredericks's deputy prosecutors turned out to be on Darrow's payroll. Darrow's waiter at the restaurant where he routinely ate was a Burns operative. Several other Burns detectives reported to Darrow on the sly for a fee. By the first anniversary of the *Times* bombing, the defense and prosecution were riddled with spies; everyone knew what everyone else was planning to do in court. On October 11, jury selection began.

Darrow's strategy was to put the blame squarely on the shoulders of the *Times'* management; he cited a leaky natural gas line in Ink Alley as the source of the ex-

plosion. To prove his theory, he had a scale model of the *Times* building constructed out of papier-mâché, which he intended to blow up for the jury.

The linchpin of the prosecution's case was Ortie McManigal, whose confession held up under intense scrutiny from Burns's detectives and Darrow's investigators. As an accused bomber himself, however, McManigal would not make the most credible witness in the courtroom. Fredericks wanted to search the Indianapolis headquarters of the International Association of Bridge and Structural Iron Workers for corroborating evidence, but Indiana authorities, who were still annoyed with Burns for his kidnapping tactics, refused. Informed of the Indiana impasse, General Otis stepped in and pulled strings that led all the way to the White House.

During a nationwide goodwill and fact-finding tour, President William Howard Taft passed through Los Angeles in mid-October. Following a Republican reception held in his honor, the rotund, mustachioed Taft paid a visit to his brother-in-law's Pasadena home. Waiting for the president in an upstairs study (the brother-in-law was one of Otis's friends as well as a fellow Republican) were the equally rotund, Republican, and mustachioed General Harrison Gray Otis and Oscar Lawler, the former U.S. attorney whom Harry Chandler had hired to work with District Attorney Fredericks's McNamara prosecution team.

For the next few hours, Lawler and Otis plied the president with brandy, cigars, and an urgent call for federal intervention in the McNamara case. Indiana would not budge on Lawler's request for a warrant to search the headquarters of the International Association of Bridge and Structural Iron Workers, but the U.S. Justice Department could easily trump a mere state attorney general, they postulated. Taft balked at first, but was eventually persuaded that nothing short of the hard proof that would surely turn up in a raid on union headquarters could keep the seething anarchic masses from ripping Los Angeles—and perhaps much of urban America—to shreds.

The following day, in a dramatic departure from his previous neutrality, the U.S. attorney general ordered federal officers to seize the Indianapolis headquarters of the International Association of Bridge and Structural Iron Workers and to remove all documents pertaining to the *Times* bombing. Incriminating letters, newspaper clippings, memos, and a basement full of dynamite cinched the prosecution's case. This was one instance when Darrow's spies did not know what the district attorney's office was up to and, for the next several weeks, Lawler and Fredericks played down their treasure trove of damning evidence.

Meanwhile, Los Angeles voters went to the polls for the mayoralty primary and, on October 30, hiked the stakes in the McNamara trial one more notch. The winner with 15,000 votes was McNamara defense lawyer Job Harriman. He was

trailed in the voting by Mayor George Alexander's 13,000 votes. A third candidate who polled 6,000 votes was eliminated from the race. If sentiment continued to hold for the McNamaras, the Socialist Party's Harriman would be a shoo-in during the upcoming December general election.

Yet, strong as public sympathy was for his clients, Darrow still wanted an extra edge in court. Whether by direct order, by implication, or merely by his chief investigator's inference, Darrow was about to have that edge handed to him in the form of bribed jurors.

In early November, while the jury was still being selected, a former U.S. Marshall's Office investigator, Bert Franklin, called upon Mrs. Robert Bain. Franklin, Darrow's chief investigator, had discovered that Mr. Bain, a Civil War veteran and an out-of-work carpenter, was being sized up at the moment by both the prosecution and defense as a likely juror. Franklin also knew that Bain had fallen far behind on his mortgage payments. If her husband could be persuaded to hold out for acquittal of the McNamaras, Franklin told Mrs. Bain, Franklin could advance her the money the couple needed to bring their mortgage current.

Not only did she indignantly refuse, Mrs. Bain told her husband, who agreed with her, that the couple had a moral duty to take Franklin's bribery attempt to the district attorney. Before they got there, however, Franklin tried rigging the jury a second time.

On November 4, Franklin similarly propositioned juror and former police officer George Lockwood to cast a vote for acquittal in exchange for cash. Franklin told Lockwood he could walk away with $4,000. Like the Bains, Lockwood balked, but he did not display his anger. He told Franklin he'd have to think about it. Then he went straight to the district attorney. Delighted by Darrow's apparent desperation, Fredericks advised Lockwood to go along with the bribe, but to arrange to accept the money in a public place where he could be shadowed.

On the afternoon of November 28, Lockwood waited at the corner of Third and Los Angeles Streets as Franklin had instructed. He was approached by C. E. White, one of Bert Franklin's operatives, as Fredericks's own undercover investigators watched. White handed Lockwood a $500 bill, then promised seven more just like it once the McNamaras walked out of court as free men. To make Fredericks's triumph even more delicious, Bert Franklin presently emerged from a nearby saloon, just in time to greet Lockwood and White; he clapped them both on the back as though they were old friends. The trio then walked west on Third Street for another hundred feet before the D.A.'s men sprung their trap.

Just as Franklin was being arrested, Clarence Darrow appeared at the end of the block. He said later that his appearance at that moment was just coincidence. The master defense lawyer watched grimly as his investigator was hauled away, but did nothing to interfere. The next morning, a dour Clarence Darrow wrote

out a $10,000 check from the McNamara defense fund to bail Bert Franklin out of jail.

But neither man's troubles were over; indeed, they had just begun.

DECEMBER I, 1911, MARKED THE BEGINNING of the end for organized labor in Los Angeles. For a generation thereafter, the nation's guilds and unions lost the hearts and the minds of an overwhelming majority of disillusioned workers in virtually every Southern California industry. Not until the Great Depression did union leaders once again make any headway in Otistown.

Fourteen months after the destruction of his beloved *Times* "Fortress," the General's worst denunciations about the violent nature of union bosses came wrenchingly true. Both McNamara brothers stood before the judge and declared themselves guilty of the *Times* and Llewellyn Iron Works bombings.

The thousands of placard-carrying demonstrators and prolabor spectators who stood outside the overcrowded courthouse could not and did not believe what they heard. At first, leaders of the throngs proclaimed that there had been a mistake. Then they angrily fixed their sights on the loathsome General Otis, who must have blackmailed the brothers and orchestrated the unbelievable news. Then, as the truth sank in, outrage, despair, and finally betrayal swept through the crowd.

The collapse of the McNamara brothers' juggernaut had begun a month earlier, when it became increasingly clear to Clarence Darrow that District Attorney John Fredericks had the goods on his clients. Darrow might have been able to destroy Ortie McManigal on the witness stand, but the documents and dynamite that the prosecution's investigators found at the ironworkers' Indianapolis headquarters was too damning. His clients were guilty, and guilty beyond a reasonable doubt, not just of blowing up the *Times* building but of staging a nationwide reign of terror for nearly four years in which they had dynamited buildings, bridges, and rail lines.

In early November, Darrow had begun working through back channels to come up with a face-saving compromise, even as Bert Franklin was busy trying to bribe the jury. Darrow even drafted that idealistic author and paragon of social justice, Lincoln Steffens, to act as a go-between. The preeminent muckraker of his time, Steffens, like dozens of other journalists, had come to L.A. to cover what promised to be the Trial of the Century; but soon after he arrived, he, too, saw the McNamara brothers' guilt scrawled all over Darrow's face. While writing a sympathetic magazine essay on the doomed case titled "Justifiable Dynamiting," Steffens agreed to try to broker a deal. He met with L.A. business leaders who might have some influence on the district attorney, including Harry Chandler. But

Chandler's father-in-law vetoed any talk of mercy. General Otis demanded that both McNamara brothers swing from the gallows for murder. Period. At least initially, Steffens's efforts failed.

Tentatively at first and more desperately with each passing day, Darrow cast into the prosecution camp for a compromise. Because the older McNamara had done the bombing, Darrow tried to keep John J. McNamara out of a plea bargain on the pretense that he had been unaware of either Ortie McManigal's career as a saboteur or his brother James B. McNamara's nefarious activities. Fredericks scoffed at Darrow's argument and demanded nothing less than long jail sentences for both brothers. Wrangling went down to the final hours before trial; Steffens, Darrow, and his defense team closeted themselves with the McNamaras in their jail cells and begged them to change their pleas. Their choice, Darrow told the brothers, was clear: They must either throw themselves on the mercy of the court or hang by the neck until dead. At best, they were told, they could become union martyrs in the face of the prosecution's overwhelming evidence.

The deal finally came down to family. As a union official who could not be directly connected with the bombings, John J. McNamara might have been able to skirt the charges at trial; but District Attorney John Fredericks could guarantee that James B. McNamara would not be executed only if the younger brother pleaded guilty too. The one concession Fredericks was willing to make was to allow John J. McNamara to plead to a single conspiracy charge, that of ordering McManigal to bomb the Llewellyn Iron Works, thus avoiding the taint of murdering twenty-one *Times* employees. To save his brother from the noose and have his sentence commuted to life in prison, John J. McNamara agreed to accept a ten-year prison sentence for conspiracy, a sentence the judge later extended to fifteen years.

With their transfer to San Quentin State Prison in December 1911, the most famous, and infamous, brothers in the United States lapsed into obscurity. Despite his ordeal, John J. McNamara remained a staunch union man even after his parole on May 10, 1921. He settled in Cincinnati and crisscrossed the nation on behalf of labor, speaking at rallies, extolling the continued martyrdom of his imprisoned older brother, and signing union members where he could find them. During a Montana mine workers' rally in May 1941, McNamara dropped dead of a heart attack. He was fifty-seven.

James B. McNamara died two months earlier than John. When he was fifty-nine, he had been inside the walls of San Quentin longer than any other inmate. In March 1941, James B. McNamara was still serving his life term for murder. He died of cancer inside the prison walls, despite repeated petition drives seeking his pardon sponsored by Darrow, Steffens, and various other progressives, including Nobel laureate novelist Sinclair Lewis and controversial novelist Upton Sinclair.

Until the end, James B. McNamara was remorseful that so many had died in the *Times* tragedy, but he was also unrepentant about the union cause. He was as adamant on his deathbed as he had been when he and his brother stood side by side in the courtroom thirty years earlier. In changing his plea from innocent to guilty that day, McNamara told the judge:

> Please say to the papers that I am guilty, but I did what I did for principle, and I did not intend to murder a man. We put that bomb in Ink Alley, just as the papers have said, and we set it to go off after all the men in the building had gone home, in the early morning, but the clock went back on us and you know what followed. Think what all of this means to us who have been fighting, fighting always for a right to live. When I set that bomb I meant only to throw a scare into those fellows who owned the *Times*.

Within a week of the McNamara brothers' stunning plea switch, Job Harriman, whose bid for mayor had appeared to be a fait accompli just two months earlier, lost by a wide margin to the incumbent, George Alexander. For all intents and purposes, socialism was as dead as labor unionism in Southern California, at least for the foreseeable future.[4]

But still the sorriest chapter in Harrison Gray Otis's stewardship as the *Times*' fire and brimstone preacher of industrial freedom was not quite complete. There was still Clarence Darrow to deal with, and if the General had his way, the Chicago champion of the oppressed and downtrodden would rot in prison along with the McNamaras.

Once he'd put the McNamaras on the train to San Quentin, John Fredericks turned his attention to Bert Franklin. The district attorney offered the defense's chief investigator a deal if he would deliver him Darrow; in exchange for grand jury testimony that he had tried bribing the former policeman George Lockwood on direct orders from his boss, Franklin would get off with a $4,000 fine.

On January 29, 1912, Franklin did testify before the grand jury and the unthinkable happened: Clarence Darrow, the personification of American legal virtue, was indicted for jury tampering. With considerable self-satisfaction, John Fredericks tipped the press to the time and place his men would arrest and book Darrow. Although the greatest living lawyer in the United States immediately posted $20,000 bail, the damage had been done. The following day, Darrow's austere visage appeared on front pages across the country beneath bleak, black headline type that accused him of stooping to bribery to influence a jury.

Clarence Darrow's trial lasted three humiliating months in the spring and summer of 1912. In the beginning, Darrow was despondent. Ironically, the man he chose to defend him was Earl Rogers, the flamboyant and foppish showman who

for six months had faced off against Darrow on the McNamara case. As a Los Angeles icon with a flair for the dramatic, Rogers turned out to be the right lawyer. Every day, the courtroom was jammed with the same army of reporters, union officials, and *Times* establishment supporters who had sat through the Mc-Namara trial; and each day Rogers gave them all a dose of his personal outrage that the district attorney would even *think* that a man of Darrow's impeccable stature could be guilty of bribery.

Eventually rousing himself from his torpor, Darrow became his own best advocate. On the witness stand, he radiated indignation during withering cross-examination and delivered a stirring oration to the jury during closing arguments:

> I am not on trial for having sought to bribe a man named Lockwood . . . I am on trial because I have been a lover of the poor, a friend of the oppressed, because I have stood by labor for all of these years. . . . Men cannot lose all their heart except by a surgical operation, and there are not here in Los Angeles 12 men without some heart. If there were they would have been in the employ of the District Attorney long ago.

The jury bought it. The twelve men took thirty-four minutes to return a verdict of not guilty. In the *Times* editorial about his triumph, Darrow was excoriated once again as an anarchist: "Darrow and his kind have chosen their colors, and those colors are not the ensign of the republic," said the *Times*. "At a dinner given to Darrow by his anarchistic sympathizers, after his acquittal, the American flag was conspicuous by its absence."

As Darrow's first bribery trial was ending, a larger East Coast version of the McNamara affair played itself out in Indianapolis. There, on the second anniversary of the *Times* bombing, trial began of forty leaders of the ironworkers' union, including Herbert S. Hockin, on similar charges of orchestrating the nationwide dynamite conspiracy. As in Los Angeles, the prosecutor's chief witness was Ortie McManigal, who testified once again that he took his direct bombing orders from the man who replaced John J. McNamara as the union's secretary.

"If ever a man had an evil genius, I had one in Hockin," said McManigal.

Hockin and McManigal were both found guilty, but McManigal got a suspended sentence and Hockin, who cooperated with prosecutors by supplying them with union correspondence and records, was convicted of a lesser charge and served no jail time.

Six months after the Indianapolis trial, Clarence Darrow was tried again on the second count of jury tampering, this time, for attempting to have Bert Franklin bribe Robert Bain, the out-of-work carpenter. The jury hung on an eight-to-four

vote for conviction. District Attorney Fredericks agreed not to retry the case if Darrow would leave Los Angeles and never practice law in California again.

In December 1913, Clarence Darrow left for Chicago and did not return.[5]

JOHN FREDERICKS WENT ON to attempt to unseat the progressive Hiram Johnson as California governor two years after the McNamara affair. Although he was bankrolled by Harry Chandler's business partner Moses Sherman, Fredericks lost the election. He did eventually win a congressional seat and finished his career in the 1920s as president of the Los Angeles Chamber of Commerce.

William J. Burns and his son, George, used the McNamara case to make the Burns National Detective Agency an international firm, with offices in Europe and South America. In 1920, Burns resigned from his detective agency to become the second director of the Federal Bureau of Investigation; when he retired in 1925, he turned the reins over to a young bureaucrat named John Edgar Hoover. Burns died seven years later in 1932 of a heart attack. In his *New York Times* obituary, the seventy-year-old Burns was remembered as being "frequently afoul of the law himself in his activities, being charged on many occasions with activities in violation of citizens' rights. In the McNamara case he was marked by many as an enemy of organized labor and in 1917 he was found guilty of committing a misdemeanor for entering a law office in this city and copying letters which he turned over to J. P. Morgan & Co."

Ortie McManigal published a book in 1913 about his ordeal. His wife divorced him, his family disowned him, and he became a pariah among his former union brothers, his name as much a euphemism for "traitor" as Benedict Arnold or Vidkun Quisling. In later years, he asserted that he had made his original confession to Burns on the strength of Burns's promise that he would support McManigal's wife and children while he was in jail. Once the McNamara uproar subsided and McManigal learned that he was all but unemployable, he left the United States to live in Honduras for several years. Although it has never been reported where he earned his income during that time, William J. Burns himself testified in 1915 during an unrelated trial in Detroit that McManigal was working for the Burns Agency in one of Burns's overseas offices.

McManigal returned to Los Angeles in 1932; he took the name W. E. Mack and finished his career as a watchman for the same County Hall of Records building that Herbert Hockin had once ordered McManigal to dynamite. On the occasion of W. E. Mack's retirement in 1944, the Los Angeles County Board of Supervisors presented him with a resolution praising him for "long, faithful and efficient services rendered to the people of this County."

Unknown to Ortie McManigal at the time that he confessed to William Burns, the detective had made a similar deal with Herbert Hockin to betray his fellow union members. According to McManigal, and later substantiated by FBI documents about the McNamara case, Burns confirmed that Hockin had, indeed, been on his payroll all along as a union informant before, during, and after the McNamara brothers' arrests.

As for the *Los Angeles Times,* Moses Sherman summed up the impact of the McNamara affair in a single sentence that he wrote to his friend and business partner Harry Chandler following the brothers' public admission of guilt and the subsequent exile of Clarence Darrow and the American labor movement from Southern California: "It will make you and your dear father-in-law the strongest men in the country."

CHAPTER 5

MAKING AN ELABORATE SHOW of the *Times'* change of command, General Otis officially retired on November 12, 1914. Age and obesity had slowed the old soldier, but his bluster and venality were intact. In full dress uniform, his medals dangling like tinsel from his breast, he ceremoniously handed Harry and Marian Chandler a "deed" to the newspaper, along with his "Ten Commandments" instructing them on the "dos" and "don'ts" of running the *Times:*

> You know, and will always bear in mind, the paramount fact that this journal is, and must continue to be, first of all a *newspaper*—a vehicle for the dissemination of current news reports and information; a faithful recorder of contemporaneous history and public affairs, of new knowledge of the tremendous daily happenings of the mighty Present around the globe, no matter of what nature or complexion the occurrences may be, provided they possess human interest.

His daughter and son-in-law humored him by publishing their equally pompous reply: "The *Times* will be conducted in harmony with the indomitable spirit, high ideals and well-considered injunctions of its great architect and builder, Harrison Gray Otis."

Whether Harry thought that highly of his father-in-law is questionable. He had never been comfortable with the General's public posturing, even if he agreed with his underlying beliefs. The General loved the spotlight; Harry did not, and

was frankly embarrassed by the General's outbursts. Where Otis strutted like a barnyard rooster, Harry Chandler preferred the role of barnyard hawk, carefully and quietly eyeing unguarded morsels.

While General Otis was alive, the *Times* did not waver much from its strident conservative verbiage. The General did not see eye to eye with his son-in-law on several key issues, particularly self-promotion. Low-profile Harry viewed the *Times* chiefly as a tool for enhancing his family's fortunes and his own capitalistic ventures, but the General saw his newspaper as a means of broadcasting his personal philosophy. While the General lived, the newspaper regularly carried his opinions on who should and should not live in Otistown. Undesirables included

Dudes, loafers, paupers. Folks who expect to astonish the natives and make money out of the resident gullibles. (They will be astonished themselves by finding smarter men ahead of them.) Folks who do not wish to obey high grounded and wholesome laws. People who have no means and no situation assured, and who trust to luck for something to do. People too near death to be saved by anything short of a miracle. Cheap politicians. Men with shady reputations "back east." People who are failures wherever they go. People who are afraid to pull off their coats. People who expect to lie on their backs and let the ravens feed them. (The ravens are all engaged.) People who haven't the patience and pocket to wait for an opening in the procession. People for whose blood the Garden of Eden is not sufficiently rich. Bummers. Scrubs. Impecunious clerks, bookkeepers, lawyers, doctors. The market is over-stocked already.

The General's acceptable list of L.A. immigrants included "Workers. Hustlers. Men of brains, brawn and grit. Fruit growers and farmers. Capitalists who seek large returns on honest transactions. Men who have a little capital and a good deal of energy. Men with a good deal of capital who wish 'to take life easy.' First-class men in almost any line of business."

Of course, the dolts, sociopaths, and charlatans showed up in L.A. anyway, despite the General's periodic harangues on the *Times* editorial pages. In his own way, Harry conspired to bring them to Los Angeles. The increasingly fat and romantic *Times* Mid-Winter Edition, which Chandler oversaw, shamelessly invited every able Easterner with a few bucks in his pocket to settle in Southern California, no matter what his background was.

And with good reason.

Without the greedy, the superficial, the venal, and the shiftless as customers, newsman Harry Chandler would probably have enjoyed minimal success in his true vocation: selling real estate. The naive and the newly arrived were so hungry for a hunk of the American Dream that they would buy any kind of property:

forty-five-degree hillsides, bone-dry gullies, flash flood plains, and disintegrating seaside cliffs. Before the turn of the century, one developer sold inaccessible lots at the top of the San Gabriel Mountains for $5,000 apiece. Another marketed saltwater wetlands that were covered by the Pacific for half the year. During the first two decades of the twentieth century, the L.A. courts saw more land fraud disputes than any other kind of case.

At the *Times*, the ebb and flow of boom and bust manifested itself in advertising defaults. Developers and speculators who could pay for their classified ad space no other way often paid with deeds, which soon began piling up on General Manager Harry Chandler's desk. Harry correctly reckoned that even the most worthless piece of real estate had some value, so he held on to the best properties and unloaded the rest for what he could get to satisfy the *Times'* accounts receivable. Soon, he was as much in the real estate business as he was the news business.

Without the saps, Harry Chandler might have amounted to little more than the General's glorified newsboy administrator. Instead, he and his partners found a bottomless cornucopia in subdividing Southern California and selling it off bit by bit on the installment plan. Even before the turn of the century, Harry Chandler's real estate wealth outpaced that of General Otis, and would continue to do so for the next forty years.

———

DURING HIS BRIEF MARRIAGE to Magdalena Schlador in the early 1890s, Harry Chandler invested $500 in a lump of land that poked out of the Long Beach flatlands twenty miles southwest of Los Angeles. Called Signal Hill by the Spanish, who set fires atop the one-hundred-foot hillock to warn clipper ships away from the shoals of nearby Palos Verdes Peninsula, Harry's purchase went for $2,000, turning a tidy profit after he'd held it for just a few months. Had he held on to the property a few more years, that profit would have been closer to $1.5 billion: the value of the petroleum that was eventually pumped from the reserves underneath Signal Hill.

In matters of real estate, Harry Chandler was rarely so unfortunate or so shortsighted. Forming syndicate after syndicate of land developers in the early part of the century, Chandler had the ersatz Midas touch. When L.A.'s establishment investors heard that Harry was in on a deal, they all wanted a piece of the action.

In 1903, Harry Chandler, Moses Hazeltine Sherman, and his brother-in-law, Eli P. Clark, bought a sixty-acre plot adjacent to a dirt road north and west of L.A. Once part of the much larger Rancho La Brea, the acreage was first sliced into city blocks. The goal was to cut the blocks into individual lots that the trio would then sell at a nice profit.

To lure buyers to the area, they built a thirty-three-room hotel, every room with its own bathroom; the building eclipsed the area's Glen-Holly Hotel, which had only twenty rooms, all served by a single bathroom. The three men built their new hotel to resemble an exotic Moorish garrison, with arched windows, muted spires, and earthen-colored plaster walls. Although its dining room did not immediately outdraw the Glen-Holly's famous $0.75 chicken dinner, the new establishment offered a Thursday afternoon tea that eventually became all the rage in nearby L.A. After his screen debut in 1914, young Rudolph Valentino earned extra cash performing the tango during Thursday tea.

In time, the hotel became a weekend destination for potential home buyers who had read about it in Chandler's *Times*. The idea was to persuade working men and women and East Coast visitors to ride Sherman and Clark's Los Angeles Railway out to tour this, the earliest of many Chandler-Sherman-Clark subdivisions and, perhaps, put a down payment on a dream home before taking the trolley back to downtown L.A.

Chandler and his partners deserve credit for being among the most successful developers of the Rancho La Brea foothills and valleys northwest of Los Angeles, but they were not the first. In 1887, Horace and Daeida Wilcox of Kansas bought the original 160 acres. They had intended to raise Arabian horses, but the teetotaling couple had already demonstrated a knack for real estate speculation. Back in Topeka, Horace had given up being a cobbler when he found he could earn more buying property for a pittance and selling it at a higher price. The Wilcoxes now saw the potential for profit in the former Rancho La Brea, where they owned a horse ranch. They advertised in the L.A. papers and began laying out a model village, which they planted with rows of pepper trees along their envisioned grid of streets and avenues. They offered free land to any Protestant minister who might want to build a church in their new township and promised discounted lots to nondrinking, God-fearing families and merchants—precisely the kind of California émigré to whom General Otis had given his blessing in the pages of his *Times*.

When Horace Wilcox died before he could see his L.A. suburb completed, Daeida could not afford to run the development by herself and began selling off chunks to other speculators. Some spurned demon rum but others saw no harm in taking a dram from time to time; thus Horace's hope of creating a safe, dry Christian community was diluted. The name Mrs. Wilcox gave their future subdivision was the only real legacy the Wilcoxes left for future generations. After she had proudly planted a pair of imported English holly bushes next to the couple's ranch house, she suggested to Horace that they call their little Protestant neighborhood Hollywood. The bushes died, but the name lived on.

Ten years later, when the Chandler syndicate's stake in the Cahuenga Valley had increased to 47,000 acres, Moses Sherman and Eli Clark wanted to abandon

the name "Hollywood" and rechristen their new subdivision in Harry's honor. But when his partners told him their intention, Harry was resolute: Hollywood would remain Hollywood. The dirt road on the south side of their development would be called Hollywood Boulevard. Even the new Moorish rooming house they had built at the intersection of Hollywood Boulevard and Highland Avenue would bear the name Hollywood Hotel, not Chandler House.

Harry preferred anonymity and attached the family name to none of his vast real estate holdings. Six years later, when the land speculating triumvirate of Sherman-Clark-Chandler began buying up the San Fernando Valley and developing roads that crisscrossed the wide expanse between the Santa Monica and San Gabriel Mountains, Harry only grudgingly accepted a skinny dirt Chandler Avenue as his sole namesake. Meanwhile, Moses Sherman lent his own name to a twenty-two-mile stretch of 120-foot-wide boulevard through the center of the valley. At a cost of $500,000, it was the longest paved roadway outside of any incorporated city in California and was inspired by Mexico City's broad Paseo de la Reforma. It was, and remains, Sherman Way,[1] named in honor of Harry's first and favorite business partner.

The promise of the L.A. Aqueduct[2] and the purchase of Porter Ranch had without question launched Chandler and his partners into the speculation stratosphere. Each successful subdivision gave way to an even bigger one. In 1909, the Chandler-Sherman-Clark syndicate formed the Los Angeles Suburban Homes Company, bought the 47,500-acre Van Nuys Ranch for $2.5 million; they transformed it from dry farming acreage to small irrigated homesites and sold all of them in seven years.[3] When the first subdivision went on sale on February 22, 1911, "thousands showed up on opening day, ate barbecue, looked around at the empty plain and, amazingly, signed up" to buy the lots, wrote William Mulholland's granddaughter, Catherine, in her history of the era, *The Owensmouth Baby.*

From 1900 to 1910, Los Angeles had more than tripled in size; it was now the seventeenth largest city in the United States, its population 319,198. The new thousands of arrivals needed somewhere to live; Chandler was ready to give it to them. During family get-togethers, he predicted that the San Fernando Valley would be nothing but block after city block of houses "before you girls die," according to his second daughter, Mae Goodan.

Although Harry was interested in moving every newly arrived Southern Californian into his or her very own bungalow, he was just as interested in buying large tracts that might never be built upon. Along with his usual cronies, he bought the hills that separated Hollywood from San Fernando Valley: a wild area that was later deeded to the city and named Griffith Park. In 1911, yet another syndicate he and Moses Sherman headed bought the vast and still untamed Tejon Ranch from the son of General Edward Beale, a former commissioner of the Bu-

reau of Indian Affairs and one of Southern California's original white American settlers. Whether by accident or design, the Tejon remained one of the few Chandler holdings that was never developed and remains intact nearly a century later—a reminder of the real *Ramona* era, when Indian, Mexican, and American culture melded in a uniquely California stew amid 281,000 acres of hill, arroyo, and seemingly endless chaparral vistas.

The original syndicate consisted of seventy participants, one of the largest groups that Chandler and Sherman had yet put together; it included such familiar names as power company magnate William Kerckhoff and members of the Van Nuys family. To raise the $1.5 million in cash that young Beale demanded as a down payment on the $3-million purchase, however, Harry Chandler had to find new investors, which included friends and rivals alike:

- Max Ihmsen, publisher of Hearst's *Los Angeles Examiner;*
- Thomas Gibbon, one of the original Los Angeles Harbor commissioners;
- Frank X. Pfaffinger, the longtime Times Mirror treasurer;
- Otto Brant, vice president and general manager of Title Insurance and Trust Company; and
- Harvey Firestone, founder of Firestone Tire and Rubber Company.

By 1916, several disappointed syndicate members who had hoped to make the same kind of instant killing that Chandler and Sherman were making in the San Fernando Valley began to drop out. Using Times Mirror equity, Chandler bought them out, gradually turning the massive property over the next twenty years into a Chandler family enterprise.[4]

Even in the earliest years, the Tejon became part of a Chandler boy's rite of passage. As teenagers, Norman Chandler and his brothers worked the orchards and drove sheep and cattle along with the other ranch hands. Norman's only son, Otis, who would eventually distinguish himself as a big game hunter, learned as a youngster how to flush quail and stalk squirrels in the remote thickets and ravines of the Tejon. Family friends and business associates fortunate enough to merit an invitation invariably remarked on the contrast between the pristine and nearly primeval conditions of the Chandlers' ranch and the wall-to-wall housing in the San Fernando Valley just fifty miles to the southwest.

During his lifetime, Harry Chandler never considered that L.A.'s urban sprawl encroached upon his Tejon Ranch. The slab-and-stucco horror slowly creeping over the San Fernando Valley might as well have been on another planet. In the years following the bombing of the *Times* building, Harry and his father-in-law saw far more menace to their lifestyle and livelihood seventy-five miles east of ranch headquarters, at the edges of the Mojave Desert.

Socialist, attorney, and failed mayoral candidate Job Harriman, one of the casualties of the McNamara trial, abandoned L.A. and his disappointment in General
Otis's triumph over labor and moved to the Antelope Valley in May 1914. There,
with five families and a $2-million capitalization through a Nevada corporation,
Harriman established a 10,000-acre socialist cooperative; he and his followers
called Llano del Rio after the Spanish name for Big Rock Creek, which ran
through the center of the property.

"It became apparent to me that a people would never abandon their means of
livelihood, good or bad, capitalistic or otherwise, until other methods were developed which would promise advantages at least as good as those by which they
were living," Harriman announced in defense of his utopian experiment.

In contrast to the sprawling subdivisions owned and developed by syndicates,
Llano del Rio was an early agrarian commune that later became a model for the
Israeli *kibbutz* and many of the post-1960s "hippie" experiments in communal
living. In Llano, anyone could join and earn $4 a day if he or she delivered an
honest day's labor in the alfalfa fields, pear orchards, and vegetable gardens; or
contributed in some constructive way to one of the many other enterprises that
grew up with the commune: cannery, warehouse, two hotels, dairy, art studio, library, print shop, shoe shop, auto repair garage, rug factory, rabbit farm, and
laundry. Everyone owned stock and everyone pitched in to make the community
function.

Llano del Rio was Job Harriman's idealistic answer to the *Times'* version of the
American Dream, and at its peak in 1916, over 2,000 people a year visited the cooperative. By incorporating and making all residents stockholders, he hoped to
sidestep the smears he had suffered as a "red" socialist during his years of practicing law in Los Angeles. But led by the *Times,* L.A.'s newspapers regularly
tested Harriman's theory that he and his fellow colonists could succeed and function independent of municipal interference. The *Times* took cheap shots at Harriman's experiment on its editorial pages and headlined every lawsuit, crop failure,
or negative report that came out of Llano del Rio.[5] In General Otis's view, Llano
del Rio's very existence was an affront to every right thinking Angeleno, and Job
Harriman was nothing less than a Godless, unpatriotic communist. The Llano
community's final ruination was not the *Times'* doing, however. As is the case
with most failed ventures in the Southern California desert, the end came because
of a lack of water: In the dry summer of 1917, the residents collectively concluded that their meager Big Rock Creek water supply could not continue to sustain a year-round population.

In December 1917, Job Harriman gathered together his diehard band and
boarded a train for Louisiana, where the New Llano colony settled on 20,000
acres of clear-cut timberland. Shortly after Harriman's departure, neighboring

ranchers vandalized the Llano del Rio buildings to prevent further socialist nesting. Except for its cobblestone foundations and a twin pair of fireplaces that still stand as a tombstone reminder of what once existed along the Antelope Valley's Pearblossom Highway, the abandoned commune reverted to desert. Although Harriman died in 1925, his New Llano in Louisiana continued to struggle against the odds for another fourteen years. The last settlers left in 1939, ending Job Harriman's utopian dream. Its passing was accorded no mention in the *Los Angeles Times*.

CALIFORNIA'S U.S. SENATOR George Hearst bought the 40,000-acre Piedra Blanca Ranch in 1865 to raise horses, but it wasn't until more than half a century later that the vast spread became known to the rest of the world as San Simeon, home to the senator's publicity-loving son and heir. With a boast heard around the world, newspaper mogul extraordinaire William Randolph Hearst launched a twenty-year building binge at San Simeon in 1919; he erected his fabled castle in the Santa Lucia Mountains. Harry Chandler's arch rival in the L.A. newspaper wars eventually spent more than $30 million on the estate that overlooked the gloomy, remote central California coastline, putting himself and his press empire at the threshold of bankruptcy.

Hearst, prototype for Orson Welles's free-spending, fictional Charles Foster Kane, used his San Simeon "ranch," as he called his gaudy hillside retreat, to showcase tons of European art and architecture. The castle incorporated some of the most bizarre and contradictory ingredients of any estate built in the United States at the turn of the century: Roman frescoes melded with plywood, Doric columns draped with chintz, and imported marble flooring covered with cheap throw rugs. Hidden passageways and secret entrances led to a medieval dining hall, a massive Victorian library, and a grand ballroom; gold leaf and lapis lazuli mosaics decorated the indoor pool and ghostly Greek statuary hovered over the outdoor pool; and on the wild foothills of the San Simeon property, the world's largest and most diverse private zoo, replete with zebra, ostrich, giraffe, and African lions, roamed free.[6]

During its heyday, San Simeon became a Hollywood satellite where Hearst played host to virtually every star of the silent era, from Charlie Chaplin and Mary Pickford to Clara Bow, Gloria Swanson, and Buster Keaton. Like many of the actors he entertained, Hearst became a national symbol of self-indulgent excess.

By contrast, Harry and Marian Chandler preferred understated socializing with the WASP bluebloods who made up the membership of such downtown L.A. establishment organizations as the California and Jonathan Clubs. In his starchy high-buttoned shirts and gray felt fedoras, baby-faced Harry Chandler

and his wife became fixtures at L.A.'s First Congregational Church, which encouraged its parishioners to adopt temperance as a way of life. Harry spent his leisure time attending Masonic Lodge meetings; Marian joined the Women's Athletic Club and, later on, became a director of the Baurhyte Maternity Cottage for unwed mothers. The Chandlers could, and occasionally did, host an infrequent teetotaling member of L.A.'s new motion picture colony, but they *never* publicized their parties unless they were for charity.

Although they were born just one year apart, Hearst and Harry Chandler were as different from each other as their respective newspapers. The flamboyant publisher of the *Examiner*, L.A.'s No. 2 newspaper, ran a nationwide newspaper chain that pandered to the working man and woman: It fed the nation's newly literate a daily dose of gossip, gore, and the most lurid headlines that bad taste could produce. The No. 1 *Los Angeles Times,* by contrast, was as stuffy, homey, and Protestant patrician as its publisher.

Despite their own and their newspapers' differences, Chandler and Hearst were always competing with each other. Whereas Harry came from poor but genteel Yankee stock and took great pride in quietly earning his immense fortune, Hearst was a rich man's son, bent on spoiling himself and growing famous at the same time. Hearst lived expansively. Harry Chandler lived comparatively modestly, quietly raising eight children with his prim but assertive Marian in their Los Feliz Hills home.

Chandler would not be chauffeured and, unlike Hearst, did not scoot from city to city in a private railcar. He paid coach fare on the train and drove himself to work each day in a 1910 Franklin convertible, which he refused to trade in for a newer model until well into the 1930s. When it rained, the Franklin's roof leaked; straight-backed Harry Chandler could be seen putt-putting from his Hollywood home to the *Times*, one hand on the wheel and the other hoisting an umbrella.

The Chandlers' retreats, unlike world-famous San Simeon, were virtual family secrets. Few knew of the sanctuary at Tejon and fewer still knew of Harry's interest in the Tres Hermanos cattle ranch or his later purchases of two sprawling ranches in New Mexico. Certainly Hollywood didn't know. The full-blown folly of Hearst's Castle would seem to make Orson Welles's 1941 classic *Citizen Kane* a natural matinee inevitability, but another thirty-five years would pass before Robert Towne performed similar screen surgery on the Chandler legend in *Chinatown*.

Hearst and Harry had similar appetites for power and money, but Chandler was far more discreet. A straitlaced Tres Hermanos fest, for example, was just as lavish as anything Hearst ever sponsored, but none except the participants knew about it.

Harry Chandler, L.A. oil wildcatter Tom Scott, and former Los Angeles County Sheriff William Rowland were the "three brothers" who originally bought the Tres Hermanos near Pomona to raise cattle, and made an annual tradition of throwing an old-fashioned, spectacular springtime round-up. Chandler invited L.A.'s elite for a barbecue, a branding, and a rodeo, but the *Times* didn't report the bash. If the gala had been covered, as *Times* columnist Harry Carr pointed out in his memoirs, the public might have cackled over Harry Chandler's bourgeois buddies: "Fat and wheezing lawyers, doctors, capitalists, bankers who came out in limousines with liveried chauffeurs, put on their bearskin caps, roped steers, branded calves. There was a certain pathos to see them teaching their young sons how to throw reatas and heat branding irons."

To Harry Chandler, such pathos was private. The reading public's sacred Right to Know ended at the front gates of Chandler's various estates. Hearst, however, invited photographers and an occasional reporter to his parties. He encouraged discreet photos and favorable mentions in the gossip columns if he believed they translated into positive public relations for his own political aspirations or were career plugs for his mistress, film comedienne Marion Davies. He viewed the teetotaling family man Chandler as a stick-in-the-mud.

"I'd say Harry Chandler was an old maid," Hearst supposedly once remarked, "except for the fact that the comparison is rough on the old maids."

One trait Hearst and Chandler shared was a romantic passion for California's Mexican heritage. Both bought into the Mission myth first championed by Charles Lummis and Helen Hunt Jackson.[7] Either personally or through their newspapers, they contributed to the restoration of several of the old Franciscan churches' crumbling remains, and raised to the status of a Southern California ritual the annual springtime dramatization of Jackson's *Ramona* in Riverside County's Ramona Bowl. But both men, too, oversaw agricultural enterprises that ruthlessly exploited Mexican labor north and south of the border. Sentiment for old Mexico ended at the profit margin. Taking different paths to get there, Chandler and Hearst had become Mexican land barons before the turn of the century.

Although San Simeon became part of *Examiner* publisher's legend, it is less well known that his father also left Hearst the 1-million-acre Babicora Rancho in the Mexican state of Chihuahua. Senator George Hearst bought the huge property, which straddled the Sierra Madre mountain range, during the 1880s at $0.20 an acre. Hearst was able to negotiate his bargain-basement price chiefly because Geronimo was waging the last of the Apache wars and driving abject fear into landowners on both sides of the border; but Mexican dictator Porfirio Díaz had also developed a policy of selling off huge chunks of the country to foreigners on the pretext of attracting U.S. capital to his poor nation. The Babicora was whit-

tled down piece by piece over the years as revolving post-Díaz régimes stripped absentee foreign owners of their property on a different pretense: The land should go to Mestizo sharecroppers who lived there. With each land grab, however, the peasants remained sharecroppers and Mexican landlords replaced the gringo tyrants. Principally through bribery, Hearst was able to hold on to most of the ranch until his death in August 1951.[8]

Faced with similar post-Díaz problems, Harry Chandler fought back, perhaps because he had bought his Mexican empire (albeit at bargain-basement Díaz prices) instead of inheriting it from his rich father, or even from his rich father-in-law.

While then-Colonel Harrison Gray Otis left to fight in the Philippines in 1899, his son-in-law paid the Mexican counsel in Los Angeles $3,000 for a three-year option to buy 862,000 acres of the Colorado River delta, which fed into the Sea of Cortez. The Mexican counsel, a retired general in Díaz's army, had paid $0.10 an acre for the land; Chandler offered $0.60 an acre.

Three years later, Harry and his father-in-law organized and incorporated the California-Mexico Land and Cattle Company, calling into service many of the usual Chandler syndicate investors:

- Moses H. Sherman;
- Times Mirror vice president Albert McFarland;
- Times Mirror treasurer Frank X. Pfaffinger;
- Otto Brant, W. H. Allen Jr., and two other executives of his Title Insurance and Trust Company.

In Mexico, they incorporated the California-Mexico Land and Cattle Company under the name Colorado River Land Company, S.A., even though the directors and stockholders on both sides of the border were identical. Together, the two companies raised $2 million in capital and began exercising the $0.60 per acre options.

Harry and his partners had originally planned to graze cattle, but a trip Chandler made to the desert altered his thinking about the acreage's being suitable only for cows. One spring, a rancher placed an ad with the *Times* to sell land in the Imperial Valley. Harry stopped the ad before it could be published. He accused the rancher of trying to sell *Times* customers worthless desert at premium prices. Not true, said the rancher, and invited Chandler to see for himself. Chandler made the two-day overland auto trip to the southeastern-most corner of California and saw firsthand how centuries of silt carried by the Colorado south to the Gulf of California had spilled a rich and plentiful layer of topsoil over thou-

sands of acres well beyond the mouth of the river. Irrigated by water siphoned off the nearby Colorado, the desert bloomed. After seeing for himself how fertile the land was, Chandler not only printed the rancher's ad but bought 1,800 acres and added it to the California-Mexico Land and Cattle Company, which abutted the Imperial Valley along the Mexican border.

The Colorado River Land Company imported thousands of Chinese coolies to construct an irrigation system, but after a major rainfall in 1905, the channel they had dug diverted the entire outflow of the Colorado River into the Imperial Valley. Unknowingly, the syndicate had tapped into one of the river's original routes; this led to the Salton Sink, a dried-up remainder of the Sea of Cortez. Overnight, Chandler's blunder created the Salton Sea, but neither his syndicate nor the Mexican government would take responsibility. At last, to protect its tracks from the rising Salton Sea, the Southern Pacific Railroad dumped enough rock into the channel to dam the Colorado River and turn its flow back toward the Sea of Cortez.

By 1907, the Chandler syndicate controlled a miniature version of the Nile River Valley just below the Baja border. Thanks to the Colorado River,[9] the C-M Ranch—the name given to the operation on both sides of the border—developed into one of the most successful agribusinesses in the West. Through a system of canals that eventually totaled more than 2,500 miles, Chandler's combined California-Mexico Land and Cattle Company and Colorado River Land Company, S. A., irrigated truck crops and cotton fields that eventually employed more than 8,000 Mexican peasants. The ranch yielded millions in produce and millions more in cotton. Peaking once with a then-record cotton crop worth more than $18 million, the ranch also boasted the world's largest cotton gin, which made Harry Chandler, Harrison Otis, and their partners the largest producers of cotton in the world.

And thus they might have remained had it not been for the Mexican Revolution. As it turned out, the *Times* building was not the only explosion in the autumn of 1910. Shortly after General Otis returned from the centennial celebration of Mexican independence in Mexico City to find his newspaper's building dynamited to dust, the President Porfirio Díaz's government also blew up. The revolution that followed brought the United States and Mexico to the brink of war.

Díaz's thirty-five years of repression and cozy deals with such absentee American landlords as Harry Chandler and William Randolph Hearst opened a decade of uncertainty, betrayal, and bloodshed over Mexican independence and U.S. property rights. Before it was over, Harry Chandler would be indicted and tried in federal court as a suspected revolutionary.

CHAPTER 6

A CENTURY HAS PASSED since a tiny, squeaky-voiced intellectual asked during a Mexican séance whether he would ever become *presidente*. A Ouija board spelled out an "S" followed by an "I." Si. Yes. Francisco Madero would one day lead his country out of its feudal malaise and into the twentieth century. The spirits did not let on then, however, that mild-mannered little Francisco's land reforms would also spark a revolution that would cost him and thousands of his country-men their lives—and Harry Chandler his ranch.

A vegetarian, teetotaler, and idealistic son of wealthy farmers from the Mexican state of Coahuila, Madero took the séance seriously. After attending college in Paris and Berkeley, he launched his political career, and by the time he celebrated his thirty-seventh birthday, the five-foot-two-inch Madero decided it was time. He declared himself a presidential candidate in the Mexican independence cen-tennial election of 1910; the candidate made the return of native lands to the Mexican people a cornerstone of his campaign.

Madero did not seem to grasp that the eighty-year-old incumbent, President Porfirio Díaz, had called the election purely as a formality. Balloting was held chiefly to satisfy Díaz's patriotic U.S. supporters—men such as William Randolph Hearst and Harry Chandler; these landowners enjoyed owning vast expanses of Mexican soil but liked to believe that they had acquired their acreage justly, from a democratically elected government comparable to that of the United States. Hailed by everyone from Teddy Roosevelt to Andrew Carnegie as a wise and courageous statesman, Díaz believed his own publicity while showing no sign that he intended to give up his dictatorship. As for the challenger Madero, he was *el loquito* (the little madman) to Díaz and belonged in an asylum, not in the pres-idential palace.

Still, Porfirio Díaz recognized a potential threat when he saw one, and he took no chances. On June 6, 1910, he had Madero tossed into prison on trumped-up charges until Díaz's government ballot counters could void enough of Madero's popular vote to assure Díaz's reelection. The *Los Angeles Times* headline of July 3, 1910, accurately, if ironically, proclaimed the outcome of the Mexican election: MASSES NOW TAKE INTEREST IN THE GOVERNMENT AS NEVER BEFORE KNOWN.

Officially defeated, Francisco Madero was released from prison the following October and immediately fled to San Antonio, Texas, where he published his rev-olutionary *Plan de San Luis Potosi*—a broadside declaring the reelection of Por-

firio Díaz an out-and-out fraud. Madero called for a national insurrection to begin at 6:00 P.M. on November 20, 1910.

As much to the surprise of his friends in the United States as to President Díaz himself, the insurrection began right on schedule. Peasant uprisings led by folk heroes Pancho Villa in the north and Emiliano Zapata in the south soundly defeated the Mexican army on Madero's behalf in a matter of months. By the following May, Díaz had resigned and fled to France. He always threatened to return, but died in exile in 1915.

Meanwhile, Hearst and Chandler and other foreigners scrambled to forge alliances with the new government; at the same time, they took steps to protect the ranches they had bought under the old régime. At first, the *Times* blubbered over Madero's revolution as "a triumph of advanced socialism"; the exiled Díaz had been "a wise and benevolent despot." But when it became clear that the insurrection was no flash in the pan and that it could soon be hitting a lot closer to home, the tone of Harry Chandler's published rhetoric and Harrison Otis's private political correspondence to Washington bigwigs grew increasingly shrill, even desperate.

For Los Angeles newspaper readers, the Mexican Revolution became a daily dose of dread. Just a few hundred miles beyond the city limits, they were told, bloodthirsty *banditos* were pillaging, plundering, and planning an invasion of the United States. Mixing the hysteria surrounding the arrest of the McNamara brothers in the spring of 1911 with mounting fear over Madero's Mexican Revolution, the *Times,* the *Examiner,* and most of the other Los Angeles dailies found homicidal radicals lurking at every turn.

Began one article, "Most of the revolutionists are either Mexican criminals or mongrel Americans who have good reasons for not risking their presence again on American soil." In a caustic editorial worthy of General Otis's own splendid malice, the *Times* clicked off a catalogue of catcalls aimed at the border rebels: "The apostles of disorder, the missionaries of unrest, the jawsmiths of closed-shop unionism, the enviers of other people's prosperity, the brawlers, the larcenists, the dynamiters, the I.W.W.'s and the friends of raising the devil. . . . The air is incaradined and made mephitic with their presence."

Brothers Ricardo and Enrique Magon, two early Madero supporters, were just such a mephitic pair. They had been living in exile in Los Angeles during the first days of the revolution, trying to drum up support for their own Baja band of rebels to defeat the hated Díaz. The Magon brothers had to endure *Times* headlines that labeled them and their followers hobos, anarchists, and chicken thieves. The brothers counseled their "Magonista" disciples to adopt the same radical action against Otis and his son-in-law that had been taken by the brothers McNamara: When all other arguments fail, persuade the enemy with force.

But the Magonistas had no interest in blowing up the *Times* again. They waged their guerrilla war against the pro-Díaz forces in the coastal towns of Tijuana and Ensenada, south of San Diego. Even more alarming to Harry Chandler, however, was a cross-border raid they made on the Imperial Valley desert town of Mexicali in January 1911. Harry paid an emergency visit to the Imperial Valley to survey the damage, just a few miles from the C-M Ranch, and found that he and his father-in-law were hated there almost as much as Porfirio Díaz.

Harry was less concerned about his popularity than he was about his property. With anarchy in the air, the C-M Ranch was the Magonistas' next logical target.

Upon his return to L.A., Harry warned the General that sympathy along the border had shifted to Madero; Otis immediately dashed off a letter to President William Howard Taft pitching for U.S. military protection: "They are a bad lot who ought to be exterminated in the interests of right, peace and order, and for the protection of honest citizens on both sides of the line," wrote the General. Borrowing from years of irrational antiunion zeal, Otis warned the president that the Magonistas' "ultimate scheme is to establish a socialistic republic in Lower California, cutting loose from both the United States and Mexico, and attempting to set up a Socialistic heaven of their own."

But the same President Taft who had helped General Otis put the McNamaras away was not persuaded this time; he did not equate the Magon brothers with socialist bogeymen and refused to intervene.

Although Harry preferred persuading the government to do the dirty work, he saw that it was time to take matters into his own hands. Chandler bivouacked with the C-M Ranch's general manager, Walter K. Bowker, to create a ranch police force: a private militia to protect the ranch's livestock, crops, and irrigation system, which, Chandler claimed, had been authorized by the Díaz régime. Armed and trained as well as any professional army, the C-M Ranch regulars began patrolling the edges of the Chandler property as if it were a small country.

On a more diplomatic front, Harry opened a correspondence with Francisco Madero to see whether the new president might be finessed. Madero did not waver from his clarion call for the return of lands sold to foreigners during the Díaz régime, but he did, indeed, turn out to be malleable, at least on Chandler's strategic ownership of the C-M Ranch. Whereas General Otis had been unable to persuade President Taft that the Magons wanted Baja to secede from the rest of Mexico, Harry convinced Madero that it was true. Thus, when the Magon brothers were indicted by a Los Angeles grand jury on charges of violating U.S. neutrality laws, Madero raised no objections on behalf of his countrymen.

Madero took the secession threat seriously enough to send an expeditionary detachment, headed by a military advisor named B. J. Viljoen, to join the C-M

General Harrison Otis, first publisher of the *Los Angeles Times*. (Photo courtesy of Sherman Library.)

Harry Chandler, second publisher of the *Los Angeles Times*. (Photo courtesy of Sherman Library.)

Charles Lummis, first *Times* city editor.
(Photo courtesy of USC.)

Harry Chandler and his first wife,
Magdelena Schlador. (Photo from
Otis Chandler Collection.)

Young Norman Chandler, astride the family pony, Spot, on the front lawn
of the Chandler home. Seated are his sisters and cousins.
(Photo from Otis Chandler Collection.)

Norman Chandler, age 5, the third
publisher of the *Los Angeles Times*.
(Photo from Otis Chandler Collection.)

October 1, 1910, bombing of the *Los Angeles Times* building.
(Photo courtesy of USC.)

Times building in the wake
of 1910 bombing. (Photo
courtesy of Sherman
Library.)

General Otis, left, flanked by his son-in-law Harry Chandler following the 1910 bombing of the *Times*. (Photo courtesy of Sherman Library.)

Labor legend Samuel Gompers posed for a publicity portrait with brothers J.B. McNamara (left) and J.J. McNamara, during their sensational 1911 trial for the *Times* bombing. (Photo courtesy of USC.)

General Moses Sherman, real estate business partner to General Otis and Harry Chandler. (Photo courtesy of USC.)

Below: The Chandler family, circa 1911: (from left, back row) May, Harry, Harrison, Ruth, Norman; (front row) Helen, Fran, Philip, Marian, Connie. (Photo courtesy of USC.)

General Otis's home, "The Bivouac," which became the Otis Art Institute shortly before the General's death in 1917. (Photo courtesy of USC.)

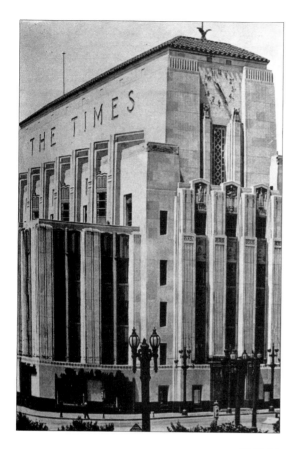

The third *Times* building, opened in 1934 and is still *Times* headquarters today. (Photo courtesy of the Sherman Library.)

Norman Chandler looks on as his father, Harry, opens the front door of the new *Times* building in 1934. (Photo courtesy of the Sherman Library.)

From left, Edward and Isabelle Emett and Buff and Norman
Chandler, 1948. (Photo courtesy of Bob Emett.)

Otis Chandler, age 10. (Photo courtesy of
Bob Emett.)

Otis's lifelong friend Bob Emett, with
Otis, outfitted in cowboy hat, holster,
and six-shooter. (Photo courtesy of
Bob Emett.)

Ranch militia. Save for the usual rustlers and poachers, the detachment saw no action during its stay at the C-M Ranch, but Viljoen had a close look at a sprawling green oasis in the middle of the desert unlike any that he had seen farther south of the border. He quit Madero's army and hired on as Walter Bowker's assistant general manager. With the C-M Ranch's new police force in place and a Madero loyalist on the payroll as Bowker's assistant, Harry Chandler at last felt confident in assuring Madero that Baja could and would remain a state loyal to Mexico.

With no objection from the new Mexican government, Los Angeles authorities arrested the Magon brothers in June 1911 and tossed them into the same county jail where the McNamara brothers awaited trial. The Magons were tried in L.A. during the first weeks of 1912, found guilty, and sent to federal prison for the next two years for their quixotic efforts on behalf of Francisco Madero's revolution.

The following year, just as Harry Chandler and General Otis began to relax, the revolution flared anew. On February 22, 1913, General Victoriano Huerta of the Mexican army staged a coup d'état and ordered Francisco Madero's summary execution, among scores of other killings. With the tacit approval of the U.S. ambassador, Henry Lane Wilson, Huerta returned Mexico to a Díaz-style dictatorship and once again, Harry Chandler saw his Baja empire placed in jeopardy.

Chandler and General Otis had at first viewed Madero's ouster as a godsend because, sooner or later, the little *presidente* would have had to make good on his campaign promise and repatriate the C-M Ranch. Despite a marked increase in government corruption and violence under Huerta, he wanted the U.S. land barons left alone. The *Times* praised him as the one Mexican leader capable of dealing with his country's "semi-barbarous population."

But neither Pancho Villa nor Emiliano Zapata read the *Los Angeles Times*. As far as they and their followers were concerned, the new *presidente* was capable only of committing wholesale murder. Unlike the unfortunate Madero, both Villa and Zapata were far more capable than General Huerta was of rallying their country's "semi-barbarous population," and they made short work of his reign of terror. While Villa's forces occupied the northern third of Mexico, Zapata's triumphant guerrilla army hammered the *federales* from the south and entered Mexico City in July 1914, just as Huerta boarded a German freighter bound for a permanent Spanish exile. Huerta's rocky régime barely lasted six months before he followed Díaz's prudent example.

Baja's politics at the time were just as volatile. The stability that Harry Chandler believed he had achieved with Madero, and later with Huerta, evaporated overnight. Following the imprisonment of the Magon brothers, Baja's governors moved in and out of office more swiftly than Mexican *presidentes*—and could of-

fer even less protection. When a handful of Pancho Villa's militants seized land on the fringes of the C-M Ranch, Chandler turned to the latest impotent Baja governor, Balthazar Aviles, who told Harry that he sympathized with the Americans but had neither the resources nor the authority to help. Only a rapid mobilization of Walter Bowker's police force drove the squatters away.

As for Aviles, his term as governor lasted only three months; in a miniversion of the Huerta coup d'état, Mexican army colonel Esteban Cantu chased him across the California border into San Diego. Aviles didn't wait around for a miracle to happen. He immediately headed for Los Angeles to ask Harry Chandler for militia money.

IN RETROSPECT, even pragmatic Harry Chandler could see that the plot to overthrow Esteban Cantu was shortsighted, overblown, and foolish. The new Baja governor publicly opposed the C-M Ranch's policy of hiring cheap Asian field labor over Mexican workers, but overall Cantu's pronouncements failed to threaten Chandler; indeed, Cantu was an improvement over the feckless Governor Aviles. Cantu was conciliatory on most issues and didn't even mention land reform.

Why did Chandler agree to bankroll the ex-governor's plan to overthrow the Cantu régime? The general paranoia of the times provided the only suitable explanation.

As 1914 came to a close, the momentary lull in the late Francisco Madero's Mexican Revolution had once again given way to chaos. The *presidente* who followed General Huerta was Venustiano Carranza, former governor of Francisco Madero's home state of Coahuila. Like Madero, Carranza kicked off his presidency by calling for a breakup of large absentee-owned ranches. This was more Mexican rhetoric, of course. As it turned out, Carranza was as lackadaisical as Madero about breaking up huge foreign-owned estates such as the Babicora Rancho or the C-M Ranch. Years would pass before government officials moved on the Americans' ranches, but Chandler did not know that at the time.

Thus began a tale of intrigue that started in the lobby of a two-story adobe hotel in El Centro, California, and ended three years later in a Los Angeles courtroom.

Besides miles of property all the way to the horizon in every direction, General Harrison Otis and his son-in-law also owned El Centro's Oregon Hotel, located in the middle of the Imperial Valley; here C-M Ranch officials recruited counterrevolutionaries for Balthazar Aviles's invasion of Baja California in August 1914. The ranch was to be the base of operations; general manager Walter Bowker and

his assistant, B. J. Viljoen, promised food and sanctuary to those who signed up for their insurgent army. The Mexican counsel in San Diego, who went by the unlikely name of Geronimo Sandoval, would supply guns and ammunition. And the man behind it all was Sandoval's good friend and former boss, Balthazar Aviles, who had found the perfect patsy in Harry Chandler to pay for the uprising.

The former Baja governor arranged through B. J. Viljoen to meet Chandler in L.A. a few weeks after Cantu's coup. There, Aviles vowed a hands-off policy towards the C-M Ranch if Harry would foot the bill for his countercoup. Once Cantu had been routed, according to Aviles, Baja could secede from Mexico and all threats of expropriating the C-M Ranch would cease. Apparently, Aviles was a more effective salesman than he had been a governor. Harry Chandler agreed. Using the cover story that he was merely paying off some back taxes on the C-M Ranch, Chandler handed over $5,000 to Aviles. In return, Aviles assured Harry that he would use the money to assemble an army, convene at the border south of San Diego, and march on Tijuana.

Harry Chandler's involvement meant more than financial backing. As one C-M Ranch recruiter put it to a prospective rebel, "You don't have to be afraid. If we get into any trouble, we have the *Los Angeles Times* with us."

Spirits of the original conspirators were so buoyed by Harry's participation that one of them began drawing up maps of the imaginary new country: One of the new states south of the border was to be called simply "Otis."

But within weeks, Aviles was back at Chandler's door asking for more money— this time, to bribe a Mexican army officer in Tijuana to conspire with the invaders once they had crossed the border; and this time, Harry refused.

"There is no reliance on these greasers," Chandler spat in disgust. Among other bad decisions, Aviles had chartered a sixty-ton steamer to haul troops not yet recruited from Los Angeles and San Diego to the imagined battlefields of Baja. Chandler told an attorney who had agreed to act as Aviles's middleman that he'd already made one bad investment; he wasn't about to compound it by making another.

"I gave him the $5,000 and he promised faithfully that he would set about at once, and now he wants more money," growled Harry. "I want to have nothing to do with him."

That might have been the end of the matter if two of Aviles's recruits hadn't run to the U.S. attorney's office with the whole sorry story. Following a two-month investigation, on February 19, 1915, a federal grand jury in Los Angeles indicted Aviles; Chandler; C-M Ranch manager W. K. Bowker; his assistant manager, B. J. Viljoen; San Diego's Mexican counsel, Geronimo Sandoval; a Mexican real estate developer named Challey Guzman; and a Dutch soldier of fortune

named Nicholas Zogg—all on a charge of conspiring to organize a revolution on United States soil against Baja governor Esteban Cantu.

Everyone pleaded not guilty and a trial date was set for November; but Chandler's defense lawyers managed to have the trial postponed five times—once because Harry had developed a sinus condition. The trial didn't begin until more than two years later, on May 28, 1917. By that time, the complexion of the Mexican Revolution had changed once again, including the policies of Esteban Cantu. In his two years as Baja's governor, the man Harry Chandler allegedly tried to depose had become Harry Chandler's best Mexican friend.

Cantu and Chandler had found common ground when it came to U.S. dollars. Harry had them. Cantu wanted them. In 1916, when the rest of Mexico was once again gridlocked in civil war, Cantu made the outrageous pronouncement that the only currency his government would recognize in Baja California was the U.S. dollar. Everything else, including the peso, was just too unstable. Cantu paid his army with dollars and collected taxes, and bribes, in dollars. When the Carranza government in Mexico City protested, Cantu threatened to secede—the very act that Aviles had proposed, leading to the conspiracy charges that had landed Harry in hot water in the first place. By the time the conspiracy case was going to trial, Chandler and Cantu were on the very best of terms: As Cantu stuffed his personal bank account with more and more U.S. dollars, he realized he needed financial advice and hired Chandler as his investment counselor.

Besides his admiration for Harry Chandler and U.S. currency, Cantu also recognized the mutual benefit to be derived from supplying prostitutes, pornography, gambling, and other libido satisfactions to the hidebound moralists on the other side of the border. It all worked out: Cantu got cash while Americans, including Chandler's wranglers and farm lads at C-M Ranch, got laid.

Meanwhile, Harry's trial in Los Angeles was over nearly as soon as it started. Although the prosecution had enough evidence and witnesses to prove that some kind of coup was brewing at the C-M Ranch, Chandler's lawyers had found a loophole in the U.S. Neutrality Act through which their client and all the rest of Harry's codefendants were able to wriggle free. Under the law as written, U.S. residents were forbidden to offer military aid to an existing foreign government. But because Balthazar Aviles was an *ex*-governor, argued the defense, Harry's $5,000 down payment on a revolution didn't count. Aviles did not represent an existing government.

As twisted as the defense's logic might have appeared, Judge Benjamin Bledsoe directed the jury to return a verdict of not guilty for everyone. The only defendant who did jail time was the Dutch mercenary Nicholas Zogg, who publicly blasted the judge for failing to recuse himself from sitting on the case because of

his own strong L.A. establishment business ties to Harry Chandler and the *Times*. Bledsoe sentenced Zogg to three months for contempt after Zogg called him a "judicial prostitute."

On the courthouse steps, Harry Chandler reveled in his acquittal and told reporters for his own and the other Los Angeles newspapers that he had been innocent all along. He found the idea of interfering with a foreign power both repugnant and reprehensible, and he only wanted to operate his ranch in peace. The jury's verdict struck a blow for common sense and free enterprise.

Privately, Chandler breathed a sigh of relief, but he never tired of broadening his normally bland rosebud of a mouth into a tight, bright smirk when he told friends and business associates, "You're not a man until you've been indicted at least once."

––––––––––––

THE MEXICAN COUPS CONTINUED WELL into the 1920s, with no real land reform forthcoming, either from Mexico City or from Tijuana. Meantime, Harry Chandler held on to his borderland and milked it for all it was worth. Once, in 1915, a communal group of Japanese farmers offered Chandler $15 million for his Baja land, but he refused after consulting Washington. The State Department advised him to steer clear of sales to foreigners for fear of triggering a response from within the confused, chaotic bureaucracy that ran the Mexican government.

Nearly twenty years after Francisco Madero's assassination, the agrarian reforms written into Carranza's Mexican Constitution of 1917 at last began to be enforced. In 1934, Lazaro Cardenas assumed the Mexican presidency and kept his campaign promise: He kicked out the foreigners. One of the Mexican government's belated confiscations was one-half of the C-M Ranch. Then well into his seventies, fighting Harry Chandler gave up. In 1935, he managed to arrange through Secretary of State Cordell Hull to salvage a token $5 million from the Cardenas government in return for the remaining half of the ranch.

That the General did not live to see his son-in-law's capitulation was some comfort. Mexico was not the only world in revolt during the final decade of Harrison Gray Otis's life. His "No Surrender!" sentiment, infused into his soul by his service to the Grand Army of the Republic during the Civil War, was no longer fashionable. The frontier crucible in which he hatched his *Los Angeles Times* in 1881 had vanished. The city that he and his son-in-law had conjured out of pueblo myth, stolen water, antiunion sentiment, streetcars, automobiles, and year-round sunshine bore little resemblance to the "Hell-Hole of the West."

Although the old warrior remained independent and opinionated to the very end, he had been winding down throughout the decade of the Mexican Revolution.

"In his last few years the old General . . . actually became senile," wrote *Times* editor Nick Williams in a 1976 letter to one of his junior editors. "He would walk around the editorial office as if it were the Pentagon and say to the telegraph editor: 'Where are the dispatches from the front?' When told there were no dispatches (and there was no front!), he would fire the telegraph editor forthwith."

Out of the General's earshot, the city editor, or occasionally Harry Chandler, would order the telegraph editor to go across the street to the saloon for a drink and stay there until the General left the building. When the General had gone, the telegraph editor came back to work until the next time Otis wanted a report from the front.

Otis's name stayed on the masthead as publisher, but Harry had been running the *Times* for at least a dozen years. Gradually, Otis set foot less and less inside the new *Times* building that had risen Phoenix-like from the ashes of the First and Broadway site of the General's fallen fortress. He had taken, instead, to the role of country gentleman.

He never quite abandoned the dream of turning Southern California into an exotic utopia laboratory for growing alien plant species or breeding Angora goats and ostriches. Occasionally, he ordered a story written about one or the other long after the novelty had faded. Otis was so set on the goats that he stubbornly maintained his own herd at Milflores,[1] his 540-acre San Fernando Valley spread where he also planted small forests of sequoias and beef wood.[2]

Politics were still his passion during his final years; he never tired of railing against such political foes as Teddy Roosevelt, Eugene Debs, or California's new reform governor, and later senator, Hiram Johnson. To Otis, Johnson was still nothing more than "a bombastic, self-assertive, conceited, dominating man." Well into his seventies, the General would still jot down his two cents worth over an issue or a candidate that caught his fancy and hand it to Harry to pass on to the *Times'* editors. When President Woodrow Wilson appointed Louis Brandeis to the Supreme Court, Otis wrote that it was "enough to make cold chills run down the spine of every patriot in the country." Dispatches from the General grew more and more infrequent, but readers knew when he was writing the words, even without reading his byline. Just as it had been in the early years, a patented Harrison Otis mixed metaphor could be as easily spotted as an ill-tempered neon whale.

In one of his final series of essays, he proposed to bring about world peace.

Before World War I broke out, Otis developed his Plan for Ending Wars. Like some aging Pollyanna political scientist, the General argued for a kind of interna-

tional strike force that would enlist all the civilized good nations to police the handful of renegades. He called his proposed organization the International Alliance of Nations and ordered his Plan published in the *Times,* translated, and sent off to world leaders as well as to Washington. He would not live to see it, but his plan did become the basis for Woodrow Wilson's League of Nations after World War I. The league failed, but the concept of Otis's International Alliance of Nations eventually found currency in both the United Nations and the North Atlantic Treaty Organization.

In 1916, he deeded his beloved Bivouac to the city of Los Angeles as a Christmas present and moved in with Harry and Marian at their new stone mansion in the Los Feliz Hills. The Bivouac became the Otis Art Institute,[3] housing a gallery of oil paintings and offering classes to aspiring artists. During the final year of his life, the General spent even less time at the institute named in his honor than he did at the *Times.*

During the spring of 1917, the United States finally entered World War I, the General's precious peace plan notwithstanding. Once the United States was in the thick of battle, the *Times* was as jingoistic as the loudest patriot. With the kind of accusatory gusto that had made Harrison Otis notorious*, Times* editorials jubilantly eviscerated local antiwar protesters like the Baptist minister Robert Whitaker and Long Beach pacifist Fanny Bixby.

The General was not part of it, however. He suffered angina and spent no time at the newspaper and less and less time out-of-doors. On the days he felt up to it, he had himself chauffeured to his San Fernando Valley ranch, to the Tres Hermanos in the Chino Hills, or to the vast and still primeval Tejon, drinking in the alfalfa fields, subdivisions, and sprouting cities along the way. The day before his death, his oldest grandson, Norman Chandler, drove the General out to Milflores and back. They drove through the village of Van Nuys on the way, population 550; it hadn't existed ten years earlier and had only recently been annexed to the city of Los Angeles. It gave Otis great pleasure to simply sit and survey the City of the Future that he, his son-in-law, and his *Times* helped to create.

"The old man was a rugged, strong character," wrote Harry Carr, who was one of the leading historians in L.A. at the turn of the century and who spent most of his career writing for the *Times.* "Tender-hearted, bitter in his hatreds and loyal in his friendships. A virile, vigorous writer, and a master printer to the end of his days."

General Otis died of heart failure shortly after 9:00 A.M. on July 30, 1917. Harry and Marian were downstairs at breakfast when it happened, but by the time the hysterical maid hurried down from the General's bedroom with the news, he had already gone.

Naturally, he was buried in his uniform.

CHAPTER 7

HARRY HAD NEITHER THE CHEEK NOR THE HEART to wrest the titles of president and general manager away from an ailing old man, but two days after the General's death, he happily accepted his well-earned due. The board of the growing Times Mirror Printing and Binding Company, led by his wife Marian, voted Harry Chandler, now fifty-four, president, general manager, and second publisher of the *Los Angeles Times* on August 1, 1917.

Harry Chandler's *Times* underwent a subtle sea change in the years leading into the Roaring Twenties. The General's personal editorial touch had died with him. Chandler's solid institutional voice, however, echoed the bland boosterism of L.A.'s Republican oligarchy, and it spread through the pages of the *Times* like a slow-growing fungus, suffocating what little remained of the General's patented outrage.

"His body was hardly cold before Chandler flopped the paper," lamented the *American Mercury* magazine's Louis Sherwin.[1] "This was, of course, an entirely impersonal business maneuver. . . . Though [the *Times*] continued to belabor the posteriors of the unions, its fulminations lost gusto, and the raciness and temper departed from its pages. The bludgeon became a bladder. The *Times* of Otis, in short, shed its character. Aside from the difference in type display and syndicate features, you would be hard put to it today to distinguish it from the *Examiner,* its only rival."

Nowhere did this loss of character seem more symbolically apparent than at the conclusion of World War I. At midnight on November 10, 1918, Harry Chandler officially marked the end of the war that was supposed to make the world safe for democracy by ordering his editors to deliver a celebratory blast from a siren atop the *Times* building. The crowds cheered and Harry Chandler beamed. The seldom-used siren, which had been installed as part of a warning alarm system following the 1910 bombing of the old *Times* building, signaled more than mere armistice for Chandler and his closest business associates. By their way of thinking, the war that had made the world safe for democracy had also made Southern California safe for no-holds-barred capitalism. The covetous Fox had at last supplanted the caustic old Walrus.

But ascendancy to the publisher's suite did not mean that it was time to relax; on the contrary, the *Times* victory siren just as certainly sounded the alarm against a new socialist threat on the far side of the globe. World War I might be over, but the Russian Revolution raged on. Some of the same American radicals[2] who had fought against the late General's *Times* were now waging war against Czar

Nicholas II. The Bolshevik revolution challenged the fundamental principles of free enterprise that Harry Chandler held so dear to his heart and his pocketbook.

Unlike his late father-in-law, Chandler was just as much a man of principal—the kind that earned interest—as he was of principle. Where money could be made, Harry made allowances. Thus, his *Times* toned down its standard Red-baiting rhetoric for several months following the Communist victory in Russia because he thought he could do business with the Lenin government. Harry and his usual retinue of coinvestors formed an oil exploration syndicate after the Revolution and made a deal to drill for oil in the Siberian province of Kamchatka.

Harry took his lumps from arch rival William Randolph Hearst, whose *Los Angeles Examiner* gleefully revealed the Russian oil deal under a headline reading

CHANDLER DENIES HE IS A BOLSHEVIK FISCAL AGENT

Harrison Otis's longtime nemesis, Senator Hiram Johnson, also chortled publicly over the late General's son-in-law and his oil exploration syndicate's latest questionable bid for cash, pointing out the obvious hypocrisy: "They prate about the "Reds," they talk of the horror of Bolshevism, they would draw and quarter every man of liberal tendencies, and yet, when they can turn a dollar and make a little profit, they will deal with anything or anybody."

Harry's sanctimony returned with a vengeance the moment the Lenin government reneged on the oil deal in 1922. *Times* editorials immediately urged the U.S. government not to recognize the renegade Reds, and accused the same Russian revolutionaries with whom Harry had wanted to do business just a few months earlier of "a thousand crimes against justice and humanity." Subjugating an entire nation through a broad Communist conspiracy and proletarian dictatorship was one thing; welshing on a deal was quite another.

Reds in Russia were a distant threat; but closer to home, the ever-present danger of trade unionism lingered. For the *Times*, communism was not just some exotic horror taking root on another continent. From where Harry sat, he could see Reds infesting Southern California next. On the issue of unions, Harry remained as firm and as rabid as his late father-in-law. When the proudly radical Industrial Workers of the World or "Wobblies," as they were nicknamed, tried to organize citrus workers in the orange groves east of L.A., the front page of the *Times* screamed

BOLSHEVIST CONSPIRACY BARED

Vigilante posses joined police in rounding up and running the Wobblies out of town, renewing the chill cast over L.A. labor following the 1910 bombing. The

IWW was in tatters, its leaders in jail or exiled, and its rank and file riddled with labor spies and agents provocateurs. Once again, unions had been put in check, and that was the way the *Times* liked it. At best, organized labor was an impediment to Harry Chandler's version of progress; at worst, it represented a vile threat to the American way of life.

Under Harry's stewardship, the *Los Angeles Times* was a pulpit for profit first, a weapon against organized labor second, and a "news" paper often a distant third. There was financial and shipping news for the businessman, comics for the kids, a daily Bible text for the Protestant faithful, and sports, murder, celebrity ogling, and scandal to titillate the working stiff, but little real information or analysis. In 1922, the *Times* began publishing a regular "Noticias Mundiales de Ultima Hora" column for Spanish-speaking readers, but killed it in 1933. The *Times* was an American newspaper for American readers and as far as Harry Chandler was concerned, Americans communicated in English.

Harry's interest in the world threat of communism did step up the paper's international and national news coverage, however, and the *Times* opened its own Washington bureau in 1916; a political functionary named Robert B. Armstrong staffed it. If a Chandler foe such as Senator Hiram Johnson spoke in Congress, Armstrong's job was either to ignore it or to write something snide. If a Chandler favorite such as Herbert Hoover made a public appearance, Armstrong hyped it to the hilt. Although Armstrong's journalism consisted of little more than parroting the Republican Party line, he served a far more important role as Harry's Washington "fixer." Armstrong saw to it that gifts were distributed to all the right people and that Harry's whims were translated into federal legislation wherever possible.

A bushy-haired munchkin named Kyle Palmer served first as Armstrong's apprentice in Washington and later as his counterpart on the state level in Sacramento.

Palmer was an avuncular snob who thrived on fine wine, rich food, and political mudslinging, and he would evolve into the single most powerful staff writer in *Times* history once he'd proved his mettle to the boss. His reporting was generally inaccurate and occasionally pure fiction, and his writing style was often indecipherable, but Kyle Palmer was a consummate deal maker and political bag man extraordinaire; it did not take long for Harry to single him out for these nonjournalistic skills. In 1922, Palmer was taking credit for engineering the election of California governor Friend Richardson, the first conservative Republican governor in control of a California Republican legislature in nearly a generation. Harry was pleased. He appreciated Palmer's willingness to do the *Times'* dirty work while keeping the Chandler name above the fray. If the odd-looking dwarf with the expensive tastes had shortcomings, they were simply overlooked.

Palmer was typical of the personally loyal but occasionally fact-bending journalists whom Harry preferred: pro-Republican, pro-growth, and proprietary about Harry Chandler's Los Angeles. Crime writer Al Nathan, his sidekick Al Rochlein, and cityside reporter Loyal D. Hotchkiss served similar functions as Harry's intelligence agents; they gathered information that could be used against Chandler's enemies at labor rallies, in the courts, and among real estate filings at the county Hall of Records. As he molded the *Times* to fit his image, Harry came to depend on his army of end-justifies-the-means, Palmeresque reporters. His reporters not only covered the city the way Chandler wanted it covered but introduced him to new and profitable business ventures.

In 1920, the *Times'* former automotive writer introduced him to a World War I barnstorming engineer who had arrived in Southern California with $600 in his pocket, an order for three experimental Navy fighter planes, and letters of introduction that the engineer hoped to use to open an airplane factory. Bankers liked his pitch, but no one was interested enough to offer a loan. Aerospace wasn't much beyond the hobby stage at the time and the hapless young pilot, thirty-eight-year-old Donald Douglas, could not convince L.A.'s blue bloods to back his venture.

Douglas rented the back room of a downtown barber shop and called upon former *Times* reporter Bill Henry for help. Henry had met Douglas when they both worked with aviation pioneer Glenn Martin at his engineering firm in Cleveland, Ohio; when Henry returned to L.A., he told Douglas to look him up if he ever decided to come to California.

By the time Douglas made the phone call, he was running out of time and money. When Henry arrived at the barber shop, Douglas explained that he had just four days left to qualify for the Navy contract. He was desperate. Henry clapped him on the back and walked Douglas down Broadway to the Times Mirror building and introduced him to his former boss. No one had to make an appointment with Harry Chandler, Henry explained. It was just a matter of catching the publisher between his endless series of schmooze sessions with the town's movers and shakers.

As Douglas and Henry settled into a pair of arm chairs in front of Chandler's massive walnut desk, Harry mentioned that he was not mechanically inclined. Fact was, Harry explained, machines baffled him. When he had learned to drive a car, he could never remember to use the brakes; he simply hollered "Whoa!" and waited for a ditch or a wall to stop the vehicle's forward motion. If something fell out of the engine and the automobile kept sputtering along, Harry didn't bother to retrieve the lost part; if the engine kept going, that was all that mattered.

Machines were mysterious entities that obeyed their own rules as often as the laws of physics, Harry reckoned. The most he ever hoped or cared to do with an

internal combustion engine was coexist. Automobiles were hard enough to comprehend; flying machines bewildered him beyond words. Turning his attention to Bill Henry,[3] Harry Chandler batted his big brown eyes; he looked more like a bashful, absent-minded diplomat than an acquisitive tycoon.

"I don't know much about either aviation or Mr. Douglas," Chandler said, looking directly at Henry, "but if you think they're both okay, I'll help. How much do you need, Mr. Douglas?"

"Fifteen thousand dollars," replied the nervous aviator.

Harry nodded. Donald Douglas then got a firsthand lesson in how to start a business in Los Angeles. Chandler scribbled the names of nine of his California Club[4] cronies on a sheet of paper and handed it to Douglas. He told him to write short letters of introduction and use the Chandler name to get in the door, then make his pitch and ask each of the businessmen to put up $1,500. Because the Navy's deadline was a crucial factor, he suggested that Douglas take Bill Henry along with him to verify that Chandler was, indeed, behind the venture. When he had gathered guarantees from the nine men, Douglas was to return to the *Times,* where Harry would sign for the final $1,500.

Armed with Chandler's support, Douglas and Henry made the rounds, handing off a short letter of introduction before they spoke with each business leader. It read:

> This will introduce to you Mr. Wm. M. Henry, formerly Automobile Editor for *The Times*, now backing a big project for the building of airplanes in Southern California.
>
> Mr. Henry wants some information from you, which I am sure you will be able to give him, and oblige.
>
> Yours very truly, Harry Chandler

Douglas and Henry gave the same spiel that Douglas had been giving before he met Chandler, but this time each meeting ended with the scribbling sound of a pen cosigning for 10 percent of a $15,000 loan instead of a polite "No, thank you."

Title Insurance and Trust Company vice president Otto Brant didn't even go through the formality of writing a letter; he scrawled "me too" at the bottom of Douglas's letter of introduction and signed his name.

With his $15,000 in capital, Douglas moved from the barbershop to a large toolshed a few blocks from the *Times,* landed the Navy contract, and finished building the three planes on time and under budget. They tested so well that the Navy ordered twenty-five more. Douglas moved his operation once again, this time to an old movie studio in Santa Monica. There, Harry came to his rescue

once more—only this time, Chandler was on the receiving end. Chandler and his old crony Moses Sherman had teamed with real estate speculator William May Garland to arrange a $42,000-a-year lease of the old Santa Monica studio for Douglas, and Douglas Aircraft Company was born, leading the way for L.A.'s sixty-year domination of America's aviation industry.

Harry's newfound interest in air travel didn't end with Douglas. When Garland came to him with another proposition to get in early on the brand-new airmail gravy train, Chandler pulled out his checkbook. Chandler and Garland teamed with Richfield Oil executive James Talbot, and the three men underwrote Harris "Pop" Hanshue, founder of Western Air Express. Hanshue had carried mail and passengers throughout the West during the 1920s, from L.A. to San Francisco and Salt Lake City, and as far east as Denver and Kansas City. At its height, Western Air had twenty-two airplanes in its fleet and its gross annual income topped $3 million.

In 1929, Western Air merged with Transcontinental Air Transport and sold one of its most lucrative routes, the L.A./Dallas circuit, to a competitor called American Airlines. Following the merger, the new company was called Transcontinental Western Air, eventually evolving into Trans World Airways, but still known by its acronym, TWA.

In much the same collaborative, coercive way, Harry helped launch and nurture at least a dozen other industries, from automobile manufacturing plants and clothing design factories to foundries and petroleum refineries. His infrequent luncheons became notorious among L.A. businessmen. When Harry invited people once or twice a year to a luncheon at the Times Mirror Building, it meant that the invitees were to bring their checkbooks, either to contribute to a Chandler cause, such as the 1921 construction of the Hollywood Bowl, or to invest in some grand Harry Chandler business venture.[5]

At the beginning of the 1920s, Chandler was instrumental in forming and driving two privately funded corporations that behaved in a quasi-governmental fashion, but without the advice or consent of the voters. Both were contrived specifically to pump enthusiasm, pride, and, most important of all, cash into downtown L.A.:

- The Central Investment Corporation, created by forty business leaders and expanded to include six hundred shareholders, built the lavish $7.6-million Biltmore Hotel, which still overlooks Pershing Square in the heart of Civic Center.
- The twenty-one-member Community Development Association, which successfully muscled the city of Los Angeles into underwriting the 80,000-seat Los Angeles Memorial Coliseum.

Football games, youth pageants, and Easter Sunrise spectacles were staged in the mammoth structure throughout the 1920s, but the Coliseum's real purpose was to entice the International Olympic Organizing Committee to schedule the 1932 Summer Olympics in Southern California.[6] Similarly, the Biltmore's underlying function was to demonstrate to visiting Olympics representatives that L.A. had a first-class hotel that rivaled the Ritz. As further mute testimony to Harry Chandler's calculated vision, L.A. had cinched the Games before the first concrete was poured; both monuments to civic pride and private profit opened for business in October 1923. Omniscient but always blithely beaming, Harry Chandler blended conveniently into the crowds, although he was on hand for each of the ribbon cuttings.

To ensure the success of all of these new ventures, Harry also saw to it that a constant supply of top-notch technical labor and engineering expertise flowed into Southern California's newest cutting edge enterprises. In 1919, Harry joined his brother-in-law, Franklin Booth,[7] and other business leaders as a trustee,[8] cofounder, and supporter of Pasadena's California Institute of Technology. Pioneer L.A. educator Amos G. Throop had opened Cal Tech as his own Throop University[9] in 1891, but Harry planned to change much more than the name of the liberal arts institution when he assumed command. He might not understand the physical sciences, basic mechanics, or mathematical concepts beyond profit/loss statements and compound interest, but Harry Chandler recognized that the future depended upon a workforce that did. He wanted a think tank that would eventually attain a national reputation equal to that of the Massachusetts Institute of Technology; to that end, he personally recruited and paid the salary of world-class Nobel Prize–winning physicist Dr. Robert Millikan to head the school and its research center. For decades to come, Cal Tech fed its graduates to Southern California's aerospace, chemical, jet propulsion, petroleum, telecommunications, nuclear power, and computer industries as fast as the school could turn them out.[10]

Few *Times* readers would have recognized Harry Chandler on the street, but his influence could be seen everywhere. Even as he approached his sixtieth birthday, his energy was boundless. He was at work by noon every day except Sunday, and he held court in his first floor office until far past midnight.

Thomas Storke, who took over the *Santa Barbara News-Press* a full generation after General Otis had abandoned Santa Barbara for L.A., recalled the *Times* publisher as a human dynamo: "Many times I visited Harry Chandler in the wee hours of the morning, and then saw him go out the next day to do the work of two ordinary men," Storke wrote in his memoirs. "I don't know when he found time to sleep. I am told that he never took a real vacation in his life."

In 1924, the *Times'* rival *Los Angeles Record* published a rare profile that was supposed to be critical of Chandler and his *Times* ("the greatest power of darkness in Los Angeles"), but the writer made Harry sound more like Santa Claus than Satan: "At 60 he is hale and hearty as a nut, with still a fairish amount of greying hair, with a twinkle still in his clear keen eyes, his cheeks rosy as a girl's, his smile ready and winning."

His enemies would testify that Harry Chandler could be formidable, even cruel if someone deliberately got in the way of his civic pride steamroller, but his timorous public persona never wavered; indeed, Calvin Coolidge displayed more charisma than Harry Chandler. It served Harry's purposes to be perceived as everyman's affable, opinionated, but bashful rich uncle.

As Ragtime gave way to the Jazz Age, Harry Chandler's L.A. juggernaut rolled on. With his encouragement—and mortgage money supplied by one or more of his various real estate syndicates—Chandler helped developers of the $5-million Ambassador Hotel and $6-million Goodyear Tire[11] plant to break ground in 1919.

Where there were tires, Chandler reasoned, there ought to be automobiles. Although he had problems keeping his trusty old 1910 Franklin in working order, Harry was a big booster of the motor vehicle; he coaxed Henry Ford, Walter Chrysler, and William C. Durant, the founding chairman of General Motors Corporation, to establish several of their assembly plants in what was already the nation's largest automobile market.

Shortly after its founding in 1900, Harry joined the Automobile Club of Southern California. The gentlemen's social organization had only forty-six members then, and there were less than 200 automobiles in the state. But by the time ground was broken in 1921 on the Auto Club's elaborate new baroque and mission style headquarters in the tony downtown West Adams neighborhood of L.A., the organization had grown to more than 93,000 dues-paying members. By 1929, there would be 124 automobiles for every one hundred families in Los Angeles County. The Auto Club had become one of the strongest political forces in the state; naturally, Harry was a stockholder, held the mortgage on the new West Adams Building, and sat on the board of trustees.

Chandler also held a virtual monopoly on the shipbuilding firms that had been rolling out naval vessels at San Pedro Harbor during the war. Harry's Los Angeles Shipping and Drydock Corporation and his nephew's Ralph Chandler Shipbuilding Company had assembled nineteen ships before Armistice Day. In peacetime, the emphasis switched to tankers, cargo ships, and reconditioned luxury liners such as the *City of Los Angeles* (originally the German passenger ship *Aeolus*) and the *City of Honolulu.*

L.A. harbor was booming as much as L.A. In the ten years between 1910 and 1920, shipping in and out of the Port of Los Angeles had increased by 600 percent, and it would double again before the end of the decade. To handle the steamer traffic and cargo vessels, Harry resorted to his time-honored solution of creating a syndicate of six familiar and unfamiliar business partners to cash in and squash the competition. The owners of Harry's Los Angeles Steamship Company included

- the ever-present Moses Sherman;
- his nephew, Ralph Chandler;
- Fred Baker, former owner of the Llewellyn Iron Works, which Ortie Mc-Manigal had blown up the same year that the *Times* building was bombed;
- petroleum pioneer Max Whittier of the Puente Oil Company; and
- two prominent lawyers, Erle Leaf and Frank Seaver.

The seven partners incorporated in 1920 with $5 million in stock. Using government subsidies and corporate tax loopholes, they locked up much of the Hawaiian cruise ship and sugarcane shipping business in and out of L.A. for the next ten years, until San Francisco's Matson Navigation proposed a merger in 1930. A stock swap ended the short life of the Los Angeles Steamship Company, but made Harry Chandler a major shareholder in the mammoth Matson shipping and cruise ship operations and promoted his nephew, Ralph Chandler, to a Matson vice presidency. Ralph, who had been so penniless that he had lived with Harry and Marian when he came to L.A., moved to San Francisco a millionaire in his own right thanks to the shipping business; later, he became a director of that city's Crocker National Bank.

The harbor was a busy place during the 1920s, but it still did not measure up to the daily frenzy of the rail terminals in downtown L.A. Tons of fresh produce—much of it grown on Chandler's C-M Ranch—were shipped out daily to the East; dazzled Bostonians and New Yorkers shivered in the dead of winter over ripe avocados, crisp celery, fresh artichokes, and fat, delicious beefeater tomatoes, all of which had just arrived from sunny Southern California. Hundreds of new residents fed up with the frozen East still arrived by train each week. The 1920 census disclosed that L.A. had surpassed San Francisco as California's most populous city: 576,000 residents to San Francisco's 502,000. And still the L.A. basin was nowhere near populated enough to satisfy Chandler.

He noticed hotel and restaurant prices climbing each winter at the height of the tourist season, and ordered the *Times* to begin regularly printing the names of the gougers as a service to out-of-town visitors. An irate rooming house owner whose name appeared on the *Times* list paid Harry a visit in 1921; she shrieked

that she *had* to raise winter prices to compensate for the summer vacancies. Harry's answer was the formation of the All-Year Club. With an initial $1-million budget, Chandler launched a three-year publicity program hyping L.A.'s climate and mountains-to-the-sea landscape as a prime year-round vacation destination.

Bolstered by the successful Mid-Winter Edition of the *Times,* which Times Mirror spread like confetti across the Eastern seaboard each January, the billboard, newsreel, radio, and word-of-mouth campaigns of the All-Year Club drove home the point again and again that L.A. was the sine qua non of American resort living. The club's original three-year mandate was extended again and again until World War II ended the hype. A final tally showed that Harry's All-Year Club had spent $6.38 million over its twenty-year existence, returning over $3 billion in tourism profits to L.A.

Harry Chandler's *Times* also thrived at the outset of the Roaring Twenties; but as good as business was, it would get even better in the years ahead. In 1921, 1922, and 1923, the *Times* led every paper in the United States in display and classified advertising lineage. In 1921, the Associated Press elected Harry its Pacific Coast director—a title that helped him corner the West Coast market on breaking news; but it was not nearly so proud an honor for the dollar-minded Chandler as the gold watch he was awarded later that same year by the Los Angeles Realty Board.

Chandler was not the kind to choke up or show the slightest emotion, but Harry did beam broadly when the board named him L.A.'s "most useful citizen." When he accepted his precious timepiece, he graciously spoke of being touched by this very public gesture of recognition and gratitude on the part of his fellow land sharks. A crocodile tear glinted in the corner of one eye as he strapped on the watch. If the founding of the Academy of Motion Picture Arts and Science had not still been six years away, Harry's performance might well have earned him an Oscar nomination.

––––––––––

THE FIRST FULL-LENGTH MOVIE shot in L.A. was Chicago producer William Selig's *In the Sultan's Power,* a sheiky potboiler filmed in 1908 outside a Victorian mansion at the downtown intersection of Eighth and Olive. The movie wasn't especially memorable, but Selig's later efforts were, including *The Count of Monte Cristo* and his discovery of Oklahoma cowpoke Tom Mix.[12] The actor came to L.A. as a star of early hayburners and became one of the most popular box office champs of early Hollywood. Selig also released the first American movie serial in 1913, *The Adventures of Kathlyn*—a thirteen-chapter soap opera cliffhanger; a print version of the story ran simultaneously for thirteen weeks in the pages of the

Chicago Tribune. The *Tribune*, which coproduced the film series, demonstrated the first synergy between newspapers and film.

The *Los Angeles Times* was neither so visionary nor so bold as the *Tribune*. Still, under the General's yoke, the *Times* had yet to grasp the full significance of the new motion picture medium. Flickers and nickelodeons were just a fad to Otis—not worthy of his attention or that of his fellow merchants and manufacturers. Only Harry Chandler understood that something important was happening in Los Angeles, right under the old guard's noses.

When a pair of New Jersey brothers, the Christies, famous for their filmed custard pie fights, came to San Francisco in 1910 at the invitation of *San Francisco Chronicle* publisher Michael de Young, Chandler paid close attention. Christie Films had emigrated from the East because of the bad weather and because de Young had promised to subsidize a studio for the brothers. When they arrived, however, the Christies found that the fog and constant overcast on the San Francisco peninsula interfered with their film shooting schedule. The climate was milder than New Jersey, but waiting for a sunny day in San Francisco was like waiting for snow in L.A.

Hearing of their unhappiness through the grapevine, Chandler sent an emissary from the *Times* with an invitation: Why not come to Hollywood, where the sunlight was eternal and the picturesque landscape ran the gamut from beach to mountain to desert, all within the distance of a few miles?

According to Harry's own account, the Christies caught the next train to L.A. and Chandler was waiting for them with plenty of studio space, which he was willing to rent at very reasonable prices.

Harry convinced Otis that movies were inevitable. Although their production companies inevitably attracted a ragtag crowd of Bohemians, hams, and emotional basket cases, the feature films could be made economically and with the greatest variety of settings: the streets of L.A. and the shorelines and arroyos of Southern California. Bright sunlight, so necessary for a moving picture camera's successful film exposure, could be had almost 365 days a year. Los Angeles was also a full continent away from Thomas Edison's New Jersey–based Motion Picture Patents Company, which vigorously prosecuted all moviemakers who did not have a negotiated agreement to use the Edison camera equipment during the first decade of the twentieth century. Renegade filmmakers who didn't want to pay Edison's premium headed for the Pacific Coast rather than wind up in court.

The *Times* could work with the new medium or against it, Harry counseled the General, but the movies were coming, and coming fast—and movies made money. Harry wanted to work with any new breed that could generate cash. In 1909, he convinced the General to publish the *Times'* first news article about moviemaking in Los Angeles; within a few years, the dateline "Hollywood" auto-

matically meant that the story was about the latest western, murder mystery, spy story, or romantic two-reel spectacle being cranked out in the Cahuenga Valley, west of downtown L.A.

Legendary director David Wark Griffith moved his famous Biograph Studios from New York to L.A in 1910 to get away from Edison, and immediately began filming his landmark *Birth of a Nation* in the San Fernando Valley. The post–Civil War Ku Klux Klan saga that reinforced stereotypes and old racial prejudices at the same time it introduced groundbreaking new camera techniques (fade-outs, close-ups, etc.) cost $100,000 to make, but grossed Griffith and Biograph more than $18 million over the next fifteen years.

Three years later, Jesse Lasky, Samuel Goldwyn, and Cecil B. DeMille paid for a trainload of actors to travel from New York to L.A. and rented a barn at Sunset and Vine. There, as Lasky's Famous Players, the trio pooled their resources, came up with $6,000 in capital, and shot *The Squaw Man,* another early mega hit that eventually earned more than one hundred times its original investment. In 1914, a British pantomimist was cast as a reporter in his first movie, *Making a Living;* its setting was the *Times* building, with *Times* Linotype machines and *Times* staff milling in the background. *Making a Living* became the first of Charlie Chaplin's dozens of hit films and made him a living in the millions by the 1920s.

Harry Chandler always grasped, almost by intuition, when there was real money to be made, and he responded to the Hollywood influx with "The Preview"—the first regular movie page published by a daily newspaper in the nation. Within months, the *Times* also launched the first Hollywood gossip columnist: Stella the Star Gazer. By 1923, "The Preview" had grown to become a separate sixteen-page Sunday tabloid.

But Chandler's main interest in Hollywood continued to be real estate, not matinee idols. Always the cautious gambler, he diluted the investment dollars he put into as risky a proposition as a motion picture with those of several dozen other investors; these were usually linked together by Henry Robinson, president of Pacific Southwest Trust and Savings Bank, or Bank of America founder A. P. Giannini. Harry always looked for real assets to secure his loans, preferably real property. Behind the scenes, where he always preferred to operate, Chandler was credited for saving Jack Warner and his three older brothers from going under in the early 1920s. He demanded their Warner Brothers Studios as collateral when they approached him for a loan years before they began developing a revolutionary new film technique that would add sound to a movie they called *The Jazz Singer.*

For the most part, Harry invested in movies sparingly. He never dreamed of going hog-wild like his rival William Randolph Hearst, who bought and subsidized Cosmopolitan Studios to produce a string of 1920s films starring his mistress, Marion Davies.

Harry preferred a more solid investment, like the original Hollywood subdivision that he, Moses Sherman, and Eli Clark had built on the old La Brea Rancho at the turn of the century. When he made business alliances in the film community, he made them with such substantial impresarios as Mack Sennett,[13] who had parlayed his Keystone Studios and the money generated by the Keystone Kops into a fortune at the dawn of the 1920s. Sennett opted to go in with Chandler and develop what remained of Hollywood. As a promotion for yet another Chandler syndicate subdivision in the Hollywood Hills, Sennett, Chandler, and Moses Sherman paid ad man John Roche $21,000 to erect a set of thirteen letters, each one fifty feet high and thirty feet wide, strung across the crest of Los Feliz. The word "HOLLYWOODLAND" could be seen from every corner of the L.A. basin. When they unveiled the sign on September 3, 1923, it was illuminated at night by over 4,000 lightbulbs. A decade later, when a little-known actress named Lillian "Peg" Entwhistle ensured her immortality by leaping to her death from the top of the "H," the lightbulbs were gone. Regular maintenance ended in 1939, and five years later, the M. H. Sherman Company gave the sign and the 455 acres upon which it was built to the Hollywood Chamber of Commerce. The last four letters were toppled, leaving only "HOLLYWOOD."

Gone too, long before the dawn of the 1940s, was Harry's brief foray into another new entertainment medium, radio. When the federal government began selling off strips of the AM airwaves, Chandler and his *Times* were first in line on the West Coast; in October 1922, they launched L.A.'s earliest radio station, KHJ, with a daily broadcast from the roof of the *Times* Building. Immediately identified by a chorus of canary tweets at station breaks, KHJ filled its brief broadcast day with everything from Professor Barclay Severns's early morning sitting-up exercises to the circuslike sermons Sister Aimee Semple McPherson[14] delivered nightly from her Angelus Temple to various autoharp recitals, history lectures, and harmonica concerts.[15]

"Rightly used, the radio is destined to become a powerful promoter of intellectual, moral and religious culture," Chandler declared at the inauguration of KHJ's broadcast relationship with Angelus Temple.

Just as important to Harry, the station was a cash cow, earning a sizable advertising profit for little or no production expense. But the one thing that could wreck radio was organized labor, just as, in Harry's narrow worldview, it could wreck anything else. Five years into the *Times'* ownership of KHJ, Chandler chose to sell the station to Los Angeles Cadillac dealer Don Lee for $50,000 rather than negotiate contracts with the American Federation of Musicians or the budding International Alliance of Theatrical Stage Employees (IATSE claimed to represent a majority of the station's personnel). No matter how lucrative a business, Chandler chose to dump it rather than deal with a union.

He had grown increasingly disillusioned with the movie and media business, and not just because of their unions. Neither Harry nor Marian made a public fuss about their Congregationalist roots, but the couple and their family were stern practitioners of biblical moderation, and the excesses that were built in to Hollywood's culture genuinely shocked and appalled them both. Little by little, the film colony's ongoing bacchanal pushed Chandler and his *Times* toward the brink of censorship. The *Times* dropped Stella the Star Gazer in the mid-1920s rather than celebrate the profligate lifestyles of Hollywood's rich and famous.

The 1921 arrest of funny man Fatty Arbuckle in connection with a lurid orgy and homicide, followed by the 1922 love nest murder of Paramount director William Desmond Taylor, and ultimately topped by the sensational 1923 drug addiction death of collegiate matinee idol Wallace Reed prompted Harry to act. The Catholic Church had already established its Legion of Decency, which urged a nationwide boycott of many Hollywood films. Like many of the early Hollywood moguls, Chandler could already see the economic impact if the studios failed to police their celebrities and the content of their movies.

As he had once done with regard to the aircraft industry by sending *Times* reporter Bill Henry out on a fact-finding mission, Chandler now dispatched *Times* reporter Chapin Hall on a nationwide "Save Hollywood" mission to persuade other newspaper publishers to participate in the *Times'* crusade. Hall invited more than forty film critics to visit Hollywood at Harry Chandler's expense to get a firsthand look at how movies were made and to ask why the isolated instances of a Fatty Arbuckle or William Desmond Taylor were not reflective of the industry as a whole.

Finally, Chandler teamed with rising Hollywood executives Louis B. Mayer, Adolph Zukor, and Carl Laemmle to save Hollywood from itself by providing its own censor. Through the *Times* Washington bureau, Chandler recruited Will Hays,[16] President Warren G. Harding's postmaster general, to set up a government lobby for the budding movie industry. Created in 1922, the Motion Picture Producers and Distributors of America[17] did more than woo lawmakers in the nation's capital; Hays established and enforced a code of conduct for Hollywood's filmland citizenry that precluded public behavior unbecoming to the industry. He also began a strict pre-release censorship regimen that stopped sex, violence, or any other action that Hays and his employers, the studio executives, considered immoral.

But even the Hays office wasn't enough. In one of the few instances where Harry Chandler let his moral outrage influence both his investment strategy and the *Times'* news policy, he and his newspaper systematically turned away from Hollywood in the late 1920s, leaving the field to Hearst's morning *Examiner* and evening *Herald*. Hearst had already gone head-to-head with Stella the Star Gazer

by hiring Louella Parsons in 1918 for his New York *Morning Telegraph*. In the early 1920s, Hearst brought Parsons to L.A. to follow the trivia and tribulations of the stars and played her up in the *Examiner*'s promotions after Chandler had given Stella the ax.

Not until the *Times* belatedly tried playing catch-up in 1938 by hiring Hedda Hopper[18] did Chandler leap back into motion picture industry coverage with the same gusto, and by then, Hearst, *Variety,* and the *Hollywood Reporter* had the advantage.

By the middle of the Roaring Twenties, Harry Chandler had little use for the made-up dramas of the silver screen or for the petty divorces, the drug scandals, and the off-screen dalliances of Hollywood's ephemeral stars. With his snow white shock of carefully groomed hair and his increasingly nearsighted stare appraising his empire through a pair of rimless spectacles, Harry Chandler in his sixties was too busy to go to the movies. The clock was ticking and his Southern California utopia was only half complete.

Although consumption and California had conspired forty years earlier to limit his college career to less than half of one semester, Harry's alma mater, Dartmouth University, saw fit to award him an honorary master of arts degree in 1922. The kudos did not come too late. Photos show Harry in his robes smiling the wan smile of a self-defined man of destiny as he graciously accepted the honor. His perpetual baby fat had finally dissolved, giving his kindly face a sallow, almost gaunt appearance. But Harry came from good stock. Both of his parents were still alive and doing well on their Burbank ranch, now hemmed in by Harry's various subdivisions, and his younger brother, Fred Chandler, prospered as a citrus grower near the Riverside County town of Perris.

Harry had created most of L.A. in less than half a lifetime. With one eye on the gold watch given to him by the realty board, L.A.'s most useful citizen figured he still had a good decade ahead of him to pound the rest of Southern California into submission.

CHAPTER 8

ON THE LAST WEDNESDAY AFTERNOON of August 1922, dewy-eyed Dorothy Buffum, draped in white crepe and pearls, marched triumphantly down the middle aisle of the First Congregational Church of Long Beach to lay claim to Harry Chandler's eldest son, Norman.

Dorothy Buffum was pretty, but not ravishing. Compact but athletic, self-effacing yet fiercely competitive, she did not stand out in a crowd. Her dark hair, bobbed in the style of the day, complemented her blue green eyes so that she looked a little like Clara Bow with apple cheeks and a rosebud pucker. Despite her ordinary looks, the future Mrs. Norman Chandler radiated ambition.

Harry Chandler sensed that Dorothy Buffum was quick-witted the first time he laid eyes on her. It had been nearly two years since Norman first brought her home from Stanford University to meet his parents. The slight, high-strung young woman oscillated between shy sophistication and a bumpkin's haughty airs—a quality Harry found oddly mesmerizing. He could see the winsome coed quietly maneuvering Norman to do her bidding. Dorothy acted the princess and her young man behaved like an adoring puppy. Harry could also tell that his future daughter-in-law was more like himself than his own daughters were. Over time, he dropped his guard and warmed to her. Marian Chandler was less welcoming.

Bolstered by her recent genealogical discovery that the Otis side of the family might have come to America on the Mayflower—or at least with one of the first boatloads of pilgrims that landed at Plymouth Rock—the elder Mrs. Chandler was not as taken with Norman's bride. It mattered to Marian that this Buffum girl had come from common Midwestern stock and had no pedigree.

Such pretenses signified nothing to Norman. The ruggedly handsome firstborn son of Harry Chandler remained proudly defiant and ignored his mother's and sisters' subtle hints that there were plenty of fish in the sea. Dorothy Buffum was just one more flounder to a Chandler. But not to Norman.

He'd met Dorothy in the usual Stanford way, during one of the autumn socials before a football game. They bonded instantly. A strapping square-jawed athlete freshly muscled from a summer of breaking horses and roping calves on the Tejon Ranch, Norman could have taken his pick from among the selection of eligible fillies who populated sorority row. In addition to being tall, brawny, and attractive, Norman was heir apparent both to a newspaper and to a fortune. There was no better catch on the Palo Alto campus, but Dorothy Buffum knew how to play the game. She refused to swoon.

"Don't ever tell a young man he is very good-looking," she once advised a friend. "It doesn't do him or anyone around him any good."

Norman admired her cool charm. From among the eligible coeds, he chose "Buff," his lifelong nickname for his twenty-one-year-old fiancée, and nothing his family could say would shake him. Now, as he waited for her at the altar, Norman studied his parents as they sat ramrod-straight and expressionless in the front pew. Always the cipher, Harry revealed none of his own positive feelings for his future daughter-in-law. As the organist struck the opening chords of "Here Comes the Bride," Norman saw Harry twisting ever so slightly in his seat to catch

a proper glimpse of the bride. Marian Chandler also turned to see Dorothy's entrance, smiling politely without making eye contact as Dorothy's father, Long Beach mayor and department store owner Charles Buffum, presented his favorite child at the altar.

When the minister asked who offered the young woman in marriage, Charles Buffum choked out his words with embarrassing affection. The Buffums found it difficult to preserve their dignity in public as the Chandlers did—a characteristic that Norman found oddly appealing. Tears and belly laughter ricocheted around a Buffum family gathering like caroms in some emotional free-for-all. The men hugged the women, the boys chased the girls, and everybody eventually gathered around the piano in the Buffums's parlor overlooking the bluffs of Belmont Shore to sing pop melodies and camp songs at the top of their lungs. The Buffums paid scant attention to how such Dickensian displays might appear to strangers. Norman liked that.

It was equally appealing to Norman that Charles, his avuncular new father-in-law, didn't care how a few tears looked as he gave his daughter away. Dorothy was his baby. He had a right to clabber up.

The youngest of three Buffum children, and always the spunky tomboy, Dorothy was the one who taxed herself, restlessly pushing beyond the ordinary. Always the irrational overachiever, she recalled years later her driven adolescence: "Many times I'd wake up with an anxious feeling that there was much for me to do. Would I ever be able to get it done?"

What nervous energy she did not expend as a sprinter, competing on the tennis court, or by playing to the hilt some hammy role in one of her drama classes, Dorothy poured into her other schoolwork.

"I didn't take to boys much except to run against them and beat them," she said.

She distinguished herself as valedictorian of her 1918 high school graduating class and Charles was obligated to let his proud young daughter go off to Stanford University. Four hundred miles north of Long Beach in the hills overlooking the San Francisco Bay, she studied history and English literature, joined the Pi Beta Phi sorority, and was voted Campus Queen. It was a given that all coeds were there first to look for husbands. To hear Buff remember it, she was there just to shimmy in a silk dress and have a good time.

"I don't think I ever missed a dance on campus," she said. "Well, I really did it up! I think I was probably the best on campus—or the worst, if you want to look at it that way."

Still, Charles Buffum only reluctantly entertained the inevitability that Dorothy would grow up and marry—and never thought she would become a Chandler's

bride. One thing Charles understood right after the engagement announcement was that his daughter was marrying above her station.

As affluent as they were, the Buffums dealt in dry goods, not in publishing newspapers or in acquiring vast tracts of real estate. Charles and his wife, Fern, were hardworking small-town merchants from LaFayette, Illinois, who had arrived in Southern California in 1904, when Dorothy was three years old. Charles joined his brother, E. E. Buffum, in opening the Long Beach Mercantile Company. They prospered, and soon the brothers had done well enough to buy out the competition—another pair of brothers named Schilling, who ran a rival Long Beach department store.

By the time Dorothy left her seaside home for Stanford, the Buffum brothers were running one of the most successful department stores in Southern California, and Charles had become a big fish in the small pond of Long Beach. In addition to serving a term as mayor, he also headed the school board and the chamber of commerce; in this way, he boosted his hometown with as much gusto as Harry Chandler and General Otis had mustered for the larger and much more voracious metropolis of Los Angeles.

But Charles ran a department store. Harry Chandler ran the most influential newspaper in California. There was no contest as to which family wielded the most power. To Marian and her daughters, snubs were in order. The General's daughter wished her oldest son the very best, but she only grudgingly accepted his choice in a wife. Only the youngest Chandler daughter, Helen, participated in the wedding of Mr. Norman Chandler to Miss Dorothy Buffum, and although Helen served as Dorothy's maid of honor, Norman's older sisters, Frances, May, Constance, and Ruth, were conspicuous by their absence; Dorothy's older brother, Harry Buffum, served as one of Norman's ushers, but Norman's own younger brothers, Harrison and Philip, were nowhere to be found among the wedding party.

Norman didn't care. Always the dutiful son, on this one point he remained defiant. He wed Dorothy Buffum despite his siblings' petty snobbery.

The previous summer, between his junior and senior years at Stanford, Norman had delivered the *Times* each morning and collected subscription payments in the afternoon, just as Harry had done when he started out in the newspaper business almost forty years earlier, but he had still found time for Buff.

"I had an old Model T and I'd pick up the papers at 2:00 A.M., wrap them, deliver them, and collect from some four hundred homes," Norman recalled in an interview years later. "After I'd caught a little sleep and gone out to take care of any complaints, I'd head on down to Long Beach, sleep on the sand all day, take Dorothy to dinner, and get back home to milk the cow."

"Whatever we did, banana splits, dinners, anything like that, I would usually have to pay at least half the bill because he was always broke," Dorothy remembered.

Norman's courting took an even more serious turn the following year at Stanford, when he announced just before Christmas that he would drop out before his final semester so that he and Dorothy could be married. Buff, too, quit Stanford at the end of her third year and did not graduate. Blame hormones or happiness, Norman and Buff returned to L.A. determined to become man and wife.

Norman was prepared to take whatever job the *Times* might offer. He overcame his parents' objections by pointing to his father's own truncated college career. Harry reluctantly had to agree: Learning the nuts and bolts of how to make a daily newspaper function was more important than any theoretical economics degree and could not be taught in a classroom. But Norman would get no special treatment. He had made the decision on his own to quit school and Harry would not coddle him.

Following a three-week honeymoon in which Norman and Buff motored up the Pacific Coast to Vancouver and back, the couple settled in the upper story of a modest duplex a few blocks from Harry and Marian Chandler's baronial brick mansion in the Los Feliz Hills. Much to the new Mrs. Chandler's chagrin, their address was 1941½ North Vermont.

"I remember being so embarrassed when I charged things, to have to list that ½," Dorothy recalled years later. "We had to scratch to make ends meet."

Norman delivered the *Times* for $16 a week. His wages were menial and the work taxing. But it wasn't all wretched in the beginning. The General had left Norman $50,000 in hotel stock, which yielded $250 a month, and the couple allowed themselves an occasional luxury during their first years together.

For Dorothy, the best times were had with Harry. She had the same passion for politics as her father-in-law, a quality that Harry found endearing, especially as no one else in his extended household, Norman included, cared who was in the White House, the governor's mansion, or even Los Angeles City Hall. When Harry and his fly-fishing companion, Herbert Hoover, paused in the front parlor to lambaste the renegade Republican senator Hiram Johnson, Dorothy sat at the top of the stairs and listened to every word. As Harry aged and his hearing worsened, he fairly shouted at times while conversing with political cronies in his study; if Dorothy happened to be there, she would race upstairs to the bedroom above the study and press her ear to the floorboards so that she could argue politics with her father-in-law later on.

Norman and Buff incessantly dropped by the Chandler mansion, but Harry rarely visited the newlyweds. When he finally did and learned that his son and

daughter-in-law slept in separate beds, he shook his head and said, "I don't approve of that. I just don't approve of that."

Chandlers were to be fruitful and populate in a biblical fashion—eight children at least, he told them, just as he and Marian had. Buff blushed while Harry deepened his frown in a weak attempt to keep a coy grin from playing over his dour face.

The Chandler women never did warm to Dorothy, but it didn't matter. She had done the impossible. She made Harry smile.

IN ITS MID-WINTER EDITIONS OF THE 1920S, the *Times* had picked up and propelled a chamber of commerce catchphrase into a national identifying logo: Los Angeles was "the White Spot of America"—no crime, no corruption, no Commies. The overwhelming problem with that description was that it was flatly untrue. Harry Chandler, and his father-in-law before him, believed with absolute conviction that their will—translated into rote for the masses every day in their *Los Angeles Times*—could overcome all obstacles. If the *Times* said that something was true, then it was true.

Having the police department in its pocket, of course, was a major asset in enforcing the *Times'* declarations. If the police said there was no crime wave, there was no crime wave. Each time a civic group discovered that L.A., like every other big city in America, had a vice problem, the *Times* editorialized against corruption, the police chief was fired, and the cycle began all over again. Continuing a tradition begun by the General before the turn of the century, Harry Chandler made a point of influencing each mayor's selection of eight police chiefs between 1915 and 1923,[1] each one more scandal-ridden than his predecessor. When L.A. reformers forced a switch to a police commission in 1923, taking the selection of the chief out of the mayor's hands, Chandler brought his influence to bear on at least three of the five commissioners. Harry's principal goal remained the same: downplay organized crime while underscoring the perpetual need to crack down on labor organizers, whom Chandler considered the most venomous of felons.

But like the rest of America, L.A.'s moral fiber marinated in bathtub gin during the 1920s. Harry Chandler's reverential voice might shake with pride and passion over his "White Spot" during the 1928 dedication of the twenty-eight-story Los Angeles City Hall or the 1924 inaugural circus at Sister Aimee Semple McPherson's Angelus Temple, but Nigger Alley's brothels and speakeasies had nonetheless found new life during Prohibition, and organized prostitution and gambling had spread even farther across the landscape, to nearby Boyle Heights, Central

Avenue, and the unincorporated county territory between Beverly Hills and Hollywood known as the Sunset Strip.

Crime bosses such as slot machine king Robert Gans, bootlegger Milton "Farmer" Page, master pimp Albert Marco,[2] and former LAPD vice detective-turned-casino operator Guy McAfee[3] had protective ties to city hall through Kent Kane Parrot, a USC law school graduate who had chosen a political career over passing the bar exam. As Mayor George Cryer's chief of staff, Parrot perpetuated the *Times'* "White Spot" myth at the same time he took political payoffs to protect bookmakers, bootleggers, and brothel keepers.

When traditional Sicilian mafiosi such as rumrunner Anthony Cornero[4] and gambling czar Jack Dragna began moving in on L.A.'s gambling and prostitution, the corruption became too blatant even for the tolerant *Times.* Wholesale murder along Darwin Avenue in the Italian neighborhood north of Los Angeles gave it the nickname "Shotgun Alley" in the *Times,* which began to warn of Black Hand terrorism in the nation's White Spot.

The *Times* also taunted Mayor Cryer on its editorial pages as "Parrot's puppet." Parrot responded by telling a reporter at the rival *Los Angeles Record* that his twin fantasies were to shut down the police commission because it had become a tool of the *Times,* and "to place tacks in spots where . . . Harry Chandler, publisher of the *Los Angeles Times*, is apt to sit down."

Harry was cautious about rising to Parrot's bait, but after Mayor Cryer's latest chief of police, Louis Oaks, was caught in the backseat of a car with a bottle of whiskey and a half-naked woman who was not his wife, prim and proper Harry Chandler could contain himself no longer. The *Times* pushed for Chief Oaks's dismissal; even Cryer and Parrot had to agree.

Always a believer in scientific solutions, Harry helped recruit a widely respected criminologist from the faculty of the University of California at Berkeley to clean up the LAPD. At the *Times'* urging, Mayor Cryer convinced Professor August Vollmer to take a year's leave of absence to translate some of his classroom theories into streetwise solutions. As the LAPD's acting chief, Vollmer introduced training, tracking, and a host of crime-fighting strategies, including the so-called dragnet sweep for the apprehension of violent criminals. Organized crime didn't end during Vollmer's régime, but it kept a low profile.

At the end of Vollmer's year, and over Harry Chandler's loud objections, Parrot rewarded his friend R. Lee Heath with the chief's job. Once again, the *Times* and Mayor Cryer were at war.

Chandler responded by putting his own friend up against Mayor Cryer in the election of 1925. Ever since his oddly favorable behavior toward Chandler in the 1917 Baja trial, federal judge Benjamin Bledsoe had become Harry's close chum; this did not go unnoticed by the *Los Angeles Record*'s political cartoonist. As the

campaign heated up, the *Record* published a popular cartoon showing portly, pompous Judge Bledsoe wielding a gavel while Harry Chandler stood grinning beside him. The caption read "Harry Calls Him Ben."

Mayor Cryer laughed and pointed out to his chief of staff that the cartoon sent everyone who saw it into spasms of grim giggles. Kent Parrot's keen political antennae picked up on the grassroots cynicism and he had the cartoon blown up and reproduced by the thousands. Chandler tried to muster a lame counterattack with a *Times* cartoon that showed a beaming Bledsoe with the cheery caption "*Everyone* Calls Him Ben!" but by then the damage had been done. The slogan "Harry Calls Him Ben" spread through the snickering electorate, the ultimate inside joke. Bledsoe was soundly defeated and Chandler had to deal with Cryer for another two years.

But the mayor and his chief of staff knew better than to goad the most powerful man in Los Angeles too far. Within months of the election, Cryer bowed to Chandler's pressure and LAPD Chief Heath was history.

The one constant through all the cycles of LAPD scandal and reform was Harry Chandler's unremitting refrain: "Keep Out The Unions!" Through Chandler's influence, California legislators had passed the Criminal Syndicalism Act in 1920; this made even the most innocuous labor organizing effort punishable by up to fourteen years in prison. Labor leaders worked to have the draconian law declared unconstitutional, but the LAPD enforced it mercilessly—no more so than under Heath's successor, former vice squad commander James Davis. Described in one news story as "a burly, dictatorial, somewhat sadistic, bitterly anti-labor man who saw Communist influence behind every telephone pole," Davis immediately became a Harry Chandler favorite. Among other union-busting efforts, Davis instituted the LAPD's antisubversive division, which evolved during the 1930s into the so-called Red Squad[5]—an intelligence-gathering division whose sole purpose was to gather damning information on labor leaders and organizers, smear them, break up their meetings, and run them out of town.

When a grand jury indicted four of his officers in 1928 for prostitution and gambling payoffs, Davis backed his men and the *Times* agreed, dismissing the jurors as "busybodies." The average citizen didn't understand the fine line between enforcement and corruption, but Chief Davis did. The *Record* alleged that "Davis quite honestly and sincerely believes that the country would be much better off if the whole question of constitutional rights was forgotten, and everything left to the discretion of the police."

Harry Chandler could not have been more in agreement. He took the opportunity of the lull in visible crime and union organizing during Chief Davis's régime to launch a "Make a Friend for California" campaign urging fellow businessmen to have their employees write letters to out-of-state friends and beseech them to

emigrate to L.A. Before the decade was over, L.A.'s population would double to 1.2 million people, most of them arriving before the end of 1923. The city would move from the nation's tenth most populous city to its fifth—and L.A.'s newest residents needed a place to live. As the largest single landowner in Los Angeles County, Chandler was once more pleased to oblige them. Before the dawn of the 1930s, his millions would multiply geometrically into billions . . . but only if he could keep water flowing into the L.A. basin.

By May of 1924, William Mulholland's almighty L.A. Department of Water and Power[6] was bleeding the last few corpuscles from the carcass that was once Owens Valley and driving the few remaining ranchers to desperate measures. As the city had grown, so had its thirst. The ever-growing urban majority defeated Owens Valley's minority rights in the courts, in Congress, and in the state legislature, and even the most liberal L.A. newspapers had adopted the *Times'* hard line about keeping the spigots wide open. Their outrage ignored, the stubborn few Owens Valley residents who would not bow to L.A.'s water lust followed Ortie McManigal's example and on the morning of May 21, 1924, they began regularly dynamiting the Los Angeles Aqueduct.

The explosions finally got the attention of L.A.'s newspapers, and even an occasional dollop of sympathy. Although critical, the *Times* editorial pages reflected remarkable restraint—a sign that it was now Harry Chandler's newspaper, not Harrison Otis's: "These farmers are not anarchists or bomb throwers but in the main honest, hardworking American citizens. They have put themselves hopelessly in the wrong by taking the law into their own hands, but that is not to say that there has not been a measure of justice on their side."

As the dynamiting continued and the confrontations between valley residents and the Los Angeles DWP persisted, however, the tone of the *Times* shifted. The newspaper applauded Mulholland for ordering machine gun emplacements at strategic points along the 223-mile aqueduct. By 1927, when the increasingly petulant master engineer issued instructions to his men to shoot first and ask questions later, Mulholland sounded more like General Otis than the General himself.

In the twelve years since his greatest triumph, the brilliant Father of the Aqueduct had come to believe his own legend and had evolved into a megalomaniac on the subject of Los Angeles and water. He told the *Times* he took the attacks on his aqueduct personally; he lamented the loss of the lush Owens Valley orchards only because too few trees remained from which to hang the vandals. All that mattered to Mulholland was that the water keep flowing. He took the DWP farther and farther north, where the department would eventually divert creeks and

tributaries that drained into Mono Lake so that they would drain instead into his aqueduct. He once half-jokingly spoke of damming up the Merced River so that he could turn Yosemite Valley into a reservoir "and stop the goddamned waste!"

Although most ranchers blamed Mulholland and L.A. for their water woes, some of the more enlightened Owens Valley residents placed equal blame on local greed and gullibility. In *The Ford,* her 1917 roman à clef about the Owens River tragedy, author and longtime valley resident Mary Austin accused Owens Valley of an "invincible rurality" that allowed men like Mulholland, Fred Eaton, and J. B. Lippincott to dupe them out of their river. None could see beyond the few dollars that they were being offered for their precious water rights. When the rubes of Owens Valley finally did understand, it was too late. Even as they began their futile counterattack, Owens Valley still might not have withered into desert had it not been for Harry Chandler's greed.

By 1922, a new generation of L.A. water bandits had turned their attention to the Colorado River where enough water flowed to slake the thirst of L.A. several times over; thus what remained of the Owens River could be left to the Owens Valley. In July 1924, William Mulholland filed for permission from the federal government to divert 1,500 second-feet of Colorado River water to Los Angeles.

Secretary of Commerce Herbert Hoover was already hammering out a plan to build the biggest dam in history to harness both the water and the power of America's third-longest river. When he enlisted the aid of his old friend Harry Chandler in pushing through the plan, Chandler was delighted at first. But when he realized that Boulder Dam might reduce the Colorado to a trickle at the Baja border and dry up the cotton fields of his C-M Ranch, Chandler suddenly became an environmentalist. The champion of the original Los Angeles Aqueduct traveled to Washington to squeal in horror before Congress at the prospect of damming the Colorado.

Once again, Chandler went head-to-head with his old nemesis Senator Hiram Johnson, who saw right through Harry's selfish opposition to Boulder Dam. Ironically, it was Johnson who now accused Chandler and his "reactionary crew" of retarding L.A.'s growth by delaying construction of the eighteen-story dam. Johnson's fulminations got full play in Washington and elsewhere in the East, but he was belittled or silenced in Los Angeles. When he sought airtime to warn the people of Los Angeles about Harry's Boulder Dam opposition, the *Times*-owned KHJ radio refused to broadcast his speech.

The *Times* gave no advance word to its readers of Johnson's planned address at the downtown Philharmonic Auditorium, but the rival *Examiner* did. More than 2,000 Johnson supporters turned out, obliging the *Times* to write about the event in the following day's editions under the headline JOHNSON RECOVERS HIS WIND.

"Harry Chandler, the public service corporations and the power companies now run the state," Johnson warned the citizens of L.A. "When Harry Chandler speaks, the ears of Governors, Senators, Representatives and financiers protrude nervously and flap attentively or apprehensively in the balmy California air."

During the ensuing battle over Boulder Dam, Johnson pilloried Harry Chandler repeatedly for spreading "fake stories, sham issues and daily malice and mendacity" to muddy his true motives. The cold facts were that U.S. farmers paid $8 an acre-foot to irrigate their Imperial Valley crops with Colorado River water, but Chandler paid only $0.86 per acre-foot on the Mexican side of the border. Boulder Dam would end that windfall by replacing the Imperial Canal on the Baja side of the border with an All-American Canal. So called because it ran along the U.S. side of the border, the All-American Canal would siphon off the Colorado before it flowed into Mexico, thereby drying up Harry Chandler's cheap water supply.

In the end, as always, Harry got what he wanted. His pitched battles with Senator Johnson effectively held up congressional approval of the construction of Boulder[7] and two other dams further south on the Colorado for more than five years. By 1928, Chandler was arranging to sell off the Mexican portion of his C-M Ranch under increasing pressure from the Mexican government, which was finally making good on Francisco Madero's promise to kick absentee American landlords out of their country. Harry invested the proceeds on the U.S. side of the border in Imperial Valley, where he now embraced the same All-American Canal that he had so bitterly opposed just a few years earlier. Chandler was now the champion of cheap irrigation on behalf of Imperial Valley farmers, which included not only himself but also his tenants.

To guarantee cheap water for the Imperial Valley and at the same time keep the Colorado wellspring flowing to Chandler's L.A. subdivision customers, Harry threw his support to the founding of the pro-growth, pro-business Metropolitan Water District in 1928. The wide-open future of Los Angeles was no longer in question. Chandler and his *Times* had arranged an adequate water supply, plenty of electricity, and a ready Imperial Valley food supply that would last for the rest of the century. When the dams were built and the All-American Canal fully functioning, L.A. wouldn't even need to tap the Owens River anymore.

But it was already too late for the Owens Valley.

Having broken the ranchers' resistance, the Los Angeles DWP tightened its death grip and bought the few remaining valley water rights. In the spring of 1927, the last of the farmers and ranchers in the desert that had once been Owens Valley pooled enough money to take out ads in the Los Angeles newspapers. They read simply:

> We, the farming communities of Owens
> Valley, being about to die, salute you!

"As late as 1945," according to historian Carey McWilliams, "the City of Los Angeles and the Los Angeles *Times* opposed state legislation designed to provide a small measure of belated justice to the ruined farmers of Owens Valley."

But justice did come to the man most responsible for bringing the Owens River to the San Fernando Valley. After transforming Harry Chandler from a millionaire to a billionaire, William Mulholland shared in none of the riches and ended his career in disgrace. After years of ranting at the beleaguered men and women of the Owens Valley, his own publicity caught up with him on March 12, 1928.

The Saint Francis Dam, a final touch in his Owens Valley aqueduct master plan, collapsed a few minutes before midnight, shooting 11.4 billion gallons of water, concrete, mud, and human debris down the Santa Clara River to the sea. The road that connected Harry Chandler's Tejon Ranch to Harry Chandler's San Fernando Valley was obliterated; over 450 people died in the flood, making it one of the ten worst peacetime disasters in American history.

At the inquest that followed, Mulholland tried at first to lay the blame on Owens Valley dynamiters, but the evidence placed responsibility on the haggard old engineer's hubris and his own poor judgment. The dam had been leaking badly at its base hours before the collapse, but Mulholland dismissed the leaks as typical minor seepage. No one downstream was warned.

Damages paid by the city of Los Angeles topped $15 million. At the inquest's climax, a broken and broke William Mulholland at last took full responsibility for the horror that his misjudgment had wrought upon L.A.

"I envy the dead," he said with typical terse understatement. The day the trial ended, Mulholland's chauffeur drove him around the city aimlessly for hours. He resigned a short time later and lived in self-imposed isolation for the rest of his life.

In 1934, Fred Eaton's family asked Mulholland to pay a final visit to his old friend. Eaton, who had been driven into bankruptcy along with his Owens Valley neighbors, had suffered a stroke and now lay dying in a Hollywood bungalow.

The two men had a lifetime of grim irony to discuss. Had they been willing to compromise twenty years earlier, Owens Valley might have been saved and there would have been no reason to construct the doomed Saint Francis Dam. Had the miserly Mulholland only agreed to pay greedy Fred Eaton his $1 million asking price, Long Valley would have become a reservoir; the need for a dam closer to L.A. to hold the Owens River water would have been negated. Furthermore, a Long Valley reservoir, built high in the Sierras due north of the town of Bishop,

could have supplied irrigation water to Owens Valley at the same time it kept the Los Angeles Aqueduct flowing year around.

A few months after Eaton's death, Mulholland died at the age of eighty-seven.[8] His body lay in state in the rotunda of the new city hall in July 1935. Thousands attended his memorial service, most grieving his passing, but a few condemning Mulholland as a scoundrel and a murderer.

Six years later, Harvey Van Norman, his successor at the Los Angeles DWP, built the Long Valley Dam. The reservoir it created was named Lake Crowley in honor of a Catholic priest who had tried in vain to quell the hostility between Los Angeles and the Owens Valley.

———————

HARRY CHANDLER HAD NEITHER THE TIME nor the sentiment to waste on Mulholland, Eaton, or Owens Valley. As his age crept past sixty-five, he grew more and more aware of his waning vitality. Taking the Bible literally, he began to breakfast regularly on milk and honey—milk produced from his own clover-fed cows and honey from the bee apiaries he maintained in the hills of Griffith Park behind his estate. He even began looking into a crackpot surgical procedure that involved goat gland transplants in the hope that he might be revitalized.[9] Chandler offered lifetime employment to any *Times* employee[10] who would undergo the $750 experimental procedure so that he could see whether it worked. When he tried to persuade longtime real estate partner Moses Sherman to go under the knife, Sherman scoffed that Harry had finally lost his marbles. Only after the *Times*' own health writer wrote an exposé about the absurdity of intraspecies gland transplants did Chandler reluctantly concede that it was probably not possible.

Despite his flagging energy, Harry's nighttime regimen at the office never let up. He continued to invite almost anybody in for a chat—a habit that only escalated with age. He listened to all moneymaking schemes, whether brilliant or ridiculous. Yet, according to Norman and Buff, eventually money meant little to Harry.

"He was always helping someone in trouble and he held more worthless IOUs than anyone in town," recalled Norman.

His absent-mindedness worsened with age. Harry bought and sold vast tracts of land, but sometimes forgot to pick up enough cash from the bank to buy a sandwich; and he constantly borrowed pocket change from his employees. Paying grocery bills also slipped his mind. His obsessive land purchases often left the family land-poor and scratching at the end of the month to make the mortgage payment on one of Harry's deals. If Marian hadn't kept track of the household utilities, their electricity and phone service would have been cut off. She bought his clothes for him because he wouldn't. In his later years, his suits and shirts

hung on his large, frail frame like scarecrow attire because he refused to take the time to go see a tailor. And yet, for all the signs that he might be slipping, Harry was forever spinning big deals with anyone who came through his office door.

"He used to waste a great deal of time interviewing inconsequential people," scoffed Buff.

But he must have found some sort of conspiratorial ego satisfaction in midnight meetings with charlatans and thieves. Harry insisted on it and Los Angeles had no choice but to obey. Business and community leaders usually perceived the eccentric beginnings of senility noted by family members as nothing more than blithe arrogance. *Time* magazine described Harry as a "white-haired and purse-mouthed . . . teetotaler" who "eschews all forms of exercise except mowing the lawn a bit. When the first drop of perspiration runs down his nose, he quits."

Harry never went to the people. The people had to come to him on his terms and in his time, as if he were some kind of municipal pope. He still did not have enough wealth, nor did he wield enough influence over the city that he had created. He would never have enough. He needed more time and more energy to gather more of both.

In its June 5, 1926, edition, the *Saturday Evening Post* profiled Harry, poetically summarizing his luck and lust when it came to owning more of California than any other individual:

When the large and passionate California moon rises majestically into the heavens and smiles a golden smile at the mocking birds and mountains and flower stands and semi-homesick Iowans that occupy such a prominent place in the California scenery, one wonders whether Harry Chandler owns 51% of said moon.

Was it Harry Chandler, one speculates, who had it changed from a silvery moon to a golden moon, so that it would harmonize more effectively with the California sunlight and the California oranges? It cannot be, one meditates, that Harry Chandler doesn't own some of the moon.

At the pinnacle of his career, Harry Chandler sat on more than forty corporate boards of directors and held large blocs of stock in several dozen companies.[11] He needed power, to be sure, but above all else, he needed more land. At nearly 1.5 million acres, Harry Chandler did not yet own enough property.

In 1927, his land syndicate bought and helped organize the Vermejo Park Club, comprised of the Vermejo and Bartlett Ranches in southern Colorado and northern New Mexico. Famous as a sportsmen's paradise, the 340,000 acres of Vermejo Park Club became an exclusive hunting preserve and cattle ranch—second only to the King Ranch in Texas as the largest privately owned spread in

America. Members ranged from Douglas Fairbanks, Mary Pickford, and Cecil B. DeMille to Andrew Mellon, Harvey Firestone, and Harry Chandler's old fishing buddy, Herbert Hoover.

Closer to home, Harry had his eye on two of the last remaining tracts of Spanish land grants in the Los Angeles Basin: Rancho Santa Anita and Rancho La Cienega. Both were owned by the heirs of Elias J. "Lucky" Baldwin, one of George Hearst's early prospecting peers; Baldwin had struck it rich in Virginia City's Comstock Lode and bought 54,000 acres in Los Angeles eight years before General Otis purchased his stake in the *Times*. By the time Harry Chandler bought the Baldwin estate, Lucky's not-as-lucky children had sold most of it, leaving only 185 acres of the 13,000-acre Rancho Santa Anita[12] and 1,300 acres of undeveloped property between downtown Los Angeles and Santa Monica—all that was left of Rancho La Cienega. Like the Harry of old, he immediately began planning subdivisions.

L.A.'s 1920s population explosion bothered Harry's son Norman, who had known some of his happiest times growing up as a cattle puncher on the remote Tejon Ranch. Norman confided more than once to his children that he would have been far more content as Harry Chandler's second or third son, relegated to watching over the family's rural properties. As the first of the Chandler males, though, he was destined to run the *Los Angeles Times*. In the early 1930s, Norman and Buff would build a home in one corner of Harry's newly acquired Santa Anita property, and there Norman would raise his family close to an orchard, horse corral, and garden: the Tejon Ranch in urbanized miniature.

But in the late 1920s, the next publisher of the *Los Angeles Times* and his department-store-heiress wife still lived modestly in Hollywood. Norman was no longer delivering newspapers for a living or getting by on $16 a week, but he was still a long way from the publisher's suite.

Through Harry's tutelage, his oldest son moved from department to department at the *Times* throughout the mid-1920s, learning firsthand how circulation dovetailed with advertising and how the daily production cycles affected both. Norman did a stint in the promotion department, too, watching Harry's master plan in action for simultaneously boosting the *Times*, Southern California, and the family's vast real estate holdings.

Norman's one blind spot in his on-the-job training as *Times* publisher lay at the newspaper's heart: the newsroom. Although his sister Constance tried her hand at reporting for a few years, even meeting her future husband, *Times* financial editor Earle Crowe, in the city room, Norman never wrote a story, covered a news event, or edited copy.

Instead, his earliest years at the *Times* were invested in following closely in his father's footsteps. Like Harry, Norman understood early that the business of the

Times was conducted as much in the private clubs and exclusive retreats of Los Angeles as it was inside the Times Mirror Building; and one of his most lucrative early collaborations had nothing to do with the newspaper.

The up-and-coming insurance firm of Emmet, Gillis, and Lee invited Norman to become a fourth partner on the strength of his ability to open the doors to L.A.'s most exclusive WASP businessmen. Open them he did, and soon all but the founding partner of the firm were invited to leave. It was renamed Emmet & Chandler. During the Great Depression, it became one of L.A.'s most successful insurance companies.

Norman also began stepping into the various family enterprises. When his cousin Ralph Chandler's Los Angeles Steamship Company needed a treasurer, Norman got the job; and Harry turned over his own directorship in the Farmers & Merchants Bank to his son and made him a vice president of Harry's Beverly-Wilshire Investment Company.

With his chiseled good looks, cleft chin, and Stanford polish, Norman also rose naturally to a leadership role among the newest generation of L.A. Brahmins. As the older patricians with whom Harry once did business began dying off, a new wave of young tycoons came to populate the exclusive mahogany-paneled grandeur of the posh California Club close by L.A. Civic Center, the near-secretive Valley Hunt Club in Pasadena, and the no-Jews/Negroes/Mexicans-allowed clubhouse of the Los Angeles Country Club west of Beverly Hills.

As one of the founding members of a select group of young businessmen who called themselves the Economic Roundtable, Norman began breakfasting once each month at the University Club with the future L.A. movers and shakers who would steer Southern California through the Great Depression, World War II, and the early years of the Cold War. They included

- "Bud" Haldeman, whose father Harry Haldeman was Harry Chandler's partner in Beverly-Wilshire Investments and the Yosemite Park and Curry Company;
- John McCone, who would go on to head the Central Intelligence Agency during the Eisenhower administration;
- Reese Taylor, future president of Union Oil;
- Preston Hotchkiss, heir to the Bixby Ranch, which would develop most of the city of Long Beach;
- Emerson Spear, whose father made his fortune through mining; and
- Frederick Warren Williamson, a prominent young attorney.

This nucleus of wealthy and powerful second-generation Angelenos were the bedrock of a new twentieth-century aristocracy who would lay down the policies

and back the politicians selected to oversee L.A.'s future. They behaved in much the same fashion as their East Coast counterparts with their own insulated neighborhoods, leisure-time activities, and social inbreeding. They lived apart from the Los Angeles melting pot that they ruled, in exclusive "White Spot" enclaves such as San Marino, Sierra Madre, and the wealthier pockets of Pasadena, and they seldom mingled outside their caste.

Like Harry Chandler, who made the politically correct decision to marry the boss's daughter, this new generation found its own marital partners within the ruling class. They met each other at the appropriate schools (as had Norman and Buff at Stanford), through the correct social introduction, or during an event at one of the right clubs, such as the annual Las Padrinas debutante ball at the Valley Hunt Club. Chance encounters were discouraged, if not outlawed altogether.

Thus, the matches of Frederick Williamson to Norman's older sister, Ruth; and Williamson's sister, Alberta, to Norman's youngest brother, Philip, were in keeping with the proper order of the new WASP oligarchy. It would continue into the next generation as well, with Emerson Spear's son, Kellogg, marrying Norman and Buff's first child, Camilla, who was born in 1925.

Camilla was their first, but she could not be a Chandler heir. Buff had suffered miscarriages and the couple feared that they might not have a son. Two years after Camilla's birth, Buff was pregnant again. This time, she and Norman felt sure the child would be a boy.

In August 1927, Harry's father and mother, Moses and Emma Chandler, celebrated their sixty-fifth wedding anniversary; even though she was six months pregnant, Buff Chandler showed up along with every other member of the extensive Chandler clan to pay her respects. The elder Chandlers were slow and stiff with age, but self-sufficient and fiercely independent. Watching her father-in-law's parents hold court in their bland Yankee fashion gave Buff some insight into how she believed her own husband would age.

Moses Chandler was ninety-one. Emma was eighty-three. The hearty New Hampshire farmer and his wife still lived on the Burbank ranch that Harry helped them purchase in 1883 when they had followed their tubercular son to California to rid themselves of their own respiratory ailments. When Harry saw his pregnant daughter-in-law arm-in-arm with Norman and congratulating Moses and Emma, he smiled. Buff's effervescence always made him smile, but seeing her so large with what he hoped would be a grandson nearly brought a toothsome grin to his tired face.

After five years as a Chandler, Buff was often loath to smile at all. The snubs from Norman's sisters waxed and waned, depending upon Buff's willingness to attend teas, garden parties, and other deadly social obligations. Buff had made it

clear to Norman early on that she much preferred sharing a good stiff martini with her husband at the end of the day to going out to one of his sisters' dinner parties. Her pregnancy had given her several months of excuses, but there was no avoiding the sixty-fifth wedding anniversary.

At the gathering, Buff saw all Harry's children, and there wasn't a black sheep in the bunch:

- Frances, thirty-seven, Harry's oldest daughter by his first wife Magdalena, had married John Kirkpatrick, a prominent physician and widower from an old California family;
- Mae, thirty-five, his second daughter by Magdalena, wed Roger Goodan, a Stanford graduate and owner of the successful Los Angeles Furniture Company;
- Constance, thirty-one, Harry's first child with Marian, went to work on the *Times* city desk as a general assignment reporter following her own graduation from Stanford, but retired early to the role of mother and society matron following her marriage to Earle Crowe, the *Times'* financial editor;
- Ruth, thirty, Buff's chief nemesis among the Chandler women, had become Mrs. Frederick Warren Williamson in 1924;
- Harrison Gray Otis Chandler, twenty-four, Norman's younger brother, was still a bachelor after Stanford, moving easily into the dull if lucrative family business of producing telephone directories for the Times Mirror Press;
- the twins, Helen and Philip, who had just turned twenty, were both Stanford undergraduates and still unmarried.

Chiefly through her husband's patience and her father-in-law's stern but tacit approval, Buff found uneasy acceptance among the Chandlers. She glanced at her protruding belly and wondered whether becoming a brood mare was all there was for a young woman of means and breeding. Although never stepping out in front of her husband, Marian Otis Chandler had certainly demonstrated that a Chandler woman did not have to be as retiring as Harry's own mother, Emma, who had spent sixty-five years in Moses' shadow. Marian showed more than once that she was the General's daughter; she never relinquished her position on the Times Mirror board of directors, not even during her five pregnancies.

But Buff had no intention of spending the rest of her own days in and out of a maternity hospital. This one was a son. She felt it, sensed it, read about it in her horoscope. This pregnancy would provide Norman with an heir, and it would be her last child. Never mind the pressure to be fertile that her in-laws foisted on

her. If they could, Harry and Marian would keep their children bearing young as long as the hormones held out. Buff was of a different disposition. She had worlds to conquer.

A son was born to Norman and Buff three months after the sixty-fifth anniversary celebration, on November 23, 1927. Honoring the Walrus and the Fox, Norman Chandler named the boy for the two founders of the family dynasty. He would be Otis Chandler.

With the weight of two legendary names and the *Los Angeles Times* foisted upon him before he was an hour old, the infant's destiny was preordained. He would have to wait seven decades before a West Hollywood psychic would tell him what he'd instinctively known from the cradle:

"You were *born* forty years old!"

PART B

Worst of *Times*

1930—1960

The *Times* is not a public institution, run in the service of the people. It is a private institution run for the personal business advantage of Mr. Chandler. . . . It is even worse than this; it is an instrument for the promotion of Mr. Chandler's unpatriotic enterprises and crooked deals. In other words, the newspaper is being prostituted for the private unworthy ends of its proprietor.

—William Randolph Hearst

CHAPTER 9

OTIS CHANDLER'S EARLIEST MEMORY of his grandfather was a visit that he and his father paid to the *Times* at the dawn of the Great Depression. Harry sat behind a large wooden desk in the fourth-floor office where he held court every day. Norman and the boy didn't have to wait in the anteroom to beg a moment of Chandler's time the way most of Harry's subjects did. They marched right in and sat before the great man.

Otis doesn't remember the conversation between his father and grandfather. He was far too busy drinking in the trappings of authority—polished brass, inlaid paneling, richly appointed furnishings. Somewhere outside Harry's heavy wooden door the steady muted hum of the printing presses were a constant reminder of the wellspring of his grandfather's power. But Otis was too young to find sermons in humming presses. From where he sat on his father's knee, the knickknacks and paperweights at the edge of Harry's desk commanded far more interest. His eyes drifted past Harry's graying head to a paneled cabinet inset in the wall behind his grandfather's chair. Harry noticed the boy's big eyes staring past his shoulder.

"Want to see what I've got in there?" Harry asked suddenly.

Otis nodded vigorously, afraid to speak. Harry swung around in his chair and pulled open the doors to the cabinet. As the old man reached his two thin arms inside, Otis caught a glimpse of the barrel of a gun. Harry turned back in his seat, facing Otis and Norman with a grim smile on his face and a ten-gauge shotgun in his hands.

"If those damn unionists come to blow up the *Times* again," he announced, bouncing the weapon on his knee like a toddler, "I'm ready for them."

Harry and Norman laughed low, confident laughs that were years beyond Otis's understanding. Still, the boy tried chiming in with his own chuckle while he studied the details of the double-barreled threat resting on his grandfather's lap. He knew it was for shooting, but he had only the vaguest notion what a unionist might be.

His next memories hazed around the celebrating of the holidays at Harry's house. During the wretched Christmas season of 1931, when the full force of the

Great Depression hit Southern California like a sucker punch, the Chandler clan gathered at Harry and Marian's Hillhurst estate in the Los Feliz Hills for the annual Christmas party. The *Times* Christmas editorial for the poor, the downtrodden, and the miserable who were out of work and out of luck that terrible year sounded much like prosperous Harry lecturing his own family on the wonders of the season: "Merry Christmas! Look pleasant! Chin up! A gloomy face never gets a good picture. . . . Faith still does the impossible . . . Merry Christmas! You have your life before you; and if you are growing old, the greatest adventure of all is just around the corner. Earth may have little left in reserve; but heaven is ahead. Merry Christmas!"

Otis and his sister, Camilla, had no concept of real economic hardship, particularly at Christmastime. Otis remembered every one of those family gatherings from 1931 on as particularly splendid moments in a life that brimmed with plenty. With its huge decorated fir tree in the entrance hall and a yule log burning in the brick fireplace, Grandpa Harry's home was a fortress that had transcended the stock market crash as if it were a timeless Currier & Ives engraving.

Before the Christmas feast, they all gathered in their holiday finery for the family photo outdoors on the tiled patio. Harry stood at the center in his finest three-piece suit, hovering over the enterprise like a kindly Zeus. By the 1930s, the Chandler children were beginning to outnumber the adults. Otis and Camilla looked forward each Christmas to seeing cousins they never saw the rest of the year. It became a ritual: Each year the children lined up for their gifts, and each year Otis picked a fight with his cousin, Andrew.

"I never knew why," Otis recalled decades later. "We never saw each other at any other time of the year. I just wound up beating him up year after year."

When Otis and Ralph Chandler's second son, Andrew, were well into their thirties, Otis learned that his cousin was gay. Always the he-man, Otis often wondered whether that was his subconscious motive for attacking the hapless boy: Testosterone-powered Otis sensed latent homosexuality the way a wolf smells blood.

Other moments in his preschool days still flash into his memory, notably the annual October ritual of visiting the artificial hills and man-made lake of Hollywood Cemetery, where stands a towering monument to twenty of the twenty-one fallen employees of the 1910 bombing of the *Times*. His mother dressed him in a little blue suit and his father held his hand; together, they lead him to the mound where the men and women were buried. There, the Reverend W. Whitcomb Brougher began the ritual every year with the same invocation: "Oh Lord, we thank Thee for the *Times*, which through all the years has championed the right to work."

Otis didn't remember the words that were said or the prayers that might have been whispered, but he remembered that it was a far more solemn moment than any he observed in church.

Perhaps his most vivid early childhood memory came in the months following the horrifying kidnapping and murder of Charles Lindbergh's twenty-month-old son in March 1932. Headlines and radio news briefs chronicling each new development in the case were so sensational and so widespread that even a five-year-old boy was aware of the crime.

Thus, even the insular young Otis Chandler knew something wasn't quite right one autumn day when a man in a business suit pulled up in front of his parents' estate[1] on Nottingham Avenue in Hollywood. Norman and Buff were away on a trip at the time and a nanny had been left to watch over Otis and his sister. Otis played in the garden while the man sat in his idling sedan and stared at him.

"He was there a long time in the car and I didn't think anything of it," Otis recalled. "I thought maybe the guy was stopped, lost, looking at a map."

In a different family, he might have been an unruly child, but by the time he was out of diapers, it did not take a paddling or a cuff to the ear to persuade Otis to comply. He was allowed neither the luxury to brood nor an occasional exercise of irrational willfulness. He was a Chandler, and neither Buff nor Norman ever let him forget it. From birth, Otis had been instructed to listen to his elders. But this time, when he looked around for one, there was no elder. Just Otis and the man in the car, staring at him.

"He must have looked and thought: There was no mother or father around, no gardener around, no nanny around. My sister wasn't there. Then he got out of the car and then I started to retreat back toward the house. And then he came running."

Otis turned and broke into a dead run himself, down the driveway, into the backyard, and through the back door, just steps ahead of his pursuer.

"The nanny must have been in the house and my sister Camilla had to have been around too," he recalled.

But in visualizing the moment, Otis did not remember anyone but himself and the man he assumed to be an abductor. All he could see when he shut his eyes was a small boy, out of breath from sprinting, his back to the door that stood between him and his assailant. After a few moments, he peered through a window at the front of the house and saw that the man and his car were gone.

And he remembered his family discussing the close call for months afterward, their speculating on how near a kidnapper or, worse, a union terrorist, might have come to snatching Harry Chandler's grandson.

Always a protective mother, Buff became a near fanatic after that incident. The

family sold the Nottingham house and moved to Long Beach a short time later, closer to Buff's family.

BUFF RAISED THE CHILDREN with a nanny because Norman didn't spend much time at home while he learned the newspaper trade. He would become third publisher of the *Los Angeles Times*, but not yet. He would have to work and learn and then wait, like a prince, for his father to die.

Like the General, Harry Chandler would always be publisher while he lived. In 1930, the American Newspaper Publishers Association elected Harry its president. He had at last risen to the top of the ultra-exclusive cabal of rich white males who then ruled over American media.

"Publishers love each other privately," observed Nick Williams, a young *Times* copy editor in the 1930s who was destined to rise high within Harry Chandler's Times Mirror palladium. "You could say that in private they fondle the balls they try to cut off in public. Harry would have supped with the Devil, even with a short spoon, had it been advantageous."

The Old Man of the Chandler dynasty basked in his glory, but he was wise enough gradually to relinquish responsibility to his heir. Harry might give up other titles to age, but never the authority that came from being the publisher of the *Times*. Contrary to what Russian and Chinese Marxists would later preach, Harry knew that *real* power did not grow from the barrel of a gun; *real* power came from a barrel full of ink.

Following his long apprenticeship in the *Times*' distribution, marketing, and promotion departments, Norman began his duties as Harry's assistant in 1929; he became assistant to the general manager five years later and took full control of the company in 1936 as vice president and general manager. For all practical purposes, Norman ran the *Times* from 1930 on, beginning with a reign of terror that the younger Chandler endorsed and ordered overseen by Colonel Guy T. Visknisski, a Chicago newspaper efficiency expert. Visknisski's economies ranged from petty (fewer typewriter ribbon changes; no personal calls on company phones) to draconian.

"Department heads were old, tired," Norman argued. "We needed younger people, more aggressive people. Times were changing. We needed to keep the *Times* abreast of change."

Production, circulation, and advertising heads rolled, but the *Times* newsroom was the least of the Chandlers' concerns. Although Norman widened the columns, enlarged the typeface, and put more pictures in the newspaper,[2] he was as uninterested as Harry about the dreck that the *Times* published. Any hope that

General Otis's fire might ever return to the *Times*' pages would have to wait. Norman's city desk edict paralleled Harry's: "Keep it Republican and don't make waves."

Thus, although a new generation of college educated reporters—Marvin Miles (who became the *Times*' aerospace expert), Jim Bassett (who eventually graduated to editorial page editor), and Gene Sherman (who won the paper's first Pulitzer Prize for reporting)—swept on to the city desk during the Visknisski housecleaning, the newsroom continued to be run mainly by traditionalist lackeys and hardworking hacks who were occasionally clever and even funny, but rarely industrious or insightful.

One infamous sportswriter from the era, for example, loved to slip off-color gags past his editors: "Angels pitcher Allen Starrett Sample pitched his initials off yesterday," or "USC runner Johnson, whose pants slipped off during the last ten yards of the 100-yard dash, led for 90 yards but then petered out." Whenever he was caught, the sportswriter was fired in much the same manner that the General used to fire his telegraph editor: The malefactor left the building long enough to down a few drinks, returned to beg for his job, and was back at his desk before the presses rolled.

A dour-faced bibliophile named Ralph Waldo Trueblood presided over the *Times* staff as its executive editor and his second-in-command, Managing Editor Loyal Durant Hotchkiss, fussed and fumed over each day's headlines.

Trueblood had inherited the editorship from Harry Andrews, General Otis's legendary alter ego; Andrews ran the *Times* after Frederick Mosher's suicide, from the turn of the century until just a few years before his death in 1926. An Otis apparatchik who mirrored the General's reactionary bluster in every issue of the *Times*, Andrews was such an integral part of the newspaper's early days that he was that rarest of employees to whom Harry and Marian Chandler awarded stock in the family-held business. By all accounts, Andrews was a bold if obedient sycophant. He won the hearts of the General and his son-in-law by loudly parroting their antiunion sentiment and pro–Southern California bias in all news stories, regardless of taste, truth, or logic. His successor, timid by comparison, was neither so revered by Harry Chandler nor so fortunate as to be cut in with a few shares of the family fortune.

In 1921, Trueblood had achieved minor fame as the inventor of a device that sent photographs over the telegraph—the fastest method available until the advent of the wire photo in 1934. Beyond that, his legacy was thin. The nearly deaf Trueblood was a devout Christian Scientist who spoke in a loud, deep voice and spent half his life wading through heavy Victorian texts or quadruple-checking trivia in the *Times* morgue.[3]

"He seemed to be personally checking out every statement of fact made by the *Times*," *Times* librarian Stanley Gordon recalled to the Chandlers' official biographer, Marshall Berges.

Hotchkiss, by contrast, was one of the *Times'* true characters.

"He wasn't what you would call a strong, biting, aggressive editor," Norman told Jim Bassett—also an authorized Chandler historian—during a 1972 interview. "He was an innovator if you put a burr under him and told him to."

One of Harry Chandler's original "fixers" who served as much as a Chandler intelligence agent in the 1920s as he did a reporter, Hotchkiss stepped up to chief newsroom executive by default. He was one of the Old Man's favorites and made few ripples among Norman's California Club friends by keeping their names out of the paper except for ribbon-cuttings and society balls. Thus, the five-foot-two-inch Hotchkiss shrieked and snarled at his staff with impunity for almost thirty years, despite committing some of the worst blunders ever published by the *Times*, including a bland whitewash of corrupt L.A. mayor Frank Shaw's notorious régime.

The avuncular and misogynistic Hotchkiss vowed that a woman reporter would never sit at his city desk, but at the same time a female clerk or typist could not pass through the newsroom without being fondled. His nickname among those women who did work at the *Times* during the 1930s and 1940s was "Old Pinch." Only very late in his career, in the late 1950s, did Hotchkiss reluctantly give into the pressure to stop touching and start hiring females.[4]

Hotchkiss also didn't want women depicted on the pages of his newspaper unless they were draped like Islamic fishwives. Any photo that could be remotely construed as "cheesecake" never left the darkroom.

"If you want to, look at it," he snarled in disgust. "But don't put it in the *Times*. You've already seen it."

Staff who were called into his office made a beeline for the couch next to his desk. It was better to sit, especially if one was tall; Hotchkiss hated any reporter who stood over five-foot-seven, and those over six feet were doomed. During the 1933 Long Beach earthquake when the *Times* building swayed with every other downtown structure, Hotchkiss beat the rest of the staff out the front door, only to turn on a gangly young copyboy who was right behind him.

"What're you doing out here? Get back to your desk!" Hotchkiss howled.

"He was a very forceful and bold and opinionated man when he was behind his editorial desk," Norman recalled to Bassett. "When he came out of his office, he was a little like a snail without a shell. He didn't have that encasement which protected him."

Colonel Visknisski's cuts and economies didn't touch Hotchkiss or his newsroom, but they did come just in time to lift the *Times'* business operations out of

the red. For all his ruthlessness outside the *Times*, Harry Chandler had always been sentimental and paternalistic toward his employees—a post–*Christmas Carol* Ebenezer Scrooge who might not pay much in salaries but held on to every Bob Cratchett who ever worked for him. In one failed experiment, the *Times* tried avoiding layoffs by shortening the workweek.

At the dawn of the 1930s, even the *Times* had to cut staff. Harry all but wept when he and Norman were forced to lay off 10 percent of their workforce. At the same time, William Randolph Hearst blithely slashed his own payrolls by almost 30 percent without a second thought. To outsiders, it appeared as though Hearst was at last getting the best of Harry Chandler.

"We were not in good shape financially, and things were getting worse," Norman recalled. "By the early 1930s, with Depression all around us, both Hearst papers, the *Examiner* and the *Herald*, had passed us in circulation. We held a slight lead in advertising volume, but they were gradually overtaking us."

What even Norman didn't know at the time was that Hearst had so overextended, chiefly through his self-indulgence at San Simeon, that the Chandlers' principal rival was in danger of losing his empire—including his beloved castle in the Santa Lucia Mountains. In 1933, Hearst couldn't even make payroll and had to borrow $600,000 against San Simeon just to keep his newspaper empire afloat.

In one of the great ironies in the long-running Chandler-Hearst rivalry, it turned out that Harry Chandler had secretly forked over the $600,000 loan, made through the Los Angeles mortgage firm of Staats & Company.[5] Harry held on to the mortgage for ten years, despite a plea from Hearst's own ruthless business manager, Clarence J. Shearn, to foreclose in 1936. To stanch the red ink the Hearst Corporation was hemorrhaging, Shearn had already sold seven Hearst radio stations, six newspapers, the Universal News Service, and Hearst's feature film production operation.

Because "land lust tempted me," Harry later told the *Saturday Evening Post*, he drove the two hundred miles to San Simeon with Moses Sherman's junior associate, Arnold Haskell,[6] to examine the property while Hearst was away. Even Harry Chandler was aghast at the majesty of Hearst's folly as he and Haskell drove up the narrow winding dirt road to the gates of the lonely outsized mansion. Much to Harry's chagrin, the master of San Simeon was at home. Hearst and Marion Davies were waiting for him and Haskell on the front steps.

Davies had invited Harry to San Simeon once before, while Norman was still at Stanford. Work on the castle had just begun when she asked Harry to bring Norman along in hopes that the young man's probity might rub off on William Randolph's eldest son, George, who had become a profligate and rake like his father. It didn't. George proved to be a worse spendthrift than his father, which didn't help keep the Hearst empire out of the red.

During the ensuing years, Harry and Hearst had drifted even farther apart. They were able to agree upon one thing only: their mutual hatred of Franklin D. Roosevelt. Still, Hearst and Marion[7] graciously asked their visitors to spend the night, but Harry begged off. He and Haskell returned to L.A. the same afternoon and told Clarence Shearn that Chandler had no plans to foreclose on Hearst's self-indulgent monument to grandiosity. In 1941, the U.S. Department of the Army bought the northern half of the San Simeon ranch land and eventually turned it into Camp Hunter Liggett. The sale gave Hearst[8] enough cash to pay off Chandler's mortgage on San Simeon.

Harry hadn't lost his taste for real estate wheeling and dealing, but he did begin to wind down in the 1930s. Following his purchase of the Santa Anita and La Cienega ranchos, he made a deal with handicapping entrepreneur Charles Strub to build a racetrack—one of the last major quasi-public works projects in which Harry participated. Although he frowned on gambling, Harry had no problem populating the board of directors of Strub's Los Angeles Turf Club with his best blue-blooded buddies[9] as a condition of helping Strub develop the property into a racetrack.

The 214-acre racetrack opened on Christmas Day, 1934, and its board went on to preside over Santa Anita in much the same exclusive manner in which they had presided over the Los Angeles Country Club or the California Club. Riffraff sat in the bleachers; Pasadena patricians held box seats and had access to the clubhouse. It didn't take long for wealthy Jews from Hillcrest Country Club and other Westside outsiders to counter the WASP snobs of Santa Anita by building their own racetrack at Hollywood Park in Inglewood.

L.A. had mushroomed just as Harry Chandler had promised, but it was not the White Spot that he and his All-Year Club had hoped for. Los Angeles had become a magnet for blacks, Japanese, and Mexicans, in addition to Jews and other Eastern European immigrants. Chandler's WASP establishment held the newcomers in check, especially when it came to swinging elections, but for all his clout, Harry began to encounter problems that even sheer wealth and years of unquestioned authority could not handle.

Harry's last big real estate deal wasn't in Mexico or some far-flung corner of Colorado or New Mexico; it was in the heart of L.A.'s Civic Center, and it revolved around the beloved *Times* Building he had personally opened in 1912. The phoenix that had grown out of the rubble of the 1910 bombing might have been precious to some other man, but when the Los Angeles County Board of Supervisors proposed razing the building in 1929 to make way for a new Union Station terminus for the Southern Pacific and Santa Fe Railroads, Harry Chandler enthusiastically agreed. He'd be happy to take a wrecker's ball to the General's final legacy if the price were right.

The supervisors' appraiser proposed paying Chandler $1.85 million, triggering outrage among a growing army of municipal activists who had begun to pay close attention to the self-aggrandizing games that Chandler and his cronies played at taxpayers' expense. Two groups, the Minute Men and the Municipal League, challenged the $1.8 million in court and got it reduced to $1.02 million. Under pressure from the reformers, the Board of Supervisors reduced the price for the old *Times* building even further, to $600,000.

Meanwhile, Harry challenged the lower price all the way to the California Supreme Court, which ordered the matter sent back to Los Angeles Superior Court for a new trial. In the spirit of compromise, Chandler magnanimously offered to drop his asking price to $1.63 million rather than go through another trial. At the same time, he secretly sent the *Times'* veteran crime reporter and fixer, Al Nathan, to the Los Angeles Police Department to riffle through the Red Squad files and see what dirt he could find on the Minute Men and the Municipal League. The *Times* then mounted a smear campaign against those who opposed Harry's $1.63-million asking price.

Such tactics had worked well in the past, but Los Angeles was entering a new era, less tolerant of Harry's manipulations and of the sweetheart deals he and his friends secured at city hall. Such rival newspapers as the *Hollywood Citizen News* recognized the patented Chandler sleight-of-hand and editorialized against it: "From the *Times* standpoint, it is better to contend that the only people who oppose the *Times* grab are radicals. The people of this city have seen for years the *Times* defend those in public office who beat the government to the demands of greedy interests."

Chandler settled for $1.19 million, but his short-term victory cost him and his *Times* dearly in long-term public opinion. At a time when half the population was out of work and makeshift "Hoovervilles"[10] were popping up in orange groves, train yards, and arroyos all over Southern California, Harry's routine real estate profit taking was viewed by many longtime residents, as well as the White Spot's latest émigrés—Jews, Italians, Irish, blacks, yellows, browns, Okies, Arkies, and Tennessee sodbusters—as the rankest brand of Midas greed.

Harry was oblivious. On April 10, 1934, he entertained civic leaders with the ceremonial laying of the cornerstone of his new *Times* Building. The concrete fortress went up across the street from the old building at First and Broadway—a symbol of *Times* forbearance in spite of the Depression. The new *Times* opened to much fanfare on July 1, 1935, a block away from city hall.

And the new Union Station that had inspired Harry Chandler's last real estate stand? Instead of waiting to build on the site of the old *Times* Building, which was torn down in 1937, the Board of Supervisors voted instead to raze the street that was once Nigger Alley and was now all that remained of Chinatown. In 1939,

when the era of rail travel in the United States was almost over, Los Angeles unveiled the last major rail station to be built in the nation; it was located several blocks east of the *Times* Building atop the crumbling ramparts of the original Hell Hole of the West. Not surprisingly, Harry Chandler owned property nearby that would climb in value and, thus, his *Times* wholeheartedly supported the site for the station's construction. A state government office building eventually went up where the *Times* Building once stood at First and Broadway.

As for the loss of Chinatown, Harry had a profitable answer for that, too. A leading society matron of the era, Mrs. Christine Sterling, urged the city to support the reconstruction of Chinatown a few blocks to the northeast of Union Station—but this Chinatown would be a kitsch version; brothels and backroom casinos were gone. Replete with Chinese restaurants, Torii gates, and red lacquered dragons, Mrs. Sterling's quaint new Chinatown would rival the similar tourist attraction that had evolved naturally near Union Square in San Francisco. L.A.'s Chinatown, however, was to be situated a few city blocks away from a second ethnic theme park: quaint new Olvera Street, also one of Mrs. Sterling's projects, which had opened as a tourist attraction on Easter Sunday, 1930, following four years of redevelopment.

Mrs. Sterling's chief ally in both projects was Harry Chandler, whom she praised for his Charles Lummis–like sense of history while he kept faith with "the finer things in life." It was Harry Chandler who had extracted $39,000 in seed money from his friends for Mrs. Sterling's Olvera Street during one of his famous fund-raising luncheons and it was Harry Chandler who helped raise Chinatown money, too. His argument for Mrs. Sterling's tourism projects was the same argument he gave for the city's continued support of his newspaper: What was good for tourism and the *Times* was good for L.A. On the day the ribbon was cut for the new *Times* Building, Harry wrote the *Times'* editorial: "The best interests of Los Angeles are paramount to the *Times*. They have always been. The city and this newspaper have grown up together. With humility, those in charge of its conduct realized that it grew because it was, in a certain sense, the voice of a lusty, energetic, progressive community. That it prospered because it echoed the call of a triumphant pioneer spirit."

Harry Chandler envisioned himself the personification of that triumphant pioneer spirit. In its July 15, 1935, edition, *Time* magazine declared Harry "an inspired capitalist."

On the occasion of Harry Chandler's seventy-second birthday one year later, gaily festooned Mexican peons pulled an old wooden-wheeled *carreta,* which carried a small children's chorale, all the way from Olvera Street to a spot beneath Harry's third-floor office window. Nearly one hundred artists, shopkeepers, and entertainers who worked on Olvera Street gathered around the children. They all

wore an odd combination of Windsor ties and bright red, green, and yellow serapes—symbolic, perhaps, of an anglicized Brooks Brothers future and a romanticized *Ramona* past. Out on the sidewalk of the new *Times* fortress at First and Spring Streets, the children burst into birthday song. Harry, who moved more slowly now than in previous years, came to his window. He smiled benevolently at all the little people and gave them faint praise for making his inspired capitalism possible.

That same year, the *Times* ran a series of editorials praising the Los Angeles police for its "Bum Blockade"—a policy of turning away unemployed California emigrants at the border before they could travel as far north or west as Chandler's City of Angels. It took the American Civil Liberties Union to point out that Harry Chandler wouldn't want Jesus crossing into California, either, unless he could show he had tangible assets.

But Chandler was unfazed. He could point out that the average weekday circulation of his *Times* had climbed by more than 20,000 since 1930, peaking at 186,423 in mid-decade. And, as always, the *Times* led the nation in ad lineage.

———————

HOW THE TIMES COVERED—or did not cover—the news of its ever-expanding constituency had become a disgrace by the mid-1930s. The front page inevitably carried dispatches of angst elsewhere in the world, from prison riots to petroleum swindles, but seldom did the newspaper reveal trouble at home. Echoing Harry Chandler's booster dictum, L. D. Hotchkiss and other senior editors at the *Times* kept bad news to a minimum, especially if it involved the publisher's pals.

But such institutional silence had its price. As Harry's monolithic power slowly disintegrated, the *Times'* nonreporting grew increasingly obvious and shameful, as in the story of Courtney Chauncey Julian and his get-rich-quick oil company— a shabby saga whose repercussions continued to resonate well into Norman Chandler's ascendancy to the publisher's throne.

By the time he cashed in his chips on March 25, 1934, C. C. Julian had already established himself alongside Charles Ponzi and P. T. Barnum in the annals of American flimflam legend. Even his suicide was a scam. Following a lavish farewell bash he threw for himself and his twenty-year-old secretary in a Shanghai luxury hotel, the forty-eight-year-old Julian retired to his suite where he downed a lethal dose of drugs without paying his hotel, bar, or dinner bill. A handful of Americans visiting the Chinese province at the time took up a collection to pay the $46 undertaking fee to bury him in a pauper's grave.

Twelve years earlier, C. C. Julian was a larger-than-life Winnipeg wildcatter who had come to Southern California with a folksy pitch and a seemingly limitless supply of stock certificates. Overnight, his Julian Petroleum Company be-

came the preeminent symbol of L.A.'s profligate naïveté during the Roaring Twenties. With considerable irony, the *Times* unwittingly launched Julian's meteoric career by publishing a June 19, 1922, headline that announced he had broken ground in an L.A. suburb on the "Gusher Field of America."

From that day until the bubble burst five years later, thousands invested in "Julian Pete" stock, as it came to be known. From the most sophisticated Spring Street banker to San Fernando Valley working stiffs who could barely afford a cracker box in one of Harry Chandler's housing tracts, all succumbed to Julian's advertised invitation to share in his bounty. He raised millions.

In his heyday, C. C. Julian also established himself as the classic free-spending L.A. big shot. According to one account, he once tipped a cab driver $1,500; according to another, he seduced a night club hostess by giving her a Cadillac. When his estranged wife decided to put one of his six lavish residences up for sale, the public got a glimpse of a lifestyle that included a Rolls Royce, a heart-shaped swimming pool, and a master bath with a tub lined in 14-carat gold.

While Julian lived it up, his company churned shares of stock and paid huge dividends from existing funds, which sucked in more and more investors. By the time the scheme blew apart on May 7, 1927, Julian had long since skipped L.A. and abandoned his company to a pair of junior grade con men who confessed to counterfeiting and selling 5 million shares of stock. When all the losses were tallied, it turned out that 40,000 L.A. residents had been fleeced of $150 million.

Asa Keyes, Los Angeles district attorney, eventually indicted forty-one "outstanding" citizens for their various roles, but Julian's name was not on his list; Keyes was never able to connect him to his subordinates' stock swindle, although Julian was indicted on separate fraud charges in Oklahoma. He skipped bail in Oklahoma and fled to China, where he planned to start an Asian version of the Julian Petroleum Company; but his luck ran out.

Following years of investigation and audit, no one discovered where all the Julian Pete money went; Keyes' at first suspected several of Harry Chandler's closest banking and investment cronies, including MGM's Louis B. Mayer, director Cecil B. DeMille, Security Trust and Savings Bank officers Henry Robinson and Motley Flint, and Chandler's longtime friend and coinvestor, Harry M. Haldeman. Because Keyes insisted on bringing them all to justice, the *Times* turned on him and labeled the D.A.'s effort to prosecute the Julian fraud nothing short of a fraud itself.

"I have been marked by the *Times* for vilification because I will not do its bidding," Keyes bitterly complained.

The *Times'* attitude toward the debacle could only be described as cavalier at best, callous at worst. Instead of applauding Keyes' vigilance, the newspaper suggested that the sorry episode was best forgotten. In keeping with Harry

Chandler's upbeat Babbitt philosophy, the newspaper's editorial position was astonishing in its disregard for those ruined by Julian Pete:

> The actual damage done by the collapse of the oil company itself is trifling in comparison to the injury which is being attempted by willful wreckers whose activities are aimed at the financial foundations of the city. The sums lost by innocent investors in the stock of Julian Petroleum Corporation are inconsiderable in contrast with those placed in jeopardy by the present effort to unsettle public confidence in institutions which form the cornerstone of the business structure of Los Angeles. . . . A large number of investors either lost their money through forced sales of stock on a falling market or are left with shares of doubtful value on their hands. But very little of the money paid for this stock actually left the community. The great bulk of it is still here in active and useful circulation.

To the *Times'* delight, about $100,000 of the lost Julian Pete boodle apparently circulated into the pocket of District Attorney Keyes, but no one knew he'd been bribed until long after the case came to trial. Keyes' deputy prosecutors had been handed a Gordian knot of fiduciary malfeasance they couldn't begin to explain to the jury. After acquitting Julian Petroleum's two principal officers, jurors threw up their hands and explained to the court that they had been too bewildered by it all to render a guilty verdict. A disgusted Judge William C. Doran threw the rest of Keyes' indictments out of court and criticized the D.A.'s office for allowing "one of the most deplorable, unfortunate and reprehensible episodes in the history of the country" to go unexplained and unavenged.

Municipal mayhem followed. Several months later, the *Times* delighted in breaking the story that a secret grand jury had indicted Keyes for allegedly taking cash, two automobiles, a set of golf clubs, a chaise lounge, and a watch as inducements to throw the case. In the cacophony of accusations that followed, a jury convicted Keyes despite his steadfast protest that he was innocent and had been railroaded by the *Times.* He spent two years in San Quentin, where he had been sending felons by the hundreds during the previous twenty years.

As for C. C. Julian's top two aides, they found that a federal jury was not quite so confused as the state court's jury had been. Both men were sentenced to seven years in a federal penitentiary.

But legal retribution meant little to those ruined by the Julian affair. They were still ruined and it made little difference to them that their lost life savings were still being circulated in the community, as the *Times* had sermonized. On the afternoon of December 11, 1931, forty-two-year-old Rosebud Harris, who had spent several despondent months in a sanitarium after having lost everything to Julian Pete, emptied a handgun into her nineteen-year-old daughter. She then

locked herself in the bathroom, opened a gas spigot, and drifted into eternity. Others reduced to poverty by Julian Pete took their own lives with only slightly less drama. Investors began jumping several hundred feet to their deaths in Pasadena's Arroyo Seco with such regularity that the city had to spend $20,000 a year just to hire extra police to keep leapers off "Suicide Bridge."

One deranged Julian investor showed up in an L.A. courtroom in March 1930 with literally his last dime in his pocket and a pistol in his hand. When Security First National Bank's Motley Flint rose to answer charges that he had engaged in usury and securities fraud on behalf of Julian Petroleum, the investor shot Flint dead.

Other victims succumbed to sustained stress. Harry Chandler's old friend Harry Haldeman suffered a fatal heart attack two months after Motley Flint's murder. His critics maintained that he died of tarnished pride and his own hypocrisy after years of holding himself up as L.A.'s leading patriot. Haldeman, a successful plumbing contractor who had risen to become Chandler's Yosemite partner and the founder of the arch conservative Better America Foundation, was only fifty-eight.

As for Asa Keyes, he maintained his innocence throughout his two years imprisonment and was applauded at the gates of San Quentin by several hundred well-wishers upon his release. He vowed to return to politics, but became a car salesman instead. As it had with Haldeman, the weight of Julian Pete showed in the premature lines in Keyes's face. He suffered a series of paralyzing strokes that culminated with his death in October 1934, just eight months after the sensational suicide of C. C. Julian. Keyes was fifty-seven years old.

CHAPTER 10

IN 1932, PSYCHIATRY HAD A VOODOO REPUTATION as bad or worse than that of Dr. John Brinkley's goat gland transplants. Thus, Buff Chandler's painful decision to enter treatment for her depression was a genuine act of courage. In addition to the criticism she suffered from her own family and friends, she had to contend with Norman's harpy sisters. Ten years after their brother's wedding, the Chandler women could now snicker and prate with perfect justification about their nut-case sister-in-law.

It was never clear to Otis or to his sister, Camilla, when Buff Chandler suffered her celebrated nervous breakdown. Buff was not under undue stress at home.

She didn't cook. There was a maid for that, just as there was a nanny for the children. On the maid's night off, the family dined at the Pacific Dining Car on Sixth Street, near the Times Mirror Building.

Otis believed that his mother was not above taking dramatic license to stretch her stay-at-home depression into a six-month-long fiction about participating in intense residential group counseling.

"I don't remember her ever being gone," he said. Mia recalled only that her mother was gone for a time.

But in Dorothy Chandler's own version, which she told fifty years later, her entire life changed as a result of her treatment at the hands of pioneering Pasadena psychiatrist Josephine Jackson. When Otis was just four years old, she checked into Jackson's group home as a last-ditch effort to subdue her raging gloom. She considered herself a failure as a wife, as a mother, and as a human being. Norman had heard about Dr. Jackson from a friend, and he asked the doctor to speak with his wife. After hearing Buff out, Dr. Jackson told her that her despondency was dangerous—might even prompt suicide.

In a pre-Prozac world, Buff Chandler had been sliding inexorably into a catch-all Freudian category known as "involutionary melancholia" ever since Otis's birth. It took Dr. Jackson's commonsense advice—"stop being a passive victim and start getting involved"—before Buff put her life back on course. She came out of the treatment armed with a declaration of interdependence. During a period when women rarely transcended their menfolk, Buff abandoned her depression in favor of acting out her wishes through her suave, drop-dead handsome—but, ultimately, prosaic—husband, Norman.[1] The mousy Buff, who had once knit and embroidered and stayed in the drawing room when she wasn't out eating cucumber sandwiches with the Ladies' Auxiliary, had now disappeared forever. In her place emerged a prim, proper, but persistently power hungry matron-in-the-making who took "no" for an answer about as often as her father-in-law did.

She took to running the lives of everyone in her immediate family, beginning with Norman, whose cocktail intake she regulated like an A.A. sponsor.

"Posture, Norman! Posture!" was a frequent Buff refrain whenever she caught her husband slumping in public.

It was *this* Dorothy Buffum Chandler who came into focus the day eight-year-old Otis was thrown from a horse and given up for dead.

With a wall full of blue and red ribbons, Camilla was the award-winning family equestrian, but little Otis was obliged to mount up on occasion, too. His mother demanded that both children develop at least the rudiments of proper breeding, and they included horsemanship. At the Pasadena stables where English-style riding was favored, the first thing young Otis Chandler noticed was that the saddles had no horns.

"There was nothing to hold on to," Otis muttered contemptuously, recalling as best he could the moments leading to his fall. "I was learning how to jump when the horse balked, and I went right over him and landed on my head, just like the actor Christopher Reeve."

From the time of impact until he woke up in a hospital bed several days later, Otis had no memory.

But in Buff's version of events—a cornerstone of Chandler family lore—she single-handedly saved her son's life.

"I rushed him to one doctor, who said it was too late—a fatal concussion," she related years later in one of her many interviews about the incident. "But I drove us to Huntington Hospital and, luckily, right inside the emergency entrance I met a doctor who happened to be an old friend. He gave Otis a shot of adrenaline and then there was pulse activity. It was just good fortune and good timing, a mother's persistence and a doctor's knowing what to do. They kept Otis in the hospital for two months."

Harry Chandler joined Norman and Buff at Otis's bedside, keeping vigil throughout that first night.

"He visited often during the next two months, and throughout his life the grandchild Harry always inquired about was Otis," Buff remembered. "Without putting it into words, Harry somehow conveyed the idea that he was counting on Otis—as the son of his own oldest son, Norman—to carry on the Chandler tradition."

Having lost so much time in convalescence, Otis had to repeat the third grade. He later maintained that the setback had no effect on him, but from that time forward, he had lost any chance of a normal childhood; indeed, a Chandler suitable for kidnapping who was now a year behind his classmates had limited adventures with other youngsters. Whether it was exploring creek beds or beachcombing; birthday parties or nibbling popcorn at a matinee—all were activities circumscribed by a cautious, overprotective mother who preferred that his playmates be limited to his older sister, a cousin, or a family friend.

Boyhood pal Bob Emmet, the son of Norman's insurance business partner Ed Emmet, recalled a selfish side of the convalescing Otis that became refined, but never diminished over the decades that followed.

"When we were both about this high," he said, holding a hand four feet off the ground, "we played cowboys, with guns and knives, but we only had one cowboy hat. So he kept the hat and gave me some damn thing to wear that was awful. He'd have two pistols while I had a little rubber knife. And even at that age, I recognized that this was a guy who had to be able to say, 'I have everything good, and you don't.'"

Otis shot backyard basketball hoops by himself, learned how to fire a pellet rifle solo at dove and quail in the Sierra Madre foothills and on the Tejon Ranch,

and pursued such solitary interests as collecting stamps and Dixieland phonograph records. His sister Mia (so nicknamed because he couldn't pronounce Camilla as a toddler), also lived a sheltered existence. As they grew up, the siblings became best friends in part because they had few other choices.

Otis's happiest memories of grammar school days were at the beach house that the family occupied on Alamitos Bay in Long Beach. There, his other grandfather, C. A. Buffum, was a small-town version of Harry Chandler, having founded the Beckoneers, a Long Beach booster club patterned along the lines of Chandler's Year Round Club. As mayor, Buffum also pushed successfully for the creation of a deepwater harbor at Long Beach, right next door to the Port of Los Angeles, which General Otis and his *Times* had fought for back in the 1890s.

But the jovial Buffums differed markedly from the stiff and formal Chandlers, especially in the eyes of a small boy.

"They hugged," Otis recalled. "My other relatives never hugged."

On the shores of Alamitos Bay, Otis had his first taste of a future passion.

"My sister was older when she learned how to bodysurf. I was probably six or seven," Otis recalled. "We graduated to little red, short, rubber inflatable belly boards . . . almost the same size as us. That was my first experience of riding any kind of a surf board and riding any kind of wave."

Home movies mark Otis Chandler's progression from inflatable belly board to the kind of hundred-pound long board favored by surfing pioneers such as Duke Kahanamoku. The first board was made of balsa, lemon tree, and redwood and stood slightly taller than the blond, wavy-haired boy who stood next to it. The board had a reverse swastika imprinted on it—the trademark of the surf board company that manufactured it and a relic of pre–World War II America.

"That was the first time I learned to ride [and] to stand up on a wave," Otis said.

Home movies show that the next board was bigger, longer, and heavier; Otis was filmed dragging the thick slab across the sand, clamoring aboard in the water, and paddling out into the Alamitos Bay channel, which was bordered by deadly rocks on one side and serene stretches of beach on the other. Those early films captured the boy's thin, pre-adolescent body as he stood atop his board for a few seconds of mist and wind blowing across his face and bare chest. When the ride was over, there was always the inevitable plunge into the saltwater when the wave ebbed. The brief experience became a kind of metaphor for the future risk taking and thrill seeking that became part of his occasionally reckless life.

He didn't deny death, but he did defy it. Even as a small boy, in the Los Feliz Hills behind the Chandlers' first house, Otis recalled shooting down the steep streets on his Flexi-Racer, a four-wheeled belly board steered by hand. When the streets close to home were no longer challenging, he moved on to steeper, more

dangerous hills, climaxing in a spectacular death-defying ride down the twisting two-lane road that led from the Griffith Park Planetarium to the park below.

Otis never attended a funeral in his preteen years, although Norman's oldest sister Francesca and her husband, John Kirkpatrick, as well as Moses and Emma Chandler and C. A. Buffum all passed away during the 1930s. He also never attended church with any regularity. When he was a young man and the time came for him to fill out various military, college, and employment forms that called for a declaration of religious denomination, Otis had to ask his father what to fill in; only then did he learn that he was nominally a Congregationalist.

By default, the outdoors and the ocean became a kind of church to Otis Chandler. He saw his first dead man there—a hapless swimmer who had challenged the sea and lost; when his lifeless body washed up on the sand, helpless friends and strangers gathered round in grief and consternation. Otis was only nine or ten at the time, but the moment didn't frighten him.

His parents might have sheltered Otis and his sister from the rituals of death and the weekly sermons preached from the pulpit of the First Congregational Church, but Otis understood his mortality. He embraced it. The moments of rising up and standing atop the big wave were fleeting and few, but they were the moments worth living for. It was a better creed to live by than any religious dogma.

HARRY CHANDLER'S ARISTOCRATIC GRIP around the throat of L.A.'s vox populi had already loosened by the mid-1930s, but the EPIC campaign—polemical novelist Upton Sinclair's plan to "End Poverty in California"—accelerated that release.

Since 1915, Sinclair—the prolific author of popular social reform novels such as *The Jungle* (1906)—had lived in patrician Pasadena, amid the cousins, in-laws, and business associates of the Chandler clan. During Sinclair's first year in California, his reputation bought him an especially nasty epithet from General Otis—a clear sign that Sinclair represented a threat to the *Times'* sleepy status quo.

"This slim, beflanneled example of perverted masculinity" was an anarchist, according to the General. In the early 1920s, when California's Criminal Syndicalism Act made virtually any kind of union action a felony, the *Times* mounted a failed campaign to have the professorial socialist imprisoned. The newspaper commended LAPD Chief Louis D. Oakes for arresting Sinclair after he had read from the U.S. Constitution at a public rally.[2] The arrest didn't stick, nor did Harry Chandler's vicious diatribes. Sinclair answered them all with his

own defiant but gracefully understated description of the *Times* as "the fountain-head of so much unloveliness in California life."

Upton Sinclair had moved to New York from his native Maryland in the late nineteenth century; he was a descendent of exiled Southern plantation aristocracy, but he forged an early identity with the working class. By the time he had worked his way through Columbia University by writing dime novels, he had become a passionate lifelong socialist whose dim view of corporate America's amoral greed shone from the pages of his books. *The Jungle* was so effective an indictment of Chicago's unsafe, unsanitary meatpacking industry that it led to the creation of the U.S. Food and Drug Administration. Hailed as America's most effective communicant of social conscience since Harriet Beecher Stowe, Sinclair's popularity might have seemed a fair match for Harry Chandler's *Times.*

But when Sinclair and his EPIC crusade became serious threats to the continued reign of Republican governor Frank Merriam, the gloves came off and fair-to-a-fault Upton Sinclair learned firsthand what it felt like to be bare-knuckled by Harry and Norman Chandler. The Chandlers' *Times* joined Hearst's *Examiner* and *Herald Express* in a campaign "remarkable for the venom, duplicity and sheer terror it produced," wrote historian John Weaver.

Even Sinclair, a novice politician, was surprised when he received more votes than his seven Democratic opponents combined in the California gubernatorial primary of 1934. Political scientists attributed the Upton upset to the perpetual threat of economic ruin that had hung over the state like a toxic storm cloud since the 1929 stock market crash. Otherwise prosaic Democrats had become angry radicals when California's record for home mortgage foreclosures and unemployment soared, with 300,000 out of work in Los Angeles alone. Dozens of labor protests ground industry to a halt—even in the Chandlers' L.A.—including a maritime walkout that shut down the Pacific Coast and led to a general strike in San Francisco.

Ironically, Sinclair's EPIC plan called for an updated version of the late Job Harriman's Llano del Rio experiment, with state-subsidized industrial and agricultural communes working hand in hand with private enterprise to offer jobs to anyone who wanted to work.

"To me, the remedy was obvious," Sinclair recalled in his autobiography. "The factories were idle and the workers had no money. Let them be put to work on the state's credit and produce goods for their own use, and set up a system of exchange by which the goods could be distributed. 'Production for use,' was the slogan."

As Sinclair's gubernatorial bid gathered unexpected steam, the *Times'* usual Red-baiting rhetoric accelerated to editorial screeds of breathtaking inaccuracy,

warning that "public enemy" Upton Sinclair would "sovietize California and destroy her business and industry."

The future managing editor of the *New York Times,* Turner Catledge, then a young reporter who was sent to California to cover the campaign, described the Democrats' candidate as a "quiet, slight figure, with a pleasant smile constantly on his lips, suggesting inner certainty rather than humor or political winsomeness."

Radio evangelist and Chandler ally Aimee Semple McPherson, however, saw "the red devil" in Sinclair and damned him as such to her vast listening audience. Harry Chandler saw in EPIC the worst form of unionism. In addition to pounding Sinclair daily in his *Times,* Harry mobilized his California Club money militia to swell Governor Merriam's reelection war chest.

He also helped hire the powerhouse Chicago advertising firm Lord and Thomas to develop a media blitz designed to bury Sinclair. Highway billboards echoed Sister Aimee's sentiment of California as hell on earth if Sinclair were to be elected. One political ad bluntly defined "Sinclairism" as "Communism, cleverly disguised . . . rooted in class hatred, fostered and fomented by radicals who boast of their hatred of American ideals and American principles of government."

Published in Republican newspapers throughout the state, the ad continued:

It will destroy California's business structure, bankrupt our families, overthrow our organized labor, confiscate our homes, wreck our industries, and rob our employed workers of their employment. Your personal security is at issue—the welfare of your home and family; your American citizenship, your rights of self-rule and freedom of worship—your job and your independence.

But MGM mogul Louis B. Mayer leveled the most effective smear against Sinclair's EPIC in the closing weeks of the campaign when he filled matinee screens up and down the state with manufactured invective. Basing a series of phony newsreel interviews on a distorted *Times* headline that read HEAVY RUSH OF IDLE SEEN BY SINCLAIR—TRANSIENT FLOOD EXPECTED, the studio staged man-on-the-street interviews with actors who wore Ukrainian whiskers and spoke with forced Russian accents; in their "interviews," they applauded Sinclair's effort to turn California into a proletarian paradise for millions of unemployed Americans. The same newsreel featured an aged widow—also an actress—who said she planned to vote against Sinclair for fear a flood of Okies would overrun the state, bankrupt her, and force her to lose her house.

"The most effective footage," wrote Weaver, "focused on Central Casting hobos huddled on the borders of California, waiting to live off the bounty of its taxpayers once Sinclair got elected."

The architect behind the brilliant MGM smear worked for the Chandlers, but was on temporary loan to Louis Mayer throughout the gubernatorial campaign. On one of his last nights in California, the *New York Times'* Catledge had dinner with the guttersniping genius of the anti-Sinclair effort—*Los Angeles Times* political editor Kyle Palmer. When Catledge asked why the *Times* carried no news of Sinclair, including where or how the candidate could be seen and heard, Palmer sighed, rolled his eyes, and told Catledge to "forget it."

"We don't go in for that kind of crap that you have back in New York of being obliged to print both sides," Palmer told him. "We're going to beat this son of a bitch Sinclair any way we can. We're going to kill him."

And they did. Not even President Roosevelt, the nation's No. 1 Democrat, endorsed Sinclair.

Yet, despite the overwhelming opposition, Upton Sinclair received 879,537 votes—most of them in Los Angeles. He might even have won had a third party not been on the ticket. Progressive Party candidate Raymond Haight, whose social reform platform resembled Sinclair's, received 302,519 votes; Governor Merriam's winning tally came to only 1,138,620.

Sinclair quit politics following his EPIC defeat. He dabbled in moviemaking and mental telepathy for a few years, returning to fiction with *Dragon's Teeth*, a novel that detailed Germany's descent into Nazism, and won him the Pulitzer Prize for fiction in 1943. In 1953, he moved from Pasadena to Arizona, where he died in 1968 at the age of ninety .

Upton Sinclair's Los Angeles legacy persisted long after his retirement from politics. Despite its overwhelming advantage in money and resources, the *Times* juggernaut was almost stalled by a single intellectual with a good and timely plan for easing human misery. Harry Chandler's political omnipotence had been tested and found vulnerable.

"LIKE TO VISIT A WHOREHOUSE?"

LAPD commander Bradford J. St. Charles sprang the surprise question on a reporter and a photographer employed by the *Times* late in a routine squad car ride along one evening in 1934, leaving the pair giddy and a little embarrassed, but certainly interested. St. Charles parked in front of a two-story building in a nondescript Hollywood neighborhood and guided the *Times*men up the outside stairwell to a side porch where he rang the bell. While the journalist poised his pencil and the photographer got ready to snap a candid shot, the madam greeted the dapper cop with the Clark Gable mustache as if he were a relentless bill collector:

"Officer St. Charles!" she snarled. "I paid you last week."

After she slammed the door, St. Charles turned, shrugged, and smiled guiltily. The mortified cop drove the *Times*men back to the precinct and the reporter raced off in his own car to the *Times*. But if he thought he was going to get a bonus for writing up this astonishing and incriminating incident, he was mistaken. *Times* editor L. D. Hotchkiss stopped him as he rolled paper into his typewriter and told him the *Times* would print no such story. A prostitute's payoff to a cop was routine stuff.

"Inconsequential," sniffed Hotchkiss.

L.A. in the mid-1930s was a bit more sophisticated than it had been in the 1920s, but it was just as much a haven for whores, pimps, con men, and gamblers. Only the police/city hall middleman role had grown more refined, intimate, and low-key. The city still played host to such renowned madams as Lee Francis, who had served champagne and caviar to visiting vice officers throughout the Roaring Twenties, and Ann Forrester, a.k.a. "The Black Widow," who took her nickname from her incriminating address book. Forrester's little black book contained the names and private phone numbers of many of the city's business elite as well as the LAPD brass, Commander St. Charles's among them.

But St. Charles's name would never see print in the *Los Angeles Times* just because he took protection money from prostitutes. The *Times* finally printed St. Charles's name after he stepped so far over the legal line that even L. D. Hotchkiss could not ignore him. A few months after Hotchkiss killed the brothel payoff story, Asa Keyes's successor, District Attorney Buron Fitts, indicted Commander St. Charles as chief informant for a gang of bank robbers; only then did the *Times* dutifully report that St. Charles would spend the next fifteen years in San Quentin.

Throughout the 1930s, the administrations of two succeeding mayors—John C. Porter (1929–1933) and Frank Shaw (1933–1938)—were riddled with corruption, payoffs, and vice, yet it took a citizens' successful recall effort against Mayor Shaw to shame the *Times* into reluctantly acknowledging municipal hanky-panky.

The bridge between the Porter and Shaw administrations was LAPD Chief James Davis. After his triumph over George Cryer in the 1929 election, Mayor Porter demoted "Two-Gun" Davis, a marksman who loved to show off his pistol-popping handiwork, to overseer of the Traffic Bureau: punishment for being a Cryer loyalist. But with the full support of the *Times* and the *Times*-sanctioned police commission, Davis rose once again to head the nation's most corrupt big city police force following Mayor Porter's ouster in 1933.

Porter's successor, Los Angeles County supervisor Frank Shaw, was a pudgy ex–grocery clerk from Joplin, Missouri, with a pencil-thin mustache, a swelling midriff, and a weak mouth. He had claimed Canadian citizenship during World War I to avoid the draft; the *Times* discovered the fraud and threatened to use it

against him following his election. *Times* crime reporter Al Nathan, Harry Chandler's hatchet man, had assembled a thick file tracing Shaw's career from neighborhood ward heeler to city council to board of supervisors to the mayor's office, all in less than twenty years—with plenty of canceled checks from hoods and bootleggers along the way. By the time he had reached the top of L.A.'s political ladder, Shaw had perfected the patronage game. Although the *Times* had supported the Bible-banging hypocrisy of Mayor Porter over challenger Shaw in the 1933 election, the new mayor knew better than to continue a grudge match with Harry Chandler. When the *Times* said that it wanted James Davis and his Red Squad back in LAPD headquarters, Mayor Shaw declared that Davis was definitely his kind of police chief—a man who could be as belligerent to bums as he was blind to vice. Presto! Al Nathan's file on Shaw disappeared.

From the reinstatement of Chief Davis forward, the *Times* applauded Mayor Shaw's ability to balance the city budget while living like a rajah; the mayor managed his lavish lifestyle through layoffs and savage cuts to city services at the same time he graciously accepted graft from both the business community and an equally grateful underworld. Shaw could not have kept his well-oiled machine running without full cooperation from the LAPD; this was accomplished through the efforts of Shaw's chief aide-de-camp and younger brother, Joe Shaw. The younger Shaw ran an LAPD boutique right out of his city hall office: plum jobs, crib sheets for the LAPD's promotional exams, and hard-to-get Depression-era raises in rank and salary, all for sale to the highest bidder.

Chief Davis never complained as long as he had autonomy over his LAPD and got his cut of the Shaws' plunder. Parroting the Chandler line, the newly reinstated chief regularly suspended civil rights when it came to protecting the *Times'* White Spot against communists, Chicanos, Okies, Negroes, Japanese, and labor agitators. Davis arbitrarily threw up roadblocks from time to time, just to roust motorists who might look suspicious, and created his personal LAPD Intelligence Division to spy on the enemies of city hall. This division, headed by an LAPD captain whose dubious repute rivaled that of the mayor, was the undoing of Davis, most of his subordinates, and the entire Shaw administration; it also served as a wake-up call to the laissez-faire newsroom policies of L. D. Hotchkiss and the *Los Angeles Times.*

The captain's name was Earle E. Kynette; his career as a sworn peace officer was as crassly cavalier and oblivious to individual rights as mayor Shaw's career as a public servant. A craggy, misshapen former pharmacist who had once worked for L.A.'s brothel meister Albert Marco, Kynette had already been fired and re-hired once since his graduation from the police academy in 1925. Like Commander St. Charles, Kynette had been caught shaking down prostitutes, but in the days before mayor Shaw, a vice officer could be suspended and/or dis-

charged for dunning whores. Fortunately for Kynette, LAPD standards had dropped since Chief Davis's reinstatement.

Before his promotion to head Chief Davis's Intelligence Division, Kynette had already achieved considerable distinction as a featured player in the chief's Bum Blockade at the California border. In a scene straight out of *The Grapes of Wrath,* Kynette took sadistic pleasure in slapping around Dust Bowl immigrants at the California/Arizona border and sending them packing back to Oklahoma along Route 66. He slapped with impunity until he mistook former Hollywood movie director John Langan for an Okie. Langan, who'd quit Hollywood to become a miner in Arizona, sued the LAPD in federal court. When the suit came up for trial, however, Langan mysteriously dropped his complaint. Subsequent news stories named Kynette as Chief Davis's strong-arm messenger and accused him of harassing Langan and his wife until they ended their pursuit of justice.

An aura of invincibility settled over Chief Davis's LAPD and his two special units: the venerable antiunion Red Squad and Captain Kynette's newer but equally insular Intelligence Division. In 1935, a U.S. Senate investigation revealed that L.A.'s businessmen had paid $145,000 to the Red Squad the previous year for after-hours strikebreaking, yet nothing was done about it. Kynette's Intelligence Division gathered damning information on city hall's enemies without interference. Meanwhile, Joe Shaw had transformed a third LAPD unit—the Vice Squad—into his personal collection agency. One detective of no particular distinction had been clearing more than $50,000 a year in vice-connected income, according to a police commission inquiry that followed the eventual collapse of the Shaw administration.

The collapse was a long time coming, however. It took a little-known restaurateur, a maverick superior court judge, and a small organization of angry young businessmen to bring down the Shaw/Davis machine. In 1937, dour and dubious Judge Fletcher Bowron appointed sober, square-jawed Clifford Clinton to the Los Angeles County grand jury. Clinton's mandate: Clean up city hall.

The son of Salvation Army officers, Clinton made a name for himself during the Depression by opening a string of low-cost cafeterias that served thousands of patrons. At one point, during the darkest hours of the Depression years, Clinton turned his eateries into virtual soup kitchens with a "pay whatever you think the meal is worth" policy. A teetotaler and unabashed do-gooder, Clinton had made a name for himself by organizing CIVIC (Citizens Independent Vice Investigating Committee), which affiliated five hundred business, church, and public organizations in a crusade to stop municipal corruption. Aided by the Minute Men, another activists' group that the *Times* openly condemned as political opportunists,[3] CIVIC hired a former San Diego police chief named Harry Raymond to get the goods on Mayor Shaw.

When Clinton and two other grand jury renegades filed their public report in 1937 showing some of the results of Raymond's investigation, the war of words in the pages of the *Times* and inside city hall heated up. Los Angeles had six hundred brothels, two hundred gambling houses, and 1,800 bookie joints according to the report, most operating with the connivance, or at least the tacit approval, of Mayor Shaw and Chief Davis.

Besides being vilified by city hall, the LAPD, and the *Times,* Clinton also suffered the wrath of District Attorney Buron Fitts.[4] Even Clinton's own grand jury foreman said the cafeteria owner was out of control and labeled him "Public Enemy No. 1." Shortly after the release of his report, Clinton's taxes climbed almost $7,000 a year, his family received death threats, and mysterious patrons left stink bombs in his restaurants. Nonetheless, Clinton continued to speak out against the Shaw régime until October 18, 1937, when his crusade climaxed with an explosion: Someone planted a bomb in the basement of Clinton's Los Feliz home, just a few blocks from Harry Chandler's mansion. Although no one was hurt, the damage was extensive.

Clinton would not be intimidated. He found allies in *Times* rivals like the *Hollywood Citizen News* and the liberal *Daily News,*[5] which gladly printed names and photos of the brothels and casinos that Clinton pinpointed for them on a map of Los Angeles. But Mayor Shaw's war of suppression had not yet peaked.

On the morning of January 14, 1938, CIVIC investigator Harry Raymond climbed into his car and turned the ignition. His car exploded, nearly killing him. With 125 pieces of shrapnel in Raymond's body and a poor prognosis for survival, he asked his doctors to call for his friend Jimmy Richardson, the newly named city editor of Hearst's *Examiner.*

"Who did it, Harry?" Richardson asked immediately upon reaching his bedside.

"That son of a bitch Earle Kynette," Raymond whispered.

For three months, Raymond said, Captain Earle Kynette had been following him.

"I've known for weeks he and his boys were shadowing me," he said. "They had my phone tapped. Somewhere in the neighborhood you'll find where they had their listening device. Kynette takes his orders from city hall and they wanted me out of the way. He's the one who rigged the bomb."

Richardson broke the story in the following morning's *Examiner*, only to see it pooh-poohed at first in the *Times*. A *Times* editorial warned that an investigation would be bad for business, especially tourism: "Has it ever occurred to any of the instigators of this Roman holiday that we are making ourselves slightly ridiculous? As large cities go, Los Angeles has heretofore enjoyed a pretty good name in the country at large. We have spent considerable money trying to maintain and deserve that reputation. Even from the sordid commercial standpoint, it is one of our chief assets."

But as the days passed and the evidence pointed more and more towards a pipe bomb built and placed in Raymond's car by Earle Kynette himself, even the *Times*' support of the Shaw régime began to fade. The Chandlers continued to give Chief Davis and the mayor more room than any other L.A. newspaper to rail against Clifford Clinton, but as public outcry blossomed into public outrage, the *Times* and its allies, including D.A. Fitts, reluctantly turned against city hall.

Chief Davis declared Kynette innocent after a week-long departmental investigation. He placed Kynette in charge of getting to the bottom of the bombing, even suggesting that Raymond might have set off the dynamite as a publicity ploy and misjudged the size of the explosion.

But Fitts's investigators found differently and less than a month after the bombing a grand jury indicted Kynette and two other Intelligence Division officers for attempted murder. By summer, Kynette and one of the other officers indicted with him were on their way to San Quentin, sentenced to spend the next decade in the company of former LAPD commander St. Charles and several hundred other felons.

The drama was far from over, however. In April, the same month Kynette's trial began, Clinton's CIVIC supporters collected 119,000 signatures on recall petitions. District Attorney Fitts's grand jury indicted city council president Howard Davis for bribery and Joe Shaw on sixty-six counts of corruption. The judge in Kynette's case repeatedly slammed Chief Davis for his convenient loss of memory on the witness stand. The only thing the chief appeared to recall for certain was that he did not order Harry Raymond's assassination.

The *Times*' editorials degenerated into a voice evocative of General Otis with a bad case of bronchial pneumonia. The newspaper would never back down completely from its support of Chief Davis and Mayor Shaw, but the arguments grew weaker and more ludicrous with each new day's edition. The *Times* even bought Shaw's shrill argument that L.A.'s underworld was responsible for the recall election: "There may or may not be grounds for the Mayor's countercharge that the real inspiration for the recall move comes from the vice interests themselves. But there is no doubt that the astute gentlemen of the green cloth and the honky-tonk will be able to make considerable hay for themselves while their erstwhile pursuers are playing politics."

On election day the following September, the *Times* alone of all Los Angeles newspapers, Republican or Democrat, endorsed Frank Shaw. He went down to a two-to-one defeat and was replaced by Fletcher Bowron, the same superior court judge who had appointed Clifford Clinton to the grand jury.

"One thing I want to make clear: Harry will *never* call me Fletch," Bowron told his supporters. It was an obvious and snide reference to the catchphrase that marked former Mayor George Cryer's successful race against the *Times*-endorsed

Judge Benjamin "Harry Calls Him Ben" Bledsoe thirteen years earlier and drew an appreciative roar from the election-night crowd.

"Just because Chandler has $60 million on the newspaper is no sign he can run this town," the new mayor continued defiantly. "He wants the kind of government he can control directly or indirectly. He can't control me, and if he attacks me, I'm not going to take it lying down."

Shaw ran once more in 1941, as did former mayor John C. Porter, but ran dead last in a field of four candidates. He took up real estate, the trade that had made Harry Chandler rich, but with far less success. He died little more than a pauper in 1958 with his brother Joe and a new twenty-seven-year-old wife at his bed side. Shaw was eighty.

As for Chief Davis, Bowron forced him into early retirement within a month of the election and fired 116 other Shaw appointments before the year was out. All told, the LAPD lost forty-five ranking officers during Bowron's first year in office. To add insult to injury, Bowron also dissolved the LAPD's Intelligence Division and Harry Chandler's beloved Red Squad.

The former chief went to work as chief of security at Douglas Aircraft briefly, then moved in with his mother, where he lived a sedentary life and swelled to 250 pounds. He succumbed to a stroke in 1949 at the age of sixty. In his *Times* obituary, there was no mention of any of the scandals that had plagued his administration, the vicious border blockades, the Gestapo tactics of his Intelligence and Red Squads, or Earle Kynette's final abuse of power that toppled Davis and the Frank Shaw régime.

THE CLERKS OF THE MAY COMPANY department store celebrated Christmas in 1937 with a strike for higher wages and better working conditions. For nearly a year, they had been trying to get more than $0.30 an hour from the successor to Hamburger's Department Store, but the new owners were as adamant about dealing with unions as the old. In the end, their strike raised nothing more than the ire of their friends and neighbors, thanks in large part to the *Times.*

While short-lived, the walkout illustrated just how little had changed in General Otis's antiunion L.A. during the half century since the first publisher of the *Times* had declared war on organized labor. In its coverage of the May Company strike, *Times* headlines described the demand for better wages as the "Assassination of Santa Claus" and "Murder of the Spirit of Christmas." That both Hearst papers were equally biased against the clerks was not surprising; but the liberal *Daily News* also disparaged the strike. The unifying factor among all the Los Angeles dailies was a full-page May Company ad they carried heralding the Christmas shopping season—precious revenue that no one, not even the mav-

erick *Daily News* publisher Manchester Boddy, was prepared to sacrifice to any union cause.

When it came to labor unions, the *Los Angeles Times* hadn't changed a jot since Norman Chandler began easing himself into position to become its third publisher. If he had made any policy shifts since graduating to *Times* general manager in September 1936, they were subtle and internal. In 1937, he created the first personnel department of any American newspaper and hired labor management expert Paul Bell to run it. The mandate remained the same for another half century: Hire the best people at wages as high as or higher than current union wages and do whatever was reasonable to keep the workers happy. Thus, when the May Company clerks walked out, no cry of solidarity rang from the rafters of Times Mirror Square. The same week that the *Times* was slamming the strike on its front page, Norman Chandler had signed off on $197,000 in Christmas bonuses for the loyal employees of his *Los Angeles Times*.

Times employees developed an almost fraternal relationship under Harry Chandler's heir apparent that was unique among the traditionally itinerant, fickle, yet driven lifestyle of men and women who made their livelihood in the newspaper trade. Reporters were still hard-drinking cynics and pressmen were still ink-stained stoics, but there existed an unmatched esprit de corps fostered by Norman Chandler's enlightened, almost paternalistic attitude toward his workers. A monthly employee newsletter, appropriately called *Among Ourselves*, announced promotions, retirements, births, and deaths. Annual family events, like the *Times* employees' picnic and the retirees' banquet, further unified "the *Los Angeles Times* family," as Norman liked to call his people. For its part, the *Times* provided a cafeteria, medical insurance, a pension plan, and office space for the Pfaffinger Foundation,[6] a special emergency fund for employees—all considered routine employee benefits in corporate America during the second half of the century, but highly unusual in the late 1930s and 1940s.

Shortly after he founded the American Newspaper Guild in 1933, *New York Tribune* columnist Heywood Broun met Norman at an American Newspaper Publisher s Association convention. An outspoken union firebrand, Broun still hit it off with the amiable and easygoing son of *Los Angeles Times* publisher Harry Chandler. Norman struck Broun as being far more reasonable than his legendary grandfather or his stubbornly antiunion father. After a few friendly drinks, Broun proposed a wager. He handed Chandler a dollar, and gave him five-to-one odds that he'd turn the *Times* into a Guild newspaper within five years.

Just before his death in 1939, Broun ran into Norman Chandler at another convention. He handed him a $5 bill without comment.

Had he paid a visit to the *Times*, Broun might have bet differently. Norman's genuine affection for his employees gave the *Times* a stability that could with-

stand a world war, a cold and troubled peacetime, and a subsequent and remarkable expansion in Southern California that would supersede even the past eras of unprecedented L.A. growth that Harry and General Otis had nurtured.

Yet the blessings of Norman's extended *Times* family would eventually prompt conflict within his own family, thanks in large part to Harry Chandler's will.

After illness took him away from the *Times* for several weeks in 1935, Harry's health began a downward spiral in the late 1930s. He became frail, his robust baby face thinning to a gaunt, grandfatherly visage. His prominent and piercing brown eyes receded into his skull and peered out through thick glasses, and his broad "howdy!" smile had been reduced to a thin, pale line between nose and chin. Foreseeing his end, the universally acknowledged patriarch of both Los Angeles and the *Times* took steps to do the unthinkable: sell the *Los Angeles Times.*

In 1935, attorneys for the *New York Daily News* and *Chicago Tribune*, which were jointly owned by cousins Captain Joseph Medill Patterson and Colonel Robert McCormick, contacted former Los Angeles Superior Court judge Isaac Pacht with a proposition: If Harry Chandler was willing to sell, the Captain and the Colonel would pay $16 million in cash for Chandler's *Times.*

It was no idle proposal and Harry did not take it as such. He had serious doubts about Norman's active interest in the day-to-day operation of the *Times* and felt that neither of his other two sons were capable of stepping into his shoes. Pacht met privately with Harry several times at his Hillhurst home before Chandler came up with the $16-million asking price. To his surprise, McCormick and Patterson agreed to pay it almost immediately.

In 1935, the *New York Daily News* and *Chicago Tribune* may have been among the most reviled right-wing newspapers in America, but they were also among the most profitable and each was operated by the last of a colorful breed of maverick publishers who were cast from the same mold as General Harrison Gray Otis.

Publisher of the *Tribune* since 1911, Colonel McCormick had developed at least as brash and idiosyncratic a reputation as General Otis. He drove to work each day in a bulletproof chauffeur-driven coupe with his pet German shepherd in the seat next to him. At six feet four inches and more than two hundred pounds, he even bore a slight resemblance to the late General; he took his military title and service with such absolute seriousness that his behavior all but demanded parody. Each New Year's Day, in a ritual reminiscent of General Otis's quasi-military ceremonies, Colonel McCormick stood at attention in the *Tribune* lobby and shook the hand of each employee as he or she walked into the building to begin another year of reporting the news.

"He liked to crack the whip and watch the serfs march by," quipped one editor.

Despite the easy sarcasm, his staff felt a kinship and warmth for the Colonel's fierce loyalty to his employees and his unwavering support for the First

Amendment. Biased or not, McCormick assiduously defended his newspaper from outside influence and backed his people against all external attacks.

"Like a benevolent Ebenezer Scrooge, he was the author of our feasts, and mighty good eating it was, too," said a longtime *Tribune* reporter.

Once, when a wealthy department store owner filed to divorce his wife, he asked the *Tribune* editors to downplay the story. McCormick was called at home and asked what to do—the department store owner, after all, was a major advertiser.

"Keep the story and throw out the advertising," McCormick ordered. "A kept newspaper is like a kept woman: no good."

The department store owner groused for a few weeks, but came back hat in hand. To reach his customers, he had to advertise in the *Tribune.*

"The minute I become friendly with a man, he wants me to keep his divorce out of the paper or something," McCormick complained indignantly. "The newspaper publisher who hangs around clubs or becomes a crony to sundry businessmen cannot run a good newspaper."

His cousin's tabloid, the *New York Daily News,* held a similar philosophy, although it was originally rooted in a slightly less virulent conservatism than the *Tribune.* Before Joseph Medill Patterson and McCormick worked side by side at the *Tribune* in the years before World War I, Patterson had been a novelist and playwright in New York, which had several competing newspapers including Hearst's *New York Journal.* None of them, however, were edited or printed in the style of the European tabloids, which catered to the working class. During the war, when the cousins were serving in France, Patterson proposed just such a tabloid for New York. In a legendary meeting with McCormick on a manure pile in the backyard of a farmhouse near the Ourcq River, Captain Patterson conceived the idea of the *New York Daily News*: It would be heavy on photos and illustrations, have thick black headlines that rampaged against everything from clairvoyants to loan sharks, and feature a little cheesecake on its front pages.

"The *Daily News* was built on legs, but when we got enough circulation, we draped them," Patterson said several years after his tabloid hit the streets on June 26, 1919.

By 1935, the *Daily News* and the *Tribune* were the largest circulated newspapers in the nation's two largest cities, respectively. Adding Harry Chandler's *Times* to their stable would give the Captain and the Colonel a lock on the nation's third-largest city as well as a presence in the nation's great Southwest—the fastest-growing region of the United States.

The deal was sealed and all that remained was the paperwork, but, as Isaac Pacht described in his memoirs, neither the publishers of the *Daily News* and the *Tribune* nor Harry Chandler had figured on the General's daughter:

To carry out these legal formalities, I arranged a conference with Mr. Chandler at his house. I sat opposite him in his very simple and comfortable living room. He engaged me in much talk about the *Times* and its place in the life of the Los Angeles community, public issues, public personalities, etc. I interrupted his recital by telling him that Col. McCormick and Capt. Patterson were agreeable to paying the $16 million for the *Times* and were prepared to immediately conclude the deal by the execution of the necessary legal documents.

At this point Mrs. Chandler, the daughter of General Harrison Gray Otis, came into the room. She had evidently become aware of the discussions which had taken place between her husband and myself. When she heard that her husband and I were about to enter upon the definitive steps for the sale of the *Times* to the McCormick-Patterson interest, she interrupted us and said to Mr. Chandler:

"Harry, you know that the *Chicago Tribune* and the *New York Daily News* are operated as union shops and if they acquired the *Los Angeles Times* the unions will compel them to make the *Los Angeles Times* a union shop. If that happened, my father will never forgive you. Do not sell the *Los Angeles Times* to the McCormick-Patterson interests or anyone who will permit the *Los Angeles Times* to be unionized."

After a few more pleasantries the conference terminated and that ended the negotiations for the purchase of the *Los Angeles Times*.

Following the near sale of his *Times,* Harry gave serious reconsideration to how he would go about passing his newspaper and his fortune to his growing pool of heirs. Because of fears that had been articulated by Marian—that his *Times* might fall into the wrong hands, perhaps even union hands—he created a complex set of secret family trusts, modeled in part after those of John D. Rockefeller. The two Harry Chandler trusts that became effective in 1938 would ensure that his enormous wealth, including an estimated 1.5 million acres in real estate alone, would not be destroyed by inheritance taxes or the inevitable infighting amongst his heirs. What was of equal importance, the trusts would preserve the conservative autonomy of the *Los Angeles Times*, provided Norman could bring his own energy and enthusiasm to running a great metropolitan daily.

The offspring of Harry and Marian Chandler's six children and May Goodan, the last living child of Harry and Magdalena,[7] were to control Times Mirror's voting stock through a wholly owned family subsidiary called Chandis Securities. As the eldest son, Norman was the first chairman of the board of eight family trustees and, as such, became chief guardian of the family fortune—a responsibility he took as seriously as his stewardship at the *Times*.

On February 26, 1941, the masthead of the *Los Angeles Times* was altered to read:

Times Mirror Company
Norman Chandler
President & General Manager

Looking ever more feeble, Harry Chandler wrapped one bony arm around his eldest son's husky shoulders to make the announcement to the *Times'* 1,761 employees. As expected, Norman was now officially in charge of the newspaper company that he had actually been running for close to a decade. He now had the title to prove it. What was more, said the old man, a rare smile playing over his slim liver-colored lips, Norman Chandler would succeed him as head of the Chandler family.

But there was one title Harry wasn't yet ready to surrender. The only name higher on the new masthead of the *Times* than that of Norman read

Harry Chandler, Publisher

CHAPTER 11

BY 1940, THE *TIMES* EMPLOYED 1,761 PEOPLE who put out 226,395 copies of the paper every day. Under Norman Chandler's leadership, the *Times* was once again leading in a neck-and-neck circulation race with the *Examiner* and soundly defeating both of Hearst's L.A. newspapers in advertising revenue. But as Norman applied his daily efforts to mastering the art of publishing and, finally, taking over for Harry at the *Times,* his cousins, brothers, and sisters lived a very different life. The Chandler women married, usually into the incestuous WASP wealth of Pasadena and its even more exclusive suburb of San Marino, and the Chandler men did their academic turn at Stanford and came to work in largely ceremonial executive positions at Times Mirror.

Norman's younger bachelor brother, Harrison, became general manager of Times Mirror Press, a cash cow that specialized in printing telephone directories, catalogues, maps, annual reports, and brochures. A leading light of L.A.'s ultra-conservative Lincoln Club, Harrison resembled the raw-boned sixteenth U.S.

president, sans beard and stovepipe hat; he spent an inordinate amount of time outside the office, schmoozing with his WASP brethren in Pasadena or talking politics at the California Club or the even more exclusive and secretive Sunset Club.

Philip, the youngest of the Chandlers, was posed to take over as *Times* general manager once Norman became publisher, although he had none of the painfully acquired polish that came from Norman's ten-year apprenticeship under Harry. Philip's own work ethic had been honed on the back nine at Los Angeles Country Club, fed by narcissistic lunches at Cal Tech's exclusive Atheneum Club, and lubricated by frequent California Club cocktails. The smallest and frailest of the Chandler brothers, he was also the most self-conscious of his own dynastic destiny. Given Philip's supercilious self-image, it was with considerable irony that Norman named the youngest Chandler in 1944 to became the first director of Times Charities, forerunner of the *Los Angeles Times* Fund, which raised money for underprivileged youths.

More so than Norman or Buff, Harry Chandler's other in-laws and heirs were likely to put on airs—usually of a Continental pretense or a Boston Brahmin's version of high society. There were charity balls, wine tastings, exclusive retreats, and social registers to occupy their waking hours. Secure in their trust funds, they took up serious English gardening, they planned for the annual Tournament of Roses, and indulged in a gentleman's brand of hunting—the kind that requires foxes and hounds. Pasadena's exclusive Valley Hunt Club may have substituted mangy gray coyotes for plump red foxes, but the baying dogs and traditional pink coats and ascots of picnicking coquettes who followed the hunters at a safe distance remained the same. In what could be mistaken as a sad parody of *Tom Jones*, they pursued their quarry on horseback throughout the arroyos of the San Gabriel Mountains.

Philip and his sisters were the hard core of the exclusive and conservative Pasadena lifestyle, forever sanctioning coming-out parties or such *Ramona*-esque occasions for celebrating a false California past as the annual Las Madrinas Ball. Of course, the organizers of the very sine qua non of the social season were more likely to hire kitchen help and parking valets of a Mexican or mestizo extraction than they were to issue them an invitation to the social debut of young, white gentile women. But the pretense of faux fiesta remained and for the Pasadena crowd, that was enough.

In this rarefied atmosphere, Otis and Camilla Chandler inched their way toward adolescence—Camilla with her show horses and Otis learning ballroom finesse as a reluctant member of Mrs. Goltz's cotillion.

Yet the more relaxed Buffum influence was equally strong, at least until Otis and Camilla were old enough for boarding school. Until 1939, when Norman and

Buff finished building their dream home at Santa Anita Oaks, just east of the stifling Pasadena haute monde, the Chandler children lived in Long Beach, where Otis attended Lowell Elementary School just like any other plebeian towhead. The patrician influence began in the fifth grade when he transferred to Polytechnic Junior High in Pasadena, a tough private school where money and family mattered just as much or more than academic grades and good citizenship awards. In the summer of 1941, after two years at Poly, Otis's life, as well as the lives of everyone in his generation, moved inexorably toward a culture shock that would reverberate throughout the rest of the century. During a late summer family vacation, Otis and his family thought they were savoring a little South Sea leisure, but instead got a foretaste of war.

"By the time we got to Hawaii, I already knew how to surf and so did my sister," Otis recalled. "I was fourteen and she was seventeen."

They sailed to Oahu aboard one of cousin Ralph Chandler's Matson ocean liners and enjoyed a week of adventure: leis, Waikiki, hula girls, poi, luaus, Diamond Head, and, most important of all, miles of cool, curling surf breaking on clean white beaches. Norman brought a 16-millimeter camera to capture home color movies of his children riding the waves. The silent films are one of Otis's treasures more than fifty years later; they show a pencil-thin Otis in baggy trunks and tall, modest Camilla in a one-piece swimsuit as they mingle easily with the beach boys, the natives, and sunburned vacationers. Though they are clearly children of privilege, glistening golden and self-confident in the equatorial sun, an innocence lives in these faded celluloid images too, as if a couple of the younger residents of Eden had found surfboards in their garden along with apples and asps. Near the end of their vacation, the Chandler family visited Pearl Harbor.

"I wasn't a journalist then and I wasn't reading the paper regularly except for the comics and the sports sections," said Otis, recalling that August visit to the largest U.S. naval base in the Pacific, "but I remember this as well as I remember what I did this morning. They were giving Norman Chandler, the publisher of the *Times*, a tour and we came along too. We were his family. There was a lot of brass there wearing their ribbons, medals and stuff."

Rumors were rife in Southern California at the time that Japan was building its air force and already had a formidable navy. As publisher of the *Los Angeles Times,* Norman Chandler felt obligated to ask about the threat.

"'Do you take the Japanese seriously?'" Otis remembered his father asking the officer wearing the most gold braid. "'Why are the Japanese building up such a big fleet? What is going on?' And this guy, whether he was the base commander or whatever, was saying, 'If those little slant-eyed bastards make any incursion

into our waters over here off the west coast of Hawaii, we'll bomb them off the map in one day.'"

One Sunday morning four months later, Otis was out shooting some hoops in the driveway at the Chandlers' Santa Anita Oaks home when his usually imperturbable father rushed out of the house with a troubled expression written in his eyes. He ordered his son indoors.

"We all huddled around the radio," said Otis. "It was a huge shock to all of us."

For Otis Chandler, December 7, 1941, became far more than a day that would live forever in infamy. Pearl Harbor Day marked the beginning of his personal cynicism, especially towards those in authority who made broad promises and sweeping statements that did not hold up over time. It also moved his interest in the *Times* beyond the comics, box scores, and the newspaper's amorphous identity as the source of all Chandler wealth and power.

"I began to follow the war in the *Times*," he said. "I was fascinated by it. I had a little map I tore out of the paper[1] and you could look at the islands, follow the progress. I forget when all the bloody battles were, but I was following the war closely, probably in the sixth or seventh grade, maybe as a class project or something. But I read about it every day."

World War II was the great equalizer. Just like thousands of other housewives, Buff carefully covered the windows each night with dark cloth and doused the porch lights for fear of a sneak attack by the Japs. Complying with U.S. defense restrictions on newsprint consumption, Norman cut *Times* advertising space while keeping editorial space wide open to accommodate a deluge of wartime news. At home, the Chandlers' clout kept the worst hardships at bay, but there was no immunity from gas rationing, air raid drills, or the awful return of the war dead to their families.

Otis recollected that his father's cousin Ralph had a son just a few years older than Otis who loved race cars. Ralph Chandler Jr. gave Otis his first real taste of a lifelong passion by demonstrating for his younger second cousin how Ralph's own souped-up speed wagon could flash over the Pasadena pavement, wheels squealing and cylinders pumping. Ralph Jr. took his love of speed to the air at the outset of the war when he joined the Army Air Corps. He flew off over the Pacific one day and never returned.[2]

Hysteria unique to the West Coast gripped L.A. in the earliest days of the war, tainting even the news coverage with terror. Scare headlines hit the newsstands several times a day, with extras following the latest rumors by mere hours. Through the dim filter of decades, Otis even looks back on the first few months following Pearl Harbor with his own recollection of "a little stinking sub" that

struck the coastline with a "podunk bomb"—a memory that was true enough and borne out by thick, black headlines in the *Times,* although the maverick Japanese submarine that delivered its isolated barrage did so far to the north of L.A.

One such scare that *Times* editor L. D. Hotchkiss and his city desk would never live down happened early in the predawn hours of February 26, 1942. The Army sent out an alert that unidentified aircraft were approaching and defensive ground forces ranged along the Los Angeles coastline were probing the dark western skies with searchlights and firing artillery for nearly two hours. The *Times* put out an extra in the morning under the headline L.A. AREA RAIDED:

> Roaring out of a brilliant moonlit western sky, foreign aircraft flying both in large formation and singly flew over Southern California early today and drew heavy barrages of anti-aircraft fire—the first ever to sound over United States continental soil against an enemy invader.
>
> No bombs were reported dropped. At 5 A.M. the police reported that an airplane had been shot down near 185th St. and Vermont Ave. Details were not available.

The newspaper went on to report that Japanese planes were sighted over Santa Monica, Seal Beach, El Segundo, Redondo Beach, Long Beach, Hermosa Beach, and Signal Hill. It would have been a remarkable scoop over the competition had it been true. Unfortunately, as the *Times'* own whimsical columnist Jack Smith wrote thirty-three years later under the headline THE GREAT LOS ANGELES AIR RAID, "There was no aircraft carrier. There were no Zeros. There were no bombs. There was no raid."

As it turned out, five people did die during the false alarm—three in fatal traffic accidents during the blackout and two from heart attacks suffered while the air raid sirens blared. But the Japanese invasion that everyone believed imminent never happened.

An invasion of another sort did disturb Otis's otherwise pastoral existence in the Pasadena foothills when Loren Thurston, son of the publisher of the *Honolulu Advertiser,* came to stay. A year or two older than Otis, Thurston was invited to live with the Chandlers at Los Tiempos, their seven-acre Santa Anita Oaks ranch, during the early years of the war as a courtesy to Thurston's father. He feared a return of the Japanese air force, this time with their awful hardware aimed at Oahu's largest city, and asked his friend Norman Chandler to watch over his boy until the danger had passed.

Loren was the polar opposite of Otis, however, and any hope that fraternal camaraderie might blossom vanished with the first Lucky Strike.

"He was a big, flabby kid who'd wait until my dad was gone and then go sit under a tree and smoke," said Otis.

Just as Harry had required Norman to do his share of chores at the Tejon Ranch when he was growing up, Norman expected Otis to grunt through his daily allotment of hard physical labor. Getting dirt beneath the nails, aches in the arms, and sweat in the pits built character, Norman said, and he had prescribed a similar regimen for Thurston when the young man moved in. But Thurston only looked busy until all adults were safely out of sight, Otis recollected. When Otis unloaded yet another wheelbarrow full of horse manure onto his father's fruit tree orchard, he resented the sight of his chubby house mate lolling beneath an oak tree with a far-off glaze in his eyes and cigarette smoke billowing like cumulus clouds from the hole in his round face. Norman must have caught on early, but never said anything about it.

"Rich boys who get spoiled don't ever develop the determination to stay with the job," Norman preached in later years. Such lofty philosophizing sailed right over Otis's young head during the Thurston years. All he knew was that he had to work while lunky Loren Thurston didn't.

Los Tiempos was beautiful and peaceful, with only the memories of muted calls from the Santa Anita Race Track announcer Joe Hernandez[3] or the lonely whistle of a Santa Fe locomotive piercing the still foothills air. It was a shame Otis only had a self-indulgent Honolulu haole with whom to share his youthful pastures. He remained as isolated in his early teens as he had been as a child, Camilla his only pal.

His real companions lived more than a dozen miles away, near Pasadena's Polytechnic Junior High where Otis rode his bicycle to school every day. He met Sylvia Morton there—his first bona fide girlfriend and matinee movie date.[4] He graduated from bike to motor scooter by the time he was in the ninth grade. He was not much of a student, but he had the makings of a terrific athlete. When coach lined the boys up for the school's annual boxing championships, Otis was none too keen about beating up on his friends; but once he had on the gloves, he learned something quite surprising about himself .

"I wanted to kill them," he said. "I wanted to knock them out. From the very first competitive athletics that I was in—and I played them all—I wanted to be the best."

His first passion was solitary sports such as the high jump, but that didn't mean Otis was such a loner that he wouldn't play soccer or basketball or some other team sport. Already over six foot tall and thin as a beanpole, he even lettered in soccer, track, and basketball. He just wasn't great in groups. When it came to standing in front of crowds, he was shy. Once, when he had to address the Poly student body, he nearly lost his lunch.

"I almost threw up, I was so nervous," he said.

But Otis got over it and won his parents' approval into the bargain. Buff ordered him to straighten up and remember who he was and what he represented. It would never do to have a Chandler male who grew nauseous every time he had to address the masses.

IN 1937, NEW YORKER HUMORIST and self-described "amateur sociologist" Leo Rosten polled ninety-three members of the Washington press corps to determine the publishers of the "least fair and reliable" newspapers in the United States. When the results were tabulated, the *Los Angeles Times*' Harry and Norman Chandler placed third, behind William Randolph Hearst and the *Chicago Tribune*'s virulent conservative Colonel Robert McCormick. Although the findings were worth a few shirtsleeve chuckles among the East Coast intelligentsia, Rosten's survey had no apparent impact on the worst of the worst. The *Times*, the *Tribune*, and Hearst's stable of yellow dailies remained stubbornly inferior. Norman Chandler had stepped into Harry's mediocre shoes without a hitch.

"We were kind of lopsided in those days," Norman conceded to *Newsweek* in 1967. "If we gave the Republicans a big story, we'd give the Democrats a small one. And we only gave management's side in labor disputes."

Yet, although he took few steps to raise editorial standards, Norman did have some aspirations beyond his father's cash and power priorities. He openly admired an odd triumvirate among American publishers, including both of his "betters" in the Rosten dud derby. Chandler spoke highly to friends and associates about Colonel McCormick's proud bluster and Hearst's tenacity—if not his politics. Perhaps most peculiarly of all, Norman looked up to the day-in, day-out top-notch quality of Arthur Ochs Sulzberger's *New York Times*. Most of the time, the *Los Angeles Times* belonged by default to L. D. Hotchkiss and his gang of Spring Street irregulars. At its occasional best, Norman Chandler's *Los Angeles Times* attempted to emulate Sulzberger's journalism, including the *New York Times*' fierce policy of standing by the First Amendment for the benefit of all American newspaper publishers. The *Times*' own steadfastness to free press and the landmark U.S. Supreme Court decision that followed paved the way for the Chandlers' first Pulitzer Prize.

The day after the bombing of Pearl Harbor, the high court had upheld the *Times*' First Amendment right to ignore a judge's gag order that barred the newspaper from spewing invective at labor unions; the following year, the prestigious Pulitzer Gold Medal for Public Service went to the *Los Angeles Times* "for its successful campaign which resulted in the clarification and confirmation for all

American newspapers of the right of free press as guaranteed under the Constitution."

Although the ailing seventy-eight-year-old Harry Chandler and all three of his sons, especially Norman, savored a proud moment, the award carried a subtle and malodorous ambiguity that left L.A.'s First Family of Industrial Freedom more than a little peevish. Their codefendant in the Supreme Court case that resulted in their first Pulitzer was an avowed socialist, probably a Communist, and certainly the most successful labor organizer in California's history. In a very real sense, the Chandlers had to share their Pulitzer with International Longshoremen & Warehousemen's Union founder and president Harry Bridges.

Australian-born Alfred Renton "Harry" Bridges arrived in California in 1920 at the age of nineteen, raring to make his mark on the San Francisco docks. For the next twelve years, he worked the waterfront as a longshoreman. It was crude but honest work, but over time Bridges witnessed unnecessary death and injury, unjust wage garnishing, and unsubtle favoritism in hiring. As he shed his youthful naïveté and grew increasingly disillusioned with the brutal greed of dockside capitalism, he took up a second profession as a renegade union organizer.

In the 1920s, shipping lines in San Francisco and L.A. controlled the Longshoremen's Association—the so-called Blue Book Union that worked in alliance with employers to keep wages low and turn a blind eye to grievances. At the dawn of the Great Depression, life on the busy San Francisco docks had grown cheap and, under the yoke of the Blue Book Union, it got even cheaper. Average longshoremen's wages dropped to $10.45 a week. Foremen forced crews to double their workload at half the pay. The waterfront was riddled with spies and stool pigeons who happily blacklisted coworkers to ensure their own job security.

After suffering two serious on-the-job injuries and being rebuffed on his own salary demands, Bridges tried to fight back but, as he later testified before the National Labor Relations Board, "I not only didn't get paid, I lost my job in the bargain."

Although he continued to pay dues to the Blue Book Union, Bridges worked feverishly to replace the shipping companies' toady labor organization with his own International Longshoremen's Association. After years of patient organizing, he had a cadre of fellow union activists soliciting new members; their efforts climaxed in the spring of 1934 when waterfront workers successfully picketed ports up and down the West Coast.

At first, shipping executives tried to ignore the picket lines, but the work stoppage grew geometrically as even the most loyal Blue Book Union members left to join Bridges' strike. The picketing gathered steam and extended into the summer; fruit and other perishable cargo rotted on the piers and several companies were driven to take desperate measures. A Northern Californian version of Harry

Chandler's militant Merchant and Manufacturers Association—the San Francisco Industrial Association—at last demanded that the San Francisco police reopen the port by any means necessary.

On July 5, police armed with gas and guns confronted picketers and began firing indiscriminately into their ranks, killing two and wounding over a hundred. Under a headline reading STREETS MADE BATTLEFIELD IN HUNDRED BLOODY RIOTS, the *Times'* San Francisco correspondent Floyd Healey wrote: "Blood ran red in the streets of San Francisco today in the darkest day this community has known since April 18, 1906, when it was scourged by earthquake and fire. One thousand embattled police held at bay 5,000 striking rioters."

Governor Frank Merriam declared martial law along the San Francisco waterfront and called in the National Guard. In the annals of U.S. labor history, the fifth of July is known as "Bloody Thursday."

But Harry Bridges's crusade was far from over. Ignoring warnings from police, more than 40,000 San Francisco strike sympathizers marched in a funeral procession honoring the two dead picketers in the aftermath of Bloody Thursday. The more the authorities threatened to crack down, the louder Bridges's followers demanded reprisal for the police killings and the governor's use of martial law. Eleven days after Bloody Thursday, Bridges declared a three-day general strike; San Francisco was brought to a standstill.

On July 13, the San Francisco Industrial Association struck back again. The Nation magazine characterized what followed as "one of the most harrowing records of brutality to be found outside Hitler's Third Reich." The shipping companies' armed vigilantes swept through the city, looting and destroying union halls; when Bridges's militant followers fought back, police arrested them by the dozen.

Three hundred fifty miles to the south, where the strike had caught on among the longshoremen of Long Beach and San Pedro, the *Los Angeles Times* followed each escalation of the San Francisco street war with shrill alarm and voyeuristic relish. Although similar violence erupted sporadically along the L.A. docks, the *Times* warned that Harry Bridges's full-blown anarchy would never be tolerated in open shop Los Angeles. For once, Harry and Norman Chandler agreed with their arch rival, William Randolph Hearst, who attacked Bridges savagely in his San Francisco and Los Angeles *Examiner*s, labeling the union leader a Communist Australian who deserved arrest and deportation, if not prison.

But Bridges persisted. When confronted by the *Times* and other news media with Hearst's accusations, the union leader would smile coyly and announce in his finest Australian brogue, "I neither affirm or deny that I am a Communist."

Besides, he continued, politics had nothing to do with earning enough to buy a child a sip of milk and a bit of bread, or working on the same unsafe docks where dozens of men died because management refused to fix its faulty cranes, hawsers, and freight elevators.

The *Times* and the *Examiner*s continued their biased reporting and abusive editorials while Bridges stolidly sought and eventually received federal recognition of his union. In 1937, over the loud objections of Hearst and Chandler, the International Longshoremen's & Warehousemen's Union (ILWU) became a legally sanctioned reality and Bridges[5] went on to serve as its president for the next forty years.

His newfound respectability as a legitimate U.S. labor leader notwithstanding, Harry Bridges remained a frequent and favorite *Times* target, which referred to him as a "non-American."[6]

In 1938, when the ILWU president wired a protest to the U.S. Secretary of Labor over yet another attempt—this time at the Port of Los Angeles—to stop his union from striking, the *Times* predictably slammed Bridges on its editorial pages. At the same time, a Los Angeles judge was about to issue an injunction against ILWU picketing. The *Times* reprinted Bridges's telegram as part of its campaign to show that Judge A. A. Scott was right to halt the ILWU picketing; but far from thanking the Chandlers, the judge believed both the *Times* and Harry Bridges were trying in their own ways to influence his ruling.

Judge Scott asked the California Bar Association to intervene. Yes, proclaimed an investigating bar committee, both the *Times* and Bridges were, indeed, trying to wield undue influence. The newspaper and Bridges were slapped with contempt citations.

The bar association did not allow its case against the *Times* to rest on the newspaper's reprinting of Bridges's telegram. The association found five *Times* editorials that had jumped the judicial gun, including a virtual love letter to one judge for convicting twenty-two strikers before they had been sentenced, and a column that urged a judge not to grant clemency for two teamsters convicted of assault. The editorial's headline read: "Probation for Gorillas?"

Norman Chandler decided to fight the contempt citation on grounds that it was a dangerous judicial gag on a free press. During the next three years, Chandler's straitlaced Republican legal team found itself huddling with the strangest of bedfellows—a crew of radical ILWU and American Civil Liberties Union lawyers who were fighting the same contempt charges on behalf of Harry Bridges. The irony was rich: The *Times* demanded the right to disparage Harry Bridges and Harry Bridges demanded the same right to disparage the *Times*. Their common enemy was a hidebound, high-and-mighty judiciary. Every court

found against the Chandlers and Harry Bridges until October 1941, when Norman Chandler's conservative lawyers and Harry Bridges's liberals jointly argued before the U.S. Supreme Court.

Justice Harry Black wrote the five-to-four majority opinion, in which he chided the California Bar Association and the Los Angeles judge for attempting to muzzle his two fellow Harrys—Bridges and Chandler:

"It is a prized American privilege to speak one's mind, although not always with perfect good taste, on all public institutions; an enforced silence, however limited, solely in the name of preserving the dignity of the bench, would engender resentment, suspicion, and contempt much more than it would enhance respect."

Justice Black's decision prompted the popping of champagne corks in the hiring halls of the ILWU and in the executive offices of the *Los Angeles Times.* The single downside for Harry and Norman Chandler was that Justice Black's stirring words would remain cited in legal texts for generations to come, not under the *Los Angeles Times* but, rather, under the name of the toughest "Communist" gorilla ever to emerge from the Australian outback.

The *Times* received its first Pulitzer Prize for fighting on behalf of *Harry Bridges v. State of California/Times-Mirror Co. et al v. Superior Court of State of California, in and for Los Angeles County.*

ON SEPTEMBER 8, 1943, a dark blanket of haze clamped over the L.A. Basin with such stifling totality that motorists had to use their headlights to pilot through midday traffic. In one of the first of many calls-to-arms about the menace of air pollution, the *Times* reported that "thousands of eyes smarted. Many wept, sneezed and coughed. Throughout the downtown area and into the foothills the fumes spread their irritation."

The *Times* got on the case immediately; it launched its own antismog campaign and assigned veteran *Times*man Ed Ainsworth to write a series about it. Norman Chandler even hired an air pollution expert to come to L.A. and study the problem firsthand.[7]

Although the *Times* echoed city hall's conviction that refineries, foundries, and other smokestack industries were largely responsible for the thick, toxic shadow cast over the L.A. Basin, everyone—including the *Times*—strongly suspected that automobiles were the real culprits. But no right-thinking Angeleno would ever be prepared to give up his or her car. By the mid-1940s, even with activity at auto assembly plants nearly slowed to a halt because of the war, L.A.'s love affair with cars showed no signs of abating, and the *Times* did all it could to nurture it.

"Southern California throbs in unison with the purring motors of its automobiles," read one *Times* editorial from the period; but such rosy elegies to the automobile were by no means new to the newspaper. As early as 1919, the *Times* rhapsodized regularly over the automobile with a fawning utopian hyperbole that anticipated none of the gas engine's future problems. The *Times* reported then that "as an agent of progress, [the automobile] has outstripped the steam engine and telegraphy, and stands second only to the printing press."

During the next several decades, the average L.A. consumer couldn't have agreed more. He looked to the *Times* for the best advertised price on new sedans and to the classifieds for used cars. Long before the beginning of World War II, Southern California had more automobiles than any other region of the country and a more highly developed system of paved roads to accommodate them. In 1934, the *Times* bragged, "In Southern California, it was the *Times* that was first and foremost in a campaign for good intercity, intercounty and interstate highways."

The *Times* also heralded a different kind of roadway that would make all others pale before it. On December 30, 1940, a revolutionary new $5-million highway with no stoplights connected Pasadena to downtown Los Angeles—the first L.A. freeway and, indeed, the first freeway in the nation. The Pasadena Freeway was followed in swift order by the Harbor, Hollywood, Long Beach, and Santa Ana Freeways and a California Department of Transportation master plan that promised to eventually link every corner of the county, and beyond.

A car had become just as much an Angeleno's birthright as sun and surf, and no one would be taking it away, smog or no smog. Los Angeles was addicted to the automobile.

And yet, years before the first smog alerts, L.A.'s automobiles had been creating havoc. In addition to having the nation's first widely recognized air pollution dilemma, Los Angeles was also the first major American city with traffic jams, parking plights, and drunk-driving epidemics. Although the *Times* duly reported these problems, the Chandlers never editorialized against the automobile. As a charter member of the increasingly powerful Automobile Club of Southern California, Harry Chandler had been as pro-automobile as he had been pro-growth, pro–real estate and pro-industry.

Norman was no different. When Los Angeles became the first major city to declare war on mass transit, his *Times* gave its tacit approval, if not its full endorsement. Freeways were the wave of the future, not railways.

As far back as July 4, 1902, when a crowd of 30,000 flag-waving Angelenos watched the first of Henry Huntington's "Big Red Cars" complete its first round-trip from L.A. to Long Beach, the Pacific Electric Railway had operated the most

extensive inter-urban transit system in the nation. Eventually, Huntington's two rail lines—the "Big Red" Pacific Electric and the Los Angeles Railway, with its distinctive yellow streetcars—linked hundreds of towns in Southern California with more than nine hundred cars that traversed over 1,100 miles of track.

But Huntington sold the Pacific Electric to Southern Pacific in 1911 and was operating only his inner city Los Angeles Railway when he died in 1927. That same year, to the editorial huzzahs of the *Los Angeles Times*, the California legislature enacted its first gasoline tax—a one-cent-per-gallon levy—to build more roads for more automobiles.

"No element, possibly, has contributed more to the fame and welfare of California than her good roads," effused the *Times*.

Another fifteen years passed before Henry Huntington's estate sold his Los Angeles Railway; its purchase was hardly noticed at the time. As the years passed, the freeways increased and became more efficient; the distinctive yellow cars of the Los Angeles Railway headed for the junkyard, followed by the long, slow fade of the "Big Red" cars of the Pacific Electric. They were both replaced by slow, diesel-driven buses that lumbered through the streets and boulevards and over the freeways under the eventual auspices of the misnamed Rapid Transit District. Neither the *Times* nor the other daily newspapers in Los Angeles showed much interest in this fundamental transformation.

Only when the air became rank with fumes and the last of the inter-urban train tracks had been idled did the driving public ask: What happened?

A conspiracy theory first revealed to the Senate Judiciary Committee in 1974 by legislative analyst Bradford Snell explained the mystery. The theory eventually became so entrenched that it become the plot line for the 1988 hit Disney comedy *Who Framed Roger Rabbit,* in which an evil industrialist destroys the L.A. trolley system to make way for automobiles.

Snell told the senators that a corporate cabal could be blamed for the wholesale destruction of L.A.'s inter-urban streetcar system—a cabal starring General Motors and Standard Oil, with the Auto Club and the *Los Angeles Times* in strong supporting roles.

"Nowhere was the ruin from GM's motorization program more apparent than in Southern California," Snell testified before the committee. "The noisy, foulsmelling buses turned earlier patrons of the high-speed rail system away from public transit and, in effect, sold millions of private automobiles."

By Snell's reckoning, the conspiracy began in 1944, when Henry Huntington's estate sold the late tycoon's Los Angeles Railway to American City Lines. American City Lines was a subsidiary of a larger consortium called National City Lines whose stockholders included General Motors, Standard Oil of California,

Firestone Tire and Rubber Company, Phillips Petroleum Company, and Mack Truck—each of which would profit mightily from an increase in bus and automobile dependence.

American City Lines immediately began replacing streetcars with buses.[8] By the time the government sued National City Lines for antitrust violations in 1946, much of the damage had already been done. National City Lines' trial, conducted in Chicago, resulted in General Motors and its fellow investors pulling out, but none of the skullduggery got attention in Los Angeles or its *Times*. Even though much of the testimony revolved around the dismantling of the L.A. rail system, *Times* readers knew nothing about the trial.

According to Snell, L.A.'s trains systematically deteriorated after that. In many cases, the track was removed and the rights-of-way that crisscrossed Los Angeles County were converted into freeways. In context, the National City Lines incident was probably more a symptom of post–World War II automobile euphoria—a universal belief that cars and buses could solve all transportation needs— than it was a scheme by big oil and auto manufacturers to wipe out mass transit. Similarly, the *Times'* poor coverage of the death of Pacific Electric and the Los Angeles Railway systems was less a conspiracy of silence than it was the short-sighted boosterism of a parochial probusiness newspaper.

Whether by accident or design, however, Norman Chandler's *Times* rationalized negative auto news for nearly a generation, applauding each new freeway as traffic congestion and air pollution went from horrendous to insufferable.

The last Big Red Car made its final run in 1962 and the yellow cars were removed from service on the downtown "P" line the following year. For the next twenty years, L.A.'s mass transit consisted of flatulent, diesel-burning buses.

ON SEPTEMBER 23, 1944, the *Los Angeles Times* really did become Norman Chandler's *Times*. At the age of eighty, Harry Chandler's heart failed and the publisher's mantle fell to the eldest son in the Chandler line.

It was a point of pride to Harry that he had been true to General Otis's antiunion edict to the end. Just seven months before his death, the National Labor Relations Board oversaw the first union election ever held at the *Times*. The pressmen, who had been solicited to join the same dreaded International Typographers Union that General Otis[9] had locked out of his *Times* fifty-six years earlier, voted overwhelmingly to reject the union. Organized labor never got a toehold inside the Times Mirror empire while Harry lived. Norman, who kept his *Times* "family" paid at least one notch above the highest comparable union wage, made the same solemn oath that his father had made: no unions on his watch.

Shortly before he died, Harry—who was unfamiliar with making requests but adept at issuing commands—handed out one final order: His and General Otis's personal papers were all to be burned. Exactly how the Fox and the Walrus who had created Los Angeles and its *Times* came to acquire and retain the family fortune would forever remain a mystery. Norman, Harrison, and Philip were left 2,694 shares each in a private California corporation called Chandis Securities, holding company for the bulk of Harry Chandler's vast fortune as described in the two Chandler family trusts that he'd established in 1938.

"With the death of Harry Chandler passes one of America's truly great," began the front-page obituary that ran beneath a clear-eyed, pursed-lipped portrait of the publisher, taken more than a decade earlier. The simple, bold-faced heading read, "HARRY CHANDLER," and began: "He helped to build an empire, and in the span of his diligent and useful years he won and held the love of those who knew him. He was a man in whom strength and courage, loyalty and duty, vision and faith held equal stature. He had many talents and these were combined with a tireless energy and an unflagging interest in his life's endeavors."

Norman Chandler's *Times* went on to praise Harry's pioneering spirit, his fearless support of the First Amendment, and his passionate dedication to his Los Angeles dream. Besides being a civic visionary, Harry Chandler was also a generous patriot, a strong family man, and a pillar of moral rectitude:

> The life and the deeds of such a man need no extended commendation from his friends or from those who loved him. Envy and malice never touched him during his busy fourscore years. They cannot touch him now. Mr. Chandler's task is done. The hands that never wearied of useful work, the great mind and heart that never failed or faltered in response to the call of need or of duty, are at rest. The spirit of Harry Chandler lives and ever will continue to live in The Times—the institution to which he gave the full measure of devotion.

Nowhere in the extensive obituary was there any hint that Harry might also have been remembered as a thief, a con man, and an unprincipled exploitation artist.

Across the country in New York, *Newsweek* was less charitable. Harry's obituary was titled "Midas of California," and it began: "He had been called the most hated man in California. Yet, paradoxically, more than any other man, Harry Chandler was given the credit for building the great city of Los Angeles from a pueblo of 12,000 inhabitants to a metropolis of close to 2 million."

Although his enemies believed him to be Midas, Mephistopheles, the ultimate Machiavellian—all of those things and more to the very end of his days—Harry Chandler went out a hero, just as he had planned.

CHAPTER 12

IN THE SUMMER OF 1937 and every summer thereafter for the next seven years, Otis Chandler and his sister, Camilla, took the train from Los Angeles to Fresno, transferred to a bus, and rode east, high into the Sierras, to the village of Lakeside on the shores of Huntington Lake. There they transferred their baggage into a waiting motor boat that took them across the water to the remote, rough-and-tumble Gold Arrow Camp for Boys and Huntington Lake Camp for Girls. They didn't return home to Norman and Buff in Santa Anita Oaks until the end of August.

"In those days, you were not treated with kid gloves as you are today," said Otis. "Now you can't push kids in their activities because they might fall and you'll get sued. It wasn't a litigious society then."

The Chandler children were pushed, and pushed hard. The head of the boy's camp played football under the legendary coach Knute Rockne at Notre Dame and neither he nor his regiment of up-and-at-'em camp counselors put up with sissies. Youngsters awakened at dawn to Indian chants and hit their cots at night the same way, exhausted and listening to the nocturnal anthems of Indians.

Not Native Americans, it should be understood. Indians. To a boy whose goal was to master the forest, the term "Indian" was anything but disrespectful. It was tinged with reverence. At the movies, Gary Cooper or Spencer Tracy racing through a western or the forest primeval as Indian companions were always a must-see for young Chandler, and his reading ranged from James Fenimore Cooper to Jack London.

"I was also enchanted with the sea and stories of heroism on the high seas," remembered Otis. "I still am."

But Gold Arrow Camp was not a place for imagining life on the water. It was a place for doing it.

"I learned how to do so many things up there that I have used the rest of my life," Otis said.

He swam, sailed, canoed, kayaked, aquaplaned, and motorboated across Huntington Lake, learning along the way how to dive deep and how to rescue a drowning person. He squeezed off his first shots from a .22 at the rifle range and made his own bow and arrows in the wood shop.

"I learned how to tie a diamond hitch on a pack mule, how to set my camp up, how to cook outside and how to saddle a horse," he recalled. "I learned how to ride horses, not English style, the way I did when I got thrown, but Western: I learned how to ride a horse ruggedly through the mountains."

And nearly every year, at some point, he wound up in the hospital.

"I'd fall on a rock or slip and bang my head," he recalled. "I didn't break any bones but they had to stitch me up and maybe I'd spend over night in the hospital. I think I got an infected leg one time from a scratch or something. But my parents would come up to the Fresno hospital and there I was. Every year before I went to camp, they'd ask, 'How are you going to hurt yourself this summer?'"

The bangs and bruises were a natural side effect of Otis's personality by his early teens. He was competitive to a fault. Even during his first summer at Gold Arrow, when he was an eight-year-old tenderfoot, he had to win more awards and merit badges than any of his peers.

"I accumulated all that stuff—I assume more than anybody in my tent or anybody in camp," he said. "In those days I wanted to be the best at this and the best at that."

Being the best was an affliction that never went away; it would cost Otis Chandler dearly in ways he couldn't foresee. But when he was a kid, the only cost was a night in the hospital and a scolding from Buff followed by a smothering hug. When his mother stifled him with comfort, the small boy blushed in awful embarrassment. Every year, Otis inevitably scuffed himself up, and every year he found himself resenting Buff's clinging maternalism just a little bit more.

"If you are going to do exciting stuff, you are going to get hurt," he said. "That has always been my philosophy."

After seven glorious summers in the Sierras, his fifteenth birthday was another turning point. At the end of his final year at Gold Arrow and Poly, Otis was packed off to boarding school.

"I don't remember any homesickness," he said. "I remember really enjoying boarding school. I played varsity soccer my first year and varsity basketball and varsity track."

The Cate School was perched on a hill overlooking Carpenteria Beach near Santa Barbara and enjoyed a long-standing reputation as a good private prep school for Southern California's affluent young males. Otis made the most of it. To woo the girls at the coed public school at the foot of the hill, he made the most of his status as a sportsman and an upper crust "Catie."

His grades, however, remained mediocre. In the spring of 1944, his parents ordered him home.

"I could tell something was on the agenda," Otis recalled. "They said, 'We have decided you are not getting the kind of challenging education we want you to have, and we want you to get into a good college, like Stanford. And you are not going to get in from where you are because we do not have any distinguished boarding schools in California the equivalent of Andover, Choate, Exeter.'"

Buff and Norman had been reading in *Time* magazine about the headmaster at Andover—a man who performed miracles with young, untrained striplings like Otis; she decided that this was just what her son needed to mold him into a gentleman.

"I'd never heard of Andover," Otis recalled. "I'd never been East except for the one summer I'd been in Colorado at the Vermejo Ranch.

"And they said, 'We are sending you to Andover.[1] It has eight hundred students. You won't know anybody there, but we think it's the best thing for your future. They've looked at your grades and they are going to insist that you come to summer school.'"

A week later, Otis was on a train to Massachusetts. He was fifteen, alone, and apprehensive about this latest adventure his parents had set him on. He would study French and Shakespeare and he would excel in both or endure the humiliation of being put back a grade, just as he had following his near-fatal horse accident.

The French class was taught in French. Otis nearly suffered another bout of crowd nausea when his teacher told him, in French, to stand before the class and describe his long train ride from Los Angeles—in French.

"So I stumbled through and it was awful," he said. "I did okay in the English course but I was failing French."

But he just barely passed and entered the nation's oldest boarding school in the fall as a junior with the rest of the Class of '46. He was six foot three and weighed 153 pounds—the epitome of a Yankee's vision of a big, dumb, blond beach bum from California. The Chandler name meant nothing in Massachusetts. If he hadn't been such a splendid athlete, Otis might have been banished as a freak. But he immediately made the varsity soccer, basketball, and track teams and lettered six times during his two years. The homemade high jump pit he'd built in the yard back in Sierra Madre gave him a leg up at Andover; eventually he was able to leap over six feet in track competition.

The old-moneyed New England clique at Andover would never brook an outsider, but most of his class accepted him. He roomed with an English transfer student one semester and a black scholarship student from Chicago the next. It didn't occur to him that the odd pairing of a big blond L.A. surfer with a Chicago janitor's son might have been designed to humiliate them both as outsiders, but if it was a sophomoric gag, it backfired. The two young men got along splendidly. Otis might have grown up in the WASP enclave of Pasadena, but he was every bit the abolitionist and racial egalitarian that his great grandfather had been. Andover taught Otis his first lesson in civil rights without his ever having to stand in a picket line or ride a freedom bus.

"Andover is not a rich man's school," Otis said. "It was true then. It's true now. I think 40 percent were there on scholarships. It is run on the English system like Eton, where you wear a coat and tie to every meal and you go to the Commons for meals. You had no choice. You couldn't cut meals. You had to wear a coat and tie to every class, too."

There was no overindulging as there is today, Otis said. He cited a recent instance, in the late 1990s, of a popular Andover senior who was caught drinking. The student committed suicide a few days later. Otis's own granddaughter, who was a student at Andover at the time, was one of the last students to see him alive.[2] The incident prompted a gathering of grief counselors to help students come to terms with their sorrow.

None of that would have happened in Otis's day.

"The school shut down for two days and they had psychiatrists and psychologists come and counsel the students and had a student day of mourning, church services and all of that," said Otis. "We didn't have any of that coddling."

Students sank or swam, and although the suicide of a classmate would be an occasion to mourn, it would never turn into the elaborate antitrauma production that schools now undergo when tragedy strikes, said Otis. The dead were given their due, but the strong survived and carried on.

In December 1945, Otis graduated with a B-minus average. He was senior class secretary and voted "most likely to succeed" by his classmates, and believed at the time that success might have to be won in the U.S. military.

"I remember my mother saying to my dad, 'Can't you get him deferred? He is the sole surviving son,'" Otis recalled. "And I think there was a deferment for that, but my father didn't want to do it and I didn't want him to do it."

Instead, Otis had taken the train to Boston the previous spring, where he dutifully took and passed his draft physical. By the time he was eligible for the draft, though, the war had ended and his military service was deferred. In the fall of 1946, Otis Chandler entered Stanford University as a freshman history major. He joined the NROTC both to avoid the draft and to help pay his way through Stanford.

BACK IN LOS ANGELES, Mrs. Norman Chandler began to insinuate herself into the daily workings of her husband's newspaper.

For several years before Otis left for Andover, Buff had already made her presence known among the social crème de la crème who were regularly noted on the *Times* society pages by becoming a diligent volunteer and fund-raiser for Children's Hospital of Los Angeles. She felt no compunction even then about in-

timidating friends and family to support her in her cause. Norman heard about the hospital's program needs nearly every night over cocktails, along with a suggestion that a story about it in the *Times* might be quite helpful. Camilla learned how to stuff envelopes, sell secondhand goods at the hospital's thrift store, and solicit funds from watching her mother tirelessly practice noblesse oblige. Whenever Buff noticed that the hospital grounds looked a little shabby, she ordered Otis to bring over a push mower and edger and tidy things up.

Otis recalled that his mother harped incessantly about Norman's tepid enthusiasm over fulfilling social obligations.

"Your father is just hopeless," she complained. "He loves to go out and get dirty in the orchard."

"But Mother," Otis protested, "he works hard during the week and he has responsibilities and you drag him out to the opening of the symphony and you drag him out to the Opera Ball. Give him a break."

Her husband did not share Buff's passion for culture, for music, and for constant self-improvement. He didn't love the symphony enough. He didn't read enough. Oddly, neither Otis nor Camilla recalled seeing their word-merchant father or their mother doing much reading, with the exception of the newspaper. He blamed their light literary diet for his own lifelong aversion to books.

"Their leisure time was made up with visiting with friends, having nice people over, or martinis and an early dinner," said Otis.

But Norman escaped to the office each day. As a result—when she no longer had her son and daughter around to hector—there was a vacuum in Buff's restless, driven existence. With both children away at school and a full complement of servants to run the household, Mrs. Norman Chandler had even more time on her hands in the mid-1940s. She decided to use it learning more about the newspaper in which she shamelessly advertised her Children's Hospital events. At Times Mirror Square, where Editor L. D. Hotchkiss still wouldn't let a woman join his all-male city room, Buff moved in. Norman gave his occasionally brassy and invariably brash wife a title (special assistant), a budget, an office next to his, and a loft on the top floor, which Buff converted into a penthouse apartment, complete with bedroom, kitchen, and bath.

The first to admit that all she knew about journalism was what she read in her husband's newspaper, Buff enrolled in courses in feature reporting, copy editing, and headline writing at nearby USC, where Norman sat on the board of trustees. While her husband was off to professional conferences in Europe or the East Coast in the years following World War II, Buff conducted her own salons in her *Times* apartment, inviting off-duty editors and other executives up for a cocktail and conversation. She became so cozy with one of her husband's editors that city desk gossip transformed her cocktail conversation into an unconfirmed affair.

"I'm sure people thought, 'Well, there is the boss's wife,'" she recalled years later. "'What's she doing here? What's she sticking her nose into these things for? She doesn't really have any authority.' So I went over and applied for my Social Security number and went on the payroll. I noticed a change immediately."

Any perceived changes in her relationship with the rank and file were purely her own opinion. As homey and cohesive as the *Times* staff had become, the line of demarcation between Chandler and worker bee was still clearly drawn. The *Times* may have introduced employee profit sharing, given staff members their own cafeteria, and admitted newspaper personnel free of charge to charity sporting events hosted by the *Times*, but still Norman, his wife, and his brothers spent little time socializing with the grunts.

Norman didn't flaunt it, but he was as much an aristocrat as his forbears. He inherited neither the febrile bluster of his grandfather nor Harry's deft talent at municipal exploitation. The grandest real estate development in which Norman played a major role was the 1940 opening of the Hollywood Palladium. Beyond that comparatively modest deal, Norman was satisfied with running a major newspaper, sitting on several corporate boards,[3] golfing (he had a 19 handicap), lunching with fellow power brokers, and sailing around L.A. in a hot late-model car, his one immodest display of personal vanity.[4]

Like Rudy Vallee or the early Ronald Reagan, Norman Chandler parted his neatly trimmed steel gray hair in the middle. He smoked a pipe and wore tweedy sports coats, looking more like a college professor than an all-powerful publishing magnate. Unlike his father and grandfather, he struck little fear in his fellow Angelenos. But Norman's benevolence remained that of an emperor, never a peer. He was reluctant to do so, but if called upon to behave as King Solomon, Norman had the will—if not always the wisdom—to order an infant divided in two. He was infinitely slow to anger, but it did no one any good to cross him.

"Everyone knew him, and no one knew him," said Buff in an interview shortly after his death.

Norman was a champion of the status quo. Outside of an increasingly shrill, irrational fear of communism that matched Hearst's virulent anti-Red hysteria, Norman Chandler's *Times* in the 1940s was virtually indistinguishable from Harry Chandler's *Times* in the 1920s or even the General's *Times* at the turn of the century. Under its third publisher, the *Times* extolled postwar L.A. prosperity with as much uncritical flourish and frequency as the broadsheets that had been published by its first two publishers. The *Times* remained a benign booster of the Southern Californian good life. Among its dubious distinctions was its becoming the first newspaper ever to enter a float in the Rose Parade. On New Year's Day of 1946, the *Times*' mobile floral display proclaimed "A Free Press . . . Guardian

of Liberty" and offered three rotating headlines: "Happy New Year," "Victory-Unity-Peace" and "Welcome Home GIs."

But its critical reporting on issues like water, housing, race relations, transportation, and urban growth remained woefully shallow. Postwar L.A.'s population exploded even beyond the late Harry Chandler's wildest imaginings. By the end of the decade, the city would swell to more than 4 million. Had Norman been more like the General, he would have been in the thick of urban planning. Had he been more like his father, he would have found new and innovative ways to capitalize on every new resident.

But Norman was his own man, and that man was bland.

California governor Earl Warren was one politician who knew and appreciated Norman for what he was. According to a 1943 profile in the *Saturday Evening Post,* Governor Warren was a "serious-minded Horatio Alger" who began his climb up California's political ladder during Harry Chandler's heyday, when Joseph Knowland, Harry's close friend and fellow Republican publisher, singled Warren out as the *Oakland Tribune*'s choice for Alameda County's district attorney. From Oakland, Warren stepped up to the state attorney general's office in 1938—but not without the editorial help of three of the strongest newspaper families in the state: the de Youngs of San Francisco, the Knowlands of Oakland, and the Chandlers of L.A. By the time Warren ran his successful campaign against Democratic Governor Culbert Olson in 1942, the future chief justice of the United States had also added the Hearst newspapers to his stable of conservative supporters.

Although Governor Warren characterized himself as an apostle of Senator Hiram Johnson's progressive brand of Republican politics, California historian Carey McWilliams described him as being much further to the right in the late 1930s and early 1940s. Political support equaled political debt, according to McWilliams, which made Earl Warren nothing more than a front man for "the smoothest functioning 'big-business' machine in the nation."

"He is completely the creature of the Hearst-Chandler-Knowland clique in the Republican Party in California," McWilliams accused.

As early as 1940, Earl Warren demonstrated a ready willingness to do the Chandlers' bidding while he was still attorney general. Then-Governor Olson had nominated liberal University of California law professor Max Radin to the state Supreme Court; there followed a firestorm of protest from the Republican right, led by the *Los Angeles Times.*

"He [Radin] has spoken at radical meetings and he has been warmly defended—without protest on his part—by Communists of the reddest hue," editorialized Norman Chandler's *Times.*

Like his father, Norman believed organized labor was the root of all evil, but Norman's generation of Republicans carried that phobia one step further: Labor unions were also the unwitting pawns of an international Communist conspiracy controlled from Moscow. It was a precept that Norman accepted and lived by through most of his adult life, and it accounted for the flagrant Red-baiting that characterized the news columns and editorial pages of his *Times.*

As an outspoken civil libertarian who refused to hide his own prolabor sympathies, Max Radin became the focal point of the *Times'* festering fear and the first in a long line of academics falsely pilloried as Communists. Norman Chandler intended to stop the professor's rise to the California Supreme Court.

In addition to labeling Radin a Red, the *Times* rallied the support of several future Republican stars to block the Radin nomination, including a young state assemblyman—a then-Democrat named Sam Yorty. As the future mayor of Los Angeles, Yorty would fight bitterly with a different *Los Angeles Times* during the 1960s, but in 1940 he and Norman Chandler were in perfect agreement. Yorty chaired a committee investigating Communist subversion in state government; in his role as chairman, he allied himself with the *Times* and condemned Max Radin on the floor of the capitol with as much venomous innuendo as any *Times* editorial.

But neither Yorty nor the *Times* had the power to stop Radin's nomination; that authority belonged to Attorney General Earl Warren, who held the swing vote on the California Bar Association's judicial review committee. Always an astute politician, Warren was not deaf to the din of iniquity spewing from the *Times.* When it was his turn to deny Radin a seat on the state's highest court, Warren blackballed the law professor and gained the *Times'* praise in the offing. In addition to securing California's next gubernatorial election, Earl Warren had also won Norman Chandler's warm personal friendship.

Thus, their voluble split a decade later over loyalty oaths at the University of California made headlines of its own, and was tinged with more than a little irony. As Warren recalled in his memoirs, his decisive confrontation with Norman Chandler happened in the summer of 1949, deep in a forest seventy miles north of San Francisco.

The two most powerful Republicans in California met beneath the redwoods in a sequoia grove, unshaven, half-naked, perhaps even a little tipsy from too much fine wine. The governor and the publisher were attending the exclusive annual retreat on the Russian River known as the Bohemian Grove, once dubbed "the greatest men's party on Earth" by Harry Chandler's good friend Herbert Hoover.

Like his father before him, Norman had been a member of the annual oligarch's retreat for most of his career with the *Times.*[5] Formed in 1872 by a group of San Francisco journalists, the male-only enclave evolved into a haven for the

West Coast illuminati. Captains of industry and political leaders could literally strip themselves of their public trappings and commune with nature in their skivvies on the private 2,700-acre sanctuary. By the time Norman joined, the founding journalists were nowhere to be seen and reporters were barred to preserve the group's secrecy. The Bohemian Grove had become the exclusive asylum of the rich and powerful, where public policy could be created free from the prying eyes and meddling opinions of the public.[6]

In a ritual more reminiscent of young Otis Chandler's Gold Arrow summer camp than a gathering of grown men, each Bohemian Grove retreat began with the "Cremation of Care" ritual, in which the club's mascot, Dull Care, was burned in effigy before a druidic owl shrine. Members were then free to wander through the woods, buck naked if they chose; they could nibble on gourmet food, sample expensive wine, and participate in or watch skits, musical revues, seminars, and speeches. Often, they gathered in groups of two or three to talk business, as did Earl Warren and Norman Chandler.

Norman began by questioning the governor's resolve in rooting out communism. After torpedoing Max Radin's Supreme Court nomination, Warren began shifting his view on academic freedom to the left. By the time California conservatives such as Sam Yorty had created the California loyalty oath as a weapon against university subversives, the governor said that the state had gone too far.

"Norman," Warren began, "will you let me tell you my story for a few minutes without interruption and then I will be happy to answer any questions you might have for me?"

With Chandler's consent, the governor began by declaring that loyalty oaths were plainly illegal and unenforceable under the state Constitution. Real Communists wouldn't think twice about placing their hands on a Bible and flat out lying about their loyalty to the United States. In fact, said Warren, the only people who *would* balk at signing a loyalty oath would be principled academics who might view such a requirement as a violation of their basic civil rights.

"Your own profession is perhaps the most vigilant in this regard," Warren lectured Norman, "and the most militant in resisting any incursion on its right to report the news as it discovers it and to interpret it as it chooses.

"I would think that you would feel yourselves very much akin to the academic community, because you consider yourselves educators in the sense that you go into every home in America for the daily enlightenment of young and old alike."

Norman began to interrupt, but Warren gestured that he was not finished.

"Because of this public service, the government gives you privileges that other citizens do not have," he continued. "You have the right to send your bulky newspapers and magazines through the mail at low postage rates that are totally

out of proportion to those required of other citizens. Now let us suppose that Congress proposed a statute that would deny such mailing privileges to all publishers who refused to subscribe to an oath denying they were Communists and swearing not to use their publications for Communistic purposes. What would your opinion be of such legislation?"

Chandler answered brusquely, "You know what our opinion would be."

"I believe I do, but I want you to tell me," Warren pressed.

"Of course we would be against it," said Norman. "If publishers subscribed to such an oath, some bureaucrat in Washington would be scrutinizing everything written and would censor it according to his views on whether or not it was in the interests of Communism."

"Norman," Warren said, "you have just made the case for the university faculty. They contend that if they sign such an affidavit, some bureaucrat or legislator or lobbyist in Sacramento will be constantly looking over their shoulders and trying to find subversion in their teaching, and this would be in violation of academic freedom. And we both know that in the present atmosphere that is bound to occur."

Chandler fell silent for a moment.

He said finally, "It looks to me as though there is too much emotion on both sides."

A few days later, the *Times* ran an editorial criticizing such undue emotionalism in the loyalty oath debate, but the paper did not otherwise alter its position. From that point forward, the Chandler-Warren friendship cooled and ultimately froze.

UNLIKE GENERAL OTIS, whose handpicked candidates frequently went down in defeat, Harry Chandler worked his political will through such *Times* reporters as Al Nathan, Bill Henry, Chester Hansen, and Carleton Williams, all overseen by the magisterial gnome Kyle Palmer. It was Palmer who rubber-stamped the election and reelection of county supervisors, state legislators, and city officials, and it was Palmer who decided which candidate measured up to the Chandler criteria. When he stepped into his father's shoes, Norman Chandler changed nothing. He allowed Palmer and his team of mandarins to perform their duties as they always had.

Thus, when the habitually jaded Kyle Palmer rushed excitedly into the publisher's suite one spring day in 1946, Norman was doubly attentive. Palmer confidently announced that he had just met with the next Republican candidate for the strongly Democratic 12th Congressional District, and he wanted Norman to meet him too: a bright, ambitious young Navy veteran from the L.A. suburb of Whittier. His name was Richard Milhous Nixon.

Palmer recalled, "My first impression of Nixon was that here was a serious, determined, somewhat gawky young fellow who was out on a sort of giant killer operation. But it wasn't too long after he settled down that we began to realize that we had an extraordinary man on our hands."

After meeting Nixon, Norman enthusiastically agreed.

"His forthrightness, and the way he spoke, made a deep impression on me," Norman said. "After Nixon departed, I told Mr. Palmer, 'This young fellow makes sense. He looks like a comer. He has a lot of fight and fire. Let's support him.'"

Richard Nixon won that November after a campaign since vilified repeatedly by political scientists and historians for its breathtaking smear tactics. The Washington Press Corps voted Nixon's five-term opponent, Jerry Voorhis,[7] the hardest working member of the House of Representatives, but Nixon flatly labeled the Democratic incumbent a Communist dupe. He even ordered his campaign workers to call voters anonymously shortly before election day with the news that Voorhis was worse than a dupe—he was Red, through and through. Only a vote for Nixon would constitute a vote for Democracy.

More than a generation later Nixon said in a moment of candor, "Of course I knew Jerry Voorhis wasn't a Communist, but I had to win."

Before he put in his first call to Kyle Palmer, Nixon had already paid $500 to a savvy L.A. attorney and Republican political operative named Murray Chotiner to find out how to win. Chotiner, who was busy working on other campaigns that year, had just enough time to give Nixon two valuable bits of advice: Con Voorhis into debating him and suck up to the publishers of every newspaper, big or small, in the 12th Congressional District.

Voorhis foolishly accepted Nixon's invitation to debate five times during the campaign, and Nixon drew blood every time. His finest moment was a shrill accusation that Voorhis was the puppet of the Congress of Industrial Organizations (CIO), which Nixon characterized as a Communist front. When Voorhis denied that he had either sought or received CIO support, Nixon pulled a newspaper clipping from his pocket that reported the CIO's Los Angeles chapter had endorsed Voorhis. Though a flustered Voorhis asked the union to withdraw its endorsement, Nixon had done his damage.

Weeks before he stepped onto a debate platform, however, Richard Nixon had gone to work courting the press.

"I called in on every local newspaper office, however small, usually spending several hours talking with the publisher, the editor, the reporters and sometimes even the printers," Nixon remembered.

His precampaign press tour paid off. Twenty-six of the thirty newspapers that circulated in the 12th District endorsed Nixon, including the *Times*.

It was a Republican year across the nation anyway, largely because the electorate blamed wartime rationing on New Deal Democrats; but L.A. voters were especially irked and they turned liberals out of office in droves. The only Democrat left in the Southern California delegation following election day was Helen Gahagan Douglas. When the 12ᵗʰ District votes were tallied, Richard Nixon beat Voorhis 65,586 to 49,994.

"Nixon never changed from the first time I met him," said Buff Chandler, who first shook the new congressman's hand the day he stopped by the *Times* to thank the Chandlers for their support. His entourage included his wife, Pat, his parents, and his brother and sister-in-law; when Norman asked them what they would like to drink, they all answered, "Milk."

"And so I went around to go into the kitchen and tell the cook everybody wanted milk," Buff recalled, "when Nixon came out into the hall and said, 'Buff, could you get me a double bourbon? I don't want Mother and Father to see me take a drink.'"

"It showed a funny, cheating quality that has never changed through the years," Buff commented.

Buff wasn't the only one who developed an early distaste for Richard Nixon. A *Times* copy editor named Nick Williams recalled a telling moment when Nixon stormed into the newsroom and went directly to the city editor.

"They began calling all over town," said Williams, who had no idea who Nixon was.

"It seemed Nixon's wife wasn't home when he got there, so he came down to have us help him track her down. I figured any guy who came running to a newspaper to help him find his wife when she'd just gone to a movie for a couple of hours had something wrong with him."

Nevertheless, the *Times* supported Nixon again two years later, praising his work as the outraged junior member of the House Un-American Activities Committee. To the delight of Norman Chandler and his editorial writers, Nixon rode the HUAC crucifixion of former State Department official Alger Hiss to an even larger margin of victory in 1948,[8] paving the way for his successful run against Congresswoman Douglas for the U.S. Senate in 1950.

Throughout the following decade, the *Times* backed Nixon's rapid Republican ascent, but as Norman Chandler came to learn many years later, he was not the first Chandler that the 12ᵗʰ District congressman had approached for support.

Twenty-two years before running for Congress, Richard Nixon had been an early student of Harry Chandler's *Times* and even thought of becoming a newspaperman himself. Before he was old enough even to deliver the paper, young Richard Nixon came looking for a job:

Times, Office K, Box 240
January 24, 1924
Dear Sir:

Please consider me for the position of office boy mentioned in the Times paper. I am eleven years of age and I am in the Sixth grade of the East Whittier grammar school.

I am very willing to work and would like the money for a vacation trip. I am willing to come to your office at any time and I will accept any pay offered. My address is Whittier boulevard and Leffingwell road. The phone number is 5274. For reference you can see Miss Flowers princaple of the East Whittier School. Hoping that you will accept me for service, I am,

Yours truly,
Richard M. Nixon

The eleven-year-old Whittier boy did not get the job, but if he had, "it could have changed American history" as Norman Chandler reflected more than forty years later.

"This is just like him," Chandler told an interviewer after reading Nixon's earliest entreaty to the *Times*. "It's a blueprint of his ambition, drive, and determination to meet a challenge."

By the time he was a teenager, Nixon had abandoned his newspaper ambitions in favor of joining J. Edgar Hoover's FBI. With that goal in mind, he graduated second in his class at Whittier College, won a scholarship, and went on to law school at Duke University, where he finished third in his class. But the FBI wasn't interested in a modest middle-class Quaker from Southern California, and neither were a host of East Coast law firms who also rejected his application.

Temporarily discouraged but never defeated, Richard Nixon served in the Navy as a junior grade lieutenant during World War II before returning home to Whittier, a career in politics, and a welcoming lift from the *Los Angeles Times*.

BILLING ITSELF AS the "easiest-to-read" newspaper in the country, in 1948 the *Times* expanded its sports and women's sections, revamped its op-ed page, and launched a full page of daily comics; it topped the 400,000 mark in average daily circulation for the first time. But Norman Chandler didn't rest on his laurels. Now the most widely circulated newspaper in L.A., the *Times* nonetheless faced a new kind of competition. Partnering with CBS, Times Mirror launched KTTV (for "*Times* TV") in the spring of 1948[9] and became the first L.A. newspaper company to dabble in the burgeoning new medium of television.

"Although I didn't want to, I thought it was the best insurance we could take out against what will eventually happen to newspapers in the advertising field," Chandler explained to *Fortune* magazine. "I am convinced that television is going to affect newspapers."

Norman went on to predict that the real competition between newsprint and television would begin when the new medium graduated from black-and-white images to color. KTTV began preparing for that inevitability by telecasting the Rose Parade for the first time the following year. Although the floral displays were broadcast in shades of gray, it was still a convincing annual invitation to the frozen East to migrate to L.A.—boosterism in the *Times* tradition that would have made Harry and his All-Year Club proud. The rapid onslaught of the electronic age became even more apparent when the *Times* hired Walter Ames, its first television reporter, and began publishing television news and features every Sunday. By 1950, daily television listings were a permanent *Times* fixture.

Norman's predictions about future media did not preclude his present-day competition, however. He met those challenges head-on in 1948, too.

Since Harry's death four years earlier, Norman had been ruminating about going head-to-head with Hearst's hugely successful afternoon *Los Angeles Herald-Express.* He took his first timid step in that direction in the final weeks of 1944, when Times Mirror quietly bought the northwest corner of Second and Spring Streets. The property would become the future home of Hearst's afternoon competition, but what would that be?

During one of his postwar visits to Europe, Norman met United Press vice president Virgil Pinkley, who became his traveling companion and fellow student of the tabloids of London and Paris.

A recent graduate to the ranks of news executives, Pinkley was everything that Norman was not in the world of journalism. A Southern California native of humble origins, Pinkley had worked his way up to editor of the USC *Daily Trojan;* then, in the 1920s, he worked his way to Europe aboard a cattle boat. He knocked around London until he landed a job with Hearst's United Press in 1929 and, once again, worked his way up to foreign correspondent. Before World War II, he had covered the Berlin Olympics and the Italian invasion of Ethiopia; during the war, Pinkley traveled 175,000 miles as a United Press correspondent,[10] crisscrossing Europe, Asia, and Africa.

By the time he hooked up with Chandler, Pinkley had become something of an expert on the unique style of journalism practiced by the Fleet Street tabloids: lurid and loaded with sex, celebrities, and crime to a degree far beyond that of even the yellowest of Hearst's American dailies. Yet tabloids sold like the proverbial hot cakes, as Captain Joseph Medill Patterson had proved with his *New York*

Daily News, which appealed to a lower-middle-class audience who would never dream of picking up Chandler's *Los Angeles Times* or a paper like it.

When he returned to L.A., Norman turned his studious eye toward the *Los Angeles Daily News*, the *Herald-Express's* only afternoon competition. Manchester Boddy's anemic and liberal newspaper was undercapitalized, tabloid-sized, and ran dead last in circulation among metropolitan L.A. dailies. And yet, to Chandler's amazement, the *Daily News* had still turned a $459,000 profit during the last year of the war.

Three years later, amid much secrecy, Norman Chandler broke ground on a building he dubbed *Times* South. In reality, the new offices would be home to the first new Los Angeles newspaper in a generation to be overseen by Norman's handpicked publisher, United Press's Virgil Pinkley. On October 11, 1948, with Pinkley at his side, Norman Chandler put the first issue of his new afternoon *Los Angeles Mirror* on the streets. At a nickel a copy, it undercut the newsstand price of every other L.A. newspaper—including the *Times*—by $0.02.

"Los Angeles had grown into an industrial and manufacturing community during wartime," said Norman, explaining the logic behind the launch of his new daily. "A tabloid paper of the *Mirror's* type might appeal to the new elements of our population more than the *Times*."

The "new elements" were blue-collar veterans who would appreciate "a good, well-rounded newspaper," according to Chandler. They were the working men and women who might not be able to afford an automobile, and rode to and from their jobs aboard what remained of the Pacific Electric rail line. They might appreciate something racy, saucy, and informative to entertain them on the long commute home.

The *Mirror* was Norman Chandler's grand experiment in a fast-changing and expanding urban landscape. But it was more than just his brainchild; it was his darling—a creation all his own, separate from the venerable *Times* that had evolved over seventy years under the careful stewardship of Harry Chandler and General Otis.

From the beginning, however, the *Mirror* was a fiscal disaster. Sales of 400,000 copies on its first day quickly dwindled to an average daily circulation of 88,000, slowly building back to 160,000 by the end of its first year. By undercutting its rivals' price and subsidizing its losses with the *Times'* deep coffers, the *Mirror* continued to creep up in circulation and ad revenue. It never did make a dent in the *Herald-Express's* strong lead, but it eventually wrought havoc on the *Daily News*. At the end of the 1940s, the once-profitable *Daily News* was posting annual losses of more than $400,000.

At first, Virgil Pinkley's emphasis on scandal, cheesecake, and grisly "street" headlines proved a little too London-like to suit Norman Chandler. But once the

Mirror's publisher toned his staff's lurid taste down a few nasty notches, the *Times* and its "bad little brother," as *Mirror* city editor James Bassett preferred to call his new home, managed to coexist through the 1950s.

"We had a lot of fun before the deadly scourge of responsibility hit journalism," said Bassett's successor Bill Thomas, who took over as the *Mirror*'s city editor in 1958.

For more than a decade, Norman protected and nurtured the *Mirror* as if it were a terminally ill but beloved child, giving it regular transfusions of *Times* staff members and capital.

"Why one will click and another won't, I don't know," Norman mused when asked during an interview in 1950 about the *Mirror*'s prospects for survival. "I'm only sure of this—if you try to please everybody, you'll go broke."

CHAPTER 13

AFTER TWO YEARS AT ANDOVER, Otis Chandler felt like a monk turned loose in a harem. He'd had his meager share of off-campus dates, of course, and even got in some occasional weekend ogling during excursions into Boston or New York. But real women in real skirts who stood in the same check-out lines at the bookstore, sat in the same cafeteria, or—best of all—worked their curvy, perfumed bodies out in the same gymnasium, tennis court, or running track as the guys....

This then was coeducational Stanford's most delicious departure from all-male Andover.

Until Stanford, Otis's lust had been pretty much confined to matinee mistresses such as Hedy Lamar, Vivien Leigh, and Dorothy Lamour. But at Stanford, it was not only a point of honor but a competitive sport to conquer and sack the best babes available, on and off campus. Otis always tried to keep more than one on his string.

"I had no high school romance," Otis lamented. "Nothing heavy, anyway. So when I got out of Andover, why it was: One is fine, two is better, and three is the best. I was a real shit. I think now: How could I have misrepresented myself to each one by letting them think they were the only one?"

But he got no complaints; during the months between Andover and Stanford, he had turned into a hunk, well worth pursuing by any woman's standards.

Otis spent that transitional summer working at the *Times* during the day, where he lugged forty-five-pound lead plates around the stereotyping department; in the evening, he went to the YMCA to exercise his newest passion: lifting weights. It was fellow athlete and weight training enthusiast Norm Nourse[1] who gave Otis his first taste of the regimen that would transform his body and his life. Otis had been a disciplined athlete at Andover, but he was pale and wiry; the inclement weather of the northeast kept the most dedicated sun worshiper indoors much of the year. California demanded something far different of a strong, young, upper-crust Pasadena thoroughbred. At one point, Otis became such a fanatic about weight training that he wrote and published a pamphlet—"Scientific Weightlifting Exercises Designed for Track and Field Events"—that he maintained had been stolen by the Soviets and incorporated into their 1952 Olympic training program.

In three months, Otis's progressive daily routine of Olympic-style lifting, plus an appetite that had increased his intake to four meals a day, added 40 pounds of muscle to his 190-pound frame. By the time he was invited to join the Stanford varsity track team in his freshman year, Otis rippled from his bull neck to his sleek loins like a bronzed California Adonis.

Otis's first stop on campus was not the gymnasium but the Deke House on fraternity row, where his "legacy" status made him a shoo-in during pledge week. Norman had joined Delta Kappa Epsilon in 1919, the first year he came to Stanford, and Otis was expected to do the same. His father had once sat upon the very same steps of the very same frat house thirty years earlier when a pert young babe from the Pi Beta Phi sorority sashayed by, flashing ankles, eyes, and enough of her well-turned calves to warrant Norman's wolf whistle.

"I had great legs in those days," Buff Chandler boasted in an interview several decades later.

During the ensuing years, sororities had disappeared from Stanford, but there were still plenty of women from the dormitories to leer at from the Deke front porch. As an underclassman, Otis did not yet warrant dates with the best of the babes, but he could leer. Deke wasn't Animal House, but there were similarities.

"That house made Animal House look like a nunnery," declared Otis's fellow Deke Ron Bishop.

Chandler's frat brother Merritt Van Zant remembered an oddball grouping of some sixty young men, half of whom were typically self-indulgent studs more than a little profligate in their drinking and dating habits. The other half were just as horny, but tended toward alcohol abstinence because they were athletes like "Oats."[2] Chandler was a strict Stanford jock, according to Van Zant—happy to cruise a Deke beer bust for any spare female who might be on the loose, but rarely tempted to drink anything harder than apple juice.

"I think what happened to Judge [his first name, not his title] Finley made a pretty deep impact on Oats," said Van Zant.

A drinking Deke, Finley was also one of Chandler's closest friends during his first couple of years at Stanford, according to Van Zant. Then, one fatal night, a tipsy Finley slammed his car head-on into another, killing several passengers in both cars in the process. Finley lived, but his Stanford career was finished. The effect on all the Dekes—drinkers and athletes alike—was profound. Otis was not averse to partying. He loved to head out on the highway aboard a Harley during the weekends and cruise for coeds with the guys on warm spring nights. But in contrast to his parents, who could not get through an evening without a martini, Otis Chandler was a confirmed teetotaler. He couldn't even be tempted on a hot day with an icy stein of lager.

"It wasn't just sports and it wasn't just being a Chandler and trying to protect the Chandler name and not do anything to embarrass my parents," he said. "It's just that something inside of me said, 'I don't want to do that stuff because it is a waste of time and it is not good for my body.' I much preferred to hike a mountain or play basketball or throw the shot."

He was in good company when it came to the serious side of his nature. Otis was part of the first post–World War II class at Stanford, which included a very different kind of freshman from the usual callow high school grad.

"We averaged six foot two and weighed 220 pounds," Otis said. "I was part of a real bunch of characters, many of them back from the war to pursue their education."

Because he couldn't decide what he wanted to do with his life, Otis became a history major, distinguishing himself with a senior thesis that departed dramatically from the Civil War blather or presidential political rehashes that all too often became fodder for dull undergraduate essays. Generally, Otis found academics a bore. As a history major, he already preferred contemporary news to meaningless antiquity. He chose the Final Solution for his senior project.

"I remember the first time I went in [Stanford's] Hoover Institute [for the Study of War and Peace] where they actually have the day books written by the commanders of those death camps," said Otis. "They listed how many they killed each day. I read through them and it was all I needed to see: 'We've got so many in the ovens today.' They would take their clothes off, put them in the showers to get clean, and then the gas would come. Then they would take the bodies out and bring in the next bunch. I . . . still get very emotional about it."

Immediately following armistice, Otis's father had been among the first American journalists invited by the U.S. Defense Department to inspect the Dachau concentration camp. Norman Chandler brought back with him horrific tales of the Holocaust and picture proof of the notorious ovens, the wretched sta-

lags, and the mass graves that branded Nazi Germany. Otis built his senior thesis upon this foundation, detailing in chillingly calm but painfully subjective prose the reasons for and results of twentieth century man's grossest inhumanity to his fellow man. Like a good news story, the paper's most blistering inclusion were the black-and-white snapshots of the ovens that Norman had brought back with him from Europe.

His father might happily give Otis a hand on his senior project, by supplying him with photos, but he was stingy when it came to cash. Otis took a job working in the cafeteria to earn enough for dates and gas; as in prep school, he could not depend on a stipend from home. Norman and Buff paid only tuition, room, and board. During summers, Otis either worked at the *Times* for minimum wage or served aboard a ship as a Naval Reserve Officer Training Corps midshipman—a hedge against future brushes with the draft. After two years, however, the draft no longer looked like a threat, and he'd already convinced himself he was not military material. He resigned from the NROTC and devoted summers to working in the *Times* pressroom and training for track and field.

The newly beefed up Otis Chandler could no longer leap six feet in the air the way he once did at Andover, but he could hurl the discus and especially the shot. Each June, for two years running, he made the touring team of the American Athletic Union.

"The State Department would send the top three finishers in the national track and field meet on these wonderful tours between Olympic years and for ten days, I traveled to England, Ireland, Scotland, France, Switzerland, St. Petersburg, and Scandinavia to compete in these international meets," Otis recalled.

His trips abroad opened his eyes to how differently Europeans regarded everything, from class to culture, and especially race.

"Half our team was black," said Otis. "They were my good buddies, but it was a real eye opener when we'd compete some place like Scandinavia, or even up in Ireland and Scotland. The girls would hang around the practice field after the meets. We wore these blue Uncle Sam track-and-field blazers—a pretty sharp-looking get up."

The routine, Chandler quickly learned, was to print business cards and hand them out to willing young groupies with one's hotel room number scrawled on the back. Unfortunately, those same young women seemed far more interested in the black athletes than they were in a California golden boy.

"In Scandinavia, they are not going to be impressed with someone like yours truly," said Otis. "But if you're a muscled black athlete from the United States. . . . Today they're not so exotic. But in those days after World War II, the world was just getting back together and for the first time these girls were seeing black American athletes. The guys used to rub it in, too. Back at the hotel room they'd

say, 'Well, who'd you get, Whitey?' And I'd say, 'Well, some 180-pound old bag. I didn't want to go out with her anyway. I wanted to read a book.'"

But Otis was not a complete loser off the field during the AAU trips. The summer following his graduation from Stanford he had one of those idylls that an old man savors when recalling the sweetest moments of youth: a stolen month in Paris spent with a nursing student from the University of Michigan who had been assigned to the U.S. AAU swim team.

The couple stayed in a tiny walk-up flat near the Arc de Triomphe and rode bicycles everywhere. They peddled along the Seine, up and down the Champs Élysées, and all the way to Versailles and back. They climbed the Eiffel Tower and went to the Paris Opera House to see *Carmen.*

And, when the summer ended, they went their separate ways.

"It was just a little fling in Paris," he said. "It didn't last very long."

Back home, trouble brewed.

"I had given Missy my fraternity pin and we were in love," he said, "but there was nothing at that time mentioned about a marriage date."

Marilyn "Missy" Brant, a pretty young blond two years behind Otis at Stanford, believed otherwise. She was perfect for Otis. Missy had a Pasadena blue blood pedigree, but even more important, her grandfather had been one of Harry Chandler's first real estate syndicate partners: Title Insurance and Trust Company executive Otto Brant. Her parents were Norman and Buff's peers and cocktail party pals. When they heard that Otis had picked Missy as his steady, the Chandlers were not only relieved but thrilled. Marriage was inevitable.

"I never remember being pushed by my mother and father into marrying within my circle of socially acceptable girls. It was never that kind of thing," said Otis, adding with a sigh: "But it was inferred."

Otis believed he'd singled Missy out to be his own, but it was she who had done the picking many years earlier. The spring before Otis had been dispatched to Andover, thirteen-year-old Missy Brant was tee-heeing in the pool house at her parents' Lake Arrowhead[3] retreat along with several other young debutantes-in-waiting when a handsome blond boy in baggy swim trunks happened by on his way to the water. Even then, she recalled, the seventeen-year-old Otis Chandler seemed to strut. He oozed self-confidence. But there were shortcomings. Otis was cheap, according to Missy. He consistently and conveniently forgot to pay back the smallest of debts, stiffing everyone he knew at one time or another.

"He also had bad skin and he was skinny," she recalled, "but he did have a good sense of humor."

A few years later, most of his physical failings had been exercised into oblivion. He was still cheap and funny, at least when it came to playing practical jokes, but his body had expanded to a degree matching his bravado. When the Stanford

freshman strutted, he now appeared to have every right and justification for doing so.

When it came time for her social debut at the Las Madrinas Ball, Missy
counted herself lucky to be able to pull the family strings necessary to get Otis
Chandler to act as her escort.

By his senior year at Stanford, Otis was cocaptain of the track team and every
bit as much a catch for Missy Brant as she was for him. They were the perfect
Pasadena couple. Everything would have come together like the thin plot of a
Harlequin romance if Otis hadn't been such a horn dog.

"I never bought a piece of ass," he said with some pride a half century later. "I
never frequented any cat houses in Tijuana or Watsonville,[4] either."

He did play fast and loose with women, though. Before pinning Missy, he'd lost
his virginity to a coed at San Jose State, "a gold mine full of very attractive girls
just twenty minutes down Bay Shore Highway from Stanford," as Otis described
the school.

Missy grew suspicious, but Otis was more concerned that Buff might find out
about his off-campus activities.

"My mother heard I was dating this girl from San Jose State and she wanted to
meet her," he recalled. "I said, 'No, I don't think I want you to meet her.' Not
that she wasn't pretty and sexy and all of that. But my mother would have asked,
'Well, do I know your mother?'"

It was understood that Otis would be seeing only the right young women—
women whose families Buff knew and approved of. The San Jose girl had grown
up in déclassé Alhambra, not Pasadena or San Marino. What was more, she attended a public university. How qualified could she be to marry a Chandler?

Otis's third-string girlfriend came with better credentials than the San Jose
coed. She attended private and pricey Scripps College, just a few miles from
Sierra Madre in the college town of Claremont. Her father was a doctor who practiced medicine in Pasadena. But because the Scripps girl's family lived outside the
city limits, she did not pass Buff's final test: Buff did not know her mother.

Otis knew what he was up against. The logistics of dating so that his girlfriends—but especially his mother—would never meet one another, had become
too complicated. He finally did what any aspiring Don Juan would do: He left the
country and spent a Paris interlude in the arms of his AAU nurse. It was good,
but when it ended, Otis Chandler accepted his fate.

"I came back and realized that I *did* want to marry Missy. That she *was* the
right girl," he said. "The Brants were socially acceptable. They were an original
historical family and my parents were glad when I decided to marry little Missy."

When he popped the question, Missy was effervescent, prattling on and on
about how wonderful it was that the two of them had both saved themselves for

each other on their wedding night. Otis fell silent for a moment, then indiscreetly spilled his guts. Missy would be the only one who'd be losing her virginity on their wedding night, he muttered.

She ran off in tears and swore never to speak to him again.

Two weeks later, she was back.

EVEN THOUGH 750 GUESTS SHOWED UP and the gala reception was staged at the Los Angeles Country Club, Otis recalled being quite blasé about his high society wedding to Miss Marilyn Jane Brant on June 18, 1951. The most memorable thing about the event for him was the problem of Missy's Catholicism.

"They had some rigid rules when a non-Catholic marries a Catholic," recalled Otis. "I had to take instruction from a priest in Palo Alto and we didn't get along because I was not religious. I had studied quite a bit of anthropology and I didn't believe in Adam and Eve. I was interested in the creation of man and I believed in evolution."

Missy also remembered the six weeks of instruction with Father Tierney, who ran the Cardinal Newman Club on the Stanford campus. What Otis recalled as debate with the priest, Missy remembered as a "spirited exchange."

"I kept arguing with him about the theory of evolution," Otis said, "and he would say, 'My boy, you have to take it on faith. We are the mother church and there is no other.' I'd bring up some of the history I had taken at Stanford, like the founding of Judaism and so on and he kept saying, 'You just have to take what I am telling you on faith. I'm serving God and we are the original ones.' We went back and forth. He was a good guy. He was just very rigid."

Eventually, Otis would prevail in the question of religion, even though he agreed at the outset to send his children to parochial schools and Sunday Mass. Otis got along by going along, as he did with Father Tierney. But over time, he imposed his will on his wife and children through the sheer force of his stubborn personality, regardless of their protests. It was the beginning of a pattern that would plague his marriage in years to come.

"He was spoiled. He always had to have his way," recalled Missy—no stranger herself to the willfulness that comes automatically with an affluent and privileged upbringing.

Strong as she was, Missy was no match for her husband if Otis felt deeply enough about an issue. She even abandoned her religion in the end. Her husband's unwavering faith in Darwin had less to do with Missy's ultimate defection from the church than her own enlightened alarm when three popes refused to sanction birth control. Despite the five children she had with Otis during the

early Catholic years of their marriage, she became a passionate advocate of zero population growth.

Catholicism was also one more wedge that drove Missy apart from her mother-in-law, whose passionate early advocacy of the Chandler-Brant nuptials had quickly soured. The first time the Los Angeles Archdiocese solicited the Norman Chandlers for a contribution to Catholic charities, Buff went through the roof. Just because her only son had grudgingly agreed to marry in the church didn't mean she and Norman had to pay to build one.

Besides, Buff had very different ideas as to how she wanted to spend her own, and other people's, charitable contributions. The edifice she had in mind might pump out as much music as any cathedral, but it would not be a church.

———————

BY 1951, anxious and aloof *Times* employees who gave Buff Chandler a wide berth in the hallways or respectfully greeted her cheery aggression by smiling weakly and averting their eyes, knew all too well who Mrs. Norman Chandler was. For those outside the offices of Times Mirror Square, however, the legend of Buff had yet to begin. Launch date for the legend was the fourth day of the Hollywood Bowl's twenty-ninth summer season.

For the first time since its opening on July 11, 1922,[5] L.A.'s unique arroyo amphitheater ran out of money. Other Bowl regulars were saddened or alarmed, but Buff was outraged. Without the Bowl, L.A. would truncate its already skimpy helping of classical music and without music, in Buff's eyes, the city's woefully lean cultural life would atrophy and die. To Mrs. Chandler, after all, music *was* culture.

"My mother was not interested in art," said Otis. "She never took me to an art gallery and she had no art in the home. Just music."

Buff loved the Los Angeles Philharmonic Orchestra; she chaired an emergency committee and immediately enlisted her husband's newspaper to aid her in her "Save the Bowl" fund drive. To sound the alarm, she sanctioned a complete shutdown of the Bowl, which resulted in a panic-driven front-page news story bolstered with *Times* editorial support. Next, she authorized two weeks of concerts in which first-rate musicians performed free to raise cash and fan the publicity flames. Finally, she worked her famous arm-twisting money magic on the miserly California Club regulars downtown and on the eager Hollywood nouveau riche who lived and worked on L.A.'s Westside and in Beverly Hills. This new, young, and Jewish constituency had been generally shunned by the old money denizens of Pasadena, but it turned out to be far more generous than the blue bloods among whom Norman and Buff lived on the east side of town. When the "Save the Bowl" campaign ended, Mrs. Norman Chandler had raised $87,000.

Largely through Buff's efforts, the Bowl reopened and the Philharmonic's "Symphony Under the Stars" again rang through the eucalyptus and pepper tree forests that surrounded the stage. But Buff wasn't finished. Any other L.A. matron might have savored her brief triumph and then settled back into a San Marino mahjong-and-crumpets routine, but not Buff Chandler. The "Save the Bowl" campaign only whetted her appetite for social power.

Amidst much fanfare, she had moved into the back pages of the *Los Angeles Times* the previous year with the first of her annual "Woman of the Year" awards. L.A.'s women weren't adequately recognized for community service, she argued, and Norman agreed. She and her husband usually "complemented each other," Buff recalled in a 1976 interview:

"I think our marriage and our lives were most unusual because I don't know anybody, really, where you have a marriage that went for fifty-one years with a husband and wife who were very compatible as far as their personal life, their sex life, their fun together . . . and who also were partners in business for thirty-five years."

The *Mirror*'s city editor during the early 1950s, Jim Bassett, put the Buff/Norman dynamic far more bluntly: "She, as the publisher's wife, carried a certain amount of weight around here."

By 1950, Norman's "special assistant" had already moved in on the society pages and the so-called soft sections of the *Times.* On New Year's Day of 1951, for example, at Buff's urging the *Times*' astrology column began a fifty-year run as a *Times* staple. A passionate believer in astrological charts, Buff later attributed many of her Taurus troubles to her incompatibility with her son's quixotic Sagittarian nature. But in 1951, while she was still in control, she hired the *Times*' first resident soothsayer: Carroll Righter, a diminutive Philadelphian who called himself "the gregarious Aquarius."

Righter had carved a reputation for himself as a Hollywood horoscope artist with a star stable that included Marlene Dietrich, Arlene Dahl, Rhonda Fleming, Joan Fontaine, and Grace Kelly. Buff was chiefly interested in Righter's readings to find out who she could approach for donations to her current favorite cause and how best to shake those reluctant donors down. Righter obliged, and even took some of the credit for her biggest fund-raising coups.

With Righter and her "Woman of the Year" awards triumph, Buff became the *Times*' de facto lifestyle editor at the same time she accepted a seven-year term as president of the Hollywood Bowl Association and the chairmanship of the Southern California Symphony Association.[6]

She shamelessly used the annual "Woman of the Year" awards to maintain control of L.A.'s cultural politics, often surprising friend and foe alike over the years by naming the wives of several of the Chandlers' worst political enemies as

"Women of the Year," including Mrs. Fletcher Bowron and Mrs. Sam Yorty. Buff shrewdly calculated that the awards could mend otherwise insurmountable fences, establish unlikely coalitions, and accelerate consensus on those issues nearest and dearest to her heart—chief of which was a post–"Save the Bowl" drive to create a permanent home for the L.A. Philharmonic. She envisioned a square city block devoted to the performing arts at the epicenter of L.A., just two blocks northeast of Times Mirror Square on a twenty-six-acre patch of Bunker Hill.

It would be a Los Angeles Music Center, she told the County Board of Supervisors when she broached the subject. It would have venues for plays and opera, and it would house her beloved Philharmonic. It would be the crowning cultural jewel in an emerging metropolis that promised to become the capital of the Pacific.

It would also cost close to $20 million plus millions more to operate, so Buff's initial reception before the Board of Supervisors was encouraging but lukewarm. Seven years and three failed bond issues later, she would finally conclude that any help she might get from the taxpayers to fulfill her dream would be severely limited. Buff would have to make it happen on her own.

Meanwhile, Mrs. Chandler learned more about the twin arts of fund-raising and playing politics. Both involved persuasion—the friendly kind and the not-so-friendly, which occasionally must be augmented by veiled threats and backroom blackmail.

Buff used both to persuade Norman to switch political allegiance to her side of the Republican Party in 1952.

Along with the rest of his family, Norman supported ultra-conservative Ohio Senator Robert Taft for the Republican presidential nomination that year, but Buff preferred Eisenhower. Her job of winning Norman over might have been easier if her arch enemy had not been in the Taft camp.

Enmity between Buff and her sister-in-law, Ruth, was brutal and relentless. Following the death of her first husband in 1942, Ruth had married a San Joaquin valley agricultural baron who owned real estate throughout the Southwest in addition to his 65,000-acre cotton ranch near Fresno. When he died in 1952, she married a third time: Sir William Charles Crocker, an obscure English knight. Her first two husbands had left Ruth richer than any of her brothers and sisters; her third husband's title had given her the pompous right to address herself as "Lady Crocker" for the rest of her life.

In many ways, Lady Crocker was Buff's perfect foil. She was aggressive, savvy, and often unprincipled when it came to getting her own way. She appropriated the family Christmas dinner tradition that had begun with Harry and Marian[7] in the early 1920s, and she made a point of inviting every relative and in-law to her English Tudor mansion save one: Buff never received an invitation.

Asked about her sister-in-law in a 1976 interview, Buff was uncharacteristically terse:

"We don't fight, but we don't see each other" was all that she would say on the subject.

An antediluvian conservative to match the politics of her youngest brother, Philip, and his wife, Alberta,[8] Lady Crocker was a formidable foe in the battle for Norman's Republican soul. Although she could pester the *Times* publisher at family functions or over the phone, however, she could never sleep with him.

"We were out in our pool house in Sierra Madre, and I remember we argued so, but I couldn't get him to change his mind," Buff recalled years later. "I said to him, 'All right, you just stay in your bed and I'll stay in mine. Don't you dare come over until you change your mind.'"

Norman did change his mind, but not because of Buff's extortion. During the 1952 Republican campaign, Norman saw Senator Taft upbraid a news photographer for taking his picture, and the usually mild-mannered publisher of the *Los Angeles Times* blew up. Journalists, he informed the senator from Ohio, had a job to do, and to berate them for doing it was unacceptable. He switched his support from Taft to Eisenhower and, according to Buff, followed it up the following evening by asking, "Can I come back to bed tonight?"

During that election year, Norman Chandler began to drift away from his sisters, his brothers, and his royalist GOP roots.

"Norman's theory was: 'If you stay with me, you and I will make it and we can't worry about them.' And so it was the two of us against five sisters and two brothers," said Buff.

Otis remembered both his parents moving "into a more liberal Republican camp," although he called his mother's tale of withholding sex "baloney." Her Taft-to-Ike tale was just another instance of Buff Chandler's reinventing herself for posterity in a slightly more interesting light.

THE REAL POLITICAL CLOUT of the *Los Angeles Times* wasn't located between the sheets of Buff Chandler's bed. It wasn't even located in the publisher's suite. Political power at the *Times* during the early 1950s remained vested in a graying, curly-haired gnome named Kyle Palmer and his small army of string-pulling assistants.

Palmer was at the top of his game during the Truman and Eisenhower administrations. The *Times'* political editor had persuaded California's Governor Earl Warren to run as vice president on the doomed 1948 Republican ticket, which

had been headed by the governor of New York, Thomas Dewey. Warren was "a fine public servant and a poor politician," wrote Palmer.

Whenever Herbert Hoover came through L.A., he bypassed the rest of the waiting press corps and made a beeline to Palmer's home, where he would regale the *Times* potentate with anecdotes and exclusive tidbits until well past midnight.

Kyle Palmer advised Richard Nixon to "slap her around a bit . . . in a political sense, of course," when the second-term congressman campaigned against Helen Gahagan Douglas in the 1950 election for the U.S. Senate. Taking a signal from the *Times*' fierce anti-Red bias, Nixon also labeled the well-respected liberal congresswoman and wife of actor Melvyn Douglas "the Pink Lady."

In his own *Times* editorial page column, Palmer backed Nixon up, demeaning Mrs. Douglas as "a veritable political butterfly, flitting from flower to flower." He didn't label her a Communist, but he did slam her as too "emotional"—but then, what did the voters expect of a female politician? Palmer, Norman Chandler's preeminent imp, shrugged off criticism of the *Times*' pro-Nixon news coverage by cavalierly pointing out that "from time to time, as space allows, news accounts of what [Douglas] has to say and what she is doing will be published."

Palmer made no secret of his absolute control of the California legislature. In Sacramento, he would literally walk a selected bill through both the Senate and the Assembly, then lay it on the governor's desk for signature. One of his many nicknames was "the Little Governor." No Republican ran for anything more powerful than dogcatcher in California without Kyle Palmer's approval.

The full extent of Palmer's dominion was illustrated in an often-repeated story *Times* reporter Fred Chase related after entering Palmer's office one day, just as the diminutive political editor had finished berating an underling. The tongue-lashee stood, his head still hanging, eyes cast at the floor, and hands folded at his waist like a chastened tot. As he brushed past Chase on his way out, the reporter recognized the man Palmer had just finished chewing out. It was Goodwin Knight, the newly elected governor of California.

If Palmer's power at the state level was formidable, in Los Angeles it was absolute. His city hall lieutenant, another *Times* gnome named Carlton Williams, instructed a majority of the fifteen-member city council on how to vote on those matters that affected the Chandlers' interests. Williams's mentor and predecessor had been Harry Chandler's venerable city hall fixer Al Nathan, who'd educated his younger apprentice in the art of influence peddling.

Depending upon the voting instructions given to him at Times Mirror Square, Carlton Williams would stand at the rear of the council chambers and point his thumb up or down. According to the *Times*' critics, the council majority cast their vote as Williams directed while keeping the Chandler name above the fray, in-

evitably rewarding big business over the poor. Williams-influenced votes included

- L.A.'s construction subsidy of Walter O'Malley's Dodger Stadium at the expense of blue-collar Hispanics in the downtown barrio of Chavez Ravine;
- defeat of federally subsidized public housing for the poor on Civic Center's Bunker Hill, where Buff Chandler hoped someday to build her Music Center; and
- support for LAPD Chief of Detectives Thaddeus Brown—whom Norman Chandler dubbed "a master detective"—as chief of the Los Angeles Police Department.

Only the Brown nomination eventually went down in defeat—a casualty of shifting politics, LAPD skullduggery, and Norman Chandler's own adulterous indiscretion.

Since Harry Chandler's heyday, the *Times* had retained control of the five-member police commission. Even following the Frank Shaw disaster at city hall, Norman held the balance of power by using his *Times* to influence the city council's selection of at least three of the five commissioners. By holding sway over the commission, Chandler could still handpick the chief of police despite objections from reform Mayor Fletcher Bowron. Thus, when LAPD interim chief William Worton[9] prepared to step down in the winter of 1950, Chief of Detectives Thad Brown appeared to be a shoo-in. The *Times* even ran a story that had been "leaked" to Carlton Williams maintaining that Brown had already been selected by three of the five police commissioners and only a formal vote was necessary to make it official.

But there was a second contender for the chief's post named William H. Parker, a veteran captain who had once worked as a personal assistant to the notorious former chief James Davis. Chief Worton took a liking to Captain Parker and promoted him to head of the LAPD's Internal Affairs Division. Unfortunately for Norman Chandler, Inspector Parker learned from a friend on the force that the *Times* publisher had become a bit too close to one of the police commissioners.

Several months earlier, Parker ally Lieutenant James Hamilton, an LAPD investigator assigned to help the police commission, had noticed a peculiarly close relationship between Chandler and the only woman who sat on the commission. It was no coincidence that Chandler and his *Times* had enthusiastically supported the appointment of Agnes Albro, the wife of Security Pacific Bank manager Curtis Albro. Agnes Albro's list of civic achievements easily vanquished

those of Buff Chandler: director of the women's division of the Los Angeles Chamber of Commerce, founder of the Woman's Tax Study Group, chair of the Women's Civic Conference, vice president of Volunteers of America, and president of the YWCA. Furthermore, she and her husband were estranged and they had no children.

Suspecting hanky-panky, Lieutenant Hamilton watched Chandler pick up Agnes Albro on the steps of city hall one evening and followed them to a beach house, where they entered at sundown and did not reemerge until dawn. Over the next several weeks, Hamilton stepped up his surveillance, installing cameras and bugs in the beach house and observing the couple at every opportunity.

As the field of candidates for permanent chief of police narrowed to Inspector Parker and "master detective" Thad Brown, Lieutenant Hamilton's dirt suddenly became moot.

Agnes Albro died of breast cancer on July 30, 1950. Her replacement on the commission was male and did not vote as he was told to vote by the *Times*. He voted with the new majority to name William Parker the fortieth chief of the Los Angeles Police Department on August 9, 1950.

Although they frequently did not see eye-to-eye, Norman Chandler worked out a truce with hard-drinking but brilliant Chief Parker,[10] who became known to his troops as "Whiskey Bill." Parker never revealed what he knew of the Agnes Albro affair, and Chandler kept a muzzle on his *Times* about all but the worst of the LAPD's indiscretions.

It wasn't merely a matter of LAPD blackmail, however. Chandler and Parker found common ground in their irrational hatred of subversive elements, whether they were minorities or union troublemakers. During the next sixteen years, Parker's anti-Communist hysteria rivaled that of the *Times;* in 1955, it gave new life to an intelligence-gathering division called the Law Enforcement Intelligence Unit, which was similar to the Red Squad of the 1920s and 1930s. It was headed by Parker's intuitive spy and ally, Lieutenant James Hamilton, who was eventually succeeded in 1963 by Parker's personal driver, Lieutenant Daryl Gates.

AS WAS THE CASE WITH HIS FATHER, Norman Chandler's fingerprints were rarely found on these local manipulations. In day-to-day operations at city hall and the state capitol, Norman remained deferential to Palmer and Williams, but he was by no means apolitical.

He'd finally had enough of the reforming Mayor Fletcher Bowron by 1952, chiefly because the four-term mayor favored low-rent, federally subsidized public housing for Bunker Hill. Chandler real estate dotted the map of downtown Los Angeles and the thought of Chicago-style high-rise housing projects adjacent to

real estate held by one of Harry Chandler's family trusts was just too repugnant to his oldest son. Norman joined a group of seven other Republican power brokers to draft a lackluster California congressman named Norris Poulson to return from Washington and run against Bowron. The Chandler committee promised Poulson campaign support plus a chauffeur-driven Cadillac and a substantial hike in the mayoral salary if he won.

A veteran observer of the *Times'* dirty politics during both the Upton Sinclair EPIC episode and the Frank Shaw/James Davis régime, Mayor Bowron saw what Chandler was up to and fought back. He singled Norman out by name in a series of attacks on the *Times* and the family that owned it. Chandler and his cronies used the *Times* "to misrepresent the facts, to suppress the news, to convince you that falsehoods are the truth, that the truth is false, that black is white," Bowron accused.

In a series of front-page editorials, Norman struck back with emotional appeals that concluded that Bowron's attacks made him no better than "the anarchists who bombed the *Times* Building forty-three years ago."

Poulson won by a slim margin and the *Times* once again was in full control of city hall. On the national level, however, the Chandlers and even the omniscient Kyle Palmer were about to witness the first near-miss in their ongoing efforts to extend *Times* influence all the way to the White House.

"I was the one who threw Nixon's name in the ring," Buff Chandler boasted as the Republicans opened their 1952 convention in Chicago.

She did so, Buff told an interviewer, by persuading the publisher of the *Chicago Daily News* just before the convention was to begin to predict in a front-page headline that Dwight Eisenhower would choose Richard Nixon as his running mate. The *Daily News* prediction gave Nixon the edge over such formidable California Republican rivals as Governor Earl Warren and Senator Joseph Knowland, the senior U.S. senator and publisher of the *Oakland Tribune.*

The popular General Eisenhower did indeed pick Nixon to run with him in 1952, but it was Kyle Palmer who had paved the way by writing many of Nixon's speeches for him and counseling him on such mundane matters as keeping a smile pasted on his face at all times, even while eviscerating a political foe. Palmer's advice was considered so key that Nixon's chief strategist, Murray Chotiner, often copied confidential internal campaign memoranda to "CC: Kyle Palmer."

A Republican victory appeared certain until one month before election day, when Ike thought about dumping his thirty-nine-year-old running mate.

The East Coast press reported that a group of California supporters secretly paid Nixon a supplemental salary of nearly $20,000 a year. During the first three

days after the story broke, *Times* editor L. D. Hotchkiss purposely buried Nixon slush-fund news on the third page. Eisenhower publicly supported Nixon, but privately suggested that Nixon bare all.

The Republican National Committee bought a half-hour of prime time on three networks for $75,000 and Nixon delivered his famous "Checkers" speech—heavy on emotion while skirting the slush-fund issue.

"Regardless of what they [Democrats] say about it, we're gonna keep it," he said, referring to a dog named Checkers that a campaign supporter had given to his two little girls.

While Washington pundits and New York literati uniformly panned Nixon's performance as the most blatantly maudlin appeal to the cheapest of human sentiment, most of the 58 million who watched the "Checkers" speech sided with the Nixons, their daughters, and their dog—including the *Los Angeles Times.*

In a front-page editorial headlined WE STAND BY NIXON that ran the following day, the same *Los Angeles Times* that had relegated the original story of the scandal to the inside pages, declared, "The personal tragedy of an upright man sacrificed unjustly to satisfy the clamor stirred by the cunning objectives of his political enemies would by no means be as deplorable as would be the loss to the public of a career genuinely dedicated to the public interest."

IT WAS UNLIKELY Otis Chandler read his father's front-page editorial or anything else the *Times* published regarding the 1952 presidential election. Except for the sports section or news of the Olympic Games, he still wasn't much interested in newspapers. He was far more interested in surfing, as he had demonstrated on his honeymoon when he saved his bride's life and made the front page of the *New York Times* to boot.

Honolulu was still exotic enough in the early 1950s to appeal to young, rich newlyweds, particularly if they were athletic, and Otis and Missy surely qualified on all counts. They spent every waking hour in the water, competing for the perfect wave. Matching her husband stroke for stroke, Missy took her board everywhere her husband went. She refused to dawdle in the shallows or remain on the beach. When Otis ventured out a half mile or more beyond the Waikiki shoreline, Missy was right beside him. One day, they went too far.

"There was an off-shore wind blowing, too," recalled Otis. "I saw her missing wave after wave and I could see she was getting tired. I was almost ready to ride another wave in, and I think if I had, she would have drowned."

He saw her fall off her board and bob beneath the waves, so he paddled to her aid.

"I put her on her board," said Otis. "She was lifeless. Then I'd push her board, and then paddle."

No lifeguard saw what was going on, so Otis struggled against the tide, pushing his own and his wife's boards back toward the beach.

"I finally got near the beach and I was screaming at the people on the veranda at the Royal Hawaiian who were having cocktails," he said. "They thought we were a couple of honeymooners playing on our surfboards. I finally got a Navy person on the beach and somebody else to get an ambulance."

The following day, newspapers across the United States reported the incident under the headline "Shot Putter Saves Wife from Heavy Surf." It was to be only the first, if the most dramatic, of many incidents in which the competitive underpinnings of their relationship led to trouble for one or the other and, eventually, for both of them.

Otis remained in school another two semesters following his honeymoon, but left Stanford in 1951 to do his time in the military.

Korea was then the world's Cold War hot spot; Otis wanted to avoid it if he could, and he meant to do so by qualifying for the Olympics as cocaptain of the U.S. Air Force track team.

As early as his freshman year at Stanford, he had been breaking records in the shot put. As a senior, he tossed the sixteen-pound iron ball fifty-seven feet, four and one-quarter inches—eight inches short of a world record. He was considered a shoo-in for the U.S. team at Helsinki during the Summer Games of 1952. But he placed sixth and didn't go.

"I had my bags all packed for Helsinki, but about a week before the trials, I hurt the tendons and ligaments in my throwing hand," he recalled. "That was a real depressing time."

An understatement, according to Missy.

"I think that was one of the biggest disappointments of his life," she said.

Instead of Finland, he went to Ohio for Air Force training to become a fighter pilot.

"Not a bomber pilot. Not a transport pilot. A fighter pilot," he said.

But Air Force jets were not made for 230-pound shot putters. He'd have to lose at least 15 pounds and even then, he might be too big. Otis simply stopped eating and lost the weight in a week, stunning Missy. It was the first of many times she would marvel at her husband's iron self-discipline.

"You could not believe it. Literally nothing but water for a week. That's how badly he wanted it," she recalled.

But to no avail. All the diets in the world could not shrink his shoulders and his hips or reduce his six-foot-three frame to where it could be shoe-horned into a cockpit.

"I just couldn't fit," he said. "They said, 'We are not going to redesign our fighter planes for you. We'll put you in bombers.' I said, 'No. I want to fly something fast.'"

Deflated, a grounded Otis now saw the Air Force as little more than a waiting game. He had to give the military a minimum of two years and that's exactly what he planned to do—no less, and no more. He was transferred to Camp Stoneman, east of San Francisco, at about the same time Missy became pregnant with their first child.

The Air Force dispatched personnel to Korea from Camp Stoneman, but Second Lieutenant Otis Chandler was not among them. As a valued member of the Air Force track team, he was rewarded with the job of Special Services officer.

"I mainly organized sports teams, softball, basketball, volleyball, dances," he said. "I had about twenty guys under me. It was not difficult duty."

They were poor, Otis insisted. He and Missy lived modestly in a tiny rental off base where they raised a pair of boxers and their first son, Norman. The Chandlers went next door to watch *I Love Lucy* because they couldn't afford a television set.

At one point, they ate horse meat, like their dogs, according to Missy. It was cheaper than steak and kept Otis's appetite at bay. When hints sent home to his eternally frugal parents produced no cash, Otis came up with a novel way to subsidize his skimpy officer's stipend. He went into the used-car business.

"Guys would get their orders and await their final shipping to Korea, and they would have a car to sell. Guess who was there?" said Otis.

If there had been such a thing as all-night television, he would have used it to hawk his cars in the fashion of Cal Worthington, but he did all right with word of mouth.

"I must have bought and sold a couple hundred cars," he said. "I would say, 'Well, I'll give you $500,' and they'd answer, 'Oh no, it's worth more than that.' And then they'd try to sell it somewhere else and come back to me when they had maybe eight hours left before they had to ship out."

In 1953, Otis and his growing family drove home to Sierra Madre. He and Missy now had a pair of boxers and two sons, Harry Brant Chandler having been conceived on a camping trip to the Sierras. Harry was thirteen months younger, but nearly as big as his older brother, Norman. Children, dogs, and a frequently absent husband conspired to turn Missy into a chain-smoker.

During his final months in the Air Force, Otis thought little of anything but his career. Medicine might be good. Sports medicine, perhaps. Having had his fill working during summer vacations in the pressroom, though, the *Times* was way down his list of possible professions.

"I thought working there was all mechanical and I didn't want to keep doing that for the rest of my life," he said.

Otis hadn't seen Norman and Buff for over a year. When he pulled into their driveway, he thought he'd at least get a hug and an invitation to stay for dinner. Instead, Norman beamed like the winner of the Irish Sweepstakes.

"I remember like it was yesterday," said Otis. "My father pulled out an envelope. . . . It was a seven-year executive training program designed especially for Otis Chandler. It was quite thorough, quite well done. It had so many weeks in this department and that department, starting salary and so on.

"I looked it over, not casually, thinking that my father might give me a day or so. But he asked right away, 'Well? What do you think?' I don't think I ever mentioned to him that I maybe wanted to be a doctor, or if I did, he wasn't listening.

"I think my mother felt that he was rushing it a bit—that Missy and I deserved a little vacation and chance to catch our breath. So I looked at it and said, 'I'd like to read it and think about it some more.' This was Friday. And he said, 'Well, I have you tentatively starting on the graveyard shift as an apprentice pressman Sunday night.' I said, 'Oh.'

"I guess I must have always wanted to give it a shot because I didn't really scream and yell at all. I guess I just said, 'Well, this is a job.' I'd be making $39 or $49 a week less than I was making as a first lieutenant in the Air Force, and we had no place to live at that time.

"We wound up renting a home in Altadena. And I started at the *Times* that Sunday morning."

CHAPTER 14

IN SEPTEMBER 1954, William G. Bonelli self-published *Billion Dollar Blackjack*—a devastating indictment of the Chandler family's greed and political power brokering throughout seven decades of the dynasty's alleged misuse of its *Times*.

Written in retaliation against a *Mirror* series about liquor license kickbacks in the California state taxing agency that Bonelli oversaw,[1] *Billion Dollar Blackjack* was the first real attempt in half a century to detail the *Times'* sins, from General Otis's successful efforts to bar unions to the rape of the Owens Valley to Harry Chandler's abortive attempt to foment a revolution in Baja. Although Norman

Chandler refused to dignify Bonelli's book with a public response, he did try to buy all 20,000 copies, according to Bonelli. Indeed, *Billion Dollar Blackjack* sold out quickly and did not reprint. The 230-page denunciation, subtitled *The Story of Corruption and the Los Angeles Times,* quickly became a cult classic.

Among the book's revelations was the unholy alliance between the *Times* and Santa Anita Park, which dated back to Harry Chandler's original deal with the founder of Santa Anita, Dr. Charles Strub, in 1934.

Since 1911, horse racing had been illegal in California until a bill allowing closely regulated racing barely squeaked by the state legislature and became law in 1934. Strub, an enterprising San Francisco credit dentist,[2] apparently grasped just how tenuous pari-mutuel betting was among the prim, puritanical, and frequently hypocritical California electorate. As he began Santa Anita's construction on land owned by the late E. J. "Lucky" Baldwin, Strub hedged his own bet accordingly. As insurance against racing's being outlawed again, he put two master Sacramento manipulators on the Santa Anita payroll: legendary lobbyist Artie Samish[3] and Kyle Palmer, the *Times'* political editor. Furthermore, Strub paid Palmer $30,000 through the *Times*, which received Santa Anita's checks, laundered them at Times Mirror Square, and then paid Palmer.

Although the Palmer payoffs lasted only three years, from 1934 to 1939, Bonelli discovered[4] a more subtle arrangement, this one between the racetrack and the publisher's wife, in the early 1950s: Santa Anita had contributed $75,000 to both of Buff Chandler's two favorite causes: the Southern California Symphony Association and an organization that became the forerunner of the Los Angeles Music Center Fund.

In exchange for these cozy cash arrangements, Bonelli suggested, the *Times* had never printed a negative word about Santa Anita, one of the only two legalized forms of gambling in California.[5] Indeed, the Chandler family owned the popular food franchise, Eaton's Restaurant, at Santa Anita, and opening day of every race season was accorded the same pomp and circumstance on the news, sports, and society pages of the *Times* as the Tournament of Roses.

Although Bonelli charged the *Mirror's* staff with libel, sued the Chandlers for $6 million, and called a press conference to denounce the family over the findings he'd alleged in *Billion Dollar Blackjack*, his anti-Chandler smear campaign fell on deaf ears. The *Times* reported nothing, of course, and its rivals, including the Hearst papers, showed tepid interest. Bonelli railed that the fix was in, but his case against the Chandlers was further poisoned when the *Mirror's* kickback allegations in its "Saloon Empire" series apparently turned out to be true: A grand jury indicted the liquor license chief for allegedly receiving $250,000 in bribes from the liquor industry. Shortly before he went to trial in 1956, Bonelli fled to Mexico, where he remained an expatriate rancher until his death in 1970.

The *Los Angeles Mirror*, however, reached its crusading zenith in the mid-1950s. It was surprisingly well written and its informative exposés, among them "Saloon Empire," had become a *Mirror* staple. Rising stars such as Bill Thomas, the *Mirror's* city editor, and the investigative team of Gene Blake and Jack Tobin had sharpened their teeth on the *Mirror's* "scandal-of-the-week" formula. Norman Chandler's brainchild was still in the red, but it wasn't hemorrhaging as much as it had been during the first couple of years. Norman and Buff both found strong appeal in their scrappy tabloid—a zest that was missing from the stodgy and hidebound *Times.*

On December 18, 1954, the *Times'* anemic but feisty little brother celebrated a major triumph when the *Mirror* managed to put L.A.'s only Democratic newspaper out of business. After a generation, the afternoon *Daily News,* launched by Cornelius Vanderbilt Jr. in 1923 and shepherded through most of its existence by former Times Mirror executive Manchester Boddy, ceased publication.

In a crafty move that would have made Harry proud, Norman secretly created a company to buy the circulation list for *Daily News* and assets for $275,000 before Hearst found out. He then cherry-picked the best of the *Daily News* staff, dismissed the rest, and folded everything into his beloved *Mirror.* Norman even briefly renamed his tabloid the *Mirror-Daily News* before permanently switching to a full-sized broadsheet format and changing the name to the *Los Angeles Mirror News.* Nonetheless, the *Mirror News* still trailed in circulation well behind Hearst's evening *Herald Express* and, although its advertising lineage outpaced every other American newspaper, the *Times* was only barely leading in the L.A. circulation wars against Hearst's morning *Examiner.* In 1955, the *Times'* average weekday circulation topped out at 434,057.

Indeed, commercial success rarely translated into great journalism. In May 1955, *Times* photographer John Gaunt won the *Times* its third Pulitzer Prize[6] for a wrenching shot of a couple on Hermosa Beach clutching each other in horrified grief moments after their nineteen-month-old son had been swept out to sea. Despite the prestigious award and the photo's profound impact, there was no follow-up reporting about the parents, beach water safety, or any other element of the story. It wasn't a *Billion Dollar Blackjack*–type conspiracy to suppress the news; it was just an especially glaring example of the *Times'* routinely poor news judgment.

When another *Times* photographer filmed police beating a demonstrator as he was waving an American flag, editor L. D. Hotchkiss burned the negative. Hotchkiss and the photographer agreed that publishing such a photo would only martyr the demonstrator, whom they both believed to be a subversive. In such a paranoid atmosphere, photographers and reporters sometimes killed their photos and stories before they even submitted them. Staff writer Bill Kiley, for instance,

took brilliant notes but often did not write the story. During an ambulance ride with a retarded mother whose illegitimate infant had just died, Kiley wrote, "Her finger was shaking as she placed it on the tiny eyelid and pushed it open. She stared into the unseeing eye for several seconds and then tears from her own swollen eyes fell on the cheeks of the lifeless infant. Suddenly a smile crept across her face. The tears in her eyes sparkled. 'That's it,' she said happily. 'I forgot to feed him. That's what's wrong.' Her hand moved to the buttons on her blouse."

Kiley stuck his notes in the back of his files and forgot about the incident. The *Times* of General Otis might have snatched up such a story and played its pathos to the hilt, but the *Times* of L. D. Hotchkiss would have shown no interest in it, Kiley reasoned.

On December 4, 1956, the *Times* celebrated its seventy-fifth birthday. After sixty-five years atop three *Times* buildings, the *Times* eagle came down from its perch. The bronzed bird—its wings spread defiantly against organized labor, subversive elements, and all nonboosters who would speak skeptically about the inevitability of Southern California—had been weakened by corrosion. Building engineers agreed that it could easily topple, land on a pedestrian, and spawn a lawsuit. Rather than go to the expense of having it rebronzed and anchored more securely, the Times Mirror board opted to bury the stubborn symbol of General Otis's *Times* in a sub-basement of the *Times* Building.

"I was the training program guinea pig," Otis groused.

Executive trainees in later years had a smoother ride, but Norman's son started at the bottom, did the grungiest jobs for the lowest wages, and gradually learned to love the *Times* in spite of every reason not to.

"My father insisted I carry my weight as I entered each new department," he said. "It was good logical thinking, but it didn't address the issue of survival. I was ill-equipped because I am not a trained engraver or a trained pressman. I didn't work up through the ranks from apprentice to journeyman over a period of years."

Because Norman wanted him to become familiar with the Times Mirror "family" as well as learn every nuance of running a newspaper, Otis didn't stay in any department for very long. Once he'd become used to working swing shift in the pressroom, he'd switch to graveyard in type setting; days in rotogravure would give way all too quickly to nights at the loading dock.

"He was always a light sleeper," said Missy Chandler, who remembered that her husband's peripatetic work schedule only worsened his insomnia. "He was always tired. He had ink in his ears during one of the children's birthdays."

Never much of a homebody anyway, Otis also became more of an absentee father. His and Missy's brood increased from two (Norman in 1952 and Harry in 1953) to three (Cathleen in 1955) to four (Michael in 1958), but his only real contact with them came on weekends or evenings. His life was not his own. He'd even given up surfing.

"I didn't have time. I was working odd hours and I didn't surf again until 1958 or 1959, when I joined the famous San Onofre Surfing Club. That's where I taught Missy and my kids to surf. Even when they were just two and three years old, I'd carry them out screaming on the front of my big tandem board."

As the ever expanding size of their family dictated, they moved from house to larger house, but their quarters were always modest. Buff offered to lend them her interior decorator, but the couple had to pay for any furnishings and construction work themselves. Missy remembered that she fainted from the paint fumes when she was pregnant for the third time and trying to spruce up a bedroom all by herself during a heat wave.

"We never had babysitters or much of a social life," she said. A big night out was a station wagon trip to the drive-in.

To hear Otis and Missy tell it, they barely lived above the poverty line throughout most of the 1950s, despite a small inheritance Missy received from her grandfather on her twenty-first birthday. Otis inherited nothing but hard work.

"I was making no progress financially," Otis said. "A few years ago, somebody found an old stub from one of my paychecks in the pressroom. I think it was for $48. I was earning less than I was making in the Air Force."

Norman Chandler insisted on Spartan financial terms for his only son so that Otis would continue to learn the true value of a dollar, just as Norman had been forced to learn this from Harry. Every time Otis switched to a new department, he started at the lowest rung on the pay scale, regardless of how many months or years he had worked for Times Mirror. He finally went to Jack Vance of McKinsey and Company, Norman's outside executive consulting firm, and asked Vance to reason with his father. Adjustments were made and Otis began to earn what he considered a living wage.

His second cousin Franklin Otis Booth Jr. (who, confusingly, went by his middle name) was also an executive apprentice for the *Times;* the two young Otises found themselves commiserating often over their stingy paychecks. The grandson of Marian Chandler's sister, Mabel,[7] Otis Booth was four years older than Otis Chandler and, like his cousin, had been encouraged by his family to become a Times Mirror executive-in-training.

The two Otises shared much in common, including a passion for the outdoors and hunting, and during those rare weekends when they were both able to get

away from the *Times*, the cousins trekked to the Salton Sea to bag as many ducks as the legal limit allowed. They even leased part of the muddy shoreline from the Southern Pacific Railroad, set up twenty duck blinds, imported an old trailer, and founded the O & O Gun Club.

Both young men agreed that they would never get rich quick—or, perhaps, get rich at all—working for the *Times*. Otis Booth persisted in his own executive apprenticeship through the remainder of the decade, rising to the rank of Times Mirror vice president of the forest-product and commercial printing group. He also dabbled successfully in real estate development on the side and was doing well enough to leave the *Times* by 1968. Through his friend and lawyer, Charlie Munger, he'd come across a promising venture in Omaha that had just been launched by a young prophet named Warren Buffett, used his real estate earnings to buy a 1.4 percent stake in Buffett's fledgling investment firm, Berkshire Hathaway, and never looked back at the newspaper business.

"He's one of my best friends to this day," said Otis Chandler forty years later. "He's worth a couple of billion dollars now.[8] But then, he was a Booth, not a Chandler."

Otis was very much a Chandler and knew full well where his duty lay. There was never a question about his leaving the *Times*. If he needed a reminder, both of his parents constantly reminded him. He was the heir apparent. Someday. Meanwhile, he earned what they were willing to pay him and he spent time in every department during those first five years, from production to circulation to advertising. His hands-down favorite, though, was editorial.

"I had no real training, so they had me doing rewrite and obits and store openings that would be easy to redo or correct," he remembered. "I guess I had a reasonably good aptitude because Bud [Lewis, *Times* city editor] would throw things back at me and say, 'Rewrite it.'"

He also took dictation from Hedda Hopper.

"I had to rewrite her copy, it was so bad."

Unlike his father or his grandfather, Otis grasped what his great grandfather, General Otis, had thoroughly understood: that the newsroom was the heartbeat of the business.

"If you don't have your editorial product, you have nothing," said Otis.

Besides, working as a reporter was just plain more fun than he'd ever had on any job in his life. There was fraternity at the city desk. He might be the publisher's son and was probably accorded a wide berth during his first few days, but such niceties fade fast under deadline pressure. Like his city desk peers, Otis developed a distaste for the "the three little tyrants" who ran the *Times* news operation with gutless temerity and a generous helping of arrogance.

"[Editor L. D.] Hotchkiss, Bud Lewis, and Kyle Palmer were all the same height," recalled Otis. "They ordered me never to stand too close to them. They didn't want to look any shorter in front of the city-side staff than they were."

Of the three, Otis found Lewis the least offensive and most professional. He even warmed to him after an initial dread of his incessant hollering.

"He had a good sense of humor, but to any reporter under his gaze, he came across as a tough guy."

Hotchkiss, however, "was anonymous," according to Otis.

"He wouldn't speak to any reporter. He hardly knew anybody's name. There was a photographer who'd been there for twenty-five years, and he and Hotchkiss were both standing at the urinal in the men's room at the same time and Hotch looked over at him and said, 'Young man, are you new here?'"

But Kyle Palmer was the worst of the lot.

"He was the little dictator," said Otis. "Kyle Palmer always felt that he was the kingmaker and that the publisher was only a means to an end."

Otis was especially disquieted over Palmer's nonpolitical acquaintances, including a furtive array of Mexican nationals who came to see the diminutive political editor at his *Times* office about secretive, sinister matters below the border. He never knew what Palmer was up to, but he instinctively sensed that it was no good.

"I just didn't like that whole scene," said Otis. "My father and mother kind of got a kick out of Kyle Palmer because he knew a lot of people, but I really didn't like any of that. My parents would have him introduce them to some of the better known political figures of their day and they were so flattered, they'd let Kyle act like he was the publisher."

Although he kept aloof from the three potentates of the newsroom, Otis developed fast friendships among the motley reporting crew who taught him how to type with two fingers and the ragtag photographers who showed him where to find the proper F-stop on a Speed Graflax. Soon, Otis Chandler became just another general assignment reporter, subject to the same front-page whims, pathos, and tomfoolery that had characterized American journalism for the better part of a century.

Otis tended to gravitate toward the younger, wilder, and more colorful denizens of the *Times* newsroom, but there was one balding, bespectacled cipher who eventually captured his attention simply because he was at once shy and witty. He was the night managing editor: an introverted, yet kindly and somewhat wry copy desk veteran who had been quietly putting in his time at the *Times* for almost twenty-five years.

"I couldn't figure him out," said Otis. "I'd met him, but frankly I felt like I didn't know him at all."

His name was Nick B. Williams, a native of Virginia who never lost his slow and thoughtful Southern drawl, despite undergraduate studies in the Greek classics at Tennessee's University of the South and a degree in government studies from the University of Texas. Author David Halberstam once described Williams's rumpled appearance as that of "someone who ought to be sitting on the neighborhood bar stool, or indeed might just have fallen off it."

His forehead was high and his fuse was long, and although he rarely agreed with "the three little tyrants," Nick Williams learned what he needed to know from each of them—and did so without belittling or upstaging their hair-trigger egos. He blandly rolled into work each afternoon just as Otis and the other day side reporters were putting the finishing touches to their stories. Nick Williams was just the kind of old-school lackey whom Otis figured he'd be dumping one day if he should ever run the *Times*.

Reporter Art Ryon, however, was Otis's kind of journalist. A brash former USC sprinter, Ryon had grown a bit too fond of visiting the Redwood Room—the *Times'* unofficial watering hole across Second Street from Times Mirror Square. Nonetheless, Ryon challenged the beefy publisher's son to a race—a one-hundred-yard dash to be conducted at Cal Tech—and made a grand show of training for the Big Event.

"He had his coaches and trainers and photographers," recalled Otis. "There were bets and streamers and all kinds of fun and games. But it was no contest because Art was only good for about thirty yards."

A few weeks after his ignominious defeat, Ryon graciously gave Otis a mounted photo. It showed Otis in the winner's circle with a Superman insignia superimposed over his broad chest. The photo staff also gave him a black-and-white 16-millimeter film that had been shot that day at Cal Tech. It wasn't until Missy ran the film for her mother and children that Otis found out he'd been had.

"Do you know what they spliced in the middle of these?" Missy asked angrily.

Otis shook his head.

"Naked strippers!" she howled.

Otis's mortification hadn't been so complete since some of the "gotcha!" pranks he'd suffered at the hands of his Deke brothers. He popped into the photo lab the following day and thanked his pals for sticking it to him. He loved the frat house camaraderie of the city desk.

"My father never worked in editorial in his life," said Otis, who moved on to the *Mirror News* in 1955 after nine months at the *Times*. "And the *Mirror* was even more fun than the old Gray Lady of Spring Street. We had much better sports writers, and the staff was just more flamboyant than the *Times*."

He worked under a different type of city editor, too, at the *Mirror.* Conservative Jim Basset had done a turn as Richard Nixon's press secretary before returning to

Times Mirror, but he had a deep, abiding respect for journalism as literature, as did Bill Thomas, who succeeded him at the *Mirror* when he later moved back over to the *Times*.

Bill Thomas was nearly the same age as Otis and several inches taller than the *Times* dour editorial triumvirate and he regarded news stories almost as if they were the raw material of legend. Like Basset before him, who had dispatched Otis to Northern California to cover a deadly flood, Thomas demanded the colorful details and the personal stories of loss and tragedy that made cold facts and casualty counts come to life. After all, he reasoned, that was the whole point of having the *Mirror*'s own man on the scene. The wire services could feed the city desk all the facts and figures any editor might ever want or need. Thomas required something more. Call it tragedy, comedy, or something in between, but he wanted that singular anecdote, narrative subtext, or brooding word picture that could transubstantiate a news report into literature.

Otis once covered a suicide for the *Times* before he went to work at the *Mirror*—a leaper from an arroyo bridge, like the wave of Julian Petroleum jumpers from a quarter century before. The dead man wore a brand-new pair of loafers; Otis watched as one of the attendants from the Georgia Street ambulance service tried them on.

"Yeah, they fit," he said. "He won't need 'em."

It was the kind of story Hotchkiss could have taken or left on the newsroom floor; it was the kind of story Bill Thomas would have loved. Bill Thomas struck Otis as a man to remember.

As a reporter, Otis's proudest achievement was a seven-part series on emotionally disturbed children at Camarillo State Hospital that began, "The hospital is a city of red-tiled roofs, blue-denimed patients, and misplaced memories."

In later years, Otis remarked that he might have profited from spending more time in editorial, but a year of writing about the weather, traffic accidents, mental illness, fires, floods, and murder seemed quite enough to Norman. He told his son that it was time to move on to circulation and advertising, where the money was made.

"When I was on the *Mirror,* I was a fighter for the underdog," said Otis. "When I left, they put together a scrap book with several of my bylined articles. It was so different from the *Times*. The *Mirror* was a gutsy paper, I liked the people, and I had a lot of hopes and ambitions for it."

Still, Otis was not so sentimental nor so naive in his newfound zeal for newspapering to forget what the family business was really all about. During a brief encounter with a couple of *Mirror* reporters near the end of his tour of duty, one of them said:

"Wouldn't it be great to work at a paper that really believed in the public's right to know?"

"Yeah, that's what it's all about," said his companion.

"No," said Otis. "The real purpose of a newspaper is to make money."[9]

To NORMAN AND BUFF, the real purpose of money was keeping it. Were it not for the extra taxes that they would have had to pay, for example, they might have owned a house instead of a trailer at Dana Point. It was certainly not that they couldn't afford the taxes; it was the principal involved. As a point of honor, Chandlers never paid a penny more in taxes than they were absolutely required to do so by law. Whenever the Los Angeles County tax assessor, John Quinn, boosted the assessed value of Times Mirror Square, for example, "they [Norman and Buff] squawked like stuck pigs," said Kyle Palmer.

Thus, when General Moses Sherman's loyal former houseboy and heir, Arnold Haskell, approached Norman with a proposal to purchase the bluff overlooking Dana Point in 1951, Chandler first wanted to know the tax ramifications. They could buy ninety-nine acres for about $250,000, Haskell said, but if they built houses or apartments, their investment would initially be eaten up by property taxes; but if they built a trailer park, the tax bill would be minimal.

Haskell and Chandler built eighty-one trailer sites and populated their property with the largest, most exclusive mobile homes along the coast. The clubhouse had a seventy-five-foot swimming pool and a pair of tennis courts and, in space no. 1, Buff installed her own custom trailer. Later on, Otis and Missy built their own four-bedroom trailer, which was designed by celebrated architect William L. Pereira, and festooned it with floating pots of geraniums. If it wasn't inviting tax trouble to label the huge homes anything other than trailers, the Chandlers would have called their dwellings what they really were: prefabricated beachfront estates. There, Buff entertained and held court very nearly as often as she did at Los Tiempos, the name that she and Norman had bestowed upon their Sierra Madre rancho.

Buff made a big deal out of "cooking" for Norman when they were at the beach—although that usually meant serving him quiche or cobbler that someone else had prepared. Back at the rancho, servants not only did the cooking but also served Norman and Buff.

After years of fighting off her own demons as well as the catty Chandler sisters, perpetually insecure Buff Chandler had finally come into her own as a doyenne. In addition to the gardener and the pool man, she had a cook, chauffeur, upstairs

maids and downstairs maids.[10] Her dinner parties were among the most sought-after invitations on the Pasadena circuit.

"She helped a lot in terms of public relations," recalled Otis. "My father didn't like to give a speech. He didn't like to be interviewed. I don't think he ever went on television or did any radio. He wasn't comfortable doing that.

"But she would say, 'Norman, you'll be fine! Let me help you with that speech.'"

While she expended much of her energy just getting her reluctant husband to meet his own social obligations ("I pushed Norman Chandler every day of his life," Buff told a friend), she had more than enough left over to conduct a mighty crusade, and that crusade formally began on St. Patrick's Day, 1955.

The Eldorado Party might seem a bit dowdy and downright bush league in retrospect, but at the time it was *the* social event of the decade: a spectacular black-tie fund-raiser for Buff's proposed Los Angeles Music Center; it was staged at the Ambassador Hotel and featured as its centerpiece a raffle for a Cadillac Eldorado, donated to the cause by General Motors. Christian Dior put on a fashion show, and the entertainers included Danny Kaye, Jack Benny, and Dinah Shore. Buff shamelessly used the pages of the *Times* to fan the flames for her party, before and after, and when the bills were all paid, she had a $400,000 nest egg to begin her quest for the $19 million she would need to build her L.A. cultural mecca.

One of the realizations she had stumbled upon during her "Save the Bowl" period was even clearer after the Eldorado Party, namely, more cash could be squeezed from Hillcrest Country Club and the Cedars-Sinai crowd than from the fat-cat WASPS of San Marino. Despite the thinly disguised anti-Semitic whining from the Lady Crocker side of the family, Buff proposed moving herself and Norman to a new, more centrally located home, somewhere west of where General Otis had once bivouacked on Wilshire Boulevard. It would have to be big enough and ostentatious enough to attract donors to dinner, the way Los Tiempos had always been, but it had to be tastefully appointed so that it would appeal to both Pasadena patricians and WASP wannabes, that is, successful Westside Jews.

Buff would have bluntly conceded that she wanted to pick the pockets of the Establishment and Hollywood at the same time. She found just the place to do it at the corner of Fifth Street and Lorraine Boulevard: a neighborhood of an old money near downtown L.A. known as Hancock Park.

First-time visitors to this new Los Tiempos usually had to check their invitations twice to be certain that they had the right address. Designed in the 1920s by William Randolph Hearst's favorite architect, Julia Morgan, the two-story mansion had originally been built for Edwin Janss,[11] one of Harry Chandler's success-

ful contemporaries in the real estate subdivision game. With its ornate Doric pillars and starkly classical façades, the home more closely resembled a bank or a mausoleum than a place where people lived. That it had sprung from the imagination of the same woman who had created San Simeon and Times Mirror Square's arch rival, the rococo *Los Angeles Examiner* headquarters twelve blocks south of the *Times* on Hill Street, lent it a sense of delicious wickedness.

With a $2-million price tag, the place was worth every penny to Buff—especially as she and Norman would be able to persuade Times Mirror to foot part of the bill because they planned to use the home for extensive business entertaining. Besides the kind of sweeping curved staircase that could have given Rhett Butler pause, there was also a pool house, which Buff renamed "The Pub," a library, and—best of all—a music room. And not just any music room. The doors, furnishings, and even the wallpaper came from the music room Wolfgang Mozart had used during his manic composing days at Vienna's Hapsburg Court. The room was an historical landmark and Buff delighted in telling her guests that the harpsichord had once been the plaything of Amadeus himself.

Using money, position, the *Times*, her piercing blue eyes, and her winning, winsome carnivorous overbite, Buff Chandler insinuated herself increasingly into public life. In 1954, California's Governor Goodwin Knight appointed her to the University of California's board of regents—a post she held for fourteen years. She also sat on the boards of Occidental College, President Eisenhower's U.S. Committee on Education Beyond the High School, and Times Mirror.

Defying the angry repercussions from Philip, Harrison, Lady Crocker, and the rest of Norman's side of the family, Buff and Norman visited the Soviet Union in 1955, after which Buff appeared before Congress to urge a more liberal student and cultural exchange program with the Soviets. The following year, Buff further scandalized the deeply conservative Chandlers by engineering a Los Angeles stopover for the touring Bolshoi Ballet and the Moiseyev folk dance company. To Philip and Alberta, Buff looked more and more like some Communist dupe and they winced at the idea that she was dragging Norman down with her.

"I'm extremely well organized," she boasted. "I'm most comfortable when I'm around men. Most women just don't seem to be competitive enough."

Through all of her public posturing—no matter whether she was well-received or whether she was damned—Buff tried to preserve an air of false modesty. While he was still night managing editor, the avuncular Nick B. Williams recalled the morning the *Times* announced that Buff had been named one of the newspaper's Women of the Year. The moment she heard the announcement, she was on the phone and she was furious.

"She said I had embarrassed her terribly by including her as a Woman of the Year," Williams recalled. "My silent reaction was, 'What the hell goes on? *She*

picks the Woman of the Year! What is she trying to do, saying I've embarrassed her?'"

All that Williams could think of to calm her was to say that she deserved the honor. She hung up and left him scratching his head. Only later did Norman confess that he had ordered his wife's appointment as a Woman of the Year and had sneaked it into the *Times* as a surprise. It had backfired on him too, he told Williams. Like most power players, Buff Chandler did not like surprises unless she was the one doing the surprising.

———————

WHEN HE WAS BEYOND THE CITY DESK, Otis began to feel his oats.

"While I was in circulation, I began to make copious notes," he said. "Wherever I went—classified, circulation, retail advertising, editorial—I wrote notes on procedures, notes on people, notes on how to do things. I made up my mind that if I ever had the opportunity to decide who I would keep and not keep, I needed a blueprint."

He shared his findings only with his father, who found his son's notes enlightening, sometimes even disturbing.

"I uncovered some unbelievably bad stuff," said Otis.

The classified advertising manager, for example, had found various ingenious ways to fleece the company. Exclusive of his managerial duties, he volunteered to host a local travel program for the *Times'* television station, KTTV. *The Open Road* offered tips to weekend travelers on Southern California's best getaways, but it also afforded special opportunities for the classified manager who used KTTV airtime to extract all sorts of freebies from sponsors, from fishing tackle to boats.

"I don't know if that's called extortion or graft or kick backs, but I didn't think it was right," said Otis.

Furthermore, the manager was smug about it, believing "he had a cushy job for the rest of his life," according to Otis. Once, the manager asked Otis if he'd like to do some duck hunting north of Bakersfield.

"I can't," said Otis, whose training program assignment at that time was soliciting classifieds over the phone. "I've got to get my ads in by tomorrow."

"Well," drawled the manager, "you're working for me, I'm the boss, and I want you to take a day off."

Otis did as he was ordered and discovered on the way to Bakersfield that the manager used a mobile radio phone to report from the field to Philip Chandler. The manager told Otis's uncle that he was tied up with an advertiser and wouldn't be back in the office, chuckling as he hung up the phone.

"He was dumb enough to include me in on the scheme, thinking I wouldn't tell anybody or wouldn't care," said Otis. "He thought it was really clever. I didn't blow the whistle on him at that time. But I made a note of it."

Otis rationalized that he wasn't merely tattling to his father. He was protecting the family business. As often as he recorded misdeeds, though, he kept notes on those who did their jobs well without getting the deserved credit.

"I think I was a big help to my father as fresh eyes and ears," he said.

In 1957, Otis was promoted to general manager of the *Mirror News,* his first executive position and, over the following year, he flexed his muscles. One of the first things he learned was that the *Times* accounting department routinely used the *Mirror* as a dumping ground for *Times* expenses, artificially driving up the *Mirror'*s deficit.

"They did it just so they could make the *Times* look good to my father," said Otis. "I thought the *Mirror* was getting screwed, so I really fought to put on some good financial managers."

It helped some, but not enough. The *Mirror* continued to operate in the red.

"The *Mirror* only made money three weeks during its entire existence," said Otis. "That's all. I was always trying to get it to a couple of thousand dollars in profit [per week], or at least to break even, but it was never a fair fight. The *Times* was big and efficient and more stately in the editorial department while the *Mirror* was fighting everyone: the *Times*, the *Herald Express,* the morning *Examiner,* and all the suburban newspapers."

Otis determined that the biggest problem was not in accounting; the biggest problem was Virgil Pinkley. The UPI executive whom Norman Chandler had handpicked to launch his new tabloid following World War II had made a habit of loading the *Mirror'*s managerial ranks with his old UPI cronies; they may have had great noses for news, but they had terrible noses for business. Reaching back to his own Deke days at Stanford where he had waited tables in the cafeteria to make ends meet, Otis drew the analogy that Pinkley and the *Mirror'*s editor, Ed Murray, "remind me of the proverbial spoiled son at college with the unlimited checking account and no idea of where the money is coming from."

Recalled Otis some forty years later, "I gave my father a twenty-five-page report that approached the problem from every way, including rates of advertising, circulation, subscriptions, and any way you cut the cake, it wasn't going to work. In the report was, 'In the meantime, before you close [the *Mirror*], get somebody in as publisher who knows what the fuck they're doing. Get rid of Virgil Pinkley. He couldn't be a nicer man, [but] he's an editorial man."

Norman read his son's findings with profound sadness. The *Times* needed new presses to remain competitive with Hearst, Otis argued, but could not afford to

purchase them while propping up the *Mirror*. Norman congratulated Otis on his detailed study, but did not act for nearly another year.

"Then he showed it to Pinkley, thinking this would spur Virgil on to greater effort. My father had a wonderful honesty about him. He figured, 'It's a good report. Why shouldn't he read it? If he's not doing his job, then this will help him.' Instead, Virgil said, 'Well, Otis is young and incompetent and doesn't know the operation and you can't listen to him. We'll do better.'"

That was not what Norman wanted to hear. In the autumn of 1957, Virgil Pinkley came to one of Buff's more intimate dinner parties where the special guest of honor was *Time* magazine's Los Angeles bureau chief, Frank McCulloch.

"I think it was set up, because Buff and Virgil got into an argument before dinner," McCulloch recalled. "Then, at dinner, Norman turned to him and said, 'Virgil, I don't think you need to come to work tomorrow.' The next day, Virgil left for El Centro."

Pinkley published several newspapers in the California desert over the next few years before moving back to L.A. in 1980 to finish out his career publishing the suburban *Glendale News Press.* He died in 1992 without ever having spoken to the Chandlers again.

At Otis's urging, Norman moved *Times* city editor, Bud Lewis, to the *Mirror* as publisher. Even with the change, the *Mirror* continued to flounder.

The *Times* never stopped making money, however. The Sunday *Times* set a new record, expanding to 268 pages, and the daily *Times* overtook the *Detroit News* as the national leader in home-delivered circulation. By 1958, the staff totaled 2,666 and the average *Times* salary was $125 per week; vacation time increased from two to three weeks. The *Times* continued to lurch forward; it put forth the same turgid and often reactionary slant to the news that had been served to Southern California since Harry Chandler's day—just more of it. More than one *Times* critic remarked that it was the only daily newspaper in America that appeared to be edited with a shovel.

In 1958, Otis moved from the *Mirror* to the *Times* as its vice president for sales. The masthead that had once read

Norman Chandler, President
Harrison Chandler, Vice President
Philip Chandler, Vice President and General Manager

now boosted Philip to the rank of executive vice president of Times Mirror, a heartbeat away from the top job held by the eldest Chandler brother.

But there were two new names added to the top of the *Times* masthead in 1958, too, and each promised to leave its indelible mark on "the Grey Lady of

Spring Street," as the *Times* had come to be known. The first name was familiar: Mrs. Norman Chandler, the newly named director of public service. The second name came out of nowhere, leaving everyone scratching his head, including Otis.

On November 26, 1958, L. D. Hotchkiss retired from his post the fifth editor of the *Los Angeles Times*[12] and Norman Chandler selected Nick B. Williams as Hotchkiss's replacement. That same day, Otis celebrated his thirty-first birthday, and he wondered out loud just what kind of turkey his father had just handed him as a birthday present.

"I didn't know Nick very well and I can tell you that I wouldn't have picked him," Otis said.

When Norman Chandler gave him the job, Williams said two decades later, he also gave him a one-line mandate. He and Buff had heard too often and too condescendingly from East Coast colleagues just how bad a newspaper the *Times* was and they did not want to put up with it any longer.

"I want the *Times* to be fair, and I want it to dig in, to investigate, and to report what it learns," Norman told his new editor.

From that day, according to Williams, "the character of the *Times* changed 180 degrees."

PART C

Best of *Times*

1960–1980

Great men are not always wise.

—Book of Job 32:9

IN THE LATE 1950S, *Time* magazine conducted a survey similar to Leo Rosten's 1937 poll, which had identified the nation's worst newspapers. S. J. Perelman, the traveling *New Yorker* wit, had heard of the survey and noted that the *Los Angeles Times* ranked second only to the *Chicago Tribune* as the most wretched fish wrap in America. When his train stopped over in Albuquerque, New Mexico, Perelman wrote, "I asked the porter to get me a newspaper and unfortunately the poor man, hard of hearing, brought me the *Los Angeles Times.*"

The inside joke that Norman Chandler's *Times* had become in Southern California spread like contagious laughter from border to border during the Eisenhower years. At a press conference in Washington, D.C., that President Harry Truman conducted in the late 1950s, reporter Don Shannon raised his hand and identified himself as a staff writer for the *Los Angeles Times*, to which Truman replied:

"Oh yes. That's the *second* worst paper in the country."

NBC News anchor Chet Huntley, part of the new television royalty in broadcast journalism, joked that he would "always read the *Los Angeles Times* and know that I can be reasonably accurate by going 180 degrees in the other direction."

The *Times'* tawdry reputation even giggled its way across the Atlantic in 1958, where the highbrow and humorless London *Economist* bluntly described the Chandlers' flagship newspaper as "a shoddy sheet of extreme right wing viewpoint."

The barbs finally stung the imperious, insular Buff Chandler into acting after she had fallen victim to one too many stage whispers and one too many lifted eyebrows at an annual convention of the American Newspaper Publishers Association (ANPA). She took the matter up with Norman and the *Times'* new editor.

"She asked if I knew why the *Times* had been named the second worst newspaper in the country," said Nick Williams. "I took it as a signal."

So did Otis. After he attended the conventions of the ANPA and the American Society of Newspaper Editors in New York with Norman and Buff, Otis adopted that signal as his own. He had tasted the same disdain that his mother had. The

newspaper professionals milling the corridors of the Waldorf Astoria had treated the Chandlers like leprous second cousins; not since his first days at Andover had he felt so second-rate.

"We were certainly excluded from what I would call the Group: the *New York Times, Christian Science Monitor, Boston Globe, Atlanta Journal & Constitution* . . . sort of the Establishment newspapers," Otis recalled. "I thought that was Eastern elite snobbism—provincialism at its worst. They couldn't say anything good about Los Angeles in those days."

Although the *Times* was "not quite as bad as its reputation," Otis acknowledged that it was only a few rungs above mediocre and light-years away from excellent. Lumped together with freeways, smog, bikini babes, and mindless Hollywood movies, however, the *Times* had also become a convenient catchall for the East Coast literati's traditional condescension toward all things Californian. The Group's ostracism stung—"a real wake-up call," according to the profoundly competitive Otis.

"I wanted to make them eat their bloody words," he said.

In his new role as the *Times* sales manager, Otis told his father that if he was going to hike ad revenue and boost circulation, he had to have a better newspaper to sell.

"Nick will do it," Norman told him.

"Well, I have some ideas," said Otis.

"Go ahead. Meet with Nick," Norman urged.

Otis still didn't know the professorial Williams well. His sense of humor was dry, quick, and often blue, and his voice came out as a high squeak: an easy parody among junior editors on the city desk. Since assuming the *Times'* top editorial position, Williams had proved himself to be abrupt and decisive. His self-effacing demeanor, born largely of his Southern upbringing, could be easily mistaken for weakness. It was not weakness. When he shoved his plastic-rimmed glasses above his bushy brows and rested them on his broad forehead, it was a sign that he meant to get down to business.

Otis hadn't made half his case to Williams before the glasses went up.

"I don't like to screw with success," he said in a soft, shy squeak.

Otis's pitch for a better editorial product was not without merit, Williams acknowledged; in fact, he'd already begun to reorganize the paper's "beat" system to free more city desk reporters for investigations and analytical journalism.

Not enough, said Otis. For five years, he'd been scribbling ideas and critiques in notebooks. Otis pointed out obvious failings, for example, the *Times* reported almost no foreign, national, or Washington news, didn't cover science or labor unless the news story damned the unions, and virtually ignored the movie business that had grown up in its own backyard.

"Here are the weaknesses that I saw in the paper," said Otis, pushing his note-books across Williams's desk.

"Do you realize what you are proposing here?" Williams asked, his squeak hiking to a soprano scold. "Do you know what you are asking? How are you going to sell this to your father? It would cost a lot of money."

Otis was insistent. Against his obsessive athletic nature, he had disciplined himself to read regularly; he pored over the local competition as well as the East Coast snob sheets that were published by members of the Group, starting with Punch Sulzberger's sacrosanct *New York Times*. He even read *Time, Newsweek, Editor & Publisher,* and *Fortune.*

"No, we have to think about doing this," said Williams.

No, said Otis. No more thinking. He'd already waited long enough and the time was ripe to build a bigger, better, stronger, award-winning *Times.*

"I don't think your father would agree and he is the publisher and he must like things the way they are," Williams said firmly, nodding to the young Chandler that the meeting was over—for the moment.

But he didn't send the hard-charging young bull packing in the same way that Hotchkiss once might have done, and Otis took note. Nick Williams knew that Norman pandered to the status quo, but he also knew passion like that of the younger Chandler would stay bottled up for only so long. The *Times'* new editor acknowledged that most of what Otis had been saying was true and had to be fixed. He told him that his door was always open to discuss new ideas, and he meant it. His tone was not patronizing. At the same time that he ushered Otis out of his office, he heaved a sigh and whined confidentially: "Can't we take it a little slower?"

Otis had found a coconspirator—older, wiser, but secretly just as fed up with the old *Times.* Over the next two years, Williams listened and adopted Otis's suggestions when he thought it politic to do so. When an idea was too ambitious or expensive or radical, he'd sit Otis down, shut the office door, and explain the facts of life to him.

"I only tried a few things on him which he didn't do," remembered Otis. "I had a set of precise blueprints for the house I was going to build, but no one was going to build it until I was publisher."

And that was not supposed to happen any time soon. Norman had just turned sixty and assumed that he had at least another decade of newspaper publishing ahead of him. Neither his father nor his grandfather had surrendered the reins of the *Times* until they were on their deathbeds. Besides, Otis was only halfway through his training program. He had yet to learn the ropes in display advertising and promotion, and he still had a year or two ahead of him training at KTTV in the burgeoning world of broadcast news and entertainment, and possibly even a turn as a mill boss at a Times Mirror paper plant in Oregon City, Oregon.

Then, in the autumn of 1959, Norman Chandler developed a stomach ailment while vacationing with Buff in Hawaii.

"My mother called to tell me Dad had to have surgery and that he was quite ill," said Otis.

His father had colon polyps—benign and not at all life-threatening, but still disturbing, particularly to Buff.

"It scared her, I think," said Otis.

At about the same time, Norman quietly launched an ambitious plan to expand the company far beyond the newspaper trade. He and Buff hired a pair of pricey downtown lawyers—F. Daniel Frost and Robert Erburu of the blue-chip law firm of Gibson, Dunn and Crutcher—to act as their personal legal advisers and as outside counsel for the expanding Times Mirror Company. There was no doubt as to which of the two men had seniority. Bob Emmet, Otis's boyhood pal, referred to Erburu as "Dan Frost's bag carrier," but regardless of their roles, both lawyers became deeply involved in the explosive growth to come.

Five years earlier, Norman had hired the well-respected management consulting firm of McKinsey and Company to start the move toward diversification. As early as 1956, Times Mirror stock split 100 to 1 expressly to raise acquisition capital. The Times Mirror board of directors, which had always been comprised of Chandler family members and one or two longtime loyal *Times* executives, grew to include three outside directors who knew nothing about newspapers, but everything about business in Southern California. They were

- Litton Industries chairman Tex Thornton;
- United California Bank CEO Frank King; and
- Union Bank founder Harry J. Volk

"We didn't have a big board of directors," Otis remembered. "It was just my father, my mother, Philip, Harrison, and the outside directors."

Despite his political conservatism, Norman had never shied away from calculated business risks, as illustrated by his bold *Mirror News* experiment. He understood as well as or better than his son that a newspaper company had to be vigilant about riding the leading edge of technology, but he also understood in ways that Otis did not that if a CEO was going to bet the company, he'd better even the odds.

Up to that point, Times Mirror consisted of the *Times*, *Mirror News*, Times Mirror Press,[1] KTTV, and a small interest in Publisher's Paper Company.[2] Norman's master plan was proceeding smoothly until his health scare. His next appearance before the Times Mirror directors was an uneasy confrontation.

Led by the three outside directors, the board demanded that Norman decide whether he wanted to be Times Mirror chairman or publisher of the *Times* because he could no longer be both. The acquisition plan for the next decade would demand a full-time executive, not a part-time publisher, he was told. Buff had been at work.

"I think my mother was pushing my father—not because of his health, but just pushing him to give his best energies to the new acquisition and diversification program," said Otis.

Buff was quoted years later in the *Wall Street Journal* as boasting, "It was time to pull my Norman pawn out and put my Otis pawn on the board." In another interview, she softened her braggadocio just a bit: "I made it easier on Norman one weekend at the beach by telling him I thought it was time for Otis to take over."

Although Otis never doubted his mother's persuasive talents, it was always his father who made the final decisions regarding the *Times,* he said. Norman came back to the board with his son's name, but added:

"I think Otis is too young. I was not given the title of publisher until I was forty-three. He's done a good job and he has been in management now and the record of *Times* sales and circulation is good. But I think he should maybe be a little older."

Pressed for other candidates, all Norman came up with was his youngest brother, Philip, but in a closeted session with King, Volk, and Thornton, he reluctantly confessed that he honestly did not believe his brother was qualified. At fifty-three, Philip was nearly too old to begin as publisher, but even more critical in Norman's view was his younger brother's lack of vision and his embrace of arch conservative politics. Instead of taking the *Times* forward, Philip would push the newspaper back to an antiquated era.

When the directors finally agreed on thirty-one-year-old Otis, Norman lit his pipe and fell into a diffident pose.

"Well, as long as you don't think that I am pushing Otis on you because he is my son," he said, puffing thoughtfully. "If he is the best that we have."

THE NIGHT BEFORE CHRISTMAS of 1959, a mysterious stranger appeared in the *Times'* display advertising department. After having been turned away at the rival *Examiner* several blocks to the west, the fellow held up a full-page ad in one hand and $2,500 in the other. Would the *Times* be willing to publish the ad the following morning?

Of course! The ad was neither pornographic nor seditious and contained not a single word supporting unions or other radical causes. In fact, it was downright

religious. The sheet that the man held up for inspection bore two-inch high letters at the top of the page that read:

JESUS CHRIST II APPEARING . . .

An announcement followed of dates and times at three Hollywood churches where the Messiah would be dropping by to preach after New Year's Day. Jesus Christ II even signed the ad.

More than 35,000 copies of the *Times* had been printed before anyone suggested that they stop the *Times* presses and tell Norman Chandler about the ad. The mysterious stranger, as it turned out, was one Thomas Lockyear Graeff, a thirty-year-old self-absorbed and self-described clergyman who had been born again as Jesus Christ II. He told his newest converts in *Times* display advertising that he aimed to have his name legally changed to reflect that fact when he found a judge who would listen to his arguments with the same level of gullible wisdom as the *Times'* ad salesmen.

After *Time* magazine got hold of the tale, Norman and his *Times* suffered further ridicule at the hands of the American Newspaper Publishers Association establishment. At the *Los Angeles Times*, where cash-in-advance advertising had been a tradition since the snake oil and desert subdivision promotions of Harry Chandler's day, Graeff's shaky credentials as the Second Coming appeared to matter less than his currency.

Nearly four months later, on April 11, 1960, some 725 of the most powerful movers and shakers in Southern California gathered at the Biltmore Hotel for a special announcement from Norman Chandler. Mayor Norris Poulson was among the invited guests, as were former Governor Goodwin Knight, the chairman of the powerful Los Angeles County Board of Supervisors, judges, college presidents, corporate CEOs, and dozens of lesser Los Angeles lights. Jesus Christ II and all the other *Times* embarrassments from Christmases past were conspicuously absent—in both body and spirit.

The ballroom of the stately old luxury hotel that Harry Chandler had helped build thirty-seven years earlier was packed. Two replicas of General Otis's screaming *Times* eagles flanked the podium and four photo enlargements of each of the successive *Times* buildings loomed over the dais. An odd mix of prospect and portent hung heavy in the air as silver-haired Norman Chandler stood, smiled, and confidently stepped to the microphone. He began:

A newspaper must be the image of one man, whether you agree with him or not. I now inform you that there is to be a new image of the *Times*, but not a radically different one. My successor is younger, serious, competent, well trained, cre-

ative, possessing character and integrity, of sound judgment, with an appreciation and warmth for his fellow man.

I hereby appoint, effective as of this moment, Otis Chandler as publisher of the *Times,* the fourth publisher in its seventy-nine-year history.

Then he turned to his thirty-two-year-old son, whose huge frame—force fitted into a stiff business suit—sat next to Norman: "You are assuming a sacred trust and grave responsibilities. I have the utmost confidence that you will never falter in fulfilling these obligations. This trust is dearer than life itself."

First, dutiful applause rippled through the ballroom followed by dead silence as Norman stepped aside and his blond, blue-eyed hunk of a son bent into the microphone. As exploding flashbulbs lit up the dais, Otis uttered his first word as publisher of the *Los Angeles Times.*

"Wow."

Otis maintained that he had no idea what his father was about to do, which accounts for his stunned one-word response; he said forty years later that it was "one of the stupidest things I have ever said."

As the flood of flash bulbs ebbed and Otis untied his tongue, his choice of words continued to be less than stellar.

"If someone were to hand me a shot put right now, I think I could put it seventy feet!" he said, following that oddly out-of-place declaration with, "If I were doing the high jump, I could jump eight feet!"

From there, his remarks moved onto the expected and the mundane: the *Times'* many accomplishments during his father's stewardship and the grand tradition begun by his great grandfather—remarks that sounded suspiciously rehearsed and that lead many of those present to doubt the impromptu nature of the transition of Chandler power. His uncles were both present, as was his mother, venerable *Times* columnist Bill Henry, Kyle Palmer, Bud Lewis, L. D. Hotchkiss, and Hotch's successor, Nick B. Williams. None of them spoke during the announcement. The dais belonged to Norman and his son.

Several hours later, after all the hands had been shaken and all the congratulations had been pronounced, Otis Chandler left the Biltmore and walked to the parking garage to pick up his car. Missy hadn't planned a party and there was work to finish at the office.

"I didn't go out and celebrate," said Otis. "I don't remember anything special that day."

He did recall that one of his Deke fraternity brothers, Merritt Van Zant, had attended the transfer of power ceremony and saw Otis heading back toward the *Times.* Van Zant caught up with him on his way to his car.

"This is a real let down," Otis recalled Van Zant telling him. "You've just been

handed the reins of one of the most important newspapers in the world and you're just heading back to work. No chauffeur, no limo, no crowd. You're just going back to work."

But Van Zant recollected saying something more to his old friend that day, which Otis did not remember:

"Do you realize how lonely it's going to be at the top?" asked Van Zant.

AS PUBLISHER, Otis was suddenly in charge of dozens of men ten and twenty years his senior, each possessing experience and expertise he could never match. Many of those senior executives, however, were tired.

"Most were probably sixty and had done a wonderful job for my father, but they were coasting," he said. "There needed to be turnover. Within the year I replaced eighteen out of twenty-one department heads."

In the newsroom, Hotchkiss had already been replaced by Nick Williams, and Bud Lewis officially retired from the *Mirror News* on July 15, 1960.

"When Otis took over, he found that not one of his top executives had a number two man—*not one of them!*" said Williams's own eventual number two man, managing editor Frank Haven. "That's the best way to keep your job, for Christ's sake—not to develop any successors."

Kyle Palmer, the last of the three "little tyrants," knew his run was nearly over, too, and didn't blame Norman's son so much as he blamed a bewildering new world. During the 1960 Democratic National Convention in Los Angeles, the sixty-nine-year-old Palmer complained that telecommunications had taken over and ruined journalism.

"There are altogether too many gadgets around," he said. "Too many intricate telephone devices, too many walkie talkies, too many microphones, too many television screens."

Palmer preferred covering the convention from the comfort of his office, where he rewrote younger reporters' copy into the same dull, doctrinaire, and biased Chandlerese that he had always produced on his old upright Underwood. He still believed, as did Norman Chandler, that the *Times* had an obligation to champion Republicans and damn Democrats.

For his part, Norman hadn't changed a jot when it came to party politics, and he still agreed with Palmer. Around midnight on July 10, the day before the convention began, Norman called Nick Williams at home to tell him that he and Buff had polished off a pitcher of martinis at their trailer retreat in Dana Point and decided they were going to practice a little journalism of their own.

"Mrs. C. and I have been thinking about Kennedy and we've written an editorial," a half-lit Norman told his new *Times* editor. Then he read a five-paragraph

welcome to the Democratic delegates, which opened with a gentle taunt: "We are Republicans over here on First Street," and ended with: "In a few more days the Republicans in Chicago will nominate their man and we think they will choose their best one—Richard M. Nixon. We know the Democrats this week will strive to nominate their best. The world will be watching."

Nick Williams cringed.

"Can I call you back?" he asked.

"Sure," said Norman.

Williams knew the editorial would accomplish nothing beyond heaping ridicule and unneeded criticism upon the newspaper he had been trying to pilot out of the Dark Ages. He knew if he told Norman he didn't like it, he and tipsy Buff would double-team him and order that the editorial be published. Not only would he lose the argument, he'd lose face to boot. After some hand-wringing, Williams heeded the sage advice Kyle Palmer had once given him:

"If he wants it, do it. It's his paper."

Nick called back and told the Chandlers he'd phone in their editorial. It did run the next day on the front page and it was every bit the embarrassment that Williams expected it to be. But, as he related the story years later to his editorial page editor, Jim Bassett, the most important element in his relations with the Chandlers had been preserved. He had their trust. He never forgot that it was *their* newspaper, even as he and their only son carefully plotted to transform the *Times* forever.

Each morning when the *Times* appeared on the streets outside L.A.'s new Sports Arena complex where the Democratic National Convention was being staged that year, the stories almost never bore much resemblance to what had gone on the previous day inside the Sports Arena. Out-of-state visitors such as Bobby Kennedy's young press secretary Ed Guthman would curse out loud after reading Palmer's glib gibberish, which described John F. Kennedy as "ultra liberal." Then Guthman would swear once more—this time, vowing that he'd by-God *never* work at such a ridiculous rag as the *Los Angeles Times*.

Five years later, after Otis Chandler had persuaded Guthman to join the *Times* as its national editor, Guthman not only violated his oath but also discovered Kyle Palmer's modus operandi for producing political pap in 1960. The *Times* had, indeed, blanketed the convention with its reporters, but—outside of their eyewitness accounts of, say, a floor riot, a shoot-out, or a UFO landing—Palmer simply tossed their notes in the trash and wrote whatever the hell he had felt like writing in the first place. The 1960 election was Kyle Palmer's last hurrah, Otis assured Guthman when he invited him to join the *Times,* and there would never be another like him at the *Times.*

"I didn't want another kingmaker," said Otis.

Palmer faced his forced retirement gracefully, philosophizing that the new publisher "was young and full of beans and I was old." Although Palmer continued to love Norman as "my own brother," he recognized that both Otis and Buff wanted the past that he represented buried and forgotten. "They want to keep the entire thing in the hands of the family," he said during a 1961 interview.

But those hands, Palmer warned, were inexperienced and a bit too ambitious.

"I think that as a young man he's altogether too sure of himself," he said. "Otis Chandler hasn't the incentives that his grandfather had, or, for that matter, that his father had. I would say that he is trying his best to be a so-called 'liberal' publisher."

From where Otis was coming from, the retiring Palmer was merely being his typically obstinate and contemptuous self. Nick Williams, however, saw in the retired Kyle Palmer a proud and loyal Chandler family servant brought low. When Williams learned that the several-times-married Palmer was retiring broke with no pension, Williams paid him $200 a month to become his "political adviser."[3] The *Times* would be "ungrateful to leave him destitute in his old age," he told Otis. Williams kept Palmer on the payroll until Palmer died of leukemia at seventy on April 3, 1962.

Palmer had called it correctly about the young publisher, though. Otis was indeed "young and full of beans," and couldn't wait for the old guard to die off.

"I am sure I was not the most popular guy among those people who were being early retired or moved to a consulting capacity," Otis reflected later. "But we had to get going. We had to start the revolution because time was wasting and the market was growing."

Shortly after moving into the publisher's suite, Otis called Nick Williams into his office. This time, Nick did the listening. Young Otis was in charge.

"Nick," he said, "I want to make this one of the world's great newspapers."

"Jesus Christ," muttered Nick, pushing his glasses back on his skull and massaging at a migraine in the making. With a Sunday circulation quickly approaching the 1-million mark and more advertising lineage than any other newspaper in America, the *Times* already *was* one of the world's great newspapers—at least in the eyes of its readers, Williams reasoned. He recited the cautionary tale of Joseph Pulitzer's *New York World* to his new publisher—a great newspaper that had produced some of the nation's finest reporters, but then lost touch with its readers and died. Move slowly, he advised. Then he recited his oft-repeated mantra once more for the ambitious young Mr. Chandler: *Don't Screw with Success!*

Williams didn't have to wait long to prove his point. In May, less than a month after Otis had been named publisher, the *Times* won its fourth Pulitzer Prize: the Gold Medal for Meritorious Public Service for the newspaper's "thorough, sustained and well-conceived attack on narcotics traffic and the enterprising report-

ing of Gene Sherman, which led to the opening of negotiations between the United States and Mexico to halt the flow of illegal drugs into Southern California and other border states."

One of the *Times'* so-called beat reporters, the ferret-like Sherman had been freed for a special three-month assignment to get to the bottom of Mexico's drug trade. He had crisscrossed the border while posing as a drug-buying tourist; he had interviewed dope dealers and international drug cops; and he had followed shipments of heroin and marijuana all the way to the streets of L.A. The result was an eight-part, 15,000-word series that generated a national furor over lax enforcement of drug smuggling along the border. The series led to a congressional resolution calling for a White House conference on narcotics and the *Times'* first Pulitzer for news reporting.

Williams emphasized that it was this gradual shift from "beats" to special assignments that would eventually create the great newspaper Otis wanted. But Otis was not appeased; one success only whetted his appetite for more.

"I wanted an excellent daily business section and I wanted a Sunday business section, because we didn't have a Sunday business section," said Otis. "But I wanted something that would put business in perspective [too]—profiles of local business leaders. I wanted an Opinion section and a daily Calendar section and a Sunday Calendar and a TV magazine."

He called for a downsizing of the paper to save the cost of newsprint, and a new type font for headlines and stories to make them easier to read. He wanted more and better regional sections that would be able to compete with daily newspapers in the L.A. suburbs. Always more: more ideas, opinions, columns, editorials, and comic strips; more explanations of trends in sports, finance, travel, entertainment, and automotive news. And he wanted stars—Pulitzer winners or popular columnists who could be lured to the *Times* from other newspapers. He wanted more bureaus, both in the United States and around the world. Every time his intercom buzzed, Nick Williams rolled his eyes and prepared to squeak in protest. Eventually, his perpetual migraine gave way to an ulcer; he kept an assortment of pills and a glass of milk always at the ready.

"Oh, Otis," Williams would mutter, "we have always done it *this* way."

Williams was "not the sort of editor who'd come to the publisher's office and hear what I wanted and go do it right away," said Otis.

At the *Times*, things were never done right away, Williams tried to explain to his young charge. The new editor recalled an incident early in his copyediting career at the *Times* when his boss upbraided him for using numerals at the end of a banner headline on page A-1. A headline could read L.A. QUAKE KILLS THOUSANDS, Nick was instructed, but not L.A. QUAKE KILLS 1000S. When Williams challenged the rule as absurd, his boss pulled a tattered yellow

memo from a cigar box somewhere beneath a pile of papers on the city desk and read from it as if it were a Dead Sea Scroll. It had been written by the long-dead *Times* editor Harry Andrews and, although the rationale behind this grammatical commandment had been buried along with Andrews, the *Times* continued to obey the rule.

"An example of the *Times'* observance of any ancient taboo, long after the tabooer had passed on," said Williams. "An almost idiotic obeisance to the past, worse than Chinese ancestor worship, often with no recall—not even a tattered memo in a cigar box—of why it was taboo."

Nonetheless, things could and would change eventually, Williams promised Otis.

One of Nick Williams's early attempts to distance the *Times* from its ultraconservative past was a five-part series exposing the hypocrisy and reactionary bigotry of the John Birch Society. Written by reporter Gene Blake and published in March 1961, the series served as an instant double entendre that attacked the secretive and ultraconservative political organization at the same time that it subtly slammed Norman Chandler's brother and sister-in-law.

Otis's Uncle Philip and Aunt Alberta had joined the Birch Society in the 1950s and, although not a member, his other uncle, Harrison, also believed many of founder Robert Welch's wilder declarations. To Birchers, Dwight Eisenhower had been a Soviet dupe, the United Nations was a Communist conspiracy, and Norman Chandler's old friend (now the chief justice of the United States) Earl Warren was nothing less than a card-carrying Red draped in black Supreme Court robes.

Without specifically naming any of Chandler's relatives, but with the tacit approval of Norman Chandler, Blake's series[4] nonetheless damaged the Birch Society and all its hyperpatriotic Red-baiting. In a signed front-page editorial that followed the last part of the series, Otis Chandler proclaimed, "The *Times* does not believe that the arguments for conservatism can be won—and we do believe it can be won—by smearing as enemies and traitors those with whom we sometimes disagree."

Neither Otis's editorial nor Blake's series could be remotely interpreted as a repudiation of Republicanism, but the *Times'* Birch Society blast did mark such a revolutionary departure from the *Times* of the past that it left many of its conservative older readers stunned. Letters and calls of protest flooded the paper, merchants withdrew their ads, more than 15,000 readers canceled their subscriptions and—in a fractious family division that would have repercussions for decades to come—Philip Chandler flew into an indignant rage and forced a showdown with his oldest brother. Within the year, Philip resigned as the *Times* vice president and general manager, and Harrison followed a short time later.

"I'm sure certain members of the family who didn't like my editorial policy and the changes in the *Times* were hoping I would fail," Otis reflected a generation later. "They were hoping that the board of directors would put in someone to take the paper back to the paper that their parents liked, that they grew up with, that their friends liked."

That didn't happen.

FREED FROM HIS PUBLISHING DUTIES, Norman Chandler went on a shopping spree.

In June 1960, Times Mirror acquired the New American Library, which was the nation's largest paperback publishing house. In March 1961, the company purchased H. M. Goushá, a successful mapmaking company. And in May 1961, Times Mirror cornered the market on aeronautical navigation charts with the purchase of Jeppesen Company.[5] A 4 percent dividend and three-for-one stock split helped boost the total number of Times Mirror stockholders from 800 to 1,800 in 1961, and—or the first time in the company's history—more than half its revenue came from companies unrelated to the newspaper business.

The *Times* remained the jewel in the Times Mirror crown, however, and Otis poured money into it faster than his father could buy new companies. When the Kennedy administration took over the White House, the *Times* became the only West Coast newspaper to retain its own news bureau in the nation's capital. The *Times* also reopened its bureau in Sacramento.

In February 1961, Otis ordered sixteen new presses installed, bringing the *Times* total to ninety-six black-and-white and fourteen color presses. He also stole his first star reporter away from the East Coast establishment: *Sports Illustrated* and *Time*'s Jim Murray, who came to the *Times* as its featured sports columnist. By July, the *Times* had opened offices in New York and Chicago, the newest fronts in Otis's escalating war on the East Coast press.

In L.A., the *Times* installed an IBM 1401, the first computer operated by a newspaper in the United States. Within fourteen months, the *Times* would switch to an automatic typesetting system built around its IBM computer, thereby moving inexorably toward a day when Linotype machines—a venerable part of the clickety-clack pressroom machinery of the *Times* since Harrison Otis's day—would be silenced forever.

In November, Times Mirror acquired the Orange Coast Publishing Company, which published the *Orange Coast Daily Pilot* on the southern fringes of the *Times*' circulation reach. It marked a major invasion beyond the Los Angeles County border and an open declaration of war against such suburban rivals as the *Santa Ana Register* and the *Long Beach Independent Press-Telegram*. The *Times*

also began publishing regional news sections every Thursday and Sunday for the San Fernando Valley, Westside, South Bay, San Gabriel Valley, and Orange County, going head-to-head with other smaller suburban dailies in a deliberate effort to move from the central city into the smaller communities up and down the coast of Southern California.

As it grew, Otis Chandler's *Times* shed more and more of its past. In December 1961, Otis dedicated an auditorium on the fifth floor of the *Times* building in the name of Harry Chandler. At the same moment, two floors below, the remaining members of the *Times* old guard waxed on about the grand years of struggle when Harry rose to dominate Los Angeles, as the *Times* staff prepared to publish its final Mid-Winter Edition.

With Norman's reluctant blessing, Otis retired the annual special issue, which extolled Southern California's virtues to prospective East Coast émigrés, that his great-grandfather General Harrison Gray Otis had instituted in 1886. With nearly 2.5 million people and more arriving every day, Los Angeles no longer needed settlers. More than enough snowbound Easterners had heeded the Mid-Winter Edition's clarion call: L.A. was now the third largest city in the country. Harry Chandler's All-Year Club had been officially disbanded for more than a decade and the *Times* booster days had come to an end.

AS CIRCULATION AND ADVERTISING for the *Times* exploded, the *Mirror* shriveled up and died. On January 6, 1962, Norman Chandler's noble experiment in afternoon tabloid journalism ceased publication.

"I am going to have to fold up the tent," a teary-eyed Norman stammered to 175 of his troops gathered around the *Mirror*'s city desk. "The *Mirror* is being combined with the *Los Angeles Times*. This is the most difficult and heart-rending statement . . . I have ever had to make. The *Mirror* was my dream."

Norman was not so moved by the moment, however, that he was prepared to reveal that he'd been negotiating for three years with Hearst's general manager, Hap Kern, to shut down the afternoon *Mirror* and the morning *Examiner* at the same time. His "dream" had cost Times Mirror over $25 million. His son's analysis of the *Mirror*'s ultimate doom had proved all too true. Figuring that one afternoon daily might still stand a chance, Norman had tried one last-ditch maneuver in 1960 to keep the *Mirror* alive by offering Hearst $5 million for the afternoon *Herald-Express*. But, always suspicious of the Chandlers' motives, Hearst had refused.

By 1962, however, both the *Herald Express* and the *Mirror* were losing millions. In its final year, the *Mirror* alone was losing over $50,000 a week. The threat of televised advertising that Norman had predicted back in 1948 when he bought

KTTV had become reality. Advertisers would no longer support four metropolitan dailies in L.A. when they could get better results from two dozen radio stations and the nation's largest concentration of television stations.

Thus, the same day the *Mirror* closed, Hearst's morning *Examiner* one and a half miles to the west also announced it was closing. Neither George Hearst nor any member of his family appeared in the city room. A notice was posted reading simply, "Economic circumstances have necessitated the discontinuance of publication of the *Los Angeles Examiner*." The Times Mirror fired 211 employees, but pulled the best *Mirror* staff members over to its *Times;* over 1,000 *Examiner* employees were told to pick up their final pay checks and pink slips at Hearst's cashier's office.

The two closures left the *Times* with a morning monopoly in L.A.; Hearst's evening *Herald-Express*[6] no longer had any competition for afternoon readers. The Kennedy Justice Department smelled a rat.

Three months earlier, on October 19, 1961, one of Hearst's attorneys, James McInerney, had written to Attorney General Robert Kennedy to seek an exemption from federal antitrust rules. Because both Hearst and Times Mirror were losing millions from their *Examiner* and *Mirror* subsidiaries, McInerney argued, they qualified under a "failing corporations" exemption that should allow them to cease publication simultaneously.

Kennedy denied permission.

"The Anti-Trust Division was not very thrilled by any kind of division of the market," said Otis. "That smacked to them of a violation of the antitrust laws, even though it happened to be purely coincidental. They didn't like it. They sent word: 'If you guys get together in any way, that's a criminal violation and you could be subject to jail.'"

The Hearsts and the Chandlers had, in fact, conspired to coordinate the demise of the *Mirror* and the *Examiner*, but were not about to advertise their collusion. Both Otis and George Hearst Jr., who had inherited the L.A. branch of the Hearst empire upon the death of William Randolph Hearst,[7] played a game of plausible deniability in the weeks leading to the shutdown of the two newspapers, according to Otis.

"Being young and naive and not being wise in the ways of antitrust I said, 'Well, okay, if I run into George, I'll see what he's planning to do and he can see what I'm planning to do and we won't use the words "division-of-the-market" or anything like that,'" Otis recalled. Twice, George and Otis just happened to run into each other in Pershing Square, right outside the Biltmore Hotel. In both instances, the young scions of L.A.'s two premiere media families agreed that shutting down the *Mirror* and the *Examiner* would certainly be advantageous to the remaining newspapers. Hypothetically, of course.

Intentionally divvying up a newspaper market as lucrative as L.A.'s violated the Sherman and Clayton antitrust acts, said Chandler, just as clearly as if two steel companies had divvied up the production of I-beams.

"You can't meet and say, 'Well, you know, we'll produce long steel rods and you produce short steel rods and we'll . . . make more money,'" said Otis.

To circumvent the law, Otis had his attorneys prepare a disingenuous formal statement that he then read over the telephone to George Hearst; it stated that Times Mirror intended to close the *Mirror* following the last edition published on January 6, 1962.

"And George said, 'Well that's coincidental. We're thinking about stopping our paper that same day.' End of conversation," said Otis.

However clever the Chandlers and Hearsts thought they were being, the Kennedy Justice Department was neither fooled nor appeased.[8] The House Judiciary Committee called Norman Chandler to testify during hearings on the simultaneous closures of the *Mirror* and *Examiner*, and Norman, Buff, and Otis expected that at some point the Justice Department would file at least a civil suit and, possibly, a criminal action against the two newspaper publishers.

"There was nail biting time. We expected it, but it didn't happen," said Otis.

During a rafting trip through the Grand Canyon many months later, Otis found out firsthand just how close he and the Hearsts had come to getting themselves into big trouble—the spectacular kind of jam in which Harry Chandler had once found himself following his fizzled Baja revolution. Bobby and Ethel Kennedy asked Otis and Missy, as well as several other young corporate power couples, on an outdoor adventure trip and, at one point as they floated down the Colorado, Otis found himself alone with the attorney general.

"I don't know what tripped it, but he looked at me and said, 'You and your father and the Hearsts could have been in jail if it wasn't for me,'" Otis remembered.

Bobby flashed the famous Kennedy smile and Otis smiled back, but said nothing.

"I let it go," he said.

CHAPTER 16

As illustrated by his Grand Canyon adventure, Otis was not so driven that he didn't take time for himself. He surfed, of course, and indulged his passion for hunting game, big and small. He took Missy, Norman, and brother-in-law Kelly

Spear on a safari to Mozambique, where Otis and Missy shot an elephant. He made trips to Canada, Alaska, and Mexico to bag what he called "the Grand Slam" of bighorn sheep—the four rarest species in North America, whose heads he mounted over his fireplace on a trophy pallet that his less reverential guests referred to as the "dead-head wall."

He reluctantly played tennis with Missy—her passion since her Stanford days. Even though she was a chain-smoker and as devoted to her regular evening cocktails as her frequently inebriated in-laws, Missy was also as competitive as her husband and regularly met him on the courts where, to his undying fury, she frequently trounced him. She had learned to fish and golf and ski on her own years before she met Otis; but he taught her to shoot, and during their early years together, while the children were still too small to accompany them, he took her backpacking into the Sierras, the Rockies, and beyond.

But Otis was a loner when it came to most sports, and his real obsession continued to be lifting weights. While still a junior executive, he had worked out alone each morning on the sixth-floor roof of the *Times,* where he had hauled up his own Olympic weights and created his own makeshift gym.

"There was pigeon shit on the ground, no air conditioning, no bathroom, no towels, no wash room, no shower," he remembered.

Once he was publisher, he changed all that; he ordered the construction of an executive workout room in the Times Mirror Building's basement. Eventually, the gym grew and other executives used it to blow off steam and keep in shape.

"I'd come in from an Eastern business trip and hit the gym at 3:00 A.M.," said Otis. "I'd feel very refreshed from my jet lag, then go down to my office, go through my mail, get home at 4:00 A.M., sleep a couple hours, go to the office, feel great until about 5:00 P.M. People would interpret that as 'Otis is a fanatic.'"

On the issue of exercise, he pled guilty to fanaticism. He even made his secretary take dictation while he pumped iron. But, Otis was quick to point out, obsessing on barbells beat the hell out of most other addictions.

"I like the feeling of having strength in my body even though I very seldom use it other than in the gym," he rhapsodized. "It's a good feeling to know that you have a great reserve of strength if you need it, whether it's carrying a heavy suitcase or whatever. I just like—and always have and still do like—having strength, unusual strength."

Now that his salary was coming closer to matching their material expectations, he and Missy developed a taste for the good life that they had been forced to put on hold throughout most of the 1950s.

Within months of Otis's ascension to publisher, the Chandlers joined Otis's old friend Merritt Van Zant in Rome for the 1960 Summer Olympic Games. Otis fixated upon the shot put and weight lifting competition while Van Zant squired

Missy around Rome's tourist attractions and finer shopping sites. Missy bought clothes and Otis bought an Italian sports car. They arranged to cruise home on the luxury liner Leonardo da Vinci. Back in L.A., they bought a series of water-skiing boats, each one larger than the former and each named "Missy."

The Chandlers had moved from their cramped rental in Altadena first to a small house near San Marino's Lacy Park and later on to a much larger home on fashionable Arden Road near Pasadena's California Institute of Technology. Their domestic staff increased with each step up the ladder; by the time Otis was named publisher, Missy had a cook and a nurse to help with her four children.

"We had two in-help when we moved into Arden Road," she said. "That was the best thing I ever did for myself. I wish more girls would spend less on clothes, less on frivolous things and have help, because that makes you able to go out with your husband. You are able to go and do volunteer work. I would have been bored to death if I had just stayed home and been Super Mom."

Unlike Norman, Otis would not allow his wife to work at the *Times*, so Missy filled her days as the manic chair for everything, from the Junior League to her own amateur tennis organization. She staged her first tennis tournament before she was twenty-six and took over Buff's spot on the Otis Art Institute board of governors, all while she fulfilled the role of dinner-party perfect corporate wife and mother of five. Her fifth and final child, Carolyn, was born in 1962 and, with the help of many an au pair, she played the role of Mrs. Otis Chandler—the do-it-all wonder woman—to the hilt.

"He did not read stories to the children," said Missy. "He did not put the kids to bed. I did. When we were very young, he changed diapers occasionally, but as he got busier and busier he did less and less. And it was very hard because he seldom went to a Little League game and he never went to a school play if it was in the day time. He would go to parent-teacher's night sometimes, but most of the time, I did it. I think that is when he was becoming selfish.

"I have more energy I think than Otis does. I can handle a lot of balls in the fire. I think you have to. All my friends who had four to nine children were all generals: 'You do this! You do that! Straighten up! Come on, it's time to go!'"

And it was time to go by 1962—this time, to a finely appointed faux adobe-and-timber manse in the epicenter of WASP San Marino, properly tailored by the prestigious architectural firm of William L. Pereira to the tastes, quirks, and wealth of a burgeoning Chandler brood. The 11,000-square-foot hippodrome had a living room with a twenty-six-foot-high ceiling, affording plenty of room for two stories of formal dining room, breakfast room, and kitchen as well as master bedroom, guest room, study, family room, servant's quarters, and a wing known as the "dorm," where each Chandler child had his or her own bedroom

that could be sealed off from the rest of the house when Missy and Otis were entertaining.

And the Chandlers entertained often. The living room, complete with a massive fireplace, was flanked by an interior garden and fountain. Outdoors were the requisite swimming pool, barbecue, pool house, gym, and tennis courts, along with more garden and terraces.

Otis found nothing especially remarkable in the move to his ideal home in exclusive San Marino; he was just a regular guy fulfilling a dream. He fondly remembered moving day because he hauled the final item from Arden Road to San Marino himself, just as if he were any other middle-class Southern Californian renting a U-Haul to switch apartments from one side of town to the other.

"The last was a big trampoline I folded up and towed for a mile or so behind my motorcycle on the street in San Marino, [my] kids hanging on," he said. "I guess that was quite a sight, the trampoline going down the street, people saying: 'There's Otis! There's that character.'"

The fourth publisher of the *Los Angeles Times* liked to see himself as a character—just an average Joe who happened to work hard and get lucky. Any sense of entitlement or Chandler privilege was purposely muted. His schizophrenic self-image wavered constantly between the prince and the pauper and may have accounted in large part for his close friendship with Jack P. Burke.

"Jack was very funny and kept Otis very entertained," recalled Missy. "On Arden Road he was my perennial houseguest and I used to dread it. He was always late and I had to have dinner for the children on time. Jack would show up an hour late and I would have to go and fix his dinner again."

Burke was one of the few non-Deke pals with whom Otis had cemented a lasting friendship during his Stanford days. Burke had been a "day student," according to Otis, meaning that he could not afford to live on campus, either as a Deke or in the dorms, and had to commute to Palo Alto every day from San Francisco to attend classes. Despite his lower status and relatively modest means, he and Otis remained fast friends long after most of Chandler's other college relationships had faded.

"I knew him the last two years that I was at Stanford," said Otis, who remembered Burke as a discus thrower with a ribald sense of humor. He was also a bitter former Catholic who had briefly attended Notre Dame and shared Otis's distaste for Missy's religion.

"He hated Catholicism," Missy said. "He told me the reasons why all the priests were phony and really hurt me, being a good little Catholic girl. I will never forget that: Jack Burke sitting there destroying all my hopes and dreams about the Church."

As Otis and Missy rose quickly past their modest college and Air Force days to their affluence and privilege as young adults, Burke clung to them each step of the way as if they were live oak and he were mistletoe.

"He was Godfather to Cathleen," recalled Missy. "He wasn't married then." It was during that period that Missy convinced herself that Jack was providing her husband with call girls—a claim that Otis vigorously denied and that Missy herself later recanted.

Jack Burke was a hale fellow, well met. He bore no external signs of pending trouble. He was the horn dog from Otis's youth who had refused to grow up—an Irish rogue of many appetites who dared to go daily where Otis never could for fear that he might violate Buff's primal edict: Remember who you are; remember what you represent. Otis might have been a good and true father, companion, and business partner, but he also ached to be as rakish as his pal Jack. Despite their outward appearance as the perfect couple with the perfect family in the perfect home, the Chandlers were cursed with a quasi-open marriage almost from the beginning, according to Missy.

"I know that Otis played around, and all my friends have told me that, all my deep friends," she said.

"I didn't, but I guess she thought I did," said Otis.

Since the earliest days of their marriage, the Chandlers had made a pact, according to Missy: "If you play around, I don't want to know about it."

"And he said, 'Well, if you do too, I don't want to know about it,'" said Missy.

For this reason, the paranoid specter of Jack Burke's call girls had as little effect on Missy as Joan Irvine Smith, Georgia Rosenbloom, or Merle Oberon had when they allegedly made a play for her husband. Smith once lived next door to the Chandlers when they rented their Lacy Park home; whether by design or by accident, the Orange County real estate heiress regularly undressed without closing the blinds to her bedroom window, which faced directly towards Otis's exercise room, according to Missy. Otis used to invite his pals over for the "striptease show," she said.

Otis boasted to buddies that Georgia Rosenbloom, the young widow of Los Angeles Rams owner Carroll Rosenbloom, had also chased him during the early 1960s, and that Jackie Kennedy once came on to him in the back of a limousine. Merle Oberon—the British dance hall hostess who starred with Laurence Olivier in *Wuthering Heights* and in dozens of other films during the 1940s and 1950s—wanted him even though she was sixteen years his senior. Oberon socialized with the Chandlers at their San Marino estate and had accompanied them on a trip to Mexico; although Otis denied there was anything between them, Missy strongly suspected otherwise.

"That's all Missy's make-believe," according to Otis.

Underscoring their incipient hypocrisy as a devoted couple, the Chandlers made their youngsters attend Mass each Sunday and study catechism for their inevitable first communion.

"My kids cried and said, 'Why are you and Mom so mean to us? You make us get dressed up and go to church and we hate it.' But I did the right thing," remembered Otis with undisguised sarcasm. "We even sent our two daughters to Catholic school in Pasadena."

Otis raised his sons to be just like their old man. They learned to hunt, surf, fish, and hike. They took calculated risks, even as children, leaping from mountain crags that were a little too high and catching waves that were a little too treacherous, especially for grade-school kids. With no small irony, Otis's older daughter, Cathleen, tended to be the most daring; the boys even nicknamed her "Crashleen" for her own Otis-like brushes with death. In a surfing mishap with the eerie overtones of her father's early horse riding accident, Cathleen was once jackhammered into the sand head first; she broke her neck and her family was convinced that she would never walk again. Not only did she walk but she ran back to the beach with her surfboard within months of her convalescence.

Like her brothers, Cathleen learned how to hold her emotions in check, the way that Otis had been taught by his own father. Cathleen and the boys could be as stone cold stoic as their father. Fortune again played with Otis's notions of gender-correct behavior, though, by making his oldest son, Norm—not Cathleen or young Carolyn[1]—the most sensitive of his brood.

In any other family, Norm might have grown up to be a painter or a poet, but as the eldest Chandler, he had to measure up to different expectations. Like his more physical siblings, he learned to be athletic, although this was not easy for him. Once, he nearly died in a waterskiing accident. Norm tried to emulate his brothers' and sisters' level of stoicism, too, but the bar always seemed a bit too high.

Perhaps because he had instinctively rebelled at some level against his own father's early drone about the manly qualities of hard work and self-discipline, Otis was able to show occasional compassion for his eldest son's emotional well-being. When Norm's dog died, the boy refused to go to school and did what Chandler men were never supposed to do. He shut himself in his room and wept. Instead of lecturing him on being a man, Otis showed rare empathy, perhaps recalling his own angst when he'd lost a pet. He gathered up the boy and took him to the *Times,* where he could stay until he was ready to go back to school; Otis deposited his son in an office adjoining the publisher's suite so that Norm could listen to the radio and come talk to Dad as it suited him.

Every Christmas, all the Chandler children got a taste of why their father behaved in such a driven, disciplined, and emotionally guarded fashion. Christmas

Eve was the only night of the year that Buff invited her grandchildren to Los Tiempos and, except for receiving their Christmas presents, "they just hated going," recalled Missy.

"Here we are, all the children in their formal best, with three butlers waiting on us and we had the first course and then the second course and after each course, the plate was taken away," Missy remembered. "All very formal. That was the only time Buff ever had her grandchildren to her house. Now, that is strange. She never had them just come over and sit and talk to them. She was never a very good grandmother. I don't think she really enjoyed her grandchildren."

Buff had no time for children, for the elderly, or for the infirm. When her own sister suffered a stroke, Buff stopped visiting her or communicating with her. Ignoring Otis's Aunt Thurleyne—who had been matron of honor at Buff's wedding to Norman—did not evolve out of anger or envy or shame, according to Otis; rather, it appeared to be Buff's genuine lack of interest and maybe an irrational fear that her sister's adversity or ill health could somehow be contagious.

Ambition riddled Buff's one-dimensional personality, leaving scant room for compassion. In 1961, when she demanded that the *Times* give Dame Judith Anderson a special award for her bravura stage portrayal of Lady MacBeth, a city desk wag pinned an anonymous note to an office bulletin board beneath a photo of the actress and Buff. It read: "Who is the real Lady MacBeth?"

Buff and Norman Sr. could be as cold as the Los Tiempos temple in which they had chosen to live out their remaining years. Even at their respective trailers at Dana Point, where the atmosphere was far more relaxed, Buff and Norman kept their distance from Otis, Missy, and the grandchildren.

"Rather than talk with the children, she would go down there to the beach with her work and she would sit and write thank you notes," said Missy. "She was very flamboyant and they were beautifully written thank you notes, but they were for the money she was raising. That's where she wrote all those thank you notes to get the money for the Music Center."

———————

"I CALLED HER 'MRS. C.' I never called her Mother all the years at the office," said Otis.

In 1961, Dorothy Chandler became Times Mirror vice president for corporate and community relations and at least once or twice a month when Otis was in town, she went to lunch with her son or had him to dinner at Los Tiempos. Mrs. C. had officially graduated to the role of Times Mirror executive, although she was always much, much more, not least of which was Queen Mum of the Music Center.

Buff Chandler's crowning monument to her drive and ambition was the Music Center of Los Angeles County, home of the Los Angeles Philharmonic and fountainhead for all of Southern California's performing arts. Her tenacious nine-year campaign on behalf of the Music Center produced more than $19 million in private donations and, when her campaign was over, *Time* magazine put her on its cover and described the fund drive as "perhaps the most impressive display of virtuoso money-raising and civic citizenship in the history of U.S. womanhood"—a line that turned Lady Crocker and the Philip side of the family green.

But the regal portraits that accompanied the *Time* elegy and the thousands of words of praise showered upon her in dozens of other flattering articles did not fully reveal how Dorothy Buffum Chandler managed her virtuoso triumph. Buff was a street fighter in satin who gathered around her a veritable pride of predators who called themselves the Amazing Blue Ribbon 400: middle-aged social climbers who learned at the paws of the grand dame just how to claw cash from unwilling fat cats, heirs, and CEOs. Dorothy Chandler proved her utilitarian ruthlessness over and over, to the point of bringing other social lionesses to tears when their efforts did not measure up to her high standards.

"Buff is the most superb fund-raiser on the face of the earth, and one of her strengths is that she doesn't under accept," said Albert Casey, a forty-eight-year-old Railway Express executive whom Norman hired in 1963 as Times Mirror's corporate acquisitions architect.

Casey wasn't alone in his awe. Watching her at her arm-twisting best could be breathtaking. Buff Chandler turned the polite game of fund-raising into blood sport as she used every weapon at her disposal to coax, blackmail, or shame her victims into doubling, trebling, or even quadrupling their donations.

When Kirk Douglas sent her his $5,000 contribution, she sent it back and demanded more. When he balked, she bad-mouthed him into submission. Charlton Heston recalled a similar incident in which "a very wealthy man gave her a check for $20,000 [for the Music Center], and she tore it up, said it was ridiculous, that she needed more than that."

When the wife of noted architect Charles Luckman begged off until she had spoken with her husband about their donation, Buff scolded her like a naughty child who was too timid and immature to make her own adult decision. Buff courted political opponents such as Democratic National Committeeman Paul Ziffren. She even pursued unlikely patrons of the arts: mob lawyer Sidney Korshak donated after Buff carelessly promised that his notorious name would never appear in the *Times* if he'd just write out a check—now.

"My mother would court the devil for contributions," recalled Otis. "Anybody who'd give her some dough."

Whatever remained of the ramparts that separated the California Club[2] WASPs from the Hillcrest Country Club Jews Buff sent hurtling to earth like so much high-toned rubble. Money mattered. Everything else was pretense. To make her dream reality, she played the name game with two of L.A.'s highest rollers: Jewish housing developer Sidney Mark Taper, and WASP savings and loan pioneer Howard Ahmanson. The Mark Taper Forum and the Howard Ahmanson Theater still stand beside the Dorothy Chandler Pavilion as marble monuments to the melding of old and new money in a communal effort to foist culture on the washed, the semiwashed, and the great unwashed of El Pueblo de Nuestra Señora la Reina de Los Angeles de Porciuncula.

A good fund-raising field general should be "at various times a psychiatrist, a psychologist, a marriage counselor, and even a sort of family doctor," Buff preached. "You have to know the family situation at all times. Divorce, illness, death—or just a routine change in the family financial situation—can inhibit contribution."

Her money-raising megalomania extended into her own family, where she openly and ruthlessly competed with her daughter for donor dollars. From the early 1960s, Camilla had nurtured her own cultural cause: the Los Angeles County Museum of Art. Tall, sedate, and polite, but as enigmatic as Norman, Mia had been clashing with her mother since her high school days. While Norman Chandler's daughter worked quietly to bring a world-class art museum to L.A. by circulating among the nonprofit boards and high-roller high teas of Pasadena and Beverly Hills, Norman Chandler's wife openly sabotaged her efforts.

"I am the grandmother of the whole thing," Mia said of LACMA, adding, "but I think you have to be [a team player]. You can't grandstand yourself."

That is, not unless you were Mrs. Dorothy Buffum Chandler who "had a newspaper behind her to photograph her every inch of the way," said Mia.

L.A. needed Mozart and Puccini far more desperately than Renoir and Picasso, Buff reasoned, so she pulled out all the stops to defeat her daughter until after Buff and her Amazing Blue Ribbon shock troops had finished putting the last coat of paint on her Music Center. She once threatened to fire managing editor Frank McCulloch for publishing a story on LACMA fund-raising—an empty threat, by Otis's account, but an uncomfortable newsroom intimidation tactic nonetheless.

"If she couldn't get her way, there would be a little tear, shouting, anger, pouting to me and pouting to Norman," said Otis. "She could absolutely destroy people if they didn't do what she wanted them to do—not in terms of outsiders from whom she was soliciting money—but I'm talking about the corporate wives, including Missy.

"If they dared to ask the wrong question or it even got down almost to the dress they had on or their mannerisms, she just nailed them. And they would go flying into the women's room in tears. Several times I said, 'Mother, that was uncalled for, completely uncalled for. Why did you do that?' 'Oh, pooh!' That was her favorite expression, which meant in effect, as guys would say, 'Oh screw them. They'll get over it.' She never used foul language ever. Nor did my father. All I heard was, 'Oh pooh! They'll get over that.'"

———————————

Norman didn't soon get over his son's disturbing lean toward liberalism—at least, not in the early years of Otis's stewardship. It was bad enough when Otis flew off to Dallas with then–vice president Lyndon Johnson on Air Force Two and spent time on the Johnson ranch, hobnobbing with such machine Democrats as Governor John Connolly. But when he took up with the Kennedys at the White House, Otis's leftward bent began to border on heresy.

"Hubert Humphrey was one of my best friends, but I didn't just associate with Democrats," Otis pled in his own defense. "I befriended Billy Graham, Liberace, Sam Goldwyn. My job was to get to know everybody, whether it be in music, art, fashion, or sports, politics, religion."

To that end, he tried following in his father's footsteps by creating the Committee of 25—a group of young movers and shakers not unlike the old California Club crew that Norman had gathered unto himself in the late 1920s and early 1930s.

"That group was still trying to hang on to its power even though they were in their eighties," said Otis. "They were more self-appointed than anything else, but they felt they could make things happen—not in terms of crime or community relations, but in terms of getting a new Sports Arena or things like that."

Otis's Committee of 25 would be more inclusive and democratic, he concluded. Agreeing to be the catalyst for the new generation of power brokers, the young publisher met regularly for lunch at the *Times* with his most influential municipal peers: young bankers, merchants, educators, the police chief, the D.A.

"I had the local head of the AFL-CIO in," Otis remembered, "and when my father found out, he said, 'My father and grandfather would turn over in their graves [with] you having the union in here!'"

But times were changing. Otis included a black church leader, a Jew, and an Asian in the mix. When it came time for his Committee of 25 to select their leader, his peers drafted Otis; he balked as his father and, certainly his grandfather, would never have done.

"I didn't think it was proper for me to assume that role," he said. "I didn't want to get back to what my grandfather and Kyle Palmer did, telling people what to do: who to pick as governor and everything else. So the group gradually fell apart."

Calling the shots, even through consensus, no longer seemed possible in a megalopolis. L.A. had grown too large for an oligarchy to control.

"It was probably too big a city to have maybe fifteen or twenty-five people sit in one room and then come to a conclusion on rapid transit, go up and see the governor, go to Washington and see the secretary of transportation, and make things happen," said Otis. "I think we all were a little bit nostalgic and maybe a little naive that we could turn the clock back fifty years when Los Angeles did have that, when my grandfather was around."

The best he could do was use the *Times'* existing strength to set the agenda for daily discussion of Southern California's future. Although Otis might have had some success inching the *Times* into a more progressive role, Norman's staunch Republican credentials still prevailed on election day. The *Times* continued to endorse only GOP candidates.

"I want the *Times* to be an independent paper," Otis told one interviewer at the time, catching himself quickly enough to modify his sentence to "an independent *Republican* paper."

Yet the rubber stamp nature of *Times* editorial policy had already slowly begun to drift toward the center. Beginning with the 1961 mayor's race, maverick Democrat Sam Yorty detected "political schizophrenia" in the publisher's suite, where Otis Chandler appeared to be "stumbling all over himself trying to support liberal positions and still stay Republican."

During a 1969 interview with *Harper's Magazine,* Yorty bitterly denounced the *Times'* biased city hall reporting during the Norman Chandler era, of which Yorty was one of the final victims: "They once had this reporter, Carlton Williams, who would run in and out of city council meetings, giving Norman Chandler's orders, saying Norman Chandler wanted this, Norman Chandler wanted that. It was a disgrace," complained Yorty.

Although Norman's kingmaking policies persisted a few years into the new régime, it was only temporary inertia. Nick Williams's new managing editor in 1961, Frank McCulloch, admitted that he erred when he "set aside my journalistic conscience" and let Carlton Williams thump on the Democratic mayoral candidate one last time, "partly because I was convinced Sam Yorty was a bad candidate."

But when Williams was poised for the kill, McCulloch reined him in. The old *Times*man's blistering libel was cut and, on at least one occasion, killed altogether over Williams's angry protests. Just as the 1960 Democratic National Convention

marked the farewell of Kyle Palmer, the 1961 Sam Yorty–Norris Poulson race for mayor became the last hurrah for Carlton Williams, who huffily left the *Times* a short time later.

To Sam Yorty's astonishment, Carlton Williams and his slanted reporting vanished. Yorty triumphed over Poulson.[3] But, Yorty complained, the *Times* filled Williams's vacuum by pouring all its reporting resources into revealing graft and corruption[4] or it did not write about city politics at all.

"They don't cover anything I do now," Yorty whined in the *Harper's* interview. "They don't cover city hall. There are twenty-seven floors here, and they have one reporter assigned."

And that was just as it should be, proclaimed Otis Chandler and Nick Williams.

"We won't become a great city until our local officials develop a little more sophistication—and indulge themselves less in small-town name-calling," said Otis.

Even as Mayor Sam was being sworn into office, the *Times* had already begun its metamorphosis into a different kind of newspaper—a kind of daily magazine, patterned after the interpretive features and in-depth articles pioneered by such national news magazines as *Time* and *Newsweek*. The collapse of the *Mirror* and the *Examiner* played a critical role in that transformation. During 1962, the average weekday circulation of the *Times* leaped 204,926 over 1961. At one point, new subscriptions poured into the *Times* at the rate of 5,000 a day. When the smoke cleared at the end of the year, the *Times* had 757,776 subscribers, making it the nation's fourth largest newspaper.

The *Herald-Examiner* did not fare so well, gaining just a few thousand subscribers over the old *Herald-Express*'s 1961 circulation.

"Hearst closed the wrong paper," said Otis. "If they had kept the morning *Examiner,* we would have been in for a much more difficult fight. They did everything wrong. I watched them and I thought, 'Thank God for those people!'"

In July 1962, the Chandlers pulled the *Times'* eagle out of storage and put it on permanent display in the *Times* lobby along with an original printing press and other artifacts from a bygone era. Otis ordered a redesign of the *Times'* banner, quietly deleting from the front page both the General's eagle logo and his venerated motto, "True Industrial Freedom, Liberty Under the Law."

The West's premiere newspaper family now had the cash and the cachet to create a great daily newspaper. If Otis Chandler had it his way, the *Los Angeles Times* would never play small-town newspaper games again.

NICK WILLIAMS WAS NOT ABOVE playing games in the newsroom. Instead of hiring a managing editor to execute the day-to-day plans that he and Otis had concocted, Williams tried a tactic that Joseph Pulitzer had once used at his *New*

York World. On January 10, 1961, Nick put in place dual managing editors whom he and Otis expected to duke it out, leaving the *Times* with the best man to lead the Chandler charge against the East Coast's journalism establishment. Thus began the short but influential era of the Two Franks:

Frank Haven, the night managing editor, was a stiff, hard-drinking copy editor who had started with the *Times* for $9 a day in 1941 and had spent most of his career punctuating and correcting grammar. Nicknamed "Lurch" by the general assignment reporters, the barrel-chested Haven kept a bottle of Jack Daniels in his bottom drawer and huffed and puffed about the newsroom like a wrestler gone to seed. His square face and square torso were squared once more by square steel-rimmed glasses, giving his gruff appearance as forbidding an air as that of the glowering Loyal D. Hotchkiss himself, but—like the retired *Times* editor—Haven could also juggle and balance all the elements of a newspaper and make them roll magically off the presses every day with precision, ease, and a minimum of libel.

Frank McCulloch, the daytime managing editor, however, was an acerbic ex-Marine who had headed *Time* magazine's bureau in L.A. He, too, had a nickname. With his clean-shaven noggin and his wisecracking sarcasm, the urbane McCulloch was dubbed "Slick" by the editorial staff. Because Norman had courted McCulloch ever since he had written his *Time* cover story about the growing Times Mirror empire in 1957, McCulloch understood that he had been hired not so much by the wunderkind Otis Chandler as he had been by his powerhouse mother and his vain but still commanding father.

Williams correctly saw McCulloch as a stylist, a field general, and a muckraker; Haven was an able administrator who would not go stir crazy handling routine matters. Both men were seasoned journalists who understood the difference between real news and a press release, but each was a journeyman with different skills.

Nick Williams expected Haven to get the paper out each night, but he gave McCulloch a blank check to hire the best writers and turn them loose on the best stories.

Cultivated and connected, McCulloch set out immediately to beef up the reporting staff. Largely through his efforts, the new foreign and national bureaus that Otis began authorizing right and left were staffed with the finest young writers and reporters that McCulloch could recruit. The median age of a general assignment reporter dropped by fifteen years and the editorial budget doubled to $7 million between 1958 and 1965. In the weeks following the *Examiner* and *Mirror* closures alone, the *Times* hired forty reporters.

Two of McCulloch's city desk pets were *Mirror* refugees: Gene Blake, who had established his *Times* credentials with his John Birch series, and Jack Tobin, an

ex-Marine like McCulloch, who had started as a sportswriter but became intrigued with the backroom deals that went on at Los Angeles City Hall; he wrote several minor *Mirror* exposés in the waning days of Mayor Poulson's régime.

In what would turn out to be the acid test of McCulloch's freedom to probe, he took Tobin aside one day in the spring of 1962 and posed a simple question: Who owned the Santa Monica Mountains?

One of the last relatively undeveloped stretches of real estate within a thirty-minute drive of downtown L.A., the Santa Monica Mountains struck McCulloch as prime territory for subdivision speculation. And, he reasoned, where there's a land rush, there's bound to be corruption, kickbacks, graft, double-dealing, and bribery.

The dogged Tobin spent weeks poring over the Los Angeles County recorder's files per McCulloch's instructions; he came up with thousands of land transactions, but no readily visible corruption. One name that did appear over and over, however, was interesting: the Central State Southeast/Southwest Pension Funds. Tobin thought at first it must be a retirement plan for schoolteachers, but a bit more sleuthing turned up a neon name. President James Riddle Hoffa of the Teamsters Union turned out to be one of the funds' trustees. Other names that began showing up in the transactions included such well-known hoods as ex-Purple Gang associate Moe Dalitz and Chicago mob mouthpiece Sidney Korshak.

At about the same time Tobin began hitting pay dirt, Otis threw a cocktail soiree to display his all-new *Times* to Washington's elite—especially the shining stars of John F. Kennedy's New Frontier. During that party, McCulloch revealed Tobin's discoveries to Hoffa's longtime nemesis, Attorney General Robert Kennedy, who nearly spit out his drink.

"He got red faced and violent," McCulloch recalled. "His voice rose. He said, 'You'd better lay off that!'"

The following day, Kennedy's press secretary, Ed Guthman, called with an explanation. Kennedy had already impaneled a federal grand jury to investigate Hoffa, he told McCulloch. Only then did McCulloch understand what kind of a corruption cornucopia Tobin had stumbled upon. Instead of backing off, he ordered Tobin to team with Gene Blake and double their efforts. The result was a series of thirty stories published over the next fifteen months; they detailed deal after deal in which the Teamsters Union apparently laundered ill-gotten mob money through its pension funds by buying, selling, and making loans on Southern California's real estate.

Frank Haven didn't like the series and said so. To a *Times*man steeped in the *Front Page* tradition, real estate transactions were dull and far too abstract to digest over morning coffee, and he said as much to Nick Williams. As the series dragged on, Williams reluctantly agreed. At one point, Haven took Williams's

waning interest to mean that he could drop Tobin and Blake back into the general assignment reporting pool. When McCulloch heard Haven had taken his two star reporters off the Teamsters story, he exploded, and the pair were back on it again the same day. It marked the opening salvo in the war between the Franks.

"Frequently, after I'd left for the day at 7:00 or 8:00 P.M., the stuff would move from page one or three back with the jock-strap ads and I'd come back and yell about it in the morning," recalled McCulloch.

Haven was adamant: Tobin and Blake produced long, dull innuendo that never paid off.

"I could never find that we got anywhere with [the Teamsters story]," said Haven. "Once you get to the point where you can get a guy to talk, then either you or he or both are going to wind up in a lime pit somewhere."

Years later, Tobin said he had been aware that he and Blake were fast approaching Haven's lime-pit stage. Instead of being sandbagged by a mafioso or a Teamster thug, however, McCulloch's two intrepid investigators were knifed in the back by their own newspaper.

One day in the spring of 1963, after Tobin and Blake had published their latest story detailing how the Teamsters had made a large and suspicious loan to Santa Anita Race Track, Nick Williams called McCulloch into his office. Nick had already pushed his glasses up above his brows, rubbing away at the wrinkles on his forehead to no avail. His headache still came, rheuming his eyes and shortening his patience. He wanted to know why Frank was still running the Teamsters stories. Hadn't they all agreed that Haven was right—that the stories were too plodding and meaningless to the average *Times* reader?

"No, we haven't agreed," said McCulloch, reverting to his military bearing. "And if you want me to stop, you're going to have to give me a direct order."

"Oh, come on," whined Williams, eyes down and fingers raking through the fine threads of hair that remained at the back of his skull. "Let's not do that."

"Nick, if you want me to stop, you're going to have to tell me to stop," McCulloch said firmly.

Williams and McCulloch sat and stared across the desk at each other in silence for several moments. In retrospect, each man described the moment as eternal. Finally, Williams slid his glasses back onto his nose and nodded an almost imperceptible nod.

"Don't run any more of those pieces," he said quietly.

Frank McCulloch was not quite finished. He demanded to know where the decision had come from. Without saying a word, Williams glanced at the ceiling, and McCulloch understood all too clearly what had happened.

Otis Chandler's office was on the second floor, right next door to Nick's. Upon being named publisher, Otis had ordered all his immediate subordinates—Nick,

General Manager Bob Nelson, and Advertising Manager Vance Stickel—to move their offices to the second floor so that they would all be near the third floor news room and Otis could call them in for a conference on a moment's notice.

But Norman Chandler still did things the old-fashioned way. His office was on the sixth floor, where he and Buff and the rest of Times Mirror's ruling class still held court over all the worker bees who labored beneath them. It was Norman Chandler to whom Nick Williams was silently referring when he nodded toward the ceiling after ordering Frank McCulloch to call off his bloodhounds.

And perhaps with good reason. McCulloch revealed in an interview with the author thirty-five years later that Tobin and Blake had found yet another Los Angeles company that had accepted yet another hinky Teamsters loan that appeared to be laundered mob money. The firm was Walt's Auto Parks, which operated several parking lots throughout downtown Los Angeles. Tobin and Blake had found that, as he was in Santa Anita Race Track, Norman Chandler was a large stockholder in Walt's Auto Parks, and that was going to be their next story for the *Times.*

IN AN EXPANSIVE ATTEMPT to establish a foothold among California's intelligentsia and create America's first truly national newspaper, the *New York Times* launched a slimmed-down West Coast edition in October 1962. The timing could not have been worse. At almost the same time, New York City's crippling 114-day newspaper strike began. The work stoppage that ultimately killed the widely respected *New York Herald Tribune* and cut deeply into the profits of every other Manhattan daily dragged into 1963.

The result in L.A. was a sorry stepsister of the great gray *New York Times* for its West Coast readers—a sheet that one of its former reporters, Gay Talese, likened to *Pravda:* reprocessed news dictated from 3,000 miles away by editors who knew zip about what made Southern California tick.

During the six months leading up to the *New York Times'* Southern California invasion, Otis opened bureaus in Tokyo, Rio de Janeiro, Mexico City, Hong Kong, and the United Nations; he also expanded the *Times'* Washington and Sacramento bureaus and launched a twice-weekly San Fernando Valley edition. Within a year, the *Times* would expand its reach even further, to Bonn, Rome, Moscow, London, and Saigon, where two correspondents were added to cover the escalation of the war in Vietnam. In addition to the international and national bursts of *Times* energy, the nation's fastest-growing daily had also expanded its suburban sections into six regional editions beyond the San Fernando Valley. One of these was the ambitious satellite operation in Orange County, where a new *Times of Orange County* printing plant, staff, and distribution system would establish itself as a separate challenge to the struggling *Santa Ana Register.*[5]

But, like New York, Otis also had his labor problems.

For decades, unions had maintained a standing boycott against the hated *Los Angeles Times* and for decades the *Times* had grown and prospered in spite of the unions. Then, in April 1962, the unthinkable occurred. *Times* pressmen voted to recognize L.A.'s Web Pressmen's Union Local 18 as their bargaining agent.

Otis was mortified. He was the first Chandler in a century who'd let a union creep into the hallowed pressroom of General Harrison Grey Otis. Over the next nine months, while the union and the company haggled, Otis fought dirty. He ordered raises for all nonunion departments, tantalizing the pressmen with the promise of higher wages if they would get rid of the cursed union. On June 27, 1963, they did vote to decertify Local 18, and Otis's honor—while tarnished— was restored with his father, his family, and his forebears.[6]

However, he was never irrationally antilabor the way Norman and Harry had been. But he didn't hate them just because his great grandfather did, either. Otis insisted that his opposition to unions was more practical: He could see with his own eyes how strong labor movements in New York and other troubled Eastern cities were impeding modernization, just for the sake of saving antiquated jobs. Instead of enduring short-term pain for long-term gain, big-city dailies were being forced to shut down forever all over America. Otis was as sympathetic about letting old-timers go as his father had been when he wept at the closing of the *Mirror*, but Otis also recognized that featherbedding could lead to bankruptcy in relatively short order because the pace of technology seemed to increase daily, and almost in a geometric fashion. One electronic innovation could lead to a hundred more and standing squarely in the path of progress were union workers who feared for the security of their jobs.

In a way, the hiring of labor writer Harry Bernstein reflected Otis's ambivalence toward unions. Ironically, Bernstein was one of several seasoned journalists the *Times* acquired from Hearst's unionized *Examiner* after supposedly labor-friendly Hearst laid off the paper's staff.

One of Bernstein's first stories for the *Times,* which involved a department store strike, provoked an outraged call to the *Times* from the store's owner. Used to Norman Chandler's promanagement slant, the store owner lectured Nick Williams that the *Times'* new labor writer was way out of line.

Williams said stiffly, "If at any time Harry Bernstein's reportage is in error, the *Times* will print, with equal prominence, a correction."

"We don't contend that Bernstein is in error," replied the store owner. "What we're saying is that we don't want this [labor] situation reported at all."

Williams took a deep breath to deliver an answer that might have had him summarily fired in an earlier generation:

"The *Times* is in the business, and has an obligation to its subscribers, of reporting the news—*all* the important news—and that includes labor news."

Nick hung up.

Norman Chandler might have winced, but he made a genuine effort not to interfere in most of his son's new editorial policies, including those regarding labor news.

"He was busy with Times Mirror acquisitions and diversification," said Otis. "He liked the publicity that the *Times* was receiving as one of the best papers, clawing its way up very quickly into the top ten and then up into the top five and above that. My mother was pleased."

Against all conventional wisdom, the young beefcake who had kicked off his career as publisher with the vapid declaration "Wow!" was now exceeding the expectations of both parents.

"Otis is an interesting combination of the two of them because he's very easy with people and polite [like Norman] but he also has his mother's drive," said Donna Swayze, who began her three decades as Otis's personal secretary in 1962.

"Otis Chandler's biggest failing was his inability to grasp subtleties," said Frank McCulloch, who quit the *Times* in the autumn of 1963 to take over *Time* magazine's Saigon bureau. McCulloch never recovered from the Teamsters series. Later regretting that what he had said had been too hasty a decision, McCulloch used the excuse of too many additional responsibilities—that is, a new Sunday magazine that Williams wanted him to oversee—as his reason for quitting.

Jack Tobin had already quit in disgust over the Chandlers' unctuous sanctimony in the Teamsters series; he took his investigative reporting to *Sports Illustrated*. As for Gene Blake, Otis and Nick had effectively silenced him on the subject by dispatching Blake to London to open the *Times*' bureau there.

Frank Haven won the War of the Franks. On December 1, he became Nick Williams's sole managing editor. Otis hated losing McCulloch, but he approved of Haven.

"Otis lives entirely in the present, with an eye to the future," said Williams, who noted that Otis once told him that he had never visited the graves of either his grandfather or his great-grandfather.

In one way, Otis Chandler was a perfect match for the incongruity of his time. He was at once concerned and detached, enthusiastic and aloof, but always—in the end—rabidly protective when it came to his family's name.

On November 22, 1963, Otis paused briefly in his constant forward motion to mourn politely, like the rest of America. Then, he moved on quickly to mobilize the editorial, production, and circulation departments of his *Times* to cover the assassination of President John F. Kennedy like a dragnet. The *Times* was all over

the story, doing as well or better than any other daily in the country. For the next three days, Otis and Nick Williams followed the events in Dallas through the eyes and ears of their reporting staff while they watched *Times* circulation leap past the 1-million mark.

Even without the *New York Times,* Otis might have pushed the paper toward "uncommon excellence," a pet phrase he would recite like a rosary for the next thirty years. But the threat of two *Times*es competing for the elite of L.A. had cinched it for the young Chandler. As far as Otis was concerned, going head-to-head with Punch Sulzberger was as exhilarating as going for the gold of an Olympic title.

In January 1964, after Otis Chandler drove the *New York Times* out of California, he celebrated with his staff, which toasted its victory repeatedly at the city desk and in the Redwood Room bar across Second Street from Times Mirror Square. Although the West Coast edition had survived for only fifteen months and never really posed much of a threat, the *New York Times* had spurred Otis and his revolutionary band to intensify their efforts to create a new kind of *Los Angeles Times:* a "mass and class newspaper" that would retain an air of sophistication expected by its traditional older readers while offering a fresh array of features, columns, and news to attract L.A.'s swelling young middle class.

Sass *and* sophistication.

As Gay Talese wrote in *The Kingdom and the Power,*[7] his classic 1969 history of the *New York Times,* "If the *New York Times* did nothing else in California, it helped to make the *Los Angeles Times* into a better newspaper."

CHAPTER 17

IT WAS A CLOUDLESS FEBRUARY DAY in 1964 on an ice pack outside of Kotsubu, north of Nome. Otis Chandler's good friend Jack Burke had chosen to remain in camp that day, eating bad food with the Eskimos while Otis flew off once more to find himself a polar bear. The place where he would meet the great white animal was southwest of Point Barrow, where all Pacific storms originate before roaring down the Canadian coastline toward California, only to spend themselves in the balmy perpetuity of faraway L.A.

Otis Chandler stood next to his pilot guide's Super Cub, bundled against the elements like a six-foot marmot in snowshoes. There was no wind, so there was no wind chill factor. But with a temperature of sixty below and a hungry male po-

lar bear for the record books already in his mind's eye—if not yet in his rifle sight—the publisher of the *Los Angeles Times* was suffering from all sorts of chills.

"Normally you're supposed to hunt up and down the Alaskan coastline and not go due west toward Russia," Otis related.

At the height of the Cold War, the Soviets did not take border violations kindly, even if it was just to bag a bear. The U.S. Air Force and, presumably, their MIG counterparts rarely patrolled the area for spies. But Otis and his guide were having no luck in U.S. waters; after some amiable sizing-up of each other as they glided over the glacial miles, the guide turned in the pilot's seat and said to Otis,

"You know, I don't really think we're gonna see what you want here. Are you willing to take the personal and political risk, if there is one, of going over toward Russia?"

Otis lived for such moments. Of course he'd defy the odds. And thus their adventure began, buzzing for prehistoric beasts in a puddle jumper within thirty miles of a hostile nuclear power's coastline. Heightening the thrill, Otis had brought along his 16-millimeter movie camera, which surely would have landed him and his pilot in a Siberian gulag had they been hunted down by the Russians.

But Otis Chandler was the only hunter that day.

"So we saw this good bear," he said, "and we landed." It was a feat more daring than it sounded, given the ocean currents and the unpredictability of the ice, which could appear quite solid one moment and present thirty-foot-high frozen spires the next. And it was all painted in disorienting shades of ivory white and blue that seemed to go on forever. Misread it once and a plane on skis could slide into water so cold that all the cold-weather clothing on earth would not save a hairless Homo sapiens.

"You're dead immediately because you can't be five seconds in that water," Otis recited from memory.

But he did not die. His bear awaited him due south about two miles from the spot where they landed. Otis leaped out and raced to the top of a block of ice to see if he could catch sight of the bear.

"Don't run," said his guide. "Just take your time. He's there, we'll find him. If you exert yourself, you'll freeze your lungs."

When they sighted the bear, the two men climbed to a position several hundred yards and some ten feet above him. Then Otis broke out his home movie camera. At first, the bear didn't see them but, within moments, the animal turned, sniffed the air, and trotted in Otis's general direction.

"I hope you aren't one of these guys that panics," said his guide, exchanging the only rifle they had between them for the movie camera.

"I think I'll be okay," said Otis.

But it was the first time he had ever faced dangerous game—an animal that could trample him, scar him, or simply eat him as easily as it could eat a caught fish. The guide stepped back and operated the movie camera, which Otis had winterized to work in temperatures as low as sixty degrees below.

The bear loped closer, sniffing the air. Otis removed two sets of gloves so that he could feel the trigger. At about seventy-five yards away, 1,200 pounds of polar bear loomed larger and larger in his sights; Otis crouched and squeezed off a single shot. The first thing he noticed was an explosion of steam erupting from the animal's fur as the rifle round found its mark. The bear's hot breath spewed from its injured lung into the arctic air and evaporated instantly into a cloud of bloody ice crystals.

The second thing he noticed was the skin of his bare hands tearing from his fingers as he left it in layers of icy dermis on the rifle's trigger housing. Half a football field away, the bear was bawling and twisting in the ice, splitting the dead silence with its deep, crazed, guttural scream.

"Well that was pretty easy," said Otis, ignoring his own bloodied fingers and standing tall with the rifle at his side. "One shot, and he's gonna go down."

His guide knew better.

"Put another shell in the chamber!" he yelled.

Only then did Otis notice that the bear's screams and somersaults had been pure histrionics—that it had been playing for time. This time, the bear did not lope. The bear charged, closing the remaining yards between himself and the two primates with angry leaps that gave Otis only seconds to reload, aim, and shoot. He said to himself, "We're dead if I don't do the right thing."

The shot caught the bear in the ribs and, this time, he went down and did no somersaults. Otis was not one to be fooled twice. He put three more shots in the beast before approaching. The black eyes shined dull in death and the blood flow from its mouth had already frozen into a crimson Popsicle.

Over the next three hours, the guide regaled Otis with tales of hunters who had panicked and run, leaving him behind to finish the kill. It took that long to skin the bear—a process the guide called "caping" because the resulting bearskin is of a single piece, peeled from the body like fur-covered rind. Only the head came back whole. Despite scrapping away the animal's substantial fat, the cape and head still weighed about three hundred pounds and had to be hauled back to the Super Cub.

Then they were faced with the takeoff. While they were hunting, the wind had picked up and the mild sixty below had dropped to seventy-five. After a few anxious moments the engine kicked over, but there was now the additional weight of a bear skin and skull in the cargo hold to worry about. As the guide gave Otis the

high sign that they were ready to go, Otis faced one final crisis. Before climbing into the plane, he unbuckled his parka and zipped open his trousers.

"No!" shrieked the guide. "It'll freeze! Just pee in your pants."

Otis shrugged, bundled back up and let loose his bladder as he clambered into the plane. A warmth bled through his long underwear. The plane's take-off run seemed to last forever before the plane lifted off like a sated carnivorous bird. Otis sat back and let himself relax for the first time in many tense hours.

The plane set back down in a western Alaskan version of civilization just before dark. Jack Burke was so jealous that he could spit, and he did.

THERE WOULD BE OTHER NEAR-MISSES as Otis tempted fate in his big-game hunter persona, like the time a dying leopard nearly got him in Kenya. A charging elephant in Mozambique missed turning his torso to Spam by inches; Otis stood his ground and shot the beast, while Missy and the Chandlers' Portuguese guide skittered up the nearest trees like the native Columnus monkeys. Otis shot four of those, too, and had a rug made from their hides.

But Otis loved best of all to tell and retell the tale of his first high adventure, his polar bear quest, refining it each time to its triumphant essence. In later years, as Alaskan environmentalists succeeded in curbing American executives with high-powered rifles from killing the beasts, his story took on the trappings of a fable, complete with a moral.

"The only place you can hunt polar bear now is in Canada, and it's not a hunt," he said a full generation after he bagged his bear. "It's a shoot, because what they do is the Eskimos take the hunter out by snowmobile and you catch up with the bear . . . and you look at the bear at twenty-five miles per hour and then decide if you want to shoot the bear, which is not hunting."

Hunting, he said, is scouting an older bear from a light plane so that the hunter minimizes the chances of blowing away a young female or even a male still in his reproductive years. Hunting is facing down one of these aging monarchs who is beyond the prime of life and engaging him in mortal combat, one-on-one, even though the odds are definitely in the hunter's favor. Hunting is a duel between a man and a matching beast. No snowmobiles. No pregnant sows. No biologists or federal wildlife officials peering over one's shoulder as the trigger is squeezed and that long, lethal phallic symbol barks death across the Alaskan icescape.

Hunting, he preached, is thinning the herd and giving the animal its final glory as surely as a matador tenders death to a prized bull. And yet, no matador stuffs his bull and mounts it in the living room.

"I was just building the big home in San Marino with Missy," said Otis. "It had just been built and I left room on one side of the fireplace."

Because the hearth-in-home was not quite finished, Otis had the taxidermist deliver his mounted kill to the *Times;* it would be a few days before he could settle his new best friend into a permanent home next to the "dead-head wall." So Otis had the fearsome-looking bear uncrated and hauled upstairs to the publisher's suite.

"It took four men to carry the bear, one on each paw," said Otis, "and Nick happened to be out of his office as they hauled it in."

The workers set it up in Otis's dressing room so that the bear stood on its hind legs, towering ten shaggy feet in the air, claws extended and fangs bared. Once it was properly posed, its agate eyes signaling danger and death to the uninformed, Otis buzzed for the *Times'* editor.

"Nick, could you come down for a minute? I have something I want to show you," he said.

He guided Williams toward his dressing room, suppressing a giggle the way he once suppressed a desire to create yellow snow in the arctic wilderness. Then he whipped open the dressing room door. All the way down the executive corridor Nick's high-pitched voice reverberated off the windows and walls.

"Je-sus Christ!" Nick hollered.

Later that night, a cleaning lady had the same reaction.

"She flipped on the light in the dressing room and there was a ten-foot polar bear growling at her," said Otis, grinning like the mischievous ten-year-old kid he'd never been allowed to be. "Thank God she didn't drop dead of a heart attack."

IN FEBRUARY 1964, *Time* magazine named the *Los Angeles Times* one of the nation's ten best newspapers. Never in the *Time*'s institutional memory had a daily paper gone so quickly from garbage to gold.

Inside the fortress at Spring and First Streets, the thirty-seven-year-old dynamo most responsible for turning the *Times* around surrounded himself with lieutenants and linemen, the finest reporters and writers that money could buy; they joined Otis in orchestrating flowcharts and goal sheets for his next big move. The first *Times* publisher to serve in the military since General Harrison Gray Otis proved every business day and in true field-marshal style that he was an Otis first and a Chandler second. Otis Chandler approached journalism as though it were a jihad.

"I think these two things," he preached. "Look at yourself, and then put yourself out there and see how others see you. Some people don't have either quality and they will try to be an executive or a leader and they will never make it."

Otis became a public figure in spite of himself. Always uncomfortable before a crowd, he had learned a hard lesson from his first major "Wow!" public appearance, when he was mistakenly shrugged off by his peers as a beach-blanket lightweight. It is never enough to be sincere in one's own beliefs and enthusiasm, he concluded. To be a leader, it is equally important always to be aware of how the troops see you.

"At public receptions, dinners, etc., I would have an out-of-body experience," Otis recalled. "And I would be out there in the crowd, looking back and saying 'Otis you're not doing well tonight. Come on, let's get going.' And I would pinch myself, and I would start working the room."

But he also kept one eye on his watch; he hurried through the speeches so that he could get his car from valet parking fast enough to make a clean getaway. There was always a secret part of himself that was ranging across the tundra, alone, even in the midst of a black-tie crowd. His gregarious and effervescent Missy, the perfect social appendage, was always present at his side, prodding, coaxing, just as Buff once had done.

"He put his heart and soul into it and I was his backup," said Missy. "I helped him a great deal because he is a very reclusive person. He doesn't like to go to anything. I would push him out the door and I had to make him go to these things."

Otis still felt awkward. The *Times* publisher was uncomfortable with small talk. He remained as restless as a caged predator, especially in a receiving line. He felt most comfortable with his people—his ragtag army of smart social misfits at the *Times* who reported the news each day to Los Angeles.

Ever since the John Birch series, his relatives thought he might be getting too close to the troops—that he'd been infected by the traditionally liberal bent of the change-the-world philosophy of most newsmen.

"How could [the Vietnam War] be liberal or conservative?" asked Otis, recalling the single most divisive political issue of the 1960s. "President Johnson told me early on we were hoping that this would stop the hordes of Chinese and that was the reason [John F.] Kennedy sent in advisors. I remember hearing [Defense Secretary James] Schlesinger and [National Security Adviser Henry] Kissinger and all those people that I had in [for editorial conferences] saying why we did what we did. We wanted to draw the line in the sand. It wasn't for the Vietnamese, but for the Allies. If we stopped them there, the Chinese might not be so eager to cross into Korea. I called it as I saw it and our correspondents called it as they saw it."

On most political issues, Otis did defer to his editors, but they, too, took each issue on its own merits—not along traditional party lines.

"In political persuasion I would say I am a centrist," said Nick Williams, from whom Otis took most of his political cues during the 1960s. "Some programs and

ideas that the Republicans might offer in an election I like, whether it be education or whatever. Others I might like on the other side."

For Norman, Buff, and the rest of the right-wing Chandler clan, the proposition that traditional Democratic-Republican divisions might no longer work in an increasingly complex world was just too much to digest. During the 1964 California primary, Otis wanted to endorse whom he pleased and base his choice on what a candidate said rather than on the political party he represented. But Norman had other ideas.

It was Otis's choice to have the *Times* endorse liberal Governor Nelson Rockefeller of New York, but when he did, Norman forewarned his son that whomever the Republicans nominated would be the *Times'* choice in November. The *Times*, after all, was a Republican newspaper. Always had been. Always would be.

When arch-conservative Senator Barry Goldwater of Arizona took the nomination, Otis cringed. He faced down his father. There would be no shouting; they were Chandlers, after all, and they resolved their differences in a quiet, tense, but always civilized manner.

"You know Barry and I like Barry and I don't think he'll win," Norman conceded. "I think Johnson will win."

And, yet, Goldwater would be the *Times'* choice, Norman said, because Goldwater, after all, was a Republican. Otis felt as though he'd had a gun put to his head.

"But that's just ridiculous!" he protested, his voice nearly rising to a forbidden shout. "I've moved the paper to this militant centrist position and now it's like this old WASP paper!'"

Otis had grown fond of the gruff, horse-trading pragmatism of Lyndon Baines Johnson since that awful day in Dallas when the vice president had unexpectedly stepped up to the presidency. He and LBJ grew to be such chums that Otis once accepted Johnson's invitation to go skinny-dipping with him in the White House swimming pool. They had first met in 1960, in the weeks after Otis had been named publisher, but before John F. Kennedy had won the presidential election. Otis had been impressed enough then to take the extraordinary step of introducing the Texas Democrat to Norman. Now, four years later, he thought that reintroducing his parents to President Johnson might change their minds about Goldwater.

He called LBJ aide Jack Valenti, arranged to fly Norman and Buff back to Washington, and had the Johnsons ask them to the White House for dinner.

"Lyndon not only had dinner—just the four of them—in the White House," said Otis. "Lyndon also—as he used to do when he was trying to impress someone—took them up to his bedroom. Lyndon was a wonderful guy but sometimes he had a little lack of judgment or taste in things like that. He just took them right

up. 'Oh, I *got* to show you my bedroom!' After five minutes, he was probably calling my mother Buffy."

Far from being appalled, the stiff and straitlaced Chandlers were charmed. The Goldwater endorsement remained firmly in place, but from that day forward, Otis saw the political crack that the Birch series had opened between his parents and the rest of the Chandler clan widen first into a gap and, by the end of the 1960s, a chasm the philosophical size of the Grand Canyon.

LIKE HER YOUNGEST BROTHER PHILIP and his Birch Society wife, Alberta, Lady Crocker was horrified when Otis began moving the paper's editorial pages toward the political center. She was equally shocked when Norman took the first steps toward trading Times Mirror on the New York Stock Exchange.

Although Lady Crocker, her siblings, or their children had anything to do with the *Times* outside of collecting their regular stock dividends, the paper was the crown jewel of the family enterprises. Shackled inextricably to nineteen of Norman's shirttail relatives through Chandis Securities,[1] Times Mirror was synonymous with the Chandler name. It should remain strictly the domicile of the Chandlers, argued Lady Crocker. Opening it to the scrutiny of the Securities and Exchange Commission and public stock trading could mean the beginning of the end of the Chandler stranglehold on Los Angeles.

Nonsense, Norman argued. Even the courtly, pipe-chewing patriarch of the family found it hard to believe how parochial his headstrong sister could be. Still, Norman made allowances. Buff might hate Ruth, and Norman might cringe at the thought of having to sit down to dinner with Philip and Alberta, but they were family—and family always came first, especially in business. Thus, the trenchant whine of Lady Crocker and her family allies could not be ignored. It remained an echo in everything that Norman attempted to do in moving Times Mirror forward.

He patiently explained to the dissident Chandlers that he, Otis, and *Times* legal counsel Bob Erburu were going to New York to pitch Times Mirror to financial analysts because the time had come to grow beyond L.A. The Chandlers' traditional distrust of all things East Coast, Democratic, or remotely organized (as in labor) had to be tempered by basic economics. In a recession, a company that owned only two or three products, as Times Mirror did, could take an awful beating and the family's all-important dividends could drop through the floor. Norman had a well-planned strategy, he explained, and it had gone into high gear in September 1963, when he'd hired as his acquisitions chief, Albert V. Casey, a former Railway Express executive who was developing a national reputation as a consummate corporate strategist.

During the previous year, Times Mirror had already acquired legal publisher Matthew Bender & Company, Kappler Lumber Company, and Cleveland's World Publishing Company, which sold *Webster's New World Dictionary* and more Bibles than any other company in the world.

Times Mirror had also agreed in principal to sell KTTV to entrepreneur John Kluge for $11 million[2]—a move that Casey argued in vain to kill. He believed the sale was nothing more than Norman's anachronistic submission to *Times* newsroom jealousy. Attempts to create a *Times*-KTTV synergy always failed, in part because Channel 11's ability to break many news stories as they were happening occasionally scooped the *Times*. The newspaper felt its primacy as the No. 1 news source in L.A. threatened.

A bottom-line man, Casey was determined to put a stop to such emotional lunacy. His strategy was to scrutinize all information companies with a profit margin of 15 percent or higher and then cherry pick, "in much the fashion of a racetrack handicapper trying to assess a field of horses," according to *Fortune* magazine. One of his first picks was Pickett, the nation's leading slide rule manufacturer: a tactical error at the dawn of the handheld computer age, as it turned out. But Casey's batting average improved. A few years later, he found a floundering Chicago company called Year Book Medical whose books Casey began peddling to physicians through a club he privately dubbed Disease of the Month.

Other acquisitions were closer to home. The New York and Pacific Coast stock exchanges listed Times Mirror common stock on May 27, 1964, and one month later, Times Mirror bought the *San Bernardino Sun*.

Unfortunately, the *Times'* first incursion into a neighboring county since its 1961 purchase of the *Orange Coast Daily Pilot* also represented one antitrust move too far in the eyes of the Justice Department. Still stung by the Hearst-Chandler sleight of hand in the suspect shutdown of the *Mirror* and *Examiner* in 1962, government antitrust lawyers who were no longer under Robert Kennedy's thumb in 1965 challenged Times Mirror's *San Bernardino Sun* bid in court. They charged that the company's strategy of buying suburban newspapers was a march toward monopoly because businesses would eventually have no choice but to pay whatever advertising rates Times Mirror dictated. The *Times* fought the Justice Department for two years, but was eventually forced to sell the *Sun* to the Gannett chain in 1968 at a $2.5-million profit.

After he was burned in the *Sun* case, Casey switched Times Mirror's newspaper acquisition focus out of state, where the *Times* could not be accused of trying to corner the market on advertising rates.

Meanwhile, the *Times* grew; its average weekday circulation now topped 800,000 and its advertising revenue had nearly doubled during Otis's tenure. By the end of 1964, the *Times* had become the first newspaper in history to publish

over 4 million classifieds and 100 million ad lines overall during a single year. *Times* reporters were now among the highest paid in the nation, grossing an average of $8,112 a year when most papers paid half that much.

Across town at the *Herald Examiner*, reporters were among the worst paid. By December 1967, the pay gap between Hearst and the *Times* had grown so wide that the Newspaper Guild and the International Association of Machinists voted to strike the *Herald-Examiner;* Hearst, in turn, locked out union members and replaced them with scabs. The dispute led to the longest strike in newspaper history, sapping whatever vitality the *Herald-Examiner* had left.

And Otis Chandler's *Times* grew and prospered.

———————

IN A SPECIAL FORTY-EIGHT-PAGE EDITION of its Sunday magazine, *California Living,* the *Los Angeles Herald-Examiner* trumpeted the December 6, 1964,[3] opening of the first of the three theaters that would collectively be known as the Los Angeles Music Center: "This is the jeweled setting of a Pavilion that, for all its height [the equivalent of six stories], has an aspect of lightness that has been artfully calculated by architect Welton Becket. It comes primarily from the slender, stemlike columns that surround the portico, extending from floor to roof. In addition, the facade is of shining glass, boldly ornamented by black granite."

Despite the striking photos and pretentious prose that characterized *California Living,* nowhere did Mrs. Dorothy Chandler's name appear in the tribute—nor had the Chandler name ever appeared in the *Herald-Examiner* in connection with the $33-million Music Center through all the years of Buff's steamroller fundraising efforts. But, with the official dedication of the new home of the Los Angeles Philharmonic, even the recalcitrant Hearsts could no longer ignore Buff.

"She did coalesce the community behind the Music Center, and that had the side effect of helping the community generally," said Otis. "I don't know how the Westside, Hancock Park, and the Eastside would have gotten together. Maybe through their own momentum as the city looked at the future of education and the freeways and whatever. But I think she brought them together earlier because she needed their help."

The Music Center's board of directors apparently agreed because, over Mrs. Chandler's own objections, they named the new wedding cake of a building for the woman whose steely eyed portrait would hang forever in its Founders' Room like a distaff portrait of Dorian Grey: the Dorothy Chandler Pavilion.

Over Buff's mantelpiece at her Los Tiempos homestead hung a different kind of portrait—Pablo Picasso's *Blue Lady*. How it got there said a great deal about Buff, the Music Center, politics, and the state of cultural morals in the land of the *Los Angeles Times,* circa 1964.

Buff's ruthless fund-raising had already reached across party lines when she blithely tried bartering the *Times*' political favor for any candidate's donation. Things had changed dramatically at Times Mirror Square, however, and she was no longer in a position to dictate the names mentioned in her husband's newspaper.

"She made the transition from sleeping with the publisher to only talking with the publisher," observed Dr. Franklin Murphy, the University of Kansas administrator who was named chancellor of UCLA in 1960 and became acquainted with Buff in her role as a University of California regent. Murphy continued, "And you know that's a big difference—sleeping with someone or talking with someone. Not just in physical terms but in psychological terms. Oh, you're sitting down in your night clothes with a martini, having a nightcap, and you talk freely and easily and it's unstructured, but when you call up your son and you say this and this, it's a highly structured exercise."

That Buff no longer directly influenced the *Times* as she had when Norman was publisher was of no consequence when it came to arm twisting. Democrats and Republicans alike believed she wielded the same power, so she exercised it boldly.

Thus, when Nelson Rockefeller sought the *Times*' endorsement over Goldwater in the 1964 California primary, the New York governor offered to donate Picasso's *Blue Lady*—which he valued at $25,000—to Buff's Music Center effort. At Buff's behest, Norman turned Al Casey loose on the presidential contender to see if even more could be squeezed out of Rockefeller.

"Picasso's *Blue Lady* isn't worth $25,000," Casey scoffed. "If you give me $4,000 in cash, I'll give you credit for a full $25,000 donation."

"You don't know your ass from your elbow about what this painting is worth," Rockefeller blustered in outrage. He was right, of course, but Casey lived up to his reputation as a ballsy negotiator when he folded his hands on his desk and stuck out his chin.

"I'm telling you, Governor, it's not worth $25,000 to me, because I need *cash* for the Music Center. Now, $4,000 is a very modest amount, and I want $4,000 in cash. Up front."

Casey later maintained that neither he nor Rockefeller had mentioned the word "endorsement" during their negotiations, but they had both understood that Rockefeller's charity was not born of a love for the Los Angeles Philharmonic.

"You can go back to Mrs. Chandler and tell her we have made a deal," Casey told Rockefeller as soon as he had grudgingly agreed to throw $4,000 into the pot.

The exchange was made and, coincidentally, Rockefeller got his endorsement. But the *Blue Lady* never made it to the Music Center.

Buff had just redecorated her living room at Los Tiempos and needed a Picasso for one wall.[4] There it remained for the next seven years until she redecorated again and shades of aqua and indigo no longer fit into her color scheme. Only then did she auction the *Blue Lady* to a Japanese buyer who paid $450,000 for the painting. Casey made sure that Buff put the money back into the Music Center's coffers.

Once the Music Center had blossomed with a nightly overture and a young Brahmin named Zubin Mehta had firmly supplanted veteran Philharmonic conductor Georg Solti as Buff's favorite maestro, she turned her attention to seeking out a world-class music critic for the *Times*.

The paper had run through several critics over the years, but most of them were like the legendary Isabel Morse Jones, who had once endeared herself to the city desk with a fawning review of a Toscanini symphony that neglected to point out that a fruitcake in pink tights had pranced onto the stage in the middle of the performance and had to be forcibly hauled offstage.

"Why didn't you tell us?" shrieked the city editor.

"Because it had *nothing* to do with the music," Jones answered haughtily.

On August 5, 1965, the former assistant music editor for the *Saturday Review,* Martin Bernheimer, officially became the *Times'* classical music critic. At first, Mrs. Chandler was ebullient. Although he was every bit as big a snob in his own way as Buff, Bernheimer was uncompromising in his tastes, idiosyncratic in his observations, and occasionally downright cruel in his reviews. He didn't mind telling Buff that her Dorothy Chandler Pavilion had the acoustics of a barn. He festooned one wall of his office with photos of topless female cellists and switched with ease from polysyllabic palaver to locker-room colloquy. He also developed an almost instant dislike for the conducting of Zubin Mehta.

Not only did Buff support Mehta; she engineered the unceremonious dumping of Georg Solti so that the young maestro from Bombay could assume his proper role as conductor of the Los Angeles Philharmonic. In her trailer at Dana Point, one of the few signed photos that she kept framed and prominently on display was that of Zubin Mehta. Thus, when Bernheimer began to heap the reviewer's equivalent of goat excrement on the unfortunate musical wunderkind, Buff was not amused and vowed to have Bernheimer's head.

"You protect Beethoven and I'll protect Bernheimer," Nick Williams had made Bernheimer promise when he hired him.

More than once, Buff waved an offending review in her son's face, tears streaming and voice as high fidelity as that of an injured cat, as she ordered him to fire the professorial Bernheimer at once. His jaw set and his huge shoulders tensed, Otis let his mother's spleen vent itself. Once her hysteria had wound down to that

of a category two hurricane, he breathed deeply to calm himself and told her to leave his office. There would be no firing that day.

Almost thirty years later, long after Mehta had abandoned L.A. for greener pastures in the East, Buff was only a memory, and Bernheimer had won the Pulitzer Prize for criticism, the cantankerous critic had nothing but praise for Nick Williams and Otis Chandler:

> Mrs. Chandler wasn't invariably ecstatic about the outside agitator who frequently carped in her own family newspaper about acoustical problems at the Dorothy Chandler Pavilion, who didn't regard the brash young Mehta as the second coming of Bruno Walter, who couldn't pretend that the rough and sometimes unready Los Angeles Philharmonic was the equal of the Berlin Philharmonic, who resisted showbiz hype even when it was supposed to serve the cause of High Art, and who griped nonstop about the absence of a worthy opera company in the land of the plastic lotus. Nevertheless, Bernheimer remained protected.

OTIS CONTINUED TO HIRE THE BEST, regardless of price or political persuasion. when the acerbic Paul Conrad joined the *Times* staff as editorial cartoonist shortly before he won his first Pulitzer in 1964 for his work at the *Denver Post,* he made enemies faster than Martin Bernheimer had.

Conrad dubbed Fred Hartley, the president of Union Oil, "Fred Heartless"; the cartoonist and the *Times* were unsuccessfully sued for allegedly libeling the business executive.

Mayor Sam Yorty also sued the *Times* following a "fact-finding mission" that he'd made to Vietnam. Yorty, nicknamed "Suitcase Sam" because of his penchant for junkets, recommended an escalation of the war at the same time that he openly campaigned to join the president's Cabinet. Conrad penned a caricature of the mayor in a straitjacket and pointing to a map of Vietnam with a caption reading "Secretary of Defense."

Yorty's $2-million libel suit was tossed out of court.

A cartoon that poked fun at the pope drew an angry letter from L.A.'s Cardinal Timothy Manning demanding that Conrad apologize to L.A.'s 2 million Roman Catholics. Beneath a caricature of the pontiff with a papal Mini-Me sitting in his lap, Conrad had printed an item he'd pulled straight off the front page: "Vatican prohibits ordination of women as priests because Christ's representatives must have a 'natural resemblance' to him."

Conrad answered the cardinal's outrage in his own letter, but he made no apology. He pointed out that he, too, was a Catholic, but considered the church's argument against women in the priesthood irrational, unjust, and wrong.

Mail poured in during Conrad's first few years at the *Times*—more than for anyone else who worked there. Nick Williams tired quickly of defending Conrad; he wrote a long form letter proclaiming that he, too, would like to "break Conrad's drawing arm" at times, but that he could not in good conscience interfere with his cartoonist's satirical mandate.

Conrad's wicked pen painted in broad strokes the liberal drift the *Times* had taken and frequently left both Chandlers—Norman and Otis—rubbing their temples with a despair equal to that of Nick Williams. Otis would press Nick to tone down their Pulitzer Prize–winning caricaturist and Nick would have a word with Conrad, but usually to no avail. Conrad did not muzzle easily. Once, during a Washington-to-L.A. flight, Norman asked Conrad how he liked working for the *Times*.

"Just fine now, although I would never have worked here in the old days," answered the cartoonist.

Norman smiled wearily.

"You're goddamn right you wouldn't have," he said.

"GENERAL OTIS WAS THE SORT of man for whom I would have detested working whereas [Harry] Chandler probably is the sort of man who would have fired me," said Nick Williams.

Norman Chandler, however, was the sort of man who mellowed with age, according to both Williams and Otis Chandler. At the beginning of 1965, Norman's plan to grow Times Mirror had mollified his avaricious relatives at the same time that it shoveled working capital into his ambitious son's coffers. The corporation earned a $12-million profit that year, which paid out a hefty $2.18 per share, effectively muting the shrill outcry from Lady Crocker, Philip, and the rest of the right-wing clan. They might hate Conrad and the shift to the left on the editorial pages, but a Chandler never argued with money in the bank. Record profits also meant that Otis had more to spend on news.

In March, he opened an African bureau with some of the windfall. In May, Otis used even more of Times Mirror's profits to seduce *Newsweek*'s Beirut correspondent, Joe Alex Morris, to the *Times*, to become its new Middle East bureau chief.

Otis caught *Newsweek*'s owner, Kay Graham, by surprise. She had just returned from spending a week with Morris, who'd given her a tour of all the East-

ern Mediterranean hot spots. Graham, who was also the new publisher of the *Washington Post,* regarded Otis as a close chum in the loose-knit fraternity of American newspaper publishers and never considered that he would stoop so low as to steal a star reporter from her. But the *Times* publisher always regarded competition as an override to friendship. There was nothing so satisfying as beating a buddy, and the secret bully in Otis Chandler got a special kick out of one-upping Katherine Graham.

"She was raving about this wonderful foreign correspondent, and then he announced he was coming to the *Times,*" he remembered with a grin. "Boy, was she mad!"

The Morris hijacking was especially vexing to Graham given her special history with the Chandlers. She and her husband, Phil Graham, had taken Otis and Missy under their wings "when we were just baby publishers," recalled Missy. During conventions of the American Newspaper Publishers Association, American Society of Newspaper Editors, and other national press organizations, the Grahams welcomed and wined and dined the Chandlers when other Eastern patricians remained aloof. Out of this close and early association evolved the 1962 founding of the Los Angeles Times–Washington Post News Service, which started with thirty subscribers and became a staple of half the leading newspapers in North America.

It was partly through Phil Graham's urging that Otis was elected to sit on the board of the Associated Press—one of the "big deals in publishing," said Missy.

"They had their meeting at the Biltmore Hotel in Phoenix that year [1963]—the one designed by Frank Lloyd Wright," Missy remembered. "Phil was acting very strangely."

An understatement, as it turned out. Graham had been diagnosed five years earlier, when he was forty-seven, as manic depressive; he and his family had skillfully suppressed his illness despite his frequent absences from the *Post.* Pharmacology was still in its infancy when it came to treating such disorders, and all that Kay Graham could do was check him into a sanitarium or stay with him at home or at their country retreat until one of his episodes had passed. With each one, they grew worse.

Although Kay Graham had been married to Phil since 1940, she did not begin to make the connection between his occasional high-wire binge drinking, which was followed by weeks of the blackest depressions, until 1957, when her husband visited the National Institute of Mental Health and quietly put himself under a physician's care. He and Kay told their friends that it was a nervous breakdown.

At first, the episodes consisted of a routine cycle of drinking, drying out, and depression followed by extended periods of relative normality. But the mood swings grew worse and harder to hide and—by the time Otis and Missy were

about to make their debut on the AP board of directors—Phil had inexplicably and publicly dumped his wife and taken up with a *Newsweek* stringer. Kay understood that her husband's open philandering was just another symptom of a worsening mental condition, but the rest of the world regarded Phil Graham's affair as some sort of wacky male menopause.

Otis and Missy knew that Graham had problems but did not know how serious they had become. Thus, when Graham offered to fly the young Chandlers to the Arizona AP meeting in his private jet, they were deeply flattered.

"We didn't know how sick he was and nobody ever warned us," said Missy. "So we got on the plane with him and, in front of Otis and in front of his girlfriend, he got on top of me on the floor of the plane and started kissing me. Somehow he wrestled me down. He wasn't trying to screw me, he was just kissing me. Otis had to pull him off."

When they arrived in Phoenix, Otis called Kay, who explained the awful truth and asked the Chandlers to look after her husband. They hired a guard to keep an eye on him during the meetings that led up to the banquet and installation of AP officers, but Graham didn't leave his hotel room.

"Finally, at the big Sunday night dinner when everybody gives speeches, Phil arrives, goes up to the podium, and starts swearing and telling off every publisher there," said Missy. "Otis had to drag him away."

Otis called Kay, who arranged to have President Kennedy send Air Force Two to pick up her husband and get him back to Washington. Graham returned to his sanitarium for the last time. Six months later, after arranging a weekend leave to spend some time at home with Kay, Phil Graham put a shotgun to his head and pulled the trigger. He was forty-eight years old.

Three years his junior and herself a one-time newspaper reporter, Katherine Graham grieved her husband's suicide, but never gave a thought to giving up the *Post*. After all, she was the daughter of the *Post*'s owner and publisher, Eugene Meyer, before Phil Graham had ever entered the picture—first, as her husband and, in very short order, as Meyer's successor. Shunning all arguments against it, she decided to step into the publisher's role herself, and suddenly she was on the phone to Otis every morning: What should she do next?

"She's just like my little kid sister," said Otis, who was ten years younger than Katherine Graham. "I mean, she looks about fourteen, but she's got a brain of a very smart lady."

But her grasp of the complex balancing act that a publisher must perform every day had atrophied during Phil's tenure. Katherine had the children, tended the family, raised the funds for charity, and arranged the dinner parties, just as Buff and Missy Chandler did, or any other publisher's wife was expected to do. As a charter member of the AP fraternity and Otis's new partner in the Los Ange-

les Times–Washington Post News Service, it never occurred to her that he might steal her employees,

"She didn't know it and thought we were buddies after Phil's death," said Otis.

Three months after hiring Joe Alex Morris, Chandler did it again. This time, he hired *Newsweek*'s Robert S. Elegant to head the new Hong Kong bureau. Fluent in Chinese, Elegant was also a best-selling novelist; his books included *The Dragon's Seed* and *A Question of Loyalty.*

Otis Chandler and Kay Graham remained business partners and cocktail-party pals, but she would never again make the mistake of putting her full trust in a Chandler.

CHAPTER 18

FEVER UNDULATED IN WAVES from the asphalt on the evening of August 11, 1965, and Los Angeles tried to slake its collective thirst with a long, cool, intoxicating drink, just as Marquette Frye had done, down in the bowels of the South Central neighborhood known since Harry Chandler's day as Watts.

Frye had no idea who Harry Chandler was and certainly no way of knowing that Watts had once been home to some of Harry's closest business associates. Most of them had moved away decades earlier and their grand old Victorian and Craftsman houses had long ago gone to seed. Once-prosperous Avalon Boulevard was now a hodgepodge of cocktail lounges, barber shops, liquor stores, dime stores, and other hardscrabble mom-and-pop enterprises. Watts had evolved into a ghetto for working-class blacks like Frye, who had been squeezed farther and farther south of the great city that General Otis and Harry and Norman and, now, Otis Chandler had imagined into being atop the vestiges of Nigger Alley.

The mercury hovered near the hundred mark for the third day in a row and temperatures barely dropped after sundown. There was no wind. Sweat only dried on bodies in motion. Half-lit Marquette Frye took his kid brother for a ride along Avalon Boulevard, rolling the windows of his Buick all they way down to manufacture some cool breeze. Another motorist noticed the Buick weaving and flagged down a motorcycle cop. He pointed out the Frye boys, then went on his way.

The complaining motorist was black, just like Marquette Frye. But the cop, CHP Officer Lee Minikus, was white, and before he could complete Frye's field sobriety test and arrest him for driving under the influence, Frye's kid brother

had run two blocks to the house where he lived and fetched his mother. Mrs. Frye hurried to the scene with several neighbors in tow, an avenging angel who railed at her no-good drunk of a son at first, but soon turned her venom on the arresting officer. She gathered support from a curious crowd that quickly swelled from forty to perhaps as many as four hundred. They had happened by at first, then began descending from their porches or wandering past cinder-dry front lawns to witness more closely the simmering proceedings out on the street.

As the crowd grew, so did its bile. After Officer Minikus's partner had sized up the cascading anger, he radioed for back up. When a battery of white police arrived, the escalation continued at a geometric pace.

According to most accounts, the crowd grew to 1,000 that night. The Frye family became so belligerent that all three were arrested. So was a woman wearing a smock who spat from the crowd in the direction of the police. The rumor raced through the assembled citizenry like alternating current through a heating coil that the woman was pregnant: a pregnant black woman being dragged into a squad car by white uniformed cops.

At that point, the crowd became a mob and Watts began to riot. Six days of looting, burning, and guerrilla skirmishes later, 34 people lay dead, 1,032 were injured, and a ten-block stretch of Watts near the ironically named intersection of Imperial Highway and Avalon Boulevard had been burned to the ground. Police made nearly 4,000 arrests before it was over, and damage totaled $40 million.

L.A. had by far the worst, but not the only race riot of the mid-1960s. With Martin Luther King Jr. counseling peaceful dissent at the same time Malcolm X argued for equality at any cost, four other U.S. cities erupted in black rage. But none of them had ever boasted of being America's "White Spot."

During the worst of the riots, civil rights activist Louis Lomax visited Otis Chandler, who admitted that he didn't even know where Watts was, according to Lomax.[1] Lomax pointed out the window and said, "Over there, where the smoke is—that's where Watts is."

Yet Watts gave Otis the opportunity to demonstrate that his *Times* had become a different newspaper from the one operated by his grandfather, or even his father. During and after the riots, reporters and photographers swarmed over a swath of L.A. that the *Times* had ignored for decades. They probed, they asked questions, they painted pictures with their words, and they captured the blistering clashes between white cops and black folk with shutters and lenses. The Watts riots were a watershed event in the world according to Otis Chandler; he tried to understand the underlying causes of the insurrection and his staff tried mightily to trace them to their roots.

When it was over, the *Times* wrote extensively about the state commission appointed by Governor Pat Brown, mandated to recommend prescriptions to pre-

vent such horror from ever happening again. Again, young *Times* reporters showed no fear nor favor in pointing out hypocrisy.

Norman's old friend, California Club member, ex-CIA chief, and WASP San Marino millionaire John McCone headed the commission. The other seven commissioners were stalwart members of the established L.A. order, including Norman's fellow Republican kingmaker, Asa Call, who showed up at one commission meeting in a chauffeur-driven limo, all duly reported with undisguised cynicism in the *Los Angeles Times*.

"Mr. McCone was the kind of guy who knew what caused it all before he started," black attorney Samuel Williams bitterly told another *Times* reporter. Williams, who worked on the commission staff, was one of its few black faces. Judge Earl C. Broady, a conservative former LAPD officer, was the sole black commissioner. Broady did not publicly dissent from McCone's tame and predictable findings. McCone and the other commissioners blamed the media for sparking further chaos by fanning the flames with sensational reporting.

Roundly criticized in South Central as superficial and unimaginative, the McCone Commission still exploded decades of *Times*-fed myth that L.A. was utopia to black and white alike. White L.A. enjoyed better housing, recreation, medical care, street repair, schools, and police and fire protection than black L.A. To prevent such tragedy from ever happening again, implied the McCone Commission, the haves and have nots would have to share city and county services more equitably; all elected officials, not just black city councilmen such as Billy Mills, John Gibson, and Tom Bradley, would have to work for the improvement of all of L.A.; and the LAPD would have to hire more blacks and train their white officers to be more sensitive to life in South Central.

But white L.A. never did talk to black L.A.; this became painfully apparent when Mayor Sam Yorty's city hall and Chief William Parker's LAPD made their grudging efforts to communicate with the leaders emerging from Watts. Meetings were stiff at best. It was ironic that white, successful, and affluent Otis Chandler became an unlikely back channel to black L.A. The former AAU champ who had toured Europe with black teammates, cocaptained the 1952 Air Force track team with L.A.'s legendary black miler, Mal Whitfield, and roomed with a black janitor's son during his sojourn at Andover turned out to have more contacts in South Central than the mayor or the chief of police.

"I went down to the colored churches, or whatever the word was then. They're called Afro-American churches now," recalled Otis. "I got to know Ron Karenga who was one of the leaders [who] picked me out to be the spokesman/intermediary so I could bring the police chief in and be in the same room so we could get some peace."

"Through Otis Chandler, the *Times* for a while was the chief conduit between militant blacks and faction leaders and the L.A. police," Nick Williams confirmed years later. "Thus, in effect, [the *Times* was] the chief conduit between blacks and whites, though with no reportage of it in the paper."

The reporting that did appear in Otis Chandler's paper was good enough to win the *Times* its sixth Pulitzer, for "a distinguished example of reporting, giving consideration to alertness, resourcefulness and high quality of writing." Bill Thomas, the *Times'* metro editor, had assigned more than fifty photographers and writers to cover it. None of them were black.[2]

That would have to change, said Otis. For years, it didn't, and neither did conditions in South Central. Eight years passed before the *Times* adopted plan for affirmative action. There was neither the advertising nor the circulation support in Watts to warrant regular reporting. Businesses did not advertise there and residents did not read the *Times*.[3]

For more than a decade, burned and looted acreage along Avalon Boulevard was left untouched, a desolate reminder not only of rage and racial divide on a hot August night but of a generation of broken promises.

RIOTS AT HOME did not slow the spread of *Times* bureaus abroad. Offices in New Delhi, Nairobi, Buenos Aires, and Bangkok opened over the following year, as well as domestic bureaus in Chicago, New York, and Houston. Otis Chandler had hit his prime at the same time as his newspaper, but at a salary of $60,000 a year, he still wasn't making enough money. His expenses began outstripping his income the day he became publisher.

"I was living off a line of credit with the Security Pacific Bank and I still have it," Otis said a generation later.

He had five children and a socialite wife to support, not to mention his own increased appetite for expensive safaris and adult toys such as boats, a fleet of Porsches, and a pristine 1931 Duesenberg Tourster for which he paid $35,000.

"When I was at Stanford in 1950 I saw Gary Cooper's Duesenberg on a car lot for sale for $500," he said. "I didn't have [the money] then."

But he did have it in 1967 or, at least, enough for a down payment. Displaying his wealth in a non-Chandler fashion, Otis drove his Duesenberg to work every so often from his San Marino estate. He sensed envious eyes resting on him and his gleaming classic as he headed south over the Pasadena Freeway, through the downtown interchange, and finally, triumphantly, into his personal spot inside the *Times* executive parking lot.

But Duesenbergs, dinner parties, and trips to Mongolia and Mozambique cost plenty, and Otis was always short of cash. When Missy suggested that they buy the empty lots on either side of their home to prevent a developer from throwing up cracker-box houses that might lessen the value of their own home, Otis snapped that they were already deeply enough in debt. He didn't need two more mortgage payments to make each month. Missy contributed from her share of the Brant Trust and Buff doled her son some dollars from time to time out of the Buffum Trust, but Otis's dividends from Chandis Securities were meager by comparison and he was too proud to ask his thrifty father for money. Fortunately, Jack Burke came to Otis's rescue.

His old Stanford buddy was a regular hunting companion by the early 1960s. He accompanied Otis on several of his more harrowing wilderness adventures; to quail and partridge weekends at the Tejon Ranch; and to the Rockies for deer-hunting trips. Burke represented something more, too: a self-made man who had tried his hand at stockbrokering for Paine Webber but had opted instead to strike out on his own. In 1964, Burke and his brother, Robert, started GeoTek Resources Fund, a consortium of oil and gas exploration partnerships that drilled wildcat wells in likely places throughout the West.

GeoTek was based on the same kind of odds that had made William Randolph Hearst's father, George Hearst, a wealthy man: Sink enough holes and, even if only one comes up a winner, the business address switches to No. 1 Easy Street overnight. To sweeten the proposition even more, GeoTek investors became eligible for a "depletion allowance," an IRS loophole that made 22 percent of income from oil operations deductible. For the affluent who hated the headache of paying their taxes, GeoTek was migraine medicine.

It all sounded good to Otis. He didn't mind at all when Burke asked him to make a few phone calls to friends, business associates, maybe some of those stuffy three-piece-suit types down at the California Club where Otis still held a membership even though he didn't use the place for business the way his grandfather and father had. Otis found plenty of early investors for Burke among L.A.'s young Establishment, including his cousin Otis Booth and his sister Camilla's husband, Kelly Spear. Art Linkletter, Nancy Sinatra, Kirk Douglas, Natalie Wood, and L.A. Lakers owner Jack Kent Cooke bought into GeoTek, as did City Councilwoman Rosalind Wyman and her high-powered attorney husband, Eugene Wyman. Even the district attorney for Los Angeles, Evelle Younger, found a little extra cash to invest in GeoTek.

And the beauty of it all was the finder's fees. Just for linking Burke to the people with whom Otis did business as *Times* publisher anyway, he received 2 percent, 3 percent, as high as 5 percent of the cash they decided to invest in the com-

pany. At the beginning of 1966, Otis's take had already come to $9,200. Before the decade was over, his finder's fees would total $109,000.

In addition, Jack Burke talked about cutting Otis in as a partner. The *Times* publisher had already invested $248,000 of his own in GeoTek. Burke sweetened the deal with an additional $373,000 in promotional stock. Otis could not see himself getting rich quick in the newspaper business, but GeoTek looked like a sure bet.

To Otis, his partnership with Jack Burke seemed like insurance salesman Ed Emmet's early relationship with Norman Chandler. Norman had schmoozed the L.A. elite and made the necessary introductions, and Emmet had closed the deals. Hence, the remarkably successful firm of Emmet & Chandler Insurance was a downtown fixture for four decades. Emmet & Chandler represented Norman's separate source of income, beyond the newspaper business, and gave him the same degree of independence from his neo-Neanderthal relatives that Buff's department-store inheritance had given her. Emmet & Chandler might have done the same for Otis had he gone into business with Ed's son, Bob Emmet, who was also Otis's oldest childhood friend.

But insurance didn't interest Otis. Shortly after he became publisher, his father sold his interest in Emmet & Chandler and it became, simply, Emmet Insurance.

Otis had different plans for his future. In 1967, when Otis celebrated his fortieth birthday, Jack came to his surprise costume party dressed as a paunchy Arab oil sheik wearing reflector sunglasses, and Otis had a seat on the board of directors of GeoTek Resources Fund.

When it came to corporate boards, Dr. Franklin D. Murphy had no match. Before he joined Times Mirror as a director in 1965, he'd already done time on every major board in his native Missouri, from Hallmark Cards to the First National Bank of Kansas City. And although he believed in free market capitalism and the all-important profit motive, he also sat on both the nonprofit Carnegie and Kress foundations and joined just about every government committee, advisory group, and study commission that extended him an invitation. Dr. Murphy had built his career on the synergy of hobnobbing.

In September 1968, Murphy parlayed a lifetime of governmental and corporate board interplay into the biggest coup of his career: the chairmanship of the Times Mirror Company.[4]

He had begun his climb not as a junior executive but as an educator. Just eight years earlier, the chain-smoking, purse-lipped Murphy had arrived in California

at the age of forty-four to accept the chancellor's job at UCLA. He came from the University of Kansas, where he had held the top job since 1951. In the rarefied world of Kansas academia, Dr. Murphy was held in the same type of wunderkind esteem that Otis enjoyed as publisher now that he had successfully faced off against the U.S. journalism establishment. Both men had steamrollered their older critics. But there were differences between them, too.

Born to a physician father and a concert pianist mother, Franklin Murphy fancied himself as something of a Renaissance man. Whereas Otis was a man of action, Murphy was a man of the mind and possessed far more refined tastes. Trained as a medical doctor, he was also an Epicurean: a collector of fine art, rare books, and old wines. He discovered early that he preferred moving and shaking to medicine.

The sallow-faced and low-key Murphy was an edgy Eisenhower Republican, equally at ease with hayseeds and high society. He was the consummate corporate creature, suiting up for directorships on Ford Motor Company and the Bank of America the moment he hit Southern California, and soon adding Times Mirror, Norton Simon, and the Ahmanson Foundation to his growing corporate collection.

Yet he never forgot why he had been brought to Los Angeles in the first place. Murphy fought fiercely on behalf of UCLA; he went head-to-head with the Northern California oligarchy, which had ruled the University of California since the turn of the century. Murphy demanded equity. No longer would the Westwood campus subordinate itself to Berkeley. So forcefully yet eloquently did he make his case before the board of regents that two members, oil tycoon Edwin Pauley and Mrs. Norman Chandler, agreed to help him set up Franklin Murphy Associates to funnel funds from the business community into UCLA.

Murphy also fought the bureaucracy of newly elected governor of California, Ronald Reagan. In 1966 and 1967, he railed forcefully against the conservative former movie star's vow to begin charging obstreperous U.C. students' tuition. Despite his own Republican politics, Murphy was a Missouri populist at heart and demanded top-notch education at minimal cost to anyone who met the tough U.C. entrance requirements. Tuition was an affront, a thinly disguised way of satisfying Reagan's conservative constituency that students were not being mollycoddled, and that the rising tide of campus unrest during the late 1960s was being stemmed at the same time. Reagan's efforts to slash the university's budget and re-institute academic loyalty oaths also smacked of political retribution, and ran headlong into Murphy's academic outrage.

At a 1967 press conference, he announced in a clear, angry voice: "I do *not* intend to preside at the liquidation or substantial erosion of the quality which fifty

years of effort have built up, and I believe faculty members stand squarely behind me."

"He sensed the future of Southern California," said Otis, who was named vice chairman of Times Mirror at the same time Murphy became chairman. Norman moved into semiretirement as chairman of the Times Mirror's executive committee.

Otis saw in Murphy a liberal Republican ally. As a Stanford trustee since 1961 and a board member at Western Airlines, Union Bank, TRW, and Pan Am, in addition to his growing role at GeoTek, Otis applauded his parents' choice to succeed Norman as chairman. A good executive ought to sit on several corporate boards, argued Otis. How else could he be privy to the inner workings of California's booming economy?

Murphy's impulsive energy did become a trial at times, however. As Otis's nominal boss, the new chairman whipped through the corridors of Times Mirror Square like a man constantly on a mission and he frequently interrupted what few moments of solitude that Otis was able to steal.

"Dr. Murphy used to storm in, you know," said Donna Swayze, Otis's personal secretary. "Otis worked with his door closed, but Dr. Murphy would come down and say, 'Otis in?' and before I would have time to say 'uh, uh, he's on the phone,' he would barge in."

Franklin Murphy and Otis Chandler formed a "troika" with Al Casey, who was promoted at the same time to president of Times Mirror, and the three of them ran Times Mirror for the rest of the decade, the best period in the company's history. Casey's acquisition program put Times Mirror into everything from paper napkins to Sunday school teaching programs. Before the end of 1968, the company had become the nation's largest publisher of paperbacks, Bibles, dictionaries, and telephone books, as well as its most profitable daily newspaper.

The *Times* continued to evolve toward genuine greatness or, as Otis liked to put it, "uncommon excellence." The newspaper inaugurated a unique front-page feature known to the public as Column One, tailor-made for a reporter such as William Touhy, the Saigon bureau chief who won the *Times'* first foreign reporting Pulitzer for his Vietnam coverage in 1968. A typical Touhy lead could go on forever and occasionally read more like the opening pages of a Faulkner novel than a news story. This was just the sort of literary journalism for which the *Times* had become famous during the early Otis years. Touhy's passionate but nonpartisan stories were also among the first Vietnam dispatches to demonstrate that the United States had mired itself in an expensive and ultimately unwinnable civil war.

Upon accepting his Pulitzer, Touhy gave credit to Nick Williams and Otis Chandler.

"The big thing that made this possible is the editorial freedom we have," said Touhy. "The fact that I am not told what to write or not write has given me the incentive to look for and develop unusual stories."

IN NOVEMBER 1968, Richard Nixon won his presidency at last on the strength of a "secret plan" to end the Vietnam war. Although that plan never materialized, the Nixon presidency appeared preordained to fulfill every fear Otis Chandler had ever had about the polyester prince of darkness whom his own parents had nurtured and then foisted upon an unsuspecting nation.

As early as 1962, Norman and Buff began distancing themselves from their creation. In his typically oblique way, Norman warned Nixon that year that the Kyle Palmer era was dead. When the former vice president tried to jump-start his stalled career by seeking Norman and Buff's pro forma blessing at a run for governor of California, Norman told him between thoughtful puffs on his pipe that he thought it was not an especially good idea. Besides, Norman said, he was no longer publisher of the *Los Angeles Times*. Otis was.

Nixon chose not to listen and woke up one day just before he announced his candidacy to *Times* headlines questioning how he had been able to purchase a $300,000 home in the Trousdale Estates of Beverly Hills for a mere $90,000.

"What's wrong with what I did?" he demanded of Frank McCulloch, then the managing editor, who patiently explained that Nixon's whopping discount looked and smelled like a political payoff.

"I'm a private citizen," Nixon added huffily.

"Well, you're not entirely a private citizen, Dick," said McCulloch. "You have been vice president of the United States and you may well have a political future."

But not in 1962. Nixon continued to play by the Kyle Palmer rules, assuming that unflattering facts would be swept under the rug while the *Times* shined a spotlight on his heroics. As Norman had predicted, however, Otis Chandler's *Times* had changed with the times. When Nixon announced he was running for "governor of the United States," the *Times*' Carl Greenburg reported the Freudian slip, underscoring Nixon's goal of making Sacramento his stepping stone to the White House. Equally hard-edged front-page coverage followed through the rest of the campaign and, despite a lukewarm *Times* endorsement, Richard Nixon lost the governorship to the incumbent Democrat, Pat Brown.

Nixon's famous diatribe against the press the day following the 1962 election reverberated with as much hurt and bewilderment as it did venom.

"He was very resentful," Buff recalled to one reporter. "Very. The blast was at the *Times* when he said, 'You won't have Nixon to kick around anymore!'"

A few days later, Nixon canceled his *Times* subscription.

But during the five years that followed, Nixon carefully planned his resurrection. In early 1967, he once again paid an obsequious visit to Norman and Buff Chandler; he told his patrons that he planned to seek the Republican presidential nomination. When Pat Nixon flatly told her husband in front of the Chandlers that she did not want the anguish of another presidential campaign, he glossed over her protests as if she weren't in the room. Instead, he implored the Chandlers for their blessing. That Nixon ignored his wife's opinion appalled Buff. Although Norman always had the last word, he was never as dismissive of his wife's wishes as she saw Nixon being toward Pat's.

Norman gave Nixon the same noncommittal reply that night that he'd given him in 1962. If Nixon won the nomination, he'd get the *Times* endorsement. It was still a Republican newspaper, after all. But the *Times* was now firmly in the hands of his son and Norman would make no predictions about how Otis would instruct his staff to cover the campaign.

Otis and Buff both thought Nixon crude and rude. Buff, who had learned early how to hold her liquor, was particularly horrified by Nixon's behavior after he had downed a few drinks. Otis didn't drink at all, and he was even more shaken when he saw firsthand just how wretched Nixon's behavior could be.

At a *Times* executives' session during the early days of the 1968 campaign, Otis invited Nixon to speak; the Republican candidate pulled a joke right out of the bathroom and laid it on the conference table just before lunch was served, proof that the new Nixon had the same lack of judgment and taste as the old one.

"I guess I shouldn't tell this one, but I'll do it anyway: Why did the farmer keep a bucket of shit in the living room?" asked the future president of the United States. As a pall fell over the room, Nixon could barely contain himself.

"To keep the flies out of the kitchen!" he burst.

After an uncomfortably long silence, Buff said:

"You're absolutely right. You should not have told that story."

But Nixon's media handlers managed to keep his taste, judgment, and unprincipled ambition under wraps throughout most of the 1968 campaign. Dominated as presidential politics were that year by the assassinations of Bobby Kennedy[5] and Martin Luther King Jr. and the antiwar protests at the Democratic National Convention in Chicago, they played directly into Richard Nixon's unctuous grasp. Vice President Hubert Humphrey, Otis Chandler's own private choice to succeed LBJ in the White House, had been tarred indelibly by an increasingly unpopular war. The third-party candidacy of Alabama's Governor George Wallace sealed Humphrey's doom. With just 43 percent of the popular vote,[6] Nixon became the thirty-seventh president of the United States, and Otis Chandler simply had to make the best of it.

"Our paper isn't read as soon as the *New York Times* or the *Washington Post* by important people in Washington," he said. "Still, Nixon subscribes."

"MY LIFE REALLY CHANGED when I started going to Washington on my own," said Missy.

As Mrs. Otis Chandler, a title she had come to treasure, the mother of five got a regular monthly junket to the nation's capital in the late 1960s to serve on the president's Commission for Population Growth in America's Future. Being a commissioner was an honor, to be sure, but all the Malthusian discussion about the earth's diminishing resources and Third World death, from wholesale Chinese infanticide to mass starvation in the Horn of Africa, gave Otis's perky, privileged little Catholic bride a very different view of the shrinking future in which her own children would live.

"She left the Catholic Church; I think it was over birth control," said Otis. "She was an advocate and worked hard in the whole zero population birth control thing."

Missy had, indeed, broken with her church over the issue of contraception, and she took her family with her. Although he had always professed a lack of interest in Missy's religion, Otis was almost relieved.

"None of my children continued as Catholics," he said. "It was so rigid and the Mass was in Latin and the bells would ring and you had to get up and down."

Missy was less concerned with having to genuflect than she was with boxing her mind into the comfortable ignorance of a kind of San Marino Eden. Living in the perfect house with the perfect family and relieving the marvelous monotony with perfect bridge games with the girls, turned out not to be enough. Unlike her husband, she read far beyond the daily newspaper. Failing to finish her undergraduate degree at Stanford had always stood as one of Missy's great regrets, and when her children were old enough to fend for themselves, she made up for lost time. Following her great awakening on the presidential commission, she undertook urban planning courses at UCLA in pursuit of the college degree she had abandoned for Otis and motherhood.

"I would put Otis and the children to bed and I would read all night, or I would read until late," she said. "I can get by on four, five, or six hours. Otis needs a lot of sleep."

Otis didn't approve or disapprove of his wife's new interests. He paid no attention. He was too busy pursuing his own.

"I was not only publisher of the *Times* and vice chairman of Times Mirror and this and that, but I was on ten boards of directors," said Otis. "I was making speeches. I was on a plane once a week to New York and Washington."

Otis had become as remote a father as he had become a husband.

"I've got kind of this romantic vision or memory of my children: We played touch football and went to Disneyland all of the time," Otis remembered a generation later. "Now I talk to them and they say, 'Dad, we hardly saw you.' I did my best."

But if his best was good enough for his children, it was woefully lacking with his wife. Fissures began to show in his marriage, although neither he nor Missy professed to notice at the time. Buff's growing dislike for her daughter-in-law didn't help.

"She and I got in several major fights down at the beach, or we would be in the car and she'd be on me over something, and I would talk back to her," said Missy. "I would get into an argument. I was the only one who did this. Otis never did."

Nor did Otis step in to stop the arguments. He was not so much in awe of or afraid of his mother as he was worn down by her. He left it to his father to separate the combatants.

"Norm adored me, and he was always on my side, even over his son," said Missy. "Otis and I didn't fight that much because Otis is not a fighter. He backs away from a fight."

Like her mother-in-law, Missy drank a bit too much and her cigarette habit had only worsened over time. Always reluctant to confront, Otis hinted his displeasure but ultimately let the matter drop; he chose a solitary bike ride or a trip to the beach over meaningful discussion of his wife's addictions. Otis remembered his indifference as merciful escape. Missy saw the middle years of their marriage far differently.

"He was always trying to form me into what he wanted," she said. "And I resisted. I said, 'You married me the way I am.' And he'd say, 'Well, I just don't like this about you.' And I got mad. So he would get mad, too. Anybody would. I didn't take criticism well. I don't take criticism and neither does he."

After years of living at close quarters, she also saw tarnish on his fearless façade. Missy caught glimpses of Buff Chandler's frightened little boy behind the weight-lifting fanatic, and not always under the most comfortable of circumstances. She accompanied him during a caribou hunting trip to the Alaskan outback once and their bush pilot dropped them off with a guide and another couple at a remote lake, promising to return in two days.

"And he didn't come back the second day, he didn't come back the third day, he didn't come back the fourth day," she recalled. "We were running out of food. We picked blueberries. We caught fish. We had flour. We had blueberry pancakes and fish. No milk, no anything."

Their born-again guide did not make matters any better.

"This crazy guide was telling us all these stories of walking on water. He wanted to be the reincarnation of Christ. He said it would take us twenty days to

walk out of there. And Otis started getting panicky. We found the wreckage of an airplane and we were going to make a boat and go down the river."

Missy saw a fear grip her husband that she hadn't witnessed before. She hated the cold and the hunger and the leering nut case of a guide just as much as he did, but she never doubted that their plane would return eventually. She never thought for a minute that she might not survive.

"He kept getting more and more worried," she said. "We didn't have radio contact. Finally, on the fifth day the plane came back for us."

Besides Otis's strong, protective image, Missy had always loved her husband's sense of humor; but she watched as it faded to sarcasm with the years. In retrospect, she began to wonder whether there had always been an underlying cruelty to his laughter.

"He was always pulling jokes on our honeymoon," she said. "He bought some firecrackers and I was sitting in the john with the door shut reading the paper and all of a sudden a firecracker came under the door. And he thought that was the funniest thing. He was always pulling jokes like that. And it was pretty funny, but in a way it was mean funny."

A similar incident shortly after Otis joined the Air Force brought corresponding peals of one-sided laughter.

"We lived in a terrible little [rented home] that had a kitchen and I had never cooked a thing in my life," said Missy. "I turned the gas on, put the match in and the whole oven exploded on me. And he laughed, and I cried because I singed my brows and hair. He thought that was funny. And I didn't."

Sarcastic or jolly or mean, laughter of any sort grew scarce around the Chandler home as the 1960s marched to a close. There was a seriousness of purpose that seemed to infect everyone. The three oldest children—Norm, Harry, and Cathleen—were teens, all kept busy and broke in the same way that Norman and Buff had once controlled the teenaged Otis and Mia. Both by word and example, Otis preached that success equaled hard work and hard play, and Missy agreed. They wanted their children to have grand adventures and self-control at the same time. There was no reason why they couldn't do both. That's what their father had done. That was what his father before him had done, and his father before him as well.

They were Chandlers, after all. It was important for them to have a good time, but it was equally important for them to remember who they were, and what they represented.

———————

In the late summer of 1969, a Mexican hurricane roared up the Pacific coast, pushing waves ahead of it the size of three-story buildings. In Southern

California, however, the sun was hot and bright. Following the burn-off of a little morning overcast, the beaches were picture postcard perfection. Besides the reporter who had to write the daily weather story, there was probably only one other person at the *Los Angeles Times* who knew or cared about the faraway storm that would fizzle to nothing along the Baja coast.

At a late morning editorial meeting, Otis Chandler appeared to be listening attentively to his editors speak of the goings-on in Vietnam and the Nixon administration. His attention shifted abruptly when a messenger shuffled in with a note about the Mexican hurricane and dropped it in front of the publisher. Otis read it, crumpled it, tossed it in the trash, and hastily excused himself.

With its leader absent, the meeting broke up moments later. As he was leaving, a new editorial writer retrieved the crumpled note from the wastebasket. It read: "Surf's up at 12:30."

It wasn't just any wave that caught the *Times* publisher's attention and rode his imagination like a boogie board all the way from Times Mirror Square to Dana Point. It was *the* Wave, coming at California like a thirty-foot locomotive, and Otis Chandler expected to be out of his Brooks Brothers uniform and into his baggies, riding atop its crest at precisely thirty minutes past noon.

Like the sun-burnished demigod that he'd become, at forty-two, Otis Chandler bestrode Southern California in every conceivable role: businessman, surf bum, diplomat, dirt biker, music lover, good son, husband, father, and newspaperman. He was a Saracen warrior on Porsche wheels, and he whipped through freeway traffic to his appointed wave wearing wrap-around sunglasses and windblown blond pompadour that always appeared fluffed but razor sharp, as though he'd just stepped out of the barber's chair.

Down at the water's edge and up on his board, Otis became just another one of the guys, waiting for the Big One. He waved at Bernie Welks, a character he'd seen many times before who took his one-eyed bulldog out in a canoe. There were other less colorful characters, skinny and thick, tall and squat, all angling for their own spot on the Wave. Otis knew them all, though most had no idea who he was.

Sometimes Otis solicited their opinions about the *Times,* never letting on his relationship to the paper. Franklin Murphy, advertising director Vance Stickel, and other titans at the top of the *Times* liked to do surveys, solicit opinions, and hire marketing experts. But Otis thought that he could get just as good a feel for how the paper was doing by shouting out questions to the mop head on the next surfboard over, or by sipping a draft with a Hell's Angel at some desert watering hole following a Barstow-to-Baker bike run.

Otis was a prince, but Otis was also a man of the people. He listened to his subjects, surfed with them, ate pizza and beer with them, and put what they told

him into his newspaper. As the most divisive decade in America since the Civil War wound to a close, Otis Chandler had mastered his own universe. On December 31, 1969, his *Los Angeles Times* reported sales of 115 million lines of advertising, more than any other newspaper in the United States. An average Sunday *Times* weighed as much as a newborn child and contained over four hundred pages. At the end of Otis Chandler's tumultuous first decade as publisher, his *Times* had an audited weekday circulation of 1,000,528, just above the magic 1-million mark.

Otis had plans to build a new Times Mirror corporate building and to decorate his masthead with yet another foreign address: a Tel Aviv bureau to track the Israeli side of the ongoing Middle Eastern conflict. And there would be a new Sunday Book Review section and a new daily features section called View instead of Women and Society. The new, expanding, growing *Los Angeles Times* would get better, bigger, richer.

His biggest plans, however, were now moving well beyond the California border. In October 1969, Times Mirror bought the *Dallas Times-Herald;* seven months later, the company paid $57.8 million to acquire a controlling interest in Long Island *Newsday,* the suburban tabloid founded in 1940 by mining heir Harry Guggenheim and his wife, Alicia Patterson.

The feisty daughter of *New York Daily News* founder Captain Joseph Medill Patterson, Alicia Patterson was credited with coining the muckraking mantra: "The business of a newspaper is to print the news and raise hell,"[7] and she vowed never to sell her hell-raising tabloid to anyone who didn't share that philosophy. Alicia Patterson died in 1963,[8] however, and her far more conservative husband let the 300,000 circulation newspaper fall into inertia for the next six years while he looked for a suitable buyer.

"[Harry] Guggenheim said he sold his newspaper to Mr. Chandler and Otis because he thought Norman and Otis had integrity," said Missy. "I remember him saying he wouldn't sell it to anybody else."

In less than ten years, the California golden boy who once couldn't get a phone call past the switchboard at the *New York Times* was literally within striking distance of its front door. Otis had no expectations of peaceful coexistence. Before he was finished with the high-toned Harvard-educated snobs of Times Square, there would be a full frontal assault from Long Island. Like the journalistic general he had become, Otis Chandler would use his *Newsday* to sack Manhattan as if it were an overbuilt Iwo Jima.

Life was good. Life was fine. He felt as if he'd caught the Big One for sure, and that the ride would just keep on going forever.

CHAPTER 19

WHEN LOS ANGELES TIMES columnist Ruben Salazar started out on August 29, 1970, he was at the peak of his career; before the day was out, he had lost his life, only the second *Times* reporter in the newspaper's history to die in the line of duty.[1] Otis Chandler recalled the story with clenched jaws and averted eyes, even dozens of years after Salazar's eyes were shut forever.

Five years before his death, on the same day that the Watts riots began, Ruben Salazar had set out for Saigon on behalf of the *Times*. A foreign war was nothing new to him, but an assignment that did not require his native Spanish tongue was. Vietnam was the bilingual Salazar's first major story for which he did not rely on his Mexican heritage.

In 1963, he had covered a coup d'état in the Dominican Republic, and in 1968 he was sent to Mexico City during the student riots that preceded the Olympic Games. Because he was a Tex Mex, born in Juarez and later raised and educated north of the Rio Grande, Salazar had landed in several other Latin America hot spots for the *Times* during the 1960s. But fluency in Spanish was not a requirement for writing about the war in Vietnam and Ruben Salazar knew that at last he had gained parity with his fellow *Times*men. He didn't go to Vietnam for a one-year tour as a war correspondent just because he was Mexican; he went as a representative of Alicia Patterson's professional priesthood: to report the news and to raise hell.

In his earliest days at the *Times,* while he was still a lone brown face in a sea of white, Salazar had reported the first of three series that Frank McCulloch, then the newspaper's managing editor, wanted written on Southern California's melting pot diversity: what it was like to be black, to be Asian, and to be Hispanic in L.A.

Although it was tame by later standards, Salazar's six-part series on L.A.'s large but silent Latin American population had an unsettling effect in the early 1960s, particularly upon Philip Chandler's branch of the *Times* dynasty. Once again, the family's Republican newspaper had publicly nosed into sensitive areas that most Chandlers believed should be left undisturbed. The *Times* did not need to be raising uncomfortable questions about political equality and undocumented workers. Since the Chandler family's earliest days in California, Mexicans with or without green cards had worked at or below the poverty line on one or more of Harry Chandler's ranches. Even as late as the 1970s, Harry's grandson and daughter-in-law employed illegal aliens as maids and other servants, a Southern California tradition that was not unique to Otis and Missy Chandler.

Salazar's award-winning series had touched enough nerves that the follow-up series, to be devoted to L.A.'s black and Asian communities, was never written. According to McCulloch, Nick Williams killed the pieces before they began, evidence to many of the younger *Times* staff who had no memory of the Kyle Palmer era that Williams could be overly cautious, ambivalent about tough reporting, and glacially slow in moving the paper forward.

Salazar was not among those critics. Although he questioned authority with the same fervor of most other young journalists during the 1960s, he recognized the radical difference between the *Times* of Norman Chandler and the *Times* of Otis Chandler, and he worked inside those parameters. Following his year in Vietnam and a stint as bureau chief in Mexico City, he returned to the trenches in L.A. Salazar understood that his reporting on the growing militancy within the Spanish-speaking barrios of Southern California could help turn the *Times* into an instrument for social change in spite of its timorous history.

In 1968, when Salazar was invited to become the news director at KMEX-TV, he accepted because he saw the position as an opportunity for him to further awaken L.A.'s Spanish-speaking population. He did not abandon his foothold at the *Times,* however; he became a regular columnist on its op-ed pages, where his voice took on a more messianic tone: a reporter whose patience frayed with each new clash between L.A.'s WASP establishment and an increasingly militant Mexican American population.

Answering his own rhetorical question on February 6, 1970, in a *Times* column titled WHO IS A CHICANO? AND WHAT IS IT THE CHICANOS WANT? he wrote:

A Chicano is a Mexican-American with a non-Anglo image of himself. He resents being told Columbus discovered America when the Chicano's ancestors, the Mayans and the Aztecs, founded highly sophisticated civilizations centuries before Spain financed the Italian explorer's trip to the "New World." Chicanos resent also Anglo pronouncements that Chicanos are "culturally deprived" or that the fact that they speak Spanish is a "problem." Chicanos will tell you that their culture predates that of the Pilgrims and that Spanish was spoken in America before English, and so the "problem" is not theirs but [belongs to] the Anglos who don't speak Spanish.

For decades, obvious perspectives such as Salazar's had been uniformly ignored in the *Times.* The often-criticized pace of Nick Williams's progress away from the *Times'* hidebound conservatism picked up following the Watts riots, however. Salazar's columns were a glowing neon sign of that primal shift.

Thus, routine police rousts in minority neighborhoods that occasionally re-sulted in a shooting and a suspect's death were no longer shrugged off by the city desk as "misdemeanor murders." The *Times*, as well as L.A.'s blossoming local television news operations, focused increasingly on violent clashes involving LAPD officers and Los Angeles County sheriff's deputies in South Central and East L.A.

In one such instance, the LAPD defended its officers' shooting of two Mexican men partially on grounds that they were illegal aliens, an excuse that might have been acceptable a generation earlier. Salazar raised a red flag in his *Times* column, however, and the officers who did the shooting were subsequently indicted, al-though ultimately acquitted.

Ruben Salazar's crusades came together on the morning of August 29, 1970, when he and a KMEX camera crew went to East Los Angeles to cover a Chicano demonstration against the Vietnam war.

Just two months earlier, the *Times* had dumbfounded Southern California with a headline on its editorial page that read GET OUT OF VIETNAM NOW. Until then, the *Times* had supported the war because Otis had been mollified by LBJ's Domino Theory; but Salazar's was one of many voices that persuaded Otis to rethink his hawkish position. The decision to condemn the war climaxed a decade of differences between Otis Chandler's *Times* and his father's newspaper, and followed by one month the Ohio National Guard's fatal shooting of four stu-dents at Kent State University.

Thus, armed with his *Times* credentials, the openly antiwar Salazar might have been lulled into a false sense of security when he and his KMEX crew followed more than 15,000 demonstrators to a rally in Lincoln Park. Sheriff's deputies had fanned out to keep the peace, but did so with a vengeance; the taunts of the crowd only heightened the tension. Months and even years afterward, deputies and demonstrators were in dispute about what had sparked the riot that fol-lowed. What could not be disputed was that three people died that day, and one of them was Ruben Salazar.

Following the initial clash, Salazar and his camera crew retreated to the safety of the Silver Dollar Café, several blocks from the riot. Acting on a report that three armed men had entered the café, sheriff's deputies shot a tear gas projectile into the building; the missile struck Ruben Salazar's head and killed him instantly.

The coroner's inquest blamed Sheriff Peter Pitchess's poorly trained deputies for Salazar's death, but none was indicted. District Attorney Evelle Younger, a close Otis Chandler ally and a fellow GeoTek investor, maintained that his office would be unable to obtain a conviction because the public could not agree about whether Salazar's death was intentional or accidental.

At the request of Salazar's family, Otis delivered his eulogy. The *Times* publisher was not easily given to tears, but his voice cracked as he spoke of Salazar as "one of our great reporters, and a great friend of mine."

Thirty years later, the sentiment had not changed. To Otis Chandler, Ruben Salazar was a fallen comrade and nothing less: a *Times* foot soldier who had distinguished himself in the line of duty and had furthered the cause, and the curse, of enlightening and informing a populace that, all too often, preferred ignorance. Salazar's death climaxed one tumultuous era at Times Mirror Square but, at the same time, it heralded a more introspective, but equally troubling new decade.

"I remember there was a cover of *Time* that questioned the very basic belief in God—whether it was a fairy tale or a myth," said Otis. "It was a time of questioning everything, and we were trying to steer our way down through all this maze."

———————————

As Nick Williams approached retirement age, Otis was certain that his editor's bad habits had gotten the best of him and that he was shriveling up.

"You know how some people, as they get older, unless they do some exercising and stretching and so on, they just shrink?" asked Otis. "It seemed, near the end, Nick was down to about five feet."

The perpetually health conscious and impeccably dressed publisher chided his relentlessly rumpled editor and warned Williams that his bad habits would kill him. Yet, in spite of his smoking, drinking, and sedentary lifestyle, Nick would live another twenty years beyond his last day at the *Times*. If Otis had had his way, Nick would never have retired at all.

Over the years, Otis had forged a link with Nick Williams that in some ways had become more of a father-son relationship than the bond Otis had with his own father. Since their earliest teamwork, when Otis asked the impossible and Nick delivered the possible, their kvetching had become so routine that the corridor outside their adjoining offices rang with dialogue that sounded as if it had been lifted wholesale from *The Odd Couple*.

"You don't realize what you are asking me to do!" Nick would begin. "How do we do it? Do you *really* want to do this?"

Right on cue, Nick would stagger out of Chandler's office, wander into his own, tap at his typewriter with two index fingers, and crank out single-spaced memos that dripped with wry wisdom and nearly always solved Otis's problem. One thing Nick did not do well, if at all, was fire people. Occasionally a dismissed employee would have to ask Nick's secretary if he or she had, indeed, been fired. When Otis ordered him to fire Bob Hartmann, the *Times'* Washington bureau

chief and one of the last holdovers from Norman Chandler's ancien régime, Nick went into his Felix Unger routine.

"But your parents like him!" he protested.

"I don't care," said Otis. "He kissed their asses when they came to Washington. That's why he kept his job."

When Williams fumed and fussed and found excuses to be busy doing anything other than fire Hartmann,[2] Otis told his managing editor, Frank Haven, to do it.

"He didn't like Bob Hartmann anyway, so he was happy to fire him," said Otis.

Hartmann's departure left the *Times'* expanding Washington bureau without a leader, so Williams was back in Chandler's office, his arms folded and his toe tapping. This time, it was Nick doing the demanding.

"Who are we going to get to replace him?" he asked.

"What about Bob Donovan at the *Herald Trib?*" answered Otis.

Nick looked at Chandler as if he were daft. Robert J. Donovan, author of *P.T. 109,* not only ran the Washington bureau for the venerable but dying *New York Herald Tribune,* he was also one of the most sought after commodities in a city where journalists were swapped like high-priced jewelry.

"We could never get him," said Williams.

"Let's get him," said Otis, slapping his desk top. "I'll go to Washington and we'll take him to a restaurant in Georgetown."

Donovan could not be bought for the price of lunch, even in Georgetown, nor was he interested in the fat salary Chandler was prepared to pay. Like any one of a select sampling of the best-connected Washington scribes, however, Donovan could be persuaded by the prospect of more power. Autonomy and authority over a bureau that had expanded to nearly a dozen reporters who worked in spacious luxury that took up one floor of downtown D.C. office space containing kitchenette, conference room, and showers for the odd out-of-town reporter who might need a bath: All that appealed to the *Times'* next Washington bureau chief. For the rest of the 1960s, suave, silver-haired Bob Donovan built the *Times* bureau into one of the most formidable in Washington, despite the three-hour time difference that kept *Times* reporters at a constant disadvantage among East Coast journalists, at least when it came to breaking news stories.

Whatever Donovan wanted, he got, often to the consternation of the *Times* staff back in L.A.

But when Nick Williams decided to retire seven years later, in 1971, and the opportunity of running the entire newspaper presented itself, the aphrodisiac of acquiring even *more* power intoxicated the fifty-eight-year-old Donovan once again. Otis invited him to L.A. and Donovan accepted.

"I did indicate to him that if he passed muster during the orientation program, he would be editor of the *Times,*" Otis acknowledged.

But orientation seemed pro forma. There was no real question that the erudite, eager, and broadly experienced Donovan would pass muster and so bring a very New York brand of literate, thoughtful, and sophisticated analysis to Southern California journalism. The *Times* had already given him the title of associate editor and helped him put a down payment on a home. Nick Williams welcomed the star of the Washington bureau with six parties and let Donovan all but run his daily news meetings as if he were, in fact, his heir apparent.

Yet, from the outset, Donovan was uncomfortable at best, mentioning to everyone from ad salesmen to copy boys that L.A. baffled him. On his worst days, he was occasionally wooden, even artificial, his sniffing disinterest in Southern California striking Otis as thinly veiled contempt.

"Donovan didn't know the territory and he and his wife weren't comfortable here," said Otis. "Some people come out here and they don't like sitting out in the sun and breathing the air or going to the beach or riding a motorcycle. They are just not comfortable here. He could have eventually learned the territory and the staff. I don't think anybody said he was terrible."

As he studied how Donovan interacted with the troops, Otis sensed trouble. The East Coast transplant would begin a conversation with, "What exciting thing are you working on?" but it invariably ended with Donovan's reminiscing about Washington, D.C., where *real* national news was made. And although he put the best face on things whenever he thought Otis was watching, Donovan, who was used to overseeing a dozen or so colleagues, was overwhelmed by the magnitude and diversity of the *Times* staff, now more than 3,000 employees.

"I couldn't sleep," said Otis. "I could see it wouldn't work."

One day after Donovan had been at Times Mirror Square for the better part of a year, Oscar Madison punched the intercom and asked Felix Unger to come into his office.

"Nick," Otis began, "this is not going to work. I watched him in his floor meetings. He doesn't know Los Angeles, he's not a Southern Californian, he's not even a Californian. It's not going to work."

Williams disagreed, told his stubborn young publisher he was making a big mistake; but finally Williams heaved a sigh, pushed up his glasses, and rubbed his forehead in concession. He understood and reluctantly acquiesced. But that didn't solve the problem.

"What are we going to do?" Nick asked, cringing at the prospect of once more being commanded to can someone, and the former dean of the Washington press corps at that.

"Well, send him in and I'll tell him," Otis said mercifully. "I know you can't do it."

Donovan professed genuine shock. Whether he was secretly relieved would never be known, but there was no question that Chandler's last-minute decision humiliated him. Jim Bellows, Donovan's former editor at the *Herald Tribune,* advised Donovan to hand in his resignation. When the *Herald Tribune* folded, Bellows had emigrated to L.A. at Chandler's invitation; he was now an associate editor for the so-called soft news of the *Times,* including the revamped women's section, renamed View, and the new Sunday magazine, *West.* Had he been courted, promised the job, and then summarily dismissed, Bellows told Donovan, his own self-respect would no longer allow him to work there.

But Donovan was too long in the tooth to look elsewhere and opted to ride out his time at the *Times* until his own retirement, only seven years away. He returned to the Washington bureau, retained his own associate editor's title and as much dignity as his great shame would allow, but he did little beyond file an occasional op-ed column for the *Times* from that day forward.

"He didn't speak to me for years and years," said Otis.

As far as who was the right person to fill the vacuum that Nick Williams would soon leave, Otis had come up with that answer, too. While observing Donovan, he had also paid closer attention to his second-tier editors, including the young Turk who had started out on the old *Mirror News* city desk at roughly the same time Otis had been a reporter there.

Bill Thomas hailed from Michigan; he had learned to play the piano by age fourteen and later hit the road with his own band. When he returned home broke, he picked newspapers over honky-tonks as a way to make a living. An apostle of the offbeat, Thomas was attracted to journalism by newspaper *writing,* not reporting. When the writing was good, it was poetry; when it was bad (and most of the time it was very bad), it was tedious bilge. He decided to wage a life-long war against bilge.

"There was not a lot of what I would call . . . flexibility in writing style and scope," he later said with typical diplomatic understatement.

After college, Thomas drifted to Buffalo, where he became a copy editor; when a friend bought a weekly newspaper in Sierra Madre in 1955, he asked Thomas to join him as his editor and business partner. After starving on weekly newspaper wages for a year, Thomas joined the *Mirror News* and moved over to the *Times* following the *Mirror*'s demise in 1962. In quick succession, he became assistant city editor, then city editor, and finally, metropolitan editor, the title he held when he directed the team that won the 1965 Pulitzer for coverage of the Watts riots. Otis liked Thomas's gruff management style. Although the promotion of a bright

young desk jockey to editor in a little over ten years might be seen by Donovan's allies as an even worse slap at the venerable Washingtonian, the decision was made and Otis did not waver.

"I called Nick in the middle of the night," said Otis.

On August 23, 1971, to Bill Thomas's everlasting surprise, Otis named him the seventh editor of the *Los Angeles Times.* Thomas had big shoes to fill. Under Nick Williams, the *Times* opened twenty-five national and foreign bureaus, won five Pulitzers, and almost doubled its circulation. Neither Nick nor his successor would be recognized outside of California the way the stars of the *New York Times,* Clifton Daniels and Abe Rosenthal, and the *Washington Post*'s Ben Bradlee were. At the *Los Angeles Times*, the publisher got the glory.

Nick Williams didn't mind. Unsung for all his efforts, he had done his duty and simply wanted out. Acting as middleman between generations of Chandlers had taken its toll. For years, he had kept his frustrations bottled up and his ulcers had steadily worsened. Never one to shy away from liquor, he had developed a habit of self-medicating with two quick belts as soon as he got home each night—"virtually a fix," he called it.

Upon Williams's retirement, the ulcers miraculously disappeared and the nocturnal fix devolved into a single regular martini, sipped at his leisure on the porch of his Laguna Beach home. He collected art, did a little traveling, wrote an occasional op-ed column, and generally tried to enjoy himself. But even then, Otis wouldn't let him.

"I don't want to lose you. I want you to help me," Chandler wheedled, pointing up the problems he was already having at his two latest fixer-uppers. The *Dallas Times Herald* and *Newsday* needed Nick's deft touch, he complained, and Nick gave it; he helped Chandler ease past the *Newsday* staff's early suspicions that Times Mirror would ruin Alicia Patterson's legacy when the new publisher replaced their beloved editor, LBJ's former protégé, Bill Moyers, with an avuncular apparatchik named David Laventhol. Laventhol, nicknamed "Clocker Dave" for his love of horse racing, hadn't the grace or polish of Moyers; but he turned out to be a capable editor in the Times Mirror tradition anyway because he kept one eye on the front page, the other on the bottom line. Fears allayed, *Newsday*'s staff continued to win Pulitzers; and the paper's circulation grew with the suburbs, which would reach the very edge of New York's fifth and final borough before the end of the decade.

Inertia at the bland, boring *Times Herald* was not so easily resolved. Rather than preserving its legacy, Dallas's afternoon daily needed a legacy worth preserving. A tossed salad of sports, wire copy, and city hall press releases, the *Times Herald* trailed well behind the *Dallas Morning News* in circulation, advertising, and prestige for good reason. Upon announcing Times Mirror's purchase of the news-

paper, as well as its sister television station, KRLD, Otis vowed "no mediocrity" to his new staff, but left it to the retiring Nick Williams to carry out his mandate.

"Nick did some very good consulting for me," said Otis.

One of Williams's tasks was to shape an ambitious young media maven from Macon, Georgia, into the next editor of the *Times Herald.*

Barely thirty when he joined Times Mirror in 1973, Wyatt Thomas Johnson had already enjoyed a remarkable career, having climbed from red dirt poverty[3] to Washington, where he had ingratiated himself early to the thirty-sixth president of the United States. Following a stint at Harvard, Tom Johnson landed an internship at the White House in 1964; he worked first under LBJ's press secretaries, Bill Moyers (later *Newsday*'s editor) and George Christian, and later, after President Johnson announced his retirement from politics, Tom, who was not related to the president, emigrated with Lyndon and Lady Bird to their ranch near Austin.

There, LBJ put the young Georgian in charge of his Texas Broadcasting Company, which operated Austin CBS-TV affiliate KTBC, its sister radio station, and a cable television system. During his presidency, the three broadcast enterprises had made LBJ a multimillionaire; advertisers stood in line to pay top dollar to a station owned and operated by the president of the United States. When LBJ left office, however, Richard Nixon's Federal Communications Commission ruled that the Johnsons owned a broadcast monopoly in Austin and would have to get rid of either the television station or the cable system. The former president opted to sell KTBC to Times Mirror and, in a side deal endorsed by LBJ,[4] Tom Johnson was to become editor of the *Times Herald* when his services at Texas Broadcasting Company came to an end.

Otis, who once remarked that Tom Johnson resembled Clark Kent, did not hire this super young man blindly. In one often-repeated story about Chandler's early enchantment with Tom Johnson, the *Times* publisher recalled his first visit to Austin as KTBC's new owner, during which Tom was working a reception line with Lady Bird Johnson. Tom stood behind the former first lady and whispered names in her ear as each of more than 1,000 KTBC advertisers passed through the line. Johnson not only identified every face but knew precisely how much each person had spent on advertising at the station the previous year; he gave Lady Bird the cue on which person to thank heartily and which to chide gently for being stingy.

"It was a remarkable performance, remembering all those names and all the amounts spent at KTBC," said Otis.

For all his quickness and shrewd ambition, though, Tom Johnson was no editor. Otis decided that a crash course with Nick Williams would be just the ticket; with a mind such as Tom Johnson's to mold, Nick could not be faced with a difficult task.

Otis was right. By 1975, Johnson had moved up to the position of publisher of the *Dallas Times Herald*, and the at-last retired Nick Williams had returned to his martinis on the veranda overlooking the Pacific Ocean, where he contentedly shrank into the sunset.

HE NEITHER CONDEMNED nor understood those who chose to fade away, but Otis would never do so himself. Fading was not his style. He consumed life like a huge buffet served from a cornucopia of rough adventure, family responsibility, and top-notch journalism. He fancied himself many things to many people: crusading publisher, dashing husband and lover, firm but caring father and companion to his children, tolerant son, loyal friend, Great White Hunter . . .

At 18,000 feet above sea level in the Afghani Himalayas, he had killed a Marco Polo sheep: "the prize of all prizes," as Otis called it. He had nailed a bongo (an African antelope) on the run in the Horn of Africa. He had bagged a Kodiak to match his polar bear, but never did kill the seven-and-a-half-foot black bear he'd always wanted for his collection.

"I not only go to rare places, but I go after the rarest and the biggest and the best," he explained. "That's part of my competitive urge. I am not your average hunter. . . . I go to Afghanistan, to Outer Mongolia, Botswana, to the jungles of Brazil. . . . and I have accumulated, I guess, one of the best collections of record class animals in the world."

Trophy hunting transformed him, freed him, gave him the will and perspective to return to bigger, broader triumphs at his *Times*. Not being publisher for a time made him a better publisher.

"You become a different person," he said, struggling to explain his annual transformation into a gun-toting hunter. "I mean, if somebody asked me, 'What do you do?' I'd have to think what I did. I'd have to think that I had a wife and children and ran a newspaper and wore suits and ties and gave speeches and shaved and all that.

"Within a day or two, I began to shed who I was, what I represented, that I was wealthy or whatever. I really seemed to fit into the landscape very easily and very comfortably and wasn't ever frightened, wasn't ever uncomfortable."

On his annual spring safari, which had grown more exotic over the years, Otis Chandler and his loyal sidekick, Jack Burke, found themselves treading the burning sands of the Sahara in 1971, as they followed the lead of their Lebanese guide, Claude Vasulet, through the desert wilderness of northern Chad. A thousand miles to the south in the Central African Republic, they had already bagged a giant eland: a huge African antelope with distinctive spiraled antlers. It would look

splendid on the "dead-head" wall over the fireplace back in San Marino. It would have been a sufficient kill on any other safari; but Otis wanted more and Claude promised to deliver.

There was big trouble in Chad. Otis might have been better prepared had he paid closer attention to the reports in his own newspaper about a Libyan dictator who was flexing his well-oiled war machine all over North Africa. Chad, a former French colony, was landlocked, poor, and due south of Libya: a perfect plum to add to the Libyan empire. Claude had already heard rumors that civil war had broken out near the capital of Chad; he began making careful plans to skirt the area, but he didn't move swiftly enough.

As Otis and Burke broke camp one day, loading their lumbering Toyota lorry with tents and victuals, Claude drove up in his jeep, a deep frown etched across his face.

"You know, we've got a problem here," he told them. "I can either fly you guys up to the airport in northern Chad . . . or you can take the chance and stay with me, 'cause I have to get up there with the lorry and the vehicles and the guides and the cooks and skinners."

Jack and Otis wanted none of this desert air travel crap. They had come to Africa to hunt, by God, and hunters did not hunt from a Cessna 1,000 feet up in the sky.

"Well," said Claude, "if you go with us on the ground, are you both prepared to kill another human being?"

Otis may have hesitated, but only for a moment.

"Well, if it means my life, sure," he said. Jack nodded in agreement. They both could be counted upon in a pinch.

"We could very well be attacked and we'd have to defend ourselves and you could get killed," said Claude, speaking very deliberately to show that he was not kidding.

"What are the odds?" asked Otis.

"There aren't many rebels. We are pretty imposing-looking and they know what we are," he answered. "I mean, they know we're a safari company going from one area to another."

Otis and Jack nodded. They were in. For the next two weeks, they were pleased that they had not been scared off by Claude's grim prognosis because they nailed some of the best beasts of their safari: Barbary sheep and more antelope in the Ennedis, a seldom-visited range of mountains at the center of the Sahara.

At the end of the two weeks, they returned triumphant and filthy to a village of lean-tos and tents assembled on a natural oasis called Um Shaluba, unmentioned on most maps. They doffed their pith helmets, plugged the holes, dipped them in the water, and stripped naked for much-needed sponge baths.

"We hadn't bathed in two weeks, hadn't shaved, we were living like animals. We *looked* like animals!" Otis said proudly.

Clean and shaven, they went shopping at the oasis market, snapped photos like tourists, and marveled at the sight of camel caravans stretching out into the desert like four-legged freight trains. They fell asleep in paradise that night and awakened at dawn like a couple of eager, overgrown Gold Arrow campers.

"It's the most majestic scene to be lying there on the ground in your sleeping bag, and wake up first light and see these caravans of camels and the men with spears riding and pulling other camels with produce and the women usually walking behind," Otis rhapsodized.

They rose, stretched, and returned to the market; but it was not the pleasant, bustling hive they had visited the previous day. While he and Burke picked through the baskets, animal hides, fruits, and other items for sale, Claude was bargaining with a pair of Bedouins, jabbering in one of the half dozen African dialects he spoke.

"So what are you saying?" Otis asked Claude.

"So far, just hello," Claude said with a grin.

But the grin faded when one of the Bedouins handed him a dirty red-stained sack.

"I thought it couldn't be watermelon, couldn't be strawberries, but they do have fruit in Africa, so I thought maybe it was some peaches," recalled Otis.

Claude's expression told him otherwise.

"Well," he told Otis and Jack in a confidential voice, "we've got real problems. There's a French Peace Corps group that were working up in the north, not too far from where we were hunting, and they were intercepted by some of the northern Chadian rebels and they cut off the head of a male doctor, took a couple of prisoners and then cut off the nurse's hands and then left. The nurse is still alive."

Claude invited Otis and Jack to come look for themselves. Otis peeked in the sack and saw that his desert peaches were actually a pair of hands and a human head staring right at him. The body parts reeked of decay. In a moment of morbid fascination, all Otis could think about was how cleanly the doctor had been decapitated: A single machete swipe had done the deed.

Otis had seen grisly human behavior before. Once, during a jaguar hunt in the Mato Grosso swamps of south central Brazil, he and his guide had come across a severed human head on a fence post. A stealer of cows, Otis was told. But the doctor and nurse who'd contributed head and hands to the Chad rebels had stolen no cows.

"We've got to get you guys out of there," said Claude.

Otis and Jack wanted to continue the hunt, but Claude cut it as short as the doctor's head. He shortwaved an S.O.S. to the U.S. ambassador to Chad; the am-

bassador called in a DC-3 airlift to pull Chandler and Burke out of the danger zone.

"Jack and I flew down to the capital and overnighted there," Otis said. "Then we flew to Paris."

At the request of the French government, Otis and Jack related all they had seen and heard. Two days later, French forces descended on the rebels; Otis and Jack were on a jetliner home. Weeks passed. Otis returned to work and forgot about the head, the hands, and the rebels of North Africa.

"Otis, you wouldn't believe what's happened since you were away!" his executives breathlessly prattled when rushed in as usual.

Invariably, the emergencies ranged around a key person's resignation or dropping ad lineage or a broken press. Otis took each issue in his stride. Weeks earlier, he'd narrowly missed being a head and a pair of hands in some camel jockey's knapsack. His hunting trips always put corporate crises in perspective.

One day some weeks after the Chad trip, Otis picked up his receiver and the voice of Claude Vasulet's wife crackled over a transatlantic telephone cable.

"Otis, they've arrested Claude!" she said frantically.

The guide had ignored the civil war, it seemed, and carted a group of Spanish hunters and their wives into Chad again. He'd seen such uprisings before and they were typically violent, irrational, and short-lived. No reason to interrupt business. But this time, the irrational violence had endured long enough for Claude's partner and his cook to be murdered, and one of his Spanish clients and his wife to be kidnapped. Claude was arrested and tossed into a Chad prison. The charge: not registering a twenty-gauge shotgun that Otis had given to him as a gift before he left Africa. The sentence: five years.

"Claude is dying," said his wife. "He's eating mice and rats. He's being beaten up by the black prisoners. They won't let me take good food to him. He's dying! What can you—can you save my husband?"

Otis could.

He called Stan Meisler, the *Times'* Nairobi bureau chief.

"You've got to get over to Chad! You've got to save this guy!" he said. "Talk to the higher ups and use the horsepower of the media and all of that."

Next, he called the *Times* reporter who covered the United Nations and ordered him to track down Chad's ambassador. Otis sent a letter on *Times* publisher's letterhead, explaining how the shotgun had been a gift to an innocent man. The negotiations were a delicate mix of abject pleading and the implied threat of the full power and resources of the biggest, richest newspaper in the United States. After several tense days, Claude Vasulet was a free man.

None of Otis's grand Chad adventure appeared in the pages of his *Los Angeles Times*. It wasn't that Otis did not recognize a hell of a story when he saw it. Un-

like his father, who'd never worked the city desk, Otis was always picking up the phone and passing on tips to his editors. He told one anecdote about himself and Norman that illustrated the difference between the generations when it came to news sense.

"He and I were coming back from deer hunting at the Tejon ranch and I saw a single engine plane go down," said Otis. "We were driving by, so I took the next off-ramp, grabbed a pay phone (didn't have a cell in those days) and called the *Times*. And my dad said, 'What are you doing that for?' And I said, 'Dad, somebody may be hurt or have died in that plane crash. And maybe it's not important, but maybe it might be, because it might be *somebody*. That's a story.'"

And surely the Claude Vasulet tale was a story too, even though Claude was not exactly *somebody*. But Otis saw no need to boast, especially if it put Vasulet's life in further danger. The saga of his last-minute rescue of a friend was known only to another friend, Jack Burke. That was what friendship was all about in the final analysis: being there when the chips were down, and damn what the headlines of tomorrow morning's newspaper might say—full speed ahead!

Of course, he could blithely make such pronouncements. As publisher, Otis Chandler decided most days what the headlines of tomorrow morning's newspaper did or did not say.

JANUARY 12, 1972, marked Norman Chandler's fiftieth anniversary with Times Mirror and, although his health was a well-kept family secret, even the switchboard operators and the secretary's pool suspected that the seventy-two-year-old *Times* patriarch was winding down. His bronze bust had already been enshrined in the *Times* rotunda at the Spring Street entrance to Times Mirror Square, along with those of General Otis and Harry Chandler. Although he was still chairman of the Times Mirror's executive committee, Norman did not put in an appearance at its 1970 dedication. The *Times* reporter assigned to cover the uncovering of the bust wrote that Norman was "eulogized by four speakers," including his son.

Colon polyps didn't get Norman, but a lifetime of pipe smoking did. By the time he and Buff celebrated their golden wedding anniversary and Norman was approaching his seventy-third birthday, the carcinoma had already been working on his throat and jaw. It was only a matter of time before the cancer would win.

Meanwhile, Buff alternately wept over and scolded her husband for contracting cancer in the first place.

"She would lose her temper at Norm," said Missy, "but Norm understood her and he was very good with her. He'd say, 'Now, now Buff, hold it down. Hold it down. I don't want to hear anything for a few minutes.' And then she would be perfectly charming and wonderful again."

Even as she ministered to her failing husband, Buff was constantly aware of her own legacy. When she granted the occasional interview to out-of-town journalists, Buff always retold her story about conjuring the Music Center into being through sheer force of will and bringing real culture at last to a smoggy frontier town. Before Norman became really sick, interviewers who could get past his secretaries, advisers, and public relations people would ask the *Times* patriarch, "Does Buff *really* have an enormous influence on you? Is she *really* as tough and great as we hear she is?" And Norman would smile beatifically and reply, "Yes."

"He had great affection and admiration for the way she raised money and brought the community together," said Otis. "He would never have met the Danny Kayes and the Paul Ziffrens and the Sidney Poitiers without her. He really loved her deeply and admired and respected her and was in awe of her in terms of her creation of the Music Center and saving the Hollywood Bowl and her charitable work."

But there was no question within the family as to which parent wielded the most clout. Even Buff acknowledged that Norman was the silent rock upon which Times Mirror had been built. She could not bear the thought of being left alone in the world to face the rest of the Chandlers, whom she had grown to loathe more than ever. Philip had already passed on, felled by a heart attack at sixty-two in 1968, but Lady Crocker was still alive and perfectly willing to snub Buff until her dying day.

"Your father has worked so hard for that family and made them so much money and made the *Times* so important and he's never received any credit from them," Buff complained to Otis at their regular weekly lunch sessions in the publisher's suite. "They've *never* said 'thank you.'"

When Otis asked his father whether Buff was telling the truth or simply lapsing into one of her typical exaggerations, Norman answered cryptically.

"I used to be a lot closer to my family than I am now," he said.

After some prodding, Norman spoke out; he even teared up once or twice when he spoke of his brothers and sisters and their never seeming to appreciate what he'd done. They were an ungrateful bunch, he told his son privately, but he wasn't bitter nor would he speak harshly of them. Chandlers did not berate other Chandlers, at least not publicly. Chandlers did not behave in such a rude fashion.

Otis prided himself on having moved beyond such trivial family bickering. He didn't have to worry about being rude. He'd hired an expert to be rude for him.

"My Uncle Harrison hated Paul Conrad," said Otis. "He hated my editorial policy. He'd always tell me, 'I'm so embarrassed when I go to the Lincoln Club once a month and they tell me how liberal that paper is.' And I said, 'Well you certainly seem to like the profit that goes through your office as head of Chandis

and distributes out to the family.' 'Yes, yes, you've done a very good job with the profit.' But how he *hated* Conrad!"

The *Times*' bad-boy cartoonist received his second Pulitzer—his first for the *Times*—in May 1971. Nevertheless, Conrad's caustic wit was occasionally banned from the newspaper, as in the case of Nixon's vice president, Spiro Agnew, during the early days of Watergate; he was drawn as a happy moron urinating on several U.S. newspapers over the caption that said simply "Leaks."[5]

Conrad's favorite target, however, was Governor Ronald Reagan, invariably caricatured to look like a Willy Loman with acrylic hair. Nancy Reagan made a morning ritual out of calling Otis from the breakfast table, always outraged.

"How could you use this terrible man?" she would begin. "He drew these awful pictures of Ronnie and is doing terrible things and Ronnie didn't do these things! Our friends are really upset with you."

Otis patronized the governor's wife for awhile, pointing out that Ronnie would have called if he was so upset. But Otis offered a solution: Mrs. Reagan might want to have the editorial section removed from the paper each morning before she and Ronnie sat down to breakfast; then she wouldn't have to look at Conrad at all.

"She never took my advice," said Otis.

While he could be tough on his editorial writers, reporters, and editors, Otis was typically tolerant to a fault when it came to his editorial cartoonist. He'd put his foot down only if something were way over the line, such as a Conrad drawing of an exuberant elephant mounting a displeased donkey from behind during a congressional session in which the Republicans were repeatedly sticking it to the Democrats. Early in Bill Thomas's tenure, the new *Times* editor called Conrad on the carpet three times in a single week over tasteless cartoons.

"Fuck you," Conrad told him. "I don't need this fuckin' newspaper."

He stomped out and almost went to work at the *Minneapolis Star-Tribune;* but Otis implored his temperamental artist to reconsider and promised to publish two of the three censored cartoons.

Norman would never have made such concessions to his editorial cartoonist, but Otis differed from his father in many obvious and not-so-obvious ways. Otis Chandler could never operate his *Times* from the sitting room at Los Tiempos, the Bohemian Grove, or the California Club. He had to be out and about in the world.

"I have to know an awful lot of people around the world and they have to know me," he said. "They have to know the seriousness of my intent and they have to know my editors. My father never did that. How are you going to write editorials and evaluate the news if you don't know people? If you don't go out like I would go out and rub shoulders with all income levels?"

Yet the view from the nose of a custom surfboard or through the scope of a high-powered rifle, from the side mirror of a Duesenberg or through the sixth floor atrium of Times Mirror Square could never be the view of the common man. Otis genuinely yearned to see the world through the eyes of a Ruben Salazar or a Bill Touhy, a Jack Tobin or a Jack Burke, or even a Paul Conrad.

But he had come to acknowledge, if not understand, that a Chandler was born wearing blinders that could be removed temporarily, but never permanently. Otis now had a good idea of where Watts or East Los Angeles were located on a map of L.A., but it would be nonsense and sheer folly for him to move there from San Marino, figuratively or literally. Besides, he had come to look upon his expensive lifestyle and enviable professional position as privileges he had earned as well as inherited; that either might be in jeopardy was impossible for him to contemplate.

He was not the kind of trust fund baby who had been born on third base and believed himself to have hit a triple, but there was no question that Otis Chandler thought of himself as having been born on second base and stolen his way home.

CHAPTER 20

GeoTek, the company that boosted Otis Chandler's income through the stratosphere in the late 1960s, came crashing to earth in 1972, and so did Otis Chandler.

While he and Jack Burke had been braving rebel terror in the Sahara, the U.S. Securities and Exchange Commission brought its own brand of terror to GeoTek Resources Fund in the closing months of 1971. SEC lawyers accused Otis's old friend of scamming investors by using GeoTek dollars earmarked for oil exploration to fuel Jack Burke's lavish personal lifestyle.

Within weeks of the SEC charges, the bond of brothers between Otis Chandler and Jack Burke disintegrated. Otis couldn't believe it at first, but as facts came into focus, his disillusion turned first to anger, and then to fear. In February 1972, a shaken Otis joined the rest of the GeoTek board in demanding the resignations of Burke, his wife Pauline, and his brother Robert. But although Otis turned against his old pal and stayed on the GeoTek board, he could not raise himself above the SEC's suspicion.

One of the first items revealed in a board-ordered independent audit that followed the Burkes resignations was a hidden agreement between Burke and Chandler: a September 1969 indemnification that held Otis harmless against GeoTek

liability while the *Times* publisher sat on the board. The unusual and ultimately unenforceable secret contract between a director and a board chairman in a publicly traded corporation such as GeoTek only heightened SEC mistrust of the Burke-Chandler relationship.

But Burke concealed far more than the indemnity agreement. As the audit proceeded, Otis learned that his old pal had mismanaged GeoTek almost from the day it was created. Since 1964, when he seduced Otis, Burke had apparently used a complex of twelve separate partnerships and corporations to milk GeoTek of an estimated $2.6 million.

In May 1972, Chandler joined the remaining board members in suing the Burkes for fraud, misappropriation, and breach of fiduciary duty. As the tawdry tale began to unfold, however, the *Los Angeles Times* reported none of it. For all of their resources and editorial independence, *Times* reporters and editors knew nothing of the goings-on in San Francisco Federal and Superior courts, or at the SEC in Washington, and Chandler did not volunteer any information to his own staff about GeoTek's impending doom.

An exposé in the *Wall Street Journal* on August 11, 1972, alerted the world that Otis Chandler, vice chairman of the $1.4-billion Times Mirror Company, had been Jack Burke's major ally in the debacle dubbed "GeoTek." Four separate deck headlines on the *Journal*'s front page said it all:

Price of Friendship

How Rich Acquaintances of
California Publisher Evidently
Lost a Bundle

Otis Chandler "Opened Doors"
for College Pal Who Ran
Oil Fund SEC Now Probes

$30 Million Down the Hole?

After the *Journal* story, in the eyes of friends, family, and his own journalists, Otis was viewed as either Jack Burke's dupe or his coconspirator. There could be no middle ground.

"Up to February of this year, I had no reason to suspect Jack of any dishonesty or self-dealing," Otis told the *Journal*'s Herb Lawson. "Jack Burke was—and I use the word 'was' very carefully and knowingly—up to February one of my oldest and closest friends."

Otis might have sidestepped further humiliation if he hadn't denied accepting finder's fees from Burke. It didn't help his case when one of the first GeoTek investors to blurt out his surprise to SEC investigators about the finder's fees was Otis's own former brother-in-law, Kelly Spear.

At first, Otis stonewalled both the SEC and the media. But his old mentor, Nick Williams, joined Franklin Murphy, Al Casey, and other ranking Times Mirror executives in urging him to come clean. The day following the *Journal* exposé, *Times* financial editor Robert Wood, who had never heard of GeoTek, interviewed a guarded Otis Chandler to get his side of the story. Even though Wood's article attempted to absolve his publisher, it was buried on page eight of the *Times* Business & Finance section under a headline that made no mention of Otis or his involvement:

SEC EXPECTED TO BRING ACTION AGAINST GEOTEK

Otis attempted to deal with GeoTek in much the same way that Norman, Harry, and even General Otis once dealt with political enemies and uncomfortable news stories: by burying them or by ignoring them.

But times, and the *Times,* had changed.

Years before GeoTek, Otis had asked Nick Williams and Bob Donovan whether they thought that accepting corporate directorships the way Norman and Harry once had might be a conflict of interest for a modern newspaper publisher. They answered, "Yes."

"We both argued strongly against his being a member of non–Times Mirror boards," said Williams.

Nevertheless, Otis went ahead and accepted seats on the boards of Western Airlines, Union Bank, Pan Am[1], and TRW, as well as GeoTek and the Associated Press. He saw his outside directorships as an extension of his personal power, but he rationalized that they also represented a source of inside information for the *Times.* Movers, shakers, and presidential advisers such as Cyrus Vance, Air Force General Hoyt Vandenberg, and Robert Anderson, former secretary of the treasury, for example, all sat on the board of Pan American Airways with Otis and shared tidbits with him that he could then pass on to his editors.

"Those were the kinds of heavyweights that were on these boards," Otis said. "I was always the youngest by far, but I found it very comfortable, very interesting, and very important to my job as publisher."

In defending himself to a *Women's Wear Daily* reporter in 1972, Otis said, "I do it to associate myself with many leaders of the country. It's a red flag out there. I'm afraid my editors don't agree with me."

His editors and his lawyers prevailed. As the GeoTek scandal escalated, the conflicts Otis encountered by sitting on the boards of companies that *Times* reporters might have to investigate aggressively became painfully clear. The same sort of dirt swept under the rug during Norman's and Harry's eras could no longer be so easily hidden. As Otis's predicament worsened, he and the rest of the Times Mirror board reluctantly concluded that no senior Times Mirror executive could sit on outside corporate boards. Otis resigned them all,[2] as did everyone else on the sixth floor with the exception of Franklin Murphy; he won a dispensation on his directorship at Ford Motor Company and the federal government's Foreign Intelligence Advisory Board.

But policy changes had come too late at GeoTek. SEC investigators wanted to know more about Otis's $109,000 in finder's fees and the $373,000 in promotional stock that Burke had awarded him and Missy for bringing more high-rolling lambs to the GeoTek slaughter. Otis had no immediate answers beyond his own ignorance of the law, an excuse that did not sit well with government prosecutors.

As the GeoTek investigation expanded, Otis began to believe that his own persecution might be politically motivated—tied to another investigation that had exploded at about the same time as GeoTek, but on the other side of the country in Washington, D.C. Just as the appalling truth of Jack Burke's deception came to light, a deception on a far grander scale had been unfolding at Democratic National Committee headquarters inside Washington's Watergate Hotel.

During the first several weeks following the infamous Watergate break-in of June 17, 1972, the *Los Angeles Times* Washington bureau played a nip-and-tuck game of one-upmanship with the *Washington Post*'s Carl Bernstein and Bob Woodward. The Academy Award–winning movie version of *All the President's Men,* Woodward and Bernstein's best-selling account of Watergate, indelibly stamped the two *Post* reporters in American legend as the only two Davids slinging stones at the paranoid Goliath in the White House.

But, in reality, *Times* reporters Jack Nelson, Bob Jackson, and Ron Ostrow were right at their heels, even pulling ahead of the intrepid *Post* a few times. At one point, five days before Christmas of 1972, Watergate Judge John Sirica even jailed John F. Lawrence, the *Times* Washington bureau chief, for two days on contempt charges because he refused to release tapes of Jack Nelson's interview with Watergate figure Alfred Baldwin.

Bobby Kennedy's former press secretary, Ed Guthman, who was then the *Times'* national editor, cited the combined handicaps of the Los Angeles Times–Washington Post News Service and the three-hour time difference between Washington and Los Angeles as key elements when the *Post* pulled far

ahead of the *Times* on the Watergate story. With rare exceptions, *Post* editors used their three-hour advantage by handing *Times* stories hot off of the Times-Post News Service wire to Woodward and Bernstein; they could either follow them up or incorporate them into their own stories in the following morning's editions. The *Post* refused to publish any Watergate story written by reporters other that its own and seldom credited the *Times* with breaking a story. Through-out the Watergate era, both papers engaged in the kind of cutthroat competition sparked by Otis in the early 1960s when he lured Joe Alex Morris and Robert El-egant away from *Newsweek*. Confident on her home turf, Katherine Graham took her turn to fight dirty.

In October 1972, however, the two papers were neck and neck, and President Nixon was well aware of their competition. In a diary entry on October 15, 1972, H. R. Haldeman,[3] Nixon's chief of staff, recorded the president's fury over a front-page *Post* story linking Nixon aide Dwight Chapin to reelection campaign espionage.

"He thinks we ought to raise hell with the *L.A. Times* if they pick up the story," Haldeman wrote in his diary. "He thinks I should call Otis and point out to him that when he was under attack on his oil deal, the President told all of us 'hands off.'"

But Nixon's crass duplicity, glimpsed in private by Buff and Norman years ear-lier, was now in full bloom. His "hands off" promise not to crack down on Otis could be seen as a veiled threat. Since moving into the White House, Nixon made and broke promises to suit his immediate needs often and with impunity.

Twice, as Norman Chandler lay dying, the president called to tell his old friend and patron that he was coming by to pay him a get-well visit; and twice Nixon stood Norman up, never offering an explanation or excuse for his broken prom-ise. Buff later sent him a handwritten note slamming the president for his gross insensitivity.

While fecklessly making empty promises to Norman, Nixon privately raged over the audacious independence of Norman's son. The no-holds-barred news policies that Otis had put in motion as *Times* publisher vexed Nixon almost daily, and he said as much to his staff. The *Times* that Richard Nixon once had in his back pocket during Kyle Palmer's reign could no longer be so easily controlled. The newspaper's reporters had to be punished; they would be denied access to the president, just as the East Coast media were. And, in the case of the *Times*, Nixon knew exactly how to squeeze it at the top.

A year before Watergate, Nixon had vowed to sic no less a prosecutor than At-torney General John Mitchell on Otis and his family. In Oval Office tapes re-leased twenty-five years after he resigned, President Nixon was heard ordering

Mitchell to direct the Immigration and Naturalization Service to raid the *Times* for illegal aliens and, more specifically, to check on the citizenship of Otis Chandler's gardener.[4]

"Now let me explain, 'cause as a Californian, I know," Nixon told Mitchell. "Everybody in California hires them. There's no law against it, because they are there, because—for menial things and so forth. Otis Chandler—I want him checked with regard to his gardener. I understand he's a wetback. Is that clear?"

At one point, the president raved to Haldeman that he wanted Treasury Secretary John Connally to turn the Internal Revenue Service loose on every member of Chandler's family.

"I want to go after this goddamn *Los Angeles Times*," Nixon snarled. "I want the whole goddamn bunch gone after."

"Mitchell says they're going after them with a special task force," said Haldeman.

"We'll just harass them," said Nixon. "I love that."

And there were any number of ways to harass Otis and his *Times*. One was to extort campaign reelection contributions. In the summer of 1972, just weeks after the Watergate break-in, one of Otis's big-game buddies who worked on Wall Street breakfasted with Al Casey, president of Times Mirror, at New York's Waldorf Astoria, and he got right to the point. He was there on behalf of the Committee to Re-Elect the President (CREEP).

"Mr. Casey, what we're looking for from the Times Mirror is a $500,000 contribution," said the man Casey would later identify only as "Mr. X."

Casey balked, pointing out that such a contribution from a corporation was illegal.

"How can you use the word 'illegal,' Mr. Casey, when we're discussing the president of the United States?" asked Otis's pal.

Casey knew the law and flatly refused to break it.

"Mr. Casey, I think you should know that your friend and colleague Otis Chandler could be in serious trouble with the SEC," the friend continued. "I could, you realize, have the SEC investigate him . . . which might prove very embarrassing."

"That sounds to me very much like a threat," said Casey.

"You may take it for what it's worth, Mr. Casey," said Otis's friend. "I should also tell you that I could, if you persist in your position, have President Nixon fire Franklin Murphy from his position on the Foreign Intelligence Advisory Board."

"That's a crock of baloney and you know it," said Casey.

But neither Otis nor Dr. Murphy took it that way after Casey returned to Los Angeles.

"Jesus, Al! They really want to humiliate me, don't they?" said Murphy.

Otis was even more upset. The *Wall Street Journal*'s story on GeoTek had not yet exploded across the country and he knew better than Casey that the threat of an SEC probe was both ominous and real.

"We really don't need an SEC investigation, Al, do we?" he asked.

"No," Casey answered. "Who the hell does?"

"It could be embarrassing, to say the least," Otis continued, real dread tingeing his voice. "I mean, Jesus, the newspapers would go to town on the story. And think of my kids, all the finger-pointing at school. That kind of thing."

But neither Murphy nor Chandler told Casey, the third member of the Times Mirror troika, that he'd erred in telling the blackmailer to pound sand. The *Times* would not pay hush money to CREEP,[5] although Franklin Murphy lost his place on the Foreign Intelligence Advisory Board and Otis's GeoTek nightmare worsened.

Following his own interrogation at the hands of federal investigators, Otis privately maintained that his crucifixion over GeoTek was Richard Nixon's personal retaliation against the *Times* for its Watergate coverage. Chandler's oldest mentor at the *Times* disagreed.

"For one thing, that sounds awkwardly like an alibi—and the GeoTek thing was just too regrettable and meriting investigation to be attributed solely to Nixon's cohorts' anger about *Times* editorials," said Nick Williams.

Otis spent days phoning or making the rounds of his relatives, trying to explain away his ill-advised participation in GeoTek. Buff tried to rein him in, and was particularly horrified by his personal apology to Lady Crocker. He was not remembering who he was, or what he represented, and she told him as much. Otis was mortified that he'd made a dismal error in judgment, but Buff found nothing but bad social form in such honest humility.

By the end of 1972, it didn't seem to matter so much to Otis that his *Times* now delivered a million copies a day, year round, and that it printed 4.3 million classifieds in a single year, a world record. While Otis watched *Times* growth records fall as each goal that he and Nick Williams had set ten years earlier was met and surpassed, the gloom of GeoTek hovered over each business day like a pox. It was hard to imagine how things could get much worse.

OTIS CHANDLER GRINNED as broadly as possible for guests and cameras on the afternoon of May 23, 1973. He'd force-fitted his lumberjack shoulders inside tailored gabardine, donned a power tie for the occasion, and mumbled his words of formal dedication for the new Times Mirror Building with as much wooden sincerity as he could muster.

The *Times* was entering a new age, he told the troops. Soon, microwave technology would link Times Mirror Square instantly to the new Orange County plant. Pages would be transmitted via the airwaves with the push of a button; hot type would soon be a thing of the past. As an experiment, editors were photocomposing the *Times* Calendar section every Sunday, and the remaining thirteen sections of the newspaper would be phased in within two years, after which the clickety-clack of General Otis's Linotype machines, which had rattled every day and night through the basement of the *Times* since 1893, would fall silent forever. Plastic printer sheets would replace the heavy stereotype plates Otis had once lifted for exercise during his summers in the pressroom.

But despite rehearsing his remarks, Otis Chandler found his words rattling as plastic as the printer sheets, and the searing pain in his gut made him feel as if he had swallowed molten lead. Deep inside his gabardine façade, the perfectly coifed and buffed-out publisher suffered from a new and inexplicable malady, diagnosed by his doctors as a spastic colon. It might be inherited, he was told, or it might be the result of stress.

"He would get up to some major event in his life that was really important, à la GeoTek or the Olympics," observed Otis's old friend Bob Emett, "and there was always some physical ailment that came out of it. Sprained wrist, a boil, spastic colon."

The odd thing was that physical activity—surfing, cycling, weight lifting, hiking up at the Tejon Ranch—was the one thing that consistently alleviated the pain. But back at his office, the agony started up all over again, growing worse by evening and becoming unbearable by bedtime.

"He complained a lot about his sleep," said Missy. "He was always tired. I've never known a man who has always said he was tired, but he did. I don't know if that is hypochondria or his mother, but he had a lot of energy, yet he was tired."

It was during this same period that Otis hit a patch of kelp while waterskiing at Dana Point, flipped, and broke his shoulder.

"He didn't get treatment right away," said Missy. "He didn't think he needed an operation."

But the pain worsened, supplementing the agony in his gut. He banished his wife from their bed so that he could roil around on its sheets alone.

"He had the whole king-sized bed to himself because of his shoulder," said Missy. "I either slept on the floor or in another room, and that is what hurt our marriage. I mean, he's demanding."

Otis eventually sought help at UCLA, where experimental treatments for pain were being run in regular medical trials.

"We did all these crazy things like putting powder in his belly button and warming it," said Missy. "We did acupuncture, biofeedback, imaging. He tried it all, but he didn't persevere. He should have persevered in all of them."

On the surface, Otis Chandler looked as rugged and ready as ever. Throughout the dedication day for the newly renovated world headquarters of a bigger, better, more powerful Times Mirror Company, none of his troops knew about his intestinal turmoil, nor did most of them know that six days earlier, he had been formally charged with wrongdoing in the GeoTek affair.

On May 17, the SEC indicted Jack Burke as mastermind of a $30-million scheme to defraud an estimated 2,200 GeoTek investors by selling $17 million in nearly worthless stock. Because he had been less than candid about his finder's fees and promotional stock, Otis also faced charges—minor by comparison, but humiliating nonetheless. It was the nastiest public stain on an otherwise spotless career; it even carried the potential of prison time: a remote possibility, but a real one. Harry Chandler's flip remark back in 1917 following Otis's grandfather's own tussle with federal prosecutors—"You're not a man until you've been indicted at least once"—did nothing to lessen Otis's anxiety.

The two most important women in his life watched helplessly, careful not to dwell on his wounded pride. Buff counseled a stiff upper lip and absolute attention to attorneys' advice. Missy not only shared in her husband's day-to-day humiliation but also suffered more of it.

The younger Mrs. Chandler hadn't been able to laugh much in the years leading up to the GeoTek ordeal. Her husband's practical jokes had stopped and he was gone from home most of the time. Except for her youngest daughter, Carolyn, who was still in junior high, the rest of the children were grown and had lives of their own. Missy still happily argued politics with Otis over the dinner table on the increasingly rare occasions when her family all sat down to supper together, but for the most part, she stayed out of Otis's way. After years as a proper corporate wife, Missy had created her own life. She chain-smoked her way to a master's degree in urban planning at UCLA and, over her husband's objections, went into partnership with another urban planner and formed her own architectural design firm.

As for Buff, her bombast hit a brick wall on October 20, 1973, when Norman Chandler died of the throat cancer that had been choking his life away for more than a year. She wept for Norman, but shed most of her tears over her own unpleasant predicament as Norman's widow.

"She went through various stages and she used to talk to Norman in a stern voice, 'Why did you leave me so early, so alone?,'" Otis remembered. "She was very mad at him."

The most powerful man in Los Angeles during the 1940s and 1950s went out with a minimum of fuss. There was a memorial for Norman Chandler at Times Mirror Square, but no funeral. He'd chosen cremation and no church service. Paddling his surfboard, Otis carried his father's ashes a hundred yards off the shoreline at Dana Point with Mia swimming along beside him. Within sight of the "trailer" in which Norman and Buff spent most of their final months together, Otis and Mia scattered Norman's remains into the Pacific.

Even during that solemn and private moment, Buff found it impossible to stifle her egocentricity. The moment belonged only to her and her offspring, she had decided. Before he left San Marino with his father's ashes to come to the beach, she admonished Otis: "Don't bring Missy."

Buff had concluded that her daughter-in-law did not know how to behave properly at such occasions. Missy could not be trusted. She would even speak openly and frankly to her friends about Otis's delicate intestinal problem, or even Norman's cancer. Buff did not approve.

"That's a no-no in this family, Missy, and I want you to know it!" she had once screamed at her daughter-in-law. "We *never* talk about illness or how we feel in this family. We are above that."

Increasingly assertive in her own right, Missy no longer took Buff's tongue lashings submissively. After more than twenty years of marriage, she had learned that she would receive no help from her passive-aggressive husband. So she gave back to the voluble Buff as good as she got, and Buff hated her even more for it.

"Buff was very mean to me," said Missy. "She was kind, and then mean."

Missy described her mother-in-law's behavior as schizoid personality disorder. She had witnessed it at least once before: a business partner in her planning firm who would lose his temper, rant for several minutes, and, later, fail to remember any of it.

"Buff was that way," said Missy. "She would scream and yell at people and then she would wonder why they were all looking at her. I don't think she realized how awful she could be."

Buff could be equally cruel by simply ignoring Missy. Until she understood what her mother-in-law was up to, Missy thought Buff had simply forgotten she was there when she talked over her at the dinner table, disregarded her contributions to a conversation, or just didn't put her name on the invitation when she asked Otis to a party.

"I blame partially Otis being unhappy with me on Buff," she said. "I think she was jealous of me because her son loved somebody else more than he did her."

Otis never completely faced up to Buff's overbearing nature, especially when it intruded upon his marriage. He didn't like the role of mediator, so he tried to

keep his wife and mother apart as often as possible; he was as blind as Oedipus to the similarities between them. One of Buff's Blue Ribbon 400 entourage once told Karen Winner, a reporter for *Women's Wear Daily,* that "Otis could have married the Virgin Mary and Buff *still* wouldn't like her."

Otis didn't seem to mind his mother's wretched attitude towards Missy, but he drew the line at her taking credit for creating the Times Mirror empire.

"My mother's star was ascending as my father's was descending," said Otis. "That's why I think this myth has arisen after his death and my mother did nothing to discourage it. Writers would say, 'Well, if she built the Music Center and was this dynamic leader in Los Angeles and the cultural world, then she must have run the *Times* when Norman was publisher. She must have been the power behind the throne.' And I'm saying that's not true."

With his father gone, Otis flexed his muscles even more. His mother's influence in society news was still powerful, but her impact on the rest of the paper was as faded as an "I Like Ike" campaign poster.

When Jim Bellows resigned as associate editor, Otis Chandler and Bill Thomas hired Jean Sharley Taylor, a respected veteran female editor from the *Arizona Republic.* Buff took it upon herself to break her in. As Taylor recalled, their first meeting took place in Taylor's new office when Buff swept in, trailed by an assistant. She briefly introduced herself, then began removing paintings from the wall. They were valuable, she explained. Then, she noticed that Taylor was eating lunch at her desk and offered a confidential suggestion.

"Get a Sego [diet drink] or perhaps a little container of yogurt, and then you can hide it in your bottom drawer!" she said.

Taylor smiled diplomatically and nodded, then went about her business; she continued to eat her lunch at her desk as work and hunger demanded, and rarely if ever sipping a Sego.

Buff still had an office at the *Times,* but it was not a symbol of her power and influence.

"She had her office because it was close to the Music Center and she could meet with all of the important people on her committee," said Otis.

She had officially retired as a Times Mirror director six months before Norman's death, but retained the titles of "Assistant to the Chairman of the Board" and "Director Emeritus." In deference to her grief, Otis tolerated his mother's meddling in the months following his father's death, but he learned soon enough that she had not grieved for very long.

"She was really in mourning the first year or two, but it didn't last," said Otis.

He knew she'd recovered fully when he met with Buff once in her upstairs sitting room at Los Tiempos and commented that Norman's portrait hung crooked against the wall.

"Why don't you have one of your servants make that nice and straight?" Otis asked.

"Oh, he's gone," his mother said, referring off-handedly to her dead husband. Then she changed the subject. Otis had to straighten the picture himself as he left the room. He concluded the period of mourning was over and took off the kid gloves: He asked Franklin Murphy to evict his mother from Times Mirror Square.

"I finally kicked her out in a nice way because there was no reason for her to take up corporate space," he explained. "So that was when she used that little outbuilding by the pool in Hancock Park. Her 'Pub,' she called it. That became her Blue Ribbon headquarters."

After more than twenty-seven years with the *Times,* Dorothy Chandler retired in February 1976. Appropriately, the woman dubbed by *Advertising Age* as "the greatest fund-raiser since Al Capone," marked her departure from the paper with a cocktail gala and vowed to continue her arm-twisting efforts on behalf of the Music Center's ongoing operating budget.

"Goodness sakes, there's the Music Center Foundation and a sizable amount still to raise to assure the resident groups survive," she said. "You don't have a family and then turn them out before they have their wings."

As soon as she was gone for good from Times Mirror Square, Otis ordered the *Times* Woman of the Year awards jettisoned and the society news cut back to twice a week. That same year, he named reporter Sharon Rosenhause as the *Times'* New Delhi bureau chief; she was the *Times'* first female foreign correspondent.

Women would never be treated in a cavalier or second-class way again at Times Mirror Square.

THE SECURITIES AND EXCHANGE COMMISSION tightened its noose in 1974. On the advice of everyone he trusted, Otis grit his teeth and put his future in the hands of lawyers, including his new brother-in-law and fellow Times Mirror board member, F. Daniel Frost.

Frost was no criminal attorney, but he was a senior partner at Gibson, Dunn and Crutcher—the largest and most powerful law firm in Southern California— and was able to retain the best defense team that Chandler money could buy. Before his GeoTek nightmare was over, Otis would spend over $1 million to fight the SEC and, what was nearly as bad, he would be beholden to Dan Frost for coming to his aid.

Despite Norman and Buff's approval of the Harvard-educated Frost, Otis had never found the Chandlers' personal attorney to be particularly helpful or likable. Since 1957, when his parents hired Frost to advise them on tax and investment matters, Otis had seen him as the polar opposite to himself: as icy and formal in

his demeanor as his surname suggested. A malformed foot kept Frost from being athletic, so he tended toward the purely cerebral. He had a California Club air of entitlement about him and his dulled sense of humor left Otis cold. Otis saw him as a high-toned opportunist and little more.

When Norman and Buff invited Frost and his fellow Gibson, Dunn and Crutcher partner Bob Erburu to join the Times Mirror board in 1967, Otis reluctantly welcomed Frost to the company's inner circle. Frost took full advantage of the opening. He married Otis's sister Mia when she was on the rebound from playboy and habitual womanizer Kelly Spear. Frost dumped his wife of twenty-seven years to marry into the Chandler clan. Otis welcomed him even more reluctantly to the inner sanctum of the family.

A right-thinking Republican with a Pasadena pedigree, Frost was readily accepted by the rest of the Chandlers, including the disaffected Philip and Lady Crocker branches. Only Otis found Frost odious. The closer Frost moved toward Otis's center of control, the more uncomfortable Otis became. If Frost managed to save him from his GeoTek blunder, Otis would feel an even stronger sense of obligation to one of his least favorite human beings.

His lawyers told Otis that he could slide out from under the SEC charges scot-free only if he took the witness stand and testified against Jack Burke. Otis balked. He hated what Burke had done and was especially angry that he'd been lassoed in as a naïve participant in his scheme, but Otis also saw himself as a stand-up guy. The idea of testifying for the prosecution tied his already spastic colon into a gut-wrenching Gordian knot.

In the end, he did as he was told. On November 7, Otis sat in the straight-backed chair to the left of the federal judge trying the GeoTek case and acknowledged that the beefy, middle-aged man hunkered down at the defense table was, indeed, Jack Burke, his friend, hunting companion, business partner, and now, perhaps, his Waterloo. The ordeal, including cross-examination, took only a few minutes. But it was seared forever into Otis's psyche.

"It was the last time I ever saw J. B.," said Otis, recalling the initials by which he once affectionately knew his close pal.

In January, Jack Burke pleaded to a single count of making false statements to the SEC and wound up with a thirty-month prison sentence, later reduced by half. Otis still faced years of civil suits arising from the GeoTek affair, but the SEC dropped its criminal complaint against him two months after Burke's guilty plea.

WHILE OTIS CHANDLER'S PERSONAL HORRORS mounted toward midlife critical mass, the "uncommon excellence" juggernaut he had set in motion at the

Times a dozen years earlier rolled on unimpeded. Two more bureaus opened, one in Cairo and the other in Johannesburg. A third would open in Madrid in 1975.

At home, the *Times* prepared to launch the new set of Orange County presses; the plastic printer sheets replacing the old stereotype plates would save Times Mirror more than $4 million a year.

Orange County and the San Fernando Valley became the *Times'* newest frontiers during the 1970s. The newspaper's real competition shifted to the suburbs, just as Otis had predicted it would when he took over as publisher. The *Santa Ana Register* changed its name to the *Orange County Register* and grew accordingly, giving the *Times* a real battle for the hearts and minds of Orange County readers. Similarly, the *Long Beach Press-Telegram*, *Riverside Press-Enterprise*, *Valley News & Green Sheet*, *South Bay Daily Breeze,* and *San Bernardino Sun* beefed up their news and their advertising and circulation campaigns to meet the challenge of an ever-burgeoning *Times.* For marketing purposes, Otis stopped calling his newspaper the *Los Angeles Times* and redefined it as the *Times:* a regional newspaper that served the Southern California megalopolis.

"Megalopolis is a word that I didn't coin, but I grabbed it from somebody and used it," he said. "I said this was going to be a market from the [Mexican] border north to Santa Barbara."

And that was how he positioned the *Times* for the growing suburban middle class: *the* indispensable news source for *all* of Southern California. The *Times* was now regularly on everybody's top-ten list, trailing a close third behind the *New York Times* and the *Washington Post*. If an individual lived in Southern California, considered him- or herself educated, and enjoyed even the hint of a disposable income, that person had to subscribe to the *Los Angeles Times*. That had been Otis's intent all along and, now, it had become L.A.'s reality.

Still badly wounded from its marathon labor strike five years earlier, Hearst's anemic *Los Angeles Herald-Examiner* barely limped along as an also-ran. Belatedly switching from afternoon to morning delivery, L.A.'s only other daily newspaper still held the edge with the racing crowd who still depended upon the *Herald*'s afternoon street-stand edition to handicap Santa Anita or Hollywood Park. The *Herald-Examiner* also excelled in late-breaking sports scores. But its home subscriptions and ad sales dropped through the floor in the 1970s, along with its overall general news coverage. On any given day, the *Times* was five times its size.

In one apocryphal but widely repeated urban legend, television's *Mission Impossible* star Barbara Bain had supposedly lost her small dog one Sunday morning when a home-delivered *Los Angeles Times* landed on top of the animal. Had she been a *Herald-Examiner* subscriber, her dog wouldn't have sustained even minor injuries.

On the evening of February 4, 1974, however, Otis and everyone else in California took a renewed interest in the waning power of the Hearst empire. The ongoing din of Watergate, which was about to break into impeachment hearings in Washington, D.C., yielded the front page of every newspaper in the United States to a mysterious band of post-1960s outlaws called the Symbionese Liberation Army who had successfully abducted nineteen-year-old Patty Hearst from her Berkeley apartment.

Otis set aside his rivalry with William Randolph Hearst Jr. to offer his sympathy and whatever services the *Times* might be able to give. He also cautioned his own children to be on the alert. Otis recalled his own brush with kidnapping almost half a century earlier and warned his brood that such things did happen to children of media moguls. Patty Hearst was no fluke. The LAPD offered immediate protection to Otis, Missy, and all five of their children in the wake of the kidnapping, an offer the Chandlers politely declined. They could take care of themselves. When Otis subsequently read an SLA communiqué passed on to him by the police that suggested he might have been too hasty, he had four-inch thick bullet-proof glass installed in his office.

"I was on the SLA hit list," he said. "I was this big publisher of a major paper, plus the Chandlers had this ongoing labor thing."

Still, he had no serious doubt that all his children could fend for themselves, especially his sons. All three boys were blond, tall, and as athletic as their father. They shared their father's passion for surfing, but also pursued generational passions of their own; Otis warned them to be cautious about whom they chose to smoke pot with.

"My kids all smoked marijuana," said Otis. "They didn't think I knew it, but I knew. I could smell it. So I guess Missy and I one time said, 'Let's ask the kids for one puff.'"

Unlike future presidents, Otis did, indeed, inhale, but he found the experience boring.

"You've got to really go for it," one of his sons admonished. "You've got to really party to get the good feeling."

Otis didn't party.

"I have no interest," he said, returning the half-smoked doobie.

As young adults, his sons were far easier to bond with than they were as children, and he began to see his own traits reflected in each of them. Otis hung out with his boys: They went dirt biking in the desert and they shot the curl at Dana Point. Norman, reflective and solitary, tended to be the most sensitive of the three, his personality influenced more by Missy than by Otis. Lusty, taciturn Michael had trouble concentrating in school and was diagnosed early as a

dyslexic. He loved girls, cars, and things that traveled fast, free, and furious, from skateboards to snow skis. There was much of Otis in his youngest son.

Harry fell somewhere between the extremes represented by both of his brothers. "Harry's my risk taker, almost equal to his father," Otis remembered with some pride. "Take the time in Montana, for instance."

GeoTek notwithstanding, the Chandlers had found enough money to purchase a 280-acre Montana ranch in the 1970s, irrigated by stream water that fed from nearby Mt. Hastings through a huge underground pipeline. For recreation on a hot summer day, Otis and his sons rode inner tubes down the stream to an open ditch, just before the water fed into the pipeline. It was Harry who decided to up the ante on the inner tube ride.

"What are you going to do?" Otis shouted at him as he headed toward the gaping maw of the pipeline.

"I'm gonna ride it and see where it comes out," he called back to his father.

"Oh come on," said Otis. "What if there's a debris gate in the middle of it? I'm not gonna be able to come get you out and you'll drown in there!"

"No, I'll be fine, Dad," he said.

And Harry was gone.

Otis and the other boys raced down the length of the pipeline to see where it ended. They got panicky when it appeared to go on forever. But a little over a mile away, the stream water emerged at the other end, and so did Harry. Once the trail had been blazed, they all climbed back to the top of the pipeline and followed Harry through the pipeline again and again. Harry became the Chandlers' Star Trekker, daring to go where no man had gone before.

The Chandler family enjoyed good times in Montana, girls and boys together. With GeoTek behind him, Otis had found a new equilibrium, and his family was very much a part of it. Thus far, the 1970s had qualified as the worst decade in his life, but the most unpleasant years now seemed to be past.

While Otis had been struggling with GeoTek, Los Angeles elected Tom Bradley its first black mayor and Richard Nixon resigned his presidency, although the *Times* was one of the few major dailies that did not call for him to resign. For the bold new *Los Angeles Times* of Otis Chandler, such faintheartedness seemed to mark an oddly disturbing editorial return to Kyle Palmer's era. From the safety of his retirement, a puzzled Nick Williams wrote critically of the episode in a letter to his old friend Jim Bassett.

"I thought the *Times* should have demanded Nixon's resignation," said Williams. "Instead, it called for the 'legal and normal process of an impeachment trial,' and this after the *Chicago Tribune* among many others urged resignation as best for the nation."

Bassett, who had retired as editorial page editor to write the official history of the Chandler dynasty, could offer no immediate explanation for the *Times'* delicate handling of the disgraced former president. A momentary spineless relapse, he surmised.

Gerald Ford assumed the presidency and pardoned Richard Nixon, and Patty Hearst turned up alive and a member in good standing of the very SLA that had kidnapped her. Her odyssey sparked dinner table conversation among Otis's children, who wondered how they might have reacted under similar circumstances. Would repeated rape in a closet strip them of their regal Chandler conditioning and reduce them to Pavlovian obedience? No one wanted to find out.

As the nation celebrated its bicentennial in 1976 by electing Jimmy Carter president and wiping the Watergate slate clean, Times Mirror celebrated yet another milestone of its own, with revenues exceeding $1 billion for the first time. The *Times* won another Pulitzer that year as well, this time for a series of editorials written by former *Nation* columnist Phil Kerby, on privacy, the press, and open government. Both the country's and Otis Chandler's long nightmares at last seemed to be over.

Thus, it remained a troubling and continuous mystery to Otis when he awakened in the middle of the night, drenched in sweat and his gut still twisted in agony. His spastic colon grew worse. He occasionally started out of bed with a howl but, more often, with a whimper.

There was no one nearby to hear. A permanent malaise had settled over the marriage bed that he alone now occupied.

CHAPTER 21

THE TIMES WAS AWASH IN MONEY in 1977. It became the first newspaper ever to print 5 million classified ads in a single year and, for the twenty-fifth consecutive year, published more advertising overall than any other daily in the world. Nearly 6,000 people worked at Times Mirror Square, many earning twice the salary of their peers at rival papers. No expense in pursuit of a story was too high. When on assignment, reporters and photographers routinely flew first class, ate at five-star restaurants, and stayed at diamond-rated hotels. When the check came, *Times*men were under strict orders never to let anyone else pick it up. Re-

porters smiled, grabbed the bill, and said: "Don't worry about it. Otis will take care of it."

Private jets were chartered, helicopters hired, and taxicab drivers ordered to drive hundreds of miles, just to return a single roll of film to the city desk before deadline. When Patty Hearst disappeared, two reporters followed a rumor to Hong Kong, where the Hearst heiress was said to have been taken and, although they came back with no story, the pair did manage to run up one of the highest expense accounts in *Times* history.

Still, the cornucopia of *Times* booty wasn't all spent on wine and wild-goose chases. Otis Chandler treated *Times* editorial employees as family; and where family was concerned, money was no object. When reporter Beth Ann Krier broke her back in an auto accident while on assignment for the paper, Otis, whom she had never met, personally took charge.

"I didn't even know this guy," she said. "I fell asleep driving on the Hollywood Freeway and I crashed. Broke my back, broke my neck. The office had no way of knowing if I were on the job or just driving home or what. But Otis got on the phone personally to the hospital when he heard. 'Spare no expense,' he told them. And the head of the department operated on me instead of some resident. I won't ever forget that."

Similarly, when Joe Alex Morris died during the week of anarchy that followed the ousting of the Shah of Iran in 1979, flags flew at half mast over Times Mirror Square; the fallen Middle East bureau chief, whom Otis had recruited away from Katherine Graham, was accorded the kind of memorial that General Otis himself would have bestowed upon a fallen comrade. When given the news of the third *Times* reporter in its hundred-year history to die while on the job, Otis broke down and cried, just as he had ten years earlier when Ruben Salazar was killed.

Times cash was also poured into modernization. Computers now tied the paper directly to Sacramento as well as to Orange County and Washington, D.C. Before the decade was over, every beat reporter, copy clerk, and editor would have his or her own video display terminal. Typewriters went the way of Linotype machines.

With the opening of bureaus in Denver, Brussels, Toronto, and Peking, *Times* satellite offices in the United States and overseas now totaled thirty-one, more than justifying its boast in the new *Times* television, radio, and billboard promotional campaign that if a reader picked up the *Times*, they'd "Pick Up the World."

Times Mirror spent its share of the wealth wisely, too. It picked up the *Hartford Courant*, the nation's oldest continuously published daily, as well as the *Greenwich Times* and *Stamford Advocate:* dailies serving two of the most affluent cities in America, both within commuting distance of New York City. Times Mirror had become so rich that Otis could publicly announce the ban of more than $3

million in sure-fire annual advertising; not only did he get away with it but he received hurrahs for his courage from staff, stockholders, and community leaders alike.

It was the era of *Deep Throat*, the Pill, and *The Joy of Sex*, and the motion-picture advertising in the back of the *Times* had become a little too raunchy for Otis Chandler's tastes. He was no prude. Otis was all for sex. But not in the loge section and certainly not up on the silver screen in big, pulsating, nipple-pink neon. He was old-fashioned and believed that such intimacy was reserved for the bedroom or, in the case of teens, the backseat of a used Buick where it was at least inconvenient and uncomfortable. It certainly had no place in the pages of a family newspaper.

In August 1977, he announced that the *Times* would no longer accept advertising for X-rated movies. Vance Stickel, his veteran advertising manager, told him he was crazy to write off such a lucrative income stream. The porn houses would pour their cash into rival papers, notably the struggling *Herald-Examiner*, which the *Times* had a good chance of finally putting out of business if Otis would just let nature take its course.

But Otis was insistent. The *New York Times* didn't carry smut ads. The *Los Angeles Times* wouldn't either. The theaters sued the *Times* for $44 million, claiming a violation of their First Amendment rights. They lost. Once again, Otis Chandler had fought the good fight and won; in the process, he rubbed off a good deal of the tarnish left on his public image by the GeoTek debacle.

But life at the top had grown just as isolated as his old Deke pal, Merritt Van Zant, had once predicted it would be. When Otis looked around, he saw himself alone. His *Times* was a well-oiled machine, perfectly capable of running on its own most of the time. His family was grown, with Norman and Harry already moved out and on their own, and the younger Chandler children so busy with school or jobs that they seldom saw their parents.

As for Missy, his wife and helpmeet had combined the Chandler name with her own raw ambition to create a new life for herself, separate from her husband and his newspaper.

As Mrs. Otis Chandler, she'd been able to land a plum job right out of UCLA, working as an executive planner for Howard Hughes's Summa Corporation. Three years later, again using the magic Chandler name, she got a generous line of credit to launch her own company, Urban Design Disciplines. She teamed up with another type A personality and began mapping out grand architectural visions from her Pasadena office.

Blending the emerging science of ecology with visions of beautiful buildings, Missy wanted to change the map of L.A. She wanted to do it on her own, as a strong professional woman, like her old Stanford classmate Carla Hills, whom

President Jimmy Carter had recently named his secretary of housing and urban development. Missy matched Otis challenge for challenge. She could do it all: be a wife, mother, and independent businesswoman who played as hard as she worked. While her husband indulged his passion for the biggest game or the most challenging wave, Missy took on the toughest tennis opponent or the steepest ski slope. Just as her urban planning business was taking off, she snapped an Achilles tendon when she went helicopter skiing in the Canadian Rockies one year; she nearly went crazy sitting at home in a cast for five months. Once she was back on her feet, she was off and running again, stumping for zero population growth, bidding for environmentally sound development projects, and meeting with city planners from Las Vegas to Watts.

But doing it all also meant pressure. Like Mama Buff, who was the antithesis of all Missy stood for, she soothed herself with a martini at the end of each day. Otis still frowned on alcohol and would not join her in her cocktails, but that only seemed to spur her on. Although Buff and Missy maintained that they had nothing in common except Otis, it was apparent to all those around them that both Mrs. Chandlers tended to drink too much.

Once, the Chandlers' secret nearly surfaced when Missy was pulled over one evening by an L.A. sheriff's deputy for erratic driving. A minor problem escalated after she advised the young man in uniform that she was *Mrs.* Otis Chandler and that he had best be on his way. When the deputy asked her to step from the vehicle, she took a poke at him and found herself temporarily under arrest. Had Otis not been friendly with Sheriff Peter Pitchess, his wife might have been booked, the family embarrassed, and the *Times'* rivals exultant. Fortunately, the incident was hushed up and Missy sobered up at home instead of in a cell at the county jail.

Otis made no apologies to his editors. He saw no hypocrisy in calling for candor in the lives of other public figures while quashing news about the more sensitive aspects of his own.

When the *Times* came under fire for opposing a federal statute that barred irrigating farms larger than 160 acres with cheap government water, Otis passionately defended his family's position. He acknowledged to the *New York Times* that the Chandlers' sprawling Tejon Ranch and the vast J. G. Boswell acreage in the San Joaquin Valley, which was controlled by Lady Crocker,[1] benefited from cheap irrigation; but he blithely denied that either Boswell or the Tejon might influence the *Times'* editorial position or its news coverage of California's volatile water politics.[2]

Manipulating or killing stories outright was nothing new to the Chandlers. Otis might have suffered a few more pangs of conscience than his forbears, but it did not stop him from using his *Times* like a sledgehammer to silence his critics. By

using the sheer power of the *Times,* he could make or break almost any book that did not paint the Chandlers in a positive light.

By the late 1970s, several authors had turned their attention toward the *Times*, including the Pulitzer Prize–winning David Halberstam. He had undertaken a tour de force that included the Chandlers as one of four American media families that dominated the national delivery of news. *The Powers That Be* profiled William Paley's Columbia Broadcasting System, Henry Luce's Time-Life empire, Katherine Graham's *Washington Post*, and the Chandlers' *Times;* it became a national bestseller despite Otis's slow burn over Halberstam's conclusion that Buff, not Norman nor Otis, was the real power behind the rise of the modern *Los Angeles Times.* Already a nationally recognized and widely praised historian and author, Halberstam could not be done any real damage by Otis or his *Times*. But others could.

Thinking Big, an equally ambitious and painstakingly researched book published two years earlier than *The Powers That Be* reached many of Halberstam's critical conclusions about the Chandlers; but its fate was much the same as that of *Billion Dollar Blackjack* a quarter century earlier. Even though it was published by G. P. Putnam's Sons and received generally good reviews outside of Southern California, *Thinking Big* was written by Bob Gottlieb and Irene Wolt, a pair of Southern California journalists-turned-academics who did not have the clout of a David Halberstam. *Thinking Big* traced the history of the *Times* from General Otis through his great-grandson's stewardship as publisher; it also documented the secretive, selfish, and often self-serving behavior of the most powerful family in Southern California and its shameless use of the *Times* to further its own interests.

A victim of the very provincialism it documented, *Thinking Big* received almost no publicity in Southern California and only a small, dismissive notice at the back of the *Times* Book Review. Gottlieb later conceded that a serious, detailed book about a Southern California institution as omnipotent as the *Times* was probably doomed from its outset if it had not received the Chandlers' tacit approval.

"I heard it sold less than 5,000 copies," Otis said derisively two decades later, long after whatever sting he thought the book had was gone.

But Otis's pique and personal vanity was not reserved just for outsiders. In 1972, he had commissioned his own former editorial page editor, Jim Bassett, to write an authorized history of the *Times* under the guidance of Nick Williams. The author of the best-selling World War II novel *In Harm's Way*, Bassett took on the assignment with gusto, riffling through the *Times* archives and taping interviews with dozens of Chandler family members and *Times* principals, past and present. During the years that followed, Bassett chronicled the origins of the *Times* and the Chandler fortune in painstaking detail, eventually producing an eight-hundred-page manuscript that he called a "no holds barred" history of the

most powerful family in Southern California and its equally powerful newspaper. Nick Williams, who read every chapter for accuracy as a favor to Bassett, heaped his own praise on the project.

A month before Bassett was due to retire in October 1977, Otis gave the manuscript to Dan Frost to review and the project was suddenly halted without explanation. Following Bassett's departure, the manuscript and all of Bassett's research lay untouched for several years until it was eventually handed off to former *Time* magazine correspondent Marshall Berges. Berges pared the manuscript down to a quarter of its size and, in the process, hacked out anything remotely embarrassing to the Chandler family.

The result was an obsequious paean to Otis and his ancestors called *The Life and Times of Los Angeles: A Newspaper, a Family and a City*. Published in 1984 to a favorable review in the *Times* and horse laughter everywhere else, the fawning Berges had attempted to absolve every member of the family of all malfeasance, including Harry Chandler and the General; the author had glossed over their naked land grabs, their rape of the Owens Valley, and their shady dealings in Mexico. According to Berges, four generations the Chandler family had lived their full and privileged lives without ever encountering a personal, a sexual, or a moral problem.

In retrospect, even Otis referred to *The Life and Times of Los Angeles* as a "kiss-ass book." Had Times Mirror not purchased it in bulk to hand out to employees and *Times* retirees, it would have sold fewer copies than *Thinking Big*.

As for Bassett, he did not live to see his final journalistic effort reduced to press release pabulum. He died of a heart attack at sixty-five, less than a year after his retirement. After having served forty-three years as a loyal reporter and editor for the *Times* and *Mirror*, he faded into history with as little fanfare as Kyle Palmer, Carleton Williams, Bill Henry, or any of the other stars the Chandlers had created then discarded when they were no longer useful.

ACCORDING TO FAMILY LORE, young Otis had zipped down Nottingham Avenue on his Flexi-Racer as a boy, rounded a curve to see a line of busy afternoon cross-traffic on Los Feliz Boulevard, and shot on through at full speed. He ducked just in time to avoid being decapitated as he flashed beneath an idling truck and came out safely on the other side. It was crazy, but it was thrilling. His own kids joked that the Flexi-Racer must have been nicknamed "Rosebud," and brought a wee smile to their father's great stone face.

Harrison "Harry" Chandler, the second of Otis's three sons, remembered several such daredevil tales that his father passed around the dinner table as Harry and his brothers were growing up. The stories were not meant to be instructive so

much as they were pure braggadocio: Take risks, he seemed to be telling his boys, but don't do anything quite so foolhardy as your old man has done.

Since his sophomore year at Stanford, when he purchased his first rolling stock, Otis had carried on a torrid lifelong love affair with anything that traveled fast on two and/or four wheels. His first motorcycle was a Harley Davidson "Knucklehead" that he and Norm Nourse, his fellow weight-lifting fanatic, had bought together; and together they boarded three-on-a-bike, some young campus honey sandwiched between them, and roared down El Camino Real at full throttle. His first used car was a 1936 Ford coupe that broke down regularly in front of the Deke house.

And his first brand-new car was a baby blue 1949 Pontiac four-door sedan, driven pristine and pretty right off the lot after Otis had made a sizable down payment that he'd earned working two summers in a row down in the *Times* pressroom. On the tight budget of a college senior, the thirty easy monthly payments that followed were anything but easy, but the gleaming Big Man on Campus ride he got out of it made every penny worthwhile.

Otis traded up over the decades that followed, always acquiring the best, the finest, and the fastest vehicles that money could buy. By 1969, he'd begun to collect the swiftest of them all: a string of eight Porsches for which he eventually had to rent a small garage in El Monte just to house them all. His shoulders were so big that he had to have special doors made to get in and out of some of them. The low-slung, German-made speed bombs were still new to the American market, and difficult to find parts for; when Otis needed engine work done, there were just a handful of places in all of Southern California where he could go, and the nearest to San Marino was a Porsche-Audi agency in the Pasadena suburb of Monrovia. There, behind the counter, he met an effervescent race car mechanic named John Thomas.

"Drive fast," advised Thomas, wearing a big "hi-howdy" grin across his plebeian face. "You're harder to hit."

No one on the sixth floor of Times Mirror Square, in the corridors of the California Club, or at the annual conventions of the American Newspaper Publishers Association had ever summed up Otis Chandler's philosophy of life quite so succinctly or so well.

Thomas dreamed of being a race car driver, not a parts salesman. J. T., as he preferred to be known, was a speed demon like Otis's youngest son, Michael. In a certain way, Otis bonded more tightly with Michael than either of Michael's two older brothers because Michael had the same yen for action and inbred disdain for book learning that Otis had: They would both rather *be* Huckleberry Finn than read about him. Despite his dyslexia, Michael wasn't illiterate, but he was definitely nonliterate. Perhaps that is why he was the son Otis always took with

him on his dirt bike adventures in the desert, and perhaps that, too, was why he took an instant shine to the book-averse John Thomas. Neither could quote a line of Shakespeare, but they survived just fine in the real world.

"Michael always thought he was dumb and he wasn't doing well in school, so he and I started to ride dirt bikes," said Otis. "We'd go and just tear ass all over the California desert and I liked the feeling of control and speed."

But Michael grew past dirt biking and took up competitive skiing, a sport Otis never got into much. In J. T., Otis sensed a fellow biker who would never grow out of it. On impulse, Otis invited the parts salesman to go out to the desert with him, and two weeks later they were hauling across endless alkaline expanses in the Mojave: the dry El Mirage lake bed that had once been fed by rivers draining the Sierra Nevada, like the sorry trickle that still wove through the lower reaches of the Owens Valley.

The two grown men frolicked and roared like boys on Schwinns racing for invisible trophies. Separated by half a football field at one point, they both spotted a hole in a chain-link fence far off on the horizon. At the same moment, they revved and raced toward the hole at top speed, neither letting up to let the other safely move ahead. Unlike Otis's near miss long ago on Los Feliz Boulevard, when he had slid his Flexi-Racer underneath an idling truck, this game of chicken ended in a wreck. Neither Otis nor J. T. made it through the hole in the fence. Instead of nursing their injuries or checking over the tangled dirt bikes for mechanical problems, though, the two men rolled around in the silt laughing like a pair of preschoolers in a tricycle crash

John Thomas came as close to becoming a best friend to Otis Chandler as any male during the guarded days that followed the collapse of GeoTek and his soured relationship with Jack Burke. Fifteen years Otis's junior, J. T. had little in common with J. B, outside of a jovial deference to Otis Chandler and a love of the great outdoors. He lifted weights, but he was no big game hunter. He didn't surf; in fact, the first time Otis took him out on a board, J. T. nearly drowned. J. T. was no Deke. He knew nothing about fraternities. Forget about Stanford; J. T. had barely graduated from high school back in his native Michigan. And although he knew "Oats" lived in a big house up in snooty San Marino, J. T. had no idea for the first year that they palled around together that his playmate published the *Los Angeles Times*.

"I was so ignorant I didn't know what a publisher was," J. T. recalled. "Oats said, 'Well, I kind of run the newspaper.' Okay, I run the back of the Porsche store and you run the newspaper. So we're even."

Except to catch up on the speed trials at Ontario or Riverside Raceway, J. T. hardly even picked up a newspaper. Only later, when he learned who Otis Chandler really was, did J. T. also understand that high-speed auto racing Meccas like

Riverside Raceway at which J. T. had worshiped every weekend since coming to California existed in part because Otis wanted them to exist. Since he began wielding his influence at Times Mirror Square in 1960, Otis had pushed for charity races and other *Times*-sponsored events at Riverside Raceway to subsidize auto sports against the encroaching megalopolis and its attendant suburban hatred of dust and high-octane noise.

"I would sit in the stands in the VIP tower at Riverside and watch all the great drivers go by and say, 'Oh, I can do that,'" said Otis. "They don't lift weights. They don't work out. They're not athletes."

Not so, said J. T. He encouraged Otis to put his prejudices away and see for himself how tough it was to handle a race car. For the first few years after they discovered their shared passion, J. T. watched from the pits while Otis got down on the track with his growing collection of Porsches and lapped at speeds that approached 190 mph on the straightaway. J. T., who had several years' experience on the track, taught what he knew to his new best friend. When Otis had satisfied his lust for speed, he would turn over one of his steeds to a salivating J. T. as if he were his loyal squire and let him pilot the high-strung machine around the track for awhile. It was a feudal relationship, worthy of Lancelot and the guy who got to carry his sword, but J. T. saw his friendship with Otis Chandler as a meeting of equals on the racetrack. It took Otis's purchase of the 917K to spell out the difference in their castes.

The 12-cylinder Porsche 917K top-ended at 242 mph. Only fifty-two were ever made and they took on legendary status after actor Steve McQueen guided the wicked vehicle through the 1971 movie *Le Mans,* a bona fide clinker about the lives and loves of the single-minded death jockeys of the international racing circuit. Despite being universally panned by critics and audience alike, the movie became a cult classic among race car enthusiasts because of the star quality of the 917K, not the wooden talent of McQueen.

Otis described the 917K as "a 113-pound tub with a little fiber glass around a 550 horsepower motor," balanced on four wheels and conceived in the minds of Bavarian engineers to move, always to move. Even at rest, it resembled a Roman candle begging to be ignited. For those racing purists who believed that only the Italians could produce a truly remarkable racing machine with their Ferraris and their Maseratis, the Porsche 917K was an "in-your-face kind of car," said Otis. Unlike everything else on the track, which tended to sound like a jet engine as it roared by, the 917K had a whining purr, like the high-decibel keen of a banshee.

"The K had a magic noise, and it was a difficult car to drive," Otis said with breathtaking understatement.

That didn't keep Otis from trying. He paid $64,000 for his super-charged Flexi-Racer and rang up J. T. to boast. It was like the day after Christmas and

he'd found a derailleur beneath the tree while his best friend's family couldn't even afford a tree. The normally garrulous John Thomas was struck dumb. He loved Otis Chandler like an older brother, but he'd never before envied anything that he owned. J. T. drooled into the receiver. He couldn't see past the gleam of the machine to the "gotcha" Schadenfreude that occasionally peeked through Otis's grand self-image and exposed the insecure little rich kid underneath.

Owning such a machine and driving it, however, were two different things. J. T. tried to explain to Otis that he had just corralled a quarter horse, not "My Friend Flicka." But Otis would have none of it. He told J. T. he would flaunt his new toy at Ontario.

"Otis, don't do it," J. T. warned. "You could kill yourself with this car. It's a fast car."

Otis blew him off. Alan Johnson, a seasoned racing veteran who had written a biography of legendary race car driver Mark Donahue, had talked him through it, he said. Otis was ready to do a little showboating. After just a few laps, the car wrenched away from him and spun out like a pinwheel. Otis crawled from the Porsche mortified but unhurt.

"I don't want you to get in that car again," J. T. scolded. "You're going to Bondurant."

Former driver Bob Bondurant had opened his driving school at Sear Point north of San Francisco and he catered mostly to young go-carters and drag strip zealots with a few races beneath their belts. His older wannabes were usually of the Fortune 500 executive stripe who had set aside their speed lust for business school and now, when it was too late to get serious about it, hankered at least to drive a land rocket a few times, usually in some relatively safe celebrity pro-am race. Bondurant training was expensive, intensive, and designed to give seasoned amateurs a taste of the big time while teaching them how best to avoid killing themselves. Otis and his son Michael enrolled for the five-day course.

Buff objected. She was less concerned with Otis's safety than she was the hundreds of orphans he'd leave behind.

"My mother hated the car racing when she found out," said Otis. "She didn't like that at all. She thought that was something I shouldn't do because so many people were dependent upon me, and she was probably right."

If he'd been assigned by the city desk to write his own obit, Otis conceded to his mother, he would have written that he'd been very selfish and didn't think of all the people who depended upon him, from his family to the men and women of Times Mirror.

"I don't want you racing," Buff chided. "You're being selfish."

But Otis didn't care. For once, he forgot about who he was and what he represented and did it anyway, changing his entire life in the process. The unexpected

happened, beginning with his week at Bondurant. The Chandlers' instructor called Michael a natural-born driver, the incipient champion that Otis was now far too long in the tooth ever to become. Otis beamed. Whatever connection he'd felt before with his youngest son was now solidified.

"He went from Bondurant to Mini Indy to Ontario and next year, to Indy," Otis said proudly, marking off the milestones of Michael's meteoric racing career. "It was a very fast progression. I'm not sure in retrospect it was smart on either of our parts."

He couldn't let his son better him, though, and he refused to let Buff guilt him into abandoning his newest reckless passion. The single-passenger 917K³ was still out of the question, but the 917-30 was a larger, more powerful, yet slightly more conventional coffin that seated two comfortably and drove even faster; it was Otis's drug of choice over the next couple of years.

Just to see how much friction and gravity his 1,100 horses could defy and to satisfy his craving for speed, Otis frequently rented the Riverside Raceway for a weekend. Once, he took Missy for a spin at Riverside to give her a taste of what he and Michael had been up to.

"She got out and vomited and almost passed out," he remembered. "Her eyes were going round 'n round."

After several months of practice and local competition, J. T. told Otis in early 1978 that he was now ready for his first professional race: an annual six-hour endurance event held each summer at Watkins Glen in western New York State. At fifty, J. T. reasoned, Otis was too old for the top-end speed sprints that attracted most race fans, intent on seeing carnage. But like a marathon that can be run as a test of stamina as well as speed at almost any age, the Watkin's Glen race would satisfy Otis the exhibitionist and Otis the speed junkie, as well as fire up his eternal competitive edge.

Racing is expensive, however, and Otis didn't want to foot the entire bill. On the strength of his name and age, he sought sponsors he thought might enjoy the cachet of attaching their product name to Otis Chandler's coattails. He found such a person in Bill Tilly, one of his old hunting pals who'd recently launched an international division of the hugely successful Shakey's pizza chain. If he could slap the Shakey's International logo across Chandler's Porsche for all to see, Tilly told him he was willing to put up $10,000 in racing money. Otis agreed. To seal the deal, Tilly dispatched his vice president for marketing to Times Mirror Square with the necessary papers.

Her name was Bettina Whitaker, and Otis liked her just fine. She didn't say much, and when she did speak, it was in muted tones. That was a perception that rang in his ears long after she'd gone: muted tones.

She was tall for a woman, and slender. She was not ravishing, but certainly at-

tractive; she showed an intense reserve that could easily be mistaken for a lack of interest. Otis made no such mistake, focusing intuitively on her keen ability to be an active listener. He watched her think before she spoke, eyes darting but never evasive. She merely needed, and took, an extra moment to formulate her thought before speaking, and Otis liked that. He found himself unconsciously testing her for inauthenticity, and coming up blank every time. She was . . . interesting.

From where Bettina sat, Otis Chandler was a hunk. By fifty, most men had already gone to seed or were well on their way, hairlines receding as waistlines ballooned. But here was as fit a specimen of the male persuasion as the twice-divorced and doubly dubious Ms. Whitaker had ever seen. If she hadn't known from the press release pitch that Tilly had handed her before she left that this was a fifty-year-old publisher who was entering the Watkins Glen race, she would likely have guessed him to be more in the forty range, five years older than she was. He was . . . intriguing.

Of course, there were framed photos of family scattered throughout his office. Sons here. Daughters there. Blonde, vivacious wife in the middle somewhere. He had obviously been spoken for long ago. Bettina shrugged it off. She was too smart and too wary to be smitten with a married man. Besides, she had just emerged from her own bad relationship back in Colorado, where she had convinced herself once again that she'd found Mr. Right only to discover within weeks that he was Mr. Uh-uh, and spent the next two years trying to get out of a bad contract.

She'd earned her marketing degree in the meantime, joined Shakey's International, and was now trotting the globe from Hong Kong to Europe, a free soul at last. She'd grown pleasantly accustomed to living out of a hotel suite and a suitcase, being her own boss for a change, with neither an immediate manager nor a smothering mate around to dictate her next move.

Still, when their business was finished and Otis offhandedly invited her down to the Ontario Speedway to take a spin in the new Porsche 935 that she and Bill Tilly were now sponsoring, Bettina didn't hesitate. Her usual polite reserve went right out the sixth floor window. On the appointed weekend, she was there with her crash helmet on.

"I remember that day," said Otis. "John took her around and tried to scare the shit out of her, and she got out and said, 'What's the big deal?'"

This wasn't ersatz bravado performed for Otis's benefit. This woman really liked speed and refused to put on any swooning airs for J. T. or anyone else. What you saw was what you got in Bettina Whitaker, and what you got was a twice-burned tomboy with tensile strength and a serious, probing nature. Down a little deeper, there might be a well-masked feminine fragility and deeper still, a hard core of insecurity tinged with New Age mysticism.

On the surface, though, she seemed tough. Not hard. Tough.

When she flew into Watkins Glen to look after Shakey's interests during race weekend, Otis met her at the airport. He was glowing and impulsively kissed her on the cheek.

"I couldn't figure out why I did that 'cause I hadn't really ever talked to her, you know," he said later. "Just that one meeting in my office."

He assumed it was just general elation because all three of his sons had shown up for the race and Missy had not. Norman, Harry, and Michael joined the pit crew, making the race a real family affair. Had Missy come to New York for the race, she would have been directing everything, said Otis. The boys would have had to straighten up, comb their hair, and watch their manners, even though they were all grown men. And Otis would have fumed, might even have told her to knock it off, but she would have ignored him and the damage would have been done.

Without Missy, the Chandler men could focus on some serious fun. Harry took the family adventure one step further by bringing along a camera to shoot a documentary of the event. He got his father's goat by repeatedly referring to Otis on the soundtrack as "a fifty-year-old grandfather," a mordant reference to the grandson that Norman and his new wife, Jane, had recently given him. Harry later sold a thirty-minute version of the documentary to cable television so that the world could watch grandpa Otis hauling ass around the track. For the next five years, strangers and acquaintances alike would walk up grinning and address him as grandpa.

They were a close and merry band, all training together down at the track, rooming at the same motel, and eating together at breakfast, lunch, and dinner. Bettina joined in easily with J. T. and the Chandler boys. All three of his sons later remarked that it was the best time that any of them could remember having with their absentee father: a belated opportunity to play with Pop long after their Golden Arrow Camp days had faded into memory.

"And Bettina and I went out after dinner," said Otis. "It stayed light late in the summer in that part of the country, and we just began to talk and talk about goals. She'd never of course associated with anyone like me, in my position, and she seemed to be very comfortable and I was comfortable.

"And I said to myself, you know, 'This is the first woman I've ever met who I think could be a friend. A good friend.' There was nothing romantic about it. And we did this every night. We just talked and walked around the parking lot and the boys saw us and it didn't raise any flags with them, 'cause there was nothing to raise."

Race day came and so did the rains. Otis started out on a wet track and witnessed crash after crash, but steered himself through. What time he may have

lost, J. T. picked up when it was his turn. The sun came out and dried the track, and Otis and J. T. continued to swap turns at each pit stop, edging up further and further in the pack. Otis couldn't believe it. He was outperforming professionals half his age on one of the toughest, best-known tracks in America. As the last laps were clocked, he and J. T. went from twelfth to third place. Had it been a horse race, they would have finished in the money, and that was more than good enough for Otis. To J. T., it was nothing short of a miracle.

It was a day full of Chandler miracles, as it turned out. Phlegmatic Norman, serious Harry, and dyslectic Michael had all set aside their sibling rivalry to put their dad in the winner's circle. Otis felt like a kid again. The cares of GeoTek, his bickering shirt-tail relatives, and Missy: All were vanquished, and so was the stabbing pain in his bowels, which had vanished the moment he set foot in Watkins Glen.

But the biggest miracle of all that weekend had to catch a plane for Japan, and did not presume to peck Otis on the cheek as she left. Bettina had another marketing assignment for Shakey's and couldn't dally. There was no mistaking her parting smile, though.

Otis caught a ride back to L.A. on a private jet and grappled with his thoughts all the way home. Other passengers slapped his shoulder and wished him well. Otis remained gracious and accepted his congratulations tersely and declined to engage in lengthy dialogue. He'd barely had time to savor his victory. His mind was elsewhere.

"I thought, 'I want to *see* that person again! I just *like* her,'" he said, wrestling with feelings that caught him on his lantern jaw like a sucker punch.

But before the plane touched down at LAX, he was in control again. He had to remember who he was, what he represented. And what was that, exactly?

The odd thing was, Missy hadn't entered into the equation at all. It was as if she were as absent from his thoughts as she had been absent in person from his triumph at Watkins Glen. The evidence of her existence was certainly there, in the persons of Norman, Harry, and Michael. But Missy wasn't. She chose not to be. Her willful absence had created a void that sucked away the residue of twenty-eight years of marriage in the blink of an eye, with no explanation as to how or why.

The idea that he might leave his wife had never entered Otis's head. It didn't even crystallize as a thought. Only Bettina occupied his thoughts as his plane touched down, and all he could see was her face. None of it made much sense. Once again, his mother had been right: Auto racing was dangerous.

"Bettina and I just seemed to fit," said Otis. "We just seemed to be on the same page."

There had been no talk about the newspaper business or what it was like to be rich and famous. Reflecting on their conversations, he couldn't even remember talking that much about himself. She certainly knew who he was, but that mattered less than the things they believed in and what they each hoped to accomplish with the rest of their lives.

"It was just that, boy, this was really a nice person," he said, trying hard to articulate what had happened to him. "I really liked being around her. She made me feel good. It was very comfortable, very surprising, very natural. I felt like I'd known her, or should have known her, for years."

He settled back into his routine at the *Times* and impatiently waited for Bettina to call; it would be unseemly for a Prince of Publishing to pick up the phone himself. As the days passed into weeks, he despaired that she might not have felt what he felt, that the magic weekend had been a fluke. His intestines once more caught fire.

Then, one day in the autumn of the same year, Donna Swayze buzzed him on his intercom.

There was a Ms. Bettina Whitaker on the line. Did he want to speak with her?

CHAPTER 22

Several weeks passed before she called again, but by then, Otis had learned far more about Bettina Whitaker.

It turned out she was a California girl, even though she had spent half her life outside the state. She had been born in Pasadena while her parents were vacationing there in 1941, but she grew up in Oklahoma, where her mother and father were schoolteachers. Raised in the fundamentalist Church of the Nazarene, she learned that a woman's role was one of service: to her family, to her God, and to her man. Her family was so devout that her brother, Paul, became a Nazarene missionary. When she was only eighteen, Bettina married a budding Nazarene minister; the newlyweds moved to Pasadena where Bettina finished school and had lived, off and on, ever since.

She'd been a teacher for several years, working with black kids in one of Pasadena's poorer neighborhoods, but she had no children herself. She and her husband tried mightily, but Bettina learned years after the divorce that the infertility problem was probably hers. When she discovered ten years into the mar-

riage that her Nazarene husband had a girlfriend who might be better equipped to bear children, Bettina divorced him and his church.

In the disillusioning years that followed, she left teaching, sold life insurance, moved to Colorado, remarried briefly, quit that marriage too, and moved to Arizona to study marketing. Shakey's International was the first job she'd had in years that she really loved, and now it seemed that it, too, was over.

The money men behind Shakey's International, Texas billionaires Herbert and Bunker Hunt, wanted to move their operation to Dallas and demanded that Bettina move too. But she'd grown to like L.A. and didn't want to go. She turned to her new amigo at the *Los Angeles Times* for career guidance.

"I really don't think I want to go to Dallas 'cause I like Southern California," she told Otis. "I'm going to have to leave the company and find other work."

"Why don't you come down and be interviewed by our personnel department and take the test?" he asked. "Maybe there's something where we could use your marketing skills in the *Times*."

Within weeks, she was in charge of the circulation department's telephone sales division.

"They're the boiler rooms, where we have solicitors set up who call to see if you'll take the paper," Otis explained.

He and Bettina ran into each other in the hallways. They lunched from time to time. Otis knew where she parked her car in the executive garage and where her house was located in Pasadena. Like millions of couples who had gone before them over the centuries, from Dante's Paulo and Francesca to Hollywood's Liz and Eddie, they believed themselves to be excruciatingly discreet. No one, they told themselves, really knew.

"Everyone knew," said stenographer Kathy Jenkins, who had recently joined the Times Mirror secretarial pool, central repository for all *Times* gossip circa 1978. A Code Red office APB vibrated across the *Times* grapevine: deal gingerly with Bettina Whitaker. She's the publisher's new girlfriend.

It was no secret to anyone who knew the Chandlers that Otis and Missy had grown apart, or that Missy had become a grand embarrassment to the publisher on more than one occasion. Missy's propensity to refer to herself in even the slightest social or business context as "*Mrs.* Otis Chandler" raked over Otis's low-profile persona like acrylic nails on a windowpane. Had she and her husband not grown so dangerously distant from each other, Missy would have known something was up just as every savvy secretary at the *Times* knew. But she did not. Over the next year, it was business as usual to Mrs. Otis Chandler, both literally, at her urban planning headquarters in Pasadena, and figuratively, at the Chandlers' San Marino compound.

Otis rationalized his behavior. He was not happily married, and hadn't been for a long time. He kept finding common ground with Bettina where it had eroded over the years with Missy, or had never been there at all.

"She's the opposite of Missy," he said. "She's smarter than Missy. She's not wealthy. She has education but she doesn't have the advantages Missy had growing up. I never met and talked to a woman who was so different than Missy, and it just seemed to be the right moment and the right time. It wasn't initially at all sexual or 'I gotta jump her bones' or anything like that."

John Thomas was one of the first in whom Otis confided his affair. J. T. was single and loved to chase the ladies: an "ass man," according to Otis—although J. T. maintained that he preferred breasts to bottoms. Over beers at the pizza parlor after a day at the track, they used to rib each other as they sized up babes' haunches and compared passing breasts to pancakes, grapefruit, and casaba melons. They were guys, and that's what guys did. Guys could talk about such matters to other guys.

But Otis was just as wrong about how his racing buddy would take the news as he was about everything else that followed. The publisher of the *Los Angeles Times* showed unerring judgment about sweeping social trends and the historical impact of national and international political events, and he could even spot a demographic shift in the culture a dozen years ahead of time; but he could not see the complex fragility of a human heart.

"I'm really serious about this gal," he told J. T., and John Thomas was furious. "You're living in sin!" he shrieked.

For all their cajoling and goofing and leering, it never occurred to Otis that his booty buddy might be a born-again Christian, or that J. T. drew the line of morality at No. 6 on the commandment scale.

"He used to claim that he was taking gals out, but he didn't touch them," said Otis. "And I said, 'Ah John, come on!'"

No, said J. T. Talk was just talk. Action was evil.

Otis didn't care. He wanted what he wanted, and what he wanted now was Bettina Whitaker. Come spring of 1979, he told Missy that he was going hunting in Mexico.

Instead, Otis took his Honda and headed in the opposite direction; Bettina was straddled across the back, her arms wrapped tight around his waist. They buzzed up the California coastline, stopping on the way back at Ventana, an upscale but quiet little rendezvous spot near the spectacular sea cliff and redwood enclave of Big Sur. They thought they'd made their tryst way off the beaten track.

"We were down there having a drink outside, the two of us, and I was hoping no one would know me and no one would see me," said Otis. "I wouldn't know

how to explain it to Missy. . . . I didn't go with a mustache or a disguise or all of that, but I was wishing I had."

Across the deck as the sun set in the Pacific, he spotted a group at a table he thought he knew. They were looking in his and Bettina's direction.

"Uh-oh," he said. A few moments later, one of them approached.

"My friends and I are having dinner and we have never met you, but we are convinced that you are Otis Chandler," said the man.

Otis looked at him as blankly as he could and smiled.

"No, I'm not," he said. "And who is that?"

"He's a famous publisher," said the man.

"Never heard of him," said Otis. "No, you've got the wrong guy."[1]

If he was not unnerved enough by the following morning, the mystery that unfolded as he and Bettina rode south along narrow, cliff-hugging state Highway 1 was a 7.5 on the Richter scale.

"It was a foggy morning, nobody on the road," Otis remembered. "We stopped at a little shop to look at some art."

There were others inside the gallery where novelist and artist Henry Miller's work was on display, but no one Otis or Bettina recognized. They bought nothing and, after five minutes, had seen enough. They put their helmets back on, climbed aboard the bike, and headed down the road. About ten minutes later, they came up behind a camper truck and had to wait for a clear, straight section of highway before they could safely pass on the left. As they gunned past the camper, Bettina stared in disbelief at the side window of the camper and tapped Otis on the shoulder. The couple driving the truck stared straight ahead, oblivious to Otis or Bettina, but a young boy inside the camper shell held up a hand-lettered cardboard sign at the window that said, simply, "Hi, Otis!"

"It wasn't funny at the time," said Otis. "It was creepy."

They gunned the motorcycle and left the camper behind. Otis never found out who had recognized him or why he had been greeted so boldly yet so anonymously at such a precarious crisis point in his life.

FIFTY YEARS AFTER the disastrous collapse of William Mulholland's St. Francis Dam, the *Los Angeles Times* won its tenth Pulitzer for a series on shoddy and unsafe dams in the United States, reported by national correspondent Gaylord Shaw.

The award represented yet another triumph for the complete daily news magazine that Bill Thomas had been developing since the first day he took the editor's reins from Nick Williams. The launch of "Business" in 1978 marked a further step in that direction and it also fattened the fattest paper in America with yet an-

other regular section. *Times* subscribers might not read even a fraction of the paper, but there was something in it every day for everyone: Sports, Entertainment, Science, Food, Health.

No longer in a position where it had to prove itself to East Coast elitists,[2] the *Times* of Bill Thomas and Otis Chandler delivered an intense, thorough, and frequently surprising brand of daily journalism rarely matched by any other newspaper in the country. Two succeeding subscription campaigns were designed around the accurate, if arguably pretentious slogan, "Stay on Top of the World" followed by, "A Special Kind of Journalism."

According to Thomas, the *Times* had evolved into a daily magazine because the television nation that the late Norman Chandler predicted back in 1950 had, indeed, come to pass. The *Times'* real competition was no longer other newspapers; it now had to offer something on its front page, every day, that television could not deliver. Hence, *Times* readers were treated to some of the weirdest, yet most enticing "news" stories ever to grace a front page:

- the comeback of Caspian caviar in Baku, Azerbaijan;
- Hugh Hefner's addiction to Pepsi and its subsequent damage to his few remaining teeth;
- a day in the life of the human residents of North Africa's largest dung heap;
- in-depth coverage of the annual One Gallus Fox Hunt outside of Eagleville, Tennessee;
- the impact of *xiuri,* the traditional Mandarin midday nap, on the burgeoning Chinese economy; and
- a visit with the underground residents of MacArthur Park who lived, homeless, in caves within a stone's throw of the site of General Otis's beloved Bivouac.

The *Times* no longer merely informed and entertained. On its best days, it could astonish as well as confound its readers with oddball, dramatic, and mundane esoterica from every corner of the globe, as well as occasionally expose scandal and corruption at home. The *Times* had evolved into that rarity of American journalism: a reporter's newspaper, where writers, not editors, dictated each day's content. No newspaper since the collapse of the *National Observer* delivered such an eclectic daily melange of genuinely intriguing information written by the finest reporters money could buy.

During the last half of the 1970s, Bill Thomas hired radical-chic journalist Robert Scheer at a then-princely annual salary of $50,000. Scheer had vaulted to national prominence for his *Playboy* magazine exposé of sacrosanct President-

elect Jimmy Carter's "lust in his heart." Scheer's arrival at Times Mirror Square brought jealous sneers from lower-paid reporters and suspicious stares from the few remaining right-wingers who still clung on from the Norman Chandler era. But Scheer soon justified his fat *Times* paycheck with a much-praised and highly critical series on the Jews of L.A. The pieces inflamed several of Buff's Music Center favorites, including financier Sidney Mark Taper, MCA chairman Lew Wasserman, and Otis's personal attorney, Democratic Party kingpin Paul Ziffren.

"Lew Wasserman yelled at me in public," Scheer recalled, after the series had publicly linked the aging movie mogul to Chicago mob lawyer Sidney Korshak.

Zbigniew Brzezinski, President Carter's national security adviser, also squawked about a Scheer profile, prompting Otis to order a reprint of the article so that it could be distributed to heads of state around the world. When former congressman, CIA chief, and soon-to-be vice president George Herbert Bush joined in the chorus of angry power brokers who had suffered from Scheer's poison pen, Otis called Scheer into his office.

"George is a very old friend of mine," said Otis.

Scheer offered to resign.

"No, I think you captured him just right," Otis said.

In another groundbreaking move, Thomas named David Shaw, an egocentric young firebrand whom he'd hired away from the nearby *Long Beach Press-Telegram*, to be the *Times'* first in-house media critic. Shaw had carte blanche to dissect and publicly censure the work of any reporter or newspaper in the world, including and especially the *Times*. Shaw answered only to Thomas, and regularly pissed off colleagues with his effete diatribes against the *Times'* weak local news coverage and uneven op-ed pages.

Thomas also dispatched two of his best city desk reporters, George Reasons and Mike Goodman, to investigate charges that the executive hierarchy of that same *Long Beach Press-Telegram* where he'd found David Shaw worked behind the scenes as the unelected dictators who ran Los Angeles County's second-largest city. According to Goodman and Reasons's findings, the *Press-Telegram's* biased news coverage and editorial favoritism—fostered by Sam Cameron, the paper's general manager, and carried out by Don Ohl, editorial page editor— amounted to nothing less than monopolistic control of Long Beach City Hall.

Although the irony of the *Times'* outrage seemed lost on its readership, Goodman and Reasons won several national awards for their "Government by Newspaper" series, and forced an overhaul of the cozy relations between the *Press-Telegram* and the city of Long Beach. But there was no similar review in the *Times'* pages by Shaw, Reasons, or Goodman of a century of equally cozy relations among the *Times,* the Chandler family, and the elected officials who ran Los

Stanford senior Otis Chandler breaks several shot put records during 1950 track competition. (Photo from the Otis Chandler Collection.)

Practicing his discus throw, Otis strikes the pose of a Greek god. (Photo from the Otis Chandler Collection.)

Buff Chandler greeting Vice President Richard Nixon at the Hollywood Bowl, 1955. (Photo courtesy of Music Center.)

Buff Chandler, circa 1965, at the unveiling of her portrait, permanently on display in the Founders Room of the Los Angeles County Music Center. (Photo courtesy of Music Center.)

Norman Chandler, with Buff seated in her Mercedes, on the front lawn of Los Tiempos, 1968. (Fred Lyon-Rapho Guillumette.)

Michael, Missy, and Otis Chandler,
early 1960s. (Photo from the
Otis Chandler Collection.)

Harry, Cathleen, Otis, Michael, and Missy
Chandler on a camping trip, early 1960s.
(Photo from the Otis Chandler Collection.)

Otis racing his boys Harry and Norman, early 1960s.
(Photo from the Otis Chandler Collection.)

Otis Chandler, newly named fourth publisher of the *Los Angeles Times,* chats with Walt Disney, left, and Bob Hope during a 1960 Olympic Games fund raiser event. (Photo from the Otis Chandler Collection.)

Otis Chandler reviewing his *Times*, 1962. (Photo from the Otis Chandler Collection.)

Otis Chandler chats with former Vice President Hubert Humphrey, 1970. (Photo from the Otis Chandler Collection.)

Otis, First Lady Rosalyn and President Jimmy Carter, circa 1977. (Photo from the Otis Chandler Collection.)

Chandler family Christmas card, 1977. From left, Harry, Missy, Michael, Cathleen, Carolyn, Norman, and Norman's wife Jane. Seated with Otis in the Porsche is one-year-old Otis Yeager Chandler, Otis and Missy's first grandchild. (Photo from the Otis Chandler Collection.)

Otis suits up with racing pal John Thomas. (Photo courtesy John Thomas.)

Otis on his 1981 wedding day with bride Bettina Whittaker Chandler, Otis's second and current wife. (Photo from the Otis Chandler Collection.)

Otis jokes with former President Richard Nixon at a 1984 newspaper editors convention. (UPI/Bettman.)

CBS legend Walter Cronkite presents press freedom award to Otis Chandler, 1986. (Photo from the Otis Chandler Collection.)

Otis entertains England's Prince Philip in the Times Mirror executive suite circa 1993. The Prince chaired World Wildlife International and Otis was one of his board members. (Photo from the Otis Chandler Collection.)

Bettina and Otis, and Chandler's prized polar bear, in front of the fireplace at the Bend, Oregon, ranch, circa 1997. (Photo from the Otis Chandler Collection.)

Otis and his Labrador, Mack. (Art Streiber.)

Otis in full beard that grated on the prim sensibilities of Buff Chandler. (Timothy Rue/Corbis.)

Angeles City Hall, the County Board of Supervisors or, indeed, the southern half of the state of California.

Well into his second term, the Chandler-supported mayor Tom Bradley rarely read a discouraging word in the *Times*. Mayor Bradley and Police Chief Daryl Gates, who seldom agreed with the mayor on most other issues, were far more likely to take issue with the reporting of the newly revitalized *Herald-Examiner*, which began operating in 1978 under the direction of a shrewd *Times* expatriate.

Jim Bellows, the *Times'* former associate editor, had moved to Washington, D.C., for most of the 1970s to oversee what turned out to be the final days of the *Washington Star*. But in 1978, when he was offered an opportunity to resurrect the *Herald-Examiner* and go head-to-head with his old bosses at the *Times*, Bellows gleefully returned to L.A. He took the *Herald-Examiner* editor's job and began building a scrappy team of young, relatively inexperienced but talented reporters who managed to scoop the *Times* regularly, especially on local news stories.

Perhaps the most glaring case of the *Times'* dropping the ball came on January 3, 1979, when a pair of LAPD officers, one white, one black, emptied their service revolvers into a thirty-nine-year-old black South Central resident named Eulia Love. The *Times* treated the shooting as routine: a single paragraph in a local news roundup. Love was, after all, a crazed black woman who had worked herself up over an unpaid gas bill and brandished a kitchen knife at two armed police officers. End of story.

Bellows saw much larger issues. He clipped the *Times* paragraph and handed it to his city editor. Sure enough, his reporters brought back the wrenching details of a distraught mother of three whose husband had recently died of sickle-cell anemia. Eulia Love, who was raising three daughters on a monthly Social Security allotment of $680, had an unpaid gas bill that totaled $69. The gas company was threatening to cut off the gas if she didn't pay $22 of the outstanding balance. Love not only refused, she snapped. She used a shovel to attack a gas company employee who tried to shut off her meter. Two more arrived and received the same shrill, angry over-the-top treatment. When police officers arrived, the standoff with the gas company had escalated to a screaming stalemate and Eulia Love had traded in her shovel for a kitchen knife. Police told her to drop it. She did not. They fired twelve bullets, eight of which hit her, and she died on the spot.

Bellows knew his reporters couldn't beat the *Times* on overall coverage, but he could throw his limited resources into a single benchmark story like that of Eulia Love. He did so, and raised the dormant profile of the *Herald-Examiner* all over the city. Before the muscle-bound *Times* could recover from its initial dismissive paragraph, the *Herald-Examiner*'s reporters had turned the Eulia Love story into

a municipal morality tale, replete with unambiguous soap opera overtones, and perfectly suited to the limited attention span of local television news audiences. Overnight, the combined punch of the *Herald-Examiner* and the L.A. affiliates of ABC, CBS, and NBC had turned Eulia Love into far more than a story of black versus white, poor versus powerful, or even inner city despair versus police misconduct. Eulia Love epitomized the inability and/or reluctance of the almighty *Los Angeles Times* to bring its newly found global focus back home to the nagging life-and-death issues of the very city it was supposed to serve first.

Bill Thomas's reporters played catch-up and covered the ensuing inquiries into Eulia Love's death, including Chief Gates's abject apology for his officers' overreaction and Mayor Bradley's indignant response to the LAPD's too-little-too-late attention to the problem of excessive force. But the damage to the *Times'* reputation had been done. The urban-and-suburban dilemma first fanned into bonfire proportions during the 1960s had not disappeared, and the *Times'* indifference remained an integral part of the problem. Its editors really did seem to care more about covering the world than Watts.

Economically, Times Mirror's reach was beginning to look limitless. The *Times* not only had doubled the size of its Orange County plant but had begun a $56.8-million upgrade that would end the century-old letterpress process and replace it with cleaner, cheaper, and more efficient offset printing. Using the Orange County edition's ongoing war with the *Orange County Register* as a model, the *Times* stretched farther into San Diego County, going head-to-head with the *San Diego Union & Tribune*. Similarly, the *Times'* San Fernando Valley section was renamed "Valley" to reflect expansion into the neighboring Conejo, Simi, Santa Clarita, and Antelope Valleys, where Harry Chandler's primordial vision of endless suburban sprawl now extended as far as one hundred miles from Los Angeles Civic Center and the *Times'* home base at Times Mirror Square. The *Times* planned yet another expansion before decade's end: a $215-million satellite plant in the San Fernando Valley to produce a separate Valley edition, similar to the *Times'* Orange County edition.

Curiously, the farther it moved away from its core audience, the less *Times'* power and might translated into automatic success. Instead of being welcomed, its high-quality presence in Orange County, San Diego, the San Fernando Valley, and beyond provoked an unanticipated reaction. Mediocre newspapers in outlying areas became markedly better, just to keep up with the *Times*, yet managed to use their hometown advantage to keep the Times Mirror superpower at bay. Thus, the *Register* beefed up its staff and grew nearly as ad-fat as the *Times*; the *San Diego Union & Tribune* increased its pay scale and its own countywide circulation and advertising reach; and a family-owned throwaway shopper in the San Fernando Valley called the *Valley New & Green Sheet* transformed itself into the

Los Angeles Daily News and, over the next ten years, seesawed with the *Orlando Sentinel* as the fastest-growing newspaper in the United States.

The strengthened suburban dailies, as well as television and the renewed vigor at Hearst's *Herald-Examiner,* posed a host of threats to the primacy of the *Times,* which now entered a new phase in its existence. The newspaper would soon begin experimenting with Ohio-based CompuServe in sending electronic editions of the *Times* to computer subscribers. Yet, as General Otis's four-sheet was about to celebrate its one hundredth birthday, new challenges arose that could not always be met by throwing money, technology, or nonunion labor into the breach. His great-grandson and namesake may have understood this better than anyone else, but Otis Chandler was not planning to be around to meet those challenges; at least, not as publisher.

"My spastic colon was bothering me night and day," Otis remembered. "I wasn't sleeping very well. I was continuing my weight-lifting and my exercise, which is probably what kept me going and saved my life. It got rid of some stress."

As often as once a week, he was off to New York, Chicago, or Washington for meetings or for making speeches. He spent half his life running on adrenaline and the other half recovering from exhaustion. Even his vacations were adventures. He'd return from flying into Afghanistan or trekking through the Sahara exhilarated, but never refreshed.

"I really was a part-time publisher the last several years in the 70s, as vice chairman of corporate, and that's not good," he said. "I was frankly wearing out with all of the jobs I was doing for the company simultaneously. I was also going to the family meetings and having to deal with difficult differences of opinion there as to what they wanted for the *Times* versus the way the *Times* was being run."

Looking to his peers in the newspaper world, he saw diminishing returns among those who were active publishers beyond two decades.

"I was looking at Punch Sulzberger. I was looking at Kay Graham and some others who, to me, were holding onto the position of publisher too long," he said. "Not that they had washed out or burned out, but they needed to move on. Give someone else a chance."

Norm Brant Chandler came to work at the *Times* in 1976; he didn't begin at the bottom as Otis had, but he did start out somewhere in the lower half of the company.

"What he really wanted to be was a surf bum," said his new bride, Jane Yeager Chandler. "His passion was surfing and if he could have figured out a way to make a living at it, I think that's what he would have done."

Still, like his father, Norm loved the sight, sound, and sweat of the pressroom. He felt ink coursing through his veins, and said as much. After a fling with off-road vehicle racing and his youthful search for the perfect wave, Norm Chandler married, gave Otis his first grandson, and decided to settle down in the family business.

"It's my career goal," Norm told Louise Sweeney of the *Christian Science Monitor,* who had been assigned in 1980 to write a profile on his famous father. "I'm going for it, in California lingo."

But Otis wasn't so sure that Norm had the right stuff. His eldest son was not particularly outgoing or resilient or aggressive. He hadn't been president of a fraternity or a senior class officer; indeed, he hadn't held any leadership positions at all during his college or prep school years. He was good-natured, but overly pensive and perhaps even a little introverted. Otis was incessantly making and re-making five-year plans, driving goals far out ahead of him like golf balls on a long fairway, but Norm putted from day to day with absolute faith that everything would turn out all right in the end.

He couldn't even make a decision about which college to attend. He started at Yale, but found no surf in New Haven; he dropped out and enrolled the following year at Stanford, where waves were breaking year-round just a forty-five-minute drive away in Santa Cruz. During summer break, Norm had never trekked back to L.A. to lift stereo plates in the pressroom. Instead, he traveled to Europe as a *Times* "junior correspondent," returning in the fall with photos that he exhibited at Stanford.

The Air Force didn't await him upon graduation either. Like most young men of his generation, Norm Chandler had prayed for and received a high enough lottery number that there was to be no Vietnam in his future. Neither he nor his younger brother Harry, who graduated from Stanford at the same time, trained as officers or acted as cocaptains of a military track team. For Harry, who planned a career in Hollywood as a filmmaker, leadership training didn't matter all that much. He had once thought about the possibility of succeeding his father as *Times* publisher, but discarded the idea when Norm made his "go for it" declaration.

"Norm always had a sense of entitlement," said Harry.

Norm wanted and deserved a shot at the publisher's suite. His mother had told him so. But his father cautioned him with the same admonition that his own father had given Otis when he, too, set out on his *Times* executive training program: There were no guarantees. It might not happen. Norm said he understood.

"So I set up a training program for him," said Otis. "I sent him back to Connecticut and he worked on the Stamford and Greenwich papers for a couple of years. Then we set up a training program at the *Times* for him."

Norm sold advertising and read balance sheets, compared circulation figures and studied type fonts, but where Otis Chandler's *Times* trainee son shone the brightest was as a general assignment reporter.

"Norman was a sweet, generous, smart, and genuinely self-effacing boy," recalled *Times* national correspondent Bella Stumbo, one of the newspaper's bona fide star reporters in the late 1970s and early 1980s.

David Rosenzweig, then an assistant metropolitan editor, was initially as doubtful about the publisher's son as anyone else. He recalled sending Norm out to cover a particularly peculiar and savage murder in downtown Los Angeles during his tenure on the city desk; Rosenzweig was pleasantly surprised when the young Chandler came back with a scoop.

Along with reporters from the *Herald-Examiner*, Associated Press, and every other major media outlet, Norm learned at the scene of the crime that a body had been stuffed into luggage left in a guest room at the new and pricey Bonaventure Hotel. All that police had to go on was that the victim might have had some association with Israeli organized crime. Seeing that there were few details to be had at the crime scene, Norm had the independence of mind to scout around the neighborhood for suitcase retailers. He found one a block from the hotel and asked the clerk if he had recently sold any luggage similar to the final resting place of the murder victim. Yes, indeed, he was told. Two swarthy-looking men in a big hurry. Norm got a full description of the suspects before the police even showed up. He called the city desk.

Rosenzweig was delighted, told Norm to write it up, and awarded him with his own *Times* byline. Norm beamed, but insisted that the byline read "Norman Brant," not "Norman Chandler."

It was not out of any disrespect for the family name. Norm had always looked up to Otis. Some might even say that he loved his father. Otis was "multifaceted, powerful—in more ways than one—and fatherly," Norm insisted in his *Christian Science Monitor* interview. Almost as if he were defending Otis, and trying to convince himself at the same time, he added: "He always spent enough time with us. His escape for many years was his family. . . . He taught us all to ski, surf, camp, hunt, swim—all five kids. He loved being a parent. And he's the world's most powerful surf nazi. That's a Southern California term for somebody who's into something."

Yet, for all the admiration he professed for his father, Norm used his mother's maiden name to identify himself as the author of his *Times* articles. Although he chose Brant partially to disguise the Chandler name and give him some small measure of anonymity in the corridors of Times Mirror Square, he also wanted to give a defiant nod of support to Mrs. Otis Chandler. Like so much Steuben glass

abandoned during earthquake weather along the San Andreas fault, Missy's well-planned life was about to be shattered.

———————

"MY MARRIAGE WAS AN INSTITUTION that was not supposed to be violated," said Otis. "I got that from everybody. 'Otis, you're not a free agent. You're a person that people look to and aspire to and you have good morals and you're a clean-cut guy, and you don't have the opportunity to be happily married if it turns out that you're not happily married. The marriage should continue.'"

But now, as the marriage of his second son loomed, Otis wasn't so sure. He was even a little envious of the next generation's freedom of choice.

Three years earlier, Norman and Jane had made what appeared to be a happy love match. Neither Otis nor Missy had towered over them à la Buff to dictate a proper melding of two of California's First Family fortunes. Jane was neither a Buffum nor a Brant; she was a Yeager from the déclassé suburb of Riverside. She hailed from no particular dynasty, but she was well bred and well educated. Her father headed a successful construction firm and her mother was related to the family that owned and operated the *Riverside Press-Enterprise.* Jane Yeager Chandler worked in a bank and wouldn't have known what to do with an upstairs and a downstairs maid even if she had possessed the wealth and real estate to justify hiring servants.

And now Harry's fiancée seemed equally as foreign to the Chandler tradition and just as unaffected as Jane. Denise Hardre's father was French, but her exotic heritage ended there. Her mother came from Illinois, and Denise had grown up middle class in Sacramento; she earned a degree in architecture at Harvard and took a job in L.A. after her graduation. There would be no grand church wedding for Harry and Denise, as there had been for Otis and Missy. They asked a retired judge to marry them.

In the summer of 1979, the wedding was still a few weeks away. Otis had just suffered such a caustic colon attack that he had no choice but to take time off from work. He hoped to get away from the stress in time to feel up to going to Harry's wedding.

"I was going to see if I could get rid of the pressure," he said.

Otis and Missy planned a trip to their Montana ranch, but started their vacation in Michigan to support their youngest son, Michael, in his debut as a Mini-Indy driver. As Otis sat in the bleachers and watched the cars roar by, he thought about the previous summer at Watkin's Glen. His already throbbing torso grew worse when he glanced sidelong at Missy sitting next to him.

"I began to say, you know, 'I really don't want to go to Montana and be with this woman,'" Otis remembered.

The hairline crack in the Otis-Missy bond that predated the 917K, zero population growth, GeoTek, the publisher's suite, the Catholic Church, and maybe even Mama Buff, had widened to an untraversable chasm. They barely talked, even when champagne flowed in the victory suite following Michael's triumph. Otis excused himself from the party, saying that he had to make a business call. He telephoned Bettina.

"I just wanted to hear her voice," he said.

In her *Times* role as boiler room supervisor, Bettina spoke with him warmly but with detached compassion. She understood better than Otis ever would that he was at a crossroads. As she hung up the phone, she could not divine whether the odds were now in her favor or Missy's.

A day or two passed and the Chandlers flew from Michigan to Montana. The rivers and lakes and forest and mountain vistas gave Otis's gut no respite. He thought lifting weights might help.

"I told Missy I was going down to buy some weights for the gym from a local store," he said.

On the drive back, he stopped at a pay phone. Bettina's secretary answered his call. Otis could barely contain himself as Bettina's voice came over the line. He burst into tears.

"I really love you," he said. "I really love you and want you to marry me."

"Yes," she said.

The worst, he thought, was over. He'd made his decision. All that remained was to tell his wife. He rehearsed his speech all the way back to the ranch, laying out his arguments calmly and carefully: a paragon of reason. He gave himself high marks for logic as he walked through the front door.

"Missy, you and I both know this marriage is not working," he began. "We argue all the time."

Missy stared as if she had just been slapped. Hard. He spoke. She could do nothing but listen, terror in her rapid eye movement and fever rising in her cheeks.

"We've had five wonderful children. We had twenty-eight good years. But this is not fair—not fair to you, not fair to me," he continued, caught up in the spirit of his delivery. Missy hyperventilated, tears welling.

Carolyn, who was about to celebrate her sixteenth birthday, was the only one of his children present. She heard her father speaking his unbelievable speech from the front porch and raced to the front room, rallying to her mother's side.

"I'm leaving," said Otis, as his daughter whipped by him, her own eyes as terrified as her mother's. "It's the only right thing to do."

Shocked sobs left Missy mute, so Carolyn spoke for her.

"Daddy, how could you?" Carolyn screamed as her father did an about-face and stepped to the porch and then, to his car, never looking back. "You're so *mean*!"

He told himself years later that the easy thing would have been to simply leave, to run back immediately to Bettina in L.A. But he did not run away, and took some solace in what remained of his personal honor. After driving a bit to clear his head, he returned to the ranch, only to discover that Missy's answer to his emotional body blow had been to swallow a bottle of sleeping pills.

"So I dumped her in the car took her to the nearest clinic," he recalled. "I made it in about two minutes, to have her stomach pumped, or she would've died.

"And I felt horrible, of course, about Missy almost dying, but I didn't feel horrible about what I'd done, 'cause I did it very nicely. I didn't scream at her. I didn't yell."

The cold, pinched genes handed down to him from Harry Chandler had taken over and Otis performed like a well-lubricated automaton. Whatever tears he would shed that day had already been left on the floor of a phone booth just outside of town. There were none remaining as he stood vigil at Missy's hospital bedside. There was only duty.

A few months later, he underplayed the crisis in the *Christian Science Monitor* profile, which lionized his macho exploits at the top of the page by suggesting that "if Otis Chandler hadn't existed, Ernest Hemingway would have created him."

At the rock bottom of the article, Otis was neither noble nor particularly macho. If anything, his inability to empathize shone through with glaring egocentricity.

"She and I are probably going to go through a divorce, which is very unfortunate after twenty-eight years," he told the interviewer, noticeably tensing up when she asked him about his marriage. "That's one of those awful things that's happened to me. . . . It happens to people. I never thought it would happen to me. But it's happening to me now."

"I have great regard for [Missy]. I think life is tough on marriages today. She's a career woman. . . . It's tough to combine my life and the expectations that I have for a wife and for her to have a career too. She's an urban planner, has her own architectural and urban planning firm."

But she had no husband. By the time the *Monitor* published the profile, Otis had moved into an apartment of his own.

TURMOIL IN HIS PERSONAL LIFE was certainly not reflected in Otis's *Times*.

More than 8,000 people now worked for the paper and its average weekday circulation totaled 1,043,028, second only to the *New York Daily News*. Times Mir-

ror was also second only to the Time-Life empire in assets, outlets, and global media reach. From 1968 through 1980, Times Mirror earnings and revenue had quadrupled. The company's buying spree continued in 1980 with its $95 million purchase of the *Denver Post*, and the Times Mirror board approved a new division to develop pay cable television programming.

The company was at the top of its game. Otis Chandler surveyed his dominion with satisfaction. It was time to move on.

"I didn't want to continue as publisher until death or retirement, and I don't care if I ever put on another tuxedo," he told Marshall Berges, the fawning biographer he'd selected to succeed Jim Bassett. "I wanted to spend a little more time trying to get my health back and trying to be maybe a better father to my children. I had some grandchildren by then."

It wasn't the hunting or the racing or the car collecting, he insisted. It wasn't even Bettina, although he maintained with increasing confidence that his instincts had, indeed, been bull's-eye accurate: She had been a missing element in his life, if not *the* missing element. Regardless of how fleeting or trivial, no time he spent with Bettina seemed wasted.

"He was doing a very, very good job in a job that he didn't like," recalled his oldest friend, Bob Emmet. "Giving those speeches was just a killer for him."

What was more, Otis told a family friend over dinner one evening, "My cousins are a pain in the ass."

It was a nagging din that only Otis heard constantly. Not even Missy or, now, Bettina, had ever been fully privy to the backbiting tug-of-war at Chandis Securities meetings and, increasingly, during meetings of the Times Mirror board as family members came of age and took their place as directors. The conservative carping that had been put in check in 1960 had never gone away; it was only muted as Otis's increasingly liberal newspaper joined Times Mirror's other properties in yielding higher and higher returns that produced a satisfying ring of the cash register each time the annual dividend checks were mailed.

And yet, as the next generation of Chandlers had grown up and replaced Otis's aunts and uncles as family spokespersons, most of them were more hidebound in their provincial arch-conservatism than Philip and Alberta,[3] or even filthy-rich Lady Crocker. Perhaps as a mark of belated humility, Lady Crocker had reluctantly given up her title in 1982, nine years after the death of Sir William. The pompous Lady Crocker remarried once more when she was eighty-five, this time to retired lumber baron Karl Godfrey von Platen, and was henceforth known merely as Ruth von Platen.

Otis's choice for his successor as publisher of the *Times* certainly would not have been his Aunt Ruth's choice, or the choice of most of his other relatives. Tom Johnson was a nice enough Georgia boy who did remember everybody's

name the first time he was told, a fine parlor trick to be sure; but he had the taint of LBJ about him and could never really be properly received at the von Platens' conservative compound, or at any of the other mansions of Otis's relatives.

But Tom Johnson did become the fifth publisher of the *Los Angeles Times* on April 14, 1980, succeeding Otis Chandler as the first nonfamily member to hold that position since 1882, when Jesse Yarnell, Thomas J. Caystile, and S. J. Mathes surrendered the title to Colonel Harrison G. Otis. The Colonel's great grandson and namesake did not simply turn the family newspaper over to an outsider, however. Otis Chandler ascended a new perch that he had created for himself for the express purpose of watching over the *Times* like his great-grandfather's eagle: he would become Times Mirror's editor in chief. Nevertheless, Johnson would run the *Times* from day-to-day, and do so autonomously, Otis declared.

"Tom had everything I was looking for," said Otis. "He was young, he was bright, he knew his way around Washington much better than I did."

Otis had kept his eye on Johnson since hiring him as editor to remold the *Dallas Times Herald* in 1973, and had moved him up the executive ladder swiftly. After Johnson had been publisher of the *Times Herald* for two years, Otis had brought him to L.A. in 1977, naming him president and chief operating officer of the *Times*. He'd been watching Norm's progress too, but his first son was not yet showing the proper executive bearing and, besides, it seemed far too early for Norm even to be considered. He was twenty-eight, and had been in the training program for only four years.

Meanwhile, Franklin Murphy was fast approaching his sixty-fifth birthday, mandatory retirement age as fixed by the Times Mirror board, and Otis would be stepping up to chairman. He needed a new publisher now. Otis had taken such a shine to Tom that he occasionally referred to him as the younger brother he'd never had, and Johnson just seemed a natural to step into the publisher's suite until Norm had proven himself.

Move carefully and with deliberation, Otis advised Tom, but act decisively to make the newspaper your own. Bill Thomas was a gifted editor, for example, just as Vance Stickel had served Otis well as advertising manager, and Bert Tiffany was as fine a circulation manager as the *Times* had ever had. But they were all Otis's executives: part of his team, not Johnson's.

"Don't just manage it status quo, 'cause if you don't move forward, it will start to slide backwards," Otis cautioned. "So, for God's sake, move it forward. Take what I did and then move it forward."

The transition of power climaxed the annual *Times* editorial awards banquet in 1980. Otis, wearing a tuxedo, stood at the podium to make a speech for what he hoped would be one of the last times in his life. His audience consisted of the

men and women of the *Times* that he had created. There wasn't a cousin among them; only the best of the best. They were there for the annual ritual that Otis had also initiated: to recognize the finest journalism that the newspaper had produced the previous year.

Otis offered up the predictable in his speech to his frontline troops, calling Times Mirror "a better company than when I came in twenty years ago," and ticking off the long list of impressive achievements of the company's flagship newspaper during his watch. Then he turned to Tom Johnson and introduced him to a standing ovation. Otis grinned proudly, and draped a fatherly arm over the new publisher's shoulders. He said to Tom, as well as to the audience who was listening in:

> As you get to know me better you will find me to be a fighter, a gambler, not on games but on people and the future, and a fierce competitor. I never stand still. I take risks. I am impatient and absolutely dedicated to excellence. But I need help.
>
> When I took over the *Times* I had no interest in the status quo, nor do I now. That's why you are here! I set out changing every aspect of the paper in order to make it the best there was. I think we are the best, but we still must get better—that's your challenge and mine. Together we are going to push the *New York Times* off its perch.

PART D

End *Times*

1980–2000

Beginning in the 1920s there was a steady stream of visitors, pundits, journalists from all points on the globe—novelists, magazine writers, etc., who came to Los Angeles in droves to report this strange new city on the basis, mostly, of overnight visits. But it was, of course, the *Times* that put the city on the map; that made it known—at the dawn of what I suppose can fairly be called the age of the media.

—CAREY MCWILLIAMS
IN A LETTER TO JAMES BASSETT,
DECEMBER 6, 1976

OTIS HADN'T DONE HIS OWN LAUNDRY or cooking since his Air Force days, but he learned how to do both all over again during the first weeks after he had left Missy. He was on his own, and so was she.

Missy had tried taking her life a second time when Otis had left her in Montana: a tragicomic attempt that involved filling her fly-fishing waders with water so that she might be dragged down a nearby river. Her abortive drowning aside, Missy was not ready to give up on her fight for Otis. When she was back in L.A., she called Bill Thomas and most of Otis's friends and colleagues, suggesting to them that her husband had temporarily lost his mind. She wrote letters to Otis, analyzing his condition as male menopause. Bettina was a fling. It could be forgiven. And, if Missy had done something to alienate him, she could change. All she needed was half a chance.

"I was very sad for her, very sad, 'cause she had been a wonderful wife, a wonderful mother for many, many years," said Otis. "But I didn't like her anymore. I didn't love her, and I didn't want to be with her."

Supported by both of her daughters, Missy conceded defeat as weeks passed into months. She shopped for a bulldog attorney who might make Otis pay for his sins in cash, if not remorse. Carolyn and Cathleen were shattered. When Otis broke the news of the breakup to each of his three boys, however, he was gratified by their understanding, and even a little taken aback by their insight.

He confessed, "There is a woman that I think I'm in love with."

"Is that Bettina Whitaker that we met back in Watkin's Glen?" asked Harry.

After Otis had moved out of his Pasadena apartment and into a trailer with Bettina at Paradise Cove, near Malibu, Michael shocked his father even more profoundly.

"There's something that I have to tell you," Otis stammered. "You met Bettina, you remember back at Watkin's?"

"Yeah, yeah," said Michael.

"Well, she and I are living together," said Otis, steeling himself for the worst.

"What, here?" asked Michael. "Dad, you old rascal!"

Even Norman, who had always been the closest to his mother, recognized what his sisters did not: that his parents had been drifting apart for years. He thought his mother's cigarette and martini addictions contemptible, and he also supported his father's departure.

Norman took Bettina out to lunch and told her that the only thing he was concerned about was more heirs.

"He made it very clear that he hoped that we weren't planning to have children," said Bettina.

None of the boys told Otis that he was making a big mistake, although all the women did. Daughter-in-law Jane sided with Carolyn and Cathleen, surprising even Norman when she boldly dressed Otis down for the way he'd dumped Missy. To blurt out his impulse to leave his wife of nearly thirty years without warning and then to walk away without looking back was unacceptable behavior, she told her father-in-law, even if separation and divorce were the best solution for both of them in the end.

Otis rationalized that marriage counseling would just be an exercise in futility and that he was saving Missy from further pain by refusing to submit to psychologists. For her part, Missy also missed the more subtle aspects of the divorce. Instead of looking at her own failings, she boiled the separation down to its competitive essence: Bettina had some ineffable winning edge, but Missy had never been given an opportunity to score come-from-behind points.

From her permanent position on the sidelines, Otis's longtime secretary Donna Swayze saw Bettina's advantage differently.

"She's willing to play the faithful handmaiden, you know, which Missy never was," said Swayze. "I remember him using that word: that she was *reflective,* and I thought that was interesting that he would respond to that.

"Missy was more of a doer, and not an always tactful doer. Bettina thought long and hard about everything and brought her ponderous nature to Otis, complementing his own hyperactive style of living. One of the reasons that he and Bettina got along so well is that she is very organized. Missy was chaos personified. She was always late, never organized, and he was always very punctual and very organized."

Bob Emmet summed up Missy's loss more bluntly, going directly to those elements in her driven personality that most repulsed Otis.

"Missy was trying to be *the* Mrs. Chandler," said Bob Emmet. "She was trying to be Buff, so she was in all of these outside activities. She was in too many outside activities, because Otis was elsewhere."

Even with the passage of decades, Missy could neither divine nor accept either the subtle or the profound differences between herself and Bettina; she knew

only that they were rivals, and somehow Bettina, the younger woman, had stolen first prize.

"I call her the yes woman," said Missy. "She yeses Otis, and that is the way he likes his life now. I don't think she has much of a life of her own. She does what he wants."

He did start off his relationship with Bettina by instructing her that she'd have to quit her job as boiler room supervisor if she was going to become the new Mrs. Otis Chandler. Otis explained, "We can't begin to court officially if you're working at the *Times.*"

Bettina liked her job and the *Times,* and she left both reluctantly.

Next, Otis told her she would have to meet Mama Buff. He had already prepared the way. Indeed, Buff's reaction to Otis's announcement that he was leaving Missy had been unhesitating. She told her son brusquely, "You know, I've never really liked her all these years."

"Oh, that's interesting," said Otis.

"Well, you see us argue a lot," she said. "I never really liked her."

With that, Buff shut the door on her son's first marriage and began planning his courtship for the next.

"Well, now you're going to be going out. Is that right?"

"Well, yes, I probably will."

"Let me think about what daughters do I have of good friends of mine," Buff mused.

"Mother, I'm fifty years old!" Otis protested.

He was a grandfather, for God's sakes. He was perfectly capable of finding his own companion.

"But that's not socially acceptable," Buff instructed him. "You haven't been out for years and you don't know the field. You don't know the game. I really need to think about who of my friends have eligible daughters."

"Well, mother, there's another thing I wanted to tell you," Otis said. "I think I'm in love and want to marry a woman named Bettina Whitaker."

Buff stopped her headlong plunge into matchmaking and fixed her son with an acrylic stare.

"You know, I don't think I've ever heard that name," she said. "Who are her parents? What does her father do? And have I ever met the parents?"

No, Otis patiently explained. Her parents lived in Tulsa. One was a schoolteacher and the other, a school superintendent. She was from a wonderful middle-class family.

"Well, you can't do this," Buff said with finality. "You're being led astray by obviously a woman who's after your money and position."

"No, she's not," said Otis, standing his ground. "I want you to meet her."

Buff tried to look as wounded as possible, but gave up on that jaded ruse in record time when her tears simply would not well up on command as they had in earlier days. Finally, following a long silence, she said, "You want me to meet her?"

"We'll come by next week," said Otis, pivoting about-face and marching out the door as if he'd just refused a direct command from a superior officer.

Bettina said her first visit to Los Tiempos was as perfunctory as it was perfidious. She and Otis entered the sterile, stately building together, but Bettina felt as if she were alone throughout the visit. She did not even rate an appearance as a written item on Buff's "to do" list, prepared daily by a secretary for the legendary Grand Dame of L.A. Buff awaited her son in her upstairs sitting room. She utterly ignored Bettina as the couple entered. Before he could introduce his intended to his mother, Buff spoke, but only to Otis and without acknowledging that the Whitaker woman standing next to Otis was even present.

"Well, I've been wanting to go over some things," Buff began, turning her eyes to the list in her lap. "I'd like for you to take care of my car. It needs fixing."

"Yes, mother," said Otis.

"I want to know if you can go to the symphony with me."

As Bettina sat helplessly nearby, Buff went over each item on the list, soliciting a "yes" or "no" from Otis on each task. At the conclusion of this exchange, Otis blurted out:

"Mother, this is Bettina. This is the woman."

Buff cast one quick glance at Bettina, then stared back at Otis, waiting.

"You know, mother, Bettina has a wonderful, a great interest in older homes," said Otis.

Bettina shot her own quick glance at Otis. She had no such interest. But she remained silent.

"I've been telling her about how you decorated this home when you and Dad moved in here," Otis continued, "and your elegant taste in furniture . . . "

For the first time, Buff looked squarely at Bettina. A flicker appeared somewhere behind the opaque irises of her eyes.

"Really?" Buff asked. "You'd like to see the house?"

Bettina gripped the opportunity with both hands. She wouldn't know a Chippendale from a chesterfield, but it mattered not a whit. She nodded vigorously.

"Oh, yes! Oh, very much!"

"Well, come on," said Buff.

And the two of them were off, examining Victorian tea caddies, rococo armchairs, Regency tables and the grand piano in the music room that had been signed by Van Cliburn.

Throughout the ordeal, Buff retained a cool politesse, quizzing her son's new love interest on her background, education, and intentions. Bettina felt as if she had gone on a job interview and she suffered a bout of abdominal distress, which Otis later described as "dysentery," as the tour came to an end. When she and Otis were finally whisked out the front door, Bettina couldn't divine whether she'd made a favorable impression on her prospective mother-in-law or not.

But Otis could tell. She'd passed her first test with flying colors. A few weeks later, Bettina returned with Otis to Los Tiempos, and this time they were given a far warmer reception. It turned out that after the first meeting, Buff had Carroll Righter run Bettina's Gemini birth chart alongside Otis's. They came up a happy love match: as zodiac-perfect for each other as Norman the Virgo had been for Buff the Bull.

"You will be best of friends," effused Buff. "It will be a wonderful union, and whatever happens—if you get married or whatever—it's just perfect."

Buff arranged for Bettina to meet with Olive Behrendt, another grand dame whose unofficial role among polite Los Angeles society was to indoctrinate middle-class wives into the customs and taboos of the ruling class. Bettina joined Andrea Van de Kamp, the wife of the newly elected Los Angeles County District Attorney John Van de Kamp, and Joan Kozberg, another young executive's wife, in what amounted to regular salons staged at the Behrendts' Pasadena home, or luncheons conducted at approved locales around the city. There, Mrs. Behrendt's charges learned the lore and absorbed the subtleties of being a woman wed to power. The small group of graduates even had a name. They called themselves the Olive Branch, in honor of their mentor.

But there was still both Pasadena and the publishing world's social debuts to contend with and, by comparison, Buff's rigid rituals were a cakewalk. During their first official outing as a couple, Otis and Bettina ran headlong into glacial disapproval.

"I remember, like it was yesterday, the first black-tie dinner at the Beverly Hilton for the Brotherhood of Jews and Christians Annual Dinner, or whatever," said Otis.

Such events were standard fare for Otis Chandler, but utterly foreign to Bettina. He arranged to arrive late so there would be minimal cocktail talk, but his timing was off and their entrance sent a hush through the ballroom. Otis and his young home wrecker had arrived.

"I mean, that's what they wanted to believe," said Otis.

Otis persevered, although his memory failed at every other introduction, names escaping him just as he was about to present Bettina. Never poised in such situations, even during his years with Missy, he now stumbled badly.

"I had never been in that position before of having a marriage break up and with a new woman," he explained later.

Still, Bettina passed muster. She held her head high, even when someone asked her if she was one of the *Whitaker* Whitakers, or merely some garden-variety Whitaker. She maintained a cool air about her that left Otis beaming, even in the face of whispers and general disapproval.

"Bettina pulled it off with such class," he said. "She looked beautiful."

He bought her clothes and had her hair trimmed and styled as he envisioned it, orchestrating her appearance as if he were Henry Higgins. Others noticed that he was dressing her almost as if she were a *faux* Missy.

"And people said, 'Oh, she's not a bimbo, she's not a cheapie.' It took quite a while though, over the next several months, for our social friends—not my personal friends; my *social* friends—to accept her," he said.

At the Annual Newspaper Publishers Association convention in Honolulu, they ran into further walls of disdain, with the likes of Katherine Graham and Arthur Sulzberger giving Bettina the slow once over. Again, Otis stumbled over names and, again, Bettina smiled graciously and picked up the conversation with warmth and skill, turning small talk into fine first impressions.

Several weeks into their strong debut as a social item, Otis began to experience an unanticipated reaction from friends and acquaintances he had known for years and, at first, he did not know how to react.

Couples began to approach Otis privately: not as couples, but as individuals. They weren't so much critical as they were troubled and more than a little astonished at Otis's behavior. Wives told him that, if a rock-solid husband such as Otis Chandler could leave his wife of twenty-eight years, what prevented their own husbands from doing the same thing? As for the husbands, they confided in him that Otis's courage to leave Missy gave them hope that they might be able to perform the same miracle in their own lifeless marriages.

Otis had no answer at first. It had never occurred to him that anyone else might have been as troubled or as unhappy as he and Missy had been. In the rarefied circles in which he traveled, such feelings were seldom afforded an opportunity to surface. Men treated their unhappiness by having affairs and women went along, frequently relieving the boredom and inattention by having affairs of their own. No one spoke of adultery or any of its attendant hypocrisy beyond the level of gossip.

Otis finally gave them all, men and women, the same answer: "Don't measure your own life by mine."

ON JANUARY 1, 1981, Otis Chandler succeeded Dr. Franklin Murphy as Times Mirror chairman of the board. Although Murphy stayed on as chairman of the

executive committee, just as Norman Chandler had done when he retired, he did not fade away with his emeritus title. He continued to act as an adviser and liaison between the $1.65-billion Times Mirror conglomerate and the outside world, in much the same way that Nick Williams had continued to consult with Otis for years after Williams's retirement.

Murphy continued as a presence on the sixth floor. Otis was grateful to the former UCLA chancellor for accepting the brunt of Buff's wrath when she had been eased out of the Times Mirror's power structure. Buff had never got over the irony of being asked to leave by the very executive whom she had steered to the Times Mirror chairmanship.

"Franklin always couldn't wait to get rid of me," Buff told Katherine Graham's daughter, Lally Weymouth, in an interview for an *Esquire* magazine profile. "I think he's really quite a chauvinistic man; I think he's very jealous of women. He was very jealous of me. He couldn't wait to get me out of there."

Responding to Mrs. Chandler's bitter accusations, Murphy said without apology, "She's a strong woman with strong opinions."

Even after retiring, the Kansas City physician with the penchant for power still had moral authority in the corridors of Times Mirror Square, and he exercised it vigorously. His office was still down the hall from Otis's and he often barged in as if he were entering a junior executive's office, even while Otis was on the phone. Tapping his foot impatiently or pacing the room, he'd wait until Otis had hung up to ask his questions. Afterwards, Otis would come out to Donna Swayze's desk and hiss:

"Why do you let him in?"

And Swayze would shrug and hold up her hands helplessly. She'd answer, "I couldn't get out of my chair fast enough, short of throwing myself on the floor in front of him."

"Oh I know," Otis would say with resignation. "That's the way it is."

Otis showed a similar deference to his new Times Mirror president in 1981: Robert Erburu, the solicitous Gibson, Dunn & Crutcher lawyer who, along with Dan Frost, had endeared himself to Norman and Buff during the early 1960s.

A California native whose Basque grandfather had emigrated from Spain in 1870, Erburu seemed destined to become a sheep rancher like his grandfather and father, but grew enamored of journalism when he was a student at the University of Southern California. Like his partner and fellow Times Mirror board member, Dan Frost, he went to Harvard Law School and then to Gibson, Dunn & Crutcher; but Erburu formally abandoned private practice in 1961 when he joined Times Mirror as assistant general counsel. From that point, Erburu considered himself a newspaperman first and a lawyer second, and Otis said and did nothing to dissuade that sentiment. In 1974, Erburu entered the Times Mirror

pantheon as chief operating officer; he replaced Al Casey, who had left that same year to become president of American Airlines.[1] When Tom Johnson became *Times* publisher in 1980, Erburu stepped up to the position of Times Mirror president and chief executive officer, and the new ruling troika at Times Mirror Square was complete: Tom Johnson, Otis Chandler, and Bob Erburu.

While Otis held the chairman's title at Times Mirror, real power was invested in Erburu, who, as CEO, quietly but deliberately began changing the company's hierarchy and corporate culture.

"Bob Erburu politicized management," recalled Times Mirror executive Pete Fernald.[2] "He put his loyal supporters in top management positions and took control of the bonus incentive system, which had been based on each unit's performance under Casey. A manager had been able to earn up to 100 percent of his salary if he produced results. But under Erburu, [the system] became subjective. He decided how much your bonus was. It was not based on uniform standards. The entire organization was demoralized."

The *Times* endorsed neither candidate for president that year, nor any year thereafter. Overseen by former *Philadelphia Bulletin* political reporter Tony Day since Jim Bassett's retirement, the newspaper's once-shrill right-wing op-ed pages had moved to the middle along with the rest of the newspaper. The *Times* had learned the journalistic neutrality lessons of Vietnam, LBJ, Watergate, and Richard Nixon,[3] and had learned them well. Otis's insistence on staying away from the right or the left by refusing to endorse presidential, senatorial, or gubernatorial races was now etched in stone, and no less a critic than Katherine Graham's *Newsweek* complimented Day's editorials as "intelligent, well-reasoned and moderate in tone." The political cartoons continued to be outrageous, but even Nancy Reagan had given up trying to have Paul Conrad fired.

Otis now began seriously to consider his legacy. He commissioned Conrad to sculpt a bust of him to place in the rotunda entrance to Times Mirror, along with the busts of General Otis, Harry Chandler, and his father, Norman. Conrad obliged and created a likeness that most who saw it appreciated for its subtlety; but Otis found sorely lacking. He didn't want to hurt Conrad's feelings, but he confided to his peers that he did not think the finished work—haggard, high-cheeked, and angular—looked at all like him. It seemed more in keeping with Conrad's satirical style than a realistic rendering. With little fanfare, Otis let Conrad down easy and found another sculptor to produce a massive bronze head that approximated a dashing, pompadoured Otis in his thirties.

"What Otis couldn't see was that Conrad had aged him, so that his bust made Otis appear as he would look when he was in his seventies," said Tony Day.

At about the same time, Otis began systematically to defer to Tom Johnson and withdrew increasingly from the day-to-day news operation of his *Times.* He

found the early years of Ronald Reagan's presidency to be as bland as Tom Bradley's dull reign as mayor of Los Angeles. Otis still liked to debate politics around the dinner table, just as he'd been taught to do by Norman and Buff when he was growing up, but he felt a growing detachment following the tumultuous era that had begun with the murder of John F. Kennedy and had ended with the resignation of Richard M. Nixon.

"The events of the 1960s and 70s were so overwhelming in terms of importance, societal issues, assassinations, the Pill, student riots and everything else," he said. "Those decades were so dynamic with changes in this country and in the world. There was just so much. It seemed like every day there was something. The intensity of the change in the world was so huge in the 60s and 70s, and there just wasn't that same intensity of change in the 1980s."

To Otis, Ronald Reagan seemed the perfect guide to sleepwalk America through the 1980s: a former actor with a good, conservative heart who was never faced with a Vietnam or an assassination. His administration was strewn with close calls, beginning with John Hinckley and ending with Iran Contra; but the Teflon president slid through the decade unscathed, just as he had slid through his California governorship, and so did the rest of the nation.

"He did some good things," said Otis. "He was very articulate when he spoke. He knew California well. I think he made some booboos too, like when he said, 'If you've seen one redwood tree you have seen them all.' Things like that.

"But he was a well-liked president. He was lucky. He just came across the radar screen at the right time. The Berlin Wall came down and the Cold War ended. He was really fortunate. He did some good things, but he also had a lot of advantages of events being on his side. Events over which he had no control."

The *Times* turned one hundred years old in 1981, and celebrations marked the occasion throughout Times Mirror Square and at the Orange County plant. The beginning of its second century began with the *Times'* full-blown entry into the computer age and the conversion of its noisy forty-six-year-old presses to the faster, less cumbersome digital whirr of offset. Within a year, the city desk would inaugurate a computerized news editing system; and word processing would make typewriters obsolete. As of July 1982, the *Los Angeles Times'* conversion to offset was complete, and moveable type, as Otis had first come to know it during his summer vacation stints in the 1940s, was history.

Times Mirror also expanded its television base with the purchase of a five-station group from Newhouse Communications. Times Mirror now owned stations in Dallas/Fort Worth, St. Louis, Birmingham, Syracuse, and Harrisburg, Pennsylvania, in addition to Austin's KTBC, Tom Johnson's old LBJ-sponsored launch pad.

Otis felt good about what he'd accomplished. Not only was his newspaper on everybody's top-ten list but Otis invariably appeared on surveys alongside Kather-

ine Graham and Arthur Sulzberger as one of the most influential and respected media moguls in the United States. There was only one group who did not share the consensus, and its uniform contempt for all that he had done continued to gall him, even after the golden climax of his triumphant reign as publisher.

"When I came into management, our pre-tax profit was somewhere around $2 million or $3 million and I took it to $100 million," Otis reflected. "I took it to $1 billion dollars in total revenues. That's one hell of a growth. And the non-Chandler shareholders appreciated it.

"But I only got one compliment in all those years from the entire Chandler family. One of them said, 'Thank God, cousin Otis, you worked so hard. We really appreciate what you did.' They're just not that kind of people. It wasn't the editorial policy. They just couldn't bring themselves to give compliments. They're not built that way."

OTIS TOLD BUSINESS WEEK IN 1977 that his beautiful blue Duesenberg, then worth well in excess of $100,000, was "my first love. Sometimes when my wife and I argue about cars, I tell her, 'Honey, I can always get another wife, but I can't get another Duesenberg.'"

Before the Chandlers' final decree was signed on July 1, 1981, the Duesenberg had, indeed, become one of the focal points of a bitter, hard-fought custody battle. Much of Otis's personal fortune was wrapped up in cars. His fleet included his one-of-a-kind Mercedes, Rolls Royce, and Duesenberg and his so-called muscle cars and Porsches, which carried the power of hundreds of horses beneath each hood. Missy demanded her share of the finest specimens in Otis's "Vintage" collection, as he had come to call the L.A. warehouse where he kept his cars. Among Missy's three choices was the Duesenberg.

"Oh, then I sold everything," said Otis. "Everything. Classics, sports cars, everything went."

He called on a rare Ferrari broker he knew in Scottsdale, Arizona, to cash out and find top dollar for his collection. He even sold J. T.'s beloved 917K Porsche for roughly four times what he'd paid for it. Besides eliminating one more roadblock in his single-minded effort to be divorced and remarried, the exercise stripped Otis Chandler down to his bare essentials: money and the *Times*. Otis's lawyers saw to it that the sordid details of the divorce were sealed so that his and Missy's net worth would not be made public, but Missy complained bitterly years afterward that she came out the big loser.

Otis married Bettina Whitaker on August 15, 1981, less than two months after his divorce was final. The wedding took place on a hot Saturday afternoon, a day

that apparently met the approval of Buff and her astrologer, Carroll Righter. The wedding was staged for one hundred guests in the stuffy, non-air-conditioned music room at Los Tiempos; Otis was nearly as resplendent as his bride, clad as he was in a white silk suit to match Bettina's white lace. Norman flew back from Hartford to take his place by his father as Otis's best man. The oldest Chandler son had entered the fifth year of his Times Mirror executive training program at the company's Connecticut newspapers, still intent on becoming the next Chandler to be named publisher of the *Los Angeles Times.* For her matron of honor, Bettina selected Judy Karns, a fellow schoolteacher from her Pasadena teaching days.

"She was so warm, honest, loving," said Karns. "She had no idea what it entailed to be Mrs. Otis Chandler."

Buff had become the least of Bettina's worries. The future Mrs. Otis Chandler had to learn how to juggle her new Jekyll-and-Hyde personas of pretty social doyenne and rugged playmate to a middle-aged adolescent. On the one hand, the former Nazarene schoolteacher studied such esoterica as couture at I. Magnin and the subtleties of managing servants; on the other, she tried to keep pace with her restless, reckless husband who was constantly on the prowl for the next big adventure. During their honeymoon in Tahiti, she began to fully comprehend what kind of an expansive, stubborn, and occasionally irresponsible dreamer she had married.

The morning after they arrived at Hotel Bora Bora, Otis awakened to the sound of thirty-foot surf pounding the reef that surrounded the island. It was a mile out and visible at low tide, and Otis meant to get beyond its bounds. He borrowed a dugout canoe from the front desk, making up a story about wanting to paddle about in the lagoon with his bride. Bettina balked. Until she met Otis, she had never even bothered to learn how to swim.

"Do you think it's okay?" she asked.

"Oh, come on," he said. "You know, a little *adventure* here!"

They paddled all the way to the reef, the hotel receding behind them in the horizon like a sinking doll's house. Otis could taste the big waves ahead when a wind suddenly came up from behind and swamped their canoe. Flushed out of the boat, the two of them got their footing on the exposed reef, but cut their bare feet on the sharp coral. Bleeding, they dumped water from the canoe, over and over again, but the wind prevented them from paddling back; at the same time, the heavy surf kept swamping the dugout, which once more began to sink beneath the waves.

Otis found a plastic sandwich bag floating in the surf and handed it to Bettina. He ordered her to bail with it while he pushed the canoe back toward the lagoon.

"It took us hours to get back and then I got chewed out for even thinking of going out to the reef," said Otis.

In a bizarre replay of the most frightening moment from his first honeymoon thirty years earlier, his second bride stumbled to shore, fell to the sand, and threw up.

Like Missy before her, Bettina had now officially been baptized Mrs. Otis Chandler. Otis said with a laugh that Bettina still was unable to share nearly twenty years later, "If I ever get married again, it's not good for anybody to go on a honeymoon with me where there's surf involved."

Otis was at the age when men of his temperament tended to slow down, but Otis Chandler sped up. He occasionally rode his bicycle through rush hour traffic the more than thirty miles from Paradise Cove to his office at Times Mirror. Not only did he take up the shot put again for the first time since his Air Force and college days but he entered senior competition for weight lifting and track and field events, taking home first prize for men in their midfifties. He noticed that competition was no longer always as friendly among athletes as it had once been. Winning was now far more important among all competitors than how one played the game.

"I surfed Point Dume when Bettina and I lived near Paradise Cove, and it was so territorial I almost got in a fight," he said. "There were not enough waves to go around and guys knew you either by name or by sight, and if you were a stranger . . .

"Now, I was big enough and my board was big enough that I never got in an actual fight, never got my tires slashed, but guys would cut me off waves or take waves that were obviously mine. They could have taken other waves, but it was just to send a signal, 'Get out of here, this is ours.'"

Preferring discretion and diplomacy to belligerence, Otis bowed out of the Malibu surf wars and, later, ended his passion for auto racing as well. He and actor Paul Newman jockeyed a few times for recognition as the nation's top senior celebrity race car driver, but Otis finally gave it up. He was still a fan, however, and sponsored a new *Times* Cal 500 race at Riverside Raceway in 1981. The race not only marked the first *Times* sponsorship of an Indy car event but also his son Michael's entry into the world of professional racing. Otis unabashedly proclaimed that he was now racing vicariously through his son.

He might no longer drive, but Otis was still passionate about collecting cars. He had held on to the legendary 917K Porsche after his divorce, for example, only selling it when he was offered a cool $1.4 million. Otis liked to brag that, although other people played the stock market, he preferred the one-of-a-kind automobile market, buying and selling like a Kentucky thoroughbred dealer. Dur-

ing the annual classic car concourse staged each autumn at Pebble Beach, the former Air Force lieutenant who had once bought low and sold high now bought high and sold even higher. Within a few years, his vintage car and motorcycle collection was as large as it had been before the divorce.

He and Bettina moved into a faux-Tudor home near Buff's Los Tiempos manse in Hancock Park, and there Bettina had an opportunity to blend her own middle-class tastes with the accepted elegance of the very rich. Her down-market furniture and art apparently met the approval of her mother-in-law, although Buff's vision and mental acuity could no longer be trusted for her once impossibly high Epicurean standards. Buff began to suffer small strokes and, although she would admit to no illness or infirmity—she was Mrs. Norman Chandler, after all—she rarely left Los Tiempos following the celebration of her eightieth birthday. Bettina and Otis might live mere blocks away, but Buff almost never visited.

Bettina used her new position in life to do something worthwhile with her little hunk of the Chandler windfall.

"I felt I wanted to find a meaningful involvement," she said. "I did not want to go into areas where Buff or Mia had been involved."

Bettina asked *Times* associate editor Jean Sharley Taylor for help, and Taylor steered her to reporter Kathy Hendrix, an ex-nun who wrote on feminist issues. Hendrix took the new Mrs. Chandler to Skid Row, where she introduced her to Jill Halverson, founder of the Downtown Women's Center. Over the next four years, Bettina volunteered regularly, cooking, counseling, and helping to raise $3 million for the homeless women who came and went at the center.

She also studied yoga, which she preferred to her husband's weight training as her daily exercise. She preferred Eastern mysticism, New Age meditation, and spiritual counselors to her mother-in-law's reliance on old-hat horoscope readings as a guide to daily living.

"I specifically wasn't interested in any religion," said Bettina, still in open rebellion against her Nazarene upbringing. "I didn't understand that you don't have to be religious to be spiritual and I floated around not having much direction or much trust in myself."

One gray day before she and Otis moved to Hancock Park, she spilled forth her unhappiness to her Malibu manicurist, who made a suggestion: Why not visit a West Hollywood psychic who had been able to put several of her upscale clients back in touch with their spiritual selves?

Bettina pooh-poohed the idea at first, but several months later, she made her first pilgrimage to psychic Bill Burns.

"I think you need to ask God for help," he told her.

"No, I kind of thought that maybe God didn't have a place in my life," she said.

He convinced her otherwise, suggesting that she jettison her traditional notions of clerics and choirs and study her own place in the world for a while. Bettina's regular sessions with Burns began moving her through the koans of Zen and the archetypal memories of Jung, eventually leading her to folklorist Joseph Campbell, a master's degree in counseling, and the layered meanings of a true pursuit of happiness.

"Otis is a man with an incredible amount of energy," she said. "It has been the grist for forcing me to become a strong person, because I could easily be so overwhelmed with his energy that I would become a nonperson. That's what made it so easy for me to lose myself in the beginning."

She learned early that she would not necessarily find happiness by simply playing quiet companion to her big, brave husband and his constant need for reassurance. Bettina graciously delivered, but it left her feeling empty. When they entertained, Bettina consciously pushed Otis to the fore and quietly helped him remember names. She moved him on to other couples at the appropriate moment, but never with the brass or impatience that Missy had exhibited during her last years as Mrs. Otis Chandler. Bettina's detractors began to refer to Bettina as "Otis's Japanese wife" because she always seemed to walk a few paces behind him.

Bettina was beginning to acquire a real taste of the single-minded Otis Chandler egoism that eventually drove Missy off into a separate world of cigarettes, cocktails, and urban planning. She might have a far different temperament than the first Mrs. Chandler, and be much better suited to deal with her demanding husband, but she had no intention of being subsumed by the enormity of his huge and sudden appetites or his needs, real and imagined.

By 1982, the young Harry Chandler was preparing to move beyond Times Mirror and begin apprenticing in Hollywood as a television and film producer. Otis Chandler's second son liked the cable television end of the family's newspaper business, but felt awkward competing with his older brother at Times Mirror. Besides, his success with the documentary he'd shot of his father competing at Watkin's Glen had infected Harry with the moviemaking bug.[4] He joined the company that eventually became Showtime and moved on to feature films later in the decade. Only Norman remained a potential heir to the publisher's suite, but Otis undercut those hopes when he began speaking out publicly about Norman's inability to handle the job of running the Times Mirror empire.

"There appears to be no disappointment in his voice when he said that neither of his sons now working for the company seems destined one day to run it," *Ad-*

vertising Age reported in May 1982, following an extensive interview that Otis gave the trade magazine about the *Times'* future.

Otis made similar cutting comments in television and radio interviews during the months that followed, prompting outrage from Norman, his wife Jane, and Missy. How could he speak so callously about his own son?

Otis didn't care. His loyalties went first to the paper he loved and not to his son, who would have to sink or swim on his own merits. Norman had not demonstrated the mettle of a *Times* publisher, said Otis. He didn't have Tom Johnson's cool decisiveness, steel-trap memory, or practical judgment, and Otis doubted that he ever would. The reports that Otis had been getting back from department heads, as well as what he was able to see with his own eyes, convinced him only that Norman's so-called people skills were excellent. He might even outshine his old man when it came to writing and reporting. But Norman had neither the aptitude nor the attitude to make the tough, pragmatic choices that corporate insensitivity demanded.

Otis appeared oblivious to the cruelty of his conclusions, particularly when they were pronounced in a public forum. Crushed, Norman redoubled his efforts. He took up marathon running and triathlon training to relieve some of his frustration at failing to earn even tacit validation from his own father.

Meanwhile, Otis Chandler's *Times* rolled on.

A Rio de Janeiro and Caribbean bureau became the paper's twenty-first and twenty-second international outposts, and the latest domestic bureau opened in Miami. Martin Bernheimer, the classical music critic and Buff's nemesis, became the first *Times* critic to win the Pulitzer Prize; and political cartoonist Paul Conrad became the first *Times*man to win three Pulitzers. In a moving tribute to Ruben Salazar, the *Times* also accepted the 1983 Pulitzer Gold Medal for public service for a long overdue series the newspaper published on the emerging political, economic, and cultural power of the Southland Latino community.

An embarrassingly underreported episode involving funds embezzled from Columbia Studios had also been belatedly repaired by beefing up *Times* entertainment news reporting.

Dubbed "Hollywoodgate" in a 1978 *Wall Street Journal* exposé, the scandal rocked Los Angeles and its *Times* after David Begelman, Columbia president and former MCA talent agent, was indicted for forging Academy Award–winner Cliff Robertson's signature on a studio check for $10,000. Not only did the crime eventually cost Begelman his job but the incident shone a national spotlight on the long-questionable business practices among the fast-and-loose deal makers who had been running Hollywood for decades. The Begelman affair sparked the best -seller *Indecent Exposure,* its author *Journal* reporter David McClintick, and a renaissance in re-

porting about the money side of moviemaking; but in the beginning, the *Times* coverage had fallen woefully short. Entertainment editor and film critic Charles Champlin ignored McClintick's revelations, eventually offering a weak apologia for Begelman after the *Washington Post*, the *New York Times*, and nationally syndicated columnist Liz Smith had all weighed in against the disgraced studio chief: "What we have here, it might be said poetically, is a culprit who doubles as a victim. It is a paradoxical and confusing situation which Hollywood and the media, including this newspaper, have been uncertain how to handle."

By 1983, the *Times'* Calendar section rebounded from a national reputation for regularly killing stories that cast a bad light on Southern California's most famous industry by delivering hard-nosed stories with some regularity about Hollywood's sleazy accounting practices, nepotism, and organized crime connections. Still, it did not seem enough.

During a 1984 press junket for *Wired*, his book about the meteoric rise and crash of comedian John Belushi, Bob Woodward confronted Bill Thomas and his editors during a luncheon in Woodward's honor over the *Times'* shocking lack of concern about a Hollywood that essentially killed its own. The newspaper investigated the seedy underbelly everywhere else, but not in its own backyard, said Woodward.

"I was embarrassed for that newspaper," Woodward said. "Why weren't they looking at the movie industry and their city and the drug plague? Their Washington coverage is terrific; they beat us a lot. But on their coverage of L.A. and the entertainment industry, I give them low marks."

The *Times'* bold progress in aggressive reporting outside of L.A. was not all marked by good news. On June 21, 1983, Mexico City bureau chief Dial Torgerson joined Salazar, Joe Alex Morris, and Tom Treanor as the fourth *Times* reporter to die in the line of duty. While on assignment along the Honduran-Nicaraguan border where Contras and Sandinistas fought for the soul of Central America, Torgerson was shot to death.

In 1983, too, the sixteen-member Times Mirror board voted to sell its New American Library, noting a slump in the trade paperback business. Legal, medical, and aviation books continued to turn high profits, but popular literature did not. With its aggressive reputation for tolerating no marginal media companies, Times Mirror pursued a policy of fast, fat returns on its money. Soon, the *Dallas Times Herald* and *Denver Post* would go on the auction block for failing to perform up to expectations. As the economy heated up, Times Mirror joined every other Fortune 500 company in dumping its short-term losers, regardless of their long-term potential.

At the *Times* itself, the next move in its suburban strategy was to create a satellite plant in the San Fernando Valley community of Canoga Park that would rival the size and press capacity of Orange County. With this newest move away from the Civic Center, critics saw the *Times* straying further and further from its roots, but Tom Johnson and Bill Thomas both echoed Otis when he answered with the tried-and-true argument that inner-city dwellers didn't read, didn't subscribe, and didn't support *Times* advertisers.

On the other hand, urban commuters who had moved to the hinterlands, now as far away as Ventura, Palmdale, and Riverside, wanted to take their *Times* along with them.

"The *Times* tried to be all things to all people and lost its focus," said veteran *Times* political reporter Mark Gladstone, who defined L.A.'s woefully underserved central city—from Watts to East L.A.—as the "donut hole" that neither the *Times* nor any other major media outlet cared to cover until riots, gang violence, or drug dealing turned the spotlight there.

"The *Times* ignored the donut hole and followed the money," said Gladstone.

But Otis Chandler saw none of this future gloom on the horizon as 1983 came to an end and the Olympic year of 1984 began.[5] L.A. was once more the home of the Summer Games, with the Coliseum that his grandfather Harry and uncle William Garland helped build in 1932 once more the focal point of the world.

The *Times* had already committed $5 million to underwrite an Olympic Arts Festival to run in conjunction with the Games. Otis lobbied the Times Mirror board to sponsor the Olympic Track and Field trials in L.A. a month before the Games got underway. He might never be an Olympic champion himself, but Otis could certainly make the L.A. Games the greatest Olympics in history.

"I'm not a mysterious character," he said. "I'm not a recluse and I'm not a conniving person. Pretty much, I am what you see and hear. I am a maverick and a perfectionist and I try to do everything I do to the best of my ability."

He had faltered in his personal life in the previous decade, nearly stumbling off course a few times. But he was now once more in the groove as a happily married man and editor in chief of the biggest, richest, and—on more than a few days every month, now—the *best* newspaper in the land.

As a writer for the Pacific Southwest Airways in-flight magazine described Otis Chandler in a 1983 article about the formidable and fortunate *Los Angeles Times*, this strapping 56-year-old titan was "the White Knight of American Journalism, a sort of Apollo in a three-piece suit, the newspaper heir who can do no wrong."

Of course, Otis was not so blown up with his own ego that he actually *believed* such blarney. And, yet, there did seem to be something to it.

CHAPTER 24

IN 1981, ROOKIE MICHAEL CHANDLER placed twelfth at the Indianapolis 500. Otis cheered him all the way to the checkered flag.

"My father lived vicariously through me," said Michael, who was then basking in the sustained glow of his father's pride for the first time in his life.

By 1984, the youngest of Otis Chandler's three sons was a seasoned Indianapolis veteran, with three races at "the Brickyard" under his belt, and over $130,000 in winnings. He'd competed on the professional Indy car circuit two dozen times across the United States, demonstrating repeatedly that the twenty-six-year-old runt of the beautiful, brainy, and blessed Chandler dynasty had a special talent that rivaled any of his brothers and sisters.

Otis recalled painfully watching his youngest son interviewed on television following one of Michael's early racing wins. Michael confessed to the viewing audience that he was the dumb Chandler. He'd barely graduated from high school. He had real trouble reading. It hurt Otis to see his son, a Chandler, speaking so self-destructively and with such embarrassing candor in a public forum. It was almost as if he didn't know who he was, or what he represented.

Michael had always been the difficult son, at once rebellious yet self-effacing to a fault. Against both his parents' wishes, he wed a beautician in 1983 and moved into an apartment in Dana Point. Michael married and lived far beneath his station, and that bothered Otis and Missy far more than his intellectual capacity.

"Michael was a natural athlete," said Otis's secretary, Donna Swayze. "Norman somewhat and Harry not so much. Harry was more the artist, the intellectual. But Michael is a natural athlete. From the time he was a little boy, he was also naturally mechanical. He could take the vacuum cleaner apart and put it together without being taught. It was just incredible."

At five-eight, Michael was shorter than either of his six-foot-plus brothers and his father, and less well educated, too. He'd graduated from a public high school in Pasadena, but Norman and Harry had followed in their illustrious father's footsteps, first attending Andover and then Stanford. His older sister Cathleen attended Princeton and the University of California at Santa Cruz, and it appeared as though Carolyn, who wanted to become a zookeeper, would do equally well in her college career. His parents explained Michael's failings as learning disorders. Michael later blamed his mother's smoking and drinking habits while he was still in the womb as the reason for his physiological limits, a theory that did not seem to have much application to any other Chandler, including his younger sister.

But college of any kind was the furthest thing from his mind when Michael headed for Indianapolis one more time in the spring of 1984. He'd discovered his niche amid a hyper-competitive family and he planned to win one for the gipper.

"I was in my mid-twenties and invincible," Michael remembered.

Just before heading off to Indiana for the qualifying rounds, he had come in second behind racing legend Michael Andretti at the Long Beach Grand Prix, a mark of how quickly he'd risen among the elite in the rarefied world of racing. All the signs pointed to 1984 as his year.

As qualifying got underway, Otis and Bettina were in Washington, D.C., for a publishers' convention, but they planned to fly into Indianapolis for Memorial Day weekend. President Reagan was staging an open house for the publishers, and the usually pensive Bettina bubbled over like a schoolgirl, thrilled at the prospect of dining at the White House. Just as she and Otis were getting ready to go, the call came in to their hotel suite: At the third turn on Indianapolis's famous oval track, Michael had hit the wall at 226 miles per hour and was not expected to live.

"Luckily, I don't remember any of this," said Michael, in reconstructing what happened. "I took a twelve-day nap. I lost my long-term memory for the one or two years before the accident and I don't remember to this day what happened for six months after."

By the time Otis and Bettina arrived, Missy was already at Michael's bedside and last rites had been administered. A four-inch gash decorated his forehead and his nose had been smashed flush against his face, but neither his spine nor the rest of his body had sustained much damage. The real damage, his parents were told, was inside his skull.

"He was out for a week and the doctors have to prepare you," said Otis. "And they tell you, you know, that your son or daughter may never wake up, or they may be a vegetable the rest of their lives if they do wake up."

Otis and Bettina took the suite next to Missy's at the hotel during the anxious days that followed, and much of the fury that had fueled the years leading to the divorce dissipated. Grudges gave way to grief and a united effort to save their son. Otis later made arrangements to have Michael flown back to UCLA Medical Center aboard billionaire Meshulam Riklis's private jet. Once Michael was back home, the vigil began.

On the sixth day, Michael sat up straight in bed and yelled. Then he lay back down and fell asleep once more. When he had recovered enough to hold a tele-phone receiver, Ronald Reagan called and spoke with him, wishing him a speedy recovery. He was well enough after a few weeks to be released into his mother's care at her new home in Bel Air.[1] When plastic surgery had repaired the forehead

and nose, his appearance was almost fully restored and only close examination revealed the scars. But his speedy recovery was a sham.

"You never fully recover from head injuries," said Michael, whose carefully articulated speech bears the peculiar effect, even decades after the incident, of one who has survived terrible brain trauma.

Troubling times followed. Michael wanted to return to racing, but his doctors warned him that the miracle of his survival would not be repeated. A secondhead injury, even a hard jostle, would be fatal.

For a time, he reviewed the videos of the deadly qualifying run over and over, trying to analyze what had happened, where he had failed. But he had done everything correctly. It was the car that had failed him.

The crash itself was spectacular. Michael viewed it slowed down to a frame-by-frame dissection of the moments that led up to the locked brakes and glancing slam into the concrete. The cause of the accident appeared to be a failure of the right front suspension. The right front tire and brake assembly sheered off on impact, flying back against the driver's helmet. By all rights, Michael Chandler ought to have been decapitated, as surely as the French doctor, whose head Otis had encountered in the middle of the Sahara Desert, had been. But he was not, and Michael often wondered in the difficult years that followed just why he had been spared.

But the wondering did not come at first. At first, he wanted to return to racing.

"I wanted to get back on the horse I fell off of," said Michael.

Although Otis was never one much given to introspection, he also wondered why his son had survived. Michael's tragedy took him back to his own coma at age nine, following his riding accident, when doctors had proffered that Otis was a goner. Otis didn't shy away from horses after that, but he was in no hurry to get back on one. Some might say that Otis Chandler had led a charmed life, and in some ways it was true. But there was method in his tempting of fate. There were lines, he said, that one didn't cross.

"I didn't feel I ever would get close to crossing over that line, and that's the judgment in life," he said. "Whether you're surfing or bicycling or doing anything, your judgment is to get up to that line and know where that line is and then not go over it and not do something stupid. I've gone through that with my son Michael."

Otis withdrew his support of Michael's racing and, for a time, they warred. Michael's first wife divorced him following the accident and he married his caretaker, a dental assistant who had been a friend of his first wife's. Mary Jean Chandler met with as much patrician disdain from the Chandlers as had Annette, Michael's first wife, and the marriage lasted only long enough to produce three children.

When he at last accepted the end of his racing days, Michael studied half-heartedly for two years at Orange Coast Community College, then followed his brothers into the family business, working first as a production mechanic at the Orange County edition of the *Times*. Belatedly, he set out on his own training program, trying to learn every aspect of the newspaper business.

"I was the sole motivator behind myself going from department to department," he said. "If there was a job posted, I'd go apply. I sold display ads for three years. It hurt me that my father never visited me once while I was at the Orange County plant. He never encouraged me at all. In fact, he'd say, 'Why don't you quit?'

"He used to say that the Chandlers had gotten to be like the Ford family. 'The *Times* and Times Mirror has become so big,' he'd say, 'that I'm probably going to be the last of the Chandlers to lead the *Times*.' My father's got an ego and he's always busy feeding his ego. It was probably his ego that contributed to his attitude toward keeping us kids from carrying on. He wanted to go down in history as the last of the great Chandlers."

FOLLOWING A TRIUMPHANT Olympics year, Los Angeles and its *Times* brimmed with hubris. Native-born singer and songwriter Randy Newman summarized Southern California's appeal in a cynical anthem that most residents and *Times* readers first heard as the soundtrack to a Nike television commercial: "I Love L.A.," sang Newman in the recurring chorus of his punchy, in-your-face lyrics, "'cuz the sun is shining all the time."

I Love L.A. could just as easily have been Otis Chandler's theme song. During his lifelong battle against the invisible demons of East Coast snobbery, he had dismissed those cautious émigrés among the Times Mirror ranks—such as Bob Donovan—who could not make the transition. Since his Andover days, Otis had never accepted the premise that hard winters and dense, dirty urban living automatically translated into intellectual depth and strength of character. Like the singer of Newman's song, Otis admired L.A.'s mountains, beaches, sunshine, and beautiful suntanned women, but had little tolerance or compassion for bums or anyone else who were "down on their knees," after several second chances.

He regularly exercised contempt for weakness. When a high-profile neighbor from his brief trailer park existence as a bachelor in Paradise Cove called on Otis for help out of a jam, for example, Otis had no time for the man once he had heard the charges against him.

"Otis, I'm in jail," said actor Dan Haggerty, who had portrayed Grizzly Adams on NBC for two years in the late 1970s. "You got to come get me out."

"What happened?" asked Otis. "Speeding?"

"No, no, no," said Haggerty. "They claimed that, when they pulled me over, I threw some little package of white stuff in the leaves."

"Did you?" asked Otis.

"Oh no, no! I wouldn't deal in drugs. No, no, no."

Otis didn't believe him. Neither did a jury. Haggerty served ninety days for selling cocaine, was no longer able to get work in television, and never had an audience with Otis Chandler again.

But there were friends, colleagues, and occasionally family members who committed far less heinous crimes and still fell into Otis's disfavor. He had little tolerance for those who could not meet his moral standards, although he could not easily define what those standards were and did not always measure up to them himself. Otis was a stranger to ambiguity, moral or otherwise, and he could not stomach philosophical debate of any kind. Eggheads left him cold, and hidden agendas always took him by surprise. As Frank McCulloch had observed years earlier, his biggest failing was his inability to grasp subtleties, and his greatest sins were those of King Lear: accepting flattery too quickly while spurning criticism, even when it was constructive, well intentioned, and deserved.

As Otis approached his fifty-eighth birthday, his ability to cut people out of his life like unwanted appendages and move on was breathtaking. If an individual did not fit his worldview, or if he believed himself to have been betrayed, he replaced the offending person as easily and with as much prejudice as Jack Burke.

He once dispatched John Thomas to snoop around the Orange County plant to investigate rumors that Michael Chandler might be carrying on an affair with a married woman. When J. T. brought him back the news that, yes, it was indeed true, Otis took out his displeasure not on Michael, but upon the wicked messenger. He declined to speak with Thomas for several weeks afterwards.

For all his faults, Otis Chandler was the undisputed Saint of Times Mirror Square. Younger staff members took their editorial freedom for granted, ascribing only token credit to the tall, fit, and shy grandfather whom they occasionally ran into while waiting for the elevators or standing in line for the daily gourmet buffet in the executives' Picasso Room cafeteria. Although the shoulders were still as broad as a barn and the eyes as blue and piercing as those of the *Times'* eagle, Otis Chandler did strike some reporters and editors as long in the tooth: a courtly presence from a kinder, gentler era.

Bill Thomas and the generation of editors who remembered the rough-and-tumble Nick Williams/Otis Chandler era knew better. Unlike his more modest predecessor, Thomas proudly boasted of his own numerous achievements while serving at the will and pleasure of Otis Chandler, but he never forgot that all his glorious efforts on behalf of the First Amendment and the public's right-to-know

would have been for naught had Otis not been the *Times*' shield against politicians, advertisers, and landed gentry, particularly and especially Otis's own family.

Through Chandis Securities, Harry Chandler's final legacy, men and women who had never set foot inside a newsroom still wielded enormous power on the Times Mirror Board. The Garlands and the Babcocks, the Goodans and the Williamsons, and the Chandlers ran the publicly traded Times Mirror Company like a shadow government, and Otis was all that stood between them and the city desk.

During the years since Norman had taken the company public, family members held fewer seats on the board as their stock was diluted, but Chandis Securities still held about 30 percent of Times Mirror's outstanding shares. Furthermore, the extended Chandler family found a way to have its cake and eat it too through a legal sleight of hand developed and encouraged by Dan Frost, the family's emerging spokesman. Using a newly opened New York Stock Exchange[2] loophole designed to protect established family businesses from Wall Street's feeding frenzy in the mid-1980s, Times Mirror shares held by Chandis Securities were declared to outvote all other stock ten to one.[3] Thus, when it came time to elect board members at the annual Times Mirror shareholders' meetings, one share of Chandis stock represented ten shares belonging to any other investor. Dividends might be paid out equally, but the Chandlers retained all the power they needed to control the board.[4]

Even with this tactic, the *Times* was no longer the family-run operation it had once been when Otis could just pop into Nick Williams's office for a chat. The publisher's job had evolved into that of referee among the disparate divisions that comprised a mammoth conglomerate.

"The best thing Otis ever did for me personally, outside of making me editor, was keep the sixth floor off my back," said Bill Thomas.

Times reporters, critics, and editors were oblivious. They enjoyed nearly absolute editorial freedom in the mid-1980s. Even at the *Dallas Times Herald*, where he literally ran the show, Tom Johnson had never witnessed an operation quite like the *Los Angeles Times*. Against constant corporate pressure to collapse the wall between editorial and advertising, Otis stood firm and advised Johnson to do the same: Advertisers could never be allowed to influence the news.

Otis had never considered his conviction a luxury. L.A.'s economy had kept humming, even during recession, because the nation's highest concentration of defense plants had been built in Southern California after World War II. Employers needed the *Times*. So did employees and consumers. Most of all, advertisers needed the *Times*. Only the rankest ad agency amateur ever asked the *Times* to publish a story about a client as a condition for placing an ad. Anyone naïve enough to make such a demand risked being banned altogether from the biggest,

richest, most prestigious newspaper west of the Mississippi.

Otis Chandler did not tolerate such nonsense. He didn't run a shopper. He ran a newspaper, and it was prestigious: a proud paper for a proud city.

Harry Chandler's Cal Tech now outranked the Massachusetts Institute of Technology and Princeton as the nation's top think tank. Mia Chandler Frost's Los Angeles County Museum of Art and the new L.A. Museum of Contemporary Art would soon be joined by the $2-billion-endowed Getty Museum as formidable rivals to New York's venerable host of art museums, including the Holy See of galleries, Fifth Avenue's Metropolitan Museum of Art. Buff's Music Center was every bit as spectacular as Manhattan's Lincoln Center or Washington's Kennedy Center. In addition to hosting the L.A. Philharmonic, the Dorothy Chandler Pavilion had also become home to the annual Academy Awards. Could New York match that?

As for the *Times,* its triumphs showed no signs of ending. Television critic Howard Rosenberg won the 1985 Pulitzer Prize for criticism and yet another news bureau opened, this one in Manila. *Times* weekday circulation hit 1.1 million at the same time that its only direct competition, the slowly dying *Herald-Examiner,* dropped below 240,000.

The *Los Angeles Times Sunday Magazine* debuted as a direct answer to the *New York Times Sunday Magazine.* Transcontinental rivalry peaked with an *Adweek* survey that now officially ranked Otis's *Times* a very close second in overall quality behind the Sulzbergers' *Times.* Universally praised for its political coverage, its editorial pages, its foreign bureau system, and even its sports, the *Times* was now at the top of every media critic's list of the best in the nation: better than the *Washington Post* and, at times, even superior to that other *Times.*

When the *New York Times* took aim once more at the West Coast with the launch of a National edition in 1985, Times Mirror answered the challenge with its own invasion of the Sulzbergers' home turf. *New York Newsday,* a Manhattan version of Times Mirror's hugely successful Long Island tabloid, leased three floors of a Third Avenue high-rise, hired 150 new reporters, and flooded New York's already saturated media market with an initial circulation of 100,000 a day. Guided by former *Newsday* publisher David Laventhol, who had risen within the Times Mirror hierarchy to oversee the company's East Coast newspapers, *New York Newsday* had a virtually unlimited budget with a $10-million-a-year cushion built in until this newest of New York newspapers got on its feet solidly enough to begin stealing both the *New York Times'* customers and its advertisers.

Back in his office at the pinnacle of Times Mirror Square, Otis Chandler beamed. The curse of the literati had turned out to be tripe. L.A. was not the land of lotus eaters. Instead of eating lotus, Otis stood at the threshold of force-feed-

ing crow to every Midtown blowhard who had ever spent a night at the Beverly Hills Hotel and tried to pass off the experience to *New Yorker* subscribers as a validation of Southern California's banality.

As Randy Newman said in *I Love L.A.*, each day did, indeed, look like another perfect day. The sun *was* shining all the time, and Otis Chandler had been born to ride. He did, in fact, *love* L.A., clear up until the moment that Bob Erburu sent a special envoy from the Times Mirror Board in the closing days of 1985 to tell Otis that his time was up.

MORE THAN A DECADE AFTERWARDS, Otis still refused to call his descent from power a "palace coup." He chose instead to perpetuate the fiction that the decision to step down was solely his own. Although those close to him say that he adjourned to his favorite Italian restaurant, downed a bottle of wine, and cried real tears following his meeting with the Erburu committee, Otis never spoke of that painful and unmanly moment. Wimps wept. Real men accepted their fate and carried on, upper lip stiff, head high. Following the announcement that he would surrender his titles and responsibilities as chairman and editor in chief as of January 1, 1986, he presented the decision as strictly his own during the ensuing flurry of interviews with the media.

"I'm very pleased to be going to chairman of the executive committee and maybe only go to the office three days a week," he cheerfully told Cable News Network's business news anchor Tom Cassidy, adding

> The Times Mirror Company is doing exceedingly well under Bob Erburu and I'm very happy to be turning over the chairmanship to Bob, so I don't really think in terms of my kids or any other members of the family coming in. I think that's gone. I think it's like Ford Motor Car Company and other companies that have been family companies, and then you bring in these wonderfully capable professional managers and they have to have their futures and they have to have their careers and I think that we owe it to them. I think the worst thing that I could do would be to insist that there be a spot kept open at some senior level for my son Norman or one of my daughters, if they were to be interested. I'm not that kind of person and I don't think that they expect that of me.

At Times Mirror Square, the transition to "wonderfully capable professional managers" was seamless. With Bill Thomas still running *Times* editorial and Tom Johnson in the publisher's suite, most employees remained blissfully ignorant of the change. Otis had been pulling back anyway since he had made Johnson the new publisher.

Times Mirror lawyers and the rest of its wonderfully capable professional managers had been softening him up for years, but it still took a facedown with peers he had known and respected for a quarter of a century to send Otis Chandler into voluntary exile. Led by Dan Frost, Erburu's dour former Gibson, Dunn and Crutcher partner and Otis's brother-in-law, the entourage included Peter Bing, a real estate heir and a Stanford University trustee, and Roger Heyns, the Hewlett-Packard Foundation chief and former chancellor of the University of California. Their message was simple: The time had come for Otis Chandler to leave.

"Otis was helped along, out the door," said one of the few *Times* staff members close enough to the Chandlers to understand or appreciate what had happened. The staff member added ominously: "That was Dan Frost's first great move."

Otis's son Harry staged a small surprise party upon his father's retirement as chairman, inviting about two dozen of Otis's closest Times Mirror colleagues. Otis was presented with a copy of a *Los Angeles Times* Extra headlined

OTIS CHANDLER WALKS

Tom Johnson was there, as were Franklin Murphy and Bill Thomas. Dan Frost was not. Following the toasts and token testimonials that were spoken through strained smiles, even Otis's most loyal longtime supporters did not think of challenging his departure. The atmosphere was that of a shotgun wedding ceremony where half the guests waxed nostalgic, unaware that anything was amiss, while the other half wanted to get through the nuptials quickly before someone came to his senses and refused to forever hold his peace.

Otis did not put up a fight. He got over his checkmate surprisingly quickly, considering the snide abuse he took from subordinates such as Noel Greenwood, the metropolitan editor, who accused him of giving up the *Times* to go surfing. He did not. Surfing was a young man's sport, like auto racing. Otis busied himself in less strenuous, if equally trivial, pursuits. Racing might suit a younger man better, for instance, but only an older, richer man could collect such automobiles. Otis poured himself into this new pastime with a vengeance.

He reinvented his Vintage Museum, buying back some of the same cars that he'd sacrificed during his divorce. Among his prize possessions were his *LeMans* Porsche 917K, the Porsche 935 that he and J. T. drove at Watkin's Glen in 1979, and, of course, his beloved Duesenberg Tourster. But Otis spent most of his time and money cornering the market on cherry Dodge Chargers, "monster-motor" Chevelles, Ford Cyclone Torinos, Camaros, Novas, and Pontiac GTOs.

These were the cars of his youth and of his own children's teenage years, the very best of the so-called muscle cars that Detroit had cranked out by the thou-

sands during the 1960s and early 1970s, before higher EPA standards, OPEC, and the threat of Arab oil embargoes diminished America's appetite for high-powered gas guzzlers. Otis's car-collecting peers thought he was crazy to invest in such rust buckets; but when car magazines began featuring his museum in their pages and publishers started printing books on the subject, he felt once again like an Air Force second lieutenant, buying low and selling high.

"By getting in it early when I did," Otis boasted to *AutoWeek* at the time, "I was able to get all the really rare stuff before it got too expensive."

His museum also featured his taxidermy collection, making the motor/mammal melange at once startling and bemusing. Like the *Times* cleaning lady who screamed when she found a polar bear in the publisher's bathroom, visitors to the Otis Chandler Vintage Museum of Transportation and Wildlife occasionally recoiled with a yelp after catching sight of a lifelike cougar through the windshield of a Pierce Arrow.

Otis still went hunting, though less frequently and with a melancholy he had never experienced before. When he discovered that he had killed a tigress after examining its genitals, he found himself wondering whether he had murdered a mother. Dressing it out, he found that the cat was not pregnant, but that didn't stop the nagging knowledge that she would never bear kittens and perpetuate the species, and that he was responsible for this tragedy.

"There's a sadness when I go to a deer, or an elk or a sheep, or even when I pick up a dead Canadian honker or duck," he mused for the first time in his life. "There's a sadness there. There's a loss, you know, like maybe I'm gonna be that animal in the next life or something.

"I don't get any joy out of seeing the animal lying there. The wind's gone out, and it doesn't have the majesty as it did when it was up there on its feet. And it's a sadness. There's no question. It's a sadness."

Belated introspection did not end his will to hunt. It never would. He knew enough about Genesis to reserve his God-given right to dominion over all the beasts of the Earth and fishes of the sea. To Otis, that stewardship would always include the right to harvest with a gun or a rod and reel.

"I still try to find the world record for this or the world record for that," he said. "But, now, I get almost the same sadness when I see a great trout that I played for half an hour and he's flipping on the ground starving for breath. There's a sadness, and I think that comes with age and . . . you wonder, 'What right do I have to kill this wonderful, majestic sheep or bear or whatever?'

"And you begin to ask yourself some real questions. And I think you hunt less, and you have more respect for the animals. . . . You should thank God that you have the opportunity in your life to hunt these magnificent animals."

OTIS CHANDLER'S ABSENCE from the *Times* did not slow the Times Mirror media machine. In May 1986, the company purchased the *Baltimore Sun* and the influential *National Journal*, which was aimed at federal officials and key decisionmakers. One month later, Times Mirror dumped the faltering *Dallas Times Herald* for $110 million.

"It was very painful personally for me," Tom Johnson told one interviewer, his voice cracking.

Johnson blamed the Texas economy for the *Times Herald*'s falling circulation, but mismanagement after he left Dallas in 1977 had a lot to do with it. When the competing *Dallas Morning News* began raiding several of its stars, the *Times Herald* refused even to match salary offers. Veteran columnist Blackie Sheridan, who jumped to the *News* for a pay boost, took roughly 10 percent of the *Times Herald*'s subscribers with him. In a similar vein, the *Times Herald* dropped its popular Sunday supplement, *Parade Magazine,* to save money and wound up losing even more readers.

By the time Tom Johnson rode to the rescue in late 1984, spending $45 million trying to clean up the mess in Dallas, it was already too late. One of Times Mirror's last-ditch measures was to install a new editor who had nearly twenty years experience as a wunderkind at the *Washington Post.*

A perpetually preppy-looking young man with square jaw and feral good looks, Shelby Coffey III was generally credited as the editor who brought a breezy, sharp wit to the *Post*'s Style section. He spoke with a Virginia drawl, ran marathons, and pumped iron, just like Otis. The two first met at a Washington, D.C., health club in 1984 while Coffey was still at the *Post* and Otis was still Times Mirror editor in chief. Coffey's mania for weight lifting so impressed Otis that it led indirectly to the Dallas appointment. After the ambitious Coffey had quit the *Post* in 1985 and spent an abortive year as editor of *U.S. News and World Report,* Tom Johnson offered him the Dallas job for the last few months that Times Mirror owned the *Times Herald.*

Although he hardly had a chance as *Times Herald* editor to demonstrate his capabilities, Coffey left as deep a first impression on Tom Johnson as he had on Otis. Besides being exceedingly trim, impeccably dressed, and regal in his bearing, Coffey was glib. If he lacked in-depth knowledge of a subject, he was usually able to muster enough superficial facts to give the impression of knowledge to most he met, at least briefly.

"He could carry on a conversation with anybody on any subject for about five minutes," said Dan Sullivan, former *Times* theater critic.

Johnson urged Bill Thomas to find a place for Coffey after the *Times Herald* was sold, and Thomas obliged. He created the title "deputy associate editor," and

put the suave young Southerner in charge of beefing up the *Times'* "soft" sections, which were still overseen by veteran associate editor Jean Sharley Taylor. No one was fooled by Coffey's sudden appearance, least of all Taylor, who welcomed his help, but she understood that Coffey was being groomed for bigger things.

Dallas was not the only newspaper war that Times Mirror lost in the mid-1980s. Since the day he first stepped into Otis's shoes, Tom Johnson had been plagued by the declining fortunes of the *Denver Post,* which fell under his direct authority, just as *Newsday,* the *Hartford Courant,* and all the other East Coast newspapers were the responsibility of David Laventhol. In the autumn of 1986, when the *Post* was running a poor second to its rival, the *Rocky Mountain News,* Johnson told *Forbes* magazine's Kathleen Wiegner that Times Mirror's Denver franchise was surging and had no place to go but up.

"In Denver we are ahead on Sunday, and we're gaining share on daily circulation," he proclaimed. "I think we have one of the strongest management teams of any newspaper in the country."

Less than a year later, he ate his words. With minimal fanfare, Erburu and the Times Mirror Board unloaded the *Post* for the fire sale price of $95 million to New Jersey–based Media News Group, the same bargain-basement newspaper chain that had purchased the *Dallas Times Herald* two years earlier.

The *Los Angeles Times* continued to expand during the late 1980s. A Nicaragua bureau opened in 1987 and Tom Johnson proudly announced the largest capital outlay in *Times* history: $405 million for upgraded presses in Orange County and the San Fernando Valley and construction of a brand-new state-of-the-art printing plant about a mile from Times Mirror Square in downtown L.A.

At the same time that Times Mirror embarked on its building binge, GTE Directories Corporation bought Times Mirror Press, the direct descendant of the Mirror Printing Office & Book Bindery that Jesse Yarnell, Thomas J. Caystile, and S. J. Mathes founded in 1873. Fittingly, with the passing of the last of Harry Chandler's sons,[5] the *Times* ended a century of involvement in the lucrative business of printing telephone directories.

Times Mirror had switched to publishing far more sophisticated books: scientific, medical, and technical reference journals, acquired with the 1986 purchase of CRC Press; maps, atlases, and automotive technical publications produced by H. M. Gousha Co., also purchased that same year; and college textbooks, published by the Richard D. Irwin division of Dow Jones until Times Mirror bought it in 1988.

The media giant had also developed an appetite for specialty magazines. *Outdoor Life, Popular Science, Golf,* and *Ski* had been Times Mirror staples since the early 1970s, but by 1987 the company had added *Field & Stream, Home Mechanix, Skiing, Yachting,* and *Salt Water Sportsman* to its stable.

Juggling assets during the late 1980s, Chairman Erburu sold off three of Times Mirror's least profitable television stations plus an 80 percent stake in Publishers Paper Company, the forest products company that Norman Chandler had acquired back in 1948 as a hedge against constantly rising paper costs. Newsprint prices were flat, Erburu explained to the shareholders. Paper was not a high-growth industry at a time when major media companies such as Times Mirror were looking for a minimum 20 percent return on investment.

The company did hold on to its four network-affiliated stations in Texas, Alabama, and Missouri, however, as well as its growing cable television division. By 1988, Times Mirror was the nation's eleventh-largest cable operator, with 825,000 subscribers in fifteen states.

NORM CHANDLER STAYED HOME on the evening of October 14, 1988. He usually got stuck with baby-sitting on Cub Scout nights, but he didn't mind. He was swim coach, soccer dad, and chief surfing and dune buggy driving instructor for four of his towheads. He and Jane had given Otis two grandsons and a pair of granddaughters, and Norm loved to spend time with all of them.

He felt nauseous and threw up that night. When Jane arrived home, he told her he felt peculiar, as though he was coming down with the flu. Norm had already put the kids to bed and now his wife felt his head for fever and then put him to bed, too. Next day, Norm hopped right up, showered, shaved, and went off to work. The symptoms from the night before had vanished.

"None of us thought anything more of it," Jane Chandler said years later.

Norman was doing his job at the time, but not much more. There were no ten- or twelve-hour days. Any professional passion for workaholism had been burned out of Otis Chandler's eldest son years earlier. He looked upon his current *Times* post, that of composing room foreman, as just part of a humdrum daily routine. At thirty-eight, his family and especially his kids were a hell of a lot more important than putting in extra hours at a career that just wasn't going anywhere.

Norm Chandler had been in "training" for twelve years. His mother raised hell with Otis about failing to promote his own son toward the publisher's suite, but Norm didn't have what Tom Johnson and David Laventhol had, Otis insisted. Even the indefatigable Missy had grown discouraged after years of running up against her mulish ex-husband.

"I think she's dead wrong, but I can see why she felt that way," said Otis. "She's an emotional mother. The Chandler family would not have accepted Norman as publisher. It just wouldn't work out. It would have been the Peter Principal if the company put him in. He would have failed 'cause it wasn't meant to be."

Norm began to think of career consolation prizes. Of all the posts he had held at Times Mirror, he liked reporting best, but despaired that he had squandered years trying in vain to become a *Times* jack-of-all-trades, and he was certainly not a master journalist. If he applied now to go back to work on the city desk and was rejected either for lack of experience or because he was regarded as some sort of Chandler prima donna, it would be the ultimate humiliation. He'd already pretty much resigned himself to his father's public prognostications that no Chandler would ever succeed Otis.

Three days after his flu scare, Norm started the day by jogging around the neighborhood. Still a triathlete, he had been training for months for his next big Iron Man test. He'd been gone for about half an hour when the phone rang. Jane picked it up. It was a neighbor. She told Jane that she had better get down to the corner right away.

"He had fallen," Jane said. "And when I went to help him up, he didn't recognize me."

This time, she didn't just put her husband to bed. They visited the family doctor and Norm tried to explain away his temporary nausea, amnesia, and loss of balance. He pushed himself, Norm explained, just like his old man. This time he may have just pushed too hard: broken a capillary, perhaps, or dehydrated himself to the point of delirium.

No, said the doctor. These weren't symptoms from hematoma or dehydration. The delirium he'd exhibited on the street corner had vanished as mysteriously as it had begun. There was something else going on. The doctor advised further tests.

Norm put his clothes on and prepared to go home.

No, said the doctor. He needed further tests *immediately*.

"I remember when Norman came down with this," said Otis. "We rushed him to the Pasadena Huntington Hospital, did a brain scan. The doctor came out and told Missy and Bettina and myself and Jane, 'He has a brain tumor. It looks like it's inoperable.'"

There was no telling whether the growth was malignant or benign. The mass was too large and too close to essential sections of the occipital lobe, and would have left him damaged, perhaps dead, if neurosurgeons tried taking it out.

"First they say it's cancerous and then they say maybe it isn't," said Otis. "We couldn't do a biopsy, but it doesn't really matter. If it's a growing tumor, it's gonna kill the person anyway, whether it's cancerous or not. So it doesn't really matter."

Jane went into shock, Missy went into tears, and Otis went looking for answers. He knew of no brain tumors among the Chandlers or the Buffums, nor had there been a history of such trouble on the Brants' side of the family. He looked at and quickly rejected Michael's theory that Missy's drinking and nicotine habits might have had some effect. Given the robust health of Harry, Cathleen, and Carolyn, the poisoned-in-the-womb hypothesis didn't carry much currency. As for Missy, she foisted the blame squarely on her ex-husband. Otis had put undue stress on all his children, she said, but especially on the oldest.

"My father-in-law was the ultimate five-year planner," agreed Jane. "When Norm and I first started dating, my father-in-law not only had his own goals set out for the next five years, he also made up five-year plans for each and every one of his kids."

Jane did not concur with her mother-in-law's diagnosis, however. She prodded Norm's physicians and learned that the tumor was of a slow-growth variety that had probably been there since birth. It had grown exponentially, increasing in size faster and faster the older that Norm got. All that could be done was to send him home with prescriptions for dilantin, phenobarbital, and a host of other anti-convulsants, and monitor the tumor's growth every few months.

Otis recalled sitting on the edge of his son's hospital bed and breaking down.

"Norman I . . . this should not be you," he stammered. "If this has to happen, I would do anything in the world to change places with you, because I've had a wonderful life and you have not. You've got half your life in front of you."

Norm refused to join his father in his grief. Although he was mystified by this sudden bombshell in what was otherwise a relatively pacific life, Norm's reaction was a carbon copy of what his father's reaction would probably have been. Norm resolved to lick it, a course of action that should have come as no surprise to Otis, but did.

"I was very, very upset about it for Norman's sake most of all, and for Jane and the family and Norman's dreams and hopes," said Otis. "I could see everything was over for him."

No, it was not over, Norm told his father. He was a Chandler, and Chandlers didn't just throw in the towel over bad news. Chandlers persevered. Over the next several months, he surprised everyone, especially his father, with his resolve: a driving force that Otis had always maintained was missing in Norm during his *Times* training program.

Norm and Jane traveled to the University of California at San Francisco, where the latest medical breakthroughs were being made in neuropathology. After exhausting the limited information about brain tumors that Western medicine had to offer, he turned to the East and read up on every holistic, dietary, or Zen herbal

therapy he could find. Finding no magic potion at the end of the New Age rainbow, he decided to create his own regimen to battle the demon inside his skull. He put the prescription drugs away and got back into training. In March 1989, he ran the Los Angeles Marathon. Afterwards, he looked himself in the mirror and saw a sleek, sharp, healthy male specimen in his prime who had just kicked ass and felt like going out and doing it all over again. He felt pretty damn good about himself.

Six months had passed since his diagnosis, and there had been no further incidents of blackout or nausea or any of the other symptoms that first led him to the hospital. Norm asked for no sympathy, especially from his father.

"He talks a lot about how he manages himself and so on, but he doesn't cry and say, 'Don't you feel sorry for me?' or, 'I'm gonna die,'" said Otis. "He's very bold in his managing of his health problem. Very. Which surprises me, 'cause Norman, as he was growing up, had a low pain-curve response. He had a very sensitive nervous system as a little boy. He broke his arm once and there were other injuries, and it really hurt him. I don't think he screamed because he wanted to be screaming. He screamed because it hurt like hell."

Norm grew braver as the weeks passed and he experienced no more symptoms. He concluded that his exercise regimen was doing the trick. Following his initial diagnosis, his driver's license had been automatically revoked, as required under California law, but after nearly nine months without further physical or psychological problems, he decided to get his license back. He hired a lawyer and set a court date. Even Jane was beginning to feel optimistic.

"And then, one day, about a year later, while we were all up at Dana Point, at Mama Buff's beach house, he had a seizure," said Jane. "It lasted for four hours. It has a name, which I have put out of my mind. Not a grand mal seizure. Worse. Much, much worse. When you go into this kind of convulsion, you usually don't survive."

Norm did survive, chiefly—and ironically—because he'd recently run the marathon and was in spectacular physical condition. A lesser heart would not have survived, his doctors told him. The prognosis was good, they said. He had been fortunate.

But he didn't feel fortunate. For the first time, the Chandler grit faltered. Norm was frightened. Deathly frightened.

Suddenly, there was a great sadness about him, like a Canadian gosling headed south for the winter, only to be shot out of the sky by a hunter's stray bullet.

CHAPTER 25

UNLIKE THE PREVIOUS SEVEN *Los Angeles Times* editors, the eighth was selected not so much on the strength of his leadership skills or his breadth and
depth of knowledge, nor for his chumminess with the publisher, or even for the
ink that might course through his veins; he was selected on his ability to write a
really terrific term paper.

In 1989, Bill Thomas would turn sixty-five, and he had let it be known several
years earlier that he planned to retire, take life a little easier, and perfect his golf
game. Once he walked out the door, he promised, there would be no looking
back, and certainly none of the postretirement consulting that Otis had imposed
upon Nick Williams.[1] Thomas's departure would belatedly force Tom Johnson to
do what he had been postponing for nearly a decade: select his own editor.

Otis remembered, "I had told Tom when I was editor-in-chief and publisher,
'You don't have to fire Bill Thomas. You can keep him as a consultant.' He'd
never done that (fired someone) in his entire career. He had been the number-
two man with us and at the [LBJ-owned] television station. I brought Tom in as
editor and publisher in Dallas, but he reported to me as the Times Mirror Group
vice president, so I made the tough decisions. He finds decisions involving people very difficult. I think he has always been a wonderful number-two man as
long as he had somebody at the top to report to. Someone who would help him
make tough decisions."

The way Johnson selected Bill Thomas's successor reflected that indecision. Instead of interviewing candidates, consulting colleagues, and making his choice, as
virtually every other publisher in America did when picking a new editor, Johnson created a rigorous collegial competition that forced candidates to behave as if
they were ambitious academics vying for a coveted university professorship. For
the better part of a year, the four finalists underwent a beauty contest. They appeared at informal panel discussions, took individual oral exams, and finally,
wrote what amounted to a master's thesis on the strengths and weaknesses of the
Times and each candidate's plans for taking the paper to a higher level. In this final test, Johnson posed sixteen questions, including: "If the *New York Times* is
intellectually stimulating, what makes it so and what does it do what the [*Los Angeles*] *Times* doesn't?"

The inside track from the outset belonged to Charles Shelby Coffey III. Not
only was he the only true outsider in the running but he also had the kind of East
Coast pedigree that had made Otis lust after Joe Alex Morris, Robert Elegant,
and even Bob Donovan. Coffey was a lean and hungry Tennessean whose grand-

father had been a U.S. senator and whose own father had been president of the Chattanooga area bar association. Like Otis, Coffey liked to pump iron, but unlike Otis, Coffey also liked to quote from Thucydides, impress lunch companions by ordering in French, and brazenly display any bit of erudition that might burnish his take-charge image to a dazzle. Even after years of banquet and boardroom glad-handing, Otis was still stiff and uncomfortable in crowds, but not C. Shelby Coffey III. He was as slick as butter-basted foie gras.

"He was my choice," said Otis. "With a lot of encouragement from me, Tom selected Shelby."

His rivals were all dry-cleaned, fluffed, and pressed *Times*men,[2] each with at least twenty years service to the fat, formidable broadsheet of Spring Street. The *Times* had grown grand in its scope and its revenue to the extent that its own journalists happily nicknamed it the Velvet Coffin: a news organization so affluent that 1,200 of the best reporters and editors in the world had ceased the eternal search for the Big Story and gone there to die.

During his own twenty years in the Velvet Coffin, Bill Thomas and his edict, "do it once, do it right, do it long," had aged with the *Times'* core readership. As the final computerized decade of the twentieth century came into view, time itself seemed to speed up and compress into smaller and smaller bytes, leaving less and less time over the breakfast table to ruminate on fascinating aboriginal lore from the Australian outback or on the clandestine Israeli airlift of Ethiopian Jews out of southern Sudan. Readers preferred news that affected their own lives and they wanted it now. Leisure time was a luxury that fewer and fewer *Times* subscribers enjoyed.

Matching the national mood, a new model for American journalism had emerged in Gannett Newspapers' decade-old experiment, *USA Today*. Although it was still far from going into the black, the country's first truly national newspaper had gained popularity among young, affluent readers by taking the opposite approach to the *Times'* daily news magazine format. Color photos, charts, and graphics created a catchy display at least as important as the written word, and the stories themselves were reduced to their absolute essence: no more than a half-dozen paragraphs for most articles and perhaps a dozen for the major front-page story every day.

Economics now posed a new and unexpected challenge to the logorrhea encouraged during the Thomas era by squeezing the *Times* "news hole"—its daily available space for stories—down to two-thirds of what it had been just a few years earlier. Ownership of major *Times* advertisers, notably department stores and grocery markets, had fallen into fewer and fewer hands; the competing retailers who had once fattened the *Times* into a lethal weapon now needed far less ad space. Throw in the ever-encroaching reach of television, whose astronomical ad

rates had been reduced considerably thanks to the growing competition afforded by cable television, and the *Times* advertising department[3] began to sense real trouble. Salesmen who had grown indolent after spending almost two decades of taking ads over the phone now had to get out in the field and hustle, just like the advertising sales forces of any other publication.

On the editorial side, Coffey appeared to be the magician who could shake torpor from the *Times.*

After graduating from the University of Virginia, he started his career at the *Washington Post* as the third-string boxing writer, rose quickly to assume control of *Potomac Magazine,* the *Post's* moribund Sunday supplement, and at the tender age of twenty-nine segued from the revitalized *Potomac* to the editorship of the *Post's* coveted daily Style section in 1976. There he earned his reputation as the *Post's* preeminent hands-on reporters' cheerleader.

Before taking over as editor and then publisher at *Newsday,* Times Mirror's other rising star, David Laventhol, had been Style's editor during the late 1960s. He turned it into the snappy, gossipy, sharply written section that gained national notoriety for its sassy . . . well, style. Coffey continued Laventhol's tradition in the 1970s, and unwittingly found a future ally at Times Mirror in the terse, rumpled New Yorker with the baby face, bloodhound eyes, and bad comb-over. Laventhol had mixed shrewd with shambling; Coffey preferred slick blended with sly. Both men opted for Style over substance.

As the *Post's* features guru, Coffey shone; and he knew how to hold the hands of such prima donnas as Sally Quinn, future wife of the *Post's* editor, Ben Bradlee. Coaching became Coffey's calling. His prep school wrestling coach once shrieked at the teenaged Coffey, "You've got to *want* it!" Twenty years later, he translated that same "can do" philosophy into a kind of pop psychology counseling service for staff writers. When his people suffered writer's block or couldn't find the handle on a story, he would follow a pep talk by reading them poetry or prescribing a little Marcel Proust to inspire and infect them. Such respected writers as the *Post's* Pulitzer Prize–winning television critic, Tom Shales, swore by Coffey's often quirky advice.

Of the four candidates for Thomas's job, Shelby Coffey was the standout. Otis mused that all he needed to do to shape Coffey into a faster, smoother, smarter, and more gregarious clone of himself was to teach this young Tennessee stud how to surf. Coffey wore a blue blazer and tie for his first visit to the beach. He replaced it with a cotton sweatshirt the second time; but throughout Tom Johnson's selection process, Otis was never able to coax Coffey to hang ten. His aversion to risk, especially in the face of the inevitable initial embarrassment, ought to have warned Otis and Tom Johnson, but it did not.

In April 1988, Johnson proclaimed that Coffey would succeed Bill Thomas, first as Thomas's executive editor and, by the end of the year, as editor. Coffey the consummate Easterner announced with gleeful grandiloquence: "The *Times* will continue to be a road map to the destiny of the West."

Eight months later, on January 1, 1989, Shelby Coffey officially became editor and executive vice president, and the *Los Angeles Times* entered a new era.

At his first convention of the American Society of Newspaper Editors, the new *Times* editor was congratulated on his winning entry in the *Times* editor sweepstakes by none other than Richard Nixon, another inveterate essayist, who had a lot in common with Coffey. Like the former president, Shelby had created a self-image early that remained unchanged for most of his life. A framed rendering of Rudyard Kipling's *If,* with its stirring advice to all boys, hung beside the young Coffey's bed when he was growing up, where it could be internalized like a rosary. And, like the youthful Nixon, Coffey learned sooner rather than later to turn the English language to his own ends, authoring an essay at age thirteen with the dactylic title: "Courage Is Needed When Tension Is High." In flawless penmanship, he had written, "The ultimate triumph is not to live a life of ease and pleasure, but to live life with courage; be remembered and revered."

It was good advice for an editor of the *Times.* Shortly before he turned over the keys to the executive washroom and got down to playing the back nine of his life, Bill Thomas told a reporter for the *San Francisco Examiner* that he had every faith in Coffey, but that his young successor was "walking on eggs."

"He has got to be careful how he handles himself," said Thomas. "He's essentially a careful fellow. He's got to get people with him."

FOR TEN YEARS, Buff had been sliding into senility. When osteoporosis snapped her hip in the mid-1980s, she took to her upstairs bedroom at Los Tiempos, never to descend again. When her old friend Olive Behrendt died in 1987, Otis and Bettina tried to coax her outdoors long enough to attend a special Philharmonic tribute to be conducted as part of Mrs. Behrendt's memorial service, but Buff refused.

"Mother, this is for Olive," said Otis. "I will carry you down the stairs, put you in a wheelchair, we'll get you a limo, and we'll wheel you in and put you in the front seat."

But Buff merely waved him off and gestured grandly from her four-poster.

"I've got everything I need right here," she said.

Her "gregarious Aquarius," astrologist Carroll Righter died in 1988 after predicting that he probably wouldn't survive once the sun entered the sign of Tau-

rus. He was right, of course, and Buff continued to believe her guru's mantra and preached it often to her son: "The stars impel, they don't compel. What you make of your life depends on you."

Otis claimed that he didn't believe in such hocus-pocus, but he wanted to humor her. He began to secretly water-down her booze to keep her alcohol consumption low. For her part, Buff continued to scold her only son, driving him farther away as her lucid moments dimmed.

"Oats came back from Alaska once and had a beard, and he went in to see his mother who had retired to the upper floor and never left," recalled Chuck Waterman, a Deke and a longtime Otis pal. "She told him that he had to shave it off, and he did."

Eventually, even dutiful Otis rarely came around. Camilla, who got along even less well with her mother as an adult than she had as a child, visited more frequently. Her husband cinched Camilla's final vicarious triumph over her mother by assuming the chairmanship of the Music Center in 1986 and badgering Bill Thomas into publishing a profile of Mia when she became president of the Los Angeles County Museum of Art. Like a cowbird who'd moved into the nest, Francis Daniel Frost now exercised silent dominion over all that his former client had built, from the *Times* to the Dorothy Chandler Pavilion.

"Frost was more or less dictatorial, which is more or less what [Buff] was, but she had more grounding than he did," said the Music Center operating company's original general manager William Severns. "She knew who to listen to."

Times theater critic Dan Sullivan learned firsthand how complete Frost's power had become when he wrote a commentary critical of a new addition to the Music Center: a separate opera house to be named for its chief underwriter, Mrs. Walt Disney. Sullivan's message was simple: Stop building more venues and start spending money to support the artists who perform there. During her final years as Music Center chair, Buff had put out the same message. What good was it to have a world-class cultural center with no substantial endowment to support singers, actors, musicians, and dancers to perform there?

"I'd heard of Dan Frost," said Sullivan. "I knew he was married to Otis's sister and that he was a conservative attorney with some interest in the arts, but I'd never met him until I wrote about the new Disney Hall. That was a mark of how we had been protected while Otis and Tom were publishers. I didn't even know who this guy was!"

Frost invited Sullivan to his Music Center office for lunch and Sullivan arrived fifteen minutes late.

"I couldn't find his office," said Sullivan, who had been writing about the Music Center for years, but had no idea that a labyrinth of administrative suites, corridors, and satellite offices honeycombed its interior. "That pissed him off right away and I still had no idea why I was being summoned. So we started eating and

he starts chewing me out, lecturing me. How did I dare write about the new Disney Hall this way? Now, I'd been with the *Times* for twenty years and nobody had ever talked to me that way. So I stopped him and said, 'Wait a minute. Why are you taking that tone? I've dealt with Mrs. Chandler. I know Otis. Who are you? My dad?'"

The reality was that Buff Chandler's beloved Music Center had fallen on hard times once she'd faded away. Whether it was for lack of Carroll Righter's prognostications or Dorothy Chandler's fund-raising mettle, the wedding cake architecture of the Mark Taper Forum, Ahmanson Theater, and Dorothy Chandler Pavilion did not pack them in the way they once had. Without flatly speaking out against the Jews and other Westside nouveau riche, Frost and his ilk had cast a pall over the ecumenicism that Buff had tried to inspire in her own vision of a Southern California cultural democracy.

"People just left," said a *Times* society writer of the era. "They took their checkbooks and went home. By the late 1980s, they'd lost an entire generation."

On the occasion of the Music Center's twenty-fifth anniversary in 1990, Otis reminisced about his mother's ability to bring "people together who'd never been together and had never expected to be together. At one point she asked me, 'Who owns the Lakers?' She'd never been to a game in her life but she went, and eventually she hit both [Lakers owner] Jerry Buss and [L.A. Kings owner] Jack Kent Cooke [for Music Center contributions]."

But the days when Buff would personally hit up Cary Grant or Henry Kissinger for a check, or follow Marion Davies into the ladies' room to solicit a contribution were gone forever.[4] None of Buff's blue-blooded successors wanted to play the role of an upscale Blanche Dubois, dependent upon the kindness of rich strangers, and her precious Music Center's fortunes declined.

At the dawn of the 1990s, Buff had only her full-time nursing staff, her live-in maids, and her kitchen help to keep her company. She had never forgiven Norman for dying first and said so over martinis, which she still shared on occasion with the few friends who still dropped by. Former Times Mirror executive Peter Fernald, who had become her public escort and companion after Norman's death, recalled that her infrequent breakdowns usually revolved around having to grow old alone.

"She'd really loved Norman," said Fernald, who remembered Los Tiempos' grand dame when she was still in her sprightly sixties. "When she'd come home late from a symphony or a fund-raiser and the front gate was already locked, she'd slip through a secret way at the side of the house just like a kid. Norman would already be in bed, but he'd leave little love notes for her on each step of the staircase, all the way to their bedroom."

It seemed as though Buff had outlived everyone and everything she'd ever

known, including the *Times'* only remaining cross-town rival. Her beloved Norman might not have lived to see William Randolph Hearst's union rag bite the dust, but Buff did.[5] The *Los Angeles Herald-Examiner*'s struggle to mimic *USA Today*'s graphs, maps, and terse approach to the news turned out to be too little too late. When the *Herald* ceased publication on November 2, 1989, it was one month and ten days short of its eighty-sixth birthday. Buff had already celebrated her eighty-ninth and was looking forward to her ninetieth. In her husband's day, or even in the era when her son ran the *Times*, there might have been a moment of silence for a fallen foe. But times had changed, and so had *Times* management.

The last *Herald-Examiner* headline read

SO LONG, L.A.

Within twenty-four hours, the *Times* had hired fourteen *Herald* staff members, grabbed thirty-one *Herald* comics, syndicated columnists, and features, and bought the *Herald*'s subscriber list and 10,000 *Herald* news racks. Nostalgia and sentiment in the form of the final edition of the *Herald-Examiner* cost a quarter, and once it was gone, the next day's edition of the *Times* took its place in every rack with a new logo that read "The best of the *Herald* is now in the *Los Angeles Times.*" Solicitors from Bettina's old boiler room operation at Times Mirror Square were on the phone night and day for months afterward in their efforts to persuade *Herald* subscribers to buy the *Times*.

Wanting to avoid the kind of Justice Department scrutiny surrounding the Chandler-Hearst collusion in the 1962 shutdown of the *Examiner* and the *Mirror*, David Laventhol flatly denied advance knowledge of the *Herald-Examiner*'s shutdown. Everything, including the *Times'* purchase of the subscriber list and the instant rack logos, were a matter of being prepared, he said with a straight face. Although admitting to regular conversations with Hearst executives for months leading up to the last day, Laventhol said, "Up until [the announcement], we didn't know if and when Hearst was going out of business."

Where the *Times* of Otis Chandler had been competitive, sometimes to a fault, the new *Times* could be ruthless. A newspaper war meant just that. Times Mirror Square evolved into a bunker with a militant chain of command bent on destroying the growing suburban dailies in Orange, Riverside, San Diego, San Bernardino, and Ventura counties. The new management rewarded good soldiers and punished dissent, but did so with cunning and stealth, best exemplified by the behavior of fifty-eight-year-old Laventhol himself, who had already demonstrated his skill in this new Darwinian corporate culture by leapfrogging past forty-seven-year-old Tom Johnson to the Times Mirror presidency in 1987.

On August 31, 1989, two months before the end of the *Herald-Examiner*, Laventhol leapfrogged again. This time, it was to the biggest prize of all: publisher of the *Los Angeles Times*.

EVEN ELEVEN YEARS AFTER HIS DEMOTION, Tom Johnson said he still didn't understand why he was "promoted" to the vacuous position of chairman of the Times Mirror Newspaper Management Committee and replaced by David Laventhol in the autumn of 1989.

"Frankly, I do not know exactly what happened to me and why," Johnson said in the summer of 2000. "That remains a mystery."

"That's bullshit," muttered Otis Chandler. "I told him what happened over and over again, and he was so emotionally caught up with this first failure in his life that he couldn't hear me."

The Times Mirror board, led by Chairman Erburu, President Laventhol, and Vice Chairman Phil Williams had ordered Johnson to not only replace Bill Thomas but to handle a long laundry list of unfinished assignments, according to Otis, including

- Fill the East Coast Newspaper Group vice presidency vacated by Laventhol when he was promoted to Times Mirror president.
- Shore up the waning fortunes of the Orange County edition of the *Times*, which was being badly beaten by the *Orange County Register,* by hiring a new editor and changing its management.
- Find a new circulation chief.
- Replace the editorial page editor, Tony Day.

As a board member, Otis endorsed most of the assignments, and told Johnson as much when he came to him for advice.

"Tom, you are not reporting to me any more," Otis recalled telling his former protégé. "I'm just chairman of the executive committee. These are your decisions that you should have made to put your own team in place and you haven't done it. And the consequences are not going to be good."

Although Johnson failed to carry through on nearly all his "assignments," said Otis, it was his refusal to fire Tony Day that cost him the publisher's suite. Neither Johnson nor any of the other top brass at Times Mirror Square would comment on the new position that had been created for the ex-publisher, but it was not a promotion.

"It doesn't sound as though Tom Johnson's job is one of those glittering steps upward," Ben Bagdikian, veteran newspaper critic and University of California journalism professor, wryly told the *Wall Street Journal*.

In retrospect, Tony Day admitted that he should have known that his own days were numbered after Coffey became editor. Like everyone else in the Velvet Coffin, Day had been lulled into a false sense of security following the twenty-year reign of Otis Chandler and nine more years of borrowed grace under Tom Johnson. Echoing Bill Thomas, Day praised Otis for "picking good people and protecting them so that they could do their job." While Otis was in charge, no one interfered with Day's operation of the op-ed pages. As publisher, Johnson extended the same protection, probably never dreaming that by doing so he would seal his own doom.

Tony Day's first warning came in the form of a phone call one night at home shortly after Coffey was named editor. Coffey wanted to know whether he was ready for a change after so many years in the same job.

"I told him no, but thank you," said Day.

He shrugged off his second warning a few weeks later as a typical and temporary mistake of a green manager. At Laventhol's behest, Coffey abolished the daily routine that Day had perfected after nearly twenty years of supervising the *Times* editorial process.

At 9:20 every morning Tony Day's staff met and hammered out a list of ideas that Day then presented to the publisher, editor, national editor, foreign editor, and metropolitan editor at a 10:30 A.M. meeting. Sometimes they would invite in an expert or a staff writer with special knowledge about a particular subject. Following a half-hour discussion, the editorial board reached consensus. The *Times* position on the topic of the day was selected, and Tony took the agenda back to his staff to be written up for the following day.

"We had a very sophisticated staff of editorial writers by then," said Day. "But sophisticated did not suit Laventhol, who is a remarkably inarticulate man."

Laventhol abolished the editorial board and the daily meetings. Instead, he ordered Day to present his daily editorial list directly to Coffey. The editor and publisher alone would decide what went into the next day's editorial page. When Day objected to this procedure, Laventhol told Tom Johnson it was time.

Johnson disagreed. He had never had his authority as publisher breached before and he refused to start by submitting to Laventhol's direct order to fire Tony Day. What happened next was a swift, clear example of how things were to be done under the new régime. If Johnson would not rid the *Times* of Tony Day, Laventhol would find someone else to do it. Tom went to Otis in a panic, but Otis had already heard from Erburu and Laventhol. They had asked him not to interfere, and Otis agreed. Otis told Johnson that he could not save him.

"You abandoned me!" Johnson accused.

"Grow up, Tom!" Otis answered.

Refusing to fire Tony Day was only the straw that broke the camel's back, Otis told the man to whom he had once affectionately referred as the younger brother that he'd never had. Tom had had his chance, and he had blown it. It was a chillingly cold side to Otis Chandler that Johnson had never seen before, and the episode left him in shock for years afterward.

"Tony Day is a good example of Tom's inability to make a decision until it is too late," said Otis. "Tom is told over and over. I told him. He didn't listen."

But Shelby Coffey did listen. Two months after David Laventhol supplanted Tom Johnson as the sixth publisher of the *Los Angeles Times*, Coffey called Tony Day into his office to tell him that he had been given a new assignment. He would be the *Times'* new columnist for ideas and ideologies.

"I told him to knock off the bullshit and at least leave me my dignity," said Day. "But it was clear with Tom and Otis and Bill gone that I was out there by myself. Laventhol was a very timid character, as was Shelby. They're afraid of their shadows and afraid of their leaders."

They did know how to carry out orders from above, though. The true leader of the new Times Mirror Company was Chairman Bob Erburu, whose strong Roman Catholic faith reportedly played a role in Tony Day's demise over the touchy issue of abortion.[6] Under Tony Day, the *Times* had presented a forceful pro-choice editorial position for years, whereas the archbishop of the Los Angeles Archdiocese, the praetorian Cardinal Roger Mahoney, took an understandably dim view of any kind of media support for *Roe v. Wade*. Not only did Mahoney rail against the *Times'* editorials but he took it a step further and leaned on Erburu.

Erburu was at the top of his game in 1989. The one-time USC journalism student whose sole claim to editorial expertise was a semester as editor of the *Daily Trojan*[7] had quietly built boardroom support since stepping up to the powerful role of Times Mirror CEO in 1980, and he now wielded enormous power. He sat on the board of the Federal Reserve Bank of San Francisco, among others, and his views about economics, politics, the arts, and the environment had begun to filter through the wall that Otis had built between the sixth floor and the city desk, coming to rest in the pages of the *Los Angeles Times*.

While Erburu presided over a below-market sell-off of some of Times Mirror's most valuable assets, including Publisher's Paper Company and its television stations, the round-faced lawyer, who bore a striking, almost fraternal resemblance to David Laventhol, continued steering a stubborn sell-off course for the *Times* that resembled that of the Titanic. With Dan Frost in the background and Chandler family members in full support of Erburu's policies, no one questioned his decision to continue pouring money into Laventhol's multimillion-dollar loser,

New York Newsday, at the same time laying full blame for failure in Denver, Dallas, and Orange County at Tom Johnson's feet.

With his cherubic grin and bland grandfatherly appearance, the Times Mirror chairman left no fingerprints during the summary dismissals of Tom Johnson and Tony Day. Still, Erburu's message, as well as that of his new city desk satraps, was as clear as a death knell. Fear and rumor raced at Mach 2 through the halls of Times Mirror Square in the closing days of 1989. If they could fire the publisher *and* the editorial page editor, they could fire anyone. There was no Newspaper Guild protection. There was no safety net at all except the one Otis Chandler had once extended, and now that had been tucked neatly away in the back of the Times Mirror boardroom. Who would be next?

Overnight, life inside the Velvet Coffin went from rosy to wretched, and most *Times*men and -women began leading professional lives of quiet desperation.

AS THE LAVENTHOL/COFFEY GRIP TIGHTENED, the *Times* introduced a new "faster format" designed to appeal to younger readers. Consisting of blurbs, news summaries, and page one "highlights" fronting all sections, the new look of the *Times* prompted unfavorable comparisons to *USA Today*, which had come to be known among journalists as "McPaper" (as in McDonald's), where fast does not always equal nourishing. Turning "A Special Kind of Journalism" on its head, the new *Times* promotion slogan was "Read This. Quick."

The *Times* also became politically correct under Coffey. He added a new page to the *Times Style Book* titled simply "Pejoratives."[8] Assuming that his own editors and reporters did not have the common sense to edit out vulgarities themselves, Coffey convened his own committee to ban offensive words from the newspaper. He announced that the *Times* would no longer tolerate racial or ethnic slurs, sexism, ageism, or homophobia. Thus, terms such as *inner city, hillbilly, handicap, ghetto, gal, skirt chaser,* or *old codger* were to be held in as equal disrepute as *nigger* or *bitch*. "At the height of the Shelby era," wrote one critic, "you couldn't swing a dead cat on Spring Street without hitting some touchy member of the Diversity Committee, who would then most likely announce that such a metaphor was offensive to feline-Americans and stomp off to organize a petition." Coffey's forbidden-word list was considered to have gone too far when phrases such as *Dutch treat* and *Indian giver* were temporarily outlawed as racial slurs.

A far more disturbing trend was to be found in the delay, defanging, or out-and-out deletion of controversy from news stories under the new régime.

In all the years the he'd served as managing editor and later, as editor of the *Times*, Bill Thomas remembered only one story that he'd been ordered to kill: an

exposé in the late 1960s involving L.A. investors who had donated counterfeit masterpiece paintings to a Seattle convent that had been run by unsuspecting Roman Catholic nuns. The donations were made for the express purpose of taking fraudulent income tax deductions, said Thomas, and although he was never given an answer as to why the story was spiked, he always suspected that some of the investors were probably friends or associates of Norman Chandler.[9] Thomas never again killed a *Times* story because he was ordered to do so, nor did he spike a story out of fear that he or his newspaper might offend a public figure.

In his first year as editor, Shelby Coffey or his subordinates spiked or sanitized more stories than Thomas had during his entire career.

When reporter Michael Cieply profiled Hollywood producer Jerry Weintraub and discovered that the filmmaker had a cocaine addiction, Coffey held the story for months until the *Wall Street Journal* published the same revelations on its front page. Only then did the *Times* publish a watered-down version of Cieply's profile in its business section.

When reporter Jill Stewart profiled Mayor Tom Bradley, she returned with a portrait of a politician who had probably been in office too long and owed too many favors to special interests.

"I was told to go back and start over," said Stewart. "I was told that the mayor was a great man and that was to be my starting premise, not that he might be a screwed-up man with problems. They said, 'This isn't about what *you* think; this is about what the *Times* thinks.'"

The recurrent theme dominating the newsroom since the demise of the *Herald-Examiner* was one of excessive caution: The *Times* was a big stick, reporters were warned, and they had to be careful how it was swung.

But even before the *Herald-Examiner* went out of business, Shelby Coffey's *Times* had pussyfooted around Tom Bradley. When reporter Glen Bunting uncovered a series of shady loans between city hall and Far Eastern Bank at a time when Bradley held a paid position as an adviser to the bank, his editors hid that glaring conflict-of-interest revelation until after Bradley had won reelection to an unprecedented fifth term as mayor. By then, *Herald-Examiner* reporter John Schwada had heard about the bank story and scooped the *Times* on the front page of the *Herald*, to the embarrassment of Bunting.

Once the story was out and the city attorney and a grand jury began investigating Bradley, a half dozen other *Times* reporters and editors joined Bunting on a task force designed to uncover all of Bradley's dirty laundry, an overreactive tactic the *Times* would employ again and again in the years ahead, each time the newspaper was scooped on a major story. Instead of admitting a mistake in judgment, *Times* editors threw reporters by the dozen into the breach, assuming that at least one of them might come up with a new angle to a story that the *Times* had already

been beaten on. Likening his reporters to locusts, Coffey called the tactic "swarming."[10]

One revelation that none in the Bradley task force expected to find was a girl-friend, twenty-four years Bradley's junior, who had used her unusual relationship with the married mayor as leverage for a lucrative public relations business. The reporters spent months confirming every detail of the relationship and even soft-ened the implication by referring to the woman who peddled access to the mayor as Bradley's "close personal friend" instead of his mistress.

"The *Times* lawyers cleared it for publication and then, the night before it was to go to press, Shelby called the desk from a skiing vacation in Aspen and or-dered out every reference to this woman being Bradley's lover," said one of the reporters in disgust. "No one would ever admit it, but we all knew that it was be-cause Bradley was black and his mistress was white."

FOLLOWING A YEAR OF SOUL-SEARCHING and job hunting, Tom Johnson re-signed from Times Mirror in August 1990 to become president of the Cable News Network. The former publisher received no credit when the *Washington Journalism Review* named the *Times* a "Newspaper to Watch for the '90s."

Similarly, Johnson was left out of the celebration in April 1990, when *Times* cir-culation reached its all-time high: 1,225,189 daily and 1,514,096 Sunday. The *Times* had at last surpassed the *New York Daily News* to become the largest daily metropolitan newspaper in the country. David Laventhol put out a management bulletin proclaiming June 14, 1990, to be "We're #1!" day, with free popcorn, coffee mugs, and T-shirts for all. The circulation surge represented the largest in-crease for the *Times* in more than twenty years, which put the lie to the Erburu-Laventhol charge that Tom Johnson had failed in the suburbs; indeed, the strongest gains of all were in Orange County and the San Fernando Valley.

Before Johnson left, the *Times* also began publishing its fourth daily regional edition for Ventura County and beefed up its San Diego edition with a new color tabloid section covering arts and entertainment. Jim Murray won the Pulitzer that year for his three decades of sprightly sports commentary, and two bureaus were opened, in Berlin and Brussels.[11]

But recession hit home in Southern California that year, too, harder than at any time since World War II. Defense plants closed. The Pentagon began to shut down air bases and naval facilities. Aerospace giants Rockwell, Hughes, Lock-heed, and McDonnell Douglas—the multibillion-dollar heir to that original 1920 pact between Harry Chandler and Donald Douglas—began laying off employees by the thousands. Real estate values plummeted. The ever-expanding L.A. econ-omy did the inconceivable: It shrank. Fast.

Instead of grappling with what was an economic emergency, Laventhol's *Times* partied on. To underscore its imagined global omnipotence, the *Times* made such sweeping gestures as the launch of a weekly World Report, described in its promotional blurbs as "a forward-looking, analytical approach to international news." One far less charitable critic labeled the ponderous section, "a weekly receptacle for all the bellybutton lint and miscellaneous dross dredged from the back pages of the *Times*' foreign correspondents' notebooks." A pair of Washington bureau reporters left on a year-long junket of twenty-one countries to interview "presidents and guerrillas, tycoons and laborers, pundits and poets" so that they could serve up two special reports loaded with even more thumb-sucking prognostications about how the rest of the world was handling the end of the Cold War.

Back home, the *Times* showed off its Shelby Coffey–inspired scholarship by publishing bilingually. A special news section called "A Land Divided: The Armenia/Azerbaijan Crisis," was printed in both English and Armenian; a few weeks later, the *Times* observed the fifteenth anniversary of the fall of Saigon with a special twelve-page section, "Legacy of War: Vietnamese in America," produced in English and Vietnamese.

As the Gulf War began to brew, one of Coffey's swarms produced the twelve-page "The Line in the Sand," to instruct *Times* readers in how the Persian Gulf crisis might change the future of international relations. As a service to the boys and girls in uniform, and because it made terrific promotional copy, the *Times* began publishing an eight-page daily Saudi Arabian edition, reproduced and distributed free to any soldier or airman who might have a fax machine in the desert.

With the *Herald-Examiner* gone, there was no critical outside opposition to act as the *Times*' daily conscience and, inside, dissent was rewarded with swift ruin. As Coffey and Laventhol identified and eliminated bellyachers and the Tom Johnson–Tony Day body count mounted, the fat and happy staff of the *Los Angeles Times* changed from pensive, analytical professionals into any other assembly line workforce: bitter, divided, and scared for their jobs.

And throughout the transition, veterans of the Otis era wondered idly if and when he might recognize what was happening to the newspaper that he'd shaped into one of the greatest in the world, and return to save it, and them, from the philistines.

Otis seemed oblivious. They might as well have been waiting for Godot.

On their tenth anniversary, Otis and Bettina took a second honeymoon to Mexico. Again, there were huge waves and, again, Otis talked Bettina into bodysurfing, going out too far, and encountering a nasty riptide. Bettina tripped,

was sucked under, and struggled to keep her head above water. Otis swam hard, screaming, "Swim, damn you!" an instant before he grabbed her wrist. He dragged her to safety, but Bettina was not aflutter with girlish gratitude. His behavior had developed into a dangerous pattern that she had come to recognize over time.

She simmered in silence for awhile, but could not sustain long-term anger toward her reckless mate. Behind his macho bluster, she sensed his terror: real fear that he had come close to losing her.

He'd done it before. He'd do it again. The full meaning of the hints and cues that she had received over ten years of marriage, that Otis Chandler rarely took personal responsibility for his mistakes, had begun to sink in. Joke slogans displayed around his auto and animal museum purporting "He who dies with the most toys wins" and "It is never too late to have a happy childhood" were, in fact, no joke.

She had married a bona fide narcissist who would always be too busy forcing himself to have fun to devote much thought to others. He bought and sold cars, motorcycles, and real estate with a passion, moving from house to house on average every two years, always expanding, adding on, redecorating, then putting up a "for sale" sign, not because he had to move, but because he wanted to try something new and different. He and Bettina were relentlessly traveling to new and exotic vacation spots. His longtime secretary, Donna Swayze, who had watched his actions for more than a generation, said that Otis had become more restless as he grew older. There would never be a genuine danger that he might stay in one spot long enough to lapse into meaningful introspection.

And, yet, like virtually everyone else who spent more than a few minutes around Otis, Bettina could not keep herself from forgiving him. He might be selfish and he might be blind, but her husband was as incapable of evil intent as a ten-year-old scooting through life on a Flexi-Racer.

In the winter of 1990, Otis trekked to the North Pole in search of musk ox. Years later, he delighted in spieling off the animal's characteristics, as if narrating a *National Geographic* television special: "It weighs about seven hundred pounds. It can go thirty-five miles per hour on the ice. They're a cousin to the African buffalo and the Australian buffalo, but there's nothing quite like them. They're very shaggy. They don't have oppressive horns . . . and they have never been known to ever be aggressive."

In February 1990, Otis and a young hunter from Kansas were escorted by Eskimo guides over the ice in the Canadian Northwest Territories on a search for musk ox.

"I got mine first," said Otis. "Got a good one, put my gun away."

Next, the Kansan picked out his. It was wandering with a second bull far from their herd, and the younger man nailed the ox with his first shot. As it fell, its companion wandered off about fifty yards, gazing off stupidly in the distance like the dull prehistoric beast that it was.

"We're not going in there," said Otis, remembering the unpredictability of jaguars and bears and countless other wild things he'd tracked and slain in his time.

"Oh, they never hurt you," said one of the Eskimos. "They'll never do anything to you."

Packing away their guns, the hunters and their guides gutted and skinned the dead ox while the live one stood stock still nearby, gazing into empty white oblivion. They started to pack up and return to camp, but in his excitement, one of the Eskimos left his skinning knife behind. Another Eskimo discovered that he'd dropped a pair of binoculars. By this time, the remaining bull had come out of its catatonic state long enough to wander over to the area where the men had butchered its companion. Envisioning himself dashing in to pluck up the knife and binoculars like O. J. Simpson in a Hertz commercial, Otis took charge.

"Okay, I'm going to run in and get your binoculars and knife," he said. "Now, you guys watch him. I'm gonna go in from the side."

Otis did find the binoculars and knife, a few yards from the ox, and bent to pick them up.

"And then the freight train hit me," he recalled. "And I was punched ten yards in the air. I didn't know what hit me."

He landed on his back, staring straight up at the woolly face of an angry ox.

"And the first thing I remember is, he's here, his saliva is frozen, he's pissed off," said Otis. His shoulder was useless, torn from its socket, and the animal appeared to be preparing to crush him, either with hooves or horns. Otis did a backward somersault to get away, and then, using his one good arm, he crawled back to the snowmobile.

"I was still in shock so I hadn't felt the pain yet," he said of the ride back to camp. He kept tasting his own saliva during the ninety-minute trip, expecting blood from internal bleeding, but there was none. The good news and the bad news was that the injuries were all external. Back at camp as he peeled off layers of clothing, he asked how bad it looked. No one wanted to tell him. As he stood erect, the fingers of his dangling, ruined arm swung so low that they touched the ground.

"Nobody'd ever seen an empty shoulder with no arm in it and they said, 'Put your clothes back on, Otis,'" he said.

It was another hour and a half by snowmobile to a little Eskimo village that had a small clinic and a nurse and doctor on duty.

"Well, we gotta put it back first of all," said the doctor. "That is the worst lookin' thing I've ever seen in my life."

There was no anesthesia. It was a matter of popping the dislocated shoulder back in place, so the nurse simply grabbed his arm while the doctor held on to Otis's shoulder and torso, and pulled until the ball slid back into its bloody socket. He called Bettina several hours later from the tiny outpost of Coppermine, en route to Edmonton.

"Honey, there's been a problem," said Otis. "I think I'm gonna make it through. No internal bleeding. But I think I need you."

Bettina flew to Edmonton, loaded Otis in a wheelchair, and took him home. Two surgeries followed. His physicians assured him that he would have a useless appendage for the rest of his life.

"No, no," said Otis. "That's not acceptable."

He began his own rehabilitation, relearning increment by increment how to use the arm again. The effort sometimes caused such agony that his craggy, robust Chandler face turned ash gray.

"Luckily I have a high pain curve," he said. "I like to rehab myself."

But there was more bad news while he was in the hospital. Blood tests came back positive for prostate cancer. Cut it out, Otis ordered. He'd just survived an encounter with a musk ox. He was not ready to die just yet.

CHAPTER 26

IN 1991, the board of directors of the Tejon Ranch gave *nouveau réalisme* artist Christo permission to erect hundreds of huge yellow umbrellas across the breadth of the Chandler dynasty's family retreat. To show L.A.'s first family his appreciation, the wealthy Bulgarian-born artist personally decorated Tejon headquarters with his objets d'art.

But cousin Otis Chandler had not been consulted.

"Oats was just pissed that all these people were stomping through his deer-hunting preserve," said Otis Chandler's old racing pal, John Thomas.

Now officially retired, even from his ceremonial duties as chairman of the executive committee, the sixty-three-year-old Otis bit his tongue and kept his distance from Times Mirror, including such artsy celebrations as the Tejon umbrella unveiling. Christo had made his debut splash fifteen years earlier when he erected a fabric fence across two Northern California counties, and now, with these heavy

metal bumbershoots, the artist expected to get the same media bounce in Southern California. Indeed, as part of the official unveiling of Christo's exhibit, the new easy-to-read *Los Angeles Times* previewed the gay yellow umbrellas. Christo got his ink and the *Times* showed off its new all-color front page.

Self-promotion symbiosis was afoot.

During the weekend of the exhibit, the Interstate 5 freeway clogged early with thousands of spectators, yet they glimpsed but a fraction of Christo's artistic vision. Roughly 60 percent of the umbrellas were erected on ranch property, which was still closely held by the very private Chandis Securities, and, thus, off-limits to most non-Chandlers. Still, what could be observed from public lands was an odd and uniquely Southern California panorama: hills festooned with massive metal mushrooms where the combined waters of the Owens Valley and California aqueducts flowed like mother's milk into the San Fernando Valley. Pragmatic Harry Chandler and General Otis before him would certainly have asked the same question Otis Chandler and much of Los Angeles were asking: What's the point?

If the Santa Ana winds hadn't picked up and slapped one of the umbrellas to earth, the media event might have been as delightfully ineffectual as Christo's fabric fence. But an umbrella *did* kill a slow-moving art lover that day, and not only was the death duly reported in the following day's *Times*, it spawned enough legal repercussions to force an immediate umbrella purge. Personnel from Times Mirror Square were conscripted to help in the cleanup, and Christo was not invited to return with a *nouveau réalisme* encore.

In or out of a museum, art could be dangerous in Southern California, and Otis Chandler understood this all too well. His mounted musk ox on display upstairs in his Vintage Museum was a menacing souvenir of death moving unexpectedly and sometimes by surprise. Similarly, the signed sculpture of the late actor James Dean's Porsche Spyder,[1] which Otis kept in a place of honor at the center of his office conference table, reminded him that not even the young and talented were necessarily safe. Things that moved recklessly, either on four hooves or four wheels, were true art objects to retired but restless Otis. With his ruined shoulder, he no longer raced, but he still liked to test-drive his art before moving it into his museum.

He had relocated Vintage to a 50,000-square-foot warehouse in an industrial park outside the coastal town of Oxnard, sixty miles north of L.A., and rarely ventured back to Times Mirror Square. He continued to sit on the board, but the other family members—Warren "Spud" Williamson, Gwen Garland Babcock, and Bruce Chandler—seldom consulted him. The rest of the Times Mirror board tended to go along with Erburu and Laventhol on most matters, as did Otis. Chain-smoking Franklin Murphy had developed cancer and stopped attending

board meetings.² Even Dan Frost, Otis's nemesis, resigned from the board in 1992, divorced Camilla, married a younger woman, and retired to a ranch in western Washington.

New forces were at work at the *Times.* The Otis era receded farther and farther into the past. Some at the paper had never even seen the legendary publisher.

"Cars are his entire life now," said a longtime Vintage employee. "More than Bettina, much more than the family. The hunt is the thrill, possession is less so, and boredom quickly sets in."

By the early 1990s, his passion for collecting had moved from muscle cars to Porsches to motorcycles, the pattern always repeating itself: He would corner the market on the best of a mechanical breed and hunt down and buy the auto du jour until he had a warehouse full. Then he would sell everything, occasionally at a loss, and start all over again. He behaved like a stingy stamp collector who triumphantly finished off the rarities of one country only to move on, unsatisfied, to the rarities of the next.

Otis was not an exhibitionist when it came to his compulsive collecting. He limited public access to his museum to just one day a month, charged viewers $7 a head, and did not advertise. He kept the museum's phone number unlisted so that his treasures could not be easily located. Otis needed to possess everything he loved, but not to show it off. Yet, once he owned the object of his affection, it diminished in subjective value and he frequently auctioned it off to the highest bidder. Then the hunt was on again for something new.

To most of his friends, buying, then selling, then buying again seemed as pointless an exercise as stringing bright yellow umbrellas across the Tejon Ranch. But those closest to him saw a sad kind of logic underlying Otis's irrational obsession.

"Cars became a necessary distraction from the exquisite pain of watching his first born wither," said a very close friend.

Otis had challenged death and survived again and again, but doctors said that his oldest son would not. Despite radiation treatments and chemotherapy, they had given Norman two years to live. Otis shouldered Norman's brain tumor like his own heavy crucifix.

"I don't think I have ever seen him so distraught as he was then," said Bettina.

Years earlier, as he began his executive training program, young Norman had written a letter to Otis about how it felt, standing in the pressroom late one night with the old presses clunking along. Ink was in his blood, he told his father then. He felt the power of the *Times,* of General Otis, of Harry Chandler, and of the *Times* itself, handed down from father to son.

Otis was moved. He kept the letter tucked away in a special place, and pulled it out to read in the hard days after Norman knew his diagnosis. As his son's life

ebbed, Otis pulled out all stops to help. When he wasn't on the phone making a deal for a rare turn-of-the-century motorcycle, he was calling all over the world looking for a miracle that would save Norman. Some "cures" were absurd, and Otis grew wary of charlatans, spiritualists, and snake oil salesmen.

"Otis has had acupuncture," said Bettina. "He is not a total disbeliever in alternative medicine. He kind of felt that, whatever Norman finds to help him, that was fine."

Norman grasped at any hope.

"By this point Norman had collected seven different therapists," said his wife, Jane. "They were all women, too. Even his doctor was a woman. One weighed three hundred pounds and told him she was taking him through the birth canal again. One was into biofeedback. One was this, one was that. Some I didn't know what they did. And the comment that Norman made at that point was that he needed to concentrate only on himself and that when he got healthy, he would be able to come back and be a father and a husband."

The tumor affected his temper, which seemed to shorten a little more each day. Norman stayed for some months with his father and then moved in with Missy; he returned to Jane sporadically in a vain attempt to keep their former family lives afloat. But Norman's tolerance level around two teenaged sons and two young daughters frayed irreparably as his condition worsened. Citing "unhappy and irreconcilable differences," Norman and Jane separated in early 1992. The following year, Norman took the lead and filed for divorce, surrendering child custody, pension, and most of his assets to Jane.

Otis's other children had all married and moved on to lives of their own. Harry, who had spent nearly fifteen years producing movies, returned to the *Times* in 1993. As part of its New Media division, he explored the emerging nexus of personal computers, cable, newspapers, and the World Wide Web. Harry thought about picking up where his brother had left off and making a run at the publisher's suite, but he received no encouragement from his father.

"What looked from the outside like a family-run business was not," said Harry. "He never said, 'Why don't you try it?' or, 'If you would like to think about it, let me have you go see someone.'"

When Harry took the initiative and found his own fast-track executive training program, Otis refused to help.

"You needed a company sponsor and I said, 'I'll pay you back, but can we use the Times Mirror to get me into Stanford or Harvard?' That's who I was looking at. And he wouldn't even reach out and do that," said Harry. "He was more about toeing the company line rather than helping his own kid out. I thought it was a little odd."

"Harry is not an editorial person," explained Otis, seeing no hypocrisy at all in his judgments of his two oldest sons. "He never worked in editorial and I don't think he would do well. He is not a good writer. He also never worked in the ad department, circulation, or the business side. He preferred only computers and the Web."

But Otis hadn't alienated only his sons. Harry's younger sister Cathleen was so angry with Otis over his divorce from Missy, and disgusted with the smug aristocratic mien of the Chandler dynasty in general, that she couldn't wait to get married and change her name. After Princeton, Cathleen had returned to the Northern California coastal town of Santa Cruz; she married a high school teacher, took up a career as a physician's aide, and lived an organic lifestyle with roots in her rebellious, semi-hippie youth.

As a direct third-generation heir of Harry and Marian Chandler, Cathleen received the same fat quarterly Chandis Securities dividend checks that her siblings got, but to her, the money was just an unearned embarrassment. She either forgot to cash the checks, lost them, or refused to acknowledge ever having received them in the first place.

For Michael Chandler, marrying within one's own class not only made sense but made life a lot easier. He divorced his second wife, the hairdresser, and remarried a third time when he worked at the Orange County *Times.* His new wife was a fellow trust-fund child, an heiress of the Hoover vacuum cleaner family, who had the additional commonality of a proper Pasadena upbringing. They had both had their fill of L.A. by the early 1990s, and when the *Times* offered an employee buyout, Michael left the *Times* in 1993. He moved his family to Oregon, where he found that he did not miss the family business one bit.

Carolyn married, too, but had always kept her distance from the *Times,* just like her older sister. She studied to be a zookeeper, and neatly segued from college into environmental causes, as well as a family of her own. Although she eventually made peace with her father, the youngest of Otis's five children never tired of pointing out to him how selfish he could be and sarcastically referred freely and frequently to his beloved Vintage Museum as "the garage."

Bettina lost her husband most days to his "garage," and most days, she didn't mind, although she had as little use for his car mania as Carolyn. Every time he bought her a new Lexus or Mercedes, Bettina had barely put a few thousand miles on it before he would sell it right out from under her and buy her a new one. It was always a better, faster, more comfortable model.

Still, Vintage had given him something to live for. Although it was imperceptible to outsiders, Bettina saw the musk ox incident, Norman's failing health, and the prostate cancer all taking their toll on her larger-than-life husband. Otis still

worked out, pushed himself to his limits, and rode his bicycle for miles each day, but he was slowing down. After his prostate surgery, he had to give himself an injection at the base of his penis so that he could perform sexually, but boasted to his pals that he gladly went through the painful process regularly to keep himself and his wife happy.[3]

His strong personal will still carried him a long way, but not as far as it once had. More and more, he awakened each day to read his *Times*, and came away depressed. It was still the best paper in the West, but to an old *Times* hand like himself, it did appear to be slipping.

"He will always spend time keeping up with the *Times* and evaluating it," said Bettina. "I think he will always read the paper with a critical eye, you know."

For the first time, Otis seemed to look beyond the purely physical for answers to life's nagging questions. The search for a shaman who might help Norman had launched Otis and Bettina on their own personal New Age explorations. They began seeing psychics as a couple.

One told Otis that Bettina had been able to step into the role of Mrs. Otis Chandler without a hitch because she had been his sister in a previous life, when they were both nobles in an ancient Roman court. Bettina believed it instantly.

"I kind of see myself born under this service umbrella and it's all teaching and helping other people," she said.

Otis was not quite so impressed.

"I said, 'Okay,'" he remembered. "If you say so, I guess."

Another psychic told Otis that he'd been a shoot-'em-up saloon keeper in the last century. He found such pronouncements amusing, but wasn't buying them. The soothsayers knew about his newspaper career and his passion for cars, but so what? Mediums who were able to pull odd bits and pieces of Otis esoterica out of thin air had done their homework; he figured they must have snooped around the library before he and Bettina came to visit and found out about his past that way.

But Bill Burns, the West Hollywood psychic whom Bettina had met through her Malibu manicurist years earlier, did not fit the usual mold. Burns didn't bother with past lives or predicting the future. He turned out to be as blunt as Otis. He began lecturing him the minute he sat down. Otis had lost his way, he said. In fact, he'd almost given up following the triple blow of Norman, the musk ox, and prostate cancer. Throw in the ongoing desecration of his *Times,* and there wasn't a lot left to live for.

"I see a lot of mental and emotional confusion," Burns told him. "A sense of just giving up, a sense of not being able to hold on to what you've had, a sense of allowing the world around you, your family, to run it, that sense of almost having lost who you are."

At first, Otis stubbornly refused to listen to all the psychobabble. Over time, though, it began to make sense. His life wasn't so much about who he was and what he represented. His life *was* what he represented.

"I think things are easy to do," he said. "You know: pick up that barbell, push that car, climb up that mountain. Because it's easy to me, and I like challenges. I like to encourage people who are with me to be with me in the excitement of this physical challenge. Bettina learned early, after a few incidents, that you don't stay with Otis. You don't let him get you with his smile and charm: 'Oh, come on! We'll climb that mountain.'"

Climbing mountains was what he represented, he decided. Climbing mountains and sweet-talking others into coming along with him. There was blood, sweat, tears, and loads of remarkably creative cursing along the way, but a genuine sense of triumph if and when they all got to the top together. That was who he was. That was what he represented.

And what he represented was not half bad.

————————

DURING THE GULF WAR, more than a dozen *Times* reporters and photographers swarmed over the Middle East, earning East Coast validation in the form of *Time* magazine's pronouncement that the *Times* delivered "the most extensive and informative coverage of the war." Similarly, the *Times* dispatched fourteen reporters to the Soviet Union in August 1991 to cover the end of the Cold War in Moscow, and the rise of Boris Yeltsin. Again, the nation's media critics heaped praise on the *Times*.[4]

Outside of L.A., the *Times* still shone like a ruby among the crown jewels of American journalism. On its home turf, however, the House that Otis Built began to quake. David Laventhol announced a virtual hiring freeze for the first seven months of 1991, in addition to a voluntary early retirement program, and over three hundred full-time employees took him up on his offer. He also slashed distribution outside of Southern California to cut costs. Weekend visitors to Las Vegas or Yosemite could still pick up the *Times* at a newsstand, but there was no more home delivery.[5]

Despite the belt-tightening, circulation did inch up in embattled Orange and Ventura counties, and in the San Fernando Valley, where the *Los Angeles Daily News* continued to win the day-to-day battle for the hearts and minds of the middle class.

For nearly ten years in a row, the *Daily News*—published by Washington Redskins, Los Angeles Lakers, and Los Angeles Kings owner Jack Kent Cooke—had been the fastest-growing newspaper in America. The *Times* grudgingly acknowl-

edged this escalating war by expanding its Valley edition at the same time that Times Mirror bought Coast Community News, operator of five small Valley papers that circulated in the heart of *Daily News* territory, including the late Virgil Pinkley's *Glendale News Press.*

On the *Times'* southern flank, Times Mirror reacquired the *Orange Coast Daily Pilot*, bought the weekly *Huntington Beach Independent*, and experimented with a new twenty-four-hour phone information service for Orange County called "TimesLink," which provided instant recorded information on sports, business, weather, gardening, mortgage rates, real estate, soap operas, and health. While Shelby Coffey's ever-increasing team of editors slapped themselves on the back for responding to the needs of the many communities they served, some veteran *Times* observers predicted disaster.

"These zoned editions further devolved what was once a unifying big-city paper into a stultifying collection of small-town rags," wrote *Buzz* magazine's Catherine Seipp." The upper middle class don't cancel the *Times* to subscribe to the *Valley Daily News* or the *Orange County Register.* They cancel it to subscribe to the *New York Times* or the *Wall Street Journal.*"

Even with the innovations and acquisitions, the *Times* barely held on to its title as the nation's number one metropolitan daily as it headed into 1992.

Shelby Coffey and Laventhol decided the *Times* needed *more*: more features, more graphics, more fun news. The *Times* gave its readers whimsical, easy-to-read columns with attractive, offbeat names such as "Cityscapes," "Laugh Lines," "Curbside L.A.," "Only in L.A.," and "L.A. Scene." "Valley Life!" was a weekly entertainment tabloid patterned after "Orange County Live!" and "North County Life!" and became the *Times'* newest offering in this emerging field of exclamation-point journalism.

Then, on April 28, 1992, an all-white jury in the suburban San Fernando Valley enclave of Simi Valley acquitted four white LAPD officers in their trial for the videotaped and widely reported beating of black motorist Rodney King. Following months of ponderous international analysis and local caprice, Los Angeles and its *Times* suddenly exploded with news of the worst racial rioting since that hot August evening back in 1965, when the *Times* won its fifth Pulitzer Prize.

Unlike Watts, 150 *Times*men and women, several of them black, responded immediately in Shelby Coffey's finest demonstration to date of the "swarm." *New York* magazine dubbed the *Times'* coverage "the best, calmest, most informed riot journalism," paving the way for the newspaper's twentieth Pulitzer.[6] A week after the rioting, the *Times* published a five-section series called "Understanding the Riots," which went on to become a 160-page coffee-table paperback that included *Times* color photos and a staff analysis of the origins and aftermath of the riots.

In the months that followed, the *Times* celebrated the city's angst, trolling for meaning and answers to the violence that had ruptured South Central for the second time in a generation. It found neither, but tried once more to be all things to all people.

As it had for a brief time following Watts, the *Times* again reached out to its damaged inner city, publishing a tri-lingual (English, Spanish, and Korean) full-page ad headlined, OUR COMMUNITY REBUILDS and a brief listing of relief organizations. Used *Times* trucks and office equipment were donated. Food banks were stocked with canned goods and secondhand clothing drives were undertaken. *Times* employees were dispatched to help in the cleanup. And to show that the *Times* had a heart, fifty inner-city youths were offered an eight-week summer work program to see whether they had what it took to become a *Times* employee. When the *Times* hiring freeze thawed, Coffey proudly announced that 60 percent of his new hires were minorities.

In September, the *Times* launched *City Times*, a new regional tabloid for South Central that contained none of the exclamation points, nor the advertising, of *Valley Life!* or *Orange County Live! Voices,* another weekly rumination on multicultural, multiethnic urban issues, also made its knee-jerk debut in the fall of 1992. In a further mollifying move, the *Times* began publishing a monthly Spanish-to-English language section called *Nuestro Tiempo,*[7] with a targeted circulation of 400,000.

All these efforts were seen by the staff as sops to an angry inner-city underclass that didn't read newspapers in the first place. Real journalism was practiced elsewhere in the newspaper. To be assigned to either *City Times* or *Nuestro Tiempo* was considered a career death knell, especially among *Times* minority staff members.

In the autumn of 1992, the death knell tolled, too, for the presses in the basement of the *Times* Building. For the first time in fifty-seven years, the *Times* was no longer published at Times Mirror Square. In another part of the inner city, a dozen blocks to the south, the new $230-million Olympic plant went into full operation and *Times* management was able to boast that it now had sixteen state-of-the-art computer-operated color presses at its three production plants in Orange County, the San Fernando Valley, and downtown L.A., more than any other U.S. metropolitan newspaper.

But despite the brave rhetoric, at the end of 1992 the aggressive, eternally expanding *Los Angeles Times* was now in full retreat. In December, David Laventhol shuttered the daily San Diego edition to shave $8 million from his annual budget, almost enough to make up for the red ink produced each year by Laventhol's beloved *New York Newsday*. The same month, Laventhol offered the first

company-wide voluntary buyout to 5,200 *Times* employees, and 668 took him up on the proposition, including Michael Chandler.

"I remember when they paid you to come to the *Times*," quipped columnist and former *Times* city editor Pete King. "Now they pay you to leave."

Nearly 10 percent of the editorial staff took the money and ran, led by such stars as national correspondents Charles Powers and Bella Stumbo.

"They seem to be methodically eviscerating the senior staff," said Stumbo.

In less than five years, the *Times* lost 30 percent of its reporters.

"It took twenty years for the paper to build up a great staff and it took just a few months to dismantle it," observed Washington bureau reporter Doug Frantz, who became one of three dozen *Los Angeles Times* reporters who eventually defected to the *New York Times*.

Chairman Bob Erburu of Times Mirror persisted in putting the best face on harsh events, blaming outside economic forces for the faltering *Times*.

"The newspaper industry is having a tough time right now," he sighed during an interview with *Forbes* magazine, hastening to point out that Times Mirror remained No. 137 on the Fortune 500. The company had just acquired college textbook publisher William C. Brown, said Erburu. That constituted good news. But when asked how Times Mirror could take in $3.7 billion a year and still report net earnings that were less than half of the much smaller Gannett newspaper chain, Erburu fell back on platitudes. Times Mirror had always built its future on long-term growth, he said, not on short-term profits.

Back in 1985, when Erburu first took over the company, *Business Week* writer Scott Ticer had him pegged as just the opposite kind of executive: an "outwardly affable" manager who promised short-term profits but ran the other direction whenever he came up against long-term risk. At the time, Ticer called Erburu "an insecure manager who is apt to blame others when things go wrong. That has bred a cautious, risk-averse bureaucracy at Times Mirror."

Erburu's waffling over the computerized future of the *Times* constituted a case in point. As early as 1983, Times Mirror had been at the vanguard of new technology, producing early databases and two-way entertainment, education, and home shopping services that the company called "Videotex" and "Audiotex." But when Otis Chandler called the two efforts "a technology in search of a market," Erburu pulled the plug.

"Our feeling," Erburu said in 1986, "is that unless you're going to concentrate on a business, you really shouldn't stay with it."

Five years later, he did an about-face. At a 1991 Newspaper Association of America convention, Erburu joined the flock of awestruck media executives who were given hands-on demonstrations of the electronic newspaper of the future.

Times Mirror, he later declared to the *Wall Street Journal*, would be one of *the* major content providers in the coming digital age.

"We plan to be in the forefront of that trend," he asserted.

But Times Mirror would be in the forefront of nothing if it didn't start earning some profit. At the end of 1992, the company reported a net loss of $66.6 million, its first loss in a century. By the end of the following year, the company had sold its four remaining television stations[8] for the bargain price of $330 million to shore up its sagging stock dividends. Argyle Television Holdings, which purchased the four network affiliates, resold them less than a year later to Wall Street entrepreneur Ron Perelman for more than $700 million.

"The family should have taken Erburu out and shot him," said Dan Akst, who had been a columnist and business writer for the *Times* until he, too, joined the growing exodus from Times Mirror Square.

Instead, Erburu kept earning praise and/or cash for his efforts. By 1994, the Times Mirror board opted to pay him a $1-million bonus over his annual salary. Those who puzzled over this seeming paradox didn't understand the vagaries of Chandis Securities or its grip on the publicly traded stock of the Times Mirror Company. They were blind to the sleight of hand at the board level of Times Mirror. Most of all, they did not fully comprehend or appreciate the astonishing greed of the vain and insolent heirs of Harry Chandler.

ONE TIMES MIRROR EMPLOYEE who understood quite clearly what was going on behind boardroom doors was *Newsday* business writer Allan Sloan. Unlike *Times* business writers, who had written almost nothing about the mysterious family-held company that controlled Times Mirror, Sloan's interest was piqued by an odd stock swap in 1994 that seemed to show a double standard between ordinary shareholders and the elite members of Chandis Securities.

The enormity of the Chandis assets and the awesome power wielded by its trustees began to come to light in May 1991, when required Securities and Exchange Commission insider-trader filings gave outsiders a glimpse into the dynasty's true wealth. Seven of the Chandis trustees, including Otis Chandler and his sister Camilla, sold 440,900 shares of Times Mirror for about $30 per share that year, which would have yielded about $13.2 million; after the sale, however, the trustees *still* controlled 19,725,488 shares as the Chandis board—and even more in their own holdings as private shareholders. According to the SEC filings, heirs of Philip, Harrison, Helen, and Ruth Chandler, who rarely set foot inside the *Times,* were worth more than half a billion dollars, at least on paper.

In addition, the ten-for-one voting power accorded to the stock held by the Chandis trustees collectively gave them a 54 percent edge over other Times Mirror shareholders. It didn't matter what other stockholders thought about Times Mirror or of its holdings, including the *Los Angeles Times*. Otis and his cousins still controlled Times Mirror and ran it as if it were their own private fiefdom. As a group, they did whatever they felt would benefit themselves first. With impunity, Chandis Securities could jam virtually any significant board action down the dissenting throat of any minority shareholder.

In 1994, *Newsday*'s Sloan zeroed in on the Chandler family's cupidity during a curious transaction in which Bob Erburu and the Times Mirror board arranged a $2.3-billion stock swap with Cox Cable, a major player in the burgeoning cable television market. The swap meant that Times Mirror shareholders would lose their cable television division, which had grown to become the eleventh largest such system in the country. In exchange, Times Mirror shareholders would receive Cox stock, making the transaction tax free.

Wall Street gave the swap its blessing, even though the consensus among securities analysts seemed to be that Times Mirror was once again spinning off a valuable division for less than it was worth.

But Sloan discovered method in the Chandler family's madness. They had opted for a different—and much better—deal than that of the average shareholder.

"I think Times Mirror is trying to address the problems of unhappy Chandler family members who live on their Times Mirror dividends," Sloan later told the *Columbia Journalism Review*.

Instead of receiving Cox shares, the Chandis trustees, including Otis, took their share of the Cox windfall in the form of preferred stock, which paid them extra dividends at the expense of the average shareholder. Thus, while most investors saw their dividend income in Times Mirror slashed by up to 80 percent that year, the Chandlers, who were already raking in about $43 million annually in dividend income, jacked up their own dividends by 80 percent with their new Times Mirror preferred shares.

In other words, the Chandlers received tax-free cash when everyone else received Cox Communications stock that might—or might not—eventually climb in value.[9]

Sloan ran his exposé of the complicated deal in *Newsday* and other Times Mirror newspapers; but the *Times* business editor, Robert Magnuson, killed it, suggesting that Sloan was "not accurate." The following year, Sloan resigned from *Newsday* to go to work for *Newsweek,* where he continued to write about the ongoing shell game at Times Mirror Square. Magnuson was promoted to president of the Orange County edition of the *Times*.

In the Times Mirror's annual report, Bob Erburu continued to blame the company's string of losses on empty biz-buzz phrases such as "restructuring charges," "nonrecurring gains and losses," and that catchall excuse that career managers the world over seem to fall back upon whenever they find themselves in deep fiduciary doo-doo: "changes in accounting methods." According to Allan Sloan, Times Mirror chalked up enough divestiture blunders to cost the company almost $1 billion during Erburu's tenure as chairman. Pretax profits peaked at 24 percent in 1985, Otis's last year as chairman, and ten years later Times Mirror's profit margin had ground down to where it was barely breaking even.

And yet, Otis stubbornly defended Erburu in later years, maintaining that the "bungling Basque," as he was known among the *Times'* own business writers, was simply the victim of a brutal Southern California recession. Otis's own sister, as well as his oldest friend, flatly disagreed.

"He wasn't minding the store," said Mia.

"He wrecked the company," said Bob Emmet.

In 1994, the *Wall Street Journal* quoted Prudential Securities media industry analyst Melissa Cook as labeling Times Mirror "the most underrated media company I follow."

In a further backhanded compliment, she added, "Their attitude that California will grow forever, is gone."

———————

BY 1994, Otis had fully recovered from cancer and musk ox, but not adolescence. He kept pulling up stakes, moving, selling, and moving again. He and Bettina lived for a while in Malibu, Camarillo, then Ojai. They kept a ranch as a second home in Bend, Oregon, but Otis never gave up his museum. He kept returning to Oxnard to oversee the correct and always shifting display of his cars and carcasses.

"I've seen other retired chief executives, where they do not have a business or a passion or a place to go, other than just an office and a secretary," he said. "Maybe they do some volunteer work or maybe they go on a board or maybe they travel a lot or maybe they play bridge, but they're bored. And their intellectual curiosity and their physical condition and their psyche just go downhill. Most, like my father, wither away and they die before their time."

He had taken up bicycling with increasing fervor since his 1991 brushes with death, and his road gear was typically always the best: the lightest, the sturdiest, the fastest. Money was no object when it came to his toys. One day as he peddled over state Highway 118 near Camarillo, he came face-to-face with a semi and

proved to himself once again that he could defy death. He was the custodian of the Chandler luck.

"He didn't hit me, but he sucked me in," said Otis.

The truck whooshed on by, leaving Otis to wobble then flip while he was doing twenty-seven miles per hour on the bicycle.

"Split my bike helmet," he said. "First thing I remember were people walkin' up, asking: 'Is he dead? Is he dead?'"

He landed on his good left shoulder, the one that had not been ripped from its socket by a musk ox. It throbbed. So did his thigh. He called Bettina on his cell phone and, when she failed to show up in a few minutes, he climbed back on his bike and started home on his own.

When she arrived a few moments later, a frantic Bettina searched up and down the highway, but could not find her husband. He had peddled home, against the pain. When she saw his bloody, broken body, Bettina rushed him to the hospital. He remained stitched up and bandaged for weeks, his leg a brackish green and blue.

"So that was close," he said with incautious pride. "But if you are going to do stuff like that, then you are going to have it happen to you. Could've gone either way if there had been a car behind the truck, because I slid on the road. So if there had been a car behind the truck, I would have been run over. So I was just lucky."

The following year, he was not quite so lucky.

During the last day of a vacation in New Zealand, with Bettina hugging him from behind, sixty-eight-year-old Otis Chandler was gunning down a two-lane country road at sixty-five miles per hour aboard a rented motorcycle, when he came up behind a John Deere tractor parked off the highway.

"From the time I started on that motorcycle tour, I had a premonition that I was gonna have an accident," he said. "And I've never in my life had a premonition about anything."

With the exception of his Camarillo bicycling tumble, he had also never had a two-wheeler accident in fifty years of riding. He ignored the premonition. He would handle things by being even more alert, he told himself. Besides, he had the Chandler luck on his side.

No one had told any of this to the tractor driver, however. In one split-second, as Otis tried roaring past him on the right, the driver, who could neither see nor hear the oncoming motorcycle, put his John Deere into a U-turn, blocking both lanes of the two-lane highway.

"It happened too fast," said Otis. "I had no place to go. Instinct took over."

He veered off, nearly missing the tractor, but clipped it enough as he passed to

go into the same kind of high-speed wobble that had flipped his bicycle the previous year. This time, he had to put the motorcycle into a slide, raking his trousers and boot against the asphalt for several hundred yards until he and Bettina came to rest in a ditch.

Otis reported, "I was stunned for a few seconds, and then I got up, worried about Bettina."

She was okay. Otis was not. There was pain in his rib cage and no feeling at all in his foot. He looked at the boot that had served as a friction brake for the speeding cycle and saw tatters of leather and blood.

"The boot took the whole hit," he said.

Bettina was shaken, but unscathed. A pretty off-duty nurse stopped and joined the gathering crowd, bending to examine the injured foot. All Otis remembered was that her breasts were spilling out of her halter top; but Bettina remembered the young woman advised them to go to an emergency room right away.

A passing motorist and his wife stopped, helped Bettina and the nurse load Otis into their backseat, then sped off to a hospital, stopping just once along the way on Otis's orders to pick up some ice for his now throbbing foot.

"I took the sock off and the blood just came pouring," he said. "The two biggest toes were just like hamburger."

Bettina blanched as she wrapped her husband's foot in a handkerchief.

"I'm gonna get sick if I have to look at that," she told him.

Otis averted his own eyes and tried visualizing something more pleasant than his ruined foot. He shut his eyes and smiled to himself. Up in the front seat, the driver turned to his wife and said out loud what Otis had been thinking since he was bundled into the car: "Dear, that was the most wonderful set of knockers on that girl I've ever seen."

At the hospital, Otis learned that his ankle was broken in ten places, six ribs were shattered, and his foot might have to be amputated. Once she was past her initial fear, Bettina grew angry. Her husband underwent two surgeries, was told that the ribs would never fully heal, and spent a week in the hospital. She had always admired his willingness to take risks, but she did not admire his behaving like a reckless teenaged fool, and she told him so.

Yet, even after that ordeal, the first thing Otis insisted upon doing when they returned home was to order a motorcycle, just like the one he and Bettina had crashed. He was still in a wheelchair when it was delivered. He wheeled himself out to the garden, climbed on board, and rode the cycle far enough around the property to assure himself that he could still ride.

"Bettina thought I was absolutely crazy," he said, adding, "which I am."

CHAPTER 27

MARK H. WILLES, vice chairman of General Mills, had the perpetually anxious look of a man on the verge of being found out.

He smiled a pinched, professional smile, undermined by a drooping sadness in his watery eyes that he hid with poor results behind rimless glasses. Willes was proudly old-fashioned and he dressed with some formality for each business day. Those who met him casually came away with the sense of a Vanderbilt-wannabe who would have worn a boutonniere and a fedora to the office had his off-the-rack tailor so instructed.

Mark Willes was square, and *darned* proud of it. He would never use the word "damn" in describing his pride, especially in polite company. His mouth was not a potty, after all, and his body was a temple. So was the Disney-like cathedral where he worshiped each Sunday. Mark Willes was a lifelong member of the Church of Jesus Christ of Latter-Day Saints, a chosen man who was putting in his proselytizing time until that better world rolled around.

It mattered little to the trustees of Chandis Securities that Mark Willes knew nothing about the manufacture or marketing of newspapers. They had met him during their search for a new Times Mirror CEO in the early months of 1995, and they had liked him. Willes even impressed Otis.

"He is very smart and very clever and very articulate," said Otis. "He told me a couple of stories about his time at General Mills which kind of caused me to wonder a little bit about what he would really be like."

There was his re-invention of Cheerios, for example. To Otis, it didn't seem like the sort of product that could, or even should be re-invented. Then there was the restaurant chain in which General Mills invested. Willes told him how he would enter incognito, order lunch, and ask to speak to the manager if he didn't find the food or service to his liking.

"'I called the manager over and told him what I'd found, and the next day, the guy would be gone!'" Otis remembered Willes telling him.

Willes's glee at telling the story bothered Otis, but not to the degree that he made an issue of his unease with his fellow Times Mirror board members. Otis was already odd man out. His misgivings would only aggravate the other Chandlers and result in his being further ostracized. The reality was that his cousins thought a cereal salesman such as Willes might really shake things up, and that could be just what the *Times* needed.

Mark Willes read two papers each day: first, the *Wall Street Journal,* then the *New York Times.* To the Times Mirror board, that seemed quite enough familiar-

ity with newspapers. If the next chairman and CEO of the Times Mirror Company were any closer to the product than that, the reasoning went, he might not be able to do what needed to be done.

In all his fifty-three years, Mark Willes had never so much as set foot inside a newsroom. He didn't have to. He had decided early that news was entertainment, intellectual Spam sandwiched between generous slices of advertising; every day it was to be devoured, digested, and flushed, once its few nutrients had been extracted. That did not mean he held newspapers in contempt. On the contrary, he wouldn't know how to start the day without business news, preferably the *Journal's*, at his breakfast table. Willes thought of his daily newspaper as a "very user-friendly, consumer-friendly thing."

But Mark Willes understood what most of the worker bees at newspapers never would: It was the *money* that they generated that mattered. Everything else, including the news, was window dressing.

Mark Willes may have been born in the shadow of Joseph Smith's original temple in Salt Lake City,[1] but his earliest interests had rendered themselves unto Caesar far more than to the Lord. The son of a banker, even in grade school Willes had liked following the stock market. After he had exhausted Utah's resources, he headed East to Manhattan for the advanced study of money and graduated from Columbia University's School of Business with an economics Ph.D. while still in his twenties. By the time he was thirty-five, he had climbed to the presidency of the Federal Reserve Bank of Minneapolis, the youngest person ever elected by the Federal Reserve governors to head a district bank. Two years later, at thirty-seven, he left the Fed to pursue "the mission of business," as he put it.

Business generated profit, and it stood to reason that a stewardship in the world of business would give him a better grasp of his primary interest: money. He joined General Mills at the executive level, bypassing the plants and warehouses where its products were created. He went straight into the boardroom where profits were projected and policy—moneymaking policy—was conceived. He spent the next fifteen years stocking America's pantries with such processed foodstuffs as Trix, Kix, Bugles corn chips, and the magical mixes of Betty Crocker. It was Mark Willes who helped Betty out of her *Ozzie & Harriet* duds and into a sensible blouse and knee-length skirt, her hair blow-dried into a neck-length bouffant, for her made-over portrait in the new Hamburger Helper ads.

As he had also boasted to Otis, Willes was the keen marketing mind behind the innovation of adding honey as well as nut flavoring to Cheerios, thus giving America its first taste of the revolutionary new breakfast treat, Honey Nut Cheerios. It was Willes who carried the gospel of Cap'n Crunch overseas, so that Europeans, Asians, South Americans, and Australians would also have a chance to start out the day with a big bowl of sugar-coated puffed grain. And, in General

Mills's consumer restaurant division, which included both the Red Lobster and Olive Garden chains, it was Mark Willes who shrewdly ordered management to have waiters and waitresses stop serving loaves of warm bread before taking patrons' orders so that they wouldn't fill up on freebies before ordering entrees.

If Willes had ever wrestled with the thorny paradox of mixing lucre with the Lord, he didn't show it. In his *Who's Who in America* entry, Willes set forth a philosophy that worked just fine for him, both as a businessman and a human being: "Be just, honest and moral. Do things not only because they are required, but because they are right. Have mercy—care enough about others to be fair and kind."

Another company might have questioned Willes's motives and background a bit more carefully, but another company was not Times Mirror in the desperate early months of 1995. At the beginning of the year, an envoy led by Bob Erburu had met with Wall Street analysts and set forth grand plans for spending $100 million or more of Times Mirror's Cox Cable capital on the digital future.

Although slow on the uptake, the Times Mirror CEO had learned his lesson about the computer age. Erburu stood rock-solid behind pouring money and manpower into on-line services and the *Times'* presence on the fledgling Internet. One of Times Mirror's early coups was its investment in Netscape; the start-up Silicon Valley company had exploded overnight into one of the earliest e-commerce giants.

Under Erburu, Times Mirror's New Media division began striking strategic alliances with other on-line pioneers, including the Prodigy network and Pacific Telesis. TimesLink, the sole surviving on-line service from Times Mirror's doomed Videotex/Audiotex, had more than 20,000 subscribers by mid-1995, making it the largest newspaper-based Web site on the Internet.[2]

Despite the positive spin that Erburu put on his bold new plans, Times Mirror's New Media division still cost far more than it returned in revenue, leaving the bottom-line moneychangers of Wall Street cold. Times Mirror stock, which had already taken a drubbing during Erburu's sell-off of the company's television division and the Chandler family's self-serving Cox Cable deal, sank below $20 a share on the New York Stock Exchange for the first time in a decade. The Times Mirror board and Otis's fellow Chandis Securities trustees went into panic mode.

At the flagship *Los Angeles Times*, turmoil also reigned at the top. After steering the paper's profits into money-losing *New York Newsday* for nearly a decade and presiding over the disastrous senior staff brain drain of the early 1990s, David Laventhol reported in 1994 that he had suddenly developed Parkinson's disease and had to step down as publisher.

His replacement was Richard T. Schlosberg III, an affable former Air Force pilot whose only previous newspaper experience was as an executive with Harte Hanks newspapers and as publisher of the struggling *Denver Post* just before

Times Mirror dumped it in 1987. Instead of firing Schlosberg when the *Post* was sold, Erburu promoted him to head all of Times Mirror's newspapers. The division posted loss after loss through most of the early 1990s, but apparently at no cost to Schlosberg's career. Under Erburu, he remained a rising Times Mirror star.

As with Laventhol, Erburu, and Coffey, Otis would not blame Schlosberg for the *Times'* continuing losing streak. He insisted on looking elsewhere, seeing Schlosberg only as a strong, pleasant, and capable executive doing the best he could with the cards dealt him. Schlosberg was handsome, dedicated, and a family man to boot, not unlike the way in which Otis chose to remember himself as a young executive:[3] disciplined, direct, smart, and forceful.

"Schlosberg came in [during] one of the most difficult times," said Otis, explaining away the paper's dwindling fortunes on recession, unemployment in the aerospace industry, riots, and even natural disasters, including the Northridge earthquake and fires in the hills above Malibu.

"That took a lot of homes out and a lot of subscribers," he reasoned. "They had no place to read the paper."

Nevertheless, the families who weren't shaken, burnt, pillaged, or fired from their jobs and homes continued to cancel the *Times* in ever-increasing numbers. Thus, the two IIIs—Publisher Schlosberg III and Editor Coffey III—bivouacked with their ever-increasing layers of *Times* middle management to ensure that Los Angeles received a kinder, gentler, all-inclusive *Times.* Again, the IIIs insisted, the *Times* was to serve all of L.A.'s diverse, dislocated populous, from the shopkeepers of Little Korea to the stockbrokers of Century City; from the Guatemalan domestics of Echo Park to the screen extras of Universal City; from the Cambodian donut store operators of Long Beach to the WASP trust-fund babies of South Pasadena.

"The paper tries to be all things to all people, but in the process it becomes very little to anyone," reporter David Freed told the *Columbia Journalism Review.* "It has no soul."

At Laventhol's urging, Coffey had created a balanced op-ed page that uniformly carried the same amount of verbiage on its Column Left as it did on its Column Right. The result, said its critics, was politically correct pabulum that infected the entire newspaper. By the time Schlosberg took over, the *Times* editorials on most days had become about as dynamic as warm spit and the newspaper as a whole was missing a distinct edge. The retired Bill Thomas paused long enough from his putting green to tell Otis that the newspaper was in trouble.

"He thinks the paper has had major damage done," said Otis. "He didn't like Dave. He didn't think Dave was a good publisher. And he doesn't think that Dick Schlosberg was a good publisher. He just feels that it is too much fluff and too

much unimportant, off-the-wall soft news. The paper has lost its national and international reputation because it no longer covers the hard news as fully and completely as it should. He really has a much more negative view of the paper today than I do."

Bill Thomas was not alone in his grim assessment. Beginning in May 1992, *Buzz* magazine had begun printing "Our Times," a regular monthly column by critic Catherine Seipp. Writing under the pen name Margo Magee she mercilessly lambasted the ongoing lunacy at Times Mirror Square. Under Coffey and Laventhol, the *Times* had developed a vacillating news policy that Seipp described as "All the News That's Fit to Print. . . . As Long As No One Gets Hurt."

Coffey, whom she labeled "Shelby the Cautious," suffered from "the Hamlet disease," eternally wavering between one point of view and, then, another, and, finally, ending all controversy by hitting the "delete" button on his editing console. She referred to Coffey's immediate subordinates as "the Stepford wives."

"He is the quintessential guilty white male: insular, kindhearted, cluelessly patronizing, endlessly infuriating," wrote Seipp. Coffey's defenders lashed out at her satire as malicious, mean-spirited, and unfair. One senior *Times* editor called her "a very, very angry woman." But to most rank-and-file reporters and editors, her wit was dead-on.

Coffey and Schlosberg did not think she was funny, nor did Bob Erburu, whom many at Times Mirror Square believed to have had his sense of humor surgically removed at birth. As Erburu approached mandatory retirement age and prepared to follow Otis into the emeritus world, his pasty, poppin'-fresh face was perpetually decorated with a scowl. Most thought that Schlosberg had now jumped ahead of everyone else in the line of succession to the CEO's position, but the unhappy heirs of Harry Chandler, now more than one hundred of them, were not so sure.

The Times Mirror board appointed an ad hoc committee to search for Erburu's successor and, for the first time since Franklin Murphy's appointment, they selected an outsider with no newspaper experience to head the company. Otis, who still sat on the board, preferred the publisher of the *Providence* (R.I.) *Bulletin,* who was one of the three finalists. But he, too, was eventually persuaded by his sister Mia and other board members to go along with Mark Willes.

"I think the directors felt that by finding Mark Willes it would rev up the whole scene again," said Mia. "He just sold the directors a bill of goods about what he could do to recharge the newspaper."

Willes was named president and CEO of Times Mirror on June 1, 1995. He would formally replace Bob Erburu as chairman of the board the following January without even having to write a term paper.

In the meantime, he put on his butcher's apron and went straight to work.

———————

WILLES IMMEDIATELY VOWED to rid the company of everything that wasn't earning at least a 16 percent profit. Gannett Newspapers, publisher of *USA Today*, was pulling down 16 percent, he pointed out in a memo to the board. The mighty Times Mirror earned a mere 8 percent return.

His first task as he saw it was to jack up the stock price and quarterly earnings, and the easiest way to do both was to slash everything that did not contribute materially to the bottom line. Times Mirror's core business was selling newspapers, just as General Mills's core business was selling processed foods. If a brand of yogurt or pancake mix didn't meet the 16 percent profit threshold, some weak-kneed General Mills marketeer might try to give it a different ad campaign or send it back to product development. But not Mark Willes. Left to the man whose nickname had quickly and appropriately became the "Cereal Killer," the brand and everyone associated with it got the ax.

On July 13, Willes flew to New York, where he toured the offices of *New York Newsday*, which had won dozens of prestigious journalism awards but lost an estimated $100 million during its ten years of existence. Although David Laventhol's baby would probably never hit the 16 percent threshold, it was now over 200,000 in circulation and on the verge of going into the black. That was a triumph, and despite Willes's grim reaper reputation, the *Newsday* staff still held out hope. When he entered the newsroom, everyone wore buttons that read "*Newsday*: Too Smart to Die." One brave staff member rushed the new CEO and pinned the declaration to his lapel. Willes smiled weakly, averting his eyes.

He completed his tour and retired to his four-star hotel. Employees who already saw the handwriting on the wall met with their new boss the following day and offered to buy their own paper. Willes smiled, nodded, took notes, and left once again for his hotel. The following day, he shut down *New York Newsday*,[4] climbed aboard a jetliner, and flew first-class to Baltimore, where he executed the ailing *Baltimore Evening Sun* with the same efficient dispatch and frigid lack of solicitude that he had exhibited in Manhattan.

Back at Times Mirror Square, the East Coast bloodletting eliminated whatever dissension that remained among the *Times* ranks. Men and women who had devoted their lives to the paternalistic paper run by Norman and, then, Otis Chandler, clamored to kowtow. Reporters and editors whose professional training involved questioning others now second-guessed themselves at every turn, and came up with fear and indignity as their uniform answer. Willes had successfully taken a page from Sun-Tzu's *The Art of War* by murdering *New York Newsday* and the *Baltimore Evening Sun*. He now had a loyal army of employees who

would do his bidding without question out of abject terror that they might be the next to lose their livelihoods.

Looking back at that moment three years later, Otis observed, "Naturally, people aren't going to tell him the truth when he asks people how we're doing. They're going to say whatever is necessary to keep their jobs."

There was still more blood work to be done back at Times Mirror Square. On July 21, 1995, known thereafter as "Black Friday," the *Times* fired 750 people, 150 of them in the editorial department. Willes had orchestrated a surgical evisceration of the staff, complete with an eight-page guide on how to terminate a *Times*man. Terminators from the human relations department were advised to show no emotion but to be certain they had a box of Kleenex close at hand. Termination tips included these:

- Do not try to make the situation lighter by making jokes or comments intended to be funny.
- Avoid too much small talk. Get to the point, communicate the decision, don't debate, don't get into fairness or the performance of others.
- If the employee becomes too emotional, acknowledge how difficult this situation must be for them and try to continue.
- If an employee becomes angry or hostile, immediately advise them that you appreciate their emotions, however, they must control their feelings or you will call Security to have them escorted from the property.

Guards did escort some reporters from Times Mirror Square. Business writer Michael Parrish was in a restaurant when he learned he had been fired; he had taken an interview subject to dinner and found his corporate American Express card had been canceled. Some wept. Some threatened to sue. Firees who refused to sign a waiver agreeing to hold Times Mirror harmless got bare-bones severance pay. Those who signed the waiver received an "enhanced package." From Black Friday forward, Catherine Seipp and every other *Times* critic ceased referring to the newspaper as the Velvet Coffin. It was henceforth known as the Pine Box.

To save even more money, Willes shut down the employee parking garage and the *Times* Employee Center, which had been operating continuously since 1966. Loyal *Times* employees who wanted to buy a T-shirt or a coffee mug bearing the *Times'* proud eagle logo now had to order via fax, phone, or mail. To show that Times Mirror was still a company with a heart, employees were offered a discount on home delivery subscriptions.

Willes set the goal of eliminating 450 more positions by the end of 1995. He also began the slash-and-burn process inside the *Times*, killing off the Washington edition[5] and the Westside section, "World Report," "*Nuestro Tiempo*," "City

Times," "Valley Business," "Ventura County Life," "Valley Life!" and "OC Live!"

In a personal slap at Bob Erburu, Willes ordered the shutdown of the Times Mirror Center for The People & The Press, which the lame-duck chairman had established in 1990 as a keystone of his own journalistic legacy. The center commissioned studies, papers, and polls in an attempt to measure popular opinion through the media. But instead of becoming the all-seeing Delphic oracle that Erburu had hoped for, the center had evolved into just another nonprofit think tank that failed as often as it succeeded in trying to outguess the public.

"Bob Erburu was a wonderful, mellow guy, but he never ran the store in recent years," said Mia. "He thought about feathering his own nest with board memberships—not corporate as much as nonprofit."[6]

On January 1, 1996, the same day Erburu surrendered the Times Mirror chairmanship to Willes, Philadelphia-based Pew Charitable Trusts saved his think tank from extinction, renaming it the Pew Research Center for The People & The Press. Erburu was now chairman of the executive committee, the same ineffectual title Otis had inherited ten years earlier when Erburu helped engineer his ouster as Times Mirror board chairman. Erburu still sat on the board, and his office was still on the sixth floor; it was just not as big or as posh as Times Mirror's newest profit prophet's office.

The ravaging at Times Mirror Square did not extend to everyone. Willes put $5 million of his slash-and-burn savings to work in renovating Times Mirror Square as a historical downtown presence. He also saw to it that he and his immediate subordinates continued to travel first-class, even if the troops now traveled tourist—if they traveled at all. He let it be known that there was to be only limited fraternization between officers and enlisted ranks. *Times* department heads, whose offices had been located on the second floor adjacent to the publisher's suite since Otis had first worked with Nick Williams, were now relocated to the cushy atrium area on the sixth floor of the Times Mirror corporate building, within summoning distance of Mark Willes's Holy See.

Willes was well aware of the jibes and the epithets. He knew what people said about him around the water cooler, or the spot where the water cooler used to be before he put his austerity policies in place. Unlike Shelby Coffey or David Laventhol, Mark Willes took with a grain of salt Catherine Seipp's column and all the other snide swipes at the Cereal Killer or his other new nickname, Cap'n Crunch. He took secret pride in being the hatchet guy. Worker bees rarely understood that sometimes drastic measures had to be taken. If a crippled limb offended, it needed to be cut away. So saith Wall Street and the board of Times Mirror; and so their servant Mark Willes performed.

Wall Street rewarded his savagery. During the first six months of Willes's reign, Times Mirror stock doubled in value, leaping above the $30 mark and continuing to climb a little higher each month. Brokers who had warned investors to sell just twelve months earlier were now recommending Times Mirror as *the* media stock to buy in 1996. Dividends were up, too. Willes left that end of the business to his chief financial officer, Tom Unterman, who made it his business to keep the endless greed of the Chandler family at bay.

Business Week named Mark Willes one of its "Managers to Watch in 1996." When he spoke of returning to the core business, getting back to basics, tearing down in order to build up—and all the other bromides brandished in business schools across the U.S.A., people now listened! Mark Willes was no longer just a fuzzy-focus economist with a Ph.D. and a lot of half-baked theories on making money. He was a *practicing* economist with a bully pulpit unmatched anywhere west of the Mississippi.

The Attila phase of Mark Willes's Times Mirror debut was over. Now it was time to show America how to manufacture a better newspaper.

DURING AN EARLY PEP RALLY with what remained of the *Times* staff, Mark Willes reportedly opened with a question: "What more can we do to shape people's thinking?"

Most sat dumbfounded. To those reporters and editors who remembered a *Times* that tried shaping people's thinking by reporting both sides of a story and letting the reader decide, Willes's question bore sinister overtones. Some even still believed that they were supposed to be objective. Willes grinned his sad executioner's smile and waited. Still no answers. He decided they just needed time to think and suggested that they get back to him with ideas.

Even at their clumsiest, the two IIIs had never been so crass as to ask the troops how best to manipulate the news. Schlosberg stayed away from the newsroom altogether. Coffey massaged his reporters, the way he had been taught back on the *Post*'s Style section. He would never come right out and tell them how to write. If they disappointed him, he had them reassigned. Shelby Coffey might have behaved with star-struck stupidity when he paraded the likes of Sylvester Stallone and Barbra Streisand through the newsroom, tacitly implying that his entertainment reporters must handle them with kid gloves, but he was never so transparent as to order a writer to skew his or her writing for the express purpose of shaping readers' opinions.

Willes dispensed with such niceties. He served the Chandlers and the Chandlers wanted the old *Times* back—the one that Buffy, Norman, and Otis had hi-

jacked from Kyle Palmer, L. D. Hotchkiss, and the ghost of Harry Chandler way back on April 11, 1960, the day that Philip Chandler was robbed of the publisher's suite. In a 1995 interview with *Forbes* magazine, Philip's only daughter, Corrine Werdel, described the situation at the *Times* as "the inmates running the asylum. They're not giving us the full news. It's one very narrow, liberal side. The paper has a responsibility to print both sides. We need to get the message across that we care."

To that end, she and her younger brother, Jeffrey, hired a publicist to help them draft a position paper and plant favorable stories, such as the *Forbes* article. They argued that the *Times'* liberal bias under cousin Otis had alienated advertisers. As the owner of a pair of San Diego radio stations, one of which was the first to air Republican talk show host Rush Limbaugh, Jeffrey slammed the *Times* for glamorizing homosexuality, for siding with consumers in product liability cases, and for opposing the construction in minority neighborhoods of factories and refineries that produced noxious wastes. Jeffrey was particularly incensed over a *Times* feature story about a gay couple who attended their high school prom.

"When you start featuring these kinds of stories the way the *Times* does," he said, "you think: 'Yes, it's important to talk about AIDS. That's something society should be concerned about and solve.' But, my God, you've got a campaign going on here!"

"Corrine was calling for a family meeting," recalled Otis. "She wanted all the members of the family who get dividends to take the paper back politically."

Although other members of the family might have agreed with Corrine and Jeffrey's politics, they did not respond to the clarion call of Philip Chandler's children to change the content of the *Times*. There was no meeting and no modification of editorial policy, either at Times Mirror Square or among the board members of Chandis Securities. By 1996, Mark Willes had established firm control, and a couple of maverick members of the Chandler clan were not about to wrest it from him. The *Forbes* article notwithstanding, he would impose his will upon the editorial side of the newspaper in a more orderly fashion.

David Margolick's *Vanity Fair* profile of Otis Chandler, however, nearly sparked a civil war.

"I only agreed to be interviewed because I was persuaded to do so by Bob Erburu and a couple of other people who thought it would be good timing because it would be pro–Times Mirror," Otis said later.

Up to that time, Otis had spurned all requests that he sit for an extensive interview. *Vanity Fair*'s Margolick compared him to J. D. Salinger, the reclusive author of *Catcher in the Rye* who had deliberately receded from public view. Otis had good reason to be reluctant. He remembered that his mother's disastrous 1977

interview with Lally Weymouth for *Esquire* had been her Waterloo: His cousins had combined forces with Franklin Murphy following the publication of "The Word from Mama Buff" and engineered Dorothy Chandler's ouster from the Times Mirror board. Her blunt quotes, critical of Murphy and the Philip Chandler side of the family, were proof enough that she had grown too old and too bold.

Just as he refused to come to the aid of Tom Johnson ten years later when he lost the publisher's suite, Otis had done nothing to rescue his mother. One of his great paradoxes was his ability to challenge a bear or a lion, but not the Times Mirror board or his own cousins. Following Buff's removal from the board, Bob Erburu began building the coalition that eventually toppled Otis and brought the *Times* to its present disastrous condition. But Otis would never face up to that reality.

In the *Vanity Fair* profile, Otis believed that he would be depicted in all his retirement glory, pitching hay at his Oregon ranch or slapping the side panel of an ancient Packard at his Vintage Museum. Otis had always been a master of denial and it was no different when he opened up his life to David Margolick, a former *New York Times* staff writer.

"I was too blunt," Otis said, trying to soften the blow with his cousins after the fact by claiming that he had been misquoted.

Otis had not been misquoted. Margolick had recorded everything on his laptop, and Otis admitted grudgingly several years later that, yes, he was a newsman and, yes, he should have known better. He unloaded years of repressed fury when he spoke candidly and with uncharacteristic venom about the "coupon clippers" who comprised the bulk of his extended family: men and women whose lives consisted of waiting by the mailbox for the next fat quarterly Times Mirror dividend check to arrive while frittering away the rest of their days at soirees, high teas, garden parties, and charity golf tournaments, perpetually complaining that they still did not have enough money.

"Their names had never been exposed in a national publication," said Otis. "It was an enormous shock. I talked to Spud [Warren Williamson, eldest son of Lady Crocker] a couple of years later and I said, 'Well, I hope you have gotten over the article.' And he said, 'Well, I have, but my friends keep bringing it up every time I run into them. They ask, "What's wrong with your cousin Otis?"'"

"I don't know. I guess in their relatively limited circle of friends on the east side of town, that was all people talked about was that article."

Williamson and the other Chandis trustees who also sat on the Times Mirror board refused Margolick's interview requests for their side of the story. They did not trust journalists, explained Otis.

They have a distrust of the press which is fascinating to me since they have lived the life that they've lived due to the profitability of the *Los Angeles Times* and Times Mirror, and yet they choose to distrust the press. That is just the way they are. That is an oversimplification, but they do have a negative feeling about the press.

A lot of the families that I grew up with in Los Angeles and in San Marino and so on feel that the press is run by Democrats and that all reporters are extreme liberals. I never asked a reporter, writer, or editor what his political persuasion is or how he votes. It is none of my business. I base my evaluation on how good they are at their jobs, not what party they vote for or what candidate they vote for. National polls indicate that a lot of older Americans judge the media ownership, reporters, and editors to be liberal and biased. The Chandler family falls into that category.

Although he was loath to admit it, Otis had grown accustomed over the years to shaping stories about himself and his family with the mighty mallet that was the *Los Angeles Times*. Even to Margolick, he admitted to killing off a critical investigative story about him and the *Times* that Mark Dowie, cofounder of *Mother Jones* magazine, had been commissioned to write for *Los Angeles* magazine. After working on his story for six months, Dowie was told in late 1995 that *Los Angeles*'s editors had changed their mind and would not publish his findings. It was only after Margolick revealed in *Vanity Fair* that Otis had spoken with Disney CEO Michael Eisner, who had recently purchased *Los Angeles*, and arranged to have the story spiked that a furious Dowie learned why his story was never published.

"The Chandler dynasty and their toadies are irresistible," said Dowie. "They're an American classic—a saga of lust and cupidity."

In truth, the truest portraits of the Chandlers had never been authorized. From such books as *The Powers That Be* by David Halberstam and *Thinking Big* by Bob Gottlieb and Irene Wolt to the probing work of *L.A. Weekly* news editor Charles Rappleye and the *Times*' own Jim Bassett, an uneven profile emerged over time of a family that wanted its cake and wanted to eat it as well: spoiled children who grew to spoiled adulthood with little sense of noblesse oblige.

But there was such a thing as family unity, Otis came to understand. Chandlers might be spoiled, but they did present a united front. With the publication of the *Vanity Fair* profile, in which Otis accused his cousins and Dan Frost of bringing down the *Los Angeles Times* that he had labored for a quarter century to build into a great newspaper, Otis again assumed the role of family whipping boy.

"I didn't realize it was built into their bones as much," said Otis.

Like a desperate kindergartner who had revealed too much during share-and-tell, Otis got on the telephone and tried making amends with Spud Williamson, Gwen Babcock, Doug Goodan, and Philip's youngest son, Bruce Chandler.

"There is this article coming out and I didn't use the words that were in the article," he recalled telling them. "You are going to read this and you are going to wonder: 'What the hell?' You are going to wonder who I am because I didn't . . . I have *never* said that you are stupid and that none of you could ever get a job and all the inferences.

"And they said, 'Well, you should know better. The press always does that to you. They always present the worst possible side, and this was a New York Jew that worked for the *New York Times* anyway.'"

What might have been a shocking admission in any other family came as no surprise to Otis. By and large, his cousins were the worst kind of bigots, paying lip service to blacks, Latinos, Jews, gays, and unions, but cringing each time they read about any of them in *their* family newspaper. That was their point of view and Otis accepted it. Everyone, he rationalized, is entitled to a point of view, even a bigot.

"If you take the spectrum to the right of the center, they are probably more to the right than to the center of the right," he said. "They are not moderate Republicans. They are fairly aggressive on certain issues [like] race.

"I told David Margolick this and it really sent him through the roof afterwards. He said, 'What was the reaction? Why was there a violent reaction?' I said, 'Because they think you are an extreme, typical, Eastern, biased, liberal Jewish Democratic reporter and that is why they won't talk to the press."

Instead of mirroring Margolick's outrage, Otis acquiesced. When his own sister scolded him for trusting the press, he behaved like a chastened child. He wrote an embarrassing retraction that was published in *Vanity Fair*'s letters to the editor section, weaseling around what he had told Margolick in a pathetic effort to disavow his own words. On the brink of his seventieth birthday, when he ought to have been fully aware of who he was and what he represented, Otis Chandler shrank back into humiliated silence, unaware of the weight of his own truth. He withdrew his honesty like a winning poker hand that had been bluffed right off of the table: a hand that Mark Willes was more than happy to replace with jokers and an array of wild cards.

THERE WAS PROFOUND SUBTEXT to Mark Willes's decision to replace the *Times'* six-year-old "Read this. Quick." ad campaign with the more homey "Get the story. Get the *Times.*" At the dawn of the Internet age, Willes was intent on

taking a giant step backward. He cut newsstand prices for the *Times* from $0.50 to a $0.25 and invested in classroom literacy, making the *"Times* in Education" program the best of its kind in the nation.

At the same time, he showed scant interest in the LATimes.com Web site or any of the other innovations of the New Media division. Willes believed in basics. He would *make* people read the *Times*. To outright laughter, he publicly announced the incredible goal of boosting *Times* circulation by half a million at a time when newspapers all over the United States were losing readers by the thousands. Even his cheerleaders in the business world suggested that he might have gone too far. Willes remained undaunted. He would once again make the *Times* the biggest, richest, most widely read newspaper in the country through the magic of marketing.

"Pardon me if I talk about it as a business, but that's how I see things," he declared with smug pomposity. "What marketers have found out is that you're more likely to have a sustainable competitive advantage if you are very clear about what you are and, then, what you have is better than anything else out there."

Indeed, circulation did begin to climb, but incrementally and at an exorbitant price. In November 1996, the *Times* posted its first daily circulation increase in five years: up 17,000 to 1,029,073. But intense boiler room activity, discount introductory offers, and an expensive door-to-door campaign accounted for most of those new subscriptions, and fully 98 percent of them were canceled after the introductory discounts ended. One report maintained that the *Times* was spending $254 just to retain a single new subscriber for one year.

"Mark Willes's predictions sounded like Harold Hill's," said the *Times'* veteran Sacramento correspondent Mark Gladstone, referring to the title character in *The Music Man*, who sold the citizens of River City on the fantasy that their children could all become master musicians.

"He had all these ideas, none of which really came to fruition," echoed Mia Chandler Frost. "He did get the stock price up. He was [one hell of a salesman]. That's what he was."

Otis kept hearing from friends and colleagues that Times Mirror had made a mistake, that Willes had exhibited just as many delusions about marketing at General Mills as he was now demonstrating at the *Times*. The stubborn, wily Mr. Willes honestly did believe that newspapers could be sold like Cheerios, and Otis could not convince him or his supporters at Times Mirror Square otherwise.

"They don't get that there is a difference," Otis complained. "Every day, the entire product changes. It changes several times during the night as you have to replate. You have different advertising every day and different editorial material every day. . . .

"There are so many things that are not like any other business. If you've got a good lively paper, if you do a good, professional job, then you present opinions that many of your readers do not agree with, and you will make them mad. Many of them may not like what you said about their favorite politician or their school or their favorite orchestra or whatever. But that is your job."

Following Otis's rant in *Vanity Fair*, no one on the Times Mirror board would listen to him—least of all, Mark Willes. The Cereal Killer continued to sell off bits and pieces of Times Mirror, maintaining that his plan was to get back strictly to the "core" business of newspapers.

"That whole diversification program at the *Times* . . . all these great companies," Mia said sadly. "It was all dismantled by dear Mark Willes."

During his first two and one-half years as CEO, Willes sold off Harry N. Abrams, the nation's largest producer of art and illustrated books; the *National Journal*; professional health sciences publishing house C. V. Mosby; and legal publisher Matthew Bender & Company to New Jersey–based Reed Elsevier for $2.5 billion in a tax-free deal engineered by Times Mirror CFO Tom Unterman. Dividends were up and the stock price was on its way to tripling its 1995 low of $18 a share. No one complained.

And while he held the Times Mirror board in rapt obeisance, Willes built his own team inside the *Times,* making it plain to the IIIs that their days were numbered. He approved the malleable Michael Parks's appointment as Coffey's second-in-command, replacing George Cotliar, the retiring *Times* managing editor who had served in the position for eighteen years.

Described by the acerbic Catherine Seipp as a squat man with "a penchant for military-ese (he schedules meetings for 1400 hours) and a buzz cut and tie right out of Jack Webb in (the motion picture) *–30–,*" Parks won the 1987 foreign reporting Pulitzer for the *Times* for his dispatches as South African bureau chief during the collapse of apartheid. Parks was well-liked, but most of his peers conceded that he was not a great leader. Although he was an indefatigable foreign correspondent with an impeccable reputation, Parks nonetheless was as poor a public speaker as Otis Chandler.

Following a Willes-inspired pep talk that Parks gave the troops shortly after his elevation to managing editor, one stupefied copy editor remarked as he left the session:

"Why do I feel like I've just been drugged?"

In the fall of 1997, Richard Schlosberg III announced his retirement as publisher of the *Times,* explaining that he had decided to spend more time with his wife and children. Less than a month later, Shelby Coffey III tendered his resignation as editor of the *Times.*

"What Willes explained was that they [Schlosberg and Shelby] preferred to move on in their careers and, in truth, what I have found out is that he made it impossible for them to continue," Otis said.

Michael Parks stepped up to the editor's position and named four managing editors to assist him: John Arthur for regional editions, John Lindsay for features, Karen Wada for projects and Leo Wolinsky for news.

As for the empty Schlosberg slot, Mark Willes filled the vacuum as easily as Napoleon Bonaparte filled the role of Holy Roman Emperor. In addition to chairing the Times Mirror board, Willes crowned himself the eighth publisher of the *Los Angeles Times*.

A week later, on September 26, 1997, Otis wrote his old secretary Donna Swayze: "Can you believe this turn of events? All I can say is I'm sorry to see Dick Schlosberg leave and I am extremely nervous about the future of the *Times*."

CHAPTER 28

"SO NOW YOU'RE FACED with this issue of finding a direction in your life," the psychic Bill Burns told Otis Chandler as he began his seventieth year.

The role of supplicant, patiently absorbing the words of a counselor, any kind of counselor, was foreign to Otis Chandler. And, yet, here he sat before this New Age guru who seemed to know him so well. He could blame this visit on Bettina, but Otis was here of his own volition. Blame it on curiosity. Once again, Otis secretly wondered if he had gone a little crazy in his old age.

From the moment he had fenced with a Jesuit over premarital catechism fifty years earlier, Otis had bristled at the thought of being told how to live. If anybody had lived life to its fullest, by God, it was Otis Chandler. He had listened to Buff harp on and on about who he was and what he represented. But he knew who he was, and he'd proved it to his mother and anyone else who had ever bothered to read his *Times*. He'd taken that crappy Republican rag that she and his father called a newspaper and turned it into a vital, breathing daily manifestation of the city his great-grandfather and his grandfather had created out of desert, stolen water, and a hopeful sense of destiny. Oh yes. Otis Chandler knew damned good and well who he was and what he represented. He didn't need to pay some shrink or shaman with a wall full of diplomas to tell him.

Still, he was bothered. Something roiled inside, and all the cars and ranches and other toys that his thick Chandler bankroll could purchase brought him no peace. It had something to do with Mark Willes and what was happening to the *Los Angeles Times*. The stock was up and Otis should have been happy, but he wasn't. Veteran *Time* columnist Jack Smith's heart had recently given out, and sportswriter Jim Murray had been diagnosed with cancer shortly after winning his Pulitzer. He wasn't expected to live more than a year. Otis had hired them both a generation earlier. Like the late Nick Williams, Frank Haven, and a host of others who had helped him conjure up a great newspaper, they were all gone now. Their faces haunted him on occasion, especially when he read or heard about the current troubles of a deteriorating *Los Angeles Times* over which he no longer exercised even token control.

But it wasn't just the *Times*. His recurrent anxiety sprang up like a ghost in almost every other aspect of his life. There was young Norman, now confined for the most part to a wheelchair, raging against his awful plight with hair down to his shoulders and his poor tortured body bloated an extra one hundred pounds by the ravages of his therapies. There was Bettina, always patient and loving, but resentful at times that Otis could not seem to settle down long enough to find himself by himself, and give her an opportunity to be something more than a nursemaid, nanny, and sidekick. And, of course, there was his mother: a shadow now, one foot in each dimension, her body and most of her mind stubbornly suspended in time as she languished upstairs at Los Tiempos until a berth could be readied for her in heaven.

"You inherited tremendous animosity the minute you were born into that family setting," said Bill Burns. "It's not really a family. It's more a series of vested interests. And you were a complication in those, from birth. A lot of your attempts to adjust to that over the years have robbed you of the option of feeling that you were okay."

Otis had spent most of his life being a hero, Burns told him. Otis felt himself nodding in silent agreement. But rarely a happy hero. Always the hero enveloped in a vague fog of guilt, as if he were the cavalry and even when he arrived in time, he was too late.

Worse, said Burns. Otis had shifted his emotions to the back burner for so many years that he couldn't even take credit for his own accomplishments. That's why he continued to display ribbons and plaques and loving cups; they were external proof of what he should have internalized by middle age, when most men dump the awards of their youth in a box and store them in the attic.

What was even more vexing was that he could no longer even be happy with what his money could buy. He couldn't buy himself a home and enjoy it. He had

to add on, renovate, refurnish, plant, enlarge, make it better and better and better. Sooner rather than later he had to sell it and move on. He couldn't savor life. He was too busy swallowing it whole, regurgitating, then swallowing something new.

"Let's talk about obligation and responsibility," said Burns. "You were born forty."

He owed nothing to the other Chandlers, Burns assured him. They were as venal, self-absorbed, and greedy as Otis had said they were in the *Vanity Fair* article, and more. His rush to apologize to each of them and his great shame at having spoken his mind publicly and in print were twin exercises in futility. His cousins were less insulted by his published words than they were affirmed in their existing dogma that, somehow, they were better than addled Otis.

"I don't think there's anybody in your life that has lost respect for you that's anybody about whom you'd care," said Burns. "You're about to generate a great deal of respect on a totally different basis from a great many more people."

Otis should concern himself less with Dan Frost and the grasping heirs of his aunts and uncles and more about those who saw who he really was, counseled Burns.

"There are people that absolutely love you, who are not related to you in anyway," he said. "That's something you're coming to see. People that would die for you. There's a reason; they're not nuts. But it's your responsibility to see why they are that way."

Otis fidgeted. Burns's office felt claustrophobic.

"You're at a crossroads," said Bill Burns. "You're not, in your sense of the word, productive, and you're not, in your sense of the word, fulfilled."

Burns spoke of the changing social order and personal responsibility and something called "popularism": a great shift in the way human beings behaved, with old forms of authority falling by the wayside. Otis was to be a part of that transformation, Burns predicted. In fact, he would be a major spokesman.

Otis interrupted, "I don't want to be on a pedestal. I never thought I was on a pedestal. I, people put me there. I didn't put myself there."

Tough, said Burns. According to his best guess, Otis was headed back to the pedestal, and soon. He had shed almost all his cloying responsibilities. His family was grown. His other relatives had underscored their own anachronistic irrelevancy, both in Otis's life and the life of Los Angeles. And Buff was a husk, clinging to life.

"On my mother, that's a very complicated issue," Otis said. "I owe enormous respect to [my parents], but she does not control. A lot of people think she controls me. She and I are very much alike. You're right about that. High energy. We work together with lots of conflict. I stood my ground, she stood her ground."

Burns assured his client that he understood. Otis need make no further protest. Buff was history. Otis was, indeed, his own man.

And once his mother was gone in body as well as spirit, just how much he was his own man would become more apparent than ever.

————————

SHORTLY AFTER Dorothy Buffum Chandler's first great-grandchild was born on October 20, 1977, Jane Chandler remembered that the family matriarch paid her and Norman a visit. That Buff would venture outside of Los Tiempos at all was startling; that she would do so to bestow her blessing on the first of a new generation of Chandlers was nothing short of a small miracle. As Buff allowed herself to beam at Otis Yeager Chandler in his crib, Jane witnessed the transformation from great grand dame to great-grandmother. Her eyes crinkled at the corners, then softened uncharacteristically, almost as if a long dormant maternal memory stirred behind them.

"She did not want to hold him," Jane recalled. "She just wanted to look at him. She got down very close."

Even at such a tender moment, however, there was Magi method in Buff's visit. It seemed that the infant had been born on a fortuitous day, consecrated by Carroll Righter and in complete harmony with the Los Angeles Philharmonic's opening that year. This child was special not just because he was a baby and a Chandler. He was special because both the stars and the symphony were in proper accord. It seemed a foregone conclusion that Otis Chandler's first grandson would know who he was and what he represented.

"She was extremely sensitive," Jane remembered. "She was very hurt by people's comments—too much so probably. She was not a touchy-feely person. She was not a person that you would touch or hug. But she was very aware of the people that she cared about."

For most of her life, Buff had been an enigma: at once regal and bitchy, prim yet girlish, histrionic one moment and ice-cold the next. She knew that she inspired respect, even fear, but she also knew the power of mercy and bestowed it judiciously, if not frequently. She saw a world of field hands, all aspiring to live in the Big House where she and the ghost of Norman Chandler held court, but her worldview was not infected with contempt. Buff Chandler was a small "d" Democrat who sincerely wanted to raise the common man high on an Aaron Copland crescendo, transforming his short, brutish life into a moment of beauty.

The common man would have to finance it himself, however. Buff never gave anything away.

"She was a tough lady," said her grandson Harry, who occasionally acted as her escort to the symphony in her last years. "She reminds me of a queen: There is

much you like, but you know not to cross them. And if you respect them, they would respect you. She liked me. I was her admitted favorite grandson."

On July 6, 1997, Dorothy Buffum Chandler passed away at Garden Crest Convalescent Home in Hollywood. She was ninety-six. A rest home was not where she wanted to die. It was not where she had planned to die. Buff wanted to fade into history in her second-story bedroom, at the top of the sweeping staircase where Norman used to leave her love notes at every step when she came home late from the Music Center. In the final decade of her life, she never left that bedroom. It was only on doctor's orders that she was removed at the very end.

Remembering a troubled Otis during those last years, his secretary Donna Swayze recalled that "sometimes she'd be very lucid and they would have a good conversation and other times she wouldn't be. And I remember him telling me one time he went to see her and they chatted and as he was going out of the room, he heard her say to the nurse, 'Was that my son?' And she would say to him, 'Now how many—tell me how many children you have?' and she couldn't remember. Men don't handle those things very well. I think his sister spent more time with his mother than he did."

Mia did what was necessary and nothing more. Too many run-ins with her mother over too many years had immunized her against Buff's complaints. She could still shut her eyes and picture a wispy young beanpole who grew to wounded womanhood during the Depression, always with the incessant maternal refrain: "Camilla! That is *not* what you do!"

A bitter, guarded childhood had made Buff's only daughter an overly cautious adult.

"She was . . . difficult," said Mia, who made a practice of always searching out just the right word. Displaying even more ambivalence toward her mother than Otis, she wavered between damnation and praise. She remembered her mother as demanding, but concerned; distant, but supportive.

"She was so forceful," remembered Mia. "I shouldn't complain, but she could be very fierce in her reprimand. And I was always kind of a shy person then."

Bettina remembered that Otis cried when he got the news. Then she remembered that he met with his sister, offering his comfort to Mia.

"I haven't cried," Mia told her younger brother. Her eyes were clear and she set right to the task of auctioning off her mother's belongings.

Tears seemed to be in short supply everywhere for Mrs. Dorothy Chandler. Every city, county, and state official with any memory of the creation of the Music Center and how it happened to land on Bunker Hill contributed his or her benediction; but although the praise flowed in stentorian tones, not one voice cracked during the delivery. All the eulogies were roughly equivalent to Mayor Richard

Riordan's dispassionate adieu: "Her imprint will be part of Los Angeles for many centuries to come. In culture, she was the most outstanding leader in the history of the city. As a person, she was a very strong, beautiful, wonderful mother and spouse, and someone we'll always remember."

"She had a lot of people who knew her and liked her and said she had a lot of character, but I don't know many people she was close to," said Bob Emmet, who had known Buff for as long as he'd known Otis—more than sixty years.

Buff had outlived most of her fan base, as well as her enemies. Even loyalists stopped paying their respects during the final years, when senile dementia took its terrible toll and Los Tiempos grew darker, more forbidding; it became a cold marble mausoleum warmed only in the kitchen, Buff's boudoir, and the servants' quarters by plug-in heaters that replaced the forced air heating so that a few dollars could be saved on the gas bill.

"She didn't really live the last, I'd say, three or four years of her life," said Bettina. "She just kind of existed."

Even Otis, whose love-hate relationship with his mother dated back most of a century, had let her go years earlier.

"That's not my mother," Otis would say. "My mother has been gone for quite a while."

His differences with Buff over how much influence she had on his career pursued him even after her death. When the *Times* reporter assigned to write Buff's obituary sent it over for Otis's approval, the only change Otis made was a line in which Buff was credited with engineering Otis's meteoric rise to the publisher's suite in 1960. Otis added the attribution "she said" to the sentence to clarify that the importance of her behind-the-scenes role was just Buff's opinion, and not necessarily shared by her son.

"I don't dote on those of the past," said Otis. Neither had his mother. Before she faded, her appointments secretary still came by twice a week. She loved to talk politics but always in the present tense. Buff had no use for memories, unless it involved Norman.

There was no public memorial service. The Music Center staged a symphonic concert in her honor, but no one gave a speech—only the printed program made note of her passing. Buff was cremated and scattered into the sea off of Dana Point, right at about the same spot where her late husband's, Norman Chandler's, ashes had been cast to the waves nearly a quarter century earlier. All of Otis's children and most of his grandchildren watched from the beach as Otis went through the short ritual. When it was over, Otis, Mia, and their children all moved on.

The grandchildren each received a memento from Los Tiempos, but Christie's Auction House inherited most of its contents. All that Buff held dear went to the

highest bidder four months after her death. A pair of interior designers bought Los Tiempos and found an estate in as ill repair as some antebellum mansion that had been left to rot through Reconstruction.

"There were five people on staff, but they did nothing," complained Tim Corrigan, one of the new owners. "They let the house go to hell. There was a Chinese couple who were the live-in cook and maid and it looked like they cooked in a wok in the kitchen and just never cleaned up. There was lard dripping from the ceiling and water damage everywhere. The windows hadn't been cleaned in so long that cobwebs had gathered in the corners of the panes."

Months of renovation brought back some of the splendor to Los Tiempos, and perhaps Buff Chandler as well.

While working upstairs one spring day several months into the restoration, Tim Corrigan heard his pet Scottie barking. He rushed into Buff's old bedroom, and there the dog sat yapping at an empty chair—one of the few that had not been sold at auction. He tried to calm his pet, but it wouldn't move from where it sat, nor would it stop barking. Later on, when he told his partner about the strange episode, they checked a calendar and found that it was May 19 and would have been Dorothy Chandler's ninety-seventh birthday.

THE SAME MONTH THAT BUFF DIED, Times Mirror sold its 31 percent stake in the Tejon Ranch to a pair of New York investment funds. Mark Willes said that the Tejon no longer fit into Times Mirror's core business profile.[1]

Losing the Tejon was one more blow to Otis. He loved the ranch as his own personal Eden, before and after the Fall. He had never been much of a history buff, but he did remember that Indians once lived there and that the U.S. Cavalry stationed camel-mounted regiments at Ft. Tejon in the middle of the nineteenth century. The Tejon was a living tapestry where Otis learned to hunt deer with a rifle and, later, a bow and arrow.

"The Tejon was a training ground," Otis said reverently.

It was where he had learned how to kill with a clean shot. He remembered his father driving him to the base of one of its mountains, leaving him, and returning hours later to pick him up at the top; his knapsack was loaded with quail and dove and his face was flushed with victory. But there wasn't always victory, even in his youth.

He remembered on occasion an unclean shot at twilight, when he and his father would stalk a deer and Otis's aim would be off the bead and he would catch it with a bullet to its gut. He knew he'd wounded it deep in its bowels by the scarlet spoor left behind, but the animal was still able to run away. His father told him to let it go. The deer would eventually lose so much blood that it would have to

stop to rest, and it would never move beyond that point. They would find it in the morning, if coyotes or a mountain lion did not find it first.

"I never slept those nights," said Otis, the memory as vivid as childbirth, or war. "I always tossed and turned and said, 'Can I find him?' And then, 'Was he dead?'"

When he was old enough to do so, he would send his father back to the ranch house alone after an unclean shoot. Then he'd lay out a bedroll and sleep on the mountain alone and wait impatiently for dawn so that he could track the animal and put it out of its misery.

"Everything's good up until the time that you're standing with the animals," he said. "There's a rush when you see your trophy up close. You look at the horns and you turn around and say, 'Yeah, that's a really nice cape and nice head and the meat looks like it hasn't been damaged.' And someone takes your picture. And then the sadness sets in and then you have to deal with that animal that you killed."

As a young man, Otis could usually heft a deer onto his broad shoulders and haul the carcass to the nearest road. There was blood to contend with, and ticks. He learned to gut the animal and tag it and hang it from a tree so that he could peel away its hide. There was no great joy in this part of the hunt, but it was every bit as much a part of the ritual as aiming and shooting the rifle. To do less, to leave the beast rotting in the fields as some hunters did, would be an unforgivable sin. Such a sin was a rarity on the Tejon.

As Otis aged, the ancient cycle of the hunt invoked pathos. There had never been jubilation in having another animal's blood on his hands, but the passing of the Tejon Ranch into other hands made his venison memories even more bittersweet. In a sense, he had evolved into an archetypal stag himself: always one lucky step ahead of a gut shot, but slowing now and keenly alert to the inevitable.

"In recent years I almost always say a little prayer for the animal that I have taken," he said. "That is not a joy to me when it's dead. I mean, I've triumphed. I've gotten maybe a good head or good trophy and I've accomplished my hunt. But the great excitement is long over."

BEING PUBLISHER WAS EXCITING, even more so than being chairman of the board, Mark Willes had decided. In his sixth-floor corner office with its long floor-to-ceiling panorama of the Los Angeles City Hall skyline just outside his window, the *Times'* newest publisher was understandably given to momentary meditation and flashes of inspiration. He had new ideas every day. Sometimes several times a day. A few of his more sardonic subordinates referred to his ever-shifting plans for his newspaper as the "strategy du jour."

In the fall of 1997, Mark Willes experienced nothing less than an epiphany: *Why not tear down the wall between advertising and editorial?*

It made no sense to Mark Willes to have an advertising sales force stumbling across terrific news and human interest stories every day, but no way to convey those stories to the city desk; and reporters who ran across great advertising leads were unable to relay them to the advertising department. Advertising and editorial did not talk to each other. The tradition smacked of the constitutional separation of church and state—a tenet that had always seemed a bit off to Willes, who lived in one nation, under God, just like newspaper reporters, ad salesmen, Mormon missionaries, and all the rest of the little people who lived and worked in the sprawling L.A. megalopolis.

There was an obvious synergy between advertising and editorial. When he first raised the issue, naturally there were protests, chiefly coming from the newsroom. Fortunately, Mark Willes had learned a thing or two about stifling dissent during his days at General Mills. He paid lip service to challenges, and then ignored them. On November 3, 1997, he commenced tearing down the barrier.

"I'll use a bazooka, if necessary," he declared.

According to the official twaddle that spewed from the misnamed Times Mirror Communications Department, the *Times* was undergoing "a top-level reorganization to align its business functions—specifically, advertising and marketing—with the sections of the paper to help the *Times* grow and connect more effectively with its readers."

What that meant was that Mark Willes would plant a sales manager in every section of the paper to work directly with that section's editor. Like some small-town weekly where the chamber of commerce could dictate the news by granting or withholding advertising, the *Times* now had a new layer of "mini-publishers" peering over every reporter's shoulder, in effect, to make sure that *Times* advertisers were given editorial priority.

The mini-publisher initiative was precisely what Otis Chandler feared most. Although he had supported the Times Mirror CEO during his first two years of bloodletting and most of the managerial experiments that followed—what Willes liked to refer to as "thinking outside of the box"—Otis finally had had enough the day that Mark Willes became publisher.

"It's simply *not* what we hired you for!" Otis kept repeating to Willes, who had crowned himself publisher during a closed-door Times Mirror board meeting while Otis was in Alaska on a hunting trip. By being both *Times* publisher *and* Times Mirror CEO, Otis warned, Willes had become his own boss—a foolish and potentially disastrous course to follow with no real checks and balances of the one man in charge of the day-to-day operation of the *Times*.

But Mark Willes didn't see it that way, nor did he seek Otis's permission to become publisher. He had all the support he needed. Times Mirror was trading at $58 a share on the New York Stock Exchange, Otis's cousins saw the family fortunes swelling toward the $3-billion mark, and, quite frankly, none of them could see what Otis was fussing about. They even liked the mini-publisher idea. That is, until it didn't work.

Over the next two years, mini-publishers and other marketing and sales executives came and went with alarming frequency, sometimes packing it in after just a few months. One Willes marketeer stayed for exactly six weeks—just long enough to assess the chaos and leave. Nearly thirty of them had left by the end of 1998. The *Times* masthead, which in the past could go for a decade or more without changing, was now changing several times a year. With no prompting from Catherine Seipp or any of the other growing army of *Times* satirists, the *Times'* own reporters and editors secretly and sarcastically began referring to the in-and-out Willes executives as "the Flying Wallendas." The tumult at the top infected the rest of the paper with growing paranoia, accounting in large part for the *Times'* increasingly insular and dreary journalism.

"The politics are so intense that all these journalists want to stay in the office and literally not get too far from their desks," observed Sue Horton, editor of *L.A. Weekly.*

The only section of the paper where Willes's "tear down the wall" experiment paid off was Business, where ad revenue grew by nearly 20 percent a year. Yet even Business mini-publisher Kelly Ann Sole left after just three years to take a job selling time on CNBC and MSNBC. She explained to reporters that she was resigning not because she did not support Willes's basic idea, but because the turf wars between advertising and editorial had finally grown too contentious even for her.

The internecine warfare at Times Mirror Square finally got to Otis's son Harry, too, who watched helplessly as Willes disemboweled his New Media division. When he came back to work at the *Times* in 1993, Harry believed that he might belatedly establish himself as the last Chandler at the *Times*—if not as publisher, then as the leading guru of the *Times'* growing presence on the Internet. But Willes would not let that happen.

"Mark Willes doesn't get the Internet," said Terry Schwadron, *Times* deputy managing editor for New Media and Harry's immediate boss. After a public showdown with Willes over the publisher's threat to kill the Life & Style section,[2] Schwadron also resigned from the *Times* in 1998. He went to work—along with nearly three dozen of his fellow expatriate *Times*men—at the *New York Times.*

Willes cut the New Media budget. It didn't matter that www.LATimes.com had made *PC Magazine*'s Top 100 Web site list five years in a row, or that the Web

site had 2 million computer "hits" the day that Princess Diana died in a car accident. Nor did it matter that the New Media division had developed Internet classifieds for used-car sales, real estate, nationwide movie listings, computer shopping, and a fee-for-download method of selling archived *Times* articles over the Web. Even Tom Unterman, Times Mirror's chief financial officer, understood how important New Media had become, but Mark Willes did not.

Said Harry Chandler, "I found Mark skeptical whereas Tom saw the sea change like the rest of us."

But Unterman was not in charge. Willes was, and to him the Internet was a fad. The newspaper was the core business and the core business would only grow if it was properly packaged and sold to the masses, like literary Hamburger Helper. Willes became obsessed with polls[3] and panels. Laventhol and Coffey had spawned a corporate dependence on the dubious results of surveys and test marketing in the early 1990s, but under Mark Willes, the *Times* became a newspaper virtually run by focus groups. Willes preferred the opinions of average folk who knew nothing of the newspaper business over the opinions of his own experienced professionals. They were the same consumers who had helped him create Honey Nut Cheerios, after all. Why couldn't they help create a Honey Nut *Times*?

And so focus groups inspired Mark Willes's second great epiphany: "Our Times."

For more than a generation, the *Times* had wrestled with the problem of providing local news to thousands of neighborhoods scattered over an area the size of Ohio while also delivering on its promise of top-notch city, county, regional, state, national, and global news. With rare exceptions, such as the days directly after a Shelby swarm through some newsworthy neighborhood, local news fell low on the *Times'* priority list.

Of course, *Times* editors had known for decades what the focus groups were now telling Willes: that they really wanted local news about the PTA, Little League scores, and Neighborhood Watch reports from the local police blotter. And the *Times* had tried to deliver the small-town bits and pieces in the form of once- or sometimes twice-weekly regional sections covering the South Bay, San Gabriel Valley, or Westside. But the effort was always spotty at best. In truth, the *Times* abandoned most of the Little League scores or shoplifting statistics to smaller independent local newspapers.

But the newest publisher of the *Times* had a better idea. When the *Santa Monica Outlook*—one of those independent local newspapers—went out of business on March 26, 1998, the Willes team launched its first "Our Times" section: a weekly round-up of local news specifically targeted to and circulated in the Santa Monica area. Although never a big advertising or circulation coup, that first "Our

Times" experiment did become a staple on L.A.'s affluent Westside, and Willes interpreted that acceptance as success.

Produced by a greenhorn staff who were paid less than half the salary regular *Times* staff writers earned, "Our Times" had farm team potential at the same time that it satisfied focus-group hunger for down-home news. The ultimate Willes master plan was to tailor "Our Times" editions for all of Southern California, eventually putting twenty-three different editions out to virtually every community in L.A., and beyond. At the end of two years, however, there were only thirteen editions in operation and collectively they had cost the *Times* between $5 million and $7 million while bringing in less than $2 million in advertising revenue. Willes was intrepid. It was his idea and it was a good one, so he stood squarely behind it.

In similar epiphanous fashion, Willes set out to win the hearts and wallets of Latinos. After axing the weekly *Nuestro Tiempo* in one of his early cost-cutting maneuvers, he discovered that Los Angeles had a large Spanish-speaking population—the largest in North America outside Mexico City. Ignoring the *Times'* many failed efforts to win Latino readers dating all the way back to Harry Chandler's *Noticias Mundiales de Ultima Hora* column in 1922, Willes got behind the newspaper's first ever Spanish-language radio advertising campaign promoting a new weekly bilingual paper called *La Opinion Para Ti.* It was to be jointly published by the *Times* and *La Opinion*, and was followed by an even more audacious circulation plan whereby bilingual subscribers were offered the *Times* and *La Opinion* on a two-for-one basis.[4]

To outside observers, the *Times'* chaos was invisible. The paper continued to look healthy, if not prosperous. *Times*men took two more Pulitzers in 1998: one for photography and the other for Shelby Coffey's final swarm, which covered a police shoot-out with two heavily armed bank robbers in North Hollywood. Pulitzers were good for circulation.

Yet, after using every subscription trick in the book, Willes still had been unable to make a dent in his hyperbolic goal of adding 500,000 new readers. Circulation still hovered just above the magic million mark, but not by much. Because most advertisers and readers did not read past the 1-million-plus circulation figures, few outside of the sixth floor realized that the *Times* had lost nearly a quarter million subscribers during the first half of the decade. The *New York Times* had now joined *USA Today* and the *Wall Street Journal* in besting the once formidable *Los Angeles Times,* which was now ranked the fourth largest among newspapers in the United States.[5] On most journalism review lists, the *Times* was also now ranked fourth in quality behind the *New York Times*, the *Washington Post,* and the *Wall Street Journal.*

"We've lost some good people who said, 'I'm just not going to wait around to see if the Titanic is going to hit the iceberg,'" Otis observed at the time. "And so some people have left. Some résumés are out. Mark Willes thinks that everything is fine. The morale is super. He just doesn't know."

Otis's misgivings came to a head in March 1998 when Willes took his master plan one step too far. It was to be Otis's last meeting as a Times Mirror director. He joined Dave Laventhol, Bob Erburu, AT&T CEO Mike Armstrong, and Getty Trust chairman Harold Williams in formally retiring from the board and ending nearly fifty years with the *Times*. Even Otis was surprised when, at the last minute, he and his fellow retiring board members learned that the meeting was to be combined with a hastily concocted farewell party that Willes had arranged to cap the Chandler-Laventhol-Erburu era and usher in his own.

AT&T's Mike Armstrong, who thought he would be addressing only the board in closed-door session, was equally surprised, but went ahead with his prepared speech anyway—a diplomatic, but quite direct appeal to the incoming board of directors to overturn Willes's wrongheaded decision to act as both *Times* publisher and Times Mirror CEO. Repeating Otis's outrage from six months earlier, Armstrong said Willes was just plain wrong, Otis's cousins notwithstanding.

"It got the room quiet in a hurry," said one veteran *Times* executive who sat through the grueling evening.

All eyes fell on Willes, whose jaws were torqued so tight they looked as though they might jut through his cheeks at any moment. Beyond his obvious displeasure at Armstrong's public upbraiding, the supercilious publisher said nothing.

Otis torqued his own jaws that night, but for very different reasons. He held a deep ambivalence about cutting his last tie to his *Times*. Although his presence at Times Mirror Square receded a bit more with each passing year, as a Times Mirror director he at least had an advisory role and was even listened to on occasion, chiefly—and ironically—by the non-Chandler members of the board. If his long association with his *Times* was, indeed, going to come to an end, he reasoned, it was at least nice to have it be among friends and peers with a chance to say farewell. He expected to receive a silver *Times* eagle and a handshake, say a few words about the noble calling of journalism, and then march into history.

"Instead, I walked in and there are four hundred people there and we are a footnote to a management meeting," he recalled.

Further, Otis Chandler wasn't lionized from the podium as the legendary publisher who had transformed a right-wing rag into a unifying beacon with global reach that reflected the disparate but dynamic capital city of the American Southwest—the proudest achievement in his overachieving life. As he stood by his chair and waited for his reward for a lifetime of Herculean effort, he listened in-

stead to a quick and dismissive address on how he liked to hunt big game, lift weights, and surf. Like every East Coast fop who had ever rolled into L.A. with a fixed vision of all that was wrong with shallow, venal Angelenos, Otis's own *Times* sent him into final retirement with the message that he was just a jock. Period. At the end of the night, he grabbed Bettina and packed it in, fuming.

"Okay, I'm out of here," he growled. "This is the current culture of this man [Willes] and I'm glad I'm not around."

When Willes executed his next atrocity and removed every executive with any newspaper experience from the Times Mirror corporate level, Otis described his fury as "ballistic," but now he didn't even have a voice on the board. All he could do was sit in his office at the Vintage Museum and rage helplessly like every other *Times* outsider who could only be heard by the man in charge if he or she happened to sit on a focus group.

"Not that these people are bad people," Otis said of the new Willes team.

Not that they can't learn. But you do not put a person in the first or second or third shift at the '24 Hours of Le Mans' when they have only driven a car on the street, and this is just about what he is doing. It's just a crazy quilt of moving present executives into new positions that they are not qualified for in terms of knowledge and experience instead of going out in the newspaper industry and hiring some experienced people to come in. It just doesn't make sense. It's going to catch up with him.

A perfect example of Willes's new untrained team was a forty-five-year-old Stanford law graduate named Kathryn Downing. Stout, formal, and intensely private, she came to Times Mirror in 1995 following a long career in legal publishing. Willes hired Downing, a fellow Mormon, to head the Mosby medical texts and Matthew Bender law books subsidiaries until the book division was sold to Reed Elsevier in 1997.

A native of Portland, Oregon, where her parents owned a landmark eatery called the Pancake Corner, Downing graduated from Lewis and Clark University before entering Stanford. She knew nothing of newspapers, but married into the profession when she became stepmother to the three grown children of Gerald Flake, a former executive of Toronto-based Thomson Newspapers.

Willes didn't want to lose Downing, so he offered her the presidency of the *Los Angeles Times,* a position held since 1982 by *Times* veteran Don Wright, who Willes moved up to the largely honorary post of *Times* chairman until Wright's retirement the following year.

Otis had met Downing and liked her, but he was "horrified" that she did not

start training on a newspaper management track at one of Times Mirror's smaller newspapers, the way his son Norman had done in Connecticut before he had become ill.

"She is bright," Otis said upon hearing of her appointment, "but she knows absolutely *nothing* about newspapers. I guess I'm old-fashioned enough to believe that it's fine to have education and intellect and commitment and be a nice person, but I also think that experience is one of the most important attributes in any business, especially a business like a newspaper. We'll just have to see what happens."

Meanwhile, Mark Willes was closing out 1998 no nearer his 500,000 circulation increase. A clueless corps of managers could offer no ideas on how to meet such a goal in what appeared to be a saturated market. Sixty percent of the ideal *Times* demographic—English-speaking high school graduates who earned at least $30,000 a year and had some college education—already took the *Times*. The remaining 40 percent had subscribed at one time or another, but did not want to renew, usually preferring the national editions of the *New York Times* or the *Wall Street Journal* instead. Maybe 500,000 new subscribers was setting the bar too high, his marketing executives suggested.

Willes went into a rage. His strategy sessions began to sound like the Caine mutiny court martial.

"I've studied generals and we're gonna take that hill," he fumed. "I don't know how. But we're gonna. Strong leaders set a goal and don't waver from it."

Meanwhile, the long-battered *Times* infrastructure continued to deteriorate. Ad sales had come in $20 million under 1998 projections, and newsprint prices were up again. Bob Erburu's shortsighted sale of Publisher's Paper Company had left the *Times* as vulnerable to paper shortages as every other newspaper in the country, forcing Willes to institute even more cost-saving measures, including

- reducing each newspaper page by an inch;
- laying out the paper tight to save newsprint; and
- adding ten more "Our Times" sections to help boost circulation and advertising revenue.

Willes had cut $350 million in overhead, but his mini-publishers were proving to be a washout, as was "Our Times"; and the impossible circulation goal, which had been so widely publicized that it now hung around Willes's neck like a half-million albatross, was faring no better.

Desperate times called for desperate measures, so at year's end the Cereal Killer resorted to what he did best. Just in time for Christmas, with what Willes hoped would be minimal fanfare, the *Times* eliminated 250 jobs in its Valley and

Ventura County editions, and laid off another six hundred people around the rest of Times Mirror.

Outwardly, the trustees of Chandis Securities continued to express confidence with their choice for CEO and publisher. Mark Willes continued to preach thinking outside the box, and so did his choice for president of the *Times*. They had new tricks up their sleeves for 1999, which they were sure would at last turn the *Times* around. Indeed, just a week before Christmas, Willes and Downing signed off on a unique deal that would mean millions in pure profits for the *Times* the following year; it was the kind of synergistic pact that the musty old *Times* team from the Otis era would have never considered.

The largest indoor sports stadium ever built in Los Angeles was due to open the following autumn, and the *Times* planned to have a big piece of the action. Named the Staples Center for its corporate sponsor, Staples Office Supplies, the sports complex would be the new home of both the Lakers and the Kings, as well as the Avengers, a new professional indoor football team. Every major concert, circus, and traveling spectacle would be staged at Staples, beginning with an October inaugural featuring the L.A. return of the indefatigable rock star Bruce Springsteen. The Staples Center could be a veritable advertising gold mine for the *Times*.

Sensing what was ahead, one of Willes's mini-publishers struck a profit-sharing bargain with the Staples Center management that called for the *Times* to publish and distribute a commemorative edition of the *Times* Sunday Magazine; it would be loaded with ads and the beauty of the deal was that the *Times* and the Staples Center would share evenly in the profits.

Mark Sande, the mini-publisher who cinched the deal, told the *American Journalism Review* a year later that "it seemed like such a great idea. It just seemed like a terrific opportunity. There was no secret regarding the deal or the profit-sharing. Mark said this is a good deal. Kathryn said this is a good deal."

And it was a very good deal, especially for Mark Willes, who was about to climax a very good year. Despite the stumbles and layoffs of 1998, Wall Street forecast strong 1999 earnings for Times Mirror, perhaps as much as $3.15 a share, and the Times Mirror board rewarded Mark Willes accordingly. Including $9.9 million in stock options, he earned $13.3 million for steering the *Times* and Times Mirror through 1998.

With his own team now in place and naysayers such as Otis Chandler and Chandler's allies on the board out of Willes's hair at last, 1999 looked as if it was going to be even better.

INDEED, THE NEW YEAR DID OPEN on a brighter note. In a long tradition of maintaining a global sweep to its coverage, the *Times* now had a bureau in Hanoi.

Echoing Otis's 1977 decision to refuse X-rated movie ads for the good of the family reader, the *Times* stopped accepting tobacco ads. Two Business Section reporters, Chuck Philips and Michael Hiltzik, won the *Times'* twenty-third Pulitzer for stories on corruption in the entertainment industry. In the future, it would be far more difficult for the Catherine Seipps or even the Bob Woodwards of the world to fault the *Times* for treading too lightly on Hollywood.

But the big news at Times Mirror Square came on June 3, when Mark Willes succumbed to months of criticism for having worn both the publisher's and CEO's hat. While remaining Times Mirror chairman, Willes surrendered the top spot at the *Times* to Kathryn Downing.

Otis went wild at the news. It was hard to imagine that Willes could do something worse than name himself CEO and publisher, but he had managed to pull it off. Downing didn't even have enough experience to assume the *Times* presidency, which remained a liaison between Times Mirror and the *Times*, and not a hands-on newspaper job. What lunacy had provoked Willes to name her publisher? No good would come of it, he warned Bettina. No good at all.

The *Times* now had seen more publishers in the previous ten years than during its first one hundred years, and the latest appeared to be the worst of the lot. Downing did not shy away for a second from Mark Willes's goal of adding 500,000 new subscribers. She immediately went him one better. She doubled the goal to an even million.

Quickly nicknamed "Calamity Kate" by a less than adoring staff, Downing explained during a series of pep rallies the ambitious plan that she and Michael Parks, the *Times* editor, had for doubling *Times* circulation. She made her point like an inspirational preacher, hoisting a bottle of Evian water high over her head and reciting an oft-repeated graduate business school vignette about Americans and bottled water. Just ten or fifteen years earlier, she patiently explained, there had been virtually no market for Evian in the United States; today, hundreds of designer water brands competed with market leader Evian for billions of consumers' dollars. How did such a market develop? Through psychology, advertising, outreach, and repetition—through *marketing!* Consumers hadn't even *known* they needed Evian until some clever marketing team told them that they did!

And that, she concluded, was precisely what her team of winners was going to do with the *Times*: convince a million consumers that they needed a newspaper just as badly as the Evian folk had convinced them that they needed bottled water. A brand was a brand was a brand—whether it be bottled water, breakfast cereal, or the morning paper.

"She really did seem infatuated with progressive management techniques," said an editor for the *Times'* Sunday Magazine. "She got groups of her employees together and smiled and talked about deadwood and bell curves, and performing

at 110 percent at all times. She was kind of a New Age conservative with an EST-like penchant for artificially boosting self-esteem."

Downing's own self-esteem gleamed like her flirtatious smile, but her self-respect she kept hidden away behind her closed office door most of the time. She was even less accessible as publisher than her immediate predecessor had been.

But she was productive and gungho. On October 10, 1999, the *Times* published her first major triumph: a 168-page Sunday Magazine about the opening of the $400-million Staples Center. *Times* sportswriters cooperated with business and feature staff to produce a slick, fat magazine with over $2 million in advertising sandwiched between the articles. That would certainly win Downing kudos from Mark Willes and the board. The cover line read "Taking Center Stage"— and that is just what the magazine did, in more ways than anyone could have ever predicted at the time.

The first hint of a problem came a little over a week later, when the alternative weekly *New Times* and the *Los Angeles Business Journal* both reported that Tim Leiweke, president of Staples Center, and Mark Willes, then-*Times* publisher, had made a deal shortly before Downing was named publisher. It was a pact to split the profits on the magazine, which, in itself, was not necessarily a problem. The *Times* published advertisers' testimonials all the time, just like any other publication. Occasionally, entire magazines or stand-alone tabloids were devoted to "advertorials": press release information combined with a sales pitch and melded with an array of display ads. *Times* staff journalists were never involved. Usually written by advertising copy writers, advertorials were always clearly labeled at the top or bottom of the page so that readers would know that they were being pitched a product and were not reading a news story.

By splitting the magazine's profits with the Staples Center and not issuing a disclaimer, however, the *Times* had broken faith with its readers. Further, Downing and Parks had broken faith with their own staff by failing to disclose the terms of the Staples deal to the editors, photographers, and writers who had contributed to the magazine. Career journalists had become shills for the Staples Center without their knowledge.

Within days of the revelation, a petition circulated through Times Mirror Square, signed by over three hundred *Times* men and women, demanding an explanation and an apology from Downing. Articles in the *New York Times* and *Wall Street Journal* that followed up on the revelations in *New Times* and the *Business Journal* further aggravated the severity of Downing's mistake. To her credit, she took responsibility for the Staples deal by apologizing to senior staff for her faux pas. But that was how she saw her error: a small to medium-sized lapse in judgment that could be corrected with a simple "I'm sorry" before moving on. She had made her second major mistake.

When she finally faced the full editorial staff during a late October meeting in the *Times* cafeteria, Downing wore contrition the way she had once worn self-esteem. She was sorry, she said, although she was not prepared to put on a hair shirt and a crown of thorns over some simple misunderstanding on her part. Her subjects were not in a forgiving mood. The docile employees who had sat bewildered or bored during her Evian rallies had turned into a rabid mob. If there hadn't been so many of them disgorging their bile, she might have been tempted to charge insubordination and fire them all.

But this mass insubordination seemed to be more of an insurrection. Downing's confident face reddened as journalist after journalist stood up and unloaded years of stifled anger. The Staples affair was merely the icing on a sour cake that had been baking for more than a decade. Perhaps Downing should take a few graduate courses in media ethics, she was told. Then she might understand what kind of sin she had committed. Perhaps she ought to just hand in her resignation and get out of the building.

"This is a major, major mistake, but I am publisher of the *L.A. Times* and I am staying the publisher of the *L.A. Times*," she said defiantly, but with new appreciation of just how far over the line she had crossed. "The question is how do I come up the learning curve faster."

She could never come up fast enough. The meeting ended after two long and painful hours, and Downing began to reassess. Michael Parks stood by her, grateful that she had taken full responsibility for the fiasco. His own knowledge about the profit-sharing deal had not been discovered, and that was good. Downing's bunker was separated from the angry newsroom mob by three floors, but Parks had to face the bellicose and the betrayed every minute of the day. Unlike the naïve publisher, he understood just how far over the line they had traveled, and although he hoped for a miracle, he knew intuitively that the shit storm was far from over.

Kathryn Downing left for the Halloween weekend, grateful for a break and hoping that this strange mutiny would all blow over. It did not.

By the following week, a second petition began circulating among the staff, calling for a complete investigation to find out how the shameful Staples episode had come about. Parks resisted.

"We know what happened," he told *L.A. Weekly.* "I don't see anything more to discover."

The Staples mess was serious and it didn't help that the *New York Times* had fanned the flames, but the staff had groused and grumbled before. Downing was as confident as Mark Willes that, if they stayed the course, the wrath would gentle down to a simmer and the uprising would pass. Parks wasn't so sure.

Then, in the morning of November 3, a Wednesday, a call came into the city desk and a thin but sturdy voice from the glorious past of the beaten, battered *Los Angeles Times* asked to speak to Bill Boyarsky, the city editor. Boyarsky took a breath. At the other end of the line was the man who had hired him off an Associated Press picket line nearly thirty years earlier and had given him the best job he'd ever had in journalism.

"I always thought the good old days were too good," Boyarsky once said of his salad days at the *Times*. "It was great. It was incredible. I always knew it would end."

But Boyarsky had stayed on at the *Times* well past his prime, through the transformation from Velvet Coffin to Pine Box, and worse. He had stayed through buyouts and layoffs and firings, through Shelby swarms, mini-publishers, and "Our Times." He had accepted the city editor's job when he was well past sixty, more out of loyalty to the ideals of good journalism than a belated scaling of the corporate ladder.

Boyarsky had become a keeper of the *Times* flame for some inexplicable reason. Until this moment, even he could not adequately explain why. Chalk it up to championing noble lost causes. But when the voice at the other end of the line asked him to take down a letter and read it aloud to the men and the women of the *Los Angeles Times,* the real reason Boyarsky had remained at the city desk through all the humiliation of recent years became clear in an instant.

Otis Chandler was back.

OTIS AND BOYARSKY WORKED over the language, faxing versions back and forth through the afternoon until they got it right. The finished open letter to the *Times* newsroom was over five pages long, rambled a bit, and belabored the obvious at times, but made its major point in the first four paragraphs:

> This is a personal message addressed today to the employees of the *Los Angeles Times*, particularly of the editorial department because they have been so abused and misused.
>
> I have been following the issues regarding the *Times* and Times Mirror very closely since I retired March of last year as a director, when I reached the compulsory retirement age of 70.
>
> Even though I have officially retired, I continue quite naturally to closely follow the events of the *Times* and the Times Mirror Company. I follow these events because most of all I am interested in what is happening to this newspaper and this company where I spent over 50 years of my life.

I care enormously about the *Times* and its survival and about the people who are there. The *Times* is in your hands. I hope and pray that somehow the forward momentum of this great newspaper will continue. The integrity, the quality and honor of the *Times* must survive.

What Otis's prose lacked in style it more than made up for in blunt, bold truth. He spoke of his great sadness at seeing his beloved *Times* slip from greatness. The Staples Center pact was "unbelievably stupid" and the blame rested squarely on the shoulders of Mark Willes and Kathryn Downing. That both top executives of the *Times* had zero newspaper experience before stepping into their roles was beyond abhorrent. He finished with a final blast at the Staples fiasco and a respectful nod to the ghosts of Times Mirror Square:

> Respect and credibility for a newspaper is irreplaceable. Sometimes it can never be restored, no matter what steps might be taken after such an event in terms of apology by the publisher and the editor.
>
> When I think back and realize the history of this great newspaper under the hands of General Otis, Harry Chandler and my father Norman and succeeding publishers, I realize how fragile and irreplaceable public trust of a newspaper is. This trust and faith in a newspaper by its employees, its readers and the community is dearer to me than life itself.
>
> Otis Chandler

When Michael Parks heard what Boyarsky was up to, he asked him not to read the letter.

"I have to," said Boyarsky. "He's the man who created this paper."

"Okay," Parks said with reluctance. "Just don't stand on the city desk when you read it."

Boyarsky read. Dozens listened, rapt. When the city editor looked up, signaling that he had finished the last paragraph, the still gathering crowd erupted. Cheers rang through the corridors and offices of the third floor, from one end of Times Mirror Square to the other.

Musty old photos of Otis Chandler began popping up throughout the newspaper, taped to windows and walls like campaign posters, and his letter exploded across the Internet. Whatever hope Parks and Downing had of containing the Staples botch evaporated overnight. The following day, every major newspaper in the United States carried the story of Otis Chandler's angry return. In a rare tribute from a worthy rival, the *New York Times* gave him praise on its editorial page.

The *Times* carried its story of the Otis letter too, notable for its "no comment" from Mark Willes. But Kathryn Downing did not remain silent; she handed her official statement to the city desk late in the day. It said, "Otis Chandler is angry and bitter and he is doing a great disservice to this paper and that's too bad because when he was publisher, he did wonderful things. It's too bad when some people get old, they get so bitter."

With Parks's approval, staff writer Tim Rutten cut her last sentence, but he still could not save Downing from herself. Her misreading of just who she was calling angry and bitter only fueled the rebellion.

"Otis is Zeus," John Arthur, the *Times* deputy managing editor said with plain-spoken reverence.

Otis was General Patton, said Bill Dwyre, the sports editor, "and you want to go out and get on the tank and ride with him. If Patton comes back and says, 'Let's go! There is one more mission,' you go with him."

Otis was also Odysseus, home from twenty years of hard sailing and not at all happy with what the suitors had done in his absence to his palace and his Penelope—his one true mistress, his *Times.*

Following the explosive national attention Otis and his letter focused on the Staples Center episode, Michael Parks gave in to the *Times* petitioners who had demanded a full investigation and assigned David Shaw to the story. The *Times* published Shaw's fourteen pages of findings in a stand-alone section of the paper on December 20. In it, Parks and Downing appeared culpable, but Willes had enough built-in deniability to defer blame to his rogue subordinates. He railed against Otis at social and business functions for weeks after, slamming the former publisher as meddlesome and out of touch. For his part, Otis began accepting invitations to speak at testimonial dinners and media panels. His message was low-key but stern: As long as know-nothings were in charge, the *Times* was in trouble.

Still, as both the new year and the new millennium approached, it looked as though the Cereal Killer would escape to fight another day and neither the publisher nor the editor who had acted as his allies before and after the Staples affair would pay a price for their transgressions. Downing and Parks codified the lessons learned from Staples, but refused to rebuild the wall between editorial and advertising. Malaise again settled over the newsroom. Cost cuts continued, with sixty-five more jobs lost through attrition; there was a tightening of the travel budget and another reduction in the *Times'* news-to-advertising ratio, which now delivered even more ads and less journalism to its readers. Just as Willes, Downing, and Parks had hoped, the furor at last settled down to a dull growl and Otis seemed to fade from view.

But the tale was not yet over, and even Otis Chandler would be caught off balance by the song the fat lady was about to sing.

THE NEWSPAPER CAREERS of Mark Willes, Kathryn Downing, and Michael Parks ended in a poetic, if rude surprise.

In theory, the beginning of their end had started years earlier, when the then-Times Mirror chairman of the board, Otis Chandler, met with the Tribune Company's chief financial officer, John Madigan. At the time, Times Mirror was flush with cash and at its most bullish, acquiring newspapers and other media companies as quickly as the board could find a bargain. The flagship newspaper of the late Colonel Robert McCormick was also in an acquisitive mood, meaning that Chandler and Madigan had much in common. That was 1981, and Chandler and Madigan had remained cordial colleagues for years thereafter in the rarefied world of newspaper publishing. When Madigan stepped up to publisher of the *Tribune* in 1990 and became CEO of the Tribune Company five years later, Otis wished him well.

The Tribune Company had become a media powerhouse, particularly in television, during the seventy years following Colonel Robert McCormick and Captain Joe Patterson's offer to buy the *Times* from Harry Chandler. In addition to the *Chicago Tribune*, the *Orlando Sentinel*, four radio stations, and two other newspapers, the Tribune Company owned twenty-two television stations, including KTLA Channel 5 in Los Angeles.

Mark Willes knew none of this background when Madigan met with him at a newspaper convention in San Diego in the spring of 1999 to discuss an invitation to merge Times Mirror with the Tribune Company.

For two months, the two CEOs bantered over a series of possibilities: a partnership, a merger, a joint venture, a buyout. In the end, however, Willes nixed a deal on the grounds that the strictures of Harry Chandler's trusts would make such a merger impossible. Willes understood that, until the death of the last heir who was born in Harry's lifetime,[6] the Chandler family was bound by the terms of the trusts not to sell, trade, or dispose of its interest in the Times Mirror Company. Such were the terms of Harry's will. Disappointed, Madigan let the matter drop.

Four months later, at the height of the Staples Center controversy, there was another meeting—this time, between Jack Fuller, the Tribune Company's president, and Tom Unterman, Times Mirror's chief financial officer. They both sat on the board of Classified Ventures, a joint Internet venture put together by Times

Mirror, the Tribune Company, and the *Washington Post* to exploit classified advertising over the Web. During a break in their meeting, Fuller and Unterman picked up discussion of Madigan's proposed merger where Willes had left off. Two days later, Unterman told both Fuller and Madigan that he thought he might be able to broker a deal with the Chandler family and bypass Willes and the Times Mirror board altogether.

Unterman left Times Mirror Square at the end of 1999 and went to work full-time for Chandis Securities and the heirs of Harry Chandler, although nominally he remained a Times Mirror employee. Outside the boardroom, his departure raised no eyebrows, hackles, or questions, and Willes even wished him well. The University of Chicago–educated lawyer had been with Times Mirror for eight years, during which time he had endeared himself to Chandis by engineering the $2.3-billion Cox Communications deal. In a more recent deal, he had created a pair of limited partnerships for Chandis which, in effect, allowed the Chandlers to sell more than half of their Times Mirror stake back to the company while retaining majority voting control and dodging every penny of capital gains tax on a $1-billion profit.

For his trouble, Unterman had earned a $10-million "advisory fee" in 1999. In 2000, as owner of 196,200 shares of Times Mirror stock and options on another 260,300, he stood to earn a great deal more.

During the first week of January, Unterman met in Los Angeles with Madigan, Fuller, and Warren "Spud" Williamson, chair of Chandis Securities. Fittingly, they held their clandestine session at the California Club. The deal was on the table.

The following month, a half dozen Chandler heirs, including Otis's sister Camilla, flew to Chicago to meet at the top of Tribune Tower with Tribune executives. The deal was halfway sealed.

By March 1, when Mark Willes and the full board of Times Mirror heard the news for the first time, it was a done deal. Willes reportedly turned as pale as a sheet and wept openly. The Tribune Company formally tendered $90 a share for Times Mirror's stock.

Over most of the next two weeks, there was much anger and bitterness at Times Mirror Square, none of which involved Otis Chandler. Willes, who in the past had banked on the support of the Chandlers against maverick outside directors such as Mike Armstrong, CEO of AT&T, or Donald R. Beall, chairman of Rockwell International, suddenly found himself on the defensive with minimal support from anyone. Unterman, once Willes's right-hand man, was now dubbed "Tom Underhand." At one point, the outside directors nearly came to blows with the Chandlers over a deal that appeared once more to benefit Otis's cousins more

than the average shareholder. If anyone saw the irony in a family attempting to sell its birthright to the highest bidder while outsiders fought mightily against it, they were not laughing. For a time, tempers flared so intensely that the Chandlers' lawyers threatened to sue Times Mirror.

"If anyone doubted it before, we know now what kind of sharks these people are," observed a longtime *Times* editor. "I wouldn't want a Chandler behind me in a dark alley."

"The Chandlers take care of the Chandlers," said *Newsweek's* Allan Sloan, who had followed the family's rapacious ways since the shutdown of *New York Newsday*.

When the tender offer crept up to $92.50 a share with a special provision that four of the Chandler family members would sit on the Tribune's board, the outside directors were finally mollified. In a further irony, the pact was sealed before Otis heard a word.

"The last week before the announcement, rumors were coming into me daily that the Tribune was going to buy us, that Knight Ridder was going to buy us, and I didn't take any of them seriously," Otis recalled.

In one of the best-kept secrets in his family's long clandestine history, Otis was out of the loop until the weekend of March 11, when his sister at last broke her silence. Since his *Vanity Fair* diatribe, Otis had been a family pariah and had even surrendered his seat as a Chandis trustee; he therefore had no direct knowledge of the machinations that Tom Unterman and Jack Fuller had initiated that fateful week following Otis's famous phone call to Bill Boyarsky.

On Monday, March 13, the merger was announced. John Madigan called Otis early, before he'd had a chance to read a word about it in his morning *Times.*

"Well, what do you think?" asked Madigan.

"I think it's great," said Otis. "You are the only ones I would be happy with. Otherwise, I'd be making a statement today saying how unhappy I was seeing the family make the decision to sell Times Mirror to company XYZ. You are the only guys. I've known you, John. I've known all the editors and publishers and chairmen of Tribune Publishing Company for over 40 years."

"We will make you very proud," said Madigan.

"I know you'll do a very good job," said Otis.

After replacing the phone in its cradle, he went for a walk. Bettina watched him go, bundled up against the cool winter morning, a solitary figure on a country road. His big yellow labrador, Mac, went with him, racing out ahead to sniff the grassy moors around their Ojai ranch. The man and his dog were gone for quite awhile. Any tears that her husband might have shed that morning were left out in the field. He came back dry-eyed.

Back at the house, he picked the phone up and called a friend. He got an answering machine and cleared his throat as the message beep sounded.

"Hi, this is Otis," he said. "I suppose you've heard the news. I guess it's good news."

He paused, his dry throat audible as he took a deep breath and let it out in a low, reedy sigh.

"The family business has sold," he said, covering the quaver in his voice by speaking quickly and forcefully. "We sold the family store."

EPILOGUE

Nothing will come of nothing; speak again.

—SHAKESPEARE, *King Lear*

THE SALE OF THE *Los Angeles Times* to the Tribune Company was consummated on June 12, 2000. Neither the Times Mirror Company nor Mark Willes survived.

Willes greeted the news that the company had been sold out from under him by publicly blubbering over his misfortune and then promptly leaving for a vacation in Hawaii. He could well afford it. During the final week of wrangling with Tribune Company officials, Chandis Securities, the Times Mirror Board, and the legion of attorneys, investment bankers, and paper pushers called in to pave the contractual way toward the $6.4-billion merger,[1] the former chairman and CEO forged himself a platinum parachute.

His other consolation goodies aside, Willes owned nearly 700,000 shares of stock, which, at the $95 price finally tendered by Tribune, were valued at more than $66 million. But there was much more. Once the smoke cleared, best estimates of the Cereal Killer's parting compensation stood somewhere between $85 million and $100 million for his five years of "work" for Times Mirror.

"He was a cereal salesman who didn't have one ounce of newspaper knowhow," said Otis's sister, Mia.

But Willes certainly knew a little something about exit pay. During his Times Mirror sojourn, he sat on outside corporate boards at Mattel, Black & Decker, and Talbot's, where he chaired the compensation subcommittee. He left the Mattel board just before CEO Jill Barad was bounced in 1998 with a $40-million parting gift after three disappointing years as head of the Barbie/Hot Wheels

manufacturer. Outraged Mattel shareholders filed a class-action lawsuit claiming that the company's directors had overpaid to dump Barad, but there was no similar outcry at Times Mirror when Willes got the boot. Everyone was apparently so happy to see Willes go that nobody seemed to mind being taken to the cleaners.

On the eve of the merger announcement, the Times Mirror Board awarded Willes a $2.2-million bonus beyond his $1-million base salary for the remainder of 2000, whether or not he stayed with the company. Because he chose to leave, he also received $9.2 million in severance pay, more stock, and a company pension, scheduled to commence in 2002, amounting to $970,000 a year for life.

But wait. There was more.

For the first two years following his departure, Willes received club memberships, physicals, and a chauffeured automobile courtesy of the Tribune Company. For the first seven years, Tribune paid for a fully furnished office, a secretary, and personal financial counseling. In case he wanted another job, Willes received $15,000 toward headhunter fees. As icing on his substantial cake, the Tribune also agreed to pay for excise tax beyond the normal income and/or capital gains taxes for which he might be responsible.

Cap'n Crunch didn't miss a bet. When he finally packed up to leave, he ordered the cafeteria to send new soft drinks to his office to replace those in his cooler so that he could take the fresh ones with him when he left the building for the last time. Despite a package that meant neither he nor his children nor his children's children would ever have to work again, Willes wept when he departed.

"Mark can cry on cue," Otis muttered.

Explaining his tears to one reporter, Willes said that his humiliating exit from Times Mirror likely meant he would never work as a corporate CEO again. He sold his home in the San Gabriel Mountain foothills for $5 million and moved back to Utah, where he took a post teaching economics and journalism at Brigham Young University in the autumn of 2000. The company that he had left in shambles was far behind the new multimedia curve, according to Mia Frost.

"There were just lots of changes, and not good changes. These were changing times in the newspaper business itself," said Mia. "People like Bob Erburu and Mark Willes were not changing with those times. We were left at the starting gate as far as becoming a multimedia company and looking to the future more."

Within six weeks of their purchase of the *Los Angeles Times*, the Tribune Company replaced Kathryn Downing and Michael Parks as *Times* publisher and editor with, respectively, John Puerner, publisher of the *Orlando Sentinel,* and John Carroll, editor in chief of the *Baltimore Sun.*

Like Willes, Downing received a sizable departure gift, estimated to be in the neighborhood of $3 million. Her newfound wealth cushioned a giant career step down to public relations chief for New Age guru Deepak Chopra.

Although easily the most qualified and admired of the trio, Parks left with the least. He, too, took up teaching, putting his thirty years experience as a much-honored reporter and foreign correspondent to work at USC, moving into the director's office of the Annenberg School of Communication.

Those who had paved the way for the Willes triumvirate in the late 1980s and early 1990s also enjoyed diminished expectations when they left Times Mirror Square.

Long accused of having made unholy alliances with Hollywood superagent Mike Ovitz and Disney CEO Michael Eisner while he was *Times* editor, Shelby Coffey went to work briefly at Disney-owned ABC-TV before finally landing at CNN, where he headed that network's financial news operation under his old boss, Tom Johnson. Johnson reportedly did not demand an essay of him before giving Coffey his new job. In January, 2001, Coffey lost his CNN job and announced that he would head a new medical research foundation.

At the beginning of 1999, David Laventhol retired from the Times Mirror board, which gave $1 million to endow the "David Laventhol Chair" for a visiting professor at Columbia University's Journalism School. His Parkinson's disease had apparently come under enough control that he was able to assume the editor's job at the *Columbia Journalism Review.*

Though retired from the Times Mirror board at the time of the takeover, Bob Erburu still maintained an office and a secretary at Times Mirror Square, even after the Tribune moved in. He continued to sit on the boards of nonprofit foundations, including the National Gallery of Art, the J. Paul Getty Trust, and the Huntington Library, but his days as a corporate bigwig were finished. As one of the last relics of a bygone era, Erburu continued to drop in at the *Times* Building with some regularity, although fewer and fewer recognized him.

"I don't think he has anywhere else to go," said one of his former executives.

Otis's own personal dismay over the sale of his *Times* did not endure. He approved of the Tribune Company's buyout as an honorable surrender that would also enrich him and his family well beyond his own parents' wealth. Chandis Securities received 2.5 shares of Tribune stock for each of the 14.5 million Times Mirror shares held in Harry and Marian Chandler's two 1936 trusts. In the grand tradition of the tax-free Chandler family, the stock swap meant enormous self-aggrandizing without paying the IRS a penny. Individual shareholders who chose to sell their stock earned more than double its market price the day that the merger was announced.

Otis Chandler came away a multimillionaire: not as rich as his billionaire cousin, Otis Booth, who enjoyed his separate Berkshire Hathaway fortune, but substantially better off than he had been before the Times Mirror sale. Unlike Mark Willes or his cousins, however, Otis felt he had genuinely earned his share.

"When I left as chairman [in 1985], I got nothing at all like what these executives like Willes get today," he said.[2]

After the Tribune sale, Otis at last accepted his cousins with some resignation as the Dickensian underachievers they had always been. Curiously, he found himself once again welcomed at his *Times* as both a conquering hero and an unofficial adviser to the "two Johns," as Otis came to address Puerner and Carroll:

"You don't have to take my suggestions at all, but I have been watching this paper for a long, long time, through all of its changes," he told the new publisher and editor.

Unlike their predecessors, the "two Johns" consulted Otis often. In the beginning, he spoke with them nearly every week. He was pleased that both were newspaper veterans as well as able managers of the shrewd, gossipy, idiosyncratic, and frequently unmanageable men and women who create a major metropolitan newspaper.

Puerner had joined the Tribune Company in 1979 after taking his MBA from the University of Colorado, where he had doubled as business manager and staff photographer for the student paper. Although he had become an astute juggler of newspapers, television, and the Internet, and a champion of Tribune multimedia synergy, the forty-nine-year-old Puerner still liked to tell about the time when, as a student, he had defied a photo ban during a campus speech by Watergate figure Jeb Magruder and was ousted by police. One of Puerner's first acts as *Times* publisher was to move his office from the corporate isolation of the sixth floor to the second floor, near the newsroom.

Similarly, Carroll rooted his own reputation in getting the news first and trifling with the niceties of how to package and sell it later. A Times Mirror employee who was acquired with the 1986 purchase of the *Baltimore Sun*, fifty-eight-year-old Carroll was credited with building the *Sun* into a formidable regional rival of the *Washington Post* during the same sorry decade that the *Los Angeles Times* descended into its malaise. Carroll once sent reporters to the Sudan on a tip that slaves were still bought and sold there. The Sudanese government officially denied that such savagery went on inside its borders, but Carroll's reporters bought two slaves.

Both "Johns" appeared to Otis to have the right credentials and instincts. He advised them to abandon the East Coast or Midwestern preconceptions they might have of Southern California. It was not the Left Coast. It was not palm trees and papaya juice on the veranda of Le Bel Age Hotel. It was not movie stars, mall rats, and John Birch Republicans. Los Angeles was more, much more.

They would have to meet the mayor and the county supervisors and countless other officials, of course, but getting to South Central and East L.A. and all the other ethnic pockets of the grand urban sprawl was equally necessary: Thai Town, Little Saigon, Little Tokyo, Chinatown, Korea Town, and beyond. In his own lifetime, Otis had seen the transformation of L.A. from frontier boomtown

to capital city of the Pacific Rim. In a single ten-square-block area of central L.A., 140 languages and dialects were spoken. In recent years, English had even given way officially to Spanish as Southern California's predominant tongue.

The new publisher and editor should read the suburban dailies, as well as obvious rivals such as the *Orange County Register* and the *Daily News* in the San Fernando Valley. They needed to watch and absorb local television and radio, with its eclectic spray of rock, talk, Mozart, and mariachi. They should visit the County Art Museum, Dodger Stadium, the Music Center, the Getty Center, and, yes, even the Staples Center. Take a walk on the beach. Cruise around town, both on and off the freeways.

"You've got to get around," he said. "You can't just focus on your own personal interests. You need to do all that stuff. Everything."

But Otis's memory isn't what it once was. His body has suffered too, always rebounding, but with less and less vigor than it had before the musk ox, the motorcycle accident, and just plain old age.

"I've never believed that there's a predestined plan for accidents and sicknesses and things like that," he said. "I just think it's the roll of the dice that life gives you and sometimes you're lucky and sometimes you're not. I don't put any great, deep spiritual or psychic or astrological significance on events. I'm not into that. Some people base their life on the astrology column. I went to a psychic and had a reading. I'm interested in that, what they say, but I don't seek it out and I don't live my life by it.

"Death does not scare me. It just pisses me off, I guess, because I've got a lot of things I want to do. I've crowded a lot into seventy years. Crowded an awful lot."

WHEREAS TIMES MIRROR was once the center of his life, his Vintage Museum had now become Otis Chandler's focus. Mixing cars with art, motorcycles, and mounted animals had become his aesthetic; he was proud of his transformation of an industrial park warehouse into a unique display of his various collections.

"Otis is a perfectionist to the extent that he likes things that function correctly," said his late Deke brother, Ron Bishop. "He is not a petty perfectionist in which he is violently irritated in any way by things that don't work immediately. But he seeks and admires things that have craftsmanship to them. He is actually a craftsman by composition himself. Craftsmanship is the key to it. He's a craftsman."

But a restless craftsman, ruled by whim, mood, and a general unease in the belly—always secretly unsure of himself and the life that he had led. His peculiar brand of insecurity still played itself out through constant one-upmanship.

"I was up at his place in Ojai not too long ago, and he's got a bunch of bicycles hanging up out in the shed, and I was saying nice things about the bicycles," re-

called Bob Emmet. "'Oh, that's nice.' And he said, 'That's $4,000.' It's kind of like, 'Look at all the possessions I have.' That is a major part of him. Everything he has, has to be the best. And, *you* can't have it!"

To be Otis Chandler's friend was to risk suffering his occasional fits of pre-adolescent cruelty: the "gotcha" mentality of the spoiled who must win at all costs, even if it meant hurting someone who cared about him. Otis likes to rub it in. When his old friend John Thomas bought ten undeveloped acres near Bend, Oregon, upon which he hoped someday to build his retirement home, Otis bought a 150-acre ranch nearby over the phone, sight unseen. It had an unparalleled view of the Cascade Mountains and a host of amenities that J. T. would never be able to afford in a dozen lifetimes. Otis recently offered to give Thomas a deal on a used RV, but Thomas did some comparison shopping and discovered that Otis's "deal" was several thousand dollars higher than Thomas would have to pay a used RV dealer.

"I don't care," said J. T. "I love the guy. How can you not?"

Despite the periodic abuse that he had to take, John Thomas was Otis Chandler's steadfast Sancho Panza. Although he lived a hundred miles south of Otis's Vintage Museum in the heart of Orange County, J. T. always kept the tank of his car no less than half full of gasoline so that, in the event of an emergency, he could drive immediately to Otis's aid without having to stop at a service station.

In his own way, Otis reciprocated. He would not pull corporate strings to get Thomas a job as a division supervisor in the Times Mirror motor pool, but J. T. still thought of himself as Otis Chandler's best friend, and probably was in many ways, although Otis would never acknowledge it because Thomas's loyalty was too blind. When anyone pointed out to John Thomas that his friendship more closely resembled hero worship, J. T. scoffed. He knew that, if the chips were ever really down, Otis would be there for him.

"It's not the number of years." he said. "It's the laps. Otis and I have done a few laps." Another of his old Deke pals, Chuck Waterman, marked his own friendship with Otis with equal fondness, but added the caveat that Chandler's self-absorption could be mercurial and frequently troubling. He recalled an invitation that he and his wife had received a few years earlier to visit the Chandlers; when they arrived, the invitation was suddenly withdrawn. Otis's dog had become deathly ill, they were told. The Watermans spent the night at a nearby hotel.

"We stopped and had breakfast the next morning, and were sitting and having a nice time, and then Otis just announced that he was going to go for a bicycle ride. He just took off," said Waterman.

Bob Emmet alternately pitied and admired Bettina, who put up with her husband's idiosyncrasies with minimal complaint.

"Whatever house he has isn't big enough and it's got to be made bigger," said Emmet. "To be married to somebody that has constantly got to *do* things is something. He is really a driven guy."

As Otis himself put it, his routine always seems to begin with buying a ranch, fixing it up, and working "my ass off."

"When are you going to enjoy yourself?" Bettina would ask.

"I'm enjoying myself, but I've got to run now," Otis would answer.

He would tire of the property, sell it, buy another ranch, plant more hay, get more cows.

"Are you enjoying yourself up there?" his Vintage manager would inquire when he called Otis late in the evening.

"I love it," Otis would answer.

"But we never can reach you except at night," the manager would persist.

"I'm out all day. I get up at first dawn and hardly come back for lunch," Otis would reply. "I can't leave anything alone and just let it run itself and not be bigger and better."

Still, he had to have land and lots of land: a genetic predisposition, perhaps, inherited from his grandfather's lust for real estate. For Otis, the land had a visceral impact and made him feel young again. He bought and sold and tended it compulsively. Possessing property was almost a religion. He felt a transubstantiation between himself and the very foliage that sprang from it. Otis could even commune with his oak trees when he spoke to them in the privacy of his own thoughts.

"Yes, yes, I am a young gardener," he would say. "Even though you are three hundred years old, the person taking care of you right now is young."

When he sold Bettina's home out from under her and told her that it was time to move on, she humored him.

"I have redone eleven houses and/or decorated eleven houses in the nineteen years we have been married," she said. "Those include second homes and trailers."

She humored him on their frequent vacations as well. When the Chandlers headed off to some exotic place, the Vintage employees posted a pool to guess the date they would return. It was never when they were scheduled to return, because Otis always came back early. Two weeks in Tahiti in the spring of 2000, for example, lasted less than a week. Otis was bored, he explained. There was nothing to do there but relax.

Bettina described him as a dichotomy:

He is very complicated and he is very simple. He has so many interests and so many things that he does well that it brings a level of complication to our life. He is simple in that he has the same needs that most of us have—that not many people attribute to him—which is, he needs to be appreciated and he needs to be re-

assured. I think that people say, . . . "Well, he has done so much and he has accomplished so much he doesn't really need to know that he has done a good job."

Bettina acknowledged that her husband could be egocentric to a fault, but she also saw his frequent tendency toward tunnel vision as the flip side of his profound ability to focus and achieve:

I admire him a great deal. I admire him for his ability to look at what he wants for himself and his life and to go for it. I don't know of anyone else that perseveres in the area of physical exercise like he does. And it is a real lesson for me because I think that too many times I say, "Oh well, somebody needs me to do this or I should do this." And I don't look enough at what is good for me. Some people say it is selfish. I think that we have to look out for ourselves because nobody else is going to. And so I admire him for that. I also admire him for what he has done at the *Times.* I admire him for his caring about other people. His calling people who are sick, calling people who have lost children, his reaching out to people.

Bob Emmet agreed. Otis was selfish, but not always to a fault, and never to the exclusion of being a friend.

"Otis has blind spots, you know," said Emmet. "He sees things as he wants to see them and he can't understand you if you may see things differently. Otis and his mother were both victims. Everything, everything that doesn't work out is somebody else's fault. He is a difficult friend, but he is a good one."

As an adult fast approaching middle age himself, Harry Chandler saw his father fondly, as the proverbial old dog incapable of new tricks:

I don't think he is really mean-spirited; I think he is a bit block-headed. I think there is sort of a WASP trait—well-to-do WASPs talk at this level. They never get down into a level of feeling and honesty. I have friends like this, not just my family. One of my best friends from college is from a well-to-do family. We met in college. I see him at least once a year. I don't know what he is ever thinking because that is just where you don't go. You are supposed to stay at a level of, "What did you do today?" and, "Wasn't that vacation fun?" I think working in Hollywood was good for me. All that raw emotion that is expressed in Hollywood. With a lot of my Jewish friends, their emotions are right out there. I think I am more that way than maybe some of my family.

When he left for Andover as a young man, Harry remembered receiving letters from Donna Swayze that Otis had dictated. When Harry chided his father for not

sitting down and writing them himself, Otis didn't understand what his son was trying to tell him about being clinical, impersonal, and dispassionate with his own flesh and blood.

"Oh, I remember my dad doing stuff like that to me," Otis told his son.

Harry just shook his head.

"He saw none of what I was trying to say which was, 'Gee, Dad do you have any sense that you and I have never been able to talk about stuff as well as we might?' Instead he went right to 'Yeah, that reminds me of my dad.'"

Even in his advanced stage of the sustained war with his brain tumor, Norman shared his younger brother's assessment of their father, who constantly carped about the expense—now nearing $200,000 a year—of Norman's medical care.

"He's lost the use of his right arm," said Donna Swayze. "He's in chemo and his memory is kind of on again, off again and his mood is on again, off again. But when I talked to him in February, he was joking about his Dad."

Michael, who stayed in Oregon after his father sold his ranch in Bend, suffered a serious heart attack in December 2000. Otis had planned to spend Christmas with Bettina, diving in a shark cage off Australia's Great Barrier Reef. He canceled his plans to be at his youngest son's bedside. Still, Michael had not yet fully come to terms with his father; Michael agreed with Missy's contention that Otis had adopted a coterie of "paid friends" who told him what he wanted to hear.

"He hasn't kept up with any of his friends," said Missy. "He keeps up with people, but not really close friends except paid sycophants."

Cathleen and Carolyn both made their peace with Otis years earlier and put the ugliness of the divorce and its aftermath out of their lives. Bettina became more of a trusted big sister than a stepmother, and the memories both daughters chose to recall were the good ones: sitting around the dinner table, holidays, family vacations.

As for Missy, she and her ex-husband remained on rocky terms: on again, off again with a truce that often seemed to resemble an Arab-Israeli peace accord. Recently married for the third time, Missy sent Otis a Christmas card in 1999 proclaiming, "The third time's the charm."

IN THE SPRING OF 2000, the *Times* launched a new branding campaign with the tag line: "Connecting Us with the *Times*." The idea was to show how L.A. connected with cultures around the world. Otis thought the campaign a little hokey and even flat-out wrong when photos of bikini-clad babes were juxtaposed with Muslim women draped in black. He blamed the tastelessness of the campaign on Mark Willes, whom he blamed for all things that were wrong about his *Times*.

Willes did get the daily circulation up, although nowhere near the 2-million mark. It crept to 1,111,785 in May 2000, but *Times* Sunday circulation during the same period was down by 1,099, dropping to 1,384,688. The new régime dumped the "Connecting Us with the *Times*" and made no visible effort to sustain the Willes-Downing circulation drive.

One of the first actions taken by the two "Johns" was to shut down Willes's "Our Times" experiment. In mid-September 2000, the *Times* eliminated 170 jobs. Like the Central City zone section that had debuted in 1973 and ended a year later because of lack of support from advertisers, "Our Times" could not sustain itself; thus, another remnant of the Mark Willes era evaporated.

In many respects, the Tribune Company was more ruthless in selling off the remaining pieces of Times Mirror than Willes or Erburu had been. The magazine division, led by the popular *Golf* magazine, spun off for nearly half a billion dollars; the perennial Times Mirror moneymaker, Jeppesen Sanderson, the world's leading maker of aeronautical maps and charts, brought in nearly four times as much. Times Mirror also turned over an employee pension fund to Tribune, nearly $800 million of which could be defined under federal rules as "excess" and suitable to move over to the corporate bottom line.

For all of its praise as a dynamic, forward-looking multimedia corporation, the Tribune Company still looked constantly at its bottom line; its directors grew nervous when the profit margin was not hovering somewhere in the neighborhood of 20 percent. By selling off the remnants of the Times Mirror empire, Tribune could quickly pay down the $95-per-share premium it had to shell out to the Chandlers. Furthermore, Tribune could still proclaim itself the only media company in the United States with a television, newspaper, and Internet interactive presence in New York, Los Angeles, Chicago, and fifteen more of the top thirty markets, reaching nearly 80 percent of all households in the country. If money had been the point all along, no one seemed to notice that Mark Willes had done a spectacular job of setting up the sacrificial lamb for the slaughter.

Nor did Willes or any of his departed subordinates receive credit for fostering an atmosphere in which *Times* Atlanta bureau chief, J. R. Moehringer, was able to win the *Times'* twenty-fourth Pulitzer for feature writing in 1999. The Cereal Killer's clumsy efforts to promote the paper's tradition of fine writing and unusual reporting went unrecognized. *Times* expatriates who had defected to the *New York Times* during the Erburu-Willes era had a ready explanation for the *Los Angeles Times'* spotty but continued excellence when it came to individual writing style and weak reporting.

"At the *Los Angeles Times*, there was reverence for the writer's every word, and no backbone," said David Cay Johnston, who spent nearly two decades at both newspapers. "At the *New York Times*, it is precisely the opposite."

In 1993, the Environmental Protection Agency determined that 300,000 tons of dust blew off the dead Owens Lake each year, enough to put 40,000 Owens Valley residents at risk of lung disease. Thus, as of 2001, the Los Angeles Department of Water and Power was ordered to release 25,000 acre feet of captive Owens River water per year into the lake to meet minimum Clean Air Act standards, and Harry Chandler must have cursed from his grave.

The wide open spaces General Otis encountered when he and Eliza and his three daughters got off the stagecoach from Santa Barbara almost 120 years ago are now wall-to-wall subdivision, many of them conceived and built by the General's calculating, devious, but utterly remarkable son-in-law: the unsung but surely the true creator of modern day Los Angeles. Times Mirror Square, the square city block of downtown L.A. that those two founding publishers of the *Los Angeles Times* claimed as their Holy See is now known as 202 West First Street; and the Statement of Ownership buried inside the A section of each daily issue of the *Times* reads "A Tribune Company newspaper." And yet it still feels like home on the infrequent visits Otis pays to the *Times.*

"It's very exciting to me, the improvement of the printing process," Otis once said. "The advent of photo composition and the advent of computer composition and the use of computers and the terminals on everybody's desk, and the new offset printing. . . . There's something very magic and emotional and exciting when the first press starts to run and the next one kicks in and you've got everything running."

He and Bettina returned to the *Times* during the summer of 2000 for a meeting in the Norman Chandler Pavilion with the new Tribune executives, but before he took the elevator to the top floor, she persuaded him to take a walk through the newsroom. Everywhere, people got up from their desks, stood at attention, and applauded. The always punctual former publisher was nearly 30 minutes late to his meeting because he was shaking hands, signing autographs, and remarking his genuine surprise to his wife.

"I want to be known as a good person," said Otis.

Not as a surfer and not as a hunter and not as a car collector. I have that way down at the bottom of the jump in my obit, I don't know where. Obviously I haven't read my obit and wouldn't want to read it. I just want to try to put my contributions to the *Times*, Times Mirror Company and journalism way up at the top. By inference, of course, the public service that you can provide if you manage a very strong newspaper like the *Times*, you are serving the broader community and that's what I want on my tombstone, not that I am a surfer and a hunter and all of that.

But he is all of those things too, even though the best rides and the finest trophy animals are well behind him now.

"I must say I come right at the end of the golden years of hunting in this country," he continued. "So I had a good run. I had a good run and I don't hunt much anymore. I was up last fall in Alaska and got a fine moose. My last moose was thirty years before that. I haven't really done much hunting in the last eight or ten years."

When he's gone, he wants his trophies in a museum, even if it isn't his own. It will do honor to the animal as much as to the hunter, he said.

There's a little hesitation there and the equal sadness when you shoot the big ram out of a band of sheep. There might be a bunch of ewes and lambs or maybe there's just a bunch of rams and you've shot the monarch. You've shot the head of the group, the one who fought with his horns. You've seen probably some of these pictures of the rams. They're lost without their leader and they stand around and look at you. They run maybe a hundred yards and they're lost.

Otis smiled sadly, a mix of metaphors crystallizing behind his tired but still crystal blue eyes.

"They have to find who their next publisher is, and it's very sad to see them standing there kinda looking at you. Lot of soul searching. A lot of questioning, you know," he said, imagining the herd asking itself what the meaning of life might be. "They have a right to be on this earth just as much as I do. This is their home and I've intruded into their home and I've taken one of their leaders."

When Harry took his father duck hunting recently at the Tejon Ranch, they had a terrific time together; but the younger Chandler wondered if it might be the last time.

"Right before sunset, these doves were landing in these walnut trees and you only had a little space between the trees, so you had very little time between seeing them, getting your gun up, and shooting," said Harry. "It was very quick response stuff and at seventy, he couldn't get his gun up fast enough. He hit one or two and I hit fifteen.

"So dove season is coming again and I was thinking of calling him, but I am thinking he will find a reason not to do it because of the competitiveness. We'll see."

NOTES

Chapter One

1. Historians of the era, such as J. M. Guinn, L.A.'s first superintendent of schools, reported that lynch mobs were organized by shopkeepers, schoolteachers, and even an early mayor of Los Angeles.

2. Harrison tried to join the regular army in 1867 and got as far as a provisional appointment as second lieutenant, but failed the written exam. Rejected and stripped of his lieutenancy, he reverted to his largely ceremonial battlefield commission in addressing himself as Colonel Otis.

3. Chandler remained in New Hampshire long enough to become a Master Mason, launching a lifetime membership in the ancient and secret order of Free & Accepted Masons. Ever the overachiever, he launched a Masonic career that garnered every significant rank or honor the fraternity bestowed, from 33rd Degree Mason to Noble of the Shrine to Most Puissant Knight of Constantine.

Chapter Two

1. In the summer of 1879, Widney also founded the University of Southern California.

2. The *Mirror* was a weekly temperance sheet that had been published by the original owners of the print shop since 1873. By the time the Otises took over, the *Mirror* was near bankruptcy and survived only a few more years as a rural supplement to the *Times*. It was revived as an afternoon tabloid in 1948 and was published for nearly thirteen years before folding for good in 1961.

3. In October, 1886, when H. H. Boyce started the *Los Angeles Tribune*, he referred to his newspaper in midsentence style as "The *Tribune*," with the T in "The" capitalized. From that point on, General Otis also insisted on capitalizing the T in his own "The," and the *Los Angeles Times* official style manual still insists on that affected form more than a century later.

4. Over the years, Harry always seemed to have one or more of his unmarried relatives living with his ever-expanding family, including a sister, Clara, a British nephew, Ralph, and his sister-in-law Carrie Otis—in addition to live-in nannies and maids to help Marian.

5. Otis did call upon Lark Ellen to sing once again at ceremonies marking the opening of the Los Angeles Aqueduct in 1913, eight years after Eliza's death. Lark Ellen took it upon herself to volunteer a farewell aria at Otis's own funeral four years later.

6. San Pedro remained a separate community until 1909, when Los Angeles officially connected the harbor area to Civic Center with an annexed railroad strip one-half mile wide and twenty-two miles long where the Harbor Freeway (Interstate 110) is located today. On February 13, 1910, the port was renamed Los Angeles Harbor.

7. Pasadena's exclusive Valley Hunt Club staged the first Tournament of Roses in 1890 to showcase the mild winter weather. "In New York, people are buried in snow," said the club's Charles Holder in announcing the first parade. "Here our flowers are blooming and our oranges are about to bear. Let's hold a festival to tell the world about our paradise."

Chapter Three

1. The nine-man syndicate that took out the original option to purchase Porter Ranch incorporated on November 28, 1904, as the San Fernando Mission Land Company and expanded its membership to include a tenth member: George Porter, owner of the ranch and brother-in-law of the late Tom Caystile, one of General Otis's original partners at the *Times*.

2. When his role was later exposed, General Otis would maintain he quit the syndicate in February 1905, just before it exercised its Porter Ranch option. Harry Chandler, however, proudly accepted the unofficial title of "Father of the Los Angeles Aqueduct" until the day he died.

3. Except for the independently owned *Los Angeles Daily News,* the only other regular daily published in Los Angeles was the morning *Herald*, the city's oldest Democratic newspaper. Harry Chandler had taught his father-in-law a lesson about co-opting the competition after putting Boyce's *Tribune* out of business. Thus, when a controlling interest in the *Herald* came up for sale in 1904, Otis secretly bought 8,051 of the 10,000 outstanding shares. For the next seven years, although nominally still a *Times* rival, the *Herald* did not print stories or editorials to which Otis was vehemently opposed. In 1911, Otis sold press baron William Randolph Hearst the *Herald* on the condition that he switch it from a morning to an afternoon paper.

4. The *Times* would tackle this problem in 1915 in a successful campaign to persuade Los Angeles to annex the valley—an area larger than the city of Chicago.

5. The painting now hangs in the conservative and private Sutter Club in downtown Sacramento—a quaint and tame artifact of California's Victorian era.

6. Fifty years hence, it would be renamed MacArthur Park in honor of World War II hero General Douglas MacArthur.

7. Managing editor Leroy Mosher, who had succeeded Charles Lummis, fell into debt and dark despair in 1904. He rode the train to Santa Monica where he found his way to the beach, wrote a note that read, "What's the use of fighting when there's no show to win?" put a .38-caliber pistol in his mouth, and pulled the trigger.

Chapter Four

1. The General later had a scale model of the Times building constructed from the rubble; he placed it on permanent display on the front lawn of the Bivouac.

2. Debs and Harriman ran on the Social Democratic Party ticket in 1900, polling just 94,768 votes against Democrat William Jennings Bryan (6,358,071) and the incumbent Republican William McKinley (7,219,530). Debs ran four more times and pulled over 1 million votes while

serving time in prison, but Harriman quit national politics and concentrated instead on Southern California.

3. The *Times* mercilessly harangued the McNamaras' defense team for years afterwards, including Joseph Scott, who successfully sued the newspaper for libel in 1915. After the state supreme court upheld the award four years later, Scott told Harry Chandler's attorney to "get a check over by afternoon or I'll have the Sheriff padlock the *Times*." A framed reproduction of the check for $47,549.71 hung on Scott's wall until his death in 1958.

4. Socialists elected a state assemblyman from Los Angeles in 1912 (their first such victory in California) and two more in 1914, but when Harriman ran again for mayor that same year, he came in third and never tried again.

5. Darrow died in Chicago in 1938.

Chapter Five

1. Sherman also lent his middle name to the San Fernando Valley's Hazeltine Avenue and his last name to a 1,100-acre subdivision in the Encino foothills, which the Chandler syndicate sold off at $780 per lot in 1927: Sherman Oaks. The present day city of West Hollywood was originally named Sherman.

2. Formally dedicated November 5, 1913, the $23.5-million aqueduct took over five years to complete and drew thousands to witness the first flow of Owens River water into the San Fernando Valley. William Mulholland's terse invocation for the event seemed to directly reflect Harry Chandler's basic real estate philosophy: "There it is," he said. "Take it."

3. The property eventually became Van Nuys, Canoga Park, Reseda, Sherman Oaks, Tarzana, and Woodland Hills.

4. On February 14, 1936, the Tejon Ranch Company was incorporated as a wholly owned subsidiary of Times Mirror and Chandis Securities, the Chandler family's privately held investment company. It remained a family holding until 1997, when Times Mirror chairman Mark Willes sold the Tejon as part of his corporate restructuring.

5. Thirty years earlier, the General used the same tactics in the *Times* to trash the socialist utopian Topolobampo Colony in the Gulf of California.

6. In 1958, seven years after Hearst's death, his castle was opened to the public and quickly became second only to Disneyland as the most popular tourist destination in California.

7. One of Harry's many land development syndicates was called the Ramona Ranch Company.

8. In 1935, Mexico expropriated 175,000 acres of the best Babicora farmland and five years later, William Randolph was forced to sell off another 117,000 acres. Hearst and his heirs were able to hold on to most of the property until 1952, when the Hearst Corporation sold the remaining 900,000 acres to the Mexican government for $2 million.

9. Chandler had no competition for Colorado River water because Arizona was a territory until February 14, 1912. From the time that Arizona entered the Union as the forty-eighth state, California and Arizona began warring over water rights; within ten years, the fortunes of the California-Mexico Land and Cattle Company began to decline.

Chapter Six

1. Following the General's death, the canyon home became the country estate of *Tarzan* creator Edgar Rice Burroughs, who turned it into a country club and subdivision he named

Tarzana. In 1922, early film mogul Jesse Lasky bought the General's "Outpost" home in the Cahuenga Valley.

2. The executors of his estate sold his six hundred goats for $2,000 shortly after his funeral. The trees lasted until 1999, when a Long Beach developer set a construction crew loose with chain saws to level the land for housing.

3. The Bivouac was razed in 1954 to make room for a larger art school campus. The scale model replica of the bombed *Times* Building that had been made from its rubble and stood on the grounds of the General's former home for nearly forty years was broken up and given to Otis Art Institute students.

Chapter Seven

1. Sherwin titled his February 1928 article "The Walrus of Moron-Land."

2. Radical journalist John Reed from Portland, Oregon, and Big Bill Haywood—one of the organizers Clarence Darrow defended in the Idaho mining strike—both supported Job Harriman and the McNamara brothers; they eventually traveled to Russia and were buried as socialist heroes in the Kremlin wall.

3. Following a stint as editor of the Auto Club's *Touring Topics* (later renamed *Westways* magazine), Henry returned to the *Times* as editor, foreign correspondent, and later, one of its best-known columnists. Henry's "By the Way" column appeared regularly until a year before his death in 1970 at seventy-nine.

4. Founded in 1888 by the leading businessmen of Los Angeles, the powerful and secretive California Club's incestuous relationship with the *Times* evolved as the city grew and the club's membership became more exclusive. Its founders included General Otis, Charles Lummis, and attorney Oscar Lawler, who helped prosecute the McNamaras for bombing the *Times*.

5. A 1939 article journalist Frank Taylor wrote for the *Saturday Evening Post* was titled "It Costs $1,000 to Have Lunch with Harry Chandler."

6. The invitation to hold the games in L.A. was formally extended to the Olympics committee in 1920 by William May Garland, Chandler's realty syndicate partner and father of Harry's future son-in-law John Jewett Garland.

7. Husband of Marian Otis's younger sister Mabel, Booth was a mining engineer and millionaire entrepreneur in his own right; he cofounded the Hotpoint electric heating and appliance business, which merged with General Electric and became a GE brand name in 1919. Mabel joined her sister on the board of directors of Times Mirror following the General's death in 1917.

8. Around the same time, he became a trustee of Leland Stanford Jr. University in Palo Alto, where his son, Norman, was an economics major.

9. *Times* Sacramento bureau chief Kyle Palmer was an early Throop graduate.

10. In 1960, the Chandler family donated the Harry Chandler Dining Hall to Cal Tech.

11. By 1927, Firestone, Sampson and Goodrich tire companies had all built plants in L.A. too, giving the city the reputation of being "the Akron of the West."

12. The star of westerns was born in DuBois, Pennsylvania, in July 1880. He died in an auto accident in Arizona in 1940.

13. While hundreds of '20s tourists made a point of stopping by Sennett's opulent Hollywood mansion to drink in the sheer extravagance of the mogul's lifestyle, none were aware that it was Harry Chandler who held the mortgage.

14. During Sister Aimee's infamous "kidnapping" in 1926, when she told police and District Attorney Asa Keyes that she had been abducted and held in a desert cabin, the evangelist was trysting in Carmel with Kenneth Ormiston, the married radio technician Harry Chandler had hired to put KHJ on the air, and later employed as the *Times'* first radio editor.

15. Chandler sold a five-hour block of time each evening from 6:00 P.M. to 11:00 P.M. to Warner Brothers, either to promote a new movie or air orchestra, jazz, or dance music.

16. Hays quickly became a close associate of the *Times'* chief Machiavellian, Kyle Palmer.

17. Changed in 1945 to the Motion Picture Association of America.

18. In a 1919 column for the New York *Morning Telegraph,* Parsons described a promising young actress who starred in *Virtuous Wives* as having "youth and good looks." The actress, Hedda Hopper, would achieve her true fame twenty years later as Parsons's arch rival.

Chapter Eight

1. In one of these scandals at the beginning of Prohibition, *Times* city hall reporter Horace "Doc" Karr was indicted along with Mayor Frederick W. Woodman for arranging to open Central Avenue to gambling, prostitution, and liquor sales. The *Times* supported Karr and the mayor, who were defended by former district attorney John Fredericks and acquitted; but the police chief lost his job shortly after his acquittal, and the *Times* fired Karr.

2. According to the Internal Revenue Service, Marco earned $500,000 from prostitution between 1922 and 1924 and Bob Gans and his brother Joe amassed a slots fortune of between $15 million and $20 million during the 1920s.

3. Nicknamed "Stringbean," McAfee joined the force after seeing a cop roll a drunk. He was fired in 1917 for running a crap game in the precinct house, but was rehired on the vice squad; here he gained a reputation as the tip-off man for the raids he and his fellow officers were planning. He was fired again when he was caught, after which he switched permanently to the other side of the law.

4. Like Marco, Cornero claimed to have cleared over $500,000 in just two years, but complained that he had spent $100,000 on bribes for police protection that he never received.

5. Named for LAPD Captain William "Red" Hynes, who infiltrated the I.W.W. and other radical unions as an undercover agent and provocateur during the early 1920s.

6. It was not officially the Los Angeles Department of Water and Power until 1929, when the Bureau of Water Works and Supply merged with the Bureau of Power and Light.

7. Harry and his *Times* successfully lobbied Congress in 1935 to name the massive dam for Harry's old friend Herbert Hoover, even though public opinion at the time held the former president in contempt for bringing on the Great Depression.

8. The third member of the Owens Valley troika, J. B. Lippincott, died at seventy-eight in Riverside, California, on November 4, 1942.

9. John Richard Brinkley, the small-town Kansas quack who pioneered the fad, once explained, "So far as I know, I was the first man that ever did this operation of taking the goat testicle and putting it in the man's testicle. The glands of a three weeks old male goat are laid upon the nonfunctioning glands of a man, within twenty minutes of the time they are removed from the goat. . . . I find that after being properly connected these goat glands do actually feed, grow into, and become absorbed by the human glands, and the man is renewed in his physical and mental vigor."

10. A decade before Chandler took an interest in the procedure, *Times* editor Harry Andrews, underwent a goat gland transplant in 1922 and died four years later.

11. A partial list of Chandler holdings at the end of the 1920s included: American Engraving Co., Beverly-Wilshire Investment Co., Big Conduit Land Co., Carmel Cattle Co., Central Investment Corp., Chandis Securities Co., Compania Industrial Jabonera del Pacifica, S.C.L., Colorado River Land Co., S.A., Esperanza Timber Co., Terrocarril Inter-California del Sur, Los Angeles Steamship Co., Mortgage Guarantee Co., Pacific Zeppelin Transport Co., Pioneer Pacific Woolen Mills, Inc., Plaza de Los Angeles, Rowland Cattle Co., Signal Mountain Land & Water Co., Southwest Co., Southwest Land Co., Tejon Ranchos, Times Mirror Co., Times Mirror Printing & Binding Co., Transcontinental & Western Air, Inc., Western Air Express, Inc., Western Construction Co., Yosemite National Park Co., Yosemite Park & Curry Co., and Crown-Zellerbach Paper Co.

12. In January 1947, the state of California and county of Los Angeles purchased 111 acres at the center of the Rancho for $320,000 and turned it into the Los Angeles County Arboretum.

Chapter Nine

1. Custom built in 1927 from a design by architect Walter Neff, the Chandlers' first home was a four-bedroom, 4,100-square-foot residence with conservatory, family room, gardens, and pool that Otis recalled as "nothing special . . . just like all the others on Nottingham."

2. In 1937, the *Times* won the Ayer Cup, a national competition for typographical excellence.

3. Trueblood retired at fifty-eight in 1944 and died ten years later of a heart attack.

4. Hotchkiss carried his hypocrisy well beyond the *Times*, keeping a mistress along with a wife. According to Buff's own account to a confidante, the mistress jumped from a hotel window and killed herself, but Norman Chandler saw to it that the woman's relationship to Hotchkiss was kept out of the newspaper.

5. William R. Staats was an early residential developer who built much of the upscale Oak Knoll section of Pasadena that abuts San Marino and the grounds of the Huntington (now the Ritz Carlton) Hotel.

6. Sherman had hired Haskell as his houseboy in 1913. Like his boss, Haskell had an avenue and a street—as well as a canyon—named after him in their vast San Fernando Valley subdivision. In memory of his boss and mentor, Haskell created Corona Del Mar's Sherman Library and Gardens in 1966.

7. Marion continued courting the stuffy Chandlers, offering a dachshund puppy to Norman and Buff for their children. According to Otis, Norman accidentally backed over it in his car. From that point, Otis raised only boxers or labradors—big dogs that could be seen in a rearview mirror.

8. *Time* magazine reported that Hearst was essentially a broken man: "At age 75, the bad boy of U.S. journalism is just a hired editorial writer who has taken a salary cut."

9. Silent film star Harold Lloyd and *Our Gang* comedy producer Hal Roach were among Santa Anita's founders.

10. Herbert Hoover got the blame, deserved or not, for forcing homeless families across the nation during the Depression to live in squalid camps that derisively carried his name. Nonetheless, Hoover remained a Chandler favorite to the end. A week before the 1932 election, Harry

ordered automobile window stickers supporting the president's reelection inserted in the *Times.* Hoover lost to Franklin Roosevelt, a target of *Times* venom for the next dozen years.

Chapter Ten

1. Rumors in later years had it that Buff might have wound up in Dr. Jackson's program because she had caught Norman with another woman.

2. Police abuses were so outrageous during this so-called Liberty Hill rally on behalf of the I.W.W. during a San Pedro waterfront strike that it led to the founding of the American Civil Liberties Union of Southern California.

3. The *Times* editorialized, "It is evident that these young men are attempting to make personal capital and heroes of themselves at the expense of responsible government. They may become a community nuisance."

4. Like his predecessor Asa Keyes, Fitts was indicted for accepting a bribe to throw a statutory rape case against a real estate developer, but unlike Keyes, Fitts had the full support of the *Times,* including the ubiquitous Al Nathan, who worked up dossiers against Fitts's enemies. Fitts was acquitted, left office at the outset of World War II, and returned to private practice in L.A. In failing health, he dramatically took his own life in 1973 by shooting himself at the southern entrance to Sequoia National Park. He was seventy-eight.

5. Founded by Cornelius Vanderbilt Jr., the black sheep son of the nineteenth century East Coast railroad magnate, the *Los Angeles Daily News* began publishing in 1923 as a Democratic alternative to the Republican *Times* and Hearst's papers. In 1926, Vanderbilt sold it to former Times Mirror executive Manchester Boddy, who continued the flip *Daily News* tradition by running a sardonic reader survey that named Harry Chandler the Boss of L.A.

6. Created in 1937 by Times Mirror treasurer Frank Pfaffinger, one of Harry Chandler's original real estate syndicate partners, the Pfaffinger Foundation's mandate was "to assist retired and current Times Mirror employees in financial distress."

7. Descendants of Harry and Magdalena's first daughter, Francesca, and her husband John Kirkpatrick, were not included. Francesca died in 1933 and John in 1936.

Chapter Eleven

1. *Times* cartographer Charley Owens once drew a map of the European Theater of Operations that seemed perfect until readers began flooding the switchboard to inform the *Times* that Owens had left out Rumania.

2. Of Harry Chandler's three sons, only Harrison served in the military during the war—a stint as a Naval lieutenant safely stationed in Washington, D.C.

3. A temporary transit center for interned Japanese-Americans dispatched to concentration camps during the war, Santa Anita did not return to horse racing until 1945. The much-beloved Hernandez never missed calling a race until the day he died in January 1972.

4. Among other films, Otis saw the 1941 masterpiece *Citizen Kane:* "I didn't know that much about Hearst, but Orson Welles was quite impressive."

5. Bridges became a citizen of the United States in 1945; was convicted and sentenced to prison for perjury in denying Communist Party membership in 1950; and was cleared of all charges by the U.S. Supreme Court when it overturned his conviction in 1953. In 1999, the San

Francisco Port Commission voted unanimously to name the square outside its new Ferry Building "Harry Bridges Plaza."

6. During a San Francisco newspaper strike a few years later, the Chandlers dispatched *Times* street sales director Jerry Cohen to the Bay area to cash in by opening a temporary circulation and sales office there. A short time later, Cohen returned to L.A., his face a bloody mess from the beating he'd taken at the hands of Harry Bridges' longshoremen.

7. As early as 1902, a Pasadena resident wrote a letter to the editor of the *Times,* complaining that "Los Angeles is becoming a smoke-making center of large proportions. The smoke comes this way about 8 a.m. in a great, black cloud and by 10 A.M. the country hereabouts is practically shut out from view." The writer attributed the problem to chimneys and smokestacks.

8. The Southern Pacific had begun the conversion years earlier. After acquiring the Pacific Electric line from Huntington, the railroad replaced the first of its Big Red cars with bus trolleys in the mid-1920s.

9. The Navy named a liberty ship for the General on January 3, 1943, but the *S.S. Harrison Gray Otis* was sunk in Australian waters on its maiden voyage.

Chapter Twelve

1. Two years his senior, Camilla was packed off to Wellesley at about the same time, where she became a biology major.

2. Also known as Phillips Academy, Andover was an all-male school until going coed in the 1970s.

3. Following the war, Norman became a director on the boards of Kaiser Steel, Dresser Industries, Pan American Airways, Security Pacific Bank, Pacific Western Industries, Safeway Stores, and the Santa Fe Railway.

4. Beginning in the 1920s, Norman drove a broad range of luxury automobiles, including a LaSalle, followed by a Cabernet-colored Rolls Royce and, much later, a two-door Mercedes 280. "Dad *loved* his cars," said Camilla.

5. Other notable *Times*men who later attended the annual retreat included Times Mirror CEO Franklin Murphy and CNN president Tom Johnson, publisher of the *Times* from 1980 to 1989. Norman nominated his son for membership, but Otis Chandler declined. "I broke my father's heart when I didn't join the Bohemian Grove because it takes forever to get in. But I just said, 'I want to spend my vacations with my kids or in Mongolia, chasing sheep around the tops of mountains,'" he said.

6. Membership remains coveted, with men routinely waiting ten to fifteen years to gain admittance. There are currently about 2,700 members. Among many other notable events, the launch of the Manhattan Project and Dwight Eisenhower's 1952 nomination as the Republican presidential candidate were allegedly conceived at the Bohemian Grove.

7. Voorhis was the inspiration for Jimmy Stewart's interpretation of the honest small-town politician in Frank Capra's *Mr. Smith Goes to Washington.*

8. On August 3, 1948, *Time* magazine editor Whittaker Chambers accused Hiss of passing State Department secrets to Chambers who, in turn, passed them on to the Soviet Union. The president of the Carnegie Endowment for International Peace and a highly respected diplomat, Hiss denied the charges; but Nixon persisted. Though it came down to Hiss's word against Chambers's, HUAC believed Chambers and Hiss was convicted of perjury for his testimony.

Hiss always maintained his innocence—a position supported by Russia in 1992 when a former KGB general reported that Hiss had never been a spy.

9. On New Year's Eve of 1950, Times Mirror bought out CBS's 49 percent share, becoming sole owner of KTTV.

10. Pinkley later wrote a book, *Eisenhower Declassified,* which combined memoirs of his war reporting with his long association with General Dwight D. Eisenhower.

Chapter Thirteen

1. Nourse and Chandler became such close friends that they proposed going into partnership in pig farming following college—a plan that Norman and Buff quashed.

2. The nickname that Camilla gave Otis when they were both still in grammar school stuck throughout his fraternity years and well into his adult life.

3. Shortly before his death in 1922, Missy's grandfather Otto Brant formed a syndicate to develop the artificial lake and resort in the San Bernardino Mountains.

4. Located approximately forty miles southwest of Stanford, Watsonville had a campus reputation as a town where the more desperate undergrads could spend their lust.

5. Hollywood pioneer Charles E. Toberman underwrote the Bowl as the summer home for the Los Angeles Philharmonic Orchestra, which had been founded in 1918. Harry Chandler's *Times* played a major role in backing Toberman's efforts.

6. In 1954, she helped raise $250,000 to keep conductor Bruno Walter's cash-strapped Philharmonic Orchestra afloat.

7. Mrs. Marian Otis Chandler died August 9, 1952. She was eighty-six.

8. Alberta was also the younger sister of Ruth's first husband, Fred Williamson.

9. A retired Marine Corps general, Worton stepped into the temporary post in June 1949 following a grand jury investigation of gambling kickback charges against LAPD Chief Clemence Horrall and his assistant chief, Joe Reed. Horrall and Reed both resigned under pressure.

10. Part of Parker's brilliance could be traced to his speech writer, Gene Rodenberry, who went on to create television's *Star Trek* and patterned one of the characters, Mr. Spock, after the chief.

Chapter Fourteen

1. *Mirror* investigative reporter Art White published an eight-part series, beginning on October 5, 1953, titled "Bonelli's Saloon Empire: Shame of California." Bonelli's State Board of Equalization selected who would be granted the limited number of liquor sales permits each year and, according to White, Bonelli and his staff took bribes in exchange for the precious licenses.

2. Strub also owned and operated the San Francisco Seals, a franchise of the Pacific Coast Baseball League.

3. Called before the Kefauver Committee on Organized Crime in 1950, the three-hundred-pound Samish testified to being a key link between big business, state lawmakers, and the underworld. "I can tell if a man wants a baked potato, a girl, or money," he boasted shortly before being imprisoned for tax evasion. His own tell-all book, *The Secret Boss of California*, was an even more scandalous potboiler than *Billion Dollar Blackjack*.

4. *Billion Dollar Blackjack* was researched and ghostwritten by former newspaper reporter Leo Katcher, who threw the book together for Bonelli in six weeks.

5. California has allowed municipally sanctioned poker parlors since statehood. The Los Angeles suburb of Gardena approved card clubs shortly after incorporating as a city in 1930.

6. Editorial cartoonist Bruce Alexander Russell won the *Times* its second Pulitzer in 1946.

7. The last surviving daughter of General Otis, Ida Mae Booth was a Times Mirror board member until she died. Booth succumbed to a heart attack March 24, 1955. She was eighty-three.

8. In 1999, Booth's 18,000 shares of Berkshire Hathaway were valued at $1.3 billion, making him the 186th richest person in the United States, according to *Forbes* magazine.

9. Years later, Otis maintained that he also added, "But the way you make money is to have a great editorial product."

10. While Chandler servants normally could count on lifetime tenure, Missy recalled one Japanese maid who became pregnant by the Chandlers' black cook. Buff fired both before her social rivals got wind of the scandal.

11. Janss was succeeded in residence at the Hancock Park home by character actor Lewis Stone, best remembered as Judge Hardy in MGM's Andy Hardy film series from the 1940s, starring Mickey Rooney. Stone died in 1953 of a heart attack after chasing an intruder from the home.

12. Hotchkiss lived six more years, and served two terms on the Los Angeles Harbor Commission before his death from prostate cancer in 1964. He was seventy.

Chapter Fifteen

1. By 1960, Times Mirror Press published 284 different phone directories for California, Colorado, Arizona, Nevada, and Hawaii—by far the largest phone directory publisher in the West.

2. Co-owned with the Mormon Church's *Deseret News* since 1948, Publisher's Paper Company began as a small newsprint plant in Oregon City, Oregon, and grew to own several paper mills and more than 400,000 acres of timberland in Northern California, Oregon, and Washington from which Times Mirror acquired 75 percent of its newsprint.

3. Shortly before his death, Palmer did pass on some words of wisdom to Williams: "You are *not* the 'friend' of Richard Nixon," he said. "You pretend to be."

4. Blake ran into Norman Chandler years later and, by way of greeting, the still handsome, if aging, patrician clapped his former star reporter on the shoulder and said, "When are we going to go after those Birchers again?"

5. A decade later, Jeppesen became Jeppesen Sanderson Inc. after its merger with Paul Sanderson Films.

6. With the close of the *Examiner*, the *Herald-Express* changed its name to the *Herald-Examiner.*

7. Hearst died August 14, 1951. Arthur Sulzberger of the *New York Times*, Colonel Robert McCormick of the *Chicago Tribune,* and Norman Chandler all attended the funeral.

8. Hearst's James McInerney contacted Antitrust Division chief Lee Loevinger informally after Kennedy denied him permission and Loevinger told him that a corporation could hypothetically shut down a subsidiary without violating antitrust law. McInerney chose not to pursue

the hypothetical any further and simply used Loevinger's opinion as the basis for advising Hearst to shutter the *Examiner.*

Chapter Sixteen

1. When his mother told eleven-year-old Norman that she was pregnant with her fifth child, Carolyn, her eldest son slapped Missy and told her that the Chandlers already had too many children. Otis had a vasectomy a short time later.

2. When former Cal Tech president Harold Brown sought membership in the California Club during the 1950s and ran into raised eyebrows because he was Jewish, Otis and Norman threatened to resign if Brown was not admitted. Norman also invited the president of MCA, Lew Wasserman, to become the first Jew to sit on the Cal Tech board.

3. Following his defeat, Norris Poulson won *Times* support for his appointment to the California State Water Commission from 1963 to 1969—a period during which the multibillion-dollar State Water Project siphoned Northern California's water to Los Angeles on a scale that made Owens Valley look like a radiator leak. Surplus irrigation water along the California Aqueduct could be had for as little as $3.50 an acre foot in 1967—a pittance that has risen one hundredfold in the years since then. Poulson joined the commission's majority in approving a route for the aqueduct that would bring the cheap water to L.A. directly through the Tejon Ranch, giving the Chandler-owned property ample irrigation for fire-sale prices. Poulson retired to Orange County in 1969, where he lived until his death at eighty-seven in 1982.

4. The *Times* won its third Pulitzer Gold Medal for Public Service in 1969 for investigating city commissioners, who were later either convicted or resigned in disgrace; widespread reforms resulted. Yorty called the investigations inconsequential, but "a masterful smear job." He threatened at one point to rent billboard space to advertise, "Just because it appears in the *Los Angeles Times* doesn't mean it's true."

5. Five years in the planning, the *Times* Orange County plant opened on February 19, 1968.

6. Pressroom employees voted to accept union representation in March 1967 and a contract between the *Times* and the union was in effect from August 7, 1967, to August 6, 1970, when, once again, the pressmen voted to decertify the union.

7. Although considered a classic, *The Kingdom and the Power* detailed the power struggle between Washington bureau chief James Reston and the *Times'* eventual editor, Abe Rosenthal, and was not viewed kindly by the *New York Times'* ranking editors. It is ironic that the best-seller was first published by New American Library, a Times Mirror company.

Chapter Seventeen

1. The family holding company that resulted from the iron-clad trusts Harry Chandler put in place in 1936 to ensure the survival of his *Times.*

2. In 1994, Rupert Murdoch paid Kluge's Metromedia Company $400 million for KTTV.

3. Others opposed opening in winter so close to Christmas, but Buff insisted upon December 6 after consulting astrologist Carroll Righter and discovering that to be the best date dictated by the zodiac.

4. Buff also needed some extra Travertine marble for her sitting room; as there happened to be some left over from the Music Center's construction, it, too, found its way to Los Tiempos.

Chapter Eighteen

1. Otis maintained that Lomax exaggerated; that he had, in fact, been to Watts frequently while he was in the circulation phase of his publisher's training program.

2. The city desk temporarily pressed *Times* ad salesman Robert Richardson into service because he was black. LAPD officers yanked him from his car, handcuffed him, and slammed him to the ground before verifying his identity as a *Times*man. Richardson characterized the insanity on both sides as "the most terrifying thing I've ever seen in my life," with black mobs equally indiscriminate in their violence, pulling whites from their cars and chanting "Kill! Kill!" as they punched, kicked, and maimed.

3. A short-lived Central zone section began appearing each Friday in the *Times* on August 3, 1973, but it served downtown L.A., Hollywood, the Wilshire district, Elysian Park, East L.A., Silver Lake, and Baldwin Hills as well as South Central. Because of a lack of support from advertisers, it was discontinued less than a year later, on July 12, 1974.

4. Before accepting the Times Mirror chairmanship, Murphy had been approached by Richard Nixon to be his running mate in 1968, according to Peter Fernald, a Times Mirror executive of that era.

5. After winning the California primary, Bobby Kennedy called Otis to invite him and Missy to celebrate at a private party at the Factory night club in Beverly Hills, but Otis declined. A short time later, as Otis and Missy were getting ready for bed, a bulletin flashed over the television announcing that Kennedy had been shot at the Ambassador Hotel.

6. Confronted by a gaggle of Youth for Nixon chanting "We Want Dick!" on a Nixon for President campaign train during the final weeks of the campaign, *Los Angeles Times* political writer Dick Dougherty, who had written about Nixon for years, muttered within earshot of *Philadelphia Bulletin* reporter Tony Day, "And you're going to get him, you fucking rubes."

7. Although Patterson popularized the phrase, it was coined at the turn of the nineteenth century by Chicago newspaper editor Wilbur Story.

8. In 1968, a foundation created in her honor began bestowing grants to career journalists who wanted to write a book. Author Joe McGinniss, one of the first Alicia Patterson fellows, used his grant to write *The Selling of the President 1968*, a best-selling exposé of Richard Nixon's closely managed 1968 presidential campaign.

Chapter Nineteen

1. While on assignment during World War II, *Times* correspondent Tom Treanor died in a jeep accident outside Paris on August 19, 1944.

2. Because the *Times* rarely fired an employee of Hartmann's stature and longevity, he was eased out of Washington and into Rome, where he opened a *Times* bureau in February 1963. Hartmann quit a short time later and went to work as an aide for then-Congressman and, later, President Gerald Ford. Of his former employer, Hartmann said, "Otis was less secure than his father, a young man on the make. Each [Chandler] son has had to outdo his father, make his own mark, and he has done it."

3. Johnson's father delivered laundry and sold watermelons and wood off the back of a truck and his mother clerked in his uncle's store. At fourteen, Johnson went to work writing high school sports news for the *Macon Telegraph and News*, earning $0.15 per column inch. Peyton Anderson, publisher of the *Telegraph and News,* put Johnson through the University of Georgia and Harvard Business School and sponsored his bid for a White House internship.

4. According to one source close to both Tom Johnson and Otis Chandler, the deal was negotiated by MCA/Universal Chairman Lew Wasserman, who began his career as a Hollywood talent agent and later became fast friends with both LBJ and Buff Chandler. LBJ press aide Jack Valenti (who later became chief of the Motion Picture Association of America) acted as go-between.

5. Twenty years later, he recycled the idea with a cartoon of Governor George Deukmejian peeing on Southern California.

Chapter Twenty

1. Otis's father, who had preceded him on the board of Pan Am, told friends—only half in jest—that he sat on the boards of airline companies and the Santa Fe Railroad so that he could always be assured of free air and rail travel.

2. He quit the GeoTek board on June 4, 1973. The company went into receivership four months later, on October 10, 1973. As publisher of the *Times* and vice chair of Times Mirror, Otis earned a salary of $229,000 in 1973.

3. The grandson of one of Harry Chandler's business partners, H. R. Haldeman came to Nixon's attention when he worked with Governor Ronald Reagan's staff to help quash student uprisings at the University of California.

4. Romano the gardener earned a special loyalty from Otis by reporting to his boss that the Chandlers' youngest son, Michael, had been cultivating marijuana next to the family swimming pool. A grateful Otis found Romano a job in the *Times* pressroom until Romano chose to take a generous severance package and return to Mexico in the 1980s.

5. Out of deference to his dying father, Otis did order the *Times* to endorse Nixon's reelection in 1972, but the partisan days of a strictly Republican *Times* died on September 23, 1973, when Otis announced that his newspaper would no longer endorse candidates for president, governor, or senator.

Chapter Twenty-One

1. Otis's Aunt Ruth had nearly as much pompous influence on him as Buff; she turned up her nose at a Chandis board meeting at which her nephew appeared unshaven. "The publisher of the *Times* shouldn't be wearing a beard," she said, and he shaved it off. She also frowned on his motorcycling, but there he drew the line.

2. Following her *Times* article decrying the Metropolitan Water District's disproportionate fee schedule, Ellen Stern Harris was fired in 1978. One of Buff's last *Times* Women of the Year, Harris had been a regular Sunday consumer affairs columnist for seven years. She had pointed out that MWD charged residential users many times what it assessed agricultural users, naming the Chandlers' Tejon Ranch as one of MWD's biggest customers. After her dismissal, she joined the MWD board as a dissenting voice and called for a grand jury probe of the agency.

3. Technically, the 917K seated two, but any passenger larger than Billy Barty or Ally McBeal would have had to hang out the window.

Chapter Twenty-Two

1. In a similar experience more than a year later during a weekend getaway with Bettina, Otis saw *Times* classical music critic Martin Bernheimer and a girlfriend out on a weekend dal-

liance of their own. Bernheimer sent a bottle of wine to Chandler's table with a note that read "I don't see you and you don't see me." Otis was shaken all the way down to his size-eleven shoes.

2. The Chandler inferiority complex still played a role in the expensive exercise of delivering 2,000 copies of a same-day edition of the *Times* to New York City and Washington, D.C. Beginning in January 1981, the paper was flown in daily to the East Coast to lackluster response.

3. Vera Alberta Chandler died at the age of seventy-seven on August 18, 1982. Her four children, Jeffrey, Steven, Bruce, and Corrine, remained outspoken critics of the *Times'* drift away from conservatism.

Chapter Twenty-Three

1. The "Kremlinologists" among the Times Mirror elite divined Erburu's anointed status at the 1973 memorial service for Norman Chandler when the eulogy was delivered by Erburu, not Casey.

2. Fernald, a close confidante of Buff, said that one of Erburu's first phone calls upon rising to CEO was to Mrs. Chandler, seeking her approval. "She was wary," said Fernald. A short time later, Otis told Fernald that he no longer wanted him speaking with Buff about Times Mirror business.

3. In the 1972 presidential election, several dozen *Times* employees signed a letter dissenting from the *Times* endorsement of Richard Nixon. "A newspaper is not a monolith," the letter began, which announced that many *Times* reporters and editors planned to vote for Senator George McGovern. With Otis Chandler's full approval and to the disbelieving chagrin of his arch-Republican relatives, Tony Day printed the letter on the *Times* op-ed page.

4. Ironically, his first made-for-television movie as executive producer was titled *Stolen: One Husband*, a comedy about an angry wife (Valerie Harper) who seeks revenge against her philandering husband (Elliott Gould) who leaves her for a younger woman (Brenda Bakke).

5. *Times* managers sought employees' suggestions on ways to improve the newspaper during the Olympics, prompting *Times* photographer Mike Meadows to drop a signed note into a suggestion box that the *Times* consider opening a foreign bureau in downtown L.A. because Asia and Africa seemed to get more page one coverage than local news. Although he maintained that he wasn't being sarcastic, Meadows was reprimanded.

Chapter Twenty-Four

1. In a divorce and remarriage scenario reminiscent of that of Otis and Bettina, Missy wed television producer/writer Malcolm Stuart on August 5, 1984, less than a month after Stuart's divorce from his first wife was final. Producer of such fare as *The Deliberate Stranger,* the television version of the life of serial killer Ted Bundy, Stuart was married to Missy for ten years. She filed for divorce on February 2, 1995.

2. The NYSE had not allowed family-dominated media companies to exercise the ten-to-one voting provision, which was why the closely held New York Times Company and the Washington Post had previously been traded only on the American Stock Exchange.

3. In 1986, Times Mirror reincorporated as a Delaware corporation; the following year, its directors adopted an amendment to the company's certificate of incorporation permitting the is-

suance of multiple series of stock with different voting rights to "preserve corporate independence and stability provided by substantial Chandler family and employee stock ownership."

4. To further ensure Chandis control and protect against hostile takeovers, the *Times* began the Employee Stock Ownership Plan in 1985, which allowed employees to buy Times Mirror stock at reduced prices, thus insuring friendly shareholders who received dividends but had virtually no voting power.

5. Otis's uncle Harrison Chandler, the last surviving son born to Harry Chandler, died April 27, 1985. He was eighty-two.

Chapter Twenty-Five

1. Nick Williams developed Alzheimer's in his final years, and died of lung disease on July 1, 1992, at the age of eighty-five.

2. The also-rans included George Cotliar, *Times* managing editor, and his two deputy managing editors, Noel Greenwood and Dennis Britton.

3. Vance Stickell, *Times* executive vice president and Otis Chandler's advertising and circulation architect, died of colon cancer October 22, 1987, ending an era on the marketing side of the newspaper that coincided with the end of Bill Thomas's rule over editorial.

4. Through Buff's cajoling, Hearst's mistress donated an emerald necklace to the Music Center.

5. Prolabor to the bitter end, *Herald* employees voted to strike just eight months before the shutdown, accepting a new three-year contract from Hearst management just before the walkout.

6. In March 1990, the *Times* banned the use of the term *pro-choice* from its pages, just as it had banned *pro-life* eight years earlier. Reporters were forced to use "abortion proponents" or "abortion opponents" in describing the ongoing controversy.

7. Virgil Pinkley, another former *Daily Trojan* editor who once figured large in Times Mirror's hierarchy, died at eighty-six on Christmas Eve, 1992, after finishing out his career as publisher of the neighborhood *Glendale News Press*.

8. Coffey began to suffer his own list of pejoratives, being addressed behind his back by staff members as "Il Cappuccino," the "Yuppie doorknob," and media reporter Jay Sharbutt's favorite, the "Light Prince."

9. Otis speculated that the story had been spiked by Franklin Murphy, who collected art and counted wealthy collectors among his inner circle of friends.

10. While frequently ineffectual in investigative efforts, Coffey's "swarms" worked spectacularly in covering disasters. An early "swarm" in October of 1989 resulted in a special fourteen-page report on the San Francisco earthquake and *Times* "swarm" coverage of the 1994 Northridge earthquake led to its twentieth Pulitzer Prize.

11. A Brussels bureau opened in 1978 but was discontinued in the early 1980s.

Chapter Twenty-Six

1. The legendary star of *Rebel Without a Cause* and *Giant* died in his Porsche on September 30, 1955, and became an instant myth in the Otis pantheon, along with T. E. Lawrence, who died in 1935 following a motorcycle accident.

2. Hailed by his peers as the "quintessential Renaissance man," seventy-eight-year-old Murphy succumbed to lung cancer on June 16, 1994.

3. Once, he shot himself up and could not turn his erection flaccid. He panicked, visited the local hospital emergency room, and waited for his member to soften. When Viagra became available, Otis became one of the first to ask his doctor for a prescription.

4. In 1991, the *Times*' own media critic, David Shaw, won the Pulitzer for his analysis of how the media covered the McMartin preschool molestation case, including what many of his fellow reporters believed to be an unjustified savaging of *Times* staff writer Lois Timnick, who indignantly resigned after Shaw ruined her career.

5. Laventhol thought nothing of the grandiose expense of flying 2,300 copies of the paper to the East Coast every day so that they could be delivered to opinion makers in Washington, D.C.

6. Within two years of the riots, six of the sixteen reporters whose bylines had appeared on the Pulitzer Prize–winning coverage had left the *Times*.

7. In one shrewd bilingual move designed to cash in on the growing Mexican and Latino middle class, Times Mirror purchased 50 percent of *La Opinion* in 1990—L.A.'s largest, oldest, and advertising-supported Spanish-language daily newspaper.

8. KTVI-TV in St. Louis, Missouri; WVTM-TV, Birmingham, Alabama; KDFW-TV, Dallas; and KTBC-TV, in Austin, Texas.

9. Several shareholders sued Chandis, Otis, and his cousins, charging conspiracy to defraud; but the case was settled out of court with the stipulation that the Chandlers' preferred stock had to be offered to all shareholders. Average shareholders who held on to their Cox stock eventually did get the last laugh. Cox doubled its value within three years.

Chapter Twenty-Seven

1. Willes was a nephew of the current president and prophet of the Mormon Church, Gordon B. Hinckley. He kept his personal life fiercely private, declining to discuss his wife, Laura, or any of their five children.

2. TimesLink eventually evolved into LATimes.com, a Web site so popular that by election day of 1996 it was recording 1.6 million "hits" every day. At the same time that the new division was succeeding, Times Mirror management cut its staff in half to save on overhead: one more symptom of the pecuniary schizophrenia that compelled the company to bankrupt its future by saving a few dollars today.

3. Schlosberg immediately ended Otis's long-standing ban on editorial endorsements for major officeholders. In 1994, the *Times* endorsed Republican Pete Wilson for governor.

4. Echoing a *Los Angeles Herald-Examiner* headline from nearly six years earlier, the final front page of *New York Newsday* read: So Long, New York

5. The *Times* resumed publishing the Washington edition in November after government officials complained that they relied on it to stay abreast of developments in California.

6. Erburu also sat on the Getty Trust board, which oversaw the $4.4-billion endowment that J. Paul Getty, the oil tycoon, established by bequest upon his death in 1976 to set up and maintain the Getty Art Museum in Los Angeles. During Erburu's tenure on the board (which was chaired by Harold Williams, a fellow Times Mirror board member), the Getty Trust lost $440 million in a single stock-market misstep in 1995.

Chapter Twenty-Eight

1. The day it sold, Tejon Ranch's stock rose $0.13 to $19; Times Mirror lost $0.81 to close at $56.50.

2. Bereft of advertising since department stores began closing in the mid-1980s, the women's pages from ancient *Times* kept switching names in a futile attempt to attract readers and advertisers. As of November 1, 1998, Life & Style (previously known as View) became Southern California Living, although its content and lack of advertising remained unchanged.

3. As of February 1998, the *Times* had conducted more than four hundred polls during the previous twenty years.

4. In early 1999, the *Times* tried similar bilingual maneuvers with *Nguoi Viet,* Southern California's Vietnamese newspaper, and the *Korea Times,* delivering the *Times* to 17,000 of that paper's 45,000 subscribers.

5. With less than half the *Times'* staff, *Newsday* won more Pulitzers than the *Times* during the 1990s and, at 570,000 readers, it was still the eighth largest newspaper in the United States, even after the shutdown of *New York Newsday.*

6. Born in 1944, Philip Chandler's fifty-six-year-old son, Stephen, was the last heir born before Harry's death.

Epilogue

1. Because the Tribune Company agreed to assume nearly $1.8 billion in outstanding Times Mirror debt, the actual cost to Tribune for the takeover was closer to $8.25 billion.

2. According to Securities and Exchange Commission documents, Otis was awarded $300,000 a year upon his retirement in 1985, in addition to his severance settlement and stock options.

SELECTED
BIBLIOGRAPHY

Adamic, Louis. *Dynamite: The Story of Class Violence in America.* Gloucester, Mass.: Peter Smith, 1963.

Ainsworth, Ed. *Enchanted Pueblo.* Los Angeles: Bank of America, 1959.

_____. *History of Los Angeles Times.* Los Angeles: Times Mirror, 1958.

Aitken, Jonathan. *Nixon: A Life.* Washington, D.C.: Regnery Publishing Inc., 1993.

American Institute for Political Communication. *Effects of Local Media Monopoly on the Mass Mind.* Washington, D.C.: American Institute for Political Communication, 1972.

Babcock, Gwendolyn Garland. *The Ancestry of Harry Chandler.* San Marino, Calif.: Gwendolyn Garland Babcock, 1990.

_____. *The Ancestry of Marian Otis Chandler.* San Marino, Calif.: Gwendolyn Garland Babcock, 1991.

Bagdikian, Ben H. *The Effete Conspiracy: And Other Crimes by the Press.* New York: Harper & Row, 1972.

_____. *The Information Machines.* New York: Harper & Row, 1971.

Baker, Robert and Sandra Ball. *Violence and the Media: A Staff Report to the National Commission on the Causes and Prevention of Violence.* Washington, D.C.: U.S. Government Printing Office, 1969.

Barich, Bill. *Big Dreams: Into the Heart of California.* New York: Vintage Books, 1994.

Berges, Marshall. *The Life and Times of Los Angeles.* New York: Atheneum, 1984.

Bonelli, William G. *Billion Dollar Blackjack.* Beverly Hills: Civic Research Press, 1954.

Bottles, Scott L. *Los Angeles and the Automobile.* Berkeley, Calif.: University of California Press, 1987.

Brendon, Piers. *The Life and Death of the Press Barons.* New York: Atheneum, 1983.

Brodie, Fawn M. *Richard Nixon: The Shaping of His Character.* New York: W. W. Norton & Co., 1981.

Burns, William J. *The Masked War.* New York: George F. Doran Company, 1913.

Cannon, Lou. *Official Negligence: How Rodney King and the Riots Changed Los Angeles and the LAPD.* New York: Times Books, 1997.

Carr, Harry. *Los Angeles, City of Dreams.* New York: D. Appleton-Century Co., 1935.

Carter, Vincent. *L. A. P. D.'s Rogue Cops.* Lucerne Valley, Calif.: Desert View Books, 1993.

Casey, Al with Dick Seaver. *Casey's Law.* New York: Arcade, 1997.

Chaney, Lindsay and Michael Cieply. *The Hearsts: Family & Empire, the Later Years.* New York: Simon & Schuster, 1981.

Chalfant, Willie A. *The Story of Inyo.* Los Angeles: Citizen's Print Shop, 1933.

Chapman, John L. *Incredible Los Angeles.* New York: Harper & Row, 1967.

Cirino, Robert. *Don't Blame the People.* New York: Vintage Books, 1972.

Cleland, Robert G. *California in Our Time: 1900–1940.* New York: Alfred A. Knopf, 1947.

Clover, Samuel Travers. *Constructive Californians: Men of Outstanding Ability Who Have Added Greatly to the Golden State's Prestige.* Los Angeles: Saturday Night Publishing Co., 1926.

Coleridge, Nicholas. *Paper Tigers: The Latest, Greatest Newspaper Tycoons.* New York: Birch Lane Press, 1994.

Commission on Freedom of the Press. *A Free and Responsible Press.* Chicago: University of Chicago Press, 1947.

Cook, Don. *Floodtide in Europe.* New York: G. P. Putnam's Sons, 1965.

Cose, Ellis. *The Press.* New York: William Morrow &. Co., inc., 1989.

Cray, Ed. *Chief Justice: A Biography of Earl Warren.* New York: Simon & Schuster, 1997.

Davis, Mike. *City of Quartz: Excavating the Future of Los Angeles.* New York: Vintage Books, 1992.

Dawson, Muir. *History and Bibliography of Southern California Newspapers: 1851–1876.* Los Angeles: no publisher listed, 1950.

Diehl, Digby. *Front Page: 100 Years of the* Los Angeles Times, *1881–1981.* New York: Harry N. Abrams, 1981.

Domanick, Joe. *To Protect and to Serve: The LAPD's Century of War in the City of Dreams.* New York: Pocket Books, 1994.

Emery, Edwin. *The Press and America: An Interpretative History of Journalism, 2nd Edition.* Englewood Cliffs, New Jersey: Prentice-Hall, 1962.

_____. *The Press and America: An Interpretative History of the Mass Media, 3rd Edition.* Englewood Cliffs, New Jersey: Prentice-Hall, 1972.

Federal Trade Commission. *A Staff Report on Conglomerate Merger Performance: An Empirical Analysis of Nine Corporations.* Washington, D.C.: U.S. Government Printing Office, 1972.

Finney, Guy W. *Angel City in Turmoil.* Los Angeles: American State Press, 1945.

Galbraith, John Kenneth. *The New Industrial State.* New York: New American Library, 1967.

Gardner, Theodore Roosevelt II. *The Paper Dynasty.* Palos Verdes, CA: Alfred A. Knoll Publishers, 1991.

Gates, Daryl F. with Diane K. Shah. *Chief: My Life in the LAPD.* New York: Bantam Books, 1992.

Gordon, Dudley. *Crusader in Corduroy.* Los Angeles: Cultural Assets Press, 1973.

Gottlieb, Robert and Irene Wolt. *Thinking Big: The Story of the Los Angeles Times, Its Publishers and Their Influence on Southern California.* New York: G. P. Putnam's Sons, 1977.

Governor's Commission on the Los Angeles Riots. *Violence in the City: An End or a Beginning?* Sacramento, Calif: California State Printing Office, 1965.

Halberstam, David. *The Powers That Be.* New York: Alfred A. Knopf, 1979.

Haldeman, H. R., with Joseph DiMona. *The Ends of Power.* New York: Times Books, 1978.

_____. *The Haldeman Diaries.* New York: Berkley Publishing Group, 1995.

Halliwell, Leslie *Halliwell's Filmgoer's and Video Viewer's Companion.* New York: Perennial Library, 1990.

Hancock, Ralph. *Fabulous Boulevard.* New York: Funk & Wagnalls Company, 1949.

Hart, Jack Robert. *The Information Empire: A History of the Los Angeles Times from the Era of Personal Journalism to the Advent of the Multi-Media Communications Corporation* (PhD Thesis). Madison, Wisconsin: University of Wisconsin, 1975.

Henstell, Bruce. *Sunshine and Wealth: Los Angeles in the Twenties and Thirties.* San Francisco: Chronicle Books, 1984.

Hichborn, Franklin. *The System, as Uncovered by the San Francisco Graft Prosecutions.* San Francisco: James Barry Co., 1915.

Hill, Laurence L. *La Reina: Los Angeles in Three Centuries.* Los Angeles: Security Trust & Savings Bank, 1929.

Hopkins, Ernest Jerome. *Our Lawless Police, A Study of the Unlawful Enforcement of the Law.* New York: Viking Press, 1931.

Hulteng, John and Roy Paul Nelson. *The Fourth Estate: An Informal Appraisal of the News and Opinion Media.* New York: Harper & Row, 1971.

Jacoby, Neil H. ed. *Corporate Power and Social Responsibility.* New York: MacMillan Publishing Co., 1973.

Karasick, Norman M. and Dorothy K. *The Oilman's Daughter: A Biography of Aline Barnsdall.* Encino, Calif.: Carleston Publishing Inc., 1993.

Ladd, Bruce. *The Crisis in Credibility.* New York: New American Library, 1968.

Lee, A. M. *The Daily Newspaper in the United States.* New York: MacMillan, 1937.

Liebling, A. J. *The Press.* New York: Ballantine Books, 1961.

Lindstrom, Carl. *The Fading American Newspaper.* Gloucester, Mass: Peter Smith, 1964.

Longstreet, Stephen. *All Star Cast: An Anecdotal History of Los Angeles.* New York: Thomas Y. Crowell Co., 1977.

Los Angeles County Pioneer Society. *Historical Record and Souvenir.* Los Angeles: Times Mirror Press, 1923.

Lyle, Jack. *The News in Megalopolis.* San Francisco: Chandler Publishing Co., 1967.

Marquette University College of Journalism, ed. *Social Responsibility of the Newspress.* Milwaukee, Wisconsin: Marquette University Press, 1962.

Marris, Robin and Adrian Wood, eds. *The Corporate Economy: Growth, Competition, and Innovative Potential.* London: MacMillan, 1971.

Mayo, Morrow. *Los Angeles: A History with Side-Shows.* New York: Alfred A. Knopf, 1933.

Mazon, Mauricio. *The Zoot-Suit Riots: The Psychology of Symbolic Annihilation.* Austin, Texas: University of Texas, 1984.

McAlister, Coleman. *A Man Unafraid.* New York: Greenberg, 1930.

McGroaty, John Steven. *History of Los Angeles County.* New York: The American Historical Society, Inc., 1923.

McLuhan, Marshall. *Understanding Media: The Extensions of Man.* New York: New American Library, 1964.

McWilliams, Carey. *Southern California: An Island on the Land.* Salt Lake City: Peregrine Smith Books, 1983.

Meier, R. L. *A Communications Theory of Urban Growth.* Cambridge, Mass: M. I. T. Press, 1962.

Merrill, John C. *The Elite Press: Great Newspapers of the World.* New York: Pittman Publishing Co., 1968.

Miller, William, ed. *Men in Business: Essays in the History of Entrepreneurship.* Cambridge, Mass: Harvard University Press, 1952.

Morris, Roger. *Richard Milhous Nixon: The Rise of An American Politician.* New York: Henry Holt, 1990.

Nasaw, David. *The Chief: The Life of William Randolph Hearst.* New York: Houghton Mifflin Co., 2000.

National Advisory Commission on Civil Disorders. *Report.* New York: New York Times Co., 1968.

Newmark, Harris. *Sixty Years in Southern California, 1853–1913.* Los Angeles: Zeitlin & Ver Brugge, 1970.

Newmark, Marcie H. and Marco R. Newmark, eds. *Sixty Years in Southern California, 1853–1913: Containing the Reminiscences of Harris Newmark.* 3rd Edition. Boston and New York: Houghton Mifflin, 1913.

Reid, S. R. *Mergers, Managers and the Economy.* New York: McGraw Hill, 1968.

Reisner, Marc. *Cadillac Desert: The American West and Its Disappearing Water.* New York: Penguin Books, 1993.

Reston, James. *The Artillery of the Press: Its Influence on American Foreign Policy.* New York: Harper & Row, 1966.

Richardson, James H. *For the Life of Me.* New York: G. P. Putnam's Sons, 1954.

Riesman, David, Nathan Glazer and Reuel Denny. *The Lonely Crowd: A Study of the Changing American Character.* New Haven, Conn: Yale University Press, 1963.

Rivers, William L. *The Adversaries: Politics and the Press.* Boston: Beacon Press, 1970.

———. and David M. Rubin. *A Region's Press: Anatomy of Newspapers in the San Francisco Bay Area.* Berkeley, Calif: Institute of Governmental Studies, 1971.

Robinson, W. W. *Lawyers of Los Angeles.* Los Angeles: Los Angeles Bar Association, 1959.

Rucker, Bryce. *The First Freedom.* Carbondale, Ill: Southern Illinois University Press, 1968.

Scherer, F. M. *Industrial Market Structure and Economic Performance.* Chicago: Rand McNally, 1970.

Seldes, George. *Lords of the Press.* New York: Julian Messner, Inc., 1938.

Shaw, Christopher and Stephen D. Isaacs. *Paper Dynasties: The Rise and Fall of America's Great Newspaper Families.*

Sinclair, Upton. *The Brass Check: A Study in American Journalism.* Pasadena, Calif: by the author, 1920.

Spalding, William A. *Los Angeles Newspaperman.* San Marino, Calif: Huntington Library, 1961.

Starr, Kevin. *Americans and the California Dream.* New York: Oxford University Press, 1973.

———. *The Dream Endures: California Enters the 1940s.* New York: Oxford University Press, 1997.

———. *Endangered Dreams: The Great Depression in California.* New York: Oxford University Press, 1996.

———. *Inventing the Dream: California Through the Progressive Era.* New York: Oxford University Press, 1985.

———. *Material Dreams: Southern California Through the 1920s.* New York: Oxford University Press, 1990.

Storke, Thomas M. *California Editor.* Los Angeles: Westernlore Press, 1958.

Talese, Gay. *The Kingdom and the Power.* New York and Cleveland: World Publishing Co., 1969.

Tygiel, Jules. *The Great Los Angeles Swindle: Oil, Stocks, and Scandal During the Roaring Twenties.* New York: Oxford University Press, 1994.

United States Department of Commerce. *Industry Profiles, 1958–1969.* Washington D.C.: U.S. Government Printing Office, 1971.

_____. *U.S. Industrial Outlook, 1974.* Washington D.C.: U.S. Government Printing Ofice, 1974.

Warren, Earl. *The Memoirs of Earl Warren.* Garden City, New York: Doubleday, 1977.

Weaver, John D. *Warren: The Man, the Court, the Era.* Boston: Little Brown, 1967.

Weber, Max. *Social and Economic Organization.* New York: The Free Press, 1947.

Weston, J. Fred and Sam Pelzman, eds. *Public Policy Towards Mergers.* New York: Goodyear, 1969.

White, G. Edward. *Earl Warren: A Public Life.* New York: Oxford University Press, 1982.

Williamson, O. E. *Corporate Control and Business Behavior.* Englewood Cliffs, New Jersey: Prentice-Hall, 1970.

Yeomans, Patricia Henry, ed. *Behind the Headlines with Bill Henry, 1903–1970.* Los Angeles: Ward Ritchie Press, 1972.

Pamphlets

Ainsworth, Ed. "History of the Times." Los Angeles: 1941.

_____. "Memories in the City of Dreams: A Tribute to Harry Chandler." Los Angeles: 1959.

"A Day in the Life of the *Los Angeles Times.*" Los Angeles: *Los Angeles Times* Marketing Research, 1971.

"Facts About the Times." Los Angeles: *Los Angeles Times* Promotion Department, c. 1969.

"General Rate Card, February 1, 1972." Los Angeles: *Los Angeles Times,* 1972.

"Los Angeles, 1973: Marketing and Media." Los Angeles: *Los Angeles Times* Marketing Research, c. 1974.

"*Los Angeles Times* Suburban Sections." Los Angeles: *Los Angeles Times* Marketing Research, 1971.

"Media Facts." Los Angeles: *Los Angeles Times* Marketing Research, c. 1972.

Lyle, Jack and Walter Wilcox. "Television News in Los Angeles, 1961." Los Angeles: UCLA Department of Journalism (mimeographed), 1963.

"Newspapers in Los Angeles, 1971." Los Angeles: *Los Angeles Times* Marketing Research, 1971.

"Newspaper Publisher's Statement for 6 Months Ending March 31, 1972: *Los Angeles Times* and *Los Angeles Herald-Examiner.*" Chicago: Audit Bureau of Circulations, 1972.

"Newspapers with Coffee—Still Around in 1990? A Study for North American Rockwell's MGD Graphic System, Printing Management." Los Angeles: Battelle Memorial Institute, 1971.

Otis, Harrison Gray. "A Letter from Harrison Gray Otis with a Reply by Harry Chandler and Marion Otis Chandler." Los Angeles: c. 1914.

"A Psychographic View of the Los Angeles Marketing Area." Los Angeles: *Los Angeles Times* Marketing Research, c. 1970.

"Retail Rate Card." Los Angeles: *Los Angeles Times,* 1972.

"Times Mirror and the Newspaper Industry." Los Angeles: *Los Angeles Times* Marketing Research, c. 1970.

"The Sixty Mile Circle: The Economy of the Greater Los Angeles Area." Los Angeles: Security Pacific National Bank, 1972.

"What the Times Stands For." Los Angeles: *Los Angeles Times* Promotion Department, c. 1969.

Periodical Articles

"The 100: The biggest winners and losers," *U.S. News & World Report*, 6 July 1987, p. 60.

"A Conversation with Otis Chandler," *Progress* 19 (First Quarter 1981).

Achorn, Robert C. "Get Ready for the Newsroom Revolution." *Quill,* November 1973, pp. 15–18.

"After a Rash of Take-overs, New Worries About 'Press Lords'," *U.S. News & World Report*, 24 January 1977, p. 54.

Ainsworth, Ed. "Early Days Difficult." *Los Angeles Times*, 4 December 1941.

_____. "Otis Chandler New Times Publisher." *Los Angeles Times*, 12 April 1960.

Alles, Fred L. "And the Job Was Done." *Among Ourselves* (*Los Angeles Times* employee newspaper), December 1931.

Alter, Jonathan. "Cruising Speed in L. A." *Newsweek* United States Edition, 26 May 1986, p. 58.

"And Now, 'Tricky Dick'," *Newsweek* United States Edition, 3 November 1997, p. 54.

Anderson, George Baker. "What the Cranks Have Done." *Pacific Outlook*, 18 and 25 May and 1, 8, 15, 22, and 29 June 1907.

"Another exec. leaves L. A. Times," *Editor & Publisher Magazine*, 20 March 1999, p. 6.

"An Automated *L. A. Times.*" *Business Week*, 28 July 1973, pp. 21–22.

"An Organization Woman Remakes the *Post*," *BusinessWeek* Industrial Edition, 29 September 1975, p. 43.

"As Leaders Size Up Their Peers," *U.S. News & World Report*, 14 April 1980, p. 42.

"Away with Trivia," *Newsweek*. 30 October 1961, p. 51.

Bagdasarian, D. R. "Power to the (Ordinary) People," *AutoWeek*, 21 May 1990, p. 16.

Bagdikian, Ben. H. "The Myth of Newspaper Poverty." *Columbia Journalism Review*, March/April 1973, pp. 19–25.

_____. "Publishing's Quiet Revolution." *Columbia Journalism Review*, May/June 1973, pp. 7–15.

Balk, Alfred. "Beyond Agnewism." *Columbia Journalism Review*, winter 1969–70, pp. 14–19.

Barovick, H., T. Gray, L. Lofaro, D. Splitz, F. Tartakovsky, and C. Taylor. "America's Most Wanted," *Time*, 22 March 1999, p. 40.

Barrett, Edward W. "Captive Newspapers." *Columbia Journalism Review*, summer 1963, p. 46.

Barringer, Felicity. "Efforts to Reinvent the Los Angeles Times Falter," *The New York Times*, 17 May 1999.

Barron, Kelly. "Charlie's Pal, Otis," *Forbes,* 12 October 1998, p. 126.

Barry, David. "Muscle Car Magnate: Ex-Newspaper Exec Otis Chandler Keeps Success Story in High Gear with High-Profit Investment in High-Performance Detroitiron." *AutoWeek*, 17 July 1989, p. 21.

Bart, Peter. "The New Look at the 'Times.'" *Saturday Review*, 12 June 1965, pp. 68, 69, and 79.

Bassett, James. "The Battle of the Analysts." *Los Angeles Times*, 26 November 1967.

_____. "Norman Chandler, Publisher of the Times for 16 Years, Dies." *Los Angeles Times*, 21 October 1973.

Battaglio, Stephen. "Is All News Good News; Cable News Network Pres. Tom Johnson; Special Television Report," *MediaWeek* 1 (8 April 1991): S16.

Bengelsdorf, Irving S. "The Adventures of Janus in Mass-Media Land." *Journal of Chemical Education* 46 (September 1969): 543–46.

Benson, Ivan. "The *Los Angeles Times* Contempt Case." *Journalism Quarterly* 16 (March 1939): 1–8.

Berman, Marshall. "City of Quartz: Excavating the Future in Los Angeles" (Book reviews). *The Nation* 252 (1 April 1991): 417.

"Bernays Reports: Top–10 Dailies Almost Same as in 1952 Poll," *Editor & Publisher*, 9 April 1960, p. 66.

"The Big Money Hunts for Independent Newspapers," *BusinessWeek* Industrial Edition, 21 February 1977, p. 56.

"The Big Show; L. A. Event Stirs Enthusiasts' Emotions," *AutoWeek*, 25 November 1991, p. 6.

"The Biggest Winners and Losers," *U.S. News & World Report* 105 (1 August 1988): 48.

Bigman, Stanley K. "Rivals in Conformity: A Study of Two Competing Dailies." *Journalism Quarterly* 25 (June 1948): 127–31.

Bird, George L. "Newspaper Monopoly and Political Independence." *Journalism Quarterly* 17 (September 1940): 207–14.

Bishop, Robert L. "The Rush to Chain Ownership." *Columbia Journalism Review*, November/December 1972, pp. 10–19.

Bogart, Leo. "Changing News Interests and the News Media." *Public Opinion Quarterly* 32 (winter 1968–69): 569.

_____. "The Overseas Newsman: A 1967 Profile Study." *Journalism Quarterly* 45 (summer 1968): 293–306.

Booth, Cathy. "Worst of Times; In Los Angeles, a Newsroom Erupts over a Business-side Gaffe," *Time*, 15 November 1999, p. 79.

Bork, Robert H. Jr. "The Price of Their Toys," *Forbes*, 28 October 1985, p. 374.

Borstel, Gerald H. "Ownership, Competition and Comment in 20 Small Dailies." *Journalism Quarterly* 33 (spring 1956): 220–22.

"The Boss's View," *Newsweek*, 30 March 1959, p. 97.

Bottini, Ronald L. "Group Ownership of Newspapers." *Freedom of Information Bulletin*, No. 190. (November 1967), pp. 4–5.

Bova, Mary M. "What is Swing Vote Value? The CPA Consultant," *The CPA Journal* 66 (June 1996): 64.

Bowers, David R. "A Report on Activity by Publishers in Directing Newsroom Decisions." *Journalism Quarterly* 44 (spring 1967): 43–52.

Boylan, James. "Alicia's Little Tabloid," *Columbia Journalism Review* XXIX (January & February 1991): 53.

Brady, James. "Otis Chandler: Always Seeking New Challenges," *Advertising Age,* 16 May 1983.

Brennan, Jody; Randall Lane; and Willy Stern. "Chandler" *Forbes* 1992 Edition, 19 October 1992, p. 222.

Brinton, James E. "Failure of the Western Edition of the New York Times." *Journalism Quarterly* 41 (spring 1964): 170–74.

Brendon, Piers. "Lords of the Jungle; 'Paper Tigers: The Latest, Greatest Newspaper Tycoons.' By Nicholas Coleridge (Birch Lane Press 592 pp. $24. 95)" *Columbia Journalism Review* 33 (September & October 1994): 53.

Brown, Christie. "Car Art" *Forbes*, 23 July 1990, p. 298.

Brown, Robert R. "Revenue Increases Outpace Expenses." *Editor & Publisher*, 23 April 1959, p. 9.

"Building the Pavilions of Culture," *Time Magazine*, 18 December 1964, p. 46–58.

"Captain Bails Out: Acquisition of *Newsday*," *Newsweek*, 27 April 1970, p. 92.

Carey, Frank. "A Quarter Century of Science Reporting." *Nieman Reports*, June 1966, p. 8.

Carr, Harry. "A Human Slant on Our Big Chief." *Among Ourselves* (*Los Angeles Times* employee newspaper), December 1931, pp. 33–37.

Carroll, Wallace. "Essence, Not Angle." *Columbia Journalism Review*, summer 1965, pp. 4–6.

Carter, Roy E. Jr. and Peter Clarke. "Suburbanites, City Residents, and Local News." *Journalism Quarterly* 40 (autumn 1963): 548–58.

"Chandler," *Forbes*, 21 October 1991, p. 278.

"Chandler Cadre Leaves Times Mirror Board," *Editor & Publisher*, 21 March 1998, p. 15.

Chandler, Constance. "A Group of 'General' Impressions." *Among Ourselves* (*Los Angeles Times* employee newspaper), December 1931, pp. 33–37.

Chandler, Harry. "Harry Chandler, 'Oldest Employee', Has Seen This City Transformed." *Los Angeles Times,* 4 December 1941.

Chandler, Otis. "The Greater Responsibility." *Seminar*, March 1968, p. 16.

_____. "Long Live the Survivors!" *Bulletin of the American Society of Newspaper Editors*, 2 April 1962, p. 15.

_____. "A Responsibility." *Los Angeles Times*, 12 April 1960.

_____. "Role of the *Metropolitan Daily* in Today's Changing Environment." *Journalism Educator*, fall 1964, p. 94.

"Chandler Winner of Vintage Car Race at Riverside Raceway," *Among Ourselves*, May 1979.

"Chandler's Change of Heart," *Times,* 28 June 1971, p. 46.

"A Changing Paper: *Los Angeles Times*," *Columbia Journalism Review*, fall 1961, pp. 31–32.

"Changing Times," *Times*, 25 April 1960, p. 85.

"Clarification Setting the Record Straight," *AutoWeek*, 11 September 1989, p. 8.

Clash, James M. and Peter Kafka. "Let Them Eat Dust," *Forbes*, 12 October 1998, p. 432.

Clemons, Walter. "'The Media Moguls; The Powers That Be.' By David Halberstam 711 pages. Knopf. $15." *Newsweek* United States Edition, 30 April 1979, p. 86.

"Comic Censors," *Review of Southern California Journalism*, July 1973, p. 16.

Conway, John A. "The Giants' Miniwar," *Forbes*, 1 December 1977, p. 8.

_____. "Hands Off at the *L. A. Times*," *Newsweek* United States Edition, 20 September 1976, p. 13.

Cooper, Marc. "The L. A. Times 7 Percent Solution," *Los Angeles Reader*, 28 July 1995.

Corry, John. "The Los Angeles Times." *Harper's*, December 1969, pp. 74–82.

Crandall, Shannon. "Memories of Men and Business in California, 1887–1931." *Claremont Quarterly* V (Spring 1958): 41–58.

Currier, Fred. "Economic Theory and Its Application to Newspapers." *Journalism Quarterly*, 37 (1960), pp. 255–60.

Dahlquist, Eric E., and C. Van Tune. "1969 Corvette ZL-1: The Most Brutal Production Vette Ever; Includes Related Article." *Motor Trend* 45 (September 1993): 98.

Davis, Jim and George Carter. "What the Times Didn't Tell You About Its Washington Bureau Changes." *Review of Southern California Journalism*. April 1973, pp. 2–4.

"Death in Los Angeles," *Time Magazine*, 12 January 1962, p. 48.

DeBaggio, Thomas. "Profits in Their Own Land." *(More)*, 21 March 1973, pp. 32, 38.

"Decline of West," *Columbia Journalism Review*, summer 1969, p. 5.

"Defining Monopoly," *Newsweek,* 23 October 1967, p. 96.

DeLorenzo, Matt. "Classic Summer Pastime Evokes Stars of Tomorrow,"*AutoWeek*, 7 September 1992, p. 10.

_____. "The Intoxicating, Addicting Allure of the Automobile," *AutoWeek*, 25 September 1989, p. 13.

Diamond, Edwin. "Multiplying Media Voices." *Columbia Journalism Review*. Winter 1969–70, pp. 22–27.

Didion, Joan. "Letter from Los Angeles," *The New Yorker*, 26 February 1990, p. 87.

Donohew, Lewis. "Newspaper Gatekeepers and Forces in the News Channel." *Public Opinion Quarterly* 31 (spring 1967): 236–43.

Donnahoe, Alan S. "Space Control by Newspapers: An Analysis and a Plan." *Journalism Quarterly* 33 (summer 1956): 279–86.

"Dubious Achievement Awards of 1997," *Esquire* 129 (January 1998): 42.

Duncan, Charles T. "The 'Education Beat' on 52 Major Newspapers." *Journalism Quarterly* 43 (summer 1966): 336–38.

Edelstein, Alex S., and Otto N. Larsen. "'The Weekly Press' Contribution to a Sense of Urban Community." *Journalism Quarterly* 37 (autumn 1960): 489–98.

Emery, Mike. "How the Times Picked Dick." *Review of Southern California Journalism*, December 1972, pp. 5–7.

"Enterprise in Los Angeles," *Time*, 13 May 1966, pp. 76–77.

"Executive Compensation: The Ups and Downs Are Sharper," *BusinessWeek*, 12 May 1975, p. 90.

"The First Outsider," *BusinessWeek* Industrial Edition, 24 March 1980, p. 60.

Fisher, Sara. "What Ever Happened to the Chandlers? L. A.'s Most Prominent Family Takes Back Seat, Gets Richer; Publishing Magnates," *Los Angeles Business Journal*, 15 February 1999, p. 1.

Fisk, Margaret Cronin. "Recyclable Plastic Printing Plate Invented by *L. A. Times*." *Editor & Publisher*, 6 October 1973, pp. 9, 16.

Flint, Jerry. "The Speedster," *Forbes*, 24 June, 1991, p. 128.

"The Forty Years War," *Los Angeles Times*, 1–4 October 1929.

Frank, Len. "1933 Isotta-Fraschini Tipo 8A SS; Vintage Automobile," *Motor Trend* 37 (September 1985): 93.

Fuchs, R. Joseph. "Newspaper Industry Review." *Kidder, Peabody & Co. Newsletter.* 22 November 1972.

Fujii, Reed. "Magnate Full of Magnetism," *Ventura County Star Free Press*, 25 February 1990, pp. 16–19.

Gabor, Andrea, Robert J. Morse, and Robert F. Black. "The U.S. News 100: Market Bonanzas," *U.S. News & World Report*, 6 July 1987, p. 48.

Gabor, Andrea, Robert J. Morse, Robert F. Black, Michael H. Gallagher, Srinjoy Chowdhury, Meegan McCorkle, and Richard Rothschild. "Hometown Billionaires," *U.S. News & World Report,* (1 August 1988), 38.

Gallup, George. "Changes in the Newspaper During the Next 20 Years." *Journalism Quarterly* 32 (winter 1955): 17–20, 38.

Gandy, Oscar H., Jr., Katharina Kopp, Tanya Hands, Karen Frazer, and David Phillips. "Race and Risk: Factors Affecting the Framing of Stories About Inequality, Discrimination, and Just Plain Bad Luck," *Public Opinion Quarterly* 61 (22 March, 1997): 158.

Gelman, David, Martin Kasindorf, and Janet Huck. "Expose Thy Neighbor," *Newsweek* United States Edition, 27 December 1976, p. 55.

Gerald, Edward. "Economic Research and the Mass Media." *Journalism Quarterly* 35 (Winter 1958): 49–55.

Gordon, Mitchell. "A Family Empire." *Wall Street Journal*, 13 October 1965.

Gottlieb, Robert. "The Forgotten History of the *Los Angeles Times*," *Review of Southern California Journalism*, winter 1974, pp. 5–11.

Gottlieb, Robert, and Irene Wolt. "The Power Broker Behind the *Times*," *New West*, 26 September 1977, pp. 29–43.

"Great Family Fortunes," *Forbes*, 18 October 1993, p. 270.

Griffith, Thomas, and Marta Fitzgerald Dorion. "Rupert Murdoch Fights to Hold His U.S. Beachhead," *Fortune* Domestic Edition, 15 January 1979, p. 66.

Gross, Ken. "Million Dollar Babies; Collector Cars," *Playboy* 37 (December 1990): 110.

Groves, David. "Power Play," *PSA*, April 1984, pp. 86–120.

Gunther, Marc, and Irene Gashurov. "Publish or Perish?" *Fortune*, 10 January 2000, p. 140.

Hachten, William A. "The Changing U.S. Sunday Newspaper." *Journalism Quarterly* 38 (summer 1961): 281–88.

Halberstam, David. "The California Dynasty," *The Atlantic Monthly*, April 1979, pp. 54–77.

Hammer, Joshua. "Look Out, the Boss Is Back," *Newsweek*, 15 November 1999, p. 76.

"Happy Chandlers," *Newsweek*, 8 June 1964, p. 93.

"Harry Chandler and Harrison Otis," *California Journal*, 1 November 1999.

"Harry Chandler Called by Death," *Los Angeles Times*, 24 September 1944.

Haven, Frank P. "*Los Angeles Times*—A 'How' Story of Journalism." *Quill*, October 1965, p. 36.

Heasley, Jerry, and John P. Huffman. "The Muscle Corvette Era, 1965–1974," *Motor Trend* 46 (September 1994): 105.

Hecht, Henry. "A Box Full of Goodies," *Sports Illustrated*, 4 April 1983, p. 84.

"Heir Apparent," *Newsweek*, 6 September 1971, p. 74.

Hensher, Alan. "No News Today: How Los Angeles Lost a Daily." *Journalism Quarterly* 47 (Winter 1970): 684–88.

Highton, Jake. "One of the Worlds Good Newspapers." *Review of Southern California Journalism*. Spring 1971, pp. 8–9.

Hotchkiss, L. D. "Times Steers Its Future Course by Beacon Lights of Experience." *Los Angeles Times,* 4 December 1941.

House, Jack W. "Lost, Not to Be Found," *AutoWeek*, 14 August 1989, p. 16.

"How a 'Milestone' Gets to Be One," *BusinessWeek*, 22 August 1977, p. 80.

"How Leaders in 13 Fields Rank Their Peers," *U.S. News & World Report*, 16 April 1979, p. 38.

"How to Build a Publishing Empire," *Newsweek*, 2 January 1967, pp. 41–45.

Hughes, Ken. "Absolutely No Sense of Humor," *American Journalism Review*, April 1997, p. 14.

Hughes, Robert. "Going Out on the Edge; Our Critic Finds Speed, Beauty and a Glimpse of His Youth at the Guggenheim's Motorcycle Show," *Time*, 17 August, 1998, p. 75.

"Hundreds Pay Tribute to Norman Chandler," *Among Ourselves*, November 1973.

"Impressive Acquisition," *Time*, 23 February 1968, p. 80.

"Insider Trading, Cable TV Stocks," *Multichannel News* 14 (13 December 1993): 63.

"It Pays to Be a Chandler," *Business Week*, 20 March 1995, p. 4.

Jacobs, Jody. "Otis Chandler Weds Bettina Whitaker," *Los Angeles Times*, 18 August 1981.

Janeway, Michael. "Breaking the Newsroom," *The American Prospect*, 20 December 1999, p. 48.

J. M. C. "Would You Buy a Used Car from These Guys? (Yes)" *Forbes*, 12 October 1998, p. 434.

"John H. Johnson Receives Communication Award During Gala in New York," *Jet*, 27 March 1995, p. 14.

Judd, Robert P. "The Newspaper Reporter in a Suburban City." *Journalism Quarterly* 38 (winter 1961): 35–42.

Kaiser, Charles, Patricia King, Donna Foote, and Nancy Stadtman. "Murdoch Buys Sun-Times," *Newsweek*, 14 November 1983, p. 117.

Kane, Pat. "Getting the Message: News, Truth and Power" (book reviews). *New Statesman & Society* 6 (16 July 1993): 38.

Karnow, Stanley. "The Newsman's War in Vietnam." *Nieman Reports*, December 1963, pp. 4–8.

Katz, David L. "Climbing the Hill: Torrey Pines Repeats Successfully," *AutoWeek*, 23 November 1998, p. 32.

Kavey, Fred. "California: Gun Control's Primary Target" *Guns & Ammo* 29 (November 1985): 28.

Kerby, P. "Most Likely to Succeed." *Nation*, 15 January 1968, pp. 80–82.

Kinter, Charles V. "Current Trends in Income of Communications Enterprises." *Journalism Quarterly* 29 (spring 1952): 141–47.

"Killing Off the Competition," *Newsweek*, 11 March 1974, p. 69.

Kirp, David L., and Douglas S. Rice. "Fast Forward—Styles of California Management," *Harvard Business Review*, January & February 1988, p. 74.

Klugman, Craig. "Good Walls Make Good Neighbors," *Editor & Publisher*, 4 December 1999, p. 45.

Konrad, Walecia, and Chuck Hawkins. "The Scoop on CNN's Bottom Line," *Business Week*, 4 February 1991, p. 70.

Krantz, Michael. "Still Setting America's Agenda; Special Report: Newspapers," *MediaWeek* 4, (25 April, 1994): 22.

Kuhn, Ferdinand. "Blighted Areas of Our Press." *Columbia Journalism Review*, summer 1966, pp. 5–10.

La Franco, Robert. "Tear Down Walls, or Hit Them?" *Forbes*, 9 August 1999, p. 56.

_____. "Vintage Vroom," *Forbes*, 3 June 1996, p. 186.

"Launching a Satellite: Orange County Edition," *Time*, 29 March 1968, p. 45.

Lawler, Oscar. "The Bombing of the *Los Angeles Times*: A Personal Reminiscence." *Claremont Quarterly* VI (winter 1959): 25–32.

Lawrence, David. "American Business and Businessmen." *Saturday Evening Post*, 25 April 1931, pp. 46, 166.

Lawson, Herbert G. "SEC Says Otis Chandler and Audit Firm Deeply Involved in Alleged GeoTek Fraud." *Wall Street Journal*, 25 March 1974.

Levin, Harvey J. "Economies in Cross Channel Affiliation of Media." *Journalism Quarterly* 31 (spring 1934): 167–74.

"Local Monopoly in the Daily Newspaper Industry," *The Yale Law Journal* 61 (June-July 1952): 948–1009.

Lockwood, Charles, and Christopher B. Leinberger. "Los Angeles Comes of Age: The City's Experiencing Rapid Growth and Big Problems," *The Atlantic* 261 (January 1988): 31.

Lorie, J. H., and P. Halpern. "Conglomerates: The Rhetoric and the Evidence." *Journal of Law and Economics* XIII (April 1970): 149–66.

"Los Angeles Aflame," *Columbia Journalism Review*, fall 1965, p. 15.

"*L. A. Times* Give Keys to Excelling," *Editor & Publisher*, 8 October 1966, p. 28.

"*Los Angeles Times* Revises Its Image to Reach Changing Market," *Business Week*, 19 November 1960, pp. 118–20.

Lubove, Seth. "Chandler Versus Chandler," *Forbes*, 20 November 1995, p. 43.

Lyle, Jack, and Walter Wilcox. "Television News—An Interim Report." *Journal of Broadcasting* VII (winter 1963): 157.

McCombs, Maxwell E. "Mass Media in the Market Place." *Journalism Monographs*, No. 24 (August 1972).

McEvoy, Poynter. "Big Advertisers—How Important Are They in Newspaper Budgets?" *Journalism Quarterly* 32 (winter 1955): 46–55.

Macaluso, Nick. "Enemy Activity" *AutoWeek*, 11 September 1989, p. 15.

MacDougall, A. Kent. "Boring from Within the Bourgeois Press; Part 2," *Monthly Review* 40 (December 1988): 10.

Macfarlane, Peter Clark. "What Is the Matter with Los Angeles?" *Collier's* 2 December 1911, p. 28.

"Making the News Two Ways," *Frontier*, June 1966, p. 23.

"Man Who Doesn't Take Sides," *Time*, 25 December 1964, p. 39.

"The Meaning of Monopoly," *Newsweek*, 12 June 1967, p. 67.

Mecklin, John M. "Times Mirror's Ambitious Acquirers." *Fortune,* 1 September 1968, pp. 155–57.

"Media Get a Message from Justice." *Business Week*, 8 June 1968, p. 110.

Merrill, John C. "U.S. Panel Names World's Ten Leading 'Quality' Dailies." *Journalism Quarterly* 41 (autumn 1964): 568–72.

"Midas of California," *Newsweek,* 2 October 1944, pp. 80–81.

"Money Changes Everything," *American Journalism Review*, January & February 1998, p. 5.

Moeller, Leslie G. "Journalism Education, the Media and 'The New Industrial State.'" *Journalism Quarterly* 45 (autumn 1968): 496–508.

Moore, Thomas, and Lorraine Carson. "Trouble and Strife in the Cowles Empire," *Fortune*, 4 April 1983, p. 156.

Moses, Lucia. "Chandler Blasts Times Execs," *Editor & Publisher*, 6 November 1999, p. 4.

_____. "Otis Chandler reloads in trying Times," *Editor & Publisher*, 11 December 1999, p. 4.

_____. "Otis Chandler: They Still Don't Get It." *Editor & Publisher*, 3 January, 2000, p. 9.

Moses, Sam. "Andretti Was Good and Ready," *Sports Illustrated*, 9 April 1984, p. 75.

Mott, Frank Luther. "Dr. Mott's Recap of Ratings." *Saturday Review*, 10 June 1961, p. 57.

"Mrs. Chandler Retires," *Among Ourselves*, February 1976.

"Nation's Editors Pick 15 'Superior' Papers," *Editor & Publisher*, 2 April 1960, p. 12.

Neal, Barbara Jean. "A Spectacular House that Carries Forth the California Heritage," *Los Angeles Times* Home, 24 October 1965.

Neiva, Elizabeth M. "Chain Building: The Consolidation of the American Newspaper Industry, 1953–1980," *Business History Review* 70 (22 March 1996): 1.

Nelson, Dean. "Back to L.A.; *Los Angeles Times* Closes Down in San Diego, California," *The Quill* 81 (January 1993): p. 20.

Neukom, Daniel. "Icky Ilk," *AutoWeek*, 9 October 1989, p. 16.

"New Edition in Los Angeles," *Business Week*, 20 November 1971, p. 27.

"New Frontier in Denver," *NewsWeek* United States Edition, 3 November 1980, p. 93.

"The New Times," *Business Week*, 26 December 1970, p. 43.

"The New World," *Time,* 15 July 1957, pp. 37–41.

"News for Advertisers: A Denver Case," *Columbia Journalism Review*, summer 1966, pp. 10–11.

"Newsday for Sale?" *NewsWeek*, 23 March 1970, p. 93–94.

"'Newspaper Proprietors; Practical Cats; Paper Tigers.' By Nicholas Coleridge. To be published in America by Carol Publishers." *The Economist*, 17 July 1993, p. 86.

"Newspaper's Death Held Exaggerated," *Forbes*, 1 October 1969, pp. 15–19.

Nixon, Raymond B. "Concentration and Absenteeism in Daily Newspaper Ownership." *Journalism Quarterly* 22 (June 1945): 97–114.

_____. "Trends in U.S. Newspaper Ownership; Concentration with Competition." *Bulletin of the American Society of Newspaper Publishers*, January 1969, p. 4.

_____. "Who Will Own the Press in 1975?" *Journalism Quarterly* 32 (winter 1955): 10–16.

_____, and Robert L. Jones. "The Content of Non-Competitive vs. Competitive Newspapers." *Journalism Quarterly* 33 (summer 1956): 299–314.

_____, and Jean Ward. "Trends in Newspaper Ownership and Inter-Media Competition." *Journalism Quarterly* 38 (winter 1961): 3–14.

"No Comment: Purchase of *Newsday*," *Time*, 23 March 1970, p. 38.

"Non-boob," *Newsweek*, 29 August 1960, p. 85.

"Nose for Corruption; Expose on City Harbor Commission Contract," *Nation*, 6 November 1967, pp. 452–53.

Olson, Kenneth E. "The Newspaper in Times of Social Change." *Journalism Quarterly* 12 (March 1935): 9–19.

"Otis Chandler Answers Some Questions," *Among Ourselves*, March 1975.

Otis, Harrison Gray. "A Long, Winning Fight Against the Closed Shop, an Account of the Seventeen-Years Conflict Between the *Los Angeles Times* and the Typographical Union." *World's Work*, December 1907, pp. 9675–79.

_____. "Where the *Times* Stands." *Los Angeles Times*, 19 September 1914.

Ottum, Bob. "A Hunk Hits the Road," *Sports Illustrated*, 14 May 1984, p. 56.

Palmer, Frederick. "Otistown of the Open Shop, the Story of Los Angeles, a City So Influenced by One Man and His Idea That Her Labor War Culminated in the Use of Nitroglycerine." *Hampton's Magazine*, January 1911, pp. 29–44.

Pogano, Penny. "The Best in the Business; The Board of Nominators; The Runners-Up," *American Journalism Review*, March 1995, p. 30.

Pogash, Carol. "The Shrinking L. A. Times," *American Journalism Review*, October 1995, p. 22.

Porter, Alice J. *The National Journal* 12 (15 March 1980): 459.

"Press Lords at War," *The Economist*, 26 March 1977, p. 48.

Presto, Kay. "Petersen Automotive Museum: A Grand Celebration of the Automobile Opens in L. A.," *AutoWeek*, 27 June 1994, p. 16.

Price, Susan. "Not Just Getting Older . . . " *Los Angeles Magazine*, January 1985, pp. 162–163.

Prochnau, William. "Down and Out in L. A." *American Journalism Review,* January 2000, p. 58.

"A Publishing Giant Takes a Long Step," *Business Week*, 14 March 1964, pp. 72–78.

"A Question of Competition," *Time*, 20 October 1967, p. 58.

Rappleye, Charles. "Are New Ideas Killing the L. A. Times?" *Columbia Journalism Review* XXXIII (November & December 1994): 49.

_____. "How Corporate Managers Wrestled Control of the Times from Otis Chandler," *L. A. Weekly*, 3 September 1993.

Rarick, Galen, and Barrie Hartman. "The Effects of Competition on One Daily Newspaper's Content." *Journalism Quarterly* 43 (Autumn 1966): 459–68.

Raskin, A. H. "What's Wrong with American Newspapers?" *New York Times Magazine*, 11 June 1967, pp. 80–89.

Rasky, Susan. "The Media Covers Los Angeles," *California Journal*, 1 July 1997.

Ray, Royal H. "Economic Factors as Forces in Daily Newspaper Concentration." *Journalism Quarterly* 29 (winter 1952): 31–42.

Raynal, Wes. "Muscle Cars Strongest Investment in Collecting More Profitable than Ferraris," *AutoWeek*, 17 July 1989, p. 24.

Raynal, Wes, and Larry Edsall. "Best Sellers" *AutoWeek*, 11 February 1991, p. 9.

_____. "The F40s Are Here! The F40s Are Here; But It's Still a Seller's Market," *AutoWeek*, 13 August 1990, p. 3.

_____. "The Fountain of Youth; Surprise! It's in Cleveland, Where Muscle Cars Get a New— if Not Authentic—Lease on Life." *AutoWeek*, 2 April 1990, p. 20.

Reagan, Ron. "While the Democrats Slept," *Playboy* 31 (December 1984): 142.

Reddaway, W. B. "The Economics of Newspapers." *Economic Journal* LXXIII (June 1963): 201–18.

Reeves, Richard. "Gray Lady Down," *Los Angeles Magazine*, August 1995.

"The Retired Publisher November 3rd," *Columbia Journalism Review*, January & February 2000, p. 27.

R. H. B. "There's More to It Than Kicking Tires," *Forbes*, 28 October 1985, p. 378.

Riley, Frank. "The Changing Direction of the *Times*." *Los Angeles Magazine*, June 1966, p. 29.

Risser, James. "The Wall Is Heading Back." *Columbia Journalism Review*, January & February 2000, p. 26.

Rivers, William. "California's Press." *Saturday Review*, 23 September 1967, p. 29.

_____. "New Winds in the South, New Splash in the North," *Saturday Review*, 23 September 1967, pp. 75–76.

Rose, Frederick. "Digital Turnabout," *Wall Street Journal*, 6 June 1994.

Rothmyer, Karen. "What Really Happened in Biafra?" *Columbia Journalism Review*, fall 1970, pp. 43–47.

Rowland, Howard R., and Donald G. Hileman. "The Inter-City Daily in the United States." *Journalism Quarterly* 37 (summer 1960): 373–80.

Rosse, James N. "Daily Newspapers, Monopolistic Competition, and Economies of Scale." *American Economic Review* LVII (May 1967): 522–33.

Russell, Ron. "Back to the Beach," *New Times*, 23–29 December 1999.

Russell, Shaw. "Tom Johnson; President of Cable News Network; N. B." *Chief Executives (U.S.)*, July 1992, p. 23.

Rutland, Robert. "Newspaper Antitrust: 'Trade Copy' Only?" *Columbia Journalism Review*, fall 1967, pp. 46–47.

Ryan, Marian L. "Los Angeles Newspapers Fight the Water War, 1924–27." *Southern California Quarterly* 50 (spring 1968): 177–90.

Sandler, Linda. "Times Mirror's Willes Expects 'Fun' to Come in Rebuilding Firm After 'Traumatic' Cutting," *The Wall Street Journal*, 14 August 1995.

Sanoff, Alvin P. "America's Press; Too Much Power for Too Few?" *U.S. News & World Report*, 15 August 1977, p. 27.

Santelmann, Neal. "Muscle fever" *Forbes*, 20 March 1989, p. 192.

Santo, Jamie. *Editor & Publisher*, 31 January 2000, p. 27.

Santry, David G. "A $160-per-Acre Play in California Land," *BusinessWeek* Industrial Edition, 19 March 1979, p. 144.

Schanberg, Sydney H. "The Murder of New York Newsday: How Wall Street's Obsession with the Bottom Line Killed One Good Newspaper—and Threatens Others." *Washington Monthly* 28 (March 1996): 29.

Schardt, Arlie, Martin Kasindorf, and Mary Lord. "Fat Times in Los Angeles," *NewsWeek* United States Edition, 22 September 1980, p. 46.

Scott, Jim. "Otis Chandler notes improvement in papers," *Editor & Publisher*, 9 November 1974, p. 14.

Scott, Michael G. H. "Hype of Muscle Cars No Match for Truth of Old American Iron," *AutoWeek*, 15 April 1991, p. 13.

Scott, Paul T. "The Mass Media in Los Angeles Since the Rise of Television." *Journalism Quarterly* 31 (spring 1954): 161–67.

Self, Thomas M. "Times Mirror Company's Otis Chandler," *The Executive*, November 1978.

Sesser, Stanford. "The Fantasy World of Travel Sections." *Columbia Journalism Review*, spring 1970, pp. 44–47.

Shapiro, Walter, and Lucy Howard. "Making It Perfectly Clear," *Newsweek* United States Edition, 21 May 1984, p. 32.

Shaw, David. "Of Obscenity, Timidity and Hypocrisy." *Review of Southern California Journalism*, April 1972, pp. 2–4.

Sheets, Kenneth R., Robert J. Morse, and Robert F. Black. "Who Owns Corporate America; U.S. News 100," *U.S. News & World Report*, 21 July 1986, p. 36.

Shepard, Alicia C. "Blowing Up the Wall," *American Journalism Review*, December 1997, p. 18.

Sherwin, Louis. "The Walrus of Moron-Land." *American Mercury*, February 1928, pp. 190–97.

Simurda, Stephen J. "Sticking with the Union? From the *New York Daily News* to the *Los Angeles Times*, The Newspaper Guild Is Fighting for Its Future; The Prospects Are a Lingering Death or a Painful Rebirth." *Columbia Journalism Review* 32 (March & April 1993): 25.

Smythe, Dallas W. "Time, Market and Space Factors in Communication Economics." *Journalism Quarterly* 39 (winter 1962): 3–14.

Spence, Steve. "Collector Cars Collecting Cash; There's More to the Action at Barrett-Jackson than a Mere Exchange of $37 Million; Many Cars Have Heritage as Rich as Their New Owners," *AutoWeek*, 19 February 1990, p. 26.

"Southern California," *AutoWeek*, 26 April 1999, p. 43.

Stapleton, Jean. "What *Does* Woman Want?" *Review of Southern California Journalism*, February 1972, pp. 8–9.

Star, Jack. "L. A.'s Mighty Chandlers." *Look*, 25 September 1962, pp. 107–10.

Stark, Rodney W. "Policy and the Pros: An Organizational Analysis of a Metropolitan Newspaper." *Berkeley Journal of Sociology* 7 (spring 1962): 23–38.

Stastny, Pat. "Water: A Vital Issue in Valley Growth." *Northridge Daily Sundial*, 18 May 1973.

Steigleman, Walter A. "Do Newspaper Headlines Really Promote Street Sales?" *Journalism Quarterly* 26 (December 1949): 379–88.

Stein, M. L. "Critic Critiques His Own Newspaper" *Editor & Publisher,* 16 May 1998, p. 18.

_____. "Good Journalism and Bottom Line," *Editor & Publisher,* 19 July 1997, p. 10.

_____. "Willes to Succeed Erburu as CEO of Times Mirror Co.; Joins the Media Company from General Mills," *Editor & Publisher,* 13 May 1995, p. 21.

Stempel, Guido H., III. "Effects on Performance of a Cross-Media Monopoly." *Journalism Monographs,* No. 29 (June 1973).

_____. "A New Analysis of Monopoly and Competition." *Columbia Journalism Review,* spring 1967, pp. 11–12.

Stern, Bernard. "How Local Government News Is Handled by Three Dailies." *Journalism Quarterly* 27 (spring 1950): 149–56.

Sternberg, Robert. "Earth to *AutoWeek*," *AutoWeek,* 21 August 1989, p. 16.

"Story of Times Coverage Told by *Newsweek*," *Los Angeles Times,* 24 October 1961.

"Suburb and City," *Columbia Journalism Review,* summer 1963, pp. 13–23.

Swaim, Will. "The *Times* That Try a Woman's Soul," *O C Weekly,* 23–29 February 1996.

Swanson, Charles E. "Midcity Daily: News Staff and Control." *Journalism Quarterly* 26 (March 1949): 20–28.

Sweeney, Louise. "Otis Chandler: Hemingway Could Have Invented Him," *The Christian Science Monitor,* 5 February 1980.

Taulolieb, Paul. "A Mirror of His Times," *Sportstyle,* 5 March 1984.

Taylor, Frank J. "It Costs $1000 to Have Lunch with Harry Chandler." *Saturday Evening Post,* 16 December 1939, pp. 8–9, 60–64.

Taylor, John H. "Betting on the Wrong Horses," *Forbes,* 12 April 1993, p. 26.

Taylor, Ken. "Harry Chandler's Crowded 50 Years." *Editor & Publisher,* 15 August 1936, pp. 7, 20.

Tebbel, John, "Rating the American Newspaper: A Journalism Faculty Survey, Part I." *Saturday Review,* 13 May 1961, pp. 60–62.

_____. "Rating the American Newspaper, Part II." *Saturday Review,* 10 June 1961, pp. 54–56.

"The Ten Best American Dailies," *Time,* 21 January 1974, pp. 58–61.

"The Ten Worst," *(More),* May 1974, pp. 16–18.

"Thank You Mr. Smith," *Newsweek,* 27 April 1970, p. 94.

"They Broke Their Trust," *Columbia Journalism Review,* spring 1962, pp. 30–31.

"They Found Newspapers Best After All," *Business Week,* 26 December 1970, pp. 42–43.

"Third Perch," *Time,* 15 July 1935, p. 32.

Thomas, Dana L. "Lord of the Press? Political and Legal Hurdles Are Mounting for 'Monopoly' Newspapers." *Barron's,* 8 July 1968, pp. 5, 18, 21.

_____. "Paper Profits: Technological Advances, Suburban Outlets Pay Off for Publishers." *Barron's,* 1 July 1968, pp. 3, 16, 18–21.

Thomas, William F. *Editor & Publisher,* 30 October 1999, p. 52.

Ticer, Scott, and Todd Mason. "Times Mirror Wakes Up with a Throbbing Hangover," *BusinessWeek,* 4 November 1985, p. 64.

"Times Mirror Acquires Harry N. Abrams, Inc." *Publisher's Weekly,* 11 April 1966, p. 28.

"Times Mirror Acquires World Publishing Company." *Publisher's Weekly,* 26 August 1963, p. 247.

"The Times Mirror Ambassadors; Marketing the L. A. Times," *Sales & Marketing Management* 136 (June 1986): 64.

"Times Mirror Company: Spreading into the Knowledge Industry," *Newsweek*, 2 January 1967, pp. 44–45.

"Times Mirror Expands Again," *Time*, 10 March 1967, p. 47.

"Times Mirror Shift," *BusinessWeek*, 30 May 1977, p. 36.

"Times Mirror to Acquire Yearbook Medical," *Publisher's Weekly*, 8 November 1965, p. 35.

"Times Mirror's Media Blitz; Five Best-Managed Companies, 1984," *Dun's Business Month* 124 (December 1984): 44.

"*Times* Stock List Sent in 31 Seconds," *Editor & Publisher*, 7 June 1969, p. 78.

"The Times, They Are a-Changin' Back," *Editor & Publisher*, 25 December 1999, p. 8.

Tobin, Richard L. "Communications: Rating the American Newspaper." *Saturday Review*, 13 May 1961, p. 59.

Towne, Jackson E. "Historical Source Material on Texas and California Papers." *Journalism Quarterly* 29 (spring 1962): 222–23.

"The Troubled Times," *Business Week*, 11 June 1964, p. 26.

Tracy, Eleanor J., Peter W. Bernstein, Susie G. Nazem, Anna Cifelli, and Renee Leggett. "Time for Digestion," *Fortune*, 7 April 1980, p. 16.

Tschucky-Daniels, G. "'White-hunter' Chandler," *BusinessWeek* Industrial Edition, 21 March 1977, p. 9.

"Two-Edged Ax," *Newsweek*, 15 January 1962, p. 26.

"Under Otis Chandler, the *Times* Has Gained Position of Eminence," *Among Ourselves*, 14 April 1980.

U.S. News & World Report. 6 July 1987, p. 51.

"The U.S. News 100," *U.S. News & World Report* 105 (1 August 1988): 40.

Van Gelder, Lindsy. "Can the Chatter, Sweetheart; Allen Neuharth; includes related article," *Business Month* 133 (February 1989): 50.

Vessell, Eugene B. "Newspaper Industry Review." *H. C. Wainwright and Co. Industry Review*, 19 January 1973.

Vier, Gene. "The Decline (and Fall) of *West*." *LA*, 30 September 1972, pp. 12–15.

Vorsatz, Mark L., and William I. Woodson. "'Swing Vote' Attributes of Transferred Stock: Implications for Minority Interest Discounts," *The Tax Adviser* 26 (September 1995): 519.

"Walter Burroughs, Former SPJ National President, Dies; Society of Professional Journalists; Convention '89 Report; obituary." *The Quill* 77 (December 1989): 38.

Wellemeyer, Marilyn, and Fay Rice. "One-on-One with the Waves," *Fortune* Domestic Edition, August 1977, p. 75.

Wells, Bob. "How the Media Covered the Los Angeles Mayoral Race." *Review of Southern California Journalism*, July 1973, pp. 2–6.

_____. "The Bleak Wasteland of Financial Journalism." *Columbia Journalism Review*, July/August 1973, pp. 40–49.

_____. "Newsday: Will the *Times* Make It Just Another Fat Tabloid?" *Review of Southern California Journalism*, April 1973, pp. 8–9.

Westley, Bruce, and Werner J. Severin. "Some Correlates of Media Credibility." *Journalism Quarterly* 41 (summer 1964): 325–35.

Weston, J. F., and S. K. Mansinghka. "Tests of the Efficiency Performance of Conglomerate Firms." *Journal of Finance* XXVII (September 1971): 919–36.

_____, Keith V. Smith, and Ronald E. Shrieves. "Conglomerate Performance Using the Capital Asset Pricing Model." *Review of Economics and Statistics* 54 (November 1972): 357–63.

White, David Manning. "The 'Gate Keeper': A Case Study in the Selection of News." *Journalism Quarterly* 27 (fall 1950): 383–90.

"Why the Decrease in Big City Papers?" *U.S. News and World Report*, 4 April 1966, p. 12.

"Why Times Mirror Wants Denver's Post," *BusinessWeek* Industrial Edition, 10 November 1980, p. 38.

Wiegner, Kathleen K. "Chandler's Johnson," *Forbes*, 31 March 1980, p. 110.

_____. "The Chandlers' Stewards," *Forbes*, 20 October 1986, p. 111.

Williams, Nick. "Manson and MyLai." *Columbia Journalism Review*, summer 1970, p. 61.

Willoughby, Wesley F. "Are Two Competing Dailies Necessarily Better than One?" *Journalism Quarterly* 32 (spring 1955): 197–204.

Wilson, Kevin A. "The Beauty of Retro-Activity is in the Age of the Beholder," *AutoWeek*, 2 April 1990, p. 15.

Winner, Karin. "Otis Chandler: The Hunt for Excellence," *Women's Wear Daily*, 18 July 1972.

Winship, Thomas. "Where Are They Now?" *Editor & Publisher*, 2 October 1993, p. 5.

Witcover, Jules. "Two Weeks That Shook the Press." *Columbia Journalism Review*, September/October 1971, pp. 7–15.

Wood, Robert E. "Geotek Allegations Wholly Unjustified Chandler Asserts." *Los Angeles Times*, 27 March 1974.

"The World's Oldest Surfer," *Time Magazine*, 13 August 1979, pp. 60–63.

"Yortytoons; Feud Between Mayor of Los Angeles and *Los Angeles Times* Publisher." *Newsweek,* 12 February 1968, p. 67.

Yu, Frederick T. C., and John Luter. "The Foreign Correspondent and His Work," *Columbia Journalism Review*, spring 1964, pp. 5–12.

Zesiger, Sue. "The Urge to Splurge; Barret-Jackson's Classic-Car Auction Gives Automotive Diehards the Chance to Buy, Sell, and Gawk." *Fortune*, 2 March 1998, p. 246.

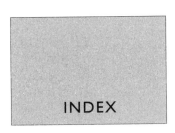

INDEX

The following abbreviations are used in subentries: "OC" for Otis Chandler, "HO" for Harrison Otis, "HC" for Harry Chandler, "NC" for Norman Chandler, *"Times"* for *Los Angeles Times*. Names of the children of Otis Chandler are spelled out to distinguish them from ancestors. In references to notes chapter number precedes note number separated by a colon. Listed streets do not necessarily indicate current names or existence.